BETHESDA

A SOCIAL HISTORY OF THE AREA
THROUGH WORLD WAR TWO

'04

WILLIAM OFFUTT

DEDICATED TO THE MEMORY OF
Mary Fulford Foster and John Adair
AND ALL THE OTHERS WHO LIVED AND WORKED AND DIED FOR US

Cover designed by Thomas Bourdeaux Jr. from a photo donated to the
Montgomery County Historical Society by Hilma Morris

Published by The Innovation Game - *Interesting Products Since 1968*
8509 Irvington Avenue   Bethesda, Maryland 20817

Group rates, discounts for schools and for charitable sales by local institutions
are available on request. Call (301) 530-4299.

Manufactured in the United States by McNaughton and Gunn, Inc.

This book is printed on acid-free paper.

second (revised) edition

ISBN: 0-9643819-2-3

Table of Contents

Appendices:

An Introduction and Foreword

In 1944 the publisher-editor of the *Record*, Bethesda's newest weekly newspaper, described what the town had been like twenty-five years before when the Bank of Bethesda first opened its doors. The village was then, she wrote, little more than "a wide place in the road."

In the whole of the district running from Rock Creek Park west to the Potomac river and north from the District Line to and including Grosvenor lane there were only 5,000 souls, or approximately 1,000 homes.

The bank was located on the southwest corner at the intersection of Georgetown road and Wisconsin avenue, in the rear of what is now People's Drug Store. Looking toward the District Line on the opposite side of the street one could see only four business establishments – Wade Imirie's garage, the Ice Plant, Lewis Keiser's real estate office, and Bill Counselman's Feed Store. To get to these businesses one had to cross the street car tracks and drive down a cinder path. There was no paved street on the eastern side of Wisconsin.

Looking toward the Capital on the western side of Wisconsin a few more business houses were visible. Wilson's store near the railroad underpass housed the Bethesda Post Office. Mr. Wilson was the Post Master and Will Dawson was the mail carrier. He used a horse and buggy. Walter Perry conducted a feed store farther down the street; there was a Sanitary Grocery near the underpass, a garage at Hampden lane and the avenue and farther down was Charlie Miller's coal yard.

Up Wisconsin avenue toward Rockville, M. E. Peake operated a dairy business in the rear of his residence and down Georgetown road Mrs. Maud Barton and Mrs. S. E. Shackleford ran small general stores. E. E. Dellinger had a store at the District Line; Mr. Sonnemann had one on Brookeville road in Chevy Chase; Mr. Canada and Mr. Tuohey each had a store on Conduit road; Tom Perry had set himself up in the coal business at Chevy Chase Lake; and Frank Wilson served the country folks from his merchandising house on Georgetown road near Grosvenor lane. Walter Tuckerman's real estate office was in the same building with the bank. With such an enterprising business community the Bank of Bethesda felt fortunate in taking in a total of $1500 on its opening day from four different depositors.

The town was proud of its schools. There was the brick building on Wilson lane (a part of the present structure); the first section of the present building at the Rosemary street school; a small frame school house on Wilson lane near Conduit road and one out near Zion Baptist Church. If young people craved a high school education they went to Rockville or the District...

The lot on which the bank now stands had been cleared of its old blacksmith shop by the Masons in preparation for the building of the Masonic Hall. Sheep and cattle roamed the fields up and down Wisconsin avenue, out Georgetown road and through Battery Park.

Transportation was furnished by a street car line which ran on a single track from just north of the District Line to Rockville. Cars ran hourly except at rush periods when 15 minute schedules were observed. There was no kicking about crowded cars.

Dr. Benjamin Perry had just come down from Frederick to take over the practice of the late Dr. John L. Lewis, but if one wanted a dentist it was necessary to go to Washington or Rockville.

Yes, it was a great young town and as the promising young cashier, Walter Bogley, built a fire and thawed out the ink well that cold December morning before slipping behind the second-hand counter to become the town's only cashier for a period of nearly 24 years, he thought to himself, "Great prospects here, Walter, my boy. Let's stick to it and see what happens."

2

My great-grandfather bought a hundred acres and built a home in Bethesda on the eve of the Civil War. In 1890 my grandfather and his bride had a home and farm on the "No Gain" land in what became Chevy Chase. The family was living on Rockville Pike just north of the Georgetown Prep when both my father and I were born. After my father's death in 1938, my mother, brother and I moved to Bethesda and rented one of those stucco, Spanish-style houses in Battery Park. All the backyards ran together, and there were dozens of kids to play with and even an old, "haunted" house to explore. I walked down to Bethesda Elementary School on Wilson Lane for second and third grade. I remember weaving around a Maypole and having to hold a girl's hand while we learned to waltz or minuet for some sort of pageant, but except for the penny candy at Emmy Lou's and the long walk home, I can't recall much else about school. In the summer of 1940, we moved into our own brick Cape Cod on East West Highway, just two blocks from Wisconsin, the bank and the intersection that still is the center of town. The village that Gertrude Bradley described was long gone and in its stead a bustling town grew faster than any old-timer could recall.

Bethesda looked forward to the 1940s eagerly, confidently. The long, tiring depression was finally over; businesses were booming, and none was doing better than home construction and its many ancillaries. Every weekend apartment renters from the city and newly arrived out-of-towners flocked to see model homes in Bradley Village and Wyngate, in Bradmoor and Woodhaven Estates. The fact that many of the streets were still muddy paths or that some prices appeared way out of line did not seem to matter. First the New Deal and now the defense build-up were vastly expanding the government payrolls, and all those people had to live somewhere. Builders offered homes from $5,000 on up to three or even four times that price. All over Bethesda families awoke to the prosperous sound of hammers and saws as wooded fields and tired farms became lots and homes and neighborhoods. Infusions of government men and money stirred even sleepy Glen Echo and still more rural Cabin John.

Chevy Chase hardly seemed to notice the building boom of the late Thirties and early Forties. Some big, new homes were going up in The Hamlet, and Rollingwood spread across the steep hillsides toward Rock Creek, but they really did not count in the view of those in the "real" Chevy Chase, old Chevy Chase, the Village. Homes sprouted west of Wisconsin Avenue and along Western Avenue, but most of Chevy Chase was sedately settled, stable, restricted and planning to stay that way. Newcomers were people who had only lived in a house for ten years or so, and they often found their home called by the name of the family that had occupied it for the twenty years before they arrived. Most families in Chevy Chase did their shopping near the District Line or down on F Street and seldom traveled west to Bethesda's multiplying shops and stores. When you could get eclairs and freshly baked bread from Schupp's and have vegetables and roasts delivered from Chevy Chase Supply or Tenleytown, why would you want to drive to a DGS or Sanitary Store in Bethesda?

Every workday morning the Capital Transit buses brought dozens of African-American women in print dresses and a few black men in sturdy shoes and well-worn work clothes to stops along the east side of Connecticut and Wisconsin Avenues while other buses picked up dozens of white men in suits and a few women wearing hats, gloves and sensible shoes on the other side of the main streets. In the late afternoon the tide reversed; the white workers headed north, and the maids, cooks, laundresses, mothers' helpers, handymen and caddies went back into the city. One group of employees paid Social Security taxes while the other received "car fare" as part of their wages. This human ebb and flow had been going on long before the streetcars stopped running through Bethesda and Chevy Chase.

Bethesda was changing. A Hot Shoppe was coming to the middle of town so young couples wouldn't have to go down to the District Line or over to Connecticut and Albemarle to get their root beers, chocolate shakes, hamburgers and fries. Some of the big, downtown stores were thinking of starting branch operations on Wisconsin Avenue, and Jelleff's was well past the talking stage. The old, white, Victorian houses that once lined the main drag were disappearing one by one, and a business district with some style as well as utility was taking shape behind plate glass windows and façades of native stone.

The town growing around the crossroads bank had seen more change in the past thirty years than it had undergone in the previous three hundred. Pastures and quarries still existed and there were horses, sheep and guinea hens right in town, but even the ten-year-old Farm Women's Market was beginning to look quaint next to the new shopping center. Now the freight trains seldom chugged through town more than twice a day, but traffic on Wisconsin Avenue had grown so much that the Commissioners had imposed parking restrictions. Bethesda now had its own County Building, and its own high school, and its own newspaper. The Chamber of Commerce was even talking about incorporating with Chevy Chase to become a real city. Progress was in the air, and the Depression was just a bad memory.

When the United States entered the Second World War, I was ten and my wife-to-be was eight. She lived in the large, brick home her family had built in Chevy Chase in the early Thirties. Although we both had only one living parent, we had reasonably comfortable lives, walked to school, went to church, played with our friends, enjoyed our hobbies and rode our bikes all over the area, from the Zoo to Glen Echo. We were children of the Depression, and we grew up with the war, and like everyone else, we were changed by both experiences, by living through both of those incredible eras.

Now fifty years later, we can still go back and visit those houses and playgrounds, wander through those childhood neighborhoods and remember the way it was. Most of Chevy Chase really does not seem to have changed very much, except that the vacant lots have disappeared, and although very little of the center of Bethesda is recognizable, most of its dozens of subdivisions remain tree-shaded, flower-rich, happy places to raise children and enjoy life.

The purpose here is to share memories of Bethesda and Chevy Chase, of Cabin John and Glen Echo, of Somerset and Alta Vista and to leave a record of the way it was. The basic data, the facts about what happened, as best we can ascertain them, were found in government records and reports, in the memoirs of past and living residents, in contemporary newspaper and magazine stories and in the history books already produced about Bethesda, Chevy Chase, the Capital, the Potomac River and life in Montgomery County. The second source, more interesting and perhaps no more fallible, was the memory of men and women who lived and worked in the Bethesda area during those years and who were, generally, older than we were. The Depression, the New Deal and the war obviously meant quite different things to parents or high school students than they did to children. A surprising number of people who were living in the region in the first half of the twentieth century are still here and have been willing to share their experiences. I am sure I heard some things wrong and certain I

left many important people out, but the reason this is called a "social history" is because it is mainly the story of ordinary people, housewives and civil servants, teachers and milkmen. The final and least important part of this story is our own. I researched and wrote this, and my wife, Eda Schrader Offutt, encouraged, advised, and read all of it in several drafts; she and our daughter Kate did the long and tedious job of editing the final draft and together they made this a much better work; daughter Caroline provided vital computer support and advice, and son Bill read, commented and advised on early drafts and on the project in general while he was getting out his own book.

This second edition is a result of the remarkable popularity of the first, 2,000 copies sold in four months, and of the corrections and suggestions provided (and in a few cases, demanded) by readers. It includes a few new pictures, a bit of improved punctuation, many changes in the spelling of names and several additional facts, stories and clarifications for which the writer is grateful. Readers of this version are invited to make the next printing, if any, even more accurate and interesting.

As for defining the area included in this study, its basic dimensions are encompassed by the Seventh Election District of Montgomery County (see maps at right), the postal zones currently numbered 20812-13-14-15-16-17 and -18 and the original high school boundaries although they also included Garrett Park and Kensington. So this mainly covers from Rock Creek to the River and from the District Line to the Beltway, the same area Mrs. Bradley described. These borders are treated with flexibility as the need to deal with, for instance, Georgetown Prep, Congressional Country Club or Tenleytown arises.

The story is divided into three sections; the first is a general background that goes through the Civil War; the next part is about the building of Bethesda and the neighboring communities from the 1890s through the 1930's, and the last part is mainly about life in the Bethesda-Chevy Chase area during World War II and the role of Bethesdans in the Charter fight and other political disputes.

I thank the Montgomery County and District of Columbia librarians who were so helpful and the folks at the Montgomery County Historical Society, the Chevy Chase Historical Society and The Historical Society of Washington, D.C. In particular I wish to express my appreciation to Jane Sween, the librarian of the MCHS, whose toleration was boundless, and to Bob Truax who provided some of the best maps and photos and a lot of good advice. Eleanor Ford read an early version of the Chevy Chase chapter; Patsy Lozupone read several WW II chapters in first draft; Anne Bledsoe read the whole second draft which ran a thousand pages; Virginia Hitchcock advised on format and publishing, and Tom and Tommy Bourdeaux made many graphic and design contributions, and I thank all of them. I have nothing but admiration for the work of Edith Claude Jarvis of Chevy Chase and for the efforts of Doree Germaine Holman and Gertrude D. Bradley who together produced the original history of Bethesda. My work is built on theirs. And I owe the deepest debt of gratitude and appreciation to the dozens of people who gave many hours of their time to be interviewed, a number of them several times.

In addition to the brave fireman and hardworking volunteer previously named, this history is dedicated to all the citizens of the Bethesda area who daily cope with paying their bills and feeding their families, doing their jobs and keeping our neighborhoods such good places to live. They are what this story is about.

William M. Offutt
Bethesda
July 1995

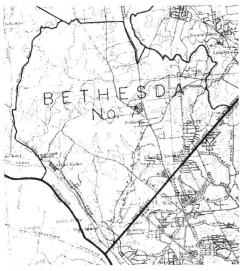

The maps on this page represent a local newspaper's overview of important places in the area at the time of the Second World War and a reasonably detailed picture of the Seventh Election District at about the time of World War I. Many more maps follow.

The interviewees - in important ways this is their story:

Leroy Allison on his family, schools and neighborhood
Stella Werner Allison on 45th Street and her mother and church
William Allman shared his research on Bethesda Park
Mrs. Herbert Angel about the Bradley Hills trolley and old Bethesda
Thomas (Loring) Appleby on his neighborhood and the high school
Charles Arnott, survivor of the `45 plane crash, several times
Alexander "Sandy" Astin on his family and school activities
William C. Austin on Woodmont and his job in Chevy Chase
Calvin Baldwin about his family, schools and the Wilsons of NIH
Thomas Jefferson Barlow on Drummond and Longfellow School, several times
Bill and **Minerva Bassett** on the Edgemoor Club and neighborhood
Leslie Bell Jr. about his family and the laundry
F. Meade Bell about his neighborhood in the late `30s
Edmund Bennett on his family, neighborhood and high school days
Robert H. Best on teaching vocational shop courses at the high school
Walter G. Birtles about his neighborhood and that plane crash
Bill Blackwood Sr. on the Chevy Chase FD and the Rescue Squad
Gertrude Bondareff on the store, her husband and their customers
Rev. William Bort on Woodmont and his hardworking family
Scott Brewer Jr. about his father, neighborhood and schools
Mrs. Ralph Broadhurst about her late husband, his family and theirs
Hugo Brooks on Bethesda in the `30s, weekly papers and old photos
Dorothy Plitt and **William A. Brown** about their neighborhoods
Mary Zimmerli Brown on sororities, B-CC HS and WW II
Howard Brubach on Glen Echo Volunteer Fire Department
Dorothy Severe Bruffey who shared her wonderful scrapbook and memories
Joseph and **Frank Cantrel** about their family and neighborhood
Austin Carlin about Bethesda when he was young
Ashby Chamberlin about Kenwood, the Club and his father
Alton Cleveland on the wartime high school and first football team
Cleveland Clipper on his family and the River Road community
Francis (Fig) Coleman about OSS training at Congressional
Kathryn Cragoe on Friendship Heights where she grew up and married
Roland W. Custer on his milk and bread routes in Bethesda
Angela Darby on the high school and the town in the 1940s
J. Slater Davidson about his family and Chevy Chase
Hartley Day on Somerset, the Montgomery Players and B-CC
Rodney Day about Woodmont, Bethesda schools and the Cavaliers
Anne Devereux about her family and life on Bradley Lane
Joseph Patrick Devereux about his father and war memories
Lois Copenhaver Dilosa on her many high school activities
Carroll "Bernie" Doyle on the Chevy Chase First Aid Corps
Shirley Dunlap and **Marjorie Solan** on the **Sonnemann** family
W. C. "Bud" Dutton about Area F and the OSS
William W. Duvall, Town of Chevy Chase historian, several times
Robert and **Nancy Hiser Eastham** about both of their fathers
Georges Edelen about the B-CC class of `42 and his leadership
Roger Eisinger Jr. on his family and the lumber business
Sumpter Embrey Jr. many times, for many hours, on all sorts of topics
Raymond L. Falge Jr. about his father's signal lamp business
Janet (Mrs. William Sharon) Farr on her mother and extended family

Charlie Federline about his father and uncle, the store and Woodmont
Earle Ferguson on Horace Smithey and the Chevy Chase Chanters
Eleanor Ford of Chevy Chase who helped and advised many times
Kenneth W. Frisbie about Friendship Heights and B-CC HS
Martha Keys Fry about public health nursing and E. M. Fry
Charlie Fuller on the Chevy Chase Dairy-Chestnut Farms story
Edward Gauvreau about life in West Chevy Chase
Arthur Gellman mainly about his father's drug store
Sister Ellen Glynn (Emmanuel Mary) on Lourdes school
Tempe Curry Grant on Battery Park, B-CC HS and local politics
Kay Greaney about B-CC HS, Mr. Pyle and the war years
Harold Greenberg on growing up in Somerset
Carroll Grenfell about the Rec Center, football and his neighborhood
Alan Hall, the sage of Battery Park, for saving hours of research
Frank Hall on the Bethesda Fire Department mostly
Loretta Tuohey Hall on Cabin John and the Volunteer Fire Dept.
Dorothy Latterner Hampton on Friendship Heights and her friends
Horace Hampton on his work and his father's contributions
A. D. "Mickey" Harris on the Glen Echo Volunteer Fire Department
Charles B. Hawley Jr. on his father's work in Bethesda
Gerald W. Hatton about his family and the River Road neighborhood
Earl Henderson mainly about the Great Falls trolley line
Ada Swigart Hess about old Somerset and her family
Lee Higgins on the Bethesda FD and living and working in old Bethesda
Earl Hill on life in Woodmont and work at the Chevy Chase Fire Department
Dorothy (Mrs. Arthur) Hilland on her mother's memoir and about her own work
Hazel Howell on her Norwood neighborhood and St. Johns, Norwood Parish
James T. Hoyle about his neighborhood and friends
Charles Hughes on Friendship Heights and B-CC HS athletics
Frederick Drum Hunt for several phone interviews about his family
John Conway Hunt who shared his research and recollections
Mrs. R. W. (Henrietta) Hunter, historian of the Newcomb Club
Mrs. John L. Imirie about her husband and their family
Millie Imirie on schools, neighborhoods, friends and family
Susan Magruder Imirie (Mrs. G. Wady) on her family and their work
Ray Jager on Leland Street, Section Four and Northwest Ford
Al Jamison, pro golfer, on Bannockburn, Kenwood and Bradley Hills
Larry Jennings about life at Leland and at B-CC HS during the war
"Mickey" (H. B.) Johnston about the Sycamore Store and neighborhood
Clarence C. Keiser Jr. mainly about his family and neighborhood
Charles Kocher on the Glen Echo VFD and the wartime newsletter
Mrs. Raymond Kohin about Battery Park and old Bethesda
Winifred Donaldson Krueger on the Shackleford store and Woodmont
Robert Lebling about B-CC High School mainly
Bill Lehr about Leland JHS, Sonoma and the Bradleys
Franklin "Zip" Lehr about the high school, his career and Mr. Pyle
Lawrence "Bootsie" Lochte about Woodmont and his family
Jane Bradley Lowe about her parents, neighborhood and schools
Frank Lozupone mainly about his family and high school days
Patsy Royster Lozupone (Mrs. Frank) about her family and friends
Louis Lozupone about Chevy Chase and B-CC HS
Isabel Gaither Lynch on the class of `44 and the yearbook she edited
Donald MacLeod (B-CC `38) on high school sports and people
Burrell Marsh on his father and his friends and schools

Peggy Evers Marsh about her parents, neighborhood and Leland JHS
Al Materazzi on OSS training at Congressional and that Italian OG
James (Rix) McAuliffe Sr. on Friendship Heights and the police force
Hon. James McAuliffe Jr. on Friendship Heights and his school days
Chet McCall Jr. on his family and high school days
Rev. William Metzel on football at B-CC and high school life
Tom Miller about Mr. Charlie Miller and his career
Thomas W. Miller (B-CC `38) about his father's driving range mainly
Billy (Mrs. Milton E.) Miles on Kenwood and many other topics
Murray Miles on Kenwood, Somerset and related areas
Betty Milne about her neighborhood, B-CC and athletics
Dr. George Mishtowt on his family and friends
Hilma Morris about her family and old Bethesda and for her pictures (see cover)
Abe Morrison, several times, for both information and advice
Kenneth Muir on his Chevy Chase neighborhood and schools
Florence O'Callaghan on Little Flower's early days
Eda Schrader Offutt, the writer's wife, about her Chevy Chase neighborhood and schools
Lillian Gloyd Offutt, the writer's mother, for stories of Glen Echo
David Simpson Orem about Chevy Chase and the Simpson clan
Kenneth Parkinson about Leland, B-CC and the first football team
Lillian Lee Philips about her family and her team sports
Carl E. "Buck" Plitt Jr. for hours on Bethesda and environs and B-CC HS
Kenny Poerstel on athletes and athletics at Leland and B-CC
Vivian Portner about her father, "Doc" Harry Gellman, and Edgemoor
Lloyd "Buzzy" Potter about his family and Cabin John
Jim Quinn on his end of Bethesda and various adventures
Robert C. Ragan about his Martin's Additions neighborhood
Robert Rickey on Leland and B-CC and the Rec Center
Celeste Lozupone Ridolfi about those houses and her family
Lois Roberts on her bookstore and other Bethesda businesses
Donald Robertson on his family's long history in Chevy Chase
Al Savage, on the phone several times, about trolley lines mainly
Mr. and Mrs. Joseph W. Scopin about their folks and neighborhoods
Henry Scott on Friendship Heights, kids' games and his paper route
William Seebold, mainly on Friendship Heights
Frances and **Leon Sherman** about the store, the war and that plane crash
Al Sherline on his high school career, athletic and otherwise
Marvin Shoemaker on Brookmont and environs, especially in World War II
Ray Shoemaker on the Shoemaker family and Bethesda in the `30s
John L. Shumate about B-CC, fraternities and basketball
Mrs. Marvin (Virginia) Simmons on the Dodge dealership and the USO
Grace and **Lewis Sims** on their volunteer work and the Charter fight
Albert R. Smith, motorman and bus driver as well as unicycle rider
John H. Smith on the trolley car conductor's job and his uncle's murder
Bill Snape about growing up in Chevy Chase and about the schools
Norma Danis Spiegel on her home, church and family
Mrs. Karl Stecher about Norwood Drive and Rollingwood
Robert Stevens on old Chevy Chase and the Bearcats
George Winchester Stone Jr. for his Martin's Additions essay and help
Reuben "Smokey" Stivers on the CCFD and growing up in Chevy Chase
John Henry Sullivan Jr. about Chevy Chase kids and fraternities
Mildred Plitt Swank on Bethesda, the Naval Hospital and the USO
Houston Swink on B-CC HS and the first football team
Mrs. Walter J. Taft and her daughter **Mary Ellen Whitcomb**

Jane Dunbar Tedeschi about Somerset and B.C.C.H.S.
Laura Tuckerman Triest on her parents, pictures and early Edgemoor
John Troth on his family, Chevy Chase and B-CC in the good old days
Robert A. Truax for maps and pictures and trolleycar lore
Ellen Bell Tuohy on growing up in Edgemoor and the USO
Mrs. C. L. "Bic" Walleigh on the old Concord Church
Mr. and Mrs. Thomas W. Walton Jr. about his father and the school
Presley Wedding about his family and the early days in Cabin John
Leonard Williams on his family, school activities and the *Thornapple Street News*
Loretta Wilson on Woodmont, the NNMC and that plane crash
Arthur Wood on getting B-CC a football team and related matters

And thanks to these folks who helped in many ways:
   Rod Alley of the Old Guard Museum at Ft. Myer on the MDW history
   Arnold "Red" Auerbach, on the phone, about high school sports
   William G. Allen who helped find Masonic information
   Larry Baume of U. S. Archives
   Pat Benton of the C&P Archives
   Max Bernhardt about the Jewish Community Group
   Thomas D. Bourdeaux, both senior and junior, for help, support and advice
   Dr. Robert Brewer on high school athletics and other activities
   Joe Burns, historian-ranger at the Clara Barton House
   William J. Cartwright, author of the wartime history of the MDW
   Kitty Clark for help and advice on the Bethesda Lutheran Church
   Betty Bender Clucas on the phone about Glen Echo Park
   Richard Cook, collector of Glen Echoiana
   Jerrod Cooper of the County Historical Trust
   Charlie Daneri who salvaged the hard disc when lightning struck
   Clarence Davis of D.C. Archives on school policies
   Michael Dwyer, the M-NCP&PC historian
   Jimmy Enright for the history of his business (and bad jokes)
   Gavin Farr for access to the Land Company records
   Wilson Lee Frazier on Sanitary and Safeway stores and John Young
   Roselle George on the Chevy Chase Land Co. maps and archives
   Jonathan Green for opening the Oakmont records
   Janice Greene who had her mother's pictures copied
   Bill Hahn of West Virginia on football in the County
   Victoria A. Harden on NIH history and tick fever research
   Joan Schrader Helms on high school life and the war
   Jan Herman of BuMed Archives for advice and photos
   LaVerne Holt of Edgemoor who wrote and, thankfully, saved
   Michelle Horowitz for help with CCLCo. records
   Milford Juten on the Brookmont Baptist Church
   Rev. Sterling King Jr. of the Macedonia Baptist Church
   Jim Kinsman, class of `40, on basketball mainly
   Jan Lazurus of the Library of Medicine for photo help
   Harry Lerch who shared his photos and interest
   Nancy Long of Glen Echo for the tour and help with the records
   Ken Luchs on the Shopping Center's history
   Harry Maginnis, historian of the Columbia Country Club
   Dr. Sam Margolis on the Bethesda Masons
   Joan Marsh of the CCHS for many kindnesses
   Hobart "Buddy" Montee, class of `41, for some high school stories
   Francis O'Shaughnessy about the Newcomb Club and library

Thomas W. Perry Jr. on Chevy Chase and his family and business
Jo Ann Pistenmaa on Kenwood and its history
West Pryce for help with TMB research and photos
Pris Reed on the Imiries and East West Highway
Jack E. Richardson and Jeff Kause of McNaughton and Gunn
Judith Helm Robinson for help and advice on houses
Miss Edith Ray Saul of Kensington who opened her memory and files
Benni Singleton of the Baptist Home for Children
James D. Sorensen, the County archeologist, for sharing resources
Leslie Strathman of Friendship Heights
Jane Sween, librarian of MCHS, generous with both advice and support
Joan McW. Weiss of Somerset for help and advice
Byron Wick for straightening out the Robert V. Bray mystery
Dr. Vivien Wiser, the USDA historian, for help several times
Marjorie Zapruder for patient help with CCHS oral histories
        and I am sure many others including the members of my family.

Finally, a note on sources. I have used a lot of local newspapers and cited them by name only. Thus *Post* and *Times-Herald*, *Star* and *Daily News* indicate Washington, D.C., papers. The *Sentinel* is a very old County paper still produced in Rockville; the *Tribune*, *Journal* and *Record* were Bethesda newspapers founded in the 1930s and `40s, and the *Maryland News* was E. Brooke Lee's Silver Spring paper. They are the source not only of much detailed information but of many photographs and opinions. The first appendix section gives credits for maps, drawings and photos.

I hope I have included footnotes for all the direct quotes that I took from other sources. Quotes without footnotes or attribution indicate material from my interviews.

CHAPTER 1

The Past, a Wooded Prologue

For thousands of years before the first Europeans came to what was to be Bethesda, men and women hunted, farmed, fished and traded along the river of swans, the brushy river, the river of trade—the Potomac. As far back as the last ice age native hunters quietly prowled the brooks and runs of the river's valley. They quarried the soapstone for utensils and flaked the quartz for weapons and tools. Before the glaciers retreated and created the Chesapeake Bay, these Paleo-Indians lived and died on the Piedmont Plateau. Perhaps 10,000 years ago, when the climate was colder and the forests were tundra-like, wandering clans built shelters in flat areas near outcroppings of valuable rock and scattered hunting camps in the nearby woods that they shared with huge mastodons, shaggy mammoths and giant beavers as well as with deer, elk and bear.

The Bethesda area's earliest human inhabitants were "selectively mobile" rather than seasonally nomadic and probably built oval-shaped dwellings near their work sites. Evidence from the Shenandoah and Delaware valleys suggests that these bands exploited various resources such as nuts, minerals, and, of course, crustaceans and fish. As the climate ameliorated, the animal population changed; the great flyways developed, and deciduous forests replaced most of the grasslands. During the Archaic period (8000 - 1000 B.C.), the population grew as food resources, especially near the Bay, increased. Notched and serrated points replaced the old Clovis or fluted types, and new tools such as axes and soapstone bowls made life easier. In the Woodland Period (1000 B.C. to 1600 A.D.), more sedentary settlements grew along river systems, and some permanent

villages developed although hunting and fishing camps were still in use. Georgetown and Anacostia were among the sites of large Indian settlements, and in the Bethesda region, archeologists have found evidence of permanent hamlets in the Glen Echo and Cabin John areas and of smaller camps along the Potomac from Great Falls to Little Falls.

As the cool, moist climate warmed toward present levels, modern fauna filled the woods, and Indians cleared some land for agriculture. Long before the time of maize, squash and European contact, Native American farmers in eastern North America independently domesticated several flood plain seed plants, and small plots of cleared land sprouted various crops before the days of tobacco monoculture.[1]

The bow and arrow entered this culture about 800 A.D., and hunting continued to be a basic activity at the time of the *Ark* and the *Dove*. Clay vessels gradually replaced stone jars and supplemented woven baskets. Late in the Woodland period, large villages and complex trade networks rose and fell. Some of the Potomac-region Indians built drying racks, refuse pits and defensive stockades along with rectangular houses of vertical pole construction which they roofed with mats. Population pressures and competition for land and resources led to conflicts between the developing tribes.

Finally the Algonquin speakers and river namers–the Piscataways, Nacostines, Nanticokes, Potopacos, Anacostans, Patuxents, Mattawomans, and Potomacs–settled in the great mixed forest and raised corn, beans and tobacco around their villages. Other members of

this large family of tribes regularly visited hunting camps or built V-shaped fish traps in the river on a seasonal schedule.

By the time the Europeans arrived, war and disease had drastically reduced the Native Americans' numbers, and they had abandoned almost all of their villages. The Indian population would decline much more rapidly thereafter as new ills and better weapons arrived in what the white men decided was a barely inhabited New World.[2]

A year after the settlement of Jamestown, Captain John Smith and his freebooting shipmates reconnoitered the land along the river as far upstream as Little Falls where "they met several Parties of Indians in Canoes, loaded with the Flesh of Bears, Deer and other wild Beasts." Smith, one of history's most self-serving and creative storytellers, wrote that the natives entertained his men at villages along the river's shore. He also claimed that the Potomac contained an "abundance of fish lying so thick with their heads above water, as for want of nets . . . we attempted to catch them with a frying pan."

In his *Generall Historie*, Smith described the river above the Three Sisters as making "his passage down a low pleasant valley overshadowed in many places with high rocky mountains; from whence distill innumerable sweet and pleasant springs." He also found a small Indian settlement below the falls on the narrow shelf along the river's northern side before he headed back to Jamestown.

The most likely candidate as first European resident of the Bethesda region is the fur trader Henry Fleet. In 1624, after deciding that he would rather not deal with "a strange and populous nation, called Mowhaks, man-eaters," he sailed up the "Patowmack" to Tohoga, generally considered to be the site of Georgetown, and then some four miles farther to Great Falls.

We came to an anchor two leagues short of the Falls, being in the latitude of 41, on the 26th of June. This place without all question is the most pleasant and healthful place in all this country, the most convenient for habitation, the air temperate in summer and not violent in winter. It aboundeth with all manner of fish...And as for deer, buffaloes, bears, turkeys, the woods do swarm with them, and the soil is exceedingly fertile, but above this place the soil is rocky and mountainous like Cannida.

The next day he took his shallop and "went up with the flood, the tide rising about four feet in height at this place. We had not rowed above three miles, but we might hear the Falls to roar..." For two years Henry Fleet lived with the Piscataways as their guest or prisoner; it is difficult to tell which. On his return to England he told stories of fur-rich tribes who sprinkled their pictures with gold. Eager entrepreneurs soon financed his return to the New World.[3]

Fleet (sometimes Fleete) found the Indians along the Potomac, especially those who had dealt with the French, hard bargainers. These people, he wrote in his journal, "delight not in toys, but in useful commodities . . . hatchets and knives of large size, broadcloth, and coats, shirts, and Scottish stockings." He called the Indians Nascotines, the basis for the names of Anacostia and Analostan.

Publication of his descriptions of the Potomac basin encouraged many to emigrate to Lord Baltimore's new colony. Leonard Calvert, the first governor, found Fleet at a village on the Piscataway Creek early in 1634. Or perhaps Fleet found Calvert. Fleet acted as interpreter for the colonists and then returned to the Potomac's mouth to build on 2,000 acres granted him by the proprietor. He was a member of Maryland's legislature in 1638, and later moved to Virginia where he won election to the House of Burgesses in 1652.[4]

In Maryland's early colonial days, relations with the Indians were reasonably good while relations with the William Claiborne-led Virginians were generally bad as settlements spread up both sides of the great Chesapeake Bay and along the banks of the streams that fed it. Many of the peaceful Piscataways became Christians, but as exploring farmers and traders moved up the Patuxent and Potomac, they bumped into the Senecas, whose way of life they disrupted. The Senecas and the Susquehannocks of the North were more warlike groups, and skirmishes with the Piscataways and the settlers led to an all-out conflict in the 1670s and to Bacon's Rebellion.[5]

Soon troops of "Rangers" patrolled the Potomac and Patuxent basins. They were led by men like the powerful, red-haired Scottish Puritan Ninian Beall, who had come to America as an indentured prisoner of war, and Col. John Addison, a gentleman and trader who built a

fort at the mouth of Rock Creek and a road to the tamer and more settled coastal plain. These men were among the first to establish land claims in the backwoods frontier, areas which were not considered safe for settlement before 1685. Troubles of various kinds continued into the 1690s, when Prince George's County was established including the New Scotland Hundred, which extended from Oxon Branch to beyond the Falls of the Potomac. The only government officials on the frontier were the Constables, the Pressmasters who rounded up men for the militia in times of trouble, and the Overseers of highways and pathways.[6]

By the time the Proprietor started making land grants in what was to become Montgomery County, the Indians' day was just about over. The few suvivors retreated into the blue hills leaving behind trails, which became the beds of roads such as Wisconsin Avenue, River Road and Old Georgetown Road, piles of oyster shells and arrow points for children to discover and wonder on, many abandoned quarries in Rock Creek Park-to-be, the remains of enough hunting camps to keep archeologists employed and a lot of place names. At the dawn of the 18th century, they were barely a memory.[7]

Generally, the Calverts did not sell their land to those who came to live in their prospering colony. At first, at the rate of fifty acres per immigrant, they parceled it out on the basis of how many settlers a squire brought with him in something like the Dutch patroon system being practiced in the New Netherlands. Later settlers could have title to one hundred acres–another hundred if married, plus fifty acres per child or servant.

The Lords Proprietor collected a "quitrent" or tax on the land each year, whether the property produced income or not. This permanent rent, unrelated to the value of the land, made Maryland less attractive than some other tobacco colonies and limited speculation on frontier territory. Because of this system, owners delayed surveying and patenting most Montgomery County land grants, and tenants worked Bethesda-area farms for many decades. Speculators sometimes held warrants for years, complicating land claims and slowing the settlement of western parts of Maryland.[8]

The first recorded land grant in what is now Bethesda was probably "Forrest," surveyed for Colonel Henry Darnall in 1694 along with "Girl's Portion," which included most of what is now Silver Spring. Darnall's 710-acre "Forrest" extended two miles west of Rock Creek across the route of both the Rockville Pike and the older road to Georgetown. About half of this grant became Andrew Heugh's "Leeke Forest" in 1772. Colonel Darnall, related by marriage to Charles Calvert, the 3rd Lord Baltimore, as well as to Thomas Brooke, the Brents and the Carrolls, became keeper of the great seal of Maryland and owner of some 27,000 acres including estates called "My Lord's Kindness," "Darnall's Delight," and "Joseph's Park."[9]

Next came "Dan," Thomas Brooke's 6,797-acre grant north of Leeke Forest, and "Clean Drinking" to the south, a 700-acre tract patented to John Coats (or perhaps Coates or Courts) in 1699. It extended down Rock Creek to the area where Walter C. Jones later had his mill and bridge, still recalled in road names.

Thomas Addison and James Stoddard patented "Friendship" in 1711. This 3,124-acre tract north of Tenleytown extended from the Potomac River to the center of Bethesda. Thomas Fletchall was another of the major, early landowners in the Bethesda area. With Charles Beale he controlled 419 acres, called "Charles and Thomas" east of "Friendship" and another 1,368 acres, also called "Friendship," to the northwest. By 1715 Fletchall had title to "Clagett's Purchase," the 772 acres west of "Clean Drinking" and south of "Leeke Forest," which included much of what became downtown Bethesda, plus a 307-acre parcel called "Huntington" along the old road to Georgetown.

West of Fletchall's property was "Contention," 620 acres patented to William Fitz Redman. North into what was called New Scotland and then Offutt's Crossroads and still later Potomac, William Offutt had the 600-acre "Clewerwell" grant recorded in 1714. The descendants of his eleven sons and daughters intermarried with the Magruders, Clagetts, Bealls and Peters. "Clewerwell" was the first of a group of Offutt properties including "Outlett" and "Bear Den" that eventually totaled more than 3,000 acres and included a Potomac island that continues to carry the family name. A bit later, in 1725, rambunctious Joseph Belt, a third generation colonist, patented his grant as "Chevie Chace," 560 acres, later enlarged to a thousand, on both sides of what would be called the District Line.[10]

This western part of the Maryland colony was still real frontier in 1700 although most of

the trappers, fur traders and would-be gold miners had passed on through by then. Behind them came some poor families, slash and burn farmers, indentured men and women who had served their time and now chanced squatters' or tenants' uncertain rights. And then the planters with their slaves and servants and the speculators with their claims and hopes arrived. What drove them all was tobacco, which was wearing out the early-settled lands downriver. For the next hundred years, tobacco was the crop, the hope, the wealth, the curse and even the medium of exchange.

Tobacco, the Redman's revenge, consumed the plantations and burnt up the soil so farmers constantly cleared more land. Woodlots also came crashing down to make hogsheads and curing barns. Farmers widened Indian trails into rolling roads that led to the shipping points on the alluvial coastal plain. Taxes were paid in tobacco; land was sold for tobacco; ministers were hired for tobacco, and dowries were offered in tobacco.

Villages along the Potomac became centers of the tobacco trade. Among the busiest were Upper Marlboro, Port Tobacco, and Georgetown. Much of the land that became Georgetown was originally deeded to Ninian Beall in 1703. Beall, commander of Maryland's Rangers and other military forces since 1699, called his 795-acre tract "Rock of Dunbar-ton." Famous Dumbarton Oaks, originally "Acropholous," was built on a small part of that grant.

In 1751, by an act of the Maryland General Assembly, George Town was laid out on sixty acres purchased from tobacco merchants George Gordon and George Beall, Ninian's youngest son. Whether the town named "George," but usually called Rock Creek Landing, honored the King or the tobacco traders was open to dispute. The colonial government authorized two annual fairs of three days each beginning on the second Thursday in April and the first Thursday of October during which those attending were to be free from arrest, "except for felony and breach of the peace."[11]

Georgetown prospered from the tobacco brought down the rolling roads from farms in the Bethesda area and farther north. Like many other middle-colony towns, it rose on the Fall Line where the rolling Piedmont Plateau met the broad coastal plain. At one time its wharves and warehouses were among the busiest in Maryland, indeed it was a world leader

in the tobacco trade. London preferred Virginia leaf, but Maryland growers found a ready market for their product in Scottish and Cumbrian ports after 1730. When Virginia adopted Governor Gooch's strict inspection system in 1730, Georgetown's trade declined, but in 1747 the Maryland legislature passed a Tobacco Inspection Act with stations at Bladensburg and at the Rock Creek landing. Trade revived, and more substantial brick houses went up along hilly streets.[12]

Of course, there soon were businessmen, factors and merchants, who served the farmers by extending credit on future crops, by buying their leaf and selling them goods and by providing warehousing and insurance. Many of these men were Scots, and it was not long before falling crop prices and growing debts led to bad blood between the planters and the merchants. Mutual distrust, followed by name calling and finger pointing, grew to be the norm of their symbiotic relationship. "The Scotch accent was regarded as an abomination, and Scotch tutors deplored." One planter swore that he would never speak to his sister should she marry a Scot and that if his daughter ever married a Scotsman, he would shoot her dead at once.[13]

It was this trade with Glasgow that brought Scottish factors to the port on Rock Creek, and soon planters could procure goods cheaper for tobacco than for gold. Bethesda's Presbyterian and suburban roots rest with the tobacco traders and other wealthy Georgetowners who used its breezy hills as a summer retreat.

The Glasgow firm of John Glassford and Company was one of the largest players in the American tobacco trade. Glassford's Georgetown factor was one Robert Peter, and both the company and Mr. Peter profited greatly from business ventures and land investments as well as from the trade in tobacco, wheat and iron.[14]

For early residents of what would become Bethesda, Georgetown was the center of economic life. Some nabobs thought the town's future rested on western development and on wheat and flour and, perhaps, on mineral riches yet undeveloped, and Scottish merchants did not overlook land speculation in the West. The Ohio County called, and various road building, river dredging and canal digging projects were soon afoot. In the 1770s in both Virginia and Maryland, legislators introduced measures to open the Potomac from Fort Cumberland to the Tidewater. One Maryland *Gazette* advertiser

sarcastically suggested that those who wanted a road to Sugarloaf Mountain were thinking too small and should instead plan a hundred-foot-wide highway to California. The whole thing was a "sugarloaf" to him.

Trustees of this early canal scheme included Thomas Johnson, George Washington and a long list of western landowners and merchants from Georgetown and Alexandria, and by 1775 British engineers were clearing some of the Little Falls obstructions, while in Boston that spring other matters regarding trade came to take precedence.

Robert Peter, Georgetown's first mayor, was born near Glasgow in 1726 and came to America as a factor representing Glassford interests. The 1756 tax list "of bachelors in Prince George's parish twenty-five years and upwards" valued his estate at £300. By 1757 he was a member of the town's board of commissioners and by 1764 a justice in the County court. Another Glassford representative, Andrew Heugh, also served on the Frederick County Court and was elected to the House of Delegates. He built and retired to a country home on his Leeke Forest property in what became the Alta Vista area of yet-to-be-named Bethesda.[15]

In 1774, as the revolutionary fever raged through Maryland, the local branch of the Sons of Liberty, the non-importation enforcers, visited Robert Peter when a cargo of tea arrived for him. He was able to satisfy the group that he was no Tory, and the brig *Mary and Jane* escaped the fiery fate of the *Peggy Stewart*. During the Revolution, both Peter and Heugh bought up their employers' property to save it from being confiscated, and during the war, Peter purchased land taken from Loyalists such as Dulaney and Addison to add to his own copious estate.

In 1776, the Maryland legislature divided Frederick County, which had been cut from Prince George's in 1748, into three parts and named the southern section for the brave 39-year-old Irishman, General Richard Montgomery, killed in the attack on Quebec on the last day of 1775. The other part was named for General Washington. At that time, perhaps two dozen families lived and farmed in the area now known as Bethesda. The ride from Georgetown to Fredericktown was mainly through woods and open fields with an occasional tavern along the way. And in 1776, in the first and only colonial census of the Lower Potomac Hundred, the area from Hungerford's Tavern (Rockville) south to the river including George Town contained 912 white persons in about 220 families plus 616 black men, women and children listed by first names only.[16]

After Independence Robert Peter became a leading promoter of Georgetown's growth. He stayed in the tobacco trade, selling on consignment for commission and buying directly from Montgomery County farmers. At the first tax census in 1782, he was by far the richest man in Georgetown and the largest property owner in the County with over 20,000 acres including quite a few farms in the Bethesda area. Only five others owned more than 3,000 acres.

In the Bethesda-Chevy Chase area, few houses remain from this pre-Revolutionary period. Most of the early planters built little more than simple cabins with slope-roofed front porches and sleeping lofts. The materials were those at hand—sometimes brick, often stone, usually timber, sometimes planked. Many homes had log sides and brick or stone ends for chimneys. Sod roofs were not unknown, but shingles were more common. Two rooms at first, with perhaps an ell added later or a summer kitchen, these plantation houses were hardly the stuff of romantic novels or ante-bellum dreams.

The oldest house in Bethesda is probably Milton, or at least a part of it. Nathan Loughborough purchased the land in 1808, and his overseer used the existing, small, granite house. Loughborough, who did not seem to mind how his name was spelled, had come to Washington as the acting comptroller of the Treasury when the government moved to the Federal City.

He bought 250 acres in the general area of what is now American University and built his fine home, which he called Grassland. There he farmed and raised horses and fought the tax collectors, claiming that there should be "no taxation without representation" in D.C. Loughborough was a stockholder in the C&O Canal and the Farmers and Mechanics National Bank as well as one of the promoters of the Rockville Pike and later president of the company that built it. During the War of 1812, he served in Major George Peter's regiment and

may have hidden a British sailor who later became an American citizen. Knowing his love of horse flesh, his friend John Randolph presented him with the great Rob Roy who sired many fine Maryland horses.[17]

When Nathan Loughborough's wife died in 1844 after bearing him thirteen children, he married Robert Dunlop's widowed sister, Mrs. John Magill Thomas, and gave Grassland to his son Hamilton. His second wife bore him two children; James, who became a minister, and Elizabeth, who married J. H. Bradley Jr., and thereby united three great Bethesda estates.

Loughborough moved to Milton with his second wife and added a large center section and a west wing for a formal dining room in 1847. He had them constructed of rough stone to match the much older, original structure, which was probably a Dutch trading post and tavern built around 1700 on an even older Indian camp site. A tunnel connected the two wings and produced some strange stories in later years. Until the Civil War, Loughborough also operated a good-sized mill on the adjacent Falls Branch less than a half mile west of the house. Drunken soldiers destroyed it, and then the "Johnstown" flood washed away what was left.[18]

Nathan Loughborough died in 1852, and his son Hamilton purchased Milton and 117 acres from his step-mother, Margaret. At the time of Lincoln's assassination, someone accused Hamilton of hiding Booth, and soon after he suffered a stroke from which he never recovered. After the Civil War his son James, who served with Jackson, Early and Lee, reportedly gave plots of land to many of the Loughborough slaves freed by the State Constitution of 1864.

The house stayed in the family until James Loughborough, utterly unreconstructed, died in 1921, and his widow sold the property and twenty-one acres to a real estate broker. Milton, once a decaying derelict and neighborhood haunted house, survived thanks to restoration work by the remarkable agricultural economist and New Dealer Mordecai Ezekial. Milton still rides its wooded hill just west of River Road tucked into a far corner of Green Acres.[19]

Hayes Manor is, according to sagacious Roger Brooke Farquhar, "unsurpassed anywhere in Montgomery County." The Reverend Alexander Williamson built the center section of this imposing Georgian brick colonial in 1762. Parson Williamson bought half of the Clean Drinking grant, 700 acres, from his friend Charles Jones and had his home built by English masons from local brick. It was about halfway between his St. Paul's Church on Rock Creek and his chapel at Rockville. The masons used the Flemish bond on the ends, but on the south-facing front and the back of the house, only the headers were exposed.

Williamson was "a learned, witty and elegant clergyman but addicted to all the vices then common among gentlemen and he built the house in order that he might entertain in a manner suited to his taste and means..." The vestrymen of Rock Creek Parish, created in 1726, had the power to levy a tax of "so much Tobacco as will enable said Parish to build a church the sum not to exceed 20,000 lbs. of Tobacco." In fact, the "545 taxables" produced only about that much tobacco each year. Loyal to King George, Williamson lost his parish in the Revolution, died in 1787, and was probably buried on the property.[20]

James Dunlop, a Scot and cousin of Robert Peter, bought the house at auction. He had come to America in 1771, succeeded in business, and married Peter's oldest daughter, Elizabeth, in 1787. It was one of their daughters who was Nathan Loughborough's second wife. (The tangled web of intermarriages among the leading families of the area has maddened many genealogists as has the predilection for cousins marrying each other.) The home stayed in the Dunlop family well into the 20th century although the Chevy Chase Land Company bought

Milton when it was the Loughborough Mansion

all but twenty-six acres of the property in 1890.

In 1894 George T. Dunlop Sr. built the two-story east wing of kitchen and servants' quarters, and his son added the west wing sunroom fourteen years later. The two wings are of matching Baltimore brick with all headers exposed. Secretary of the Interior Harold Ickes rented the stately home during Franklin Roosevelt's administration.

Of Hayes Manor's original neighbor, Clean Drinking Manor, nothing remains but the owner's name in Jones Bridge and Jones Mill Roads. The property, granted to Colonel John Courts by William and Mary, was patented in 1699. Courts' grandson Charles Jones, who became one of Montgomery County's first justices in

1776, built the house of two and a half stories with brick ends for the fireplaces. Originally there was one large room on the ground floor of the manor plus slave quarters, a sunken garden, a detached kitchen, a family burial plot and, of course, a mill. George Washington may have rested there on his way home after Braddock's 1755 defeat, and some government officials took refuge at the manor when the British burned the capital in August 1814.

The last Jones on the property was Nicholas, a stubborn recluse who would not allow visitors or repairs but kept the huge, brass doorknobs polished. When he died in 1911, the house, which had long before lost its top floor to a fire, was tumbling down around him, but its chimneys stood along the lilac-bordered road long after the home disappeared.

Edith Claude Jarvis, an early chronicler of Chevy Chase, remembered the small manor house in "its decaying stages."

As a small child of five, I remember driving by horse and carriage with my mother, who frequently packed and delivered a market basket of food for the lonely old and unkempt man. I remember his yellow cat, "Lancaster," a creature as odoriferous as his master. On the other hand I remember too the wonderful fragrance of the lilacs and the pungent smell of the ancient box as we approached the house...

Today my two lilac bushes; a white and a lavender, which were transplanted from "Clean Drinking Manor" in 1918, bloom each spring, and I never fail to associate them in my mind with my childhood visits to old "Nick" Jones, the lonely old hermit.[21]

Another late visitor to the old manor house was Ada Swigert Hess who was born in Somerset in 1903:

My cousin Ada King, who lived in Georgetown, had a horse and carriage, and she used to come out and get my mother and me and drive us over to Clean Drinking to call on Mr. Nicholas Jones. We never got inside the house, but we got to sit on the porch. I was a little girl.[22]

In 1916, Captain and Mrs. Chester Wells purchased a hundred acres of the old grant and had John Russell Pope, who had designed the National Gallery, the Archives building and the Jefferson Memorial, build them a fine, 10,000 square-foot mansion, which they called Woodend. Some essence of Clean Drinking Manor survives at Mount Vernon where part of one of the outbuildings was constructed of ancient bricks salvaged from the site.[23]

The most fortunate survivor of these old Bethesda houses is Samuel Wade Magruder's Locust Grove which still stands just west of Montgomery Mall. By all rights, it should be no more than a memory. The house very likely holds the Bethesda-area record for the number of times it was sold at auction. Magruder, like Jones, was a justice in Montgomery County's first court and a leading member of a large, complex and rather contentious family. He probably built his house shortly after his marriage and just before the Revolution at the center of his 300-acre farm.[24]

A descendant of the Alexander Magruder shipped to America in 1651 as a Scottish war prisoner, Samuel Wade served in the French and Indian Wars and was a major in the War for Independence. He married Col. Ninian's granddaughter, Lucy Beall, and his name and hers ring through all local histories.

We know much of the early days of this house because William Wirt, later Attorney General of the United States, boarded there while a student at nearby Tusculum Academy; and kept a remarkable journal.

The Magruders, at that time, formed a numerous family in that county. The original name, I have heard, was Macgregor of Scotland, and the ancestors are said to have sought a refuge in this country, after the defeat at Culloden. The Major showed marks of Highland extraction. He was large, robust, and somewhat corpulent, with a round, florid face, short, curling, sandy hair, and blue-grey eyes...He was a magistrate and ex-officio a conservator of the peace, which, however, he was as ready, on provocation, to break as to preserve...

I remember (his voice) as the loud north wind that used to rock the house and sweep the snow covered field. The mansion was a large, two-storied brick house, built not long before I went there (in 1783). In this his family proper lived. Within a few feet of it stood the old house, which had been the former residence of the family, but which was now occupied, at one end, by the overseer, and in the residue of its chambers by the school boys and the two apprentices. Here, at night, we got our lessons and more frequently played our pranks.

When the leader of the Tusculum School, the Reverend James Hunt, had his mind set on it, the whole school would go trooping on foot through the woods with the Master in front leading the way to Rockville. When they arrived at the Courthouse, they entered the courtroom very gravely and sat down in the empty jury box. Government and the law were studied firsthand.

In the summer of 1939, piano teacher Doree Germaine Holman, who was writing a series of articles about "Old Bethesda" for the new Bethesda *Journal*, went looking for signs of the old school.

Last week under the guidance of Mrs William Renshaw, who used to own the farm, and her daughter Miss Mamie, we drove around the place.

To reach it one can go to Alta Vista and turn on Cedar Lane or go out the Boulevard and turn in the road marked National Skeet Club. The skeet club leases part of the farm from the present owner, Mr. Fleming Newbold, and the clubhouse was once the Renshaw barn.

We went on past the clubhouse and turned West beside a corn field to the ridge where tradition says the school was located. The Hunt house was to the East of the club house and up to a very short while ago its big brick chimneys stood in the grove, mute reminders of an active past.

Miss Holman also visited the Magruder home.

If one follows Old Georgetown Road to what used to be called Beane Post Office and turns left, he will find himself on narrow, twisting Bell's Mill Road. There is a saying in Maryland that if a road is very crooked it shows that it is descended from private roads that took their way carefully between fields and were thrown together as need arose. There used to be a number of very old houses on the

road and one of those still standing is the red brick house of Major Samuel Wade Magruder...

Today the old house looks inviting. It is approached by a long straight lane and sits in a green lawn with towering trees. A string of barns and out-buildings gives it the appearance of a little settlement...

Locust Grove, with its typically Southern center-hall design, was built of red brick laid in the Flemish bond. Three fireplaces served the first floor, but none were built on the second which must have made for cold winter mornings in the bedrooms. A kitchen wing was added sometime in the 19th century.[25]

By 1783, Samuel Wade Magruder owned more than 1,100 acres in the new Montgomery County. The mill on the property, located on Cabin John Creek at about Seven Locks Road, was, according to the *Star*'s Rambler who photographed it in 1919, "grinding wheat and corn and sawing timber long before the American Revolution." Samuel Wade died in 1792. His estate included twenty slaves, two of whom were carpenters, seven horses, a number of other animals, three looking glasses, one old still, a weaver's loom and six linen wheels. His quiet, gentle wife died three years later leaving the house and land to three young sons.

Problems arose over guardianships and executors of the estate, and in 1801 a court order divided the land into three unequal portions. Lloyd, the youngest of the heirs, received Locust Grove and three hundred acres. In 1803 he married Elizabeth Magruder, became involved in the sale of tobacco abroad, and began living in a high style on borrowed money with his front door, literally, almost always open.

After his death at 55 in 1836, leaving behind seven minor children, his second wife's relatives forced the sale of his property to satisfy his debts. In February 1838, John A. Carter, who had married Lloyd's daughter Mary Catherine, bought the house, the grist and saw mills and 300 acres for $4,500 at public auction with three promissory notes. In 1853 Locust Grove was again on the sheriff's auction block, and the Carter family was somewhere in Arkansas. William Orndorff bought the property for $7,850 and worked the mills and the farm profitably with his slaves and sons through the Civil War. According to the 1860 census his property was worth $14,000.

After the end of slavery in Maryland and the end of the Civil War, the farm and the house deteriorated rapidly. In the 1870 census it was valued at only $1,000, and by the time Orndorff died in 1874, Locust Grove was falling apart. Appraisers found the brick in very bad condition with the "east end propped to be kept from falling out..." Orndorff's nine children and their wives quarreled over the property, and the court finally ordered it divided and sold to settle the estate.

The mill went to George Bell, and his name stuck to it and the road that survives in that area although some sources suggest that it may have been Beall's Mill at one time. Miss Holman traced the succession and marveled, "It takes an old resident to point out the mill site. An account of its sales takes on the rhythm of 'The House That Jack Built': Maj. Samuel Wade Magruder to son Lloyd; Lloyd to John Carter; Carter to Orndorff; Orndorff to Bell; Bell to Bradley; Bradley to Williams. And that's the way Bell's Mill Road got its name."

After two unsuccessful auctions, the trustees sold Locust Grove and 260+ acres to a Tenleytown farmer for $4,835, which he borrowed from a Georgetown miller. The miller sold the house and land at auction in 1890 for $7,057.10 to a couple of entrepreneurs who were planning a trolley line and a new town with Locust Grove at its center. This sale was the old house's luckiest break. The walls and chimneys were repaired; a new roof was built over six new courses of brick, and very likely, the front porch was added.

But the grandiose plans of the Tenallytown and Rockville Land Company collapsed along with Bethesda Park and John E. Beall's hopes, and the house was auctioned again in 1898 and went through a series of owners in dizzying succession until it was purchased by Robert D. Weaver of Georgetown in 1901.[26]

Stoneyhurst, another Bethesda house that is probably pre-Revolutionary, was built by a Magruder who acquired the land from his father, who had inherited about 300 acres, parts of "Honesty" and "Samuel's Delight," from Ninian Magruder Senior. The Magruders were, in Roger Brooke Farquhar's words, one of the most vigorous clans ever to come from Scotland, "and they have made, and are still making, history." Samuel Magruder of Ninian, sometimes called

Samuel the Third, was a leader in the patriot cause, and his son, Samuel Brewer, served in the Continental Army.

When Samuel of Ninian died in 1786 he left his wife, Margaret, "my dwelling plantation with 200 acres of land" plus some slaves. His son, Samuel Brewer, inherited the tract later called Stoneyhurst. The rough stone building there has walls twenty inches thick, paneled window jambs, and a wide porch and dormer windows on the third floor. The property passed through several hands and then in 1904 it went from Joshua N. Offutt to Lilly C. Stone whose family operated four quarries in the Cabin John Valley.

On the same property at Seven Locks and River Road is a small, stone blacksmith shop that may be a bit older since there is some evidence that Ninian Magruder built it. His initials are cut into the chimney. The shop or house has had many owners since his time. The area was once called Embrey's Corner for a Maria Embrey who owned the place for many years in the late 19th and early 20th centuries. Like the Magruders, their houses are survivors.

There is at least one other house in Bethesda that can claim roots in the Revolution, but it is more famous as the site of Uncle Tom's cabin. The house to which the cabin that may have been Josiah Henson's home is attached was probably built by a Revolutionary War soldier. Its construction certainly places it in that time period. It has the typical, large stone fireplace, oak cellar beams with bark on three sides, and wide, white pine board flooring.[27]

The Luxmanor Corporation acquired the farm about 1920 and sold it to William and Levina Bolten in 1936. The Boltens had the house remodeled with the help of Lorenzo Winslow, one time architect of the White House.

Colonel Joseph Belt's property, which he named after a ballad commemorating a bloody 1388 border battle between the Percy spearmen and the Douglas archers ("Of fifteen hundred Englishmen, went home but fifty-three; the rest were slain in Chevie Chace, under the greenwood tree."), included an Indian trail that became the route of Belt Road. Belt's brick home, at about Connecticut and Oliver, stood until 1907, and the large, frame house that his son

Thomas built on the Maryland side of the line lasted from about 1747 until it burned in 1921.

In 1815 the Bradley family purchased that house and some 200 acres from trustees Philip Barton Key and John W. Clagett for $3,250. Chevy Chase, as the house was called, had a mansard-style roof and a large second floor porch. Abraham Bradley V, who was Assistant Postmaster General at the time, helped move the Post Office and all its records from Philadelphia to Washington in 1800.

According to Bethesda historian Doree Holman, the Bradley's home "became famous for its quiet, cordial hospitality. We can be sure that men in official life became familiar with the hills and turns in the road leading out to the farm." During the British invasion of 1814, a number of cabinet members stayed there along with their departments' papers.

Joseph Bradley inherited the house and farm on his father's death and lived there until he died in 1884. He was a graduate of Yale, a Washington lawyer, a good farmer, and president of the Rockville Fair credited with restoring the fair's buildings after the Civil War. Eventually the Bradley's manse became the home of the Chevy Chase Club. A fire destroyed most of it after the new clubhouse opened, and only the large chimney, a few hand-hewn beams, and some of the wisteria survived.

Joseph Belt and his father-in-law are remembered on two huge stones. One is in Georgetown and the other rests in front of All Saints Church on the west side of Chevy Chase Circle. Attached to this large, grey-brown boulder is a bronze plaque placed there in 1911 by the Society of Colonial Wars of the District of Columbia. It reads:[28]

COLONEL JOSEPH BELT
1680 Maryland 1761
Patentee of " Cheivy Chace"
Trustee of the First Free Schools in Maryland
One of the Founders of Rock Creek Parish
Member of the House of Burgesses
Colonel of Prince George's County Militia
During the French and Indian War

[1] Four plants underwent morphological changes to become full domesticates: *Curcubita pepo*
-squash, *Iva annua*-marshelder or sumpweed, *Helianthus annuus*-sunflower and *Chenopodium
berlandieri*-chenopod or goosefoot plus three others: erect knotweed, little barley and
maygrass. See Bruce D. Smith's work summarized in *Anthro Notes*, Spring 1993.

[2] In *The Potomac* (1949,`77,`86) Frederick Gutheim wrote: "The very name Potomac in the Algonkin
tongue is a verbal noun meaning 'something bought,' and as a designation for a place, 'where
something is bought,' or more freely 'trading place.'" Potomac, spelled more than a dozen
different ways, also suggests river of small fry where fishes spawn, traveling traders, and the
burning pine or council fire (cf. Burning Tree). See Paul Metcalf's *Waters of the Potomac* (1982)
and "Pre-Contact Indians of Montgomery County" by Mark Walston, *Montgomery County Story*,
Vol.29 No.1, Feb. 1986. See also James D. Sorensen's paper "The Piedmont and Coastal Plain
Provinces of Maryland: A Culture History," (1982) Catholic University of America.

[3] The woodlands' Piscataways were also called Conoys, or Konoi, Kanawha, Canawese and Ganawais,
which says something about both the English ear and Elizabethan spelling.

[4] Labeled "unscrupulous" by historian Aubrey Land, Fleet or Fleete tramps off into the unexplored
West. See MacMaster and Hiebert, *A Grateful Remembrance* (1976).

[5] The remains of a very old (circa 1600 B.C.) Susquehanna Soapstone Culture camp have been
excavated on Ruppert Island near Glen Echo, and in 1983-86 a small, tool-making camp was
found near Wisconsin Avenue on the Medical Library campus by builders of the Woodmont
Avenue extension. Lloyd "Buzzy" Potter excavated a Rock Run village on high ground east of
TMB (Site 22 in the State list) which is now covered by the Carderock interchange.

[6] Beall fought for Charles II at the Battle of Dunbar in 1650, and Cromwell sold him into servitude.
As a political prisoner he may have been sent to Ireland or the Barbados first, but he was in
Maryland by 1658 and at the time of the Restoration commanded the colony's forces. For more
see Guy Castle's "The Washington Area between 1608 and 1708" in the *Records of the Columbia
Historical Society*, 1963-1965. For a list of those officials in the early days see Castle's essay.

[7] Descendants of the Piscataways still live in Montgomery, Prince George's, and Charles counties.
See Henry Scarupa's "New Identity for Maryland's Indians" in *The Sun Magazine*, Jan. 11, 1976.
For more on local Indian sites see *AncientWashington* by Robert L. Humphrey and Mary
Elizabeth Chamber in the GW series, n.d. For more on Ninian Beall see Caleb Clarke Magruder
essay "Colonel Ninian Beall" in the *Records of the Columbia Historical Society*, 1937.

[8] See the first chapter of *A Grateful Remembrance* and of *Montgomery County: A Pictorial History*
by Coleman and Lewis (1984) for more on early colonial history.

[9] "Col. Henry Darnall and His Family" by Elizabeth Duhamel in the *Records of the Columbia
Historical Society*, 1924.

[10] Scharf's *History of Western Maryland* (1882) has many land grant descriptions with surveys that
often start with phrases such as "beginning at a bound hickory, standing on a ridge between the
branches of Rock Creek and Potomac River, near a great rock..."

[11] For more on land grants see the 1882, two volume *History of Western Maryland* by J. Thomas
Scharf and T. H. S. Boyd's centennial history and directory of Montgomery County issued in
1879 and reprinted in 1976. Beall's claim was a Scot's pun and was changed to Dumbarton about
1800. By the time of his death in 1717, Beall owned some 25,000 acres.
Doree Germaine Holman is one who argues for it being named for the two Georges who had the
land "convenient" for a town. See Bethesda *Journal*, September 1, 1939. The Rock of Dumbarton
property was added to the town in 1783, and Georgetown was incorporated in 1789 with tobacco
merchant Robert Peter as its first mayor. In 1792 it became part of the District of Columbia.

[12] *A Grateful Remembrance*, Chapter 1. "Georgetown and the Tobacco Trade" in the *Records of the
Columbia Historical Society,* 1966-1968, for Scottish factors and business practices.

[13] Gutheim, *The Potomac*.

[14]Frederick County including all of Western Maryland and Montgomery County was divided from Prince George's in 1748.

[15]The same list shows "Willm Offut the 3 ^d Near the Upper falls Potomac" worth £350 and "Zachariah Offut Near the great falls" with an estate of £100.

[16]There are at least a dozen other Montgomery counties in the U. S.

[17]Loughborough's first home in the region was built on lot #2 in Georgetown, which he purchased from the Claggets for $1,684, and on which he had constructed a three story, brick home which still stands as 3039 M Street, the offices of the Junior League.

[18]The *Journal of Jasper Dankearts 1679-1680* printed by Charles Scribner's Sons in 1913 and reprinted in 1969 is a good source on Dutch trade. Dankearts concluded that the "lives of planters in Maryland and Virginia are very godless and profane." Loughborough's mill was opposite the huge boulder near Massachusetts Avenue.

[19]Amazed at the remarkable stories of survival, the writer can hardly help pointing them out.

[20] Much of the information in this section is from Roger Brooke Farquhar's 1952 work of love, *Historic Montgomery County Maryland, Old Homes and History.*

[21]"Nick Jones, The Hermit" by Mrs. Wm. T. Jarvis, Mar. 1977, in the Chevy Chase Library.

[22]When interviewed, Mrs. Hess had four fine water colors of the home on her dining room wall. Mr. Jones at one time conducted art classes, and Clean Drinking was a favorite topic for his students. The water colors and the drawing shown are signed W. K. Fisher and dated `95.

[23]"Four loads of old brick, numbering about 6,500, were hauled from a homesite near Bethesda, Maryland. They have been stocked in Hell Hole for use in the exhibition area, possibly in the rebuilding of the Coach House foundation." Mount Vernon Ladies' Association *Minutes of the Council 1970.* Later diary entries indicate that the foundation of the Coach House was built of this Bethesda brick.
The Wells' home and some forty acres were donated to the Audubon Society in 1967, and that organization and twenty-eight species of resident birds now occupy the site.

[24]Other members of the first court: Elisha Williams, Richard Thompson, Edward Burgess, William Deakins, and James Offutt.

[25]The house is now used as a branch bank. WMAL's radio towers are about where the school was.

[26]Most of the above from "The Turbulent History of Locust Grove" by John M. Walton Jr. in *The Montgomery County Story*, November 1983. Holman quotes from the Bethesda *Journal*, Aug. 11 and 18, 1939. The Weaver family used it as a tenant farm until 1954 when Dr. John H. Solomon bought it. The Manor Investment Company, a subsidiary of Chevy Chase Savings and Loan, purchased and preserved the old house and a bit more than an acre of ground.

[27]The cabin at "No Gain" just off Brookeville Road, a house built by the McCubbins in 1789 and used as an inn until 1920, occupies the site of a much earlier, perhaps 1760, cabin that burned in the mid-1920s. Neighbor Robert Ragan who saw it burn and help salvage melted-down loving cups from the ashes. See *Post*, Nov. 2, 1969.

[28]The other half of this huge stone, which was found and blasted in two during 1909 railroad building, is on the southeast corner of Potomac and O Streets on the grounds of St. John's Church and it is dedicated to the father of Belt's wife, Esther Beall:
COLONEL NINIAN BEALL
Born Scotland 1625   Died Maryland 1717
Patentee of Rock of Dumbarton
Member of the House of Burgesses
Commander in Chief of Provincial Forces of Maryland
In Grateful Recognition of his Services 'Upon All Incursions
and Disturbances of Neighbouring Indians' the Maryland Assembly
of 1699 Passed 'An Act of Gratuity'
The "act of gratuity" was the price of "three good serviceable negro slaves." Beall gave a receipt for the slaves John, Sarah and Elizabeth in May 1699.

Chapter 2

Rural Roots and Branches

When General Edward Braddock was headed for Fort Duquesne to put down the trouble young George Washington had started the year before, he may have stopped his six-horse coach in Bethesda on the night of April 19-20, 1755, but there is no record of it. The road he traveled is now called Wisconsin Avenue and Rockville Pike, but in those days it also included part of Belt Road from Tenleytown and followed what is now Old Georgetown Road from Bethesda. Part of Braddock's force went up the Virginia side of the Potomac and some units may well have traveled north on River Road; in fact, the Daughters of the American Revolution are sure of it. For many years folks claimed that the ghosts of that ill-starred army tramped past the Loughborough property along River Road's hills.

During the French and Indian War, the County suffered a number of Indian scares, but there was no real fighting in the Bethesda area. Several local men, notably the Magruders, served bravely, and Marylanders played an important part in the 1759 capture of what became Fort Pitt in that "miracle year."

The lure of new land along with the despoiling of local farms led many to head West over the next hundred years. And much of the travel began along the twelve-foot wide road Braddock's men built or improved to carry his artillery and heavy wagons to defeat, the one the Madonna of the Trail watches today.

All of the early explorers and fur traders had noted the beauty and richness of the Bethesda area. But Smith, Spelman, Argall and even Henry Fleet may not have been the first Europeans to see and praise the country. French Jesuits mapped and described the upper Potomac and the Shenandoah well before the Calverts claimed the land and attempted to establish their palatinate. Swiss prospectors had searched for minerals as far north as Harper's Ferry and established a settlement on the Monocacy long before Baron Christoph de Graffenried surveyed the region from Rock Creek to Sugarloaf in 1711 and discussed buying land at Little Falls from Ninian Beall. Trappers and traders from New Sweden and New Netherland built log outposts along the river and trails years before English-speaking farmers started clearing Bethesda's woods and planting their oft-shared crops.

The first families to farm what would become the Bethesda region of Montgomery County were, for the most part, tenants. Scots, English, Welsh, and Scotch-Irish migrated up the river from the earlier-settled Tidewater when the land there became too dear or too exhausted. Germans, Swiss and Dutch moved down from Pennsylvania through Frederick and along the trail later called the Great Road. They rented farms from the usually-absentee landlords who had surveyed but seldom settled their grants from the lord proprietor. The farmers, Celtic or Germanic, paid their rents in tobacco, sired huge families and cleared more land.

These early farms averaged about a hundred acres, but the common practice was to

open and cultivate only a small fraction of the land at first. Often they girdled the trees, killing them, to let sunlight onto their fields. Tobacco crops annually required thousands of hours of backbending labor, and it was an exceptional worker—free, indentured, or slave—who could tend much more than three or four acres of the weed.

In 1729 Lord Baltimore was informed that tobacco:

. . . leaves no room for anything else; it requires the attendance of all our hands, and exacts their utmost labor, the whole year round; it requires us to abhor communities and townships, since a planter cannot carry on his affairs, without considerable elbow room, within his plantation. When all is done, and our tobacco is sent home, it is perchance the most uncertain commodity that comes to market...the most liable and subject to frauds, in prejudice to the poor planters.

In early spring the tiny, black seeds sprouted in well-protected beds where they had to be carefully tended until the danger of frost passed and the rains were due. Then the young plants crowned rows of hills spaced a yard or so apart, and with sharp hoes and constant sweat, men and boys kept the fields of pungent Orinoco free from weeds through the hot summer. Many planters developed an identifying misshapen and green-stained thumb from topping the plants to prevent blooming. Women and children pinched back the suckers and picked off the bugs and the large, striped caterpillars, the dreaded hornworms.[1]

All this work produced plants with large, clean leaves which were harvested and hung on rods in the drying barn. These distinctive barns with their wide set, unchinked side boards were sometimes heated by smoky fires that also called for constant tending. Once the leaves were dry and yellow, planters removed them from the long sticks and then stemmed, stripped, and tied them into "hands." They packed the cured tobacco into huge hogsheads that could hold up to a thousand pounds.

Tobacco merchants tried to discourage the planters from rolling their casks to market because that broke up the leaves, but the practice was common until all-weather highways replaced the "rolling roads." Most farmers soon recognized that the "sotte weed" debilitated their soil, and so they rotated their crops or cleared new land, and many raked wood ashes into their seed beds, but yields steadily declined.

Frederick Gutheim concluded:

The tobacco civilization stamped the landscape, originated social habits, gave birth to ideas, and created a type of personality that gave the people of the lower Potomac region a distinctive personality . . . . Good manners and sharp trading, hard riding and soft living, have gone hand in hand.

The depth of tobacco's "stamp" varied from place to place in Maryland. In the Bethesda area, although some "gentlemen farmers" from Georgetown were early inhabitants, tobacco dominated the land for almost a century.

Only a planter with a large family or a few slaves or indentured workers could successfully take up a tobacco farm in the early 18th century. The contract he signed forced him to raise the crop year after year, for his rent was to be paid in leaf or its equivalent in hard-to-come-by currency. Tenancy made possible land speculation on the scale practiced by Robert Peter and his few peers. Owners also required tenants to clear a certain number of acres and to plant a set number of fruit trees. Many landlords demanded that farmers plant wheat and corn on a certain percentage of the land and increased their rent for each slave or hired hand in an attempt to control tobacco production.

For some one-time servants or farm hands, especially those newly freed from their indenture, the system was too expensive and too risky. Many of the poorest people moved on west while others competed with the growing population of free blacks as hired farm laborers. Numerous poor farmers and their families, and often their descendants, became permanent tenants or sharecroppers.

As tobacco devoured the land, more acres were cleared, and the original fields reverted to scrub or were turned into pastures. The farmers cut trees for fuel and barrels as well as to construct houses, sheds, furniture, and even the platters from which they ate. So, when President George Washington traveled the road to Frederick in 1791, he saw, in the region now called Bethesda, a much more open and settled area served by taverns and dotted with farm houses rather than the relative wilderness he had traversed with Braddock only thirty-five years before.[2]

By then the government Washington headed under the adolescent nation's second constitution was negotiating the purchase of land for the new capital city, and the tobacco market was at the height of its post-Revolutionary boom. Georgetown, south of the planned District Line but by far the largest town in Montgomery County, had a population of perhaps three thousand. It was a thriving port at the wide mouth of Rock Creek that was beginning to have a silt problem because of deforestation upstream. Bethesda's hills had become the site of a few wealthy families' summer homes as well as of several dozen prosperous farms.[3]

Once Thomas Jefferson and Alexander Hamilton reached their famous compromise in 1790 and George Washington chose the site, all that was left to do was acquire the property, lay out the boundaries, and create the capital city. Planned was a diamond ten miles square with its southern tip at Alexandria and the new Federal City, soon called "Washington," laid out in the center of the "District of Columbia." Pierre L'Enfant, an obstinate French officer Washington met during the Revolution, took on the task of planning the city to be established in the boggy wilderness between the Eastern Branch and Rock Creek south of a Boundary Street that lay, generally, along the fall line.

The President's Commissioners chose two Marylanders to survey the boundaries and plat the city; the third generation-free, African-American Benjamin Banneker, a self-taught astronomer from Baltimore, and Andrew Ellicott, a respected surveyor of some experience as well as a veteran of the Revolution. In order to include the ports of Alexandria and Georgetown within the District's square, they set the south boundary stone, based on Banneker's calculations, at Jones Point with Freemasonry brio and appropriate libations on April 15, 1791.

While the Commissioners, shocked by the acreage disappearing under the Frenchman's broad avenues, dealt with Davy Burns and the other recalcitrant land-owners, Ellicott and his crew of brush-clearers and tree-fellers headed northwest to mark the first ten-mile side. He measured the line with a sixty-six foot chain and the best available instruments but still did not get it quite right. It took him eight months to reach Little Falls planting a sandstone marker-stone at each mile in the

forty-foot wide path his men cleared. In his spare time Ellicott helped the dilatory L'Enfant draw lot-lines on his city plan.

In 1792, after having several of his ax men killed by falling trees, Ellicott crossed the Potomac and began installing milestones along the tamer Maryland boundary. The work went faster, but it still took almost two years for him to finish the job. On the south side of the stones in the Bethesda area, "Jurisdiction of the United States" was carefully carved, on the opposite side, "Maryland," on the third, "1792," and on the fourth the variation between magnetic and true north.[4]

With the establishment of the Capital, Montgomery County lost its biggest town as well as the stage stop at the River Road junction where the Tennallys had a tavern. It also lost the taxes of a few big farms in what became Washington County. Most people in the Bethesda area hardly noticed the difference, and neither did those in the new "County" that was still under the jurisdiction of Maryland law. For the area farmers, however, some changes were in the making.[5]

Across the river in Loudoun County a young farmer named John Binns, a veteran of the Revolution, watched his neighbors abandoning their farms as the land wore out. He also observed a Quaker farmer renew his fields with limestone. Binns pounded some chalk stone to dust and spread it on his own corn hills. He experimented, kept records, and year after year his crops improved. He bought abandoned farms then rehabilitated and sold them. He built a mill to grind limestone, and by 1800 he was a rich man and people had stopped leaving Loudoun County.

North of the river some farmers had adopted the improved machinery and innovative methods that were starting to sweep across Europe. Most of these planters lived in the Sandy Spring area where the Quaker Thomas Moore spread the Loudoun County ideas. Moore had crossed the river to marry into the Brooke family and brought with him an understanding of deep plowing and of the use of clover, manure, and gypsum or "plaster of Paris."

In the environs of Bethesda, James Dunlop of Hayes Manor adopted many of the ideas the Quakers espoused, and by the time of the War of 1812, he was using limestone on his

fields, sowing clover and spreading the word of John Binns, who in 1803 had *A Treatise on Practical Farming* published in Frederick.[6]

Soon County landlords required tenants to change their methods, and some even supplied clover seed and plaster. New breeds of sheep and cattle were also introduced, notably Merinos and shorthorns. Soon agricultural societies and clubs organized and held the first County fair in 1822, a cattle show which also encouraged keeping sheep and swine. But as the censuses showed, the County had entered a period of steady decline until mid-century.[7]

	White	Black	%	total
1790	11,679	6,324	33	18,003
1810	9,731	8,249	45	17,980
1840	8,766	6,690	43	15,456
1860	11,349	6,973	38	18,322
1870	13,128	7,434	36	20,563

Note that these figures do not differentiate between free and slave African-American residents of Montgomery County, nor do they identify the numbers of indentured or apprenticed whites and blacks of which there were many.

Three distinct classes of workers existed in Maryland in the ante-bellum period: whites, slaves, and free blacks. And despite the loud and continuous efforts of the State legislature to discourage manumission and to make it difficult for freed men and women to remain in Maryland and the almost equally strenuous efforts to establish a resettlement colony in Liberia, their numbers steadily grew. Not surprisingly, the "rights of blacks in Maryland declined just as quickly as their numbers increased."[8]

By the middle of the 19th century, Maryland had more free blacks than any other state, slave or free, and only countries such as Brazil and Cuba had a higher percentage of free blacks. In 1850 Maryland had almost 75,000 free African-Americans, about forty-five percent of its total Negro population. In other border states such as Missouri and Kentucky, more than ninety-five percent of the blacks were slaves at that time.[9]

In Montgomery County, which was about forty percent black in 1850, 8.3 percent of that population or 1,311 individuals were

free. The free black population of Washington, D.C., was even greater. In 1830 there were 4,604 free blacks and 4,505 slaves out of a population of 30,261. And by 1860 the number of free blacks in the District had increased to 11,131 and slaves decreased to 3,185. For the two-dozen-or-so Bethesda-area slave-owning farmers, the nearness of the Capital only increased the irritation and labor problems produced by a large free-black population.

Free blacks became tenant farmers, hired hands, and, in a few cases, skilled workmen such as blacksmiths and coopers. In 1832 the County's freedmen owned only 1,773 acres, but by 1841 blacks owned 5,371 acres, and in 1860 there were more than fifty listed as landowners with holdings of 17,142 acres. A few free blacks even owned slaves.

By the time of the Civil War, there were two Marylands. In the northern part of the State, which included fast-growing Baltimore and German-influenced Frederick, free labor dominated; on the Eastern Shore and in Southern Maryland, slave labor was the rule. Montgomery County fell about halfway between its grandfather, Prince George's, and its mother, Frederick County. Just before the "War Between the States," as most slave-owning Bethesdans would have called it, slaves were about a third of the County's population while the figure in Frederick County was seven percent and in Prince George's fifty-four percent.

While the spirit of the Revolutionary Era and religious scruples certainly played a part, the majority of free blacks came from owners who turned from labor-intensive tobacco to highly seasonal wheat needing only harvesting crews. Some impoverished planters simply allowed their slaves to wander off to Baltimore or to the North; others sold them "down the river." But it was agricultural reform that produced a new and growing problem for the politically dominant planters as well as the dilemma that those who needed the new methods most could least afford to apply them.[10]

Very few farmers in the Bethesda area owned more than ten slaves, and most of the tenant farmers owned none at all. Slaves often slept in lofts built over the kitchen or in the rafters of one of the outbuildings. Some of

the larger and more prosperous farms had separate slave quarters usually built of logs but sometimes of native brick or, as on the Bohrer farm, of stone. By the middle of the 19th century, the slave-sex ratio, which had been about two to one male in the colonial period, was about even, and that led to more marriages and the construction of more detached quarters for slaves and their families.

Of the County slave owners enumerated in 1790, only two owned fifty or more slaves, and eighty percent owned ten or fewer. Of the 929 owners listed, 192 had one slave and 111 just two. In 1860, census takers counted 770 Montgomery County slave owners, and only one owned more than a hundred slaves while seventy-six percent owned fewer than ten; 173 had one and 107, two.

Certainly the best known slave to have lived and worked in the Bethesda area was Josiah Henson who claimed to be the model for Harriet Beecher Stowe's "Uncle Tom." What may have been his "cabin" still exists near Old Georgetown Road in the Luxmanor subdivision of Bethesda. Henson visited Mrs. Stowe in 1849-50, and although she never actually stated that he was "Uncle Tom," she did write an introduction to the second of his three autobiographies in which she praised his work: "Among the singular and interesting records to which the institution of American slavery has given rise, we know of none more striking, more characteristic, and instructive than that of Josiah Henson."

The third of the dictated memoirs, *Uncle Tom's Story of His Life,* was published in 1877. In it Henson named and described several County residents, both slave and free, who, he claimed, were models for the characters in Stowe's incredibly popular and influential 1852 book. There is no doubt that *Uncle Tom's Cabin* made Josiah Henson famous, but he was certainly no "Uncle Tom" as that pejorative came to be used.

Henson was born in Port Tobacco, in 1789 and described his move to Montgomery County: "My brothers and sisters were bid off first, and one by one, while my mother, paralyzed by grief, held me by the hand. Her turn came, and she was bought by Isaac Riley, of Montgomery county. Then I was offered to the assembled purchasers." Henson told how his mother begged Riley "to buy her baby as well as herself" and how he refused.

Adam Robb, a Rockville tavern keeper and stage line operator, owner of thirty-four slaves in 1810, purchased Henson, then five or six. He soon became ill, and Riley bought him from Robb in return for some horse shoeing. Reunited with his mother, "I recovered my health, and grew to be an uncommonly vigorous boy and man."

The Riley plantation adjoined the Magruder's Locust Grove land along the main road to the Montgomery Court House, which was what most people still called Rockville in those days, and the families became linked by marriage. George Riley, Isaac's father, was a blacksmith as well as a farmer and local politician.

Henson's detailed depiction of the slaves' daily life certainly must have had an effect on Harriet Beecher Stowe. "We lodged in log huts, and on the bare ground. Wooden floors were an unknown luxury. In a single room were huddled, like cattle, ten or a dozen persons, men, women, and children . . . Our beds were collections of straw and old rags, thrown down in the corners." Their food, wrote Henson, was mainly corn meal and salt herring plus whatever the slave might raise on his small truckpatch.

In ordinary times we had two regular meals a day: breakfast at twelve o'clock, after laboring from daylight, and supper when the work of the remainder of the day was over. In harvest season we had three. Our dress was of tow-cloth; for the children, nothing but a shirt; for the older ones a pair of pantaloons or a gown in addition, according to the sex. Besides these, in the winter a round jacket or overcoat, a woolhat once in two or three years, for the males, and a pair of coarse shoes once a year.

By the time he was fifteen Henson said that he could out-hoe, out-reap, out-husk, and out-dance every competitor. "Slavery did its best to make me wretched, but, along with memories of miry cabins, frosted feet, weary toil under the blazing sun, curses and blows, there flock in others, of jolly Christmas times, midnight visits to apple orchards, broiling stray chickens, and first rate tricks to dodge work."

They grew wheat, oats, corn, tobacco, barley and potatoes on this Bethesda farm, and by the wagonload Henson took their harvest down to the markets of Georgetown. He

also sold enough windfall apples to buy a speller and tried to teach himself to read and write. Riley caned him when he discovered the book, and Henson did not learn to read until he was forty-two. And it was also in Georgetown that he heard of an anti-slavery baker, a Methodist named John McKenny, and Henson found him at Newport Mill, stood outside the meeting house, and heard him preach Christianity and equality. He was 18 and he was converted.

I early learned to employ my spirit of adventure for the benefit of my fellow sufferers. The condition of the male slave is bad enough; but that of the female...is one that arouses the sympathy in every heart not dead of all feeling... No white knight, rescuing a white fair lady from cruel oppression, ever felt the throbbing of a chivalrous heart more intensely than I, a black knight did when running down a chicken to hide in an out-of-the-way place till dark, that I might be able to carry it to some poor overworked black fair one, to whom it was at once food, luxury, and medicine... I felt good, moral, heroic.

Henson also told of being beaten by Bryce Litton, a white overseer who worked for Isaac Riley's brother. The beating caused permanent damage. Henson wrote that from "that day to this I have been unable to raise my hands as high as my head." When Henson returned to work, he rebroke his shoulder when his plow blade struck a rock.

At twenty-two he married "a very efficient, and, for a slave, a very well-taught girl, belonging to a neighbouring family reputed to be pious and kind. I first met her at the religious meetings which I attended." Henson's first wife bore him twelve children.

George Riley died in 1815, and Isaac married young Matilda Magruder and then proceeded to get in deep financial problems with his in-laws. Riley sent Henson and his family to his brother in Kentucky. Henson returned to Maryland and with the help of Mrs. Riley's brother, bought his freedom for $500, $350 cash and $150 to be paid later. He received his manumission papers in 1829, but Riley sealed them "for safety." He returned to Kentucky for his wife and children to find that Isaac Riley had written his brother Amos that Henson still owed $650 for his freedom.

A year later Henson escaped to Canada with his family, and he lived there and worked against slavery. He established a farm, two mills, a brickyard and a school at the northern terminus of the Underground Railroad and became the leader of a large colony of former slaves. Henson personally led more than a hundred slaves to freedom. In 1851 and 1852 he visited England and told his story to Queen Victoria.

After the Civil War and the period of Reconstruction had ended, Henson and his second wife were guests of President Rutherford B. Hayes at the White House and then traveled out the old Georgetown road to the Riley home for a visit. Isaac Riley had died in 1850 but his widow, Matilda, still lived. The dilapidated house, stripped of its fences and outbuildings, sat in overgrown fields. He found Matilda Riley, whom he remembered as a young bride, a feeble, old woman who did not recognize Henson.

He came closer, and she felt his broken shoulders and is reported to have said, "Why, Si, you are a gentleman."

Henson proudly replied, "I always was, Madam."[11]

T. H. S. Boyd in his 1879 history of Montgomery County summarized its agricultural past:

Montgomery County has witnessed three phases of civilization. . . . . First, were the old Tobacco Planters, with their baronial estates and armies of slaves. They felled the native forests and planted the virgin soil in tobacco and Indian corn. This did very well as long as there was timber for the axe, and new land for the hoe . . . . These days are known as "the good old times."

In less than a century after this system of denuding and exhaustion began, there were no more forests to clear, and no more new land to till. Then succeeded the period of old fields, decaying worm fences, and moldering homesteads. This sad condition of the County reached its climax about the year 1840 . . . . Montgomery County lands became a synonym for poverty. The lands bordering the Turnpike were . . . but a succession of unenclosed old fields.

Boyd marked the second period from the introduction of Chicha Island guano in about 1845 and called it the cereal growing period. New fences and barns went up, and the decade before the Civil War was "one of universal prosperity to the people of the County. Towns and villages sprung up, stores were established at cross roads, while internal improvements were progressing in all parts of the County."

The Civil War was hard on the County, both physically and emotionally, but the end of slavery, Boyd declared, ushered in the era of free labor, "and now, with a larger and increasing population, the people are making rapid strides towards an advanced state of enlightenment and material property."[12]

The collapse of the tobacco markets, the silting of the Georgetown harbor and the exhaustion of the land combined to leave much of the County poverty stricken and many Bethesda farms abandoned by the middle of the 19th century. Historian Roger Brooke Farquhar concluded that "Montgomery County suffered from tobacco-depleted soil more than any other county in the state . . . ."

The roads to the West were much improved, and the land there was cheap. Some farmers headed south to tobacco and cotton fields, but more trekked toward Missouri, Kentucky, Tennessee, Illinois or even to California when the gold fever called. Almost the whole town of Barnesville moved to Ohio.

It was a Sandy Spring Quaker, Edward Stabler, who saved the County's agriculture. In 1844 on his Harewood farm, he placed spoonfuls of Peruvian guano around some of his hills of corn and found that the treated area's yield increased 300 percent. Stabler mixed the nitrogen-rich bird droppings with lime, bonemeal, and manure and watched his wheat yield grow from three or four bushels per acre to twenty-five or thirty bushels. "A new golden era for the county dated from that moment on" concluded Farquhar whose ancestors helped establish farmers' clubs. It was the Virginian Binns and his Quaker neighbor Israel Janney, concluded Gutheim, who put "the wheatlands of the Piedmont on a solid basis that lasted a century."[13]

Other innovations in pre-Civil War agriculture included the introduction of many new varieties of apple, pear and other fruit trees. Again, Edward Stabler of Sandy Spring played a role as agent for a New York nursery. The 1820s brought improved varieties of wheat, and by the 1840s "Zimmerman," the Frederick hybrid, flourished throughout the County and grain yields improved steadily.

Also in the 1840s reaping machines became popular on the large and more prosperous farms. In 1851 Robert Dunlop of Bethesda, a leader of the Montgomery County Agricultural Society, was using one to cut his wheat and oats at Hayes. The County farmers' support for an agricultural high school led, eventually, to the establishment of the University of Maryland, and local farmers also encouraged the development of a Federal agriculture department, which found an early home in Bethesda for some of its work.

But it was improvements in transportation that really changed the County. The old road that led through Bethesda to Georgetown had limited what County farmers could grow and to whom they could sell. Then, in historically rapid succession, came the turnpike era followed by the canal building epoch and the railroad's ascendancy. By the middle of the 19th century, Montgomery County farmers could reach many different markets and had access to a much wider world of knowledge as well as trade.

Even then, Bethesda was still barely a village. It would take one more transportation revolution before the suburbs emerged. After all, until the Civil War, many considered the Capital to be just another small, muddy Maryland town with some extra-wide streets and a seasonal and highly transient population of out-of-town lawyers living in rooming houses.[14]

Congress authorized the National Road, the eastern section of which became US 40, in 1806 as part of what would later be called the American System of internal improvements. This pike, most often called the Cumberland Road, was to connect the Ohio County to the East, and the already existing road from Fredericktown to Georgetown was to link up with this first national highway. Despite recessions, bankruptcies, Presidential vetoes, and another war with England, the road from Cumberland to Wheeling opened by 1819 and the section to Baltimore in 1825.

The old road that became Wisconsin Avenue rose straight out of Georgetown to Tenleytown and then followed Belt-Brookeville Road's path to the District Line and Old Georgetown Road's route out of Bethesda. What became well-traveled Route 355 then went north to Rockville and past Gaithersburg and on to Frederick. In 1805 investors chartered the Washington Turnpike Company to improve what was then called the Rockville Turnpike. Twelve years later they had still not sold enough shares to begin

work, but a reorganized company began grading, widening and macadamizing in 1818, and the road was in operation and making money within ten years.

The fourth milestone on the Pike stood near Cockendorfer's tavern just south of Bradley's lane; the fifth, north of "five points" at the stone inn where the old Georgetown road and the new turnpike split to give Bethesda its main intersection, and the sixth, on the new route near the Presbyterian Church that gave the town its name. Nathan Loughborough, president of the road building company, stated that the construction to Rockville had cost $46,000 but that he planned to recover the expense through the sale of stock as well as by collecting tolls.

Stage lines ran a regular schedule from Georgetown, but in bad weather their jarring coaches could take a full day to reach Frederick. Several inns, including a large, stone one in the middle of what became Bethesda, prospered along the route. Tollgates went into operation in 1829 with rates for cattle and sheep (a score of sheep or hogs for twelve cents) as well as for carriages (12 cents) and a horse and rider (6 cents). Wagons with wide-rimmed wheels paid lower rates than those with narrow rims for obvious reasons. The road's owners exempted local residents from paying tolls, and the gate keepers usually knew who they were.[15]

The company began work on a new section of road from Tenleytown to the District Line about 1840 and moved that part of Wisconsin Avenue to its present, hilly location. The stage lines declined in popularity but continued to operate until the 1870s, and the toll-gate keepers were still collecting nickel fees into the 1880s. By then the all-weather road had become rough and uneven as rains washed away the smaller stones used in the macadamizing process. In some places road crews patched holes with tree stumps or corduroyed problem areas with logs. Most travelers used the narrow dirt roads along side the highway except during muddy periods when they had to endure the juddering ride on the poorly maintained pike.[16]

Another important early road, built over the so-called Seneca trail, was River Road. The improvement of this road, authorized by the Maryland Assembly in 1774 but delayed by the Revolution, was not completed until 1779. By then many Scots and Irish including the Magruders, Edmonstons, Bealls and Offutts had moved into what would become the western part of Bethesda.

The road builder was Jacob Funk, a well-known German entrepreneur who had planned a new community called Hamburg on the edge of Foggy Bottom and later founded Funkstown, Maryland. In the middle of this highway, also called Great Falls Road among other names, Funk erected poles every hundred yards, and only wagons with wheel rims at least five inches wide could travel on the north side of these poles. At Gloria Point in Tenleytown, hilly River Road met the old pike just as it does today. Farther north, a trail that followed the general route of modern Greentree Road connected River Road and Captain (Cabin) John.

Along the old Indian trail a small community called Concord developed on a grant known as "Brothers' Industry." Bethesda's first Methodist church was built there about 1819 on a piece of land purchased from Thomas Clagget. It was a simple log structure in a grove of trees with benches along the sides and a slave gallery that covered half of the auditorium. The Methodists soon set aside a burying ground, its boundary marked with trees.

The church may have been a way station on the Underground Railroad, but by the Civil War it was under the control of the Methodist Episcopal Church, South, and the Rockville Circuit. When the old log church decayed, services took place in the adjoining one-room school house, but the church seldom saw or heard a preacher, and finally the Reverend George Tyler from Rockville recommended that the members go elsewhere to worship.

About 1880 the Baltimore Conference, North, sent the Reverend George M. Berry to Concord, and he saw to the building of a new, plain church. "It was by no means an elaborate structure. The walls were not plastered, and there was no pulpit. The pews consisted of three long stout pine poles with boards laid across them to serve as seats." The Wheatly brothers contributed most of the lumber.

A Reverend James completed the construction, and the church served as a "point" of Tennallytown Station and a Methodist church called Mt. Zion. That church later became Eldbrooke taking its name from Acquilla Eld and Philip L. Brooke, both early

Bethesdans. In the 1890s, according to Nettie Embry whose family had long been Concord congregants, "the church was going full blast, with large attendance every Sunday."[17]

Other than Wisconsin Avenue, River Road and the road to Brookeville, the major routes between D.C. and the Bethesda area, such as Conduit Road, Connecticut Avenue, and Massachusetts Avenue Extended, all came later. Conduit Road, now MacArthur Boulevard, was a concomitant result of the great aqueduct and bridge completed early in the 1860s. The road sashayed back and forth as a result of the palisades' geography and because its designer had set sections of the aqueduct at oblique angles to slow the water's flow. Stewart and Newlands' Chevy Chase development brought about the bridging of Rock Creek and the extension of Connecticut Avenue in the 1890s, and another real estate boom in the 1930s led to the growth of Massachusetts Avenue. Most traffic from very early in Bethesda's history went more-or-less north and south.

On the 4th of July in 1828, the race for the trade of the Ohio River Valley and the coal of the Cumberland began with the turning of two shovels full of dirt. In Baltimore, the last living signer of the Declaration of Independence and perhaps the richest and best known man of Maryland, Charles Carroll of Carrollton, signaled the start of what appeared to be the more risky venture, the Baltimore and Ohio Railroad. The President of the United States, embattled and embittered John Quincy Adams shed his coat to inaugurate the Chesapeake and Ohio Canal.[18]

The canal story started with the dreams and plans of George Washington and his Patowmack Company, which tried to make the river navigable with pass canals around the thirty-seven-foot rise of Little Falls and the seventy-six-foot climb to get above Great Falls. In 1784 the State legislature approved support in a bill endorsed by Washington and Horatio Gates, but by 1795 the company had to petition for a new stock issue to continue its work.

In 1799 the canal company was broke again, and the Maryland legislature bought 130 shares to keep the work going. In 1802 the canal paid out its only dividend and began work to improve the channels in the Po-

tomac and Shenandoah Rivers. It claimed that the Potomac was open for navigation, but droughts, floods and ice regularly closed it. Some County wheat growers and millers began shipping by water to Georgetown while most of those north of Seneca used the toll roads and turnpikes to Baltimore. The original canal company foundered in 1819.

The Maryland General Assembly appropriated $500,000 for the C&O Canal in 1826, the same amount for a lateral canal from Baltimore to D.C. and for another canal to Pennsylvania plus $200,000 to improve rivers on the Eastern Shore. Despite financial and engineering problems, the new company completed the twenty mile stretch of the C&O Canal to Seneca Creek by 1830, some of it atop the old Patowmack work. Meanwhile, the railroad, still horse and gravity powered, had reached thirteen miles to Ellicott City. Round one to the canal builders.[19]

In the next phase the railroad jumped ahead with steam power. By 1831 it had seventy miles of track in operation and reached Frederick, which welcomed it with donated land. The B&O then began a court battle with the canal over the route through the forty-foot-wide pass at Point of Rocks.

The canal builders, who decided to use contracted, indentured Irish laborers rather than slaves, had constant problems. First, the Irish they hired were of two warring clans, the Corkonians and the Longfords, who fought each other even when it was not pay day. Then cholera hit, and mass graves soon lined the canal between Captain John and Great Falls. Surviving workers fled the river. Nearby towns, including Rockville, prepared for the worst, liming their streets and filling their churches. It was also during this period that the great Crommelin House, the tavern at Great Falls, opened, and at the Seneca aqueduct a short-lived boom-town called Rushville prospered. The canal reached the Monocacy in 1833 and crossed that river on an impressive aqueduct.

After the court approved joint construction at Point of Rocks, the canal company, almost bankrupt, sold stock to the B&O and went to the State legislature for help. In 1842 Cumberland welcomed the railroaders with the help of capital contributed by local mine owners, but the canal was broke again having

spent the $16 million it raised on repairing damage caused by ice, floods and Irish fights.

The canal company decided to sell. There were no bidders. By 1842 the State itself was bankrupt, mainly from over-investment in transportation companies, and there was talk of repudiating Maryland's debts. The railroad bought more shares to support its previous investment and keep the canal solvent, but in 1845 another disastrous flood roared down the Potomac. The canal company finally completed the 3,118 foot Paw Paw tunnel, reached Cumberland in 1850 and had its grand opening on October 10. It had come 184.5 miles, about eight miles a year. And it had lost the race but built a masterpiece of 19th century engineering that included seventy-four lift locks, eleven stone aqueducts, seven diversion dams, fifty lock-keepers' houses and dozens of other structures including 200 culverts.

While the railroad rumbled on west through a series of eleven great tunnels, the canal company spent the next ten years making its system work and continuously repairing flood damage. By the Civil War the canal was in good condition, but then it took until 1869 to repair the damage done by Confederate raiders. The canal's busiest time was in the 1870s when its chief cargo was coal.[20]

Shortly after the C&O reached Cumberland, some Georgetowners admitted it was a failure by joining with Montgomery County leaders to seek a charter for a railroad from Washington to the Monocacy. It was that railroad, the long-sought Metropolitan Branch of the B&O, that would bring the first suburbs to Montgomery County, but Bethesda was not one of them.

Who were these farmers in Bethesda in the era of turnpikes and canals, in the tumultuous period before and during the Civil War? They included the gentry: the Dunlops at Hayes Manor, leaders in agricultural reform employing the latest methods and machinery, including the Hussey reaper. The quarrelsome Magruders at Locust Grove and the horse-breeding Loughboroughs at Grasslands and Milton both operated mills as well as large, diverse farms. The Bradleys of Chevy Chase had a farmstead admired throughout the area. In addition there were the Dodges, immensely successful Georgetown merchants, and the Davidsons on the other side of the Pike, both with huge tenant-farmed estates and various members of the Peter family whose farms spread betwen the Pike and the old road to Georgetown.

In 1810 John Counselman bought 450 acres along the Maryland-D.C. line on the east side of what became Wisconsin Avenue. For more than a century there were Counselmans farming or storekeeping in Bethesda.

In 1819 on the other side of the Frederick Road, Samuel Shoemaker, a Quaker from Montgomery County, Pennsylvania, where his family had farmed since 1683, bought 102 acres from Clement Smith. Over the years the Shoemakers enlarged their holdings near the District Line to take in most of what is now Yorktown Village and Westmoreland Hills as well as Friendship Heights. The census of 1860 showed that Jesse Shoemaker had nine children living at home. He valued his real estate at $2,800 and the rest of his property at $5,000, and those figures put him well ahead of many area farmers.[21]

By far the most prosperous Bethesda farmer on the eve of the Civil War was slaveholder Greenbury Watkins, a 52-year-old widower, whose four young children were in the care of a hired governess. The value of Watkins' total estate, including land spread on both sides of Coquelin Run, was over $100,000. Robert Dunlop at Hayes, who listed his occupation as farmer and judge, placed the value of his land and other property at $55,000.

Much more the norm was Watkins' neighbor Madison Gingell (Gingle in the census); he and his wife, Artemia, had five children, $4,000 in land, and $1,200 in other property. Farmer John Counselman out on River Road supported a wife, and seven children with the help of two free blacks, a washerwoman, a white farm worker and seven slaves on land worth $10,800. The miller William Orndorff and his wife had eight children, a white servant, and nineteen slaves. Their property had a $9,000 value and the rest of their estate $14,000.[22]

Bethesdans were leaders in the early agricultural societies and in the establishment and operation of the fair at Rockville. Otho Magruder headed the committee that drafted a constitution for the Montgomery County Agricultural Society in 1846 and, among the other Bethesda-area farmers on the commit-

tee, were Nathan Loughborough, G. M. Watkins and some members of the Peter family. The first elected officers were John Parke Custis Peter, president, and Robert P. Dunlop, vice-president. In September of 1846 the Society held its first fair in front of the courthouse in Rockville.

The social aspects of the fair and the very popular horse racing led many Quakers to leave the association, but the Fair prospered. The Agricultural Society awarded prizes in various classes for the best horses, cattle, sheep, poultry, vegetables, fruits, hams, harnesses, jams, and quilts. In the days before the Civil War, slaves won prizes for their owners in plowing contests that were among the most popular events.

The major goal of both the society and the fair was to promote the restoration of the tobacco-depleted land which had led some to call the County the "Sahara of Maryland." By the end of the 1850s, the *Sentinel* reported:[23]

Fields once turned out as unworthy of any further attention of the plough and the hoe, have again been gathered under the farmer's protecting fences, and bear evidence of great productiveness.

Some blamed fanatics, but in 1856 Francis Blair of Silver Spring was censured and removed from the vice-president's office for his anti-slavery activities. The Society's membership, like the nation, the State, and the County was sharply divided on the issue of slavery, but most of the leaders were slave owners.[24]

By the 1870s, the Fair was back in business, better than ever with a third-of-a-mile track, a two-story exhibit building, a speakers' stand, stables for fifty horses, and numerous cattle and stock pens on its sixteen acres. And in 1872 hundreds came to the fair on the first passenger trains run on the newly opened Metropolitan Branch of the B&O.[25]

One of the great engineering and construction projects accomplished in the 19th century in the Bethesda area was the building of the Washington Aqueduct and its Union Arch Bridge. With four major interruptions, Captain, later Brigadier General, Montgomery C. Meigs completed the work in ten years, and it is still in operation bringing 185 million gallons of Potomac River water each day about twelve miles from Great Falls to Georgetown.

After continuing complaints about the water supply of the growing capital city and a number of studies, including a plan to dam Rock Creek, in 1853 Congress appropriated $100,000 for a survey and the first steps of the aqueduct project. Maryland approved the Meigs plans in May 1853, authorized land condemnation and ceded jurisdiction over the property. Obtaining the right-of-way proved to be both more expensive and more time consuming than anyone expected. It was especially difficult in the Great Falls area where the water power was important. The Great Falls Manufacturing Company, for example, had a 1839 charter granting it use of the Falls, forcing a change in the plans for the dam in that area.[26]

Ground was broken in November 1853, and a work force of between 300 to 400 men began building a dam and tunneling under the C&O Canal. The rip-rap dam at Great Falls raised the river level five feet, to 150 feet above mean tide at Georgetown. A feeder tunnel ran from the dam, under the canal to the gatehouse some 250 feet away where huge, sliding, cast iron gates controlled the flow.

Meigs's men dug and built all through the winter, and by June 1854 they had exhausted

Montgomery Meigs, about 1855

their funds, and the work stopped. By then they had acquired all the necessary land in Maryland, started the first three tunnels, and built a small piece of the nine-feet-in-diameter brick conduit itself. All this work, and all that was to follow, proceeded slowly and with constant supervision and inspections in accord with detailed specifications for the grading, the brick work, the concrete work and the sand, cement, and mortar. Meigs opened a sandstone quarry at Seneca to produce the stone for culverts, the gate house and the bridges. For the next two years menial Congressional appropriations limited the work accomplished.

In 1857 Congress approved $1 million for the project and the next year added another $800,000. Work went forth steadily on all phases until funds ran out in June 1859. At times, the monthly payroll was over $36,000. Masons, stonecutters, plasterers, carpenters, and painters were paid two to three dollars a day, and unskilled laborers, $1.00 to $1.25 daily. In May 1858 the payroll listed five assistant engineers, fifty surveyors and inspectors, 700 unskilled mechanics, 1,100 laborers, 40 teams, sixty cooks and waiters, thirty overseers, twenty clerks and twelve slaves. At the same time, outside contractors probably were hiring about 1,000 men bringing the total to about 3,000 working on the project that May. [27]

Many of the men boarded along the route or lived in housing the government provided for $10-13 per month, deducted from their wages. Obviously the building of the aqueduct brought hundreds of workers, both skilled and unskilled, to Bethesda and provided jobs, at certain times, for almost any who sought them. The few slaves employed, never more than fifteen, were paid for at the rate of $1.20 per day.

Despite doing all the work by hand, Meigs and his foremen found it cheaper to drill tunnels than to make open cuts in hard stone, and they constructed seven tunnels totaling 5,392 feet. The 1,427-foot tunnel at Great Falls was the longest, and the eighty-six-foot Bear Den tunnel at Widewater, the shortest. Meigs's men also built twenty-six culverts to allow creeks to pass under the aqueduct. They did all the fill work a year ahead of time to allow for settling. The only steam powered machines used were hoists or derricks. [28]

The work also attracted other businesses, and Meigs complained about those who leased land to "groggeries." He blamed several deaths on excessive drinking. At times the work slowed, occasionally even stopped, because of sickness, especially malarial fever, particularly in August and September. The crowded government boarding houses probably contributed to the problem.

In 1858 workmen laid pipe from the just-completed receiving reservoir to a fountain at the base of Capitol Hill. On January 3, 1859, Meigs proudly watched water spurt thirty feet into the air to the applause of appreciative Congressmen. By the time the money ran out again in 1859, the job was ninety-eight percent complete, and the only major project unfinished was the bridge over the valley at Cabin John Creek.

From his office in Georgetown Meigs traveled out almost every day on his horse "Corbo" or in the Washington Aqueduct carriage, which in winter could be equipped with runners. Along the way he and his sons collected snakes, which, to the consternation of visitors, he kept in his office. Sculptors used some of Meigs's snakes as models for the Capitol's door rings and handles.

The cost of the project attracted numerous lobbying efforts to take it away from the Corps of Engineers and solicit bids from private contractors. But after a year's stoppage, Congress appropriated $500,000 with Meigs's name tied to it. This act precipitated a clash with Secretary of War John Floyd that led to Meigs being transferred to the Dry Tortugus at the rocky tip of the Florida Keys to build Fort Jefferson. He was there from September 1860 to February 1861.

Meigs returned to his project, examined the books, and refused to pay out the $157,745 obligated by his replacement, Captain H. W. Benham, during his absence, believing "that all persons are bound by the laws and that contracts made in defiance of them are void." Shortly after he was recalled, Meigs was promoted to captain of infantry and then, almost immediately to brigadier general and quartermaster general, titles he held until his death. During the Civil War he oversaw the spending of $1.5 billion for army supplies and accounted for it to the last cent.[29]

Of all the work on this great project, Montgomery Meigs was proudest of his two

remarkable bridges, the iron span over Rock Creek and the longer, stone arch at Cabin John. Work began on the Rock Creek Bridge in the spring of 1858, and it opened for traffic in 1862. Meigs described it in one of his reports as the "only one in which (cast iron pipe) arch ribs are utilized to convey the water supply to the city and at the same time support the roadway." Resting on masonry abutments, two 48-inch cast iron pipes reached two hundred feet across Rock Creek in Georgetown.

Meigs's bridge replaced a wooden structure on M Street, but since it was only seventeen feet wide and the road was 50 feet wide, it also created a longtime bottleneck for traffic between Washington City and Georgetown, especially for the first ten years when railroad tracks shared the roadway. A new bridge, completed in 1916, covered the old water pipes but did not rest on them.

Near the other end of the giant conduit lay the beautiful Cabin John Valley which was about a hundred feet deep and two hundred feet wide. Meigs had originally planned a multi-arched bridge, but after studying several examples decided on a single masonry arch, the longest in the world.[30]

With the C&O Canal only 1,000 feet away, the first step for Meigs's resident manager Alfred Landon Rives was to dam Cabin John Creek and build a lock to connect it to the canal. Then construction materials, first the wood for the framework and then the stone, came by barge right under the work site to be hoisted up to the growing span by derricks and a traveling crane. Meigs built most of the bridge's inner and outer arches of local stone, granite from Port Deposit and sandstone from Seneca, and the arch ring itself of dressed granite from Quincy, Massachusetts. His workers quarried the

abutment stone a few hundred feet up the valley.

The work began in 1857 when Congress made its first substantial appropriation. The masons keyed the arch near the end of 1858 and completed the stonework by July 1859, except for the spandrels that filled the space between the arch and roadway. Hidden behind these side walls are five arches at the west end of the bridge and four at the east end.

It was, on the "striking of the center," the world's longest stone arch, spanning 220 feet with a rise of fifty-seven feet. The brick conduit, nine feet in diameter and enclosed in stone, rested on the top of the arch. The work was completed with red sandstone from Seneca after Meigs returned from Dry Tortugas, and he finally finished it in 1863. Although the bridge was under construction for over six years, work was stopped or delayed about half the time mainly due to lack of money.

After the firing on Fort Sumter and Lincoln's call for volunteers, Alfred Rives crossed the river and joined the army of the Confederacy. His name never appeared on the bridge, and in 1862 a master stone-cutter named John Bobinger was ordered to chisel the name of Meigs's benefactor, Secretary of War Jefferson Davis, from the bridge's dedication plaque. For the next ten years the official name of the bridge was the Union Arch. It was not intended for traffic, but the engineers and workmen used it from the start, and it soon became a roadbed for both the farmers and the military. In 1872-3 stone parapets were added to the great bridge, and the road was macadamized.[31]

In December 1863 water was let into the Washington Aqueduct for the first time and two days later into the reservoir at Dalecarlia. After two weeks the water was shut off, the system drained, leaks repaired and the conduit "pointed up." With the final repair work finished the system was put into service in July of 1864 and was not drained again until 1891. It did not leak.[32]

At mid-century, farms in the Bethesda area, as throughout the County, varied in both size and value. Most had a woodlot for fuel; many were only partially cleared. On some, especially in the northern parts of the County near Clarksburg, tobacco

A turn-of-the-century souvenir postcard view

was still the chief money crop. However, change came with the turnpikes, the canal, the railroad and the growth of the Capital.

Wheat gradually became much more important, but corn flourished on almost every farm. Dairy herds were growing and many farmers were raising both sheep and cattle and becoming interested in improving their herds through breeding. Hogs and chickens and other fowl were common, and killing and cleaning fryers and broilers were as much a part of the farmwife's life as churning butter and making cheese.

She also kept a kitchen garden where she raised peas, beans, squash and, perhaps, some flowers. The men did the cold-weather hog killing, but the women made the sausage and were in charge of smoking the hams and bacon and producing the scrapple and lard. The pace of farm work slowed in August and deep in the winter, but even after corn replaced tobacco, life was not much easier– especially for women. They made clothes, did laundry with homemade soap and dried or canned fruits and vegetables. They doctored the sick, buried the dead, often went through a dozen or more pregnancies, taught their children, and died young.

Some things common to almost every farm home are easy to forget because old houses like Locust Grove or Milton now sit alone amidst their trees. The outbuildings are gone, but originally every farm of any size had a barn or shed in which to keep hay and animals and a buggy or wagon. Most farms had a corn crib on short stilts, which like the tobacco barn, had open spaces between side boards to help dry the product inside. A chicken house or coop and run were common with a separate place for "broody" setting hens to hatch their chicks. Many farmers also kept ducks, geese, guinea fowl, and turkeys, and some had a fattening pen where they overfed young birds for the supper table.

Tossing the chickens their cracked grain and scratch was usually a child's job as was gathering the eggs, often the farmwife's medium of exchange. The hog lot was important with its wallow and trough for the skimmed milk and kitchen scraps. Many farms had windmills and almost all had pumps; some had a pumphouse with a cistern to keep milk and butter cool. A few farms had a deep icehouse where the family stored pond ice between layers of straw, a smokehouse where hams, bacon and sausage hung for months was common, and all had a cellar big enough for storing apples and root crops. And, of course, there was the necessary or outhouse where the hollyhocks and trumpet vines seemed to grow extra well.

For most residents of what became Bethesda, farming was the way of life well into the twentieth century, and at least a dozen barns remained in the middle of town when the New Deal began. Some families had tenant houses on their property or hired others to do much of the hard work and, perhaps, thought of themselves as gentleman farmers, especially after real estate speculators started buying nearby property. They built some grand homes and involved themselves in politics and civic enterprises. On the other end of the scale, there were poor farmers in Bethesda, both black and white, whose hardscrabble life was much like that of the first settlers two-hundred years before them.

Along the Pike and the older roads, a small store would sometimes appear on a slope-roofed front porch, and a blacksmith might find enough trade for his forge and anvil and settle down. William Darcy started Bethesda's central business district when he opened a general store on the Pike a couple of hundred yards south of the Y formed by the old road and the toll road. He soon attracted competition in the form of a blacksmith and another store-keeper.

These early Bethesdans built churches and schools and complained about the roads. In 1860 a County school system began, under the leadership of William H. Farquhar, and during the Civil War a school opened in Bethesda just north of the Presbyterian Church. In the same era another one-room school served the Concord-Cabin John communities. The war soon closed both of them.[33]

A few Bethesdans were only summer residents, professionals or businessmen fleeing the city's heat and humidity and enjoying large, frame homes with big verandahs and spacious lawns and gardens. But most lived quiet, rural lives affected more by the seasons and the weather than anything else. Change came slowly as did almost everything else.

[1]See Chapter Four of Gutheim's *The Potomac* for more on colonial tobacco culture.

[2]Like Jefferson, Washington urged the cultivation of wheat and other crops.

[3]The old Continental Congress had surveys made of sites near Georgetown on the Potomac and Trenton on the Delaware and discussed having two Federal towns.

[4]Some Bethesda area boundary stones can be easily seen. NW6 at River Rd. and Fessenden is in bad shape, but resurrected NW 7 is in almost perfect condition at 5600 Western Avenue. NW8, with a benchmark, is at Pinehurst Circle (7 and 8 are the only two without the DAR's protective fences). NW9 is in the park near the end of Western Avenue, and the North Corner Stone is 20 ft. south of East West Highway within a round enclosure on the outskirts of Silver Spring. It used to be three feet high. For more see Fred Woodward's "Ramble," *Records of the Columbia Historical Society*, 1907, and Edwin Nye's "Revisit" in the 1971-72 *Records*, and "On the Borderline" by Bill Gilbert in the *City Paper*, March 21, 1993.

[5]The Census of 1800 gave Georgetown's population as 2,993. Washington County's was 1,941. Together they were about 68% white and 29% slave.

[6]Subtitled "The Use of Plaster of Paris, with Directions for Using it, and General Observations on the Use of Other Manures. On Deep Ploughing, Thick Sowing of Grain, Method of Preventing Fruit Trees from decaying, and Farming in General."

[7]See *A Grateful Remembrance*. These innovations were part of a period of agricultural reform which swept Europe changing life, increasing productivity and laying the foundation of the Industrial Revolution.

[8]See Robert J. Brugger's *Maryland A Middle Temperment* (1988) on the free black "problem."

[9]Only Delaware had a higher percentage of free blacks: 2,290 slaves and 18,073 free in 1850.

[10]See Barbara Jeanne Fields' *Slavery and Freedom on the Middle Ground* (1985).

[11]In 1883 Josiah Henson died at Dawn, his home in Canada, at the age of ninety-four. For more, see Mrs. Neal Fitzsimons' long article "Uncle Tom in Montgomery County" in the February and May 1975 issues of *The Montgomery County Story* and Cyril O'Brien's unpublished paper "Josiah Henson, the Real Uncle Tom" in the Maryland collection of the Rockville library. Uncle Tom's Cabin Museum is near Dresden, Ontario.

[12]Boyd's *History of Montgomery County, Maryland, from its Earliest Settlement in 1650 to 1879* (Clarksburg 1879, Baltimore 1968) is a very valuable document.

[13]See Chapter 6 of *The Potomac* for more on the Loudoun system and Chapter 9 of Farquhar's *Historic Montgomery County* for much more on Sandy Spring and the farmers' associations.

[14]Until the New Deal era, many considered the County a rural backwater and referred to it as "Egypt."

[15]There were toll gates at the top of the hill in Tenleytown, in Bethesda where the Metro airshaft now rises by the railroad bridge, and near Georgetown Prep at Garrett Park. Gatekeepers kept a "shot bag" of coins to make change for travelers. See Farquhar, p. 72.

[16]"Old Bethesda" by Doree G. Holman in Bethesda *Journal*, September 22, 1939. Bethesda's toll gate was under a big oak that survived into the 1930's. "The last toll rate was five cents, but there was rejoicing when even that was abolished."

[17]See "A History of Concord Methodist Episcopal Church 1819 to 1976" by Malowe Ausen and "Our Church and Its Members Through the Years" by Louis E. Reid Jr. in the Concord-St. Andrews archives.

[18] The story is only summarized here and there are many good books about both ventures. I like Capt. Tom Hall's *The C&O Canal: An Illustrated History* for its drawings by Diana Suttenfield-Abshire (1981) and Herbert H. Harwood, *Impossible Challenge: The Baltimore and Ohio Railroad in Maryland* (1979).
Also see Douglas R. Littlefield's "Maryland Sectionalism and the Development of the Potomac Route to the West" in *The Maryland Historian*, Fall/Winter 1983.

[19]The Peter family's sandstone quarry produced building material for several canal locks, the Smithsonian castle, and the Major's Seneca home.

[20]The canal also played a role in Maryland politics during the Gilded Age as the base of Arthur Pue Gorman's powerful machine. Its golden age lasted from about 1870 to 1889 when it was wrecked again by floods. The B&O finally took it over and used it to haul coal during World War I. The 1924 flood finally put the canal out of business. In 1935 the B&O sold what was left to the U.S. government, and it became a park on George Washington's birthday in 1939 and by 1940 had been restored to Seneca only to be wrecked again in the great 1942 flood. In the 1960s many people, led by Justice William O. Douglas, worked to save the canal from the road builders, and in 1971 it became a National Historical Park. Then came "Agnes."

[21]Some Shoemaker descendants still live in the area and maintain the only known private burying ground in Bethesda. See Chapter 6 for more on this family.

[22]The writer's great-grandfather, Hilleary Offutt, had not moved to his Bethesda farm in time for the census.

[23]*Sentinel*, July 1, 1859.

[24]They had asked for $8,300. Both Union soldiers and Confederates had caused the damage.

[25]Much of the information on the Fair is from Mary Charlotte Crook's article "The Rockville Fair" in *The Montgomery County Story,* August 1975. The Metropolitan Branch was not finished and opened for traffic until 1873. See Chapter 4.

[26]Under the rules, twelve local inhabitants summoned by the sheriff made the land evaluations, and almost all of the property went through the condemnation procedures.

[27]The work done under contract was at a unit cost basis:

earth excavation	$0.15 per cu. yd.
hard rock excavation	1.25 "
soft rock excavation	0.75 "
laying brick	2.25 "
laying stone masonry	3.00 "
furnishing Seneca sandstone	0.26 per cu ft.
concrete in place	3.25 per cu. yd.
furnishing brick	8.25 per thousand

[28]Most of this information from the 1953 Corps of Engineers' booklet,"Washington Aqueduct 1852-1952" and Harry C. Ways's recent history for the Corps.

[29]For more on this brouhaha see Sherrod E. East's 1939 paper in the *Records of the Columbia Historical Society,* vol. 40-41, "The Banishment of Captain Meigs" and "Captain Meigs and the Artists of the Capitol" by Russell F. Weigley in the *Records* of the CHS, 1969-70.

[30]Some dispute exists over the role of Assistant Engineer Rives, but most scholars now agree that the idea and design for the Cabin John Bridge was Meigs's. See Harry C. Ways, *A History of the Washington Aqueduct* (Corps of Engineers, 1994).

[31] Jefferson Davis' name was restored in Teddy Roosevelt's time.
During the Civil War, Meigs finished the Capitol's new dome, and after the war, he directed the planning for the new War Department building which is now called the Old Executive Office Building and the 1876 extension of the aqueduct. He retired in 1882 to his home on Vermont Avenue where he designed the Pension Building, one of Washington's finest structures, now the National Building Museum. (Gen. W. T. Sherman regretted the place was fireproof).

[32]A second conduit was authorized in 1921 and built between 1922 and 1928, and until early in World War II the route above the big pipes was known as Conduit Road. For an excellent overview of D.C.'s water system see Michael Dolan's "By the Waters of the Palisades" in the *City Paper*, June 7, 1991.

[33]These two schools were still operating in 1869 with Henry Badgely teaching in Bethesda and Maggie Heaton at Concord. Jewell, *From One Room...* p. 56.

Chapter 3

War, Both Civil and Uncivil

The first combat in the Bethesda area, of which we have a record, dates back to the 1680s, the days of the Rangers who operated from a fort at the mouth of Rock Creek when Maryland was the Calverts' colony and the Potomac was the western frontier. Certainly there were numerous wars and bloody conflicts between the Susquehannocks, the Iroquois and the Piscataways long before Europeans plowed the land, but their historians sang songs and told tales that disappeared with the smoke from their campfires.

Often led by Scots with a well-developed taste for brutal warfare, the settlers sent out armed bands of young men who "ranged" along the river and through the forests and pushed the native hunters and traders back toward the blue hills in the West. These light cavalry companies, captained by men such as Ninian Beall, drove most of the remnants of the native tribes north of the Falls of the Potomac by 1700.

In its early stages, the long struggle between England and France for control of North America left Maryland almost unscarred although Indian attacks near Rock Creek in 1692 kept the Rangers alert along the frontier. In the colonies, the first two intercontinental wars of Louis XIV flamed along the Mohawk and the St. Lawrence and raged from the Carolinas to Newfoundland. Late in 1697 Indians tricked the Rangers out of their fort below Little Falls. John Baker was killed, and the Indians took his head and right arm as trophies. It was at about that time that Colonel Addison acquired "a good Quantity of Fusees & Musquets" for the poor people of the frontier. In those days what became Bethesda was the frontier.

After the War of Jenkin's Ear, the French lost their great fortress at Louisbourg for the first time, and then William Johnson, the British Indian agent in the Mohawk Valley, stirred up the Iroquois again in King George's War. In 1704 Lt. Charles Beall, one of Ninian's many sons, took command on the Potomac frontier, but by 1708 the woods were so quiet that the Rangers were disbanded. All of these events were mere overtures to the final act, the Seven Years War or the French and Indian War, as it is known in American history books. It began in 1754 when 22-year-old George Washington had his militiamen fire on a French diplomatic party they surprised near Fort Duquesne. Washington quickly built a small fort he called Necessity where the French overwhelmed and defeated him and his 150 men on the 4th of July.

On his way back to Virginia young Washington may well have visited his friend Charles Jones at Clean Drinking Manor, but Bethesda hardly had a role in this war either. The next year Braddock, on his way to defeat and death, rode up the Pike, rebuilding the highway and commandeering every wagon he saw. Bealls and Magruders and others with ties to what would become Bethesda served on the frontier against the threat of the French forces' Indian allies, but no fighting took place in the County.

In the American Revolution, a number of Bethesdans made their fame, and several others, such as Robert Peter, greatly improved their fortunes. But except for the Bay, Maryland was spared as a battleground. All

Marylanders can proudly boast of the service of the Maryland Line in Washington's army and later under Nathanael Greene. No American troops fought better. The list of those who served in the war for independence is long, and it is amazing how many Magruders were officers. Also on that list, however, stands a private called William Offutt.

It was during the Revolution, as has been noted, that Montgomery County was born, and among the first justices of the first County court were two Bethesdans, Charles Jones of Clean Drinking Manor and Samuel Wade Magruder of Locust Grove. A number of Georgetown merchants and some manufacturers and millers contributed to the patriotic or rebellious effort. A Bethesda innkeeper, Michael Cockendorfer, set up a stocking mill with a £300 advance from the State legislature to become proprietor of the area's first defense-related industry.

A salt-petre works operated near the tobacco inspection house at the mouth of Rock Creek. Fishermen on the Potomac above Little Falls produced large catches of shad and herring that they salted and shipped to Washington's troops. In the final stages of the war, County farms near the port of Georgetown became an important source of wheat, hay, forage and entrenching tools for the armies of Washington and Rochambeau as they moved toward Yorktown to hear the British band play "The World Turned Upside Down."[1]

After the war hundreds of Bethesda acres that had belonged to the Addisons and other Tories as well as the property of numerous Glasgow and London merchants went on the auction block under the Confiscation Act of 1780. The old order gave way to a new, but equally landed, and usually slave-owning, aristocracy.

The continuation of the American Revolution called the War of 1812 almost brought fighting to Bethesda's streets after the remnants of the army that had failed to defend the Capital on August 24, 1814, gathered on the Tenallytown hills to watch the city burn. All that night stragglers shambled up the road through Bethesda and on toward the Montgomery Court House (Rockville) amid rumors that the British were not far behind.

Congreve's rockets had terrorized the hastily assembled and poorly led militia who had stopped retreating that steamy day on reaching the western banks of the Eastern Branch. Hissing and trailing twisting tails of black-powder smoke, the rockets exploded over, among, and through the American ranks. Only the sailors and marines, who had dragged 24-pounders from the ships they scuttled in the upper reaches of the Patuxent, and the small group of local artillerymen, who stood their ground well past the point of discretion, carried their heads high when the White House and unfinished Capitol burned after what came to be called the disgraceful Bladensburg Races.

Alongside Commodore Joshua Barney's men, in the second line, were some well-served six-pounders and two companies of riflemen, part of the light artillery of the D.C. militia, whose rolls included Francis Scott Key, on detached duty that day, as well as Nathan Loughborough. Their commanding officer was Major George Peter. The petite President and a number of Magruders and Bealls were there leading both Maryland and District troops, but from the debacle of that afternoon, only stiff-necked Major Peter emerged as a local hero.

Much of the government fled north toward Rockville and then Brookeville, but some flustered bureaucrats stopped when they reached rural Chevy Chase. Dolly Madison made it across the river with the silver and the Gilbert Stuart. Government papers by the wagonload and government officials by the carriageful were deposited at Bethesda-area homes such as Hayes Manor and the Bradley farm.

The Renaissance man who was head of the Patent Office and designer of both the Octagon House and Tudor Place as well as the Capitol, Dr. William Thornton, packed up everything portable at his F Street residence and with his wife fled toward their farm in Bethesda. Mrs. Thornton watched the "conflagration of our poor undefended & devoted city" from the hills of "Tennely Town" before going to spend the night with the Peters at Tudor Place. The next day Dr. Thornton returned to the nascent city and faced down General Ross's men as they were about to set fire to Blodgett's Hotel that housed the patent records as well as the Post Office.

"Are you Goths or Vandals, or are you British officers?" asked the doctor who had just rescued his self-designed violin. He claimed the patents and models were all "personal property" protected by General Ross's orders and that "to burn what would

be useful to all mankind would be as barbarous as to burn the Alexandria Library, for which the Turks have been condemned by all enlightened nations." The Patent Office was spared.[2]

The next day what was left of General William Winder's American army straggled out the Pike toward Rockville, but the British, drenched by the torrential rains that put out most of the fires and then frightened by the storm that roared through town, declined to follow and turned to attack Baltimore where Ross was killed and the "Star Spangled Banner" written.

George Peter parlayed his fame and his influence as a property holder in Georgetown and Bethesda as well as Montanverde, his summer home at the far end of River Road, into political power. Peter led and dominated the Democratic Party and the slaveowning decision-makers of Montgomery County until the Civil War, and members of his family carried on that seigniorial role through World War I. Their general political position involved a stout defense of property and the status quo.

George Peter was born in September 1779, the son of wealthy Robert Peter. He tried to serve in the Whisky Rebellion, but Washington sent him home since he was only fifteen. A few years later he received his lieutenancy from Washington's hands at Mount Vernon and embarked on a successful military career that included service in the Louisiana Territory. He resigned his commission as a major of artillery in 1808 to manage the family business and considerable property he had inherited from his father.

After the War of 1812, Peter recognized that his Federalist Party was moribund and became the first Democrat elected to Congress from the Sixth District in December 1816 by winning a special election over Judge Charles Kilgour, a respected barrister and potent vote getter later called the "ploughboy of old Montgomery." The fact that George Peter lived at 3017 N Street in Georgetown did not seem to matter. He used his summer place near Darnestown as a voting address and won a second term before he moved there permanently. With his three wives he fathered sixteen children, nine of whom survived to adulthood, including several judges, numerous politicians and one well-known doctor, Armis-

tead, who married into a life at Tudor Place with his remarkable mother-in-law, Britannia. One notable grandson, among many, was G. Freeland Peter, Canon of the Washington Cathedral, whose Bethesda summer home became the seat of the Woodmont Country Club.

The Peter family's major Bethesda holding lay between the Pike and the Old Road, just north of the Woodmont Triangle and Battery Lane in the area later occupied by the medical library and NIH. The Peters and the Dunlops, the Magruders and the Bradleys, the Loughboroughs and the Bealls intermarried and became the political leaders and acknowledged "aristocracy" of the Bethesda area in the period before the Civil War.

In 1848 Major Peter entertained the young Whig Congressman from Illinois, Abraham Lincoln, at Montanverde and made speeches at Seneca and at Rockville that year for Whig candidates. When the Whigs died out, the Peters reverted to their Democratic loyalty and fought the Know-Nothing American Party for power and positions.

"In the political battles of these stormy

Major Peter, probably from a St. Memin drawing

decades," concluded the County's bi-centennial historians, "a majority of Montgomery County voters adopted the defensive, somewhat self-conscious conservatism of a declining rural backwater. Their attitude was reflected in their preference for leaders from the planter aristocracy." In one election of this period three of the five County candidates for the House of Delegates were members of the Peter family which led one observer to conclude that "we may expect soon to be Petrified with a full ticket." Before the War Between the States, George Peter Jr., replaced his father as a Democratic Party leader and spokesman for the ruling, slave-owning class.[3]

Major George has one other distinction at least. He is undoubtedly the County's best-known ghost. Many witnesses have provided colorful accounts of his spirit's antic behavior which includes moving chairs so they face the fire and enjoying a late night drink. Here is Roger B. Farquhar's version which relates to a later owner of Montanverde, Frank P. Harman of the Hamilton National Bank, who bought the home in 1916.

There is a tradition among the descendants of the Major that in his older years he had a toddy or "night cap" brought to his bedroom before retiring. When he had drained the glass, he made it a practice to throw the glass violently into the fireplace. One evening when there was no one in the house but Mr. Harman and a local mechanic discussing some plans, they heard a loud shattering of glass upstairs. Mr. Harman asked in surprise: "What can that be?"

The man with him replied: "That is only the ghost of Major Peter throwing his last toddy glass into the fireplace."

The only words Mr. Harman found adequate to express his feelings after that experience were (from Virgil's Aeneid) "opstipui steteruntque comae et vox faucibus haesit." ("I stood amazed, my hair stood on end, and my tongue clung to the roof of my mouth.")

It is difficult to fear or dislike a ghost who only returns to his home for an occasional drink.

"Marylanders wanted slavery protected and maintained, but they also wanted to preserve the Union." Concern over the effect of ending the slave trade in Washington also worried County leaders although many admitted they were happy to see the slave

pens opposite the Smithsonian dismantled. As the cancer of slavery devoured the Whig Party, other political forces rose to fill the vacuum, and it was the Nativists, the haters of immigrants, Jews, and Catholics who called themselves the American Party but were yclept Know-Nothings, that bubbled to the top in Maryland's fetid, political stewpot. They had simple answers to all of society's problems and seemed to see themselves as born-again Federalists. Many in their ranks were upwardly mobile, first-time voters whose candidates wrapped themselves in the flag while spreading venom and prejudice[4]

Democrats attacked the American Party's candidates as un-American, as anti-Catholic, and finally, as abolitionists. The ultra-violent 1855 campaign resulted in Know-Nothing control of the House of Delegates and the re-establishment of the Democratic Party in Southern Maryland and Montgomery County. The American Party soon dissolved in the mire of the slavery question, but elected Thomas Holliday Hicks governor in 1857 over the divided Democrats. He, as much as Federal bayonets, kept Maryland in the Union.[5]

John Brown's raid on Harper's Ferry and the resulting tide of negrophobia finally swept away the Know Nothings. By 1860 the American Party had collapsed except in a few backwaters such as Montgomery County.

An Eastern Shore slaveholder's convention in Cambridge in November 1858 dealt with the concerns caused by a large, free-black working force which, it was claimed, "corrupted and demoralized" the slaves. In some places, free blacks had real leverage especially at harvest time. Besides, "they affronted the established order by possessing a degree of independence altogether unsuitable for black people." And increasingly the problem was not what might be seen as "uppity" behavior, it was fear.

In the Bethesda area the 1860 census lists more than a dozen individual free blacks, mainly as farm workers or servants. These included the household of Levy Offutt, 55, who headed a family that consisted of Almira, 22; Bella, 16, both washerwomen, plus Lucinda, 2, and Alice, four months. Margret Lee, a 30-year-old laundress, had three children: Charles 6, Ann 4, and Josiah 2, and a mulatto washerwoman named Charlotte Baptist had four children in her home.[6]

On the Bethesda farms the number of slaves decreased sharply as wheat, cattle, and

diversified farming replaced tobacco. The largest slaveholders at the time of the Civil War included Greenbury Watkins with thirty-three, thirteen of whom were under ten years of age; miller William Orndorff with nineteen; Robert P. Dunlop owned fifteen (nine men, three women, and three children) and James Dunlop only one; John Davidson had fourteen slaves including eight children (one 10-year-old was listed as a fugitive); Elizabeth Bohrer was the owner of eleven slaves on the farm that became the Naval Hospital; the Luf-broughs, as the census taker spelled it, owned seven as did John Bean with a man, woman and six children which may or may not be a family since the census listed only the sex and age of slaves. P. S. Posey on River Road owned twelve slaves including six children

The various Counselman families owned eighteen slaves between them and the Magruder clan held three-dozen slaves. At the other end of the scale, Joseph Bradley owned a 16-year-old boy as did Henry Renshaw, and C. F. Willett owned two 60-year-old men and a 56-year-old woman. Old Major George Peter topped the list with a hundred slaves to mark both his political and economic status.[7]

In the period just before the war the County was recovering from the economic depression and depopulation of the 1840's. In a divided nation and state, Montgomery was becoming a divided county, but the leaders were still, for the most part, slave owners. County Democrats swept to victory in the 1859 election and sent slaveholders to the House of Delegates and the very well-to-do physician Washington Duvall, owner of more than sixty slaves, to the State Senate.

In response to the not-too-distant rumblings from Harper's Ferry, a mounted rifle company started exercising at Rockville. Robert Peter Jr. was among the company's officers. In general, the northern parts of the County seemed more "Southron" and more sanguinary as the fatal 1860 election approached.

The Whigs and Know-Nothings reorganized themselves under the banner of the Constitutional Union Party and nominated John Bell of Tennessee for the climactic Presidential election of 1860. Republicans were few in number in Maryland, but in Montgomery County they had a notable representative in Montgomery Blair who lived at Falkland near

his father's mansion, Silver Spring.   The younger Blair, who had been Dred Scott's counsel, made a number of poorly received speeches for Lincoln. The nominee of the regular Democrats in their second try at Baltimore, Stephen A. Douglas, had little support in the County or in the State, but Vice-President John C. Breckinridge, choice of the Southern wing of the party, was clearly a favorite of the slaveocracy.

In the *Sentinel*, editor Matthew Fields cried that "God had placed Maryland in the South," and as the election day neared, the tone of his editorials and columns attacking the "Black Republicans" grew more strident. On the 26th of October 1860 the *Sentinel* concluded that the contest was between Lincoln and Breckinridge and that the other candidates were "mere cyphers." And on November 2, under the headline "Democrats to the Work!" Fields wrote, "We would earnestly remind every democrat in the County of his duty on Tuesday next. Let him remember that never before, in the history of his county, was his individual exertions more required in defense of his very liberty, than at the present moment."

The election took place on November 6, and both the State and County's voters divided almost equally between Breckinridge and Bell. Statewide, Breckinridge gained Maryland's eight electoral votes, but the final tally in Montgomery County was Bell 1,155, Breckinridge 1,125, Douglas 99, and Lincoln 50. Obviously Lincoln was not acceptable to the voters of Maryland and did not have enough adherents in the County to fill a tavern while Bell, the overt symbol of compromise, was a local favorite.[8]

In the County, after the election of Lincoln was assured, the Breckinridge supporters were those who talked loudly of secession. Some suggested the "reversion" of the District of Columbia to Maryland if the state should secede, but even among the most rabid, states-rights slaveowners were few willing to follow South Carolina's intemperate lead and declare immediate secession.

On the first day of 1861, 300 men gathered at the Courthouse in Rockville to proclaim their sympathy for the South. A series of unanimously adopted resolutions supported slave owners' rights, but two more radical proposals failed, and the secessionists blamed the Sandy Spring "Friends" for their defeat.[9]

With the collapse of the Constitutional Union Party and the virtual disappearance of the Know-Nothings, the newly organized Union Party filled a vacuum and by the end of May 1861 was ready to enter the elections statewide. Its platform supported military efforts to preserve the Union, and it happily took in all Democrats opposed to secession. In the special June election the Unionists carried every Congressional district against the States Righters and Independents who protested the presence of soldiers at the polling places and soon disappeared as political forces. The 6th District, which included Montgomery County, chose Union candidate Charles Calvert. In November the Unionists would elect a governor, Augustus W. Bradford, and win control of the General Assembly with the unsolicited and embarrassing help of Federal troops patrolling the ballot boxes in the counties of Southern Maryland and the three-day passes given members of the Potomac Home Brigade to go vote.

In shattering succession Fort Sumter had been fired on; seven Deep South states claimed to have seceded; blood had been shed in the streets of Baltimore, and General Benjamin Butler, yet to earn the sobriquet "Beast," had become Maryland's military protector in charge of keeping the trains running and the elections peaceful. Governor Hicks, "a man trying to keep his footing on a log swirling in a midstream rapids," finally did call a special session of the Maryland legislature, but to meet in pro-Union Frederick, not occupied Annapolis.[10]

By the time they reassembled, a number of leading secessionist spokesmen, including two Baltimore newspaper editors, members of both the House and Senate and a half dozen legislative clerks had been arrested, and the writ of habeas corpus had been suspended. They protested these acts in the strongest terms. And again they adjourned. "Most Marylanders probably wanted to be left alone," and the State "government, roughly reflecting that wish, appeared paralyzed. Neither the governor nor the assembly found any decisive course appealing."[11]

On the day that mobs attacked Union soldiers in Baltimore, the Confederate flag flapped above the Courthouse in Rockville, but soon thereafter a local observer wrote that George Peter Jr., and the other "mad ones of our village are cooling down somewhat." Mary Anderson noted, "Several northern families have left hurriedly but I believe of their own free will. Some may have felt fear but most I reckon from guilty consciences."[12]

In the Capital, real estate values collapsed while the cost of foodstuffs soared. The "experts" predicted that the District would have to be abandoned or would surely become a battleground. Some Southern-sympathizing families had already moved from Washington City to the Bethesda area. For example, Alfred Ray transplanted his farming operation to what would later be called North Chevy Chase or Kensington, and Hilleary Lyles Offutt abandoned Georgetown for a large farm just north of Dr. Davidson's place in the middle of what became Bethesda.[13]

While the politicians ducked and dodged and debated, young men went to war. Along with hundreds of Marylanders, some of the Capital's largest and best equipped militia units, including many members of the National Rifles, marched over the bridges and joined the army of the Confederate States of America. But within a month more than thirty loyal, volunteer infantry companies and two new cavalry troops were drilling in D.C. with many Montgomery County residents in their ranks.[14]

Some County detachments joined the Southern cause en masse, and the First Maryland Cavalry grew out of George Gaither's First Virginia Cavalry. Ridgely Brown of Unity, a neighbor of the Sandy Spring Quakers, became their captain. T. H. S. Boyd in his *History of Montgomery County* listed five Confederate colonels including brigade commander "Lije" White, four captains, a lieutenant, surgeon Edward Wootton, and "a host of other officers, non-commissioned officers and privates, all of revolutionary descent, and who, whether in a good or bad cause, illustrated the valor of the race and well maintained the reputation of the old Maryland Line."

Boyd could not bring himself to print the names of any local Union officers, but J. Thomas Scharf for his *History of Western Maryland* found three, and Francis Preston Blair's son Frank became a general in the Union Army and a son-in-law, Samuel Philips Lee, was promoted to admiral in the U. S. Navy.

Nathan Loughborough's grandson James Henry Loughborough served in Lee's army as a

cavalryman and then in the Signal Corps in most of the major battles of the East including Jubal Early's 1864 "raid" on Washington. He was with the Army of Northern Virginia when it surrendered at Appomattox, and his young wife, Margaret Cabell, worked for the Southern cause in Richmond all through the war and returned home on a flag-of-truce ship in March of 1865 only at her husband's insistence. After the war Loughborough and his family rebuilt ravaged "Milton," and he lived in Bethesda and served as a justice of the peace until his death in 1921. When his son returned, in his blue uniform, from the Spanish American War, he is supposed to have said, "Suh, I don't allow any damn Yankee near me in uniform, so you better take it off quick, or I might shoot!"[15]

And one more. Walter Gibson Peter was the youngest surviving child of Major George Peter, who died at age 81 in June of 1861, and of his third wife, Sarah Norfleet Freeland. Eighteen-year-old "Gip" Peter crossed the river soon after his father's death, collected several bullet holes in his clothes at the ghastly battle of Ball's Bluff, and in early 1862, despite his sister's warnings that the man was "foolhearty and rash," he joined his cousin Capt. William

"Gip" Peter

Orton Williams, whose mother was America Peter Williams, sister of Britannia Kennon. Together they traveled to Tennessee, and on the evening of June 8, 1863, dressed as Union officers, they entered Federal lines at Franklin, Tennessee, carrying forged orders as Colonel Auten and Captain Dunlap. When suspicions were raised, someone drew "Capt. Dunlap's" sword and found it engraved "Lt. W. G. Peter, C. S. A." Another officer then recognized Williams as a West Point classmate. Orton claimed it was all a joke, but a court martial met that night.

The next morning they were given time to write letters and visit with the chaplain and then, despite their request to be shot, they were both hanged from a hastily constructed gallows near a wild cherry tree. They were buried in the same grave, and about a year later their families had the remains exhumed and reburied in the Peter family's plot at Oak Hill Cemetery in Georgetown.[16]

As young men rushed to answer Lincoln's call for troops, Washington became a sprawling campground that soon spread out into the fields and farms of Bethesda, and one of the first decisions made by the Union's military leaders was to fortify the Capital city. The volunteer soldiers, itching for a fight to cap their exciting summer holiday, were put to digging trenches and cutting trees. Partly it was the ancient dictum of "keep 'em busy and keep 'em happy," and partly the fear of attack from just across the river.

Some bridges were dismantled, others heavily guarded, and Lee's home was occupied. Meanwhile, detachments of soldiers protected the C&O Canal and the Washington Aqueduct and established a screening picket line. In May General Charles Stone marched his men through Bethesda and on north to establish outposts at Great Falls, Clopper's Mills, Darnestown and Poolesville.

Along the river, Confederate pickets exchanged a few shots with Union volunteers. A skirmish at Seneca Mills, was followed by a number of horse stealing raids into the County. On June 17 Confederates fired some twenty ineffectual rounds of light artillery at the New Hampshire men stationed at Poolesville, an act probably applauded by most residents of that area. Two men died in an early July skirmish at Great Falls involving Company B of the Turner Rifles, which included a number

of Germans and was part of the 8th Battalion of D.C. Volunteers. But as the fort building and the training continued, the general cry that first spring and summer was "On to Richmond!"

Many of the boys and young men from the Bethesda end of Montgomery County who answered Lincoln's call did so in D.C. volunteer organizations, and they too were put to digging and building and clearing fields of fire while old Winfield Scott tried to make an army out of a polyglot mob. By July the 90-day enlistments were running out and the pressure for a battle to end the conflict was mounting. Irving McDowell took command of some 30,000 barely trained men wearing all sorts of different uniforms and carrying many different calibers of weapons. His force took five days to traipse the twenty miles to Manassas, straggling, getting lost, and picking berries as they went.

On Sunday, July 21, they met and almost defeated the equally unprepared army of Pierre Gustave Toutant Beauregard. But Joseph E. Johnston's men arrived from the Valley, and Thomas Jonathan Jackson, who hated fighting on Sunday, won his nickname, and the Federal army disgraced itself before a crowd of picnickers who had come down from the Capital to see the war.

That night McDowell's men scattered all over Washington and through the surrounding countryside including Bethesda's farm fields. They had "skedaddled." The Rebels could have ambled into the city and, perhaps, ended the war, but as Lincoln noted they "were all green together." In Bethesda the distant thunder and rolling boom of cannon arrived all day on the western breeze. The sagging telegraph wires hummed, and the pickets were extra nervous that night.

The two armies now camped even closer to each other. Within a month nearly 40,000 Union soldiers spread along the Potomac from Point of Rocks to Georgetown. Skirmishes continued especially at the fords and ferry crossings. And soon two other things happened around Bethesda and all along the river, fences and slaves began to disappear. The fences went into soldiers' cookfires and the slaves into their camps.

The first forts around Washington went up in May 1861 on the Virginia side of the Potomac starting with the hills on which Robert E. Lee's fine home stood. All through June and well into July almost no thought was given to constructing defenses on the northern side of the city. But after the embarrassing disaster at 1st Bull Run and the arrival of the "Young Napoleon," Gen. George Brinton McClellan, all that changed. McClellan endorsed a plan for a "beltway" of forts mounting three hundred cannon and put Major, later General, John Gross Barnard, Corps of Engineers, in charge of construction.[17]

Barnard first had the Arlington Heights positions improved and extended. The soldiers felled acres of trees and moved tons of earth as the fort line grew south to cover the important port of Alexandria. By the late summer of 1861 with the river low and increasing reports of skirmishes and raids as far north as Harper's Ferry, the sweating engineers turned their attention to the wide northern approaches.

The first, huge, Bethesda-area bastion went on Rockville Pike in Tenallytown and was originally called Fort Pennsylvania because most of the men who built it hailed from the Keystone State. It was later renamed Fort Reno. A lookout and signal tower soon rose on the highest point in the District of Columbia, some 429 feet above sea level. To the east alongside the Seventh Street Road, Fort Massachusetts soon stood along with

Gen. John Barnard

Forts Slocum and Totten to its right and Fort DeRussy and several batteries to its left in the Rock Creek Valley. Fort Massachusetts was later renamed for General Isaac I. Stevens, who was killed in Virginia in 1862.[18]

Still farther to the east on the road toward Baltimore, Barnard built Fort Lincoln to protect the highway and the railroad to the North. Then he began the work of filling in the spaces between the forts and protecting the C&O Canal, the Aqueduct and the bridges. In the fall of 1862 engineer battalions built a military road to connect the forts, keep them supplied and make possible the rapid movement of troops.[19]

By the winter of 1861-62, forty-eight earthen forts encircled the city, each with a magazine to protect one hundred rounds of ammunition for its massive 24-pound and 32-pound cannon. Fourteen of the forts faced northward between the Potomac and the Anacostia Rivers. In the spring of `62, Stonewall Jackson's bloody dance through the Shenandoah Valley dazzled three Federal armies and led to the call for stronger defenses. After the slaughter at Sharpsburg in September 1862, the system was re-evaluated. The Secretary of War appointed a commission. Its recommendations were to fill the gaps between the forts, to mount better guns, to build a few new forts, to replace antiquated Fort Washington with some real river defenses, and to train and house 25,000 infantry and 9,000 artillerymen plus 3,000 cavalry at the forts to protect the city against any invader from the south or north.

The soldiers themselves did most of the early work of fort building, but as more and more slaves escaped to Union lines, these "contrabands" were put to work. The engineers handed axes and shovels to the walking wounded, and finally, as Barnard tried to fulfill the commission's plan, he hired laborers for a dollar a day.

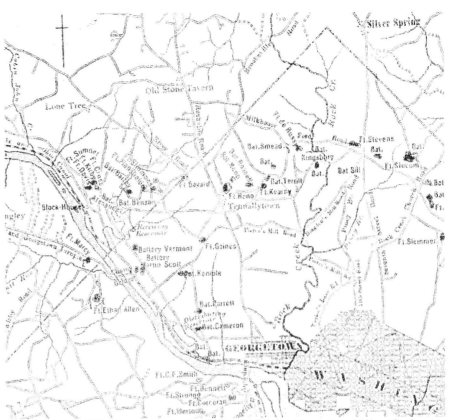

The defenses of Washington in the Bethesda (Old Stone Tavern) and Silver Spring areas

According to one observer, fort building did more "to clear the country of its primeval timber . . . than two centuries of occupation." At times up to a thousand civilians were on the payroll, slowing the construction of the Aqueduct and other area projects. By the end of 1863 there were sixty forts in the network including the huge river defensive works called Fort Foote and Battery Rodgers both of which mounted 15-inch guns and 200-pounder Parrotts and had walls twenty feet thick. Two ranks of rifle pits connected the whole system. Barnard, satisfied with the work, asked Stanton for a transfer to active service.

In the Bethesda area, very little is left of the Civil War forts. Above Chain Bridge are the remains of Batteries Cameron, Parrott and Kemble, which mounted huge, rifled cannon to protect the bridge. On the Potomac Palisades was Battery Martin Scott. A Rhode Island lieutenant wrote that he and his men seemed to be isolated and forgotten there but "do not grieve for us. We lived on the fat of the land — and the water too. From the Potomac we had shad, herring, and catfish; by energetic foraging in the neighborhood we obtained milk, butter, eggs, chickens, cornbread, sugar and coffee." The lieutenant and his men were un-

happy when they were transferred to Fort DeRussy on the wooded fringe of Rock Creek. Most soldiers assigned to heavy artillery companies or to the infantry manning the forts' trench lines considered it good duty with many fringe benefits.

Under the parking lot behind Sibley Hospital, lie the remains of Battery Vermont that, with Fort Marcy across the Potomac, controlled the river and protected the water supply of the Capital with their seacoast cannon. The only big fort in Bethesda itself was Fort Sumner, the remains of which were easily seen well into the 1950s but have now all but disappeared under the lawns of up-scale subdivisions and the Defense Mapping Agency.

Sumner was a huge fortress composed of three connected redoubts called Kirby (Fort Franklin), Cross (Fort Ripley) and Davis (Fort Alexander) built on three small knolls with a total perimeter of about 850 yards. The fort was named for General Edwin Vose Sumner, a veteran of the Black Hawk and Mexican wars and the bloody disturbances in Kansas. Its cleared fields of fire spread from present-day MacArthur Boulevard to Massachusetts Avenue north of Little Falls Branch and included the homes of the Loughboroughs and the Brookes, who like most of their neighbors were Southern sympathizers.

For most of the war years hundreds of soldiers camped at the complex to man the twenty-two large cannons, the battery of mobile 6-pounders, and pair of Coehorn mortars as well as the trenchlines between the gun platforms. Widower Edmund H. Brooke of "Oak Hill" and his daughters, Maria and Anne, all Rebels at heart, learned to tolerate the attentions of the First Maine Heavy Artillery.[20]

The fort was built on the property of one Albert Lodge whose family had acquired part of the old "Friendship" tract in 1817. New York volunteers did much of the construction, and at various times, New York infantrymen, Ohio militia, and heavy artillery companies from New Hampshire and Maine manned the complex. Most lived in wooden barracks also built by the troops with the hundreds of trees they cut.

The First Maine Heavy Artillery was stationed at the fort from the summer of 1862 until May of 1864. Then Grant pulled them out of the defenses of Washington along with many other well-trained artillery regiments,

converted them into infantrymen, and threw them into the attacks on Lee near Richmond. Fighting only in the last ten months of the war, the 1st Maine "heavies" had the sad distinction of suffering more battle casualties than any of the other 2,047 Federal regiments.[21]

Many of the men stationed at Fort Sumner wrote home about the beautiful countryside and their view of the peaceful river and distant Sugarloaf Mountain. H. T. Chace of the 10th Rhode Island praised the "pure air, spring water, wood, cut and dried; excellent drainage, good bathing facilities, little policing, hardly more guarding, and a drill which offers a pleasant change." But Chace also noted, "Some of the boys call one tent 'The Smithsonian Institute' on account of the variety of bugs and insects it contains."

The surrounding woods disappeared into construction of the forts, and north of the works, the soldiers cleared huge fields and built abatis with the sharpened and entangled tree branches. In their spare time some of these men prospected for gold and dug a series of exploratory tunnels. It is likely that the "gold mines" youngsters from Glen Echo and Bethesda crawled into early in the 20th century had at least their beginnings in the leisure time of soldiers.

The horseshoe shape of Battery Bailey may still be seen in Little Falls Park. This small fort and Battery Benson to the east once controlled the Powder Mill Valley; the creek now called Little Falls Branch. Two other forts to Bailey's east, Mansfield and Simmons, built mainly on Shoemaker property, have disappeared as have Fort Gaines and a camp the soldiers simply called "Mud," part of a second line of defense on the hill where The American Univesity now sprawls. Gaines won some local repute when red jacketed Zouaves of the New York 55th had Lincoln to dinner. Afterwards the President told the officers that if their Frenchmen "could fight as well as they could cook, the regiment would do very well indeed."

Fort Bayard was built on what Barnard called "a very peculiar knob of rock" on a ridge long a source of soapstone. Members of the local Shoemaker families aided in the construction of this fort and operated a small store to sell provisions to the soldiers. Bayard was part of the Fort Reno complex, and its powerful guns could sweep the River Road approach to the city.

Fort Reno itself, although not as large at Fort Sumner, was a major fortress that contained twenty-seven heavy guns and mortars and guarded the important roads to Georgetown. Pennsylvania volunteers built it on property purchased from the Dyer brothers, and the fort was home for large numbers of troops throughout the years of the Civil War.

All the way to the District Line the soldiers cleared fields of fire in front of Reno. They felled acres of timber, including a number of orchards of peach, apple, and crab apple trees, and turned their tangled branches toward the expected enemy. A large campground spread behind the fort, and by September of 1861 it was ready to welcome President Lincoln for a review of the troops and presentation of colors.

A forward redoubt grew at about Fessenden and 39th Streets, and by the time the fort became "Reno" in 1863, the complex included barracks, officers' quarters, two hospitals, several kitchens, stables and a number of other structures for the 3,000-man force. Soldier mail overwhelmed the post office at Tenallytown, accustomed to handling a few pieces of mail each day, and, according to a Rhode Island soldier, when the postmaster began to receive "upwards of a thousand, he didn't know 'what on airth' to do with them. They say he has been in the hospital ever since."[22]

Bethesdans living in the neighborhood of Sumner and Reno and the other forts found themselves with, at best, a mixed blessing. They had a ready market for their milk and produce and were able to sell meals and pies as well as vegetables to men who were sick of salt pork and hardtack. But apples and chickens often vanished, tombstones became oven walls, and fences fed campfires. The forts became a magnet for runaway Maryland slaves, and soon there were black men and women working as laborers and cooks, carpenters and washerwomen behind those thick walls.

And the soldiers had to drill and practice. So the cannon cracked out regularly, and the rounds whirred a mile or more to land in the fields or the river. Doree Holman reported that Miss Hester Counselman, whose home was on what is now the Kenwood golf course, found "the target practice from the forts near the District Line very trying. She used to tell the writer: 'The cannon balls went flying over our heads.'" When the Shoemakers went to complain, they were told that "the safest place to be was in the line of fire since the soldiers never hit the target." It was not long after that that a cannon ball splintered a tree in their yard.[23]

The forts' sentries constantly interrupted traffic along the roads and regularly harassed local "Secesh" sympathizers, of whom there were many. The soldiers bathed in the river or in Rock Creek whenever they could, and they fouled many local streams with their waste. The digging of hundreds of wells and latrines played havoc with the local water supply.

Young men far from home for the first time drank in Georgetown and at the rural taverns, flirted with the local girls, and attracted a constant stream of prostitutes and sutlers. In slack times the soldiers sometimes engaged in rough horseplay or even wanton destruction. A carousing bunch of drunken volunteers tore apart the Loughborough's mill, just south of Fort Sumner, and even churches were not immune from ransacking and damage as the vestrymen at St. Albans discovered.[24]

East of Fort Reno stretched trenches, rifle pits, field gun batteries and small forts, one located at a place once known as Rudolph Kauffmann's "Airlie" and now St. John's College High School Next was Fort DeRussy high on the edge of the Rock Creek Valley where a great deal of the earthworks may still be seen. In 1863 this fort received a Parrott 100-pounder that, although difficult to handle and operate, fired thirty-two shells on Early's force near Silver Spring at ranges up to 4,500 yards in July of 1864.

Next to the east were some smaller batteries and then Fort Stevens itself on 13th Street two blocks north of Military Road where Lincoln came under fire during Early's 1864 "raid." Here men of the Sixth Corps fought and died to save the Capital. Lewis Cass White, a veteran of that battle, saved the fort and formed an association to mark the spot. However, not much is left but their marker, a plaque and the walls restored in 1937-38 by the young men of the New Deal's Civilian Conservation Corps.[25]

In 1913, at his request, Virginia Campbell Moore wrote her grandson about her family's life in Bethesda during the Civil War. She was a very proper Southern matron with all the

manners and prejudices that station entailed, but she was also a careful observer.[26]

First of all, you must know how it happened that Grandfather and I found ourselves in a border-Southern state during the Civil War — we, who had always lived in Washington City since our Ancestors, or mine at least, came here in 1799, one year before the Capital of the Nation was transferred from Philadelphia . . .

As you doubtless heard, we married when your Grandfather was about twenty years of age and I was nineteen. His health had never been very robust since an attack of Typhoid Fever a few years before, and when he was about twenty-two, the Doctors advised strongly that we try Country life for a few years — anything that would keep him out of doors. All his Father's relatives were in North Carolina, Georgia or Alabama and they urged his coming there to live, but my Father offered to give us any plantation we would select, if we would settle at some not distant place from Washington. The Doctors, too, preferred this to a more enervating climate, so we fixed upon the pretty place seven miles out, in the Bethesda neighborhood, near the Church, in Maryland, which you know as "Wildwood." It was situated on the main "Turnpike" road from Washington and Georgetown. Just at the upper end of our place, the "County Road" [Cedar Lane] came in, this road passing from the turnpike across to the Potomac River.

Grandfather and I, bought our plantation in Maryland, a small one, less than a hundred acres, for we were new to country life, and were pleasantly established there with our three baby girls, Ella, Julia and Eloise who died four months later. Our house stood on a high hill, in a beautiful grove, back of which was a fine pinegrove, which was particularly adapted to our needs, as lung trouble was then feared to be Grandfather's cause of ill health.

As he sits by while I am writing this, not far from eighty years old, you may judge that our selection of locality was a wise one. The hill on which our house stood was about a quarter of a mile from the Main road, the Turnpike, over which troops constantly passed, and was approached by two long winding roads from two gates, one at the lower end, one at the upper, close to the County road of which I have spoken which leads to the Potomac River. The house commanded a full view of the road, so that when troops passed, sometimes in disorderly fashion — well, we knew it!

The first visible intimation we had that War was declared, was when we waked one morning to find a "picket station" established at our upper gate, and they were there to stay, day and night, until peace was declared four years later. What those four years brought, in mind, heart and nerve strain, only those who lived and struggled through them can ever realize.

At first we felt angry — bitter — for here we were, Southern people by birth, education, environment, forced to remain in a State held down by our enemies, into whose hands we had fallen without a moments warning and from whom we did not know as yet what to expect. Truly we could sing the song — "The despot's heel is on thy shore, Maryland, My Maryland." Had we left our home it would have been destroyed as "Rebel" property, or confiscated by Federal Officers, so there was nothing to do but occupy it ourselves and take what came.

Of course, they, the Pickets, were as suspicious of us as we of them, as you will see. The first day after selecting their camping spot, depositing their knapsacks, cooking utensils, etc., two of them sauntered up to the house and, as I stepped towards the open door, asked if I would "give them a little milk and something to eat" — pie preferably. I told them "we had no pie," "we do not keep pie on tap as you Northern people do, but I will give you milk and good Southern cornbread." Their faces brightened — they thought we might be good neighbors.

I called the cook, who brought the milk and bread and they sat down at my invitation, on the broad wooden platform over our large cistern, just outside the back door, between it and the Cook's quarters in which was our kitchen, connected by a covered way with the back door. I poured a glass of milk and handed it to one of the men, who took it shyly, turned it about and looking sideways at me, said, "lady would you mind tasting it first?" I laughed and said: "Why of course not, it is good milk, I don't want to poison you though, perhaps I ought to as you are going to fight my friends." So I drank the milk and they gladly emptied the pitcher and ate all the cornbread, thanked me and said they "hoped all the Southern ladies were like me." Then they left.

After that as the nights grew chilly and we thought of those poor men out in the cold and often rain, and even snow — we forgot they were "Yanks" and used to send them hot coffee and something better than "Hardtack." So we got to be quite good friends with our enemies and were sorry when the pickets were changed and we had to begin all over to convert the new ones.

We talked a great deal with many, many common soldiers who came to our place during the war and I often asked them why they came. Generally it was because there was no work. Once or twice it was "the love of excitement — adventure" — not once did I hear one say it was "love of Country, patriotism." Now and then an Officer or two would come to the house and ask if we would give them a meal — always offering to pay for it, which we declined as we did not wish to "open a Restaurant," as some around did.

Only once did we take pay for a dinner — and that because a coarse, ungentlemanly Officer tried to force us to express strong Southern sentiments — in the argument — and finally became personal and insolent. We all kept quiet and when he offered to pay for his dinner, Grandfather took it turning to our waitress, handed it to her, at the same time declining pay from his two companions, telling them they were "welcome to our table." Don't you think we were right good "rebels"?

I recall a Minnesota regiment camped near us for a while, who, though knowing our sentiments, respected them and were most friendly, expressing themselves gratefully for our hospitality. There was also a Massachusetts regiment we recall with pleasure. Returning one Sunday from the little country church in sight of our house, we found two Officers, I think three, sitting on the porch, awaiting us and much to our relief, they only wanted their dinner.

In those troublous times, men were imprisoned in the old Capitol on the merest suspicion of disloyalty to the Federal Government, so one who was known to be a Southern sympathizer, out of the fight only because he could not pass the physical test, as was your Grandfather, was closely watched; so when more than one official bluecoat appeared, we felt more or less anxiety until we knew their errand. We had a good dinner, fried chicken, etc., and we also had company, but there was nothing to do but share it with the self-invited guests, and when those three hungry men got through, there was a shortage of chicken for the "Company." However, they did not suffer, for you know our habit of always having cold ham and we wisely checked our hospitality when it reached the frozen custard which was not put on exhibition until the "Yanks" had gone.

Perhaps we do not merit the commendation which we claim, for our hospitality was somewhat compulsory, it not being wished to antagonize declared enemies backed by U. S. Government. Sometimes it was hard to be polite when we knew that on their way to our house, some of these men

had questioned our servants in the field, or at the Quarters, as to our political views. This however, did not often happen, though I recall three occasions when it did. Unfortunately there were in our neighborhood several Northern men who had bought small places and some of them curried favor with the Military by pointing out Southern sympathizers as people who would "bear watching;" yet when McCausland's Confederate Brigade came down our road, rushed to us for protection.

In one instance a family of five quartered on us until we declined to entertain them any longer. They needed no "protection" since no outrages on life or property were committed on any of the Southern raids excepting that they took horses for army use, of course. We lost several horses but Grandfather recovered them as they were stolen by Federal soldiers without the knowledge of their Officers, and carried to a livery stable in Washington, whence they were being shipped to New York when Grandfather discovered them and the thieves were caught and punished.

The Confederates were going off with my fine riding-horse, but were persuaded by a neighbor to leave him to the "Southern lady" at whose table they had just been entertained. He was strictly a lady's riding-horse so would have been of little use to the army. When troops from either side were about, we had the horses in the woods and then were in terror lest their neighing should betray them. Horses were legitimate Warspoils of course, since they were needed by both sides to replace those killed or disabled in battle, but we preferred to have our go to our friends if they must.

One day in July 1861, which was as you know early in the four year war — Grandfather, driving home from the City in his buggy, found the road blocked by hundreds of disorganized soldiers. Federals in full retreat, after the battle of "Bull Run" and "Manassas," where they had been badly beaten by the Confederates, and those not taken prisoners were escaping into Maryland, worn, bloody, dirty and hungry clamoring for food and water. In a few hours, every spring and well in Tenallytown — where was a tollgate on the pike — was drunken dry and all available food consumed.

They had thrown away their guns, after twisting and bending them all out of usefulness, in the Railway tracks as they ran. One of these guns is now on one of the tall bookcases in our library, as you may remember. It was picked up and given to Grandfather after they had been organized and marched off to some other point. I shall never forget the excitement of the days on

which that dreadful battle was fought — on Sunday, particularly. The firing was terrific and we sat with clasped hands and anxious thoughts and hearts — almost starting from our seats as the roar of cannon reverberated over the hills, telling of the carnage, the suffering, just across the river. A hush seemed to fall upon all, even the children and servants paused to listen, wide-eyed and awe-stricken.

Seated on the porch with us was our dear old friend, Judge Robert F. Dunlop, who lived alone, a bachelor in the Colonial home of his Ancestors, about a mile from us. Every Sunday he spent with us returning to us after the morning services in the little church just across the road from us. He was a Democrat in politics and afterwards a Representative in the State Legislature, strongly Southern in his affiliations, as were many others, opposed to secession, feeling that it would have been wiser for the South to fight for its rights in the Union. While we, believing this to be hopeless, felt that since we could not live peaceably together, we had no alternative but secession; therefore we had agreed not to talk about the war — so, whenever he appeared, often two or three times a week, we and he put on our muzzles and so friendship remained unbroken till the day of his death. Well! This dear friend as I have said, sat on our porch during that battle, neither of us daring to say what was in our mind.[27]

At first we tried to make conversation, but finally fell into silence, each respecting the feelings of the other too much to express the bitterness within. Perhaps the self-restraint was good for us, but it was hard work to keep still and for the first and only time we were glad when supper was over and he rode home.

By this time we had grown accustomed to war conditions — the high prices which compelled us to give up many hitherto essentials; the daily restraints as to the hours allowed for passing up and down the road, for after the "countersign" was out, none could pass the pickets without it, or a pass after dark. We seemed to get into a rut where nothing excited — we expected the "unexpected": the searching of the house for rifles, never there; the orders to put out our "signal" lights which were not signal lights, all those were constantly happening and taken as a matter of course. Because of the nightly alarms caused by the passing and repassing of troops, heavy army wagons, horses and artillery the children would rouse in terror and needed soothing to quiet their nerves enough to sleep and so we all slept in rooms opening into each other on the first floor and house

being on the hillside, the windows in some of these rooms were only a few feet above the ground.

One night as I sat by one of these windows with the closed outside shutters, but the windows open — holding in my lap your Father, then a babe a few months old and not expected to live from day to day, I thought I heard a rustling of fallen leaves, but thinking it was one of the negroes returning late to the Quarters, paid no further attention, when suddenly against the shutters there came a crash and a rough voice gave the order: "Surround the house," and instantly a detachment of Cavalry dashed around to obey.

By this time, Grandfather, who had been asleep, sprang from the bed to a window opposite and in no gentle terms called out "what the thunder do you want?" Quickly there was a change as the Colonel who had partaken of our hospitality, recognizing the voice, said, "Why Mr. Moore, I did not know this was your house. I was ordered to go up to that house on the hill where a signal light was kept burning every night and find out what it meant. I am very sorry, but will you tell me why the light burns. You know I am compelled to obey orders." "Certainly Colonel, you can come in and see for yourself, we were sitting up all night with a child we believe to be dying — we cannot sit in darkness. The shutters are closed — I do not see that we are giving out light for a 'signal' to those across the Potomac. We certainly have no such intention."

And so the Colonel, after glancing into the room to "see for himself," with many apologies, and the assurance that we "should not be again so disturbed," galloped down the road. Some of his men however, not relishing so "much ado about nothing" dashed through the orchard and thrashed off the fine crop of peaches upon which we were relying to pay for flour at $12.00 per barrel and coffee to replace toasted rye, of both of which we had been destitute for some weeks.

One morning we waked to find an armed man standing at each of the many trees encircling the house. Grandfather asked why they were there and was told their Officers were approaching and would tell him. Just at that moment our magnificent Newfoundland dog, the protector and companion of our children on their daily walks, as well as our house at night — dashed, barking loudly, up the hill. A shot rang out and he lay at the door, howling and bleeding before our eyes. The screams of the children, the cries of the servants and our own grief and anger at the cowardly act — for he was not attacking the men — almost frenzied us and some of the soldiers themselves

turned away with sympathy and shame at the lawless act and the loss and grief it had caused. Fortunately the ball had done its work well and our faithful, loving, almost humanly intelligent friend "Carlo" in a short time was relieved of his sufferings. The Officers on their arrival, were most indignant, not only on our account, but because of the breech of discipline by "firing without orders" and took the guilty man under arrest. This however, did not return our valued dog nor ease the heartaches of the little children who so loved him.

As to Grandfather and myself on that sad morning, we nervously waited through the tragedy to see what was to come when the Officers appeared. I was possessed with the idea that they had come to take him to the "Old Capitol" prison, as had been done to other Southern men, altho no charges had been brought against him, so I packed his valise, we each took a dose of nerve tonic (Hoffman's Anodyne), and then tried to eat our breakfast, so that he would not go off hungry, at least! In about an hour, three Officers appeared, crossing the field between us and our nearest neighbor and friend, the Rev. Mr. Cumpston, upon whom also they had been making an early morning call. Finding they had not arrested him, a Virginian holding our own sentiments, we took courage and calmly waited.

They saluted us courteously and then the Major, "regretting his necessity to perform an unpleasant duty, but you know we are compelled to obey orders," etc., etc., informed us that "information had been given that we were storing and forwarding ammunition to the enemy and that he had been ordered to search the house!" The relief was so great that we would have given him the house, but we did not let this be seen. Grandfather told him that he was at liberty to search, but that we were entirely guiltless of such charge and that he trusted that it would not be necessary to take his thirty men with their mud covered feet through the building on their fruitless search.

Signalling to his men to guard the house closely and be within call, he began his inspection, accompanied by four men and Grandfather, who led him upstairs first. Realizing that they would confiscate even a small pistol, which with a rifle for shooting squirrels, constituted our armament, I secured the former and slipping it into my old fashioned dress pocket, greeted the Major when he came down stairs as innocently as tho' not amenable to the law against "carrying concealed weapons."

The rifle was up over our door in the sleeping room into which the Major merely looked through

the door over which it hung — so we were safe! They examined most carefully, every closet and wardrobe where they had been told they might find "arms awaiting transportation to the Confederate line," they also ran their bayonets through hair mattresses, but found nothing of course. The Major then sent his men, under his Lieutenant, to examine barns and dairy, and, in the latter, after drinking all the cream and milk they wanted, they turned all the long rows of full milk pans upside down into the raised water trough, whence it ran out into the escape pipe. Why did they do that? Were I as young as I was then, I would say from pure deviltry — for they gained nothing by it — I think I'll say it anyhow! Meanwhile the Major made himself agreeable to us, sitting on the porch, and sincerely sympathized with us at the loss of our friend, the dog, his whole manner being apologetic and regretful, but it was some time before the children went to sleep without tears in their eyes!

The next event which I recall was the coming of the "Billy Wilson" Zouaves, to camp in a field just back of our plantation, where they were sent to be sufficiently trained before going to the front. This regiment was from the lowest slums of New York — the "Five Points," and was composed of the worst criminals — many of them liberated from prison upon condition of joining the Army. Their very dress was enough to convert them into savages. As I remember, their pants were bright red knickerbockers, over high tan leggings, blue jackets highly decorated with yellow braids, and their closely shaven heads covered with a blue and red fez with its long hanging tassel, the whole tending to heighten the diabolical expression which drink and crime had stamped upon many of their faces. Their coming struck terror into the neighborhood, for they were utterly lawless and before they had camped many days, pits were dug, covered with log huts, patrolled day and night by sentinels — into which they were put as punishment, when becoming unmanageable.

One warm summer day when windows and doors were wide open, I was sitting alone in the middle room, sewing and singing, when a shadow falling upon the floor, showed me one of these creatures about entering the side door opening into the adjoining room. Instantly realizing the danger, I advanced towards him, at the same time getting nearer the kitchen (connected with the house by a covered way) there was the cook, the only person within call. Fortunately at my advance "the foe retreated," until I had him outside the door, when Nancy the cook, hearing my voice calling her, ap-

peared. He demanded bread, pie, milk, eggs, potatoes, etc., etc., and I gave him what was within our reach, for we dared not leave him a moment, not turn our backs lest he should strike us, for he was evidently under the influence of liquor. Finally, seeing that we had nothing more for him, he seized his gun, killed a chicken nearby, snatched it up together with what we had given him and amid a torrent of oaths and foul language, wandered back to his camp. Had we reported him our lives would not have been safe.

When Grandfather came home from the City and heard of my fright, he wanted to attack the whole regiment, but on second thought, decided not to so, but after several such incidents in the neighborhood, the gentlemen took the matter to headquarters in Washington and the regiment was sent to the front. It was after this that I learned to shoot with the pistol which I had saved when the house was searched, and was very proud when once or twice I hit the target!

Now and then, as I have intimated, the Pickets were changed and then for a while we knew not what was coming, and until they realized that we had no evil intent and would not poison the milk for which they asked, they seemed to think it their duty to cause us annoyance at least. So, we learned to sit closely on the veranda and see them fill a blanket with "roasting ears" or potatoes, wasting double the number consumed for the mere pleasure of destruction. Once only Grandfather remonstrated, offering to have ripe ears gathered for them, but was told, with a long string of adjectives, that he might be thankful his life was spared and that they would take what they choose! So, another situation was accepted.

For the first half of 1862 there was little military action in the Bethesda area and "all quiet on the Potomac" became an accusation as well as a cliché. In March, Congress adopted as an article of war forbidding the Army to return fugitive slaves. The military in the Washington area had become one of the chief employers of contraband labor. And on April 16, Congress abolished slavery in the District of Columbia with compensation for slaveowners. Several men drove their chattels into Maryland to prevent their emancipation, and some Marylanders put their slaves in jail to preclude their escape.

By the end of the month the Baltimore *Sun* was reporting that up to two hundred slaves a week were escaping into Washington from the neighboring counties. Maryland slaveholders sent delegations to meet with Secretary of War Stanton and General McClellan and even with Lincoln and continued to try to use the civil law authorities to reclaim their runaways. In May when constables seized two Maryland runaways attached to a New York company as servants, there was nearly a riot on Seventh Street. The Fugitive Slave Law was still in effect but almost impossible to enforce. The *Sentinel* predicted a slave insurrection.

Numerous conflicts developed between the D.C. authorities and the military with Attorney General Bates eventually ruling that civil authority outranked the military in the Capital. A few days later William H. Offutt of Offutt's Cross Roads, now Potomac, recaptured one of his runaway slaves in the Capital with the help of the deputy marshals and took him back to Maryland. General James S. Wadsworth, the military governor of D.C., sent out a squad of soldiers to reclaim the slave. Mr. Offutt, a respected if irascible citizen in his mid-70s, told the officer in charge that the slave was no longer there. The old man had sent him to another farm at Poolesville so he would have a longer walk to freedom should he want to try again. Offutt was arrested and taken to the Old Capitol as a prisoner of state, and it took some time for Montgomery Blair to secure his release.[28]

Military action that affected life in Bethesda picked up again after 2nd Bull Run. Lee decided to invade the North in the hope of persuading England and other foreign nations to recognize and aid the Confederacy and to give Virginia farmers a chance to bring in their harvest. Many Southerners also expected hundreds of Marylanders to rally to the "cause," and some even hoped the State would still secede even though Governor Bradford and the legislature had clearly stated their loyalty to the Union. General Bradley Johnson C.S.A., the former Frederick state's attorney whose name had appeared on the Union ticket in 1861, believed that "Maryland's heart was with the Confederacy, but her body was bound and manacled to the Union."

As Lee's Army of Northern Virginia moved down the Valley, Stuart's cavalry crossed the river at White's Ford and swung out into Maryland to screen its movements. For several days detachments of blue clad soldiers moved through Bethesda. McClellan's 2nd and 12th Corps marched out Rockville Pike

and passed by Mrs. Moore's plantation while the 6th Corps and part of the 4th traveled out River Road and then on north along Falls Road.

Stuart established his headquarters at Urbana where a number of "very charming and pretty young ladies" congregated around the dashing cavalrymen, and a short social season followed which was crowned by a ball at the academy on the evening of September 8. The dance was going very well, although the young ladies declined to polka, when artillery fire crashed nearby. The officers charged out and helped repel a Union attack before returning to the frivolities.[29]

Lee's victorious troops moved into the Old Line State with the brass bands playing "Maryland, My Maryland," but their disheveled and often barefoot condition, while it may have inspired sympathy, begat few recruits. "A most ragged, lean and hungry set of wolves" was the way one Marylander saw them. On the 10th and 11th the sound and smoke of battle came from Sugar Loaf Mountain where a Confederate signal station operated. In those days the mountain could be easily seen from Fort Sumner and Fort Pennsylvania, soon to be renamed for Jesse L. Reno who was killed at South Mountain.

Lee, as was his wont, divided his forces, and McClellan, out of incredible luck, soon had a copy of the Reb's orders, but still he moved slowly and carefully while he studied the outnumbered Confederates dug in at Sharpsburg. The ghastly battle of Antietam raged along the lanes and through the cornfields and across the creek all day on September 17, and by sunset more than 23,000 men had been killed or wounded in the bloodiest day of American military history. Lee tenaciously held his lines on the 18th while his engineers threw pontoon bridges across the Potomac. That night he re-crossed and headed for Fredericksburg where he licked his wounds and dug in for the winter.[30]

The battle had been a tactical draw, but since the invasion of the North failed, the President counted it as victory enough to issue the preliminary Emancipation Proclamation. Thus Lincoln changed the nature of the war and likely ended whatever chances the South had of receiving increased foreign support. Despite the double disaster the Rebels suffered the next July at Vicksburg and Gettys-burg, this was the turning point of the Civil War.

Lincoln visited McClellan at Sharpsburg but could not convince him to pursue the retreating Confederates, so he relieved him of command. The President's unfortunate choice to lead the battered Army of the Potomac was Ambrose Burnside who could not convince Lincoln that he was the wrong man for the job. He proved it at Fredericksburg in December.

Mrs. Moore remembered that fall:

On September 17th, 1862, was fought the battle of Antietam, Md., or Sharpsburg as often called by Southerners. To reach this point the Federal Army passed up our road and for three days we were kept busy feeding the men who demanded food and helped themselves even to the family dinners which they took from the stove. One of our neighbors, an aged woman, had to apply for a guard in order to keep enough for her family needs. Her descendants now have in their possession a black silk apron through which was fired a bullet when she went out to remonstrate with marauders. After the Army, with its troublesome Camp-followers had entirely disappeared, we found that we had only food enough left for two days, the medicine for our ill baby had given out; we had brandy, which with codliver oil, was all that kept him alive.

Then arose the question of how we were to get supplies from the City. If Grandfather went for them I would be left alone with the children, and excited, timid servants and this could not be thought of. At last it was decided that Mr. Carroll, our Overseer, a respectable white man, who with his family lived in our tenant house, should drive me to town in a big three seated carryall where my father and brother would gladly attend to all my commissions. We started early in the morning and when we reached the toll-gate at Tenallytown, I was surprised to be halted by an Officer who recently had dined with me. He recognized me and expressed regret that I must be on the road at this unsettled time, because he had just received orders that a pass would be required or they could not return in the afternoon; hence I must go to the office of the Provost Marshall to secure such a pass. This was not a pleasant duty for a young woman of twenty-six, *who might or might not be treated discourteously.*

I quickly decided to go to my Father and be advised by him. My brother at once undertook to attend to the pass matter, while my dear father filled the carryall so full of provisions, meat, flour,

etc., etc., that I had to sit in front with the driver on the return trip; but in those times conventionalities were not considered and I might have returned on the back of one of the horses without much comment! I recall my father paid $16.00 for the medicinal Brandy for the baby. In a little while my brother came with the good news that it was announced at the Provost Marshall's office that the order had been rescinded and no pass was required; so, with an easy mind, I spent several hours with my Mother and Sister and at four o'-clock started on the journey home, knowing that I must pass the last picket station before sun-down or not be allowed to pass even tho' within sight of home.

As we passed the toll-gate we found the road filled with returning vehicles of every description, men lashing their horses and swearing, and dust flying and general pandemonium reigning. One of the men, recognizing us, told me to go back as quickly as possible and get a pass. "But none is required," I answered. "Yes, Madam, it is — they told me so too but the order is again changed. Turn quickly and go to the Provost Marshall's Office."

I said to Mr. Carroll, "There is no time to go to my brother," so putting the horses to their speed, we dashed back into the City. Reaching the said office, I mounted the steps and told the Sentinel pacing before the door my errand. "Proceed to the rear door and you will find the office." I "proceeded," opened the door and entering a large room filled with men, some of them rough looking — and stood aghast for a moment — when out from the crowd sprang a man who had a little farm near us — a rich livery-stable keeper whose little daughter had recently died, and I being her Sunday-School teacher had been attentive, so he was eager to do me a service. He drank heavily but was a brave man, afraid of nothing, and with as kind a heart as ever beat. "Let me get your pass for you," he said, and turning to the crowd, called out "Men, will you give way and let this lady have her turn first?" Yes! Yes! Yes! from all over the room and they opened a line for me to pass to the rail at the end of the room, behind which sat a much bedecked Major with his Lieutenant at his shoulder.

I approached him saying, "I should like to get a pass up into Maryland." He looked at me most insolently, waved me aside and said, "The lady may wait her turn."

"I'll be damned if she shall, " said my protector — and there came a hoarse growl from the crowd: "No, she shan't wait."

The Major saw he had gone too far, intoxicated tho' he was, and acceded to the request of his gentlemanly Subaltern that he "might be allowed to attend to the case." As quickly as possible, the Lieutenant wrote the pass, and bringing me a little book like a checkbook, told me "to kindly inscribe my name on the stub," which I kindly did with neatness and dispatch, writing merely "Mrs. Moore" without my initials.

My protector, Mr. Burch then escorted me from the room amid the cheers of the crowd! As he put me in the carryall, he said, "Do you know that by writing your name there you took an oath to the Federal Government?" "No," I said, "but since I did not know I was taking an oath, I shall not know when I am breaking one, should the necessity to do so ever arise."

And so we started for home and when reaching that same Tenallytown toll-gate, were met by our kind enemy friend, the Major who had been anxiously watching for us, as he knew of the little ones and the ill baby, and told me to drive quickly and so get through the picket station. This you may realize we did and an anxious, nerve-straining ride it was.

Just as we got into safety, the sundown gun boomed out, after which we would have had to give the countersign, or sit in the carryall till daylight, as did a neighbor, on one occasion, while her husband paced the floor all night with their two months old baby. The pickets had been watching for us too and told me that "Mr. Moore had been pacing up and down like a caged lion, with one eye on the house and children and the other on the road."

What would we have done in those days without our dear, faithful "Mammy" to aid us in the care of our helpless little ones! She too was carrying her heartache. Her husband, from a nearby plantation, when having a day's holiday in Washington, was accosted on the street by a man — a white man — from the North, who invited him into a saloon where he soon got him under the influence of liquor, and when, some hours later, poor Wesley came to himself, he was in uniform as a regularly enlisted recruit in the Federal Army!

He was heart-broken and begged to be released but all to no avail, and he would have been treated as a deserter had he escaped. He was allowed to communicate with his wife, so Grandfather took Mammy to the camp, just across the Potomac, to see him. Every effort was made to secure his release but all failed. He was killed in his first battle — at Petersburg, June 19th, 1864 — in a few months. After the war Grandfather secured a

pension for Mammy and this helped in building the home on the lot just back of 1680 31st Street, Washington, which we gave her.

On January 1, 1863, the Emancipation Proclamation went into effect. It had no direct, legal impact in Maryland, but it greatly increased the number of runaways to Washington, D.C., and to the Union lines. It also paved the way for a movement to do away with slavery in Maryland, a topic once politically taboo. By spring a faction calling themselves the Unconditional Unionists was tub thumping for abolition and producing a rupture in the coalition that was the Union Party.

In March of 1863 the first Conscription Act passed, and the coming of the draft, even with the opportunity to hire substitutes, forced a decision on a number of Montgomery County men who immediately headed South. The draft took white men and "colored" and even slaves. All three were listed among those conscripted from the Bethesda area of Darcy's Store in the last two years of the war. All through this period the market price of slaves steadily declined as recruiting squads of black soldiers had little trouble persuading field hands to win their freedom by putting on a blue coat and fighting for Old Abe.

The war went on. In early May near the Rappahannock and not far from the old battlefields near Bull Run, Lee bamboozled and then smashed Hooker's huge army in his tactical masterpiece, Chancellorsville. It cost him Stonewall Jackson.

While Grant pounded away at Vicksburg, Marse Robert, hoping to encourage the Copperheads and other peace advocates of the North, moved quickly into the Valley, crossed Mason and Dixon's Line, cut the main trunk of the B&O and was soon scouring south-central Pennsylvania. Hooker pushed his demoralized army across the Potomac and moved to make his headquarters at Frederick where he waited for supplies. Once more Bethesda homes became the targets of stragglers and bummers.

Now the third player entered from stage left. By moonlight on Saturday, June 27, 1863, James Ewell Brown Stuart with three Rebel cavalry brigades crossed the dangerously high river at Rowser's Ford near Seneca and

paused to burn and loot some canal boats and damage the locks as much as possible. On Sunday morning while the horses and soaked cavalrymen rested, Wade Hampton rode ahead and had Rockville cleared of Union troops by dinnertime when Stuart arrived.

According to one Rebel cavalryman "flocks of pretty maidens congregated on the front to greet us, showing strong sympathy for our cause, and cutting off all the buttons they could get hold of from our uniforms as souvenirs." These were the students from the Rockville Seminary, whose "doors and windows were full and running over with the fairest specimens of the gentler sex that eye ever beheld." The girls ran to cheer the cavalrymen waving lacy handkerchiefs and sheets of music emblazoned with Confederate flags. "It was Sunday, and the beautiful girls in their fresh gaily colored dresses, low necks, bare arms, and wildernesses of braids and curls, were 'off duty' for the moment, and burning with enthusiasm to welcome the Southerner; for Rockville, in radical parlance, was a 'vile secesh hole.'" They traded hair ribbons and handkerchiefs for uniform buttons and pulled hair from the horses' manes.[31]

Stuart was between the Army of the Potomac and the Capital and having a wonderful time when the head of a wagon train appeared on the Pike just south of Rockville. Then the day got even better. The Reserve Forage Train of Hooker's army contained 150 new army wagons each drawn by six sturdy mules. Most wagons carried bags of grain and bales of hay, but they were also hauling every imaginable type of provender to Federal officers at Frederick. When the head of the column reached Rockville, the tail of the long line was just entering Bethesda as young Mrs. Moore and her family went to church. Stuart quickly sent the 9th Virginia to capture the wagons and the small guard detail accompanying them.

Panic followed as the teamsters tried to get turned around or crashed off into the woods. Every team at full gallop, every wagon whirling onward, rebounding from rocks and jouncing into the air—one crashing against another "with the noise of thunder"—here one overturned and lying with wheels upward, the mules struggling and kicking in the harness; then one toppling over a steep bank and falling with a loud crash; others burning, others still dashing to the trees for shelter—

the drivers cursing, yelling, lashing, blaspheming, and howling amid the bang of carbines, the clatters of hoofs, and cries of "Halt! Halt! Halt!"

As Stuart's men charged over what is now Pook's Hill, they could see the gleaming but still unfinished Capitol dome in the distance. For a change, Jeb Stuart resisted temptation.

Mrs. Moore and her husband had gone to the Presbyterian church on horseback.[32]

Everything being peaceful and quiet on the road – with Pickets at the gates as usual. Suddenly, in the midst of the service, a Federal Officer burst into the church, calling out: "Get these horses away from here and get to your homes – the Rebs are coming." Rushing to our horses we galloped off, fearing we might be caught in a clash and prevented from getting to our children. Reaching our gate we found the pickets had gone, falling back to Fort Reno – two miles below – and wagons before our place loaded with supplies for the Federal Army were being hurriedly fired by their soldiers to prevent their seizure by the Confederates, the horses having been cut loose and sent towards Washington for safety.

The Confederates reached the tail end of the wagon train in the middle of Bethesda, disarmed the few guards and began enjoying the captured booty. The *Star* described the action under the headline "ONE HUNDRED AND SEVENTY-EIGHT WAGONS AND OVER ONE THOUSAND MULES GOBBLED UP" and reported that Captain Page, who had been in charge, "was at about the middle of the train and, as the rebels rode up, he hastily jumped on his horse, over the fence and struck for the woods amid a storm of bullets, and thus escaped, and arrived in this city yesterday evening." Soon smoke marked the route of the Pike from Bethesda to Rockville

Many years later Miss Holman told about journeying up to Middletown to see an old family friend, Mr. Frank Maught:[33]

. . . the only person we know of who was living on the Pike at that time and whose memory of that dramatic raid is still vivid. The house where he lived still stands at the gate of the Georgetown Preparatory School and is sometimes referred to as an an old inn. . .

What a melee must have taken place up and down that stretch of the pike between Montrose and Bethesda; frightened animals threshing on the road and falling off all tangled with harness and wagon; men shouting, swearing and shoot-ing in the hot June sun; running back and forth — and a ten-year-old boy taking it all in with the keenness possessed by most children of that age.

At that time the Maught family was living with Mr. Frank's grandfather, Mr. Osborn Sprigg Willson, who had quite a place; farm, house, stables, quarters, and to the north, blacksmith shop and wheelwright shop. There was a large family and when the "women folk" became alarmed over the swarms of soldiers passing the house and walking in unceremoniously, complaint was made.

Stuart, "the gay cavalier" who cheered his men with music, gave strict orders that civilians were to be treated with respect and a guard was stationed at the Willson house.

Horses and mules were invaluable to an army in those days so the Confederates went up and down the Pike looking for salvage in the teams that had fallen off (remember it was high in the middle with rough stones). The injured animals were shot, the sound ones taken off, the wagons burned. All this within a short distance of Ft. Reno at Tenallytown. The unfortunate farmers were relieved of their stock and Mr. Willson had five horses taken. One of these was the favorite mount of his daughter, Miss Lucinda. She begged and pleaded for its return but the officer was obdurate. After a while he sent her two hundred dollars, not in the good U. S. Money taken from the Quartermaster, but in Confederate bills and that made her feel worse than ever.[34]

By supper time Stuart was in possession of 125 wagons and most of their mule teams, two ambulances and several hundred prisoners including a number of civilians such as Sam Perry of Bethesda. Perry, a slave-holding Union-sympathizer, had been stomping around some wrecked wagons that were practically in his back yard and cursing the cavalrymen rifling through them for wasting brand new equipment and all the fodder and foodstuffs when he got in trouble. "There ain't a rebel within miles," Perry had insisted, thinking these soldiers were the same ones he had seen a few minutes before setting fire to their own wagons down near the Moore's place. The smiling Confederates finally tired of listening to farmer Perry rant and marched him off to Rockville where they turned him loose to hike back home, his pro-Union opinions unchanged. Stuart told one of his prisoners, Engineer Captain James C. Duane, "but for his

jaded horses–he would have marched down 7 Street Road–took Abe & Cabinet prisoners."

Many of the teamsters, for the most part black men, had escaped. "The wagons were brand new, the mules fat and sleek and the harness in use for the first time . . ." While a brief skirmish broke out near Offutt's Cross Roads, the Rebels feasted on bread, hams, bacon, and bottled whiskey intended for the officers of the Army of the Potomac and their horses enjoyed the oats and hay the wagons had carried. That night Stuart, after cutting the telegraph lines, paroled his prisoners, divided his forces, and set out to find the Union Army, stripping the countryside of horses as he went. He had no idea where either army was.[35]

For more than a hundred years, soldiers and historians have argued about the Battle of Gettysburg and about the failures of Ewell and Longstreet, about the luck of Sickles and Meade, the courage of Armistead and Warren. Lee took the blame and offered Davis his resignation, but "Beauty" Stuart's absence and the lack of information that went with it were much at fault.

So those laughing Rockville girls in their frilly dresses and that summer-Sunday wagon chase into Bethesda, and the roistering picnic that followed played an important part in what the *Star* headlined:[36]

GREAT AND GLORIOUS NEWS
The Union Arms Victorious In The
Greatest Battle Of The Century.
The next day, July 4th, Pemberton and his 30,000 men surrendered to Grant at Vicksburg after a six-week siege. That July was the beginning of the bloody endgame in the American tragedy.

In three days Lee had lost about one-third of his army and Meade about one-fourth of his. Despite howling thunderstorms on the 4th of July, the Rebels held their positions expecting an attack and then slowly pulled back toward Sharpsburg using Jeb Stuart's captured wagons to carry the wounded. Lee found his bridge destroyed and for the next week, while the river was too high to ford, fought off disaster.

"Our Army held the war in the hollow of their hand, and they would not close it," said Lincoln. He said that Hooker's replacement, George G. Meade, reminded him of "an old

woman trying to shoo her geese across a creek."[37]

In Maryland in 1863 the Union Party, and in particular its Unconditional wing, swept to victory with the help of blueclad soldiers and enforced loyalty oaths. Only in the Fifth Congressional District, including Montgomery County, were the Democrats able to elect their candidate. Most of the district was under the jurisdiction of the Department of Washington and General Christopher Augur, one of the most luxuriantly bewhiskered men of an extremely hirsute age, who used more restraint in policing the polls than did his compatriots in the rest of Maryland. The State legislature, dominated by emancipationists, called for a constitutional convention and scheduled an election on the first Wednesday of April on the question. The delegates would be required to take an "iron-bound oath" of past and future loyalty, and voters, if challenged, would also have to take an oath.

By the time Bethesda-area voters reached the polls in Rockville on election day, they found the polling place closed. That morning a captain with orders from General Augur appeared to decide who was and was not a qualified voter. The election judges stated that they planned to follow Maryland law and to call on the army for help only if it were needed as Governor Bradford and General Wallace had agreed. The captain insisted on following his orders. The judges refused. The election was cancelled.

A similar scene was enacted at Poolesville, and the polls in Medley's District were also closed. In the other three Montgomery County districts, the convention was defeated, and before the governor could order new elections in the closed districts, the Union forces led by Preston Blair, conceded.

Throughout Southern Maryland the convention was voted down and Democrats were elected as delegates, but state-wide the vote for the convention was an overwhelming 31,593 to 19,524. The Democrats chose thirty-five delegates and those pledged to emancipation, sixty-one.[38]

The convention assembled on April 27 in Annapolis to do what had been unthinkable to most Marylanders only four years before. With a short break for the Union (Republican) Presidential Convention in Baltimore, the debate on the emancipation clause, with every

imaginable argument from the Bible to the budget included, lasted until June 24, and then the vote was 53 for abolition and 27 against.

The "peculiar institution" was finally ended, and Maryland went on record as opposed to "slavery or involuntary servitude, except in punishment for a crime." The convention then adjourned until July 6 to allow its farmer-delegates to harvest their crops. When it tried to reassemble, the brothers' war intervened.[39]

Occasionally in the midst of war, people found something to smile about. Mrs. Moore remembered one such event:

In the spring of 1864, newly promoted Lieutenant General Grant, now in charge of all of Lincoln's armies, was urging Meade's Army of the Potomac relentlessly toward Richmond while Sherman battered his way across Georgia. It was an election year, and the President's re-election was no sure thing as many of the infantry companies from the forts around Washington headed south, and Grant pledged to "fight it out on this line if it takes all summer." Lee's "miserables" dug miles of trenches, and Grant's men began writing their names on slips of paper that they pinned to their uniforms. In one month Grant lost as many men as Lee had mustered when the year began, but his army still numbered over 100,000. However, Grant's army began suffering from what historian James McPherson called "a Cold Harbor Syndrome" and did not want to make any more frontal assaults on Lee's trenches, so Grant issued new orders. David Hunter was to move up the Shenandoah toward Richmond and cut Lee's supply lines while Sheridan's cavalry was to tear up railroads to the west and Meade would quickly move south of the Rebel capital and seize the rail hub at Petersburg. Grant hoped these efforts would get Lee out of his trenches and force him into the open.[40]

Hunter started well and tore up a great number of Valley properties, not all of them military. His men burned both V.M.I. and the governor's home and moved toward Lynchburg. Lee sent Early to block Hunter, and he frightened him clear out of the Valley. After what was left of Jackson's "foot-cavalry" drove Sigel out of Martinsburg and Mulligan out of Jefferson County, the old route lay wide open for the third annual invasion of Maryland if Lee wanted to use it.

Discouragement swept the North. The price of gold reached an all-time high, and Lincoln's chances of re-election, an all-time low as newspapers posted the long, long lists of those killed in action. Now to encourage the Copperheads and relieve pressure on his lines, Lee sent General Jubal Early and what was left of Jackson's and Ewell's corps down the Valley and into Maryland. Old Jube, who had opposed secession with all his heart, had about 13,000 experienced infantrymen, many without shoes, and some 4,000 cavalry when he splashed across the Potomac again on July 5. Kyd Douglas, who rode with Stonewall, believed that "no other general in either army would have attempted it against such odds." Mosby led the way at Point of Rocks, and Early moved through Shepherdstown and on toward Frederick with many of his men seeking retribution for Hunter's depredations.[41]

On July 5 the Confederate cavalry under John McCausland attacked the Union forces at the supply base of Hagerstown and took the town the next day. McCausland gave the city fathers three hours to raise $20,000 in U. S. money and to produce clothing for his men and an additional 1,900 pairs of pants. The ransom was paid, and McCausland galloped off toward Frederick.

Bradley Johnson, a respected lawyer and longtime resident of Frederick, led the Confederate push through the Middletown Valley on July 6th to the suburbs of Frederick City where Lew Wallace's reinforcements stopped him. When word of Early's movements reached him, General Wallace had gathered up every fighting man he could find in the Middle Department including the Potomac Home Brigade and some hundred-day militia from Ohio and wired Grant for help.

On the evening of the seventh, shoes arrived for Early's men while units of the Union Sixth Corps were on the B&O cars and moving toward Frederick. Wallace dug in south of the Monocacy River and ordered the city abandoned on the night of July 8. The Confederates quickly occupied the town.

As had happened several times before, Maryland men faced each other on opposite sides of the stream. Bradley Johnson had in his command the First Maryland Cavalry, the Baltimore Light Artillery, and the Second Maryland Battalion of Cavalry. Wallace threw into his line troops from the Third Maryland Regiment, the Baltimore Battery, the

Baltimore Home Brigade and the Maryland Cavalry.

About 8 am, Frederick's mayor, William G. Cole, received a terse note from Gen. Early. The Rebels wanted "$200,000 in current money for the use of the army," or they would burn the city in retaliation for Hunter's work in the Valley. It was about then that McCausland realized that he had misread Early's orders. He was supposed to have demanded $200,000, not $20,000, from Hagerstown. Early's commanders enjoyed a good laugh at young McCausland's embarrassment while waiting for the Mayor to convince representatives of Frederick's five banks that the citizens would agree to be taxed to pay back the ransom.[42]

Lew Wallace did not know which way Early would jump, so he had to spread his 6,000 man force very thinly along the Monocacy to cover the roads to Baltimore and Washington. Jubal Early hit Wallace with Ramseur's division and McCausland's cavalry beginning at about 9:30 am. A rather desultory fight continued until early afternoon when Early ordered Gen. John B. Gordon's infantry, who had been watching and criticizing the dismounted cavalrymen's fight, into the battle. Gordon sent in charge after charge, and the Monocacy ran as red as his shirt as the men of the Sixth Corps slowly gave ground but then finally broke. The Union line dissolved. Lew Wallace reestablished some order around New Market, but most of his little army melted away. "I am retreating," he reported, "with a foot-sore, battered, and half demoralized column." At Ellicott's Mills he reorganized what he could find to defend frightened Baltimore. Soon word spread along the streets of Washington that Old Jubilee was coming down the road from Frederick in a mean mood with at least 30,000 foot cavalry.[43]

The road to the Capital was open, but the sun outlined the trees on the ridges of the western hills. Early, not wanting more prisoners than he had already accumulated, did not pursue the fleeing Federals. He also was not sure just what forces Wallace had and finding veterans of the Sixth Corps facing him had been a surprise. On the other hand, if the Sixth was near Frederick it meant he had taken some pressure off Lee's Petersburg lines and achieved his basic goal.[44]

The next morning, Sunday the 10th of July, as two divisions of the Sixth Corps boarded steamers down at City Point, Early sent Bradley Johnson and his cavalrymen toward Baltimore with orders to cut telegraph lines and disrupt the railroads as much as possible. Led by former Vice-President Breckinridge's Corps, Early's small army marched south almost thirty miles through terrible heat and choking dust until the men fell and slept in fields from the fairgrounds at Rockville to prosperous farms of Gaithersburg. Urbana, Clarksburg, and Hyattstown had welcomed them with buckets of lemonade and punch. Girls rode for miles to see them pass, and a few Marylanders even joined their ranks. In some towns the prisoners in the nine-mile-long wagon train were also cheered and given crackers and water. McCausland's tired troopers pushed a small detachment of Federal cavalry back through Rockville and then off the hills just south of town.[45]

Ahead of them ran panic. Farmers in Bethesda and the surrounding area packed their valuables and their families on wagons and fled the countryside to get within the line of forts that had made a treeless arc a mile wide and fifteen miles long from Chain Bridge to the Eastern Branch. Wives buried their silver or dropped it in their wells, and husbands ran their horses and cows into the woods.

The size of Early's army grew with every telling, and as the traffic increased in Tenallytown people began to notice that the forts' garrisons contained invalids and convalescents, untested militia and recent draftees. Even to frightened civilians, the difference was obvious. Barnard now estimated that instead of the 34,000 needed, the defenses of Washington were manned by 9,600 men, and about half of them were in no condition to march. Adjutant General Montgomery Meigs, builder of the aqueduct and the new Capitol dome, organized more than 2,500 clerks and bookkeepers and sent them into the trenches. The canal boats huddled together in Georgetown as they always did when the Rebels crossed the river. And the thrilling panic spread.[46]

At 10:30 pm Chief of Staff Halleck wired Grant at City Point, Virginia, "It is the impression that one-third of Lee's army is with Early and Breckinridge, and that Ransom has some 3,000 or 4,000 cavalry. If you intend to cut off this raid, we must have more forces here."

The Confederates were a half-day's march from the Capitol. Early and his officers spent that Sunday night as "guests" on the Summit Hall farm of John DeSellum, a Unionist slave owner who had suffered at the hands of his neighbors for his views and the fact that he had drawn the names of draftees. By the time they dined, his farm and the surrounding countryside were quite thoroughly plundered.

Nothing stood between General Jubal Early and President Abraham Lincoln except a few cavalry units, ten miles of dusty roads, and the thick walls of thinly-manned forts.

From Petersburg, Grant wired the agitated General Augur to hang on, he was sending two divisions of the VI Corps and the XIX Corps would follow. Lincoln and Grant exchanged wires on the advisability of Grant coming to the Capital himself. Halleck sent a general in New York a telegram that read: "We have five times as many generals here as we want, but are greatly in need of privates. Anyone volunteering in that capacity will be thankfully received."

The District of Columbia Militia was called up, a sure sign of desperation. A company of artillerymen and another of 100-day men (Halleck knew most of them could "scarcely fire a gun") plus all the reserves in sight were sent toward Fort Reno where the attack was expected to hit. The soldiers at the Chain Bridge forts did not even know how to load their cannon, but the experienced Ninth N. Y. Artillery was at Tenallytown. Newly promoted Brigadier General Martin Hardin, USMA `59, who had lost an arm at Catlett's Station and been wounded four other times, arrived about midnight to take charge of the big fort on the hill whose guns commanded the road from Bethesda into the city.

That night Hardin's force consisted of 1,818 infantrymen, another 1,834 artillery, and sixty-three cavalrymen. Early's army was estimated by reasonably reliable sources, both then and after the war, to be at least 15,000. Early himself later wrote that he had 8,300 infantry, 3,800 cavalry, and 1,600 gunners with forty pieces of artillery, the largest were 12-pound Napoleons, and a few pieces of horse artillery.[47]

Under pressure from Stanton, Lincoln and his family returned that night from their summer retreat at the Soldier's Home to the fetid White House. At the Treasury, clerks spent the evening filling canvas bags with bank notes and other securities and kept a small steamer ready at the docks. The history-minded recalled that it had only been fifty years since the British scattered the Capital's defenders and burned many of the public buildings.

July 11, 1864, dawned bright and hot as had every day so far that month. Patrols were alert to keep Southern sympathizers from slipping out of town to describe the weak defenses to Old Jube. Dust devils twisted along the roads and through the yellowing fields of corn. "Early's rag-tag army was only a hair's breadth from achieving the greatest Confederate triumph of the whole war. It all depended on the events of that Monday morning."[48]

Early roused his tired men, gave them a chance to eat, and got them on the move as the temperature climbed into the 90's. It had not rained in the Washington area for forty-seven days. Early recalled that the "day was an exceedingly hot one, and there was no air stirring." His topers fired on the pickets at Great Falls who withdrew to the walls of Fort Marcy as the sun rose.

Early was sending McCausland south to test the defenses from Fort Reno to the river. His troopers had taken a battering on the Monocacy but had spent a good night and eaten well at the espense of Ignatius Fulks' farm. Now the rebel horsemen jangled cautiously down the Pike toward Bethesda.

The rest of the small Confederate force marched southeast along the road toward Vier's mill and Leesborough, raising a towering cloud of dust visible to the lookouts high on the signal towers at Forts Sumner, Reno, and Stevens. The procrastinators among the suburban farmers now clogged the roads and spread more stories of Rebel depredations as General Hardin ordered his cavalry out to meet the threat.

From Fort Reno came Colonel Charles Lowell and three squadrons of the 2nd Massachusetts Cavalry and two of the 8th Illinois. They had been stationed across the river at Falls Church and Annandale and were quickly moved into the northern defenses. The horsemen clinked and clattered through Bethesda and on out the Pike through the unfamiliar countryside to relieve Major William Fry of the 16th Pennsylvania Cavalry who, with remnants of the veteran 8th Illinois, had been

trying to hold the turnpike since Sunday night. From two miles south of Rockville, Fry had sent a message to Augur the previous afternoon telling him that Early's column was a mile long and aimed at the Tenallytown forts.

Now low on ammunition, the mixed company was happy to pull back and join the rested units in establishing a thin hilltop line on the ridge where Georgetown Prep and the Corby mansion (Stratford Hall) were later built. McCausland's men harried them back down the Pike and threatened to flank them with a move toward River Road. Horse artillery and one heavy field piece supported the Rebel infantry, and after a few shots, the blue-clad horse soldiers had to give ground. On the older road to Georgetown, McCausland's cavalrymen ran into another small company of Union soldiers near Rabbitt's store at Bell's Mill Road and exchanged a few carbine shots.

Past the new school, the Bethesda Meeting House and Mrs. Moore's farm they retreated, and then low on rounds for their Sharps carbines, disengaged and fell back toward Tenallytown. The Perrys, having learned from the Jeb Stuart raid, hid their young colts in the cellar of the house and stayed out of sight. Rebel cavalry struck sparks from the turnpike's white stone as they jangled into Bethesda, rummaged through the abandoned

Gen. John McCausland, C.S.A.

homes and the empty toll house and cleaned out Postmaster William Darcy's store and Mr. Franck's blacksmith shop.[49]

The big guns at Forts Bayard and Reno opened up at long range and soon the cannon of Simmons and Mansfield and the rifled Parrotts from Sumner joined the fray. Many of the rounds, stored too long, did not explode, but enough did to keep the few left-behind Bethesdans, like the Moore family, in their cellars worrying about their horses.

While Early tried to keep his hot and tired infantry moving toward the Seventh Street Road, McCausland with perhaps three hundred men skirmished all morning along the fort line looking for weak points. His cavalrymen rounded up several small herds of cattle which had been abandoned by their frightened owners when pickets at some forts would not let them into the city without a pass. Then about noon he sent a galloper to Early with the message that the forts between the Georgetown Pike and the river were manned, ready and too strong for any frontal attack.

Obviously the forts looked a lot more impressive than they were, and only Reno atop its hill was really prepared for an assault. McCausland pulled back to Bethesda and made his headquarters on the Bohrer farm and took over the Presbyterian's meeting house for a barracks. The guns reached out from the big forts after three years of waiting, and the heavy shells whirred and hissed over Bethesda and into the fields beyond. Late in the day a shell from Reno killed four Rebels who had camped across from the Moore's plantation.

A Federal infantry picket line was reestablished in front of the forts, and cavalry scouts were sent out to the river and up the Aqueduct road to see if the enemy was moving in that direction. The President visited Tenallytown during the morning and then drove down to the Potomac to wait for the Sixth Corps to arrive. Behind him the guns boomed and behind their shutters some Washingtonians sewed feverishly on silken Stars and Bars with which to welcome Early's liberators.[50]

General Early rode along his straggling divisions. He promised his men he would have them in the Washington saloons by nightfall. He told them they were going to put General Breckinridge back in the Vice-President's chair. The soldiers responded with the usual cheers and waved their hats, but by noontime even

the most experienced were dropping out of line and looking for shade and water. They were lean, ragged, sunburned, and played out.

The cries of "close it up, close up" died, and Early slowed the pace as his vanguard reached Silver Spring, the Blair family's handsome farm. Through the haze the recently finished, gleaming dome of the Capitol rose before him. He had done it. His men, led by Imboden's cavalry, moved across the District Line and toward the cleared fields around Fort Stevens driving the Union skirmish line back into the ramparts. Beyond lay the Treasury and tons of supplies. "General Early," wrote Margaret Leech, "hunched in his saddle before Fort Stevens, knew a flash of hope more dazzling than the noonday sun."

Early harried what men he could find, most of them from Rodes' division, forward as skirmishers and sent runners back to doubletime the rest into the fight. But it was too hot; they were too tired. Many soldiers were busy looting abandoned as well as the few still occupied houses or just resting in the shade, avoiding the noncoms and waiting for the heat of the day to pass.

One of the farms the soldiers picked clean was "Highlands," owned by a man who had just been hunted down by the Pinkertons and jailed as a Confederate sympathizer, Alfred Ray. Mr. Ray, whose large country home was built by a grandson of Daniel Carroll, had sold his land in the city and bought property far out into the country shortly after the war began. When the cavalrymen arrived on her front lawn, Mrs. Ray provided them with welcoming buckets of water and was delighted to find among them her young brother, Tom

Skirmishing in the Capital's suburbs. From *Frank Leslie's Illustrated* Aug. 13, 1864

Gatch, who had been a student and D.C. militiaman. Her husband had never believed that Tom would amount to anything—"not fit to drive a hill horse," was the way he often put it—and here he was a Confederate officer. On their way out of the city, some of Early's men stopped again at the Ray home to requisition hams, quinine, and two mules and to leave behind a flimsy quartermaster's receipt.[51]

Nearer the District Line Kyd Douglas took possession of "Silver Spring," the elder Blair's house, and chased out the stragglers who were tearing it apart looking for food and whiskey. Both Francis Preston Blair and his son Montgomery were on a fishing trip in Pennsylvania while their wives and children were enjoying the New Jersey shore. Douglas reported what he had done, and Early made the large home his headquarters. Douglas stated that although the officers were considerate of private property, "I feel compelled to say that the wine cellar of Mr. Blair was much depleted before they got away."[52]

A prisoner being hauled along with Early's corps remembered seeing "mortar shells sent up from the defenses, and the curves described by them were most beautiful. Exploding high in the air at times, they gave a

superb display of pyrotechnics, though I must confess that our admiration was somewhat tempered with apprehension lest 'some droppings might fall on us.'" A member of Gordon's Division recalled their approach to the Capital:

> *When we were several miles from the city, the enemy in the works around the town opened on us with their big guns. As these shells passed high over our heads our boys in the ranks laughed at the marksmanship of the "melish" behind the guns. We knew then that our enemies were a set of fellows untrained and badly frightened. When these big shells came over and exploded in the rear, I suggested to my comrades that the enemy was shelling our wagon trains, but none of them did us or the trains any harm.*[53]

On the wharfs at Sixth Street Lincoln watched and waved from his carriage as soldiers in faded blue, their caps marked with the Greek cross, clambered from the steamers and assembled in the dusty streets. The Sixth Corps had been here before and helped build the forts. Many of them had learned to be soldiers here. Washington knew them, and those who feared Early cheered their arrival. Under the command of General Horatio Wright, who had taught French and engineering at West Point, seized Arlington Heights early in the war and aided Barnard in building the forts, the VI Corps had survived the bloody campaigns of '64.

Now they swung out toward Chain Bridge and Fort Reno until Halleck and Augur got them all headed out Seventh Street. By midafternoon Early could watch the dusty blue riflemen filing into Stevens and taking over the rifle pits. His men were within one hundred yards of the fort, and Federal cannon began to search out the houses where his sharpshooters hid. As Frank Wheaton's division took over the ramparts and began to serve the big guns, Early must have known his opportunity had vanished. It was about 4 pm. No one within earshot ever forgot the explosive content and imaginative syntax of Jubal Early's long and colorful curses.[54]

All night the ships arrived at the foot of 6th Street, and the men of the VI Corps marched out to Brightwood and replaced Meigs' clerks in the lines from Fort Slocum to Fort Stevens. Early met with his officers, and according to Douglas Southall Freeman, the "decision was to attack at earliest dawn the next morning unless some new development came."

After the meeting, one of Early's aides, James Henry Loughborough who had also served on Jackson's staff, followed creek beds and animal runs he knew well and made his way through the Union picket lines and past the forts to his parents' home, "Grasslands." During what has been called the longest night in Washington history, he enjoyed a brief visit and a hasty meal behind shuttered windows before making his way past the nervous Federals and back to his own lines before dawn.

Meanwhile, Bradley Johnson with Major Harry Gilmor's Marylanders was headed toward Baltimore burning railroad bridges and rousing the countryside as they went. The plan, at its ultimate, was for Johnson to cross 200 miles of occupied Maryland in four days and liberate the prisoners at Point Lookout while the C.S.S. *Tallahassee* steamed up from North Carolina with 20,000 weapons for the prisoners and a detachment of marines under Custis Lee.

By the 11th, Johnson was on the outskirts of Baltimore City and lunched with "Ex Parte" Merryman whose arrest had brought Taney and Lincoln into direct conflict over habeas corpus in 1861. On the morning of the 12th at Owings Mills, Johnson's men discovered a boxcar being loaded with ice cream, a delight many of the cavalrymen had never seen, and using every utensil imaginable enjoyed what was likely "the largest ice cream social held by either army during the Civil War." In response to Hunter's burning of the Virginia Governor Letcher's Lexington home, Johnson ordered Governor Bradford's house on North Charles Street destroyed, left Gilmor to raise hell in the Baltimore area, and headed south to camp at Tridelphia.[55]

Back at Silver Spring, Early looked into Washington and found the forts and other defenses strongly manned on the morning of the 12th of July. Ten years later in a letter to the Baltimore *Gazette*, Early wrote that "it would have been madness to attempt an assault, and I therefore determined to remain inactive in front of them until night and then retire."

Inside the city, with the railroad and telegraph to the north cut in several places, unrestricted rumors spread like ground fog. All night, in front of the forts, houses burned brightly near Silver Spring and Bethesda, and

refugees moved deeper into the city. Except for an overabundance of beef from the cattle driven into town as the invading army neared, the city's markets were almost barren, and some merchants were posting highly inflated siege prices on potatoes and flour. Newspaper extras were gobbled up as fast as they were printed. Many people believed that there were spies in the city signaling the rebels about weak places in the defenses, but the curious clogged the roads trying to get to Fort Stevens and Tenallytown to see the rebel horde, and in many places business went on as usual while the District militia was called to arms without much effect.

A reporter from New York who walked out toward Fort Reno from Georgetown wrote:

> *It looked like Sunday on Tuesday. I met twenty rebel prisoners under guard of a corporal and four men. Work on three houses was suspended but an old negro was vigorously shingling his cabin. . . Down the hill thundered a great wagon loaded with household goods of a refugee and a little after I met cattle and negroes fleeing from the enemy.*

Confederate sharpshooters fired from houses and trees at any target that could be seen within the forts, and all day the cannon boomed out and shattered their hiding places. From Forts Reno and Sumner came companies of cavalry and infantry to skirmish with McCausland's troopers who probed for weak places from Rock Creek to the river. A few men fell and several were captured by both sides in these small fights. The Rebels pulled back to the hills of Bethesda.

But on that hot Tuesday, the main attraction was on the Seventh Street Pike and not on the road to Rockville. Lincoln probably visited Fort Stevens twice, the second time with his wife and some high government officials. He may not have noted the confusion in leadership that existed in the Federal lines, but it is certain that he mounted the parapet and watched the action for a time.[56]

About 6 pm guns from Stevens, Slocum, and DeRussy pulverized the fields between Fort Stevens and Silver Spring. Then Colonel Daniel D. Bidwell led out his brigade of the VI Corps and joined General Frank Wheaton's men in an attack on Rebels' skirmish line. Early sent in Rodes' men to hold the line, and a fierce, concentrated, fire fight ensued.

Near Lincoln on the wall of Fort Stevens a doctor was wounded, and General Wright ordered the President down and the parapet cleared. Lincoln, an inviting target for sharpshooters in his black coat and tall hat, watched the soldiers move forward in the fading light for a moment more and then stepped down, much to Wright's relief. The President sat on an ammunition box and bobbed up now and then to peer over the wall. The oft-told story of young Colonel Oliver Wendell Holmes Jr. shouting, "Get down, you fool!" at Lincoln is a pleasant one, but Holmes never claimed he said it nor did General Wright report hearing it.

Early described the Battle of Fort Stevens as "quite a brisk engagement" and stated that it "was in that affair that nearly my whole loss in front of Washington was sustained." The fighting went on until 10 pm with some eighty Confederate casualties and more than 200 Union killed and wounded. The skill of Early's sharpshooters resulted in the death or wounding of every Union regimental commander involved. Even before the Federal advance, Early had begun withdrawing his army, moving his wagons and the unused artillery back toward Rockville.

Forty of the Union soldiers killed in this battle, mostly Pennsylvanians and New Yorkers, were reburied in the little Battleground National Cemetery on Georgia Avenue. Thirty years after the fight, sixteen or seventeen of the Confederate dead were reinterred in the cemetery at Grace Episcopal Church on Georgia Avenue in Silver Spring and some years later, a marker was erected. Early sent a $100 check to help in this work.[57]

Margaret Leech wrote that the capital was "too sophisticated for panic. No city ever heard the noise of cannon in its suburbs with greater appearance of *sang-froid*." But it had been a near thing. If Lew Wallace's little army had missed the train to Frederick or if there had been a cooling rain that Monday, Early might have done it.

He could not have held the city, but he might well have captured Montgomery Meigs who spent the night under a poncho with his clerks, or "Old Brains" Henry Halleck, whose Georgetown neighbors would surely have applauded, or even Lincoln. And then what? As it was, some foreign experts were more astonished by Early's exploits than most in either the North or South who brushed it off as

a "raid." The London *Times* concluded that the "Confederacy is more formidable than ever."[58]

That night McCausland's men were still looking for horses in Bethesda. They ransacked the old stone tavern near the crossroad, the No Gain farm, the Bethesda Meeting House on the hill and the nearby school house. Women's clothes and picture frames lay scattered around many homes.

Disappointed, General Early and his officers met at Blair's home and planned the retreat. Then came one of those incidents no story teller can resist, and Kyd Douglas wrote it first with typically Victorian reserve.

> Some while after dark that night I was sent for by General Early. Generals Breckinridge and Gordon were with him. He seemed in a droll humor, perhaps one of relief, for he said to me in his falsetto drawl:
>
> "Major, we haven't taken Washington, but we've scared Abe Lincoln like h———!"
>
> "Yes, General," I replied, "but this afternoon when that Yankee line moved out against us, I think some other people were scared blue as ———'s brimstone!"
>
> "How about that, General?" said Breckinridge with a laugh.
>
> "That's true," piped General Early, "but it won't appear in history."

And thus he and Kyd Douglas assured that, of course, it would.

Early folded up his little army after burying some of his dead and finding homes where he could leave his eleven wounded officers and about ninety badly injured men. Douglas, grumbling that Marylanders always got the dirty duties, commanded some two hundred men as a rear guard, and Jubal Early headed north hoping to get to the river before Union forces blocked the fords.

The signal lights at the Retired Soldiers' Home flashed all night as the dust cloud rose beyond the District Line. About midnight, Kyd Douglas gathered up his sentries and followed. When he looked back, he saw that Montgomery Blair's home, Falkland, was burning. Early did not order that action although he understood it, and Kyd Douglas suggested that it might have been done by one of Blair's neighbors.

"Silver Spring," Francis Preston Blair's home, on the other hand, was spared, and Gideon Welles, Lincoln's Secretary of the Navy, who visited the house soon after the battle, declared, "The place was damaged little more than it would have been if occupied by Union troops.".

General Breckinridge, a longtime friend of the Blairs, likely played some role in protecting the house. In fact, when a Confederate cavalryman was found to be carrying some of Blair's "notable silverware" during Early's retreat, it was returned to the family through Breckinridge. Nothing but the smouldering chimneys was left at Montgomery Blair's, but he rebuilt his home after the war.[59]

Meanwhile, Bradley Johnson had burned B&O cars, torn up the telegraph at Beltsville, driven off some cavalry from D.C. and captured several hundred government mules before he received word from Early that the Point Lookout raid was off. He then started west across the line of forts and rejoined the rest of the small army around midnight near Rockville. Early put him in charge of the cavalry rear guard. Near Baltimore, Gilmor's men burned several trains and bridges and even captured a Union general before heading back across the state, his men often asleep in their saddles, to join the retreat.

In Bethesda, McCausland's troopers rounded up the horses they had found and packed up all the food they could carry. Before dawn some of them were moving out River Road toward Offutt's Cross Roads while others left the way they had come, past Mrs. Moore's and Sam Perry's and up and down the hills to Rockville. Along the Old Road, flour, hams and sacks of coffee lay spoiling in the fencelines and drainage ditches. At the ransacked church on the Pike, the front door hung crookedly from a single hinge.

At many Bethesda-area farms, clothes and books were scattered about the yards, windows and doors were shattered. Pots and pans had disappeared, sheets and other linens had been torn up for bandages, and little was left in the pantries, cellars or chicken coops. In some homes the destruction was wanton with all the crockery broken, obscene messages scrawled on walls, furniture and pianos smashed.

At about eight that morning, Lowell's Massachusetts cavalry ventured out from Fort Reno to find Bethesda empty. While most of the men of the Sixth Corps enjoyed a "loafer-like, gipsy style morning," cooked their breakfast and filled their canteens, the cavalry

spread out and searched for the Rebels who had skedaddled in the dark. Out from the forts came squads of soldiers and contrabands to gather up the stragglers and bury the bloating dead. One badly injured Rebel was found near the Bohrer farm where there were several new graves.

About mid-day Lowell's cavalrymen found the Confederate rear guard at Watt's Branch outside Rockville. The First Maryland Cavalry had two of their officers captured in a melee, but Bradley Johnson ordered another charge and recaptured one of them. Gilmor caught up with Early at Poolesville, and on the 14th, while Johnson's men held off the Union cavalry, the Confederates recrossed the Potomac at Edward's, White's, and Noland's Ferries with the wagons, prisoners, and livestock they had accumulated. At about sunset, the rear guard followed.

The scene of battle changed to the Valley where there was a brisk fighting near Winchester until the Confederates broke and ran at the end of what the soldiers called the "Snicker's Gap War." Once again a Rebel army had invaded the North, been stopped, and then was allowed to escape. At the end of the month, John McCausland was in the news again. He and his men burned Chambersburg, Pennsylvania, to the ground when the town council refused to pay a ransom. And then Grant sent Phil Sheridan into the Valley with orders to follow Early "to the death."

Mrs. Moore at her home on the Pike was much involved with Early's raid.

The Confederates appeared, played "Dixie" under the guns of Fort Reno and for two days and nights after, we slept in Confederate lines, breakfasted in Federal lines, dined in those of the Confederates and so on until the Sixth Federal Army Corps was rushed to Washington up through Maryland and the Confederates were compelled to retreat and recross the river at Edward's Ferry thirty miles above, where they had entered. From this point they had come down with forces intact, as far as Rockville, there detached McCausland's Division of Cavalry which came down our road, while General Early's men crossed over to the Seventh Street road leading to Washington.

There were constant skirmishes going on and the balls were flying so fast and shells bursting so near our house, that we collected the family in the cellar for safety, a ball having passed through the

house of a neighbor. Soon Grandfather went out to watch the bursting of a shell, as it described in its fall a perfect letter "S" and seeing him between the well and the tree nearby, I too slipped out and soon all were watching except the children who were young enough for Mammy to hold on to! The excitement of these times was so great that we thought not of danger and this we were told by many soldiers is the case in time of battle.

Soon a powder blackened Confederate dashed up to the well for water and told us they must fall back as strong reinforcements were coming up from Washington which they could not meet, having come over for a "raid" rather than for an actual engagement with the enemy. We had kept our table spread and always had food ready when they came to the well for water.

That night they recrossed the river and the next day the "Yanks" were coming to ask for milk and "pie." They got the milk only for we had little left to give them. Except for such foraging and the taking of such horses as were needed for their army, no depredations were committed by the Confederates.

The morning after the retreat The Sixth Army Corps passed up and the papers rang with their deeds, how at "Duffy's Run" they had charged on the retreating enemy and forced them to fall back, and the Country believed it! But we who were there were only amused, for "Duffy's Creek" was a tiny steam running across the pike, over which our little children often stepped from stone to stone when out with Mammy, and by the time the Federals had reached Duffy's Run which had never before had a name but was on the place of a Mr. Duffy, the Confederates were across the river, having retreated in the night while the Sixth Corps passed our house on the morning and day following. So much for newspaper reports!

The most thrilling of our War adventures occurred just at this time for Grandfather came near losing his life. After the Army had all passed up, as we thought, he walked around the plantation to see if the fences had been destroyed and was met by the Overseer of Mr. Dick's place adjoining and asked to come over to his house where lay a wounded Confederate. A ball had passed through his body above the hips, he was bleeding profusely and they had no proper bandages.

There were no telephones in those days and no Doctor could be reached until the road was cleared of troops, so Grandfather came home for lint, bandages, ice and whatever was needed and started back to the Overseer's house near the dividing line. Just before reaching the fence in an

effort to put the barn between himself and the road from which the firing came, but when about springing over, a ball came between the fence rails, fortunately not striking him. He quickly dropped to the ground and crawled to the shelter of a large tree, where he sat, waving with both hands the white bandages he carried.

Finally the firing ceased and he was soon surrounded by a squad of armed men, demanding who he was. He told them a "Citizen." By this time an Officer rode up and asked the men "what they got." "He says he's a Citizen but he looks mighty like a 'Johnny,'" was the reply. The Officer after questioning Grandfather told him to go on to do what he could for the wounded man who of course was his prisoner, and at Grandfather's request, sent a soldier to the house with him, whose blue coat protected him from further danger from balls from the road. In a few hours an ambulance was brought and the poor wounded prisoner was carried to the Hospital on Judiciary Square in Washington, where in a few days he died.

The nerve shock told heavily on Grandfather, and indeed on all of us as you might imagine. As the last of the Sixth Army Corps passed up, two of its men appeared, leading a comrade who had dropped in the road and asked if he might lie in our barn and rest as he was too ill to go on. So we made him a comfortable bed of straw and hay, covered him with a blanket and for two or three days fed him with such food as he could eat, milk and cold, ripe tomatoes being his great desire. Finally we were able to report the case to one of the Hospitals in Washington and they sent an ambulance for him but we heard that he lived only a short time, being far gone with tuberculosis.

In Annapolis the Constitutional Convention reassembled on July 18 angry over Early's raid and Bradley's depredations near Baltimore. The delegates were particularly incensed by the number of Marylanders involved in the raid. Into the new constitution the Unionist majority inserted a provision for an ironclad oath of past and future loyalty that could have had the effect of leaving no voters except the Unconditional Unionists and even a few of them would have been suspect. Certainly the intent was to disenfranchise permanently anyone who wore the butternut or grey uniform of the C.S.A. The loyalty oath was also to be required of teachers, lawyers, and corporation heads.

The only provision the old slave areas salvaged was one that allowed minors, incapable of being supported by themselves or their parents, to be apprenticed by the Orphans Courts. Also, blacks were not granted the vote nor the right to testify against whites in court. And finally, the new constitution provided a method for soldiers in the field to cast their ballots. The constitution passed by a vote of 53 to 26 on September 6, 1864, and was sent to the voters for their approval.

The minority members, including those from Montgomery County, published a protest "To the Voters of Maryland" condemning uncompensated emancipation, Federal superiority over the state, the increase in Baltimore's representation, and the test oaths. These States Righters claimed that the abolitionists wanted Negro children to go to white schools and black men to vote. The Democrats, feeling brave, held a September convention and stated their unanimous opposition to the new constitution. Soon the issue became tied to the upcoming Presidential election and "either you were for the constitution and Lincoln or you opposed both."

As election day neared, violence flared and threats of military intervention were heard. The Copperheads were meeting. The Negroes were plotting. The barrooms were full.

But the election was peaceful and the voting was heavy. Test oaths were sworn, few observers suggested the possibility of perjury, and state-wide only thirty-three voters were rejected. In the fourteen slave counties, where the new constitution was crushed, there was a record turnout, and in some places, an extra day was given to swear in all the voters. And as the votes piled up it was clear that the constitution had been defeated. The official total was 27,541 for, 29,526 against; in Montgomery County the vote had been three-to-one against, 1,367-422. But the soldier vote, mainly from men stationed in Virginia, was still coming in and had yet to be counted. Most of their votes were just slips of paper with "for the constitution" or "against the constitution" printed or hand written on them.

The Court of Appeals ducked and the Governor examined the votes and the manner in which some were cast and began throwing out many. The First Regiment had voted in the wrong place, and Eastern Shore regiment had illegally reopened its polls. In all Bradford rejected 285 absentee votes for the constitution and five that were opposed. The soldiers

voted 2,633 for the constitution and only 263 against it. On October 29 the governor announced that the constitution had been approved by 375 votes out of almost 60,000 ballots cast and would go into effect three days later.[60]

Maryland had freed its slaves. The guns boomed from Fort McHenry. "Property" with a pre-war value of at least $30 million had been wiped out. Lew Wallace quickly created a freedman's bureau and placed all the celebrating former slaves under military protection. And some slave owners hurried to the Orphans Courts to tie black children to them as apprentices. For three years, the Constitution of the Free State declared that "all men are created equally free; that they are endowed by their Creator with certain unalienable rights, among which are life, liberty, the enjoyment of the proceeds of their own labor, and the pursuit of happiness." And then the basic law was again rewritten.

The next month, Thomas Swann, an opportunist, Know-Nothing running as a conservative Unionist, was elected governor by a slim majority, and Lincoln received Maryland's seven electoral votes by an even slimmer one, 7,432 ballots. Both had been defeated state-wide but had rolled up impressive majorities in Baltimore City and had counted almost all the soldier votes into their column; 2,799 soldiers voted for Lincoln and only 321 for McClellan. In Montgomery County Lincoln lost 1,542 to 496.

Bethesdans had found the war very difficult, but occcasionally there was something to smile about. Mrs. Moore remembered:

The only diversion we "Citizens" living as were we, in a border state held by our enemies, was an occasional dining out among our neighbors, and always the whole family was invited, as we never knew what might happen on the road to prevent our return to the children should we leave them at home.

One evening as we were returning from a pleasant day spent with our friend and Physician, Dr. Davidson, about two miles below, we were delayed by a little accident to the carriage and were not able to reach home until after the countersign was required, so expected trouble with the Pickets, although on pleasant terms with them.

It was quite dark so we could not see that the Pickets had been changed since we had passed down the road in the morning, a new set of

strangers — their Officer a rough German, having replaced those we knew. Suddenly a harsh order — "Halt!" came close to us and followed by the demand for "Countersign" which we did not have. But Uncle Lawrence, then about four years old, hearing the word "Countersign" and rousing from a nap, quickly responded, "Secesh!" — the answer he was in the habit of giving in play-drills in which our children were sometimes trained by a young boy in the neighborhood. Fortunately the German knew but little English, so did not take in the meaning of the word and we escaped trouble on account of it. After much argument through translation by one of the men, and the discovery that there were four small children in the party — for your father was the baby asleep in Mammy's lap — we were conducted to our gate and allowed to go to our house at the top of the hill, which was unknown to the new Pickets...

And the war ground on. In early October while the convention delegates were still debating, a small group of Mosby's rangers was surprised just north of Rockville by a posse, and their leader Walter Bowie, was killed in an exchange of shots. All through the war there were raids along the canal and farther inland by elements of Lige White's cavalry, and a number of irregular units and some just plain thieves.

On April 3rd Lee abandoned Richmond, and on the 9th surrendered at Appomattox. Soon after that the raiding forces of White, McNeil and Mosby disbanded.

The news of the war's end came to many in Bethesda with the shock of cannon fire. One after another the big guns in the forts and the lighter field artillery in the redoubts between them fired their salutes. The wave of thunder went around and around the city for several hours, always in the same direction, fading away and then approaching again from the river until the booming changed to crashing bangs with clouds of acrid smoke and then the sharp, flashing cracks from the rifled cannon.

At Ford's new theater at about 10:30 on the night of April 14, using a laugh line he had often heard in "Our American Cousin," Maryland-born John Wilkes Booth stepped into President Lincoln's box and shot him in the back of the head. At about the same time Lewis Paine attacked Secretary Seward with a knife, and George Atzerodt left his card and his courage at the Vice-President's residence.

The next morning Atzerodt pawned his pistol in Georgetown and bought a bottle of whiskey and a ticket on the stage to Rockville. As the coach bounced into Tenallytown, he saw the soldiers blocking the road. He got out and traded drinks and jokes with the guards at the toll booth and then hitched a ride with a farmer from his neighborhood and rode through Bethesda and past blue-coated men searching for Lincoln's killer. Three days later a soldiers brought him back down the Pike to a military trial and a gallows.

The military and the secret service entered many homes in Bethesda and questioned a number of known Southern sympathizers during the confusion following Lincoln's death. Nathan Loughborough suffered a stroke after he was interrogated, and his homes, and especially that tunnel between the kitchen and the dining room at Milton, were roughly searched.

Mrs. Moore watched the end of the world she had known:[61]

On April 14, 1865, Grandfather started on horseback for the City, but reaching a blacksmith shop was stopped by the owner with the news that President Lincoln had been assassinated at Ford's Theater the night before and that the road was closed, as were all exits, in hope of arresting the murderer.

Of course, Grandfather returned immediately home—for the Country had gone insane and no Southern man's life was safe although all realized that no greater misfortune could have come to the South than the death of President Lincoln. No such "Reconstruction days" would have cursed the country by widening the breech between the South and the North, as did those following the honorable surrender at Appomattox.

"Bethesda takes its name from the Bethesda Presbyterian Church which stands on Rockville Pike a little north of the Naval Hospital. This was built in 1850 to replace the church on the site which was built in 1820 and destroyed by fire."
Doree Germaine Holman in *Old Bethesda*

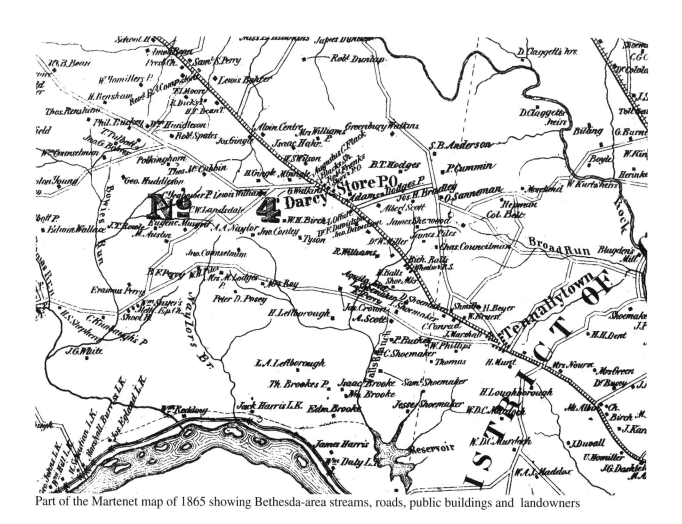

Part of the Martenet map of 1865 showing Bethesda-area streams, roads, public buildings and landowners

---

[1] One of those surrendering was Robert Peter's nephew, Thomas, a British captain.

The other original County justices were Edward Burgess, William Deakins, Elisha Williams, James Offutt, and Richard Thompson.

[2] Two popular works on the burning of Washington give slightly differing accounts. See Walter Lord's *The Dawn's Early Light* (1972) and Andrew Tully's *When they Burned the White House* (1961). The "Diary of Mrs. William Thornton" is in the *Records of the Columbia Historical Society*, Vol. 19, 1916.

The Patent Office served as the Capitol for a year while the Madisons stayed at Blair House, and the "Brick Capitol" went up on the present Supreme Court site.

[3] See *A Grateful Remembrance*.

[4] "Politics and Democracy in Maryland, 1800-1854" by W. Wayne Smith in *Maryland A History* edited by Richard Walsh and William Lloyd Fox(1974). The Know-Nothings were also responsible for interrupting work on the Washington Mounment in the mid-1850's so that it ended up with two colors of stone.

[5] "The Era of the Civil War" by Richard R. Duncan in Walsh and Fox's *Maryland*.

[6] Most of this from Barbara Jeanne Field's *Slavery and Freedom on the Middle Ground*.

The 1860 census listed race or color as "w, b, or m."

[7] 1860 slave census for 4th District. Because there was no Bethesda district at the time, the slaves owned by Bethesdans can only be estimated at about 300. The value of a working-age slave is porobably equal to the value of a present-day piece of farm equipment such as a

tractor or a truck. The dozen or so Offutt families in the Rockville election district owned a total of seventy-two slaves. George Peter Jr. owned thirty.

[8]For more, see Dr. Carolyn McCreesh's "The Secession Crisis of 1860-1861" in *The Montgomery County Story,* August 1977, and Brice Claggett's letter in the same edition.
It is difficult to swallow all of MacMaster and Hiebert's conclusion that "Most people wanted to stay in the Union and end slavery."
State vote: Breckinridge- 42,482, Bell- 41,470, Douglas- 5,966, Lincoln- 2,294.

[9]For more of these times, see Jane C. Sween's *Montgomery County: Two Centuries of Change,* 1984, and Chapter 10 of *A Grateful Remembrance.*

[10]In *Governor Thomas H. Hicks of Maryland and the Civil War* (1902), George L. P. Radcliffe concluded that delaying the meeting of the State legislature until public opinion cooled and Federal power coalesced was Hicks's greatest contribution. For more on Gov. Hicks and the times, see Chapter 22 of Donald Marquand Dozer's *Portrait of the Free State* (1976).

[11]Robert Brugger, *Maryland: A Middle Temperament* (1988).

[12]From the Anderson family letters cited in *A Grateful Remembrance*, p. 169.

[13]Grocer Hilleary Offutt bought the property in March-April 1860 but at the time of the census was living with a fellow merchant in Georgetown. He evidently did not own any slaves in 1860, and his mother had freed hers in her will. See land records: JGH 8/71. In *Divided Town, A Study of Georgetown, D. C., During the Civil War* (1968), Mary Mitchell wrote that "The Offutts were a large family group in Georgetown and came from Maryland. Various members occupied seven different houses, most of which are still in use today. It was a divided family, four of them remaining throughout the war, and three, among whom was the Hilleary branch, disappearing south." In many ways Bethesda in 1861 was Southern.
For more see *Washington: Village and Capital, 1800-1878* by Constance McL. Green (1962).

[14]On April 10, 1861, the National Rifles could only muster fifteen men, but after heavy recruiting was the first company to enter national service under Lincoln's April 15 proclamation. In all 4,720 District men volunteered. See "Military Activities in Washington in 1861" by Elden E. Billings, *Records of the CHS*, 1960-1962.

[15]From Roger Brooke Farquhar's wonderful book of old homes and history, p. 214.

[16]See Rick Griffin's "Gip Peter - Spy?" in *The Maryland Line*, n.d., *Divided Town* (1968) by Mary Mitchell, and David N. Hughey's unpublished work in Franklin, Tenn. "Tragedy of Two Cousins - Adventures or Spies?" by Patrick J. Griffin, III, in the November 1991 *Montgomery County Story* offers a sympathetic and detailed view.

[17]Barnard's own *A Report on the Defenses of Washington* (1871), is still the best source.

[18] Despite the work of the CCC at Stevens in the 1930's not much is left of what should be the best known of all of Washington's forts. The remains of Fort DeRussy at Military Rd. and Oregon Ave. are worth seeing as is reconstructed Fort Ward in Virginia.

[19]Most of that wide, well-built road has disappeared into Grant Road; today's Military Road is generally north of its path.

[20]See Shaw and House's regimental history cited by Cooling and Owen.

[21]They had 476 casualties in their first fight and then lost 632 of 900 men, including 13 officers killed and 12 wounded, on June 18 attack on Lee's Petersburg lines.

[22]In *Tenleytown, D. C.,* Judith Beck Helm used William Spicer's *History of the 9th and 10th Regiments, R. I. Volunteers* (1892), for many of her anecdotes and quotes.
The park north of Wilson HS is about the size of the fort.

[23]See page 43 of *Old Bethesda* for more about little Miss Hester. Sumner's big guns could reach from Glen Echo Heights to, in modern terms, the American Legion Bridge at Cabin John or the parking lots of Montgomery Mall, and Fort Reno's from the NIH campus to Chevy Chase Lake and beyond.
Shoemaker story in August 22, 1941, *Journal,* when the family still had the cannon ball.

[24] For more on the effect of the war on Washington see Green's *Washington Village and Capital,* Chapter X. The *Star* denied estimates of 15,000 prostitutes in the city and counted only 2,300 white and 1,600 "colored" in 1863.

[25] Benjamin Franklin Cooling III is the local expert on the defenses of Washington. For more on the forts, see his 1975 book *Symbol, Sword, and Shield* and the 1988 work produced for the Friends of Fort Ward with Walton H. Owen, II, *Mr. Lincoln's Forts*, which contains directions to all the forts as well as many illustrations.
Although Lincoln is said to be the only President ever under fire, James Madison came very close at the time of the Bladensburg Races in 1814.

[26] The full text was published on November 1984 in Vol.27 No.4 of *The Montgomery County Story* by the Montgomery County Historical Society. It has been used and edited with permission.

[27] The Dunlop home was Hayes Manor. His brother James Dunlop was chief judge of the Circuit Court in D.C. and kept a home and office in Georgetown. His Southern sympathies were also well known.

[28] Old Capitol Prison was at First and A Streets, N. E. and was a big brick barn built in 1815 and used as the Capitol while the British damage was repaired. Margaret Leech's *Reveille in Washington* (1941), is the classic source for information about the Capital in wartime and this story. William H. Offutt owned 24 slaves in 1860.

[29] See Emory M. Thomas's *Bold Dragoon* (1986) for more of Stuart's exploits.

[30] The best recent history of Antietam is Stephen Sears' *Landscape Turned Red,*(1983).

[31] Kyd Douglas, *I Rode With Stonewall* (1899, 1961).

[32] Mrs. Moore confused this incident with Early's raid the next year, but surely it refers to the wagon chase since that was on a Sunday and Early arrived on a Monday.

[33] "Old Bethesda" by Doree Germaine Holman, Bethesda *Journal*, Oct 13, 1939. Soon after this event the Maughts moved to their new home at Montrose and let themselves in for more excitement when they took the Montrose teacher to board. The teacher was John Surratt.

[34] The Willson place which became the Morrison place and then the Offutt place, ended up being mostly Georgetown Prep.

[35] Duane quote from July 1, 1863, letter from Elizabeth Blair Lee, Montgomery Blair's sister, to her naval officer husband in *Wartime Washington: The Civil War Letters of Elizabeth Blair Lee*, edited by Virginia Jeans Lucas (1991).

[36] Douglas Southall Freeman concluded a chapter, "The Price of 125 Wagons," with "Other adventures would be his, but nothing he had achieved and nothing he could hope to accomplish with his exhausted men could offset the harm which the events of coming days were to show he already had done his chief and his cause." See *Lee's Lieutenants*, Vol. 3. James McPherson in the *Battle Cry of Freedom*, concluded that Lee was deprived "of intelligence about enemy movements at a crucial time."

[37] Richard Wheeler's *Witness to Gettysburg* (1987), has many excellent eyewitness accounts.

[38] The final vote in Montgomery was 716 against and 516 for the convention. In Southern Maryland the totals were 5,406 against and 1,927 for. Eastern Shore: 6,008 against, 4,508 for. Northern counties: 16,056 for, 8,023 against. And in Baltimore City, only 87 voted against the convention while 9,102 supported the call.

[39] See Charles Wagandt, *The Mighty Revolution* ,(1964), and Fields' *Slavery and Freedom on the Middle Ground* for more on this convention and its work.

[40] James M. McPherson's *Battle Cry of Freedom*, which is part of the Oxford series, deals with both the conflict and its chroniclers.

[41] See *I Rode With Stonewall* by Marylander Henry Kyd Douglas, the first horseman into Frederick that July. The number of soldiers Early's "raid" is uncertain and disputed.

[42] The banks received 4 1/2% bonds and the debt was finally repaid in 1951, but all efforts to have the town reimbursed, including "Mac" Mathias' last act as a U. S. Senator, have failed.

[43] July 9 was remembered as a very pleasant day in Frederick, warm and sunny, see Judge, p. 171. It is almost mandatory to note that after the war Wallace wrote the very popular Christian novel, *Ben Hur*.

[44] For more on the important battle at the Monocacy, see D. S. Freeman *Lee's Lieutenants* Vol. 3; Frank Vandiver's *Jubal's Raid* (1960); B.F.Cooling's *Jubal Early's Raid on Washington, 1864,* (1989), eyewitness Glenn Worthington's interesting *Fighting for Time* (1932, 1985), and Joseph Judge's *Season of Fire* (1994). Judge calls the battle "one of the hinges of our national fate.".
If Bradley Johnson had liberated the Confederate prisoners at Point Lookout and they had joined Early's men in attacking the city, it would have been a very interesting time. The capture of Washington may not have been Early's "basic goal," but had he been 12 hours faster, he could probably have done it and certainly would have tried.

[45] A Confederate cavalryman, who lingered several days before dying at the Clopper's home, is buried in the front yard of the St. Rose of Lima Church.

[46] In December `63 cannon boomed from all the city's circling forts as the bronze statue of Freedom finally stood atop the Capitol's cupola.
Tenleytown was Tennally's Tavern, Tennallytown, Tenley Town, Ten Alley Town, and Tenallytown, which I like for this chapter, and probably several others. Judith Beck Helm in her 1981 *Tenleytown, D. C.*, prefers "Tennallytown" for the 19th century because the people who had the tavern were the illiterate Tennallys or Tennelys or Tennolys.

[47] Judge estimates 15,000 effectives plus forty cannon in three battalions and lighter artillery. See p. 122 of *Season of Fire* for a full list of units.

[48] Benjamin Franklin Cooling's estimate. It reached 94° at the Farquhar's Olney farm later that day.

[49] *A Report on the Defenses of Washington* by J. G. Barnard is the basic source and contains excellent maps and drawings of forts.

[50] See *Reveille in Washington* and Mitchell's *Divided Town* for more on who the Washington Sesech were and how they behaved.

[51] The Ray home was about where the Mormon Temple is today. Edith Ray Saul, Alfred Ray's granddaughter, still has the quartermaster's receipt. And she still recalls Tom Gatch's stories of the charge of the VMI cadets and other oft-told tales of the Lost Cause. Miss Saul is Kensington's respected historian and keeper of the town's memory.

[52] See Coleman and Lewis's *Montgomery County* and Douglas's *I Rode With Stonewall*. Some early historians made much of the drinking and other debauchery as the cause of Early's failure. It is highly doubtful since the Stonewall Brigade was well disciplined.

[53] Alfred S. Rowe of the 9th N. Y. and Georgian I. G. Bradwell in Worthington's *Fighting for Time*.

[54] After the war Leesboro was renamed Wheaton to honor the general who brought the first of the VI Corps reinforcements to Ft. Stevens.

[55] See Daniel Carroll Toomey's *The Civil War in Maryland* (1983) for a day-by-day chronology and Mark Walston's article on "The Ballad of Ismael Day" in the Feb. 1994 issue of *Maryland* for an interesting sidelight.

[56] See Vandiver's *Jubal's Raid* for more on Lincoln's movements and for the assessment that, at the time, he "seemed the only one who thought in offensive terms" and was eager to see that Early not escape as Lee had twice.

[57] The Rebel dead had been accidently disinterred during the building of a trolley line. See *The Forest Glen Trolley and Early Development of Silver Spring* by Louis N. Markword, 1975.

[58] In his *Personal Memoirs*, U. S. Grant concluded that Lew Wallace's leadership of a "forlorn hope" contributed "by the defeat of the troops under him a greater benefit to the cause than often falls to the lot of a commander of an equal force to render by means of a victory."

cannot see he would have failed –   had he tried it, until 3 olk at night there were only one hundred men at the Guns at Fort Massachusetts." She thought Early had 40,000 men.

Some of President Jackson's papers ended up in Richmond and were returned to the Blairs some years after the end of the Civil War.   See Farquhar, *Old Homes and History*, p. 31.

[60] Much of the foregoing from Wagandt's *The Mighty Revolution* .

[61] Mrs. Moore was a day off on her date, but she was surely right about the effects of Lincoln's death although not in Montgomery County as that Confederate statue in Rockville attests.

G.W.Hopkins' map of 1874 courtesy MCHS

CHAPTER 4

Rail Revolution and Evolution

The forts stood silent. Bethesda's farm families repaired their houses, restored their fences, replenished their livestock, and replanted their corn and rye. According to storekeeper Alfred Wilson, there were only a dozen or so large, area farms when Darcy's store became the post office.[1]

The Shoemakers owned property on both sides of the Pike at the District Line. Coming toward Bethesda one passed the Williams farm where Somerset is now, the Bradley estate where the Chevy Chase Country Club greens are today, the Davidson farm north of what is now Drummond, the Offutt farm a bit farther up, with the Dodge acres of corn and wheat directly across the Pike.

Greenbury Watkins had a large farm where East West Highway now runs, and he also owned 200 acres in Edgemoor. Several Gingell families farmed the Woodmont area, and they also had a farm across the Pike where the Pumphrey Funeral Home is today. On up the Pike the Lewis Bohrers lived on what is now the U. S. Naval Medical Center reservation, and still farther up was the farm of Sam Perry, directly across from the old church.

On the west side of the Pike, coming back toward Five Points, lived the Moore, Buck, and Bean families. Out Battery Park way was the Lewis Williams farm. Augustus Franck's blacksmith shop stood south of the intersection of the Old Road and the Frederick Pike. There were two stores on the east side of the Pike -- Darcy's and Frank's, while on the west side was a little toll house operated by Jake Stadler. It was Jake's job to collect five cents from every vehicle which traveled the rutty, rocky road toward Georgetown.

Simon J. Martenet's 1865 map of Montgomery County was supposed to contain the names of all landowners. A close examination of the Bethesda section of that map at the end of the previous chapter shows that Judge Wilson's memory was pretty accurate. G. W. Hopkins' map of the Bethesda District on the facing page is about ten years later and, while not as inclusive, does show the school at the Grange Hall and some other changes

By the time the fences were rebuilt and the barns repaired, life in the Bethesda area returned to much the way it had been before the war. At the forts, the government sold off or gave away the lumber and logs and then auctioned off the land or returned it to its pre-war owners. Soon the trees and the grass along with the rains and the snows softened the ramparts and trenchlines. In even less time the ante-bellum political leaders returned to their accustomed places as the former slaveholders, mostly Democrats led by the Peter family, re-established control of Montgomery County.

In 1867, after another constitutional convention, political power in the State flowed from north to south. The General Assembly refused to approve either the 14th or the 15th amendments, and what passed for "reconstruction" in Maryland came to an early end despite the outraged protests of disappointed Union Party leaders and former slaves.

Attempts of compromisers such as Montgomery Blair to build a middle-of-the-road coalition ended in ruin, and Blair himself rebuilt "Falkland," returned to the Democratic

fold, and went down fighting for Tilden in 1876. For the next twenty-five years the Old Line Democrats controlled the County as well as the State.[2]

Even with the Federally mandated right to vote and to testify in court, social, political and economic equality were a distant dream for the black men and women of the Bethesda area. One study showed that in all of Southern Maryland including Montgomery County only 1,078 African-Americans owned land in 1870. Blacks were supposed to know and keep their "place," and rarely was a black man called by his last name. No "gentleman" allowed conduct that he considered "uppity" to pass without at least verbal rebuke.

The irrational fear of "Negro domination" was a common theme in post-war political dialogue. Violent acts against African-Americans were few and even fewer were reported, but they happened. "Philip Brown was shot in the head while riding along a public highway in Montgomery County. One of his assailants had urged the other to 'shoot the d——d son of a b—h, he is nothing but a union soldier.'" And black churches, often the only schools for African-American children, became particular targets; several burned. When a Rockville doctor attacked a black man with his cane because he did not like his attitude, the *Sentinel* was "outraged" that the doctor was jailed on the complaint of a black.

When the State legislature appropriated some money for black schools in 1872, the County Commissioners merely added to it funds from a levy on the few black property owners. White taxes were not to be used for black education, at least not in Montgomery County. The first school for black children in the Bethesda area was Moore's School, a one-room building opened in 1880 on a half-acre between River and Conduit Roads in Cabin John.[3]

Farmers sought white hired hands whenever possible and, around the stoves in country stores and in alarmed letters-to-the-editor, regularly castigated their black workers for their indolence and greed. Politicians encouraged immigration, but few Europeans seemed willing to work on Maryland farms. "This waiting upon the negro . . . will not be borne with by the independent farmers of the State," declaimed the *Sentinel*. But despite higher wages for white workers, they continued to flee to the cities or to the homesteads of the West.[4]

The Nation's Capital had permanently changed. The sleepy Southern town with the muddy streets that Lincoln came to in 1861 had but 75,000 inhabitants, and beyond Boundary Street and Georgetown, it was all country; Washington County it was called and much of it only roughly surveyed. In Grant's time, the population reached 132,000, and real estate speculators bought up acreage and platted subdivisions pell-mell. In ten years the white population increased by forty percent and the African-American by more than 200 percent. By 1880 the total passed 178,000 with the black population stabilized at about one-third. By then Montgomery County's population had finally rebounded to Jackson-era levels growing, since 1860, from 11,000 to 16,000 whites and 7,000 to 9,000 African-Americans.

During the dynamic rule of Alexander "Boss" Shepherd, the city was modernized whether or not it wanted to be. Kalorama Heights, Massachusetts Avenue, Washington Heights, Cleveland Park, LeDroit Park, and Uniontown sprawled out from the Capital, and property values increased exponentially, nearly 500 percent in some areas of Washington County by the 1880s. D.C. added almost 2,500 buildings in 1887, and at least a hundred real estate firms flourished.[5]

This boom almost ignored Georgetown although it was still a busy port and the cynosure of Bethesda's social and economic life. The city used the Rock Creek estuary as a dump, but each year, through the 1880s and `90s, hundreds of three- and four-masted ships arrived at the canal company's Mole to load cargoes of coal and wheat. Georgetown suffered greatly at the hands of Shepherd's road builders, but sank slowly toward a quiet dotage. In Capital-area agriculture, the movement was toward truck and dairy farming for the multiplying markets of the nearby city.

The C&O Canal struggled along despite business reverses and almost regular floods. Its new president, County-native James C. Clarke, improved the dams and lift locks and raised the dangerously low pedestrian bridges in Georgetown. When Clarke, who was making an unprecedented $10,000 annually, left for an even better paying job, the board

replaced him with Arthur Pue Gorman, political boss and Speaker of the Maryland House of Delegates. In 1875 the canal carried a record 973,805 tons of freight on some five hundred boats. The increase in traffic helped some Bethesda-area farmers, but many complained that the barge families' "perception of the right of property was very dim."[6]

Some Georgetown leaders, admiring Alexandria's success since freeing itself from D.C., petitioned Congress for retrocession claiming that "Maryland stands with open arms and loving heart to welcome her plucky son to her bosom again." Congress not only ignored their petition, it passed the Organic Act transforming old Georgetown into West Washington. Until 1871 the County, as it was usually called, had its own, separate government and was not even considered part of the City of Washington. Georgetown began a long but steady swoon toward not-so-genteel impoverishment that would not end until the advent of the New Deal.

In 1888 Congress imposed the L'Enfant street-grid plan on the subdividers, but the building boom continued until the Panic of 1893. Although some early real estate ventures in the Bethesda area collapsed, what was happening in the rest of the country did not strike home until Populist Jacob S. Coxey's "Army" came down the Pike and the canal in the spring of '94 demanding relief from Congress.

The first big change for Montgomery County farmers, and for its few townspeople, arrived with the long-awaited railroad. The Metropolitan Branch of the Baltimore and Ohio was chartered in 1865 and completed in 1873. It ran diagonally northwest to southeast across the County and into the Capital and originally had twenty-six stations between Point of Rocks, or Washington Junction as the railroad men called it, and the B&O station at New Jersey Avenue and C Street.

In 1879 Boyd 1879 rhapsodized:

As the location of Washington seems to be on ground prepared for the site of a seat of Government of a great Nation, so Montgomery County seems prepared to furnish supplies of all kinds for the inhabitants of such as city; Milk, Butter, Poultry, Hay, Fruit and Vegetables, in fact, every thing which will not stand long carriage. Also by means of this road to furnish locations for country residences for those who can afford it, the whole line from Washington to Sugar Loaf Mountain furnishes sites for cottages, where abundant water is of first quality, shade trees and soil most favorable for gardeners can be found.

In the fall of 1872 the first passenger train on the Metropolitan Branch carefully brought fair goers from Washington to Rockville, covering the fifteen miles in an hour on the newly ballasted track. Hundreds made the trip. Joseph Bradley of Chevy Chase had overseen the completion of the repair and renovation of the fair grounds, which enjoyed another boom of popularity.

Regular service began in May 1873, with two passenger trains and two freights in each direction daily. By 1880 about a dozen trains passed each way every day, by the turn of the century over twenty. The first real suburbs developed in Takoma Park and around Knowles' Station (Kensington), and soon many men and a few women were commuting to jobs in the city from Gaithersburg and Rockville, especially after the passage of the Civil Service Act. For County truck and dairy farmers, the railroad meant access to new markets and a much easier and more reliable route to fast-growing Baltimore as well as to Washington, and it also meant tons of cheap fertilizer and limestone which, at the time, were probably more important.

Farmers cleared fields abandoned since

Metropolitan Branch			
Stations	Miles	Stations	Miles
Washington	0	Rockville	16 1/4
Metropolitan Junction	1	Derwood	19
Queenstown	3 1/4	Washington Grove	20 3/4
Terra Cotta	4	Gaithersburg	21 1/2
Stott's	4 1/4	Clopper's	24 1/2
Brightwood	6 1/4	Germantown	26 1/2
Silver Springs (sic)	7	Little Seneca	28 1/2
Linden	9	Boyd's	29 1/2
Forest Glen	9 1/2	Barnesville	33 1/4
Ray's Quarry	9 3/4	Dickerson	35 3/4
Knowles	11	Tuscarora	39
Windham's	13 1/2	Sugar Loaf	41 3/4
Halpine	15 1/2	Washington Junction	42 3/4

the death of the Whig Party, and millers, seed merchants and equipment dealers all prospered. The nation celebrated July 4th, 1876, the centennial of American independence, with a huge fair in Philadelphia, but the leaders of Montgomery County studiously ignored the holiday as a Northern victory party. However, they glorified the County's hundredth anniversary in September of the same year with speeches of self-congratulation for the progress that had been made, especially since the coming of the Metropolitan Branch.

By the County's centennial, according to Thomas Anderson, half million dollars worth of "lime, bone-phosphates, and other fertilizers of kindred character" had been spread on the County's farms, and yields were up to thirty bushels of wheat and fifty bushels of corn per acre. Certainly the Metropolitan Branch did not deserve all the credit, but it became a symbol of a renaissance.

The Boyd's *Directory* gave the following estimated population for towns and villages, and it is not difficult to note the relationship between proximity to the railroad and size of population: Barnesville 175, Bethesda 25, Boyds 100, Brighton 150, Brookeville 250, Clarksburg 250, Damascus 100, Darnestown 200, Dickerson 100, Four Corners 125, Gaithersburg 200, Germantown 100, Hyattstown 150, Laytonsville 100, Offutt's + Roads 125, Olney 75, Poolesville 275, Rockville 1,000, Sandy Spring 100.

And Boyd described Bethesda this way:

On the Frederick and Georgetown Pike, five miles from Georgetown, D.C., and three miles from Knowles' Station on the Metropolitan Railroad. Soil fertile, selling from thirty dollars to one hundred and twenty-five dollars per acre. Products — Wheat, 25 to 50 bushels, Corn, 45 bushels, Hay, two and one-half tons per acre. Presbyterian Church and Public School. Population, 25.

For Bethesda's farmers and shop keepers, the new railroad meant very little. "Bethesda" was now the post office name, with the counter in Robert Franck's store since January of 1871. The change was much to the satisfaction of the Rev. Edward Henry Cumpston of the Presbyterian Church, who never liked the name "Darcy's Store." In 1878, out of parts of the Rockville and Berry Districts, the County Commissioners created the Bethesda Election District of some thirty-five square miles, then and now District Number 7. Its eastern boundary was Rock Creek, and the southern borders were the Potomac River and Washington, D.C. The western boundary ran from what is now Persimmon Tree Road to Thomas Creek and to Bell's Mill Road, the northern boundary, and to Old Georgetown Road and across to the Pike just north of the present Grosvenor Lane. (The map at left is of the WWI era. Another, similar map is in the Foreword.) So by 1880 the name "Bethesda" was well established even if the district's borders lacked definition in the minds of most residents, another condition still true today.

The Seventh Election District of Montgomery County

Bethesda also had its own Grange or Patrons of Husbandry. The members built the two-story Grange Hall on the west side of the Pike across from the lane that led to the Bradley farm. Montgomery County Grange Number Five was in existence from 1874 until at least 1879, and various Bethesda-area groups were still using the Hall as a meeting place well into the Nineties. The Grange Hall was also the location of one of the early, post-Civil War public schools in Bethesda with classes being held on the second floor.

Boyd's list of Bethesdans in 1879 named only the heads of families, but this incomplete list suggests that there were a lot more than twenty-five residents at the time of the *Directory*'s publication:

Postmaster- Lester, R.C.
Attorney at Law- Bradley, Joseph
Blacksmiths - Kirby and Loehte
Carpenter - Beckwith, Benedict
Carriage Maker - Austin, James
Merchandise - Lester, R.C.
Physician - Davidson, James H.
Farmers: J.Hopkins Anderson, A. H. and B. F. Bean, E. H. and Jas. M. Bean, J. T. and John G. Bohrer, Joseph Bradley, H. G .Carroll, Wm. Counselman, James H. Davidson, John Davidson, J. H. Dodge, George Dunlap, James M. Gingel, Joseph Gingel, John Gleghorn, Geo. and Wm. Hudleston, L.C.Jones, Cyrus Keizer, Eli Keizer, C. Kisner, Henry Kisner, David Lawrence, R. C. Lester, H. L. Offutt, Z. Owens, James Powell, Henry Pyles, Henry Renshaw, Thomas Renshaw, William Renshaw, Frank Spates, George Spates, Robert Spates, Theophilus Tolbert, Edwin Wallis, E. P. Watkins, Spencer Watkins, John C. Williams, Lewis Williams, John N. Willson, Michael Willson.[7]

In the upper part of the County, exhausted land, scrubby lots and piney woods metamorphosed into wheat fields, acres of corn and rolling pastures. Frederick lime, brought in at a reasonable price by the railroad, renewed the farms, and the *Sentinel* crowed that "lands which thirty years ago would not grow enough wheat to pay for the harvesting now in favorable years yield as much as forty bushels to the acre." By 1880 the County ranked fourth in Maryland wheat production, and the increased value of the land showed in the tax assessment that grew steadily through the 1870s and `80s. The first of several seemingly endless real estate booms had begun.[8]

At first much of the talk was of summer residences for office workers in the steamy capital with its malarial flats, and there was a brisk sale of building lots near the Rockville station as some enthusiastic entrepreneurs tried to promote the county seat as a resort town complete with hotels, including the popular Woodlawn.

The Methodists bought 268 acres north of Rockville and incorporated a camp meeting association in 1874 with a new station on the B&O called Washington Grove. Takoma Park developed in the 1880s as the first real suburb under the leadership of New Yorker Benjamin Franklin Gilbert, a friend of D.C.'s great modernizer and bankrupter "Boss" Alexander Robey Shepherd.[9]

In the 1890s the Seventh Day Adventists built a sanatorium and their church headquarters in Takoma Park. The town incorporated in 1900 with more than a thousand residents and elected Gilbert its first mayor. Woodside was developed on a hundred acres near the intersection of Georgia Avenue and the B&O where the promoter, a bank director and dean of the Howard law school, built a station for commuters. A resort hotel and some summer cottages sprang up at Forest Glen, and the developers of Capitol View dug out a five-acre lake and stocked it with trout at their hopeful rural retreat.

Kensington grew at Knowles' Station under the leadership of Brainard H. Warner, a real Horatio Alger, who headed the biggest real estate company in D.C. by the time he was thirty and was president of Washington Loan and Trust at forty-two. And one of the most interesting of all the County's suburban communities, Garrett Park, with its winding streets and odd-shaped lots was designed and sold in the 1880s by Henry Copp who named it for the powerful, long-time president of the B&O. A similar Copp project in "Peerless" Rockville, West End Park, foundered in a title morass.

Through the `80s land prices boomed along the railroad, and by the early `90s some $50-an-acre farmland was going for $500. The golden dreams of most of the speculators ended with the Panic, but the stability brought by civil service legislation had produced a growing number of long-term government employees looking for a place to live if the train could get them to their desks on time.[10]

But all this was along the line of the B&O and had little or no effect on the farmers of Bethesda. Although some were going down to Market Place and other venues in the central city, for the most part they still shopped and sold their produce in Georgetown. In the 1880s George Peter, by then a Pue Gorman ally, came close to promoting a railroad down the C&O Canal right-of-way until the B&O squashed his plan with its General Assembly power. For Bethesdans the "rail revolution" came with the electric trolley car.

In the Capital the development that was to make Bethesda a suburb was taking shape. When the Civil War began, a single horse-car line crossed Washington. It operated omnibuses from Georgetown to the Navy Yard by way of M Street, Pennsylvania Avenue and 15th Street with feeder lines on 7th Street and 14th Street. By the summer of 1863 Gilbert Vanderwerken's Washington and Georgetown Railroad was profitably running seventy cars at five-minute intervals (headway). The Pennsylvania Avenue part of this route became the heart of the Capital Traction Company lines, and thanks to parades on the Avenue, the most seen and best known trolley line in all of America.[11]

In 1864 a competitor emerged from a carbarn where the Corcoran now stands. It was the Metropolitan Railroad Company whose horsecar routes became the basis of the Washington Railway and Electric Company lines. Several other companies rose and fell, merged or disappeared during the 1870s and '80s until only two, Capital Traction and WRECo remained.

In Richmond in 1888, Frank Julian Sprague built the first electric-trolleycar route, and the horsecars' days were numbered. Sprague, an Annapolis graduate who had worked briefly for Edison, invented the "troller" that came to be called the trolley, a grooved metal wheel, usually brass, which conducted electricity from an overhead wire. By "the turn of the century half the streetcar systems in the United States were equipped by Sprague, and ninety percent were using his patents."[13]

The first electrics in Washington were those of the Eckington and Soldiers Home Railway Company that began operation in October of 1888. The *Star* described the novelty:

The cars do not differ materially from those found on other lines - except that there is no place to hitch the horse . . . . Flying along New York Avenue, which is brilliantly lit at night by clusters of electric lights at the top of iron poles, the occupants of the car become conscious that they were creating something of a sensation . . . . The Star can be read in any part of the car."

And the race was on. In the next few years a line was chartered to Chevy Chase, another to Tenallytown and then on through Bethesda, two to Glen Echo, and later a line to Kensington and then another from Bethesda to Great Falls. At the ends of many of these lines, amusement parks and summer hotels blossomed. Along these lines, planned subdivisions appeared and disappeared, fortunes grew and vanished, and life changed gradually but permanently.

In five frantic years, from 1887 until the

Trolley Lines of the Washington Area[12]	
charter date	company name
1862	Washington & Georgetown RR Co.
1864	Metropolitan Railroad Company
1868	Connecticut Ave. & Park Railway Co.
1870	Columbia Railway Company
1872	Union Railroad Company
1872	Boundary & Silver Spring Rwy Company
1872	Anacostia & Potomac River RR Company
1875	Capitol, N. O St. & So. Washington Ry.
1888	Eckington & Soldiers Home Rwy Co.
1888	Georgetown & Tenallytown Rwy Co.
1888	Brightwood Railway Company
1888	Rock Creek Railway Company
1889	Glen Echo Railroad Company
1890	Tenallytown & Rockville RR Company
1892	Columbia & Maryland Railway Co.
1892	Md .and Washington Rwy Company
1892	Wash. & Great Falls Electric Railway
1893	Belt Railway Company (name change)
1894	Baltimore and Washington Transit Co.
1894	Ch. Ch. Lake & Kensington Railway
1895	Capitol Railway Company
1895	Wash., Woodside & Forest Glen Ry.
1895	W. Wash. & Great Falls Electric Ry Co.
1895	Capital Traction Company
1896	Washington & Glen Echo Railroad Co.
1897	Washington & Rockville Railway Co.
1898	City & Suburban Railway of Washington
1899	Washington Traction and Electric Co.
1902	Washington Railway and Electric Co.
1902	Kensington Railway
1912	Wash. & Great Falls Ry and Power Co.
1933	Capital Transit Company(merger)

end of 1892, much of the land in the Bethesda area changed hands several times until some of it was valued at $350 to $500 an acre just before the bubble burst in the Panic of 1893. In the speculative process several nascent suburbs collapsed, and a number of local nabobs and real estate promoters lost their shirts as well as their families' land.

Georgetown chronicler Mary Mitchell, concluded that

(T)he impact of the electric trolley, whether one went to work or play, shop or pray, cannot be overemphasized. Along with electricity, the motorcar, and the telephone, it was one of the turn-of-the-century changes that erased the District's old city boundaries and particularly gave women wings and seven-league boots. The yeasty input of the Nineties prefaced a revolution in lifestyle and social emancipation unequaled since.[14]

Silver lobbyist Francis G. Newlands, the vastly wealthy leader of a group quietly buying up farmland between Calvert Street and Jones Bridge Road, acquired the charter and became the president of the Rock Creek Railway in 1890. It was basically a simple line up 18th and Calvert Streets to Connecticut Avenue and on north to newly created Chevy Chase Lake. It crossed very undulating and stream-cut topography with two major defiles, the Rock Creek Valley and the Klingle Valley. His company spanned the creek valleys with two iron-trestle bridges, felled hundreds of trees for ties, dug numerous deep cuts, filled several stream valleys, and then laid a double line of T-rail tracks. Between the two tracks for the first mile outside the city, poles of metal pipe with ornamental bracing under the crossarms held the wire. Farther out square wooden poles, painted black, carried copper lines for the electricity generated at the new power plant at the Lake. The work crews set the poles 125 feet apart and ballasted the roadbed with crushed granite taken from the hills along the line.

On August 1st, 1891, the *Star*, in its feature-filled Saturday edition, reported that the construction was making "favorable progress" and went on at some length about the distant and rural real estate project.

In fact, the greater part of the work is finished. All that remains to be done is to complete laying the rails and to erect the power house. This building is to be located at the northern terminus of the road, and when it is stated that it will be just seven miles from the southern terminus, which will be at the head of Connecticut Avenue and Boundary, some idea of the magnitude of the enterprise will be gained. The building of this road, which was begun almost a year ago, would have been completed by this time only that it was decided to wait until the Baltimore and Ohio had constructed its southern branch, which is to be run in a westerly direction from the Linden station, on the Metropolitan Branch, to the Conduit road above the Chain bridge. This road is now being constructed, and the engineers expect to have that portion completed between the Linden Station and the junction with the Rock Creek road by the later part of this month. The power house, where the electricity will be generated, which will be used as the motive power of the Rock Creek railroad, will be located at this point, which is two miles from the District line in Montgomery County. The rails for the northern portion of the new road are to be brought over the southern branch of the B. and O., as well as the fuel supply for the power house. This will save the great expense of the long haul from the city. As is well known the Rock Creek railroad is being constructed along Connecticut avenue extended, which has been opened and graded at the expense of the syndicate owning large tracts of land along the line of the road and also owning a controlling interest in the railroad company. Connecticut avenue is now opened in a straight line all the way from Woodley Park to the District line, a distance of three and one-half miles. Owing to the broken and rugged character of the country, immense fills and cuts were made, some of them as much as fifty feet in depth, and two long and expensive bridges were built. The first part of the road near the city passes over city streets as it starts at the intersection of Boundary or Florida avenue with Connecticut avenue and goes thence along Boundary to 18th, thence along 18th crossing Columbia road, and thence through the subdivision of Cliffbourne, which lies between Lanier and Washington Heights, to Rock Creek.

To make the crossing at Rock Creek an iron bridge has been built a 180 feet high and 750 feet long. It is seventy-five feet higher than the new Woodley road bridge, which is just to the south, and twice as long. The bridge, including the masonry, has been built at a cost of $85,000. It passes over the south end of the Zoological Park. Another bridge has been erected to

carry the road over the Klingle road at an elevation of seventy feet. This bridge is 400 feet long and, including the masonry, has cost $42,000. When the road reaches the District line it turns at a slight angle to the northeast and extends through Montgomery County for two miles until it joins the new branch road of the Baltimore and Ohio. Mr. W. Kesley Schoepf, the engineer in charge of the work, thinks that road will be completed early next spring. The vice president of the road, Mr. Edward J. Stellwagon, during the absence from the city of the president, Mr. F. G. Newlands, has the general direction of the work. It is estimated that the road when completed will cost a half a million dollars. After this expenditure is made, which must be added to the $1,500,000 already laid out in the purchase of the land bordering on the line of the road, the owners of the property will only have fairly begun the execution of their plans. It is proposed ultimately to develop the country all along the line, but just at present the operations will be confined to establishing a town in Montgomery county, just across the District line. The Chevy Chase tract is to be subdivided, a system of water supply and sewers to be introduced and the streets are to be macadamized.

By September of 1892, cars were running to Boundary Street, and at the growing "lake," B&O steam engines were switching from the new Metropolitan Southern Branch onto the trolley line's tracks to pull flatcars loaded with rails and other building materials southward as the work continued. The superintendent of the construction phase of the Rock Creek Railway was A. J. Warner of Ohio, a Union general in the Civil War who was a free-silver political ally of F. G. Newlands, Esq. Late in `92 his memo to Newlands had nothing but good news.

The electric conduit line on U Street is now completed and, I think, may be pronounced a success. The Rock Creek Road from Boundary to Chevy Chase is well ballasted and has been much improved by cutting down summits and raising low places, and the tracks I consider now to be in first class order for operation. The steam plant comes fully up to our expectations, and in coal consumption comes considerably within our calculations. On Sunday last, with ten cars on the line, but 4,400 pounds were consumed in twelve hours. For economy in coal consumption, I do not think this showing can be surpassed anywhere.

I see nothing therefore now in the way of the safe operation of the entire line, including U Street and the line to the Zoo Park. Special cars will be required in the operation of the Zoo Branch, and I suggest that to insure entire safety, the speed of the cars when descending the grade, should be limited to 3, or at most 4, miles an hour.[15]

The road formally opened on September 16, 1892, with cars full of company officers and city dignitaries. The whole line was in operation by the end of 1892, although the spur to the bears' den at the Zoo was never used due to its steep grade.

There must have been some sort of working relationship between the politically powerful John Garrett's influential B&O and lobbyist Francis Newlands' little, electric railroad, but it may have existed only as a "gentlemen's agreement" between the men involved. The Chevy Chase Land Company and the railroad made two contracts regarding the tracks and sidings at the Lake and freight charges. The B&O's directors had at one time believed that the Southern Branch, which reached Chevy Chase Lake in 1892, would "develop some important suburban settlements in the vicinity."[16]

For whatever reasons–the cost of right-of-way land was the one given–the B&O stopped at Connecticut Avenue for almost eighteen years helping the Chevy Chase builders get a good start and perhaps slowing development to the west. Then track laying commenced again through a series of cuts following the creek to Bethesda in 1910. The line curved gently toward the river along Willett and Little Falls brooks and near the Canal at the District Line joined the tracks of the Washington and Western Maryland connecting it with those of the Georgetown Barge, Dock, Elevator and Railroad Company laid along the riverfront in 1889. The whole three-company, single-track line was only about eleven miles long, but it carried a great deal of fuel and building materials in its time and helped build Bethesda.

Newlands *et al.* had originally intended to extend Connecticut Avenue straight into Montgomery County and join Rockville Pike south of the old Presbyterian Meeting House, but problems with land acquisition forced a turn due north at the District Line. This decision, along with the intersection of Belt

Road and Brookeville Road and other planned streets at the entrance to the new subdivision, led to the creation of Chevy Chase Circle. The Maryland half of the 200-foot diameter circle was, with some difficulty, ceded to the federal government, and the whole circle put under the jurisdiction of the D.C. parks department.[17]

Cows grazed on the Circle in the early years, bands played there, and it was the goal of many D.C. bicycle clubs, both black and white, who picnicked there in the Gay Nineties. Unlike Dupont Circle, where both trolley tracks ran on the western side much to the consternation of many already baffled tourists, the Rock Creek line's tracks divided at Chevy Chase Circle where riders could watch boys playing on the broad, flat, grassy expanse in all seasons. Willow oaks were planted around the circumference in the early 1930s, but the Circle remained one of the area's premier baseball, football and playground fields until the fountain honoring Newlands was installed in 1933.[18]

In 1893, under continuous pressure from Theodore Noyes of the influential *Star*, who had seen and admired an underground system in Budapest, Congress outlawed overhead trolley wires in the City, south of Boundary Street (Florida Avenue). At first the Rock Creek line tried the Love two-wire system with a "plow pit" at 18th Street to switch from overhead wires. When this proved unreliable, they installed thirty-one-foot, u-shaped copper bars. They worked and became the basis of the in-town, underground D.C. system.[19]

The Rock Creek line had two powerhouses, one at 18th and Champlain for the conduit and the other at Chevy Chase Lake for the overhead lines. The Chevy Chase facility was less than fifty feet from the B & O tracks, and two coal chutes stood on a siding beside it. The original brick powerhouse measured 55 by 100 feet and contained divided boiler and engine rooms. Four, belt-drive, 90 kilowatt generators produced the power, and a separate alternating current generator provided incandescent home and street lighting.

Above and in front of the power station was the 60 by 130-foot, frame carbarn with five tracks and room for all twenty-five of the cars the line had when it began service. Two of the tracks extended over pits five feet deep

and sixty feet long where motors and trucks could be repaired. The car house sat on a slight angle to Connecticut Avenue (extended) and the two-track main line so that turns into it were on a gentle radius.[20]

The "Lake" was a creation of the trolley company to supply water for the boilers and condensers by way of a large cistern on the east side of the building; the small amusement park, hot dog stand and famous dance pavilion came later. A couple of hundred yards east of Connecticut Avenue, a small dam stopped Coquelin Run, which had its beginnings as a fine spring in the middle of Bethesda. A muddy swamp eventually produced an oval, weedy acre or two of water and a lot of mosquitoes, but it did become a fashionable and popular place to picnic or go for a row in a rented boat (5¢ for half an hour and don't forget your parasol). Skaters used it at their own risk in the winter until several reports of drownings kept many of them away. It was never fit for swimming although diving exhibitions were held there on several occasions.[21]

William Duvall, chairman of the history committee of the Town of Chevy Chase, remembered the lake as a place of high adventure for young explorers who usually worked their way up from the muddy eastern end. "As people approached, the turtles hurried down the banks to safety. Small fish rippled the surface and tadpoles abounded along the shores. Snakes of questionable species sunned themselves and were viewed from a prudent distance. Pieces of wood were pushed out from the shore and became warships of fancy to be bombarded with an artillery barrage of stones." He also noted that to the local parents "the lake was a source of continuing despair."[22]

The powerhouse at the lake, after being rebuilt and enlarged once, was abandoned in 1920. All the power then came from the city with a booster station on a Connecticut Avenue hillside at about Davenport Street. The company removed the Chevy Chase generators, salvaged other useful equipment, and left the rest simply to rust and decay. The broken pipes soon filled the powerhouse with water, but there was still a frightening buzz in the old electrical switchboards. Over the years a number of Chevy Chase youngsters peered through its broken windows, but only the most daring explored the ravaged interior.

The Rock Creek Railway also built a row of brick houses on the west side of Connecticut Avenue, across from the Lake and an odd-shaped office building with terra cotta trim. Conductors, motormen, and the steam engineers who had to rise before dawn to fire the boilers in the building behind the carbarn and get the first cars out on the tracks rented the modest homes or boarded with those who did. Some of the trainmen on the "extra" board who filled in for absent trolley car operators also lived there. The street, officially Watkins Lane, came to be called "chinch alley." Between this row of houses and the loop at the end of the line, which had a hot dog stand on the Lake side and the waiting station and office on the other, land for a swimming pool was leased in 1925.

Operation of the trolley line began with both open and closed, single-truck passenger cars and trailers built by Lamokin and one very popular Westinghouse freight car. The open cars had striped side-curtains that could be pulled down in case of rain, and some had an extra wheel in the center on each side to help them safely negotiate the Circle and other sharp curves. The passenger list for the inaugural trip included Gen. A. J. Warner, Spencer Watkins, Magruder W. Offutt, J. J. Malone, H. L. Wyman, W. A. L. Graham, G. E. Disney, District Commissioner Douglass, and Assistant Postmaster General Hazen. The conductor was C. O. Shubert and the motorman William Thrift. The run from Boundary Street to the Lake took thirty minutes, a speed never equaled once scheduled runs began.

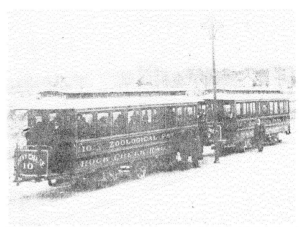

Two Rock Creek cars - note center wheels which helped on curves especially at Chevy Chase Circle

The trolley became a part of life in Chevy Chase. For years one of the sure signs of spring was the Marine Band playing its way up Connecticut Avenue to the Lake on one of those wooden seated, open cars with the wide running boards. The Band's leader, Captain William Santlemann, had a fine, turreted home in Chevy Chase, D.C.[23]

The trolleys to Chevy Chase were maroon until 1909 when the great, olive-green Cincinnati "pay-within" cars began running (below). These wooden, two-man cars with their rounded fronts, big sliding doors, fold-down steps, and swaying ride are ones still affectionately remembered by older residents.

In 1895 the company acquired the old Washington and Georgetown line and changed its corporate name to Capital Traction with the unlimited capitalization possible under Newlands' charter. The first

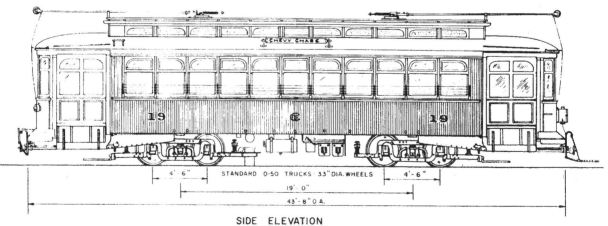

4' 6"   STANDARD O-50 TRUCKS 33" DIA. WHEELS   4' 6"

19' 0"

43'-8" O.A.

SIDE ELEVATION

Cincinnati car

president of the Capital Traction Company, and the man some credit with bringing about the merger that created it, was George Thomas Dunlop, born at Hayes Manor in Chevy Chase in 1845.

After the Civil War he established his agricultural equipment and supplies business in warehouses near the canal on the west side of Wisconsin Avenue south of M Street and became one of the most successful fertilizer dealers in the area. He employed more than forty men and had sales totaling $165,000 in 1880. "One can only hope his office at 3200 M. Street was insulated against the odors produced by mixing and bagging Peruvian quanape lobos, guano, ammoniated bone, super-phosphate, and acids," wrote Mary Mitchell who thought Dunlop's career had a bit of Horatio Alger in it. Dunlop built a fine, big home on Q Street at 31st and directed the operations of Capital Traction from his offices in the Car Barns, the still-standing fortress on M Street completed in 1897.[24]

Beginning in 1895 the single track Kensington Railway ran from the trolley barn at the Lake to the bank near the B&O station in Kensington. It had one siding, called Ray's Turnout, about midway along the line just past Rock Creek and got its power from Capital Traction. Herbert Claude, superintendent of the Chevy Chase trolley line, was one of the construction engineers. "The contour of the ground was followed as far as the limits of the right-of-way permitted in order to avoid grading, which accounted for the many curves," and the cars usually stopped anywhere along the route to pick up or discharge passengers. The friendly motormen hauled ice cream down from McKeever's store in Kensington for many a Chevy Chase party.

The line was sold in 1902 to a company headed by R. Henry Phillips who planned an extension to Ellicott City and actually built a bridge across the B&O tracks and laid about 2,500 feet of track toward Wheaton. To improve service into Washington, the line was leased to Capital Traction in May 1923. The people of Kensington bought $13,500 worth of five percent bonds, and the Capital Traction Company paid an additional $8,700 to repair and improve the system and replace the wooden trestle over Rock Creek with a steel one to carry the heavier cars.

It was in its last years when young Bob Truax was allowed to handle the controller and the air brake on some late summer runs while the tired motorman sat and chatted with the straw-hatted passengers. The line died with the Chevy Chase electric railway in 1935. Bethesda-area folks who had been enjoying Fontaine Fox Jr.'s comic strip since the Great War often called the Kensington line the "Toonerville trolley."[25]

George Winchester Stone, who grew up in Martin's Additions, claimed that "all of us kids knew how to run the streetcars just by watching, and when a new man would come on and the old one would teach him, we could tell him how to put the airbrake on and release it a little so the car wouldn't stop with a jerk." And Bill Duvall recalled that it was not only on Hallowe'en that a group of boys would stand at a streetcar stop so that a couple of their friends could pull the trolley pole off the wire when the car slowed. Then

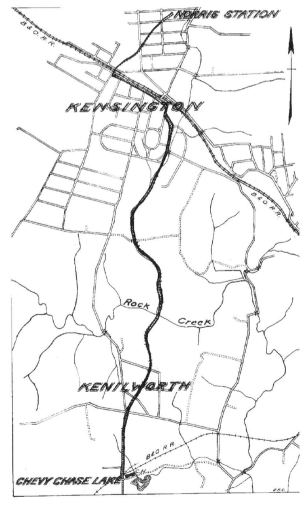

Route of the streetcar line to Kensington

they all hooted, laughed, and ran as the car went dark and the long-suffering conductor, careful of his language if there were ladies on his car, got down to put them back on the wire.

The Washington and Georgetown Railroad Company constructed a very successful cable system on Pennsylvania Avenue, 7th Street and 14th Street that became part of the Capital Traction operation in 1895. The cables ran at 9.9 miles per hour and the cars, often operated with a trailer, had grips beneath them that grabbed the moving cable through a center groove between the tracks. On September 29, 1897, a fire destroyed the central powerhouse and marked the end of the experiment with cable cars, but a lasting result of the installation of the expensive but short-lived system was that D.C.'s trolley lines used a centered third rail when they were converted to underground electricity.

By 1899 within the city, the Capital Traction system was all on the underground copper conduit. A sliding shoe or plow, as the railway men generally called it, rode under the car and collected electricity from the conduit. The system did have problems in heavy snows and sometimes leaves or other debris clogged the third rail.

One motorman vividly remembered having a car full of commuters stuck in the middle of 14th and New York Avenue one snowy, winter morning at rush hour when his front trucks went through the switch to get him on the tracks to the Navy Yard, but his plow did not. Most streetcar riders from Bethesda can recall the plow pit in Georgetown where the trolley pole atop the car was lowered and the shoe attached beneath during a thirty-second, or sometimes much longer, pause on the narrowest part of Wisconsin Avenue.[26]

The Georgetown and Tenallytown Railway Company was also a pioneer, chartered in 1888. Its first double-track line ran out Wisconsin Avenue from the canal to the District Line. It went down the middle of the road to Calvert Street, and then along the east side of Wisconsin Avenue to River Road on the Tenallytown Hill where it switched to the west side. In 1920 the whole line was moved to the middle of the repaved street. The coal-fired generating plant was mostly

below grade at Calvert and Wisconsin. C&O Canal barges brought the Cumberland coal into town and then up Rock Creek to High Street where it was loaded into freight cars.

The outbound route to Tenallytown was mostly uphill, and in the summer of 1899, one of those coal cars loaded with five tons of bituminous got away and came whizzing backwards toward Georgetown on the northbound track. It met car No. 12, which seconds before had been loaded with passengers, on the steep hill between Dumbarton and N Streets. All of Georgetown heard the crash. The open passenger car, still holding the purses and packages of many of the women passengers, was filled with big lumps of coal and knocked backward forty feet, and the coal dust lay half a foot deep in places. Big baulks of timber crashed through the plate glass windows of Carter's barber shop and Weaver's grocery store. This was the third runaway car to rumble through Georgetown. A stout trolley pole stopped the first, and the second crashed through a boat house and almost ended in the river. Georgetown citizens soon petitioned the G&T to have safety brakes installed on all its cars.[27]

The Tenallytown and Rockville line, chartered in Maryland in 1890, laid track as a continuation of the Georgetown and Tenallytown line to Alta Vista by way of the Rockville Pike and Old Georgetown Road. The Maryland section's incorporators were John E. Beall, Dr. Ralph Walsh, Gen. Richard C. Drum, H. Bradley Davidson, Spencer Watkins, J. Heath Dodge, and James B. Henderson. Heavy grades on the Pike led the engineers to select the Georgetown Road route where property owners agreed to the sixteen foot right-of-way.

The double-track line ended with a spring-loaded Y switch near Somerset and the single track proceeded up Wisconsin and the east side of Old Georgetown with the first siding at the intersection by the blacksmith's shop, later the location of the stone Bank of Bethesda building. At each siding the motorman reached out to a switch on the power pole with a hoe-handle-shaped stick, which had a half-inch female socket on its end. By turning the switch, he set the block lights to red so that a car coming the other way would not enter the section of single rail track he was on. By the spring of 1891 the tracks and power poles had reached the top of the long

hill up from Somerset, past "Langdrum," the retirement farm of General Drum, the line's nominal president.

The first trip on the newly completed line took place on the last Saturday of June 1891. The *Sentinel* reported that "There were on the car General Manager Watkins, John E. Beall, Dr. Slaywater, Messrs. George W. Drew, Z. H. Denham, W. Turner, Thomas Boucher and Misses Watkins and Dodge." Among the other passengers were Gen. Drum's two young grandsons, Fred and Harry Hunt. The trolley line obviously expected heavy summer business since it began with three open but only a single closed car.

The Bethesda Literary Club advertised an entertainment for the evening of June 9, 1891, with talent from both Washington and Rockville providing "music, recitations, declamations, etc." at the Grange Hall and refreshments at moderate prices. "The committee will make an effort" stated the announcement, "to have cars running to the door that night." The trolley age had begun for Bethesda, but because the line was single track, the service was never as good as that offered to Chevy Chase by the Rock Creek Railway.[28]

At the end of the line, the developers built a short-lived but very successful amusement park in the neighborhoods now called Sonoma and Oakmont. Bethesda Park, which opened in the summer of 1891, challenged both of its local, popular, end-of-the-trolleyline competitors at Chevy Chase Lake and Glen Echo-Cabin John. Cars had to run well into the night to take happy revelers back into the city from its midway attractions, bright lights, theater and dance floor. Entrepreneurs Richard C. Drum and John E. Beall, an important stockholder in the trolley line as well as a lawyer and real estate speculator, built the park on fifty acres of woods and pasture land they had acquired only two months earlier from one Annie Vance, who may have fronted for Beall and his cohorts in the purchase of this and other properties.

Beall made his home on Old Georgetown Road, past Sunnyside and Woodmont where the Lutheran church now stands on its hill. He bought up or acquired options on a number of farms and soon owned or co-owned more than a thousand acres of Bethesda-area real estate. He probably was the moving

force behind both the trolley line and the park. Other Bethesda Park investors included M. Willson Offutt, Spencer Watkins, and Ed Watkins—all long-time owners of large blocks of local acreage as well as allies of Beall in the trolley line. It is reasonable to assume that all expected the value of their property along the electric railway to increase.[29]

On the 4th of July with a fireworks display and a front-page ad in the *Post*, Bethesda Park opened The advertisement also stated that building lots and acreage were available along the route of the trolley line and boasted that the "country through which it passes is the most beautiful and salubrious in Montgomery county."

The park was an almost immediate success despite being little more than overgrown picnic grounds, and it was not long before a different kind of news story ap-

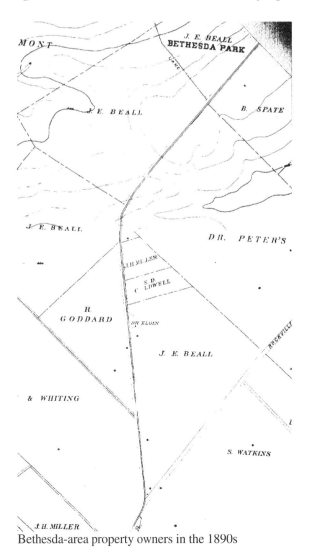

Bethesda-area property owners in the 1890s

peared reflecting complaints about the lack of transport, "especially on Sunday when hundreds who come from all parts of the District to enjoy a pleasant ride in the country are unable to obtain either sitting or standing room."

By the end of the summer of 1891 the Park was already attracting local organizations. The St. Ann's Society of Tenallytown held a jousting tournament and picnic there, and several announcements such as the following appeared in the *Sentinel*.

The Women's Aid Society of Mt. Zion Baptist church at Beane will hold a festival and supper for the benefit of the church on Tuesday July 30th at Bethesda Park, the present terminus of the Rockville and Tennallytown Electric Railroad. Refreshments will be served at moderate prices from 3 to 10 P.M. The music will be furnished by a band from Washington, and a good time is expected. All are invited to attend.

At the Park a steam-heated botanical garden in a sixty-by-twenty-foot hot house displayed exotic plants from all over the world, and a menagerie held caged panthers and other beasts that rivaled the collection of the newly opened zoological park. From time to time visiting animal acts included trained lions. The park also had a shooting gallery, quoits, swings and "flying horses." Dance music was provided almost every night, and concerts by the Marine Band were scheduled on Wednesday and Friday evenings.

In September the promoters laid on extra cars for the appearance of Grace Shannon, "the world's greatest Lady Aeronaut," and her balloon ascension and parachute leaps. Her work drew big crowds, many gasps, and great cheers. It also left a durable memory for one of old Bethesda's best known families.[30]

From all accounts the feature of greatest interest to the young employees of the concessionaires at Bethesda Park was the inflation of the bag. A crowd of men and boys would gather around the fire, add kerosene to the fuel to increase the intensity of the heat, and watch for the first quiver of the big bag. There was usually a tangle of men, fuel, and ropes and when the shout "Look out! Let 'er go!" came they scrambled out of the way.

One night things seemed to be going as usual when suddenly yells of horror were heard. The balloon and the man in the parachute went up, but dangling headdown foot entangled in a rope was Howard Gingell!

The wildest kind of excitement took possession of the spectators. Men, women, and children ran back and forth in the woods trying to keep in sight the balloon and its passengers.

"He'll be killed!" cried a group.

"If that boy comes back alive I'll give him a hundred dollars," said Spencer Watkins one of the prominent business men of that decade.

The balloon had so much extra weight that it did not rise as high as usual and the unfortunate man in the parachute, who had no way of knowing that he had an extra passenger, was dragged through the tree-tops in imminent danger of serious injury or death. Sensing this, he pulled the release rope and came down in the clear space where the Reeside house now stands opposite Oak Place.

By one of those quirks of fate that make people believe in luck or Providence, Howard Gingell was in less danger than the professional in the parachute. When the balloon was relieved of the weight of the other man it rose and Howard followed by a pack of men and boys on foot, on bicycle, on horses, or in vehicles, had a nice ride almost to Garret Park. He liked it so much that he applied the hundred dollars Mr. Watkins gave him on the purchase of the balloon and made the ascensions himself the rest of the season.

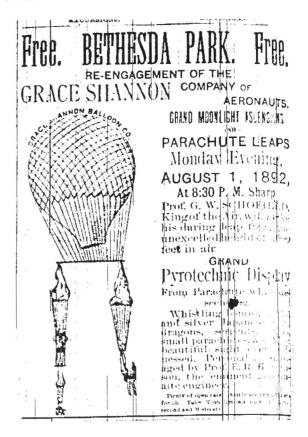

In the spring of '92 the trolley line purchased a double decker car with side entrances, and the *Star* reported that the improvements at Bethesda Park "have changed its appearance greatly. The switchback railway is up and in running order; the merry-go-round, which is now at the depot and which is said to be the largest and finest ever made, will soon be in working order; the grounds are being abundantly supplied with arc lights, the pavilion has been enlarged and the cafe is rapidly nearing completion."

Soon the ads boasted of the "$10,000 Steam Carousel, accommodating 150 people at one time and accompanied by a costly German Orchestration Organ." The park opened in late April with railway service every half hour during the week and every fifteen minutes on Sunday. It advertised that a deputy sheriff was always on duty, that no liquor was permitted, and that it was "Beautiful Bethesda, Queen of the Pleasure Grounds." In May the *Sentinel* reported, "The managers of Bethesda Park have determined to make that place a popular resort for picnicking parties and many appropriate improvements are being made. A roller coaster has already been constructed and an electric fountain that will very much beautify the

grounds is now receiving the finishing touches."[31]

A Ferris wheel contested for the visitors' coins; and later a razzle-dazzle, the latest in rides, which threatened to make its passengers joyously sea-sick, joined the attractions. One building held four bowling alleys, another the shooting gallery. A prize bazaar, musical phonograph, electric battery display, photo gallery, coon game, magic lantern exhibit, baby game, cane board game, and electric target were along the midway. An illuminated electric fountain was a highly praised addition in the second year of operation, and the cafe, managed by Alexandre Fortin, "the White House chef under the Arthur and Cleveland administrations," did a booming business.

The Park included tennis and baseball grounds and lots of room for rustic picnicking. At the western end, on the higher ground, where Hempstead Street cuts across today, hot-air balloon ascensions drew big crowds on summer weekends.[32]

A regular patron of the park told Miss Holman about:

. . . the Jolly Fat Men's Picnics at which games calculated to make any fat man puff and pant were featured. And the double-decker cars. Whether the fat men and the thin men went on the double-deckers we were never told. In fact, this one person is the only one we have found who remembers this particular type of car, but she always referred to the double-decker as extra-special means of transportation. According to her, they were very popular and certainly the top deck must have been exceedingly pleasant on a hot night. (Excellent preparation for an evening of whirling around on the dance floor.) The open-air dance pavilion was on a hill in the grove of oak trees between Oak Lane and Sonoma Road and was one of the most popular places in the park.

The League of American Wheelmen met at the Park, and Wichita Jack's "Wild West" show drew appreciative crowds. Prince Leo, "King of the Tight Rope Walkers," strutted across his wire blindfolded, then with his feet in market baskets, and finally carried a stove to the center of the rope, lit a fire and ate a meal. Other attractions in 1892 included Professor Hampton's dog circus, "Mlle. Electa, the greatest living illusionist and Mons. Du Gay, the equilibrist performing mid air feats," illustrated lectures on the Holy Land and a

tour of Paris, a sacred vocal concert, and at the end of the season, a giant free barbecue to attract the participants in that year's GAR convention.[33]

On the other side of what later became Sonoma Road, in 1892, John E. Beall invested $15,000 in a three-story, wooden, Queen Anne style hotel built that was "highly decorated on the outside with rustic work" and had a broad veranda circling both the first and second floors. The 230 and 75-foot frame building had partially enclosed dining rooms and parlors on the first floor and guest rooms above. Behind the hotel an elaborate springhouse covered a deep well.

The next year the park added a summer theater, which cost some $3,500 to construct and could seat a thousand spectators. Operettas, band concerts and minstrel shows brought well-known singers and dancers to the Bethesda Park stage. A large pavilion and bandstand provided dancing every Tuesday and Thursday as well as on the weekends. Arc lights and many strings of colored bulbs illuminated the whole park with power supplied by the trolley company. The hotel's laundry, and perhaps some other attractions, were hidden away under the switch-back roller coaster.

Bethesda's then-resident historian, Miss Holman, who often visited the nearby Riley farm where her grandfather lived, wrote:

There were great crowds each night during the park's heyday and special excursion cars were run for various groups . . . . One of our most successful business men got a lot of valuable experience when he was a boy by working at various jobs up there. The one that made the most lasting impression was operating that sensational, unbelievable, new invention, the phonograph, for the man who had the concession. It was very, very new. Very, very wonderful. And no extra strict parent could possibly object to it as a means of entertaining Daughter Sue. Round cylinders, beeswax brown, were put on the machine and those who wished to listen to the latest tunes, paid their nickels, fitted the ear plugs into their ears, and listened delightedly to the strains of music. If one liked the first tune he paid another nickel and got a different one. In those days the most popular ones were "Only a Bird in a Gilded Cage," Sousa's marches, "A Bicycle Built for Two" and "The Band Played On." Just think of the pathos of "A Bird in a Gilded Cage" being ground out on a revolving machine while

Doree Germaine Holman

one tightened the earplugs and squirmed to a comfortable position for listening. After that a quiet stroll though the greenhouse should have been soothing to body and spirit.

Miss Holman also recalled the small zoo.

The poor animals were chained to posts and must have endured enough teasing to ruin the disposition of even the best natured beasts. One of the men who enjoyed outings at the park used to laugh and tell us of the time he got too close to a bear. The bear swiped a wicked paw down the man's trouser leg and ripped it to shreds.

"Did it hurt you? What did you do, go home?" we asked.

"No, I just pinned it up. I thought it fun — it caused a lot of attention. All the ladies were asking me about it.""

Even during the popular Chautauqua at Glen Echo, Bethesda Park drew bigger crowds according to Albert Shoemaker who lived in Friendship Heights and could see the passing cars of both railways. He complained,

The people will frolic on Sunday, Many thousands of people went to Glen Echo, but many more went to Bethesda Park. So many that a large number had to walk home . . . some as late as four o'clock in the morning.

That summer Grace Shannon returned with Daisy, the parachuting dog, and a moonlight ascension with fireworks. To challenge the Glen Echo attractions, Bethesda Park had lectures on the Holy Land complete with stereopticon slides, concerts by a gypsy band, and a succession of "daring" tightrope walkers. Many guidebooks for tourists of the Gay Nineties, including "A Glimpse at the Night Side of Washington, A Guide-Book to Night Amusements by One Who Has Been There," listed Bethesda Park as one of the Capital's prime attractions.[34]

Like Chevy Chase Lake, only a couple of miles to the east, Bethesda Park promoted itself as a high-class operation where the riff-raff were not welcome. But the operation did not please everyone. Law student, staunch

Methodist and vigorous Prohibitionist Albert Shoemaker wrote in mid-June 1892,

"I feel very much disappointed in Bethesda Park for it has come to be a very degrading place, there is so much to amuse people on Sunday. They even have dancing on Sunday. I am surprised that the men at the head of the company would permit such things . . . and to make things worse I understand that our local option law is being violated up there."[35]

Six weeks later he wrote his wife-to-be that he had planned to go to Glen Echo "to live again some of the happy events when we were together," but the streetcar was late so he decided to go to:

the Park and see the baloon go up and to get some beer. The baloon ascended before I reached the grounds. But I found beer in fifteen minutes . . . . They sell it very quietly indeed in a little box arrangement under the roller coaster. There are no windows, only a door which is kept closed all the while, is only opened to the initiated man. I sat watching this secluded place so long that I have reached home just in time to write you . . . .

Five days later Fannie Fern Brown wrote Albert from her home in Delaware, Ohio. She told him "whenever you mention Glen Echo or I think of it, I always feel a thrill of happiness and joy in my heart." But then as she started a new page, she wrote of her fear. "Dear Albert, I <u>do</u> wish you would not have anything more to do about the beer up at Bethesda. I feel sure someone will kill you." The foreigners were dangerous, she wrote and advised him "you can't fight these things single handed and alone."[37]

In the depression year of 1893, the parachute jumpers and wire walkers gave way to traveling concerts and stage shows as John Beall and company leased out much of the Park's operation. Both Beall and the railway were even more deeply mortgaged by then. The new management's ads claimed that up to 24,000 people visited in one week, and emphasized that they catered to "only the better class of people" or "to only the best classes." They held free concerts, and trained lions put on three shows a day on Sundays in July. In mid-June the Park stirred up some anger when it posted signs stating that the grounds were open to whites only. On July 2, 1893, in an ad featuring the appearance of Col. Boone's Lions, they made it absolutely clear that they were "Catering to White People Only."[38]

Neither the Boston Comic Opera's production of *H.M.S. Pinafore* nor the appearance of Cyrene, a dancer said to earn $350 a week, could pay all the bills. Some of the Park's attractions were repossessed, and as the depression deepened, the sale of real estate in the suburbs all but ceased.

In the fall of 1893 the rumors of bootlegging evidently reached the County authorities and the Park was raided. On Monday, October 9, the *Post* reported under the headline "Bethesda Park Wide Open":

A. H. Hart of the company of Christie & Hart, lessees of Bethesda Park, yesterday skipped town, leaving behind him a good many people who would be anxious to make a settlement with him.

Last Friday the officials of Montgomery County, Md., made a raid on the place to secure evidence that intoxicants were sold on the grounds. The park was deserted at the time and consequently the raid was a failure. Knowing that the place would be well patronized on Sunday, they determined to make another raid yesterday. Every thing was planned to a nicity, but in some manner Manager Hart got a rumor of the proposed scheme on Saturday.

Accordingly he locked up all buildings and made a farewell bow early Sunday morning. The officials did not hear of his plans

Dick Mansfield, "Those Were the Happy Days"[36]

and swooped down yesterday. They were dismayed to find the hotel closed and no one around, but they lingered until late in the afternoon.

The people who visited the park yesterday had a rare time. Some urchins had started the roller coaster and all enjoyed free rides. The razzle-dazzle and the theatre were running free and the bowling alleys were used. The conservatory was stripped of all flowers and all the privileges of the place were gratis to those who cared to avail themselves of them.[39]

In 1894, Ernest McCobb, a Tenleytown builder, and William J. Mullin, a grocer on Broad Branch Road, leased the park and promised a "first-class" operation with the cafe and all amusement attractions in operation. The theater opened only on special occasions, mostly for "sacred" concerts on Sundays. Dancing was cut back to two nights a week, but large crowds still came out to have a good time and enjoy the country air.

A typical event was the Bricklayers Union Labor Day picnic after their parade up Pennsylvania Avenue to Georgetown. Members of other trades and crafts participated, and soon "Every car was pressed into service by the Georgetown and Tennallytown road, and the picnickers, happy in the thought of a day's holiday in the woods and in the cessation of their tasks, were transported to the pleasure ground as quickly as electric facilities would allow."

The leaders of both the Knights of Labor and the Federation of Labor were there in addition to the officials and members of the tinners, carriage and wagon makers, house painters, carpenters, plasterers, cigar makers, stone masons, and granite cutters associations along with their wives and children.

Many of the eccentric engineers had to work in the afternoon, but a number of them got a day off, and the bakers, No. 2389, who had worked for twenty hours steadily to keep Washington from eating stale bread on their holiday, shared the enjoyment of the afternoon and evening.

About 700 of the revelers wore the brick layers' blue badge with white ribbons and perhaps a thousand other working men and their families took part.

"The entertainment was devoid of speeches on labor topics, as was intended, because of the absence from the city of Con-

gressmen who had been invited," and most of the men and their families simply enjoyed their lunch on benches along the pathways and in the woods. From two until eight in the evening the ten-piece Fourth Artillery Band, which had marched in the parade, played Sousa marches and other tunes in front of the hotel while the nine-piece Bethesda Orchestra led by Daniel Immich performed "waltzes, polkas, glides, and quicksteps" for those who "wished to pass the time in tripping the fantastic toe."

In the evening the Park awarded $10 gold medals in the shape of sixteen-pointed stars to the best male and female dancers.

The merry-go-round was kept running at full blast to meet the demands of the children and shared good fortune in this respect with the swings, the razzle-dazzle, and the great switchback. The marksmen patronized the shooting gallery extensively and prize bowling offered its allurements to the lovers of that exercise.[40]

On October 8, 1894, at about 7:30 in the evening, the Park electrician, a Mr. Stadler, spotted smoke coming from the northwest corner of the hotel's roof. He gave the alarm and with some fellow employees started for the top floor only to find the stairs ablaze. Stadler sent for the hotel's proprietors, Ernest McCobb and William J. Mullen, and then he and the other help began carrying out the dishes and furniture from the open dining room on the first floor until flames drove them out of the building. As in the Baltzleys' ill-fated restaurant near the river, the rustic style used in the constrcution contributed to the conflagration.

Within ten minutes the whole, huge structure was blazing and flames were roaring through holes in the roof. A shower of sparks blew through the trees. Trying to keep the fire from spreading, volunteers began throwing buckets of water from the well at the rear of the building and chopped a hole in a wall to attempt to douse the burning floorboards. The only other water available was from a small garden hose used in the hothouse. The fire jumped to a small cottage and the roof of the summer house over the well, and the heat drove the firefighters back again. Then the decorated front of the story-and-a-half theater burst into flame and within minutes that whole structure, along with the chairs and scenery flats within it, blazed.

By this time the large crowd of spectators included a number of patrons who had been in the park when the fire began and had helped in the futile firefighting and many others who had just arrived on the streetcars from Washington. They watched from Old Georgetown Road as the buildings collapsed on their stone foundations leaving only the massive central chimney of the hotel standing in the smoking debris. The fire had lasted only a bit over an hour.

To prevent injuries, Edward Watkins, a stockholder in the park as well as manager of the trolley line, had the electricity to the tangled strings of broken lights cut off soon after the fire was out of control. Because several wires ran through the part of the roof where the fire was first seen, faulty electrical wiring was blamed although the exact cause of the fire could not be determined. One report speculated that the culprit was "a wire suspended near the building, that had its insulation worn, owing to being repeatedly tossed against the structure by the breeze."

The owner's loss was put at $20,000 and may have contributed to the failure of the trolley company in less than two years and to the collapse of all of John Beall's real estate ventures a few years after that. Mullen and McCobb, who leased and operated the hotel, estimated that their uninsured loss would be about $2,000. For the next two years, the Park operated without a hotel or a theater but continued to draw big crowds.[41]

In April of 1895 a syndicate headed by electrical engineer Oscar T. Crosby and his partner Charles A. Lieb purchased the Georgetown and Tenallytown streetcar company and used it as the basis for forming the consolidated Washington Railway and Electric Company. A year later, in June 1896, the creditors of the Tenallytown and Rockville line precipitated a foreclosure sale, and Crosby bought both the streetcar line and the amusement park for $36,500. Crosby now controlled the whole route from Georgetown to Rockville, although the track still ended at Alta Vista. He operated it as one line from that time on although the two streetcar companies were legally separated until 1926. In 1897 he rechartered the Maryland section as the Washington and Rockville Railway Company of Montgomery County. Somewhere in this corporate morass the plans for a subdivision at the end of a trolley spur to Locust

Grove vanished as the recession following the Panic of `93 deepened.

In the summer of 1896 Crosby and company leased the park they had acquired with the trolley line to Thaddeus Green and Ephraim Keiser. They finished cleaning up the fire damaged areas and reopened it late in the summer as Electric Park and still drew profitable crowds even without the once-popular theater.

The storm that was to end the Park's short history had first been reported southeast of Cuba on Sunday, September 26, and the weather map in Monday's newspapers showed heavy rains from the Gulf to New England with a threatening storm off Florida. On Tuesday the big story was a visit to Washington by Democratic candidate Williams Jennings Bryan, but it was noted that the barometer was falling along the coast and that the Gulf storm was now in Georgia.

On Wednesday evening, September 29, a devastating hurricane, the biggest and most destructive storm in the memory of the oldest inhabitants, smashed through the Washington area tearing the new copper roof from the Pension Building, destroying the tower of the Grand Opera House at 15th and E, and toppling church steeples from Rockville to Alexandria as well as within the Capital.

The broad roof of the Metropolitan's new carbarn collapsed on about fifty street cars on 4 1/2 Street and the outfield fences at the ball park blew down. The grove of old elms on the White House lawn was almost completely destroyed. Streets throughout the area were impassable, and the city was cut off from the world as most telegraph and telephone lines were down. The *Star* reported that the center of the city was as "dark as Egypt." The underground trolley system, however, proved its worth.

In the Bethesda area, the winds uprooted thousands of old trees and twisted others off five or ten feet from the ground. The high water tower at Major George Armes's "Fairfield" on Connecticut Avenue fell and smashed into a nearby cottage, and he also lost his largest cherry tree. Out along the Rockville Pike the storm destroyed numerous trees, smashed windows with slamming shutters, and flattened out-buildings. Many houses, including Hilleary Offutt's on the hill near Garrett Park, lost their roofs and suffered heavy damage.

All over the area, out-houses and corn shocks simply disappeared. Hundreds of windmills collapsed. Most of the trees at the Rockville fair-grounds went down. The *Sentinel* reported, "The waiting shed at the Balti-more and Ohio depot was lifted up bodily and de-posited upside down in the adjoining field."[42]

The Brill Rockville car

At Bethesda Park little was left. What the howling winds and driving rains had not destroyed, the falling trees smashed. Strings of broken electric lights dangled from branches, and all that stood were the solid stone gate pillars on Old Georgetown Road. The local McKinley supporters, known as the Bethesda District Sound Money Club, had rented the Park for a Republican mass meeting on Friday night, October 1, "to hear the issues of the campaign intelligently discussed" as well as to enjoy the music of a big brass band. But the park never reopened.[43]

The storm also seems to have wiped out the last vestiges of the Tenallytown to Rockville streetcars, although some recall a derelict car on the west side of the road for a number of years, and later, up on the G. Wady Imirie's property in Alta Vista, an abandoned trolley car from the old line was used as a home and then a chicken house well into the 1930s. After the hurricane the Georgetown and Tenallytown cars carried the trade on the Bethesda line, and in 1908 the company began buying the "incomparable" Rockville cars and operated them until the line was abandoned. These big cars had a long-remembered air horn, a two toned whistle — ooooOOO — that was used out past Alta Vista. At first the Rockville cars were a dark olive green color all over, later they were painted dark red.

Crosby reorganized the trolley company in 1897, but he kept the fifty acres that had been Bethesda Park as his own personal property. Seeking a new summer destination, the company began acquiring the right-of-way to extend its line to the County seat where there were summer hotels as well as the fair grounds. Several property owners refused the railway's offer and condemnation proceedings

finally concluded in August of 1899 when the jury awarded $112 to Albrecht Mense for his half-acre and Hilleary Offutt settled for $4,200 for a sixteen acre strip at the back of his farm.[44]

By April of 1900 the line extended to the fair grounds in Rockville, and later, under pressure from the city fathers, through town to the Woodlawn Hotel, which later became well-known Chestnut Lodge. Many Bethesda-area children went out to the annual field day in Rockville on the streetcar. For several years during the days the County Fair was open, the old, open trolleys operated with trailers for a long ride through woodlots and farmland.

From Alta Vista the tracks left the route of Old Georgetown Road and plowed straight across country on a right-of-way that can still be hiked in several other areas. A long trestle spanned a creek near Tuckerman Lane and, covered with weeds and saplings, it is still there too. The line ran through Beane, crossed Bangarter (Bangerter) Road, which became Transformer Lane before it was Grosvenor's lane, passed a transformer station and went between the Edson's land and Offutt's farm where Georgetown Prep was built. It then rejoined the Pike south of Montrose and generally followed the Pike northward.[45]

The whole sixteen mile trip from George-town to Rockville could be made in fifty-five minutes. Streetcars did not have speedometers, but passengers and experienced motor-men have estimated that 60 mph on this route was not uncommon in the open country between Alta Vista and Rockville, and the closer the cars came to the transformer, many riders noted, the faster they went. Accidents were few, but early in the line's history a car did leave the tracks near Halpine.[46]

In the late Nineties, Crosby and his partners worked at consolidating Washington's trolley lines and in 1899 chartered the Washington Traction and Electric Company combining thirteen street-railroad lines, the United States Lighting Company and the Potomac Electric Power Company. In June of '99, Washington Traction issued $20 million in bonds but could not make the second interest payment and was foreclosed in November 1901. The newly reorganized Washington Railway and Electric Company, generally called "wreck-co," acquired its holdings in 1902.

While this high-level financial maneuvering was going on, Crosby split his Bethesda Park property along Old Georgetown Road into three parcels. He kept the northern sixteen and three-quarter acres, Mr. Lieb the center share, and Frederick C. Stevens, another partner in Washington Traction, the southern portion in deeds recorded in December of

1900. The next year Stevens bought Lieb's land for a reported $100, and those thirty-five acres became the Sonoma subdivision in 1913 under the ownership of Joseph Burkart and Karl Heurich. Crosby sold his land to Alonzo O. Dille in 1901 for $5,000, and after another transfer of ownership, to E. Baker Evans the same year, this became the Oakmont subdivision in 1903 and in 1918, under the leadership of O. O. Kuhn, the smallest township in Maryland.[47]

Roland Custer recalled a late trip on the Rockville line.

One time, I was about twelve, I had been out with my brother shellacking floors at the Prep school, and I got on the trolley to go home. I forget the man's name; he just let the car run and came back and was talking to us, and the car was rocking along and going tah-don, tah-don, ta-dah, tah-don, and he saw a light ahead and then it went off. So he said, "What the hell was that?" He went up front, and the light went on again, and a guy was working on his streetcar trying to get the trolley back on the line. We would have run into him full speed.

Generally these cars just went back and forth from Georgetown to Alta Vista or Rockville. At the end of each run the motorman would remove his controller handle and walk to the other end of the car, turning over the seat backs as he went. Outside, the conductor would pull down one pole and raise the other trolley, and on some cars, change the "cow catcher" to the other end, too. Then with the back of the car having become the front, they would go the other way. Boys from Alta Vista enjoyed hiding in the woods and making owl and coyote sounds in the gathering dusk and then watching the wide-eyed trainmen hurry though their paces on the side of Old Georgetown Road.[48]

The triangular terminal building at Wisconsin and Willard Avenues opened in August of 1891 with "comfortable rustic seats" and an Italian couple who lived in the back and operated a refreshment stand. The trolley line from Georgetown to

LINE MILEAGE. WASH. & ROCKVILLE RWY. FROM D.C. LINE TO ROCKVILLE TERMINUS.

The Glen Echo Railroad barn and powerhouse

Rockville shared the small building with the Glen Echo Railroad. It was chartered in 1889 and began operation in 1891 as a part of the Baltzley brothers' grandiose plans for developing the Potomac Palisades as the American Rhine.

That line did not reach its Glen Echo destination until 1896 mainly due to the delays caused by the Army engineers who controlled the Conduit Road and were concerned about both the safety of travelers along the right-of-way and effects of trolley cars crossing Washington's aqueduct. The original route followed Willard Avenue and Walhonding Road to the Sycamore store where it turned north, and from there the double tracks were laid on stone ballast with center poles.[49]

A two-story, stone carbarn and powerhouse, with a tall smokestack at the rear, stood just east of Conduit Road at the Walhonding intersection. The building, completed under the direction of Washington Railway and Electric Company engineer William Folsom, was about 150 feet long with a metal roof and a white oak floor. In the back were the steam generators which drew their water from the river despite the opposition of the Corps of Engineers who did not like the idea of a conduit running under theirs. Stacks of interconnected storage batteries stood ready to provide emergency power.[50]

In May of `96 after a protracted battle for securing the right-of-way, the line ran a loop to Cabin John, and later built a spur from Chevy Chase Circle along the path of Oliver Street and then across the tracks of the T&R and beside the creek between Somerset and Friendship Heights. After 1897 this became the main route and the tracks along Willard were abandoned. The line changed its name to the Washington and Glen Echo Railroad

Company and made arrangements for its riders to transfer to the cars of the Rock Creek line at Connecticut Avenue.

Despite all this effort and a cooperating arrangement with both Capital Traction and the Georgetown and Tenallytown, which hauled coal to the powerhouse and painted and repaired the cars of the Glen Echo line, the company ceased operating in the fall of 1900. Crosby's operation took over the outer end of its double tracks.[51]

From the Capital Traction Company's Georgetown terminal came the competing West Washington and Great Falls Railroad which began service almost to Cabin John late in the summer of 1894. At 36th and M it used an old horsecar as a waiting room, and when it first opened, its tracks passed right through the middle of an operating dairy barn before reaching the popular wooden oval of the International Athletic Club's cycling track near the District Line. Just beyond the Maryland line on Conduit Road was the Cycle Clubhouse, a popular destination for many black Washingtonians in the Nineties. "There were a number of high trestles, very few road crossings, and lots of heavy wooded countryside interrupted by delightful and impressive views of the Potomac River Valley."

This line's brick-red cars ran along the palisades above the river and canal before reaching the huge buildings of the Chautauqua at Glen Echo or the most popular resort hotel ever operated in the Washington area, the Bobingers' Cabin John Hotel, just across the great Union Arch. The WW&GF was originally built as a single track line in the middle of the right of way with Y switches at the passing sidings. This system led to a few frightening accidents such as the head-on collision near the District Line between two cars

An open car on the WW&GF

loaded with passengers in August 1899.

By the turn of the century the wooden trestles were replaced by steel ones, and the route was double tracked all the way to Glen Echo after taking over the northern end of the Baltzleys' line. This ride along the river became the best-loved trolley line of all, and its open cars carrying happy crowds to and from Glen Echo are still fondly remembered.[52]

Joseph Bobinger came to America from Alsace-Lorraine and found work as a stone mason on Montgomery Meigs's impressive bridge over the Cabin John Creek. His fellow workers envied the lunches his wife fixed for him, and Rosa soon found herself preparing numerous chicken dinners each day for her husband's chums and some of the engineers as well. Soon Mrs. Bobinger opened a refreshment stand where she sold cigars, snuff, candles, cold drinks, and pies, and then she and her husband leased and renovated an old construction shed, and they were in the restaurant business. It was Joseph who was chosen to chisel Jefferson Davis's name off the Union Arch's cornerstone after the Civil War began, but it was Rosa's "chicken a la Maryland" that made the Bobingers famous.

Cabin John, by then a permanent corruption of Captain John, the original name about which there are numerous interesting stories but no discernible facts, was long recognized as one of the most pleasant regions of the Washington area. Even the McMillan Commission, which produced the 1902 plan for developing the Federal City, admitted that "The best scenery lies beyond (the District Line), especially in the neighborhood of Cabin John Creek and in the region just about and below Great Falls."[53]

Thomas Fletchall had been a pre-Revolutionary property owner in the area with some sixty-five acres on the east side of Captain John

CABIN JOHN BRIDGE HOTEL—BOBINGER BROS., Proprietors.

Run and twice that on the western side. In 1784 Joseph White bought into the area, and in 1793 Thomas Beall patented twenty-five acres called Hallifax. In 1802 Robert Peter established Carderock. Some unclaimed land remained, and a number of protracted boundary disputes reached the courts.

The Bobingers borrowed from the Riggs Bank in 1870, bought one hundred acres south of Conduit Road and west of Cabin John Bridge, and built the central part of their wooden hotel, modeled after a German tavern and painted a creamy yellow. As business prospered, the inn grew turrets and porches with stained glass windows and gingerbread scrollwork. According to John Clagett Proctor, the hotel was "one of the most delightful places to rest and refresh one's self after pedaling a bicycle for about seven miles" out from the city.

The Orchestration at the hotel's rear with the gazebo-bandstand at the left.

Forty acres of shady lawns dotted with fancy gazebos, summer houses and elaborate gardens connected with white, chipped stone paths swept away to the canal and the river. One of the summer houses was a two-story rustic affair with a stairway which wound around a large poplar tree and boasted a fine view of the Potomac. John Harper, a local carpenter, designed and built those from cedar. The Bobingers filled the lawn with magnolias and flowering shrubs. At the bandstand on the lawn, during a party for the newspaper's staff, Sousa and his twenty-one smartly uniformed musicians introduced his "Washington Post March."

The Bobingers secured permission to have an entranceway constructed right over the aqueduct just north of the bridge and, even more remarkably, to draw their water from the conduit itself and run it through their own purification system.[54]

When they acquired more property, outbuildings spread to the other side of Conduit Road. They soon had their own ice house, smoke house, dairy buildings, poultry coops, stables, grooms' quarters, and a gas house, the only surviving building of the huge complex. Mrs. Bobinger also maintained a large garden north of the aqueduct which included what was said to be the largest asparagus bed in the country.

Soon the hotel and its dining rooms became the favorite destination for many of the crowd that made the Nineties gay and for the politically powerful such as Speaker of House Uncle Joe Cannon, who was a frequent guest. Until Harding's time, the elite of Washington came to be wined and dined at the Cabin John Hotel.[55]

Built of wood on a granite foundation in a kind of German-romantic-Victorian style, the hotel was mainly a summer place with forty rooms for guests. A hundred diners could be seated in each of its splendid banquet halls. The main ballrooms boasted ceilings decorated with gold leaf and multitudes of flowers in hanging baskets. There were also several private dining rooms, two parlors, two bars, a barber shop, and a pool hall. At one time the hotel employed seventeen bartenders and forty waiters. Joseph's basement rathskeller and Rosa's fried chicken had brought a steady stream of customers even before the arrival of the trolley cars.[56]

The Bobingers' "electric" bridge

When electricity arrived with the streetcar line, a thousand electric lights glowed among the trees. The Bobingers added a narrow lover's lane bridge over the canal and later a fancy, $25,000 iron bridge over the creek for trolley passengers. Its arches sparkled with five hundred colored lights

On the back of the hotel they built a huge, imported, octagonal "orchestration" with large stained glass panels above bevel-edged windows and an electric-powered organ which used big rolls of punched paper like a player-piano. It could be heard throughout the grounds. In general, the hotel was dressed out with German furnishings and woodwork while the gardens were manicured in the English manner and filled with every kind of flowering shrub. The family and the help lived on the third floor, which was covered with green shingles.

The cool breezes, broad verandas, cold beer, and noble Union Arch bridge brought out the crowds from the city first by horse and buggy or bicycles and then on the electric cars or in automobiles. One ad promised that "picnic parties will find fishing tackle for their use at reasonable rates."

When the trolley loop was built on ten acres donated by the Bobingers, huge weekend throngs descended on the hotel. The Bobingers built a theater and later added a small amusement park. And they had many slot machines. Willie Bobinger, grandson of the builder, remembered:

The customers all played the slot machines. On the way out of the bar or the men's rest room it was convenient to stop by and put a quarter in the slot machine. This was legal in Maryland. They used to collect the coins from the slot machines by the bucketful. They didn't count it, they weighed it."

But it was the food, served on the Bavarian china decorated with the image of the Union Arch surrounded by dogwood blossoms and marked "BB," for Bobinger brothers, that brought them back. The head waiter, John L. Smitz, who spoke seven languages and remembered all the notable guests by name, trained his staff to impeccable service. A quarter-century after the hotel closed, Mrs. Warren Gingell of Bethesda wrote:

I can remember how it looked with its white table cloths, spic and span colored waiters, and crowds of diners. The hotel served excellent food and often there would be such crowds that you would have to wait to get a table . . . . They had a beautiful grove and the over-flow crowds would be served out-of-doors."

Rosa's recipe for "chicken a la Maryland" was always in demand. She laid strips of bacon over each piece while it was being fried "to keep it moist" and then served it with a heavy brown gravy and corn fritters. The Bobingers baked their own breads, and operated their own laundry, and offered fine wines from their well-stocked cellar. Some of the wines came from the vineyards maintained by the Readings in the valley of Cabin John Creek. Wine was served in red and white or green and white crystal which matched the chinaware.

Down by the creek they built special enclosures where they kept Potomac black bass. "As they needed the bass," Harry Bobinger recalled, "they'd go down and get them out of the creek, kill them and fry them right away." The bass was served, split down the middle, fried golden brown and garnished with tartar sauce, with boiled new potatoes."[57]

Competition soon arrived. Twin brothers Edward and Edwin Baltzley were Ohio businessmen who had opened a small factory in Pennsylvania. They became fairly wealthy from the invention and production of an improved mechanical egg beater that reversed beater direction halfway through each turn of the crank. Edwin lived in Northwest Washington, on G Street and later on 28th Street, and served on the staff of Senator Sherman of Ohio in the early 1880s. Edward came to the Capital area in the boom year of 1888, and they sold the factory and patent and established the firm of E. and E. Baltzley Real Estate in Room 7 of the Sun Building.

They lived on Pennsylvania Avenue and began buying real estate along the river including most of William Reading's 516-acre tract on the south side of Cabin John Creek opposite Sycamore Island where a rather rowdy "Pleasure Club" was just getting started. Eventually, Reading was paid approximately $92,000 for his property. The names of both Edward Baltzley and his wife Laura are on all the early deeds.

The brothers invested perhaps another $50,000, increased their holdings to over 900 acres, subdivided some of their property and, after scratching out a few roads, started selling lots in Glen Echo Heights. Their fancy deeds contained a number of restrictive covenants. Buyers had to agree to a set-back of forty feet and to construct a "substantial brick or stone dwelling house of not less value than three thousand dollars." No taverns, hotels, blacksmith or other trade shops were permitted, and no steam mill, tannery, glue works, livery stable or other building for "offensive purpose or occupation" was allowed. Home owners were expected to construct a walkway in front of their property, keep their wells, drains and cesspools covered and build their privies of brick or stone. And they could not quarry stone for commercial purposes. These 1890 deeds are among the first recorded in the Washington suburban area with covenants of this type. Similar restrictions were to be found in Chevy Chase Land Company deeds when it began selling lots about two years later.[58]

At first the property sold well, and many people bought several lots, evidently as investments. The Baltzleys saw the Potomac as a potential "American Rhine" and began pouring money into a series of flamboyantly speculative investments, all of which eventually failed. The quarter million they received for Edwin's eggbeater did not last long. They founded and promoted the Glen Echo Railroad to bring customers to their property and organized a half dozen other companies. But they kept only one set of books and paid for their wives' dresses, the milk bill, real estate transactions, Edward's cigars, the purchase of mules from Joseph Reading, and their multiple and growing payrolls, all from the same account.

They began the construction of their castle-homes high on the hills above the river,

One of the Baltzleys' castles

and advertised their often vertical and nearly inaccessible lots with promises of granite in a variety of colors and grades for the cost of quarrying, the novelty of electric lights for all who desired them, and, of course, the best in electric railroad comfort and service. The Baltzleys envisioned a series of mansions marching along the cliffs above the river.

Early on, Edwin Baltzley's florid brochure, "Glen-Echo-on-the-Potomac, The Washington Rhine" stated its thesis:

And we of Washington, the most beautiful of cities, where have we been wandering that our eyes have not come to see and our hearts to know the rich treasures our own Potomac has been tendering us these many years? Here we have our own Rhine, our own Hudson, but we knew it not. Here we have scenes of beauty, altitudes of health, and regions of promise and pleasure, where we may take our wives and children, and build them homes, and rear them, that when the afterday comes their faces shall shine with the beauty that the loveliness of Nature has implanted in them, and their hearts will glow with the tender love and gladness they have learned from the delicate leaf, the eloquent smile of the arduous sun on the distant hills, the music the water makes gainst rocky isles, and shores made stately by the dignity of ancient trees; these and ten thousand voices will teach the child those divine secrets that make pure men and women, and implant the wellspring of genius.

Looking across the creek at the Bobingers' highly successful hostelry and dining rooms, the Baltzleys constructed an incredible restaurant of 30,000 cedar logs which they called the Pa-taw-o-meck Cafe. It opened on July 25, 1890, and it represented the zenith of the Victorian back-to-nature movement in the Washington area. The weekly payroll ran about $800, the furnishings were from Julius Lansburgh, John Wannamaker, and Woodward and Lothrop, and the groceries from local farmers and the finest stores in the area including G. W. and H. W. Offutt's market in Georgetown.

Beyond the fancy gateway and even fancier porte cochere, the cafe stacked dining rooms and towers, porches, walkways, and overlooks. It also contained the real estate offices of E. and E. Baltzley. The ceiling of the huge, main dining room was "cathedral like, arched over by trunks of bark covered logs, woven in complex embrace." Above was the "Tower of Babel" which had two dining rooms on its "first two stories while perched on the roof of the Sleepy Hallow is the Minnewawa, a mid-air building approached by a curious stairway which leads you on a pretty, covered porch . . . ."

Some of the private dining rooms had electric fans and lights, but all were as rustic in style and decoration. On the river side of this "Air Castle," as the Baltzleys called it, was "Cañon Eyrie" from which diners could let their "eyes escape into the beyond to drink in the rapture of the matchless river scene."

The aerie of the fanciful Pa-taw-o-meck Cafe

Less than four months after it was completed, on Saturday, November 29, 1890, the Pa-taw-o-meck Cafe burned to the ground in one of the Bethesda area's most spectacular fires. As part of the rustic style, the bark had been left on many of the cedar logs out of which the sprawling restaurant was constructed, a pretty effect that doubtlessly contributed to the speed and thoroughness with which the building was consumed. The Baltzley families barely escaped with their lives. According to the *Star*, the loss was $85,000, only partly insured, and nothing but the gate structure survived.[59]

Edwin Baltzley's description of the fire reflects some of the pain he and his brother must have felt.

At two o'clock in the morning the inmates were aroused from sleep by a loud, roaring, crackling noise, and a brilliant light streaming through the windows. The main hall of the great structure was in flames, and there was barely time to escape. The fire ran rapidly from balustrade to minaret, from balcony to tower, until soon the whole building was a filigree of fire outlined against the dark sky of the night in all the magnificence and intricacy of the vast, poetic building. In one short hour all was reduced to ashes. Nothing remained but the recollections of what so short a time before was the most unique cafe in the world. It was an air castle, a dream with a rude awakening. It will be rebuilt in stone.

It was not, and neither was the planned, castellated hotel called The Monican which, granite and fireproof, was supposed to surmount one of the hills. But the Baltzleys still hoped to "have a good house put on every lot sold," and sought to insure the creation of a model, up-scale community. Benjamin Harrison, Grover Cleveland, and Navy Secretary William C. Whitney were among the prominent names mentioned as purchasers of land along Washington's Rhine, and some sources suggest that before they were through, the twins had sold a million dollars worth of lots.

The Glen Echo Railroad made it through the Little Falls Valley and the Loughborough's property, crossed the creek on stone abutments just east of present-day Massachusetts Avenue, and went into operation from the terminal at Wisconsin and Willard to Conduit Road in 1891. Its first class cars from J. G.

Brill of Philadelphia brought sightseers and potential customers to the property even while the various conflicts with the Corps of Engineers involving the carbarn and tracks beside the aqueduct were being resolved. At one time the Baltzleys had some three hundred masons and about 600 laborers working on their various projects. The sale of lots was quite brisk in this ambitious suburban development, which was second only to Takoma Park on the Metropolitan Branch of the B&O at the other, less fashionable, side of the County.[60]

But then, while the Baltzley's stone castles continued to rise in the hills above the ruins of their wondrous restaurant, a rumor began to spread. Some in the Glen Echo area blamed it on the promoters of the Chevy Chase Land Company, then pushing Connecticut Avenue northward with pick, shovel and mule power, but like most rumors, proving its source is almost impossible. "Malaria," said the whispers, sickness in the land near the river. "Remember what happened to those poor men that dug the canal?" asked the doubters with a knowing nod. And lot sales dried up; the books record barely a sale per month. Some buyers even sold their lots back to the Baltzleys at a loss. Almost nothing was built on the land that had been sold.

But the Baltzleys did not quit. They had one more card to play, their trump ace — Chautauqua.

The Chautauqua movement developed from a summer program for Methodist Sunday school teachers which began in 1874 on the shore of a narrow lake not far from Jamestown in western New York. Dr. John Heyl Vincent, later a bishop in the Methodist Episcopal Church, and Lewis Miller, a Midwestern businessman long active in church affairs, started an institution that, by the turn of the century, had more than four hundred local assemblies and influenced the lives of millions of Americans. Vincent and Miller's goal was to unify the increasingly factionalzed Protestant churches through a broad democratization of learning. They also hoped to combat the heresies and controversies raised by the disciples of Darwin and Marx. Chautauqua stimulated the development of adult education and extension programs and encouraged the growth of correspondence courses and "great books" discussions.

The first "Assembly" met for ten days in August of 1874 and attracted about a thousand Sunday school teachers with a variety of classes, discussions, entertainment and physical activities. Within five years Hebrew, Greek, German, and French as well as the study of English literature had been added, and the Chautauqua, which never identified itself as "Methodist," was offering in-service courses for public school teachers. Then came the home reading and study program with its four-year plan and the *Chautauquan* magazine which was filled with discussion questions, literary excerpts, and inspirational essays. At its height the correspondence program had 60,000 enrolled and issued respected diplomas to its graduates.

The Sunday school offerings also expanded under the leadership of Dr. William Rainey Harper, a Yale Hebrew professor who became president of the University of Chicago in 1892. Courses in music, speech, theater, theology and, under the direction of Melvil Dewey of the famous decimal system, library science were great successes.

Early in the 20th century some 12,000 men and women were living and studying at the Chautauqua Institution each summer. Several groups were active in the D.C. area, and a Chautauqua Union sponsored winter activities. The Chautauqua "circuit" developed, and booking agents sent politicians, preachers, and musicians out to the hundreds of locals. Traveling Chautauquas brought the "show" to smaller towns, and while the programs sometimes were little more than vaudeville, they did expose a multitude of Americans to good music, new ideas, "old time religion," and lectures on everything from astronomy to zoology. The circuit of summer programs peaked in the 1920s when radio and the movies began gathering in a large audience, but the summer sessions for teachers continue on Lake Chautauqua.

Chautauqua, the Baltzleys decided, was the answer to their business slump. Even before the restaurant opened, Edwin's wife had convinced the brothers to begin promoting the Chautauqua assembly and to set aside some property for it. They planned a huge real estate development in concentric arcs around the great meeting hall they would build. On March 24, 1891, with as much publicity as they could muster, the brothers deeded eighty acres to the National Chautauqua of Glen Echo which was incorporated to "promote liberal and practical education, especially among the masses of people; their several pursuits and professions of life, and to fit them for the duties which devolve upon them as members of society."

Whether the land was eventually sold, a price of $300,000 was commonly put forth, or donated is not clear. And it does not matter because in reality Chautauqua was just another Baltzley enterprise operated out of the same set of books although the twins did their best to make it look separate. The incorporating board of directors included a number of prominent Washingtonians and Bethesdans such as General Drum, H. Bradley Davidson, George Peter, John Wesley Powell, Hattersly W. Talbott, Arthur B. Cropley and, of course, the Baltzleys.[61]

By 1891 there were fifty-two Chautauqua assemblies that met for two-week sessions each summer in tent camps scattered across the nation, but this assembly at Glen Echo was to be a "permanent seat of culture" with two annual sessions of six weeks each in large, impressive, stone buildings. The founding members subscribed thousands of dollars, and the Baltzleys borrowed more for the estimated million dollars of planned construction. Dr. A. H. Gillett, field secretary of the Chautauqua Literary and Scientific Circle, who had more than sixteen years of experience in the enterprise, became the chancellor. Other trustees included the U.S. Commissioner of Education, William T. Harris; the president of the board of the Homeopathic Hospital, Adam S. Pratt; attorney James Henderson and Edwin Baltzley.

Theophilus Parsons Chandler, the Philadelphia architect of the Baltzleys' castles and incredible cafe, designed the Amphitheater and, in what was called Glen Vincent along Naylor's Run, construction began on the huge structure and, some 200 feet away, on the Hall of Philosophy, which overlooked the river. When the Amphitheater was finished, Chandler modestly called it "The greatest feat of building on record."

Facing the Conduit Road and the route of the slowly growing electric railway, the Baltzleys built a large gateway arch with a round tower and adjoining buildings of native stone. Victor Mindeleff, a local architect, designed the domed Hall of Philosophy and the gate

complex that contained a number of offices and a set of chimes which could be heard "for miles around."[62]

The impressive Amphitheater was the prideful centerpiece, 206 feet in diameter and built of locally quarried granite topped with a wooden superstructure and metal roof. The amphitheater seated at least 6,000 people (Chautauqua literature claimed 8- or 10,000) in semi-circular rows facing the huge stage, which was large enough for a chorus of one hundred plus an impressive organ that cost a reputed $10,000. Behind the stage were a gallery, dressing rooms, and a number of committee meeting rooms. Under the building ran what was now to be called Minnehaha Creek née Naylor's Run, which dove beneath bridges and along a cedar walkway through two floors of cool and picturesque grottoes lit with dangling electric bulbs. The tumbling creek also powered the huge organ and air-trumpet speaker system above.[63]

On May 27, 1891, the *Star* reported that "Since the laying of the cornerstone at Glen Echo, work has gone steadily forward on the great buildings. The last arch of the stone work of the amphitheater is now completed and the tinners and roofers are making the hills echo the noise of their hammers as they push the work through." The sale of lots picked up again along the newly platted streets, all named for famous colleges and universities, where 488 homesites awaited the construction of year-round dwellings. The Baltzleys had recorded 111 deeds in 1890 and followed that with a whopping 300 real estate transactions in 1891.

Despite seventy-eight days of rain between February and June of 1891, the thousand-man work force graded roads, opened nine stone quarries, built the railway and powerhouse, constructed water and sewer systems, almost completed the huge stone and wood buildings and then raised an eight-foot wire fence around the whole enterprise. The payroll was over $2,000 a week through the whole period and hit $3,500 in the first week in May. According to the Baltzleys' accounting, 12,958 cubic yards of stone at $2.50 a yard went into the Amphitheater, and 760 cubic yards into the Administration Building, 512 in the Hall of Philosophy and 275 in the Public Comfort structure. The total cost for stone was over $36,000 with another $2,500 for sand.[64]

With Miss Clara Barton as its president, the Chautauqua Woman's Department organized with offices in the Sun Building at 14th and F Streets. The wives of well-known clerics, politicians and academics lent their names to the enterprise which published a brave prospectus for this "permanent seat of culture" which, its promoters hoped, would outshine even the mother assembly in New York. Among the planned activities were:

1) a series of three "first class Lyceum lectures," concerts, or entertainments each day,
2) a school for English Bible instruction,
3) special classes in the New Testament, Greek and Hebrew,
4) Sunday school normal classes,
5) class work in both vocal and instrumental music,
6) a school of physical training,
7) a school of methods,
8) university extension courses in history and English, and
9) literary and scientific lectures.

The "talent" engaged to lecture and entertain at the first session included some of the best known platform performers of the day, plus poets, preachers, Egyptologists, bell ringers, quartettes, an orchestra, a band, and the "famous Ben Hur Tableaux Company."

Tiny, stubborn Clara Barton, seventy at the time, was one of the few who purchased land from the Baltzleys and actually built on it. On July 31, 1891, she paid the brothers $2,300 for 7,684 square feet on a high spot just upstream from the Chautauqua property. Although the bookkeeping records are unclear, it appears that the Baltzleys advanced Miss Barton the money with which to make the purchase so that they could use her name in their publicity.

After the Johnstown Flood of 1889, Miss Barton gave away most of the wood out of which emergency housing had been constructed until the local lumber dealers protested. She then transported a few thousand board feet back to Washington by train and had it stacked at her property in Kalorama Heights where she planned to built her Red Cross headquarters. But D.C. building codes required steel for the kind of structure she planned, and she did not have any of that nor could she afford any. So she accepted the Baltzley-Chautauqua offer of land near the canal, and the Baltzleys paid $25 to have her lumber hauled out to Glen Echo.

Her three-floor home with its white canvas ceilings, stained glass windows, thirty-six rooms and thirty-eight concealed closets was based on standard designs of the time and originally looked a lot like the emergency hotels built at Johnstown. But it was modified to meet her needs and the storage demands of the Red Cross. The house also had a Chandler-designed, yard-thick stone front so that it looked like the nearby Chautauqua structures and, from Conduit Road, appeared rather pyramidal. The Baltzleys paid for the stone front as well as some of the running expenses, and indeed, they may have paid the whole construction bill. In July of 1891 the *Star* reported that:

> The unsightly scaffolding has been removed from the front of the Red Cross building and the great red brick cross set deep in the grey stone facade can be seen as far as the building itself . . . . The interior consists of the wide hall draped in the flags of all nations which have been presented to Miss Barton in acknowledgement of her services in the Red Cross Society. Flanking the hall are the large, airy bedrooms and pleasant sitting rooms through which there is a constant cool breeze.

The building, 48 by 98 feet, served as a warehouse for the Red Cross and as its headquarters from 1897 until 1904. The thick stone facade was removed in 1897, except for the corner towers, because it gave the interior a "prison like chill." After the Spanish-American War, during which she directed relief activities from Cuban battlefields, Clara Barton was pressured to resign as leader of the growing Red Cross which she unwillingly did in 1904. She continued an active life, founding the National First Aid Association and working for feminist causes.

Clara Barton died at the Glen Echo home she loved in 1912. Her associate, Dr. Hubbell, gave the house, which he had inherited from Miss Barton along with all her other local property, to a very attractive spiritualist named Mrs. Mabelle Rawson Hirons, who claimed to be in touch with Miss Barton's spirit. Hubbell won it back in a protracted court case that lasted from 1920 until 1926. Clara Barton's secretary, Daisy Sweitzer, encouraged the doctor to seek legal assistance and helped finance the long fight.

By then the home was a boarding house with a cement front porch. Roomers could stand on the screened sleeping porches in the back and wave to riders on the Derby Racer as they plummeted down the nearby tracks in what had become an amusement park. Rena Hubbell, the doctor's niece, inherited the house in 1929, and she added central heating and converted it into an apartment building in the 1930s. Like Locust Grove, another survivor.[65]

Although only the business school's building was finished, the Glen Echo Chautauqua opened at the almost completed Amphitheater on June 16, 1891, with more than a thousand in attendance. A line of horse-drawn herdics and carettes waited at the end of the Baltzleys' uncompleted trolleyline to transport people to the gates. Many turned back at the Wisconsin Avenue terminal because service was slow and overcrowded due to a power plant problem. Others came out from town in hacks or aboard a talley-ho (roundtrip fare: 50¢ inside, 75¢ outside). All made their way through the heat, dust, and hurrying workmen to gawk at the stonework and to dodge the wagons of the campers coming for the Chautauqua "session."[66]

"Masses of purple flower vine cascaded from stone wall and trellis. Everywhere was blooming shrubbery. Directions were conveyed by wood carvings." The *Star*'s reporter noted that even during the hottest portion of the day, the amphitheater was "cool and comfortable" and that the big organ "formed an effective background for the ladies and gentlemen seated on the stage" alongside a "a well-drilled chorus." The colorful crowd waited in long, hushed rows beneath an impressive number of electric lights.

At 2:30 in the afternoon Chancellor Gillett began the dedication, and the Rev. S. H. Greene brought the greetings and good wishes of the Christian churches of the Washington area. In his brief remarks the Rev. Dr. Elliott of the Foundry Church mentioned the problems of getting to Glen Echo but praised locating the Chautauqua in Washington "where to live was a liberal education in itself."

Dr. T. Dewitt Talmage gave the principal address. He eulogized the Chautauqua, at some length, as an ecumenical device for harmonizing contesting Protestant factions and as "sunshine and gospel, mathematics and poetry." His recipe for a Chautauqua in-

cluded "a mixture of Presbyterian catechism, the Episcopal prayer book, the Methodist love feast, the Congregational liberalism, and enough Baptist water to mix well." He placed a flag sent by Dr. Vincent across the lectern and declared the Chautauqua at Glen Echo open. According to the Baltzleys' account books, Dr. Talmage earned $500 for his speech, and other participants in the program received lesser amounts.

The *Post* quoted James A. Green, who had been on the Chautauqua lecture circuit for five years, as saying,

Its auditorium or amphitheater is by far the best in the country. Even the famed Albert Hall of London has not the splendid aisles and perfect acoustics of the Glen Echo Amphitheater . . . . That it will be a success there can be no doubt.

The Marine Band and the Rogers Band filled the afternoon and evening with concert numbers, and Professor Harry Brown of the famous Brooklyn Tabernacle played the chorus organ which, according to local reports, could be heard for miles. By dusk hundreds of tents lined the streets around the Amphitheater. More than three hundred families planned to stay for the first two-week session.

That night and early the next day an extremely heavy rain washed away the newly laid trolley tracks, chased tent campers out of the lower areas even though most tent floors were six to eight inches off the ground and prevented many of the spectators from returning home. Quite a few spent the night in tents or in the still unfinished buildings. It was not an auspicious beginning for such an ambitious undertaking, but it was typical of the Baltzleys' luck.

"With all its pranks, however, the rain was welcome," reported the *Star*.

It cooled the air, and laid the dust, and as the canvas roofs did their duty manfully no one was the worse for the outburst. Chautauqua this morning, however, is decidedly English. The male portion of the colony have their trousers turned up to the man.

Workers cleared brush along the river for swimming and boating while another crew erected a huge hotel tent that boasted a dining hall measuring sixty by ninety feet and forty-eight rooms for rent, all under canvas. Many families brought their own tents while others leased them from the Chautauqua operators. The rent for a ten by twelve foot tent, 4'6" high, was $8.00 for the assembly session, $10 for a month, $20 for three months, or $25 for the whole season. Wooden floored tents and their furnishings could be rented at higher rates by those who wished to "rough it" in style. Among the tents was one near the Amphitheater "manned" by representatives of the Women's National Press Association, and across from it were the Baltzleys themselves, complete with "artistic rockers, fur rugs, and pretty drapery."

The schedule showed exciting speakers and programs for every day of the week except Sundays when religious activities predominated. In what must have been a shock to some Bethesda-area veterans of Lee's army, who had barely recovered from the erection of a Maryland monument in the Union lines at Gettysburg, the Grand Army of the Republic had control of the 4th of July plans. The Women's Christian Temperance Union took charge of activities on July 5th.[67]

Lecture topics ranged from "Shakespeare's Home" to "Our Kitchen Interests" and from "Bimetalism" to

Looking toward the stage in the Amphitheater at Glen Echo's Chautauqua

"Pray and Grow Fat." In a popular one, Peter Von Finklestein, in costume, with five men, five women and five children, also in costume, gave a picture of life in the Holy Land and put on exhibition his "magnificent collection of curiosities."

The trolley car from Tenallytown was thirty-five cents, round trip, and admission to the Chautauqua was forty cents daily, two dollars for a week and five dollars for a season pass. Children under fifteen were half-price. In good weather, the crowds steadily grew, and the promoters smiled and twirled their mustaches— land sales had picked up, too.

THE FOURTH AT GLEN ECHO

Last night was a parody on "All Quiet Along the Potomac Tonight." Promptly at midnight all the bells and tin whistles and firecrackers combined to make night hideous, then just as people were dropping off to sleep again they were treated to the most diabolical serenade imaginable. For wild hilarity and unique and classic music the Chautauqua serenade stands alone. You are dazed with a glare of torches and a babel of voices, then the cry breaks forth "What's the matter with Mr. Jones - He's all right - Who's all right - Mr. Jones - Rah, Rah, Rah, Fourth of July at Glen Echo - Rah, Rah, Rah," then an infernal confusion of tin pans, horns, pistols, and Indian war-whoops. The treasurer and secretary of the association led the procession, which embraced all the male members of the camp, and no one could accuse them of partiality, for they treated almost every tent to the same ear-splitting melody. Most people took it good naturedly, but at one tent some of the serenaders were not quick enough and succeeded in getting pretty thoroughly drenched by several buckets of water.

Today was everything that could be desired for a Fourth, cool and clear and no dust, and the crowd that swarmed beneath the great flag over the gate increased in numbers every hour. The secretary of War ordered out a battery of six guns and they were met at the entrance by the band and escorted to their position on the knoll overlooking the river so they could fire toward the river and thus avoid the danger of breaking any windows. The salute was fired just at noon and was of twenty-one guns.[68]

Because of all the canvas, firecrackers were prohibited on the grounds, "so boys had to go to the river bank, where they could burn their clothes and themselves as much as they wanted." Every tent was flag decorated and the "hotel tent was gaily bedecked with bunting and everything possible was done to accommodate the hungry crowd."

The grottoes under the amphitheater became a very popular attraction, and a young man was quoted as suggesting that the ministers "should take a slice of stock in the grottoes, for they would probably lead to more weddings than all the rest of the Chautauqua put together." The Washington press reported almost daily on the activities at Glen Echo, and one *Star* reporter urged his readers to come out and view the feminine charms of the many young ladies who graced the grounds.

The organizers had planned to end the first session of the Chautauqua at Glen Echo on the 4th of July, but attendance was so good that it was extended to the first of August. A weekly newsletter called the Glen Echo *Chautauqua* published a list of all the programs, activities, and lectures. The *Star* called it "a very interesting little sheet."

Band concerts and lectures on topics such as "Bible History and Geography in the Sunday School" vied with discussions of peasant life in various parts of the world complete with participants "dressed in the different costumes of the peasants in different periods." There were tennis matches, bicycle races, and duets by Giuseppe Vitale on the violin and Vincent Fanelli on the harp. Dr. Gillett showed a large number of stereoptican views when he lectured on his specialty, Egyptology, in a continuing series of well-attended talks. A baseball team was organized, lost its first game, but improved as the summer wore on. Children played in the creek, enjoyed an enormous swing on "Faculty Hill" and had taffy pulls in the evenings.

On July 14 violinist Vitale paid the Baltzleys $850 for lot 7 of block 24 on Wissioming Road in Glen Echo Heights. Chautauqua insiders made a number of real estate deals, and the Baltzleys' companies issued a larger number of demand and short term notes and satisfied some creditors, including William Reading, by assigning mortgages on their real estate. The Maryland Tent and Awning Company, for example, agreed to take a two-month note for $2,500 and a three-month note for the same amount in payment for the huge canvas hotel and restaurant.

On one of the last nights, about fifty residents dressed up in sheets and table cloths to visit Dr. Gillett and present him with some souvenirs. Spirits were high, and the chancellor had the "nerve wracking " responsibility of

two young ladies in his cottage. It was reported that they did not always adhere to his 10 pm curfew, "and then anyone who happens to be in that vicinity will see the very amusing sight of two dignified damsels climbing in a window higher than their heads. There are a great many young people on the grounds and, of course, where there are young people there are moonlight strolls, but moonlight walks by electric light are not romantic, so at all times of the evening stray couples may be seen meandering through the gates and up the Conduit road."

Belva A. Lockwood "with her accustomed energy" conducted a program featuring peace advocates and arbitration representatives on July 28. On July 30 a talk on "Raphael and his Works" with views of his paintings and frescoes was followed by a party at which a "collation was served and the guests unanimously voted it the most brilliant reception of the season." Clara Barton was honored in the domed Hall of Philosophy which was decorated with "flags, flowers, and electric lights" on Friday the 31st. The final day's main lecture was on "Matthew Arnold, Poet and Critic" and that was followed with elaborate and musical closing ceremonies of the "first annual session of the Chautauqua at Glen Echo . . . now a permanent institution of Washington and the nation."[69]

According to one set of figures the Chautauqua at Glen Echo had employed more than 300 musicians, 900 singers, sixty lecturers and readers, and seventeen full-time teachers during the summer had drawn over 100,000 participants and raised and expended $550,000. It was, by almost any standards, a very successful enterprise.

The first session was also the last.

Late in August the well-known head of the Chautauqua business school as well as of the Spencerian Business College, Dr. Harry Spencer, died of pneumonia. The rumor mill once more spun into action, and his death was attributed to malaria and was multiplied until dozens, perhaps hundreds, were reported to have died at Glen Echo during the construction of the buildings and as a result of attending Chautauqua programs. Some people blamed the way Naylor's Run had been channeled, but more pointed as the water filled pools at the stone quarries.

The Baltzleys advertised that more than forty cottages, valued at $2,347 to $2,914, would be sold "to desirable purchasers" on the installment plan for $500 down and monthly payments of $20 to $30. But again lot sales dwindled to almost nothing and building stopped. In fact, there was some sickness, a fever, among the workers in the spring of 1892 and according to one of the Baltzleys' timekeepers, George Pollock, it probably was malaria. By then Baltzleys' books reflected an investment of $383,558.57 in real estate and improvements.[70]

Into this vacuum came Philadelphia real estate plunger William McGeorge Jr. who formed the Glen Echo Land Association and began buying up the Baltzleys', and others, property, outside the Glen Echo Heights and Chautauqua subdivisions. The Baltzleys' ledgers recorded receipts from December 15, 1891, to January 15, 1892, of $2,000, $2,000, $14,917, $2,000, $300, $21,946.52, $50,000, $25,000, $25,000, and $10,000 for a total of more than $150,000 in a month. The brothers paid off some of their loans and made a full settlement of the William Reading land purchase. They also bought $4,000 worth of stock in the Glen Echo Land Association.

In the next two weeks McGeorge poured another $60,341.48 into the Baltzley coffers. Again E. & E. Baltzley retired some notes, but, oddly, they also made two $25,000 payments to William McGeorge Jr., "on account." By spring, McGeorge was the principal owner of what had been Reading's Cabin John Farm and of the land that later was developed as Fairway Hills and Bannockburn.[71]

In the spring of `92 the organizers reported that "work had been commenced on the houses and grounds" and that an early opening was planned despite the storm that washed out the trolley tracks. The Baltzleys hired John A. Blundon to clean up the grounds and grade the roads. The newly completed buildings along Conduit Road had an open arcade on either side, and "the two stone towers that guard the gateway to the Chautauqua grounds are nearing completion, and give an imposing aspect to the entrance. Their upper stories will be utilized as schools during the next session." The Hall of Philosophy above the river needed only decoration and the finishing of a "rustic lookout from the tower."

The W. H. Houghton Manufacturing Company was providing tents with flies for rent, but the railway company was still dealing with the Congress and the Corps of Engineers about laying its tracks to the park. Therefore, Mr. Blundon contracted to run barges on the C&O Canal, which would make the trip from the foot of High Street to the new dock at Glen Vincent in fifty minutes. "Ten boats are ready and ten more are under construction and will be held in reserve for special days." The canal boats, according to the Glen Echo publicity, could move 10,000 people an hour. More than a hundred workmen were finishing the forty-three Mindeleff-designed cottages while the "Philadelphia syndicate" was laying out roads. A public comfort station was promised near the Amphitheater.[72]

But the only use made of the great Amphitheater that summer of `92 was during a 4th of July celebration that featured a tenor, a contralto, and a soprano, a female orator, an elecutionist, Signor Vitale's violin solos, plus the Chautauqua Oratoric Chorus and the huge organ and two choruses of "The Star Spangled Banner." A few concerts disturbed the birds and chipmunks during the rest of that summer, and a series of musical programs attracted some old soldiers during the GAR convention in September.

The Cedarcroft, a rustic cafe next to the orchestra pavilion, built in the "spirit of the one destroyed in 1890," struggled to stay open. Albert Shoemaker wrote his sweetheart that "there is nothing going on at the Chautauqua ground this season," and concluded that "it was 'hung up' for lack of funds."[73]

In 1893 concerts echoed through the trees at Glen Echo almost every summer weekend. At the "terminus" of the trolley line, the advertisements promised:

A BEAUTIFUL GROVE. Under the trees are rustic benches for hundreds of people. An ORCHESTRA PAVILION and a BEAUTIFUL RUSTIC CAFE are also there. The appointments of the cafe are first class and every thing served is of the best. The most select people in Washington patronize this resort.

On Sunday, July 9, the "grand concert" featured "a fine orchestra under the leadership of Prof. Charles B. Donch Jr." and the singing of "Mr. Morrison of New York and Miss Barbara Reitmayer, the celebrated prima donna of New York, formerly with Gilmore" and a male quartet. The performance lasted from 3 to 8:30 pm.[74]

The Baltzleys' corporation foundered, and the Baltimore Building and Loan Association, holder of the first trust, grew restive and gathered in the other notes. For five years the Baltzleys tried to get the Chautauqua restarted and for five years they failed. Finally, after fighting off several legal moves, they could not pay the bills. The gate tower complex including the administrative offices had been mortgaged to the Ohio manufacturer of the giant organ, the Carl Barckhoff Church Organ Company, which held a $3,900 one-year note and a two-year note of $2,000. It foreclosed, sold the buildings at auction, and eventually the Washington trolley company purchased them.

During the next several years there were occasional concerts at Glen Echo, and in the late `90s vaudeville acts and fight promoters rented out the Amphitheater, and a few motion pictures were shown there, admission five cents. For a time a spur of the trolley line ran down into the park grounds. This announcement in the *Star*'s entertainment section in the summer of 1897 was fairly typical.

GLEN ECHO — The list of new attractions for the amphitheater at Glen-Echo-on-the-Potomac next week includes the following high class vaudeville artists direct from Keith's New York and Philadelphia theaters: Van Leer and Barton, the kings of black face comedy; the Brownings in a refined sketch; Baker and Rajidail comedians and dancers; Caswell and Arnold the electric acrobatic duo, and

Some of the permanent buildings of the Chautauqua

Emma Francis, the terpsichorean marvel. The famous Fadettes, Boston's lady orchestra of twenty-five trained and skilled musicians, will also be heard in grand concert. Wonderful improvements have been made at Glen Echo under Manager Middleton's care and attention, and thousands of Washington's best people avail themselves nightly of the opportunity of witnessing the high class attractions offered at Glen Echo.[75]

John Clagett Proctor's memory of Glen Echo went back to the Spanish American War. In 1898, he attended a light opera performance at "this place shortly after the call for volunteers for this war."

A New Jersey regiment had just arrived in Washington, and as it was probably a warm night, the officers, in seeking a cool spot, took the trolley to this amusement park and listened to the opera, after which they entertained the chorus girls with champagne. Naturally the folks back home thought their loved ones were having a very lonesome time in Washington while waiting to be sent to the front, but not so with these brave soldier boys for they were having the time of their lives.

Big excitement was planned for the 4th of July that year of the "splendid little war." A balloon ascension and a parachute drop were added to the program which already included the Parry Opera Company's 'Ermine' at the amphitheater. Later that summer vaudeville returned bringing with it the arena scene from "The Gladiator" -—adults 25¢ children 10¢.[76]

LeRoy King Sr. recalled in remarkable detail two trolleys serving the area:

When I was a small boy, I went to Glen Echo one summer afternoon with my mother and grandmother. When time came to go home, we went thru the gate, just as you do now, to board the street car. There were two cars waiting. In front, No. 19, the 8-bench Jones going to Georgetown and behind it one of the 12-bench Jackson & Sharps headed for Chevy Chase Circle. They followed one another out. When we got off the Cabin John Line and past the Glen Echo Barn and Power House, the race began.

The little 4-wheeler was light and very fast. The motorman was red headed and had on one of the brown straw caps of the period. His coat tails stood straight out behind with the breeze. The heavier car pounded along behind us until we reached the turn off for Tenleytown for which the switch was set so that we went right

thru and the motorman of the following car had to stop and reset the switch.

That was the end of the race, which was an exciting one while it lasted and gave me something to think about for quite some time afterwards.[77]

The extension of the trolley line to a loop at the Cabin John bridge was delayed by Edwin Baltzley who owned two hundred feet of the right-of-way, but eventually that dispute was settled despite injunctions and several court hearings to condemn the land. The Glen Echo Company leased the Chautauqua property in the summer of 1899. They installed a merry-go-round, a bowling alley, and some other attractions and advertised a picnic grounds. They also built a "charming, quaint, little band pavilion" out in the center of a lake where free concerts were performed before minstrel shows and other attractions in the big amphitheater. That summer Simmon's and Slocum's Minstrels attracted and entertained crowds of up to 3,000, and the *Star* reported that the audiences included "well known society people and evidenced how popular the resort is becoming with the better sort." After the shows an orchestra furnished dance music at the pavilion.[78]

By then Glen Echo was an established, if struggling, community with many year-round residents other than the famous Miss Barton, who became rather disgusted with its fall from grace. Rena Hubbell, the doctor's niece, described it as "a quiet, almost lifeless place, with uninhabited houses falling into various stages of decay." In the fall of 1900 the trolley line stopped operating from Chevy Chase, and in 1903 the bank took over the remaining Chautauqua property for the foreclosure price of $13,000. Edward Baltzley went west to seek a new fortune in the gold and silver fields and died of mercury poisoning in 1907. Edwin stayed in the area, living first at his castle and then in D.C., where he had previously served as private secretary to Senator Sherman. He died in New Jersey in 1919.[79]

At the urging of attorney John Garrett, the Town of Glen Echo incorporated in 1904 and became semi-self governing. Mr. Garrett was elected its first, "boy" mayor, and the town adopted ordinances exiling pigs and hogs, outlawing wandering cows and goats, making gambling illegal and ordering that the Sabbath be strictly observed.

During Garrett's two terms as mayor, the town secured lights and trolley stations from the Washington Railway and Electric Company and convinced property owners to build boardwalks by providing $175 worth of lumber and nails. A fire brigade got started, and the council appropriated $125 for apparatus including a hose and reel. The school house became the town hall, and the council approved a dollar rental fee for its use by the Catholics for church services and by other groups for dances and socials. The town hired a paid clerk-treasurer and a health officer, and Mayor Garrett set up a court to fine the out-of-town speeders his officers apprehended in a very profitable, warm-weather speed trap.[80]

The turn-of-the-century amusement park started Glen Echo down a new, and somewhat gaudier, trail. In 1906 manager Alonzo P. Shaw, who had built the huge elephant at Coney Island, decided he wanted to live in Miss Barton's house and turn it into a hotel, so he ran his scenic railroad through her front yard where the Ferris wheel was already located and had his roller coaster, The Dip, rumbling by her side windows late into the night. Clara Barton rejoiced when he was replaced.

After several high-stakes deals among the street railway barons, the Chautauqua grounds and buildings ended up belonging to the Washington Railway and Electric Company, and the very experienced Leonard B. Schloss became manager of the park in 1911, a position he held until 1948. It was Schloss who converted the operation into a mechanical amusement park, and under his direction Glen Echo became popular and successful. Coney Island's Luna Park, which opened in 1903 and which Schloss managed, and the successful St. Louis fair of 1904 had energized the development of various types of "rides" that involved the customer in active participation beyond the old, staid merry-go-round or the Ferris wheel, introduced on the Midway at the 1893 Columbian Exposition. Schloss was a pioneer developer and exploiter of these rides and of amusement park operation.

Throughout the country, trolley car companies found that building amusement parks at the loop ends of their lines increased their business on weekends and at times other than the normal "rush hours." Picnic groves and dance pavilions gave way to shooting galleries and bowling alleys, to midways with games of chance and penny arcades. Then came the thrill rides, and each year they got faster and more frightening. The switchback roller coaster of the kind built at ill-fated Bethesda Park was introduced at Coney Island in 1884, but the type typified by Glen Echo's well-loved and oft-feared Coaster Dips was "state of the art" until after World War II.

Four roller coasters preceded it: Shaw's "The Dip," which screeched past Clara Barton's bedroom window; the $50,000 (advertised price) Derby Racer, which had two three-car trains that ran from WWI until the late 20s when it was closed as unsafe; the short-lived Gravity Railway of 1912 took customers along a mile of track on a "ride among the tree tops"; and about 1915, the Hydraulic Dive, which had roofed cars with a six-inch pipe running through them. It was supposed to spray a curtain of water over the riders from a trough it ran through.

They designed and built the ride, and ran it through a test with a couple of people in the thing, and it worked perfectly. The first day, it was packed, loaded up with people. And the additional weight helped to increase the speed as it went down the hills. It shot through the trough, the water went up in the air, and the cars were

The Hydraulic Dive in action

gone before the water came down. You didn't get this nice effect of the water raining over the roof.

So they tried redesigning it to slow it down and nothing worked if the car was full. Finally they installed a brake on the front car and had a man ride it all day long. When it came down the hill to the water, he pulled on the brake. All day long.[81]

Only very experienced men worked on the roller coaster. In 1945 Thomas J. Muck, who had sweated for the Park for twenty-one years, was superintendent of the Coaster Dips, and Reason Prather was the brakeman. He had worked at Glen Echo nineteen years by then. According to Muck, three people had died on the roller coaster in his twenty-one years, all from not observing the safety rules. The first was a 23-year-old Marine named Walter Dobbs who was killed in August 1927. By the time of World War II, 10,000 people a day were riding the rumbling Coaster Dips and screaming as they fell down that first, great hill.

The Gravity Scenic Railway, Hydraulic Dive, and the Coaster Dips were all designed and built under the supervision of Frank Finlon. By the time he was finished, Mr. Finlon hated roller coasters.

The Coaster Dips, the biggest of the roller coasters and the one that most people now recall, was constructed in 1921 and increased to its final height in 1926. It had about 3,000 feet of track on a white-painted wooden framework, and its clattering cars reached almost 60 mph from a sixty-three foot summit. The wooden framework, which flexed and creaked, did not look very substantial or well maintained, adding much to the thundering ride's thrills.

Under Schloss's leadership, the park rapidly developed as a popular Washington summer attraction, for white patrons only, of course. However, there were some festering problems. Conduit Road speed limits and the continuing problem with auto license tags led to several embarrassing arrests of foreign dignitaries. Cars sporting D.C. tags could safely use Conduit Road since it was Fedral property, but if the driver pulled off to visit the park or one of the summer hotels, he might receive a summons from one of the town's eager deputy marshalls unless his car also had a Maryland license plate.

Town Marshall Charles P. Collins, astride his bicycle, operated a notorious "speed trap" unconcerned about who had jurisdiction on the winding road over the aqueduct. "Burners" exceeding six miles-per-hour found themselves facing a $25 fine or three months on the rock pile. Sheriff Viett seldom saw the humor in the attitude of the Capital city press over these incidents.

And there were some other problems, and in 1911 they suddenly boiled over in a combination of civic zeal, moral fervor, energetic law enforcement, and a water shortage. The "boy mayor" of Glen Echo, John Garrett, had, from time to time, threatened the previous park managers with enforcement of Maryland's old, but seldom-a-problem, "Blue Laws." In May the forty or so voters of Glen Echo had chosen Louis C. Witkowski as mayor, and the town council had divided into factions favoring the new man who promised reform and independence from the influence of the amusement park and those supporting the Garrett brothers. By August 1911 tempers were short and the tension exacerbated by lack of rain and very little water in the spring-fed town reservoir.

On Sunday, August 23rd, Mayor Witkowski, after asking Schloss to close the park to save water, wrote out warrants for the manager's arrest which Deputy Marshall Walter P. Snow, who also ran the Ferris wheel, refused to serve. The mayor then took the large brass key and a pistol and attempted to enforce the blue laws by shutting off its water supply. He was stopped by the Garrett brothers and one or two town councilmen who sat on the water main.

Witkowski pulled his revolver and backed away to try another entrance. There he was jumped by Garrett and the others. His glasses were smashed, and he was rescued and hustled out through the woods by park employees. The next day warrants were sworn out in all directions as Witkowski charged that Garrett was the "boss of this section" and a tool of the park corporation. The mayor wired the governor for help.

Meanwhile, Sheriff Viett and Judge Joseph Reading came to Glen Echo Park and arrested manager Schloss, park superintendent Finlon, and eighty other park workers for violating the Sunday labor laws and fined them a total of about $1,000. Schloss paid the fines of the thirty who were Park employees. The soda

'THE TROUBLE OVER THE BORDER.

hand on his head and the other on the book of Moses and then be sworn."

"I am not a Hebrew," shouted Witkowski. "I am a Baptist."

Also on Saturday the WR&ECo. shipped 2,500 gallons of water to the town, and Glen Echo advertised that it would be closed on Sunday. "Tomorrow will be a 'Blue Sunday' because of 'Blue Laws' which deprive the public of innocent recreation and throttle good will toward men, women, and children. Therefore Glen Echo Park with its 57 high-class attractions will be closed TOMORROW ONLY reopening with all its wealth of beauty at 1 pm Monday July 31." In court the mayor lost, and the case against two of the town councilmen was dismissed.

The next Sunday, the Park had a program of religious music and an illustrated talk on the passion play. That day the Blue Law enforcers hit the Cabin John Hotel and Chevy Chase Lake and later even the Chevy Chase Club fell under the sheriff's eye. At the Park a compromise was reached. The Soldiers' Home military band was allowed to perform and the restaurant to stay open for the rest of the summer. But no ice cream cones or pop, only full meals were to be sold on Sundays.

In September, Witkowski resigned and moved to Kensington, urging that Dr. Hubbell be chosen to replace him. The town council elected Robert Garrett, WR&ECo. motorman and brother of lawyer John, as mayor. It rained that fall, the reservoir filled and the little town settled down for the winter.

The Park's popularity steadily grew, and the following "news" story, probably written by Schloss or one of his minions, reflects the image the Park sought to attain.[82]

One very potent reason for the high class of patronage that Glen Echo Park enjoys is the fact that the best of order is maintained, no rowdyism or objectionable conduct being tolerated, with the result that only the better element cares to visit the resort regularly.

fountain manager, Charles Winslow, put up $200 collateral and said he intended a court fight. A reporter wrote that "all that escaped the clutches of the law's minions were the whirligigs, the Ferris wheel, the creek, the trees and benches, and a couple of dogs."

The town council asked the mayor to resign and refused to sit with him. John Garrett, among other things the Park's attorney, blamed the arrests on spite. The Capital's newspapers had a wonderful time reporting the internecine warfare.

The dry spell continued, and the Park brought in barreled water by way of the trolley line, but in Glen Echo the pipes ran dry and many people left town. Mayor Witkowski's request to tap into the Aqueduct was rejected, so he proposed a bond issue.

On Saturday the first case from the fight came to court. When Witkowski was sworn in, Garrett objected. "Your honor, this is not the usual way of administering an oath to a Hebrew in this court. He ought to put one

In the dancing pavilion the ban has been placed on the "trotters" and "raggers" and the new floor manager, Maury Wolf, will allow none of the objectionable dancing that certain elements of the modern school consider permissible.

Glen Echo's popularity as an outing place is rapidly increasing and scarce a day during the next few weeks but has its special outing scheduled. Possibly the largest of these is that of the Royal Arcanum on Monday, June 23, which promises to be one of the largest days of the season. A special program has been arranged and there will be something doing every minute. The big event comes at 6:30 in the afternoon, when two companies of the District National Guard compete for a silver cup offered by the park company. Another feature will be the championship ball game on the Glen Echo diamond.

With the new gyroplane added to the long list of attractions, Glen Echo offers every inducement to amusement seekers, and a more delightful form of recreation during the hot weather is hard to imagine.

Admission is always free and free motion pictures are a daily offering.

On Sundays the special drawing card is the series of concerts by the Soldiers Home band, under the direction of John S. M. Zimmerman, possibly the best known band leader in this section.

Over the years Schloss claimed that he invested more than a million dollars in the park and took pride in having at least one new attraction every year. In 1921 in a twelve-sided building with a domed roof that echoed some of the Chautauqua construction, the Dentzel Brothers of Philadelphia installed the well-loved carousel with its three rings of fifty-two hand-carved animals including a stag with real antlers, and two chariots. The animals circled, and some went up and down, to the tunes from a Wurlitzer "duplex orchestral organ" installed in 1926.[83]

The bumper car pavilion, with its swooping roof, dates from 1923 when it was called the Skooter and was one of the first dodge-em operations in the United States. Sparks flew from the ceiling in some teeth-jarring crashes despite the "no head-on collisions" signs, and sweating operators often had to untangle jams involving a half-a-dozen cars. The 1936 motor boats were popular with both couples and little kids, and the miniature golf layout was a long-time favorite as was the airplane ride. At first, passengers on the wooden airplanes that circled a tall tower just sat and enjoyed the breeze under a high wing, but later brave riders could grip the big, front-mounted rudder and pilot their fat, metal planes in swooping dives and climbs that almost touched the sycamores.

Curved mirrors produced smiles. You could stamp out your name on a lucky coin or get three pictures of your sunburned face and mugging friends for a quarter. Claw machines devoured pennies. Under the fun house in what had been the Chautauqua grottoes, the Old Mill or The Tunnel of Love was popular despite breeding tales of water moccasins instead of mosquitoes; it later became the World Cruise with the same chain-pulled small boats. The Whip broke down many shy couple's inhibitions as did the Cuddle-Up that came later.

At any given time in the Park's history, more than half of the rides and almost all of the food stands were privately run concessions. For most of its years, the park itself owned and operated the Coaster Dips and its predecessors, the carrousel, as they spelled it, and the ballroom. Everything else was a concession, and in the early years, many Park officials also owned some of the rides. The Park did the bookkeeping, paid a majority of the "take" to the concession's owner, kept twenty-five or thirty percent for itself and took care of maintenance and painting under the direction of the Park superintendent who was in charge of the day-to-day operation.

On a typical hot day in the early twenties, August 11, 1923, the Park had an estimated crowd of 5,000. All ride tickets were 10¢ and 2,776 tickets were sold to the Coaster Dips, 1,673 to the carrousel and, despite the hot weather, 139 couples, 285 gentlemen and 368 ladies paid to enjoy the ballroom (75¢ for couples, 50¢ for gents, 25¢ for ladies). The Park made $745 from these three attractions while the concessions brought in $1,260 of which the Park took about $320. Daily gross receipts ranged from $1,500 to $3,000 with the Park net about half of that. In 1923 the gross was $184,648 and the net $92,809. That is a lot of dimes.

In the whole history of Glen Echo as an amusement park, there were only three superintendents. Frank Finlon had the job from

Frank Finlon

1911 until about 1921. Among his lasting contributions was the construction of the still-admired building housing the Dentzel carousel which replaced a smaller merry-go-round. Joe Hart then took over and was superintendent and assistant manager until the end of the Second World War. In 1945 Emory Crouch, who had worked at the Park since 1924, at one time overseeing both the merry-go-round and the World Cruise, became superintendent and kept the title until a year after the Park closed.

Hundreds of people worked at Glen Echo over the years, all of them white and most of them part-timers. Betty Bender Clucas grew up in Glen Echo. Her father's regular job was at the NIH, but on summer evenings and weekends he took tickets on the Coaster Dips to build up his Social Security credits. Betty started riding the roller coaster with her father when she was about five. She recalled that she always looked over at the swimming pool just before roaring down that first hill, and she believed it was one of the best roller coasters ever.

Lillian Gloyd came down from Gaithersburg for several summers just after the First World War and stayed with her aunt, Mrs.

James Riley, who ran a rooming house where most of the summer boarders worked at the Park. The borders gave Lill and her cousin Helen Ogle free strips of tickets. They took a nap at Aunt Fanny's insistence, and then ran for the Derby Racer and rode the front car of the roller coaster until their tickets ran out. The front seats of the other train were held down by Frank Finlon's daughters.

The four of them smiled hello to big, bluff Mr. Mulligan who took tickets at the fun house, and they played there for hours, watching carefully for the holes in the floor through which air would blow up their skirts and never figuring out where the boys who hit the switch were hidden. They ate ice cream and rode the merry-go-round over and over, hoping to grab a brass ring. At the end of the season when they had to go back to school, the man who ran the carousel said he would have to put new tails on all the horses because the girls had worn off the old ones.[84]

Through the period of the First World War and into the 1920s the dance pavilion "was thronged, and the tango, hesitation, and all other modern dances took their turn with the waltz." The Park advertised "NO WAR HERE ONLY FUN" and "PHURE PHUN PHRUM PHIFTY AMUSEMENTS." By 1921 the posted dancing rules and warnings including the following:

Don't dance with cheeks close or touching.
Don't hold your partner improperly.
Don't dance in one spot.
Don't dance against the line of direction.
Don't attempt the "shimmy"
    or its variations.

The plinks from the shooting gallery and the klunks from Deebo's Skee-Ball games mixed with the strange glee of the laughing lady at the entrance and the tinny cymbals of the carousel's caliola and the clack-clack-clacking followed by squeals from the roller coaster where brave adolescents raised their hands as they rounded the curve at the top of the long hill. Glen Echo had a sound.

And a smell. Warm buttered popcorn overpowered the sticky-sweet cotton candy and the burnt powder smell coming from the shooting gallery. Axle grease, graphite, and spilled beer added their odors to those of the chlorine, leaf-mold, disinfectant, asphalt, sweat and sunburn lotion.

Entrance to the big roller coaster

In February of 1931, while the Depression deepened, local contractors Skinner and Garrett broke ground at the site of the old Derby Racer and began building a huge, complex and expensive concrete swimming pool. Five years earlier the Chevy Chase Land Company had constructed and leased a big pool across from the Lake and dance pavilion at the end of its trolley line. It was the first public pool in Montgomery County and was immediately popular and advertised in newspapers and on the front of the Rock Creek line's trolley cars. This pool would be much bigger.

It was designed by Alexander, Becker and Schoeppe of Philadelphia, who specialized in this kind of work. It measured 150 by 250 feet, and cost $250,000. The Crystal Pool had two main swimming areas, a large wading pond and a diving pool. A unique 10,000 square-foot sand beach and an observation platform attracted non-swimmers, and there were wood-floored locker rooms for the 3,000 swimmers the pool could accommodate. Most people who enjoyed the pool remember the cold sprays of water that hit them from all directions at the locker room exits. In the main pool area stood a long, fast sliding board, two central "rafts," and a powerful fountain that, like the rest of the pool, had lights on the bottom. The pool circulated, filtered and chlorinated one and half million gallons of water a day.

A view of the pool with the Midway in the background

Many families brought lunches to be quickly eaten at the weathered tables under the trees. Sunday schools and employee associations planned regular outings. Glen Echo, called the cleanest park in America in 1940, was proud of its reputation and of its numerous long-time employees. Many business and church groups staged outings at the

park, and the cry "Let's go to Glen Echo!" was regularly heard in Bethesda homes as it was in white households throughout the region. The popcorn was the best, the candied apples the gooiest, and the cotton candy the pinkest. And almost no place else had soft ice cream.

Almost everyone who went there has a story about Glen Echo. While he was in college, Winchester Stone drove a Ford truck for Bethesda's Suburban Ice Company. With a smile of anticipation he said,

One afternoon we were delivering ice to Glen Echo. I had to put a 200-pound block into a great wooden bin of fruit punch. I was sweaty and had cinders on my feet, and I got up on the edge and fell in - and they sold more juice that day then they'd ever sold before.

It was the self-proclaimed Glorious Galaxy of Gorgeous Gleeful Gayety. And it was never expensive. Through World War Two most of the rides were a dime as were the soft drinks and hot dogs. Swimming was fifteen cents for kids, 44¢ for adults. Meals were available on the terrace restaurants from 60¢ to $1.25, and a roundtrip trolley ride from D.C. was a quarter. A dollar would last many children a whole day at the park, parsimoniously doled out by the penny and nickel.

The roller coaster cost more; Stone and his friend Gus Winnemore recalled spending five tickets in a row on that. Bill Duvall first went on the roller coaster when he was eight; he talked his reluctant father into going with him. As they crested that first big hill, Bill was scared and looked as his father beside him only to see that he was, if anything, even more frightened. They gripped the bar and made it through the curves and coasted to a welcome stop, but Bill was later surprised to overhear his father describe how frightened his son had been and claim that he was only afraid the boy might fall out. Bill stayed away from the roller coaster for the next ten years, but then a date got him back on it one evening and he found he loved it. A lot of people rode the Coaster Dips only once.

Next to the Crystal Pool, on the site of the old Crystal Ballroom, Schloss had the Spanish Ball Room constructed at a cost of about $50,000 in 1933. The 90-by-145-foot structure was also designed by Edward Schoeppe and held a 7,500 square-foot maple floor that could accommodate 1,800 dancers. The roof tiles, stuccoed walls, tower, projecting beam ends and decorated interior were, like the

The Park about 1930 - Carousel at left center and Derby Racer at top left

had to be careful you didn't put your hand down on the slide because you'd burn a blister on it."

"Uncle Billy" May used to sit up in the crows-nest with the push buttons which controlled the sixteen air jets in the floor. He never bothered the young mothers with children, but he seldom missed the girls with dates. Under the fun house adventurous boys explored the grottoes with flashlights looking for coins dropped through cracks in the wooden floor above them and trying to frighten Old Mill riders or catch couples smooching in the dark. In the winter some of those same boys took their sleds roaring down the tracks of the roller coaster and pried pipes from the old organ to blow mournful notes at each other in the woods.[86]

park's entrance gate at that time, a mix of faux Spanish and Art Deco elements.

The ballroom drew almost all of the "name" bands of the big band era before the war, and many people thought Paul Kain's house band was as good as any of them. Young Kate Smith sang at Glen Echo as well as at Chevy Chase Lake and most of the other, local dance pavilions. Dancers at the Spanish Ballroom were expected to be well-mannered and properly dressed to pass through the terrazzo-floored arcade and enjoy their music.[85]

In 1940 a new, art deco entrance building and gates rose near the trolley tracks, but at the other end of the park the great Amphitheater still echoed with laughter of the "fun house" or Midway. There you could take a spin in a whirling tub, try to make your way through the rolling barrel, race down a huge sliding board, ride scooters on the catwalk above the crowd, watch girls have their skirts blown up over their heads, and enjoy dozens of other activities all inside the cavernous walls of Chautauqua's temple of learning.

Pres Wedding, whose family lived in Cabin John, recalled that his mother loved the Coaster Dips and that in the Midway "they had the roulette wheel that spun around, and you'd get on it and try to see how long you could stay on it. And they had the slides coming down, all waxed and everything. You

Several developers tried to invigorate the Glen Echo area, but real estate prices continued to fall. One lot, bought for $1,250 in 1890, was sold, by the original owner, for $250 in 1920, and ended up going for eight dollars at a 1927 tax auction.

At the District Line, Aaron Bradshaw subdivided Dalecarlia Park in 1915 on a little over nine acres. The slow but steady growth of his Brookmont subdivision, which totaled 870 lots in two sections, was encouraged by having the Glen Echo trolley line running through the middle of it. Brookmont was where two locks of the old Patowmack canal were located and about a quarter of a mile upstream President J. Q. Adams had, with some effort since he ran into a tree root, doffed his coat and turned a spade of clay to start the C&O Canal. Lock Five, the waybill lock where tolls were collected, was here as was Lock Six, once called the Magazine Lock because blasting powder was stored there.[87]

Brookmont became a quiet, almost hidden community, but the area was an early "hot spot" known for its beer joints, dancehalls, gambling, fighting, and occasional shootings. Despite Prohibition, the Silver Spider and, farther down the road, Sunset Hall, earlier known as the Rock Spring Club, and a number of other roadhouses made this part of the Glen

Echo region a loud and busy area on weekends. Many locals cheered when the Silver Spider, sometimes known as the "Bucket of Blood," burned down.

Marvin Shoemaker of Brookmont recalled his father's description of the area:

At one time, in the late `30s, there was more bars and things along here and more beer sold along this stretch of road from the District Line to Seneca than any place in the County.

Start right up there where the new gas station is, that was the Hilltop Inn, then there was Texas Tavern and Rock-a-way Inn but before that there was a guy from Prince George's County started that place, up by Bonfield's, that was the only place that the Liquor Board ever owned, right next to Bonfield's, where the parking lot is.

You come down the road, off Maryland Avenue that was Eddie Colleens, Eddie Fontaine, that was a gambling joint. My father said that used to be the gambling house and there was another up there at the castle. Up the road at the turn used to be a bar, Sunset Hall, my cousin owned at one time. He was the first County policeman ever killed on duty, Everett Shoemaker, him and his wife owned that.

Before Sycamore Store on right was place called Annie B. Lewis's. She ran like a store where you could buy a can of beans. She was probably the first one, she would close the door and serve blacks. They would sit on a bag of potatoes in there and drink beer. She used to keep her money in her sock.

On the north side of dusty Conduit Road along the flank of old Fort Sumner was a small black community that supplied many of the cooks, waiters, and other workers at these now long-forgotten roadhouses and the ice cream parlor that later became Callison's gas station. Up on the hill where the fort itself had been, children played war games in the ramparts of Redoubt Kirby (Ft. Franklin), and the Messerlis rented out the old, wooden, barracks-like tenant houses to several African-American families, some of whom worked on their 100-acre farm.[88]

"I was born right up where the map service is," Marvin Shoemaker said.

That was the old Brooke farm. My father and his brother and father came over from McLean about 1900 and rented 242 acres alongside Sang-amore Lane, which was just dirt and ashes. The whole rent was about $20 a month. They farmed it, mostly truck farming. George Thomas Shoemaker was my grandfather; Jesse was my father's name.

We lived in a house without electricty or running water until the Army map service came and took it during the war. We had to walk across the road and down the hillside to where that shopping center is to the spring to get the water and bring it back to the house.

We didn't have a car or anything; we had horses, and if you wanted milk you went and milked a cow. We did get ice delivered. We could sleighride from up there all the way across MacArthur Boulevard to the trolley tracks in Brookmont.

My Uncle Ernest built this house (in Brookmont). They panned this house out with a team of horses named Dick and Harry, scooped this basement out in 1920. You could see nothing but a cornfield on down the street.

Carlock built a lot of these houses through here. Royal Carlock, he was a delegate to Annapolis. He owned a photo shop down on F Street. He built a row of houses on Broad Street and lived on Ridge Drive.

Nettie Burgess was a great lady. She lived in here. She used to come in here in a Model-A Ford with trash container on the back with the black man that worked for her. She owned a lot of different properties.

Except for Brookmont itself with its square Victorians and several models of Sears homes, just about the only reminder of the old days is Bonfield's "historic" Garage, a two-and-a-half story frame building that began life as a store in 1921 and was converted into a gas station that has been in operation since 1927. Mr. Bonfield claimed that in those days "it took you twenty minutes to get across the road on a hot Saturday night. People parked all the way out here and walked to Glen Echo."

Between Brookmont and Glen Echo, and for the most part between Conduit Road and the Canal, grew a small neighborhood, now vanished, which included a number of summer houses and a small artists' colony. No road came down into this community known as Kenton Station for stop 27 on the trolley line and later called Potomac Valley. Visitors and residents left their cars parked and locked along Conduit Road. Norman Danis rigged his

with a primitive alarm system, and his eldest daughter, Norma Spiegel, remembered him grabbing a gun and and then running out and firing shots into the air when the bell went off.

Danis, a long-time PEPCO employee who rose from lineman to, as he said, as close to administration as a non-Mason could get, made his home there in 1918 and became a leader of the community. He built a spring house on the hilly far side of the road and brought a pipe through the culvert and supplied water to a half dozen homes in addition to his own. Two houses on the far side of the canal, where Andrew P. Talmadge and Dr. Fred, a dentist, lived, also got water from this system through a pipe that ran down into the canal and under the tow path.

Danis also built a rough bridge of heavy pine planks over the canal with a lift section across the tow path and extended Potomac Drive from Brookmont into his neighborhood to make it easier for the firemen to launch their boat when unwary canoers got in trouble on the Little Falls dam. His house below the brow of the hill grew over the years by the addition of several rooms and a screened porch plus a concrete swimming pool with two twelve-feet-high sliding boards. A number of summer people including several scientists had cottages in the Danis's neighborhood. The large lots, roughly ninety by two hundred feet, were rented from the trolley company.

The Baltzleys' stone castles up in the Heights were operated for a time as part of gambler Jimmy LaFontaine's extra-legal empire under the name Mohican Lodge. The rumored escape tunnel built between the houses by LaFontaine's associates has never been found, but when the current owners took over the "castle," there were still big holes in the floor where the bar had been in the speakeasy days. In the New Deal era, Edwin Baltzley's thick-walled, fourteen room mansion with its six fireplaces was rented by one Thomas Gardiner Corcoran, FDR's speechwriter and crony, "Tommy the Cork." During WW II, naval officers, a dozen at a time, billeted at the castle. The turreted stone mansions have survived.[89]

The oldest home in Glen Echo has a history almost as remarkable as the Magruder's Locust Grove. The white, stone, Greek Revival house sheltered by ancient oaks at 44 Wellesley Circle was once called Oakdale Villa but is now usually spoken of as the "Reading house." Charles Lilly Coltman, who had built the Treasury Building downtown, designed the house and the slave quarters next door at 42 Wellesley Circle. They were constructed in 1853 by William Reading with walls twenty-six inches thick in the first floor of the main house and eighteen inches in the rest.

Reading had purchased a major part of Magruder's and Beall's "Honesty" for $3,389.65. He planted orchards of apple, pear, and other fruit trees on the part of his 500 acres that stretched up toward Bannockburn, had his barn and stables on what is now Cornell Avenue, cultivated grapes on both sides of Cabin John Creek and made locally famous wines that were proudly served at Bobinger's hotel.

About 1890 the property was deeded to the Baltzleys who lived in the house and enlarged it after the fire at their rustic restaurant. In 1906 Jacob Decker acquired the houses, added a four-story, thirty by fifty foot frame addition plus porches and a cupola tower, and opened the Oakdale Villa summer hotel. It became a very popular place to come for good meals on the lawn or porches and before or after a round of golf at hilly Bannockburn.

Locals sold vegetables to the "Decker Hotel," and Ronnie Vine, a Glen Echoian since 1919, remembered Decker as "a real aristocrat. He had a Reo touring car." Decker was elected mayor in 1919 and again served from 1920 to 1926. Guests stayed all summer at his hotel, played croquet and often dined on tables set out under the oak trees. Eddie Deebo, who operated several concessions in the Park, arrived in Glen Echo in 1926. He recalled that the town held dances in the Oakdale ballroom and that Mr. Decker, who then lived there alone and rented out the upstairs rooms, "was a good old man and let the children play on his lawns."

Later it was more of a rooming house with long-term tenants. In the Depression the house fell on hard times, and by the outbreak of World War II, it was a wreck condemned by County authorities who found no water or electricity but a number of chickens and alcoholics in the building. Just after the war, long-time real estate saleswoman cum local historian Nettie Mae Burgess bought the property for $2,800, tore off the dilapidated frame additions and saved the house. For

several years after the war, Roger Tory Peterson lived and worked in what had been the slave quarters. Today the field stone house still stands behind the pillars of its two story front porch, another survivor.[90]

On the east side of Conduit Road on three-quarters of an acre purchased from William Reading for $100, John Dugan built the Morgan Spring Hotel in 1885. It was the forerunner of the three-and-a-half story, shingle-style Rock Spring Club which, like Oakdale Villa, was in direct competition with the Cabin John Hotel. It had awning-shaded verandas on the two lower floors and a large stable to accommodate the carriages and horses of its guests. The hotel operated through the turn of the century, was sold in 1905, had a short but lively career as a roadhouse and burned to the ground in 1909. One of the Rock Spring Club's small claims to fame is that, like the Cabin John Hotel across the creek, it had a Bell System pay phone in 1895, one of the first in the Bethesda area.

Clara Barton's friend and aide, Dr. Julian Hubbell, speculated in Glen Echo property with her money and, very likely, her permission. He also imported a small herd of Swiss goats that wandered through the town for some years. Miss Barton had extended her holdings near her house until she had about one acre and then purchased several building lots through the Baltzleys' Sun Building office which were recorded in Hubbell's name in the Rockville records.

Richard Cook, an inveterate collector of Glen Echoiana, maintained,

Clara Barton felt very sorry for Edwin Baltzley because he had tried so hard to make a success of the Chautauqua, and she believed in what they were doing. She basically supported Baltzley for a number of years by buying lots from him . . . . And Hubbell ended up owning close to half of what is now the Town of Glen Echo.

John J. Carow, who claimed to be the first person ever arrested in Glen Echo Park for breaking the Blue Laws by selling soda pop on Sunday, told Morris Fradin that his father bought two houses on Harvard Avenue from Hubbell, one for $600, the other for $800, about 1902. Carow recalled that` all eight children in his family came down with malaria at once and that at that time building lots had fallen to $50 or $60 each.

His daughter, Dorothy Carow Merrick, recalled that when her father tried to start his

Pope-Hartford, Miss Pace, who taught five classes in five rows in the town hall across the way, declared "recess" until Mr. Carow got the car started or gave up. John Carow also remembered the dances in the hall over the one-room school that often ended in brawls between young men of Glen Echo and tough guys from Concord, the community up at River Road and Wilson Lane where there was an old Methodist church.

The first church right in Glen Echo, the Episcopal Church of the Redeemer, began with the efforts of the David Houghton family and several other summer residents to establish a chapel so they would not have to take that long trolley ride. Prayer services, sometimes led by the curate of St. Paul's, took place in Mrs. Sally Bogue's home around the turn-of-the-century, and the Sunday School banner with the date "January 3, 1903" has been used to mark the birthdate of the parish.

In 1904 Doctor Thomas Duncan was "called" to the Norwood Parish in Bethesda, and after attending a prayer service at the home of Mrs. William Roach and a series of meetings, he agreed to lend $500 to build a chapel in Glen Echo on land donated by Walter Carroll. Students from the seminary in Alexandria, Virginia, led the services and spent Sundays in various parishioners' homes. Hattie Roach headed the Sunday School and Minnie Houghton led the choir and was the first organist. If it was muddy, she made the boys tie newspapers over their shoes when they came to her home for choir practice.

Early on, the Ladies' Guild, with Mr. Carroll as an honorary member, raised money with bake sales and minstrel shows. Leonard Schloss contributed two tons of coal a year, and it was welcome since cold winds blew through the unsealed walls in the winter. In 1907 the property was deeded to Bishop Satterlee and became a Cathedral mission, but in 1915 St. John's, Norwood, once again was made responsible for monthly services, and the Reverend James Kirkpatrick saw to adding a Sunday School wing and sealing the walls while the congregation raised money for a brick chimney.

By 1925 the Chapel of the Redeemer boasted forty-four communicants, thirty-three Sunday School pupils, an active Ladies' Guild, an Everyman's Club, a small Altar Guild, fourteen members of the Girls' Friendly Society, and two scout troops. The Deacon-in-charge

was paid $480, but the total receipts were only $432.12 that year.

The Rev. Manlius Mills Perkins, one of the many seminarian lay-readers who served the mission in the 1920s, worked especially hard to secure full-time services and a new church on a better site. In 1929 Perkins himself installed a new roof on the old chapel with only the assistance of a local schoolboy. The Ladies' Guild with lawn parties and bake sales raised $290 for the shingles and other supplies.

In the mid-Thirties, bus service helped the Sunday School grow to more than 150; Deaconess Ellen C. Camp began her work, and with Harry T. McCuen as treasurer, the little church became financially stable. By 1939 Dean Powell from the Cathedral and Mr. Perkins, who also served Grace Church in Georgetown, settled on a new site to be purchased with income from Old Trinity whose choir stalls went into the new building.[91]

In the early days most Glen Echo Catholics took the streetcar down to the Jesuit's Holy Trinity Church to attend Mass. The Catholic Church of the Little Flower began as a mission of parishes in D.C., but its roots go back to little St. Gabriel's church at Offutt's Cross Roads (Potomac) built by the Rev. John Barry of St. Ann's in old Tenallytown. A single carpenter and local volunteers built that church and a small school in 1890, and it lasted until the canal company collapsed. It was abandoned in 1926, but its cemetery remained as a reminder of its existence. By the time St. Gabriel's closed its door, the Little Flower chapel, which had had an off-and-on beginning, was becoming more stable, and the altar, pews, organ, and Stations of the Cross were moved down to Glen Echo.

In 1906 Father Malachy Yingling founded Our Lady of Victory parish, and his bailiwick extended all the way to Rockville. His Glen Echo congregants built a small hall on land donated by the local inn-keepers, Mr. and Mrs. Jacob Decker. To raise money, the building on Vassar Circle was rented out for various purposes, and when attendance at Mass grew so small that the mission was abandoned, the chapel served as the school and weekend dance hall for many years. Meanwhile Father Yingling attended to the building of Our Lady of Victory parish.

One former resident remembered the church's start:[92]

Father Yingling

I had a girlfriend, Madie Moran; her parents were very devout Catholics. Madie and I persuaded the Morans to write the Cardinal's office in Baltimore asking if it would be possible to have a priest come to Glen Echo to say Mass. Consent was given and the first Mass was said in the Morans' living room. I do not remember the month but the year was 1906. Madie and I were both twelve years old.

We all worked very hard to start a church; we gave parties, dances, and plays, did everything we could think of to raise money. As time went by we had enough to start to build a hall. It was not consecrated as a church because we had to use it to have entertainments in to raise money, but it was called The Little Flower, and we had a "pastor," Rev. M. L. Yingling. He called the future church Little Flower because of Madie and me being so young.

The Moran family moved away. I missed Madie very much. I did all I could to assist Father Yingling, of whom I was very fond. I do not know why the attendance dropped. I guess there was too much to do and too few to do it.

I taught the Sunday School, played the organ, sang. I asked some of the ladies to keep the altar linens laundered; in the summer, when there were flowers, I put them on the altar; on Saturday I swept and dusted the church. In cold weather I went early in the morning and started a wood fire in the stove. I helped Father Yingling with his vestments before and after Mass.

One day he said to me, "Someday I expect to come here and see you saying Mass!"

The original Little Flower Church

The chapel was reactivated and consecrated in the late-1920s through the efforts of Father Joseph Buckley, founder of St. Francis Xavier Parish in Southeast. He sent his assistant to say Mass. Ed Sonntag, who moved the equipment from St. Gabriels to Little Flower and built the confessional and altar railing, shuttled priests and distant parishioners back and forth in his car. By 1931 when Our Lady of Victory Parish took over the mission again, there were about two hundred who regularly attended Mass at the little, white chapel.

The Methodist church at Concord, founded in a grove of trees almost a hundred years before, was revived and a new frame building erected in 1912 only to be abandoned again in the 1930s. One of the church's problems was that it had no recorded deed for the land it stood on and therefore could not be incorporated. William McGeorge Jr. of Philadelphia acquired title to the land, and the Reverend Merritt Earl, who had been assigned to Concord in 1908, opened a long and complex correspondence and negotiation which resulted in 1910 with the church finally receiving a clean deed to its one and a quarter acres.

Rev. Merritt Earl was viewed by church members as "the first preacher one can really call our own." In April 1912 George Broadhurst contracted to build the third Concord church. Edward Stacks, William H. Embrey and John Harper donated their labor to the construction while services continued to be held in the old schoolhouse nearby. The Rev. John Fort was the first to preach in the new church, and sixteen-year-old Jesse Benson made a speech at the dedication of the building. Strawberry festivals, lawn parties and church suppers, prepared in the basement and handed out through the windows to be served at tables under the trees, soon paid off the building debt. But by the mid-1930s, except for an occasional funeral and burial, the church was all but abandoned.[93]

Among those who walked to the Concord Church on River Road were several families from Cabin John more-or-less led by "Judge" Charles E. Benson. In 1920 through the Concord pastor, Rev. Silas E. Robb, thirty-six of these Methodists signed a petition to the Baltimore Conference asking for a branch of the church in Cabin John. The petition was approved and while services were held in the Benson's, Davis's and several other homes, funds were raised, a lot purchased (lot 51,

section 1), a tent was erected under an elm tree and then a church built at 5th and Conduit Road (now 77th and MacArthur). The one-room, frame church with its square bell tower served served for both worship and Sunday school classes.

The church was incorporated and named, in honor of a Philadelphia Bible class teacher, the G. W. Shaler Memorial Methodist Episcopal Church of Cabin John in July 1921. The building was ready for worship in the fall of 1921. The Ladies Aid Society, led by Mrs. Benson, raised most of the building fund with strawberry festivals, church suppers, and the sale of Mrs. Jesse Baker's extracts.[94]

From 1921 until 1943, the community was served by visiting pastors and student ministers. Rev. J. M. McCauley followed pastor Robb and performed the first marriage, of Hazel Wilson to James Lyle. Harry Wedding led the choir in the early years and his young daughter, Helen, played the organ. By the late 1930s the church had about seventy members, more than sixty Sunday School participants and, like most other local churches, a lot of trouble meeting its budget and paying its bills. At the end of 1939, however, conditions had improved enough that a building committee

The Methodist Church in Cabin John

including the pastor, Rev. J. E. James, started discussing the remodeling of the church.[95]

The Blue Laws were irregularly enforced in the Bethesda area, but in 1931 Charles W. Ballenger of Glen Echo Park was arrested for driving nails at his home on Sunday. Most folks assumed that one of his neighbors had become annoyed with him and called the police. Mr. Ballenger took the case to court, and when he was found guilty despite his explanation that he was a Seventh Day Adventist who did not consider Sunday his day of rest, he refused to pay the five dollar fine and spent five days in the Rockville jail. During the `30s the laws were modified and weakened for several counties and for many activities such as ballgames and movies, but they stayed on the books for another generation.

After the collapse of the Baltzley enterprises, the hills became home to squatters who built rough shacks, many on stilts, some from abandoned horsecars, and conducted various illicit businesses in the neighborhood. Later many people bought lots in the heights over the river and built cottages as summer homes; others became permanent residents. Earl C. Toone Sr. came to Glen Echo Heights in 1913 when his father purchased two lots and built a home for his large family.

Mr. Toone told local historian Morris Fradin about the neighborhood's narrow dirt roads, big old trees, and of the good water from the three free-flowing springs in his area. He had picked wild plums and fox grapes and gathered walnuts, hickory nuts, hazelnuts, chestnuts and chinquiapins in the woods. He fondly remembered the blackberries, dewberries, raspberries, huckleberries, and even wild strawberries that were plentiful when he was young. Toone said he played in the old abandoned streetcarbarn on Walhonding where the ticket office had been turned into a tiny store, and each summer he watched the gypsies who gathered in the valley beneath the carbarn with their horses. He collected flint points from Mount Misery and lead bullets at Fort Sumner. He explored the long, cool and exciting tunnel of the gold mine and helped build a swimming hole near Massachusetts Avenue. The Carows and the Toones and a lot of other folks including a small black community up off Wissioming Road found Glen Echo Heights a fine place to live.

Harry Klopp, who moved to Glen Echo Heights in 1921, said:

A man could come up here, buy a lot averaging eighty-five by a hundred feet for $10, if it were somewhat swampy, and up to $40 for a prime piece of property. The owner could then get the trees on his land sawed down with the help of his neighbors, and have the timber hauled down to a nearby sawmill. When the dressed lumber was returned to his lot, the landowner could secure nails, roofing, and plumbing supplies, and aided by friends and neighbors, he could erect a home for his family . . . ."

There were restrictions: homes had to cost at least $3,000 and no pigsties were allowed. "Chickens? Horses? Cows? Goats? They were all okay. We would often have to shoo

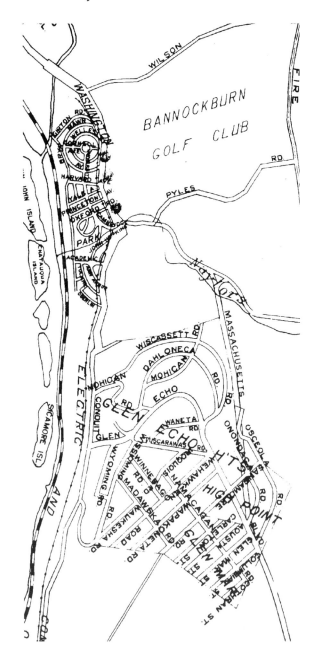

away coveys of partridges. The fool wild birds would feed with our chickens." In the 1920s and `30s Mr. Klopp was active in the citizen's association that conducted many community activities including popular block parties. And like many other residents of both Cabin John and Glen Echo, Klopp remembered the visits of Woodrow Wilson to the area where Mrs. Galt had relatives. The big Pierce Arrow always got waves from the kids along Conduit Road, and sometimes the ailing ex-President waved back.[96]

Orville Kile came to Mohican Hills, the area west of Walhonding Road, and built his home in 1923. Building lots sold for about $500 at that time and there were still many small, weekend cottages when he moved into the neighborhood filled with all those Indian names that were the Baltzley twins' legacy. Mr. Kile remembered with pleasure shopping at the old Sycamore Store Hugh Johnston opened in 1919. In typical Bethesda-area tradition, he seemed to think that his part of Glen Echo Heights was better than some other sections.[97]

The Sycamore Store developed a loyal clientele for its groceries and delivery service in the 1920s. The store also earned a reputation for high quality meats, and its long-time butcher, the oversized Mr. Layton, soon was as well-known as storekeeper Johnston whose home was right behind his place of business. His truck was generally out two-thirds of the day delivering orders from Cabin John and Wood Acres to Brookmont and Glen Echo Heights.

The weekends brought heavy traffic, and by most summer afternoons cars were parked alongside Conduit Road from up towards the Hilltop beer garden and past Annie Lewis's small store all the way into Glen Echo. The Sycamore Store did a steady business of soda and snack sales, and a group of neighborhood youngsters, both black and white, found a unique way to make some money. Mickey Johnston, who worked in his father's store, remembered:

Where Sycamore Store sits was the Sycamore stop, and there was a bunch of kids in the area that used go down there and dance. As the street-car would come up and stop, people would pitch out nickels and dimes. The kids would sing and dance, and the car would stop and watch them for five minutes or so.

This was a big thing. Many people would come out in the evenings to see it. They used a harmonica and sang, and they could really dance. I used to sit in the store and watch, and they were really good. This was in the late `30s mainly.

Slowly, the various communities of the Glen Echo area stabilized and by the time of the First World War, when the Bannockburn Country Club arrived, a homey tone had been established; the post office was no longer just a summer operation, and a couple of stores and churches were in business. Otto Kumfert, in the tavern later called Trav's, and Donald Canada were selling cold drinks and sand-wiches. By the end of Prohibition three stores were operating including Miller's where the miniature golf layout was later built. They all quickly turned into bars.

Canada's mother took over as the post-mistress once he started selling beer, but Don would usually fetch a patron's mail long after the little post office was closed. Oldtimers enjoyed playing checkers by Canada's pot-bellied stove but noted that sometimes it gave only the illusion of warmth since Donald, who was "tight," just had a candle lit inside it. The Canadas kept the postmaster job in the family for about fifty years. The mail came out from the city in the morning on the #20 streetcar along with bread and other supplies and went into town on the 4:30 car.[98]

The Bannockburn Golf Club, named for The Bruce's bloody victory over the English in 1314, organized around the turn-of-the-cen-tury and used the Kirkside links west of Chevy Chase Circle. The club incorporated in D.C. in 1910 and, by the time America entered World War I, had purchased 123 2/3 acres from the William McGeorge group, built a club house and laid out a hilly, 18-hole golf course. The trolley line and nearby summer hotels helped make Bannockburn a popular destina-tion for area golfers. In the boom of the 1920s, faced with competition from newer country clubs with snazzier layouts, the club borrowed heavily, in part from the McGeorge interests in Philadelphia, and added to the original, hip-roofed, two-story clubhouse. Its clientele, however, remained decidedly middle-class and its dues-paying membership relatively small.

Al Jamison had been caddying and playing semi-pro baseball before he came to Glen Echo and the golf course.

I came right to Bannockburn from Wilmington, Delaware, in 1928 as assistant pro. It was the hilliest golf course around. The members were mainly government employees that lived out that way. The pro was Tony Sylvester. He had been assistant club maker for Tommy Armour when Tommy was at Congressional.

Armour was the one that showed me the proper grip for holding a club. He came over to have lunch with Tony. I was out hitting some balls, and he came out and watched me and said, "Son, let me see your grip" so I showed him, and he said, "You're holding it wrong." So he showed me, and it felt like hell, but when he left I stepped away from the ball and said, "Who am I to question him? He's National Open Champion and I'm nothing," but it made all the difference, and I've never changed my swing.

It was a hilly golf course. From No. 2 green you could look over to Virginia, and it went over to Wilson Lane. At 18 there used to be a cat that sat alongside the green, and you drove blind to that hole, it was elevated. If you got on the green, the cat would be sitting there, and as soon as the ball would come up there, she'd get up and play with the ball and push it into the hole. There was more damn eagles on that hole, so we had to get rid of the cat.

Par was 70. It was fairly wooded, with a creek running through the back nine and sand traps, but no white sand in those days.

Sylvester was club maker for Tommy Armour and Bobby Jones. At that time, it was all we did, made our own stocks, wooden shafts. I'm one of the few around that broke a course record with wooden shafts after they started using steel shafts; in 1929 I shot a 67 at Bannockburn. There were few ready-made clubs, a company down in Chattanooga made some.

The Scots thought they were really club makers, but we got tired of them telling us how it should be. We made them all ourselves. You got the forged heads, from Stewart, no chrome. Stewart iron they called it. We'd get the hickory shafts from Chattanooga. Then we shaved them down to get the feel they should have for that person, what they do today with the tru-temper step down, to give you the feel where you want it. We used to shave them to get the right feel, did it with a piece of steel saw, cut a piece about four inches long and filed it to get a sharp edge on both sides.

I only got $40 a month when I started at Bannockburn and paid $30 a month for room and board in Glen Echo. I was twenty.

In 1930 the Bannockburn club could not pay the interest on its loans, and in 1931 when the $75,000 McGeorge note came due, it still could not pay and received extensions. The tax bills to Montgomery County were a different matter, and after a series of law suits and delaying actions, the club's treasurer began slicing off pieces of land to meet annual tax assessments. In 1931, for example, the delinquent tax list contained a ten acre Bannockburn parcel at $1,401.61 and a twenty

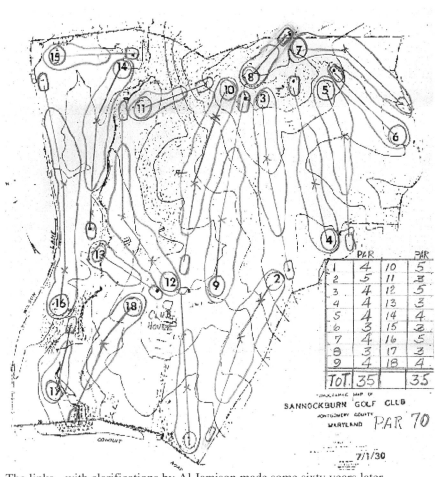

PAR		PAR	
1	4	10	5
2	5	11	3
3	4	12	5
4	4	13	3
5	4	14	4
6	3	15	3
7	4	16	5
8	3	17	3
9	4	18	4
TOT	35		35

SANNOCKBURN GOLF CLUB
MONTGOMERY COUNTY
MARYLAND   PAR 70

7/1/30

The links - with clarifications by Al Jamison made some sixty years later.

acre piece owing $2,529.34, which were "bought in" by the Commissioners.

Eventually, most of this tax delinquent acreage was bought up by John J. Shinners of Norristown, Pennsylvania, who took possession of the club in the late 1930s and usually rented it out. For some years Bannockburn operated as a public course with very reasonable greens fees while the McGeorge and Shinners' attorneys fought through a series of Circuit Court law suits which were finally settled in 1942.

"Mickey" Harris felt Bannockburn was "never too successful, but they had the best hamburger for a quarter anywhere. If you carried two bags for eighteen, you got two dollars and the first thing you did was to go to the back door and get Mr. Lumsden, the greenskeeper who lived in Glen Echo, to get the cook to make you a hamburger." Harris also made money by picking crabgrass out of the greens for twenty-five cents an hour.

And Banockburn always had the best sleigh riding hill in the Bethesda area, at least in the opinon of most "river rats." Mickey Harris and his friends would get a running start near the pro shop or off the first tee. They raced down the steep hill toward the first green and flew across Conduit Road, bumped over the trolley tracks and dragged their toes as they headed for the canal. Then walked back up the lane to do it again. In fact it had been a favorite place for sleigh riding at least a generation earlier. Pres Wedding, who came to Cabin John with his family in 1919, also caddied there and brought his sled down when it snowed to go bellywhopping across the fairways.[99]

The volunteer fire department in Glen Echo had its genesis in the unforgotten May 1930 Moxley fire. A mother and her four children, ages 14, 11, 8 and 5, died when the neighborhood's hand-drawn hose cart and lack of ladders were tragically exposed as inadequate. The father, a one-armed watchman at the amusement park next door, survived after jumping from a second story window. The Moxleys' home was completely destroyed, and the Riley house next to it was damaged.

The volunteers, with a great deal of local help, built a cinderblock fire station on Vassar Circle, and acquired one of the Bethesda fire department's 1926 LaFrance pumpers and a hose truck and began training. Bethesda fireman Sumpter Embrey remembered that fire

truck well. "It had left-hand steering and chain drive. That was a six-cylinder truck we called Leaping Lena. I recall my coat brushing a stop sign when we crossed River Road on Wilson Lane going to a fire and that thing bounced into the air."

When the reconditioned, repainted and relettered 750-gallon pumper arrived, Glen Echo, according to the *Sentinel*, had the "greatest community fete in the town's history." As part of the celebration, maple trees were planted around the circle by Mayor H. T. McCuen and citizens' association president Mrs. J. L. Loveless.[100]

Those who drove "Lena" never forgot the experience. Driver #1 was Willard Alban who lived next door to the fire house at 21 Vassar Circle and Driver #2 was Ronnie Vine, who therefore seldom got to drive, but when he did he considered it "the thrill of a lifetime." Al Jamison and most of his brothers became volunteer firemen, but Al did not remember that they received much training in those early days. "They weren't into that. It was more of a social thing," Jamison said, "but they were all trained to drive."[101]

I was there when they first got a fire truck, one of those La France trucks. Man, those boys went crazy. They deliberately set fires and called in false alarms early in the morning. They set a fire down in Glen Echo Park. They called in one night at two o'clock in the morning and said there was a train hit a car on River Road and, of course, these boys that did this, they would be the first ones there to drive the fire truck. We just drove on that fire truck to River Road, and it was a false alarm. And I started thinking, boy, I must be dumb. Here I work at Kenwood, and I know there's no train at that time of the morning. This boy, he was always the first one on the driver's seat, and I began to catch on.

But, Jamison said, "they went after a fire like they were going after their last meal and competed for fires with Cabin John." They may not have trained much in those early days, but the boys from the Glen Echo VFD won three hook-up contests in a row in the summer of 1931. Jamison decided he had enough of firefighting when "one boy, a good driver, was going down Conduit Road so fast, I'm hanging on the end and my feet left the board. No more of that I said." And "Mickey" Harris recalled being on a fire truck when it passed a car going the other way on the Cabin John Bridge. He remembers the solid "tick" of

fenders striking. It was, he said, the Cabin John postmistress taking bags of mail down to the trolley at Glen Echo.

In 1933 the Conduit Road Fire Board was established to operate one or more fire departments in its region and was given taxing power by the State legislature. The elected board, unique in Maryland, included representatives from Green Acres, Glen Cove, Fairway Hills, Sycamore Hills, Glen Echo, Woodburn, Glen Echo Heights, and Wood Acres. The first president of the Fire Board was Henry T. McCuen who served until his death in 1948.

"Mac" and his wife, Beulah, came to Glen Echo in 1922. By 1925 he was on the town council and in May `26, Harry McCuen became the town's mayor, a job he held until he was "Hatched." in 1939. During his time in office he worked for both the town and the fire department paving the streets and acquiring the site and funds for the new fire house while also serving as the postmaster of the Friendship station.

In 1935, with WPA funds, a new, two-story brick firehouse and meeting hall was constructed in the middle of Vassar Circle on the land set aside back in Chautauqua days for the Women's Temple. It had room for the equipment on the lower level and a large auditorium with an entrance facing Conduit Road on the upper level.[102]

The fire company soon became an important social institution with an active women's auxiliary. The ladies, mostly firemen's wives, made curtains for the firehouse windows, ran many small carnivals and bingo games, and became famous for their fried oysters. The firemen distributed baskets of food at Christmas time, held dinner dances, and staged turkey shoots and ball games. The various fund-raising activities paid off in 1937 when the company purchased a triple-combination truck built by Peter-Pirsch on a big Diamond T chassis. The whole town turned out to admire the big engine with its 500 gallon-per-minute Hale pump and Indian pumps for brush fires. Because of the number of river rescue calls the company received, the Glen Echo firemen, like their "river rat" brothers across the Cabin John Bridge, acquired a heavy wooden boat and built a trailer for it from an old Model A rear end. Wrestling that boat into the river was one of the hardest parts of being a fireman.

The volunteer fire department's operations were the responsibility of an annually elected chief who reported to the Fire Board. By far the best known of all the chiefs of the Glen Echo VFD was Joseph A. Giammatteo who was first elected in 1939 and served for some thirty years. Giammatteo had been brought down to Glen Echo about 1930 by his brother, Bannockburn golf pro Al Jamison. He finished high school and played basketball at B-CC and then secured a government job as a messenger at $900 a year. He studied accounting and started getting promotions at the ICC then at the FCC. His big brother Al eventually had brothers John, Art, and Paul rooming with Joe and him at Alma Lynch's.

Fire Chief Joseph Giammatteo

Giammatteo (JAH-mah-tay-oh) soon developed a well-earned reputation as an innovator as well as a teacher and disciplinarian. He worked as an accountant for the Federal government during the day, but his nights, his weekends, and much of his leave time were given to the fire department. He became a University of Maryland-certified instructor and taught courses in both basic and advanced fire fighting techniques for volunteers from many local companies. The long-time chief also maintained excellent relations with the D.C. fire department and shared his expertise with them. Some of his experiments, especially with inch-and-a-half hoses and new types of nozzles, were widely adopted.

It was Giammatteo who convinced the Glen Echo firemen to paint their equipment white. He claimed that white made for cleanliness and easy maintenance as well as for

visibility at night and recognition. When "Mickey" Harris, a Glen Echo volunteer for fifty years, talked about that first white `41 LaFrance with its gold leaf trim and blue striping his eyes lit up and he smiled with pride. Harris also recalled when the firemen added a used Packard ambulance with a twelve-cylinder engine and "a gear-shift lever a yard long." It was later replaced by one of Pumphrey's funeral-home Cadillacs, quickly painted white.

The Glen Echo VFD siren was hooked to a pay phone, BRadley 0012. When the phone rang, the siren sounded until a volunteer got to the firehouse and turned it off and answered the phone. It woke up a lot of folks in Glen Echo, but those who recalled the Moxley fire did not seem to mind.

Its one-time Mayor, Bill Herson, once WRC's early morning deejay, called Glen Echo "the greatest little town in Maryland," and for Bethesdans, for a long time, it certainly was the most popular one to visit in the summer.

Meanwhile north of the creek and the castellated gingerbread hotel that the Bobingers ran, Cabin John was also slowly growing. Among the first to settle in the area were Irish laborers hired to build first the canal and then the great bridge. Some of them established squatters' rights in ramshackle cabins near the river or in converted canal barges. They scratched out little farms which floods regularly washed away. High above the stream, off the trail that became Persimmon Tree Road, in 1853 John Saunders built his home, called Ellerslie, on a thousand acres with a right-of-way to the canal.

Persimmon Tree Road itself was laid out in the spring of 1869 and became the unofficial western boundary of Cabin John. The eastern border is the creek or perhaps what used to be Cohassett Road but since 1928 has been called Wilson Lane. Cabin John does not lend itself to boundaries. One Washington *Post* reporter wrote that you were no longer in Cabin John when it did not "look" like Cabin John.

In 1876 Thomas Tuohey bought twenty six and a half acres south of the aqueduct and west of the Bobinger's big tract and built a two-story house that still stands. For the next hundred years, the Tuohey clan was considered by many to be Cabin John's "first family." Nine years later, Thomas's son Dennis pur-

chased part of the Peter family's Carderock land and built his well-remembered home and store. It was the store that became the "beer joint," Tuohey's Restaurant, when beer "came back" in the 1930s, and his son David reclaimed his parents' place. Norman Tuohey, who later operated the beer joint as did his brother Gordon, described his grandfather's place.[103]

The old store was just like what you see in the mountains today . . . as long as we had it, it was grey. I think he built it in the eighties . . . . Only one room was store, the rest was house. The big steps out front that went into the lunch room at the beer joint, that was the entrance to the store. Now, that one big lunch room was divided up into three rooms. The store was out front; then the dining room; then the kitchen. It was a very small store, but he had a lot of stuff packed in there. Where the beer joint had its bar, that was considered the parlor. Which was never used. Upstairs there were three bedrooms.

By the turn of the century, almost all the rest of the land that is now considered Cabin John belonged to Amanda Dowling. The first real "subdivision" beyond Cabin John Creek was made by J. D. W. Moore who sold five-acre plots along Seven Locks Road to ten black families working on his farm. "Miss Lena" Brown was 93 in 1975 when she talked to Elizabeth Kytle about her father, Henry Brown, and the farm he bought for $300.

She remembered working so hard and well that "he used to call me his boy. Oh, I worked in the garden! I'd get out there and sweat! I had a whole yard full of chickens; I used to look after them. Turkeys and ducks too." Miss Lena called the small farm a vegetable garden.

There was cabbages, potatoes, tomatoes, broccoli, sweet potatoes, and corn. *I love corn. There were peppers, watermelons, cantaloupes. Everything. Everything they have at the market. This is way back there; my father died in 1912. He took all these things to market in Washington — Center Market, Georgetown Market, P Street Market, and K Street Market. K Street Market was his main market.*

Miss Lena also worked at the scrub boards in the laundry at the Cabin John Hotel and remembered the Bobingers fondly. The government bought her property to build public housing in 1940. Miss Lena was living in one

of those wartime houses and could see the land where she was born and raised when she was interviewed. [104]

Mrs. Matilda Bowles was born in the Brookmont area in 1884 and "worked at the Cabin John Hotel for many a year. It was a beautiful place . . . . I used to dip ice cream in the hotel's ice cream parlor." Like Miss Lena, she also worked in the laundry. "I used to do the laundry, carry it up to the hotel— roll it up there in a wheelbarrow—take it out and carry it inside, and put all the clothes away . . . . I did shirts and things like that, the fancy clothes. I ironed them too . . . . The Bobinger men used to have beautiful shirts."

The Bowles family lived at the corner of Palisades and Seven Locks, which was called Number 10 Road then because it had ten houses on it, and walked to work at the hotel. But on Saturdays she rode her gray mule, Dolly, bareback to the markets in Georgetown to do the shopping for her family. The African-American community of which she was a part is one of the oldest and most stable in Montgomery County.

Among the other early residents of the area were the lockkeepers who lived in small stone houses along the canal. Otho Swain, whose father, Jess, was a lockkeeper as well as a canalboat captain, was born on a barge at Great Falls in July 1901. He recalled his grandfather, who had helped to build the canal, telling of cholera outbreaks and of how the contractors tried to cheat the immigrant workmen. When he was eight, Swain's father quit boating to become a lockminder, and he began boating himself when he was 15 or 16, made his home in Cabin John and worked at Bannockburn and other golf courses, and then at Burning Tree "for a long, long time" as a greenskeeper.[105]

The men that tended the locks before the First World War got only $22 a month — for working seven days and seven nights a week. . . . In the winter months he got $11 a month. In the winter most of them used to work on the canal, wheeling out mud and stuff like that. They couldn't do any extra work during the summer because they had to be on duty all the time. My father tended lock for 35 or 40 years.

I helped him open the gates, turn the paddles up and leave the water in or out. I helped him do anything that's supposed to be done around a lock. . . . And we always kept the lock whitewashed to make it look good. I helped do that too.

My father had a pet goose named Jimmy and that goose lived to be 27 years old. My father would get in the buggy to go to the Potomac store, and Jimmy would get right up beside him and ride out there and back . . . . If my father would go fishing in the boat, Jimmy would get in the water and swim right out to him and stay there as long as he stayed . . . .

One of the last lockkeepers in Cabin John were Charles Spong, who tended lock number eight at the foot of Hallifax Street, and the twins, Victor and Virgie Hall, who took care of locks nine and ten. The canal closed for good after the flood in May of 1924, and no longer were the sleepers in Cabin John awakened by the insistent horn or the call of bargemen approaching a closed lock.

Down at the sprawling hotel by the bridge, changes were taking place. Joseph Bobinger, who had become the area's first postmaster shortly after receiving his citizenship papers, died in May of 1881. His wife, left with two small boys, operated the popular establishment until her death in 1893 at which time George and William, her sons, took over but stopped renting out rooms to overnight guests.

After his brother's death, William, who had married Mary Ellen Ogle in 1902, ran the hotel through both its best and then its declining years when more modern attractions such as country clubs and the rides at Glen Echo drew customers away. The restrictions

William and Mary Ogle Bobinger with William, Harry and Edith Rose on the porch of their hotel about 1910

imposed by local-option prohibition laws and later by the enforcement of the so-called Blue Laws cut deeply into the business.

He tried building his own small amusement park and was one of the first in the area to show motion pictures, but business still declined. William Bobinger rented out the hotel and others ran it from 1914 until he died in 1926. His widow padlocked the place and first took up residence in one of the summer houses and then in a small cottage on the other side of the creek. She and her sons Harry and William and her daughter Edith Rose, ran a taxi service from the end of the streetcar line, and Mrs. Bobinger had a refreshment stand there for many years with, one regular recalled, a slot machine and some punch board games. She refused numerous offers for the hotel's register with its many famous guests' autographs.

On Tuesday night, April 7, 1931, the hotel burned, still full of its furniture and antiques, most of its silver, china and glass, and its bulging register. Sumpter Embrey recalled that they could see the red glow in the sky long before they got to Conduit Road with the

Cabin John Hotel Ruins

MARYLAND FIREMEN INJURED FIGHTING BLAZE TODAY.

THE old Cabin John Bridge Hotel, famous landmark of the National Capital of 70 years ago, was destroyed by fire of undetermined origin early this morning. Seven volunteer fire companies and an engine company from Washington were unable to save the ancient structure.

—Star Staff Photo.

Bethesda fire trucks, the first on the scene, and Bootsie Lochte, who drove one of the pumpers, said that when they got there, "It was just a ball of flames."

Loretta Tuohey Hall recalled lying on her bed in Cabin John and seeing the flames shoot into the air. Harry Bobinger said,

I remember looking out the window the night the hotel burned. I could see it all from the porch, and man, it was —. The fire started in the orchestration, in the back part of the hotel. The fire departments all came and they thought they could save at least the front end of it, but they couldn't. Gone. It was terrible. Awful. We couldn't get near it. It kept getting hotter and hotter. And it all went, every bit of it.

According to Harry's brother, Willie:

Someone set a fire and burned the whole thing down. Someone must have set the fire. It was such a terrific blaze you couldn't tell too much. There were thirty-three fire engines there. They had come all the way from Bethesda. They drew water from the Washington aqueduct. The fire had plenty of chance to get going, and not only that it was a frame building — and frame, of course, in an open area, it just went straight up.

There was no insurance. The company had refused to renew the policy on a vacant building.[106]

Ten acres of the Bobinger property north of the conduit were purchased for the Cabin John School and the recreation field behind it, and in 1940 the U.S. Housing Authority bought nineteen acres where the hotel had been for a public housing project called Cabin John Gardens and built small homes with cement floors for workers at the model basin and map service. Later the U.S. Government acquired the land along the creek for a park.

On display at the Clara Barton House are a teapot, creamer, and saucer from the Cabin John Hotel. They were donated by Edith Martin "Bin" Armstrong, a long-time Cabin John historian, who had been given the pieces of china by Mary Bobinger. Except for the gas house across the road, not much else is left.

In 1907 Charles E. Benson bought part of Thomas Tuohey's land and built a home, store, and blacksmith's shop that is still a local landmark. His house was even used briefly for church services and later housed the first fire engine. "Judge" Benson, some people called him Gene, under authority given him by the Federal Commissioner, operated a small

courtroom by the soda fountain in the back of his store and meted out justice to those caught by Roy Ferguson and Eddie Bissett for breaking the laws on the federal property along Conduit Road. By then Benson had rented out the blacksmith business to Jimmy Williams who was still smithing well into the 1930s.[107]

According to Norman Tuohey, in 1910:

> There were only about six houses in Cabin John. I'll start at the bridge, with the old Cabin John Bridge Hotel. The next thing you hit was Benson's store. On up the road, close to the road, an old house sits down on the bank to your left, just on the curve of where you get to the fire house. That, as far as I know and was always told, belonged to my great-grandfather. That's one of the oldest houses. It has two rooms downstairs, stone basement, then frame construction — then two rooms up. That's three places.

> The next place is the house I was born in, between the old beer joint and the fire house. The next place came down by the side of our place, and all that property from 79th Street clean over to Persimmon Tree Road was Dowling's farm. A big dairy farm, and the old house is still standing. It was remodeled when Roy Carlock bought it during World War II. There was an old quarry right across from Dowlings, I think on 80th Street . . . was the old Gray farm. And that house is still in existence.

> That's six. But no, there was one more. I'm a little vague on this, but I think this was a Dowling house too. It's right there by the water tower. Now, all of that used to be a big farm, and that old house is still standing, I think. It was a big old mansion with tall columns. All of that was a farm clean down to the Bobinger place . .

The modern era of Cabin John dates from 1912 when J. S. Tomlinson, who was the American Land Company, bought the Dowling's 600 acres for $50,000 and laid out the four sections of Cabin John Park and began selling various sized lots for $10 down and $10 a month. All lots were advertised to have at least 100 foot frontages with the smaler lots 15,000 to 40,000 square feet and the larger lots one to five acres.

Tomlinson's terms offered many choices:

> 1. deposit of $10 is required when the lot is selected

> 2. a cash payment of not less than 6% is required at settlement

> 3. monthly payments on the basis of 2% of purchase price

> 4. a discount of 8% will be allowed for full cash payment

> 5. settlement is made by contract for monthly payment plan

> 6. settlement by deed and trust notes when one-third cash payment is made

> 7. settlement by deed when full cash payment is made

> 8. no extra expense on account of insurance feature.[108]

Tomlinson's well-illustrated sales brochure showed that the Baltzleys' bravura literary style lived on. "The first sweep of the eye over these undulations brings an involuntary exclamation of admiration and a closer examination confirms the first impression that this is

3 Dozen Attractive Features
Cabin John Park

1. Near-City Homes	19. Grapes and Melons
2. Profitable Investments	20. Ginseng, Golden Seal
3. Splendid Location	21. All Garden Crops
4. Beautiful Home Sites	22. Chicken Farms
5. Villa, Bungalow Sites	23. High Elevation
6. Pleasant Surroundings	24. Monument in Sight
7. Attractive Scenery	25. Refreshing Breezes
8. Magnificent Situations	26. Sunshine and Shade
9. Surface Undulating	27. Abundant Shade Trees
10. Perfect Drainage	28. Healthy Community
11. Southern Exposure	29. Good Neighborhood
12. Fertile Land	30. Pure Spring Water
13. Suitable Truck Patches	31. Running Streams
14. Fruits and Vegetables	32. Best Public Roads
15. Fine Soil for Apples	33. Splendid Car Service
16. Peaches, Pears, Plums	34. Elec. Light, Telephone
17. Sweet, Irish Potatoes	35. Free Life Insurance
18. Lettuce, Kale and Cabbage	36. Cheap Prices and Liberal Terms

WRITE FOR FURTHER PARTICULARS

a beautiful and meritorious situation from one end to the other." The American Land Company claimed that the "natural scenery is more romantic and fascinating than that in Rock Creek Park and where there are more beautiful sites for country home, villas, and bungalows than can be found at Cleveland Park or Chevy Chase."[109]

The first to purchase one of Tomlinson's well-advertised lots were David , one of Dennis's sons, and his wife, Mary, who built their home on Woodrow Avenue (79th Street) in 1913-14. Next were Mr. and Mrs. Percy Redden who eventually built three houses near the firehouse and the Tuoheys, including the Sears bungalow where Buck and Irene Worsham lived well into their nineties and raised four of the best golfers the area ever saw.

According to Mrs. Redden:

It was my husband who got electric lights in Cabin John. When we first moved here, we were using kerosene lamps. He went down to the electric company and they told him if he got, I think it was 15, signers as promised customers, they'd put electricity in for us. You know, there weren't many people around here then, and, I mean to tell you, it wasn't easy for him to get 15 signers. But he did. Three of them didn't have any money, and Mother and my husband paid their way and later were paid back.

Charles R. Smith came out to Cabin John on Sunday afternoon in 1913 when Tomlinson was having an auction sale and bought four lots at what he considered bargain prices. "The roads were laid out but not paved. Conduit Road was paved. In a way. It was quiet here, no houses." Mr. Smith built his own home with a great deal of local help. His neighbor Joe Lynch dug the foundation with a horse and scoop. He got sand and gravel free from the creek as Mr. Tomlinson had promised, and Jim Royce hauled it for him.

After he finished building his own house, alone, Tomlinson had him construct several other homes in the area. Mr. Smith was also a charter member of the Citizens' Association, but was not very active. After the first meeting he decided "This is a good place to get either blessed or cussed." He recalled Tuohey's store as "a place where people could let off their political opinions. People would go after their mail, and they would meet here casually, like around a cracker barrel in the old days."

One house that is outstandingly different is the so-called "mud house" built by Harry and Olive Humphrey on two acres bought in 1919. Mrs. Humphrey, an architect in Minnesota, designed the house and supervised its construction that was accomplished, in part, by her husband and sons. They dug the basement, set the concrete block foundation, and then rammed a mix of sand, gravel, clay, and just plain dirt into wooden forms set eighteen inches apart to form the walls of the first floor, leaving room for doors and windows.

The USDA, where Dr. Humphrey was a plant pathologist, had experimented with this type of construction before World War I. A builder added a conventional, dormered second floor, and the Humphreys moved in for Christmas 1923 and enjoyed their ten-room house with its giant, stone fireplace for the next twenty-five years and were among the leaders in the campaign for a new school.

In 1917 in the same neighborhood William Case built a small restaurant and,

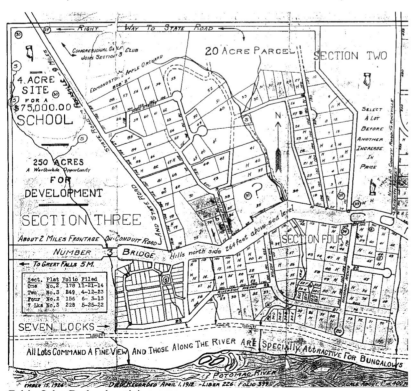

Cabin John Park advertising map

like the big hotel down the road, specialized in black bass and Maryland fried chicken. Jimmy Williams, the blacksmith, moved his operation from under Benson's store to the corner of 79th and Conduit and was still there when the community got together and built the firehouse next door on part of the Tuohey's land.

Another early homesteader in Cabin John was carpenter Harry I. Wedding and his family. They had lived in Southeast Washington and had been hit hard by the flu at the end of World War I. Presley Wedding recalled:

It left my younger sister very weak, and the doctor recommended that we get out of the city. So we moved out next to my great uncle's place in Cabin John. His name was Benson; we called him "Uncle Earl." He was U. S. Commissioner for the Conduit Road property and had a store. His wife, Aunt Addie, was my grandfather's sister. I think I was in the third grade.

My sister regained her strength, and we were there for about ten years. We located a farmer up on Number Ten Road that sold milk. One time we didn't get up there in time to get the milk, and when my dad came home, we went up there and my dad herded the cows in so the farmer could milk them so we could get some milk. It was a big change from living in the city.

We moved into a two-room cottage for the summer and then into another house just east of the store. The living room had been Benson's original store, but it's no longer there. We lived there for two or three years while my dad built our own house just to the west of the store. That street is 78th Street–used to call it Halifax Street.

There was a blacksmith shop up at Seven Locks and Conduit Road, his name was Williams, and on summer mornings when the windows were open and I was in bed trying to get some extra sleep, I'd hear that old hammer banging against the anvil. Judge Benson was a blacksmith too. He had a row of sheds there. One was a blacksmith shop and another was a garage and another was a store room and then there was a stable. He shod horses, and remember him grinding up that old forge. He was quite a capable individual.

He built that store himself, and he had a residence down on 78th Street and a sizeable tract of land, six or eight acres. He had a big cornfield, and he'd hire a couple of us kids to plant corn. He'd plow a furrow and drop a bit of fertilizer, and we were supposed to drop three or four kernels in the hills, and he'd have a horse pulling some sort of implement along and he'd cover it up. So we'd carefully count out three or four kernels and

drop them in each hill, but when he'd begin to catch up with us with his horse, we stopped counting and just tossed in a few.

Down at the bottom of the hill was a spring, and when we first went out there, we'd have to go down there for our water. Good water. The house that my dad built, we had a well there with a electric motor later. It was covered over with the concrete slab that was the back porch. You had to drill a hole in the concrete to get the pumping rods out.

We kept chickens and had a cow once, and my uncle kept a herd of pigs down by the spring. He had several pig pens down there, and very year around Thanksgiving time when the weather began to get cold we waited to hear the squeal of pigs being slaughtered. We'd go down and watch 'em. They'd string `em, up on a crossbeam, eviscerate `em. Had a big tub of boiling water to get the hair off and a barrel of boiling water they put scraps in to make scrapple. Then they had these sausage making machines. Used everything but the hoofs.

We enjoyed the canal; every Sunday afternoon we'd take hikes along the towpath. There were some summer people that came out there. Halifax Street led down to a lock, and the canal boats were running. Mostly hauling coal. Once in a while the excursion boats came out from Georgetown, and they were fun to see.

One of the summer people, a fellow named Lanning, built a water wheel for the canal race that by-passed the locks, hooked it up to a generator and had electric lights. We just had oil lamps. We swam in the canal some but mostly we swam in the creek.

In the winter we went sledding at Bannockburn right across from the school. And we used 78th Street too. It was a sizable hill and when it was sleeting or the snow was packed real well, we'd have a grand ride. We'd get down almost to the hill before it went down to the canal. We were taking a chance crossing Conduit Road, but there was very little traffic. One winter it snowed six inches or something then thawed on the top and froze enough to hold a sled. And when you started out you had no control whatsoever. I remember a sled coming down at Bannockburn as I was going up missed me by about a foot.

Dennis Tuohey served as Cabin John's postmaster for thirty-five years, until he retired in 1925. Then Mr. and Mrs. Charles Scott ran the post office out of their general

store at 77th and Conduit across from the Methodist Church until 1936. The Carpers, Wilbur and Irene, bought out the Scotts and took over both store and post office until 1942 when Ruth Tuohey Shuff brought the post office back to the family where it started. Laura McKelvey was postmistress from 1944 until 1972 in a small frame addition to her home on 77th.[110]

The first building used for community meetings, other than the old store, was the Junior Order of United American Mechanics Hall which even housed the third grade for one term. The "Juniors," as locals called it, was the site of many dances, dinners, parties and meetings until the firehouse was built in the early 1930s.[111]

Cabin John Park VFD was organized and incorporated in 1930 by Charles Benson and ten charter members who met at Mr. Benson's store cum court room on Conduit Road. The minutes of the first meeting were made on a brown paper bag, and later meetings were moved to the Clara Barton School. As it did with their neighbors to the south, the tragic Moxley fire provoked action in Cabin John.[112]

The first apparatus was a Model T pickup with a 100-gallon portable pump housed in a shed at 77th Street. That 4th of July the new fire company took part in the parade on Conduit Road featuring fire apparatus from many other companies. Then the Cabin John Boy Scouts, Troop 105 under P. T. Hannon's leadership, beat the Scouts from Bethesda in baseball.

The early years of the Cabin John fire department were marked by acrimony and division much of it a long-term dispute between Dennis Tuohey and A. A. Potter, which "Buzzy" Potter still remembers.

Tuohey was one of founders of the fire department. He and my dad went round and round. Dad was a teetotaler, and he wanted to put that beer parlor in there, and Pappy fought him. They locked horns. They both were in on organizing the fire department originally, but father finally bowed out. The records are downstairs. He was the fire department's letter writer, so he kept the records, the earliest ones.

The Cabin John Fire department had a problem about starting fires. We'd know from the inside grapevine who the hell did what. One served time for setting abandoned houses on fire. The hotel was another one of them, but nobody knows who did it.

In the spring of `31, the *Sentinel* reported that the fire department was "torn by internal dissention," and some communities along Conduit Road had asked to be put in the Bethesda fire district. Through the summer of 1933, the various fire department disputes tore the association apart, and Judge Benson and fire board president F. O. Day asked for increased and broader support. Reorganization was underway by mid-July after several officers resigned. At one point the board considered whether or not to ask all of the firemen to resign and start all over. By fall things had started to stabilize, and in October Donal Chamberlin, vice-president of the Cabin John Park Citizens Association, announced that the reorganization was almost complete.

Loretta Tuohey Hall and her younger brother Gordon Tuohey, the last of his family to run the beer joint, grew up with the fire department; it is in their blood.

Gordon said:

After they got started with a '29 Brockway that was built for Cabin John, they moved into a garage behind Scott's store across from the Methodist Church, to get it out from under the store on the other side of Conduit where you had to go down a hill and it was hard to get out in the winter.

Then my grandmother donated ground on the corner of Seven Locks Road and MacArthur, or Conduit Road at the time, for the construction of the old firehouse . . . . They owned about two acres from Seven Locks to 79th street where the shopping center is. There was $300 involved in it for the survey and the paper work. She was on her way to a meeting to sign the papers, when she had an attack and died.

"She and another friend had started walking," Mrs. Hall added. "She had a goiter and died on the back seat of a car."

Gordon Tuohey continued:

It was approximately sixty by ninety deep for old Company Ten. The fire companies are private corporations chartered by the state of Maryland. That's how the companies are numbered, in the order of incorporation. Cabin John is Company Ten; Glen Echo is number eleven. It was built by a lot of volunteer labor in `31-`32, even the bricks were donated. Later they added another bay. The cornerstone was moved to the new building, and the County got the money from selling the old building.

'The fire department used to be the hub of the community," Mrs Hall said. "You had the dances, the dinners, everything. You don't have that any more. We could have banquets at our old firehall for 200-250 people."

"Cabin John didn't have a fire taxing district until '42 or 43," Mr. Tuohey recalled.

"Daddy and Mr. Hanks went to Annapolis and got it," his sister said.

"Until then all the funds were raised by projects, even the apparatus was bought that way. The siren was hooked up to a telephone and when the phone rang, the siren took off."

"During the war," Loretta Hall said, "the siren was moved over to the beer joint."

Her brother nodded:

My father ran a beer tavern, which used to be my grandmother's store and the Cabin John post office, next door to the fire station. During the war, with the air raid drills and so on, you couldn't have someone calling the wrong number and that siren blowing until somebody pushed the button to turn it off. So my father had the phone moved over, and he intercepted all calls, and if it was a fire, he'd blow the siren.

Civil Defense in World War Two was the fire service. He had two phones behind the bar, one to Chevy Chase; they had a switchboard. Later they moved the phones to Glen Echo before the central alarm was put in. And then Glen Echo and Cabin John did runs together.

I was training officer for a number of years. A volunteer was issued equipment, and then it was on-the-job training and every Wednesday night was drill night.

Some times we'd get together with Glen Echo and burn a house down to drill on, one that was going to be torn down. We put out the word for anybody that wanted to come to a house burning if it was big enough.

We voted new men in. We could have only fifty by the original by-laws. And you had to be eighteen. And there were University of Maryland courses. Chief Giammatteo at Glen Echo taught some. If he was teaching the basic course, he let it be known, and we could send our men up to him. He had to have so many to make up the class. I've taken them over and over just to fill up a class. If we took in five volunteers, we might get one to stick after they found out how much work it was.

Only monies from the County, other than tax monies, back in the days of County Commissioners, was a maximum of $1,500 but you had to have one piece of apparatus with a 350

gallon pump or better for each $500. Cabin John had only one piece of equipment, back when my father was chief, this '29 Brockway, that could meet specifications, so we only could get $500. So he went down in the District and rigged up with the fire department to buy two old American LaFrance, solid tire, chain drive, right hand steering; they were 750 gallon pumpers. And he set them in our fire station, and we got $1,500. I think he got the two for $500.

In Glen Echo and Cabin John, at certain places on MacArthur Boulevard, and they used to be marked with a piece of round pipe, you had to dig down a foot or eighteen inches to get to a manhole where you could draft water out of the conduit.

"They gave us permission to go to those manholes," Mrs. Hall added.

"Or you went to the canal or a creek," Gordon remembered, "and run into relaying water. Of course, we are all river rats along Conduit Road. They called us that.

"The ladies' auxiliary, they'd get out and make us sandwiches and coffee if we were working a night fire. Most of the companies had good ladies auxiliaries, but Bethesda and Chevy Chase didn't when they were paid companies."

Mrs. Hall said, "We had a 4th of July parade and ham and chicken dinners. We had a ten burner stove, a double oven."

"Back when they would have chicken dinners, the only thing they had to buy would be the meats," Mr. Tuohey emphasized, "the rest was donated."

Said Mrs. Hall with a smile:

Daddy would go down to the market and buy chickens, no more than two pounds. And we'd cut them in half and fry them.

We won the trophy in 1931 in our beach pajamas. We won a big loving cup at a county convention. At the old fair grounds where Richard Montgomery High School is, they'd have a county meet. We competed with Gaithersburg. F. O. Day's wife drove the fire engine. He was working for the King Construction Company, building roads, and he brought trucks out and bulldozed the bank for the firehouse.

We fed the men off our back porch. That ramp in front and beside the fire station belongs to the Corps of Engineers.

The firehouse should have been on the corner, but there was a blacksmith on the corner and my grandmother wouldn't tell him to move,

and he died before it was built. That was Jimmy Williams, and he was in the fire company."

Gordon Tuohey laughed:

People who moved out here weren't used to those sirens, Cabin John was even accused of making a man's wife pregnant because the siren woke him up in the middle of the night. He blamed the baby on the siren, a man who lived down in Cabin John Gardens.

I joined at eighteen, in '43. When I was a kid I couldn't wait to join. I don't mind telling you that at one time it was known as the Tuohey fire company all through Montgomery County.

"My father and my two brothers," said Mrs. Hall, "and my mother was in the auxiliary and I was in there. My mother formed the auxiliary; we are charter members of the association."

"At one time my father was president, I was vice-president, and my brother was chief. And we were voted in by the membership. I'd say ninety percent of my leave was taken by the fire company. The volunteers did it because they enjoyed it," Gordon Tuohey concluded.[113]

By 1919 there were enough people in Cabin John to form a citizen's association which was reorganized in 1924 and in 1926 began collecting trash in the subdivision and dumping it in a gully behind the ballfield off Persimmon Tree Road. The association also organized scout troops, lobbied for street improvement and lights on Conduit Road, and worked to get a new school built. Charles H. Godbold, Walter B. Armstrong, Ellis R. King, and Andrew C. Wilkins, the first leaders of the Association, were known as "The Four Horsemen of Cabin John."

A. C. Wilkins said:

We talked with E. Brooke Lee, the political bigshot of the county, who had just returned from World War I. He was a Democrat. We let him know that we were all Republicans, but told him we were interested in the locality and in the people who were doing things for this locality, regardless of their political affiliation. He worked with us, and we petitioned to have a school of twelve rooms built.

It was also Mr. Wilkins who got the final piece of property needed for the new school.

When we did get the authorities to buy four acres from Mrs. Bobinger and were going to erect a school house there, we hit a snag. We

found out that J. S. Tomlinson had reserved ten feet outside the street area so that nobody could enter the acreage owned by Mrs. Bobinger — because she hadn't sold to him. The authorities had already sunk a well before they discovered this restriction barring access to the school site. They had bought the land, but they couldn't cross Tomlinson's footage in order to build the school. Tomlinson was critically ill at the time, but I talked with him, and he signed a deed granting the ten feet along First Street to Montgomery County.[114]

Cabin John's first school had been built in 1867 on a plot used as a cemetery for Irish laborers who died of cholera while digging the canal. The land, useless for farming, cost five dollars, and the community built and paid for a one-room log schoolhouse. A large, one-room, frame school known as Friendship was built uphill from the old building in 1885. It served as Cabin John's school until 1914. Edwin Broome, long-time superintendent of the County's public schools, had his first teaching experience in that school.

After 1914 Cabin John children walked across the bridge, some of them on the parapets to, as Pres Wedding put it, "test our nerve." They went to the Glen Echo School on Wilson Lane (then Cohasset Road) opposite Bannockburn where a Presbyterian church is now located. This building, remodeled in 1908, had been called the Concord School or Crockett's Academy.

One of its long-time and best-remembered teachers was "Old Man" Crockett who started teaching at 19 and retired in 1916 after thirty-five years of service. Dorothy Carow walked there by cutting across Bannockburn and fording the creek. She recalled a two-room school with a dark center hall. Crockett taught both Norman Tuohey and his father. All his ex-students recalled his strict ways.

Presley Wedding said that in 1919:

The principal's name was Mrs. Kramer. She had the fifth, sixth and seventh grades, I think. Her sister taught the lower grades, Miss Pyle. I went out there in the second or third grade. After a few years they built an additional room, and they hired a new teacher whose name was Miss Howard.

I graduated from there, and my mother didn't like the county schools too much so she sent me in town. Sometimes I'd get a ride with a neighbor who worked at the Bureau of Standards.

He always left late and went up Cohasset Road to River Road and went seventy, seventy-five miles an hour. First I went to Columbia Junior High at 7th and O Streets and then to Tech at 7th and I. Dad worked for a contractor in the District so we didn't have to pay any tuition.

Although many children attended D.C. schools at the time, "Crockett's Academy" soon became overcrowded. Classes were held at the Mechanics Hall in Cabin John and the Little Flower church/town hall in Glen Echo. The principal-teacher from 1925 was Guy Jewell, who worked for the Montgomery County Public Schools for fifty years. He rattled from one classroom to another in his Model-T touring car with an occasional stop at students' homes for a cold drink and sometimes a treat such as a slab of Mrs. Potter's gingerbread.

Jewell remembered the school well if not lovingly:

> *Three rooms heated by pot bellied stoves. The only ventilation system were little draft boards angled in at the windows and there were two exits, one front and one back. There was a wide center hall where everybody kept his coat in bad weather, and there was a pump out in the yard where you went to get a drink of water, and the toilet facilities were two little buildings at the far corners, at the back, of a one acre lot. There was not grading whatsoever. We had room to play dodge ball games or a softball game.*[115]

The bickering between Glen Echo and Cabin John as to the need for and location of a new school stopped after D.C. began excluding Maryland children. The Maryland House of Delegates passed Appropriations Bill 663 in 1927, and the area had its long-sought school. Guy Jewell came along as its principal. The six-room school house for eight grades, two met in the auditorium, won awards for its architect, Major Howard Cutler.

The invited Congressman never showed up, but, although he was late, E. Brooke Lee, the long-importuned leader who had listened to Cabin John's petitioners, spoke at the May dedication in front of the dark red velvet curtains the ladies of the Homemakers' Club had made with the help of upholsterer David Tuohey and his wife. Among the first graduates were Charlotte Smith, daughter of Mr. and Mrs. C. R. Smith, Loretta Tuohey of the best-known family in town, and Neal Potter, who had accepted the flag presented to the school

by the O.U.A.M. The next year the frame "Practice House" was finished but never used as it was intended, and in another year a second story was added. In 1942 Cabin John became a K-6 school, and junior high students were bused to Leland JHS in Bethesda.[116]

The first school for black children was built on Conroy Road in 1880 on a half-acre purchased for $10. Three years later the site of what was called Moore's School was enlarged when another quarter acre was purchased from J. D. W. Moore for $32.50. Teachers in this school, prior to the turn-of-the-century, included Edwin Gant, Celonia Offutt, Florence Johnson, William Luckett, Jennie Peters, A. J. Neverson, and Sadie Lyvers.

The Gibson Grove AME Zion Church was founded by ex-slaves in 1898. The original log cabin church stood south of the present building on Seven Locks Road. Sister Sarah Gibson, who donated the land for the church, started a one-room school there around the turn-of-the-century, and in 1911 the school board rented the Gibson Grove school and changed its name to Cabin John Elementary School. In 1922 the school was closed, and the community's twenty-four black children were left without a school. At parental request, in 1926 the school reopened at Moses Hall, and five years later the children were transferred to the new River Road School where Margaret Dorsey taught for a number of years.[117]

By then there was even a County high school for "colored students" if they could get to it. Of course it was only two rooms and some people said it looked like a chicken house.[118]

In 1922 Mrs. Anna Bartlett, who lived on Tomlinson Avenue, began the Cabin John Demonstration Club. Blanche Corwin of the Department of Agriculture, who had been doing home demonstrations at the County Fair, helped them get organized. Mrs. Smith recalled that "We were all people from town mostly, and she taught us how to start gardens and raise chickens. I'd never done any of that. Neal Potter's mother was an active member."[119]

By 1925 the Cabin John group had attracted twenty-five members and joined the Council of Homemakers Clubs. It not only actively participated in the ongoing campaign for a new school but also, with the help of spe-

cialists from Johns Hopkins, sponsored a series of baby clinics. "We had a clinic in the Glen Echo Fire House, and we had a regular nurse in charge of it–Miss Bodenhook," according to Mrs. Smith. "Every so often they'd have a doctor come over and examine whoever needed it, and the fee would be whatever they thought was right. I think this may be the most important thing we did."

In the 1930s the club operated a summer school for girls and spun off the Conduit Road Public Health Lay Committee. In 1941, with its membership increasing from the Brookmont and Mohican Hills areas, the organization changed its name to the Potomac Valley Homemakers Club.[120]

The Potters of Cabin John had originally come from Minnesota where both had graduated Phi Beta Kappa from the University. Alden Archibald Potter and his wife moved to Cherrydale, Virginia, when he took a job with the Agriculture Department. Neal was born there in 1914 and Lloyd in 1917. In August 1919 the Potter family moved to a thirty-five acre farm on the northern edge of Cabin John to raise a few crops and cows as well as their boys.

When he was old enough, Lloyd had a milk, butter, and egg route that reached down to the District Line as his father concentrated on the dairy herd after he left the government. A small inheritance from family-owned property in Minnesota insulated the Potters from dependence on the farm as well as from much of the Depression's pain, and when government regulations on the sale of raw milk became onerous, they quit farming.

A. A. Potter became a gadfly critic of the New Deal for its failure to deliver on its promises, and his stinging letters appeared regularly in the columns of the local papers and the in-baskets of bureaucrats. He even ran for the U. S. Senate once as a write-in candidate. Mrs. Potter was active in the school and other community affairs including the Homemakers Club of which she was president in 1930 when discussion of a farm women's market began.

In 1924-26 the Army Corps of Engineers laid a second conduit through Cabin John and down to the Dalecarlia Reservoir. This pipe was ten feet in diameter and could carry 100 million gallons a day into the growing capital city. Pres Wedding recalled:

It came right through our front yard. The steam shovels used to wake us up in the morning. They left manholes for access and built it all the way down to Cabin John Creek and then built this inverted siphon down across the creek.

Fortunately they left ladders out there so we'd climb down through a manhole and walk all the way through the conduit till it came out at the creek on the way to school. One morning there was a lot of mud at the end of this pipe, and it was real cold so I thought it was frozen over. I wasn't going to be chicken; I was going to walk across that mud up to solid ground. I got about halfway across and down I went up to my knees. I couldn't go back home so I scraped it off, got to school and made a point to sit by the old potbellied stove to dry off.

Traffic was detoured through the town and over a temporary bridge at the foot of Wilson Lane. The Corps ran the second pipe down into the Cabin John gorge and put the old creek in a pipe too. The two aqueducts are interconnected in three places to permit repairs without completely cutting water service. That odd traffic circle where Goldsboro Road meets MacArthur Boulevard at Glen Echo contains a set of pipes and valves connecting the two aqueducts.

For Cabin John the worst part of this experience, other than a smallpox scare, was that the pipe layers cut down the long row of fine cedars that had lined the old road from Benson's Store to the Cabin John Bridge. A lot of people never forgave the Army for that. On the Potter farm they had to blow up the sycamore roots with dynamite. The Potter boys gathered up the shattered sticks for kindling. By 1928 there were street lights on Conduit Road and a fight began for water and sewer service from the recently organized WSSC.[121]

Presley Wedding had a *Star* newspaper route in Cabin John in the `20s.

It started at the streetcar terminal where I picked up my bundle of papers and put them in my coaster wagon. Then I went up Conduit Road and did some houses in there, Wilson Avenue I think, and I served my own house, of course. I might have had fifty papers at one time. It was spread out, and I had to collect, too. The papers were two cents.

The Star sent the papers out in my uncle's name, Uncle Gene. Had to have somebody responsible, but I did the collecting and paid for the

papers. Didn't even have a receipt book. Sometimes I was successful and sometimes I wasn't. The Lanings down on the canal, whenever I'd collect from him, he'd give me a big tip, but whenever I collected from her, she asked for change. I served the Spongs, the lockkeepers. I delivered a paper to the Tuohey's store and sometimes spent a nickel there on a candy bar.

In 1929 the Bucolston Quarry opened at the bottom of Main Street. It was operated by Commerce Department attorney Hugh White, who had hoped to build houses on the stony ground. He produced stone used in many area projects including the underpass in Silver Spring and in the Calvert Street bridge. At one time about a dozen men were employed blasting, digging and delivering the rock. Complaints from the neighbors about the noise and the effect of blasting on their wells and the two-ton limit on Conduit Road ended the business in 1943, and Nettie Mae Burgess bought the fourteen acres.[122]

The Depression of the 1930s was made harder in the towns near the river by several destructive floods. Norman Tuohey recalled, "Practically nobody in Cabin John was working. They managed to get along somehow. Same as it was every place else. Hard hit. I know a dozen people lived there in Cabin John without paying rent. People just let them stay."

Knicker-clad, Buzzy Potter and his brother Neal pedaled bicycles to school in Bethesda every day. Buzzy noted:

It was very tedious all winter long on those long hills. I had printed a little newspaper when I was 10 or 11 years old, then went to raising white rabbits; then I went in the bicycle business, when I was 14-15, on the farm. When I turned 16, I got a motorcycle I could drive, had one when I was 15.

So I got interested in motorcycles with another guy, Austin White, and wrote a couple of letters, and they referred us to the dealers, so we got a pickup truck and went through Chevy Chase offering to clean out garages with old motorcycles in them for five dollars, and if that didn't work, sometimes paying them a couple of dollars for one. At 15 I'd saved about $110 dollars at 10¢ an hour to buy an automobile, but I put the money into buying and selling motorcycles, mostly in high school.

The other guy dropped out. He was very formal, wrote billheads and letterheads. In the de-

pression, no boy had any money, and you had to sell on credit. Motorcycles on credit had a high fatality rate, but we managed to struggle through getting documents signed in blood. The down payment was whatever I'd paid for it, the rest was gravy. By `42 I had a $5,000 profit, and I was cutting wood all winter and plowing victory gardens.

Mrs. Isaac Marshall, who came to Cabin John in 1923 when her husband was a foreman helping to build the second conduit, remembered the Depression:

When the depression came along, I think I had about thirty-two cents. My husband came home and told me he had no work. The banks were closed and the contractor he was working for -- F. O. Day -- they couldn't borrow money . . . and we had four boys . . . . It happened that we had a lot of stuff canned and put up, and we had our chickens and we had our eggs -- that was before feed got so high -- and that's what kept us from going hungry.

The Marshalls and the Tuoheys were among the leaders in getting the fire house built. After the flood of '36, dozens of area people were housed and fed at the fire house, and Mrs. Marshall recalled that some of the firemen did not like the Red Cross and the women's auxiliary taking over their building; "some of them got very cantankerous about it."

The flood of '36, which left many people homeless, is also recalled for one daring rescue. More than fifty years after the event, Al Jamison remembered it clearly. He had come to the area in the `20s as assistant pro at Bannockburn before moving down the road to work with Wiffy Cox at Kenwood, and he rented a room in Glen Echo.

I was in Glen Echo in the '36 flood. You could hear that water at night, the last night. I heard that roaring and got the hell out of there. They were getting people off the banks, and in the morning we were running all over in the fire trucks. And this woman was out there on that island off Glen Echo. They had told her not to go out there. She was a swimming instructor at the Shoreham, and she got stranded out there.

Next morning the water's up so high, she's setting on the roof with a board, a dog, and a newspaper. As the water came up she moved to a tree next to the house, put the board across the limbs and sat there with her dog and newspaper. And she kept going higher as the water rose. Finally it took the house down the river. And she's at the top limb and the water's a foot below her

feet. They called the Navy and they sent up six sailors with a steel boat. And they looked it over and told the fire chief, "I'm not going to take a chance of losing six lives for one."

And here a couple of drunks from Cabin John were standing around, and one says, "I can get that gal off that tree." And the other says, "I'll bet you a case of beer your can't." "You've got a bet," the first one says. He goes up to Cabin John where he's got this row boat, and he comes down through the trees rowing backwards.

The bet was to take the woman off the tree and bring her in at Sycamore Island. So he gets her off the tree, lots of people are watching now, and gets her into the rowboat, and the dog, and comes in to shore with all the people there. And the drunk is there waiting and yells, "This is not Sycamore Island."

"It isn't," he says. "Push me out again." He goes down to Sycamore Island with this gal. And the whole romance of this thing is she finally marries him.

The woman's name was Eva Dell Myers, and the man who got her out of the tree and married her a year later was William E. Swanson, an accountant from Cabin John. Swanson, described as a boatman with many years experience who had rowed on the varsity crew at college, and a younger man that Mr. Jamison forgot about, John McCann, did come down the roaring river at an estimated thirty miles an hour among the tree tops and amid the tumbling debris and rowed the woman to safety. There was nothing about a bet in the newspaper stories, and the word "drunk" was often lightly used when men from Glen Echo and Cabin John talked about each other in those days. They took pride in being called "river rats" and claimed that only out-of-towners ever drowned in the river or the canal.

The great flood of '36 almost wiped out the Sycamore Island Club, which had started in 1885 as a rather rowdy place for young men to enjoy the summer and had become a retreat for canoeists and their families to boat, roast oysters, and play tennis. It then had rules against firearms, alcohol and gambling and some forty stock-holding, dues-paying members. A letter from club secretary Rodger Gessford brought the bad news along with a reminder that the river had not reached such heights since 1889.

At this time, the flood waters at Sycamore are receding, but it seems quite certain that when in a few days they have dropped to a stage ap-

proaching normal, whatever is left of our club buildings will be scattered about the Island in wreckage. Practically all of the members' canoes had been moved into the clubroom, the highest point on the Island, but with the club-room torn loose and wrecked, it seems probable that most of the canoes and other personal property have been lost.

The secretary suggested that members who lost canoes "should be able to obtain one fairly reasonably in Georgetown—possibly your own." Despite the ongoing Depression, members pledged loans totaling $3,525 by the time of the April issue of "The Sycamore Islander" and eventually paid $4,205 into the rebuilding fund. The new, steel reinforced clubhouse was finished by August 1936 and withstood the floods of 1937 and 1942. The Club, more Washingtonian than Bethesdan, with its consistently bright, tongue-in-cheek newsletter, is another amazing local survivor.[123]

The 1936 flood also ended the odd relationship between the Town of Glen Echo and the inhabitants, some would say "squatters," on Cabin John Island and smaller Cedar Island. Cottages had been built on the islands prior to the First World War although the land belonged to the C&O Canal Company. Around 1917-18, without any legal authority, the Town "took in" the two islands as part of its territory at the request of those who lived and fished out there in the summer.

During Prohibition, two stills operated openly on Cabin John Island and one cottage became a much-too-popular speakeasy. The town fathers began regretting their de facto jurisdiction, fenced off some river landings and posted "no parking" signs on Cornell Avenue. The March `36 flood covered both islands and washed everything away, and when the islanders requested permits to make repairs and rebuild, their requests were rejected by Glen Echo which continued to act as proprietor until the Park Service acquired the canal and all its property.[124]

Late in the 1930s the U. S. Navy began looking for a site for a new basin in which to test models of ship hulls. At first the Bobingers' property appeared promising, but when that proved unsuitable, the Navy searched farther north where a residential community with a golf course was being planned for the old Robert Peter tract called Carderock.

Glen Echo and Cabin John, both to a major extent trolley line communities, never grew as

fast or as big or as successfully as did Bethesda and Chevy Chase or even the communities down Wisconsin. They disappointed their promoters.

Phyllis Theroux wrote of Cabin John that "no other town so close to D.C. looks less like a town close to Washington" and the same applies to Glen Echo. And that is how most of the people who lived there liked it. Some of those who came to these communities before the First World War were "rusticators" seeking an escape from the pressures of city life. They may not have found Arcadia, but what they built lasted.

*   *   *

It was the Baltzleys' and then Crosby's and WRECo's trolley line that helped build Glen Echo and Cabin John just as other electric rail lines encouraged the growth of many other Bethesda-area communities. But of all the streetcar lines, partly because it lasted so long, the Glen Echo line seems to hold a special place in the roster of long-abandoned tracks. Morris Fradin, one of the most diligent of Cabin John's historians, remembered the trolley ride better than many.[125]

At 37th and Prospect Streets in Georgetown, the motorman rapidly cranks his manual brake chains tight by whirling a large wheel. The car screeches to a halt over an underground pit. The heel of the motorman's shoe comes down hard on a floor button: GONG-G-G-G! There's a dull thud under the car and the third-rail plow is extracted. Like a decayed old tooth.

Lights and power go off and the passengers sit quietly in the gathering dusk, then blink their eyes when the current flows again, this time from the overhead copper wire, contacted by an outside worker who hoists a spring-loaded pole and wheel from atop the car roof. The air compressor motor for the brakes cluck-chugs alive.

Clang! Clang! There goes the all-clear gong in the pit beneath the car trucks. The motorman releases his hand brake with an ear-shattering crash, and the trolley rattles off into the woodlands of suburbia.

In its unique, never-to-be-forgotten fashion, the car lunges and bounces, jerks, creaks, sways, squeals, bobs, rocks, and rolls over rickety wooden trestle bridges, over culverts, through wooded areas, with glimpses of the Potomac River far below the hill of Georgetown University.

A cautious stop to cross MacArthur Boulevard in Foxhall Village, then clickety! clickety! Clack! through the Potomac Palisades.

You stare out the windows on the same Potomac River valley landscapes your grandparents viewed since 1896, when trolleys first made the breathtaking, picturesque sights possible. Then there were open "summer cars" -- until the 1930s -- with long, varnished benches running the width of the vehicle, while the conductor scurried the length of the outside running board, jingling his large leather purse and mysteriously searching out riders who had not paid their fares as they leaped up and into their seats at stops along the route.

(Need a transfer, punched to ride on another line -- like the Capital Traction Company transfer to the Washington Railway and Electric Company cars? That will cost you another cent.)
(*Punch, conductor, punch with care;
Punch in the presence of the passenger!*")
When "Old 701" screeches around the turns at high speeds, the wheel flanges squeal in the rail slots. And later, as the locked wheels shoot sparks, skidding up to a car stop sign, the smell of hot, ground sand comes up from the rails.

"All aboard!" calls the conductor, ringing off the fares of the boarding passengers as they scramble for seats or standing space, and the car creaks ahead. (One reads his newspaper, book, or magazine on once-upon-a-time streetcar rides. Or he would scribble notes for a thesis, study textbooks, snooze, or wink at a baby or a pretty girl across the aisle. Or gaze through the windows at ever-changing sights. It was quite restful. Even though your innards complained at the "bucking bronco" jolts. Yet --"the galloping ride among the trees gave many a child the thrill of a momentous excursion" rhapsodized the *Washington Post*, apparently unmindful that even its hardboiled reporter had grown lyrical, recalling his experience.)

Past the Georgetown Reservoir, the woods give way to quiet, quaint Sherrier Place. The perspective of glistening tracks stretches in parallel lines down the middle. And tall, wooden poles, supporting overhead wires, march down the sides of the street.

Then the car picks up speed. It whizzes past the backyards of Palisades homes, past greenhouses, pigeon cotes, fenced gardens, clotheslines fluttering with intimate apparel scarcely visible in the near darkness.

Past Dalecarlia with its reservoir. Through sleepy, quiet Brookmont. Swirling, streaky glimpses of the roiling Potomac at Little Falls. Then the sweet smell of honeysuckle. The young romantics aboard exchange glances. His hand seeks hers for an extra fond squeeze . . . .

Stops are made at sheltering shacks alongside the rails, where passengers sit and wait.

Past Glen Echo Heights. Then a final, swift race..clickety, clack!...clickety, clack!...across a trestle bridge, and through some woodland punctuated with hillside cottages. Around a bend -- and there, up ahead, glow the bright lights of the Glen Echo Amusement Park! -- land of enchantment for the young and young at heart.

A long pause at the gaudy entrance, while excited passengers stream off the car and enter the park to the strident tunes of the carousel. Its

crashing cymbals, wheezing pipes, and booming drum vibrate the heavy summer air.

There's the aroma of pink, cotton candy and "sticky" apples, the tantalizing scent of hot, roasted peanuts, buttered popcorn, and hot dogs -- even the smell of clean, chlorine-dipped humanity, fresh out of the swimming pool.

There's the whimper of tired children, the sleepy squalls of babes in arms, the excited jabber of youngsters gripping kewpie dolls and teddy bears: prizes won at the shooting gallery, the hoop throws, and knock-'em-down stalls.

The car jerks ahead again, empty now except for a few end-of-the-liners residing in Glen Echo, Fairway Hills, Bannockburn, and Cabin John.

A wooded island, girded by a loop of tracks, appears at the east end of the Cabin John Bridge. It serves as the terminal of the Route 20 line. Here, Mrs. Mary Bobinger operated a refreshment stand. Ever since her famous Cabin John Bridge Hotel burned down in 1931. The car conductor drops off a case of potato chips for her stand. Also mail sacks for the waiting Cabin John postmaster standing by his flivver.

The conductor twirled the car's destination signs to "Union Station." Then he goes outside for a breath of fresh air, a smoke, or a chat with the waiting passengers.

[1] *Bethesda Not So Old* by Gertrude D. Bradley, Chapter 23.

[2] Relying on States Attorney W. V. Bouic, the County refused to even pay the 1865 registrars.

[3] *A Grateful Remembrance*, McMaster and Hiebert (1976) Chapter 11. See p. 142.

[4] Much of this from Field's *Slavery and Freedom on the Middle Ground* (1985)

[5] See Chapter II of *Washington, Capital City, 1879-1950* by Constance McLaughlin Green (1963).

[6] See Capt. Thomas Hahn's *The Chesapeake and Ohio Canal: Pathway to the Nation's Capital* (1984) and his *The C&O Canal: an illustrated history* (1981).

[7] H. L. Offutt was one of the writer's great-grandfathers, Hilleary Lyles. The spellings are Boyd's.

[8] For many years "County Day" rather than the 4th of July was the "official" holiday.

[9] The Methodists, by far the fastest growing denomination in the County, are credited or blamed for making the County legally "dry" until 1933. See *A Grateful Remembrance*, pp. 196-7.

[10] Civil service employees: 1861-2,000; 1871-6,200; 1881-13,000; 1890-23,000; 1910-39,000

[11] Extra "hill" horses helped haul cars up the 15th Street hill and Capitol Hill.

[12] A modification of John White's chart, see p. 222 of the *Records of the CHS*, 1966-68.

[13] Kenneth T. Jackson, *Crabgrass Frontier* (1985), p. 108.

[14] See *Chronicles of Georgetown Life 1865-1900* from Seven Locks Press (1986), p. 108.

[15] From "A Trolley to Chevy Chase" by Walter E. Beach and Allen E. Beach, grandsons of A.J. Warner, 1983, in the collection of the Chevy Chase Historical Society.

[16] The contact with the B&O may have been through Nevada's Senator William Stewart.

[17] The "Lodge," would have been on Connecticut Avenue had it been extended straight from D.C.

[18] *The Town of Chevy Chase Past and Present* (1990). Probably the Bohrers held them up, see the early minutes of the Chevy Chase Land Company.

[19] See *The Electrical World*, Jan. 14, 1893.   Note Warner's previously quoted memo to Newlands.

[20] The office building on the same site beside the B&O tracks sits on the same angle.

[21] The dual drowing of 1912 was the biggest shock.   See footnote #93 of Chapter 5.

[22] *The Town of Chevy Chase; Past and Present* (1990).

[23] For more on the trolley line see *The Electric World,* Jan. 14, 1893. *Star*, Sept 15, 1935.

[24] Mary Mitchell, *Chronicles of Georgetown Life* (1986), p. 88.

[25] "The Kensington Line" by LeRoy O. King, Sr., Bulletin of NRHS, 1959.

[26] See John H. White Jr.'s article "Public Transport in Washington Before the Great Consolidation of 1902" in the *Records of the Columbia Historical Society*, 1966-68.
    The stuck motorman was Sumpter Embrey, a part-timer in the mid-thirties.

[27] *Star*, Aug. 28, 1899.   Bethesdan Warren Gingell, "Jingle," as the *Star* spelled it, was the conductor of the double-truck car that tried to pull the coal car up "pole hill" and out to Glen Echo that day.   Gingell was later a well-known local plumber, see chapters 7 and 8.

[28] In the 1890s and later there was much talk of double-tracking the line, but despite promises, it was never accomplished.   See *Sentinel*, July 22, 1892, and March 31, 1893.
    In January 1892 the Georgetown and Tenleytown RR Co. elected an interesting board of directors: Francis Newlands, Spencer Watkins, J. B. Henderson, J. E. Beall, John C. Davidson, J. Hite Miller, J. E. Mitchell, M. Willson Offutt, and Robert D. Weaver.

[29] See William G. Allman's "Bethesda Park: 'The Handsomest Park in the United States'" in *The Montgomery County Story*, August 1991

[30] Bethesda *Journal*, Nov. 10, 1939.   Miss Holman wrote that Howard later walked across Chevy Chase Lake on a tight rope when the scheduled acrobat was late arriving.

[31] *Star*, May 23 and June 7, 1892. *Sentinel*, May 13, 1892.

[32] Allman, *op. cit.*, who deserves much credit for his search of old newspapers.

[33] See the ads almost every week in the *Post* and occasionally in other papers.

[34] See *Old Bethesda*, p. 51, and the A. E. Shoemaker papers at Georgetown University.   Most Holman quotes from Oct. 27 and Nov. 3, 1939, editions of the Bethesda *Journal*.
    In September `92, Beall, Spencer Watkins and James B. Henderson were visiting the Park when the trolley frightened their carriage horses.   They bolted, the vehicle overturned, and Henderson was injured and treated at Beall's house.   *Sentinel*, Sept. 9, 1892.

[35] Local option, which divided the Peter-led Democrats, finally passed in 1880. See note 9 above.

[36] *Sunday Star,* Feb. 22, 1931.

[37] Shoemaker papers at Georgetown University.   That is how he spelled "balloon."

[38] *Sentinel*, June 18, 1893.   The proprietors' signs read "Private park for white people only."   They claimed that "the presence of colored people would cause the whites to discontinue their patronage."   On the first Sunday of the new policy "the cars brought up the usual large crowd of colored people from the District, who were so thoroughly mad when they reached the park and learned of their exclusion that an impromptu indignation meeting was held on the roadside and white people in general were denounced."

[39] See *Post* ads in June and July `93 and *Sentinel* of Oct. 13, 1893.

[40] *Star*, September 5, 1894.

[41] Most of the fire information from the *Sentinel* , Oct. 12, 1894 and the *Star* of Oct. 9, 1894.

[42] Katherine Peter Offutt, Hilleary's wife and the writer's grandmother, had three young sons she put to bed in the potato bins in the cellar as well as a five-month-old daughter to care for when the storm hit the house on the hill and deposited its roof a half-mile up the Pike.   The story of this long-ago hurricane is one of the few from that time still told in the family.

[43] The pillars were still there bracketing Sonoma Road until Old Georgetown Road was widened in the 1960s.   Leon J. Kosofsky ("Oakmont and Sonoma: Two Bethesda Neighborhoods and Their Common Heritage," 1981) claims to have found the foundations of the razzle-dazzle in his

research and has pictures to back up his assertion.   Millie Imirie recalled the glass insulators on back yard trees, and Kay Keating's family found pieces of stained glass on their Sonoma lot.

[44]Offutt's Station on the trolley line was at Georgetown Prep/Golf Lane.

[45]And the route and alternating schedule of Metro's Red Line seventy years later.

[46]There is an undocumented story of a motorman who leaned too far out where the tracks turned sharply and was tossed from the car which proceeded on into Rockville without him.

[47]From Mr. Kosofsky's research at MCHS, used with permission.

[48]When the Capital Transit streamliners and the PCC cars were introduced with one-man operation, loops such as the one at Wisconsin and Western had to be built.

[49]See *Sentinel*, August 28, 1891, and April 1, 1892.

[50]Its vandalized walls lasted well into the Sixties, and large stones in yards throughout the area came from its remains.   The forty-foot retaining wall and a few stone fragments remain.

[51]Mark Shoemaker recalled "many happy hours riding a forgotten hand-car down the tracks along now Willard Avenue – also many unhappy hours pushing it back up again."

[52]The quote and most of the trolley car information from Leroy King Jr.'s *100 Years of Capital Traction*. (1972), the undoubted "Bible" on these many companies.   The collision on the Great Falls line occurred on the evening of August 22, 1899, and later that evening a car was derailed near the Rock Spring Hotel - *Star* Aug. 23, 1899.
The last Glen Echo streetcar run was early on Sunday, Jan. 3, 1960.

[53]Ann Paterson Harris in *The Potomac Adventure* (1976) makes a good case for Captain John Smith, see pp. 35-36.   But the Justice Department concluded Captain John stated it referred to "an Indian of prominence who lived in the valley where the stream runs."   *Sentinel*, Nov. 19, 1926. Or he may have been a pirate.   Until the 1930s land purchasers agreed to give up half of any treasure they found buried on their property.

[54]In 1911 the Corps of Engineers ended this practice, surprised to find that it had been going on.

[55]The gas house, a small red brick building now used by the park service as a storage shed, was where calcium carbide was mixed with water to form carbide gas that was pumped to the hotel for illumination before electricity arrived with the trolley cars.   It was later converted into a springhouse. The other outbuildings, like the hotel, were made of wood.   Also see Edith Armstrong's paper, "The Cabin John Community" (1947)   and Edith Armstrong and Rev. Willis Bergen's "Cabin John and the Bobingers" in *The Montgomery County Story*, August 1964.

[56]Until the 1920s the enforcement of local option prohibition was very loose, and even during national Prohibition,   Maryland was known as the Free State for its attitude.

[57]Quotes from Kytle's *Time Was*.   Gingell story from MCHS collection.
The best description of the closed hotel is in Virginia Burbank Angel's article in the Sunday *Star* of Oct. 6, 1929, illustrated with two of the Bobinger's photos.

[58]See Montgomery County land records, libers JA 20-25, and the microfilmed Baltzley ledgers at the Clara Barton Historical Site which are the source of all references to the "books."
According to long-time resident Sarah Canada, Edward Baltzley named Glen Echo after he and some friends walking through the area found that their "voices echoed continually" in the glen; see her letter in the *Journal*, June 7, 1940, and J. Manuel Espinosa in "The Echo," May 1984.

[59]The following insurance payments are recorded in the Baltzleys' ledger at the Clara Barton house: Guardian Assurance Co. $2,475, Liverpool & London Ins. Co. $4,950, North American Ins. Co. $2,475, Phoenix Hartford $1,980, Niagara Ins. Co. $4,950, Eliot of Boston $2,475, and a handwritten note refers to a total of $24,255 for the Patawomeck.

[60]All the Edwin Baltzley quotes and descriptions are from his 1891 pamphlet *Glen Echo on the Potomac, The Washington Rhine*.

[61]See liber JA 25 folio 253 of the Montgomery County land records.   Land was reserved along the canal and the aqueduct for railroads.

---

62 The tower of the gatehouse complex, along with the first floor of the Chandler-designed "caretaker's house," is almost all that survives from the original Chautauqua construction.. The Baltzleys may have paid Mendeleff in building lots or perhaps the architect invested in Glen Echo Heights. Lots one through six of block one, valued at $8508.98, were deeded to him in June 1890 and another 45,000 square feet at a dollar per square in August 1890.

63 In 1956 what was left of the rotting amphitheater was burned and local firemen were allowed to practice on the ruins. The remains of the huge building along with the creek were buried under a new parking lot. Some 33 years later, in May 1989, fragments of the old stonework were revealed when Minnehaha Creek had the last laugh and swept away the parking lot and sixty-eight automobiles, some of which were carried all the way to the Potomac.

64 March 1891 had a record setting nine inches of rain.

65 *Sentinel*, April 10, 1925. Hubbell lived over Canada's store during the court battle and sometimes tended the counter. See "The Echo" July 1976 and August 1977.
The house and grounds are now administered by the National Park Service, which received the home from the Friends of Clara Barton in 1975. The amusement park had offered the Franks sisters $50,000 for the property with the intention of tearing down the house and enlarging their parking lot, but a volunteers saved it in 1964.

66 Letter from Sarah E. Canada in Bethesda *Journal*, June 7, 1940. Henry C. Spencer, purchased Lot 9 of block 22 from the Baltzleys in April (JA25/343).

67 A new Maryland statue with both a Northern and Southern soldier represented, the only one of its kind, was dedicated in 1994.

68 *Star*, July 5, 1891. This is just the start of a much longer story.

69 Mostly from the *Star* of June and July 1891 and Benjamin Levy's 1967 National Park Service study, "Glen Echo: Chautauqua on the Potomac" republished by the Town of Glen Echo in 1968 which also reports some popular misconceptions.

70 See George Freeman Pollock"s *Skyland* (1960). He was a timekeeper for the Baltzleys.

71 Obviously the Baltzley books need the attention of a historian/accountant which the writer is not.

72 *Sentinel*, March 18, 1892, and April 22, 1892.

73 July 9, 1893, letter in Shoemaker papers at Georgetown University.

74 Washington *Post*, July 9, 1893.

75 The *Evening Star*, July 24, 1897.

76 The *Evening Star*, June 20, 1937, Holman in the Bethesda *Journal*, April 26, 1940.

77 Unpublished reminiscence used with permission of LeRoy O. King, Jr.

78 *Star*, Aug. 15 and 17, 1899. Some of the right-of-way can still be traced near the Glen Echo post office and town hall.

79 Interview with Rena Hubbell in "The Echo" April 9, 1949. See Louis Jacobson's historic houses articles in the Bethesda *Gazette*, Oct. 26, 1989, and the essays on "significant" Glen Echo houses in "The Echo" in 1982-3-4. See also Echo articles by J. M. Espinosa in Aug. and Sept. 1986.
At least one of the "castles" had secret passages hidden in its thick walls, great for games of hide-and-go-seek as Mickey Johnston remembered.

80 Garret won the first election with 36 of the 38 votes and re-election in 1906 with 36 of 41 ballots. See "The Echo," August and September 1986. The other early mayors: 1909-10 William H. Roach, 1910 Clarence Wilson, 1910-11 Oltho James, 1911 L. C. Witkowski, 1911-13 Robert Lee Garrett, 1913-14 F. Lombard Woodward, 1914-16 Wm. H. Roach, 1916-18 Oltho James, 1918-19 Harry Houghton, 1919 Jacob J. Decker, 1919-20 Harry Houghton, 1920-26 J. J. Decker, 1926-39 Harry T. McCuen, 1939-48 Beulah H. McCuen.

81 In 1926 Clayton Lambert, 19, was killed on the Derby Racer when he stood to catch his hat, fell out of his car and had his right leg cut off by the next car. One of Frank Finlon's daughters told Richard Cook the story about the Hydraulic Dive. Her father, who hated roller coasters, had to ride the thing hundreds of times until they got it right.

[82] *Sentinel*, June 13, 1913.

[83] The style 165 organ, the largest model, is one of only ten survivors of the type. It has 256 wooden pipes and a multitude of metal ones, including reeds, plus drums and a glockenspiel. A deer, a tiger, a giraffe, a lion, a zebra, thirty-eight horses, four ostriches, and four rabbits also grace the merry-go-round.

[84] Lillian Gloyd Offutt is the writer's mother and most of this is her story.

[85] During the final stage of park operation the ballroom became the Jungleland ride, but it is now being restored and enjoyed as it was in the 30s and 40s.

[86] See the National Register of Historic Places - Nomination Form at the MCHS and "The Glen Echo Amusement Park" by Mary Charlotte Crook in *The Montgomery County Story*, August 1986 and "The Glen Echo - Cabin John Area" by Roger S. Cohen, Jr. in the August 1964 issue of *The Montgomery County Story*.
A few of the Chautauqua pipes ended up in Keith's big organ downtown.

[87] Originally all this land had been part of "Friendship," which was purchased by Thomas Brooke about 1817. A number of Brookes and Shoemakers farmed the area by the time of the Civil War.

[88] "Mickey" Johnston: ". . . back over the hill were ten or fifteen two-story wooden like-barracks, 60-70 feet long, over toward Glen Echo from the fort, on the other side of a ravine from the house. Janet's father had leased them all out to black families, must have been a hundred people in that area."

[89] Baltzley Castle and Charles Castle, named for the Treasury Department official who bought it, are owned and have been restored by a doctor and his wife, and the third house, known as "Blue Stone," is also privately owned.

[90] "Oakdale Villa" by Carlotta Andreson and Nettie Mae Burgess in "The Echo" April, May and June, 1976. Burgess, who lived in a Brookmont cottage, spent forty-eight years in the real estate business. She also wrote the "Along Conduit Road" column of social notes for County weeklies.

[91] "History of the Congregation" by Senior Warden Maude Rollins Pryse in the Gold Anniversary pamphlet published in 1953 and *Historical Sketches of the Parishes and Missions of the Diocese of Washington*, 1928.

[92] Mrs. Atkins to Mrs. O'Callaghan in Little Flower's, "Rose and Thorns," September 1974.

[93] See Chapter 3 for early history. Mostly from Mrs. Julius Ausen's "A History of Concord Methodist Episcopal Church."

[94] Other charter members: Bakers, Selby, Weddings, Davis, Eicketts and Paul Connelly.

[95] Edytha B. Weil, "Cabin John United Methodist Church 1921-1971."

[96] Much of the above including the Toone, Klopp and the Carow materials is from Morris Fraden's papers at the MCHS and used with permission. For more on life in Glen Echo in the early days see the series of 1980 articles by Dorothy Carow Merrick in *The Echo*.

[97] *Sentinel*, Aug. 21, 1975.

[98] There had been a post office in operation during that one Chautauqua summer, which was re-established in 1897. Van B. Canada became postmaster five years later. The Canadas are also remembered for donating the land across from their store and home for the town hall. See "The Echo" November 1975 and March 1982.

[99] Mostly from Appendix I of *Bannockburn*

[100] *Sentinel*, June 6, 1930 and Dec. 4, 1931.

[101] See "The Echo" April 1987. Writer Ronnie Vine was better known for his long conversations with the town's resident ghost, Mr. Weems. See "The Echo" April `78 to June `79 *et. seq.*

[102] The well-constructed building with new windows and the fire engine doors bricked up is now a Methodist Church.

[103] To Mrs. Kytle, see below.

[104]This material and all the following interviews credited to Mrs. Kytle are from *Time Was* published by the Cabin Johns Citizens Association in 1976 and are reproduced by permission of Elizabeth Kytle who holds the copyright.

[105]See pages 6-14 of *Time Was*. Otho Swain built Ike's putting green at the White House. Lock 21 is Swain's Lock; it and the road were named for Otho Swain's father.

[106]Kytle, *Time Was*, pp. 58-59. The fire was called in at 2:45 am and eventually seven County fire departments and No. 29 from D.C. fought the blaze.

[107]The Washington Aqueduct police began in 1916 and continued until Montgomery County took over the road in 1975, a move long desired by the Corps of Engineers.

[108]*Cabin John Park*. The "insurance feature" offered the deed or full cash refund on the purchaser's death before full payment was made. Lots went for one to four cents a square foot.

[109]See *Chautauqua '76: The Bicentennial in Cabin John*, a souvenir program.
Cabin John Park: 7 Miles from the White House. A Picture and Paragraph Story. Facts and Comments. Prices and Terms. n.d. MCHS from Morris Fradin collection.

[110]After all its moves, the post office is still in hollering range of where it started.

[111]Much of this from long-time resident Edith Armstrong's *Cabin John Community* (1947).

[112]Other charter members, see plaque in the firehouse, were B. G. Brann, L. Atwell, H. T. Davis, N. Lynch, J. Lynch, J. Lowe, C. Magruder, N. Hunt, J. Sipes, and E. Magruder.

[113]A bronze plaque in the new firehouse lists the early chiefs: 1930-31 - N. Lynch, 32 - G. Sullivan, 33 - D. S. Tuohey. 34-5-6 - C. Kipps, 37 - J. Sullivan, 38 - W. Curtain, 39 - N. Hunt, 40-41 - K. Tuohey, 42 - N. Hunt, 43 - D. Tuohey, 44-45-46 - D. S. Tuohey.

[114]Kytle, *Time Was*, pp. 47-48.

[115]Oral history at County Archives.

[116]See E. Guy Jewell's *From One Room to Open Space* (1976), Mrs. Armstrong's "Cabin John Community," and the Morris Fraden papers at the MCHS.

[117]Gibson Grove's "new" church was built in 1923. Nina Clarke's *19th Century Black Churches,*.

[118]*History of the Black Public Schools of Montgomery County, Maryland 1872-1961* by Nina H. Clarke and Lillian B. Brown (1978) contains some valuable first-hand accounts.

[119]Other charter members: Mrs. C. R. Smith, E. W. Maxim, Edith Armstrong, Charlotte Potter, Loretta Norton, and Lelia Kenney.

[120]See Mrs. Kytle's interview with Mr. and Mrs. Smith in *Time Was*.

[121]See Michael Dolan's "By the Waters of Palisades" for a good description of laying the second pipe and of the whole system. *City Paper*, June 7, 1991.

[122]See Peter Camplair's story in the Cabin John *Village News,* Aug. 1971.

[123]A fine collection of the papers of The Sycamore Island Club, including its bulletin from Vol.1 No.1 in Dec. 1921, may be found at the Historical Society of Washington, D.C.

[124]"Cabin John Island" by J. Manuel Espinosa in "The Echo" December 1988.

[125]From the Morris Fradin papers at the MCHS, reprinted with permission.

CHAPTER 5

Chevy Chase Is Different

Shortly after the inauguration of President Benjamin Harrison, Major George Augustus Armes, USA (ret.) found himself in trouble again. While concluding another highly successful real estate transaction at one of Washington's best hotels, he noticed that a reception hosted by Governor Beaver of Pennsylvania was in progress. The Governor had been chief marshal of the inaugural parade, and Major Armes had served as his volunteer aide and had been named a colonel in the Pennsylvania militia, a title he often used thereafter.

Somehow Armes's name was omitted from

Major George A. Armes

the list of those to parade up the Avenue, but Governor Beaver arranged that Armes, resplendent in his best uniform, should greet the new President and accompany him to the Capitol for his speech. It was after the Harrison's address, when Armes mounted his horse and the parade began, that two of Beaver's staff, in Armes' words "charged upon me," and ordered him off Pennsylvania Avenue and out of the parade. "My first impulse," wrote Armes, "was to shoot them both." But he withdrew and the next day demanded an explanation and apology from Governor Beaver.

Washington historian John Clagett Proctor produced a more colorful description of the event:

> In the course of the parade, which was held during a cloudburst, Gov. Beaver had discovered Maj. Armes caracoling up the Avenue in the rain, resplendent in his handsome uniform of major of cavalry of the grand old Indian-fighting army of the `70s and early `80s. This uniform included a yard-long yellow horse hair plume, which was a white hair plume dyed a brilliant yellow. Gov. Beaver had ordered Maj. Armes removed from the parade and that retired officer was furious at the rebuke.[1]

Now, three weeks later and after an exchange of increasingly terse notes, the smiling governor swung his wooden leg across the carpeted reception room and shook the hand of his war-time friend. The unsmiling Armes dropped the governor's hand and preemptively demanded an apology. The jovial governor suggested that they "let it drop." Armes then stated his opinion of the State of Pennsylvania and of that commonwealth's officials,

both appointed and elected, and commented loudly to the governor that there was nothing that could be done about it because of the difference in their stations.

Beaver, jaw clenched, growled that he would put "himself down on the same platform" with Armes and that then he "could do his damnedest." Armes snarled that he resented that, and while the dignitaries stood amazed and the ladies gasped behind their ivory fans, Armes reached out, grabbed Governor Beaver's nose and gave it "a vigorous twist." Pandemonium ensued. Women screamed, glasses crashed to the floor, and Armes struggled with the men who had grabbed him and were threatening to thrash him then and there.

Cooler heads prevented more violence as James Beaver, who lost a leg at Gettysburg during the repulse of Pickett's charge, stood red-faced, held back by two of his aides. Armes shook himself to straighten his clothing, and amid a buzz of voices as people who had seen the insult explained what had happened to those who had not, he stomped from the room as if he were on some dusty parade ground. Order was restored, chairs were righted, glasses were refilled and the music began again.

A generation earlier, although it would have been illegal almost everywhere in the U.S., that nose tweaking would have called for some sort of satisfaction and, in many cases, a sub-rosa duel. It was, as Armes and Beaver and certainly all gentlemen south of Mason and Dixon's Line knew, a dreadful and almost unforgivable insult.[2]

Armes was court-martialed less than two weeks later for behavior unbecoming an officer and a gentleman and quickly found guilty. As part of his punishment, he was restricted to the immediate vicinity of the Capital City and had to obtain written permission to travel more than fifty miles from Washington. And he was prohibited from wearing his uniform for five years.

Major Armes protested the negative effect the travel restriction would have on his thriving real estate business, but it may well have been the loss of the uniform that hurt more deeply. George Augustus Armes loved the Army, and he reveled in the polished boots and gold braid, the colorful aigrettes and swags of aiguilettes, the tasseled epaulets, and French lace frogs framing big, brass buttons.

Most of his adult life had been spent in the U.S. Army fighting various of his country's enemies as well as numerous friends and superior officers like Governor James A. Beaver.

A few days later Armes received a $300 gold medal from a group in Pittsburgh inscribed to him "in approval of his pulling Gov. Beaver's nose." The Army demanded that he return it and threatened another court martial, but Armes said he would not give it back for $10,000 and then went on to use the medal and his stated position in real estate ads. The Army gave up.

In his self-published autobiography *Ups and Downs of an Army Officer*, Armes kept track of his wounds, awards, arrests, enemies and court martialings. During the Civil War he took part in most major eastern actions from First Bull Run to Early's attack on Washington and finally to Appomattox, and emerged wounded twice, arrested eight times and, in 1865, court martialed.

He stayed in the Army, secured a commission in the 2nd Cavalry, and went to the Kansas frontier to fight the Indians and the U.S. Army. He was arrested eleven more times by 1869 when he was dismissed from the Army after his fifth court-martial despite being defended by Yellow-hair, the "boy general" George Armstrong Custer.[3]

Having exhausted his savings in his defense, Armes came to the Capital to plead his case with the War Department and the politicians. He entered the local real estate business just as the boom of the early 1870s began and prospered almost at once. In 1873, for example, he made $24,662.50 on a single transaction and cleared $63,000 for the year at a time when few government clerks made $1,000 annually, few Federal officials $2,000, and there was no income tax.

He waded deeper into the real estate business while he sought to regain his commission. By 1874 Armes owned fourteen houses in the city, hundreds of acres and dozens of building

lots in Maryland, and $25,000 in stocks and bonds. At age thirty, he married Lucy Hamilton Kerr of Maryland and began siring his large family.

My Children.

During Grant's administration, Armes, according to his own account, helped to bring down Secretary Belknap, and in 1876 President Hayes restored his commission. At Fort Stockton, Texas, after several more arrests and two more courts-martial, a medical board forcibly retired Armes in 1883. He then returned to his real estate business full time while again trying to clear his name and regain his command through political means. By 1885 Armes was dealing with the likes of Washington McLean, Secretary of the Navy W. C. Whitney, and Judge Dean who authorized the sale of his prime Washington Heights property for $100,000. Then came the Harrison parade, the Beaver imbroglio, and the ninth and final court-martial.

It was while he was under broad house arrest, perhaps while pacing the fenced walk on the roof of the large, country house he had recently purchased, that the idea arose. Without much success, he had been trying to convince his farmer-neighbors to build a long driveway some two miles into the city. His new home, "Fairfield" was on a Grant Road hilltop, and it was in that isolated, rural retreat that feisty Maj. George Augustus Armes invented Chevy Chase. At least that is what his granddaughter, Edith Claude Jarvis, believed. She called him a "dreamer" and told Town of Chevy Chase historian William Duvall that the idea came to him "between court martials."

Armes stated that by December 1889:

I was trying to find capitalists to purchase a tract of land that I have secured the prices of in order to get Connecticut avenue extended to the District Line. I have talked to a number of men of means in New York, Boston, Chicago, and Philadelphia, trying to induce them to go into the enterprise, and have figured up the cost of the land, the building of a road and stocking of it, including bridges, and it will require $3,500,000, but I propose to persevere until I succeed.

Armes received written permission to travel on business at the time, so he may have done just what he said. In his diary entry for the day after Christmas 1889, he wrote "took a drive with Sen. Hearst this afternoon, trying to get him to take hold of my Connecticut avenue project. He gave me considerable encouragement."[4]

Sometime during the night of New Year's Day 1890, Armes awoke with the thought of Senator Stewart of Nevada, who had made a name for himself in Washington real estate circles almost twenty years previously by building in the then-remote Dupont Circle area. The Senator's five-story, castle-home on the circle with its seventy-foot ballroom and dining room that seated 200 was long called Stewart's Folly, but now the land he and his California friends had scooped up and built on was worth ten times what they paid for it. Armes lit his bedside candle, wrote down Stewart's name and went back to sleep.[5]

The next evening he called on the tall, silver-bearded Senator at the Shoreham and finally got in to see him at about 11 pm. He

Senator William Stewart

laid out his Connecticut Avenue plan and his cost estimates for the land and a cable or electric railroad and said that he believed the senator "could clear $10,000,000 or $15,000,000 within fifteen or twenty years." According to Armes's account, Senator Stewart, who had a well-earned reputation for fast dealing in dubious mining stocks, looked over the maps and figures and stated that it was the "best scheme that had been proposed to him in years, but that he could not raise over $100,000 individually."

He thought over the names of several of his capitalist friends, and finally stopped at the name of F. G. Newlands, who represented the Sharon estate, and wrote a dispatch suggesting to him if he would take hold of it we could carry the scheme through. After some little talk on the details and the price of land, and agreement that this must be kept perfectly secret and out of the newspapers was made, I parted with him at 3 o'clock, with his request that I call on him at 10 o'clock that evening.

So late on January 3, 1890, it began. Newlands, a leading lobbyist of the silver interests, approved the plan, and Stewart wrote out a $35,000 check, payable to bearer, and told Armes to hire his own lawyers and to title the property in his own name and to keep both Stewart's and Newlands' names out of the transactions and the land records. Armes leased a building at 1405 F Street, had it "nicely furnished," hired clerks, stenographers, and two young lawyers with solid real estate backgrounds and some connections to Stewart's coterie.[6]

And then with Newlands' fortune behind him, Major Armes began buying property along the line of Connecticut Avenue extended from Florida Avenue to Jones Bridge Road and as far west as Tenleytown. "What a hey-day he must have had," his granddaughter wrote, "spending other people's money — going from farmer to farmer, bargaining and making settlements left and right."

Armes, under a written agreement made early in the negotiations, received a ten-percent commission on the sale of the property accumulated and could keep whatever commission he might get from those who sold property to the syndicate. Day after day, all that winter, he traveled the country lanes with attorney Edward H. Thomas bundled in a fur lap robe beside him. He paid Thomas twenty dollars a day to close "each transaction with

an iron-clad agreement" that no court could break.

Night after night he met with Stewart and Newlands, who authorized the purchases in huge chunks, often early in the morning. Some offers were rejected or counter-offers made. Some land owners refused to sell or wanted too much and were passed over. Some desirable land was tied up in estates, in the hands of dilatory executors. But piece by piece, farm by farm, parcel by parcel hundreds of acres quietly changed hands in just a few months.[7]

The generally accepted story of the start of Chevy Chase involves the same dramatis personae, but the script, the time and the setting are a bit different. In the summer of 1886 or perhaps `87, according to two of Chevy Chase's early and respected historians, Edith Claude Jarvis and Thomas E. Robertson, as well as Newlands' authorized biographer, Albert Atwood, Maj. Armes invited Senator William M. Stewart of Nevada and his friend, Francis Newlands of San Francisco, to visit Fairfield. Armes took these gentlemen upstairs and showed them the view from the top of his remarkable home. Over the trees and fields to the south they could see the Capitol, the White House, and the recently completed Washington Monument with the Potomac River shining behind it. To the west rolled away the misty hills of Virginia, and to the north and east stood nothing but woods and farmland dotted with isolated red brick chimneys and slowly turning windmills.

Armes, the stories go, observed that if Connecticut Avenue were to be extended into Washington County and then on out into the wilds of Maryland, the road would pass almost directly by his home. He suggested that a suburb could be built near the District Line at the end of such a road, and a model community created that would increase the value of all the property between it and the city. The acreage was relatively cheap and available in large parcels, affirmed the Major. It would involve a huge land purchase and the construction of a railroad, but it should prove extremely profitable.

According to the now-much-told tale, Armes pointed to the north and with a dramatic and sweeping gesture said, "Here, gentlemen, is where you should develop the finest suburb in America." And Newlands decided to do it.[8]

It may have happened that way, but if it did, Armes forgot to put the event into his diary-autobiography, and he was not shy about making ex-post-facto claims for his own farsightedness. Armes did not move his family from the Wormley house, which his wife did not like, into his greatly enlarged Fairfield home until September 10, 1890, and by then his relations with Newlands and his syndicate were much cooled if not severed. Of course, he could have used the roof of the home while it was being remodeled since he acquired the property in May of 1886 for $15,000 cash and a lot in the city. In his printed diary there is no mention of buying any other property along the Connecticut Avenue line until early 1890.[9]

If, as Atwood and Professor Roderick French suggest, Newlands "was possessed of a vision" of limitless suburban development back in the `80s, he does not seem to have told anyone except for his oft-quoted belief that all development was westward. So it is not clear when the decision was made, but in January and February of 1890 Major Armes was astride one of his fine horses or in the rig behind an impressive matched pair visiting homes from the Rock Creek Valley to the Clean Drinking tract expressing his interest in purchasing farmland.[10]

Inside the city, other strawmen led by Edward Stellwagen, an agent as well as son-in-law of the president of the Thomas J. Fisher Company, bought up property north of Boundary, or as it was now being called, Florida Avenue, and had it registered in their names. C. C. Glover of the Riggs Bank recommended Stellwagen to Newlands. Glover himself had more than an academic interest in the Newlands-Stewart project since he owned a good bit of land just west of the proposed extension of Connecticut Avenue. Out in Montgomery County, George Hamilton, a rising young lawyer, seems to have acted on behalf of the syndicate in the purchase of 140 acres of the No Gain property from Hilleary and Kate Offutt in March 1890 and others undoubtedly bought land for the Sharon syndicate.[11]

The Dean property at the top of the hill at Kalorama posed an early problem, but out in Washington County and across the line in Montgomery County, land was being gobbled up for as little as three or four hundred dollars an acre. However, Captain John F. Rogers

rejected a $100,000 bid for the 300 acres still in the Belt or "Chevy Chase" tract before selling when the offer increased by fifty percent to a bit over $500 per acre. The ownership of the large Bradley farm was so tied up in a will and estate settlement that its unavailability may have determined the due-north route of Connecticut Avenue in Maryland and the creation of Chevy Chase Circle.

Secrecy was the key to the operation, but as deeds were recorded and transfers were noted, the real estate industry and the Washington press corps began to talk and wonder who was buying and why. Since G. A. Armes's name appeared on a number of the early transactions, the reporters came to him. As much as he loved publicity, he turned them away and refused even to speculate about what was happening beyond Dupont Circle. He was just enlarging his holdings, he told the curious.

But a fever burned in him, and he must have loved the story in the *Post* that March that named him the "Napoleon of his calling" under the headline "King in Real Estate." The article, complete with a three-quarter length portrait of the Colonel in full dress uniform including the plumed helmet, said his operations were "enormous, and his transactions, especially of late, are the heaviest ever reported in the District." The paper concluded with a list of some forty sales Armes had negotiated in the first two months of 1890 including the purchase of the Belt tract and a number of other properties that later became part of the acreage owned by the Chevy Chase Land Company.[12]

Meanwhile the promoters of Rock Creek Park and those interested in finding a home for the Smithsonian's growing menagerie (grazing buffalo on the Mall was becoming a problem) were pressuring Congress for action. They built their case on the foundation laid by Major Nathaniel Michler's 1867 report and on the work of Olmsted and Vaux in New York's Central Park. Senator Stewart, whose almost thirty years in the halls of the Capitol made him an extremely influential figure, could see double-barreled advantages in the proposed park. It would doubtlessly increase the value of the land being acquired for his and Newlands' speculative venture, and it would also take "2,000 acres out of the market."[13]

So while Charles Carroll Glover of the Riggs Bank and Crosby Noyes of the *Star*

pushed, Stewart and his colleagues in Congress pulled, and in 1890 created Rock Creek Park with space for the zoo firmly established at its southern end. Senator John Sherman of Ohio, a D.C. land developer in his own right among whose close acquaintances were the Baltzley brothers, proposed and supported the legislation. Rock Creek's great, meandering watershed gave Chevy Chase the best possible eastern boundary and a buffer to settlements on the "wrong side of the Park."[14]

Some Democrats called the park a land grab for privileged Republicans and inserted an amendment ordering property owners to pay the city a special assessment for the amount they benefited. Senator Stewart recognized the amendment as a gesture, called it "absurd," and accurately predicted that the assessment would never be made.[15]

By mid-March, Stewart announced that his friends were giving up their proposed cable railway and instead were planning to build bridges across Rock Creek for an electric trolley line. Soon "progressive businessmen" such as W. K. Ryan, John F. Waggaman, and Edward Stellwagen were said to be "willing to cede the right-of-way." Francis Newlands had "discovered" the Rock Creek Railway Company and its 1888 charter to build an electric railroad out Connecticut Avenue extended.

Actually, the undercapitalized company had barely started construction despite an eighteen-month time limit in its charter, and Newlands' agents convinced the railroad's president, John F. Waggaman, to seek an amendment to extend his route and his time limits. This was done by the Fifty-first Congress in May of 1890, and the road gained the right to bridge Rock Creek, to issue more capital stock, and to dedicate a 130-foot-wide street to the District of Columbia.[16]

Newlands quickly bought up the Rock Creek Railway Company's outstanding stock and within a year owned 1,438 shares; Senator Stewart had 942 shares, leaving only five other shares outstanding. Construction began almost immediately, and the railroad's friends in Congress amended the charter to allow it unlimited capitalization and the use of other lines' tracks while the proposed right-of-way through Washington Heights dragged through the courts.[17]

In early January 1890, Armes was writing in his diary with proprietary élan about the decision to bring our railroad out Seventeenth Street. Congress also gave the Rock Creek Railway unique authority to acquire other transit lines, which eventually led to the creation of the Capital Traction Company. Having friends and fellow stockholders in Congress did no harm to the goals of the new president of the Rock Creek Railway Company, Francis G. Newlands.[18]

Although he was only four years younger than George A. Armes, Frank Newlands was of a different generation and a quite different world. Too young to serve in the Civil War, he was a college-educated lawyer who had developed his tastes and come into his fortune in California among some of the grandest plungers and most wondrous rascals in all of American history.

Francis Newlands was born in 1848 of Scottish parents who had immigrated to Troy, New York, and then moved to Natchez, Mississippi. His father died when Francis was only three, and his mother, left with four young sons and a daughter, soon remarried. Newlands' stepfather was Eben Moore, a banker who had been mayor of Quincy, Illinois. After being all but wiped out in the Panic of 1857, Moore found a government job and moved the family to war-swollen Washington, D.C., in 1863.

Young Newlands entered Yale in 1867, the year after his stepfather's death, but returned home halfway through his junior year, for reasons both monetary and academic. He took a job at the D.C. post office, attended classes at Columbian College and was admitted to the District of Columbia bar in 1869, age 21. Attorney Newlands, handsome and clean-shaven, moved to San Francisco, hung out his shingle and within a few years was handling the cases and private papers of many wealthy men. He made friends in a fluid, fast-moving and flamboyant society. His mother joined him in California after the death of an older brother who had been wounded in the Civil War.

California was in the midst of a second gold rush. Fortunes were being made and lost overnight. Some uneducated and uncouth miners went from tattered shirts and broken boots to dollar cigars and gold vest chains in less time than it took their oft-forgotten wives to bring forth another child. Huge homes, each one grander and more ornate than the last, soon crowned the hills. If he had pewter door-knobs, then I must have gold. If his library has

ten-thousand unread books, then mine will have twenty thousand, equally unread but leather bound. If his daughter can marry a duke, mine will marry a prince. In this world where neither refined taste nor business ethics counted for much, the movers and shakers included Charles Crocker and Mark Hopkins, Collis Huntington and Leland Stanford, James Flood, John Mackay and the rest of the Irishtocracy–the unfortunate Ralston and the fortunate Giannini, and the Stewarts and then the Sharons and, finally, the Newlands.

One of the newly minted millionaires for whom Francis Newlands did legal work was a "reserved, shrewd, and cynical man," William Sharon, the so-called King of the Comstock. Irving Stone described him as "beady-eyed, pale-faced, black-mustached" and "a thoroughgoing scoundrel," and in *The Wasp* (1885) Ambrose Bierce called him an "unthinkable vulgarian." Sharon had come overland with the Forty-niners to sell at incredible prices the tons of merchandise he had shipped around Cape Horn. He plowed his profits into San Francisco real estate, developed a reputation as a canny poker player, invested heavily in mining stocks and by the end of the Civil War lost almost everything; some said he was cheated out of it. Fortunately he had married the daughter of a man who was a friend of William Ralston.[19]

"Ralston," wrote Stephen Birmingham, chronicler of America's monied elite, "must certainly be classed among the robber barons, but one tends to forgive him because he was such a pleasant man." He had built the huge and impossibly expensive Palace Hotel and an incredible home called "Belmont" with a hundred bedrooms all sporting silver doorknobs. Ralston headed the Bank of California, which he founded after making fortunes in real estate and railroads. He was the city's financial wizard who studded his white linen shirts with black cameos and gambled on a hundred fronts at once.

Now Ralston hired the impoverished and embittered Sharon, lent him $15,000, and sent him to Nevada to investigate the slowing of the Comstock Lode's production and the value of related mining stocks. Sharon established a branch of the Bank of California, lent money at low rates and invested heavily in the Comstock for both Ralston and himself. He developed practically a milling monopoly, and built the Virginia and Truckee Railroad that paid for itself in the first year and made piles of profit thereafter. Sharon helped make the mines more efficient in processing low-grade ore, acquired an interest in most of them by foreclosing on his low-rate loans and soon had an income of $2,000 a day. By then Will Sharon and his wife were regular house guests of the Ralstons at their fabulous mansion.

After the silver rush, Nevada had been admitted to the Union in 1864, in part to insure the passage of the 13th Amendment ending slavery. Much of the impetus came from the assertive William Stewart, another Comstock millionaire who as the territory's first Senator pushed through the lode statute in 1866 protecting miners' rights. He also helped to draft the 15th Amendment.

By the 1870s Nevada was, in one of the region's historians, "hardly more than a satrapy" of the San Francisco millionaires' club. In 1874 Sharon, rich again but labeled a "hyena" by the *Territorial Enterprise*, may have been seeking social status when he "purchased a United States senatorship by bribing the Nevada legislature with shares of one of his silver stocks." During his whole term as senator, from 1875 until 1881, Sharon never visited Nevada and came to Washington, D.C., only three times. On the first of those visits, he and another of his California attorneys and a Yale classmate, Curtis Hillyer, bought farmland between Dupont Circle and Florida and Massachusetts Avenues with the help of his friend and associate, the former senior senator from Nevada, who was given the site for his home on the Circle as reward. They goodhumoredly called their Dupont Circle development "The Honest Miners' Camp." Soon Senator Stewart's "castle" and Judge Hillyer's mansion attracted other wealthy men, and their property boomed in value.[20]

On November 19, 1874, Francis G. Newlands married Clara Adelaide Sharon, the younger daughter of the czar of the Comstock Lode. The Newlands lived in the Palace Hotel for seven years, and two of their three daughters, Edith and Janet, were born there.

One of those events that suddenly and completely change many lives occurred on August 26, 1875. Much of the fortune that built Chevy Chase can be dated from the run on the Bank of California that began that day. Ralston, according to one source, had to sign over his rights to the Palace Hotel to borrow two

million cash from Sharon to keep his bank afloat. Runs were not uncommon in those days, but the Bank of California was in rather tender condition from the loans Ralston had made to himself for the construction of the Palace and his ornate homes.

The bank closed early, leaving an unhappy mob of clamoring depositors and stayed closed on the 27th. Ralston signed a document making William Sharon trustee of all his property and then called a meeting of the bank's board of directors, men he had made rich. He explained to them that he owed about twice as much as he had including some four million to the bank. He left the room at his board's request, and almost immediately Sharon demanded Ralston's head. The board voted, and Ralston signed a letter of resignation, went to North Beach, put on his bathing suit and, as he did almost every day, swam out to sea. His body was brought to shore that afternoon.

Suicide? There was no water in his lungs, and the New York Life Insurance Company paid his widow $65,000. A few days later John Mackay asked Sharon, "Couldn't they revive him?" Sharon's reported reply was, "For a few minutes I was afraid they would."

Now historians diverge. Albert Atwood, the official biographer of Francis Newlands, seems to agree with the contemporaneous California press that Sharon was a hero who saved the Bank, paid off Ralston's debts with his own money, and provided his friend's widow with $800 or $900 a month until her death in 1912. Stephen Birmingham calls Sharon's action the betrayal of a friend and "one of the most stunning instances of business treachery in the history of California." He states that the widow "sued Sharon over the deed of trust, in an out-of-court settlement of her lawsuit she was persuaded to accept $250,000. That plus her insurance money, was all she ever got."[21]

Sharon took over the bank, the Palace Hotel, and Ralston's home and assets as well as his debts. The panic passed, and the bank reopened quietly and profitably. Soon Sharon was said to be San Francisco's number one taxpayer, contributing one-fiftieth of the city's revenue. By the late-1870s, his income was estimated at $800,000 a year.

Through this period Newlands traveled back and forth from California to the District of Columbia to represent the Sharon interests and those of his other Western clients before the committees of Congress and in the Federal courts. Senator Stewart's Adolph Cluss-designed castle on Dupont Circle was no longer being called "Stewart's Folly," and Curtis Hillyer's place, which was later to become part of the Cosmos Club, was no longer alone on Massachusetts Avenue. Both homes were, of course, open to Counselor Newlands who moved in rather rarefied, if not pedigreed, legal circles in a city he had long known.[22]

In 1880 Sharon's other daughter, Flora, married Sir Thomas George Fermor Hesketh in the seventy by twenty-four foot, mirrored music room of Belmont, the huge white palace her father had "inherited" from his friend Ralston. One hundred and fifty guests attended the ceremony and eight hundred more the reception. Despite rainy weather, hundreds lined the streets or stood under the estate's trees to watch the proceedings. Flora thus became the first in San Francisco society to acquire a title, which put Sharon at least one up on the railroad magnates and the Irishtocracy.

Her father contributed a five-million-dollar dowry and staged a memorable wedding . The *Examiner* carried column after column describing its lavish excess and garish display. When someone had the courage to criticize Sharon for the money wasted bringing the Metropolitan Opera Company from New York to play at the reception, the Senator from Nevada replied that it had not cost him even one day's income to do so.

Sometime during the period in which he was marrying off his daughters, William Sharon acquired a lady friend. His wife had died in 1875, and he had become "acquainted" with a beautiful, hot-tempered woman of twenty-seven named Sarah Althea Hill. Sharon openly lived with her at the Grand Hotel and took her to Flora's wedding reception. She called herself Althea, but the newspapers soon named her "The Rose of Sharon." When Senator Sharon decided to end the affair, with suitable gifts, Miss Hill went to court seeking half of his assets and instituted a series of divorce litigations that lasted more than six years and involved twenty court decisions. The Rose's chief piece of evidence was a purported marriage contract signed by William Sharon and dated August 25, 1880.

Sharon hired William Stewart, the man he had ousted from the U.S. Senate, as his chief counsel. He admitted paying Althea $500 a month but insisted he had never promised marriage. All of Sharon's enemies, and there were many, laughed at the stories of his offers to buy Althea's love and happily supported the wronged damsel. After sixty-one days of evidence, the California Superior Court ruled in December 1884 that Sharon had been married to the young woman and granted her the requested divorce, $2,500 a month in alimony and her share of their common property, half. Sharon took his appeal to the Federal Court, and even his death did not end the affray. It outlived him by three years.

On February 18, 1882, Clara Newlands died shortly after bearing a son, Sharon, who died almost at birth. The prosperous, 34-year-old lawyer was left with the care of three young daughters as he continued to handle much of his father-in-law's legal affairs, both business and personal. When Sharon died after a long illness in 1885, Newlands became the executor and trustee of his estate as well as inheritor of his late wife's third of the vast fortune and wide-spread property. A small part of the Sharon estate, for example, made Newlands the second-largest property owner in the state of Nevada.

William Stewart decided to try to return to the U.S. Senate and turned over the Hill-Sharon case to Newlands in 1885 but continued his interest. In 1888, convinced that the Sharon heirs could not win in California courts, Stewart suggested "The first and most important step, therefore, is for both Mr. Newlands and Fred Sharon (the late Senator's son) to become *Bona Fide* residents of some other state. The change in residence must be positive and in good faith, as you know."

Francis Newlands took Stewart's advice and established his residence in Nevada soon after marrying Edith McAllister in England in September 1888. The move of the Sharon estate out of California helped put the case into Federal courts, and finally Supreme Court Associate Justice Stephen J. Field, sitting in the California circuit, ruled that the marriage contract was a forgery.

Althea jumped up and screamed, "How much did Newlands pay you?" When the judge ordered her removed, her husband and lawyer, former Confederate General David Terry, a longtime enemy of Judge Field, sprang to her defense and knocked out several of the marshal's teeth. The other guards subdued Terry and managed to take his Bowie knife away from him and then relieved Althea of the revolver she carried.

Terry, who had killed a friend of Justice Field in a duel and served on the Supreme Court of California before marrying his attractive client, was sentenced to six months and his fiery wife to thirty days in jail. After Terry's release from prison, Judge Field traveled with a body guard, and when Terry attacked him on a train, the guard, a notorious gunman named David Neagle, shot Terry dead and was rewarded with a gold watch. Althea spent the last forty-five years of her life in an institution for the insane.[23]

In the spring of 1890, the news that the California or Sharon syndicate was behind the acquisition of property along the line of Connecticut Avenue extended became common knowledge. The story's source was soon identified: Major George Armes. That was the end of the petulant officer's relationship with Francis Newlands but not of his family's influence in Chevy Chase. Armes feared that Stellwagen and others might try to cheat him out of his commissions, but he must have received most of them. His income for 1890 was more than $200,000.

With himself as president and Edward Stellwagen vice president, Newlands quickly organized the Chevy Chase Land Company in June of 1890 for the purposes of:

. . . buying, selling, mortgaging, leasing, improving, disposing of, and otherwise dealing in the lands in the State of Maryland, and lands partly within the District of Columbia; and also, the construction, equipment and operation of a passenger railway. . . .

Almost all of the properties previously purchased by Armes and the other strawmen were retitled to the Company for a reported $330,000 in capital stock of the one million authorized (10,000 shares, par value $100 per share).

The company name came from the largest single tract, the one that straddled the District Line where either Armes or Newlands had suggested a high quality suburb be built. Belt's old, brick home still stood, and the ancient battle's name had been on the property since 1720 when Lord Baltimore gave the land grant

to the rambunctious colonel. The fact that Newlands was of Scottish descent also may have played a part in the choice.[24]

The Chevy Chase Land Company of Montgomery County, Maryland, soon acquired a charter to build the Maryland section of the Rock Creek Railway. The value and asking price of farmland north and west of the city rocketed up, but some property continued to be purchased. It was at about this time that a few eager investors such as John Beall and Dr. Ralph Walsh even considered that sleepy Bethesda might be a good investment.

The large Ryan, Clark and Richmond Park properties, purchased after the CCLCo was formed, brought premium prices, especially the land just opposite the newly located zoo, which opened for business at the end of April 1891. In Maryland the Bradley farm and a large portion of the Dunlop's Hayes Manor property were also acquired later. A few sellers tried to break or renegotiate their sales agreements only to find that Armes's lawyers had done a good job of sealing their contracts. Armes himself took almost the top price, $4,800-an-acre, for a right-of-way and about two-and-a-half acres of his twelve-acre Fairfield estate and wrote no more about his part in the project.

The Land Company became the umbrella organization for the building and management of the railroad and for the buying and selling of land. In February 1895 Newlands accepted the Thomas J. Fisher Company as the sole agent to manage his real estate business with a sales commission of five percent. All three companies operated out of the same office where one could find Francis G. Newlands almost every morning, if sometimes only briefly. Newlands reportedly always carried a Land Company bank balance and bookkeeping summary with him. By then he had sold the $160,000 worth of lots, which Sharon had bought near Dupont Circle, for ten times what was paid for them.

When the company issued stock, William Stewart invested $300,000 and stayed actively interested in the project until he retired, under pressure, from the Senate and left the area in 1904 having served in Congress for almost forty years. Stewart's influence in the Congress in relation to the establishment of Rock Creek Park and in gaining charter changes for the Rock Creek Railway was certainly more important than his investment.

The ownership of most CCLCo stock was and is in the hands of the extended Newlands family although at one time Stanford University owned 187 shares, H. E. Huntington 94 shares, and various trusts held others. At the time of her death in 1927, Dame Florence Louise Fermor-Hesketh owned almost 800 shares.[25]

On June 11th, 1890, a committee composed of Edward J. Stellwagen and J. Kelsey Schoepf reported to the president and board of directors of the new corporation "on the proposition made to this Company by Mr. Francis G. Newlands, on his behalf as Trustee of the estate of Wm. Sharon, and on behalf of Senator Wm. M. Stewart" and showed the properties offered and the cash expenditures made by Newlands and Stewart. In all 1,572.74 acres were included in the list, and Newlands and Stewart held clear title to all except for four parcels owned by J. H. Ralston for the Sharon trustee. "Exhibit A" attached to the report showed the expenditure of $330,000 and deferred payments totaling $545,568.51. The committee concluded that "said proposition is fair and just and its acceptance is recommended."[26]

The first job for the Chevy Chase Land Company was pushing the railroad and its broad, accompanying street, 150 feet wide, through heavily wooded and extremely uneven terrain. A lake to supply water for the steam powered electric generators and a power house and carbarn were being built some two miles north of the District Line at the end of the B&O's recently completed spur. At the same time, the Edgemore Bridge Company was hired to construct the Calvert Street and Klingle Valley bridges on the planned right-of-way.

In April 1891, the Metropolitan Southern Railroad and the Rock Creek line signed memoranda of agreement. The B&O's southern branch received a hundred-foot-wide right-of-way through CCLCo property and land for a depot and siding in exchange for a $4,000 passenger station and a siding to the trolley line's powerhouse. The agreement left the intersection of the railroad tracks, the trolley tracks and Connecticut Avenue extended unresolved. The related agreement with the B&O, addressed to the Hon. William Stewart, granted the CCLCo half-rates on building materials such as stone, lumber, and bricks.[27]

Carbarn and power plant at Chevy Chase Lake

By February 1892 trains loaded with ties, rails and other building materials made regular trips to the new powerhouse at the growing lake on what had been the Laird property. This freight must have been intended for Newlands' growing trolley line because the B & O had run into the same problem that stymied the Land Company's goal to have Connecticut Avenue intersect with Rockville Pike, the cost of land in Bethesda. The only part of the B&O's right-of-way toward the river secured by early `92 was "two or three acres right at the toll gate on the east side of the Georgetown turnpike."[28]

By the time the builders finished the railroad and roadway, they had removed 454,198 cubic yards of earth including 242,195 cubic yards of solid rock. That was about twenty times the amount of stone that came out of the quarries and went into the huge Chautauqua buildings at Glen Echo. The previous chapter included much of the story of building the Chevy Chase trolley line, but former CCLCo president Edward Hillyer's memoirs lend some detail:[29]

The hills had to be cut down by pick and shovel and the valleys filled by horse drawn carts. A good illustration of that operation was the cutting down of what was known as Soapstone Hill on the west side of the Avenue at Albemarle Street, and the earth had to be taken across the Avenue and filled in where the Ice [Palace] Shopping Center is today, a fill of forty or fifty feet. In some places a train of small dumping cars with a donkey engine carried the dirt on very narrow gauge rails.

Stellwagen was in charge of the Land Company's day-to-day operations, and one of the men he hired to help construct the seven-mile, million-dollar rail line was a young civil engineer from Annapolis named Herbert Claude. He worked under the direction of A. J. Warner of Ohio, a Silverite political ally of Newlands who had been president of the Toledo, Walhonding Valley and Ohio Railroad Company. On many warm days in the spring of 1890, the grandly mustachioed Claude stopped at a multi-porticoed hilltop house for a drink of cool water and a polite word or two with the beautiful, teen-aged girl who lived there. She was Cecily Armes, oldest of the nine children of Lucy and the Major.

Her father may have discovered the budding romance for soon Cecily and her sister Edith accompanied their mother aboard a steamer in New York and did not return from England until September. By this time Armes had a reputation among his neighbors as a wild man who occasionally galloped one of his foam-mouthed horses across the fields to Tenleytown firing off two cavalry pistols as he went. Only a young man with great courage would court his daughter.[30]

The building of the electric railway continued. Claude's position improved until he was second in command, and his parents moved to Chevy Chase as the first full-time residents of the village. His visits to the large house at yet-to-be Connecticut Avenue and old Grant Road resumed.

Herbert Claude

One day shrill blasts scattered the birds from the trees and set the dogs to howling. A close-coupled, shining-black steam engine belching smoke appeared on the newly laid tracks in front of the Armes' home. Between the tender and the caboose, the engine towed a rattling line of flat cars and carried construction supplies back and forth all day. When it became clear that the engine was there to stay and was left near their house in the evenings, some of the Armes children went to visit it. They decorated Number 178 with flowers, met the fireman, and were given a tour of the cab. Within days they were riding along regularly.

The next step was obvious:

We came thundering down the grade from Pierce Mill road, one hand on the throttle and one on the whistle cords, and as we rush nearer Soapstone Hallow, I would let forth a terrific blast which echoed its shrill notes for miles around.

The whistle brought the few neighbors to their doors to see the engine and its girl engineer, Ethel Marie Armes, yellow hair flying in the wind, chuffing down the tracks through the deep cut in front of her house beside unfinished Connecticut Avenue.[31]

The electric road formally opened on Friday, September 16, 1892, and after enjoying the seven-mile trip out from the city and admiring the new power plant, the company's officers and their guests, including the District Commissioners, lunched sumptuously at the weedy lake on the northern end of the line. Connecticut Avenue itself was a long way from finished.

Meanwhile, despite her father's best efforts, Cecily Armes and Herbert Claude had fallen in love. Armes refused to consent to their marriage and finally asked for a six-month postponement, but it was too late. On October 1, 1894, Lucy Armes smuggled her daughter out of Fairfield, and with the help of some cooperative priests and a nun, the young couple married and moved to a small house near the end of the streetcar line. Before the month was over, Armes's wife and children were also gone, and Lucy began divorce proceedings.

The Major blamed Francis Newlands and Herbert Claude for breaking up his family. After long and bitter legal tangles, his wife gained an absolute divorce in 1896. Armes enlarged Fairfield to fifty rooms and leased it out as a summer hotel. He also made one last try to get his brevet commission restored.

"Fairfield," Armes' home on the new trolley line

Mismanagement doomed the hotel that young Edith Claude visited and recalled looking like a merry-go-round with piazzas piled one atop another. Armes remarried, gave up Fairfield in 1912 and left the area. He died in New Jersey in 1919 at the home of his third wife.[32]

Herbert Claude became an officer in the Land Company and superintendent of the Maryland section of the streetcar line until his death in 1933. For forty years, Claude's office was in the oddly-shaped, waiting-room building with the twin C's on its chimney beside the track across from the carbarn.[33]

According to Chevy Chase historian Eleanor Ford:

During all the years when Newlands and the Land Company receded into the background, Claude kept things going on the spot and deserves a lot of credit for that. Herbert Claude was the key man operating between the Land Company and the residents. Any time a resident had a complaint or the Land Company wanted something adjusted, they would call on Herbert Claude.

In 1902 Herbert and Cecily became the parents of Chevy Chase's favorite, early historian, Edith McAllister Claude, named, obviously, for Newlands' second wife.[34]

Historians and the CCLCo may denigrate Armes's role in the creation of Chevy Chase or dismiss him, as Roderick French does in his comparison of Chevy Chase to Boston's suburbs, as vain and paranoid, but he lived on in the Claudes' contributions. It is indeed a wise child that knows its own father, and Chevy Chase may have had at least two. Newlands,

the anointed if somewhat detached visionary, is remembered with a street, a biography and the thoroughly refurbished fountain in the Circle. No Armes Street runs through Chevy Chase, but then there is no Stellwagen Drive either. However, on Wisconsin Avenue near Tenley Circle is a small subdivision called Armesly (or Armesleigh) Park including eight of the row houses the major built in 1890 while all of this Chevy Chase business was going on. And his granddaughter remembered him and wrote the first history of Old Chevy Chase. She even recalled her father burning a trunk full of copies of her grandfather's autobiography thus making it a rare book.[35]

The Washington *Evening Star* on New Year's Day 1891 reviewed the previous year's activities in various fields. Among its summaries and conclusions:

> *The most notable transaction that has ever been known in the history of suburban property was the extensive purchase of land along the line of Connecticut Avenue and for two miles beyond the District line by the representatives of the Sharon estate and others. The purchase of the land involved the expenditure of about $1,500,000. Under the same auspices the building of the Rock Creek electric road was begun, involving tremendous engineering work and an outlay of about a half a million dollars...*

The plans of Newlands and his compatriots were strikingly similar to the dreams of the Baltzley twins who were building their castles in the Potomac Palisades at about the same time as the invention of Chevy Chase Circle. A model community for the rich was their common goal. The best of everything for those who could afford and appreciate it seems to have been their motto. A plan? Naturally. Newlands and Frederick Law Olmstead had discussed the need for a comprehensive, coordinated effort. Restrictions? Of course.[36]

Both Glen Echo Heights and Chevy Chase prohibited commercial development and established required set-backs and substantial, minimum house values. Both used respected architects and planners; both published elaborate promotional literature; both built high-quality electric railroads, and both had summer hotels and seasonal attractions at the far end of their streetcar lines. Had it lasted, the Baltzleys' labyrinthine restaurant might have tipped the scales. Chautauqua outdrew anything planned for Chevy Chase Lake which re-

ally was not even up to the entertainment standard set at unfortunate Bethesda Park. The Chevy Chase Hunt went down with the *Titanic*, and golf at Bannockburn was as least as good as that at Columbia or "Chevy" in the early days. The two developments were roughly equidistant from the Capitol and, on paper, Glen Echo and Chevy Chase looked very similar. The Baltzleys' deeds were on even heavier stock and had fancier seals.

Two factors left Glen Echo deeply depressed and Chevy Chase slowly prospering. The first was the death of Professor Spencer and, even worse, the rumor that he died of malaria. That killed the Chautauqua after one spectacular season and collapsed land values near the river like an earthquake.

In those days Washington was still a marshy bog in many areas and regularly had summertime problems with bad water and yellow fever as well as tropical weather. Those who could afford to had always escaped the city in the summer months. Congress and the courts shut down. A succession of airy homes above the fall line became known as summer White Houses—Lincoln had been at Soldier's Home when Early came to town, and Cleveland's Red Top set the standard in the 1890s. The healthy breezes of the Potomac and the pure air of the hills above it had been one of the Baltzleys' main selling points. The specter of sickness ruined them. As has been noted, some Glen Echoians blamed the Chevy Chase Land Company for spreading the rumor.

But the greatest advantage Chevy Chase had was money—the Sharon fortune, Newlands' money, barrels and bushels of gold, silver and greenbacks—and the ability to borrow more. Newlands' signature on most early CCLCo papers was a reminder:

Francis G. Newlands
Trustee of the Estate
of Wm Sharon

The Baltzleys mortgaged everything and "hung paper" everywhere as their enterprises outstripped their resources. They discounted loans and paid multitudinous creditors with

their debtors' dubious notes. Undercapitalized, quickly land poor, and deeply in debt, their glorious Rhineland on the Potomac collapsed much more easily than the charred hulk of the Hall of Philosophy yielded to the demolition teams in the 1920s. But at Chevy Chase, Newlands was able to shake off the Panic of 1893, the greatest financial collapse in American history to that time, and keep on building, and even buying, evidently without concern for profits.

By the end of 1893, Newlands had spent over $1,254,000 on land, another million and a half on road building, interest, and an electric railroad, and was in the process of sinking another million or so into turning farmland into his distant suburb. The Chevy Chase Land Company would not pay its stockholders a dividend until 1922, five years after the Senator's death. Echoing the earlier Stewart castle at Dupont Circle, some of the Newlands' family, with a smile, came to call Chevy Chase "Uncle Frank's Folly."

Newlands became interested in other things, especially after winning a seat in Congress in 1892 with the help of Senator Stewart and under the aegis of the Silver Party. In 1898 Newlands found himself labeled a traitor when he challenged his mentor, Stewart, for his Senate seat in a thoroughly corrupt campaign that Newlands lost. The tangle of Nevada politics eventually put Francis Newlands in the Democratic camp and returned "Old Bill" Stewart to the Republican fold. With the help of Will Sharon, Newlands finally won his Senate seat after the 1902 election during which he was labeled a sickly hypocondriac and frequent absentee as well as a tool of the railroad interests.[37]

Unlike some of the Californians who had represented the Silver State in the Millionaires' Club that was the Senate of the United States, Newlands was a hard-working and unusually conscientious law-maker who labored for the benefit of the Southwest. His public papers, collected at Yale, show a man in constant touch with Nevada politics and affairs.[38]

Then the great California earthquake of 1906 drew his attention to the extravagantly expensive rebuilding of the Palace Hotel, a property that stayed in his family until the 1950s. The Palace had cost Ralston about $6.5 million to build, and Newlands invested $8 million in its restoration.

Soon the opportunities in the West from reclamation programs and irrigation projects must have seemed much more vital and interesting and worth more time and attention than sewer problems at that small suburb at the end of the long, bumpy, gravel road and trolley line. And regulating the nation's railroads was certainly more important than overseeing the development of Capital Traction although, unlike the Maryland subdivision, it was making money.

During his twenty-two years in Congress, Newlands actively served on nineteen committees; in 1912 his name arose as a possible Democratic candidate for President, and he was a friend and advisor to Woodrow Wilson. Newlands also became involved in the growth of Cleveland Park and with Olmsted in the beautification of the Mall and the plans for Washington's public buildings.[39]

And certainly his wife and daughters had other interests, particularly in the more airy realms of Washington's high society where cliff dwellers "womaned the ramparts." His grandchildren claimed that "Uncle Frank was always on a horse," and his grandson and namesake, Francis Newlands Johnston, concluded that Chevy Chase was just a "side project" to his grandfather. Newlands stopped by the CCLCo office almost every morning, and there were a number of letters from him on Senate stationary regarding Land Company affairs, but if Chevy Chase did not end up as he had planned, one wonders if he noticed. To his biographers, his lasting monument was the Reclamation Bill of 1902.[40]

He was the first president of the Chevy Chase Club, which he helped to create out of the Dumblane Club three years before the first house was built, and he did enjoy riding to hounds or just plain horseback riding. One of his daughters recalled that while he often took the children riding, he sometimes went out by himself and "lost in thought forgot he was on a horse." When the horse came back without its rider, "we went looking for him in Chevy Chase, but he often came back on the streetcar, genial as ever . . . ." Newlands was always carefully dressed, often in well-cut, English-tailored suits, but his grandchildren remembered him most often in his red riding habit and shining boots.[41]

Newlands earned praise for his perspicacity, his insistence on doing things right, and his patience in gaining profits from the sizable

Sen. F. G. Newlands

Chevy Chase investment. These undoubted virtues may have resulted from the fact that he and his family simply did not need the money. Roderick French admired Newlands' continuing "interest in shaping the form and quality of the development." In stating that he was able to forego profit for thirty years to achieve such control, French noted, "He had or had at his disposal, the capital necessary to such a comprehensive, long-term undertaking." After all, he spent more restoring the Palace than he had on Chevy Chase.

The original plans for Chevy Chase Village harkened back to the time when only the rich could afford to indulge in the "rural ideal" and then, in the days before the railroad, only by having a summer cottage. By the 1890s the development of streetcar suburbs was bringing a more modest modification of that ideal within the reach of the middle class just as the building of the Metropolitan Branch of the B&O had done for Takoma Park and Rockville twenty years before.

Once the civil service workers and the transportation systems were in place, the suburbs bloomed. Coming home from work in the city to your own bungalow or "colonial" on your own little plot of land and to your children playing on your lawn became an attainable goal of many wage earners. It was the rural ideal, according to Sam Bass Warner, that turned the middle class against the city and led to the creation of the modern, suburban way of life.[42]

But, at first, the developers of Chevy Chase were not interested in the middle class. What Newlands and company seem to have had in mind was a small number of large "cottages" on expansive lots along beautifully landscaped streets at some distance from the hoi polloi. To some extent, they succeeded. A study of the 1910 census concluded that, unlike the capital city, Chevy Chase was a white, literate community of extended families, many with live-in servants, where a high percentage of household heads were in professional and other white-collar occupations and with a high rate of home ownership and other characteristics of a prestige-status area. "Chevy Chase," Kenneth Jackson summarized, "was to remain a tightly controlled enclave of upper-income Americans long after its great growth in the first half of the twentieth century."[43]

Setting aside the question of authorship, Land Company leaders decided to first develop a "village" of some 250 acres just north of the District Line in Maryland and to divide the rest of the property into four large sections to be developed later. Out-of-state buyers could work in the city and keep their right to vote while living out in the country if building and sales began in Maryland. Montgomery County taxes were lower, but then so were County services. The CCLCo would have to do something about supplying such amenities as streets, sewers, schools and churches, if the subdivided farmland was to sell. They left the other property between the Calvert Street Bridge and the District Line in its rural state in

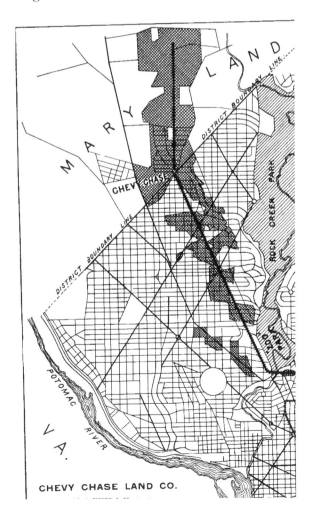

CHEVY CHASE LAND CO.

the hope that the success of Chevy Chase, Maryland, would make it easier to sell. Until the end of the First World War, this decision looked like a mistake.[44]

The covenants and restrictions laid down by the CCLCo through the Thomas J. Fisher Company specified that houses on Connecticut Avenue had to cost at least $5,000 and those on other streets a minimum of $3,000. All lots had to be at least sixty feet wide, and setbacks of thirty-five feet on Connecticut and twenty-five feet on side streets applied to outbuildings as well the main house. No businesses, rowhouses, apartments, or alleys were allowed.

Although the word "restricted," in an ornate typeface, almost always appeared prominently in newspaper ads, in the early years Land Company deeds contained no overt racial or ethnic covenants although they were in the legal papers of other Bethesda-area subdividers. None was needed; those restrictions were simply understood. By the time carpenters raised roofs in Chevy Chase, Washington had become a thoroughly segregated city. The truth was that "cultivated Negroes, even those who looked almost white, discovered that each passing year made it harder for them to purchase or rent comfortable homes without paying exorbitant prices; by the 1890s they could rarely buy at all in a conveniently located, orderly neighborhood."[45]

As for Jews, except as shopkeepers, they were almost nonexistent in the suburbs under a long-term "gentlemen's agreement." Builder Sam Eig estimated that there were only ten Jewish families in the whole County in 1920. Even Italians raised some eyebrows as the Lozupones noted when they arrived on Connecticut Avenue in the mid-1920s. Baltimore's Roland Park had written covenants against blacks, Jews, and European Catholics, but its mirror image in Chevy Chase did not need them.[46]

One of the oddest aspects about the early life of Chevy Chase was that the people who moved there as well as the governments of the District of Columbia and the State of Maryland behaved as if there were no District Line and that the new suburb was part of the Capital City. Belt Road, Broad Branch Road and the trolley linked Chevy Chase to the city. Jackson Road, soon Bradley Lane, was a narrow trail to Bethesda, but except for a couple of stores and a blacksmith's shop there was

not much there, and Brookeville Road eventually did get to Brookeville but almost no one had gone there since Madison's time. Neither a good reason nor an easy way to get to Silver Spring existed unless one hopped aboard a freight train at the Lake.

Many early D.C. directories list Chevy Chase residents, not those in Friendship Heights or Bethesda. When phone service began, Chevy Chase homes received a "Cleveland" number like their neighbors across the District Line. The D.C. Fire Department regularly beat the Chevy Chase volunteers to fires in the Village much to the chagrin of Judge DeLacy. Even after Montgomery County opened a school in Chevy Chase, most children went to what became E. V. Brown just south of the Circle. Chevy Chase, born a true bedroom community, had a thick and enduring umbilical cord.[47]

Once the decision was made where to build and sell property, the Land Company hired first-class people to design the village and its necessities and amenities. Newlands' friend Frederick Law Olmsted, busy in Baltimore with his own subdivision, recommended Nathan Barrett who came down from New York to design both the street layout and the landscaping for $3,600 plus expenses for one year of his services. The cross streets in Barrett's plan paralleled the comprehensive street grid of the District of Columbia, but the parkways curved in graceful arcs from the circle. On the original plans the street names all ring American: Houston, Kansas, Lexington, Plymouth, and Quincy. Perhaps they did not carry the cachet Newlands and the CCLCo wanted; they substituted Kirke, Lenox, and Primrose, as well as one for Lord and Lady Hesketh and another for Newlands himself. Quincy survived.

The tree planting and other landscaping amounted to a façade in the beginning since they were undertaken mainly along Connecticut Avenue and only a block or two deep near the bare and treeless Circle. By 1910 the landscaped area had tripled. The CCLCo planted many fine trees, both domestic and imported, some in double rows. Mrs. Jarvis listed the principal shade trees as elm, pin-oak, linden, sycamore, and maples, especially the Norway.

Philadelphia's Lindley Johnson contributed to the planning, sketching out a series of home designs to set the style, and Washington-born

Leon Dessez, best known for the Admiral's House on Observatory Circle, supervised the building of the first houses. Dessez, who designed the Raleigh Hotel and was a pioneer in the use of reinforced concrete, became a Land Company director and served as the its chief architect until his death in 1918.[48]

The Land Company hired D.C. assistant engineer W. Kelsey Schoepf as its chief engineer to supervise construction of the transportation facilities and the subdivision. Samuel M. Gray, a consulting sanitary engineer from Providence, Rhode Island, designed the sewer system and based the water supply network on a series of artesian wells, a large pumping station and a 300,000 gallon standpipe built by David J. Howell on Rosemary Circle just north of Bradley Lane. Gray charged the Chevy Chase Land Company $1,500 for engineering the sewer system for the 1,100 acres north of the District Line and $700 for designing the water works plus an additional $2,000 for drawing the plans, inspecting the materials and superintending the construction of the systems.

In August of 1892, Gray submitted his plans along with a letter to General Warner complaining that the promised grades had not been furnished and that "numerous and frequent changes have been made" and the "layout and grade of streets has never been fully determined upon." He asked for $2,400 a year for future consulting and travel expenses but agreed to work for $50 a day plus expenses and ended up getting $200 a month plus expenses for the rest of 1892. By October of 1892 John A. Grier of Bethesda had drilled

The water tower at Rosemary Circle

and tested four wells at 68 feet, 100 feet, 150 feet, and 168 feet, each of which produced about ten gallons per minute. He pronounced the water clear and excellent in taste. Work on the water tank accelerated, and it became, as Professor G. W. Stone of Martin's Additions was later to note, "one of the most remarkable and highly visible things in the area."[49]

The tall, graceful, 130-foot high water storage tower was conically-topped, twenty feet in diameter and had a spiral stairway winding around its exterior that was a continuing dare to local youngsters for almost forty years. Walter Kemon, who grew up just west of the tower on Elm (now Stanford) Street, and three of his friends, including Rick Imirie and Tristam Devereux, decided to be parachutists shortly after World War I and jumped off the side of the tank holding on to the corners of a big piece of canvas. It did not work, but the ground was soft and they all survived. A generation later "Clackie" Walker and his buddies bragged about being able to see the Washington Monument from the top.[50]

Until the Naval Hospital's steel framework rose in 1940, the tower was the only thing in the Bethesda area that could be seen from the top of the Washington Monument, and on a good day, one could view Sugarloaf as well as the city from the tower's walkway. A smaller water tank on four metal legs stood near Leland Street at about where West Avenue is now and in the very early days another graced Chevy Chase Circle.

The whole middle of Section Four was left unplatted for water development and even today many of that area's storm sewers constantly rustle with the flow of buried springs. Old-time residents still claim their water was much better than WSSC's. For years a number of Washingtonians rode the streetcars to both Chevy Chase and Bethesda carrying empty bottles so they could bring back fresh well water for their households.

To survey Barrett's street plans and Gray's sewerage, drainage, and water works, A. J. Warner created an "Engineer Corps" consisting of civil engineer Edwin Reynolds and three assistants. Reynolds earned $125 per month, his assistant $90, transitman $55, and chainman $40. His first survey of Section 2 showed ninety-six and a half acres in lots and fifty-nine acres of streets, parkways and parks.

When Stellwagen's construction gangs started felling trees, grubbing brush and laying out streets in Maryland through what had been corn fields and pastures, a number of people already lived in what would be called Chevy Chase. Beautiful Hayes Manor, the scaled-down Clean Drinking manor house, and the big house and log cabin at No Gain were the oldest homes on the northern extremes, and on a part of the Clean Drinking land, John Simpson, an immigrant from England by way of the James River plantations, had settled after the Civil War. According to the family story, he bought the land that later became Small's Nursery for $35 and a load of hay. William Orem, Methodist minister with his stake at Forest Glen, also built a home there and married into the Simpson family. Closer in along Brookeville Road, the Sonnemanns had constructed a large, plain home at Broad Branch about thirty years earlier and were now contemplating the subdivision of their farm property.

George Frederic Ludwig Ottmar Sonnemann, a well-educated native of Giessen, Germany, immigrated in 1849, married Rebecca Cox of Wheeling, Virginia, in 1851 and began siring a large family. Rebecca had approximately eighteen confinements and raised ten of her children to adulthood. An architectural engineer, Ottmar Sonnemann found work on the Cabin John Bridge and moved his rapidly growing family to Maryland several years before the Civil War. He worked with Montgomery Meigs on the Capitol dome and in the building of the Library of Congress and then designed bridges for the B&O and a small Virginia railroad. In the late-1880s, Sonnemann added a dairy farm in Tenleytown to his holdings in what became Chevy Chase. His oldest son, Theodore, eventually opened a successful

Ottmar Sonnemann

Rebecca Sonnemann

general store on Brookeville Road and, after his father's death in 1904, took over most of the property, which he subdivided.

A number of black families, mainly farm workers, including the Davis, Harris and Moten families, and the Hinsons who had been Bradley tenants, also lived in the area. Joseph Bradley had died in 1887, but that house and farm were still there. Others were planning to build homes along Jackson Road/Bradley Lane, which led to Bethesda where the trolley line climbed the hill toward the Grange Hall.[51]

Farther out were the Cummings and Williams farms on opposite sides of Brookeville Road. The Irish-immigrant Cummings brothers had arrived in the area in 1848 and divided their large farm when one married. Oak Grove, home of the last "straight goer" rider to the hounds, 6'6" Andrew Jackson "Cy" Cummings, survived in Martin's Additions.[52]

In 1830 Richard Williams bought 212 acres on the west side of Brookeville Road from the owner of No Gain, and erected a good-sized barn and a small shed. About 1840 he built a two-story frame house on a semi-circular drive which he lined with pear trees. The house had a square front porch and a carved wooden door, central stairs and two front parlors with bedrooms above. In the back was a large kitchen and a porch that could be used as a summer kitchen, and there was a stone-lined storage room under the kitchen. Williams married about 1845, and the census of 1860 showed Richard Williams, farmer, 59; real estate, 212 acres, value $5,500; wife-Julia, children-Clayton 14, Richard 13, Bettie 11, Douglas 7, Ariana 5.

When Bettie Williams married at 19 in 1868 her father built her a frame house with large front and side porches, now 3807, on high ground west of his home and barn. He extended the Lane beyond his barn, and then Ariana married, and her father built a second large frame house, 3806, across from her sister's. J. M. Williams, who had inherited the property, sold all but thirty-three acres of his land to the Chevy Chase Land Company but kept Williams Lane's access to Brookeville Road. He used the money to install an indoor bathroom over the side porch and a small furnace to replace the Franklin stoves.[53]

In 1892 Connecticut Avenue was still two years away from being a passable route into the city, but the trolley was running, spitting

sparks with great crackling sounds when there was ice on the power line. In Chevy Chase, the eight-inch water pipes laid under the main street fed four-inch lines which ran down the middle of secondary streets. Connecticut and Magnolia Parkway had been graded and graveled. The installation of curbing, gutters, and sidewalks proceeded as well as the building of storm drains and water lines to the houses and the placement of a few fire hydrants. Sewer drainage fields would be located in undeveloped areas particularly out near the Lake and toward the west along the creek that ran between Friendship Heights and Somerset.

First houses on the Circle (l-r) The Lodge, Claude's, Nyman's, and Newlands'/Corby's (under construction) - note landscaping and trolley line

The first four houses in Section Two, as the CCLCo called it, were intended for company officials and stockholders, two on the circle and the other two right behind them on Connecticut, "intending thereby to set the standards of home-building for subsequent residents." Johnson and Dessez designed the four large "cottages." The Lodge had been intended as Stellwagen's home, but he evidently never lived there. The large, square house may have been leased or lent to prospective investors or hunt club members before May 1893 when Dessez and his family moved in.[54]

The 125,000-square-foot lot northeast of the circle was intended for Senator Stewart, but he decided to stay downtown although his "castle" had become the Chinese embassy. The house sketched for Stewart was never built, and Congressman Francis Newlands and his wife and daughters agreed to "rough it" and moved out to the $32,000 Jacobethan house that replaced it in the spring of 1893.

Shortly thereafter, despite the gold panic which led to a stock market crash in June and the failure of almost five hundred banks and 15,000 businesses, Newlands purchased the thirty-acre Woodley estate for $140,000. Philip Barton Key built that house about 1803 on part of the Rock of Dumbarton grant, and Presidents Van Buren, Tyler, and Buchanan were among those who had used it as a summer residence.[55]

Connecticut Avenue was still a muddy, unfinished trail beside the streetcar tracks; Broad Branch Road wound down to the creek and led to Georgetown, and Belt Road went to Tenleytown while Milk House Ford Road seemed to just wander from farm to farm. It was difficult to be "at home" when your home was out in the wilderness even beyond the Washington County where some of the upper crust kept tenant farms or summer places.

Mrs. Newlands could, of course, ask her friends to come visit on the trolley. But at midnight the cars stopped running. Maids with candles guided sometimes unwitting guests to unprepared rooms for when the railway shut down so did the houses' electricity.

Janet Farr remembered that occasionally Edith or her mother, Janet, would be called down to eat with dinner guests and "even up" the table especially if there would have been thirteen at the meal.[56]

My mother had many memories as a little girl of entertaining there. One never knew whether grandfather was going to bring one guest home or five or six. They had to keep a very well stocked larder because there were not any grocery stores anywhere near.

It did not take mother and daughters long to figure out that Chevy Chase just would not do and to remove themselves, during the "season," to the former summer White House in Cleveland Park, the family's Washington home until 1916. There the daughters grew up, received their education, and "came out."[57]

Newlands invested in and promoted the growth of Cleveland Park which was also much more convenient for him once he was in Congress. His presence and the trolley lines on Wisconsin and Connecticut Avenues accelerated its growth. Many of the architects and builders of homes in Chevy Chase found work in Cleveland Park where there was, perhaps, an even greater variety of houses. For years

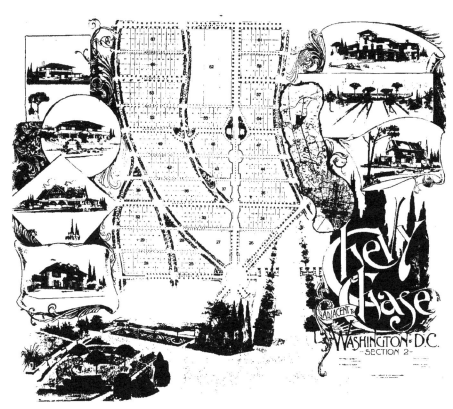

An early ad featuring landscaping plans and drawings of some never-built houses

during the hunt seasons. From the time he moved to Reno, Nevada, in 1888, Francis Newlands claimed that state as his home. It was, he said, "a real, a genuine, a valid residence and citizenship," and after being elected to Congress in 1892 as a candidate of the Silver Party, he stated that he only remained in the Capital while the legislature was in session. In what is now called the Newlands Heights section of Reno in 1889, he had built to his new wife's design a fine, stylish home. The shingle-style, fourteen-room, two-and-a-half story, redwood house sat on 2.2 acres and looked much like some of the homes that would go up in Chevy Chase over the next ten years. It was the Newlands' legal domicile until his death in 1917.[60]

He planned a suburban development north of Reno on 300 acres, and he also invested in similar projects in Phoenix, Arizona, and Burlingame, California. It is difficult to say how long Francis Newlands lived in Chevy Chase or how much of his undivided attention he gave to it, but it is likely that the winter of 1898-99, the coldest and snowiest on record, convinced his family to abandon the distant suburb.[61]

When Newlands gave up the house on in 1898, it reverted to the ownership of the Chevy Chase Land Company. Over the next ten years the Company rented it out to summer boarders including President McKinley's Treasury Secretary Lyman Gage. In 1909 William Corby bought the house and lot #1 for $35,000 with the CCLCo keeping the right to get to and use the well on the property.

Over the next five years Corby massively remodeled the house both inside and out under the supervision of architect Arthur B. Heaton and named the Tudor-style, half-timbered result Ishpiming, "high place" in Chippawa. Heaton added a thirty-foot-tall, Medieval-style music hall to the center of the house, and at one end of this twenty-three by

the Newlands' home was, according to the *Star*, the "center of the most exclusive social life in Washington."

When Newlands' daughter Edith married Charles H. L. Johnston, they moved into the old farmhouse next door at 2920 Cathedral Avenue which they "modernized" and called Single Oak. A year later Janet Newlands married Charles's older brother, Dr. William B. Johnston. The men were sons of Dr. William Waring Johnston, Senator Newlands' physician.[58]

For a time, it looked as if the Washington Cathedral might be located in the area. When the price of Mount St. Albans proved a bit rich for the Episcopal committee's pocketbook, Newlands offered land on Connecticut Avenue and accepted a $5,000 down payment on the $40,000 parcel where Cathedral Mansions was later built. Negotiations reached the Cathedral Commission's engineer, Henry B. Looker, who agreed on a division line between the Evans and Clark tracts in the fall of 1892. When the hilltop's owners came down in price, Newlands refunded the deposit.[59]

Newlands owned the big house on Chevy Chase Circle until 1898, but it is likely that he used it mainly in the summer and perhaps

fifty foot room, Corby installed an Aeolian Duo-Art organ with pipes that ran up to the third floor through five rooms. Mrs. Corby enjoyed music. For the next half-century the Corby family lived and entertained there on fortunes generated by bread and yeast.[62]

Almost certainly the long-gone Nyman house at Irving

Howard Nyman, secretary of the Chevy Chase Land Company, moved into the house on the northeast corner of Connecticut and Irving, which had probably been intended for the CCLCo treasurer, Thomas Gale, but it is difficult to say how long he lived there. The Claude family from Annapolis was the first to occupy the $10,000 "Cottage G" west of the streetcar tracks. The Claudes, whose engineer-son encouraged their move, were the first family in what is now the Village, although the Land Company used their first floor as an office for some time.[63]

Most of the other early lot sales were made to investor-speculators and few of the purchasers' names showed up on lists of early residents. The smallest and most popular lots were generally 7,500 square feet, 60 by 125, along the side streets, and many of the early sales at twenty or thirty cents a square foot were of pairs or groups of lots. Some of the large, corner lots were later subdivided while a number of smaller lots were combined before houses were built.

Some of the planned parks disappeared, but a few triangles and the half circle where Newlands Street almost meets Connecticut remained. The Club, of course, ate up much of Barrett's original plan. The land company cut the huge lot of Newlands' house on the Circle almost in half and carved four new building plots from its north side, and after using part of The Lodge's property for a Fisher Company parking lot, sold lots for houses on the Circle side, which have made Dessez's house difficult to see.

Earle and Meline cooperated with the Land Company and built a number of early houses with the Earles occupying one and the Melines another. The Land Company itself was directly involved in the construction of a few other houses including the building of a small home for Superintendent Claude on the Laird property north of the Lake. Thomas Cowling and Frank Sonnemann built that house in 1894 under the supervision of Leon Dessez for $1,643 with few problems.

Cottage "Z," however, was a large and continuing pain for both the Land Company and the client, Henry A. Cozzens, who purchased lots 14 and 15 of block 33 on "Kirk Street" and for whom the house was built. Dessez had to fire the first contractors, hire their replacement and fend off the irate customer for months. The file still contains a large envelope stuffed with unpaid bills and this final, plaintive note from Mrs. Dessez:[64]

> Dear Mr. Nyman,
> Mr Dessez asked me to send you the following message: Mr Hughes will deliver to you to-day the keys of Mr Cozzens house you must use your own discretion about giving them to him.
> Very Sincerely
> Bessie S Dessez.

Chevy Chase grew at a painfully slow pace. The records show sixteen houses built in 1894 and eight more the next year, but after five years, only twenty-seven homes were occupied, and some of those only in the summer months. Thomas E. Robertson, later U.S. Commissioner of Patents and an early historian of the community, moved into his W. Melrose Street home in 1895 when he was 24, two years before he married.

He recalled other pioneering residents:[65]

The year before saw a number of home owners move into their new residences: Mrs. Mackrille and her two daughters, the Wm. Richards family, Dr. Compton and his family, the Couzens family and the Fisher family all on W. Kirke Street; the Birney and McCubbin families on E. Kirke Street; the Brown family on W. Irving street, the Lemly family on Laurel Parkway, and the Porter family on East Lenox Street. The same year I moved to Chevy Chase also saw the Lewis family occupy their new home on W. Melrose Street and the Portman and Verrill families on E. Melrose Street. . . .

In February 1897 the Secretary of the Chevy Chase Land Company had very bad news for the few stockholders, but he tried to sugarcoat it as best he could :

Sales of lots for the year amounted to $15,166.50, which though smaller than any year since the Company placed its land on the market, and seemingly disastrous, is easily explained by the universal depression of business throughout the country during that year, affecting the locality to a marked degree, and does not signify, as would appear, a depreciation of the enterprise.[66]

The census of 1900 showed that more than a third of those living in Chevy Chase were renters. Army officers, government clerks, carpenters, painters, and proprietors of boarding houses who rented their homes mixed with attorneys, scientists, plumbers, and real estate brokers who were buying their houses. Morris Hacker owned his home, but geologist George Eldridge was renting. The German ambassador rented as did black coal-yard worker Julian Jones.

Across Connecticut Avenue from the Lake, boarding houses thrived on Watkins Street in brick homes the railway had built. The street came to be called "Chinch Row." Motorman Eugene Fling and his wife had eleven boarders, seven conductors and four motormen, while Mary Turner had six boarders and Jennie Denty three, all railway men. Conductor Reinhold Springirth, his wife and children shared a rented house with two boarders who worked for the trolley company.[67]

By then some of the churches had begun to get organized; Newlands gave the Episcopalians land on the circle in 1897, and St. John's in Bethesda established a mission there under Reverend H. Allen Griffith who served until 1899 and started the building committee. The cornerstone of All Saints' granite church was laid on June 4, 1901, and the first service was held on Advent Sunday of that year by the Reverend Thomas S. Childs. He was succeeded in 1911 by Canon John W. Austin who saw the size of the congregation steadily grow. Canon Austin served until his death in 1923 after building the Guild Hall, later Kingan Chapel, the rectory, and a much larger church. The old church became a parish hall.

Other denominations met in homes or at the Village Hall built in 1901 and made into a lending library by Newlands' older daughters, Janet and Edith, and the Misses White and Birney. The Free Library Association met monthly at members' homes in social gatherings to raise money to buy books. In 1912 the Village Hall cum library was expanded to house the post office, which moved into the north end of the building.

The post office had been in a small room at the side of Postmaster Claude's house along with the Land Company, which occupied most of the first floor. Jessie Claude became the postmistress when her father died and held the job until the New Deal. She was famous for never missing a day of work, even if she had to be pulled to the post office on a sled, and for her little bow ties.[68]

Parked under the post office was a hand-drawn hose cart that served as the town's first fire "engine." According to one story when there finally was a fire in the Village and the volunteers hauled the cart to Dr. Grey's home on Grafton Street, the unused hose burst to pieces when the "brigade" pumped water into it, and the house burned to the ground.

The twice-daily trolley freight car was a much anticipated and appreciated service used for delivering groceries, medicines and other supplies including furniture. The railway built a Spanish-style, stucco, freight terminal at the "loop" near the Rock Creek Bridge and established a schedule of fees.

Some city grocery stores sent order-takers through the neighborhood before telephones were more common. The motormen put the orders off in front of the post office or at other "stations" along the route. In the early days there was a free delivery service, but generally people were responsible for picking up their own goods before the dogs got to them. There was a box on the power pole at Irving Street where motormen could put prescriptions ordered from drugstores downtown. In fact in the early days, if someone was ill and a request was made, the electricity was kept on all night. The developers also contracted for the regular delivery of coal and ice.

In January 1893 the Land Company hired Morris Hacker to replace Kelsey Schoepf who had resigned in August 1892. Hacker was the first village engineer or supervisor, and he is credited with designing the Club's first golf course in 1897 with greens on both sides of Connecticut Avenue. George Dunlop, who played golf with a feather ball brought from England in 1894, was blamed for or credited with bringing the game to "Chevy."[69]

In May 1893 the County sheriff agreed to appoint Benjamin F. Shank as a deputy sheriff for Chevy Chase after the Land Company posted the usual bond. "An early nightwatchmen was a Mr. Osborn with a white beard to whom some residents, but not all, paid a dollar a month for his services. Ed Wise and later Springirth took over in succession." Some of these men slept at the post office and were on twenty-four hour call to deal with barking dogs or other disturbances.

Curtis Hillyer, who grew up on Quincy Street, recalled "Capt." Springirth catching him stealing a piece of lead pipe from a house under construction to melt to make toy soldiers and warning him never to do that again. John Powell, who later lived in what had been the Hillyer's house, said that boys enjoyed hiding the little ladder Springirth used to climb up to light the Village's gas lamps. The old watchman later sold vegetables from his North Chevy Chase farm through the same neighborhoods he had patrolled.[70]

Reinhold Springirth, the son of Prussian immigrants, came to Chevy Chase with the trolley line in the 1890s and worked fifteen years as a motorman and five as a conductor before being sworn in as the town constable in August 1914, a job he kept until 1939. He then became, at age sixty-eight, the night watchman of the town offices, a sinecure. His job as constable was to walk the streets of Section Two every night from six until eleven. He usually ended his tour at the Circle where he offered to walk home with those arriving on the last trolley. Then he was "on duty" in the Library until six in the morning to answer the phone and handle emergencies. When the fire equipment was stored in the office basement, one of Cap's duties was to sound the fire alarm by striking the iron wheel that hung by the front door. If no volunteers appeared, he and Mr. Wise, the janitor who slept in the basement, would haul out the hose wagon and attend to the fire. In all his years on the job, "the genial old German," as the *Journal* called him, never had to use his revolver.[71]

North of Bradley Lane, the Chevy Chase Land Company attempted to emulate the success of the Bobingers in Cabin John and Bethesda Park's summer hostelry with the construction of the Spring Hotel in 1893, one of the company's more public failures. The two-story, frame inn was designed by Lindley Johnson and built by Joseph B. Williamson of

the District for $24,000 plus $875 for the added front porch. Soon renamed the Chevy Chase Inn, it featured spacious lawns, comfortable rooms and outdoor bowling. The Inn advertised "Music every evening. Plenty of amusement, Lovely surroundings. The Great Specialty is the Dollar Table d'Hote dinner, served from 5 to 8."

But it was still a wintertime white elephant despite the attempt to establish a Young Ladies Seminary under the leadership of Miss Lea M. Bougling in 1895. One year later the hotel was leased for $1,500, but the owner's books showed only a $353 profit after paying the upkeep on the building and bowling alleys. Except for the four months of the year when the "Inn" was in operation, the bowling alleys in the back were open free of charge to the residents of Chevy Chase and became the village Bowling Club.

By 1903 the hotel's days were over, and the Chevy Chase College for Young Ladies appeared. The name later became the Chevy Chase Junior College although most people called it the "School for Girls." A brick façade soon covered the white, frame, colonial structure, and two new buildings sprouted on either side. In 1927 a high school division opened, and the school survived until 1950. The girls were long a decorative part of the landscape as they walked down Taylor Street to get sodas at Doc's on Brookeville Road.[72]

A small, temporary school operated briefly at the Circle, but the elementary school that would be called E. V. Brown opened in 1898 south of Chevy Chase Circle on land donated by the CCLCo. When classes began there, the only other building in sight was the old Belt mansion. A raw plank walk led across a muddy lawn to the front door and to four classrooms behind the impressive pillars. Beside the school was a pump and behind it two toilets and a lot of woods for nature walks.

It was the community's good fortune to have as the Chevy Chase School's first teacher and long-time principal Miss Ella Givens. "No one else wanted to teach in such a lonely spot," she said. The next year Miss Hendry arrived, and the program expanded to seven grades. Children came from as far north as Kensington and as far west as Glen Echo, wherever the trolley lines reached. Kathryn Frisbie and most of the other children in Friendship Heights walked through the Kirkside golf course while Ada Swigert and the

Somerset students wore a path along the Club's fence north of the sewer outlets to get to school.

William Orem Jr. rode his horse down from the Clean Drinking home of his minister father, and Miss Givens strapped his left hand behind him and insisted on him writing with his right. After he left school, he wrote a beautiful script, lefthanded. Brockett Muir recalled Miss Givens and Miss Rogers as "great teachers." Another of his teachers lived in the Chevy Chase apartment house and at noontime she would walk her students over and make biscuits and butter and pass a jar of milk around as they sat in a circle. Mr. Muir also remembered that he sometimes put bullets on the car tracks before he went back to class and then waited for the explosions that came a few minutes later.[73]

Despite later governmental restrictions, this was the school of choice for most Chevy Chase families for a quarter-century, and many of its Maryland graduates went on to D.C. high schools to finish their educations. Miss Givens, who roomed in the Village at Mrs. Shields' home, worked at the school until 1933, and John M. King was the janitor for almost as long. The school went through a long period of over-enrollment, growth to sixteen rooms, dark portable classrooms, and was last used for pupils in 1942.

On October 6, 1915, the D.C. school board renamed the Chevy Chase School for Elizabeth V. Brown. Miss Brown was a locally-educated primary school teacher in the District, teacher of methods in the Washington Normal School and director of primary instruction from 1904 until her death in July 1915. She was also the author of several collections of stories for children and an active member of the Audubon Society, the Y.W.C.A., and several other organizations.[74]

Schools for Chevy Chase, Maryland, accumulated a long, sometimes bitter, and often confusing history. Public schools, both elementary and secondary, existed in a number of places before they settled on Rosemary Circle and East West Highway, and there have been several private schools in the area. The CCLCo built the first public school at the Circle between Grafton Street and Magnolia Parkway as a Land Company office. The Episcopal church later used that small, yellow building for Sunday afternoon services.

The second school on the Maryland side of the District Line in Chevy Chase was near the northwest corner of Bradley and Connecticut on land donated by the CCLCo, "that lot with a walnut tree thereon, and located on Bradley Lane, with a front of 100 feet and a depth of 150 feet." The Land Company built the two-room school, and the Board agreed to pay "$350 on the completion of the foundation; $600 when the building is roofed and shingled; $600 when the second coat of plastering is finished, and the remaining $608.50 when the building shall have been completed. . . ."

The school opened in the same year as Chevy Chase School in D.C., 1898, and was in operation for five years until it closed because of low enrollment. After the first year a pot-bellied stove replaced the furnace, which had gobbled up six tons of coal. The Chevy Chase School south of the circle was much more popular, and Miss Givens' reputation much better than that of the County teachers. The school was sold for $1,700 and became a private home.[75]

In 1911 the D.C. Board of Education began enforcing its tuition charges for non-resident students, and the next year, because of continuing overcrowding, banned Maryland students from the primary grades. There were, of course, exceptions; Winchester Stone recalled his father being urged to buy a D.C. dog license to show he was a taxpayer in the city, but there was immediate agitation for a school on the Maryland side of the line.

Not everyone was convinced it was needed. Cy Cummings said he did not think there were a dozen children who would attend such a school. But Dr. Ryan Devereux, president of the County school board, organized a Home and School Association, a County first, and in September two teachers were hired and the Cromwell house at 6812 Delaware Street rented, and soon more than a hundred students were in attendance.

The parents elected Thomas E. Robertson, the father of three sons, as the first president of the Home and School Association, which worked to develop support for the new school. Even young Edith Claude, age ten, tried to go to school there because a number of her friends were going, but when her father learned she had enrolled herself, he said, "Indeed, you are not going to that public school" and paid tuition for the D.C. schools. After

finishing at E. V. Brown, Miss Claude attended Central High School and then the Normal School before returning to E. V. Brown as a teacher. Jeannette Hall, née Troth, forced out of E. V. Brown by the changing law, attended the school on Delaware Street and then graduated from the school on Rosemary.

The Delaware Street school was, Mr. Robertson noted, "merely an unsatisfactory makeshift."

The Chevy Chase School and Home Association made an arrangement with the County School Board, to have the Chevy Chase Public School Corporation borrow $5,000 on individual notes, and erect a four-room school building on Rosemary Street on a lot lent by the Land Company; the County School Board was to pay rent to the local corporation until the notes were paid off, when the building was to be the property of the school board. This was accomplished through the assistance of such residents as Colonel Clephane, Guy Camp, Eugene Stevens, Clarence Dawson, and others. [76]

During that school year, 1912-13, the various sections of Chevy Chase contributed $1,500, the County appropriated $2,500, and mortgaging the lot Newlands donated produced the rest, and four, wooden, "portable" classroom buildings measuring twenty by thirty feet went up on Rosemary Street at a total cost of about $5,000. The County hired four teachers with Florence Barksdale as principal, and the school opened in September 1913. It soon expanded to include the first two years of high school although few students above grade eight ever attended.

By the 1914-15 school year thirty-eight of the 185 students enrolled at the Chevy Chase school were in the high school division. The upper grade pupils shared the efforts of "household economics" teacher Effie Barnsley and "manual training" teacher Edgar Thompson with the grammar school. The two high school teachers that year were Elsa D. Muench for English and foreign language instruction and James R. Daly, who taught math and science and coached the boys' teams.

Bobby Stevens was one of the first students at the new school. His parents had both been active in getting the school started. "Those portable buildings were all on one floor, but they kind of snaked around," he remembered.

In first grade I had Miss Washington, and my second grade teacher was Miss Tracey. I

Mr. Daly with the school's baseball team[77]

remember them because I was always in trouble. Once in first grade, I was having trouble with the kid in front of me, and she brought in a pair of boxing gloves and put us out in the middle, and we banged each other. I was losing until this boy's nose started bleeding, and she got scared and stopped it.

A political battle between Kensington and Chevy Chase over the location of a down-county school ensued with Harry M. Martin charging Chevy Chase with operating an illegal high school. The trustees of the Chevy Chase School urged residents to send their children to the Maryland school. "Every child of this community attending the D.C. schools will serve as an argument against our needs," said a letter signed by Guy W. A. Camp, Mrs. Eugene E. Stevens and Vernon E. Hodges.

Suburban demands, especially for schools, reached Annapolis in early 1914, and up-county Delegate Eugene Waters the first to clearly enunciate the growing split between the rural "upper" County and the fast-growing "down" County. He urged dissatisfied suburbanites to move back to D.C. if they were unhappy, and when someone suggested that the County would starve if they did, Waters replied "Let the south end cut itself off and make a little county of its own. We'll be mighty glad to give all the help we can if the people of the south end want to do this."

When a proposed $30,000 bond issue for a high school in Chevy Chase stirred up a storm, Delegate Andrew J. Cummings of Chevy Chase proposed a ten cent increase in the County tax to pay off the existing school debt. Despite a post card campaign asking Chevy Chasers to petition their representatives in the State legislature for a new school, the proposed bond issue and tax increase failed, and while some in

Chevy Chase blamed Kensington, more blamed Rockville. By then the Bethesda election district was providing twenty-three percent of the County tax money, but the only "real" schools were in Glen Echo and Bethesda.[78]

Despite the disappointment, the young school closed with a flourish:

The commencement exercises of the Chevy Chase public school were held last Friday morning, commencing at 9 o'clock, on the lawn before the school building. Immediately following the exercises was the oratorical contest for gold and silver medals offered by Dr. Ryan Devereux, president of the County school board and resident of Chevy Chase, for which there were 17 entries. Medals were won by Miss Helen Hodges and Miss Ruth Pierce. The assembly was addressed by Dr. Devereux, also by Charles D. Frailey, Esq., president of the Chevy Chase Home and School Association, after which light refreshments were served. Athletic sports by pupils closed the events of the day, well attended by parents and friends and marking the close of the second year of the new school established in 1912.

The next year a $1,500, one-story annex added three classrooms to the school. In June the high school division reported three graduates: Helen Elizabeth Hodges, Charles Shoemaker, and Thomas D. Servis.

In 1915 Congress changed the rules so that those employed in the city could send their children to D.C. schools free of charge. Sometimes everyone south of Melrose was allowed to go to E. V. Brown, and at other times Maryland students were excluded from that school but allowed to attend other, less crowded Washington public schools. In Febru-

ary 1917 the County school board awarded an $18,204 contract to Roy W. Poole of Frederick to build a school in Chevy Chase.

In the spring of 1917 work began on Valley Place between Meadow Lane and Rosemary Street for the first permanent school. The dedication of the two-story, red brick building took place in November 1917. The school, which some called "Valley View," operated with a high school for a year and then became a seven-grade elementary. The principal, Mrs. Barksdale, established one precedent when she hired the first known Montgomery County Public School school secretary, Margaret Owens, in March 1918.

The only thing Bobby Stevens recalled about the new school was the big assembly room on the top floor where they sometimes went to sing. It was also the last place he saw a pupil really whipped:

It was one of the Dellinger boys. Miss Ankers took him to the back of the room, and she had a belt, and she was giving it to him. She really had that boy jumping.

Elsie Irvine came to work there as a third grade teacher, and then she taught the 4th grade until her son was born in 1939. Myrtle Anderson was the principal when she started. She recalled that her classes sometimes had forty-five or more students, and that the old building had a central hall with a piano where the classes assembled for sing-a-longs. She remembered Helen Stephens as the first teacher in a tuition kindergarten, which began in 1926, and that the other members of the staff at that time were Savilla Burns 1st grade, Margaret (Peg) Hyson 2nd grade, Miss Perry 5th and Marion Swartz 6th grade.

Among the best remembered activities were the field trips classes took downtown on the trolley cars to visit the Smithsonian and other museums, and the field days in Rockville to which parents transported children in their cars for many years although sometimes they walked over to Bethesda and took the trolley.

Ed Stock, who hiked from his home on Bradley Boulevard from 1916 until 1920, recalled:

We used to go up to Rockville on the streetcar. We used to chant "Ice cream, soda water, ginger ale, pop! Chevy Chase, Chevy Chase, always on top!" They had races and that sort of thing. We had a good time.

Of course, the water tower was still there in the circle, a constant dare to a lot of boys

Chevy Chase HS 1913 - (l-r) Fred Imirie, Helen Hodges, Mark Shoemaker, Mr. Daly, two unnamed girls, Buddy Dawson, Chick Shoemaker

and several girls. Helen "Sister" Smith (B-CC `35) gained long-term fame by hanging by her knees from the top of the winding stairs at every opportunity.[79]

Enrollment declined in the early 1920s, but by 1926 the building boom was well underway, and the trustees met to discuss a bigger school. Mrs. Irvine said she did not think Tom Perry or Horace Troth or the other trustees paid much attention to what the teachers wanted, but soon delay became impossible. The overcrowded school turned away twenty-five children in 1927, and the Chevy Chase sixth graders moved over to the newly built high school at 44th and Willow at mid-year.[80]

In 1930 the school board built a twelve-classroom, brick building facing Rosemary Street beginning at a cost of $94,000. It almost ended Valley Place as a street and gave the school a new, informal name–Rosemary School. A lunch room serving soon operated in the basement with the help of volunteers supervised by Mrs. Irvine, the treasurer of the PTA. When the Chevy Chase Bank closed in the Depression, she recalled worrying about how she was going to pay for the produce or get the cafeteria manager her $20 a week.

In 1936 the BOE demolished the old Valley Place school and built a $100,000, nine-room addition connected to the back of the older structure by a long, white, clapboard wooden hall. "The 'Long Hall' had a row of windows on each side, and no pretense of insulation or heat. A ten-year-old, running hard, could shake the whole structure. In the large square enclosed by the school buildings on three sides was space for the annual May Day dance and for graduation ceremonies, weather permitting." The enlarged school had a health

room and a music room, and well into the 1940s, a room used by a cooperative nursery school.[81]

Of the private schools, the Chevy Chase College for Young Ladies, later Chevy Chase Junior College, was, by far, the most enduring and most successful. Miss Rose Mactier and her sisters operated a short-lived school at her family's large home on Connecticut just north of Bradley. Her father was an inventor best known for the Atlantic City rolling chair. Edith Claude attended what she called the "little French school" but said:

It was dubious as to how much French we learned, but the cookie jar which Miss Mactier kept filled on the sideboard remains in my memory more significantly than the French I absorbed.

She recalled going there on the streetcar with her Irish setter, and said there were "probably no more than eight students."

Another pupil of the Mactiers was Don Caffery Glassie whose family built the third house on Bradley Lane in 1910. He said there were three kids in three rooms with three teachers when he attended, but remembered even better playing in the barn out back, which was filled with Colonel Mactier's inventions.

Over the years the Village Hall was the site of many dancing classes. Among the dancing teachers were Prof. Zebele, Mrs. Murphy, Miss or Mrs. Chase, Miss Minnie Hawke and Miss Libby. Back on Brookeville Road, Dr. Frank Hood Schultz purchased and remodeled the No Gain farm. He sold roses and peonies to D.C. florists and grew grapes and made his own wine during Prohibition. In 1928 with the local public school becoming crowded, he built the Bradford Home School. Many children in the Martin's Additions area attended, and some remembered playing in an old streetcar in the school's backyard. The Depression and the opening of the new building at Chevy Chase Elementary in 1932 put this school out of business, and then Mrs. Schultz opened the Brook Farm tea room, the first of many restaurants in that structure.[83]

The Cobb School, sometimes called the Chevy Chase Country Day School, began in the Village Hall, and when enrollment increased, rooms were rented in Miss Mackrill's home on W. Kirke.

Kindergarteners practicing for the big May Day celebration in 1939.[82]

Dr. Cobb tested applicants and placed them according to their abilities, and among the more prominent students were the Tuckerman girls from Edgemoor. It was a "progressive school" in the early `20s which had the children taking nature walks on the Kirkside golf course and doing exercises on the porch, rain or shine. Later the school with programs from grades one to eight moved to a home at 3 Grafton Street with both boarders and day students, and according to a later resident, "the house practically fell down."[84]

Blessed Sacrament opened a three-classroom school for sixty-two students in 1923. The school, like the parish, grew rapidly and within ten years was building a new convent for a dozen sisters of the Holy Cross. By the end of the 1930s the sisters taught more than 650 students at Blessed Sacrament. The parish became locally well known for its numerous large families, including the nine children of Joseph and Helen Devereux, and there were joking references to the growing membership of the "Seven-Up Club."

Then there was the short-lived Peniel School run by Mrs. Clotilde Cunningham at Brookeville and E. Lenox in the late 1920s. It was a very small school for children of all ages that precipitated one of the first major legal actions under the zoning powers of the M-NCP&PC when the local citizens' association and the County Commissioners tried to close it down as a non-conforming use.

Miss Libbey's School operated in the Chevy Chase Library beginning in 1935. It was a very small "progressive school" with a kindergarten for children ages four to six and offered grades one to six plus transportation. Bertha Belt started an outdoor nursery school at her home on Meadow Lane in 1933 which was still going sixty years later at "In the Woods."

In 1897 the Chevy Chase Club, which Newlands, C. C. Glover and others had held afloat so they could ride to the hounds in a proper manner, bought the 9.36-acre Bradley place for $22,000 after almost being tempted away by a twenty-acre offer from Bethesda Park's John Beall. The Chevy Chase Club became important to many early residents and investors but never to a majority. Herbert Claude, for example, was asked to become a charter member, but according to his daughter Edith, "he, being a young married man with

quite a family said, 'I'm sure I can't afford to be a member of the Chevy Chase Club,' so while his dues and his initiation fee would have been paid for, he declined the opportunity." While Dr. Devereux was a very early member, his eldest son Joseph, who lived next door, never joined. In many ways the exclusive Club was never a part of the community.

Golf was immediately popular, and before the turn of the century the foursomes were out on the links by six o'clock in the morning during the summer. The early morning trolley cars carried many illustrious Washingtonians out to "Chevy" for some country air. Associate Justice John Marshall Harlan, noted for his dissents, was often on the first car to reach the old clubhouse on Saturday morning. "Golf attire" was not allowed at Chevy; most men played in flannels and wore scarlet coats with black facings.

By 1905 the baying hounds and the horsemen and women who followed them had stirred up enough complaints that Clarence Moore, who had succeeded Henry Earle as master of hounds, took his horses and dogs to Virginia leaving behind a bill for $25 for "manure left, about 50 loads." He returned to a farm near Kensington in 1906 and that fall there were rides almost every Monday, Wednesday, Thursday and Saturday; however, the golfers were slowly but persistently taking over.

An August 1899 *Star* story on "Golf at Chevy Chase" reflected the attitude of the Club and of most of its imitators.

The Chevy Chase club, looked at from a purely practical point of view, is of decided benefit to the working classes. It employs half a dozen men regularly to keep the green in its perpetual state of velvety smoothness, numbers of small boys find employment as caddies, the waiters, caterers and other purveyors and employees receive a livelihood from the annual dues of the 300 members.

The expense attached to the playing of golf may to a certain extent be governed by the player. The entrance fee of the Chevy Chase club is $25 and the annual dues $30 – not a large sum truly when one considers the benefit to health, both of mind and body. The absolute relaxation from business cares and the good, healthy bodily fatigue resultant from a game of golf is a sure cure for insomnia and all its attendant ills.[85]

In 1903 the club reincorporated and purchased sixty-five more acres to meet the needs

of golfers. Then in 1908 it acquired the long-sought, 118-acre Dodge property along Wisconsin Avenue, had its first 18-hole course laid out, and hired a pro and a clubmaker. Tennis was popular from the beginning, and sixteen courts were in use by World War I. The club also had bowling alleys and sponsored a baseball team.

Henri deSibour designed the new, Potomac gneiss clubhouse built by the Page Construction Co. for $105,580.50, occupied in June 1911, and labeled by William Howard Taft a fine example of "early penitentiary colonial architecture." The restored Bradley farmhouse served as sleeping quarters but, except for a chimney and some wisteria, disappeared in a 1918 fire.

By the 1920s the Club had relaxed its restrictions on admitting anyone "in trade" but still continued to be highly selective. Prohibition caused little change in the operation of the taproom or in the ministrations of one of the best-known bartenders in the area, Henry William Thomas. The behavior of President Harding and some of his cronies, both on and off the golf course, scandalized some of the more abstemious members.

In 1926 Waddy Wood redesigned and added to the clubhouse, and County Commissioner Benjamin Perry made plans to widen Bradley Lane. The Club refused to deed a strip ten-feet wide along the road because of its effect on the entrance, tennis courts and trees. The plan was abandoned. No one was really surprised. Although its membership represented the Capital cave dwellers much more than its neighborhood, the Club was undoubtedly responsible for the view many outsiders had of Chevy Chase.[86]

About twelve years after the Chevy Chase Club began operating, a group of businessmen established the Columbia Country Club on 126 acres of Hayes plantation property purchased from the Land Company for about $700 an acre. The Columbia Golf Club had started in 1898 on Georgia Avenue on land that later was Morris Cafritz's first great real estate development, Petworth. The initiation fee then was $2 and membership, originally limited to twenty, soon grew to about 400 before the club was forced to move.

The new club, incorporated in Maryland in 1909, soon had 200 members who paid $100 each to join. Henry L. West was the first president, and H. Bradley and John C. David-

son were both members of the original board of directors. Edward B. Eynon Jr., of the Washington Baseball Club was one of the best recruiters of new members and sellers of bonds, and William Corby was one of the club's early members and supporters. He joined Columbia, it was said, because he heard that the Chevy Chase Club had turned down the applications of men in business. Like Chevy Chase, Columbia built its $50,000 clubhouse, designed by Frederick B. Pyle, close to the trolley line; it opened New Year's Day 1911.[87]

By the turn of the century the Land Company had accomplished much to make its "model suburb" livable. It had provided a railway, roads, sidewalks, gutters, and electricity, later taken over by PEPCO. It had landscaped near the main road, provided water and sewer service (although the latter was becoming a problem) and had given land for schools, churches, clubs and a meeting hall. It built a lake and amusement park, a hotel, and even tolerated an apartment house. But still the sale of building lots proceeded sluggishly and in some depression years would not pay the taxes.

In 1898 the T. J. Fisher Co. sold sixty acres south of Cleveland Park to New York investors represented by H. P. Waggaman. The price was $4,500 per acre for the land west of Connecticut and $4,000 an acre for the thirty-five acres east of Connecticut. It was, the *Star* noted, "a handsome advance for Mr. Newlands over what he paid for it." But big sales such as this were not what the CCLCo had in mind.

Edward Stellwagen and B. Frances Saul founded the Union Trust and Storage Company in 1899 so that loans on Newlands' undeveloped real estate could be secured from the Deacons Bank of Manchester, England, and the heavy investment of the Sharon funds released for other purposes. Ten years earlier Washington Loan and Trust had been incorporated in West Virginia and American Security and Storage in Virginia to aid in the financing of real estate development. Union Trust's charter was the first granted in D.C. under the 1890 legislation that encouraged the establishment of well-capitalized, responsible, local, lending institutions.

The bank, next to the Willard on F Street, along with the Thomas J. Fisher Company, the Capital Traction Company and the Chevy

Chase Land Company moved to the site of the old Wormley Hotel and built their offices at 15th and H. In 1907 the bank occupied the new building and changed its name to Union Trust Company and funded some of Newlands' later interests in municipal improvements. By the time of the crash in 1929, deposits were approaching $10 million.

About 1900, the Land Company opened up Sections Three and Four in Maryland and sold a number of lots, often in multiples, in both of those areas. Section Three was the land north of Bradley between Brookeville and Connecticut, which some thought of as the "working man's" Chevy Chase, and Section Four was west of Connecticut and now makes up most of the Town of Chevy Chase.

The census of 1900 showed that Chevy Chase was going to be different from other streetcar suburbs in the Bethesda election district in several ways. The majority of early families, for example, were from out-of-state while most households near the river and along Wisconsin Avenue were full of Marylanders. Chevy Chase families tended to have more servants and very few of them were farm laborers. Only a handful of farms remained and those were mostly dairying operations such as the Cummings and Callaghan places. "Otho" Sonnemann listed himself as a "gardener," and John Green, an African-American, and his large family had a dairy farm in northern Chevy Chase. There were very few black families and a larger proportion of foreigners, mainly English and Germans, in Chevy Chase.

At the turn of the century some thirty Chevy Chase and North Chevy Chase families had about thirty black and fifteen white live-in servants. Professor Elmon Gates, ensconced in the Lodge with his wife and three young children, had an assistant, a cook, a janitor, and two governesses while several households included two or three servants. At the Club, the manager listed four black waiters living on the premises, and at the inn, the proprietor, Charles McDermoot had his wife and daughter, eight boarders and fourteen employees under his roof. The Chevy Chase area had almost forty percent of all those listed as servants in the Bethesda census district in 1900.

In 1907 the CCLCo also began selling building lots south of the District Line. Three houses were built on Oliver and Northampton Streets as models of the type of construction that was expected. Brainard W. Parker had the old Belt mansion southeast of the circle at about 3734 Oliver Street demolished to make way for a more modern house. When the north wall fell, the English ivy stood "as firm as a board fence" and had to be chopped down with an ax. Some bricks from that old dwelling went into the foundation and chimneys of the new house on the same lot. The Belt cemetery east of the home vanished in the building of the Chevy Chase Parkway area.

In D.C. the lots east of Connecticut went for 25¢ a square foot and those west of the Avenue for 38¢ with a ten percent discount offered to the first fifty buyers and an additional 10 percent if construction was begun in three months. In 1911 after a rather noisy dispute between the young Citizens' Association and the CCLCo, Doc Armstrong's drugstore and Willard Folmer's grocery and post office opened in the first block south of the Circle, and by the mid-20s the theater that became the Avalon was in operation and the Beaux Arts arcade had opened.[88]

Of all the early decisions and actions of the Chevy Chase Land Company perhaps the oddest and most inexplicable was the construction of the Chevy Chase apartment building which opened in 1910. It was designed by the director and chief architect of the Land Company, Leon Dessez, and built just opposite the Corby mansion and fifty feet from the Maryland Line. The building was not only an obvious violation of the covenants in the Chevy Chase deeds, it was also a queer use of one of the prime pieces of Land Company acreage at the entrance to its slowly developing, high-class suburb. Across the Circle the Episcopalians had already built their first stone church, and the Presbyterians and Catholics, meeting at the Library, were both talking construction on the Circle. And there rising in its white stucco, Spanish splendor under the wide eaves of its red-tiled roof was a four-story, sixteen unit, walk-up apartment house in the middle of a broad lawn.[89]

The apartments originally rented for $40 to $60 per month. James Goode called it "the first true suburban Washington apartment building." Half of the rental units have four rooms and three exposures; the smaller one-bedroom apartments face Western Avenue. Balconies and taller windows add to the second and fourth floors. The halls and stairwells boast marble floors and wainscoting,

and the apartments have walnut-stained, chestnut woodwork.[90]

The next year Dessez designed and built himself and his family a large, pebble dash stucco home with big, bay windows on Jenifer Street in Chevy Chase Heights, D.C., and left the Village and the apartment house across from the Lodge. That house was then occupied by a Professor Gates who, according to Mrs. Jarvis, had a theory about the migration of the soul, which he studied in a steel lined room he built inside the Lodge. The Catholic Church bought the land to the east of the apartment house in 1911 and constructed a small, wooden chapel. In 1925 services moved to the large, stone Shrine of the Most Blessed Sacrament.[91]

In July 1908 the Chevy Chase Land Company leased twenty acres at Chevy Chase Lake to Herbert Claude for ten years. According to the lease the renter was to erect "such improvements upon said land as are necessary for its use for pleasure purposes, charging a reasonable compensation to all persons availing themselves of the same. . . and will pay the Chevy Chase Land Company ten percent of gross receipts. . . but not less than $600 per year." The lease included use of the lake, and all structures were subject to CCLCo approval. Claude was also given the option to purchase the land for $1,500 an acre, and the Land Company agreed not to lease adjacent land for similar purposes.

The Lake had been a popular place to visit before 1908 with rowboats on the still waters, a band stand, shady picnic grounds and at night "thousands of fairy lights" of various colors flickered along the water's edge. Occasionally all the bulbs were replaced with those of a single color. In August 1899, an ad proclaimed, "the tiny lights along the shore, the big set pieces and the legends in letters several feet high will be of the uniform color, red."

But the big attraction in the early days was the Marine Band which appeared in "full and colorful regalia. They played," according to Mrs. Jarvis, "semi-classical numbers much like the pop concerts of Boston. . . For the last half of the program, which was dance music only,

the musicians had walked down the hill from the band stand to the large, rustic dance pavilion, overlooking the lake."

In competition with Bethesda Park and Glen Echo, the Land Company's trolley line brought vaudeville and circus acts to the Lake from time to time. In the summer of 1899, for example, the big attraction was the "marvelous aquatic feats of the famous Meiers family" which included 13-year-old Bessie, "the most graceful child diver of the day," 10-year-old Tommie, both a diver and trick swimmer, and three-year old Elma who "rows about the lake in her tiny boat and manages her craft with wonderful skill." The Meiers' act featured a high dive of sixty feet and a "mimic drowning" at 5 and 8:30 pm. The admission was free.[92]

Herbert Claude soon added attractions to rival the growing popularity of Glen Echo. As a youngster James H. Pugh, who lived in the Chevy Chase area for more than seventy years and served as both State's Attorney and Circuit Judge, worked for Mr. Claude.[93]

My family moved to North Chevy Chase in the year 1906. As a young boy about 4 years of age I grew up a short distance from Chevy Chase Lake. In those early years and later as I reached the age of 10 years I visited and worked in the evenings at the amusement park in the summer. My duties were to row the boats on the lake, set up bowling pins on the bowling alleys, attend the shooting gallery, attend the boat swings (on shore), was the ring boy on the merry-go-round (the carousel), was the hat check boy on the dancing pavilion, along with my four brothers, Mike, Ed, Charlie and Robbie. . . .

To reach the amusement park people would have to cross, by foot, a large wooden bridge. There was a second wooden bridge which was seldom used.

From the Lake to Columbia CC in the early `20s with B&O across the bottom

In the park there was a cafe where ice cream was served, boat swings, pulled by long ropes to make them swing, a band stand, where the Marine Band played and also where John Philip Sousa led the Marine Band a few times.

A merry-go-round, as it was called in those days (1910), but now known as a carousel, a shooting gallery, three bowling alleys, row boats for hire on the lake, at 5 cents for 1/2 hour and a large dancing pavilion [where] the Meyer Davis Orchestra played for many years and Kate Smith got her start there as a singer and Irene Castle danced there many times.

In the early days, just after the turn of the century in 1900, there was a small pony track at the upper end of the amusement park and band stand. The ponies were housed by Mr. Herbert Claude, superintendent of the Capital Traction Streetcar Co. which operated the car line from D.C. to Chevy Chase Lake. In 1910 Mr. Claude's house on Manor Road burned to the ground and that was the end of the ponies and the track at the amusement park. The track was replaced by the merry-go-round which was operated by Harry Mullendorf. The red, white and blue lights that surrounded the lake gave it a beautiful outline. As young boys we would "gig" bull frogs around the edges of Chevy Chase Lake at night after the amusement park closed, using flash lights we caught frogs and we sold the frog legs to the Columbia Country Club nearby for 10 cents a pair.

The lake had one bad fatality in the winter of about 1916 (see note). The lake was partially frozen over from the cold weather but part of it would not freeze because the hot water from the power plant would prevent it. A teenage couple was skating on the frozen part of the lake at night, not aware that part of the lake was not frozen. Both were drowned. Swimming was never permitted in the lake.[94]

Chevy Chase Lake and amusement park had a wonderful reputation as a high class amusement park, no rowdyism, no drinking or smoking or carousing....

Mrs. Jarvis, and others, recalled the bandstand as "a mammoth seashell, with hundreds of electric lights sparkling from its interior, which

was painted a pale and delicate blue." Along with dozens of other Chevy Chase children, she also learned to skate there with her father standing on the shore shouting instructions: "Use the outside edge. Use the inside edge." Mr. Powell remembered not only skating there but also playing "shinny," pick-up ice hockey, and falling through the ice into chest-deep water and then riding the trolley back down to Quincy Street in his stiffening clothes.

Of course, on holidays there were special events, and one 4th of July "all the fireworks caught fire on the barge. It went up all at once in a terrific noise and the man who was working the fireworks had to swim to shore." As at the Cabin John Hotel and Glen Echo Park, silent motion pictures became an added attraction as early as the summer of 1904.[95]

The high fence around the Lake and amusement park was no barrier to determined boys. One of their favorite sports was riding bicycles or roller skating on the dance pavilion's huge, hardwood floor. Bill Duvall had one of the oddest experiences there:

One day we went underneath the dance floor and there were a whole lot of slot machines in there, small ones, a little bigger than a typewriter. So several of us decided they would be real nice to have at home so somehow we got these things out and balanced on the handlebars and took them home, and our parents all agreed that they better go back where we found them, and they did.

Band leader Meyer Davis took over the lease in 1918 at $1,500 a month, and one by one the various amusements disappeared, even the merry-go-round, and the operation became dances only. It continued into the 1920s as a rendezvous for the younger crowd,

In the `20s - looking south from the Lake, powerhouse and carbarn, with the dance pavilion and carousel above them, and across Conn., the trainmen's houses on Watkins Street. Note streetcars on Conn. Ave and trains on B&O tracks (detail from photo on p. 169)

and a number of name bands played there including Russ Columbo's. Kate Smith, as well as numerous other local talents, entertained at the Lake. Fires in 1925 interrupted the dances, and the dam finally collapsed or was destroyed in the late `20s. The country clubs and hotel terraces became the places to go.

Across the street from the Lake and its attractions, the Chevy Chase Land Company leased several acres of land for a swimming pool operation in 1925. Much of the bottom land where the pool was built had been the gardens of the conductors and motormen who lived in the row of brick houses just up the hill. Long after the dances at the Lake and the trolley cars were gone and the carbarn apron a used-car lot, the pool behind the arched gateway and wooden fence was still a popular if somewhat shabby summer attraction.

Chevy Chase Swimming Pool

Generally there was so much chlorine in the water that the complaints about the condition of the locker rooms, the crumbling concrete, and the cinders that passing trains blew into the pool were suppressed since adding chemicals seemed to be the management's answer to all suggestions. The cost was low, but since the fence was seldom in good repair, a lot of kids swam for free with a "borrowed" key on the elastic band around their ankle as proof they paid. Like the apartment building on the Circle, the swimming pool at the Lake seemed an anomaly, but a well advertised one.

Together with Edith Claude Jarvis' more organized work, the recollections of early Chevy Chase residents make a lively patchwork quilt. Vida Ord Alexander wrote:

Early Chevy Chase had a distinctly rural flavor. Nearly every one kept chickens, the cause of minor neighborhood feuds, because they would get loose and scratch up gardens and croquet grounds! Several stables were maintained — Sen. Newlands, now the Corby estate; Dr. Childs, the first rector of All Saints Church, on Conn. Ave. be-tween Kirke and E. Irving; John L. Weaver, Brookeville Rd. and E. Kirke, and Dr. Frank Evans, 16 W. Kirke. A few had cows — one was famous for being pastured on Chevy Chase Circle!

The Chevy Chase Hunt used to ride through the village and surrounding fields, its pink coated huntsmen and pack of hounds, an impressive spectacle. Clarence Moore, the famous sportsman who lived at Briarbank on W. Lenox, was a member of the Hunt. Several annual horse shows were held on the Club grounds. . .

Another member of the Hunt, banker Samuel J. Henry has left a reminiscence as has his youngest daughter, Anne, born and reared in Chevy Chase.

We had only been in the house a month when we were shocked by the news of Mr. Clarence Moore's death in the Titanic. As M.F.H. of the Chevy Chase Hunt, he had mounted me on his fine hunting horses to follow the hounds on fox hunts and drag hunts.

My first recollection of Chevy Chase, is of the village major domo, one Spencer Hays, a medium sized colored man of atomic energy and uncanny resourcefulness. He had charge of a dozen men engaged in road repairs, garbage and trash removal. Unofficially, Spencer bossed the colored maids, cooks, chauffeurs and yard men and seemed to maintain an inexhaustible reserve of these minions which when occasion demanded, he called up with military dispatch. Let one of our domestics resign, or was fired, my wife sent for Spencer and told him her requirements. "Don't you worry, Mrs. Henry," Spencer would say: "just you leave it to me; I know exactly where to find the person to fill the bill." And sure enough next morning bright and early, there would be Spencer on the back porch, grinning from ear to ear, with a candidate ready and willing to go to work.[96]

Inordinately proud of his talents and always busy as a jay bird in a cherry tree, Spencer never doubted in the least his capacity to execute any commission that had been entrusted to him. Whether it involved an order for a cord of firewood, a new laundress or a sewing woman, a job of white washing or retrieving a lost dog, bicycle or children, he proved to be a go-getter of unbelievable puissance. Spencer liked to tell about his early life. He said, "When I was growing up I worked on a farm near Rockville. I helped with corn and potatoes and we raised chickens, hogs, cows and horse. I brought water from the spring with one bucket on my head and another in my

hand. *These people coming along now, don't know nothing."*

Mr. Henry went on to describe his neighbors, Judge DeLacy with his nine children and noisy Model T on one side and the quiet William D. Henrys, no relation, on the other. "Mrs. Henry kept a small flock of hens; I never heard a cackle from one of them," he noted. His other neighbors included the Colts and the Beales and their four children, the youngest of whom was called "Baby" all her life.

Mr. Beale also displayed a fondness for shooting and, since the Village was infested with screech owls, he and I often hunted them at twilight with a .22 Winchester, a harmless sport calculated to improve one's marksmanship. . . The artillery I used was the same .22 Winchester I had taught our children to shoot with, the range being the garage driveway and the distance fifty feet to a paper target.

Another neighbor was Bob Yellott, who was involved with the Bradley Hills Syndicate, and Mr. Henry recalled riding that trolley line "to Great Falls and return, the car swinging and swaying in the most exciting way." Henry also rode horses through Edgemoor with Walter Tuckerman, General Billy Mitchell and took part in the numerous horse shows. Horses were kept on the Club grounds, tended by "Old Mose," and when they got loose and charged through the Village, mothers and maids ran to gather in their children.

Samuel Henry's memoir also includes his views of Prohibition:

In 1918, that silly piece of legislation, the Dry Act, hit the country and all hands were supposed to stop drinking. At the Chevy Chase Club you placed a bottle of whiskey and gin in your locker and when you wanted a drink you got the bottle out and called for a set-up. Sometimes both bottles were empty. Henry Thomas, the black-eyed, black-haired bartender, was always helpful. He had an icebox which contained cheese and rye breads, also olives and cherries, contraband so to speak, for in those days food could be obtained only in the dining room or men's porch upstairs. When a fellow's private stock of liquor became non-existent and that fact was communicated to Henry, he always managed to scare up a drink, thereby saving many a life which would otherwise have been a sacrifice to the ridiculous dry crusade. At home I built a locker in the sewing room and by contacts with bootleggers and not sparing the cash managed to ride out the storm.

Mr. Henry succeeded Justice Stanton J. Peele as head of the Chevy Chase Citizens' Committee and was responsible for acquiring the land north of the library that provided space for the new post office; the southern part of block 37 had been deeded to the Free Library board in 1901. He stated that this was done was to keep the CCLCo from "commercial exploitation" of that land.[97]

Anne Henry called her reminiscence "Six West" and provided a child's eye view of the same world:

My sister Billie and I shared a room together, my half crib snug next to her old fashioned brass bed. Holding her hand until I drifted off to sleep I woke early to hear the clop, clop of the milkman's horse in the early dawn. Later in the day the ice man and his cart and horse. We always received a sliver of ice to chew. Too, there was the breadman, his cart held a most delicious aroma of freshly baked bread and rolls.

Both my parents complained to each other of the DeLacy's hen house which contained one large red rooster, who crowed each morning, rain or shine. But still worse, and not on their side of the house, was the manner in which Judge DeLacy backed his Ford from the garage. If one held his breath until his Honor was out of the narrow drive, he would perish. Such forward and backing by the kindly man was nerve racking since he would put forth all steam on the gas peddle and even the soundest sleeper would wake to the large roar of the small engine. . . .

One of my earliest memories was the summer concerts played at the Chevy Chase Circle by the Navy Band. The Circle then had no fountain — completely bare. What a treat it was to see the sign "Navy Band Concert Tonight." It was well attended, barking dogs, excited kids and crying babies. But everyone enjoyed it.

Numerous reports exist of football and baseball playing on the Circle, which was a good bit larger before the street was widened, and of children who rubbed Ivory soap on the streetcar tracks to watch the trolleys blow bubbles. After the Scouts erected the flagpole in the center in 1918, there are even stories of boys competing to see who could put the biggest dents in the brass ball on top. Everyone knows about the Marine Band at the Lake, but only young Miss Anne seems to have remembered the Navy musicians at the Circle.[98]

Another Kirke Street memorialist—the street seems to have bred them—was Connie

Weaver Thompson whose father built a house designed by her uncle, Arthur B. Heaton. She described the Village Hall in detail with the tall pole in front on which was the makeshift fire bell that the Cobb School children enjoyed ringing at recess, then the post office, and then the library with bookshelves on one side and a stage for theatricals and a kitchen behind and a "powder room." She wrote that the fire fighting equipment included a chemical unit and a length of hose kept under the kitchen, and that after church on Thanksgiving a fire drill was held with all the VIPs participating. She remembered "Dad rushing around and trying all the fire plugs—all four of them."[99]

The village movement spawned a slick, coated-paper magazine, *The Village: A Journal for Village Life*, which looked at Chevy Chase in August of 1907. It noted that "the deeds drawn by the original founder had an eye to the well-kept, ideal village" and concluded that "a prettier or better kept village could not be found." Not everyone was equally impressed by what was being achieved just north of the Circle.

When the *Star*'s long series, "Improvements Seen From A Trolley Car Window," got around to assessing Chevy Chase in June 1910, the view of Newlands' prize real estate was hardly flattering.

It is only a little farther along to the north and one reaches the southern extension of Chevy Chase where the tide of building has crossed over from Maryland territory into the District. Here is found the bungalow, and in addition to the conveniences and advantages which evidently belong to this style of house, it is readily apparent it fits in with the landscape and does not thrust great, hulking, awkward masses of brick and stone and sometimes of wood into the soft harmonies of foliage and lawn and sky.

There are larger houses and of different style not only in that section of the Connecticut avenue region, but beyond and throughout Chevy Chase proper and also in the newer region of the vicinity of Bradley lane. A good many of them are designed with some regard to their surroundings, while there are also houses that are entirely out of place and look it. They fly in your face if a

figure can be used implying the possibility of life and movement in such dead masses of material almost without form and certainly without any grace and having no manner of relation to the setting in which they have been placed.

The suburb grew slowly and unevenly but tended to develop along the trolley line and Brookeville Road. In 1910 the T. J. Fisher Company summarized its sales and announced that "sales continue active" and that there were a half-dozen buyers waiting for water connections to start building. The price of land in Section Two was raised five cents per square foot. Based on the Land Company's records, the chart below is a summary of the sales through March 1910:[100]

1910 SUMMARY section	II	III	IV
Acres subdivided	136.5	70.0	69.0
Proposed lots	440	223	333
Lots sold	264.5	145.0	176.0
Percent sold	60	65	53
Improvements	$1,350,262	$927,657	$14,832
Sq. Ft. sold	2,710,294	1,644,649	471,208
Value per sq.ft.	20¢ - 50¢	10¢ - 25¢	20¢ - 35¢
Net sales to 3/31/10	$514,127	$205,791	$169,374
Value of unsold land	$310,560	$111,318	$423,127
	@ 23¢	@ 12¢	@ 24¢ per sq.ft.

In 1910 the census taker enumerated 166 households with 753 inhabitants within the statistical area labeled Chevy Chase. The decennial count found 429 women, 57 of them black, and 324 men, 14 of them black. In that count were 245 children and 85 servants. But, of course, not all of these people lived on land purchased from the CCLCo. Some, such as the Williams and Cummings, had been there long before and others were building on the lots sold by developers such as Harry Martin.

Between Underwood and Thornapple streets west of Brookeville Road a subdivision called Otterbourne found a way to survive surrounded by the Chevy Chase Land Company. It laid its own sewer pipes and even received Land Company permission to construct a boardwalk from the trolley line to its property. The plat for Otterbourne in the County land records was filed by John Frank Ellis in July 1894 on his purchase of 14 1/2 acres of the Williams' "No Gain" property. He laid out streets called Douglas (Underwood)

and Percy (Taylor) and sixty-nine lots ranging from 12,000 to 6,250 square feet. Otterbourne, with its own citizens' committee, survived until Section Three gobbled up most of it when it was incorporated. Even then it retained its identity in census and election records. According to Thomas Robertson the name, which he spelled Otterburn, referred to a Scottish border town connected to the Ballad of Cheivy Chace.[101]

Robert Stevens, one of the best baseball players ever to come out of the Bethesda area, remembered the neighborhood:

My father, Eugene Stevens, came to Chevy Chase in 1902. They started building in 1901 and moved in to 3 West Lennox in `02,. My father was from Ohio. He was a patent and pension lawyer. Following the Civil War that was big business, getting these old soldiers their pensions, up until the Twenties. Then soldiers started dying off, and he branched into patents.

"Patents, Pensions, Government Claims" he had on his window. He had an office in the old Barrister Building at 7th and F and an office in Cleveland and Chicago.

We lived on that end of Chevy Chase for about thirty, forty years I guess. We were four years on Underwood and five years on Thornapple and twenty-four years on Williams Lane. Otterburn is what they called it when we moved out there. Originally we lived on Douglas Street and then Thornapple was Percy Street and there was another connecting street called Melrose. All named after that poem, that Ballad of Chevy Chase. They took all the names. Douglas was the leader of the Scottish troops, and Lord Percy was the leader of the English troops, and they had a big fight. I forget how Melrose got in there. It was just those three or four streets. Just frame houses with coal furnaces and a well we had to pump.

They had a little citizens' association for a while, and then all of a sudden after we had been up there a few years, they changed the street names to correspond to the streets on the other side. The Williams Lane people wouldn't change their name. It's Virgilia on the other side.

Lyles Offutt lived on Williams Lane in two different spots. He was a great guy; he'd wander around and talk to you. My brother, when the Mexicans started raising hell in 1915, he was in the National Guard, and they pulled him out of Western High School and sent him to the border. When he came back, about the time we got

in the war, it was about 1917 that they changed the names. We were four years on Douglas Street, and it seems to me about when we moved to Thornapple Street, they changed the names.

Chevy Chase became the home of numerous large families who contributed to its stability. "Daddy Frank" Simpson who lived on Brookeville Road, headed one of the largest extended families. It eventually included numerous Orems and several generations of Troths; almost all of them engaged, in one way or another, in building Chevy Chase. Janet Troth Hall was born on Jones Mill Road in 1900, grew up in the home her father built on Raymond Street in 1907 and as a married woman lived on Spring Street in the last house her Grandfather Simpson built in 1925, and counted thirty-two first cousins.[102]

As a single surname the Devereuxs (the last syllable is more like *roo* than *row*) did more to populate Chevy Chase than any other family. They eventually occupied the first two houses on Bradley Lane, and between them Dr. Devereux and his first-born, Joseph, and their wives reared nineteen children there. John Ryan Devereux, a graduate of the University of Pennsylvania medical school, married Annie Sinnott of Rosemont near Philadelphia in 1897. His uncle Archbishop Ryan performed the ceremony assisted by her uncle Rev. James P. Sinnott. Both families were more than well-to-do.

After a honeymoon, their first of several, at the Waldorf Astoria and a wedding tour to Colorado, the young couple made their home on S Street in the Capital, and the new Mrs. Devereux recalled "the first large reception that I attended in Washington was given by the Misses Riggs at 1617 'I' Street, a wonderful old house built by their father, a famous banker." She pronounced the gathering " a real cavedweller's party."

Dr. Devereux lectured at Georgetown, and in 1898 their first child, Joseph, was born. After serving as a contract physician during the Spanish-American War, Ryan Devereux became a surgeon in the Army Medical Corps; Margaret Mary was born in 1899, and the new family became highly peripatetic. After serving in Havana, where their second son was born in 1901 and their third, James, in 1903, Dr. Devereux was transferred to the 6th Cavalry in South Dakota. Daughter Anne was born there in 1905, and Joseph, Margaret and John began a long love of horses on small In-

dian ponies. Their next post was Ft. Logan near Denver where their fourth son was born. After working with the survivors of the San Francisco earthquake, Dr. Devereux was ordered to Washington, D.C., where Edward Winslow Coffin Devereux made his appearance in 1907. By then the family had both an American and a German nurse to help with the seven children.

In ill health, Dr. Devereux resigned from the Army and took his family to California where he and his wife enjoyed a "honeymoon" trip up the coast. After his health improved, the family sailed to Europe on the *Carpathia*, visited Naples and had an audience with the Pope before settling in Vienna where Dr. Devereux studied at the hospital and the older children attended a German school. After a bout of measles and a case of diphtheria, the family visited Cologne, Brussels, Paris and London before returning to Philadelphia where daughter Mary Frederica arrived in 1909.

When Dr. Devereux accepted a teaching position at Georgetown, they bought the home at 3 West Bradley Lane and undertook a major renovation.

The house we bought in Chevy Chase was of stucco construction, built by Mr. Ford, who was a great scholar, and the largest room in the house was his library.

We decided to remodel the house, having Clarke Waggerman as our architect. He designed a Georgian brick house and while we were living in the old house, the front of the house was covered with brick and two wings were added. It was very interesting to see the house gradually change from one type to another. We added a large ballroom, which is four steps lower than the entrance hall and has a small raised platform at one end.

Agnes was born in Chevy Chase in 1910 and Tristram Coffin in 1913. Some summers the Devereuxs took over a dormitory at the Woodbury Forest School where the children gathered up most of the prizes in local horse races on their horses and a Shetland called Dynamite. Several of the children attended school in Chevy Chase and most entered Catholic schools when they were older.

In World War I Dr. Devereux became a major in the Medical Corps while Joseph served with the Ambulance Corps in France. Mrs. Devereux rented her house and moved into the city where daughter Margaret drove an ambulance during the flu epidemic. At the war's end they moved back to Chevy Chase and soon the weddings began and grandchildren multiplied.

In 1922 Joseph married Helen de Chantel Kemp of Catonsville, and soon moved with his growing family into what had been the old school house next to his father's home on Bradley Lane.

The senior Devereuxs' daughter Mary made her debut in January 1929 in what her mother called "the last large party" and then was married at the Chevy Chase home in June of `29 with a wedding procession "from the ballroom, down the steps of the porch to the lower garden around the mirror pool and up the path to the brick archway where we had an altar arranged."[103]

To supply the needs of the builders and the home owners, who burned coal in their furnaces and kept chickens in their back yards, Kensington-born Thomas W. Perry started a small building supply and fuel business at the Lake in 1910. With the encouragement of the Senator from Nevada, young Perry bought fifty feet of land along the B&O tracks, which he

From the left - Joe on High Flyer, James holding Dynamite, in pony cart - Margaret, Ashton, Agnes, Mary and Edward, Ann beside the cart, Father, Mother, and Tristram with John on Mingo in front of the big house on Bradley Lane.

later expanded to two acres with his own spur or siding. He brought his brother-in-law Howard Griffith into the business and soon Griffith-Perry trucks were dumping coal into basements all over the area and a separate feed operation was growing in Silver Spring. T. W. Perry eventually became a member of the board of several banks, joined the Columbia County Club, and was a pillar of the Methodist Church that was next door to his home on Shepherd Street.

The Methodists, who had first met in the Williams' barn, started holding services in the small, brown-shingled Baptist church on Shepherd Street in 1912. The next year, led by Dr. Lucien Clark, Bruce Bielaski, Dr. John Sumwalt, and a number of Troths and Simpsons, they purchased the building for $3,960. In October 1912 the trustees signed the articles of incorporation of the First Methodist Episcopal Church of Chevy Chase. The Baptists moved down to the Circle.

The little, brown church on Shepherd Street

The congregation's growth led to the construction of a new wing and then a new center section of the church after the old one had been cut in half. In 1922 they built a parsonage next door and added a school wing behind the church. In 1924 they excavated a basement and built a school and kitchen under the church, and ten years later Edward L. Simpson built a new sanctuary for $20,000, and it was dedicated Palm Sunday 1935.[104]

Delivery trucks, and before them horse drawn wagons, were common in the suburbs. The ice man came regularly, and was often a local hero in the summer. Some houses had a pantry built so that the ice could be put into the box from the outside, and every son and daughter spilled the drip pan on his or her mother's linoleum at least once. Groceries

were delivered, sometimes daily, often in a cardboard box that could be made into many playthings or simply used as a sled on the nearest grassy hillside.

Hucksters patrolled the streets with vegetables and fruits, and the melodic call of "stra-a-a-a-berries" or "waaatamelon, ice-cold wahtahmelin" rang through many a warm afternoon. The milkman seldom knocked and also brought butter and eggs right into the kitchen; the insulated box came later, and some folks did have a separate "egg man." Bread trucks competed with the milk wagons and laundry trucks and the vans from Palais Royal and Lansburghs on narrow streets.

The only real traffic problem of the era seems to have been the delivery trucks, and there were a few tragedies despite 15 mile per hour speed limits. And the streets were where some games were played, even ice hockey once in a while, but usually kick the can and capture the flag, dodge ball and football and stickball with trees for bases. On snowy weekends some fathers dragged a train of sleds through the narrow streets behind their chain-equipped cars.

Trash was not a big problem in the 1920s and `30s. In the first place there just was not as much and many of the packages were saved and reused. Everybody learned "waste not, want not" and had a ball of string, a pile of gunny sacks, and lots of folded brown paper. Some trash was buried; a lot was burned, and there were ragmen and scrap dealers who, like the knife and scissors grinders, drove slowly through the neighborhoods ringing a bell or calling out their trade.

But the ashes from the coal furnaces and kitchen stoves were a problem. Everyone used the cinders to patch the roads and driveways, but the ashes remained, so the ash man came around. In the early days, he usually drove a wagon pulled by two large horses. He and his partner would roll the heavy cans to the street and dump them into the wagon. By the driver's seat stood two levers, one for the brake and the other for the dumping mechanism. One day young David Orem and a friend ran into an irresistible temptation.

We were watching this operation and noticed that both men had left the wagon and gone into a driveway to get the ashcans. What an opportunity! We jumped up in the driver's seat to play "Ash Man," and there in front of us were these two huge horses. The reins were lying across

the brake handle. The horses sensed that it was time to pull the wagon to the next house, and they began to move. We were panicked. The ash men heard the wagon start to move and shouted to us to get down. One of them said "Pull the brake," and we reached for it and got the dump lever by mistake. Of course the load dumped right there on Williams Lane. The horses stopped, and the ash men came running, but it was too late. We were over the fence and gone.[105]

Of all the memoirs of life in the early days of Chevy Chase, none is better than Winchester Stone's. He called his "My Local Habitation and its Name: Reminiscences of the Quality of Life in Martin's Third Addition to Chevy Chase 1909 - 1930."[106]

Expansion north of Bradley Lane came into being after 1905, when the lively Harry M. Martin, a business man from Washington, D.C. (Investments, Real Estate, Insurance) developed his "Additions" to Chevy Chase. This genial bachelor seems well to have known potential real estate values north of the Circle, for he began buying up parcels of from 35 to fifty acres from the Chevy Chase Land Company and others in 1896. (Others include Willson Offutt and Henry N. Griffith.) He also knew the value of association with an attractive name, so he registered his parcels as "Additions to Chevy Chase."

In 1909 my family moved into Martin's Third Addition, land for which Martin had bought from Henry M. Griffith. The Addition was surrounded by six working farms east of Brookeville Road and north of Bradley Lane, belonging to the Cummings, Wise, Callaghan, Ghormley, Brook, and Dunlop families. The Land Plat (#170 recorded in 1906) refers to the Brook farm, the oldest and by then perhaps the smallest, as a piece called "No Gain." The Cummings farm stood a bit to the South East. Cy Cummings had inherited his fifty-acre spread from his father James. James Cummings and his brother Patrick had emigrated from Ireland in about 1848, had purchased 100 acres, and divided it into two equal parts. Patrick, a bachelor, left his to a niece who married Mr. A. P. Wise. Wise, Ghormley, and Walter(?) Dunlop (dairy farmers largely) served milk to neighbors and to large distributors in the District of Columbia. Their distribution was taken over in the 1930s by the Oyster and Chestnut Farms dairies, later taken over by the Lucerne/Sealtest outfit. But, as developer Harry Martin and other moved to northerly parts, the herds dwindled and vanished. Cummings and Callaghan tilled the soil.

Closest to Bradley Lane lay the Cummings farm. To me as a boy it seemed a large one with crops of wheat and corn produced in alternate seasons. A lane from the farmhouse led west to Brookeville Road, gave a jog south to Bradley Lane, offering passage out to Connecticut Avenue, and ultimately over to small and sleepy Bethesda. Bradley alone of the planned cross streets was a paved road in the early days. Various builders, Horace Troth, Albert N. Prentiss, and John Reid, built modest houses to sell to solid federal government employees of middle-income status who were beginning to move out from the District. A double lot, with 100-foot frontage and great depth, with a house on it cost $6,500.

My family moved into No. 410 on a dirt-and-gravel surfaced Cummings Lane in 1909. The house had been built by Albert Prentiss, situated fifty or sixty yards from Brookeville Road, past a field of grass and briar patches. The Lane was lined with large, old Cedar trees, which prompted the inhabitants (for a time) to call it officially "Cedar Lane," and Harry Martin had designated it on the original Plat as Cedar Avenue. Both attempts failed to stick. After all it had long provided egress from the Cummings farm. (Book No. 1, Plat 70.)

The Lane boasted only eight houses, compared to the thirty-six crowded along its sides today. At the east end stood the large Cummings homestead and fields leading down to Meadow Brook, the same that passed below the Brook farm and ultimately emptied into Rock Creek. The homestead remains standing on a small plot engulfed by the late sprawl of smaller homes.

The north side of Cummings Lane provided homes for William P. Montgomery, Major George W. Burke, John Harvey and William Orme — with large expanses of fields and good air in between. Strictly speaking, according to the registered plat the Third Addition extended only to the South side of the Lane. On this South side stood four dwellings, those of Miss Bertha Erdmann, John H. Dynes, R. Palmer Teal, and George W. Stone. William Orme bought (and much enlarged) the original house of Harry Martin. . . (He was) one of six brothers, who were partners in the Emerson-Orme Buick Distributors in D.C.

At the farm end lived Miss Berthe Erdmann, a government employee but also a seamstress of skill long over from Germany who owned a two family structure. She never lost her heavy

Germanic accent, so was a puzzle to us as young-sters. "Guten Morgen," she would say as she walked past to the street car. Agnes Cummings, one of Cy's sisters walked daily (as did all others) to the car on Connecticut to attend her office in the Treasury Department. My Aunt, Faith Bradford, who lived with us, catalogued books in the Library of Congress, and later headed its Division of Serial Records.. . . Three excellent practicing physicians served the neighborhood — Dr. Gary Morgan (Bradley and Connecticut), Dr. John Ryan Dev-ereaux (Bradley just west of Connecticut), and Dr. Chester D. Swope (Raymond) an osteopath, held in greatest respect in the District even by medicos of the day whose stock in trade dealt mainly with pills, potions, and scalpels. Major Richard D. Clayton, retired from duty in the Spanish-Ameri-can War, Captain Redway (a Civil War Veteran), a patent lawyer Roy F. Seward, a dentist Dr.Wilbur E. Evans, a jeweler William H. Groverman, two builders Horace Troth and John Reid, the investment banker (A.B.?) McLaughlin, a blacksmith John Stone (who hammered a toy sword for me at his forge on Broad Branch Road) made up some of the healthy social mix of reliable occupations among the neighbors.

Then there was Dennis Cohane, an eccen-tric Irishman who lived in a tent stretched over a wooden frame (or it may have been a squatter's hut) amidst his lush garden of roses on a patch at the corner of Brookeville and East Quincy Street. I never knew what he did for a living. He heated his quarters in winter by a small two-burner kerosene stove. He was a pleasant, well-spoken individual from the auld sod, with an Elizabethan vocabulary and a heavy brogue accent.

Places, People and Things! The most remarkable and highly visible thing in the area lay not in Martin's Third, but in the Rosemary Circle area — across Connecticut Avenue — namely a huge, tall Water Tower, rising some 100 feet, bearing an external circular iron staircase, which we used to climb to the observation post aloft from which we could view the whole Chevy Chase/ Bethesda area — houses and club grounds in Chevy Chase,

The water tower

and a sleepy country village in Bethesda, but mostly farm land and woods all 'round.

Perhaps the "Thing" next in prominence was the Chevy Chase Lake, much hyped in adver-tisements during the early years of the century. Actually it was a not-very-large pond — man made — for water dammed up to provide steam for the generators of the electricity that moved the trolleys of the Capital Traction Company as they went down to the "loop" (at Calvert Street Bridge) and thence to Potomac Park. The water surface, however, was large enough to do a mod-icum of boating on, and for ice skating in winter-time. On a hill above the water stood a dance pavilion which drew numbers of young couples (because the band music of Meyer-Davis was in-deed fine) on summer evenings. It was host also to free Marine Band concerts. The thing to do was to take a summer trolley (open cars with straw seats, and running boards on which we kids loved to stand) and ride for a nickel from Chevy Chase Circle to the Lake, wander about a bit, ride to Raymond Street, then walk home.

The third "Thing" was an institution — The Chevy Chase School for Girls, occupying con-siderable space and grounds on upper Connecticut Avenue (west side) just above Shepherd Street. There young ladies were boarded and taught some Latin, some music, much etiquette, some literature, and a course in art. We attended open air spring festivals on the lawn, where the girls performed short plays and dances. . . .

The fourth "Thing" occurred in a bulge in Rock Creek, just south of where the East West Highway now crosses it creating space and depth enough (in the eyes of the young) to constitute a swimming hole. It got the name of "The Two Dollar Hole" because someone whose name has long dropped into oblivion lost a two-dollar bill there. I learned to swim in that hole, and used to walk (with bathing suit wrapped in a towel) from 410 Cummings Lane across fields, up past the Minnick and Essex houses (he a Veterinarian, whose dogs barked and animals made noises) down through the woods on a long path through the Ghormley and Dunlop wood lots past what now makes up Rollingwood, then spent an hour or two with several boys of my age playing games of Mumbly Peg on the hard clay shore of the creek, then swam. One summer I performed that routine daily until I came down with an illness, called then the "summer complaint," but surely brought on by swallowing too much creek water, into which had seeped waste from Kensington and North Chevy Chase sources. Quite a fever it was.

Parental proscription followed as to swimming there. Townships were not fastidious in the 1920s. In fact farm and community waste seeped into many a streamlet tributary to Rock Creek from the Martin's Additions-and-beyond areas. 'Twas thought it would clear itself before it reached the Creek. At the foot of East Raymond Street stood a primitive "cess pool" and wooden slatted sewage tank treated with lime which I often wondered about.

I was a very short boy but possessed a prize pair of hip boots in which I used to spend hours walking and wading down several streams from Brookeville Road through the woods to Rock Creek. Those leisurely poke-about trips nature's plentitude piqued my curiosity — the stream banks loaded with bluets, violets, moss, and water-cresses, the stream beds alive with tadpoles, frogs, turtles, and young harmless water snakes.

The fifth "Thing" (for a few of us anyway) was the Cummings Farm, though our elders might have stipulated the presence of two Clubs: Chevy Chase (attended by presidents and out of reach by many of us), and Columbia (which edged the Lake and was within means of many on the middle income level). As boys we did occasionally slip into the Chevy Chase Club grounds back of the tennis pro's shop, to watch Big Bill Tilden or Vincent Richards take on French or Japanese tennis stars. The sport was still for amateurs only.

But I spent hours in my youth at the Cummings Farm — watched the pig killing in November, the wheat harvested in July and the stable activity at other times. There I learned to ride a horse, and to see how a large pack of hounds was maintained. For Cy was Master of the Hounds for the Montgomery Hunt Club, and kept its barking pack. On hunt days the hunters in red coats, black caps, riding boots and white pants moved up Cummings Lane past our house and off over the fields to the north, with a long line of hounds trailing behind them.

Occasionally the Cummings' horses and a cow or two would get loose and wander through our yard cropping grass and munching from our garden. At times a few of his chickens wandered in. Everyone in the area kept chickens for fresh eggs and an occasionally fryer—even the Ormes. We would chase the stray birds off. The law in Maryland at the time specified that if you wanted no alien livestock to enter your property you had to fence it out yourself, a farm being too large to fence it all in.

Cy Cummings was a jovial, land owning politician who had played football, I believe at

Georgetown, the school of his youth. His arch political rival in the county Democratic party was Blair Lee of Silver Spring. My mother, excessively community minded and certainly persistent, pressured Cy to lay on a sidewalk from Turner lane south along Brookeville Road to the Sonneman's Store at Quincy Street so that matrons and children would have safe passage from gradually increasing traffic. She mobilized the "Community Club" getting members to put on ice-cream and bake sales every Friday at the juncture of Bradley lane and Brookeville to raise some venture capital (or matching contributions). And she kept the heat on Cy. "Mrs. Stone," said he on one occasion, " if we didn't spend so much on the darned schools we'd have more for streets, roads and sidewalks." He was more broad-minded than that irritated comment bespoke, yet sidewalks appeared, and Cummings Lane together with Raymond and Shepherd Streets became paved—great joys indeed for the roller-skating generation among others.

Cy early on had an automobile, as well as horse and wagons. We school children walking down Brookeville to the Circle and the E. V. Brown elementary school thumbed rides whenever a car passed. Cy would always oblige, and when prompted sang out in his rich baritone some stanzas from the "Soldiers" chorus, or "Anvil" chorus. We in our squeaky tenors joined in.

Cy had an arrangement with the Columbia Club to pick up its table and kitchen scraps for his hogs. Hank Sonneman, an eccentric who worked for him as a farm hand and handy man, drove a wagon to the Club once a week to collect the barrels and haul them to the pig-stye behind the barn down along one of the streamlets mentioned above. Hank used to let me ride one of the draught horses on those missions.

The sixth "Thing" constituted more of an event or happening than any object such as a water tower, an institution, and entertainment center, a swimming hole or a working farm. It had to do with <u>fire</u> — the annual burning of the fields in the area. The large fields between Cummings Lane and Raymond Street and on up to Thornapple lay uncared for from early spring until late fall—save where a junior baseball area was trodden out. The grasses grew abundantly and rattled in the dry September air. Often in the Fall (occasionally in early Spring) at eventide after the men had returned from the their offices downtown, someone would drop a match, purposely, and soon the territory would be ablaze. Word passed and soon men and boys came out with brooms, rakes, and

dampened gunnysacks to tend these field fires and keep them from encroaching on gardens or spreading to buildings. The exercise was exciting, the sight was beautiful against the dark sky, and the result probably beneficial to the ground and its scrub foliage. The land, we felt, was never scorched, just fertilized.

Two pick-up baseball fields were worked out by those of us who enjoyed a game of one-knocker, or three-knocker ball. Nothing fancy, just some sacks laid out for bases 'round a large enough diamond with some sort of outfield to set up a game. One such space on Cummings Lane stood just opposite the Orme house. Later we young-sters with great effort and some help from a neigh-boring contractor, Joe DeVoe, turned it into a rough version of a community tennis court. The other stood on the west side of Brookeville between Shepherd and Taylor streets, on which those of us who called ourselves the Chevy Chase Midgets played. We learned the ways of the market by or-dering baseball gloves from Sears and Roebuck. We marveled at my father who had played sand-lot ball in Cincinnati never using a glove. Some-times in the early evenings a parent or two would join in the play for an inning or two. The space doubled in the Fall for pick-up football games. Our bodies were healthily tired and our appetites splendid as a result.

The children of both sexes were a busy and self-occupied lot. We climbed trees, chewed sas-safras leaves imagining them wads of tobacco, cut paths through briar patches making a maze with difficult passages, caught butterflies for a collec-tion, skated, biked, played (on cool evenings) dodge ball, or red rover in each others' front yards, learned to dance, did the leg work for the weekend ice-cream sales (McKeever's vanilla from Kensing-ton was delicious and special), explored the sur-rounding woods, and jumped from shed-roof to barn-top at George Medler's playing cops and robbers. We played step-up school on any family's front step when the girls were around.

All of us were committed by our parents to work stints spading and weeding individual gar-dens. Public water came late. Each house pos-sessed a large circular or oval tank with a capacity of 500 gallons aloft in the attic. Filled and refilled periodically it started the gravity flow of water through the pipes below stairs. Water source came from dug or drilled individual wells. At our house in 1909-1911 the well-water arrived top-side by aid of a small wind mill. But by 1912-13 tank-filling ceased to rely on the vagaries of wind power

as we broke-in a gasoline engine in a pump house shared with neighbor Teal. Whenever that failed we worked man and boy at 100 strokes each on a large pump handle before going to school or to work.

A certain regularity found its way into boys' work (as it may still) in daily and Sunday paper-routes, with guaranteed delivery in all weather. The <u>Washington Evening Star</u> as well as the <u>Post</u> comprised the staples year in and year out. Both were handled easily, for then they were less bulky with ads, and specials, and inserts of all sorts. We learned to "box" them (i.e. to fold them into eight-inch squares) load them into coaster wagons and make our rounds. Thus boxed we could easily sail them from the sidewalk to the cus-tomer's porch hoping our aim was good. Occa-sionally one carried aloft to a porch roof or into bushes flanking the front steps. If we failed to cor-rect such an error our parents were soon informed, bringing on sharp lectures about workers' respon-sibility. Good discipline this. My route embraced Raymond (west and east), Cummings Lane and Shepherd (east and west) for which I received 25¢ a week. The Cummings Farm was my last stop, where the hounds always barked at me, but where on cold evenings Cy's sister Alice would ask me into the ample kitchen to have a warm cup of milk, or cider as I put my feet on the hearth and looked at the pictures of hunting scenes over the fireplace.

Seems hard to believe, but entertainment for adults was largely home made. Radio news and music had arrived and spread gradually in the 1920s, but television existed only as a scien-tific dream. What to do! Plays, music, art gal-leries, and opera occurred in season downtown. They were indeed events. Movies were spreading in popularity, and a picture house "The Avalon" finally came to lower Chevy Chase in the 1920s. But the small hall in the Village Library (Connecticut and Kirke) which also housed the Post Office became host to two sorts of entertain-ment (between occasional dances). The one, for those interested in the intellect, came into being as "The Chevy Chase Roundtable." There once a month a program of papers on lively subjects, stereoptican-slide lectures (of the Burton K. Holmes type), many of them illustrated travel-ogues, and book reviews occurred. The other ex-pressed itself in pageants prepared and acted out by family members for occasions such as Thanks-giving and the Fourth of July. Participation was wide. Dr. Mauchly, grave scientist from the Bu-reau of Terrestrial Magnetism, made an outstand-

ing Indian Samoset in a pageant celebrating the first Thanksgiving. Dr. R. D. Harper, from the Bureau of Standards, acted an impressive Robinson Crusoe in another one.

To keep the money-changers out of the temple the Church Bazaars even for charity held forth in that Library. Occasionally progressive suppers involving seven or eight families were laid on purely for sociability. They killed time (most enjoyably) for a whole evening, as groups moved from soup on Shepherd Street, to salads at a home on Raymond, to a main course on Brookeville, dessert on Bradley, and coffee at a home on Quincy. Took some planning, but the spirits of all participants seemed raised by the exercise, the company, and the food.

The Fourth of July held possibilities for further experiments with powder. Occasionally, after a long trudge to Bethesda to Tom Perry's Feed Store to buy fifty cents' worth of crackers, torpedoes, Roman candles and other noisy explosives, we would set off a number, some of which were duds. Once I carefully collected the powder from some 4-inch salutes which had failed to blow, poured it into a used cardboard tube attached to a small wooden base, and decided to drop a match into the concoction. Nothing happened so (a complete innocent) I looked in to see what was amiss. In a flash the powder exploded, and there I stood in Brookeville Road with a scorched face, no eyebrows and much pain. Mrs. Joe Devoe, in front of whose house I was yelling, took me in, rubbed sweet butter all over cheeks and forehead, and sent me home. . .

My earliest memory of what might be called joint parent and child entertainment comes from Sunday afternoon excursions with father, mother and brother by horse and buggy up and down Brookeville and over Bethesda way. I sat on the buggy floor and couldn't see much forward except the tail and belly of the horse, but I liked the motion and regular clatter of four hoofs.

Although the Cummings hounds outnumbered other dogs in the neighborhood they could not compete with the canines throughout the "Additions." The area abounded with them. If a leash-law was on the books it was honored by ignorance and universal non-compliance. Some dogs affable and friendly in temperament pleased. A few snappers and growlers jumped at anything that moved—a plague to salesmen, mailmen, icemen, paper boys, and delivery clerks. I got bitten three times — once by a John Cummings stray on Thornapple Street, once by a jumper (who was probably reaching for a rolled magazine I was

holding high), and once by Major Clayton's pesky beagles. On each occasion Dr. Devereaux came to the house (Doctors did so then) to clean and cauterize the slight wounds — no sulfas, no penicillins, no anti-toxins then). But my bête noir was the Norcross' (Raymond Street) rude Airdale, which I learned to steer clear of. My own dog Tweezer, friendly and loveable, a mix of Collie and Shepherd, ran with the children everywhere, and even played with my aunt's large cat well-known to the neighborhood, called Mr. Bittenger, named, I believe, for an elder in the Presbyterian church.

An annoying factor of hard-topped roads in the early days lay in their tendency to crack off at the edges each Spring. The County found relatively inexpensive ways to correct this action and to offer some work for strong boys. It laid cement shoulders three feet wide along each side of thoroughfares such as Brookeville and Broad Branch roads, incidentally widening each by six feet. Contractors scraped the sides with small tractors then hired strong-armed fellows to dig out the channels eight inches deep. One could earn four dollars a day at this. Some youngsters hired on.

The stoves on which meals were prepared were, throughout the community, wood or coal ranges, but by the early 1920s a gas line was put on Cummings Lane, enabling us to have a fancy coal range with a three-plate gas burner. The advantages lay in the fact that we had quick heat for cooking, but constant heat for the uninsulated household hot water boiler, which stood beside the stove in the large kitchen and helped keep it warm in winter. Food was semi-preserved by use of a cold pantry equipped with an ice-box filled thrice a week.

I recall the minor brouhaha when apparently a zoning waiver was obtained by Doc Evans to set up a competing service area for Sonnemann's store. Many an old timer disapproved, but events took their course. The block seems useful to neighbors now, though Doc underestimated need for adequate parking in order to make the enterprise "take off." He was a practical man, with little sense, I thought, for neighborhood aesthetics or attractive landscaping. Sonneman's became the "Lakeview Market" (with no sight of a lake within miles and miles) and now lies as a grassed-over spot...

Trash, in the early days, came to be collected on a weekly basis in the Additions only in the late 1920s. We buried garbage and burned paper trash on our own deep lots, and most things we saved (might be of use sometime) rather than casting out.

The minds of parents in Martin's Additions were divided as to schooling. An elementary school came on line at Rosemary Circle shortly before World War I. Some children attended there. Others, including my brother and me, walked down to the E. V. Brown school at McKinley and Connecticut Avenue. It was a fine one with good teachers. During that War what with the influx of families of war-working families several grades had to be housed in portable buildings — three in number set up in the rear school yard. When time arrived for high school choice, groups from both the District and Maryland elementary areas had to choose an institution down town — as did those from Kensington and Bethesda. For a general education the predominant selections were for the New Central High or Western High. For those headed for science or engineering careers (the practical subjects) McKinley Tech was the magnet. We all remained friendly competitors in sports and cadet drills. Once a week we kept up our old home-and-neighborhood ties in the young people's groups at the churches.

Educational needs met, spiritual ones followed. A cluster of churches sprang up around Chevy Chase Circle — All Saints Episcopal, Chevy Chase Presbyterian, and Most Blessed Sacrament Catholic. After a time a Lutheran one came into being on Ellicott, and a Methodist one appeared on Shepherd and Connecticut. Matter of fact the genial Harry Martin gave the first thousand dollars to purchase the land for the Presbyterians in 1908 to insure that no other denomination, or no business would snap up the location. His arm was long, from developer to churchman. In that early Presbyterian building he taught some of us in Sunday school. Once he invited his boys' class out to his home (somewhere on Rockville Pike) for ice-cream and strawberries — feeding both soul and body at a single clip. . .

In the late teens one morning appeared a man with a donkey and a scoop-shovel at the corner of Cummings Lane (south side) and Brookeville. Then came Horace Troth, the carpenter-builder, a soft-spoken and gentle man who lived on Raymond Street (west). Soon the cellar space for a new house was underway. The owner-to-be, Mr. Helmuth, had planned for a large bungalow spread over one floor. Curious Winchester Stone was soon watching the process. Several weeks later as it began to be floored (over its Belgian blocks foundation) he hung around again, as Mr. Troth, with single-handed skill set the plates and began to fit the beams. The boy dates his first gainful employment from that day,

for Mr. Troth asked him to hold upright one end of a two-by-ten, to steady it while he toed it onto the plate on the opposite side. We did this for several, then the builder came 'round to affix the loose but standing ends. "Thank you, young man, and here's for your work," said Mr. Troth as he pulled two dimes from his overall's pocket.

The lots on Cummings lane and east Raymond Street ran deep, very deep the farther they stood from Brookeville Road and the terrain was not level. The back areas from both streets ran down to a mild gully where a stream began which ultimately wound its way to Rock Creek. The depth of John Dynes' lot enabled him to have a large chicken yard and two chicken houses at the foot. On the Stone lot (No.11) stood a similar house, small and fenced in by Mr. Prentiss. My father expressed little interest in the birds, save when fried or roasted on a platter at table. Hence his sister-in-law Faith Bradford asked to have the structure while she lived with us. Lyles Offutt in his carpentering mode (he was basically a house painter) fixed it up for her, put in a brick fireplace and chimney, trimmed, squared, and shingled it to make a cozy cottage. She named it "Chickalow" as it seemed cross between a chicken house and bungalow. There she lived and slept in the summers, moving to her room in the big house when the snow fell. There she entertained her friends at tea. There she had a brick walk laid, edged with small box-wood plants imported from Mt. Vernon sprigs (one brought back each time anyone visited the first President's home). They were sold there in pots from the garden house for 25¢ apiece. When our house was sold (1958) the plants were very large. She donated them, about six, to the Octagon House in D.C., home of the American Institute of Architects, in memory of her brother-in-law George W. Stone.

Faith also raised flowers, especially Van Fleet pink roses in beds around her little "estate." She kept count of buds and perfect blooms, some summers amounting to more than three hundred. She took a bouquet each week to her desk in the Library of Congress, and filled a basket of them on Memorial Day for the graves of her father and brother in Arlington Cemetery. Her fame, however, lay in the doll house which she had built to perfect scale, and furnished over a period of half a century. It now stands as an exhibit in the Smithsonian Museum of American History.[107]

Large fields lay in the backlands to the south west of the Stone property. Though vacant, they supported half a dozen stray persimmon trees scattered around, and a lone plum tree. Mar-

velously sweet plums. But we initiated each new child in the area to the pitfalls of eating persimmons. Many a puckered mouth resulted, but when the fruit was wrinkled and ripe (after the first frost) the taste was sweet. Most of us on the Lane had apple and pear trees in our yards. We had three splendid apples of the Black Twig variety. I never heard of the variety elsewhere, but its fruit was the tartest yet sweetest I ever tasted until I met up with the Macoun variety of upper New York State. Cummings' horses occasionally munched on the culls.

The Teal-Reichmuth-Birch lots supported a long grape arbor, from which hung capital bunches of Concord sweet grapes — too many for any family to absorb, so we all helped ourselves to a bunch any time of day when we passed by in late July or August. The Dynes family raised berries with bushes of currents and gooseberries aplenty, along with black caps and red raspberries in abundance. All were readily available to the neighbor children.

Mrs. Stone did dahlias and peonies to brighten the scene. I found it a great chore to dig up the bulbs each fall to save over the winter. Mrs. Harvey did tulips in a double line on each side of the long, straight walkway to her house. As a very young child I once cut a whole row of red ones, took them to the front door and presented them to her. She was gracious but not amused. I was forbidden to carry scissors out of the house thereafter.

We were free spirits, and community living was really communal among the young as I remember it, before 1930. Another illustration, a Mr. Cutter on Raymond Street (east) had his single garage torn down to build a larger one. My father bought the lumber, thinking to build one himself (which he did many a year later when we had a Model T Ford, in 1927). Meantime he stacked the boards on the rear of the vacant lot next, planning to use them soon.

But there they remained for ten years, forming a play place for numbers and numbers of children. Now the pile was a ship, again a train, another time (with slight re-arrangement) a fort, then a school, then a council-sitting place. Children from Quincy, Raymond, east Bradley, Shepherd and the Lane used it to the full capacity of their imaginations. Open air, no breakage, relatively safe, and within the watchful eye of anyone in the Stone household. My mother on several occasions wanted to take us down to the museums in town to expand our cultural horizons, but had a hard time weaning me away from the "lumber pile."

Occasionally the urge for an exploit of daring-do came upon us. Often the locale lay in the Jones Bridge Road and upper Rock Creek area. Near the former stood the B&O trestle over which the scheduled trains moved west. There was also the spur trestle for freight going to Georgetown (over which rolled the huge cut stones for the slow-building Cathedral). Once in a while we would mount the tracks and place a penny or two on one of them, then watch the train roll over flattening them "like gold to airy thinness beat" (as the poet John Donne remarked so long ago on another occasion). When parents got wind of such activity it stopped. The thinned penny became a thin souvenir in a boy's collection box.

Another act of semi-prowess involved a walk on the thin ice-cakes in Rock Creek where it widened below the Forest Glen Seminary cliffs. The winter of 1917 was extremely cold. It found my brother and two cousins from town doing the ice bit with some joy and sense of daring.

But the trip I recall came during the January thaw. Ice at the edges was thin and unstable. A cake extending to mid stream broke free when one jumped from it ashore. Happened to me and I landed thigh deep in mighty cold water. I clambered ashore, with cousin William Bradford's assist, and contemplated the long, long walk back to Cummings Lane, and to dry my pants. Nothing to do but run, at least in a steady jog. By the time I reached home my corduroy knickers were frozen stiff. "Winnie," my mother said, "learn from this to gauge your capacities. You must be cold. Now warm up and dry off." My free spirits took a bit of a check. I was never partial to corduroys thereafter, nor to the long, heavy black stockings we then wore. . .

Dairyman Wise and his wife (a Cummings) in the late 1800s built a house split by the District line along Western Avenue. In the dining room (so the story went when I was young) he at the head of the table sat in Maryland and she at the foot sat in the District of Columbia. . . Mike Callaghan's pumpkin fields adjoining, along with the house of his farm hand John Green — the only black in the area then — and his large family of daughters have given way to another large cluster of small houses. One other black, Jeff Freeman, janitor for years at the Chevy Chase Presbyterian Church lived in that region, either in the woods off Pinehurst Circle, or with John Green—I remember not where.

Pinehurst Circle upon which we used to pick strawberries and violets each Spring seems to be a circle only in name now. All the brooks (branches we called them then) have long been filled in. . . Fashionable Rollingwood acres occupy portions of the Ghormley and Dunlop farms on which a large old stone-lined well once existed. In my youth I spotted deep at the bottom a long gone cow which had fallen in and never made it out. . . .

The Wise family described by Winchester Stone included the proprietors of what came to be the Chevy Chase Dairy. George A. Wise, who lived in Chevy Chase, and his brother Joseph had dairy farms on Belt Road and Murdock Mill Road in the 1890s and joined together as "George A. Wise and Brother" in 1905 and later "Wise Bros. Chevy Chase Farm Dairy" at 3310 P Street NW. In the 1920s the company was owned by Joseph A. Wise, George's widow M. Edith Wise and general manager Raymond J. Wise who made his home in Chevy Chase, Maryland. The dairy then had a large plant with an office on the upper level at 3206-3208 N Street in Georgetown and the garage on Prospect Street.

By 1930 the Wise name was associated with butter, eggs and a high quality mayonnaise, and the Chevy Chase Dairy had branch offices on both Connecticut and Rhode Island Avenues and a stand at the Center Market. The president-treasurer was Raymond J. Wise and the vice-president Spencer L. Wise of Chevy Chase. In the mid-1930s Chestnut Farms bought them out and combined the names and operations under the ownership of Henry Brawner of Potomac. The Wise name survived as the brand of mayonnaise handled by the delivery men, and the Sealtest name referred to the type of bottle and cap the dairy adopted.[108]

One of the Wise's milkmen was Roland Custer from Halpine. After leaving school at 15 and apprenticing as a carpenter with his brothers, Custer went to work for the Chevy Chase Dairy when home building slowed in the late Twenties.

I drove a horse and wagon from Georgetown way across town to 5th Street Northeast for the Wise brothers. I was going with this girl, and we got married when I was 19, in 1928.

The horse knew the route. That horse would go from Georgetown clear to Northeast and

stop at the first customer, and when he'd hear the bottles rattle, he'd start off and stop at the next place. When I finished I'd take the horse, put the feedbag on and put a weight on it and go eat my breakfast and come back and go collect the bills and then go in. Joe Wise, he tended to the horses and he treated the horses better than the men. If you didn't take care of your horse, you'd get some old plug the next day.

I was on that thing for fourteen months. Raymond Wise asked me if I had a permit and I said yeah, and he said, "You did a nice job on that so I'm going to give you a truck route where you can make some money." So it was in Bethesda with a jumper. I had all Bethesda and Kenwood and down River Road and out to the Congressional Country Club, Bradley Boulevard.

I started building it up in Battery Park and other places. We worked seven days a week, not a day off. I worked two years without a day off, and then Roosevelt came in and that's when I got Mondays off. Got $18 a week and then a commision if your route paid enough.

"Punks" Dove, all you had to do was be late one morning and you were fired. There were forty guys waiting out here for your job. "Milk," he says, "has to go every day. The cows give it and we deliver it." Meanest man in the world. He fired a man who stayed home when his wife was having trouble delivering a baby. He said, "You wasn't having the baby" and the guy had been there five years. We had to go to work at 12:30 in the morning, started loading then.

I had some weekly bills in Woodmont, but mostly monthly and some people mailed the checks in or put them in the milk bottle. A few you had to go collect, and we went around and sold butter and eggs and cottage cheese.

When I would build it up, they would divide it, and they cut it about seven times in the fourteen years I had it. Then I'd lose my jumper for a while, but I was making money, about $60 a week at the end. I started with a Diamond-T, then a big White truck; that thing would haul some milk. I had 400 customers and it was everyday service then.

An early inhabitant of Martin's Additions was Robert Ragan:

When we first moved here, I came with my mother when my father died in 1920, I was four, and the only houses on Chestnut were this house and the house across the street. There were two houses on Delafield and two houses on

this block of Summit and two houses on the deadend of Summit and about three houses on what was then North Central Avenue but is now Delafield Street. The Cummings had a big farm that came right down to Taylor Street. They had a big barn there.

This house was built by a man named Wells. My grandmother bought it in 1914, and I think she paid about $6,000. Those little shoebox houses down on Taylor Street, there's about six of them all identical. They cost $2,500, and I remember that Mr. Peters was very indignant when they put them up there and said they are going to ruin the neighborhood

Mrs. Corby was my mother's sister. I spent a lot of my childhood in that house. When I first went to the E. V. Brown school, my mother was working then, and she would take me down on the way to work and drop me at the Corbys and when it came time for school, their black butler would walk me to school. At noon, kindergarten was only a half day, the butler would come down and pick me up. I'm sure all the kids thought that he was my father.

We played all over the place. It was nothing but fields and an awful lot of sumac bushes. We'd go play in the wood and down to the creek. And Rossdhu Castle, that lake was much bigger originally, I served papers there. I climbed around over it when it was being built and probably stole a little bit of lumber - that was a favorite thing.

I started serving the Star when I was about nine or ten. I would get my papers at the corner of Shepherd and Thornapple Streets. I had a hundred papers and that covered everything east and north of Shepherd. Nearly everybody got the Star. The last house on Connecticut Avenue was just beyond Woodbine, and there were no houses beyond Summit.

In 1916 the Thomas J. Fisher Company produced a large, slick, well illustrated pamphlet called "Chevy Chase for Homes." It modestly admitted that Chevy Chase was "The Best Suburb of the Nation's Capital" and set out its basic premise.

In ordinary real estate development too frequently everything is sacrificed for quick financial returns, but this has not been done in Chevy Chase. Back of the development, so far as it has progressed today, is a big, comprehensive plan, and the men who formulated that plan believed that the best results could be obtained only where

things were done right. . . . The fixed purpose of the Chevy Chase Land Company was to provide the National Capital a home suburb, a community where each home would bear a touch of the individual owner, where each home would possess an added value by virtue of the beauty and charm of the surrounding homes.

Pictures of the new Presbyterian and Episcopal churches and the two clubhouses were bracketed by photographs of Chevy Chase streets and of a dozen individual homes, each with its own slogan in quotes: "Not Without Art, but Yet to Nature True," "If Thou Would'st Read a Lesson That Will Keep, Go to the Woods and Hills" or descriptions such as "In Chevy Chase Nature and Man have Combined Their Efforts with Charming Results."

The pamphlet then presented a brief history of Washington, D.C., and of the efforts of the CCLCo in land acquisition and road and trolley line building. Under "development," the three subdivisions in Maryland and two in D.C. were briefly described. Sections II, III and Chevy Chase, D.C., it was noted, "are practically sold out," but sites in Section IV and Chevy Chase Heights, D.C. are available "to suit the purchaser." The two country clubs were praised, and the reader was reminded that "the best suburban section is always surrounding or adjacent to the leading clubs." The brochure maintained that while Chevy Chase "was designed and has been maintained to meet the requirements of discriminating people" that did not mean only the rich could afford to live there. The restrictions were to "maintain or increase values and protect property holders against the encroachment of undesirable elements."

The Presbyterian church on Chevy Chase Circle

While it was true, as the census of 1910 showed, that many of those who lived in the large, frame houses built before the Great War could afford to keep live-in servants and it was equally true that many heads-of-household worked in the professions or for the government, there were others who did not fit this picture at all. Of the 166 Chevy Chase families in 1910, fifty-seven had live-in servants; thirty-four of those had only one, usually a cook, and a live-in cook could be hired for $12 or $15 a month in 1910. Of the eighty-five inhabitants of Chevy Chase who were resident servants, sixty-two were black and twelve were men. The Corbys had a waitress and a gardener from Germany, a cook from Austria, and a maid from West Virginia–all white. The Dessez family with two grown and two young children at home had no live-in servants.[109]

The 1920 census of expanded Chevy Chase, including Martin's Additions, Otterbourne, Norwood and other developing areas, showed about twice as many households but only fifteen percent with live-in help. Of the seventy-one resident servants, forty-three were black women and nineteen white women. William Corby still had his white-European help, but his brother Charles out on the Pike employed three African-Americans.

On the other hand, in 1910 twelve households were taking in boarders with the wonderfully named Missouri Kessler, a single, 28-year-old from Illinois, leading the way by renting rooms at her Grafton Street home to eight residents including a lawyer and his family. A number of people, such as the house painter Henry Wolford, shared their home. He and his wife plus his son, who worked at the zoo, and his son's wife and three young children all lived together. Sara Campbell, a 66-year-old Treasury Department clerk, had Grace King and her 15-year-old daughter as boarders. Susan Sipe, 45, shared her house with Catherine Lowry, 21; both were teachers. Not everyone in Chevy Chase was enjoying the life of the rich and famous.

The census of 1920 showed about the same picture with some thirty roomers or boarders in Chevy Chase homes including a family of three living with Thomas Robertson whose household also included a white maid and her six-year-old child. Solidly middle class was an appropriate description of the first generation in Chevy Chase.[110]

Very early in the history of this sprawling suburb the residents of the various neighborhoods felt a need to band together for reasons social and political as well as religious. Isolated on the southern extreme of Montgomery County, many dusty miles from the courthouse where decisions were made as well as several somewhat easier miles from the busy streets of the Capital, the families who came to live in Chevy Chase found they had common problems and concerns. Many of them were Northerners and city people, and Montgomery County was still rural and quite Southern. A lot of them were rock-ribbed Republicans in a County run by unreformed Democrats. Most of them found their entertainment and did their shopping in the city. Suburbanites subscribed to the Washington papers, read the latest novels and rode the trolley to work. County farmers read the *Sentinel*, the *Bible* and the almanac and went to town, be it Poolesville or Damascus, only on Saturday.

In 1910, eighty-two percent of the County's 333,440 acres were farmland, and of the 2,432 farms, three-quarters were owner-operated. The County's population grew from 27,000 in 1890 to 32,000 in 1910, but the Bethesda/Chevy Chase district, although the fastest growing part of the County where the population had tripled in the same period, still had only ten percent of the population in 1910. Suburbanites soon discovered that, as far as the rest of the County was concerned, their problems and views did not matter and their behavior, both social and political, was obviously aberrant.[111]

Mrs. Jarvis noted that "in the early days everyone was interested in either the Literary Society or in the politics of the day." The Literary Club of both male and female Chevy Chase Association members got started in 1907 at Eugene Stevens' home and met on fourth Tuesdays from October to May. Travelogues, dramatic readings and very light refreshments were the usual fare. The Ladies Reading Class was for women only and met in the afternoons. Some of the ladies' husbands, in self-defense, organized the Honorary Economical Epicureans who cooked one evening a week at someone's house. Tom Robertson was a leader of this group, which included Cliff Richards and C. D. Parker.[112]

The Chevy Chase chapter of the Y.W.C.A. began in a meeting at the home of Mrs. W. K. Butler on Quincy Street in December 1909 and

became one of the largest in the D.C. area. Its annual spring luncheons and fall bazaars were soon "institutions." At first they were held at Mrs. Butler's home and then at Mrs. Corby's and later at the Presbyterian church. The chapter supported Camp Winona on Rockville Pike and Kamp Kahlert where it furnished a cottage for seniors. Later presidents included Mrs. Thomas Robertson and Mrs. G. W. Stone.

The Women's Club of Chevy Chase began in Section Three in 1913 pledged to "promote the welfare of the community and of the state of Maryland" and met in churches and at the elementary school until its clubhouse was built. The first president was Mrs. George F. Mikkleson, wife of one of the area's best-known builders, and originally membership was limited to thirty.

The organization, then led by Mrs. Joseph Travers Maguire, celebrated its twenty-fifth anniversary by moving into the $30,000 building on Connecticut at Dunlop Street in October 1938 and by honoring its founders; Mesdames Burkhart, Beattie, and Bielaskie. E. Burton Corning designed the building, and Willard Warthen of Kensington was the builder.

The Chevy Chase Garden Club with Mrs. Hugh Southgate as the first president was organized in the 1920s and was considered by some more exclusive than any of the country clubs. It often met at the Corby's home where there was bell ringing at Christmas time.

Christmas led to one of the Women's Club's more embarrassing moments. In the winter of 1927, the Club decided to erect a community tree on the Circle and secured rather informal permission from Dr. Benjamin Perry, head of the Board of Commissioners, to cut a tree along a County road. The first one the club's work gang attacked was a big spruce on William Parker's property on Jones Mill Road. Parker was in Florida and when his neighbor, Mrs. George E. Philips, saw what was happening, she put her body in the way of the workmen and saved the tree.

Contractor Lincoln Peter's men moved down to the Dunlop estate and felled an "old and prized" juniper or red cedar that had stood for about seventy years and hauled it off to Chevy Chase Circle. Outraged, North Chevy Chase called in the law. When the case reached Judge Samuel Riggs's police court, the charges were dismissed because it was shown that one member of the Christmas tree committee, William H. Gottlieb, was also an au-

thorized forest warden for Chevy Chase. North Chevy Chase remained outraged.[113]

There was even a very early Chevy Chase Boys Club that held a track meet on the field behind the post office in the spring of 1915. Contestants were divided into three classes by age with juniors under twelve and seniors over sixteen. They staged both running and field events with the help of older boys including Ben Carpenter, Cliff Richards and Frank Weaver, who was the official reporter. For the "seniors" Tommy Robertson was the winner. He set records in the pole vault (10' 4") and running broad jump (17' 10") and won the high jump with a leap of five feet one inch. Clarence "Buddy" Dawson was second; he won the 50 yard dash and finished second in several events, and Nevins Gardner of D.C. was third with victories in the 220 and quarter mile. Nate Robertson, Tom's younger brother, was the winner among the juniors with Miles Imlay second. Mrs. J. T. Martin of Grafton Street awarded the prizes.[114]

At first, loosely organized and informal, neighborhood organizations dealt with petty annoyances such as wandering farm animals and met social isolation with sewing circles and the literary and bridge clubs on a casual basis. But continuing problems with unpaved and poorly repaired roads and smelly septic systems led to the formation of more formal citizens' associations. The "Chevy Chase Association" started as far back as 1895 and maintained the library, began the fire service and supported the night watchman idea.

In December 1906 the residents of Harry Martin's "additions to Chevy Chase" organized the Chevy Chase Home Association for the "advancement of the public interests of the membership" and assessed themselves twenty-five cents per year dues. By 1909 the residents of Sections Three and Four had also formed citizens' associations and were dealing with safety, education and road repair concerns. A Chevy Chase Taxpayers' Committee soon became active and most associations included both a health officer and an ad hoc building inspector.

Martin's Additions had fewer amenities than much of the rest of Chevy Chase since there were no sidewalks, sewers, piped water or lights, just a great deal of mud. As Wallace Janssen noted in his history of those early days, action was what they needed, and the

second meeting produced the first big project–a 350-foot boardwalk to the trolley tracks.

> *After a general discussion . . . the following estimate was submitted: $14 for lumber, $2 for a team, and $4 for stone. Moved by Mr. Martin and carried that the committee on Roads and Streets be authorized to spend $20 if necessary on the path.*

Homeowners were asked to chip in $1.50 per family and to help split logs and nail down the planks. The finished path was one board wide and it helped, but the mud was still there. Folks expecting to come home late often hid lanterns with their rubbers in the shrubbery near the car line. Later, another committee named the streets, and Lawrence Troth, the treasurer, painted the signs, black letters on white boards, and posts.

The biggest headache for the committee was the cooperative sewer and septic tank. The residents regularly "shelled out" for lime, for cinders, for the roads and for every other expense, and, of course, some people did not pay. It was this problem that led to talk of incorporation so that expenses could be fairly shared through taxation.[115]

While the ladies of the "Community Club" raised $350 in a series of lawn parties, progressive suppers, and food sales to build a sidewalk from Turner Street to Sonnemann's store after Brookeville Road was macadamized, some of the men met with other Chevy Chase associations to push for incorporation. The Chevy Chase Improvement Association of Martin's Additions joined with a group from Section Two led by William T. S. Curtis to push a home rule bill in the State legislature, and after a compromise, the "Municipal Control Act" passed in 1910.[116]

A taxpayer's suit brought an end to the first attempts at incorporation in 1914, and the various sections as well as the General Assembly had to try again. Edith Jarvis remembered Mr. Curtis as the first Mayor of the Village and "among those who steered the affairs of our own little government" in the early days, but she also called him a "single dictator" who ran everything his way. W. T. S. Curtis' most important contribution may have been convincing Asa Philips of the D.C. government and representatives of the Maryland Board of Health that an area-wide sewer and water system was needed. Eventually his efforts, and those of a number of others, led to the creation of the Washington Suburban Sanitary Commission.

In April 1914, Section Two along with part of Section One became a Special Taxing District now called the Village of Chevy Chase. Section Three followed, and in 1916 Martin's Additions also became a special tax area. In 1918 the State approved the applications of Sections Four and Five, and in 1924 North Chevy Chase and Chevy Chase View also became special taxing areas. Section Four expanded several times over the years and eventually became the Town of Chevy Chase.[117]

North Chevy Chase, as a subdivision, began life called Kenilworth on a 64.5-acre tract platted for Redford W. Walker in 1895. Cinder walks lit by kerosene lamps ran beside dirt roads, and the developer put 118 lots of varying sizes on sale.

By the early 1900s there were about fifteen homes and sixty residents in the area. Originally, a well on the Lanning's property on Kenilworth provided water, first by gasoline engine and later by an electric pump. Many housewives used the two cars of the Kensington trolley line, operated by friendly motormen Bob Shepperd and Ed Kelly, as a free delivery service. In the spring of 1920, a Citizens' Committee was organized at Magnus Thompson's home and the property owners were assessed fifty-cents a month to support its work. In February 1921, the Committee invested $600 for twenty Firefoam extinguishers to be placed in homes and a hand-operated fire siren.[118]

The internationally best known house in North Chevy Chase was almost forgotten for a number of years. In 1910 Dr. David Fairchild, a world-famous plant explorer and horticulturalist, built his home, "In the Woods," just north of Jones Bridge Road and landscaped it with a wide variety of plantings. The rustic house, designed by Edward Clarence Dean and built of hollow tile covered with tan stucco, was a "successful blending of Japanese simplicity, European permanence, and American materials." It was often visited by Gilbert Grosvenor and by Fairchild's father-in-law, Alexander Graham Bell, who had a small workshop on the property. It was later rented to Wilson's Secretary of War and still later, during the flu epidemic, by Herbert Hoover.

Fairchild was best known locally for introducing Japanese cherry trees to America from

the one he brought back in 1905 and "naturalized" in Chevy Chase and was credited with importing more than 75,000 edible, ornamental, and useful plant species to this country as well as a few undesirables such as kudzu. What is left of the original thirty-four acre site contains unique plants and many of the largest and rarest trees in the East. Some like the Siberian elm at the front door are well past their prime, but they once included outstanding examples of the Nikko maple, Dove tree, Turkish cedar, Chinese fringe tree, Oriental spruce, Korean pine, and Oriental oak and numerous varieties of flowering cherries.

The house looks like a transplanted Californian, with floor-to-ceiling glass doors and a handsome, craftsman-style central stairway. The property was acquired by Dr. E. A. Merritt, a radiologist, in 1927, and after his death leased to family-friend Bertha Belt for her nursery school. Yet another survivor.[119]

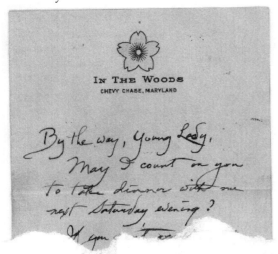

"In the Woods" notepaper

All the "towns" in Chevy Chase operated in similar ways. They all had an elected board and an annual meeting at which the tax rate was set. Most were concerned mainly with road repairs and trash removal, with health and safety, and with preserving their neighborhoods and their property values. In their early days most had a resident doctor as a health officer and a paid, part-time building inspector.

For the County government in the period after World War I, they served to protect the rural majority from paying higher taxes to meet the needs of a fast growing, and often very vocal, minority. Until the 1920s men held all the elected and most of the appointed jobs.

Elizabeth West, Mrs. Millard F., was the first woman elected as an officer of the Citizens' Committee of Section Two, as secretary, and Mrs. Thomas E. Robertson, who was in charge of the library, was the second.

Section Five wrote rules and regulations that were reasonably typical. The original citizens' association leadership became the town's Committee until an election could be held in April 1923. Matthew T. Moomaw was the chairman. Staggered elections were established for two-year terms and six-month residency was required to vote.

In general, the Committee controlled the streets and sidewalks, the collection of trash and garbage, the erection of buildings, snow removal, traffic and health regulations. It also had the power to borrow money up to ten percent of the property value, to assess front-foot benefits, and, of course, to tax and spend money, with bids needed for expenditures over $500. The Committee also had the right to appoint a health officer, quarantines were still common then, and a building inspector, each for two-year terms.[120]

Similar rules may be found throughout Chevy Chase and in Martin's Additions. There was to be no firing of guns or throwing of stones, and no drunken, lewd, vulgar, or violent behavior. Disturbing religious services was outlawed as were loitering and dumping trash on the roads. Hedges, gates, and porches were protected by law, and the keeping of cows, swine, or goats was no longer permitted. Fowl could not be allowed to run at large. There was to be no song bird trapping or killing, and rules were set down for dealing with mad dogs, vicious dogs, and female dogs in heat. Hedges and vacant lots were to be kept trimmed; barbed wire fences were verboten.

The building regulations were quite specific. Only single-family homes were allowed, and no trade, business, or manufacturing was permitted. Building permits, $5, were needed to erect or modify a structure and $50 deposits required to cover possible street damage. Deed restrictions were to be enforced. The lifestyle of suburbia was being citified and codified.

One of the early problems of the taxing areas was the Chevy Chase Land Company itself. When Senator Newlands died in 1917, Edward Stellwagen became the president of

CCLCo with the understanding that there would be no interference from the Newlands or Sharons. He contracted encephalitis in 1922, and Edward Hillyer was the acting president for the next ten years although he was generally following Stellwagen's instructions. When Newlands was in Washington, young Hillyer had visited his bedroom every Sunday morning from 1909 until Newlands' death to discuss company matters. He was chosen as the third president in 1932.[121]

The Company, by the end of The War to End All Wars, had paid out $172,396.46 more than it had taken in partly to meet the demands of English bondholders, but part was simply due to the continuing dearth of land sales. During the years of continuing red ink, the CCLCo made a small payment each year, usually six percent, of the capital value of the stock and by 1926 had reduced the par value from $100 to $68. Losses, which had run as high as $40,000 a year, were reduced to $28,600 in 1918, $19,000 in 1919, only $878.50 in 1920, but were up to $8,648 in 1921. After total losses in the ten-year period 1913-22 of $277,777.30, in 1923 there was a profit of more than $50,000.

The Land Company was in no mood to be taxed on its undeveloped lots by these new towns its old customers had formed, but eventually it paid. And the Land Company in the 1920s created another contretemps when it made several attempts to solve its money problems by erecting fashionable apartment buildings on some of its vacant land on the east side Connecticut Avenue. These planned violations of the covenants led to vigorous and cooperative opposition from the special taxing districts. Other problems were more minor.

For example, in June 1924 George P. Hoover, attorney of the Chevy Chase Citizens' Association, wrote George E. Fleming, secretary of the CCLCo, that Mr. Fred R. Parks, the recently appointed Village manager of Section Two "is desirous of obtaining access to the office rooms now being occupied by the Chevy Chase Land Company in the Library Building." He suggested a joint occupancy. This matter had come up ten years previously, and Claude had checked the County land records and found no covenant or conditions in the 1901 deed regarding the office, but Fleming put Hoover off suggesting that they "let it drift" while he contacted Stellwagen at the Poland Springs resort in Maine.

Stellwagen wrote, "I think we will have to let the Chevy Chase people occupy the office room jointly with us, if you have not found where we have any title to it." Hoover pressed with repeated phone calls,

E. J. Stellwagen

and Fleming finally wrote "we are willing to permit this use by Mr. Parks of this space" but insisted that "when this real estate was donated many years ago, there was a restriction on the part of the Land Company" to keep an office in Maryland. It was not so, but they agreed to share. Usually the Land Company used the office only once a year for the annual stockholders' meeting.

Meanwhile, as Winchester Stone noted, over on Brookeville Road a popular commercial area developed that held two small grocery stores, a DGS and a Sanitary. The early tenants included a small dress shop and yard goods store, a barbershop and Lois Reynolds' "beauty parlor" that later moved upstairs, a drug store, and Evans gas station, which gained the reputation of selling the best fireworks in the area.[122]

The pharmacy became almost a neighborhood coffee-house as well as a source of big cones of Breyer's ice cream, and "Doc and Mrs. Doc" Shapiro "were sort of the heart of the community for quite a long time." Elsie Irvine, longtime Chevy Chase Elementary School teacher, recalled being asked to sign a petition against the Shapiros moving in next door to her on Brookeville Road. She refused and found them to be "lovely neighbors."[123]

The Roaring Twenties also saw a boom in land sales and prices, and in several years the Thomas J. Fisher Company sold more than a million dollars worth of property. Most lots doubled in value and some tripled. In April 1926, for example, the bookkeeper's report reflected an active market.

Land sales reported by Rankin on 5-20-26	
Land sales	86,087.96
Value of land (1913)	51,305.85
Gross sales profit	34,782.11
Expenses	7,671.90
Net sales profits	27,110.21
Interest income	7,091.43
Total net profit	34,201.64

During the period from 1918 to 1931, the company took in more than $7,500,000, held more than $2 million in first and second mortgages and the subdivision of Chevy Chase was completed. Hillyer and the CCLCo then decided to retain the commercial land rather than subdivide it further.

Chevy Chase kept growing. In the summer of 1918 John L. Warren's Addition blossomed at the northeast corner of Leland and Wisconsin and added fifty-five building lots. Surveyors laid out the four blocks and thirty-three lots of Section Five between the Williams and Otterborne tracts in 1922. The Sonnemann property between Brookeville, Broad Branch and West Oxford was subdivided as Section Six in June of 1923 as was Section Seven to the east. There were originally five blocks and eighty-four lots of varying sizes in these two areas.

Early Bethesda-investor Dr. Ralph Walsh, after whom the street was named, designed Section Eight on Wisconsin Avenue between Leland, East, and Stanford Streets in 1923, and Monroe and R. B. Warren added to it two years later on the border of Section Four with Sections 8-A, which included the Leland/B-CC junior-senior high school site, and 8-B which ran up to the railroad tracks. The Warrens called theirs the Leland subdivision.

Just to confuse things, another Section Two of fifty-seven lots averaging 7,500 square feet was added east of Wisconsin between Grafton and Cedar Parkway in 1924. The triangular tract between Grafton Street, Western Avenue, and Cedar Parkway became Section One in October 1925 and Section 1-A, which ran over to Wisconsin Avenue opposite Friendship Heights and the Bergdoll tract was added in 1927. These included what had been the Kirkside golf course, the old quarry and dump site, and the sewer "farm." A good bit of replatting took place inside Section Four including Mikkelson's Subdivision and Shannon and Luchs's 150 lots. Prices were going up, and it seemed that everyone wanted to build a home in the suburbs.

The Lozupone brothers decided to move to Chevy Chase.

They bought the lots on the west side of Connecticut between Underwood and Thornapple and built three, square, Italianate homes of stone and stucco. The end houses had flat-roofed, two-car garages behind them and the one in the middle a large porch. Oldest brother Steve was on the south, youngest brother Frank in the middle and Constantine on the northern end of the block. The houses were all slightly different but shared certain design features including marble staircases, tiled kitchens, fancy chandeliers, oil burners, trash incinerators and lots of decorative, molded plaster work, which was how the Lozupones made their living.

Patsy Royster Lozupone originally saw the houses when she rode the streetcar out from Cathedral Mansions to swim in the pool at Chevy Chase Lake:

When we got out there, the car listed to one side, and everybody said look at those three houses. They were pink and yellow and orange. Then the car listed the other way to see a Spanish-style house built by the Seventh Day Adventists who worked on Sunday. But everybody knew where the three Italian brothers lived.

Stephano came to America about 1904 with no English but the skills of an ornamental plasterer. He worked on Union Station and soon made enough to bring over his younger brothers and the older generation. After the Great War, the brothers did plastering jobs in the Capitol and many other government buildings and in the movie palaces, office

The three, new Lozupone houses; note trolley tracks

The interior of Frank's house

buildings, and department stores that multiplied in the 1920s.

It was Stephano who bought the lots on Connecticut Avenue and built the houses. His son Frank remembered carrying water to the workers and learning to burnish the plaster pillars so the black and white stones would shine through. By the time the families moved into their Chevy Chase homes in 1925, Stephano and Constantine were spending more time as foremen than they were up on the scaffolding, and Frank was handling the office work. Obviously three large and very Italian families moving into Chevy Chase at once attracted some attention and talk. Constantine's oldest son, Louis, remembered hearing about the gossip after he helped carry big cartons of grapes into the basement where his father had a press and kept barrels of the wine he made. They used the grape skins to fertilize their gardens, and guests always took home a gallon jug of homemade red drawn from the Lozupone's casks. In those Prohibition days, that was sure to cause talk.

Louis's younger sister Celeste did not recall any problems, but her brother had some fights at Chevy Chase Elementary and remembers being called a "wop" a time or two. Celeste said that when she and her sisters walked over to the grocery store on Brookeville Road, "We were a big family, and the girls would go and each buy two loaves because we didn't want to say six loaves of bread. We paid ten cents for Wonder Bread."

Louis's family bought chickens a half-dozen at a time, kept them in the backyard under the grape arbor and killed them for

Sunday suppers. Louis's uncle built him a pigeon cote on top of the family garage, and he raised birds there for several years. For a long time he could not figure out what was happening to his baby pigeons although Celeste claimed that the rest of the family knew. Finally, he discovered that his grandmother, who lived with the family and spoke only Italian, was putting a ladder up against the garage and then climbing up and taking the young birds and cooking and eating them. Grandmama loved squab. Frank and his brothers sometimes slept out on the roof of their garage on hot, summer nights, and there was a side porch the girls used.

Louis had worked as a water boy when his father's crew did the Fox Theater ceiling, but he much preferred his *Star* paper route:

I'll never forget the first year I went around with the calendars to sell at Christmas time. I thought the people would give me like a dime or a quarter, and they were handing me dollar bills.

We had that big wagon with the iron wheels, and when they were building East West Highway, before it opened, I used to go down that hill in that wagon, and we used to swim in that creek down there. It was a good swimming hole.

Sometimes Celeste would go with her big brother and pull the wagon on his paper route. Her mother did not like it when they came home with apples or pears picked from customers' trees. They also used the wagon to haul gallons of water from the spring at the bottom of the hill on Underwood Street. "Momma liked fresh spring water," Celeste recalled, and her brother said the water piped into the houses tasted awful.

Celeste smiled:

We used to sit on the wall and count the cars going by, and sometimes we'd get up to ten cars, and we'd tell people, 'We saw ten cars today.' That was a lot. And on the corner where the trolley stopped, there was dirt there and we played marbles where all the maids got off the streetcar.

The large Section 5-A, which Mr. Armentrout called "beautifully planned," included land acquired from Senator Stewart and land owned by Edward H. Jones. When it was subdivided in 1928, there were 211 lots between Connecticut, Brookeville, Dunlop and Woodbine to build on. Section 4-A across the street from the Lake was platted in the late

`20s while Section 4-B was a Warren property divided in 1930 and bordered by Maple, Cypress and East West Highway.[124]

In the 1920s and `30s direct racial covenants began to appear in Chevy Chase deeds. The standard paragraph read:

That no part of the land hereby conveyed shall ever be used, occupied by, sold, demised, transferred, conveyed unto, or in trust for, leased, or rented, or given to any negro or negroes, or any person or persons of negro blood or extraction, except that shall not be held to exclude partial occupancy of the premises by domestic servants of the grantee, his heirs and assigns.

Another boilerplate paragraph in the files of the CCLCo added to the above, nor to "any person of the Semetic race including Armenians, Jews, Hebrews, Persians and Syrians" and excluded domestic servants.[125]

Another sign of changing times was the organization of the fire department, which began with a meeting in July of 1926, shortly after Bethesda had begun to organize and had urged Chevy Chase to join its effort. The Chevy Chase and Martin's Additions leaders formed the "Association for Fire Protection for the District of Chevy Chase" and by the end of the year, raised enough money to order a $3,000 American LaFrance pumper and to make space for it under the Village office building at a cost of $1,690.[126]

In February 1927 the fire department went into service with six paid men, all former D.C. firefighters led by Chief William F. Lanahan, and about two-dozen volunteers under the direction of Paul Grove and Robert Dunlop who became deputy chief. By June the special taxing area had been authorized.[127]

Martin's Additions' home-made hose wagon on a old Overland truck chassis became No. 2 Hose Company and stayed at the end of Georgia Street near Taylor. Its equipment included a twenty-foot extension ladder, 350 feet of hose, two axes and two plug wrenches. In January 1929 this volunteer company acquired a new Chevrolet Hose Wagon with a fifty-gallon chemical tank and a lot more hose.

Winners of the Bethesda Cup Hook-Up Trophy for 1929 on 1926 Brockway-American LaFrance - top row on apparatus: Chester Schaffer, Paul Alexander, Lawrence Winnemore; standing (l-r): Supt. Marcellus Shields, BVFD Chief Dudly Brown, Capt. Robert Dunlop (CCVFD), Chief William Lanahan (CCFD), John G. Adair Jr., Robert Beall, Horace Troth Jr., Bernard Cassell; kneeling: (Geo. Medler or Geo. Offutt), James Garrett, Arthur Ricker, Eric Savage

The first officers of the Chevy Chase Fire Department were Dr. C. C. Clark president, Paul Sleman treasurer, William Orem Jr. secretary, and Marcellus Shield superintendent. Chevy Chase was the only fire department in the area to begin with a basic cadre of trained, experienced and paid men. It was also the only department with a "superintendent" who acted as liaison between the firemen and the fire board.

In 1931 the incorporated fire department, which was answering about a hundred alarms a year, authorized the construction of a fire-house at Connecticut Avenue and Dunlop Street. The engine house, designed by R. H. Berry and built by Alfred T. Newbold, cost almost $36,000 and was opened and dedicated in February 1932. It contained, in addition to space for the fire engines, a dormitory, locker room, showers, lounge, kitchen and a basement game room.

Chief Lanahan resigned in 1932 and Phillip H. Buehler, a D.C.F.D. lieutenant, replaced him. The No. 2 Company moved to the new house, and despite the ongoing Depression, the department took delivery of a new Seagrave pumper in early 1933. The next year the board authorized raises for its eight paid men: chief $1,500, deputy chief $1,380, privates $1,320, and housemen $600. In `35 North Chevy Chase was added to the taxing and basic coverage area. When Chief Beuhler's request for a raise to $1,800 was denied in mid-1935, he resigned, and Deputy Chief Edwin J. Sackett replaced him. In 1938 T. Marshall Duff succeeded Robert Dunlop as deputy chief of volunteers.

The fire department received generous community support and usually had a long list of volunteer applicants. Mrs. Charlotte B. Randall, named honorary battalion chief for her efforts, donated a silver cup that became the most desired trophy of local companies in hook-up contests. In Chevy Chase these were usually held at Oliver Street and Cedar Parkway and were much anticipated, summer-time celebrations.[128]

Most Chevy Chase homes date to the 1920s and `30s, and carpenter-entrepreneurs built many of them. They used stock plans in creative ways and dealt with local subcontractors from Kensington, Cabin John or Bethesda to complete electrical, sheet metal, and plumbing work. The First World War pretty much marked the end of the large "California cottage" and H. H. Richardson-influenced, shingle-style houses which made the old Village a target for historic preservation, but it also marked the beginning of almost everything else.

According to Judith Helm Robinson, "Virtually all of the late nineteenth- and early twentieth-century styles are represented today, including the Shingle, Colonial Revival, Tudor, French Eclectic, Spanish Eclectic, Mission, Neoclassical, Italian Renaissance, Prairie and Craftsman styles." To that add Dutch Colonial, Georgian Colonial, Mediterranean, and Federal style plus a number of Sears' sturdy, pre-cut, kit houses of various sizes, and numerous versions of the classic bungalow, at one time "the most fashionable houses built in America."

In Section Four about eighty-five percent of its one thousand houses were finished by 1941. But by the time the war came, almost every block in Chevy Chase still had at least one vacant lot; a place for football and capture the flag, cowboy and Indian fights, clubhouses, and long-term trash disposal. On those once treasured vacant lots stand the sometimes incongruous ramblers, split-levels, and ranch houses built after WWII.[129]

The Warren brothers, Monroe and Robert Bates, best known for their pioneering, luxury, co-op apartments, were among the big bungalow builders of the `20s in the fifty-seven-acre development, which they, but almost no one else, called "Leland." The Chevy Chase Club had purchased most of that land when negotiations for the Dodge tract seemed at an impasse and then sold to the Warrens at a profit when it was no longer needed.[130]

In the mid-`20s the brothers built Bethesda's first shopping center, a row of stores on the east side of Wisconsin Avenue between Leland and Walsh Streets with a vaguely English-colonial, Tudor-revival appearance. They dedicated the front part of their property for the old highway's widening. The shop roofs were steeply pitched, painted boards crisscrossed the stucco façades, and the doorways were set back into shallow arches. It was one of the first developer-planned, neighborhood shopping centers in the region.

The Leland Pharmacy was an original tenant and eventually a Sanitary grocery store oc-

cupied the south end and an A&P the north end with the Warren's office at 4606 Leland Street. At about the same time the Warrens were putting finishing touches to this local landmark, they were capping their apartment building in D.C. with the $3 million Tilden Gardens project, their 1927 masterpiece.[131]

In the *Star*'s Spring 1929 edition of "The Book of Model Homes," the Warren's advertised a basic change in building style after praising the bungalow:

The first houses constructed in Leland were attractive and picturesque bungalows containing a spacious living room, a well proportioned dining room, a well equipped kitchen, two handsome bedrooms, and an adjoining bath, the excellence of which was appealing to all. This type of house was extremely well proportioned, compact, and conveniently arranged, so that one would not be embarrassed because of the great shortage of domestic help immediately following the war.

According to the brothers Warren, "Very few reached completion before they were purchased." But now they were switching to the six-room, two-story home with three bedrooms in "English and Colonial designs" priced from $10,000 to $12,000.

Their 1929 "Star Model Home" was a colonial at 4509 Elm Street designed by Harry L. Edwards and built of white-painted, reclaimed brick on the first floor and ten-inch siding on the second. On the back of the 60-by-117-foot lot was a detached garage plus a rustic bridge over a small stream. The 13-by-23-foot living room had a fireplace, a radio-antenna outlet and a door that led to the side porch. A finished kitchen with a tradesmen's entrance in the pantry was behind the dining room. On the second floor were two large bedrooms and a nursery plus a bath and a cedar-lined closet. All hardware and fixtures were brass, the screens were bronze wire, and all the walls papered. The full cellar had five windows, laundry tubs, and a hot water heating plant.

"Leland Homes can be purchased by the average salaried man without causing a strain on his income." The Warrens wanted at least ten percent down "with the balance over and above the first trust arranged for payment in monthly installments over a definite period of years."[132]

Along the streets of Chevy Chase north of Bradley there are often groups of three or four houses of similar design and construction. Al-though a number of skilled architects such as Arthur Heaton designed homes in Chevy Chase and several prestigious builders such as Harry Wardman put them up, there are few homes of really unique design. Plans could be obtained from many sources for a few dollars and flipped over or turned sideways and easily modified. While it is true that Waddy Wood and Dan Kirkoff and a number of other designers' work can be found, it is also true that houses right out of the pages of *The American Builder* or *The Ladies Home Journal* are more common. In the building permits issued by town governments in the 1920s and `30s, often only one name filled the four spaces marked for owner, builder, architect, and contractor.[133]

And among the primary builders of Chevy Chase was that large and talented clan, practically a cartel, of Simpson, Troth and Orem. Contractors, carpenters, painters, electricians, insurance brokers, bankers, hardware store owners, real estate salesmen, pillars of the Methodist church, and civic-minded citizens, the community's growth fed their children and seemed to run in their blood. They worked with and for each other and tended to intermarry or to marry into the trade as Horace's daughter Lillian Troth did when she wed house painter-carpenter William Lyles Offutt, who in the early `20s could advertise "30 years in Chevy Chase." He lived in the old Williams farmhouse, rotated to face Williams Lane, and served as the County's assessor for Chevy Chase during most of the 1920s.

Simpsons lived in the nearby house made out of the Williams' barn, which Horace Troth had turned ninety degrees and moved back from the Lane, #3713. No one was surprised when Edward Simpson was awarded the contract to build the stone sanctuary of the Methodist church in 1934 or that William Orem Jr. headed the committee to plan a larger church in 1944 under the leadership of Coordinator Horace E. Troth Jr.

In 1940 the Simpson-Troth combine built a series of four brick colonials on Maple Avenue, and Bill Duvall's father traded in his Brookeville Road home on one of them. In a time when a builder's reputation was his only warranty, the Simpson kith and kin were trusted and successful as well as prolific.[134]

When David Orem was growing up in Chevy Chase, the favorite hobby of boys in his

neighborhood, as well as in many other parts of the area, was watching houses being built and then playing on the construction sites after the workmen left and "borrowing" whatever they could to build tree platforms and clubhouses in the woods. Older boys often became apprentices to their father or one of their uncles at an early age. If you did not like to paint, there were always jobs within the family for carpenters.

David Orem, who followed in his father's footsteps as head of the Edw. H. Jones Company and who lived in the house on Williams Lane that Simpson and Troth built for his father and who had two double first cousins, said that every time he came home after being away at school or in the service "there was a crowd of people, all related to me" and most of them involved in building, painting or repairing houses. His father, with the help of some other men from the Methodist church, where he was Scoutmaster, salvaged most of the Edw. H. Jones Co. in the Depression although Riggs took over the failed banking operation. His mother started pushing greens such as kale and okra during those dark days, and they ate a lot of chicken during the Thirties, but the Simpsons, Troths, and Orems did more than just survive.

Frank Simpson, the patriarch, had his home and business on the east side of Brookeville Road across from Williams Lane, now 7315. Just south of his property was the home of Horace Troth. Both lots went back for hundreds of yards to a ravine and creek and woods. Horace Troth's land had the better sleigh-riding hill.

The Troths stored and mixed paint in a large barn later converted into a four-car garage. John Troth thought his father had enough paint shelved there to cover the whole town. He said they really did not notice the Depression because there were all those big Chevy Chase houses to paint. Beyond the two-story barn was a chicken yard and a small garden, and then a big garden, then an orchard, and well beyond that, retaining walls framed a Troth-built tennis court and then the land went down across a ravine and another hundred yards to the back of the lot which was wooded.

"When I was growing up," said John Troth, "I thought that was the end of the world back there." Behind the Simpson home was a large

pump house, a small forge, and three other spacious outbuildings one of which held a huge, circular table saw while another was a two-story barn used to store lumber. David Orem, and many others, remembered that "those of us growing up on Williams Lane spent many hours, many delightful afternoons, playing around behind Daddy Frank's house where there were things you could build with and the smell of rosin and turpentine and watching the workmen cut and do mill work. So it was manufacturing as well as an office for the Simpson people."[135]

Growing up in Chevy Chase, both before and during the Depression, was a pleasurable experience for most children with many places to play and lots of kids to play with. By 1923 four Boy Scout troops were in operation. Troop 52 at All Saints had forty-one boys with Charles M. Marsh as the Scoutmaster. At the Presbyterian Church, Major F. B. Downing led Troop 57 with twenty-seven members, and Troop 90 at Blessed Sacrament, Scoutmaster W. S. Hull, had enrolled sixteen boys. The new Troop 55 at the First Methodist Episcopal Church with William Orem as Scoutmaster and hardware store owner Lawrence Troth as assistant Scoutmaster included Richard Beall, Harold DeVeau, Walter Gard, Everett Leonard, George Medler, Courtney Offutt, Chester Shaffer, Robert Troth, and Jack Davenport.

Even after the flagpole and the pin oaks were planted, ball games enlivened the Circle until October 1933 when the fountain was finished. It was built mostly with Newlands' money and designed by family friend Edward Donn. The three Scout troops at the Circle continued to play wild games of capture-the-flag into the night, and Robert Stevens recalled the D.C. police chasing baseball players off the circle from time to time.

The Kirkside Club, which followed the Bannockburn group and the English Cricket Club on the rolling property behind All Saints, provided acres to sled and play on, and the better players used a good ball field over on Wisconsin Avenue about where the trolley became single-tracked. Children played in the streams all over the area, trapped muskrats near Hesketh Street and built a swimming hole in the far corner of the Columbia Club. Columbia also had a fine sledding hill, as anyone who has been in an automobile on the section of East West Highway between Con-

necticut and the high school in icy weather can attest. On a really cold day and with a good sled you could fly down that hill and across the fairways to the creek, skid to the right and go on under Connecticut Avenue to the Lake. It was a long walk back up past Columbia's clubhouse, but it was worth it.

Ball games went on behind the post office, across from it on Chanlee's field, and at the corner of Western and Broad Branch even though the pitcher had to throw uphill. Games were played on Burr Edwards' field and in the small, semi-circular park, which some called the Newlands Street swimming pool. Another field was on Quincy Street at Sonnemann's store where the horse trough sometimes provided a cool dunking after a hot game.

Bobby Stevens: *When I was growing up, it was the main field. Visiting teams would come out and dress in his stable. He didn't think much of it. During the first war Sam Rice was in the Coast Guard, and they came out to play a local team at that field. Sam and them came out and beat our team to death and gave old man Sonnemann some trouble when they were dressing in his stable.*

Meddler's Field out on Brookeville Road, where the outfield still had ridges from the corn rows was also called Calhoun's field because it belonged to the same man that built long remembered Rossdhu Castle at the end of Woodbine Street in 1927, a favorite skating place for many Chevy Chase youngsters. Captain and Mrs. Clarence Calhoun had Philip Gormley and his son George build their fireproof castle on a ninety-acre tract in what was called Braemar Forest. Cornerstones came from ancient Scottish castles. Mrs. Calhoun designed the house with the help of Joseph W. Geddes.

A great hall sixty feet long and forty feet wide dominated the center of the "castle" and ended in a conservatory. A stone paneled fireplace faced the great stone stairway which led to curved gallery that sometimes served as a stage. To the right of the great hall lay the long, brown mahogany dining room with Mackart's "The Judgment of Paris" over the fireplace, and on the other side stood the huge living room which opened onto a stone terrace and bowling green covered with Scottish turf. Beneath the living room was a beamed billiard room with a tiled floor.

From the top of the home's square tower, called "The Chapel," one had a fine view of Rock Creek Park and the Capital city. In front of the gateway lodge, intended as a guesthouse, lay "Wee Loch Lomond" surrounded by willows, laurel and flowering shrubs. The Crash of `29 brought down the socially prominent Calhouns who retreated to the gatehouse while the castle became a popular nightclub in the 1930s and then was cut up into thirty apartments in 1937.[136]

Like Bethesda and Glen Echo, Chevy Chase supported a baseball team in the County league from time to time. The Bearcats flourished with a loyal cadre of ballplayers. They played at the Chevy Chase playground on unfinished Western Avenue, took on both D.C. and County teams and did not lose many games. Bobby Stevens, a charter Bearcat, remembered the only time they played a local African-American team:

There was this black team at Brighton, and we went up to play them. Some of them worked at Columbia Club, and a couple of us worked down there picking crab grass. They beat the hell out of us. They came and got us in a truck and took us out there, and got a couple of our boys full of wine. They gave us an awful thumping. I pitched that game. I was 16 or 17.

Stevens, who later played professional baseball for several years and even had a short stay in the big leagues, recalled how the team got its first uniforms:

I think it was John McAuliffe, he was our leader, he got somebody to donate a ton of coal, and then we went around and sold all the merchants in Chevy Chase tickets on this ton of coal, and we got about $100, and you could get uniforms for that. That's how we got our first set. All the merchants were pretty good about it. After a while it got so we got guarantees to go somewhere and play. We got twenty or thirty dollars. We had a treasury and had $100 in there usually.

The second set, Johnny McAuliffe went down and talked to Clark Griffith, and we got their old uniforms, the 1926 uniforms. I wore Cobileski's uniform. We had a big pitcher named Monkey Claude, and he had Walter Johnson's uniform. He was the son of superintendent of the trolley line. His name was Irving, and he was our ace pitcher. He played professional ball somewhere. He was a good pitcher. Henry Gichner was one of the best receivers I ever saw, the best amateur catcher I ever saw. If he could have hit, he could have played professional baseball. Could talk, he'd drive the batter crazy talking.

Chevy Chase Bearcats of 1925 (29-9) Top (l-r) - J. S. "Rix" McAuliffe, Bert Adelman, Irving "Monkey" Claude, John McAuliffe, Don Goodman, Tom Tribby Bottom - Mike Stevens, Henry Gichner, Doug Frisbie, Bob Stevens, Lewis "Duke" Oldfield, Charles Burdette [137]

Duke Oldfield had a chance to play professional but his mother would not let him go. Rix McAuliffe was our general utility man. He played infield, outfield, did a little pitching. He usually was in the game. He managed the team after his brother was killed. It kind of disintegrated after Mac was killed.

The Bearcats started out as fifteen- and sixteen-year-olds. We put ads in the paper for games. Then we went up to seniors and finally got in an unlimited league. When the Avalon went up, they didn't show movies on Sundays at first, and John McAuliffe, he was a real go-getter, he had the manager put a sign on the screen advertising our Sunday games. We had a football team too but seldom the same guys two weeks in a row. When the Episcopalians at the Circle built a new church they turned the old church into a gym, and they let us play basketball in there. They had radiators along the walls and somebody was always getting busted up. They didn't call many fouls.

Our clubhouse was down in McAuliffe's basement. His father kept some wine he made down there. He still had the old brogue. We played cards on Saturday night; in high school and afterwards, there was always a card game at his house.

In the early `30s the local team was called the Chevy Chase Grays and the usual line-up went Hieder, cf; Valanza, 2b; Wilson, 1b; Burdette, lf; Manville, ss; Pierson, c; Hall, rf; Kline, 3b; and pitchers Clark and Young.

Some more dangerous games were also common. The railroad tracks attracted a lot of boys, and there was a fair amount of bird and rabbit hunting or just plain shooting in the woods. David Orem and his friends never told their mothers when they waited at Tom Perry's spur and then hopped a slow freight to Georgetown or just saved a walk to Bethesda.

For many boys, crossing the long, timber trestle over Rock Creek was a rite of passage. The stream seemed a long way down when viewed between the open ties. Then halfway across an older boy would put an ear to a rail and a finger to his lips. "It's coming!" he would yell, and everyone ran to get off the trestle trying not to slip a foot between the splintered, creosoted ties. A lot of skin, a few tears, and some blood were left on that old bridge by small boys with fast-beating hearts.[138]

"We had sling-shot wars in Chevy Chase," said Jack Sullivan (B-CC `43) who grew up on Stanford Street.

We got sling-shots down to a science. We used to use marbles for ammo, and I remember we took the windows out of a house one time. We divided up three or four on a side, and we were in an oak tree, and they were in a vacant house, and they started shooting so we fired back and took out the windows, screens and everything.

We made them out of inner tubes and coat hangers. You take a pair of pliers and snip off the sides and bend and twist them around and had a neat slingshot, but you had to use a heavy coat hanger. I cut out the center out of an old wallet to hold the marble.

We played down around Oakridge at Thornapple where there was a great big piece of property. It was our turf, down at the bottom of that hill. We played cowboys and Indians, climbed trees, built underground hideaways, crawled through the storm sewers, and climbed the big oak trees. We climbed from tree to tree eighty feet off the ground. We played baseball at Oakridge and

Stanford, and another place was behind where we lived where Rosemary Street deadends.

There were lots of vacant lots, and we had so much to do that we didn't need any supervised activities. In the winter we broke into Leland to play basketball.

Jack Sullivan's buddy Joe Cantrel recalled that Dean Almy lost a front tooth in one of those slingshot wars. He remembered not only the vacant lots on Oakridge Avenue, but:

That whole block back of Gummel's farm. And right across the Maple Street from our house was vacant lot, and I had a pipe between two trees over there that I chinned and spun around on.

We went sleigh riding on Stanford Street's hills and down Oakridge. In those days, when cars had bumpers, a car'd come by and we'd grab hold of that bumper and swing out to the side cause they had chains on the wheels spitting snow back at you. Sometimes if they knew you were back there they'd speed up, and you had to watch for traffic coming the other way.

A number of children, especially in the long summers, set up small businesses selling lemonade or used toys and comic books at card tables or orange crate stands in front of their houses. A lot of boys and a few girls had paper routes, and some youngsters sold magazines or chicken and duck eggs door-to-door. Quite a few Chevy Chase homeowners were keeping chickens, guinea hens, rabbits and other animals well into the 1930s despite restrictions in some areas. Brockett Muir stabled his horse on Woodbine Street well into the `20s when he was riding out to visit a young lady at the National Park Seminary.

Helen Wolcott's family moved to 19 W. Kirke, a Simpson-built house, when she was an infant, and one of her worst memories of growing up in Chevy Chase was the next-door neighbor killing one of his chickens every Saturday and it flopping around in the yard. Even Mrs. Deming, the prosperous architect's wife, kept a flock of chickens on Oxford Street.

One of the more unusual enterprises was the neighborhood newspaper. Several had short runs, but one became an institution. In October 1931 the first edition of the *Thornapple Street News* hit the neighborhood with an editorial on the danger of burning leaves. Mimeographed, two-columns on both sides of legal-sized, pulp paper, the weekly sold for ten cents a month and went from forty copies

of the first issue to eighty by the end of the month.

The editor was eight-year-old Larry Williams Jr., of 128 E. Thornapple, and the associate editor was Dixie Fowler, who was nine. Larry's mother, a biologist who had worked on butterflies at the Smithsonian, cut the stencils and, some suspected, acted as copy editor at least. "I know that neither of us could operate a typewriter in those days, but somehow it got typed," admitted Leonard Williams.[139]

The paper carried world news when there was room, which was seldom, and had advertising right from the start. The first ad was for Brookeville Pharmacy. In late November the editorial warned readers to watch out for people with guns because "right in our neighborhood some boys shot near some children and a house. Boys with guns should not shoot at birds . . . ." One of the themes that ran through the *Thornapple Street News* was respect for wildlife.[140]

By 1932 the editor was complaining about the cost of paper, $1.50 per edition. He was printing 250 copies each week and offering mail service for 15¢ a month. Eventually the *Evening Star* contributed the ends of rolls after its press runs, and that solved the paper problem. Leonard Williams recalled that ads sold for twenty-five cents an inch and remembered one of the regular advertisers.

Mrs. Schultz started the Brooke Farm Tea House in the barn on their No Gain property. We always had a competition to see who would get the copy for their ad. Every week you had to go physically to the Tea House, and every week the routine was identical. You'd go in the middle of the day when they were setting up to serve, and you'd see Mrs. Schultz and she would tell you how sorry she was that it wasn't ready and could you wait. So you sat at a table, and she went back to the office and without exception she always waited long enough that the hostess would come out with a dish of ice cream and by the time you finished the ice cream, she had her copy ready. It was a ritual.

The big story of the Jan. 9, 1932, edition was the school:

The new Chevy Chase Elementary School opened on Monday and all the classes have gone into the new building except one fourth grade and on up. The new building has new desks and new everything nearly except the children and they don't all have new pencils. There is a new

fountain to wash our hands in, and my, how the towels disappear because the children wash their hands for fun and not because they are dirty.

The cafeteria at the new school is lots different from the old one and it is lovely. It has a place to buy the food you want, and you can get almost anything to eat. There is a certain table for each class and two girl scouts to watch the children so they will not be throwing paper. Anybody who saves dixie tops can get plenty of them if he walks around and looks for them.[141]

On Sunday morning Jan. 17, 1932, a long-remembered extra hit front porches with BROOKEVILLE PHARMACY HELD UP LAST NIGHT as a banner headline. In February the editor toured the new firehouse, and in March the mailman delivered all the papers one week when the Williams boys had colds. By then Larry's brother Leonard, 6, was listed as a reporter and Graeme T. Smallwood Jr. as a special reporter from Washington. The paper was up to four pages. By April they were printing 400 copies a week and decided to mail them on Fridays so made the price 15¢ a month for everyone.

They went up in a blimp, put out an extra on the Lindbergh baby's death, saw the Bonus Army downtown and took a three-week break in the summer for a trip to Canada. In one editorial the paper noted that there were two number eights on E. Underwood Street "and we think they should change it."

Leonard Williams said, "We were poor in the Depression days, but we didn't know it. We didn't have the clubs and the camps to keep the kids busy in the summer time. I think our mother wanted something for us to do that would be fun for us, besides being a good experience." By the fall of 1932 they were publishing 800 copies of a six- or eight-page paper weekly and stated editorially: "We are glad Mr. Roosevelt was elected. . . . And we hope he will make better rules for our country."

The ad rate was still 25¢ per inch, and plenty of ads appeared each week, often with illustrations. In December the editor pointed out a serious need:

Some of the boys at school want the teachers and some of the other people to have the Janitor build another jumping bar because there are a great many people that like to jump on the jumping bar. And they have two and there are about 59 or so people that want to jump on the two, and you all know that that many can't

jump on just 2 bars because they only have 5 or 10 minutes for their recess and one whole hour to eat lunch and come back.

That same week the editor pleaded with his readers "We wish that people's children would not bite the reporters when they come to get news. It is bad enough to be bitten by dogs sometimes." Despite the hardships they went on telling about pets and hobbies, awards and discoveries, and enjoying the snow. Then in February 1933:

NEWSPAPER FOR SALE
including complete equipment
reason for selling, a baby sister
price very reasonable
call Wisconsin 3791
Larry Williams Jr. publisher

Evidently no buyer was found, and by April they were back in business after the Washington *Herald* let them run some stories during the interregnum. Contributors came and went. Jack Lipscomb was listed as circulation manager at one time and Donn Tucker as sports editor at another. The editor once wrote "We wish the roosters around here would keep their mouths quiet real early in the morning," and at another time his "wish" was that people would not pass their copies of the paper around to their neighbors.

The editor pleaded, "When one of our reporters went to some houses for news and maids came to the door, the maids looked at him as if he were crazy. Please tell your maid that when we ask for the news, we are not crazy." The request provided some idea about how the operation worked.

The abandoned trolley right-of-way received a good bit of attention in 1936 as did the visit of the 17-year cicadas. In the last issue before they went away for the summer of 1936, a news item read: "Larry Williams' owl ate a lot of locusts. He ate a live one that was singing and you could hear it sing in the owl's stomach for several minutes."

The Williams family moved to Virgilia Street and that was the end of the *Thornapple Street News*. Both the Chevy Chase Historical Society and the Montgomery County Historical Society have bound collections of many of the paper's issues thanks to the efforts of

Wallace Janssen and a number of Martin's Additions and Chevy Chase residents who had saved one or two yellowed copies for half a century. As Mrs. Moore's letter gave readers insights to life in Bethesda during the Civil War, so the *Thornapple Street News* is a time machine to a neighborhood in the 1930s.

Another Thirties enterprise was the cookbook produced by the Rector's Aid Society of All Saints Episcopal Church. "Culinary Secrets," was dedicated to Mrs. William H. Heron who evidently did much of the recipe collecting. The Publication Committee produced 120 pages of recipes from "distinguished hostesses of Chevy Chase Parish" and sold dozens of ads. The recipes, for the most part reflected a slower-paced time and the ubiquity of "help."

Mrs. Northrup's recipe for tomato soup:

Chop fine 1/2 turnip, 1 carrot, 2 small onions, 1 stalk celery, 3 springs parsley, and mix with one can tomatoes (qt.) and 1 quart water. Season with one teaspoon each of sugar and salt and add a little pepper. Boil gently for 1 hour. As water boils away add more to keep the quantity constant. Mix 1 tablespoon flour with an equal quantity of butter and thin it with some of the soup. Mix it with the soup and boil 5 minutes and add parsley. Strain tomatoes before mixing with vegetables.

The cookbook contained three recipes for chop suey and three for chow mein along with two for spaghetti, one with pork and the other with bacon, and Mrs. J. B. Bowen's directions for making watermelon pickle:

Peel rind and cut firmer part in pieces. Soak for 24 hours in a salt solution made by dissolving 1 cup salt in 4 qts. water. Soak another 24 hours in alum solution (10 c. box), then an additional 24 hours in cold water. Boil 2 hours in strong ginger tea, remove and cool. To tea add 1 lb. sugar for each lb. of rind and one pint apple vinegar for each 3 1/2 lbs. sugar, then 2 tablespoons cloves, 2 tablespoons whole mace and 3 to 4 sticks of cinnamon. Into this syrup drop the pieces of rind and cook 1 hour. Color if desired with red or green vegetable coloring.

Chevy Chase somehow managed to stay reasonably isolated from Bethesda. Leonard Williams said, "Chevy Chase kids learned Bethesda existed when we got to Leland. I didn't know it was over there. We went to Chevy Chase Circle to get a haircut, down to the Safeway or Doc's." And they maintained their own teams. "We played ball in Tommy Perry's side lot on Shepherd Street," Williams said. 'That was everybody's baseball field." Thomas W. Perry Jr. recalled one day when his father came home from work and did not notice all the bicycles lying in his driveway and ran over a dozen or more.

A team grew out of that neighborhood playground, and the Land Company put up a good backstop on the Blackthorn Street vacant lot. Perry remembered Earl Elliot, Jimmy Trimble, Clackie Walker, and Buddy Speis as being "regulars" along with himself and Leonard Williams. Williams said:

When we were at Leland, we got a team up and played in the D.C. recreation league down on the Ellipse. We were the Chevy Chase Wildcats. Nobody sponsored us, but most of the other teams were from D.C. and were sponsored. Every team we played had bats and balls and uniforms. We had one criminal, a boy from Glen Echo, and on the way to every game he would come through Bethesda and go through Sears and steal two or three baseballs. You couldn't play if you didn't supply some balls.

The fellow who got the team together was Ned Ferren who lived next door on Thornapple. His father owned West End Laundry on Pennsylvania Avenue. There was a Little Tavern next to the laundry, and after every game we went in there to have a hamburger. We had a good time.

Donald Robertson grew up in the same neighborhood just a few years later. He remembered his grandfather, Thomas E. Robertson as a rather intimidating figure who dressed quite formally even in retirement. Don's father was newspaperman Nathan Robertson, and he and his family lived on Shepherd Street until 1939 when they traded houses with his father who had been on East Melrose since 1895.

Don learned about football from his father and played softball on the empty lot next to his Shepherd

Thomas E. Robertson

Street home. He and his friends also played on the lot behind the post office, and Don recalled being chased off by Bill Austin, the village policeman, after he built a pitcher's mound there. They also had games on the Cummings' farm field that later became a playground, and Don and his buddies put together a pickup team to play football and baseball against his friends down at the 41st Street playground. "We all wanted to play on the Perry's lot, but Mrs. Perry wouldn't permit it. She had gardens there. I recall in fall of `43 several of us played football there while Tom Perry stood in the driveway watching and knowing we were going to get kicked off."

They did a lot of their sleigh riding right there on Shepherd Street although they also tried the hills at both Chevy Chase and Columbia County Club. On the back edge of his memory, Donald Robertson recalled the trolley cars.[142]

Over the years the long, double-track Chevy Chase line had undergone almost constant maintenance and improvement. Most of the steep hills had been regraded: the Crushen Hill at Ordway and the Zoo Hill in 1900, the Pierce Mill Hill in 1902, and the Armes Hill in 1906. The original wooden ties were replaced and new rails laid by 1909 when the line acquired fifteen large, new Cincinnati cars, which seated forty-four in rattan comfort. Five more of these big, 48,260 pound, olive-green cars arrived in 1912 and they provided a comfortable if increasingly swaying ride until the line was killed. Some other, lighter street-cars served the line including the Kuhlmans and Brill-built cars, but the Chevy Chase car was the big Cincinnati.[143]

With the arrival of the new cars, the bridges had to be strengthened, and in the mid-1920s south of Chevy Chase Circle, iron poles marched along both sides of Connecticut. The tracks around the Circle were completely rebuilt and brought up to the street grade, but north of the Circle the old tracks marched to the Lake and sometimes the swaying cars barely missed the wooden center poles; in fact, No. 20 reportedly hit one and was retired to the back of the carbarn. By then a paved road ran on both sides of the tracks with an experimental brick section on the hill between the Lake and Columbia Club. In 1922 the power plant at the Lake closed down, and PEPCO supplied all the power for the trolley line. It did not take long for the generator room to flood.

Capital Traction replaced its one-man, late-night cars with "night owl" buses north of the loop at the Rock Creek Bridge, and in 1925 instituted a deluxe, extra fare and almost instantly popular service called the Chevy Chase Coach Line using small buses that looked like oversized limousines. The service ran every twenty minutes from the Circle through the mid-town area to Union Station in about a half-an-hour and offered buses every ten minutes from eight to nine am and between 4:30 and 5:30 pm. Once the license-plate dispute between Maryland and the District was finally settled, the Coach Line of Capital Traction went to the Newlands Street-Chevy Chase Club circle to pick up passengers.

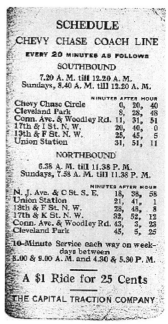

In 1929, when he was 21, John H. Smith came down to Bethesda from the farm near Walkersville where he and his eleven brothers and sisters were born and reared.

My uncle was living down here. He was a line man on the streetcars, Lawrence Emory Smith, went by Emory, worked with Frank Fling. They were two linemen for Capital Traction from down at Rock Creek bridge. They'd tie their ladder on a streetcar, always took a ladder with them, and ride to where they had to work as far as Calvert Street Bridge. So my uncle said why don't you go over to the Lake, he always called it "The Lake." The superintendent that was retired, Mr. Claude, was there and asked, "What are you doing down here?" I said I thought I might find some work around somewheres. He wrote a letter and sent me over to Georgetown and that's how I got my job. .

Claude had bought boxwood bushes from my father; that's how I knew him. He brought a box of candy to my mother when he came out to buy the boxwoods. If you go over to Newlands

Street right now, right near Brookeville Road, you'll see some boxes that came from Frederick. He bought twenty-six of them for $100 and gave his sister half of them.

In November I broke in on the streetcars as a conductor for thirteen days. You stood there and did exactly what the conductor was supposed to do, and the conductor sat there and watched you; that's how you broke in. Out in Maryland they had a three-cent ticket or a five-cent fare, you had to collect those and ring them up; if you didn't collect one but rang it up you had to pay for it. Anyhow when you'd get to Irving Street, you'd clear that register and then go through and collect the District fares and ring them up, think it was seven cents then, and you had to account for them. You wrote it down on the manifest.

You counted the people when you got to the District Line. You had to make sure the people who said they were getting off at the District Line got off, or you had to collect fares from them. One time I started collecting fares at Irving Street, a block before Chevy Chase Circle, and I was still collecting when we got down to Ellicott Street. They were standing, but you had get through somehow. The run went to Foggy Bottom, to 26th and G and F, went around the two blocks and back up Pennsylvania Avenue past the White House and up 14th and U and over to Calvert and out Connecticut Avenue.

When you got in the District, everything went in the farebox, and you had to grind that out and reuse it, grind that out and reuse it. It had a counter, and you had to take a reading off that when you changed ends. You signaled the motorman: two bells - go, one bell - stop, three bells was an emergency. In D.C. if they wanted a transfer to another line, 14th Street, New York Avenue; you gave them a transfer, and you had to punch the time, date and what line they were going on. You could punch the day and time ahead of time, but you didn't want to do too many. The transfers on the Washington Electric Railway were a cent extra. The only thing I kept was my punch; I had to buy that.

I was an "extra" when I went to work, had to report at 5:25 when the first car went out. There were eight of us on the extra board and eight on the motormen's side. One day you'd work and the next day you had to report, and if you didn't "catch anything" you stayed until the last run went out, and you might have to come back in the evening. They had a day and night

John Smith and I. Vincent Elmore - 1935

board. You were paid "half fare." If it was fifty cents an hour, you got twenty-five cents an hour.

You were paid every day. If you worked the streetcar when you'd come in at night, you'd deduct your pay and the motorman's pay from what you took in that day. I was the bookkeeper for myself and the motorman; I had to pay him, and you turned in what was left and a manifest. That thing had to balance every day. Sometimes you had someone standing on the rear of that car watching what you were doing. J. L. Murph, they had him on the carpet so many times for missing fares, he quit. The basic pay was about fifty or fifty-two cents, after three months it was so much and after a year, you got top rate, fifty-two cents. It got down as far as forty-five cents in the Depression.

November 22, 1929, was my first day of working by myself. Now you imagine a new guy and all those maids that come out to Chevy Chase on Thanksgiving. I was on the extra board until the two companies merged in `33. Then I got a regular run from about six in the morning, then go back in the evening and work again. Sometimes I had the run to Kensington or to Norris Station. You had to collect fares out there by hand. It went about every hour to Norris Station, on the half hour to Kensington. Someone went out there every day. I remember a motorman named Fones; he'd go so fast on that line I thought he was trying to see if the car would jump the tracks.

Another motorman I recall was Bill Gittings. He was all bent over. He would sit in the

station window and watch people swim. He had been with the line since `06. He'd pull one of those benches over and set his lunch on that bay window and watch them swim.[144]

Under governmental prodding the two, competing trolley companies had been attempting to effect a merger for more than a decade. Public Utility Commission findings and threatened lawsuits followed Congressional hearings and investigations. The basic fares had increased slowly, creeping up from the nickel rate at the end of World War I to a dime, four tokens for 30¢, by 1930. Beginning in 1931 school children could buy books of three-cent tickets for trolley or bus rides. Transfers were a problem as were track-congested intersections. At one time the government threatened to take over the systems, and finally in 1933 the Capital Transit Company was created and brought all of the street railroads under one management.

Despite discussions about abandoning the suburban lines, the once-reinforced, 750-foot-long Calvert Street Bridge came under study. The engineers decided to build a new bridge, but since trolley traffic was much too important to stop, a way had to be found to move the old bridge and use it as a detour while the new one was constructed. Rails were laid down in the Valley and wheels were welded to the base of the 1,200-ton steel girder bridge, and using horse and mule power it was pulled eighty feet downstream in two days, from 4:30 am on June 7th to 5 am on June 9th, 1934; the tracks were reattached and service continued. The new bridge included streetcar conduits, but they were never used.

"One cold morning the police came to my door," John H. Smith said fifty-six years after it happened.

I was living on Woodmont Avenue where the Holiday Inn is now, and they knocked and asked, "Know where Emory Smith is?" I said he left last night to go to work at 12 o'clock. In 1935 Pulliam was the night man and on his night off my uncle would go over there from until 8 o'clock in the morning and take his place as a watchman.

They said, "Well, we can't find him this morning. The man in the office was murdered. Your uncle's car's over there." So I said I don't know where he is, and I got dressed and went over there and in about an hour's time someone came in

and said they found him in Rock Creek. His clothes caught a snag, or he'd've gone down the creek that makes a sharp turn there.

A Saturday storm produced the heaviest snow in five years. The temperature fell to five degrees and would drop even farther in the next few days.

At about five o'clock on the morning of January 21, 1935, one or more people who seemed familiar with the trolley line's operation and routines, entered the car barn at the Lake and shot depot-clerk James M. Mitchell several times in the head while he sat at his desk. A pair of work gloves rested on the top shelf of his tall desk above an ink bottle, a Mr. Goodbar box, and rows of pigeon holes. In the top drawer was a loaded pistol.

The sixty-eight-year-old night clerk had worked for the transit company for forty years. The robbers got away with an estimated $1,800 in receipts from the Saturday and Sunday operations including the sale of weekly passes and, after a struggle, took 40-year-old lineman-mechanic-watchmen-handyman Emory Smith with them. His broom was lying by the tracks, and when his badly beaten body was dragged from Rock Creek, he had four bullet wounds in his head including one in the face.

The crime was discovered at about 5:30 am when Parker H. Hanna, an "extra" trainman reporting for duty in the foot-deep snow found the door open when there was no response to his knocks. He saw Mitchell's bloody body on the floor of the "cage" and ran outside. Hanna heard a car coming and hid until he saw that it was another employee. They called the police from the Chevy Chase firehouse.

Officers McAuliffe and Soper arrived and then called for Volten, Rodgers and Chief Garrett. They pried the locked cage open, and at 6:45 am, Pumphrey's men removed Mitchell's body. The police found no fingerprints, but collected four empty .32 cases and one unfired .32 steel-nosed bullet from the shop floor. The money had been in a company bag waiting for the Brinks' pickup, and Mitchell's neat accounting showed it contained $650 in $50 packets of ones, $325 in fives, $100 in tens, one twenty dollar bill and nineteen loose ones plus $31 in half-dollars, $60 in quarters, $10 in dimes, $10 in nickels and three dollars worth of pennies plus some checks.

While firemen joined the search for the missing watchman, McAuliffe interviewed Charles Henry Smallwood, T. W. Perry's watchman from next door. He reported hearing some loud voices when he was shaking down the furnace at 4:35 am. A carbarn employee, who had finished work about 1:30 am, slept through the entire affair on a bench in the back room. Everyone said Frank Gregory slept like a horse.

About 8:30 that morning a school bus driver reported seeing something near the Kensington Bridge. The police discovered drag marks, blood stains and pieces of auto window glass along with a paper bag containing an empty, quart milk bottle. Wet-footed searchers soon found Smith's body bobbing in the creek. Bethesda firemen dragged out the corpse. The police concluded that he had been killed in the getaway car since only Mitchell's blood was found at the carbarn. The wound on Smith's cheek showed powder burns, and a bullet had severed his jugular vein. A lookout was broadcast for a car with a broken window and a bloody interior.

Superintendent D. S. Schmidt of the transit company told reporters that he suspected a former employee. It was an opinion shared by many of the men who worked at the Lake. By lunch time D.C. police joined Corporal Theodore Volten, Pvt. James McAuliffe and other Montgomery County officers on the case, and within twenty-four hours they arrested a woman and four men, including two former transit employees while $1,500 in reward money was posted.

The next day produced some bloody clothing hidden away near the carbarn, and the arrest of two more Capital Traction employees. State's Attorney James H. Pugh took control of the investigation, which had grown to include Baltimore detectives. The murder weapon was identified as a .32 caliber pistol.

As foot-deep snow and below-zero temperatures hit the area, the authorities freed all the suspects by the end of the week, and sought new witnesses and a blood-stained car. A tip from Baltimore led to a search for three D.C. men, and a County policeman, Jerry Hobbs from Colesville, went undercover posing as a Baltimore criminal and spent the next two weeks in the Washington underground chasing various clues and eventually identifying the prime suspect.

The investigation went on, and although no one was ever charged with the crime, the police were reasonably sure that a former employee was involved. The story soon disappeared from the newspapers which were filled with the Lindbergh trial. The men who worked at the carbarn, including Emory Smith's nephews and young Bob Truax, thought they knew who did it but had no proof. "It had to be somebody who knew him," Albert Smith concluded. "They had to make sure he was dead, or they wouldn't have shot him so many times in the head."

The case (#130B) rests, technically still active and occasionally stirred, in the Bethesda police department files. In the big, worn manila folders are photos of footprints in the snow, of the desk, three pictures of Mitchell's body and wounds and one of Emory Smith's body after the post-mortem. The file also contains the expense report totaling $1,182.35 including $15 in fees paid to informers and such items as "dinner for 7 $10.50, lunch for 5 $4.00, hotel for 3 in Phila $9.00" and five payments to Officer Hobbs totaling $24.

Transcripts of the questioning of prime suspects and copies of some of their intercepted mail are in the files. A small tan envelope with "Wm. Reuben Pumphrey Colonial Funeral Home" printed on it contains three shell cases, two clean and one deformed bullet, and two broken teeth found in Mr. Mitchell's mouth. A note signed "Mrs. Edith Smith" and dated Jan. 25, 1935, states "received property of Emory Smith - 1 open face watch, $1 in bill folder & drivers permit Md. and other cards, $1.66 in change, 8 car tokens, 1 large brass key, screw driver, tobacco pouch, 4 lead pencils." Emory Smith's watch was still running when they pulled his body from Rock Creek.

After Emory Smith's funeral, another nephew, Albert Smith, went down to stay with his widowed aunt in Woodmont "for a while."[145]

First thing you know I went over to the Lake to see about getting a job, and they hired me right away, and I went to work the first day I went down there. I only got forty-one cents an hour. I was on the extra board for three or four years, and then when they drafted me, I had a regular run. They had all old farm boys driving for them when I went down there.

Harry Craver broke me in, and I thought, my gosh, have I got to go through all this the rest of my life. If somebody got on the track in front of the old streetcar, you know, they had a little gong you stomped on with your heel. Boy, when he stomped on that thing those cars would get over to the right. They had me almost scared to death, but I stuck to them and I liked it after a while. Craver was a smooth operator, and he made me the same way. I learned to stop so it didn't jerk and the same way with the buses. When I got the hang of it, I could pull up and let that air off so easy.

I never wanted to be a conductor; I liked being the motorman. I hated to leave the street-car. But you know when those leaves in the fall of the year got on the tracks you couldn't stop them things for anything. I didn't mind the ice, but I hated the leaves. I was only on the trolley cars six months, and I was surprised when they closed it down.

The first suburban line closed by the new Capital Transit Company, in August 1935, was the one that ran from the District Line through Bethesda to Rockville. The next was the Chevy Chase Line, and its last day of operation came on Saturday, September 15, 1935. Bob Truax spent the day photographing the crews as they finished their runs. He stayed until the last car left.

The five and a half miles from the Calvert Street Bridge to the Lake then became bus routes 4, 5, 6, 7, and 8, and some sixty buses seating 35 passengers each went into service. The trolley line itself closed rather quietly with few protests of its passing. Some folks said they had trouble reading their paper on the buses, and others complained about their smell, but considering how long it had been running and the fact that it usually provided a car every five minutes south of the Circle and every ten minutes in Maryland, few noted or mourned the trolley's passing.

The Kensington Line died with it. That line had been running as a mostly one-car operation under R. H. Phillips for the two years since the Capital Traction lease expired in 1933. For a while the question of the location of the station at Chevy Chase Circle added to the confusion, and buses used Oliver Street to turn around until a child was killed in 1942.

All of the conductors, motormen, and other employees went to other trolley lines or to the expanded bus operations. They had

had two weeks, with seniority the rule, of course, to pick their runs. From the Chevy Chase Division, forty-two conductors and motormen (twenty-two regulars and twenty on the extra board), including both John Smith and his motorman brother Albert, transferred to the Western Bus Division of Capital Transit.

The regular trainmen with the most seniority, plus a few younger men who could not qualify as bus operators, moved to other street car divisions. These included the sometimes irascible Gene Fling with his wonderful handlebar mustache, with the company since 1895; George Pulliam who was second in seniority with a date of Feb. 18, 1904 and who sometimes sold corn, squash and tomatoes to his "regulars;" popular Tom Marshall from the 1905 class, and mustachioed Charles Beaver whose 1917 entry date concealed his long service with WRECo until the strike of that year. They all chose the 14th Street Division.

The transferees to the Navy Yard run included Charlie Terrell, Herbert Claude's assistant before being transferred downtown; Mr. Abersold and Mr. Fox of the Kensington Line, who got no seniority credit because that operation was non-union; conductor R. M. Chinn, the shop steward with twenty years of service, and Frank Fones, who finally did qualify for the buses and drove the loop at Chevy Chase for years. Henry E. Gibbons, who had replaced Mr. Claude as superintendent in 1933, continued in Capital Transit's administration and eventually piled up forty-two years of service.[146]

The fate of the abandoned tracks was uncertain although in the District of Columbia repaving the streets was the goal and the question was only who paid for what. In Maryland the first question was who owned the right-of-way and how much it was worth. The Chevy Chase Land Company, the State Roads Commission, the County Commisioners, the Civic Federation, and, of course, all the sections of Chevy Chase became embroiled. Some wanted the center of the road used for parking, others wanted to plant trees, and the garden club proposed a compromise, landscaped parking area, but most commuters wanted more street to drive on. In February 1936, the *Thornapple Street News'* poll showed that out of ten people asked, seven said parking and three said more road space. "As it is now," wrote the editor, "it must give everyone riding through a bad impression of Chevy Chase, Maryland."

The arguments continued for more than a year, and the middle of Connecticut Avenue became a skinny field of weeds, clover and mud. The fight went on into the late 1930s with Robert Hagner and the Democrats blaming the Fusion dominated County Commisioners for delaying acquisition of the right-of-way. The task was finally turned over to the State Roads Commission. In November 1938 the Chevy Chase Land Co. contributed $2,500 to help buy the trolley right-of-way. The State's final offer had been $7,500 while the transit company wanted $15,000 but settled for $10,000. Of course, that still did not get the road repaved.

One of Eda Schrader Offutt's first memories of Chevy Chase is of sitting on the curb on the west side of Connecticut Avenue and watching the men and steamrollers repave the street after the removal of the trolley tracks. The tracks "everyone says" were sent to Japan as scrap metal and returned to Pearl Harbor on Dec. 7, 1941, as bombs.

Eda's father was Dr. A. Lee Schrader, professor of pomology and head of the Horticulture Department at the University of Maryland, and in 1931 he and his wife decided to build a sizable home in Chevy Chase. Dr. Schrader sketched out a house with space for his own growing family plus his mother-in-law and her German cousin, who had come to stay, and his brother Bill, who had returned from the First World War permanently quiet and withdrawn, plus, of course, room for a maid or housekeeper.

Then he bought a suitable lot on Woodside Place, a quiet, short and dead-end street, and found an architect to draw up the plans. After inviting bids on his new home from several local builders, the Schraders chose an old friend of the family, "Uncle Billy" Beahm, and the work began in the fall of 1931, and by the end of 1931, the house with its field stone front and fireplace, its scattering of clinker bricks, and two-car garage was almost completed and ready for decorating, landscaping and the finishing touches. In March of 1932 the Schraders and their extended family moved into their new home. Including the lot, it had cost about $25,000.

In June 1933 their second daughter was born; they named her Eda after an artist-aunt. As Eda grew and explored her neighborhood, she found a small, safe and interesting world. Houses were still being built on Connecticut Avenue almost in her backyard, and she could wedge through a hole in the fence at the end of the street and visit the horse in the small barn behind the Junior College.

She named housekeeper Flora Moyers, "Tommy," and the family as well as the young woman adopted the name. Tommy took the child exploring in the city as well as the neighborhood, and except for one year when a pay dispute over her $12 a weekly wage led her to quit, was with Eda's family in Chevy Chase until 1942. Tommy's room was on the third floor as was quiet Uncle Bill's, her father's oldest brother who bought the *Times-Herald* on Sundays and always shared the big, colored funnies with Eda. He called her "Peaches," smoked a pipe and played the horses.

Joan Schrader in the front yard of her family home

It was a street with a fair number of children most of the time and many interesting neighbors, both human and four-footed. Behind the Schraders on Connecticut lived Mrs. Hord who had a granddaughter named Audrey Cook, who played with Eda when they were little more than toddlers. Next door lived Tommy Collings and his folks, Banks and Maude. Tommy and Eda became best friends as they grew up, but Tommy died of pneumonia, perhaps from meningitis, when he was only six years old. About a year later, Charles and Lucy Bell and their three beautiful, teen-aged daughters moved into that house. He was an assistant Secretary of the Treasury and later ran the celebrity war bond drives. On the other side of the Bells lived the Phillips whose son, Howard, went to Landon. They had a small dog that yapped a lot.

On the north side of Eda's home, past two wooded lots where children were not allowed to play, lived the Crawfords. Mrs. Crawford seemed to attract stray cats and kept them in her basement where they multiplied. One day Mr. Crawford went down to the cellar and tried to count the cats. He was not sure of the total, but it was more than thirty. He told his wife "It's them or me," and the cat population on Woodside Place decreased rapidly.

Across from the Crawfords lived the Ofensteins and later the Woodruffs, who had several blond little girls. Next door were Mildred and T. Stanley Holland and their two handsome sons, Stanley and Griffin, and a daughter, Betsy. Mrs. Holland always collected for the Red Cross in the neighborhood, and it was Griffin who buzzed the street during the war. Next were the "Dutch" Bergmans with daughter Susie, who was about Eda's age, and an older son. They moved to Rosemary Street before Dutch coached the Washington Redskins to an NFL Eastern Conference championship in 1943. When Dr. Schrader developed a large gold and dark red peach, he named it "Redskin."

The Schiffs replaced the Bergmans, and Eda learned about Judaism and many other important things from them. Jeanne was a bit older, Walter a year younger than Eda, and the twins Carol and Helene were little more than babies. Eda spent a lot of time at the Schiffs, playing games and looking at *Life* magazine, not allowed at her house.

During the war, Mattie and John Hoskins lived in the house directly across the street from the Schraders. He was the Assistant Surgeon General and wore an admiral's uniform during the war. They had two large, pampered cats that Mrs. Hoskins cooked liver for. In the late afternoon, the older cat walked to the end of the street and waited for Admiral Hoskins and then rode home on his shoulders. Eda played Russian Bank with the Admiral who puffed his pipe and accused her of constantly making up new rules.

On the corner lived the Potts who had a large outdoor cage connected to a basement window on the side of their house where a big monkey with a very red rear end lived. Not many neighborhoods could top that. On the other corner was a small, stucco house with many windows in the back, which some said had been built for a TB patient.

In the summer the hurdy-gurdy man with his monkey came around playing his tinkling tunes. And the Holmes bread man, the milkman from Harvey Dairy, the man from Tolman's Laundry, and Mr. Copp, the egg man, they all came to Eda's house regularly. The Fuller Brush man and the Realsilk hose salesman came less often, and once in a while, the linen merchants from Syria arrived with their bulging metal suitcases filled with beautiful, handmade linens. Occasionally a man looking for work or food came to the back door.

Eda enjoyed Chevy Chase Elementary and liked her teachers, but joined her friends in giggling when they called the principal "Anna P. on the rose." Miss Fell was the kindergarten teacher and then Miss Kenny in second grade; she enjoyed Mrs. Hazel Phillips in both 3rd and 4th grade and Agnes Kain's combined 5th and 6th and Creative Club. She missed being a princess one time because of mumps. Eda finished up with Miss Ocie Dodd in the 6th grade.[147]

The Depression hit Chevy Chase hard, fast and briefly. Some builders failed, and some lenders such as the Edw. H. Jones Company collapsed under the weight of valueless second mortgages. Two of the three Lozupone brothers lost their houses as business evaporated and banks failed. Stephano, the oldest, stayed and paid off all the company's debts.

"My parents lost our house in Chevy Chase," said John Henry Sullivan Jr. "They foreclosed on it. I remember standing on the lawn on Stanford Street and they auctioned off the house for about $6500. My mother ar-

ranged for someone she knew to bid on it, but we had to leave."

But it was also the time when Janet Newlands Johnston's daughter, Janet, married William Sharon Farr. She had known her third cousin, who was then the Land Company's landscape architect, since adolescence. They had Dan Kirkoff design a large, French-inspired home for them in the raw and treeless Hamlet near East West Highway.

"The Hamlet was my mother's idea," Janet Farr said:

Nonna and Aunt Edith were very conservative, but mother had become a businesswoman in helping to run the Palace Hotel. She found Kirkoff out West and had him design some houses to be built in Reno. Then she sent him here, and he laid out the original Hamlet with no houses right next to each other and entries from courtyards.

Mother decided it was ridiculous to sell lots as the Fisher company had been doing. She came up with the theory of leasing land. She also suggested that the Land Company hold on to the houses it built in the Hamlet, rent them out instead of selling them for $15,000.

But the Chevy Chase Land Company was seriously considering going out of business. In 1937 it sought advice from T. Howard Duckett on methods that might be used to accomplish liquidation. The next year the Company reorganized, "borrowing" its officers from the Union Trust and Thomas J. Fisher companies and paying president Hillyer $250 a month, treasurer Miller $50 and secretary Fleming $25. The CCLCo's proposed budget for 1938 was $123,840 ($92,000 for taxes). Two years later, however, sales totaled more than $450,000 and filled the books with black ink.

A DEVELOPMENT OF THE CHEVY CHASE LAND COMPANY
at Connecticut Avenue & East-West Highway, Chevy Chase, Maryland
THOS. J. FISHER & CO. INC., AGENT - 738 15 STREET, WASHINGTON, D. C.

While the CCLCo recovered slowly, most of the Washington area felt a resurgence in home building in 1936. On the 4th of July the *Star* reported that Washington-area builders had enjoyed their best June in six years. The Western Suburban toted up $1.5 million in construction in the year's first six months, the greatest building boom in its history.

Shannon and Luchs started the year with a campaign "announcing" Rollingwood and offering many floor plans to prospective buyers. In West Chevy Chase new basements appeared with the robins and the violets, and carpenters, plumbers, and bricklayers soon found all the work they wanted. In 1937-38 Section Two budgeted $22,900 for trash removal, street repair, and public safety. By the end of the decade the Land Company shared in the feast as it began promoting its upscale Hamlet on East Leland Street.

By December 1939 a twenty-foot Christmas tree glowed with two hundred blue lights in front of the Land Company's office, a symbol of renewed prosperity.

---

[1] J. C. Proctor, *Star*, Nov. 17, 1946, and *Star* July 30, 1891. Note that the staid *Evening Star* chronicler, never known for his choice of colorful verbs, here used "caracoling."

[2] See "The Nose, the Lie, and the Duel in the Antebellum South," by Kenneth S. Greenberg in the *American Historical Review*, Vol. 95, 1990.

[3] While participating in a pseudo-knightly tournament in New York, Armes became involved in an exchange of insults over a young lady, twisted a Virginian's nose and was challenged to a duel. The next morning the other young man went back to Virginia.

[4] His book was published some ten years after the facts were known.

[5] See *William M. Stewart: Servant of Power* by Russell Elliott (1983).

[6] Stewart's own memory of the financing is much more convoluted. See Elliott's *Servant of Power*.

[7] Most of this from Armes' own account, *Ups and Downs of a Soldier* (1900), which, while full of spite, seems to have the basic facts right. His diary entries for January and February 1890 record almost nothing but real estate acquired along the line of Connecticut Avenue extended. Also Edith Claude Jarvis' "Old Chevy Chase Village" in *The Montgomery County Story,* Nov. 1969, has both this story and the one that follows. There seems to be no contrary evidence in the land records of the County or of the District or of major purchases in 1886-89.

[8] According to Atwood, "In one of his many trips to Washington in 1886 or 1887, Newlands decided to launch a great plan of land purchase, amounting altogether to more than 1,700 acres, along with a comprehensive, imaginative and yet practical plan of suburban development." "The Romance of Senator Francis G. Newlands and Chevy Chase," *Records of the Columbia Historical Society,* 1966-68, p. 298.

[9] The home stood about where Ellicott Street crosses Connecticut Avenue today,

[10] Senator Stewart also used the 1890 date for his original purchase of 200 acres, and the Stewart Papers in Reno contain letters from both Armes and Stewart on this sale. See *Servant of Power.*

[11] The writer's paternal grandparents kept a couple of acres around their home but then gave that up when, according to family tradition, it looked like Connecticut Ave. would come through their dining room. They got a much better price for the last two acres. See land records: EBP 10/300, JA 118/7 & 35. George Hamilton will re-emerge in the 1942 Charter fight.
Mrs. Glover was the niece and friend of the second Mrs. Newlands.
Boundary Street became Florida Avenue in 1890. D.C. adopted its street-name system in 1905.

[12] *Post,* Sunday, March 2, 1890.

[13] Stewart to Newlands, Oct. 2, 1890, in the Stewart manuscript collection.

[14] See "Rock Creek Park, Emerald of the Capital City" by William Bushong and Piera M. Weiss in *Washington History,* Fall/Winter 1990-91. Also see Don Hawkins' "Unbuilt Washington" in *Washington History,* Fall/Winter 1993-94.

[15] William Lilley III, "The Early Career of Francis G. Newlands 1848 - 1897" Yale PhD, 1965, p. 210, based on the *Congressional Record* and the Stewart to Newlands letter cited above. Lilley had access to Land Company records and interviewed Edward Hillyer in 1963.

[16] Lilley, p. 209, cited by French (note #18), p. 320. *Post,* March 18, 1890, on the railway. Lilley: "Newlands had two bills introduced in Congress" for Rock Creek Park and his railway.

[17] Stewart's "political" biography is unclear on the actual amount of his investment.

[18] See footnote 40 in Roderick French's "Chevy Chase Village in the Context of the National Suburban Movement, 1870-1900" in the *Records of the Columbia Historical Society,* 1973-1974. Emphasis added. Also see Lilley dissertation, pp. 211-213.

[19] Rodman W. Paul, *Mining Frontiers of the Far West,* 1963, p. 76.

[20] This Hillyer is, as far as the writer can tell, no relation to the Hillyers of Chevy Chase.

[21] Atwood says $800 in "The Romance..." and $900 in the biography.

[22] Mark Twain's *The Gilded Age,* which skewered this society, was a product of both his time in Nevada and his brief service as Senator Stewart's secretary. They parted over Twain's habit of smoking cigars in bed.

[23] Most of the above from Albert W. Atwood's "The Romance of Senator Francis G. Newlands and Chevy Chase" in the *Records of the Columbia Historical Society,* 1966-68, *California Rich* (1980) by Stephen Birmingham, and *Men to Match My Mountains* (1956) by Irving Stone. Stone quoted Sarah as crying, "You have been paid to render this decision."

[24] Rising attorney George Hamilton may have been one of Newlands' agents in Maryland. In March 1890, he purchased the 140 acres of No Gain that belonged to the writer's grandfather, young Hilleary Offutt, and in May of the same year transferred the property to Stellwagen and Morsell and the CCLCo. See JA 118-7 in the land records. Hilleary and Kate Offutt then bought the 138-acre farm on the Pike, most of which became the campus and golf course of Georgetown Prep, the site of the Red Barn summer theater and Ed Offutt's/Dietle's Store.

[25]Archives of the CCLCo. In 1898 trustee Newlands held 13,627 shares, William Stewart 968, May Bell Stewart 100, and Stellwagen, Ralston, Dessez, Nyman, and Hacker, one share each.

[26]Modified from M. R. George's thesis (note #44), original report and source in CCLCo archives.

[27]A contemplated railroad bridge over Connecticut Avenue never got past the preliminary stage.

[28]Both signed contracts are in the CCLCo archives. The going shipping rates from Baltimore were 82¢/ton for stone, $1.10/ton for lumber, 86¢/ton for common brick.

[29]Atwood, "The Romance of Senator Francis G. Newlands," *Records of the CHS*, p. 299.

[30]Cecily's daughter Edith said "they became enamored of each other" and told the story of her mother being sent abroad but also said her father did not arrive until 1891.
Starting with this chapter "Tenleytown" replaces "Tenallytown" as the spelling of that area.

[31]*Post*, Oct. 9, 1892. Since the story was Ethel Marie's and since it appeared on the "children's page," it need not be taken without salt, but it is too good to leave out. If the story is true, #178 was probably a 0-8-0 Camel engine according to the B&O Railroad Museum in Baltimore.

[32]His front-page obituary described his Civil War and Indian fighting service and his real estate dealings in NW, D.C., but did not mention anything about Chevy Chase. *Star*, Dec. 19, 1919.

[33]Probably built by the B&O as part of their deal with Stewart and Newlands.

[34]The Claudes' "cottage" cost $1,643 in 1894. The trolley station cum waiting room was taken apart and moved to Hyattstown and rebuilt there in 1980.
The second Mrs. Newlands, "Nonna" in the family, bore him two sons who died in infancy.

[35]See "Old Chevy Chase Village" by Edith Claude Jarvis in *The Montgomery County Story*, Nov. 1969 and the Jarvis oral history of July 16, 1971, by Paula Locker.

[36]Lilley, p. 211.

[37]Stewart in the 1902 campaign: "I never heard of Mr. Newlands being well a week at a time; it is either rheumatism, gout from English high living, bladder trouble, headache, indigestion, or all of these combined, that not only requires a syndicate of puffers to navigate his political balloon but a syndicate of doctors to keep his feeble heart in motion . . . ." Elliott, *Servant of Power*.

[38]Stewart died at Georgetown Hospital in 1909.   Newlands was silent amid the encomiums.

[39]On January 27, 1893, after taking his seat in the 27th Congress, President Francis G. Newlands of the Chevy Chase Land Company signed General Order No. 1:
From and after this date and until further orders, Mr. Edward J. Stellwagen, Vice President of The Chevy Chase Land Company will have the active management of the affairs and conduct of the business of the company under the general direction of the Board of Directors, and in all matters ordinarily pertaining to the office of and requiring the action of the President his decision shall be final and considered the same as if that of the President.

[40]Johnston quote from a CCHS oral history interview, May 1988. Granddaughter Janet Farr recalled Senator Newlands riding a fat, old grey named Molly when he visited her family in Normandy.

[41]See Albert W. Atwood, *Francis G. Newlands: A Builder of the Nation* (1969). Janet Farr: "He loved shoes. My mother said he couldn't resist buying boots or shoes. Like some ladies buy hats, he had a weakness for shoes." MCHS oral history 1976.

[42]*Streetcar Suburbs* (1978) by Sam Bass Warner, Jr. There were about 23,000 civil service workers in D.C. in 1890, with their families, perhaps 80,000 people. The question of the creation of the middle class is more than this writer can handle as is what makes up "the American dream."

[43] See Mary Roselle George's 1989 U. of Md. MA thesis, "Developer Influence in the Suburbanization of Washington, D.C.: Francis Newlands and Chevy Chase" and Kenneth Jackson's *Crabgrass Frontier* (1985) p. 124.
Donald Robertson, among others, recalled the Chevy Chase of his youth as much more middle class than Chevy Chase of the 1980s and 1990s. And Eleanor Ford of the CCHS also thought "it was middle class. Comfortably off but not 'wealthy.' Income was from salaries, not from inherited or earned capital. Corby was an exception, not typical."

[44]Until 1912 when a precinct was opened at the Library, Chevy Chasers had to trek over to a house near the blacksmith shop in Bethesda to vote. Probably one of the few times they went that way.

[45]Paragraph five of an early Martin's Additions' deed read: "That the property hereby conveyed, either before or after improvements are made, can not be sold, rented, leased, or otherwise placed in the possession of a colored man, or one of the African race." By 1910 the CCLCo covenants prohibited the building of anything but single-family residences costing at least $5,000 with a 25' set-back. See MC land records. Constance Green, *The Secret City* (1968).

[46]In the early 1940s when William Orem sold a house to the Bernhardts, the first Jewish family in Section Five, he was visited by a small delegation of neighbors, but we cannot know what happened because David's mother sent him to his room. When the first Jewish family moved into Woodside Place, also in the early `40s, there was no remembered comment from neighbors.

[47]The writer has no idea when or how Brookville Road lost that middle "e." It may well have been a County sign painter's error (cf. Viers). The writer put it back.

[48] Dessez's father designed forts for the Confederacy although his family remained in Washington.

[49]From correspondence in the CCLCo archives.

[50]From 1985 interview by the Chevy Chase oral history project.

[51]See Vita Alexander's "Recollections" at the CCHS.

[52]See the Washington *Times*, Nov. 21, 1933, for more on Cummings.

[53]"Brookville Road and Williams Lane: Oldest Streets in Chevy Chase" by Hallie Lou W. Blum and Francis X. Emmet, 1972, in the collection of the Chevy Chase Library.

[54]French, "Chevy Chase Village," *Records of the CHS*, 1973-74, p. 327. Professor French concludes "In this intent they were rather successful." Note the word "rather." Miss Givens wrote that these houses "struck the keynote for the community which was to grow up around them."

[55]The Spanish-style house designed by Johnson for Stewart was replaced by the Dessez-designed house used by Newlands according to Eleanor Ford. "Woodley" at 3000 Cathedral Avenue became the Maret School. Stewart lived at 1906 H St. NW in 1893.

[56]James E. Scull's interview with Mrs. William S. Farr, MCHS 1976.

[57]Janet Farr: "They didn't go to school. They studied at home. Their father allowed them complete control of their education, and they chose the subjects they wanted to study. They were provided with professors. . . . (My mother) decided she would like to be an architect and there my grandfather was the old school and said no." Scull 1976 interview, MCHS.

[58]Dr. Johnston gave up his practice shortly after the birth of his daughter Janet and moved to France to become a painter. Janet Newlands also painted, "but the minute she married she stopped painting," her daughter said.

[59]Single Oak became the Swiss ambassador's residence. Atwood is the source of the Cathedral story, and Mrs. Jarvis is one who said that the Newlands left because of the electricity shutoffs.

[60]"Francis G. Newlands completed last spring a very comfortable residence, office and out buildings on the bluff overlooking the town . . . that adds greatly to that part of the suburb. The buildings are something after the Queen Anne style of architecture, and still in its artistic design it is purely original. Mrs. Newlands was her own architect, and the structure speaks well for her taste." Reno *Evening Gazette* Dec. 24, 1890. Janet Farr labeled it "uglier than anything in Chevy Chase."

[61]The thermometer stood at zero on Jan. 2 and reached the all time low of fifteen below zero on Feb. 11. Thirty inches of snow fell on Feb. 13, and snowfall for the year was 54 feet 4 inches.

[62]County land records Liber 202 folio 376. The deed was signed by Stellwagen and witnessed by Herbert Claude. Today the house is still generally called the Corby mansion or "place."

[63]Remarkably three of these first four houses still survive in modified form and on much smaller lots. Nyman's house was torn down and four brick houses built on that land.

[64]See Thomas Robertson's "History of Chevy Chase" and the CCLCo archives. Kirke Street was often spelled without the final "e" in the early days. The CCLCo has in its files the complete

specifications and the correspondence of the Claude job which went well until the very end when 2,250 shingles somehow were lost by the trolley line's freight service.

[65] "History of Chevy Chase" by Thomas E. Robertson, *The Record*, Jan. 5, 1945.

[66] From the Atwood biography, p. 38. Much of the above from Jarvis, Atwood and George plus J. H. Robinson's "Chevy Chase" chapter of *Washington at Home* (1988) edited by K. S. Smith.

[67] This was very likely the "row" built across from the carbarn and the Lake.

[68] The original part of the Village "Hall" was built for $5,000 by the Free Library Association on land donated by Newlands and exempted from CCLCo restrictions. (See "A Brief Summary" in CC Village files.) The first area phone was ordered by the Land Company for the trolley line in the summer of 1893, and the first private phone was Robert Dunlop's at Hayes the next spring.

[69] Mr. Matthewson, a Norwegian with a small office at the Village Hall, was in charge of the landscaping and also read the water meters at this time.

[70] From Vida Ord Alexander's "Some Recollections of Old Chevy Chase" in 1952. Mrs. Jarvis called him "Captain" Springirth. The Hillyer memory from a 1986 oral history and John E. Powell's from a 1983 interview, both by the CCHS.

[71] *Journal*, Sept. 6, 1940. More Austin interview in chapter 8. He did not find Springirth so genial.

[72] The site is now the home of the busy 4-H Center.

[73] Brockett Muir oral history in collection of the CCHS.

[74] From the Charles Sumner School museum and archives, D.C. Board of Education. Ada Swigart Hess and some of the other older students still called it the Chevy Chase School.

[75] The unused school property later became the site of a short-lived proposal for apartment development in 1925.

[76] See letter from Mr. Robertson in *The Record*, Feb. 5, 1944, and his "History of Chevy Chase" in *The Record*, Jan. 12, 1945. What now seem very odd arrangements with the BOE evidently were not, see Chapter 7 regarding the Masons. The notes were all paid off within four years.

[77] 1914 photo at Sonnemann's Field by Gertrude M. Stevens – top: Daly, M. Shoemaker, Thompson?, F.Imirie; middle: G. Stevens, Dawson, Lewis, R. Stevens (who made ID); lower: Max ?, C. Shoemaker, Robertson, Caldwell.

[78] See Chapter 13 of *A Grateful Remembrance*, E. Guy Jewell's *From One Room to Open Space* (1976),*The Town of Chevy Chase*, Mrs Bradley's "Vignette" of Mrs. Robertson in the Apr. 4, 1941, Bethesda *Journal*, and the oral histories of the CCHS.

[79] From a CCHS interview.

[80] Robert Ragan, who climbed the water tower more than once, was in the class that moved from sixth to seventh grade at mid-term after a short stay at Bethesda Elementary.

[81] Elsie Irvine oral history at the CCHS. One of the temporary buildings at the old school may have become part of Imirie's Garage, see Chapter 7.

[82] That is Eda Schrader front and center with the bow in her hair. Prior to 1939, the sixth graders did the Maypole, and Eda's big sister, Joan, had been looking forward to the honor.

[83] See the Jarvis and Glassie oral histories and Janssen's "Notes" on the Bradford school.

[84] Chevy Chase oral history of Blanche M. Wilson, who moved into #3 in 1935, and of Louise Knowles who was born on Newlands Street in 1911.

[85] *Star*, Aug. 26, 1899, by F.T.

[86] Samuel J. Henry, *The Old Days with Horse and Hound*, 1960, and *Sentinel*, Dec. 4, 1926. For more on cave-dwellers, see C. McL. Green's *Washington Capital City, 1879-1950*.

[87] *The Columbia County Club as it was in the beginning* by Henry Litchfield West, 1938.

[88] For more on early days in Chevy Chase, D.C., see Edward T. Stafford's "Fifty Years in Chevy Chase 1909-1959," which was produced by the citizens' association.

[89]It may well be that the apartment house was built by Dessez over Land Company objections. At the time of James Goode's inspection, the woodwork had been painted white except in apartment No. 21 which had had the same tenant since 1929.

[90]James M. Goode, *Best Addresses* for the Smithsonian (1988). Ralph Crawford, who lived in the basement apartment was born in the building and succeeded his father as janitor in 1935.

[91]CCHS oral history 1986. Gates eventually owned the whole block. Blessed Sacrament purchased the apartment building in 1962.

[92]*Star*, Aug. 16, 1899.

[93]From the files of the Chevy Chase Public Library.

[94]Actually Jan. 16, 1912. Marguerite E. Kauffman, 17, a Central HS junior, and 6'2" Norman T. Locke, 18, a clerk at Lowdermilk's book store, took the trolley from 14th and U to the Lake that evening and, heavily dressed, skated into open water about ten feet deep. Herbert Claude helped find the bodies on the morning of the 18th after the Lake was lowered overnight. JP Alfred Wilson certified the deaths as accidental.
See *Star* Jan. 17, 18 and *Sentinel* Jan. 26, 1912.

[95]From the Jarvis and Powell oral histories and *Origins II* (N.P.C.2&3, 1976).

[96]Other early residents also remembered Spencer Hayes, as Mrs. Jarvis spelled it. She wrote that he cleared snow from the sidewalks with a horse-drawn, homemade plow and the "straightness of the path he left may have depended on the quantity of alcohol inside of Spencer!"

[97]For much more on the Chevy Chase Hunt see Samuel J. Henry's *The Old Days with Horse and Hound* published by the "Coursestormers" in 1960 and "The Potomac Hunt" by Valentine C. Wilson in the MCHS bulletin of Feb. 1990. The *Journal* was still carrying hunt news in 1940.

[98]Robert Ragan, who has lived on Chestnut Street since 1920, also recalled that the Marine Band played concerts on the Circle. Monkey Claude was credited with the most dents.

[99]From the files and oral histories of the Chevy Chase Historical Society, which are stored in what were the maids' rooms on the third floor of the house where Connie Weaver grew up.

[100]See U. of Md. MA thesis of Roselle George, p. 138. On many old CCLCo maps unsold property on Connecticut Ave is marked 30¢ and off the Avenue 25¢ per square foot.

[101]The area, now part of Section 5, was once labeled "Chevy Chase Section 7."

[102]Chevy Chase oral history project interview by David Secrest in September 1985. Patrick Devereux counted 51 first cousins at the time of his 1993 interview.

[103]Mostly from "Our Happy Marriage" by Annie Sinnott Devereux, n.d., which ends with her husband's death in 1936. In the collections of the MCHS and the CCHS.

[104]"75th Anniversary: Chevy Chase United Methodist Church" (1987) - history by Homer Smith.

[105]David Orem, in CCHS oral history.

[106]Edited and printed with permission from his 1990 essay on deposit at CCHS and MCHS.

[107]She is also remembered as the lady in purple - which is all she wore and used. She had violet stockings and purple ink and a purple blotter on her desk.

[108]For the most part from Washington, D.C, directories at the HSW. The Dunlops did have a dairy operation right in Chevy Chase and for a time operated a small retail store in Dr. Evans' row.

[109]In 1900 the Dessez ("Desay" in that census) had a live-in cook and another servant, both black.

[110]Censuses of 1910 and 1920 and R. George thesis. Edgemoor in 1920, had eleven black and five white live-in servants in twenty households, but the Doves and Tuckermans had seven of those.

[111]See Chapter 13, "Clinging to Rural America," in *A Grateful Remembrance*.

[112]First officers of the Literary Club were R. P. Teale, president; S. S. Paschel, secretary, and E. E. Stevens, program chairman, with the assistance of Miss Mackrille and Tom Robertson.

[113]*Sentinel*, Dec 30, 1927, and Feb. 3, 1928. The Montgomery Club, organized in October 1929, devoted itself to good works–at first mainly in support of the Methodist Church.

[114]Nathan Robertson found the summary of this track meet when he moved from the house where he was born on Melrose Street and wrote Mrs. Bradley about it. See *Record*, Sept, 17, 1948.

[115]This almost ubiquitous situation may have had as much to do with the incorporation of Bethesda-area suburbs as did the disinterest of Rockville in the suburbanites' problems.

[116]Wallace Janssen, Annual Report "Notes on a Neighborhood Birthday" (1946) which also appeared in the *Record*, August 2, 1946.

[117]*The Town of Chevy Chase: Past and Present* may still be available for $8 at the Town Center on Willow Lane where Leland JHS used to be. It has an excellent history of early "town" government and its problems and many fine photographs.

[118]"A Brief History of North Chevy Chase" by Robert Simpson and Edward Yardley, 1953. The first elected officers after the 1924 incorporation were chairman Robert Gangwisch, Vaugh Bowley, A. G. Durham, Robert H. Simpson, and William L. Lanning.

[119]*Country Life in America*, Oct. 1914, Elinor Horowitz's Washington *Post* article, Apr. 19, 1979, the report of the Maryland Historic Trust, and Linscott Hall's essay in *The Town of Chevy Chase*. "In the Woods" became the site of the Chevy Chase Recreation Association and its pool, and in the 1990s the children in the Outdoor Nursery School drown out the Beltway traffic noise.

[120]The other founders: Frank Simpson, Ralph Daskam, Frank H. Shultz, and Handley D. Dale.

[121]In the CCLCo archives are puzzling letters of resignation from both Newlands and Stellwagen both dated December 20, 1893.
Stellwagen's 1932, front-page obituary in the *Star* (June 2) said very little about Chevy Chase.

[122]In fact the fireworks stand may have preceded the row of stores by a year or two.

[123]Margaret Bruce and Elsie Irvine, CCHS oral histories.

[124]John B. Armentrout, "History of Land Subdivision Development in Montgomery County, Maryland, Adjacent to the National Capital," U.of Md., 1936 Tau Beta Pi thesis.

[125]See land records, 658-417 and 664-89 for the sale of lots 41 and 42 of block 5 of section 5-A to William B. Johnson in 1937. Antisemitic clause applied to block 9 of section 5-A.

[126]Chevy Chase Fire Department archives.

[127]The original paid men and their monthly salaries: Chief William F. Lanaham $62.50, J. H. DePirini $52.50, C. F. Mullineaux, J. D. O'Connor, J. Mosby Wooster and G. L. Hogan $50 each. Sixteen volunteers were listed as "active and have uniforms," including Private George C. Offutt, who became a paid man in 1932, and another ten "inactive."

[128]In its first ten years the department responded to 1,053 alarms with 4,406 "volunteers to fire."

[129]Robinson, op. cit, p. 200. The excellent section on "Houses" in *The Town of Chevy Chase* was written by Susan Goodman.

[130]In 1908 the Club purchased the Dodge tract for about $117,000 after leasing it for several years. See land records, 202-92.

[131]The row, at this writing, is still there with some of the entrances and façades basically unchanged, especially 7011. For more information see the Historic Trust.

[132]All of this from "Leland, A Community of Distinctive Homes in Chevy Chase, Md." in the *Star*'s "The Book of Model Homes"(1929). See also the *Star* real estate section Nov. 9, 1929.
In the 1930s Monroe Warren survived the bankruptcy of his partnership with E. S. Kennedy, formed Meadowbrook, Inc. and built many successful home and apartment projects. R. Bates Warren became a leader in the co-op apartment movement.

[133]In 1913 Harry Wardman was selling the house at Oxford and Connecticut, seven rooms with sleeping porch on a 50 x 140 lot opposite the Club, for $9,000.

[134]At this writing, Bill and his wife still live there.

[135]CCHS oral history project interview and interviews with the author.

[136]*Star*, April 16, 1927 and July 28, 1945. Also see *The Town of Chevy Chase*, p. 67.

[137]Picture and identification from Robert Stevens.

138 The trestle was originally 1,400 feet long and all wood, the biggest thing of its kind on the B&O, but it was rebuilt in 1904 and again in 1928 and shortened with fill to 281 feet and a steel center span added. But it was still sixty-seven feet high. See *Impossible Challenge* (1979).

139 Cuba Tracewell whose husband, Charles, was a well-known *Star* columnist, called it "a paper kids put out with a lot of help from their mothers." CCHS oral history 1985.

140 Mrs. Tracewell identified ninety-five species of birds in her backyard in the 1930s.

141 Under the lid of the five cent Dixie cup of vanilla and chocolate ice cream was a picture of a sports, radio, or movie star, usually Shirley Temple or Tom Mix, and later pictures of war planes and ships, which kids saved and mothers threw away thus destroying a possible fortune.

142 Because, on the way to work, his father would sometimes take him on the streetcar down to Melrose Street to spend the day at his grandfather's house, Donald Robertson remembered the trolley cars on Connecticut Avenue. Few others of his generation do.

143 See "History of the Capital Traction Company" by Flavius Morrill in Crockett collection at HSW. One car which served on this line may be seen and ridden at the Trolley Museum on weekends. It was #27 then but is now marked 766. All of the Cincinnatti cars, which cost $2,175 new, were taken to the yard at Benning Road, tipped on their sides and burned in the fall of 1935.

144 John Smith worked for the streetcar and bus companies for thirty-nine years and for Community Paint and Hardware thirty-five years, the last eighteen full-time after he retired from Capital Transit. He was 79 at the time of his second retirement when the hardware store closed. He was an usher for the Bethesda Union Methodist Church for more than fifty years.

145 Some will remember Albert Smith in Sixties parades riding a unicyle with four auxiliary sets of handlebars on its ladder-like frame and a seat twelve-and-a-half feet off the ground. After serving in the 29th Division in World War II, he was with the transit companies until 1973.

146 Capital Transit Company, Order #427-A, from Robert Truax collection. The Kensington Railway treid to convince the B&O to institute electric service from Georgetown through Bethesda.

147 Don Robertson, who graduated from "Rosemary" in `42 could also recall all of his teachers; Miss Fell kindergarten, Miss Kemp 1st grade, Mrs. Daly in the 2nd grade, Miss or Mrs. Phillips in the 3rd, Norris Wise in the 4th grade, a combined 4-5th grade class, the only male teacher in the school, Miss Dodd in 5th and Mrs. Smoot in the 6th grade.

CHAPTER 6

Down Wisconsin

During the "Gay Nineties" south of the Episcopal chapel at Bradley Lane and the Offutt farm across from it, lay the properties of Georgetown's Dodge family and the Chevy Chase Land Company on the east and Dr. Davidson's old place called "Montrose" and General Drum's big home on the hilly land to the west. Then the Pike went down a steep hill to the Little Falls Branch and rolled up past the blacksmith's rundown collection of sheds to the Eld and Shoemaker farms and the District Line. Until the carbarn and power station went up on Wisconsin Avenue in 1903, the tavern at Gloria Point in Tenleytown, as it was now usually spelled, was the next landmark.

The Rockville-Georgetown Pike itself had really become two roads for much of its length, the original hard-surfaced, poorly maintained one where horses' shoes struck sparks from the flinty stone and a secondary, soft, dirt track along both sides of it, deeply rutted, now often ten or twelve feet lower than the old road, but preferable in good weather to the spine-jarring remnants of the tollroad. In some places, folks traveling north could not see those headed south on the other side of the old turnpike.

As for maintenance, the turnpike company was moribund and the State of Maryland derelict. In the 1890s the State was spending only about $200,000 annually on all its highways, and it was not until 1908 that the General Assembly created the State Roads Commission with authority to borrow five million dollars. Until then, it was the job of the County Commissioners to build and maintain the roads, a task that consumed much of their budget, involved many bartered decisions of shared patronage, and devoured a major part of the Commissioners' meeting time.[1]

At the turn of the century Montgomery County had only forty-five miles of hard surfaced highways (stone, gravel, or macadam) and about 800 miles of dirt roads. Even the best were not very good, and a Maryland Geological Survey report labeled the Rockville Pike "one of the worst pieces of main highway in the state." Many travelers preferred to risk the narrow "old road," Old Georgetown Road, in and out of Bethesda.[2]

In the summer of 1891 the *Star*'s itinerant columnist, a sort of pre-Rambler, walked from Tenleytown, a place-name he discussed at length, to Bethesda. He found little except a bad road between the two.[3]

Emerging from the town, the vision is treated to fine landscape views.

The remains of old Fort Reno are visible on the right, while on the left, over on River road, a line of well-preserved rifle pits are seen. North of these pits, a half mile distant, at the Maryland line, stands old Fort Bayard. Fort Reno occupies the highest ground in the District of Columbia, being 439 feet above tide level.

Crossing the District line into Maryland at the Glen Echo electric railway junction, a decided change is observed in the condition of the road, which is good up to this point. It now becomes a rough, apparently neglected thoroughfare.

Ball's blacksmith shop is soon reached, and you presently cross the east fork of Falls branch.

Langdrum, the pleasant county home of

Gen. Drum, is a half mile farther on, west of the road.

Another half mile brings you to Bradley's lane, Bethesda post office being visible a quarter of a mile beyond, where there is a toll gate. Two miles further north is the old village of Bethesda church. The proposed new villa of Bethesda Park is west of Bethesda Church...

This is an excellent agricultural neighborhood.

Turning to the right along Bradley's lane, which has a good smooth sand and gravel surface and lined on either side with stately old cedars, three-quarters of a mile brings you to the Brookville Road....

But in the 1890s the trolley line builders made their way uphill from Georgetown to Tenleytown and then on toward Bethesda, and as they did, they catalyzed the development of suburbs like those that had sprung to life on electric rail lines near the river and along extended Connecticut Avenue. Enterprising men with visions of handsome villas in an ideal rural setting, as well as of handsome profits, purchased land by the acre and sold it by the square foot. Until the mass-produced Model-T and its many cousins replaced the electric railway as the basic mode of suburban transport, road upkeep suffered, and new homes clustered near the trolley stops, some on extra-long first blocks so that subdividers could advertise their nearness to the tracks.[4]

At about the turn-of-the century, farmer-prohibitionist Albert Shoemaker and developer-banker Henry Wootton Offutt platted adjoining subdivisions near the District Line called "The Hills" and "Friendship Heights." Montgomery Street or Eld Street, depending on whose plat one read, divided the two. The street was originally part of the wandering farm lane that led from the Pike to the already-old Eld farmhouse. Much later a third subdivision, also of Shoemaker property but on the River Road side, became part of the village.[5]

Henry W. Offutt was born near Offutt's Cross Roads, now Potomac, in 1862, a descendant of the William Offutt who had settled in that area more than fifty years before the Revolution. Henry and his brother George Warren built up a successful grocery business at the corner of Wisconsin and M Street in Georgetown on the healthy foundation their older

brother had established. Both were leaders of the Potomac Savings Bank, and when G. W. died in 1923, H. W. succeeded him as president of the bank. He was active in the D.C. real estate boom of the '80s, and he and his second wife often spent their summers in the Holly Cottage on the hilly Eld Farm, acreage Offutt had purchased on the high land just across the District Line.[6]

Aquilla Eld, an English-immigrant, had established a hilly homestead about 1854 on twenty-two acres purchased from Isaac Shoemaker, a family the Elds later married into. The census of 1860 showed Eld and his wife Louisa with three daughters and two sons on property valued at $700.

The sixteen acres that Henry Offutt subdivided and built on was mostly Eld farmland; the only other existing house at the time was the Ball's small place on the rise beside the old turnpike, which served as home, blacksmith shop and stagecoach way station. The survey of Offutt's subdivision by William J. Latimer, filed in June 1901, included three sections nearest the Pike of platted building lots averaging about 6,000 square feet each and six, large, undivided lots on both sides of High Street.

By the 1890s the Shoemaker families had owned much of the land near the Pike on both sides of the District Line for about a hundred years. Their burying ground "containing 6 1/4 square perches and which shall never be appropriated to any other purpose and there shall at all times be a convenient right-of-way to and from the same" was established by the 1846 will of Samuel Shoemaker Sr. Within its black, wrought iron fence are stones marking the graves of Jesse Shoemaker, born in 1815 and died in 1887, Jesse Jr. and his brother John, and Elizabeth, wife of George Shoemaker, who lived from 1859 until 1890.[7]

In 1839 Isaac Shoemaker bought the creek-cut farm that included "The Hills" and the property along the Maryland border from Wisconsin Avenue to River Road. Shortly before the Civil War he sold ten acres to smithy Hilleary Ball and forty to Cyrus Perry as well as the land he conveyed to the Elds.[8]

The plat map of the Shoemaker subdivision showed a triangular area with a wide variety of lot sizes and shapes north of the hypotenuse labeled Willard Avenue where the Glen Echo trolley had originally run. The largest of the

forty-three lots was two acres and the most common size 6,250 square feet.

Richard Ough & Son, who had constructed both commercial and residential buildings in Georgetown, Tenleytown and Somerset, built many of the primary houses in Friendship Heights, and Albert Shoemaker himself raised some of the first homes in The Hills on what became the 4500 block of Willard Avenue. Later, William Collins built many of the others.

Mark Shoemaker, Albert's son and the earliest Village historian, called Collins a good carpenter and "a colorful personality. As an ex-cavalryman, he kept a riding horse for a number of years. No western movie ever depicted greater horsemanship than he did in coming home from work as he guided his horse around the dusty bends of now High Street. He rode at full gallop, and at the same time, vaulted from one side of the horse to the other, his feet touching the ground but for an instant." Other old-timers recalled the Collins family as one of the last to move all their plumbing indoors.[9]

A number of prominent Bethesdans called Friendship Heights home. Perhaps the best known family in the last half-century was the McAuliffes including County police chief Col. James McAuliffe and his respected judge-sons, Jim and John. At one time William Tyler Page, the rotund Clerk of the House of Representatives and author of "The American's Creed," would have stood in first in fame with the Bogleys, banker S. Walter and attorney Emory H., close behind.

However, Annie Garrett Ferneyhough Sheiry holds a special spot in the history of the Village. She came to Friendship Heights as a young wife and mother in the spring of 1903 and lived there until her death in 1969. She was, as Mark Shoemaker put it in his *Brief History of the Special Taxing Area*, "one of our earliest and most loved residents." She left her children a thick, genealogical scrapbook that included dozens of photographs of the neighborhood before World War I and a long, handwritten document she called "Memories from Lamplight to Satellite."

Written between the late 1940s and the 1960s at her home on High Street, the old Eld farmhouse, it is a reminiscence of everyday life. Like Mrs. Moore's homey pictures of Bethesda during the Civil War, it celebrates the ordinary– the trials of parenthood, the triumphs of children and the tragedies of families in pain. "Book 2" begins:[10]

On Tuesday, April 21st, 1903, our little family, consisting of John Slater Sheiry, our two sons, Edward Slater Sheiry and Russell Coleman Sheiry, and myself, Anne F. Sheiry, moved to Friendship Heights, Md.

We first heard of Friendship Hts. through a Mr. Allison, an artist who bought his supplies from my husband, who was working at the E. Morrison Paper Co. at the time. He told my husband that he was eager to sell his home as he wanted to move away from the city and from his in-laws, who lived to the rear of his home. They were the Ough family, and Mr. Ough was the builder of most of the houses in the Heights, until he and his family moved to California some years later.

5511 Prospect Street - Note boardwalk and daisies growing in the street

My husband was interested in Mr. Allison's proposal and came out to see the house and liked it and the country very much. It is now numbered 5511 Prospect St. When I came out to see it, I, too, fell in love with the house & surroundings, so we decided to buy it, the price being $2,500 for the eight room house and lot 50 x 110 ft.

On the day we moved, we realized, in the late afternoon that we had no lights as we had not had the electricity turned on, so we went over to the Ough's house and used his phone to call the store in Bethesda and ordered lamps and kerosine oil. The store, owned by the Wilson Bros., was one of the two buildings in Bethesda, the other being a blacksmith shop on the present site of the bank, "Bank of Bethesda." The grocery store was what is now the Community Hardware Store by the bridge, or overpass, on Wisconsin Ave. You could buy anything in that store, groceries, dry goods, farm supplies, hardware, china, etc., etc. A young man

by the name of Lyles Offutt drove the grocery wagon & horse and was a clerk in the store . . . .

There were three houses on Wootten Ave. and three on Prospect St. Mr. Ough & family occupied the middle one on Wootton, Prof. Rice & family lived in the one to the north of the Oughs. Prof. Rice worked at the Naval Observatory, and later taught at the Naval Academy in Annapolis. In May 1903 Mr. Offutt and family moved out from Georgetown to the other house on Wootton, on the corner, 5500.

On Prospect, besides our house, was the one on the far end of the block, occupied by Mr. Falstitch & family. Across the street and exactly like it, was a vacant house which later was occupied by Mr. Frost and family, and which much later, burned to the ground. The Frosts rebuilt it on the same foundation but from a different plan. Our son, Edward, had two playmates, John Falstitch and Mark Shoemaker, who was about three years older than Edward, but who became a life-long friend. His home was down the hill from us, in "The Hills" section.[11]

Our streets were just mud roads and the sidewalks were board-walks. The streetcars had double tracks to Somerset. A single track, with sidings, went to Rockville. Several years later the terminus of the railway was put at the District line, & my husband, John, was instrumental in having the signs on the streetcars changed to "Friendship Hts.". . . . The cars ran on a half-hour schedule from about five thirty am to midnight. Just missing a car was very disconcerting to say the least, as there was such a long wait. The residents of our little community built a waiting station at the entrance to afford us shelter while waiting.

We continued to deal with the grocery store in Georgetown, and would phone our orders the

day before delivery. There was a freight streetcar which left Georgetown at 11 am which we could use for delivering things which did not come in the grocery wagons. Our phone number was Cleveland 690.

There was no gas out here then, so we used oil cook stoves in the summer and wood and coal ranges in the winter. We had a coal furnace (hotair) and our water was piped to a tank in the attic from a well on Mr. Ough's property. Later it became necessary to furnish more water as more houses were built, so the community drilled a well next to our house & built a very large tank and windmill. When Mr. Wm. Tyler Page came out to live here, he said it reminded him of Holland. Mr. Page's house was built between Mr. Ough's and Prof. Rice's. When Mr. Ough made plans to build three houses between Mr. Ough's and ours, we bought 25 ft. on our south line and Mr. Offutt extended his western line, forming that jog in the line, and squeezing what had been three lots into one, as we did not want three houses in that space. We paid $500 for the 25 ft.

In August of 1903 the Sheiry's year-old son Russell died from a head injury after falling from a hammock on the front porch. In October 1904 Dorothy Virginia Sheiry, who much later helped her mother assemble the scrapbook from which this section is taken, was born in the house on Prospect Street and life went on.

One day I was sewing in the north window of the northeast room where Dorothy was born, and I heard Edward's voice close by, so looked out to see where he was. I didn't see him on the ground, so called and asked where he was. I was astonished to see him on the top of the big water tank! I went to the foot of the ladder, hoping I could catch him should he fall, telling him all the time to come down slowly and to hold on tight. I surely was relieved when he touched ground.

As more houses were built and the population increased, so did the number of dogs! Both children were afraid of them & were not happy playing outdoors alone. John & I decided to fence in our yard to keep the dogs away & ordered wire fencing & posts. The neighbors objected to the wire fencing, so we hesitated about putting it up. For some time we had been admiring the shade trees around the old house across the hill from ours. Also we had become dissatisfied with the arrangement of our living room and hall . . . . Mr. Offutt owned the old house and used to live in it in the summer, until he rented it to the Pyles family. We approached Mr. Offutt about making a trade and after

The Ough families - note water tank

some dickering and the addition of a sum of money and against his advice, we made the deal. He was afraid we would regret the move, but we never did.

We had electricity and water put into the house and a bath room. Our idea was to live in the house while we were building one on the knoll behind the house. Besides the large black walnut tree, there were five large aspen-poplars around the front of the house. Also a holly tree and a boxwood bush in the front yard. It was an ideal place for the children to play. We moved here in 1906. At that time our houses were not numbered and we had to have our mailboxes at the sidewalk so that the rural free delivery mailman could put the mail in them without getting out of his vehicle. Our first house

Dorothy and (l-r) Prof. Rice's, William Tyler Page's and Mr. Ough's houses in Friendship Heights

number was 401 High St, which we had until very recently, when it was changed to 4531, to conform to the numbers in the District of Columbia. Soon after we had our first house number, we were given regular mail service to our door.

High St, which was named Montgomery St for the first three blocks, now includes those three blocks and begins at Wisconsin Ave (which used to be called Rockville Pike). It is the old wagon road to this house and ended here until Mr. Offutt subdivided the property.

Just across the street from us was a pear orchard and the old well which supplied this house until we had water put in. All the nearby neighbors used that water for drinking as it was so good

and cold even after we had a community water system. Part way down the field, in the middle of what is now Willoughby St, was a large apple tree, which had two kinds of apples on it . . . .

This house was just a white-washed weather board house with a wooden shingled roof, some of which was covered with moss an inch thick. We lived in it just as it was for nearly three years, while trying to decide on a plan for the new house which we hoped to build. When we finally had the plans drawn up and estimates given on the cost, we knew we couldn't afford so much. Rather than curtail our plans and do without some of the things we wanted, we decided to take the advice of our architect friend, Mr. Lacey, and remodel this house as it was strongly built., which we did at about one-fourth of the cost of the estimate of the new one during the summer of 1909.

Soon after moving here, my husband left E. Morrison Paper Co. and went to work for the District of Columbia Paper Mfg. Co. as a traveling salesman. His territory extended from Canada to Cuba & Mexico and as far west as Denver, Colorado.

So at the time of the remodeling, he could not be here all of the time, and I was glad to have Mr. Lacey's advice. For instance, the contractor, Mr. Hazard, tried to make me accept four-light window sash in place of the twelve-light ones we ordered & had them delivered here. I called Mr. Lacey, who told me to insist on the ones we had ordered, as our plan to keep the home as colonial looking as possible would be spoiled with four-light windows. The original windows were small and when raised had to be held up with a stick. So all of the windows except the ones in the store-room which are half size, were much larger. We turned the main stairway around, thus making the living room larger & lighter as we cut a window in the west wall where the stairs had been. We faced the old fireplace with new bricks and made a new mantel piece. This fireplace was in what was originally the kitchen and was used in cooking and the pothook is still there . . . .

When the stairway was turned & the partition torn out between the old hall and our room, it gave us a lovely, bright room. There were no closets, so we built some in the new hall. I think the Murdocks must have used our present bathroom for a large closet and trunk room, as there were nails on a strip of wood all around the room to hang clothes on. There was no partition there at that time, as we had it built when we put the bathroom there. The new floors downstairs are edge-grain Georgia pine.

On the outside, we had pebble-dashing put on over the wood siding, had the front porch extended around the side, & the back porch shortened to uncover the window so as to make the dining room lighter. That window had been a door opening on to the porch. We decided on a slate roof as being more durable than shingles. That was our reason too for using the pebble-dashing instead of wood as when we lived in the Prospect St. house we dreaded the time when we would have to paint that big house & porches, as we knew it would cost so much.

One day, after the workmen had left, I was shocked to discover they had torn off the old shingles all along the east side of the house for the depth of about three feet and had left it all open. Storms had been predicted for that night, so I was very worried. I couldn't get hold of Mr. Hazard, so I called Mr. Huddleson who had contracted to put on the slate roof. He was a friend of my husband's, also a brother Mason. He rounded up some of his workmen & brought them out & covered the open space with tar paper. I couldn't thank him enough especially when the storms did come as the whole house would have been flooded.

We had more trouble with Mr. Hazard & finally had to call in another man to finish the job, Mr. Simpson, who did a fine job, making us wish we had had him in the first place. The china closet in the dining room and the railing in the hall were part of Mr. Simpson's work . . . .

Going back to 1906, when Edward was six years old, he was due to start school, the nearest one being the Jackson School in Georgetown on R St several blocks from the carline. We decided he was too young to go that far alone, so I taught him his first grade work and entered him there in the second grade when he was nearly seven and a half years old. The John Eaton School in Cleveland Park was built before Dorothy and John had to go. The first grade teacher, Miss Miller, lived here in the Heights, so Dorothy went with her and when John entered school, Dorothy took care of him. Edward transferred to the John Eaton, and both he & John went, later on, to the E. V. Brown School.

When Dorothy was beginning fourth grade, a law was passed requiring out-of-District pupils to pay tuition. Edward was then attending McKinley Manual Training School (Tech High) so we felt it was more important to keep him in school than to keep Dorothy in the grade school as we couldn't afford both. (Mr. Rippey, a teacher at Tech & a neighbor saved us many a car-fare by taking all

three of my children to the school in his automobile.) . . .

Maryland authorities decided to start a school here and rented two rooms in Mark Shoemaker's parents' home and engaged one teacher who had to teach all grades from first to eighth. We entered Dorothy there, but she didn't stay long, as the teacher had too much to do and couldn't give each pupil proper attention. I took her out and taught her through that grade, keeping in touch with her former grade at the John Eaton School. The next fall that tax was rescinded and Dorothy went back to the John Eaton and with her class to the fifth grade. That two room school was the beginning of the Somerset Elementary School.[12]

Up until about 1907 we had continued going into town to our church, the Metropolitan Presbyterian church at 4th & B, S.E. I couldn't go often but John went every Sunday as he was an officer in the church, a deacon. The trip took about a half a day as it was at least an hour each way on the cars in addition to the length of the services. So when several Presbyterians living out this way conceived the idea of starting a church, we heartily agreed. We began by having cottage prayer meetings on Friday evenings. I couldn't attend many, as there were no baby sitters in those days, & I could get my sister-in-law to come out & stay very seldom as they worked & had to get in town early. When enough people were interested, we secured the use of the Chevy Chase Library for our Sunday morning services which were conducted, at first, by a Mr. Samuel Johnson, who was living at the time at the home of Mr. and Mrs Feezer and I think was a Methodist. It wasn't long until we secured the services of our beloved Dr. Hubert Rex Johnson in 1909. He & his family lived in Washington, after retiring from his pastorate in Pennsylvania. He accepted the office of pastor of our little flock but doubted that he would be able to serve long on account of his health.

There were twenty-three of us who were charter members, and at the time of the organization of the church there were 274 families scattered over about eight square miles of territory around Chevy Chase. That was in 1908. Two ruling elders were appointed -- Mr. Grant Leet and Mr. John S. Sheiry. We soon realized we had to have a church building, and when Mr Martin, a real estate dealer and member of the congregation, said he could buy the lot at the corner of Connecticut Avenue and what is now Chevy Chase Parkway for $2,975, we bought it and were delighted to get it at that price. Plans were made for the chapel, ground for which

was broken on July 7, 1910, corner stone laid Aug. 1st 1910, dedicated Jan. 8, 1911. I could not attend the ground breaking ceremonies as my dear little son John Jr. was about to make his appearance which occurred on Sept. 24, 1910. Edward acted as my proxy and lifted my shovel full of dirt!

It so happened that about five or six weeks before John Jr. was born, that my husband had to travel to Cuba & Mexico for the paper company. He didn't want to leave me alone, so we asked my father, who had retired, to come and stay here with me, which he did. In order to give him something to do, we suggested that he raise chickens and sell eggs for pocket money, which he did. He had quite a business before he left here about a year later to go home to Richmond where he was living with my sister, Laura Belle Fleming. I remember an egg-laying record his flock of eighty hens made in the short month of February -- 1,200 eggs!! My dad used to go to market in Georgetown every weekend and would always bring back a bag of chocolate drops for the children -- Edward and Dorothy....

Henry Latterner and his wife Letitia moved from Georgetown to a new house on a hilly one-acre lot facing Willard Avenue in 1904. His German-immigrant parents invested wisely in Pennsylvania Avenue property and operated a busy cleaning establishment near the Capitol. In Friendship Heights, the Latterners had the usual outbuildings plus a windmill and built a chicken coop down near the street for their small flock of birds. The location proved a temptation to would-be chicken thieves, and the squawking and flapping occasionally brought Mr. Latterner running from the house, shotgun in hand, but his daughter Dorothy could not recall that he ever fired the gun. The Latterners planted a large number of apple, pear and cherry trees on the hillside which produced many hours of fruit picking and canning for both wife and daughters.

Mr. Latterner rolled sections of leftover pipe from a sewer project in Somerset to Willard Avenue and made a culvert so the creek would run under the road instead of washing it away. Mrs. Latterner, who was called Lettie, had been almost deaf since she was sixteen. She was an enthusiastic bridge player, but neither of the adult Latterners was very active in community affairs.

Their older daughter, Helen, was a beautiful girl who enjoyed reading. But her sister,

Dorothy, was usually to be found playing baseball on Mr. Offutt's empty lots near the entrance gates, chasing down the boys in a game of tag or keep-away, or roller skating on Wisconsin Avenue after it was resurfaced. She and her friends often skated down the long hill to Somerset and then waited for a slow-moving truck to get a tow back up to Friendship Heights.

Dorothy Latterner Hampton remembered William Tyler Page as her always-prepared and very proper Sunday school teacher at St. Columba's where he conducted a class for fifteen teenaged girls. For years he sent all of his students a silver dollar on their birthdays. Mr. Page later headed the Sunday school program for the Episcopalians at St. John's, Norwood Parish.

When the *Evening Star*'s real estate reporter looked at Friendship Heights in the spring of 1910, he noted,

The smaller cost of land is manifest in the greater liberality of the allowance of ground about the houses. There are spaces on either side as well as large back yards where chicken runs can be put and still leave space for a garden plot. The houses are, of course, of frame and are supplied with water and lights, and for the most part they are occupied by people whose business is in the city.[13]

In fact it was common in many of these early suburban communities for homeowners to purchase more than one lot and to preserve a side yard for gardening. In some neighborhoods the pattern of building on every other lot can be noted by examining the age of the homes (see Drummond). By the late 1930s this practice was generally abandoned, but at one time almost every Bethesda-area neighborhood had several residences built on double lots.

Another early property owner in Friendship Heights, whose home and holdings fit the model, was Henry S. Frisbie, a Treasury department accountant from Alabama with a growing family. In 1906 he purchased five of the Shoemaker's fifty-foot wide lots on Wisconsin Avenue and three lots behind those on Mercer (Wootton) Avenue and began to build his home while he rented nearby. He planted thirty-two apple trees and several cherry and peach trees on the side lots and built a large chicken house behind his square, frame home. The Frisbies' property on the Pike was below

the grade of the road, and it was not uncommon for a wagon or buggy to fall into their front yard on dark nights.[14]

The Frisbee children all walked to school at E. V. Brown. They crossed the by-then macadamized highway and the trolley tracks, trotted along a well-worn path past the old stone quarry which became a dump, cut through the golf course called Bannockburn and later Kirkside to McKinley Street and trudged on to Connecticut Avenue. Crossing two major thoroughfares was seldom a problem nor, evidently, a parental concern.

Kenneth Frisbie, who was born in Friendship Heights in 1909, attended first grade at General Hunt's home up the hill toward Bethesda, walking there with friends from Somerset including Robert Horne and Margaretta Moore, but when that makeshift school closed, he followed in the sometimes muddy footsteps of his brother and sister and enjoyed the ministrations of Miss Givens, Miss Berry and Miss Athey. He remembered E. V. Brown's dark, portable classrooms and their glowing stoves. One of his classmates was Emilio Ferrari whose father operated a small grocery store on the corner of McKinley Street, long popular with the elementary school crowd for its penny candy.

The High Street "dog leg" - a good while later

The Irish-immigrant McAuliffes, Mary from County Cork, John from Dingle, moved from D.C. to one of Henry Offutt's large lots on the western end of High Street and built a home in 1908. They had three sons at the time, Joseph, John, and Jim, who was only a year old, and added daughters Mary and Ellen. They cultivated a large garden and fed a big flock of chickens, raised some hogs and, according to James McAuliffe Sr., "had fruit trees galore." The McAuliffes' children walked down Wisconsin to St. Ann's School at Tenley Circle.

On the Maryland side of the District Line, as in Chevy Chase, school continued to be a problem. Dorothy Hampton recalled attending the John Eaton School in the morning and, since it was on double sessions, County public school classes in the Shoemaker home in the afternoon. In 1912 the County school commissioners allowed pupils four cents daily to take the trolley to Bethesda or Chevy Chase schools but most still went into D.C. In the summer of 1913 C. W. Rippey and W. B. Kirkpatrick, representing Friendship Heights, Somerset, and Drummond, requested a school for the region from the County school board. A committee composed of Dr. Ryan Devereux and Superintendent Earl B. Wood promised to investigate.

In 1914 the school board paid Cyrus Keiser Jr. of Bethesda $12.50 a week to transport children from Friendship Heights and Somerset to Chevy Chase Elementary in his car, but the school commissioners balked at financing transportation to the high school in Rockville. "Let 'em take the trolley!" was their motto, and most Bethesda area adolescents attended D.C. high schools. The school problem was not solved until Bethesda Chevy Chase Junior-Senior High School and Somerset Elementary opened in 1928, the last full year of the Bethesda-area's second building boom.[15]

The only grocery store in the Friendship Heights neighborhood was Dellinger's located across the Pike from the trolley station on the northwest corner of Willard and Wisconsin behind a large concrete apron. It was an old fashioned general store previously run by a man named Palmer Page, a dark and dingy frame building with coils of flypaper dangling from its dim lights and a wide front porch overlooking the Willard Avenue creek.

Dellinger, originally from Front Royal, headed a feisty family who lived above and behind the store. The Dellingers had two boys, Aubrey and Curtis; more generally called "Hans and Fritz" after the troublemakers in the popular comic strip. Former County police chief McAuliffe recalled shooting marbles with them and even remembered one day when they got into the basement of the store and found some hard cider. Dellinger sold the cool, potent apple jack for five cents a glass to the laborers who trudged across Willard to their homes on River Road after a long working day. His

African-American customers from "Crow Hill" knew to go to the back door.

Ken Frisbie and the Dellinger boys built one of the local swimming holes on a small stream wandering through the fields south of Willard, and the McAuliffes and Mark Shoemaker helped build another. According to Mark, these "were safe places to smoke corn silk and grape leaves."[16]

Bill Seebold recalled Mr. Dellinger as "a nice little man" who always wore a stubbly beard and a bloody apron and who had one of the biggest and busiest 4th of July fireworks stands anywhere. But Al Savage, one-time vice-president of Capital Transit, said, "He and my father thought each other the biggest thieves around." Mr. Dellinger had sold Mr. Savage a bushel of seed potatoes that lacked eyes, and the feud started when he tried to take them back. Al Savage also remembered the fireworks stand and the fun of putting torpedoes on the tracks of the Rockville trolley line.

Henry Scott grew up in Friendship Heights in the 1920s when there were lots of kids, he estimated twenty or thirty, within two or three years of the same age, and he remembered Dellinger's as:

the life blood of the area - you'd go up and sit there and wait for the taxi drivers to give you a sip off their Pepsi Colas, or try to charge a soda to your family's grocery account. You never had any money.

Self-service was unknown at Dellinger's. He waited on everybody for everything from behind his wooden counter. It was a dark place, just a couple of lights.

Smiling, Mr. Scott said that he spent one-fourth of his life at Dellinger's, and recalled that behind the store, well back from the street, was a frame two-story building with two flats and a big upstairs porch, and that later two small stores were built next to Dellinger's.[17]

Charlie Hughes, a bit younger than Scott, remembered Dellinger's store at a slightly later period.

I never went in there. Some real lowlifes drank in there and hung out the window over Willard Avenue. My dad said it had been a nice place in the Twenties, but he allowed people to run up a tab and the Depression broke him.

In Friendship Heights, before the coming of the WSSC, to the youngest son usually fell the job of pumping water up to the big tank in the attic. Mark Shoemaker claimed it took 375 strokes to fill the tank at his house. He occasionally hired Henry Scott to do the pumping for him, and sometimes, as he worked the pump, young Jim McAuliffe envied the Latterners their windmill, but, as Dorothy Hampton said, "The wind didn't always blow."

The boys and girls in Friendship Heights had chores to do almost every day, cleaning chicken coops seemed to be the one disliked the most and remembered the longest, and many of the boys had paying jobs including caddying at Kirkwood for fifty cents a bag. Ken Frisbie pulled a wagon up and down the hills selling vegetables from Warren Shoemaker's farm, and Jim McAuliffe took one of Dellinger's *Post* routes and made around $5.50 a month. The job started at 5 am and took Jim and his St. Bernard about an hour and a half. In the 1930s Bill Seebold's *Times-Herald* route stretched north to Drummond and included all of Somerset, but he still had only thirty-seven customers. Henry Scott's *Star* route was Friendship Heights, and he remembered banker Dulin fumbling his change and never quite having enough when it came time to pay.

Cherry trees dotted the area and the remains of a peach orchard enriched the old Eld place. Many farm animals lived in Friendship Heights in the early days including a number of cows, horses and mules. Ken Frisbie recalled trying to ride one of the Shoemaker's mules, and Colonel McAuliffe remembered them, too.

There were streams where Willard Avenue used to be, from Wisconsin to River Road, and there was another creek that ran into that. It had walnut trees around it, and I used to go down there to pick walnuts. The Shoemakers had two mules; one was nasty, kicked the barn out. That's where I got my St. Bernard dog, got one of the pups. After the pup got pretty big, I used to go to a swimming hole over there on the creek that had a rope you could swing out on. I went over there one day and the mother of my dog remembered that I had taken one of her cubs, and she kind of growled at me, a gentle dog usually. I was surprised she remembered.

Mark Shoemaker wrote that "One of the biggest commotions ever experienced in the area came yearly at hog killing time at the McAuliffes." Colonel McAuliffe said:

I didn't participate in the hog killing, but I remember it. They used to heat the water with

some hot irons, red hot irons. My daddy and Dellinger would be around for the killing. They used to shoot the hogs with a .22 rifle. Wasn't much pain involved; they just keeled over and that was it. We'd have some of that meat for years. We had a little house adjacent, underneath the big house, where my daddy used to keep some of his homebrew during Prohibition.

By the time the Seebolds moved to Prospect Street in the mid-1930s, there were few animals left, just dogs and cats and the McAuliffe's chickens and Shoemaker's bantams that seemed to produce an unending supply of pullet eggs. The times were changing.

In the Twenties, "Woodies" came to Friendship Heights by a roundabout route. When Isaac Shoemaker died in 1883, his son Louis, who had married 18-year-old Mary Eld in 1862, inherited the farm. When he died in 1915, it became the property of his seven children and grandchildren with his oldest son, Albert Shoemaker, Mark's father, as trustee. Most of the Shoemakers wanted to keep what was left of the land in the family since property values were increasing, but, according to Lillian Shoemaker Brown, "one of the brother's wives disagreed, and made it so unpleasant for all, that in the name of peace, they sold the entire farm to Mr. Woodward of Woodward and Lothrop."[18]

At least that is what Mrs. Brown thought had happened. The heirs actually sold 59.91 acres including seven acres of what had been Eld property to Francis Bennett Poe for $150,000 in January 1925 with a deed signed by eighteen Shoemakers or their representatives who evidently believed that the land was going to be almost instantly subdivided and built on. A month later Poe transferred the deed to Walter R. Tuckerman who secured a loan from Walter Bogley of the Bank of Bethesda to pay him off. Six months later Tuckerman and Bogley, with his note subordinated to the money still owed the Shoemakers and all the covenants and restrictions related to Poe's supposed subdivision wiped out, sold the property to Donald Woodward and Irene W. Parker who rented out the land for various uses for the next twenty-five years.[19]

So by the early Thirties while Mark Shoemaker's long, shady grape arbor still produced impressive crops next to the Latterners fruit trees on Willard Avenue, the Shoemaker's fields of corn, now owned by Woodward & Lothrop,

had given way to a mowed golf driving range along Western Avenue with a parking lot right at Wisconsin and Western. The range with its fifty-seven "box" tees, and tall light poles was the idea of Preston Miller who moved his family to DeRussey Parkway in 1931 after the failure of his D.C. interior decorating business. The range stayed open year-round except when there was snow on the ground, and in the summer people lined up to hit a bucket of seventy-five balls for 50¢ or a half-bucket for a quarter. Miller built a small "shack" near Wisconsin Avenue where he sold soft drinks, snacks, and when it became legal, beer. He also rented claw machines and pinball machines from E. O. Likens, and several winters he drove down to Florida and came back with a load of oranges and grapefruit to sell on his corner.

Preston Miller's son Tom (B-CC `38 and nicknamed "PE" from the initials on the gearshift of his father's Chrysler) remembered his father as "not a golfer himself. He hardly ever hit a ball, but I did and got pretty good at it. Peter Jackson and Monroe Hunter were the pros at the range and gave lessons. Walter Johnson, Sam Rice and some other well-known locals came down for lessons from Jackson."

The Millers kept a horse on the place to help even out the rough places and drag the mowers until they got a small tractor. A couple of black men worked more or less full time picking up the balls out on the range. Miller mounted a forked stick on the end of an old golf club and as his son remembered, "The men went right-left, right-left and flipped the balls into a bucket or one of those bags over the shoulder that paper boys used. They got paid by the bucket."

Bill Seebold and his friends built chicken-wire dams in the creek that ran through the middle of the field and sold the golf balls they collected back to Mr. Miller at the driving range. Henry Scott used to watch John Sheiry Jr. chip nine-iron shots at the tractor out mowing the grass or picking up golf balls. He seldom missed. Neighborhood children played on the far end of the range, beyond the 300 yard sign and the ability of most of the duffers who came to hit a bucket of balls.

The rock "mountain" on the old Shoemaker farm was still a favorite place to play, and when it snowed, boys and girls sledded across the fields "for miles" and then walked back up Willard to do it again. They dug caves into the

hillsides at Willoughby and Willard, and when it rained, somebody always dammed up the creek and made a pond you could swing across on grape vines. And it was not just the boys out playing and exploring although girls were never allowed at the swimming holes. Kathryn Seiler Cragoe, née Frisbie, remembered her adventures and skinned knees, and Colonel McAuliffe recalled Dorothy Hampton, née Latterner, as perhaps the best tomboy of his generation. "She could run as fast and climb a tree as well as any boy," he said.

Before the advent of the bi-county Sanitary Commission, the community sewer system emptied into the creek that ran along Willard, the same one the brooks with the swimming holes led to, and the community water supply centered on individual, deep wells and the large tank and windmill Mrs. Sheiry described. She also remembered:

> One dry summer, when there wasn't enough water to keep the tank full, the boards dried out & shrunk, allowing the water to leak out. Someone told Mr. Offutt to put some bran into the tank and it would swell and fill up the cracks. Instead the bran soured making the water unfit to drink.

Mark Shoemaker called it the town's first, large-scale still. North of Friendship Heights, shortly after the Frost house burned, the men built a dam on the creek that ran through the Bergdoll property and produced a pond they hoped would help with fire fighting.[20]

As the hilly community grew, the need to keep up the roads and the boardwalks, as well as the desire for schools and the fear of fires, resulted in the formation of a citizens' committee, and by 1912 there was a full-fledged Friendship Heights Improvement Association with A. E. Shoemaker, president, and Maj. B. M. Purssell, secretary. In addition to improved fire department service from D.C., the association requested a deputy sheriff and constable for the southern suburbs from the County and petitioned for a branch post office. In 1914, at the request of the community leaders, the State legislature created a unified special taxing area combining Friendship Heights and The Hills and named the members of the first council with Henry W. Offutt as chairman.[21]

In April 1919 for the "peace, health and welfare of the community" the Friendship Heights committee produced an eight-page

pamphlet containing a list of rules to which the County Commissioners had given their imprimatur. The first "Article" dealt with animals and made it unlawful "for the owner of any horse, mule, swine, cow or other cattle to permit such animal or animals to run at large within the limits of the taxable area." If a resident wanted to keep pigs, he had to obtain a license, and the applicant could be required to "submit a petition signed by 75 per cent of the actual residents within two squares of all sides of the place where the swine are to be kept..." If the County health officer approved, a license good for one year would be issued. It was also made "unlawful for any person or persons to permit fowl to run at large" and the owners of dogs which disturbed the "peace and quiet" by "barking, biting or howling" could be fined up to $5.00 per day.

Article II prohibited the "offensive accumulation of animal, vegetable, stagnant or other offensive matter" and the growing of weeds "likely to become dangerous or unwholesome to the public." This section also outlawed privies and cesspools and the obstruction of the sidewalks or streets including "bushes, grass or other growing matter" that interfered with the "free passage of pedestrians." It was also made it unlawful to "throw, cast or deposit" on the village streets or vacant lots "any litter, trash, refuse or debris." The selling or discharge of firecrackers and other fireworks was made illegal by Article III, and the last article stated that "All offenses herein mentioned shall be tried by the justice of the peace sitting in Bethesda District."[22]

REGULATIONS

FOR THE

GOVERNMENT OF THE SPECIAL TAXING AREA

KNOWN AS

FRIENDSHIP HEIGHTS AND THE HILLS

The minutes and treasurers' reports of the Citizens' Committee show that streets, sewers, and lighting as the community's major concerns. In 1923, to improve the roads, the committee borrowed $1,850 from the Potomac Savings Bank, where it had some influence. With its annual income of $300-350, it took several years to get out of debt.

The 1926 committee sent a letter to all residents proposing street and drainage improve-

ments based on the payment of front-foot benefits, a system eventually instituted after much debate. The committee also dealt with the problem of chickens running at large, presents for the Tenleytown firemen, paying $250 a year for lighting and keeping sidewalks repaired. By then taxes were bringing in over $600 annually.[23]

On May 19, 1927, S. Walter Bogley swore in the newly elected committeemen and the first elected woman. William Tyler Page was chosen chairman, and the other members were Nellie B. Ross, H. W. Offutt, James C. Dulin, E. E. Dellinger, Alfred G. Seiler, who had married Kathryn Frisbie, and Albert E. Shoemaker, who often acted as chairman during Mr. Page's absences. This was the group that took on major road work, fought PEPCO over its ugly poles on Willard, and forced Mrs. Archie Montgomery to get a sewer connection and clean up what had been the blacksmith's property on the northern edge of town. They also argued with the post office over being considered a part of Chevy Chase and asked milkmen to deliver more quietly early in the morning.

The committee borrowed $3,500 from Potomac Savings for road work and staged a long-remembered "fun-fest and carnival" complete with dancing pavilion, fire-fighting exhibition by the newly organized company in Bethesda, and eleven booths on Montgomery Street which was closed for the event on June 30, July 1 and 2, 1927. The excuse for the celebration was the completion of the concrete east side of Wisconsin Avenue.

The citizens' committee continued on into the Thirties trying to slow down speeders on Willard and nagging B. W. Parker to clean up Woodies' property. A grand gateway project at Wisconsin and Western took up many meetings but dissolved in the Depression, and in `34 the committee even turned down Dellinger's request to sell fireworks.[24]

On March 29, 1916, a group of women met at the home of Mrs. Albert Shoemaker to organize a Friendship Heights Women's Club. Mrs. Getzendanner, the Bethesdan who at the time was President of the Montgomery County Federation of Woman's Clubs, attended, talked on the different activities of various clubs, and provided helpful ideas in regard to forming one. According to Mrs. Sheiry's history, written on the Club's twenty-first anniversary, "A Nominating Committee was appointed, also one on

By-laws, and the first regular meeting was held on April 4, 1916, at Mrs. Fraser's."[25]

The first activity of the newly formed Civic Club, as the women called it, was a drive against flies and mosquitoes, particularly on the vacant Bergdoll property where many residents burned their trash. "Funds were solicited to purchase kerosene, and with the aid of the local Boy Scouts, a successful sanitary campaign was carried on. Several days were spent cleaning up the adjacent dumps and burying old tin cans. The ladies served lunch to the boys and a friendly good time was had by all."

"Reading matter, games and bandana handkerchiefs were sent to Comp. K, 1st Maryland Infantry, along the [Mexican] border, and special days were given over to sewing and making surgical dressings for the American hospital in France during the World War." The ladies provided milk for poor children in rural areas, sponsored Better English contests in the schools, and helped a "stricken family in the immediate neighborhood."

When the Somerset Public School was built, the women helped to establish a cafeteria, bought a refrigerator and an electric clock, and presented the school a Maryland flag in honor of Mrs. Jervey, a former club president. In the community the club went well beyond the purview of most women's organizations and erected street signs, kept the grass and hedges trimmed, contributed to the fund applied to the road improvement debt and placed the brass Friendship Heights signs on the stone gates at the High Street entrance.

> *While we have worked we have played, and many a picnic and party have been enjoyed, especially the picnics at Herring Bay under the hospitality of Mr. and Mrs. George Warren Offutt Jr. Each year a Christmas dinner, or party, has been given, followed by a community sing, and the members, each and all, have done their best to make them a success...we are proud of its twenty-one years.*[26]

So Friendship Heights became a neighborhood where people enjoyed their large, frame homes and their shady porches and where not much happened. In the village's published chronology, there are no entries between 1914 when the town was incorporated and 1951 when the Woodward and Lothrop store was finally built. Mrs. Sheiry's memory of one kind of event probably represents the norm:

While Mr. and Mrs. James C. Dulin lived next door to us in the house on the hill, they had an egg-rolling party every Easter for the neighborhood children. Mrs. Dulin (Leila) would make a lot of cookies which they would serve with ice-cream cones and peanut-butter sandwiches.

The parties were gay and colorful affairs to which my grandchildren were always invited.

When the games were over and the eggs rolled, smashed or eaten, Mr. Dulin brought out the big freezer of ice cream in his wheelbarrow and had the children line up. As he served each child, they would run to the end of the line while eating their cone and go through again - some of them several times - until the cream was all gone.

This was always Mr. Dulin's party and was looked forward to by the children from year to year.

And Henry Scott recalled that for several years Mr. Dulin took all the boys in the neighborhood out to his hunting lodge for the weekend once the ice cream was gone. Mrs. Dulin was remembered for her many years as a member of the choir at St. Albans and service in the Music Section of the Woman's Club of Chevy Chase. A Bogley before her marriage, Mrs. Dulin was president of the Woman's Club of Friendship Heights for several years and very active in the work of the Red Cross.

In July 1927, John S. Sheiry, 62, was killed on Wisconsin Avenue when he was struck by a car driven by a Montgomery County policeman who was transporting a prisoner to Washington, D.C. Mr. Sheiry walked into the side of the police car while crossing the street just north of the gates of Friendship Heights. His death, like the sale of the Shoemaker farm, was a symbol of change.

Along Wisconsin Avenue, as traffic increased on the widened, graded and repaved road, the houses south of High Street all found themselves behind a wall and several feet lower than the new street level while the homes north of the gates rose higher and higher on the bank above the busy highway. Bill Seebold recalled that the old smithy's house was still there in the 1930s with its rickety, front-porch roof held up by posts made of tree trunks with the bark still on them. One by one the big, old Wisconsin Avenue houses, plus several new ones built by Sam Bogley, became tourist homes with "vacancy" signs hanging in their front yards. By World War II the Frisbie home was among them.

The combination of the Depression, the New Deal, and the automobile produced this phenomena, a change one observer called "natural."[27]

Election Notice!

Notice is hereby given that, pursuant to Chapter 131 of the Public Local Laws enacted by the General Assembly of Maryland of 1914, entitled "An Act to create a special taxing district to be known under this Act as the villages of 'Friendship Heights' and 'The Hills'; * * * for the selection and succession of a committee to be named and known as 'Friendship Heights Citizens Committee,' etc." an election will be held on

Monday, May 13, 1929
DELLINGER'S STORE

in said villages for the purpose of electing seven members to be and constitute the "Friendship Heights Citizens Committee," for the ensuing period.

All resident taxpayers upon real or personal property situate in the said villages shall be eligible to vote at such election.

Such election will be conducted by the following Judges and Clerks, duly appointed as required by said act, namely:

Judges: HENRY LATTERNER, ROBERT L. HUGHES, CHARLES W. RIPPEY   Clerks: FRANK B. GERMON, CHARLES H. ROESCH

The Polls will be at the said Dellinger's Store, and will be open at 7 o'clock p. m., and closed at 9 o'clock p. m., when the ballots shall be counted according to law.

Any person desiring to become a candidate or to nominate another

At the District Line in the mid-1930s the unified Capital Transit Company, after abandoning its trolley line to Bethesda and Rockville, built a new, brick terminal and a tight loop of tracks with a forty-foot radius that needed constant applications of graphite. For the next thirty years the screech of trolley wheels was part of the background music in Friendship Heights. Across the street a small beauty parlor and a dressmaker joined Dellinger's old store, which still had some worn rocking chairs on its shady front porch. Thomas Jefferson Barlow remembered that he and most of the other young "masters" at St. Albans piled into the coach's station wagon and rode out to Dellinger's for a few cold ones the day beer became legal again in 1933. It was Barlow's first "legal" beer, and it cost him fifteen cents.

Preston Miller tore down his frame "beer joint" in the mid-Thirties and built a new and much bigger restaurant at Wisconsin and Western. Tom Miller, who "jumped cars" at the drive-in with trays that hooked on the windows and served his customers beer as well as Cokes and shakes, remembered the new place as "similar to the Hot Shoppes that Marriott was

putting up then. It had metal sides, orange and yellow. It was just called Miller's."

In the spring of 1937 "Bill" Marriott rented the square, drive-in restaurant Miller had built. Young men, Marriott called them "running boys," trotted out curb service when drivers flashed their headlights, and hamburgers soon replaced chili at the top of the Hot Shoppes' menu. It was not long before the Running Boy became the logo for the whole, growing chain. An experiment putting the waiters on roller skates was short-lived, but hiring girls to car-hop proved very successful. Male or female, they worked for tips.[28]

Across the street Mr. Mulligan pumped gas at the Lord Baltimore station, and Mr. Miller pounded out dents at his one-man body shop. In D.C., Cities Service and another Lord Baltimore gas station took over the other corners of Wisconsin and Western as the traffic increased past the brown stone marker planted in 1932 by the Garden Clubs of America. An increasing number of accidents at Wisconsin and Western led to requests for a traffic light in 1937, but Washington Cleveland, responding for the D.C. Motor Club (AAA), wrote 200 intersections needed lights and that the one at the District Line was well down the list.[29]

Despite the city's growth under the impetus of the New Deal, in Friendship Heights life went on much as it had before except there were fewer roosters to herald the dawnings. For children, there was always lots to do. In the winter the sleigh riding on Prospect Street was good, but the more adventurous dragged their sleds down to Tenleytown's longer hills, some of which the police roped off. When the snow melted, boys built coaster cars with baby buggy or old coaster-wagon wheels and orange-crate bodies and raced them down the hills toward Willard Avenue. Bill Seebold recalled that when that got too tame they armed their "cars" like tanks, got out their water guns and invented a game in which the goal was to prevent the other guys from reaching the bottom of the Prospect Street hill. Dick Hurtle's cars with a superior broomstick-and-clothes-line steering system were often the survivors. [30]

Henry Scott remembered the great day when he and his friends found they could sneak into the carbarn at Jenifer Street and "get at the old cars in the back and cut the best lariat rope from the cord you pulled to ask for a stop. One day Mrs. Hurtle caught us. We said somebody

gave it to us, but she rounded up nine or ten guys and marched them down to the office." When Shorty Davis, who supervised the carbarn for Capital Transit retired, Al Savage went to his party. Shorty told the crowd that he would not have chased young Al out of the carbarn so often if he had known he was going to grow up to be his boss.

One of the favorite tricks on Hallowe'en was stealing shutters from neighbors' houses and hanging them in the trees. Mr. Offutt, whose big house had dozens of windows, usually caught up with the tricksters a few days later. "Come on, boys," he would say, "you've had your fun. Now put the shutters back." And Dorothy Hampton, who was there and may have done some shutter hanging herself, averred that they would.

Across Wisconsin Avenue and the trolley tracks, youngsters grubbed and stamped out a homemade playing field on the Chevy Chase Land Company territory where pick-up baseball and football games filled sunny afternoons. Down at Dorset there was a better diamond where real ball games were played almost every Sunday except when the field was soggy. Children regularly used a Bergdoll-estate acre at the end of Wootton, and another small field on Mr. Offutt's vacant lots right by the gate was popular for many years.

Teams, although there was never a coach, played boys from Chevy Chase and Bethesda. They stayed away from the Tenleytowners who had earned a tough reputation. Boy Scout Troop 37, with Henry Scott's father as scout-master, had a shack down on Willard Avenue and somewhat better organized activities.[31]

Charlie Hughes's family moved out near Friendship Heights in 1935 when he was six years old.

We lived on a street that was just cinders, and people kept the street going by taking out the ashes from their furnace and putting them in the street. It was called Shoemaker Lane and there was Perry Place, those were the two prominent names; it was all farmland with the exception of four or five houses. It was near River Road and Western.

Ruth Shoemaker, who was a delegate to the State legislature, lived in a little farmhouse surrounded by peach trees, and we were about a hundred yards away. We had a well and septic tank and a coal furnace. The guy that lived next door was a carpenter, John Mosedale, he had a big

family, and he built that house, he and his sons. It wasn't weather stripped, and the winter of 1936 was terrible. It was cold and there were snow drifts on that little road. We moved to Brookdale, about four blocks away, in 1939 on Andover Road.

> *One of the places we played, we followed the creek over to Loughborough's Bottom near Massachusetts Avenue. We just called the place "Big Rock." It was just a huge rock half the size of this house. We played there and then we'd go over to Loughborough's Bottom, and it was all sand, an acre of clearing and all sand. We played football and softball games in my backyard.*

> *That creek came through the golf course and went down Willard and then, half way down, on the other side of Willard. We used to patrol this creek and harvested balls that came through the nets. Once we went up to see the guy and tried to sell them back to him, and he told us to go to hell.*

> *Hardy Sorrell was a good friend of mine, in my class but a year older. We went to Somerset Elementary, which was a great school, and he lived off Western Avenue about a mile from me in what was called the "hollow" on the other side of River Road. He came from a large family and his father worked down in the Bahamas. He had a brother named Curtis, Curty we called him, and we always had a baseball team and tried to find games around the area. We played over at Fort Bayard Park or where the golf balls stopped coming on the driving range and sometimes over in Chevy Chase. Hardy was very good, a natural athlete.*

Friendship Heights' informal playgrounds produced a number of fine athletes and one of the best was a gangly young man that most people called Rix or Ricksy, James McAuliffe. His brother John helped organize and lead the Chevy Chase Bearcats, one of the best baseball teams of the 1920s, with Rix as a speedy utility man. And it was probably some of the Bearcats, who met regularly in the McAuliffe basement for a game of cards, that gave Jim Senior his nickname.

Shortstop Bobby Stevens told it this way:

> *There was an old washer woman, an old black wash-woman there in Friendship Heights called Mrs. Rix. And somehow we kids started calling him "Liza Rix" and then later dropped the Liza. Everybody knows who you are talking about when you call him "Rix," but McAuliffe's wife and family said it more like "Rex."*[32]

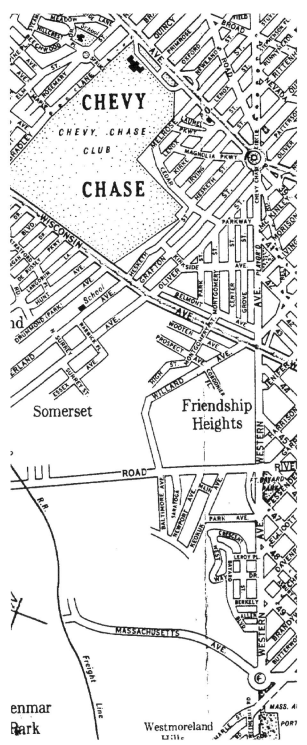

Part of Vaucher and Pirola map, circa mid-1930s

North of Friendship Heights a big creek, Little Falls Branch, ran through a Chevy Chase sewer field, under Wisconsin Avenue, across a scrubby woodland and joined the crooked Phillips Branch that meandered along Willard just where that street turned sharply before reaching River Road. This wilderness was the 132.4-acre property beer baroness Emma C. Bergdoll of Philadelphia bought from the trustees of John E. Beall's estate for $36,000 at a foreclosure sale in April 1900.

Despite her oft-stated intention to build a home on it and except for the right-of-way for the Baltzley brothers' trolley line from Chevy Chase Circle to Glen Echo, the disputed property stood empty for almost a century. During World War II, Victory Gardens flourished along its Friendship Heights' frontier, and small scale farming continued there for some time after the war was over, but it was mainly a dumping ground for neighborhood trash. It was also a place for children's games and expeditions despite their parents' constant admonitions.

Some, like Henry Latimer, followed the ballast trail and ties of the old trolleyline across River Road "looking for a blazed tree at the edge of the deep forest, which marked the path to an old gold mine." Mr. Latimer wrote that the mine tunnel near what was left of Fort Sumner "was an irresistible attraction to me and my pals, and we would explore it with fear and trepidation." Kathryn Cragoe and her younger brother Kenneth Frisbie both recalled crawling down that long, dank tunnel, something few girls did. Even though they carried a candle, "it was kind of spooky" and an adventure long remembered. Mr. Latimer thought the tunnel was near the Glen Echo fire station while Mr. Frisbie placed it closer to the Westbard shops, and Mr. Scott thought it was just across the railroad tracks at Massachusetts Avenue. It is likely there were several mines.[33]

The land that became Somerset had long been a unit. An early map showed that a part of the tract known as "Friendship" belonged to Richard Williams, "farmer and patron of the Bethesda area," and contained 211.5 acres with boundaries almost exactly the same as the present town. The Loughboroughs owned most of the southwestern part of Friendship, and much of the rest had been carved up into farms such as the Shoemakers'.

In February 1888 Thomas Hyde paid $32,148 for a tract of some 217 acres and in June sold off twenty-two of those. In March 1890 entrepreneur John Beall, one of the powers behind both the trolley line and Bethesda Park, bought the rest of Hyde's land for $72,500. Then in August, Beall and is partner, Dr. Walsh, sold fifty acres of their planned development between River Road and Rockville Pike to Messrs. Wiley, Crampton, Salmon, Fuller, and Horton of Washington, D.C., for $19,000.[34]

The *Evening Star* reported their plans:

The Agricultural Department Colony: After considering various propositions made by land owners, the committee representing the scientific men of the Department of Agriculture, who had in view the establishing of a suburban colony, have selected a tract of rolling land on the Tenleytown road adjoining the property of Gen. Drum, just across the District line in Montgomery County, owned by John E. Beall, esq., and Dr. Ralph Walsh. The tract is part of the so-called Somerset Heights and consists of fifty acres sloping to the south. The company will begin operations by providing the property with a good system of sewerage, a bountiful supply of water and electric lights from the Georgetown and Tenleytown Electric Railroad Co.

During the coming Summer and Autumn steps will be taken in preparing the property for building. Mr. Beall, through whom the property was purchased, will build a broad avenue from the Pike along the border of the property, plant shade trees and lay a sidewalk. The initiatory steps in house building have been taken by Dr. D. E. Salmon, Dr. H. W. Wilie, Dr. C. A. Crampton, Mr. H. E. L. Horton, Mr. Miles Fuller and others. The lots are to contain not less than one acre, with the view to insuring the building of a cluster of villas, forming a suburb fashioned after the very pleasant ones of Boston and other northern cities.[35]

The founders were a remarkable group led by Crampton and Fuller. The most illustrious of the "scientific men," the "father of the Pure Food and Drug Act of 1906," Harvey Wiley, for twenty years chief of the Bureau of Chemistry of USDA, was both a medical doctor and a Ph.D. He was a "zealous advocate of a plain

simple diet and pure and wholesome food. Among his friends he was known as a connoisseur of delectable viands. When he dined with friends where the food and drink satisfied his discriminating taste, he consumed them in quantities commensurate with his body weight of over 200 pounds." At one dinner where he was billed as the "star," he rose after the meal and a florid introduction to say, "Mr. Toastmaster, I am not a star. It would be more appropriate to liken me to the moon, for the fuller I am the brighter I shine."

Hoping to bring his parents from Indiana, in 1891 he built a house at what became 4722 Dorset Avenue. In the late 1930s this became the home of Arthur and Dorothy Ringland. Mr. Ringland worked for relief organizations after World War I and was a founder of CARE after WW II. Although he visited the town many times, Dr. Wiley never lived in Somerset, but his house survived, if just barely.[36]

Dr. Harvey Wiley

However his assistant, Charles A. Crampton, built and occupied the house at 4807 Dorset in 1893, and a year later the town's first baby, Carl Crampton, was born there. Dr. Crampton, a graduate of Columbian College, also became the first mayor in 1906 and owned the first auto in Somerset, a Cadillac. He built a number of other early houses for speculation and planted many of the community's original shade trees.

Dentist-photographer Dr. Sidney Jaffe bought Crampton's property in 1918 and built several houses on it including his own unusual ten-room, stone and Siberian cedar-log home which had to be located far from the street, in the center of the four-acre tract, because of the town's opposition to a "log cabin." The Jaffe's annual open-house Christmas party became a much anticipated ritual. Remodeled in the mid-1930s, the original Crampton home is another survivor of the first five.

Dr. Daniel Salmon built his home at 4728 Dorset and called it "Clover Crest." He was "a brilliant scientist of international repute" who led the fight against pleuropneumonia and Texas tick fever as head of the Department of Agriculture's Bureau of Animal Husbandry. He did much of his work just up the road at the Bethesda experimental farm established by USDA in 1897. While there is no direct evidence, it is likely that the Research Station was located in Bethesda in part because so many USDA types were making their homes in Somerset.

In 1902 John William Stohlman, proprietor of the Georgetown bakery and confectionary founded by his German-immigrant father, purchased Salmon's house as a summer place for his large family and moved there year-round in 1916. The Stohlman children, all nine of whom attended Immaculata Seminary, were about two years apart in age and all had birthdays in the summer. Their ice cream and cake parties were long anticipated by the town's other children. Mr. Stohlman was the fifth mayor of Somerset, serving from 1919 to 1938. His house still stands, rivaling the Sutliffe's long lost home as a showplace.[37]

At about the same time as the Stohlmans, in the early 1900s, Jesse Swigart moved his growing family to the eight-room frame house built by his brother-in-law Alf Ough on Essex Street just behind the Stohlmans. Ada Swigart, the youngest of the family's three daughters, was born there in January 1903. She was not sure of the date they moved in but knew that the Somerset Wednesday Club was picking out a name for her before she was born.

Her father had come to Washington when his father, an Indiana elector for Harrison, accepted a Treasury Department appointment. Instead of returning to school, young Jesse took a Civil Service exam and became an apprentice plate maker at Printing and Engraving in 1891 at $320 a year. By 1897 he was well enough established to marry Rebecca Daw, the daughter of a renowned Georgetown builder. Jesse rose

to be assistant director of the Bureau and retired in 1941 on $1,320 a year after fifty years of service. He and Rebecca lived to enjoy their fiftieth wedding anniversary.

Miles Fuller, the nominal leader who handled most of the business details for the partnership, built at 4723 Dorset and lived there until about the turn of the century. Fuller also built several other houses on speculation after he resigned from the Bureau of Animal Husbandry in 1889 and opened The Drillery, his school for secretaries.

Dr. E. A. de Sweintz, chief of the Biochemic Division of the Bureau of Animal Industry took over Horace Horton's interests in the project. DeSweintz's home at 4721 Essex was destroyed by fire shortly after it was completed in 1895. Another house was built on the foundations for James and Ella Tibbetts and their family who were long famous for their gardens.[38]

The "nucleus" of the community became the four large, white frame homes at Dorset and Surrey. Like the pretentious neighborhood to the east, the partners agreed on English names for their streets and on covenants prohibiting alleys and establishing 30-foot setbacks. They also agreed on a $2,000 minimum home cost, and each promised to build five houses in short order. In 1899 they platted the rest of the fifty acres into ninety-six building lots of various sizes. The partners then divided them up by lottery and set out to make some money, but the census of 1900 showed a bare dozen families established in the community. However, the community was running a close second to Chevy Chase in servants-per-household and probably led in advanced degrees-per-breadwinner.[39]

John Beall and his partners, who still had 192 acres of farmland to sell, printed up a fancy brochure that emphasized the nearness of Somerset Heights to the Capital, the recent investment by a group of men of high standing in the government, and the convenience of the three nearby electric railways and the promised arrival of the B&O. Like the Baltzley brothers and J. S. Tomlinson to the west and the California Syndicate to the east, the real estate speculators and the scientist-promoters saw a bright future for the Capital and a profitable and pleasant one for the fast-growing northwest suburbs.

Somerset Heights, its investors claimed, "lies in the heart of that active real estate movement and march of improvement northwest of Washington." The land was a "beautiful ridge" sloping toward the Potomac and "400 feet above tidewater, absolutely free from malarial influence..." Beall, who dealt in real estate, loans, and insurance from his F Street office, assured prospective buyers of his square, one-acre lots, "There is no cheap property in the neighborhood," and land values were rapidly advancing. Ghostly street tracings for roads never graded show up on many old maps, but neither Beall nor Bergdoll filed a plat for a subdivision.[40]

Lots sold well, at least in the "Colony." More houses went up along the dirt streets; many of those the Oughs built looked a lot like the ones up on the hill south of the creek, and within five years there were about three-dozen families living in Somerset Heights. The promised water supply was inadequate, the sewer "system" drained to the creeks and fields through fractured terra cotta pipes, and the roads were three dimensional when it rained. People going into town after dark hid lanterns in the bushes near the trolley stop so they could find their way home on the paths and boardwalks.

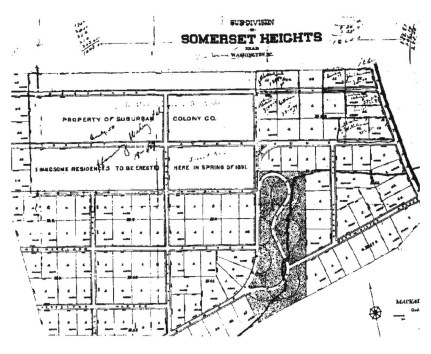

But as the *Star* noted "the region of country in all directions presents delightful views and prospects, so that the residents are able to enjoy the benefit of a much larger domain than that in which they hold the legal title."[41]

In August of 1902, Dr. Crampton and four other men founded and incorporated the Somerset Heights Water and Power Company of Montgomery County for the purposes of "dealing in land" and for procuring and selling "a supply of water" in Somerset and nearby towns, and also for producing and selling power and light and "constructing and maintaining a system of sewerage...." They dug deep wells in the woods, and at first a windmill pumped the water up to a big tank at 4718 Cumberland from wells at 4822 Cumberland. Later a gasoline engine did the job, and finally an electric pump replaced it. Until tuberculosis forced him to leave the area, carpenter-contractor W. A. Ough remained the water company's sole employee whose main duty was keeping the big wooden tank on stilts filled. Ada Swigart Hess recalled her Uncle Alf having to leave bridge games and go home to turn on the pump.[42]

When the Dudleys lived at 4721 Cumberland, they took on the task of watching the gauge mounted on the side of the water tank across the street. Seventy years later Henry Dudley helped locate exactly where the water tower and wells were since "he and his brother Frank went down the hill at all hours to start the gasoline motor to pump the water up the hill to the tower. His father was a plumber and paid by the town to keep the pump working." The original hookup fee was $200 and in the coldest weather the shallow pipes froze, but the demand generally outran the supply as carpenters framed more big houses.[43]

About 1902, Willis and Amelia Davis built their home at 5800 Warwick at the corner of Dorset on one of Miles Fuller's lots. They operated a small store from the north side of the house where they sold bread, candy, tobacco, and kerosene. Later the town's first telephone switchboard was here with Mrs. Davis' older daughter Louise as the operator who said, "Number please." Bessie Swigart's sisters were also her neighbors, Mrs. Henry (Lettie) Latterner in Friendship Heights and Mrs. W. A. (Lilly) Ough on Cumberland Street. When telephones were installed, the three of them and Mrs. John R. (Louise) Cox were on the same

party line and used to pick up their receivers at nine each morning for a free visit.

William A. Ough built three houses on Warwick for Edward Halliday in 1901. Mr. Halliday bought twenty-four lots from Fuller some of which he further subdivided. Many folks thought these smaller houses "cheapened the neighborhood."

At least two outbuildings were later turned into houses, the smaller one at 4910 Cumberland, now a handsome, yellow, frame farmhouse, may have been part of the Phillips farm and the other at 4719 Dorset started life as a barn for a small farm, and some oldtimers even remembered that the Biggs family kept a Jersey cow there.

But in general, it was a neighborhood of large houses on big lots, and when the *Star*'s series on Washington suburbs reached Drummond and Somerset on May 20, 1914, the story was headlined "Artistic Garden Spots Enhance Suburbs' Beauty" and praised Somerset for its "stately" trees and the rolling nature of the ground "just uneven enough to permit artistic development."

Several dairy farms, most with windmills marking their centers, were operating more or less successfully when the men from the Agriculture Department started building homes in Somerset. Joshua Callahan had a farm at Cumberland and Warwick, and its broad front yard, once a popular sleigh riding hill, later became the site of the elementary school. The Voigt's small place was closer to the Pike, but they had a windmill, too. William Voigt huckstered produce in Drummond as well as in Somerset and was the topic of many letters of complaint from both Drummond and Somerset leaders about the state of his privy and premises.

Just south of the Callahan's was an open field, often full of daisies, where Somersetters held 4th of July celebrations, which included pie-eating contests and all kinds of races. A well-worn diagonal path crossed the field, ran past a popular baseball field and out to Wisconsin Avenue.

The Kirby farm house was at 4910 Cumberland where a chicken house stood into the 1940s. On the far side of town, John W. Phillips had a farm extending west to the B&O railroad tracks with his barn beyond the creek in what is now part of Kenwood. He became the local milkman, and Ada Swigert Hess

remembered that on some snowy mornings he gave children a ride to the Chevy Chase School in his horse-drawn wagon. His tenants' home was at 4914 Dorset, and his own small house just across the street at 4915. Joseph S. Hardy, whose dairy farm had been in the Kenwood area, bought that house in 1917. Mr. Hardy "kept pigs, drove a mule wagon, and did odd jobs in Somerset."

The Town fathers had a terrible time trying to get the Hardys to hook in to the sewer system and to pen up their hogs. Cleveland Clipper, who grew up on River Road, said that Simmons Hardy was "passing" and that the Hardys "powdered their children every morning and sent them off to the white school" until they were found out. "People in Somerset would say we know what Frank Wood is," Clipper said with a laugh. "He's as dark as these shoes, but we don't know what this man is. Hardy had a milk route, too, but they cut that out."

Harold Greenberg, who grew up in Somerset in the 1920s and `30s, recalled that the Hardy father and son lived across the street from each other on Dorset and were still farming then.

Their bread and butter came from landscaping, grading and digging foundations. They had these dump wagons (the bottom would open up) and two teams. The main part of their business was selling topsoil to all these houses that were being built in the area.

I guess I was attracted to them because of the horses. I loved horses. They were very kind to me and permitted me to hang around there and help cut hay, rake hay, help them drive the wagon - not that they needed my help. They were lovely people. It was like going to camp in the summertime. The barn was almost at the railroad track and they grazed their horses on Kenwood property.

The Kirbys' dairy farm on Cumberland was all there was on that end of town at one time. Their chicken house lasted a long time as well as the huge white oak, some said the largest twin oak in the County.[44]

Farther north on the other side of competing Drummond was Gen. Drum's big house and, of even more importance to Somerset's children, the General's ice pond where they skated "as late in the season as he could allow before it was necessary to cut the ice for his needs during the summer following." Water pumped from the ice pond was used to fight the fire at Dr.

Milo Sutliff's large, handsome red house with the big porches and white trim. But Somerset's "showplace," despite the efforts of the firemen and their horsedrawn fire engine from Tenleytown, burned to the ground in July 1909. Ada Swigert was only six, but she remembered the fire well and that her mother barely escaped from the burning kitchen just before the ceiling fell. Dr. Sutliff built a small bungalow on the site which he used only in the summer.[45]

South of town, the "Great Woods" and the wandering stream on the Bergdoll property lured children to build tree houses, play cowboys and Indians, wade in the creek despite their parents' direst warnings, and explore the shady wilderness of the mountain laurel-covered hill that led up to Friendship Heights. When they were young girls, Dorothy Latterner and Ada Swigart looked forward to the times when that hill was dotted with beautiful violets, which they gathered in huge bunches.

In Somerset, most youngsters practiced their piano lessons and their elocution pieces, and many attended dancing classes in various homes where there was enough space, and there were many of those in the early days. Asked for her memories of Somerset, Mrs. Elizabeth Allen, who as Betsy Watkins grew up at 4709 Cumberland, wrote:

I remember when the streets were paved with concrete from stone beds and straw was put on the wet concrete to help it dry and when riding my bicycle around the corner of Warwick Lane and Cumberland I slipped and scraped my knees considerably; skating and playing hockey on skates in Drummond because it was flat enough for two teams; playing games like Run Sheep Run on Cumberland Avenue in the evening with the neighborhood gang; 4th of July putting thunderbolts under tin cans to see how far they would blow, Roman candles and sparklers at night; hopscotch on the sidewalk in front of 309 Cumberland Avenue, leaf houses in the fall in our yard; playing house, with stuff garnered at Laurel Hill, in the woods next to the Dunbars where the Bradys live now; playing at Laurel Hill in the stream, picking pansy violets and dogtooth violets, swinging on a grapevine swing across the creek; when the trees were planted in front of our house, tiny things; the Dunbars' Model T Ford; coasting on Cumberland Avenue when it snowed and having the fire at the top of the hill; the pageant we all participated in; walking across the fields to E. V. Brown to school every day and back . . growing up we did all those things.[46]

As in other early Bethesda communities, people worked together to maintain the dirt streets, filling the holes with ashes and cinders, and tried to keep the boardwalks passable. Children always looked forward to the walks being lifted for cleaning so they could recover toys dropped through the cracks as well as a having chance to find a few lost coins.

Unfortunately, not everyone pitched in to share the work. Of the thirty-five families living in Somerset in 1905, only about a dozen regularly contributed either work or money for the common good. It was not long before the lack of County services such as schools and fire protection and the need for a better water supply and sewer system led to the formation of a citizens' association. As in Martin's Additions and many other neighborhoods, those who sweated to keep up their community grew tired of those who refused to do so, and in 1906 the Town of Somerset was incorporated by the State of Maryland. Its boundaries expanded to about those of the old Williams' tract and took in several existing farms and most of the property acquired by Mrs. Bergdoll.[47]

Somerset elected its first Council on May 7, 1906, with Dr. Crampton as the first mayor. Property assessment and taxation were almost the first order of business when the Council met at Dr. Crampton's home on May 14th. At their second meeting, three days later, the Mayor appointed Dr. Sutliff, Mr. Moore, and Mr. Howell to be the Board of Assessors. Mr. Elbert Richmond was chosen Town Marshall. At its third session on May 21, the Council heard a report from its special sewer committee, brothers-in-law Swigart and Ough:

Your committee has investigated the conditions of the outlet to the main sewer which empties into Little Falls Run and finds that the pipe is broken in several places as far as 200 feet from the outlet, due to washing away of the earth from under the pipe. This causes the sewerage to run out on the ground into several large pools which are a menace to the health of the community . . . .

The Council approved its first three ordinances prohibiting the breaking of street lights, the defacing of property and letting "any animal of the goat, horse, cow, or hog kind, or any fowl such as geese, ducks, turkeys, or chickens to go at large" except when being driven. In less than a month the Town Board of Assessors completed its task, and the tax rate was set at the maximum, fifty cents per hundred dollars of taxable property. The Council approved a 1907-1908 budget calling for expenditure of $511 of which $350 was for street maintenance and lighting.[48]

A health officer, Dr. Thomas A. Griffin, was appointed, and inspection of the dairy farms was made a part of his job. The Council spent $75 to repair the sewer pipes and extend the one on the west past the cesspool to an open field. A dollar went for a padlock for the yellow, frame trolley waiting station, and Council discussed fire protection with the captain of Station No. 20 in Tenleytown. The Council dispatched a letter to the WRECo managers asking that the "West Chevy Chase signs be removed from the Cars on the Rockville and Georgetown Line and that the name Somerset be used instead." Searching for new sources of income, the Council placed an unpopular two-dollar tax on dogs and ended its first year with a cash balance of $81.70.[49]

In 1910 Jesse Swigart, of the Bureau of Engraving and Printing became the second mayor, and in 1912 he was succeeded by Warren W. Biggs, a steam heating contractor who was first in town to have radiators in his home at 4718 Cumberland. Mr. Biggs raised cows and bees and was remembered for playing his coronet so loudly that everyone in town could enjoy it.

Next came SEC lawyer Charles S. Moore in 1916. The growing town of about two hundred residents elected J. William Stohlman mayor in 1919, and he served for almost twenty years. In 1938 W. B. Horne, one of the organizers of the County Civic Federation who played a role in promoting both the M-NCP&PC and the WSSC, became mayor, and Irving M. Day, who with his wife, Doris, founded the Montgomery Players in 1929, was elected in 1940 and then re-elected six times.[50]

With the men of the town reasonably well organized and busy with their water company and Council, the women could turn their attention to other important concerns since they had little direct voice in governance. Women did not vote in town elections until 1921, and in 1928 Mrs. Oliver H. Gish was the first woman elected to the Council. In the mid-1920s Dr. June Madison Hull became Somerset's Health Officer, the first woman to serve in an official post. By the end of World War II only two other women, Mrs. Marquis Childs and Mrs. R. E. Miles, had been chosen as Council members.

THE WOMAN'S CLUB OF SOMERSET

Presents the Following Program

SOMERSET SCHOOL HOUSE

SATURDAY, MARCH 23, 1935—8:15 P. M.

PRINCESS TENDERHEART

By GITHA SOWERBY

CHARACTERS

PRINCESS TENDERHEART ....BETTY GRAHAM
HER PAGE ....KATE JOHNSON
THE KING, her father ....IDA MARY SHEPARD
PRINCE CUTANDRIED ....ANN SHILLINGER
DR. SADCASE ....CLAIRE RICE
LADIES-IN-WAITING ....MARIANNA BRADY
                                                                               JOAN RICE

Act 1—Scene: A room in the Palace

Act 2—Scene: The Throne Room

MUSIC

Trio from the Newcomb-Bethesda Community Singers:

Mrs. Ruth L. Morgan
Mrs. Caroline Baldwin
Mrs. Edith Loomis
Mrs. Margaret Hyson, Accompanist

The Countess Dances ....Mozart arr. by Tillotson
The Japanese Maiden ....From the Toy Shop by Gaynor

'OP-O'-ME THUMB

By FREDERICK FENN and RICHARD PRYCE

CHARACTERS

MADAME JEANNE MARIE DIDIER.............................KITTIE WOOD
ROSE JORDON ....NANCY DOWNS
CELESTE ....JEAN SMITH
AMANDA AFFLICK ....JANE RICE
HORACE GREENSMITH ....STEPHEN ROBERTS

Scene: Working room at Madame Didier's Laundry in Soho, London

Plays directed by JANE PLUMMER RICE

Maryland My Home.................Words by Louise C. Morell; Music by Hill

You are cordially invited to have coffee and cakes in the school cafeteria immediately following the program. Cakes donated by Lorraine Pastry Shoppe. Coffee donated by Gills Coffee Company.

Right from the beginning, the women who moved to this isolated community, far from everything except the trolley which rattled past every half hour or so, cooperated in order to survive and keep their sanity. Finally Maybelle Michener, Mrs. Perry G. Michener, "who was a sort of mother to the neighborhood," organized the Wednesday Club to provide a regular, social meeting place for tea, friendship, and an exchange of ideas. The Club continued, rather informally, through the First World War as a busy Red Cross unit and had occasional meetings into World War II.[51]

In October 1916 five Somerset women felt the need for a more active organization and founded a "civic" club. They were Mrs. Everett F. (Mary G.) Phillips, Mrs. J. A. (Annie J.) Nelson, Mrs. G. C. (Laura E.) Spencer, Mrs. Lynn (Dora) Haines, and Mrs. A. W. (Carrie P.) Starratt, who as the first secretary not only kept the

minutes but preserved them. Town historian and archivist, Dorothy O'Brien, called Mrs. Starratt "the true founder."[52]

The first meeting at Mrs. Phillips' home featured two speakers, Mrs. Johnson and Mrs. Getzendanner, from the Federation of Women's Clubs. Thirty-six women voted to organize a club and became its charter members. At the second meeting two more names were added to the list of charter members, and it was agreed that regular meetings would be held at 7:30 pm on the first Friday of each month. Officers were elected: president, Mrs. Anne E. Howell; vice-president, Mrs. Phillips; secretary, Mrs. Starratt; treasurer, Mrs. Spencer. The club voted to apply for membership in the Federation and named Dora Haines as its delegate.

The first items discussed, including the question of having a school in Somerset, trolley fares for school children, and the continuing sewer concerns, showed up for many years in the minutes. Soon they organized card parties and a rummage sale as fund raisers, and gathered papers and magazines to be sold to a junk dealer. They used some of their money to repair the wooden sidewalks with husbands dragooned to do the work. By the next spring Club members led a community clean-up campaign with the Boy Scouts, planned a 4th of July celebration, and began exchanging menus. The Woman's Club of Somerset was also an early and continuing supporter of the Social Service League of Montgomery County.

During World War I, the Club mailed magazines to army camps, encouraged the cultivation of "war gardens," and sent out singing groups to entertain the soldiers. In 1918 they acquired a steam pressure cooker, which the members shared. They tried to get Grafton Street cut through to Chevy Chase so they would not have to worry about their children playing in the creek, or worse yet in the fetid "sewer farm," on their way to and from the E. V. Brown School. In the early 1920s they formed a tennis club and for one dollar a year rented the proposed school lot on which the Voigts had been dumping trash.

Mah-jong and card parties, ambitious pageants and one-act plays became fixtures of the yearly schedule. The music division staged

concerts, and in 1925 the Club presented "Somerset, a sylvan drama in one act" as part of a carnival and parade to celebrate the paving of the streets. The stone gates at the entrance to Somerset were also a contribution of the Women's Club in the 1930s when the old gateway disappeared with the widening of Wisconsin Avenue. The Club continued into the war years with a popular book club section, an annual benefit Christmas party, and a June garden party for all residents of Somerset that boasted of never being rained out.[53]

Jane Tedeschi: "In back row, that's me, Margaret Balcum, Louise Watkins, then a Cremins, Margaret, the youngest one we called Googy, then Harriet Balcum, Lois Gish, and Margaret Saylor." A Somerset pageant.

When Mary Phillips, wife of the bee expert and author of childrens' nature books, was asked to take part in a founder's day celebration in 1940, she replied:[54]

Little did I dream that I would ever be celebrated for being a founder! I have no idea what year it was that we who lived side by side in the rural village of Somerset got together and started the club. But I do remember very well some of the wonderful times we had together.

We once were ambitious enough to put on an evening of Dickens' tableaus, when men, women, and children were dressed in the costumes of the day and posed as some Dickens' characters. I remember some of the famous cakes made for our parties by members, and in that day we beat the batter by hand! We had serious programs sometimes too, as I imagine you still do. We shared the first vacuum cleaner and the first pressure canner owned by a Somersetter.

Oh, yes, we had a song too, that began, "Some are set, and some are setter."

In that day the nearest store was down at the District Line, and there was much borrowing back and forth. Once when I saw my husband coming up the road with a man with a suitcase and realized we were having an overnight guest, I was in despair for the main dish for our dinner was a can of salmon!

I dashed next door to Mrs. Van Dine, who was just lifting a roast from her oven. "Here," she said, "you take the roast and send one of the boys over with the salmon." I hope you are as neighborly as that still . . . .

Change was constant. In 1913 new ordinances prohibited driving across sidewalks, discharging firearms and the use of licentious or obscene language. Gas mains were laid; the ramshackle waiting station was replaced; a school lot was acquired, and a 12 mph speed limit was posted. The USDA established its bee lab at 4823 Dorset, the Nelson house, and filled the sideyard with hives about 1917. Other than Mrs. Bergdoll's property, Dr. James Nelson's house, which had dozens of stuffed birds on the shelves of the den, had the highest assessment ($3,500) in the early days.

The Entomological Division of the Department of Agriculture had conducted apiculture studies and research since the 1880s. The third floor of a home in Drummond originally housed the project, but it slowly outgrew that space. In 1907 the bee lab scientists began a study of bee diseases, in 1908 of the physiology of bees. When the project moved to Somerset, the work accelerated under the leadership of Dr. Everett Phillips. In the summers local students, including Elizabeth Swigart and some of her friends, hired on at $5.00 a month to help with the bees. By 1930 the Bureau had issued nineteen publications on bee behavior and claimed that almost "every advancement made in this country in the study of bee diseases is directly attributable to investigations which have been made by the Bureau." In 1930 the annual payroll was over $26,000 for the five full-time scientists, two clerks and a librarian at the Somerset laboratory and apiary, which housed the administrative office of the bee culture division.[55]

In 1928 the big push by the Citizens' Association, the Woman's Club and the Town Council was for an elementary school. As early as 1913 a school census had been made and transmitted to the County school board, and Mrs. Bergdoll was approached about a site. The result was classes in the Shoemaker's house and the appropriation by Somerset of a sum

"not to exceed ten dollars...for the construction of a bridge across the stream between Somerset and Friendship Heights for the convenience of school children."

Some children may have attended classes earlier at the Grange Hall on the edge of Bethesda and others briefly at General Drum's home where the BOE used four rooms in 1915 for $35 a month. Conway Hunt remembered that "in World War I the school board rented the second story of my house and they put me and my sister on the porch. We had to crawl through a window to get into the house."[56]

Most Somerset children walked more than a mile across the fields and the creek and through growing neighborhoods to Miss Givens' Chevy Chase School, later E. V. Brown. The path cut diagonally past the Watkins' house and their beautiful flower garden and then went on out to the highway. On the other side it followed the fence of the country club to Grafton Street to avoid the sewer farm. Even after World War I, when elementary schools were well established in Chevy Chase and on the car line in Bethesda, the thought of going to school in Maryland was anathema to many Somerset parents. Ada Swigert Hess said they would no more have gone to school out there than they would have lived in Kenwood, on the wrong side of the tracks.[57]

The women centered their attention toward securing a neighborhood school. Mrs. Oliver Gish and Mrs. Parker Dodge formed a School Committee. They met with Superintendent Edwin Broome and found that he favored small schools within easy walking distance for most children. "The women canvassed the entire neighborhood in a school census, demanding a school nearer than Rosemary Street or Wilson Lane. The board of education was astounded that so many children lived around here."[58]

On February 9, 1928, the Somerset Council, hearing that the BOE was contemplating a new elementary school, adopted the following resolution and sent it to Rockville:

Now therefore be it resolved that the Mayor and the Council of the Town of Somerset endorse the plan for the erection of a new elementary school, and recommend that it be located as near as possible to the center of population of the area bounded by Bradley Lane, Western Avenue and the B & O freight line, and in support of such recommendation shows that this area is the most

thickly populated in the Chevy Chase district, having in excess of 330 children of elementary school age; that there is no school in this area and that the rapid growth of the community and the constant increase of property values renders immediate action imperative....

Despite the best, and at times devious, efforts of some of the Chevy Chase parents, who wanted their school enlarged instead of another school being built, George Farrell presented the Town's case and the census data collected by Mrs. Gish and Mrs. Dodge. The Board agreed to place a school in Somerset.

In May 1928 the school board purchased the Callahan land from Mrs. Grace Meadows for $38,500, and in June let the contracts for the construction and furnishing of the school for a total of $40,849. Parents registered their children on the front porch of Mrs. Merchant's house. Classes took place in the gym at Bethesda Elementary until October when 138 students began working in the still-unfinished eight-room building with their six teachers and 25-year-old teacher-principal Kathryne Bricker. She led Somerset Elementary School for the next thirty-seven years. Their square, unpainted, red brick building with its oiled floors and two lavatories faced Dorset in the early years. The women's clubs in Friendship Heights and Somerset continued their support helping to create a cafeteria and donating many useful items such as a clock and flags to the school.

Harold Greenberg was in the first graduating class at the Somerset Elementary School. His family had moved from New Jersey to 410 Surrey in 1927, and he went to school at Bethesda Elementary for a year. He remembered Miss Poole and Mrs. Bricker fondly and had nothing but good memories of life in Somerset despite the fact that, as Jews, his parents, brothers and sisters were isolated and practically ignored in the community.

We had a great life growing up there. It was a beautiful way of raising children. There was only one other Jewish family in Somerset, the Jaffes, and in all the years we lived in Somerset, although their property was only one lot from ours, we never met. We never saw them. We were never in our next door neighbors' homes. It was a beautiful place to live, but it was a lonesome place. It's a good thing I had four brothers and sisters.

Mayor Stohlman, their neighbor, visited the Greenberg home only once, the first time they

had a party. The Mayor stated his expectations about how loud the music should be and how late the lights should burn. Harold Greenberg was not sure what his father said, but they never saw or heard from Stohlman again.

Jane Tedeschi née Dunbar was a member of Somerset's second graduating class. Her father and mother, PhD chemists Paul B. and Alice Davison Dunbar of the FDA Bureau of Chemistry, moved to Cumberland Avenue with their three, young daughters in 1921. They found a neighborhood full of children. Jane, the youngest, recalled trudging across fields or roller-skating on the brick sidewalks over to E. V. Brown from kindergarten on. She remembered "Miss McCubbin in 4th grade. I loved her. She taught long-division." She also remembered the sledding on her street:

Cumberland Avenue flattens out by our house and then it starts down and it levels then it goes a big down and then it levels, then a short down, and then a hill all the way to the creek, or we'd go through the woods or the other way where there was a guy wire we had to duck.

My father bought a Tuxedo racer. It was the top of the line like the Flexible Flyer. It was long and narrow, and he got it for ten dollars. We used to pile on that sled on top of each other, boys and girls together, and then sometimes we'd had two sleds going side-by-side, and at the bottom they'd steer in opposite directions, and there would be people all over the place.

The Voights had a farm down here, and we used to play in haystacks and make a house in there, and they chased us one time, and Louise and I ran and hid under the bed in her bedroom, and they came to the door.

When one of their boys was injured sledding my father took him to the hospital in our Model-T, and he threw up all over the thing.

We played croquet and played tennis on street with a tar line for a net, and you tried to hit so you would not have to run down the hill after it. When we played hide and seek or kick the can with identical twins Dick and Don Hamilton, all we had to say was "twin."

Henry Scott of Friendship Heights was another of the early students at Somerset Elementary who recalled his experiences there with pleasure.

I went to D.C. schools until they opened Somerset when I was in 2nd or 3rd grade. I remember all those teachers. Mrs. Bricker, she was the principal, the most wonderful person, supposed to be the person you feared, but she was wonderful, and Mrs. Souder, and my 6th grade teacher that I thought was the smartest person in the universe, Miss Morningstar, tall, skinny thing. Miss Poole from Poolesville left an indelible mark on me.

When Miss Morningstar was our 6th grade teacher, every Friday we would have game day. She'd pick a subject, most popular one was capitals of states, and she'd divide us up, A team and B team, and one side asked questions of the other. If you missed you had to sit down. We looked forward to that, and to this day I know all the capitals.

The school organized Halloween parades and May Day festivals, field days and picnics up at the recreation center on Norwood Drive, safety patrols and grade-level teas. Classes competed with each other in projects to beautify the grounds. The PTA held its meetings in the evenings, and soon Somerset had an unusual number of fathers involved.

Mrs. Bricker recalled that the"PTA Executive Committee for years met in the home of one of the officers. This was good. We took care of business and had a pleasant social

Somerset's first 5th and 6th grade class[59]

Mrs. Kathryne Bricker

time too—even a drink or two which was forbidden in the school building." Summer programs sponsored by the PTA began in 1935, and during WW II, victory gardens extended from Warwick Place to Dorset Avenue and the fathers built a log barricade in front of the first-floor windows to protect the shelter areas in case of air raids.

Along with the creation of the volunteer fire department in Bethesda, the school at Somerset helped loosen the ties those communities "down Wisconsin" had with Tenleytown and Georgetown. Although much of the shopping was still done in D.C. and that was where most people went to find work, the school made a difference. Some students even continued their education at the new high school in Bethesda.

Throughout the years the town government spent more time on streets, sidewalks, sewers and gutters than on all other topics combined. Occasionally another issue galvanized the Somersetters into action. In 1927 it was the noise of all-night stone cutting by the Fuller Construction Company on River Road. Letters and petitions did not get results and neither did an August mass meeting. With the coming of winter the problem seemed to disappear only to be replaced by the question of Kenwood.

At the council meeting of December 7, 1926, "Messers Chamberlain and Pissano, engineers, appeared and were given an opportunity at this time to explain the plans for improvement of the 200-acre tract west of Somerset owned by the Kennedy Brothers." The suggested improvements included a bridge over Willett Creek and the extension of Dorset about two miles to River Road. Kenwood's emissaries assured the Council that they planned to build houses on large lots costing about $20,000 and "that the deeds would be given to white people only."[60]

For the next year the town fathers regularly postponed the discussion of the Kenwood proposal and the extension of Dorset. In January

1928 Donal Chamberlin appeared again with two letters requesting the extension and paving of Dorset Avenue to the western boundary of the town. More delay ensued but in May the mayor was empowered to discuss Dorset's extension with representatives of the Kennedy-Chamberlin Development Company.

At the end of May the Council promulgated a proposed ordinance authorizing the paving of 583 feet of Dorset and assessing adjacent land owners the estimated $4,500 cost. At a hearing on June 11 Chamberlin explained his plans and answered questions. Despite a petition signed by forty residents who feared increased traffic and opposed the extension, the council adopted the ordinance and signed a contract with Kenwood.

The Town's engineer, Captain Cockey, formerly of the WSSC, hired young Horace Hampton, fresh out of the University of Maryland, to supervise the extension of Dorset Avenue and cope with Donal Chamberlin who was building the Kenwood side. Hampton, who knew the land from the time he roamed it and swiped pumpkins from the local farms as a boy, built to the specifications.

Here I was a kid right out of college, and he wasn't that much older but had been an engineer for some time. When the concrete trucks showed up and the mixture wasn't right, they tried to tell me it wouldn't matter. But I said, "Dump it. You live by the specifications." And they dumped it. You should have heard Donal Chamberlin scream.

It was not until February of the next year that Capt. Cockey pronounced the work completed and authorized payment.[61]

When the Council undertook the writing of a new book of regulations, there were disputes over whether or not the keeping of chickens really should be outlawed along with hunting within town limits. The building code, no home of less than 14,000 cubic feet was allowed, took up ten of the fourteen pages of ordinances. It was not until 1940 that Somerset outlawed the keeping cattle, horses, or swine, and in 1942 it made it unlawful to allow fowl to run at large.[62]

Along with the families in Friendship Heights, Somersetters kept ties with stores in Tenleytown and at Chevy Chase Circle for many years and seldom went up Wisconsin although some had their groceries delivered by Bethesda markets in the 1930s. A Saturday

ritual saw troops of kids tramping across the fields toward Chevy Chase Circle to raid Garrison's and Peoples and then loudly enjoy the matinee at the Avalon.

Marquis Childs, was likely Somerset's best known resident of the 1930s. He and his wife, Lou, bought 4901 Dorset, the house built for Dr. George Spencer, the USDA chemist, and his wife, Laura. The Childs remodeled the home to a more "modern" appearance and landscaped the adjoining lot. Murray Miles remembered the house. "I bicycled home from school past Childs' where an evil chow dog, a white dog with a black tongue, chased me every time I went past. It was never chained."

Childs wrote that the Town "seemed to me in many ways a typical American community. Its shaded streets with the overarching trees. The friendliness of neighbors. Yes, our town meetings and their direct democracy. The more I have lived there, the more I feel that Somerset sums up a great deal of the best that is America." And now, Mr. Childs told the readers of the *Record* in 1944, that rezoning threatened all of that.[63]

Walker Lith. & Pub. Co. Automobile Map 1909

Long before Kenwood's day, a small, vibrant African-American neighborhood lay west of Somerset centered on the River Road hill near the B&O tracks. The roots of this community may have rested in the homes of freed slaves for there is a dim memory of a "slave school" on the Loughborough land west of the road.

The Counselmans and the Shoemakers owned much of the land on the east side of the old road to Edward's Ferry. The 1860 census listed John Counselman as having seven slaves and two free blacks, William and Virginia Martin, working on his property. One of the Counselman slaves, Mary Ann Wood, worked for the Shoemakers. In 1873 the land records show that Counselman sold two-acre lots to John Burley and to Nelson Wood for $200 each. In 1900 the census taker enumerated a dozen black families in the area including the Browns, Jacksons, Rivers, Warrens, Burns, Robinsons, Burleys and four Wood households and about fifty people not counting the eight Willetts or Jacob Wilbert and his wife and servant.

Cleveland Clipper, born in 1908 and reared on River Road, spun out the family stories he heard from his father.

My father would tell me what his father, John Clipper, had told him. He came out of Hanover, Virginia, Louisa County. When he left down there it was `64, 1864. He was a slave, and the Union soldiers told him, "Boy, you're free," and put him on a steam ship to Baltimore. My father's father told him, "I tried my best to get in the quartermasters to help to steal stuff for the Union soldiers."

Anyhow he got to Potomac, Maryland, in the big woods, "Big Pines" they used to call it back there, and that's where he met his wife. She was from the Johnson family from over in what they called Beantown in Lincoln Park. His mother-in-law was a mid-wife with ten grandchildren. She took care of white and colored. She'd be up in Darnestown, and they'd tell her don't go home, the stork is

Cleveland Clipper

coming to my house. She'd be gone a couple of months.

My grandfather had something like thirteen children, right on that canal, out in Seneca where River Road ends. They lived down in there and had these gardens and raised hogs almost right in the river. He could get a load of wood for cutting a load of wood.

My father, Bill Clipper, worked on the canal, drove mules on that thing, worked on the canal boats. They went to Cumberland to get lime, and they would come from there right to George-town, 29th Street. He worked driving the mules, and they had cabins on the boat where they sleep at. They'd drive them mules four miles and then rest them, put them on and take off two more. When I was a kid, we used to see them every day hauling coal, hay, cordwood.

We moved from old Captain John to River Road. My father had his house built by a man named Zeke, a carpenter for the Agriculture De-partment at the experimental station. He built four or five houses in there. My father was the first Clipper that lived there. He came down there, in 1906 he told me.[64]

When I was young on River Road it was just one lane and there wasn't but about five fami-lies, the Duvalls, the Henrys, and the Woods, they was the oldest family there, Clippers, and Hawkins on Clipper Lane there. Wasn't no stores, no tele-phone, no electric, no sewage. When the house was built, Poppa dug the well and had the kitchen porch come out right over it so when you come out you could get everything right on the porch; had one of them pitcher pumps and a little, cutoff barrel to keep water in.

For many years the biggest business on that River Road hill was quarrying and finishing stone. Several companies worked in that area just as they did out at Seven Locks and Per-simmon Tree Roads. The quarry grew in the hillside to the west of the road and the finishing operations, for the most part, took place east of the road in the area later used by Briggs Clari-fier in World War II. Cleveland Clipper recalled the neighborhood quarry about the time of the First World War.

Albert Walker was quarrying rock for the Federal Government. He had some boys working for him exempted, keeping the tools sharp and watching out for this and that. They asked him to drive down to St. Marys, 90-some miles, in a Day-ton wagon with a horse and brought some boys

there that weren't old enough for the draft. They lived in a shanty. I got my hide whipped two or three times for being down there smoking.

Once I thought my poppa had gone to a prayer meeting when he came down there where we were smoking, and he knocked on the shanty door. I throwed my stump out there, and he caught it and put it out and carried it all the way to church and showed it to my mother. He didn't whip me, but I tell you my mother'd tear your tail up.

My father used to tell me, "Ain't you smoking?" I thought he could smell it. He'd say, "Sit down there a minute. You know I ain't always been a man." I hadn't given that no thought; he was a man when I came. "I used to chew tobacco on the sly," he said. "You know how I kept it? I'd bore a hole in the back and put it around my neck and slip it down in my bosom." I said, "How you think I'm smoking?" He say, "I picked your hand up and looked at your fingers." My eyes got as big as that pan. He'd searched me when I was sleeping. He had a big laugh and said, "I been a boy. You can't fool an old man; he's been up the same road you're coming up."

The shanty was on other side of River Road down near the railroad tracks. Walker's quarry was around there. They dug rock out till they struck water. It was grey granite. We used to go up there on Sunday and watch them polishing it. The ones too old for the draft, they was the bosses, all colored bosses in that stone quarry. Mr. Walker lived down on Cleveland Avenue in Cleveland Park. He had a son, named Albert, too, that built houses in Green Acres. He was a big time sport and womanizer. I see stone in a lot of cemeteries like that stone.

They pumped water out of the holes, but it got so bad they had to stop quarrying rock. My brother, closest to me, like to got drowned there. My father was going to show him how to swim, and he was sitting on the edge and slipped off and went way out in that thing. My father went down, and he couldn't catch hold of him and went back down, and he got a hold of him. Since then he ain't been in no more water than you use washing your face, this was William.

It was forty feet deep, and they say still wa-ter is hard to swim in. They had ladders that went all the way down, but the pumps couldn't keep the water out.

This old man Henry Jackson, that's where he lived, in an old slave cabin, built stout, nice and warm inside. He had a big white mustache. Then, after a while, more people moved there. All those

that lived on Clipper's Lane, Mr. Hawkins, Mr. Coleman, Issac Clipper, Cleve Clipper, Bill Clipper, they were working for the government. My uncle and them were working at the Naval Observatory. The uncle I'm named after worked at the District Property Yard. I worked down there cleaning lanterns. They walked over Willard Avenue to catch the streetcar, about a 12-13 minute walk.

Where the buses go around, it was a hole, with a little green station there where one track went to Rockville. They had that hole stay there till they filled it up with trash, a dump. That hole was big enough to put three or four of these houses in, where all them stores are built up there, a regular dump. We used to go out there and sell balls to Miller at Wisconsin and Western. We'd fool around at the driving range and find some balls. This Miller was a tall man. They said he hit the longest ball off the tee than anybody else, that's what _he_ said. Up there a ways was Kirkside, a woman's club, between Belt Road and Kirkside Drive, but men used to play there, too. It didn't come down as far as the dump. I used to cut school and go over there and caddy, make twenty-five cents, but I was scared of that because if my father found I missed one day, you look out, boy!

I went to school at Fort Reno in Tenleytown, and I went to a Maryland school right there in the house where the Woods raised their family. They leased that to Counselman. I think he was a Commissioner, and he sold everything to the schools, coal and wood and chalk and stuff like that. Frank Wood had three brothers, Dan, Alonzo, Andrew Wood. They was the oldest family on River Road. The county rented the house where Andrew and Lilly raised Margaret, George and Mary Wood for the first school, on the right hand side going north. The school on the Loughborough property was a slave school. My aunt went to school there, my mother's sister, Stella.

Old man Loughborough he was a magistrate. I worked over there when people from Chicago bought that old home place, Mordecai Ezekiel. They had it remodeled. He was an advisor to Henry Wallace. He was a Arab, too, see. He'd work the shit out of you.[65]

I went to River Road School first, where the Woods had leased it, then to Tenleytown, old Fort Reno school. When they built Alice Deal down there, they moved our church to make room for the road. I went to school down there to the 6th grade, and then my father bought a team of horses, and I went to driving them. He said you can go to school at night, but following that horse around digging

them cellars — we dug most all of them cellars on Fessenden Street for a fellow named Johnny Skinner. We plowed it with two horses and then scooped it out, scoop held a quarter of a yard, called a slip pan —time you get done throwing that back in and out, you didn't want to go nowhere but bed. He was paying us two dollars and half a day. I was about 13. I was doing a man's work, but I didn't know how to hook them up, but I liked horses see. People do go to night school but they ain't following this thing around and around and around eight hours a day. Sometimes you'd almost go to sleep in the hot sun, and July them horseflies were on you, too. My father bought some horses afterwards. We had a shed out back behind the pump. Poppa bought them for me. I took them down to the branch across the tracks where the Rivers lived.[66]

The County built a school on River Road, and my younger brother went to school there. They had a teacher there named Miss Bundy, and I think Miss Ford was the first one, a big six-foot woman. The school was just one floor with a flat top like a shed and a basement to keep things in. Another teacher was Miss Howard, and Margaret Wood was the last one.

It was nice inside, and the County dug a well right on that school ground. My uncle used to live over there. John Garrett, who owned that place after my uncle died, he owned down to the branch, but he had to leave a road for the funerals to take bodies up there to that graveyard, to the left of that school toward Westover, it was all high. They moved them bones to Lincoln Park. I had a brother and grandmother and uncle buried there. When they dug them hills out to make Westover, they dumped all that dirt in there, they were paid for that. Kenwood got some of that dirt, too. I worked for them people, cleaning out along Brookside Drive.

The cemetery belonged to the Moses Lodge; they was in charge of that. One branch of it was in Number 10, just across Cabin John Bridge, one of them old houses. They gave $50 at their death. It came from Howard Street in Tenleytown, started down there years ago. Old Moses Hall was at 28th and Dumbarton in Georgetown first, like Masonic, like the Elks or Masons, but had men and women in it.

The 1910 census showed that about thirty black families of widely varying sizes lived on or near that part of River Road, many included in-laws, other relatives or boarders. Based on

the census and other documents such as Cald-well's *Directory*, eighty adults and fifty children seems a reasonable estimate of the neighborhood's population.

For the 1912-13 school year, the River Road Colored School was opened in a rented building on the Loughborough property. For many years one principal-teacher taught more than forty students in what had been a farm shed. In 1914-15 the school board expended $269.30 including the teacher's salary, $14.50 for fuel, $3.80 for "sanitary expenses and incidentals," and $11 for books on fifty-nine students. The trustees of the River Road school for 1916-17 were Frank Wood, Cleveland Clipper, and Peter C. Harriss. In 1919 the parents offered to build a new school house to replace the decrepit rented one if the Board would supply $60 for materials. The parents were ignored.

In 1924 the school board purchased a site on the west side of River Road and built a school for a total of $5,390. This "colored" school on River Road remained in operation until integration and was used as a community center for a variety of activities. In 1931 the principal-teacher was Maud Howard and her assistant Margaret Wood, and by school year 1939-40, seventy-five students attended the River Road school.

To Cleveland Clipper the community seemed filled with relatives, and he remembered most of his other neighbors as well.

Frank Wood was an excavator. He had horses and dug cellars. I used to work for him, and he owes me eighteen dollars now. I dasn't sass him cause he'd whip me.

My father worked at the experimental farm and Cleveland Clipper, my uncle, worked at the experimental farm, too, and went from there to the District property yard until he retired. My uncle Ike worked at the Naval Observatory, drove the big admiral around; he was a coachman. One of the neighbors was Edward Turner, lived next door to us, another was the Burleys. Now Octavia Burley, she was some kind of Muscovie Indian. They was black but they still were Indians. The Burns, they were my mother's kin, too.

Sarah Rivers was some kin. From slave time everybody was kin. We called most everybody aunt this and uncle that. Henry Jackson, he was a short, older man; he said his master was Booker Washington. William Brooks and his half-brother Dave Hawkins worked at the experimental farm. They all lived on River Road.

On the other side there was just one house, a man named Frank Matthews. Fanny Matthews she used to make bread; she had a little store so you didn't have to go clear to the District Line to get a loaf, but it was hard stuff, like hardtack. He worked at the experimental farm, and they found out after he died that he hadn't married her.

Cassius Parker, they were kin to my mother; I called him Uncle Cash. At the railroad tracks lived a lady named Della Turner. William

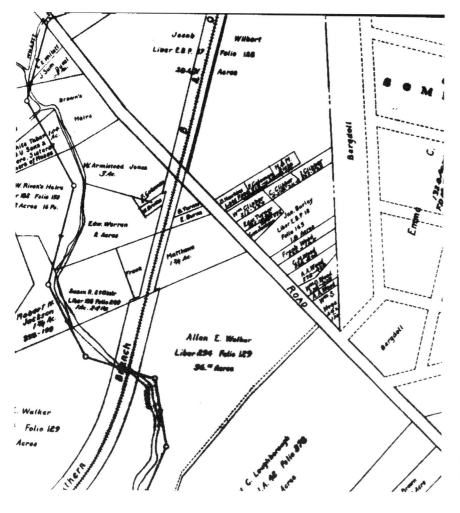

Brown lived across the tracks. He was older than Uncle Henry Jackson. He lived in the slave house up there across from Wilbert Yakum (Jacob Wilbert) that sold him that ground.[67]

"Yakum" owned it. All Loughborough ground was on the other side of the road. This side was Yakum and Shoemakers. They was kin to this Yakum. They were German or something, too. Wilbert, his wife was buried up there. As you're going north before the tracks there's a big place where they cut the stones for the Washington Cathedral. I had a job in there, helping stack them. All that ground there belonged to one German from where we lived, where that church is, clean down to Little Falls Road.[68]

His name was "Wilbur Yahcum," a one-eyed German, looked like the Kaiser. He couldn't see very good, but if you'd go down there to get ten cents worth of something, like turnips or a head of cabbage, old man Yakum would take your quarter and feel in his bag of pennies and dimes. You couldn't cheat him. He would put it in his mouth and feel them to get the right size.

By the time of the census of 1920, the little community had contracted to eighteen African-American families including thirty-seven children of school age or younger. That census also showed that 86-year-old James Loughborough, his 79-year-old wife and three adult children were still on their property and that Jacob Wilbert, age 77, lived alone in the middle of the black neighborhood. Two generations of the white Willett family were listed as one household in that census.

In the Twenties Cleveland Clipper and his brothers got new neighbors on the other side of their family lane.

Hatton was a hostler at the Naval Obser-

The Hattons' home

vatory. That house was a Sears and Roebuck house they put together, the biggest one on River Road. His brother-in-law did all the cement work and putting that house together. He was a smart feller. Hatton started out hauling for Piggly Wiggly and A &P, had a truck, stake body with a canvas over it.

He drove from Washington up to West Virginia and places like that, made good money out of it, and later got another bigger truck and got his wife's brother to help him. I remember him saying, "I can stop working now and spend a dollar a day as long as I live." They came out from around 35th and O, belonged to Mt. Zion, the oldest church in Georgetown.

Gerald, his son, the youngest one, anything in arithmetic, he can run through it like a chicken picking up corn. They smart like their uncle.

Gerald Hatton remembered River Road and his neighbors, too:

My parents moved there, I'd say, in 1922. I was born in 1921 at Georgetown Hospital. My father's name was Pinckney C. Hatton Senior. He was hauling for A&P; they used private trucks at that time, from the warehouse to the store. That's where I got some of my Social Security as a teenager. We left the stuff on the street in front of the stores in those day, imagine! He did that for a long time until they put a tax on A&P in this area, and they closed the stores in the District.

River Road was just two lanes, and then they put cement shoulders on the sides. He had the house built for him, two-story with four bedrooms. It was a big house, had a coal furnace and then later oil. It was about the largest one out there. Had a big lot in the back where he kept his trucks. My mother had a store on the property, she told me. I can't remember.

There was a well with a hand pump. We had to heat water for a big tub, but we had indoor plumbing later. We had outhouses first. We raised chickens and hogs, and one of our neighbors had a cow. I remember when people made white corn liquor during Prohibition, and they used to hide that stuff in my father's basement. We made home brew, beer.

After A&P, well, he'd always had some other trucks for moving and things like that, and he had hired help. That's why I studied business; I guess I was ten or twelve when I was typing and doing payroll. After A&P went out, he had dump trucks. That was a good business for five or six

years, and then he went into cabs. That's what he did until he died. Basically he hauled the maids and the children. He did that up until his eighties.

You had to cross the railroad tracks to get to school. The tracks go on down to Georgetown, K Street. We used to hop that train, and we walked the tracks to Bethesda. The school was wooden, two rooms on the same floor. The teacher's name was Maud Howard; Margaret Wood came later. Miss Howard taught us up through the seventh grade, and we couldn't bring any funny grades home either.

Sometimes we carried a lunch, and sometimes we walked home. There wasn't any kitchen until later. They had two outhouses, for boys and for girls. Our desks were where three kids could sit, bench type, and the top opened up. We had one row of single desks. In the center was a round, pot-bellied stove. It was a wood stove, but eventually we got coal, kept it down in the basement. The school was used for all kinds of meetings.

The teacher, she lived in the city. Sometimes when the weather was bad, my parents would pick her up and bring her to school. She taught both my brothers and me. I was the youngest. Just had one teacher all those years. We had about four or five per grade, I guess about thirty-five kids most of the time. They came from Glen Echo, Potomac, Cabin John; bus brought those kids down. Those off Massachusetts Avenue and in Bethesda walked, walked the tracks.

A lot of them, that was all their training. There were some poor children. It was the end of school for many kids. They were old enough to work, some of them. Some would start to school in the District with new clothes and all, but by October and November, they couldn't keep it up. They couldn't dress, kids would laugh at them.

D.C. schools, even segregated, were better quality than the system in Maryland. And it was easier than going to Rockville. I finished 7th grade about `32. We walked to Wisconsin and Western and had three-cent tickets for the streetcar. It was illegal to go to D.C. schools without paying tuition, but we used friends' addresses in Tenleytown. By the time we finished, they used the correct address, but it didn't matter.

Francis Junior High School in Georgetown was new at that time. We had chemical labs, science; I learned to type in the 8th grade. We walked Willard Avenue at night to get home from school. I skipped grades at River Road and went to Howard at 16.

We played all over that neighborhood. We had skateboards, take a pair of skates and put them on a board, right on River Road, and sleigh riding. We had good hills. We used to roll up snow and make a jump and run two sleds together. One of the Christian family was killed sleigh riding. His brother Richard was my best buddy; I called him Puddin. We didn't have any hospital or ambulance, no fire department. People's homes burnt up. They were wooden and once they caught on fire all people could do is just get outside and watch.

The stone quarry, there used to be a grave yard back in there, it was a dangerous hole, but we used to play there. I was afraid of it. We used to walk through the woods over to Massachusetts Avenue or Glen Echo and went fishing in that creek and so-called swimming until it got polluted. It was an open sewer.

I caddied at Kenwood, got fifty cents for nine, a dollar for eighteen. We knew people that would tip. They used first-come-first-served. They had what we called a caddy pen. If you got there early and put your name on the list, then they went by your name unless someone called for you special. Had a caddy master, Al Jamison, I think. It was the only course where they let Japanese play. The caddies played on Monday morning, free, until 12 o'clock. Kenwood wasn't but nine holes, then they expanded across River Road.

The big boys pushed the little ones around. They gambled, smoked but not pot, shot craps. All that was a learning experience. A lot of caddies came from the city. They had a bus, and Congressional had trucks to pick them up at the District Line, and a lot of them walked.

Some people called the River Road community "Crow Hill," and Gerald Hatton said, smiling, "There were a lot of crows there sometimes." It had two institutions, other than the school, which spread its fame beyond the Seventh Election District. One was a semi-pro baseball team and the other was a beer joint. Hatton and his older neighbor, Cleve Clipper, remembered both of them.

Gerald Hatton:

The River Road Lions started when I was about 14 or15 . I remember because they wouldn't let me play in high school because I was consided a semi-pro. We got a little money, wasn't much; the winner got 60 percent and the loser got forty.

They had a team before, that had patched

up uniforms, but ours was the first to have "River Road Lions" on it. To raise money they had a dance and other things. We had to pay for the uniform, and we bought our own gloves. We got money for equipment at the game, by playing. Passed the hat around. We would travel in one of my Dad's vans to Rockville, Gaithersburg.

I played left field all the time. Milton Matthews was our catcher; Richard Christian, his brother-in-law, was a pitcher. My brother Roosevelt played first base. Dutch Matherson played second base. We had Lorenzo Price from Tenleytown, some lived in Scotland.

Cleveland Clipper was a member of the older team as he recalled:

The ballfield was right between where that George A. Fuller Company was and then the Hot Shoppe took over, in between that. The ballfield belonged to Albert Walker, the stone man. They had old Ford trucks to haul them stones, flat body with chain drive. We could play ball there, but they didn't want us to cut the sod off; it was good clover and stuff.

We had a team, the River Road Lions, in the late `20s and early `30s. We went all up in there, to Olney, Maryland, and Mt. Zion. They had a diamond up there like they got at Griffith Stadium almost, with a scoreboard in the outfield. We played down in Georgetown, 37th and Prospect, and way out on 61st Street at Huntsville.

I was a back catcher and knocked my knee out of place. One of the pitchers was Richard Christian. He's a preacher now. I showed him how to throw a curve ball, and I taught him in Sunday school, too.

At that time there were families around there that wanted a team, like Mr. Hatton and my father and Frank Woods. We used to have lawn parties, cooking pigs feet and potato salad on the diamond. The mothers would do this while their sons were playing ball, and then we got money from Mr Hatton and two or three men who liked ball; the Christians would donate, too.

Then we'd go play ball for fifty dollars, and if we won that, we had a hundred now. We put up the money because we thought we could beat them, but we got fooled once or twice. It was winner-take-all. One team's umpire called the strikes and the other ran the bases.

Neither Mr. Clipper nor Mr. Hatton remembered Willie Smith's Sugar Bowl fondly, but it was the other institution that spread the fame of Crow Hill. Hatton said, "That's where I learned what not to do." Cleveland Clipper wryly recalled the place, and Willie Smith.

The Smiths came from Frederick with Dr. Perry. He brought them down here. Willie Smith was the chauffeur for Dr. Perry. Anything he done, Dr. Perry give it to him. He was the Commissioner; he could get you out of it, then Bob Hagner after that. Dr Perry built a hospital up there with Dr. Bauersfield, built a hospital for himself for special treatment right next to the station house, and he brought some people from Frederick, John Russell and his wife, and another one they called Bo Peep, they worked down there.

Milton Smith replaced Willie as the driver, and when Dr. Perry was so big, they would give the police a whole lot of lip, but when Dr. Perry died, they didn't even allow them in the liquor store in Bethesda, that's the truth. They wouldn't let them in the coffee spot by the railroad bridge to get nothing to eat.

Willie bootlegged, but my father helped him out with that beer garden. He had a little store, like a convenience store, and they gambled in the back, maybe three, four hundred dollars in the pot, all against the law. This was up on Bethesda Avenue.

I said, "Poppa, he's not going to be a community merchant. His business is whiskey and gambling." He opened it in the `30s, and he had a lunchroom first. He bought that River Road bungalow, the last house before you cross the railroad, for the mortgage. The same man that built ours built it. The man that had it built couldn't keep the mortgage up. He lost an eye working. He got $2,200 for losing that eye, but he couldn't get a job with one eye.

There was a fellow living on River Road, he came from down in North Carolina, and he had killed a boy. This was Bill Smith's right arm, his muscle man, big, tall, half nuts. He could hit you with his fist and knock you out, if you tried to cheat playing poker.

Smith's caused trouble because we got the people after other places closed up at 12 o'clock, and they come to River Road and stay to two, four o'clock in the morning. They'd come out there and cut that ball diamond up on those muddy nights. They'd come out and had wide open sex parties out there. They'd pick up gals and bring them out there. Dr. Perry was behind it. He give the police them jobs. He could put you back on the street walking or take the job away from you.

Bill Smith was going to help give us some money when I got the ball diamond to draw some crowds out there because Scotland always brought a big gang down when they came. Drinking beer, the rooters they stayed in the beer garden, and when they do come out they couldn't see the ball. But the beer was good, and they had whiskey, too.

"They sold it after hours," Gerald Hatton said.

And the guys were out on the street shooting crap. My parents were among those that were really concerned, working people trying to raise a family. I went down there, and learned how to dance. It was about as big as the house, had a bar in the back and booths on both sides and a juke box. It was open late every night. He paid off too many people, even police officers. They did a lot of fighting down there.

Saturday nights sometimes got a little noisy. Colonel McAuliffe remembered that when he was a young Bethesda policeman, the Sugar Bowl was one of the places he visited to with some regularity on hot summer weekends.

Said Charlie Hughes who lived nearby:

When you went by there on Saturday night, I mean that place was jumping. I used to feel so sorry for the kids that lived there. They had to walk from Crow Hill to Wisconsin and Western to get a bus or streetcar to go to school.

When the Kenwood and Wood Acres communities formed citizens' associations, one of their first areas of concern was Willie Smith's noisy tavern, and they began putting pressure on the County to close him down. In April 1937 the Montgomery County Liquor Control Board, after hearing from the Congressional Country Club and Keystone Auto Club as well as from Kenwood and other local communities, refused to renew Willie E. Smith's beer license. This action was overturned at the state level, and the Sugar Bowl continued to operate in its usual lively manner. The Fusionists had temporary control of the County government, but the Brooke Lee machine still operated smoothly at the State level, and Dr. Benjamin Perry was Lee's Bethesda lieutenant.

Bill Austin recalled the Sugar Bowl from the time he was Chevy Chase's one-man police force. "Dr. Perry used to go over there at election time to make a speech," he said. "Once when he reminded them he'd gotten them a school bus, one guy jumped up and yelled that it was just an old Model T."

Austin often rode late at night with one of the Bethesda officers.

I went there once with Ernie Thompson, backing him up. A guy had emptied the Sugar Bowl, and when one guy was tough enough to do that; well, the owner of it was a rough man. This big black guy was there with his head down on the table, and the customers were all outside. So Ernie put handcuffs on him and then yelled, "Get up you so-and-so," and we took him away.

Women from this small neighborhood worked as nannies, maids and cooks in many homes in Friendship Heights and Somerset, some as live-in servants and many as day-workers. The men found jobs at the nearby quarry and at the USDA experiment station. Many of the construction laborers who dug the basements and raised the walls of homes "down Wisconsin" came from the community some called Crow Hill.

The Posey home on River Road

Just a little farther north on River Road, past the railroad tracks and George A. Fuller's noisy stone works, Willett Creek crossed River Road. For many years the large Willett family lived near the creek on both sides of the road, and when the *Star*'s Rambler visited the area in 1915 they had long resided in an old tavern called the Spinning Wheel. According to Shannon, the tavern had been there "a good many years before the coming of the American Revolution" and was the subject of much interest among local "antiquarians." The head of the family at that time was Jehu Willett and his wife was the daughter of Rachel Shoemaker and Thomas Dean and a direct descendant of the tavern's 1775 owner and of the Shoemakers who had been in the area almost as long. She recalled when the tavern had been very busy

and there were trains of wagons on River Road. On the left side of the next hill the Rambler visited the steep-roofed, grey-stone house known as the old Posey place and noticed the cluster of white buildings belonging to a dairy farmer named Hardy on the right.[69]

Cleveland Clipper said he remembered:

> *Ed Willetts, trash collector, he lived where you turn into Kenwood off River Road, Brookside Drive, but he didn't own it. Dick Willett, his son, had a trash route. The creek was where they gave their horses water. We used to go down and dam it up and swim in it and drag along the bottom. I guess that's why I never learned how to swim, crawling the bottom. I had to lie to my children sometimes.*

And Gerald Hatton also knew the family. "That's where I learned to play golf, at Kenwood. I knew the Willett boys. They lived a quarter of mile down from Kenwood. We caddied together." Like the Worshams from Cabin John, the Willetts turned out to be some of the Bethesda area's best young golfers.

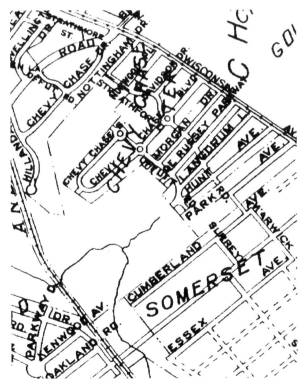

Section of unidentified local real estate map ca. 1933

General Richard C. Drum entered the United States Army in 1846 as a private in Company K, 1st Pennsylvania Infantry, and retired from the Army in 1889 after nine years as its adjutant general. After serving with Scott in the Mexican War and spending most of his military career on the Western frontier, then-Captain Drum accompanied General Sumner to California in 1861 to replace secession-minded leaders in that area. Drum spent the Civil War there fighting the Indians and trying to keep peace with the Mormons.

His wife, Lavina, daughter of Gibbs Morgan of Baton Rouge, bore him a daughter, Henrietta, while they were living in San Francisco. The Drums also adopted young Susan Drum, daughter of the captain's brother, an artillery officer killed on the last day of the Mexican War. It may have been his in-law's well-known Southern sympathies that kept him in the West, but he did well there for both the Union and himself. When he left California in 1866, deeply invested in mineral rights, the grateful citizens paid his debts and presented him with a gift of $30,000.

After the war, he served under Meade and Sheridan, and in 1880 became Adjutant General and moved from I Street to a more fashionable K Street home between 15th and 16th. His neighbors included General Sherman, Mr. Corcoran, Governor Shepherd, and Mr. Riggs. *The Republic* found the front room on the second floor of his new, brick home very interesting:

> *It is furnished wholly in old mahogany — I don't know how many hundreds of years old — handed down from Mrs. Drum's ancestors. From the grand old bedstead with its immense high posts and canopy to the "dresser" and "chest of drawers," the old-fashioned brass mounted bureau and table and the queer chairs, it looks more like an old picture than a modern chamber. In this room hang many portraits of Mrs. Drum's ancestors. One, a picture of her father, is particularly interesting. It was in the family mansion at Baton Rouge, Louisiana, and when the Union army reached that city the mansion was sacked, mostly by old servants of the family. The portrait referred to is full of bayonet holes.*

Susan Drum Tarr, "Trudie" in the family, a 29-year-old widow in 1880, moved quickly into fashionable Washington circles. Less than a year later President Arthur attended the wedding of Blossom, as the 18-year-old Henrietta

was called, to Henry J. Hunt Jr. The groom, anchor man in his class at the Naval Academy, was the son of Meade's famed artillery commander at Gettysburg, and his first wife, a DeRussey. Generals Hunt and Drum were also friends as well as Army compatriots.[70]

Henry and Henrietta had two sons, Richard Coulter Drum Hunt in 1883 and Henry J. Hunt III in 1885. Their father died of tuberculosis in 1886 after having been lost for almost two years during the second Arctic expedition seeking the Greely party. Blossom and her children moved back in with her father. The General's wife, "one of the most accomplished and popular ladies in refined Washington society," and her two stylish daughters cannot have been altogether happy when the general told them of his plans to move out of the city after his retirement.[71]

He decided that the farm at Friendship, which later became the McLean estate, was not far enough out in the county for his retirement home and, despite his wife's protests about the wilderness he was taking her to, bought the southern half of Bradley Davidson's Bethesda property, some 212 acres, for $15,000. He built a 20-room house, including two inside bathrooms, on the crest of a gentle hill, laid down an impressive wine cellar, named the place "Langdrum," (his mother's people were the Langs), installed his multi-layered family plus seven live-in servants, and then looked around for something to keep himself busy.

He took on, without pay, the nominal presidency of the recently reorganized Tenleytown and Rockville trolley line and saw it through to completion at Bethesda Park, in which he also invested. His business associates included C. C. Glover of Riggs Bank, Robert Weaver of Washington Gas, and John E. Beall, the real director of the electric railway. The general settled down to the life of a gentleman farmer and said that he was "learning to be a good neighbor." He continued to work with the American Mutual Aid Association, which he had helped found and of which he was president for twenty years, and he was also active in the Aztec Club for Mexican War veterans and in the Loyal Legion.

The census of 1900 found 75-year-old Richard Drum at home with his wife, 68; Susan Tarr, 50; Richard C. Hunt, 16; Harry Hunt, 13; Margaret and Marion Oliphant, seven and five (re-married Henrietta's children by Hughes Oliphant whom she divorced); four female servants, two black male servants, a white farm laborer, and an Irish boarder and his wife. At the end of 1900 General Drum had some sort of disagreement with his insurance company and refused to renew the policy on his home. Before he could venture downtown and have a new policy written by another company, his mansion was destroyed by a fire, which began near the furnace on the night of February 14, 1901.

Home and Contents Lost — The residence of Gen. R. C. Drum, on the Georgetown and Rockville turnpike north of the District line, was Thursday night of last week totally destroyed by fire. The flames were discovered about 11 o'clock by Mrs. Drum as she was about to retire for the night, the other members of the family having already gone to their rooms. Mrs. Drum saw smoke coming up the stairway from the cellar, and she at once aroused the people in the house. Her prompt action proved to be fortunate, for it was only by the greatest haste that the members of the family were able to get out of the burning building.

The fire made such headway that the occupants were obliged to leave with only the scantiest apparel, and it was impossible to save the contents. Those in the neighborhood were aroused by the light of the burning building, and a telephone message was sent to Georgetown for a fire engine, which soon afterward arrived on the scene, but little could be done, and the fire burned itself out.[72]

Beer and real estate baron Christian Heurich put the family up at his hilltop Tennallytown Inn while Drum rebuilt the house on a somewhat less grand scale. In 1903, to recoup his losses, he decided to subdivide some of his land and sell some lots. As in Somerset, many of the first buyers in Drummond purchased two lots and developed large gardens in the side yards next to their sturdy, Victorian homes.

The San Francisco earthquake and fire of 1906 was also a disaster for the General who had invested in a mutual fire insurance company that assessed its members heavily to cover its losses. The sale of building lots accelerated. The General also presented each of his grandsons with a large lot and a house when they married. Dick's home was at the Wisconsin Avenue end of what came to be Hunt Avenue and Henry's on Langdrum Lane.

The Latimers were one of the first families to move into Drummond. Henry Latimer recalled, "Some of the happiest moments of my

boyhood were when I could ride behind the saddle on Gen. Drum's horse, with the reins in the hands of the general's faithful employee Mack, as we rode to the store-post office to get our mail." Mr. Latimer also fondly remembered his parents ordering ice cream from Stohlman's in Georgetown. It "came packed in a metal box, surrounded by salted ice, all contained in a wooden bucket. The motorman put this off at the Drummond stop where we lived. Some members of my family would meet the trolley to pick it up, usually using my hand-drawn wagon as a carrier."[73]

General Drum died in 1909, and his growing subdivision and other properties then passed to his widow, Lavina Morgan Drum, in whose name the plat map of Drummond had been drawn. "Momanee," as the General's wife was called, died in June of 1912. The property was left in trust for Susan Tarr and was not divided or developed until after her death in 1926.

Drummond, all three blocks and forty-three houses of it, became a special taxing district in 1916. It took over its own street repair and trash removal with a three member council headed by a "mayor." Its concrete street, which ended at the top of the hill, and its smooth sidewalks made it the favorite location for young roller skaters for many years and still mark the division between the township and the county. Dogs and cats may roam freely, but the town has rules against allowing "any horse, mule, swine, cow or other cattle" wandering about. Debate over adding the fourth block at the "bottom of the hill" has been just about the only continuing issue in Drummond's very local politics.[74]

North of Drummond, after the General's estate was finally settled, the Hunt brothers began developing the farm property. Richard C. D. Hunt built a number of fairly modest houses on Hunt Avenue in the late 1920s. His brother, Henry, paralyzed from the waist down by polio since 1910 when his infant son was stricken and Hunt slept with him to comfort the child, set about having somewhat larger homes raised on Langdrum Lane. In 1928 they filed subdivision plats for two sections of Chevy Chase Gardens, the first ending at Stratford and the second just past Offutt Road. The Hunts sold some land to Morris Cafritz, who had come a long way from his bowling alley start, and to Jacob Shapiro,

"Builder of Homes" and successor to Slye & Watson. Much of this land was later repurchased in the spring of `29 as the real estate market boomed in the hectic months before the stock market crash. That property became the third section of Chevy Chase Gardens and included the somewhat smaller lots laid out on Morgan Drive and DeRussey Parkway.[75]

The first blocks were extra long and they preserved the old home on the hill between Hunt and Langdrum for several years. The lots on Wisconsin remained vacant in the hope that the property might go commercial. Eventually teams of mules dragged the General's house, with its wing cut off, through the woods to Wisconsin Avenue where it served as an inn and later a tourist home. From 1930 on, Henry P. Kerner operated the Chevy Chase Inn at 6208 Wisconsin Avenue. He began by charging a dollar a night for a room and bragged that his front door had never been locked. The Hunts cut the site of the old house into six, large building lots.

For a number of years, tenant farmers had grown crops on much of the General's property, some of which was leased to the Department of Agriculture. Hay, alfalfa, oats, and corn were rotated in the fields. J. Conway Hunt, Henry's younger son, used what became DeRussey Parkway as a landing strip for the single-place Aeronica he bought for $300 after he learned to fly out at Congressional Airfield. He kept the plane in the shed where he had stabled the boyhood pony his father bought from Bethesda fireman George Gummel.

When the bottom dropped out of the real estate market, the crash wiped out the Hunts' development. The debacle caught Henry Hunt with a number of half finished houses, especially in section 3, and a collection of notes he had endorsed to finance their construction. The Hunts sold off the rest of their property, and Henry Hunt tried to pay off the Tuoheys, Oldfields, Gummels and other workers who had been building his houses. His own home had to be sold, and Conway Hunt recalled, "It practically killed my mother when that house was auctioned off." Conway's sister bought a lot on the corner of Wisconsin and DeRussey, but the creditors took the rest.

Depressed, Harry Hunt went back to his hobby of raising show chickens and fancy pigeons. Horace Hampton recalled, "He and I raised chickens and went to fairs when I was a

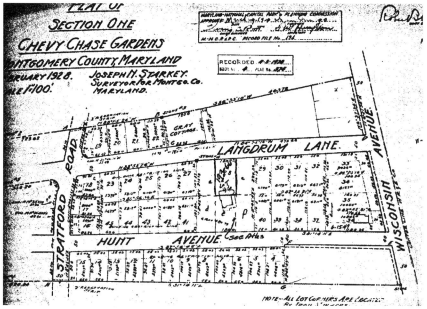

1928 plat map showing the location of General Drum's house

kid and showed our chickens. I could make more money out of a cock or hen by showing them than you could raising a dozen chickens."

Later the County's Democratic "boss," Brooke Lee, gave him a job as an assessor in a "dismal little office" in the Courthouse. He rose as part of the Lee machine to become a County commissioner and for three terms Judge of the Orphans Court. A few remember Hunt from those days as something of a poet.[76]

The first Davidson in Bethesda was John , a direct descendant of James Davidson, a member of the Maryland Line in the Revolution who, according to family tradition, was with Washington when he crossed the Delaware. John Davidson was an extremely successful merchant who came to Georgetown in 1814 and became a partner of Francis Dodge Senior and Junior in the wholesale grocery business. They owned at least two ships and in 1860 constructed a successful flour mill later operated by Tenney and Son. Davidson built a summer home on a large farm he had purchased from John Marbury in 1839. It was diagonally across from the chapel of St. John's, Norwood Parish, and directly across the Pike from the Dodge property which eventually became the golf course of Chevy Chase Club.

John Davidson, one-time president of the Washington and Rockville Turnpike, sired twelve children at his home at 28th and N Streets. The first son and fourth child was James Henry Davidson, born 1828, who became a doctor. By the time of the 1860 census, Dr. Davidson, his young wife and semi-retired father were ensconced on the Bethesda farm, "Montrose," where they entertained the Moores from the other side of Bethesda and where the doctor remained until his death in 1886.

The doctor's wife, Sarah Slater Bradley, daughter of Henry whose farm was on the other end of Jackson Road (Bradley Lane) at Chevy Chase, bore him five children; two daughters who died in infancy and three sons: Henry Bradley, John Cumpston, and James Slater. Dr. Davidson was a vestryman at St. John's, but his wife was active in the Presbyterian church.[77]

H. Bradley Davidson, who tore down most of his grandfather's house and built a new home on the same site with more room for entertaining, was born in 1860, educated at Hunt's Academy and then graduated from Princeton University in 1880. He gained a law degree from Columbian in 1882 and founded the real estate firm of Davidson & Davidson with his younger brother John the next year.

By the turn of the century, he had become a gentleman farmer noted for his horsemanship and his investments and was developing a reputation as something of a ladies' man. In the spring of 1900 he and his brother moved their active business into the newly constructed Davidson Building at 1413 G Street, N.W., and profited from financing improvements in older structures and from the construction of office buildings and homes such the row houses on S Street between 19th and 20th.

He bought one of the most notable early cars in Bethesda, a red Stutz Bearcat with which he regularly frightened the carriage horses at the Presbyterian church and supposedly decreased egg production all over town. Davidson sold about half of his Bethesda farmland to General Drum and leased and then later sold another large portion to the Department of Agriculture before he became deeply involved in the Bradley Hills venture.

H. Bradley Davidson's daughter Louise remembered being sent down the lane by her mother to wait for the trolley and pick up the groceries the conductor would have for her. She said her mother was shocked when she learned that the Rockville road was going to be renamed Wisconsin Avenue because "that was just a dirty little street coming out of Georgetown and didn't deserve to be called an avenue." The Davidson's sold the last of their land in 1924 and moved to Edgemoor and a large home that took up the western half of the block of Fairfax Road between Edgemoor and Moorland. Louise accompanied her parents and lived on in the house after their deaths.[78]

Davidson Drive was developed quite early in the boom of the 1920s with the first four homes completed, most with extra lots, in 1922. Much of the rest of the property and what had been the Hunts' land was used for less expensive and less grand houses built from the mid-thirties on. George W. DeFranceaux, founding president of the local Junior Chamber of Commerce, built many of them as the head of the Permanent Homes Company.

Edward Gauvreau and his wife moved to their new home behind the Davidson house at 4901 Chevy Chase Boulevard in April of 1936 when only a few other houses in that area had been finished. There was, he said, a lull in building about them. He paid $6,750 for his brick home and got a mortgage at two and a half percent.

He and his wife were both D.C. natives and moved to the suburbs from an apartment in Northeast. "Ed," asked his worried wife, echoing many women from a generation earlier, "why are you taking me way out here in the country?" That first summer he thought he had made a terrible mistake when he and his wife could not see through their screened door because it was covered with flies from the USDA farm just across the way.

The first major government installation in Bethesda, other than the Civil War forts and the post office that moved from one general store to another, was the Department of Agriculture's Animal Disease Research Station operated by the Bureau of Animal Industry. It moved its operations to eighteen acres leased from Bradley Davidson in July 1897. The experiment station, as it was usually called, had been established in 1883 on a seven-acre tract near 18th and Benning Road in Northeast Washington, a site it quickly outgrew.

"D. F. Salmon, Chief of the Bureau of Animal Industry, was anxious to expand the work into the broader field of animal husbandry and wanted space to permit such an additional workload." The Bethesda area was well-known to a number of high ranking USDA scientists making homes in Somerset including Dr. Salmon, one of that town's founders and the holder of a number of vacant building lots.[79]

Dr. Ernest C. Schroeder was the superintendent of the experiment station when it moved to Bethesda. He established his wife, Florence, and young son, Robert, in a home on Rockville Pike and turned the small house on the eighteen acres rented from Davidson into a temporary headquarters. Carpenters soon completed a frame laboratory, a breeding house for small animals used in experiments, four stables with thirty box and twenty open stalls, and a carriage and tool house, and the research work began. In 1899 the Government purchased the eighteen leased acres plus two more for $20,000, and three years later added an additional thirty acres for $10,000.

The operations outgrew the original, frame lab building and moved into the basement and first story of a fireproof, brick laboratory in 1906. Three years later, when further funding was available, they added the second floor and a permanent roof. The total cost of the red-brick building was about $25,000. In 1910 a larger and better breeding house, which the USDA claimed paid for itself annually by producing cheaper and better lab animals, went into service. Over the years the government built several more large stables and about two dozen smaller ones to hold three or four horses or cows for a particular study. A number of other USDA scientists pursued their own experiments, including work with silk worms, in various corners of the sprawling "station."

When King Menelik of Abyssinia gave President Theodore Roosevelt a male zebra, TR sent it to Bethesda and encouraged a project to develop a superior, cross-bred farm animal. The zebra was mated to a local mare and the result christened a "zebhorse." One of Bill Clipper's boasts was that he "broke in a couple of zebras and drove them up Wisconsin Avenue in triumph." The project continued for about five years before being abandoned by the Animal Husbandry Division.[80]

Because the experiment station was becoming crowded and to separate the work on animal husbandry and dairying from the work on diseases, the government leased a nearby sixty-acre farm beginning in 1907. This farm was likely in the Kenwood area although there is also some evidence that USDA pastured horses and perhaps cattle on farms between Bradley Lane and the Columbia County Club for some time before this. Another government farm was located about two miles north of Bethesda near Rock Creek.[81]

In 1909 the $25,000 allocated to buy the 60-acre farm in Bethesda proved insufficient because of the inflation of land prices generated by the filing of sub-division plats. The government purchased a 475-acre farm at Beltsville, and moved the dairy herds and other animal husbandry work out there.

In its 1910 annual report the USDA described the Bethesda facility.

It is equipped for and conducts investigations regarding animal diseases with a view to their control and eradication and their bearing on the public health, and investigations in animal breeding, with special reference to the laws of heredity and the development of increased resistance to disease. A small farm is maintained in such a manner as to provide the other divisions of the bureau with facilities for making observations for which large domestic animals are needed.

The first work at the experiment station was on the contagiousness of pleuropneumonia in cattle, a serious problem since ante-bellum days. Work on swine plague and hog cholera continued at Bethesda, and Drs. Theobald Smith and F. L. Kilborne completed their investigation of Texas or southern cattle fever. This "epochal" work showed "why a truly infectious disease may in no respect be contagious." Their study demonstrated how ticks transmitted the disease and how infected immune cattle could carry it.

Other experiment station work included the study of glanders, anthrax, blackleg, sheep scab and poultry diseases and a major investigation of tuberculous, its spread, diagnosis and treatment in cattle, hogs, and humans. This work also involved the standardization of tuberculin and the supervision of commercially prepared tuberculin. At Bethesda, USDA scientists tested "alleged cures" of many infectious diseases and numerous sheep and cattle dips and

other preparations. They also studied unusual outbreaks of animal diseases, examined infectious abortion disease in cattle and produced valuable tests for hoof and mouth disease.

The research farm became a favorite haunt for many youthful Bethesdans. Horace Hamp-

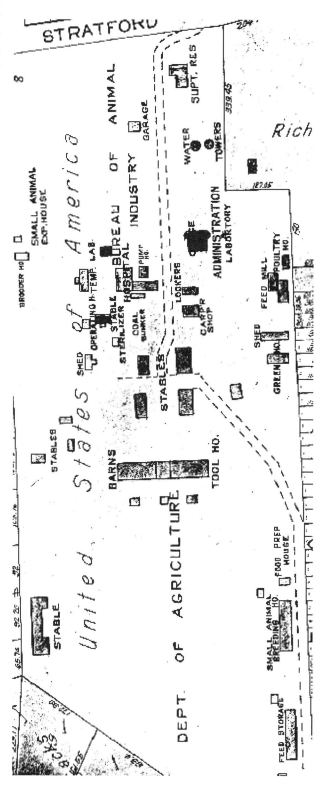

ton took his .22 and hunted rats there when he was a schoolboy. J. Conway Hunt remembered playing there when he was young, eating lunch with the workmen, riding the wagon with them and listening to the men talk about their home life. Oats and corn from his family's fields fed the hundreds of guinea pigs at the station.

When an experiment was over, Hunt recalled:

They'd pull a cow, after they made sure she was not going to recover, they'd pull her nose down, and a big guy like Charlie Norris hit her with a sledgehammer. Then they'd hang her up and later put her in the wagon and take the body back to the incinerator. Where the swimming pool is today, that's where they burned those cows.

Bill Clipper's son Cleveland remembered the "station."

We walked up the railroad tracks to the experimental farm when we lived on River Road. The field was full of pretty horses, and they were going to kill them–belonged to the 2nd and 3rd cavalry over in Virginia. We used to watch on the 4th of July, those cavalrymen would ride up Wisconsin Avenue to Sharpsburg and have sham battles.

Poppa worked right around the clock. Somebody had to be there all the time, to feed the animals. My father worked in the guinea pig house, raised guinea pigs, rabbits, and white mice. He got off per-diem and got on regular-with-pension money. They were paying him twice a month, thirty-some-dollars a month in the Teens. It was just like a big farm with corrals like you see these Western places have with fences, and some in pens that they are going to use for something. And they had discarded animals they killed and burned them up right there.

When Henry Wallace was Secretary of Agriculture, when they killed good beef or pork, they would cut it up and give it to the men.

The same thing with milk; they'd give you a two-gallon can every day. I'm talking about contented cows; there'd be cream on there the next morning like that, yellow cream.

They separated the sick ones, that had anthrax or syphilis, the horses. My father worked with doctors, taking temperatures. It tickled me. I asked where do you take their temperatures. He'd say put it up their rectum, and some of them would do their business. They poop right on you.

And then he had to be with them when they'd drop an animal like a cow or a bull or some-

thing right down to the floor and bore a hole into his brain and get some of that and then stop that hole back up. Chickens the same way, pigs.

As the scope of the work at the experiment station increased and the development of the land in West Chevy Chase and along Bradley Boulevard also accelerated, the two uses came in conflict. Early in the 1920s residents of nearby homes began pressing for the removal of the farm with its flies and its smells. In 1923 the Department of Agriculture bought thirty more acres of land back near Willett Creek and the complaints increased. The station was no longer welcome in Bethesda. In 1930 thirteen civic groups met and asked the Federal government to stop work at the site and to turn over the land for park use.

Mrs. John Werner, president of the Bethesda Elementary School PTA, where her husband ran a boys' club program, was one of the moving forces behind this drive. Stella Werner admitted that in the 1930s "recreation was my hobby." Emory Bogley badgered the politicians and drafted the bill, which Senator Tydings introduced, to give the land to the Maryland-National Capital Park and Planning Commission. The bill failed three times but was finally passed and signed in 1936, and by September most of the supplies and animals had been moved and only a few men were left to salvage equipment and care for the few remaining animals. USDA vacated the experiment station by early `37 leaving behind fences, sheds and pens and not much else. The heating plant, electrical wiring, and plumbing had all been removed. Civilian Conservation Camp boys from Garrett Park helped to clear the land along with workmen from the new M-NCP&PC.

If it had not been for the boom in real estate produced by developments along the trolley line and the Bradley Hills extravaganza, perhaps Bethesda and not Beltsville would have been the site of the Department of Agriculture's great farm and library. Then again, if it had not been for the USDA's experiment station, there probably would not be a Bethesda-Chevy Chase Recreation Center and there certainly would not have been the stolid, brick building that still stands at the end of Norwood Drive, another survivor and a reminder of an agricultural past.

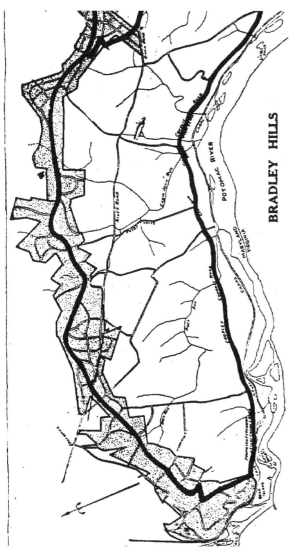

Map showing property owned by Bradley Hills syndicate -
see Caldwell map in next chapter for another view.

M*y father came to this county in 1876 or
'78 and went to Macomb, Illinois, where
an uncle of his was staying at the boarding
house of a lady whose husband had recently died.
At the age of twenty he married her daughter, who
was also twenty. His uncle was in the clay products
business and made some of the original blue china
that was made in England.*

*Father traveled the United States looking
for kaolin and fine clay, and I had brothers and sisters born in Georgia, Paducah, Montana –he had
many stories to tell about the Indians out there–and
they traveled across the country and ended up in
Pennsylvania where I was born.*[82]

Horace Hampton went on to say that his
father, Thomas Hampton, sold his successful
clay pipe and brick making business in Pennsylvania and moved to Washington, D.C.,
about 1908. The Hamptons made their home in
the Trinadad section of Northeast and built a
brick yard near Florida Avenue. Within four
years Thomas Hampton was advertising himself as a contractor as well as a brickmaker and
had moved his home from Montello Avenue,
NE, to 2517 Wisconsin Avenue in Georgetown.
He was listed in the city directories as president of the Pittsburgh Kiln Company and of the
Pittsburgh Construction and Supply Company
located at 734 15th Street, NW. Then he came
to Bethesda.

With some luck or perhaps with a lot more
capital and patience, Thomas Hampton and
the men and women with whom he was associated might have made Newlands, Stellwagen
and company look like small time operators.
Doubtlessly the Bradley Hills entrepreneurs
modeled their enterprise on the development of
Chevy Chase. The Bethesda group acquired
more than twice as much land and, as in Chevy
Chase, bought it quickly and quietly in the name
of several different purchasers and for the most
part in large hilly chunks.

They drove a first-class trolley line through
their land followed by a potentially wide road
that ended with a small amusement park at the
Great Falls of the Potomac. A small group of
large homes on well-landscaped lots stood
proudly near the entrance, and a richly illustrated brochure promised the good life among
neighbors of breeding and taste–the rural ideal
personified. "An acre of ground at less than the
price of the average city lot," declared the ads.
Of course there would be a country club, and of

course, one could ride to the hounds as well as enjoy a round of golf. By the spring of 1913 the Real Estate Trust Company, with the trolley line still under construction, offered prospects the opportunity to "motor through beautiful Bradley Hills -- our autos are at your service."

The Bradley Hills land development involved at least five separate corporations–two in Maryland, one in D.C., one in Virginia, and one in Maine–and several others materialized and vanished with disturbing frequency and a recurring cast of officers. Most early historians such as Miss Holman and more recently Mac-Master and Hiebert have tied Thomas Hampton's name along with M. Willson Offutt's to the development, but the source of the capital behind this sizable enterprise remains as hard to ascertain as the actual value of the investment.

Horace Hampton believed it was mostly "West Virginia money" and said that he did not think that his father or his brother Thomas Earle lost anything. Magruder Willson Offutt was deeply involved, at least at the beginning, as were H. Bradley Davidson and several other local nabobs. Bradley Davidson and his brother, John Cumpston Davidson, were in the real estate, insurance, and loan business with offices in the Southern Building (Davidson and Davidson, phone Main 1512) and seemed to have been at least nominally, and perhaps deeply, involved in Bradley Hills to its quiet end. The Davidson and Offutt names lent the enterprise a certain antiquarian cachet and local legitimacy.

Circumstantial evidence suggests that both Offutt and Davidson lost substantially in the collapse of the putative subdivisions. But many of the names that appeared on transactions, boards of directors, and deeds remain a mystery as does the rather abrupt demise of Bradley Hills. If it was a "bubble," it was a beaut.[83]

In 1912 the development began on land at the intersection of Wisconsin Avenue and the new Bradley Hills Boulevard where the Offutt's windmill marked what some considered Bethesda's southern border. M. Willson Offutt had obtained this property by court order in 1888 and in 1912 laid out a road system and then subdivided the eighty-some acres into several large lots near the old turnpike and many smaller ones westward toward the B&O tracks and a planned Hillandale Road. The Offutts had owned a hundred acres of the adjacent

property on Wisconsin Avenue since 1860 when, as one historian put it, M. Willson's father, Hilleary Lyles, and his family left Georgetown and "went South" on the eve of the Civil War. The Offutt tract became Section One of Bradley Hills with a strip thirty feet wide reserved in the middle of the new street for the trolley tracks, which would run just southwest of the Offutts' home.[84]

Bradley Hills Boulevard and Wisconsin - Davidson home at far right, Offutt's house in trees at left center (ca. 1925)

Now, for the first time, appeared the name of the Chevy Chase to Great Falls Land Corporation of Maine, H. Bradley Davidson, president, which received the deeded right-of-way. Why this corporation was chartered in Maine, like many other aspects of this project, remains unknown.[85]

Two of the less-well-known leaders of the Bradley Hills development were Eldridge E. Jordan and one J. Walter Long, whose name first appears in 1912 as the general manager of the Chevy Chase to Great Falls Land Corporation. Not much is known about Mr. Long except that he was active in the real estate business and made his home at 2616 Woodley Place, NW. When the Real Estate Trust Company was organized in 1913, he was listed as its secretary. That company, which within a year was advertising itself as "Washington's Largest and Most Progressive Real Estate and Insurance Office" was to Bradley Hills what the Thomas J. Fisher Company was to Chevy Chase. H. Bradley Davidson was also its first president, but Eldridge E. Jordan, the original vice-president, headed the company from 1915 until it disappeared in 1920.

Mr. Jordan, who must surely hold some sort of area record for irons-in-fires, had also been

president of Jordan and Company and of the United States Trust Company as well as vice-president of the Commercial National Bank and vice-president and treasurer of the National Assurance Company. The president of National Assurance was H. Bradley Davidson, who also spread himself rather thinly. Another player in this morass of interconnected enterprises was Bert T. Amos, briefly an officer of both Real Estate Trust and National Assurance, whose name appears in the Montgomery County land records as an owner of Bradley Hills property.[86]

Then there was Augusta C. Grossart, purchaser of record of the Widow Haney's forty-acre tract in 1917. She was the bookkeeper of the Real Estate Trust Company. In 1919 when the Bradley Hills adventure began its meltdown, she ended up as secretary-treasurer of the Safety First Manufacturing Company, E. E. Jordan, president, which may have been the successor of the Quantico Company of which Eldridge Jordan was president, J. W. Long vice-president, and A. C. Grossart secretary and treasurer in 1918. Obviously, printing business cards and lettering office windows were growth industries at 14th and F Streets in the Teens.[87]

Thomas Hampton's Pittsburgh Construction and Supply Company came in to build Bradley Boulevard, the trolley line and a half-dozen large houses in late 1912. His son Horace recalled:

The road was built with no mechanical equipment. It was built with plows, scoops, dump wagons. Where the Safeway is located (at Arlington and Bradley), just past the railroad bridge, that was built as part of the project; that's where father's stables were. And he had a hundred horses and mules there, and that's what he used to build Bradley Boulevard. At Great Falls, Maryland, he built an amusement park that lasted a couple of years. Later it burned down. The whole idea was to get people to come out from Washington.[88]

Three of the houses Hampton built were on large lots on the triangle of land between Bradley Blvd., Offutt Road and Chevy Chase Drive. George Sacks' house was the largest and faced up toward Wisconsin Avenue. Behind it were the houses of the Stocks and of the builder, Thomas Hampton, who moved his large family to Bethesda in 1914. Arthur A. Chapin bought the big house on the corner

George P. Sacks' home at 101 Chevy Chase Drive

where the Grange Hall had been. The two behind it were harder to sell but eventually Dr. R. B. Wiltberger, and Vernon M. Dorsey bought those. Later George Sacks, in tandem with Chapin and E. L. Stock, bought up most of the empty lots in this subdivision, and during the Second World War the land became part of Bethesda's largest concentration of apartments.

"The houses were finished, and we moved in in 1914," remembered Horace Hampton.

The Stocks, he represented a boiler company from Ohio, they had three sons, Ed and Charlie and Steve, they moved in. Eckart Sacks built between George Sacks and our house. He was the father of George Sacks, and he had a butter and egg business at Centre Market. Then his daughter and her husband, his name was Ellis, he was connected with the Fussell-Young ice cream people. Sacks and Chapin opened up an ice cream business and dairy, and then they sold out to the National Dairy and took the money and bought out here. Chapin was the nicer one of the two but not a businessman.

In April 1912 the twenty-one sections of property and trolley line right-of-way were transferred from the Chevy Chase to Great Falls Land Corporation of Maine to the Washington to Great Falls Railway and Power Company of Maryland in a deed signed by H. Bradley Davidson to J. Walter and Eleanor H. Long. A deed of trust was recorded from the W. & G. F. Ry. & Power Co. to Fidelity Trust of Baltimore in December 1912 to secure payment of $500,000 in bonds and interest. The Maryland Public Services Commission approved the issuance of the bonds in the denomination of $1000 each with interest at five percent paid semi-annually with the proviso that the railway be completed within two years.

That winter the *Sentinel* reported:

Those behind the project declare that it will be in operation long before the expiration of the two years. The work of constructing the road has been in progress for some time, but now that all obstacles have been removed, additional workmen will be engaged and the work pushed rapidly.

By February of 1913 another corporate name joined the growing list when the Washington Utilities Company appeared to operate the railway. That same month Fidelity Trust announced that it had sold $300,000 of the authorized bond issue. Building continued on the first five homes, the road and the trolley line.[89]

Newspaper stories extolled the merits of the new suburban development.[90]

With the completion of the electric road which bisects the extensive subdivision known as Bradley Hills from its eastern extremity at Wisconsin avenue west of Chevy Chase to its western extremity at Great Falls, a territory heretofore practically inaccessible will be thrown open to the public. It will be but a short time now before the road is completed, according to present plans.

With the exception of a short stretch, not more than a 100 yards in length, the road is practically completed. The tracks have been laid, the trolley poles erected and the wires strung, and all that yet remains to do is the ballasting. This will be a comparatively easy task, for the crushed rock for this purpose can be shoveled from the freight spur of the Baltimore and Ohio railroad, near the eastern end of Bradley Hills, into flat cars on the electric line which passes beneath the railroad tracks. It can then be transported to any section of the road and dumped on the tracks.

The only uncompleted section of the electric road is that portion which passes beneath the tracks of the Baltimore and Ohio. A culvert through which it is to pass is now nearing completion, and soon the 100 yards of track connecting the already finished sections of the road can be laid.

Besides making accessible the 4,000 acres of ground included in the Bradley Hills tract, the electric road will also make it possible to reach the Maryland side of the Great Falls of the Potomac without using an automobile or carriage or walking up the Conduit road from the terminus of the electric road at Cabin John bridge. With its completion both sides of the falls can then be reached by trolley.

The ride through the Bradley Hills section from Wisconsin avenue to Great Falls will be as picturesque as any trolley trip around Washington.

All of Bradley Hills is rolling country. In some places it is thickly wooded and in others there are large open spaces. Because of the absence of flat stretches the natural drainage of the tract is excellent.

The land for the most part is fertile. Much of the territory was formerly devoted to farm purposes. When once the development of the territory gets under way, the fertile nature of the soil will prove a big factor in the beautification of the grounds surrounding the homes.

Varies in Width

This sub-division varies in width from one-half to more than a mile and is ten miles in length. It is the largest sub-division around Washington, and is said to be one of the most extensive in the country. The electric road winds its way through the center of the property and will make accessible countless numbers of the home sites. The electric road is to occupy the center of a boulevard 100 feet in width, which is to extend through the entire length of the tract. Lateral roads will traverse all parts of the suburb.

Already a narrow roadway runs parallel with the electric road throughout its entire length and eventually this will be widened into its full width of one hundred feet. When completed and properly surfaced, it should be one of the most picturesque drives about Washington. It will follow a series of valleys which broaden out as they near the river.

In Bradley Hills there are many outcroppings of rock which is well suited for masonry walls. In practically all of the suburbs lying to the northwest of the city quantities of good building rock are to be found. Already in Bradley Hills it has been used for several residences the walls of which are entirely of stone. It has also been used in constructing residences which are half stone and half frame.

In clearing the right of way for the electric road and boulevard many cords of oak and chestnut timber have been cut. A sawmill was installed and all the ties needed for the electric road were prepared.

Unusual Feature Planned

Several unusual features in suburb planning are contemplated for Bradley Hills. Among these will be a so-called English village, a section in which the old English type of architecture will be followed exclusively in the designing of homes. A large site on top of a hill which commands a view both toward the river and Wisconsin avenue has been set aside for school purposes. Close to this an

open field will be reserved for athletic purposes.

Only recently an announcement was made that a large tract toward the western end of Bradley Hills had been reserved for use by the newly organized Montgomery County Club, an exclusive organization in which a number of prominent society leaders are interested. The clubhouse is to occupy the top of a gently sloping hill. The surrounding territory is well suited topographically for a golf course. The electric road and boulevard wind around the foot of this slope, so that the proposed club will be accessible both by automobile and trolley.

Bradley Hills, together with the other extensive subdivisions which lie close to it, will be benefited by reason of the transportation facilities offered by the freight spur of the Baltimore and Ohio railroad. . . . This branch freight line makes it possible to transport coal, building materials and other articles to the very center of the section from Chevy Chase to Bethesda which is fast becoming developed. Formerly it was necessary to haul such material from the city at considerable expense.

The trolley line went into operation on July 2, 1913, on a single track 10.2 miles long. The line was built to steam railroad standards and used six signal blocks with spring-switch turnouts at Offutt Drive, Wilson Lane, and at the Kefauver, Bradley, and Lynch properties. It employed ten "state-of-the-art" Nachod automatic signals, which permitted a car to follow onto the same tracks but not opposing traffic, and had a double wire, bracket catenary overhead power-supply system of the type later used by the Pennsylvania Railroad. Thirty and thirty-five foot chestnut poles supported the grooved trolley wire and messenger cable. The line began with 6,600 volts, later doubled. While it was under construction, a spur ran east of the Pike about 1,000 feet to a stone quarry in Chevy Chase.

From the Offutt properties near Wisconsin Avenue the tracks ran on the north side of the new road, navigated a narrow culvert under the B&O tracks, looped through a corner of Edgemoor, then switched to the south side of the road near the new country club until they reached Bradley and River Roads where they went across country, behind the old Angel home and on across Brickyard (formerly Offutt) Road to a loop at Great Falls that can still be seen if one is willing to search a bit. Although the

right-of-way was designed for the middle of a street 100 feet wide, only one side of Bradley Boulevard was built.[91]

The trolley trip to Great Falls took forty-three minutes, and first operated with one Washington Railway and Electric car shuttling back and forth. During its short prime, the line's Pullman green cars ran every hour and half from 5th and F Streets on a regular schedule. Some Sundays larger cars provided transport to the Falls and brought many potential customers through the building sites.[92]

Many Bethesda and some Chevy Chase residents used the line for excursions to the river. Bootsie Lochte and his father, Roy, Bethesda's last blacksmith, often rode to Great Falls to go fishing. Some Potomac residents commuted to work or school. Many riders, including Anson Ball, called it "a regular Toonerville Trolley. The conductor and motorman used to shoot rabbits, pick up chestnuts and gather a few blackberries along the way." Within two years, however, the amusement park was gone and the trolley line cut back on weekdays to end service at about Hillmead, but while it ran it was reasonably popular.[93]

Mrs. Angel rode the trolley to and from school in the District from her Potomac home.

The car ran right by our house and up to Great Falls. The conductor would sometimes get off at our place and repair our old 490 Chevrolet, and the motorman would go on up around the loop and come back. Sometimes he would come in and get a bag of apples or pears, and they'd take those on the car when the motorman got back. There was a small wooden structure on the corner of our property at Offutt Road that served as a waiting room. It was covered with pornographic graffiti, and I wasn't allowed to go in there.

When I first went into John Eaton in Cleveland Park, they had these side seats. We had tickets; I'm not sure what the fare was. People would get on all the way down the track and finish dressing. There were people at the next stop at Oakland Drive called Ingalls, Richard and Norman Ingalls, and they would get on putting on their ties. We were sitting on these long seats and people would be doing their nails. The trolley only ran every two hours, so if you missed it you were really late. I read my fairy tale books that I got from the public library on 9th Street.

At Seven Locks and Bradley Boulevard was the Leland stop, and a lot of children got on there.

It was an old cornfield, and we pulled up one rainy morning and there was not a child to be seen. The motorman hit his footbell –dong, dong, dong. And out from every corn shock came a child, maybe ten of them. Then there was Bessie Case, the Case family, he was called "Little Brother." Their houses are still there; they had to walk down Persimmon Tree Road and got on where Avondale Farms is today. She was a beautiful young lady. Then Miss Johnson, Miss Erner, Mr. Phillips got on almost every day. At Bradley and Wilson Lane, English Village, a man and his daughter got on and her name was Uranium. He was a miner and when I asked, I was told that "uranium" was a precious metal.[94]

At first it ran down to 5th and F, but then it only ran to Wisconsin and Bradley, a shuttle, and we had to change cars to the Rockville line.

We got stuck in the snow once. I must have been in the 5th grade, that would make me ten or eleven or something like that. Sometimes I would come out on the earlier car or I'd wait for my aunt on the car with working people on it. There wasn't much of a store in Potomac, so they had all the food they bought in big bags, vegetables and so forth. Somewhere along the line, pretty far out, we got stuck in the snow. The car couldn't go any farther, so they got out their food, and we had dinner on the car. And somehow they got some dry sticks and made some coffee; I didn't get any, but they had hot coffee. They must have built the fire on the back platform.

I went to sleep on one of the seats and the motorman covered me up with his coat. Somehow a message was sent back and toward morning a snowplow came out, and we went back down to the carbarn in Tenleytown where we tried to keep warm around a stove. The snowplow went out and cleared the tracks, and they sent us home in another car that followed the plow.

Edward O. Henderson, a sharecropper near Great Falls, sent six of his ten children to the Chevy Chase School on that trolley. Earl Henderson remembered that they had to walk a long way to the stop on Brickyard Road.

That was in 1918, I guess. At the Chevy Chase School the teachers said I was so little they were going to let me out at twelve o'clock if it was all right with my mother. I was six years old, and I'd come home by myself. Most of the time I would be the only one on the car at that time of the day. They had some little cars with seats along the side.

Sometimes the trolley wheel would come off; it was solid brass about four, five inches around, and they'd have to struggle to get it back on the line. And that darn thing was light and would jump the tracks if you looked at it.

One day the car jumped the track coming down that hill by the power station, and it throwed me down on the floor. And it bumped along and finally got stopped, and I remember the guy's name, it was Tommy Entrussle, he was the conductor, and Tommy wanted to walk home with me. He said it was too far to go by myself, but I said, "I can make it," and I walked home.

And then another time right there at that old power station there had been a big storm somewhere, and I was on the early car, and when it got to the creek, it couldn't get across. The water was up over the tracks a foot or so. When the next car come through, we walked across on the railroad ties and that car went back to Bethesda.

This Tommy Entrussle had a rifle in that streetcar all the time, and he'd tell the motorman, "Stop the car. Back up a little" when he saw a rabbit out the back, and he'd sit there and shoot. He said he got one now and then, but I never did see him get one.

On Sundays they brought a lot of tourists out. We used to have visitors at the house all the time on Sundays.

The County furnished us with books of tickets, and the people down at Seven Locks Road, kids there, had books with half-tickets, but I don't remember what the tickets were worth. The County had to furnish those tickets as a way to school.

That many kids, to get them ready for school was a pretty hard job. I remember one time walking out that old Brickyard Road, and I wanted to miss the car. I tried my best. I was draggin' my feet. But my sister pushed me along, and I was a'crying and the old motorman said, "I'll wait for my little boy." I thought to myself I was beat.

The car we rode to school on was always full. After all there were six of us. At Seven Locks Road, a lot of black people got on there. Some of those big women would sit on a seat and wiggle and push the kids out. After you left Seven Locks, there wasn't too many got on anymore. It went pretty good out there. In the evenings they'd have the big trolley cars, but in the middle of the day they had little dinky cars with seats on the sides.

When we got to Bethesda we had to walk across Bradley Lane and down to Rosemary Street

to the school. There were some tremendous big houses through there. Those people had money and used to play tennis. When they knocked the ball in the street, they never came out. We got there too early for the school so we had to look around for things to do, and we got those tennis balls.

And sometimes we'd walk down Connecticut Avenue and on the left hand side there was a store, like a little country store. And we used to walk down there and get these licorice sticks. It was down past the Club a little bit. Sometimes we'd walk out to Counselman's store and then go across the field where there was broom sage growing up higher than we were, and we had a path through there.

My sister and her husband, Bill Clagett, lived on Leland Street. He was working for Kennedy and Warren at the time. He built his own house. There was five carpenters built houses there on Leland Street–Dick and Bill and Leo Clagett and a fellow named Frank Pyles. Don't recall the other one, but there was five of them on that curve. It was mostly an abandoned farm when we went through there.

I remember some kids climbed on that big water tank near the school and about got expelled. I never did that.

There was one boy name Curtis, he had some .32 bullets in his pocket one time, and he went on out to Connecticut Avenue and he laid some of those bullets up on the streetcar track. And when the streetcar came we run and hid, and that thing went off. That was risky. I just went there two years. The line closed shortly after that.

My father used to fish over there at the canal along with us; there was four boys. I remember coming up from that old hotel to the circle, and if we come up at the right time, we could get a ride out to Brickyard Road and get off. I recall those cars had great big headlights, and the bugs were always swarming around. The conductors and motormen knew us all so there was no trouble hitching a ride.

The last piece of equipment that come out on that trolley line was when they were building that tunnel into Washington, water tunnel. They brought a crane out there that had a yard-bucket on it, and they had a lot of trouble. The old railroad ties were pushing out under all that weight. And then when they got it over to the circle, they had to go down over that hill, and they let it down with pulleys and cables.

Meanwhile, through the Real Estate Trust Company, the Montgomery Country Club in-

corporated in Washington, D.C., with Joseph Leiter as president and purchased 150 acres of rolling land including the old Sylvester Jones homestead tract. They set about converting the late Mr. Jones's home into a club house and by 1915 had laid out an eighteen-hole golf course. The membership, although still small, was increasing.[95]

The club's publicity stated that it intended to have a national rather than a local following and that it would be difficult to gain admission; "only the ultra fashionable will be permitted to join." The promoters expected polo, golf, and tennis to be popular, and promised that "particular attention will be paid to hunting, and the new club is expected to develop this sport, already so popular in this city to a degree where Washington will be one of the most widely known of the hunting centers."[96]

As part of the promotion, C. W. Long, likely a close relative of the company's general manager, wrote the words and music of a song called "In the Land Where the Sun Never Sets" which was "Dedicated to Bradley Hills." A few lots were sold and a few houses were built. Horace Hampton concluded that the time and the distance were both wrong. There was a lot of competition and not many buyers in the Teens. The country suffered a twenty-month depression in 1913 and `14 that did not really end until the Great War was over, and then the flu epidemic hit.

As for his father, Hampton said:

He was a contractor but he didn't own any property out there. It didn't take my father down, and it didn't take George Sacks down. Father did well, he came out all right.

One of the subdivisions built on Bradley Boulevard was called English Village. They had some houses built in there, but it was never successful. One large frame house that was built on Bradley Boulevard near Wilson Lane later became a night club and then in Prohibition days they couldn't keep it going. A roadhouse. I went there several times before I was married and heard some of

the most risque songs I've ever heard. It didn't attract people. It was at the wrong time.

Horace Hampton also recalled that his father did not spend all his time trying to make Bradley Hills go:

In 1916, now remember he was an Englishman; England was going under because of the German submarines. So father got backing, I've never learned how he got the backing, and they formed the U.S. Maritime Corporation, and he went down to Brunswick, Georgia, and built a shipyard. And he built the largest steam-powered ships ever built, and they saved England by taking supplies through to them.

When he came back from there, he and my oldest brother built houses in the Rosehill section of Baltimore. Then he came back to Wisconsin Avenue and laid out the streets and sold lots in the Rosedale section of Bethesda, the property that goes back to Columbia Club. He was quite an entrepreneur and finally became the secretary-treasurer of the Park and Planning Commission.

Thomas Hampton also returned from the South with the honorary title of "colonel," which he used in certain social circles for the rest of his days. Thomas Earle Hampton, Horace's brother and his father's assistant at the shipyard, stayed on in Georgia for a while after the war and found time to fall in love. He returned to Bethesda, developed a successful insurance and real estate business, entered politics and in 1943, when he was president of the County Commissioners and for all practical purposes mayor of Bethesda, to the surprise of almost everyone, married Miss Helen Branham, the girl he had met during World War I.[97]

By the end of the First World War, the Bradley Hills trolley line suspended service, and the money and interest seem to have dried up together. What were called "franchise runs" were made annually for the next few years just to legally retain the right-of-way. Al Savage recalled being at the Congressional Club one Sunday and seeing an old single-truck car, probably a yellow 100-class car, making its way down the tracks toward Great Falls with men wielding sickles preceding it

Service ended on February 12, 1921, and the Maryland P.S.C. approved track removal in October 1926. For many years a curved piece of track could be seen buried in the macadam of Wisconsin Avenue at Bradley Boulevard and the wire hangers remained under the B&O tres-

tle even longer. The National Capital Trolley Museum preserved one car that ran on this line, #0509. The stone powerhouse on Bradley by the creek just west of Seven Locks Road, long a private home, is another survivor and reminder of this venture.

On September 28, 1920, the directors of one-year-old Bradley Hills, Inc. of Maryland agreed to sell their assets to the Bradley Hills Corporation of Virginia. Rudolph B. Behrend, president of Bradley Hills, Inc., signed the deed which included fourteen parcels of land subject to liens to Harvey T. Winfield and James Mullen for $150,000 and $200,000. The Virginia corporation's charter lasted until 1923.[98]

The boom of the 1920s brought a rebirth to the name when developers and agents advertised acreage and building lots in the "Country Club District " of Bradley Hills. The main street became just Bradley Boulevard. The country club site went through several incarnations and was in the news once more near the end of World War II when new owners attempted to make it into an aviation club with a grass landing strip.

Then, of course, there was Kenwood. Originally this tract of high and hilly land, abandoned farms, scrub pine, sassafras, and briar thickets north of Willett Creek was part of the huge Friendship land grant. Kenwood's progenitor, Edgar S. Kennedy, president of the Kennedy brothers' construction company, was already well known for his row houses and apartment projects. Some family trouble developed in the 1920s, perhaps over the problem-plagued Meridian Mansions project, and after his brother William died in the mid-20s, E. S. Kennedy decided to try his hand at a prestigious suburban development.

In 1926 he acquired a large piece of undeveloped land east of River Road known as the Montgomery Park Syndicate Property for about $1,100 an acre. The owners had been considering an amusement park project to rival the increasingly popular Glen Echo. Most of the 200-plus acres had been part of the old Counselman farm where Miss Hester and Miss Amanda lived during the Civil War when the batteries at Fort Reno fired practice rounds over their heads. The Counselman's frame house and the nearby slave cemetery were about where the fifth green was built, and the nearest community down River Road was Crow Hill.

To gain access to Bradley Boulevard, in 1927, Kennedy bought two parcels of Bradley Hills land from widow Annie P. Gaynor for about $8,000. When Kennedy and his wife, Alice, deeded all this property over to the newly formed Kennedy-Chamberlin Development Company they held first trusts of $222,558, $5,340, and $2,700.[99]

Edgar S. Kennedy took as his partner a brash young engineer and promoter from Princeton, Class of '21, Donal L. Chamberlin. After college Chamberlin had wandered a bit designing bridges for railroads and dabbling in city planning before performing various engineering jobs for the Kennedy brothers. He married Ellen Lyle Fay, who had grown up on Kendall Green, the campus of Gallaudet College which her father, Allan Bradshaw Fay, had helped to found.

The Chamberlins' first home was a house acquired at a tax sale in Cabin John. The previous owner had been a moonshiner and bootlegger who ran a still in the basement. Chamberlin had to put in a new concrete floor and a better drain because the smell of mash permeated the house in damp weather. There were also occasional late night knocks at the door by the previous occupant's would-be customers. The Chamberlins moved to a new home on Highland Drive in Kenwood early in World War II.

Chamberlin oversaw the clearing of the underbrush on building lots and the transforming of the meadows along River Road into a golf course. Meanwhile, Kennedy hired Charles H. Jerman as his sales manager. Jerman was a Virginian from the Difficult Run area whose father had been an enlisted man in the Confederate army. "One of the few, everyone else was at least a colonel," according to Mrs. Milton E. Miles, his granddaughter. Charles Jerman had been in the grocery business with his father, Middleton G. Jerman. They operated both a small store at 11th and I, NW, where they lived, and a space in Centre Market when he married in 1902. He and Will Corby, who also had a stall in the market, had used Will's bread delivery wagon to court girls on the weekends.

C. H. JERMAN

In 1904 Jerman went broke, partly from extending too much credit to boarding houses, and entered the booming real estate business with the firm of Willoughby, Gibson, and Daniels. He was very successful. He once accepted Analostan (Theodore Roosevelt) Island in trade, and on another deal became the proud possessor of a half-dozen Pope-Hartford automobiles. Charles Jerman became known as the "Cadillac" salesman because he was one of the first to take customers out in a car. He was also a member of the influential Chain and Sprocket Club, which gave him contacts with men like the Milans brothers who could afford to build in Kenwood. His weakness was the horses; "My father thought betting on races was an investment," said Billy Miles.

The first street plan presented by engineer Chamberlin showed a grid of lots similar to Somerset's plan. Both Kennedy and Jerman suggested larger lots and more contoured streets, and the results were platted in 1927 as Sections One and Two of "Kennedy."

In Section One, at the top of the hill nearest Bradley Boulevard most of the lots had 75-80 foot fronts; a few were only 90-100 feet deep,

but most had a depth of 120-30 feet. South of the circle, where the community Christmas tree later glowed, and nearer Dorset Avenue, the only named street on the first plat maps, the lots were smaller, averaging 70-75 by 122.5. The building restriction or set-back line was twenty-five feet. The strip of land near Dorset and the railroad tracks showed on the plat maps as a long, narrow park.

Within a year the same two plat maps were refiled with the subdivision name changed to "Kenwood," and the addition of street names and several wide, shallow lots near Bradley on Kennedy Drive. When Section Three was platted about a year later, the lots of Brookside, Shadow, and Sunset were much larger, many 150 by 175 and all with at least 120 foot frontage. All the later Kenwood plats, most in the mid-1930s, showed lots in Sections Four, Five, and Six at least 110 feet wide, a few with thirty-five foot set-backs.

By the winter of 1927, the woods had been cleared of underbrush; water and sewer pipes had been laid along with gas lines; several miles of roads had been graded, and concrete paving had begun on Kennedy and Chamberlin, the first two streets to be developed. Near the intersection of those streets rose the first house, designed by Alexander H. Sonnemann, K-C's resident architect and son of Ottmar and Rebecca Sonnemann of Chevy Chase. The big, red-brick colonial with the semi-circle of pillars in front is usually called the Ferry house for its first owners, the A. Montague Ferrys who were constant Kenwood tub-thumpers.[100]

Across from it a small sales office went up, and Charlie Jerman hired a black man, whom he dressed in colonial costume including knee pants, to greet prospects on the weekends. Sonnemann kept one of his drawing boards there and was seldom without a commission. He had been born in 1872, late in his fecund mother's long child-bearing years. His twin brother died at birth, and he inherited a congenital heart defect which left him very spare and deliberate. He attended area elementary schools including the one at the Grange Hall in Bethesda and then was educated by his father before apprenticing with an architect. He and Louis Justement became partners in 1923 and designed many apartment buildings as well as private homes.

The Kenwood work gangs began planting a double row of trees along all the streets. Kennedy himself was generally credited with the idea of the neighborhood's famous cherry trees, but salesman Jerman may have suggested them, as his family believes, and David Fairchild, who had imported dozens of varieties, was doubtlessly consulted. The crews planted flowering Yoshino cherries grafted onto American stock near the unfinished streets, even those to be developed some time later, and installed a line of maples between them and deeper on the lots to provide shade and color in the fall. When the Japanese cherries matured and proved to be healthy, most of the Norway maples were "sacrificed," some on moonless nights. Within five years almost 2,000 cherry trees lined Kenwood's streets.

Meanwhile Kennedy had a nine-hole golf course laid out and plans for a clubhouse drawn with the promise of tennis courts and a swimming pool. His workers accomplished almost all the grading work with animals, mostly mules, as they rerouted streams and created

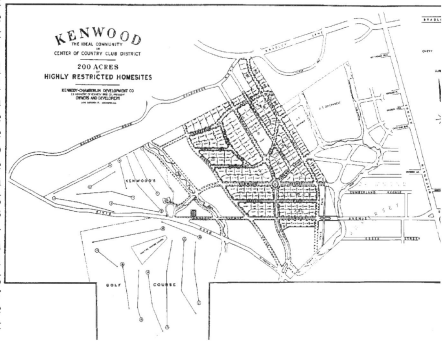

fairways. The golf course opened as promised on June 28, 1928. The lockers and showers in the still-unfinished stone-faced clubhouse were ready by September, and on November 1, 1928, meal service began. Right from the start, no community in Bethesda was more closely identified with a county club than Kenwood.

In the early Thirties the club rented the Posey land on the other side of River Road and built a second nine holes. Miss Holman suggested that the Posey's old stone house might be haunted, but that did not seem to bother the golfers, and since there was almost no traffic on River Road, neither did having to cross that street twice on each round. By the mid-1930s Kenwood was prepared to host the National Capital Open.

While the credit for the cherry trees in Kenwood may be shared by Mr. Jerman and Mr. Fairchild with Mr. Kennedy, there is no doubt that the dogwoods that beautify the golf course were E. S. Kennedy's. "Most of them are his trees," said Ashby Chamberlin, Donal's younger son. "I remember him with his white hair and his cigar in that area where the pump house is now. He had the whole area covered with little, dinky dogwoods, and guys would be weeding around them. They were later planted out on the golf course."

Originally, club membership came with home ownership in Kenwood, and the obvious purpose of the club was to promote the sale of lots and of homes. At one time the developers contemplated a ring of extra-large lots around the golf course.

The Kennedy-Chamberlin Development Company would gladly sell you a lot, and then you could hire your own architect and builder, or they would provide both of those services. In the deed K-C held the right to approve your plans, and their deed restrictions included several relating to styles and sizes of homes to be constructed. In 1934 the first "committee on plans" included Raymond F. Kyle, Harold F. Clemmer, F. Irwin Ray, and A. H. Sonnemann, all chosen by the residents.

The words "restricted" and "restrictive" appeared in Kenwood publicity as often as they did in that of the Chevy Chase Land Company a generation earlier. The Kennedy-Chamberlin deed, which property buyers had to agree to, included the usual racial restrictions plus rules having to do with architecture, price and the re-

sale of homes. Garages could not face the street; clothes lines were verboten, and fences needed the neighbors' approval. In 1927 Mr. Kennedy told the *Star* that the "section is to be highly restricted, with emphasis placed on the beauty of the houses."[101]

At first, lot sales were brisk, and Mrs. Coolidge even came out one weekend to see "Kenwood, the beautiful" as it was advertised. The patent attorney Milans brothers, Joseph H., Robert McP., and Calvin T., built their big stone and brick houses on adjacent lots, and Donal Chamberlin convinced several of his Princeton friends to invest.

In 1929 a Kenwood house was one of the *Star*'s model homes and was held open for a month beginning mid-May. The Sonnemann-designed, French Provincial-style home on Kennedy Drive had a brick facade with stone ornamentation. The 110 by 130 foot lot featured oaks and poplars on the rear of the site, a driveway to the rear of the house and a large, paved auto yard plus a two-car garage in the basement, which also had a cold storage closet, laundry chute, built in ironing board and servants' quarters. The L-shaped house had a center hall, four bedrooms, two baths, and a living room measuring 17 x 22 feet.

Then came the crash.

Once Kenwood was up and running, E. S. Kennedy gave over the day-to-day management

to Donal Chamberlin and turned his attention to other projects. In 1930 he and another young builder, Monroe Warren, formed an ill-fated partnership. Warren and his brother had become very successful home builders in Chevy Chase and had put up several, luxury co-op apartments in the District. Now Warren and Kennedy began a huge apartment house project just north of the Zoo, the Kennedy-Warren, with its unmistakable central tower featuring geometric rows of aluminum panels and limestone griffins and the main lobby containing huge golden marble pillars and elevators doors decorated in the Aztec style. Built on the side of a Rock Creek Park hill and fifteen stories high in the back, the art deco masterpiece has two dining rooms plus a ballroom featuring friezes of aluminum dancing girls, fluted columns and artistic wall sconces, and if it had been completed, would have had 442 apartments and fifty hotel rooms.

But when the crash came, even their joint financial resources were not enough to keep it going, and the B. F. Saul Company, the mortgage holder, took over in 1932 when the construction was about half finished. Then the Washington developers' favorite, the Park Bank at 14th and Park Road, failed in 1933 destroying what was left of Kennedy's resources. The Metropolitan Life Insurance Company took over Meridian Mansions, and Edgar Kennedy and his brother's widow both had to vacate their large apartments and move to much meaner quarters out on Connecticut Avenue where they managed to hang on to several small apartment buildings. The Kennedy finances were in such inchoate condition that clear title to some Kenwood lots was in questions for several years.[102]

Donal Chamberlin claimed that he asked a "veteran realty man" what he thought of the Kenwood project and was told "I think you will lose every dollar you put into it." He also said, more than ten years after the fact, that the company had planned for the onset of bad economic conditions around 1930. But things got very bad indeed. A few lots were even auctioned, and Kennedy-Chamberlin mortgaged parts of Section One through H. L. Rust Company and kept on going. Land prices fell.

In 1930 E. W. and Nell Shinn bought a lot on Brookside Drive that was about 118 by 160 feet for $4,000 paying $40 a month and six percent interest. When the Miles and Jerman fami-

1930 model home - 5 Woodlawn Avenue

lies, with resale in mind, built their big Sonnemann-designed home on Shadow Road in 1931, the total cost including land was $34,000. Mr. Sonnemann had specified whitewashed bricks, Mrs. Miles remembered:

It was the beginning of the bad depression, and the stone man that owned the quarry came to my mother and said, "I have Italian stone masons here, and we've no work for them, and they don't know anything else. They'll go back to Italy if I can't find them work. If I give you stone will you pay their wages?" It came out pretty close to what the brick was.

Mrs. Miles, she was called "Billy," and her admiral husband, who carried the Academy nickname "Mary," were Kenwood pioneers.

When you asked friends for dinner you gave them a map and maybe even kept them to morning light so they could find their way back to town. Bradley and River Roads were both narrow two lanes and winding through woods with edgings of pokeweed and blackberries. In fact, the summer of `31 I picked all the blackberries my family of six needed for cobblers just along the dirt track later to be Sunset Lane.

The Miles's middle son Murray recalled being pushed through the brambles and prickles to collect blackberries up where the skeet shooting range was. His mother made some of them into wine. The Miles boys, Bill was the oldest then Murray, who was called Boots, and Charles known as Sea-going as in "where's he going?," were Kenwood's paper boys for years. They carried all the papers both morning and afternoon and followed each other in sucession. If a customer cancelled one paper and took another, he still got a Miles coming to his door to collect every month. Murray said that collecting in Kenwood was sometimes difficult because people were not home. "I remember some

always had a lot of tickets in my collection book. They were obnoxious. You had to go back several times to get paid." Murray Miles estimated that the *Post* and *Star* routes in Kenwood had about seventy customers each in the late Thirties and during the war.

Another Kenwood paperboy took over a route and inherited the help of a small collie named Silver which belonged to his neighbor, Mrs. Bryce Blair of Highland Avenue. The sheltie had learned his job with her son and kept up the work when Bobby Sullivan served the route. The 12-year-old pushed his bike along rolling papers, and the dog delivered them to the door steps. When a customer complained that she had not received her paper, Bobby told her, "That's impossible. I definitely remember giving your paper to Silver."[103]

Much to architect Sonnemann's displeasure, relaxed building restrictions during the Depression allowed the construction of some smaller houses south of Dorset and two homes of very modern design, the most notable of which was Studebaker dealer Lee D. Butler's big, white, Bauhaus-inspired pre-fab on a huge lot at Brookside and Chamberlin. Its flat roof invited Halloween pranksters, but Mr. Butler countered by waiting for them on the roof with his garden hose. The back of Butler's lot became one of the favorite playgrounds for Kenwood kids as did the Somervilles' big front yard.

The Lee D. Butlers' "modern" home at 101 Brookside

In the 1930s almost the whole middle of Kenwood was mainly weedy fields and broom sage where there were occasional neighborhood get-togethers and ball games. Murray Miles recalled letting out a mile of string flying a kite from there. This area, especially between Elmwood and Brookside above the circle, was turned into a large plot of Victory Gardens during World War Two.

Topography blessed Kenwood with good sleigh-riding hills. Sometimes Chamberlin Avenue was blocked off; Kennedy was a shady street where the snow stayed for a long time, but the real daredevils went flying down Brookside. One of the best sledding routes started across the street from the Mileses on the Pardoes' hilly front yard, went across Healys' and Boltons' lawns and then down Shadow Road. Numerous sleds wrecked there, and in the spring the patient Mr. Pardoe often had to resod his terraced lawn.[104]

For the adults there were a couple of clay tennis courts, usually covered with leaves, and the popular sport of walking about on Sunday mornings to inspect the new houses that were going up. "Billy" Miles remembered meeting half her neighbors around these foundations "speculating on where would be the kitchen and how many baths or what in the world was the purpose of the 'peek-through' hole between two bedrooms." Once a month, most of the residents got together for a dinner at the Club. They pulled numbers out of a bowl for table partners and sometimes had entertainment by their neighbors. Mrs. Miles enjoyed sitting with Charlie Ross because he could talk about everything, but she found that most of the other men stuck to golf and the Redskins.

In 1935 Thomas Somerville III, representing the home owners, and Donal Chamberlin signed a concordat granting residents half-price memberships, free social membership, free swimming on Mondays and Tuesdays ('35 was the year the pool opened despite grumblings of some golfers that it would just attract more women and children), and waiver of the cash deposit for owner-residents. The Kenwood Citizens' Association replaced the Residents' Association in 1937 "to promote civic matters." Its first president was George D. Horning. Relations between the development company and the community were often strained and sometimes even stormy.[105]

Community traditions developed including the annual "show," for years written mainly by Willard and Grace Egolf and often directed by Judge Prettyman. The cherry blossom festival became an unavoidable event, which produced some unlikely lemonade stands, a photo contest sponsored by the Club, and numerous residents escaping for the beflowered weekend. On Christmas Eve many neighbors met at Brookside Circle to sing carols, and at one memorable

Christmas party at the Club the women all dressed in green and the men in red.

The postman, followed by a pack of dogs, was another institution as was Admiral Miles's "What-the-Hell?" pennant which read "???!!!***" and showed that he was "at home." Several very active bridge groups developed, and during the war a Red Cross sewing unit met at the Club to roll bandages. To relieve the monotony of the tasks, Betty Sears began to read to the women assembled by Leonie Moffitt. That was the start of Kenwood's first women's organization, the "Sewing and Reading Club," which started meeting on Thursdays in 1942.[106]

Quite a few Kenwood children attended private schools and their buses were regular

visitors to the neighborhood, but many went to Somerset Elementary.   Neither Leland nor B-CC was as popular. Murray Miles remembered bicycling up the hill on Dorset to school and worrying about the Childs' "evil" chow as he headed toward his patrol post.   The Miles boys played in the Somerset band, and their mother was very active in the PTA, but, Murray Miles recalled, "They wouldn't let a woman be the head of it in those days." Ashby Chamberlin walked to Somerset school and sometimes played in the barns near the creek on his way home.

The Kennedy-Chamberlin Development Company struggled on and survived the Depression. It printed big, slick promotional brochures full of romantic photographs and florid prose that labeled Kenwood "a choice bit of nature's canvas upon which she has painted a beautiful picture of hills, streams, and forests" and promised that "residence in Kenwood carried with it social prestige as well as investment

security." From the very early days single, sepia-toned pages of Club News circulated with announcements for golfers, tennis and bridge players, and word that "That good Georgia ham is still being served in the club dining room." On the back of one was advice from "Al" Houghton, the first golf pro, on playing the first hole, which he called by far the most difficult.

Starting in 1933, Kennedy-Chamberlin produced a monthly magazine to promote the sale of homes. Edited by Ruth H. Farnham, K-C's long-time office manager, the magazine included monthly columns on skeet shooting and one called "Dainty Divot Diggers" about female golfers. Eventually the magazine, which lasted about five years, ran serial romances and tips for homemakers, but it always featured a newly built home and a full page ad for "Kenwood, the Beautiful."

The many communities down Wisconsin grew up along the trolley line and expanded with the growing popularity of the automobile. Held together at first with common concerns related to pioneering in then remote, suburban outposts, the residents of Friendship Heights, Drummond, Crow Hill, and even Kenwood slowly became Bethesdans.

Like their sisters and brothers in Glen Echo and Martins Additions, they tended their gardens, supported their schools, and worked to make their neighborhoods safe places for their children. The African-American community had its school and its baseball team and would soon have a church in Bill Clipper's old house. The white neighborhoods shared the Somerset school and the recreation center on Norwood Drive. The neighborhoods grew, prospered and took on a confident outlook.

Detail from Hopkins' 1894 map of the Washington area showing development "down Wisconsin."

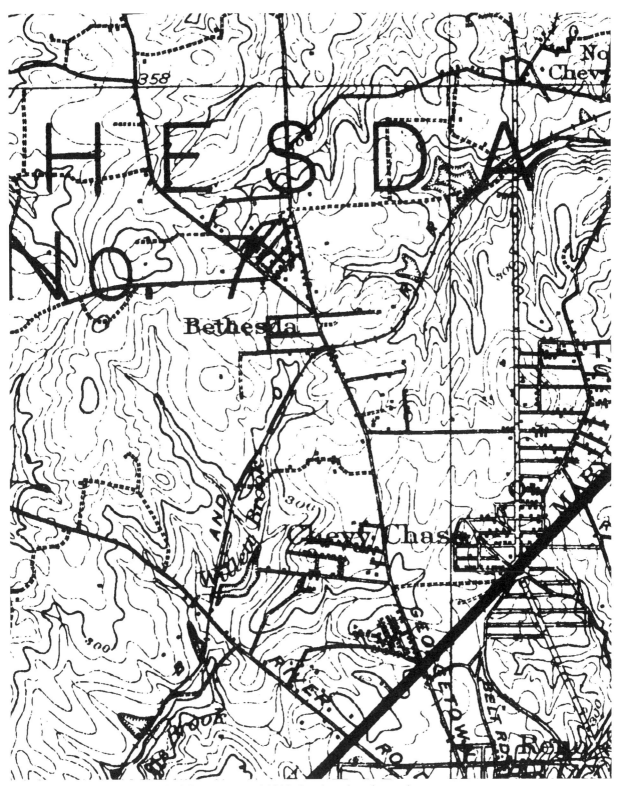

Deatil from Maryland Geological Survey map of 1910 showing elevation and water courses

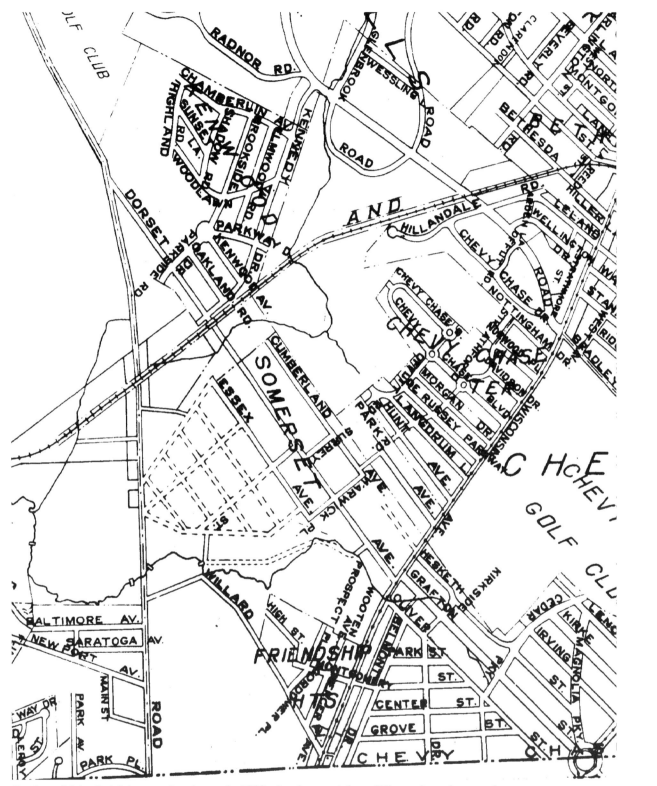

Section of John Imirie's map showing early 1930s development down Wisconsin and some plans.

A page of ads from the Kennedy-Chamberlin Development Company's magazine in the fall of 1933

[1] This had been going on since 1777 when the first County roads were laid out and divided into thirty-six sections, each with its appointed overseer.

[2] See Chapter 13 of *A Grateful Remembrance* for more on the good roads movement. Maryland's well-earned reputation for bad roads continued for another half-century.

[3] "Roadside Sketches," *Star*, Aug. 15, 1891. J. Harry Shannon, the *Star*'s first "Rambler," began his pieces in 1912 and wrote them until 1927.

[4] For more on the trolley line to Bethesda, see Chapter 4 and, of course, the basic source, King's *100 Years of Capital Traction*, available for purchase at the trolley museum on Bonifant Road.

[5] Streets in Friendship Heights have had several names. See Mark Shoemaker's "Brief History" in the Village information booklet (1989).
John Murdock, who purchased 400 acres of the old Friendship tract, probably built the Eld house along with its barn and outbuildings about 1760.

[6] Based on the biography by his nephew, G. W. Warren Jr. in the Offutt genealogies at the MCHS. For more on the Offutts of Potomac, see Ann Paterson Harris, *The Potomac Adventure* (1976).

[7] See Liber HH folio 1 for the will of Samuel Shoemaker dated Feb. 4, 1846. At the time of the 1860 census Jesse and Elizabeth Shoemaker had three daughters and six sons at home.

[8] County land records, liber BS9 folio 533 for the original deed. The Village of Friendship Heights has a complete title search of this property in its archives.

[9] All Mark Shoemaker quotes from his "Brief History" in the Village booklet, first printed in 1959 and reprinted in the 75th anniversary edition of 1989.

[10] A photocopy of the scrapbook and photographs is in the collection of the Montgomery County Historical Society, a donation of her daughter, Mrs. Arthur Hilland, with whose permission the following is excerpted and through whose kindness the photographs are reproduced with the help of her daughter, Janice Greene. Mrs. Sheiry was fond of ampersands.

[11] Mark Shoemaker: Residents had been burning off the Bergdoll tract "as customary" and Mr. Frost's smouldering broom was left on the back porch. The house burned to the ground "with the help of the D.C. fire department."

[12] According to Mark Shoemaker, classes were for only the first three grades, and later classes were held at the Oughs' and in other homes.

[13] *Star*, April 9, 1910.

[14] It still is; see the entrance of the Barlow Building. Most early Friendship Heights residents seem to have called it the "Pike" as did many in Bethesda until WW II.

[15] Although the Maryland Constitution of 1864 had led to reorganization, the law of 1868 made the counties autonomous but required high schools. By 1910 the illiteracy rate had been cut to 7.2 percent (African-American 23.4 percent), but not until the equalization fund was established in 1922 was real progress made. By 1930 white illiteracy was 1.3 percent, and black was 11.4.

[16] This creek, now Jenifer Run, is mostly underground and a recurrent source of pollution.

[17] An annex of Miss Corwin's market where farm women who had not joined the Bethesda co-op sold their produce, cakes and pies occupied that second store in the late `30s. See Chapter 8.

[18] See Lillian Shoemaker Brown's 1988 handwritten autobiography in the collection of the MCHS.

[19] County land records: 368-203 & 206, 378-135 & 139. Not until the 1960s and '70s was the Friendship Heights land subject again to such chicanery and paper shuffling.

[20] See Mark Shoemaker's "Brief History."

[21] Shoemaker's "Brief History" and the *Sentinel*, Dec. 12, 1912. Other members of the first council: Walter Balderson, Charles E. Roach, John A. Garrett, Emory H. Bogley, J. Walter Bogley and William Tyler Page.

[22] "Regulations for the Governing of the Special Taxing Area known as Friendship Heights and The Hills" in the archives of the Village of Friendship Heights and the MCHS

[23] 1926 committee: chairman J. A. F. Farnham, H. W. Offutt, G. W. Offutt, E. H. Bogley, Ernest E. Dellinger, John D. McAuliffe, and Earl S. Haines, secretary,

[24] The Shoemaker family papers at Georgetown University contain A. E. Shoemaker's scrapbook with most of the minutes and many treasurer's reports from 1925 to 1935. Were it not for this collection, saved only by happenstance, the early history of the Village would not be, since the town's records were lost or destroyed in the acrimonious autocannibalism of the 1960s out of which the modern village emerged phoenixlike with feathers ruffled.

[25] First officers: "Pres. Mrs. Rippey, First Vice-Pres. Mrs. Henry W. Offutt, Second Vice-Pres. Miss Anna Smith, Secy. Mrs. Shoemaker, Cor. Sec. Mrs. Constantine, Historian, Mrs. Sullivan."

[26] All quotes from Mrs. Sheiry's pictorial genealogy.
One of the brass entrance signs is still proudly displayed in the Village. It was salvaged by Henry Latterner from the rubble of the stone gates and cleaned, polished and presented to the town by Horace and Dorothy Hampton to whom it had been given.

[27] *Star*, May 23, 1914. The land records show that Isaac Shoemaker sold Hilleary Ball ten acres in 1846; the *Star*'s peripatetic reporter called it a blacksmith shop in 1891.

[28] The Marriotts did traffic surveys, "rented the properties in the busiest sites, and secured permits to alter curbs . . . ." *Marriott Hot Shoppes Cookbook* (1987).

[29] See minutes and correspondence at MCHS. The Garden Clubs' obelisk, now much shorter and switched to the other side of the street during Metro building, survives.

[30] For some reason the name Tenallytown or Tenleytown, the preferred spelling after 1920, seemed to be disappearing in the 1930s with the designation "Friendship" replacing it in news stories and post offices. See J. B. Helm's *Tenleytown, D.C.*, p. 500.

[31] Tenleytown's Grant Road gang had a well earned reputation for nastiness, and that area's football team, the Bonecrushers, often found it hard to schedule games. *Ibid.*, p. 502.

[32] McAuliffe does not dispute the genesis. The spelling remains unsettled.

[33] Henry A. Latimer, "Memoir of an Oldtimer," Bethesda *Gazette*, Jan. 25, 1984. Other Bethesda-area mines were found along the creek near Landon School.

[34] Land records, JA9-230, JA17-151, and JA19 folio 489. Dorothy O'Brien's "In the beginning."
After establishing criteria, the scientists, as one would expect, had worked through several committees before agreeing to the purchase by their company.

[35] *Star*, May 17, 1890.

[36] "Federal Food and Drugs Laws" by Fred B. Linton in the *Food Drug Cosmetic Law Quarterly*, Dec. 1949, p. 451. The date of his house is often given as 1881, but `91 is more likely.

[37] Part of the Stohlman's store is now an admired Smithsonian exhibit.

[38] Fuller's house was torn down in the mid-1960s and three new houses built on the lot.

[39] In plat book #1 of the County land records, plat #30 shows the faintly penciled names of the "winners" of various lots, and Somerset has in its archives a "blueprint" showing lot ownership, early houses, and the original sewer and water lines.
Information on early houses mostly from the Town's diamond jubilee publication, especially the section by Donna Williamson. Much of the rest from the 1956 history by Dorothy O'Brien.
The 1900 census listed eight black and two white live-in servants in Somerset out of the district's total of 170, about fifty of whom worked in Chevy Chase.

[40] Quotes from "Somerset Heights Land Co." booklet, 1895. The company's officers were listed as "Ralph Walsh, president; Chas. M. Barrick, vice president, and John E. Beall, sec. & treas."

[41] *Star*, April 9, 1910. Ough is pronounced "oh."

[42] Incorporation papers in Somerset archives at MCHS. Frank Millis, Jesse Swigart, William Benham, and Edwin Gibbs were the other incorporators.

[43] "Heritage" by Dorothy O'Brien, 1976 ms at MCHS. The Maryland Historic Trust lists the following as some of Somerset's most interesting examples of Victorian architecture:
5800 Dorset - for its porch and balustrade, its two-story Italianate tower, and its millwork;

4719 Cumberland - a "nice example of Colonial revival style" with very tightly overlapped clapboards;

4723 Cumberland - a 1901 construction by Ough and/or son once owned by the town clerk and later the home of town historian Dorothy O'Brien and her husband;

4824 Cumberland - a more recently built but seldom-locally-seen Greek Revival home with a pedimented portico and a central chimney.

[44]Much of the above from Somerset's diamond jubilee publication, by Joan McW. Weiss, Donna Williamson, and Helen Jaszi, 1981.
It is very likely that Mr. Hardy was an African-American, possibly a "mulatto" as the census used that label. See also minutes of town meetings, 1913-1917 and 1924-1926.

[45]Irene Rice's memory in the 1981 town publication. Her family lived on Warwick Place.

[46]From her 1976 letter in the Somerset archives at MCHS.

[47]"Town of Somerset Maryland 1906-1956," the history credited to Dorothy O'Brien.

[48]The original Council members were Jesse E. Swigart, C. Fred Cook, W. A. Ough, and John R. Cox.

[49]Minutes of the town council meetings, 1906-1909. Unlike Friendship Heights, Somerset has been able to preserve most of its history. See also Helen H. Jaszi's "Somerset; Beginnings" in the 1981 Town publication.

[50]Mr. Moore, who invested early and wisely in the Woodmont Triangle, was the father of Margaretta who walked to school with Ken Frisbie.

[51]Notes on "What the Women of Somerset Did" by Mrs. Wilber (Carrie) Starratt, ca. 1940, in Somerset archives, MCHS.

[52]These women were among the few to use their own names in public rather than their husbands'.

[53]From Mrs. Jesse Swigart's scrapbook and Mrs. Starratt's collection of minutes in the Somerset archives at the MCHS. Both saved and donated by Dorothy O'Brien who also collected pictures of all the mayors but one and did a number of title searches. Somerset's history rests on her work. See also Jane Russell Snyder's "Know Your Own Community" *Record*, April 27, 1945.

[54]The letter is in the archives at MCHS and in the 1981 diamond jubilee booklet.

[55]Gustavus A. Weber, *The Bureau of Entomology*, The Brookings Institution, 1930.

[56]See "Somerset School 1928-1988." No direct evidence places any Somerset children in any of these early Maryland schools.

[57]Ada Swigart Hess also wanted it clearly understood that she attended the "Chevy Chase School" and did not approve of the name being changed to E. V. Brown. Later she went to Central High, Wilson Normal, and was graduated from GW before starting her teaching career.
Chemist Howard Watkins once was national secretary of the Iris Society.

[58]Somerset archives at MCHS and "Somerset School 1928-1988."

[59]The class - ID by Jane Dunbar Tedeschi: Alice Ellsworth, John DeJarnett, John Dodge, John Amiss, Dorothy Stevens, Rose Beard, Bertha Fawcett, Edmund Amiss, Norman Grady, Harry Anderson, Harold Greenberg, Ella Willet, Katherine Loudermilk, Annie Mae Rodman, Austin Milans, Emily Bogley, Louise Watkins, Caroline Hummel, Charles Davis, Howard Bryan, Alex Clinton, Billy West, Billy Swingle, Betty DuPre, Mary Kuster, Paul Williams.

[60]For more on this, see Kenwood section in this chapter and footnote 98.

[61]Somerset town council minutes, 1927-1930.

[62]"Charter and Ordinances of the Town of Somerset, 1930," as amended.

[63]For recent history, as well as more on the colorful past, see "The Town of Somerset" by Dorothy O'Brien and Helen H. Jaszi in *The Montgomery County Story* (vol.20 no.2) May 1977 which also contains an up-to-date map. The Child's piece is in the Jan. 29, 1944, *Record* .

[64]The land records show that William Clipper purchased a lot measuring about 60 by 185 feet from Jacob Wilbert in March 1910 for $150, 212-159.

[65]For more on "Milton" see Chapter 2. New Deal economist M. J. Ezekiel purchased Milton in 1932 and restored the abandoned house with love, care, and a lot of money.

[67] Jacob Wilbert bought 25 acres from the Counselmans in 1877 for $1,200. See EPB 17-128 in the land records. Wilbert was 67 in 1910 and his German accent probably made Clipper hear his first name as "Yakum" or "Yahcum."

[68] By "the church" Clipper meant the present-day Macedonia Baptist Church, which occupies what was, at one time, his family home. It moved there from Miller's Flats during WWII. After several lengthy attempts, the writer gave up trying to learn its history.

[69] *Star*, March 14, 1914.

[70] Viewers of the famous cyclorama at Gettysburg will find Henry Hunt hard to miss.

[71] Mostly from *The Republic*, Dec. 4, 1880.

[72] *Sentinel*, Feb. 22, 1901.

[73] "Memoir of an oldtimer" by Henry A. Latimer in the *Gazette*, Jan. 25, 1984. He was Dick Latimer's grandfather (see Chapter 8).

[74] Jane Dunbar Tedeschi recalled, "All through junior high school, I had skinned knees from playing hockey with the boys on Drummond." See Washington *Post* article, March 24, 1990. Most of the town's early records have been lost; others were stored in Mr. Barlow's garage beside a lovely old Packard when this was written.

[75] See the plat maps in the County land records and liber 78 folio 130. The source of almost all these street names should now be clear.

[76] For more on one of Bethesda's most interesting citizens, see Doree Holman's sketch of Hunt's life in the Apr. 26, 1940, Bethesda *Journal*.

[77] See *James Davidson of the Maryland Line and Some of His Descendants* at the MCHS.

[78] Article by Verla P. Richtmyer in Western Bethesda Community Planning Association's *News Carrier*, November 1959.

[79] "Background for Plenty: A National Center for Agricultural Research" by Vivian Wiser and Wayne D. Rasmussen in the *Maryland Historical Magazine*, Dec. 1966, pp. 298-299.

[80] "Clippers Along the C&O Canal" by Michael Kernan, *Star*, n.d., at MCHS.

[81] Several interviewees including Kathryn Cragoe and Thomas Barlow said they thought that the Chevy Chase area was used by the Dept. of Agriculture, and Horace Hampton played on the farm near the Grosvenor Metro station.

[82] Horace Hampton was the youngest and the last survivor of Thomas Hampton's nine children. Hampton and his wife of more than sixty years, Dorothy Latterner Hampton, lived in Potomac at the time of this 1990 interview. He was a long-time telephone company employee and expert on communications security.

[83] J. Slater Davidson, whose father later worked for his brothers' company, said H. Bradley Davidson "died a wealthy man" and doubts that he lost much in the Bradley Hills venture.

[84] See plat maps 148 and 152 and liber JA 11 folio 196 in the County land records. For the 1860 purchase from the Batemans, see LGH 8/71. H. L. Offutt also purchased 90 acres of No Gain land from Benjamin Hodges for $3,645 in 1873, see EPB 10/300, which became part of the CCLCo acquistion twenty years later when his son (the writer's paternal grandfather) sold it. See also footnote 14 of Chapter 3.

[85] Jos. Williamson of Augusta was the registered agent and E. M. Leavitt of Winthrop, the treasurer according to the records of Maine's Secretary of State. The company was incorporated in 1911 and suspended in 1918.

[86] See plat map 234 and PBR300-163 regarding the Hillmead section.

[87] The writer has been unable to ascertain what either the Quantico Co. or Safety First Manuf. Co. made or did and has been unable to create a clarifying, two-dimensional chart of these many companies with few people and their relationships to each other. Most of the information is from Boyd's D. C. directories in the collection of the HSW.

[88] Hampton also hired teams from farmers along the way to speed up the work. Abe Morrison recalled that his father and older brothers took horses from their farm on Cedar Lane (Greentree

[89] Road) over to the road building but that he was too young to go watch the work.

[89] County land records liber 230 folio 458; *Sentinel* December 20, 1912. The CPI was very low in 1912, so if one triples the 1912 cost and adds a zero, the result may be in the ballpark for now.

[90] *Star*, June 14, 1913.

[91] Which helps explain those fire plugs that seem to be in the middle of some folks' lawns and why houses are set back so far on one side of the street.

[92] See *The Electric Railway Journal*, Jan. 10, 1914, pp. 89-90. In 1915 the schedule called for cars to leave Great Falls for 5th and F at 7:15 am, 9:00, 10:45, 12:30 pm, 2:15, 4:00, 6:06, 7:40 and 11:52 with the last three only to the District Line.

[93] Ann Paterson Harris, *The Potomac Adventure*, p. 67.

[94] Charles W. Miller, his wife Annie and daughters Genevieve and Uranium lived on Wilson Lane according to Caldwell's 1915 Directory.

[95] Col. Frank L. Denny USMC (ret.), vice-pres.; R. S. Reynolds Hitt, secretary; and George Howard, treasurer.

[96] *Sentinel* June 13, 1913 and S. D. Caldwell's 1915 *Directory*. Other incorporators included John F. Wilkins, Paul F. Pearsall, Frederick E. Chapin, William B. Hitt, Huge E. Legare, J. Henri deSibour, and Edward A. Mitchell.

[97] The site was on Back Creek, now the Riverside development. The marsh was filled, siding was laid, and a yard built that employed about 2,000 men and built the S. S. *Euharlee, Fernandina,* and *WeQuahic* and tugs *McClintic* and *VonEzdorf* under Hampton and Gen. Mgr. A. N. Shelander.

[98] County land records: 289-340, 289-350, 300-163. Records of State Corporation Commission, Commonwealth of Virginia.

[99] See plat maps 359 and 360 and the deeds recorded at 392-441, 424-363, 458-1, and 458-4 in the County land records. Among those consulted by K-C in planning the subdivision was Jesse C. Nichols who had designed a similar development in the Kansas City, Missouri, area.

[100] Sonnemann, an architect for sixty years, designed many homes and apartment buildings in Washington, including Kew Gardens and Meridian Mansions. He also designed the Kenwood clubhouse and was K-C's resident architect until his death in 1956.

[101] *Star*, Nov. 27, 1927. Much of the above from Kenwood's golden anniversary publication of 1978 and the Washington *Post* , Sept. 13, 1931, and various issues of *The Kenwood Magazine* in the 1930s. There was nothing covert about Kenwood's racial restrictions as Chamberlin had told the town fathers in Somerset.

[102] See James Goode's *Best Addresses*, p. 152-3 and the *Post* "Where We Live" article of May 25, 1991. Goode lived at the Kennedy-Warren. For more on the Warrens, see the *Town of Chevy Chase* chapter section on "Leland." Monroe Warren's new venture, Meadowbrook Inc., lasted from 1932 until 1966 and built many excellent, low-cost houses.

[103] *Journal,* May 21, 1943, *Record*, Aug. 4, 1944, and Kenwood archives.

[104] Ed Pardoe is remembered as the organizer of bus trips to Redskin games and as the community Santa who not only gave out the presents but opened each one, vigorously.

[105] Other original officers: H. H. Moffitt, vp; J. D. Sears, secretary; Claude W. Dudley and M. M. Daubin, general counsels.

[106] Much of the above from Jo Ann Pistenmaa's history presentation and letters from Ibby (Mrs. Benjamin A.) Powell and Marcia Ely, which were in the archives maintained by Mrs. Pistenmaa. For the story of the "What-the-Hell?" pennant see pages 103-6 of *A Different Kind of War* by Vice-Admiral Milton E. Miles, which was published in 1967 by his widow.

CHAPTER 7

Old Bethesda

When the sweating work gangs laying track for the trolley company reached Bethesda in the spring of 1891, they found a crossroads village not much changed in the generation since the end of the Civil War. At what became the center of town, they turned the tracks northwest alongside the old road where General Braddock's men had marched and away from the hilly, deteriorating turnpike where Stuart's troopers had captured the wagon train.

The big Watkins farm spread from east of what would be the high school campus across the intersection of Rockville Pike and the old road to Georgetown. Spencer Watkins' fields covered most of what became Edgemoor with one barn sitting just south of the 1938 post office site and another near the Bethesda Elementary School playground-to-be. What later became the western end of East West Highway was then Watkins' tree-shaded lane. His spring house stood on what is now Pearl Street.

A blacksmith's shop marked the point of Gingell's land that later became the Bank of Bethesda's lot. In the twenty-some years he

The blacksmith at Old Georgetown Road and the Pike

had been there, William Lochte had added a substantial wheelwright business to his farriery and had built a sizable shed beneath a huge willow tree where his oldest boy, Leroy, shod horses and his younger son and namesake learned the smithy's art. Lochte settled in Bethesda just after the Civil War and apprenticed at Flack's forge about where the B&O tracks later cut the hill. The electric railway builders placed the first siding of the single-track trolley line where passengers could watch the sparks fly and hear the blacksmith's hammer ring while they waited in an open shelter for the car to Alta Vista or the one going down into the city.

Across the Pike from Lochte's sheds was a big stone house that had long been a tavern. No one seemed to know how old it was, and of course, there were stories of Braddock stopping there and of Washington's visits. James Madison Gingell was the one-time owner. The rooms were huge and the fireplaces devoured immense logs. Heath Dodge, after he finally sold off his Norwood property to the Chevy Chase Club, tore down this old place and built the foundation of his fine Victorian home from its stones. His house would later become home to the town's undertaker.

The Gingell family had owned much of the land in mid-Bethesda. At one time their holdings, which dated back to the 1840s and were said to have cost about eight dollars an acre, included almost all of Woodmont and a good bit of Edgemoor. Their name sounded like "jingle" then, but some softened it later and changed the stressed syllable.

Madison Gingell and his wife, Artemesia, had six sons and seven daughters. He built

homes for three of his sons, all of whom worked for the trolley company, on the opposite side of Old Georgetown Road from his ten-acre farm. That part of the old road and trolley line came to be known as Gingell's Curve and was later the location of the far end of Battery Park. Son Warren lived next to his father's place in the Woodmont Triangle and went into the plumbing trade, and one daughter married into the Lochte family.

Darcy's store beside the streetcar tracks

William Darcy's place on the east side of the Pike was the oldest store in Bethesda and had once given the village its name as far as the U.S. Post Office was concerned. The Darcy family lived where the County Building and police station were later located, and the general store was at 6811 Wisconsin Avenue in the old numbering system, in the middle of the present 7200 block, which, of course, was no block then because there were no side streets. A Mr. Pierce operated the store after Darcy and then came the Counselmans—John, Amanda, and Hester—after they abandoned River Road. The old store with its "easy, slender railed stairway" survived well into the 1930s and a number of businesses used it after "Uncle Billy" Counselman finally gave up storekeeping.

Diagonally across the street to the north Jake Stadtler had lived and worked the gate at the toll house collecting the five-cent fee. The turnpike fell into disrepair after the opening of the Metropolitan Branch by the B&O, and the company abandoned the toll gates in 1887. Two years later, after a brief apprenticeship at Counselman's, young Alfred Wilson gave up teaching, bought the old, four-room toll house and a piece of J. Hite Miller's land and opened a general store.

Within a short time he dragged the old place back from the road, built a new store in the style of the time with a sloping roof over the porch out front, and married Minnie Poole.

They made their home over the store later known as Community Paint and Hardware.[1]

Alfred's father, Michael Wilson, and his family had emigrated from Canada about ten years before and bought a farm called Mountain View where the wealthy McLeans later built a home that still later became the Landon School and then the Whitehall School. The mountain they could "view" was Sugarloaf. The road to the house, which some old-timers called "Wilson's lane," turned off near present-day Moorland Lane and wound through pastures and past a line of English cherries.

A granddaughter recalled:

(The lane had) a pear and apple orchard on one side, and peaches on the other and came to the crest of the hill where the house stood among huge swaying oaks. The area was so sparsely populated it was an event to see a horse and buggy pass on Wilson Lane. The family knew every horse and vehicle and I can remember being stationed at the kitchen window when a new buggy appeared in the distance—to identify it when it came close."[2]

Alfred's brother Herbert soon moved down from "Mountain View" to live in the house behind the store and go in partnership with his busy brother and make most of the deliveries until they hired Lyles Offutt. From 1895 to 1905, Alfred ran the post office from his store with Will Darcy as one of his RFD men. The electric railway hired Alfred to keep the books for Bethesda Park and act as paymaster for the motormen and conductors on the Bethesda line. He was one of the busiest and best known men in town long before he became a justice of the peace and gained the title "judge."

The store stocked everything from groceries to kerosene, from dry goods and notions to harnesses and hardware. The Wilsons had to fetch their stock on horse and wagon trips to the Centre Market and to Georgetown because most wholesalers refused to deliver so far out of town. Doing it in an hour and a half each way was making good time.

Annie Gingell, who set up housekeeping by the tracks in Woodmont with her plumber husband about ten years after the trolley line arrived, remembered the Wilson brothers' establishment as "an old-fashioned country store with the post office in a corner, groceries on one side and hardware and dry goods on the other. There was also a telephone–one of the few within miles. If someone wanted to get in touch with a Bethesda resident over the telephone

they rang Wilson's store. Mr. Wilson then gave the message to the first person going past."[3]

Down toward the city, past vacant fields and a creek-cut countryside were the late Hilleary Offutt's large, square home and sprawling farm. There Magruder Willson Offutt, who was deeply involved with the trolley enterprise, and his wife, Dixie, were just getting their family started. Across the rough road and the newly ballasted tracks stood the small Episcopal church with its fancy memorial windows, fifteen years old by the time the trolley came to town.

Cater-cornered from the church, on the west side, rose the two-story Grange Hall. School kept on the first floor for a while but was soon given up because of lack of students. Upstairs the local Patrons of Husbandry met behind green baize doors to discuss their agricultural problems and plan political solutions. Beyond, toward the distant city, lay the rolling land of the Davidsons and the Dodges.

From the several Shoemaker farms at the D.C. line to often impassable Jones Mill Road and Cedar Lane a mile north of the Wilsons' store, only narrow Bradley Lane connected Bethesda to the old Brookeville-Tenleytown Road and the farms to the east where rumors of land speculation proved true and Newlands' two-track trolley line clanked toward a growing lake and a newly laid spur of the B&O.

That was downtown Bethesda when the electric railway arrived for the first time in 1891: two country stores across a wide, wagon-worn street from each other, a couple of blacksmiths, a few farm houses, some barns, several windmills and an old tavern. The rest was farmland: cows, chickens, creeks, corn and alternately dusty or muddy lanes.

In 1940 historian-piano teacher Doree Germaine Holman wrote that "the biggest single event that ever took place in Bethesda was the passage of the first electric car, which opened the section to the commuter and provided rapid transportation to the city." Alfred Wilson and several other young men walked down to General Drum's lane, boarded the first car there, and appeared in Bethesda "with the air of world-travelers."[4]

Bethesda did grow, but in a leisurely and spotty manner and, until the 1920s, in very low gear. A few more houses went up along Wisconsin Avenue, several more in Woodmont. Isolated summer places such as the Wheatleys'

stood here and there, and some folks lived beside the old road as far out as Alta Vista and Beane, where there was also an old, one-room school house and the Mount Zion Church, "the little church in the wildwood," both established before the Civil War.

The small, frame house of worship that first stood on Spider Hill had a gallery at the back for the slaves. The Rev. J. S. Teasdale became the first pastor after it separated from the Rockville congregation in 1881. A new building in 1910 was a prosperous sign of the growing community, but Beane itself had never grown although a post office existed there in 1884 with Bernard Rabbitt, the local storekeeper, as postmaster.

In 1917 the Star's Rambler, Harry Shannon, walked by on his way to Locust Grove and noted just the "country store, a ruinous shed that once was a blacksmith shop, two dwellings of colored folks and close by the road a pump." Two years later another small store, operated by Turner and Franklin Wilson, appeared across from Rabbitt's at the end of the improved section of Old Georgetown Road.[5]

Of course, much of the property in the Beane area had once been part of the oft-divided Magruder holdings. Beane itself as a post office and "wagon turn around" was founded by John and Anna Bean who married in 1840, acquired property there, and raised five children on their Georgetown Road farm. Descendants of this family divided and farmed the land and lived in and around Bethesda from that time on.

Susan Magruder Imirie, one of whose great-great-grandfathers was Samuel Wade Magruder, was born in 1897, grew up on her father's small farm, and lived all her life on Old Georgetown Road. When she was very young, one of her brothers brought scarlet fever home from the water at Bell's Mill, and it raced through all the children. At seven, she walked with her older sister to the Beane School and began learning to read and write.

Sue Imirie remembered it.[6]

A one-room school, just plain with black-boards all around and a stove in the middle. The teachers had charge of everything, but the boys would help to bring in wood. Julian Griffith taught me to write. He made us toe the line on penmanship.

Sometimes Mr. Weaver who had an automobile, a Studebaker, he went by the school and knew Papa, so he'd stop and pick us up, and we were in heaven.

When my sister and I finished school, this teacher, Mrs. Thomas, a grand person, she finagled a scholarship for us to a secretarial school. A man over in Kensington named Brainard H. Warner paid for it. We went to Wood's Commercial School, and he paid for it.[7]

We both graduated in shorthand typing. I took shorthand, typing, rapid calculation, spelling and English–five courses. I got the streetcar at twenty minutes of eight, and I went to work when I was 16 and took the civil service examination when I was 18. You couldn't take it `til then, and I got a job at the Agriculture Department almost the very next month, and my salary was $900 a year. And we thought that was wonderful. I was a millionaire.

Alta Vista itself was Bethesda's first real neighborhood as well as the name of the oldest home there. The tall, green, frame house at 5506 Beech Avenue is, according to the Maryland Historic Trust, "either a completely new house constructed in the later Victorian years, circa 1880, or an extensive remodeling and alteration" probably by Lewis Keiser, of a much earlier, likely pre-Civil War home or of one built just after the war to replace an even older, tenant house.

The land that became the subdivision of Alta Vista had been the part of Leeke Forest purchased by Georgetown merchant Andrew Heugh who retired there after serving in the Maryland House of Delegates until 1770. The property was among the McCubbins family's holdings in the first half of the 19th century, and the Keisers owned it from 1875 until 1896.

With the coming of the trolley, the land changed hands several times, and new owners cut it into smaller and smaller "villa and cottage sites." The plat of 222 acres by the Bethesda Land Company resulted in the streets being named for trees and the creation of thirty-eight lots of from two to eight acres.

Residence of Mr.M. E. Croxall about 1915

Between 1907 and 1937, "Alta Vista" and its three-acre lot were owned by Mary Perry, and her heirs modernized the old house and brought in running water. Its admirable two-story bay window and shady, wrap-around porch guard the abandoned trolley right-of-way.[8]

More typical of the square, hipped-roof houses built in Alta Vista early in the 20th century is the handsome, eight-room, "four-square," Colonial-revival frame and stucco home built in 1914 by George W. Norris on three acres at 5420 Beech Avenue. It has a wrap-around front veranda as well as a back porch and hipped dormers on its hipped roof. Its 1915 value was $2,100, and it is as handsome as any of Chevy Chase's frame or stucco dowagers of similar years. A few, smaller bungalows were built in Alta Vista by World War I, and later, of course, many of the big lots were redivided and other types of homes constructed.

Surely the most impressive early home and farm was that of Mr. and Mrs. Harry T. Newcomb. At the time of the 1910 census they and their eight children under ten, including the two-

The Newcomb estate with the trolley line to Rockville at the far right (west)

month-old twins, plus Mrs. Newcomb's parents and three servants lived in Alta Vista. Their home filled the center-spread of the sales brochure, which claimed that Alta Vista "is the only subdivision around Washington which is laid out according to the topography of the land, giving each lot a good building site with a fine view of the surrounding country, the beauties of which are second to none."

The neighborhood sat atop its hill on both sides of Georgetown Road and enjoyed the breezes for many years before the rest of Bethesda began to grow. Neither the promoters of Alta Vista nor the Newcombs next door made mention of the Washington Hospital for Foundlings, which bought nine acres of the old Lyddane property and moved part of its operation out of D.C. in the winter of 1898 to become a fixture at Cedar Lane and Old Georgetown Road.[9]

The Keiser family was one of the first to see the potential of the Bethesda area and to seek to develop it. Lewis Keiser, born in Ohio of German-immigrant parents, came to Montgomery County in 1875 with his 24-year-old son, Cyrus, and bought a 145-acre farm in Alta Vista just north of Cedar Lane, which included the farmhouse at 5506 Beech. Keiser then purchased an old farm at Georgetown and Montrose Roads and moved there leaving his son on the Alta Vista property.

"The first Lewis," as the Keisers called him, died in 1886 and was buried in the family plot at Mt. Zion. Cyrus subdivided and tried to develop both the Montrose property, called Ingleside, and Alta Vista. He built his new house on the west side of Georgetown Road in 1892 after selling the Alta Vista farm for $28,000. The first buyer defaulted on his loan, and three years later Keiser sold the property again for the same price.

To back up his sometimes unsure real estate income, Cyrus operated a very successful ice plant in Bethesda with his son Lewis, who later succeeded Alfred Wilson as the town's postmaster. The deep well on the east side of the Pike had a long reputation for producing cold, delicious water that brought jug-carrying people out from the District on the trolley. To their ice business the Keisers soon added a lumber yard as Bethesda expanded. Later Cyrus Keiser with Alfred Wilson as treasurer incorporated the Bethesda Ice and Lumber Company on this property.

Clarence "Bud" Keiser: "That's Cyrus, his wife Elizabeth, my grandmother Lois who lived to 104, me, Lewis, then Clarence, my father, about 1932."

Cyrus senior was also the enumerator of the entire Bethesda area, the Seventh Election District, in the Twelfth Census of the United States made in June 1900 and was a founding member of the Bethesda Masonic lodge. Cyrus junior entered the history books by driving children from Bethesda and the communities down Wisconsin over to the school in Chevy Chase for $12.50 a week. He later moved into the District and also entered the real estate business.

Lewis became an incorporator and director of the Bank of Bethesda and was active in Republican political circles, small though they were. He died in 1936 with a reputation as being the friendliest man in town. His son Clarence took his father's place on the bank board as well as in the real estate and insurance business and, also like his father, was a leader of the local Masons.[10]

Among those building houses in Bethesda shortly after the trolley's arrival was the president of the electric railway and the town's first great promoter, John Beall, owner of some thousand acres of prime residential property. His empire collapsed in the Panic of 1893 and the hurricane of '96, and after his death at the turn of the century, much of his property had to be auctioned off. His big Victorian house crowned a knoll above the tracks on Old Georgetown Road where Glenbrook Road was later cut through. It stood empty for a decade, and some early Battery Park denizens remembered it as the local "haunted" house. Then the Presbyterians used it in 1925-26 and finally it became the home of the Lutheran church

In 1911 St. John's Norwood Parish built a rectory on a lot donated by Joseph Bradley.

John Beall's Old Georgetown Road home

The Rev. Thomas Lewis, the original full-time rector, was the first to live in the manse on Old Georgetown Road, which was later purchased by Walter Perry. It was located just north of George Sacks's Commerce Lane.

Other builders followed in Woodmont and Northwest Park. Small subdivisions such as Highland Park briefly blossomed, but the building was sporadic and scattered even though the land speculation of the `90s just about ended farming in central Bethesda. Long before World War I began and the Bradley Hill venture took wing, the first Bethesda boom evaporated. Some marked its end with the sudden demise of Bethesda Park in the hurricane of `96. By the time John E. Beall lost his shirt, the town's pre-trolley population of about one thousand had tripled.[11]

Many early Bethesdans worked in the building trades. The 1900 census showed more carpenters than attorneys and as many other skilled workers (plumbers, bricklayers, painters, well diggers and stone masons) as there were government "clerks," a very broad term then.

One outgrowth of the first boomlet was the establishment of the Bethesda Citizens' Association. It met monthly starting in 1904 and included representatives from neighborhoods in Chevy Chase. The Association had committees on Law and Order, Roads and Highways, Education, Health, Transportation and one called "Farms, Gardens and Domestic."[12]

Bethesda boasted its first real schoolhouse since the Civil War shortly after the trolley line arrived. The plain, square, one-room school with a chamfered cornice was built in 1894 up the hill northeast of Gingell's Curve. This was the same year Chevy Chase's school opened on "that lot with the walnut tree" on Bradley's lane. According to Miss Holman, the first teacher at the new Bethesda school was Miss Eleanor Chambers "who had a great deal of difficulty in finding a place to live." Another early and long-remembered teacher was Miss Ida Dove who planted an ash tree beside the porch on Arbor Day and recalled the excitement caused "by the sight of Judge Harry J. Hunt 3rd, then a daring youngster, riding a mule backwards around the school grounds."

The girls cleaned the room and collected the books, and the boys stoked the iron, pot-bellied stove and kept the water buckets filled. Mrs. Gingell wrote that in the winter many children would not be able to get to school and sometimes "when Miss Dove did not have more than a half-dozen children, she would go through the lessons quickly and dismiss class early." At least one male, a Mr. Venable, taught there. It was he who tutored "Judge" Alfred Wilson for his teacher's examination.

Schoolhouse on Gingell's Curve as a private home

Miss Holman's list of those attending this one-teacher school included the Jones, Lochte, Hunt, Offutt, Bohrer, Keiser, Owens, Green, Moyer, and Renshaw families. Both Bethesda Presbyterian and Mt. Zion Baptist used the school for choir practice with an expert instructor brought over from Virginia. By 1905 forty pupils squeezed into the little school on the hill, and the school board was considering the addition of another room when it was approached by the just-then-organizing Bethesda Masonic lodge with an alternate plan. [13]

William Chitty, Esq.

The first "Worshipful Master" of the Bethesda Lodge, William Chitty, stated:

We induced them to buy an acre in a new sub-division near the junction of the two Rockville roads, and erect thereon a good two-story, four-room school building, the upper floor to be left unfinished, for which we agreed to pay as rent interest on the cost of this enlargement. This gave us ample space where we rattled around like a dozen peas in a bushel basket.

The first meeting of the new Lodge at the Bethesda School was on June 6, 1906. The Masons paid the school board seventy-five dollars per year and invested in "three lanterns to light the board-walk to the (trolley) car." Their furniture was "largely home-made."

Our good ladies covered a dry goods box with red cloth for an altar, and leading to the East was a piece of straw matting. An important duty of the Senior Deacon was to carefully watch and see that no candle grease ran down from the Lights to set the matting afire. He never missed.

In 1912 James Henderson (Henny or sometimes Ham) Peter bought the abandoned school with its bright blue door at auction, and he and his wife and her sister, Miss Hodges, lived there behind a fine oak and in a grove of poplar, gum and hickory trees for many years. However, their barn and sheds were on a corner of the Bohrer farm at Jones Bridge Road and the Pike.

A Bethesda teacher (Miss Brown ?) and her well dressed, lower grades class about 1916.

The Peters never were able to do much with those rough, plank, schoolroom floors. [14]

The new frame school on Wilson Lane, some called it the Woodmont School, was painted yellow and opened with just the two rooms on the first floor finished. The large second-floor room became sort of a town-hall as well as the Masonic Lodge and later the school lent it to other organizations.

For example, on Friday evening, May 28, 1915, at the school house hall, Fidelity Lodge No. 326 of the Independent Order of Good Templars presented "The Heart of a Hero," a domestic drama in four acts. The printed program carried advertising from the Alfred Wilson's store, W. E. Perry's Feed and Hardware, Clarence Keiser's Bethesda Ice and Lumber, Francis Day's Bethesda Garage, Miller's Coal Yard, and Stohlman's Bakery. The cast included George Reid, Fletcher Everhart as the hero, Neale Franklin as the villain, young Ruth Wilson as a village belle, and Calvin Owens as the office boy. Calvin's father, W. Thomas Owens of Highland Park, also took an ad: "Contractor and Builder, Phone Bethesda 6."[15]

That year, 1915, the "white" schools in the Bethesda area enrolled 469 students including thirty-eight in the Chevy Chase high school division, and the "colored" school on River Road had fifty-nine pupils. The cost-per-pupil in the white schools was $29.96 and in the colored school, $4.56. The River Road school had 110 books, or about two per student, while the white schools had more than six textbooks per enrollee. The teacher at the "colored" school earned $160 for the school year, while the average "white" teacher made more than $400. Only in one measure was the school for African-American children superior; average daily attendance there was seventy-six percent while at the "white" schools it was only only sixty percent.

As the enrollment at the school on Wilson Lane grew, the Masons moved out, and the large, second-floor hall was divided into several classrooms for older students, including a domestic science room for which the Newcomb Club donated a sewing machine. "This was fitted as a kitchen and the girls got a real thrill when they were able to try their hand at cooking. We were very proud that our school was making such progress," recalled Mrs. Gingell. She also remembered that they soon organized a PTA and attempted to provide an occasional lunch for the students.

Our first school luncheon went over with a bang! We sold out entirely and the mothers on the committee in charge did not even have a crust of bread left over for their own lunch that day. I was the chairman for the first luncheon and I remember how most of the mothers did not have any idea of how to plan for so many children as they were used to their own little families.... Almost everything was made at the school and served cafeteria style... It was this early beginning that paved the way for the cafeteria that our school knows today.

Mrs. Gingell also found herself serving the Bethesda School, in several other ways.

In those days I lived very near the school on Wilson Lane. Schools did not have offices in those days, and the principal usually served as a teacher as well. Whenever the teachers had to call the Board of Education at Rockville, they would send the message by a pupil to my house. I would telephone Mr. Broome, the superintendent, and write down the reply and send it back to the school house.

In case of an accident on the playground or in the school, the teachers would rush him over to my house for first aid. Once one of the little boys received a very bad gash on his head. He was brought to my house bleeding very much. I had to shave around the gash and apply a dressing. He was kept on my parlor couch until he was better. I usually had the spare room rented out to one or two school teachers each season, and a great deal of school business was carried on from my house. I always felt that I had the duty when school was in session, as I never knew when I would be called on in some sort of emergency. Those were some really happy days, too.[16]

By school year 1916-17 the Seventh Election District had four schools for white children and the one "colored" school. Ruth V. Poe was the principal teacher of the school on Wilson Lane, and her assistants were Bruce Colton, Irene Brown, and Ruth Beall. Helen Pumphrey taught domestic science to the girls. For Chevy Chase, listed as a high school that year, the school board paid $1,200 in rent. Florence M. Barksdale was principal, and her high school teacher was Gertrude Lane. The other teachers were Mary Tracy, Emma Washington, Lillian Morgan, and Corinne Anderson. Effie Barnsley taught domestic science and Wilson Ward manual training.

At the Glen Echo school Edward E. Crockett was principal and Maud A. Carlile, "assistant," which is how teachers were listed. At the rented Friendship Heights school Mary Easton was principal and teacher just as Margaret Dorsey was the only staff member at the rented River Road school.[17]

The earliest subdivisions of Bethesda included Miller's Addition (1892) from Wisconsin Avenue west along Bethesda Avenue to Arlington Road. It originally had about 140 large, rectangular lots measuring 50-by-200 feet and was developed mainly for business with some of the property redivided into smaller lots in 1925. J. Hite Miller and his wife, Anna Offutt had inherited the property from her father, Hilleary Lyles Offutt, whose original Bethesda farm covered a hundred acres.

Here, as Bethesda developed, and especially after the arrival of the railroad in 1910, spread the coal and lumber yards, machinery sheds, several of the auto dealers, and a low, yellow tile apartment house filled with black men and women who worked as laborers in the coal yards and as domestics in Edgemoor and Battery Park. Later the fuel oil distributors, an African-American church, Willie Smith's store, Maloney Concrete, a laundry and some very secret World War II industries would thrive there. The area, widely called the Flats, boasted, at one time or another, several good ball fields and a "blind pig" or two. Miller's Flats was also

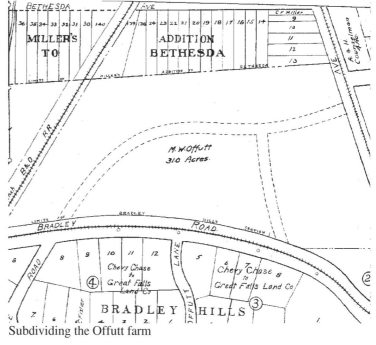

Subdividing the Offutt farm

the source of all that weekend noise that later worried Mrs. Tuckerman. According to Cleveland Clipper, whose father knew Charlie Miller pretty well, "Miller went down to North Carolina and got these fellers to come up there to work in the coal yard, wild bunch. Several of them got killed down in there."

But in that same area, Clipper remembered:

That's where that church got started, too. Will Mason used to be up there in Miller's Flats, built a church right there on Bethesda Avenue. It was a house church, but they raised the roof and put a steeple on. Deacon Thomas, lived in Scotland, used to come down there. It was there for some time.[18]

Clipper said that he and his friends "used to play ball down on the flats along Fairfax Road," and he recalled that some men lived in a cave cut into the side of a big hill.

They were living in a hole as big as this room, and you couldn't tell it until you went back in there. That hill was cut down when they put Arlington through. We used to go and slide down it and make holes and play Indian.

Charlie Miller, some young gal broke him. He got her pregnant, and she got them lawyers who said this is a good time for you to get on your feet, see. He lost his coal yard and got down till he didn't have nothing but mules to pull that coal wagon.

Clipper smiled and shook his head.

East of the Pike, E. W. Haights had the land from Bradley Lane to Leland Street subdivided in 1893 into six blocks having 138 50-by-150-foot lots. He called his proposed neighborhood Norwood Heights, and although little was built there, several houses from that era still stand. The most prominent, on Leland Street, was the home of William Grindage (Willie G.) and Bettie Offutt and their children William Lyles, long-time teachers Viola and Virginia, and house painters Fred and Richard.

In the mid-1920s much of this land was re-divided and with the addition of Dr. Ralph Walsh's property (he was still living there at the time of the 1900 census), it became part of Chevy Chase and the Monroe's "Leland" development. Dr. Ralph Walsh's big home on the lot between Walsh and Stanford became a boarding house, which attracted summer guests with good meals and a breezy porch.

Woodmont, another early subdivision, was platted in 1894 for Charles E. Wood between Northwest Park along Battery Lane, then called

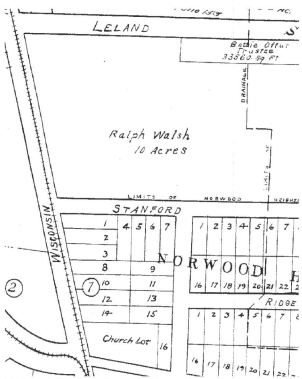
Early subdivisions from Bradley to Leland

Michigan Avenue, and the Pike and Old Georgetown Road. The basic road network of Fairmont, St. Elmo, Melrose (now Cordell), Del Ray, Auburn and Rugby crossed by Norfolk and Arlington (now Woodmont) resulted in fourteen blocks with 584 small lots, most only twenty-five feet wide. Just about all the buyers here purchased more than one lot, and by the turn of the century a scattering of homes, both large and small, lay among the trees on its hilly dirt and cinder streets.

On St. Elmo Avenue in 1899, attorney William L. Chitty built the fourth home in Woodmont. It was considered a mansion in its day. Mr. Chitty helped to found Bethesda's Masonic Lodge No. 204 in a series of meetings at his home in 1906. Chitty was involved in the Masons' purchase of what became the site of the Bank of Bethesda and the property back where the Masons built their hall and library. Chitty and his wife, Mary, left the area in 1913 after helping to initiate the Bethesda Citizens' Association with H. Bradley Davidson as its first president.[19]

The smallest of the early subdivisions, Sunnyside, spread across six and one-half acres of the Gingell's land where the old road and the Pike met just north of the point where Lochte's forge glowed and the Masons staked their claim. Here four big lots, two of one and three-

tenths acres and two of two acres each were platted in 1901. Five years later Joseph Bradley carved lot four into two one-acre lots. Both Dr. John Lewis and his successor, Dr. Benjamin Perry, lived here. They were just across the Pike from "Heathcote," the Dodge's spacious residence that was later sold to George Bradley Jr. and, still later, it was moved toward the highway with a horse-powered winch, faced with brick by Morrison Brothers, and became Pumphrey's Funeral Home.

The long promised B&O finally made it to Bethesda from Chevy Chase Lake in 1910, following the creek bed and cutting through the hills, creating a gully near the end of Watkins' lane, skirting Highland Park's cesspool, burrowing under the Pike beside the Keiser's ice house and erecting a small freight station down in the "flats" where J. Hite Miller's son Charlie established the first coal yard with his father's help. Despite some real estate developers' promises of commuter service, the railroad failed to reach its anticipated potential in Bethesda, but a small industrial area did spread across Miller's Flats and later near River Road where quarrying and stone cutting went on for years.

Although there was never any passenger service, innumerable boys and quite a few adults hopped slow-moving freights for free rides to Georgetown or the Lake. It was a "coal and construction" railroad carrying mainly fuel, cement and lumber. Its biggest customer was the power house in Georgetown, and in later years the daily trips in and out of Washington were the only trains passing through Bethesda.

The freight train to Bethesda passes Columbia's golf course

Despite parental warnings and a few fatal accidents, children played along the unfenced tracks and under the bridges where the graffiti were sometimes mystifying ("Margy is a hoer"). With their engine puffing black smoke and cinders, the trainmen smiled and waved to boys and girls along the weedy right of way and mashed a multitude of pennies as they passed. A youngster who was on the bridge when the train came through always considered himself very fortunate and bragged of his good luck. The sulfurous smell of the smoke was wonderful, and it clung to hair and clothes all day.

Isabel Lynch, neé Gaither, whose stepfather was a Bethesda policeman she called "O. T.," grew up on Montgomery Avenue at Pearl Street in the 1930s. "I climbed a lot of trees and did forbidden things," she said.

The railroad track ran behind the lumber yard, which was behind our house, and we were all forbidden to play there. This was circumvented because the banks were nice clay banks, ideal for Tootsietoys. Betty Plitt and I walked down Montgomery Avenue past Mr. Rosenthal's yard, looking back to make sure that no parent or child who might tattle was around, and then you would go through the yard to the tracks and walk back up to where you wanted to go and play Tootsietoys. We also used to find crayfish in that stream, and when you were really being adventurous, we would sometimes go down to the bridge over East West Highway.

Sometimes when I was late for Leland, I would go across the creek back there. I remember one Eastertime we were going on a field trip, and I had a lovely purple skirt. To go across the stream you had to swing on a grapevine that had been cut to a point so I hopped on the grapevine and put a hole through my brand-new Easter dress.

To most Bethesdans the railroad was more a nuisance than an asset, and some neighborhoods managed to pretend it did not exist. During WWII the freights served the OSS and war industries such as Briggs Clarifier, and the B&O managed to resist the constant attempts by the Chamber of Commerce and local newspapers to have it fenced or shut down.

But whatever its importance, it certainly was—and is—one of the most picturesque railroad lines anywhere in

the area. Within its 11-mile length is a long trestle, a short tunnel, street running, canalside running, an impressive curved truss bridge, the ruins of a masonry canal aqueduct, a wooded reservoir, fine views of the Potomac and a general off-the-beaten path atmosphere.[20]

As the result of a 1910 land survey Northwest Park came into being on what had been forty-two acres of John E. Beall's Bethesda empire. Thirty-four large lots of about a hundred by 400 feet lay along what is now Battery Lane from the Pike to the older Georgetown Road. A number of large homes soon graced this curving street. Later one of Bethesda's earliest and busiest builders, Sam Robertson, had lots ten and eleven resubdivided and created a new street, Glenbrook Road, where he built on eight lots, and then he cut Keystone Street through at the dogleg curve adding more drainage problems for the "village."[21]

Among the first newcomers to live on Michigan Avenue/Battery Lane were the newlywed Fred Keplingers who built a home at 4805 in 1909 and then a tennis court, which they shared when they acquired neighbors. In 1916 they staged the first of their invitational tennis tournaments that became a Bethesda institution. They planted large gardens and many fruit trees, and in the 1920s built a small studio complete with fireplace where Mrs. Keplinger painted. She had studied and taught art before her marriage and enrolled at the Corcoran when she moved to her new home. Bethesda's flowers were among her favorite subjects. Mrs. Keplinger also led the fight for kindergartens as a member of the Bethesda PTA and as chair of the Federation of Women's Clubs' education committee.

Another popular family on Battery Lane was Wharton Moore's whose large home near Georgetown Road featured a goldfish pond that became a favorite of all the neighborhood children much to Mrs. Moore's dismay. Nursemaids even brought their charges to play while they rested in the Moore's shady garden.[22]

In May 1918 Masonic leader Philip A. Rosendorn, who had become a resident of the community in 1910, and two other Northwest Parkians, H. O. Gould and A. L. Vandercook, with the support of their neighbors, had the subdivision incorporated and made a special taxing district. The three incorporators became the first village council with Rosendorn as chairman. The taxing area, in common with similar down-county districts, took on the trash and garbage collection, snow removal, and the repair and improvement of Michigan Avenue. It was the sorry condition of the street that led to the creation of the "town" of Northwest Park.

The council's first act was to borrow $200, pay $27 to have the road planed, and then $41.22 to build a heavy, wooden "drag" for road maintenance. In February 1919 the council received a petition signed by twenty residents asking for the construction of a twelve-foot cinder road and sidewalks. After hearing Mr. Moore's protest of their planned front-foot assessment, the council borrowed $2,000 and solicited bids.

In their first annual election, as prescribed by their charter, they set the pattern of having the person with the highest number of votes become chairman and the second and third vote-getters becoming "associate members" of the council. Treasurer J. H. Eldridge was elected chairman and Gould and Rosendorn were second and third in the balloting.

The new council offered the job of secretary-treasurer to Mrs. Keplinger and when she declined chose E. K. Ellsworth. This was as close as a woman came to serving in this mini-governmental structure. The council rejected all road-building bids as too high, took on the job itself, assessed property owners 40.5¢ a front-foot and then ran over its budget. The minutes soon filled with reports of men hired at $3.50 or $4 a day and teams rented for $8 a day and then of buying cinders to replace washouts.

During its first decade, the village of Northwest Park was concerned almost entirely with improving the road and getting PEPCO to install lights along it. However by 1920, with

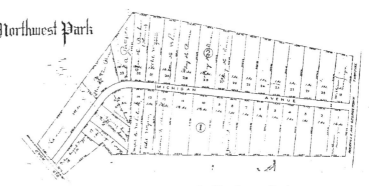

The original plat map for Northwest Park

Rosendorn as chairman again, they did adopt some ordinances prohibiting the driving of a horse drawn or motor vehicle on or across the sidewalks, setting a 15 mph speed limit, requiring building plans be submitted for council approval and prohibiting the construction of houses costing less than $4,000.

Through the Twenties the taxing area fought with Woodmont over the sewerage and stench coming from the hog pens in that area and then with the Suburban Sanitary Commission when their road was not properly restored after the sewer was built. In the mid-20s PEPCO installed street lights and the town paid $12.82 each month for that service. In 1926 in order to get the post office to provide "city delivery," Northwest Park changed the name of its main street to Battery Lane.

Into the 1930s with Mr. Rosendorn usually secretary-treasurer and Wharton Moore taking an active role, the village coped with Sam Robertson's road building and serious drainage problems. From the mid-Thirties William Ovington led the council as Northwest Park planted more trees, tried to clean up the neighborhood garbage dump, paid Archie Phillips $5 every other month to cut down the weeds, worked to keep the drains and culverts clear and dealt with the new problems caused by the building of Keystone Avenue. The council became much less active, sometimes met only once a year, but kept up the annual elections, set the tax rate and met problems, such as the building of Soper's Esso station, as they arose.[23]

Some of the earliest suburban clusters of dwellings had been built out in Oakmont and Sonoma. Here the trolley had left the memories of the lights and music of Bethesda Park and a large oily stain beside the highway from the days when that was the end of the line. Oakmont, all eighteen acres of it, became arguably Maryland's smallest, chartered municipality. Led by the *Star*'s managing editor, Oliver Owen Kuhn, GPO printer Charles A. Read, and insurance broker James C. Adkins, Oakmont, platted in June 1903, became a special taxing area on April 10, 1918. The three-person committee that governed the tiny township regulated building construction, maintained Oak Place, collected garbage, provided snow removal and street lights, and had the right to establish it own health and traffic regulations.

Oakmont began with twenty-one homes on sixteen-foot-wide Oak Place with its northern boundary Walter Johnson's farm where he raised horses and foxes when he was not busy firing strikes for Clark Griffith's Washington Senators. Kuhn lived in a converted farmhouse that dated back to the Civil War, but most of the other clapboard homes with their wraparound porches and big dormers date from the time of the Great War. It was a quiet little neighborhood where nothing ever happened. "Daddy" Read, as he was called, had a knife switch on the outside of his house, and when he went to bed, usually around nine, he would pull the switch and plunge Oakmont into darkness. If a citizen was throwing a party and promised the lights would be doused when it was over–no later than 11 pm–Read would grant a dispensation. In the late 1930s and early `40s, with the help of young attorney E. Austin Carlin, this little community put up a terrific fight against the County commissioners and powerful developer Eugene Casey over the right to control its streets.[24]

Out on the old road, Huntington Terrace was born on surveyors' maps in 1910 and included those "president streets," Roosevelt, McKinley, and Madison as far back as Garfield, but very few houses went up on these hilly and unpaved lanes until the mid-1920s. Today one can find a few good examples of World War One-era Bethesda homes in the first block of McKinley, Lincoln and Southwick Streets as well as in Sonoma. Roosevelt Street west of Old Georgetown is a living museum of almost every type and style of single-family housing built in D.C. suburbs in the 1920s, `30s, and `40s at about a decade a block.[25]

Right in the middle of this development lived one of Bethesda's best-known couples. The former County sheriff and his wife, Mr. and Mrs. B. Peyton Whalen, moved from their Seven Locks Road home to live in her parents' house, which stood at the end of a winding driveway bordered by maple trees on fifteen acres between McKinley and Lincoln Streets. Mrs. Whalen's father, Masonic leader Jed Gittings, built the house in 1900 on what had been a part of "Needham's Discovery."

The *Star*'s Rambler called it a "place of ancient charm" marked by hewed oak, wrought nails, mossy shingles and dormer windows in the garret. Both the Gittings and the Whalens were movers and shakers in early Bethesda society, and tiny Edith Gittings Whalen, one of the most remarkable Bethesdans ever. Their

land became the home of Suburban Hospital, but not without some dispute over the price.[26]

Publicity for the Chevy Chase Land Company operation and the success of various builders down Wisconsin after the coming of the trolley line stimulated this early property acquisition and subdivision. Bethesda saw very little actual building until well after the First World War, which some historians believe changed the Capital permanently, but land values did increase. The 1900 census showed that one-fourth of all the Bethesda-area households were still farms (about 85 of 300 white and 8 of 50 black householders called themselves farmers or gardeners) and the vast majority owned their property. Farm labor or day labor was by far the chief occupation of the election district's African Americans as well as of many whites.

But subdivision was in the air. Rosedale Park, for example, dated from 1908 with ten blocks and some 300 lots between Maple and Chestnut Streets east of the Pike, but until the 1920s few house were built. West Chevy Chase Heights, platted east of Rosedale Park in 1910, had a similar hiatus. Highland Park, created in the middle of Bethesda at about the same time grew a bit faster. Cyrus Keiser and Charles Kincheloe, who built their big, square houses side by side in Alta Vista, owned this rectangular, eighteen-acre tract between the railroad and what became East West Highway from Wisconsin to now-abandoned Cloverdale Street.

Builder W. Thomas Owens lived in Highland Park as did Will Counselman and longtime Chevy Chase mailman Charles Hurley who often went home by way of Watkins Lane because Montgomery Avenue was little more than a muddy path. In the late-20s the subdivision became the site of Dr. Perry's skinny brick office building, Bethesda's first, and of the proud, stone County Building, which most folks called the police station.

But despite these young subdivisions, in Bethesda's early days most people lived rather scattered and isolated existences on what was left of old farms. The bad roads were part of the problem. In 1898 the County Commissioners finally took over the decrepit turnpike, which, said the *Star* in polite understatement, "has not a very enviable reputation among those who are obliged to drive over it." The Commissioners planned to cut down many of the hills and macadamize it as soon as they could get the State to authorize a bond issue. Promised roads, improper drainage and irritating bottle-

necks were part of the Bethesda story from the beginning.

By 1895 phones jangled at the Cabin John Hotel, the Chevy Chase Inn, and the Chevy Chase Land Company, but the directory also included numbers for the Dunlops at Hayes Manor and for H. Bradley Davidson, Amanda Counselman, and John E. Beall. It was not until 1910 that the phone company installed the Bethesda Central switchboard in the spare bedroom of Ada Cunningham's home at 106 Melrose Avenue in Woodmont for the fifty or so local customers. The phone company paid her $30 a month, and she soon knew the numbers of all her customers as well as those of most of the D.C. stores they called.

By 1920 the number of phones had jumped to 1,000, but the switchboard stayed there, with her daughters (and sometimes their beaux) manning the plugs, until 1928 when the first part of the Chespeake and Potomac's impressive stone building on Wisconsin at Stanford opened. By then it was a six-position switchboard, and 2,855 subscribers used the BRadley and WIsconsin exchanges.[27]

Up in the center of town Walter Perry opened his first feed store in 1910 in what had been the home of plasterer John Worthmiller. Dr. John Lewis convinced young Perry to move down from Kensington with his view of Bethesda's bright future. When Perry went into D.C. with $300 to buy supplies, he found, as had Alfred Wilson twenty years before, that wholesalers would not deliver "that far out in the country" so he ended up purchasing his nails, harness, rope, and other goods in Alexandria.

W. E. PERRY

DEALER IN

FEED, HARDWARE, FARM AND GARDEN IMPLEMENTS

AND POULTRY SUPPLIES

Telephone, Bethesda, 31 B
Cleveland 563   BETHESDA, MD.

The next year Perry built a brick store just past the Wilson brothers and moved his growing business. In 1915 Perry brought his bride, Sally Fontaine, to the house on Old Georgetown Road that he had purchased from the St. John's vestry. He and his wife joined the Presbyterian Church on the Pike. In 1922 with the town showing signs of progress, he tore down his old store and built a new one on the same site. He kept his two phone lines.[28]

In 1914 the Washington Railway and Electric Company made two moves that recognized the growth of the suburbs "out Bethesda way." First WRECo initiated express service with limited stops to such distant destinations as Alta Vista and Rockville during the evening rush hours. This was a very popular improvement. Second, a new branch line from the old Tenleytown route was built along Macomb Street and out Massachusetts Avenue all the way to the District Line. They abandoned the route in 1925 and replaced it with bus service.

Meanwhile as automobiles became more common and more of the suburbs accessible, the Wilson brothers' old emporium was becoming a tight fit. Mrs. Gingell described it:

> Wilson's store carried a full line of almost everything from nails and horses' harnesses to cheese and bedding. But there were no green vegetables for sale. People either grew their own or bought directly from a neighbor. The store carried fresh meats, but only a few cuts. Smoked fish was kept in an open barrel and salt meat and hams were hung from the ceiling.

> In Wilson's we bought our food, our "wrappers" (as ladies' dresses were then known), our red flannel underwear, gingham, sewing materials and novelties. We had all of the essentials but little variety. Candy, most of which was the stick kind kept in large glass bottles on the counter, was a delicacy appealing to all.

> In the winter the store supplied our coal and wood. From it we also obtained oil for our lamps, gasoline for the stove, feed for the chickens and tools for the farm....

> In the evenings the young men of the community walked to the country store and parked themselves around the huge "iron belly" stove which was placed in the center of a large metal wagon tire. The space around the stove was filled with sand and as the men sat there for hours telling stories of hunting, fishing and farming, they dyed the sand red with their tobacco juice.[29]

About 1910 the Wilson brothers dissolved their partnership, and Herbert built a big, brick, two-story store about a hundred feet south of Alfred's and kept the grocery business while his brother specialized in hardware and dry goods. For a while, J. Herbert Wilson's store was Bethesda's pride and "town hall," replacing the Grange Hall and rivaling the school as a meeting place, and much later it became the first Sanitary Grocery Store in town. The Masons moved to the room above the new store and met there until their own building was completed in 1923.

Woodmont was also growing and attracting men with building skills such as Charles H. Viett, a contractor and builder who advertised houses for both sale and rent before the Great War. By 1910 four of the six sons of George Broadhurst, a long-time tenant farmer of the Damascus area, had settled in the Triangle and were building and painting homes and investing in land. By 1915 contractor George A. Broadhurst and his wife, Valley, were raising four children in Woodmont. His brother Joshua, a house painter, and his wife, Elizabeth, were starting a family just a block off the Pike. William Broadhurst, his wife Ollie, and their children Lansing, Liston, and Odessa, had also made a home in Woodmont as had his youngest brother, James, who began his large family on Fairmont Avenue.

Much like the hardworking Simpson-Troth-Orem clan in Chevy Chase, the Broadhursts prospered in Woodmont. They helped to start the Methodist church there in a tent in 1913 and were mainly responsible for funding and constructing the church building at Norfolk and St. Elmo in 1916. George built the stone foundation, and James paid for and erected the church itself. The Rev. W. W. Beasley was the first full-time minister. He was very popular and received so many dinner invitations that, according to Mrs. Gingell, "it was necessary to honor one family by coming to breakfast." Later, a dispute led the Broadhursts to change their allegiance to the Eldbrooke congregation.

As James and Artie Christina Broadhurst's family multiplied, the house in Woodmont soon became too small, and they moved out past Alta Vista and bought part of the Bean farm, about twenty-two acres with 400 feet of frontage on Old Georgetown Road just across from "Edland" Stellwagen's big, model dairy farm. There James Broadhurst built the first of several houses and planted a large grove of Stark apple trees. Broadhurst apple butter soon became locally famous. By the 1910 census the family included Roscoe, 9; James, 7; Henry, 5; Carl, 2; and Ralph, almost one year old.

Veterinary surgeon James F. Morris moved his young family from D.C. to a new, Broadhurst-built home at the southwest corner of Fairmont and Rockville Pike in 1910. He paid his mortgage on the frame house and four narrow lots to neighbor Joshua Broadhurst. The two-and-a-half-story home had no basement, electricity, or inside plumbing, but it did have

four bedrooms upstairs, and a pleasant parlor, a big kitchen and a long hall to the back porch where the pump was located. The "facilities" and a small barn were in the back yard where there was plenty of room for a big garden as well as for goats and pigeons. Dr. Morris pastured his horse, Lovetts, on the east side of the Pike in broad wheat fields where the children sometimes gathered dewberries.

Looking west toward the Moores' house

The veterinary kept his $60 per month job with the D.C. government, but established a practice in the County and was soon treating most of the horses, cows, and mules in Bethesda as well as a number of dogs. His general fee for "professional services rendered" as well as for examinations and most treatments was one dollar, surgery might go $2.50. Among his clients were storekeeper Alfred Wilson, entrepreneur H. Bradley Davidson, and developer Walter Tuckerman, who had Morris look after his sheep as well as his horses.

He dispensed powders and medicines of various types to the Bohrer's cows out on the Pike, the Newcomb's horses in Alta Vista, the Wheatley's cow, the Hunt's ponies, Cyrus Keiser's horse, Will Counselman's mule, and the Wilfong's cows: Queenie, Flossie, and Kate. Even the Rev. Flourney's horse became Dr. Morris's patient. The minister with his flowing white hair and beard was a familiar figure in Bethesda as he drove his buggy making his rounds.[30]

Dr. and Mrs. Morris's older son Frank, who was called A. F., went on the trolley to Western High School, but the two younger children, Hilma and Lex, whose given name was Lars James, attended the new Bethesda School on Wilson Lane for four years. Then their parents transferred them to the District schools, which were less crowded and had, in their opinion,

better programs. For several years, Mrs. Morris rose before dawn in the winter to take her husband and younger children by horse and buggy to the carbarn at the District Line so they would not have to wait for the trolley at the Edgemoor switch.

In 1920 Mrs. Morris, at a time of family upheaval, borrowed money from the newly organized Bank of Bethesda and built a small store on the Pike right next to her home. A Swedish immigrant, she had run a successful catering business on Massachusetts Avenue before her marriage. Now she opened a general store with groceries, meats, chewing tobacco, and canned goods, which soon became a regular stop for the farmers bringing milk to Peake's dairy just down the street and for the deliverymen who gathered for a cup of coffee. The store evolved into a popular soda fountain serving Fussell-Young ice cream and featuring small, white tables and bent-wire chairs.

The Morris children worked there after school as well as helping to keep house, and daughter Hilma, who became a teacher in the City, lost her taste for ice cream from all the cones she dipped. Much later her brother Lex ran a beer and sandwich shop in what had been his mother's store. He was the kind of storekeeper who would run his customers out and close the place if one of his buddies showed up and suggested a hunting trip.

Horace Hampton and his parents along with his six brothers and sisters moved to Bethesda from Georgetown in 1914 as part of the high flown ambitions of the exuberant Bradley Hills impresarios. He was the youngest, eight years old. It was his job to make sandwiches each morning for the many school lunches. The Hamptons had a

The Woodmont switch in the winter of 1915-16

stone, three-car garage, but Horace grew up in an age of horses. His father liked to use a little sulky with a pacer, but his mother kept a riding horse at the stable, which she occasionally would let Horace borrow. And, of course, there were dozens of work horses.

His mother also liked gardens, and his father hauled in four feet of top soil so she could have them. Horace made twenty cents an hour pulling weeds at home and for the neighbors. "On Saturday," he recalled with a smile, "I would ride the old mare up to Bethesda and buy a barrel of gingersnaps. Then I'd ride over the countryside talking to people."

Across from the Hamptons on Wisconsin Avenue extended, as it was often designated, stood the small, stone chapel of St. John's, Norwood Parish, which had been built in 1874, and the parish hall, which was added in 1899. The founders included the Dodges, the Davidsons, the Offutts, the Watkins and the Bradleys with Hilleary Offutt and Dr. James Davidson the first trustees. It was by far the best building in town with fancy windows honoring the founders and their families.

The Hamptons moved into one of large homes Thomas Hampton built on Willson Offutt's land at the entrance to Bradley Hills. Horace grew up there and remembered his "stomping grounds."

South of us was the agriculture experiment station and the Davidson house and property. Across the street on the corner was the little Episcopal church, St. John's. It burned down in 1914 (May 13th). I had been down in Washington, and I came out and got as far as the District Line and looked up towards Bethesda and saw the sky all red, and I ran out to Bradley Boulevard thinking our house might be on fire. The fire engine they had then was a 500 gallon tank on the chassis of a farm wagon pulled by a rope. It was kept in a barn up behind the store, where Community Hardware later was. When I got up to Bradley Lane, everybody was sitting down watching the church burn down because they'd used up the water and there wasn't anything else.

On our side, father had built a little stone office, and George Sacks bought that. Mr. Offutt lived next door and he had a great big booming voice, and he'd holler at me and Ed Stock playing down on Bradley

Boulevard; all that land had been his farm and he had a smokehouse up there.

Across the street up at Leland Street, which was the only street that went through to Brookeville Road, north of Leland wasn't much, up there was Colonel Offutt, little man that wore a goatee, and every Saturday night he got drunk in Georgetown. In the family there were three children I recall. The two girls became teachers and their brother, a painter. Miss Offutt was my third grade teacher.

Up where the farm market is was Uncle Billy Counselman's place. As a kid I'd ride my bicycle up there, and you'd see pheasants along the street. It was a two lane macadam road with the streetcar track on the east side. Across the street, the Perrys came in. Now the first doctor in Bethesda was Latane Lewis, and he had a house right behind where the bank was built. He had two sons, Tom and John, who was about my age. Anyhow across the street was Walter Perry, Dr. Perry's brother. He had a feed store that was the dirtiest place I ever saw. But he was a sharp guy. He didn't have any children, and he sort of adopted Fontaine Hall.

Next to Perry's was a brick building, the first major grocery store in Bethesda. Before that the only grocery store was up on Old Georgetown Road about Norfolk Street. People used to buy from Booker and Harry in Georgetown.

North of the railroad track was all heavy pine forest on the east side up to the Watkins' place. On the other side, Charlie Miller had a coal and wood place on the railroad track where the old freight station was. He built a half dozen little row houses for blacks that worked for him. And the people raised hell.

On Wisconsin Avenue at the bridge was a gas station and automobile repair shop. Later, one was built across the street. But that was the only gasoline station in those days. On the bank corner was a blacksmith shop with a barn in the back where I saw the first birth of a calf I ever saw.

Going on out on the west side, out two or three blocks, was the dairy. On the other side of the street was a big vacant piece of property that went all the way back to Columbia Country Club.

There wasn't much at all on Old Georgetown Road. On the corner of Wilson Lane was the school

ST. JOHN'S EPISCOPAL CHURCH.

with a big lot beside it that my father bought and gave to the school as a playground. The school was a four room, frame school. In the fall of 1914 we went there, my brother and two sisters and I, and I think it was on the opening day one of my sisters didn't behave, and a teacher took a ruler and whacked her with it. My father blew up and said you are not going to school there. So the John Eaton School had been built in Cleveland Park near the Cathedral, and they did not have many students there.

We went down there to school on the trolley. The trolley was expensive, five cents, six tickets for a quarter. We used to walk from Cleveland Park back out to save a nickel and go in Dellinger's store and buy a pickle. And that's where I met my wife, in the third grade at the graded school, John Eaton. We could have gone to Tenleytown, but that was a pretty rough place.

We played ball on Sam Boyd's old farm out there, he was quite a baseball player. We did try to form a Boy Scout troop, but we couldn't get enough boys together.

Beyond there was very little, just farms and a few big houses. The agriculture department had a place out on the Pike. The superintendent was a man named Rankin, and his son and I were the same age. I used to go up there on weekends because he owned a billy goat. We'd hook the billy goat up to a wagon and ride around out there. Back down from there was a wide water in Rock Creek and that was a swimming hole for us; we used to up there and go swimming right by a bridge, and there was a girls' camp up in there. It was across from Grosvenor. So when we were skinny dipping and the girls came by, we had to stay in the water.

By the time the Hamptons moved to Bethesda, just before the outbreak of World War I in Europe, the town was on the edge of major change. The framework of the old rural crossroads was still there, but the arrival of the railroad and of men like Walter Tuckerman, who had a clear vision of a different kind of community, marked another turning point. Somehow they could see past Lochte's blacksmith shop and the Gingell's old farm. They could ignore the fact that Bethesda was barely a wide place in the turnpike with Mandy Counselman's old store on one side and Alfred Wilson and Lewis Keiser, the new postmaster, on the other. Progress was coming out from the city, and while the Glen Echo developers might have failed, Somerset and Friendship Heights were steadily growing, and Chevy Chase was

finally starting to look like more than just a summer success.

The electric railway line had also changed. Gone were the old, single truck trolleys as well as #099, the freight car, which had been a very popular innovation. The trolley line's managers had hoped that it might become a major hauler of milk and produce from the local market farms when the line reached Rockville, but that trade never developed. In the summer of 1908 a rider had complained to the District electric railway commission that the Rockville and Tenleytown was the "worst, most ill-managed, dirtiest, out of date line" in the area.[31]

Now the big, arch-windowed interurban cars built by J. G. Brill were in operation even during the Fair in Rockville when open cars with running boards and even two-car trains had been used in the early days. The fifteen "magnificent" Rockville cars, as LeRoy King Jr., and most other fans of Washington street railways called them, began arriving at the shop on P Street in August, and on September 9, 1908, #585 and #586 began operating on the Maryland line.

They were thirty-four feet long, weighed 52,000 pounds, were powered by four fifty-horsepower Westinghouse engines and seated forty-eight passengers. Originally cadmium orange and lemon-yellow with light green art glass in the fake arch windows, the cars were soon repainted olive green and then briefly in the 1920s bright red with gold striping and finally maroon and cream with maroon striping just before the Capital Transit merger. Slightly lower, bigger, and faster than most of their contemporaries, these cars with their rattan seat coverings, mahogany woodwork, and high

Interior of the Brill "Rockville" car

"empire" ceilings with dangling straps for the standees were the mainstay of the line until it closed. Compared to their competitors, they were, as Virginia Angel of Potomac and many other riders recalled, "big and beautiful."

The general manager of the Washington Railway & Electric Company, described their route to the readers of *Brill's Magazine* in 1908:[32]

> *This line, operating northwest from Washington to the Montgomery County seat— Rockville— 4 miles, serves a territory that has been selected by prominent men of the city for the location of their suburban homes. To the man of business whose work requires more or less constant attention during the summer months, as well as to the man of leisure, this region is equally charming. In altitude it is some hundreds of feet above the city. The contour is rolling, and viewed from the cars, the constantly changing panorama of open fields, valley and woodland makes the ride a pleasant one, and after a hot day in the city affords welcome relief. No pleasure resorts or parks are operated along this line, and the company directs all of its efforts to the maintenance of a speedy, comfortable service for the benefit of its patrons residing in the adjacent territory.*

Despite it being only a single track line, accidents were rare. Just before America entered World War I, during a prolonged strike against the Washington Railway and Electric Company by the Street Railway Employee's local, two cars collided head-on near Gingell's curve. Both cars were heavily damaged and several people slightly injured. The *Star* reported that WRECo employees "are investigating a report that signal wires had been tampered with."[33]

On at least one occasion the trolley became an ambulance. Dr. Lewis had a young patient who needed an emergency appendectomy, and the streetcar was obviously the fastest way to get the boy to Georgetown Hospital. The stretcher was placed across the backs of seats and arrangements were made to switch the car off the main line and right to the front door of the hospital. "The operation was successful and the boy's life saved by the ingenuity of an old country doctor." Dr. Lewis was also one of the first in town to own a car, but for quite a while when his Ford would slide toward a telephone pole, he would cry "Whoa! Whoa!" before he remembered to stomp on the brake and reverse pedals.[34]

Bethesda's prettiest and most influential subdivision grew slowly in the middle of the town. Originally called Edgewood, it was laid out for Walter R. Tuckerman by surveyor J. H. Starkey in 1912 on 183.5 acres of what had been the Watkins' farm. After post office confusion, Tuckerman renamed it. Edgemoor contained about 250 lots, mostly large, and four, big, undivided plots.[35]

Tuckerman built his own home, bravely called "Tuxeden," at what is now 5215 Edgemoor Lane and raised the social and economic level of Bethesda by about a factor of ten when he moved in. Colonel Theodore Boal, soon the Tuckerman's next-door neighbor, designed the house. "We added to it by fits and starts as the family grew," Tuckerman said, and the house finally grew to ten bedrooms and six baths as his family expanded to five daughters. The ballroom was forty-four by twenty-two feet with maple hardwood flooring while in the large dining room(14-by-24 feet) and in the library, which was even bigger, the flooring was herringbone oak and the trim mahogany. The carriage house held a two-car garage, a three-stall stable, a feed loft and two very small rooms for the gardener and driver. It became a separate home during World War II.[36]

Tuckerman planted fruit trees, mostly apple, and raised acres of corn and wheat. There was a large kitchen garden, and the Tuckermans also kept pigs, chickens, pigeons, and for a short time, guinea hens. And he stabled an "indeterminate number" of horses in the carriage house and at a nearby barn.

South side and front of Tuxeden about 1916

Sleigh riding in Edgemoor in the Teens

Tuckerman often took his daughters and their friends riding. "If there weren't enough horses," he recalled, "why, we'd put two children on a horse." Occasionally they rode down to the back of the USDA experiment station. "Sometimes when we were on our way back from the blacksmith in Tenleytown," his daughter Laura, now Mrs. Triest, recalled, "we would ride slowly through the cattle, and I would pretend I was a cowboy, but we had strict orders not to annoy the cows." Her sister, Else, enjoyed racing the freight train along the B&O tracks.

Mrs. Triest also remembered horse shows on the empty lots across from her home, riding with her father to the Rockville Fair where he bought her a pony, and then riding her pony to lay a trail for paper chases through the neighborhood fields and woods. For a while the Riding and Hunt Club used the estate as its headquarters, and it was not unusual to see a group of men galloping across the fields of Edgemoor after a pack of hounds. "Mother was the least athletic person in the world," said her oldest daughter, "but she was a good sport about riding with us." Laura Triest also recalled, "One of our horses was a genius at getting out of the pasture. A neighbor on Glenbrook used to call in the middle of the night, 'Come and get your blankety-blank horse off my lawn!'"

Walter Tuckerman and his Edgemoor Land Company were the principal players in the subdivision although other corporations such as Abner Ferguson and David Ely's Security Land Company and Maddux, Marshall and Company, which developed Battery Park, participated in the development. Eventually, Tuckerman said, "the city came out and swamped us," and he had to abandon farming. He harvested his last wheat in 1920.[37]

Large shade trees, many planted by Tuckerman and his hired hands, legions of azaleas and other attractive shrubbery, carefully planned streets, and, for the most part, well-built and expensive houses marked Edgemoor's early years. Tuckerman's workmen installed a water and sewer system and carved out the streets which he named. The sewer pipes emptied into the spring-fed streams on the eastern and western edges of his property, which joined behind Somerset to form Willett Creek and then fed into Little Falls Branch. The deep well, electric pump, and big, metal water tank on four sturdy legs were at the western end of Hampden Lane. "It was up by the Wheatleys," daughter Laura said. "I remember going out with Daddy because he would get calls at all hours saying it wasn't pumping or doing something. It was pretty rugged country, and we had copperheads in there, which I didn't like at all. I climbed almost to the top once."

Where Edgemoor Lane met Old Georgetown Road, Tuckerman built a set of brick gates and a small, stuccoed office building, painted both white, and asked his first clients to exercise a great deal of imagination. He also created "five points," one of the most complex intersections ever to test a novice driver's nerve.

Many of the first houses, like Tuckerman's own and J. Maury Dove's, were small mansions on very large lots, but economic stresses changed that construction pattern. Abe Morrison and other builders noted that Tuckerman had a hard time selling his English-style manor houses and put up smaller, more conventional, brick colonials.

The thirty-foot right-of-way and the trolley cars of the Chevy Chase to Great Falls Electric and Power Company briefly looped along Glenbrook and through the southwest corner of the subdivision turning back to Bradley at Oak

The "Hunt" clatters past Tuckerman's new office building.

Lane, but the Bradley Hills gamble seems to have had little impact on Edgemoor. Edgemoor, on the other hand, changed the direction of Bethesda's growth and style.[38]

Walter Rupert Tuckerman, a fine rider, champion golfer, excellent tennis player and well-bred lawyer, was a tall, spare, quiet and gentle man. His family's pedigree reached back to Puritan Boston and included participants in the famous Tea Party and a signer of the Declaration of Independence, but his family had been in Washington since 1879. He was Harvard `03 and GW Law `07. Although he had worked for Union Trust prior to being admitted to the bar, before he settled down, he had also prospected for gold, managed cattle ranches in Nevada for two years and participated in the Alaska Boundary Survey as a rifleman to keep the crew supplied with fresh meat.[39]

In 1910 he married Edith Abercrombie-Miller, daughter of Commander F. A. Abercrombie-Miller USN. She was a member of the first graduating class of the National Cathedral School. "I think they knew each other from the time they were young," Laura Triest said.

They knew each other socially and had fun together at parties. Mother and her parents went to Europe together nearly every summer. They were in New York waiting for the boat to sail, and she was walking along the street, and a carriage and horse came whirling around the corner and it was Daddy. He had rented it for the day. He saw mother so he stopped, and they chatted, and he said, "Let me give you a lift." They began talking, and all of a sudden, with mother anyway, something clicked. Mother told her parents she didn't want to go to Europe. Mother was twenty-seven and Daddy was twenty-nine when they were married.

Tuckerman brought his wife and their infant daughter Laura to his new "Eden" in 1913 along with four maids, a German gardener and a chauffeur. They had to walk in and leave the car on Wisconsin Avenue because of the muddy condition of Edgemoor Lane. Not much else was there. At the time, Mr. Tuckerman said, "You couldn't buy a cup of coffee in Bethesda."

During her married life Mrs. Tuckerman scheduled her hours carefully, worked tirelessly for both St. John's and the Washington Cathedral, became an active club woman, helped to found and was the first president of the National Women's Country Club. She actively supported her multitude of charities including the Working Boys' (Newsboys') Home in the city and British relief activities in both world wars. Somehow she also found time to rear and oversee the debut and weddings of five daughters: Laura Wolcott, Edith Elizabeth (Elsie then and Else now), Ruth Hollingsworth, Alice Noel, and Margaret Cary. Unlike the Chevy Chase Newlands, the Tuckermans lived in their suburb, reared their children there and learned to enjoy a house often filled with their daughters' many friends.[40]

"Daddy used to ride his horse into town to his office," Laura Triest recalled.

He used the stable of the Riding and Hunt Club at 22nd and P Streets. He would ride across country. I don't think it took him any longer than it does to drive today with all the traffic. There was one bad fence, but he had a very sure horse. He took a large linen napkin with him, and when he came to the fence, he put the napkin on the top wire and jumped it. He didn't always go that way, but he told me that was what he did. Screwdriver was the name of the horse, a wonderful horse.

Tuckerman put aside his love of the West and his golfing trophies, including the Mid-Atlantic Championship of 1907, and organized the National City Real Estate Corporation, later renamed the Edgemoor Land Company. He was treasurer of the Real Estate Investment

Laura on Quaker, Tuckerman on Screwdriver

Company, the exclusive agent for Edgemoor, and during World War I, a leader of local Red Cross activities. Typhoid fever, which almost killed him, prevented him from serving in the Army and affected his health for the rest of his life. Tuckerman became president of Union Savings Bank in 1915 and a director of National Metropolitan Bank in 1917.

And in 1919 Tuckerman helped to found and was the first president of the Bank of Bethesda. "Its success was largely responsible for the rapidity of growth here," he told an interviewer. By the 1920s he was master of the hounds of the Riding and Hunt Club, head of the St. John's church orphanage association, active in the D.C. Harvard Club and the Middle Atlantic Golf Association, a founder of the Burning Tree Club and respected at every other club in the area. Unassuming and generous but never a self-promoter, Tuckerman helped bring Bethesda up toward his own high standards.

The copy in his original advertising brochure listed the subdivision's "proprietors," and began, "Those of refined taste, demanding a better social atmosphere than surrounds the usual suburb; a more picturesque environment for an all-year-round home out of the city, without the expense and responsibility of a large estate; will find these qualities happily realized and united in 'Edgewood.'"

The brochure promised that each building site would be provided with "pure artesian water; sanitary sewerage; gas for cooking, heating and lighting; electric light and telephone service;

macadamized roads and sidewalks accessible everywhere, doing away with the dirt nuisance, yet not interfering with privacy." The "village" of Bethesda was described as "near at hand, with markets, stores, churches, schools and physicians' residences" but the nearness of the City was emphasized with a map that showed the Capitol only six miles away. Agents of the Real Estate Investment Company "will be glad to motor you out at your conveniences to judge for yourself on the ground." The Company listed W. H. Hilleary as president and Charles S. Robb as vice president.

However in the early days, Edgemoor was hardly the idyllic "Eden" the sales brochure pictured. It was mainly acres of corn, hay and scrubby second growth, and the town was not much to brag about either and included some rowdy neighbors as his eldest daughter recalled:

Over by the tracks they had a gang of men working on the railroad. They had a camp there, down toward Kenwood behind Perry's store. They frequently fought on Saturday night, and it would get pretty raucous. Daddy would go out on the lawn with his gun because he was worried about them getting too close, and mother would sit shaking by the telephone waiting for his shot in the air that meant for her to call the police.

On the next two pages is the map produced as part of S. D. Caldwell's 1915 *Directory* of the Bethesda District showing "Country Between Washington City and the Rockville District."

Looking west through Tuckerman's entrance gates at Edgemoor Lane and Old Georgetown to acres of empty fields   The "old road" and the trolley line to Rockville are at right in this panorama from the winter of 1915-16.

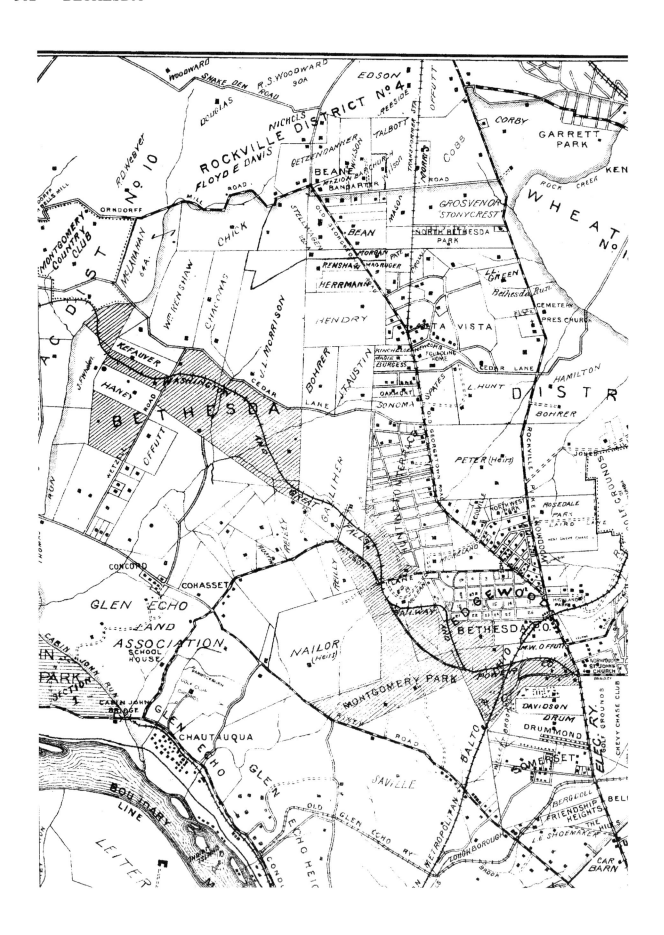

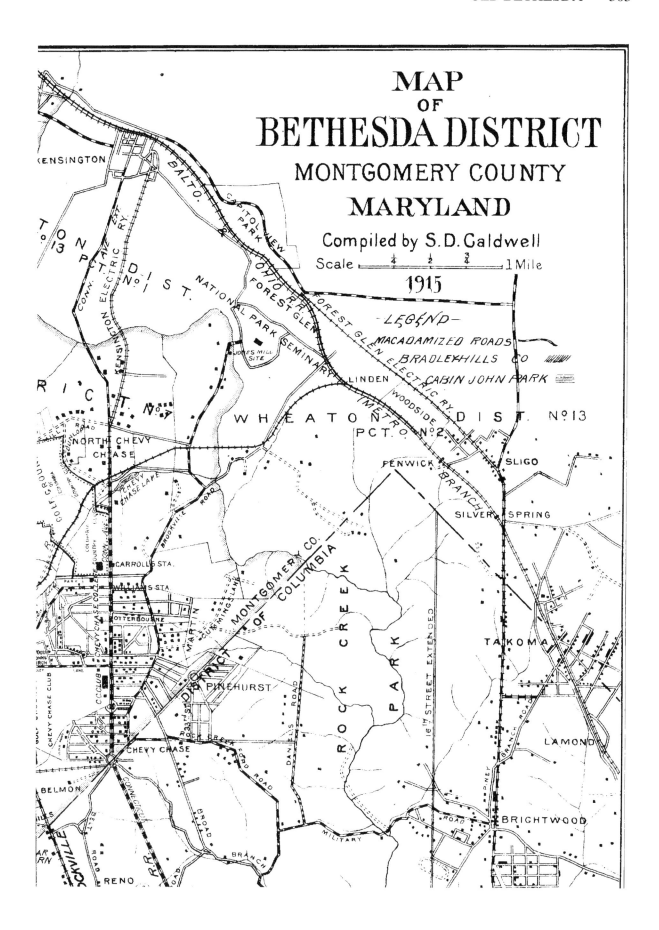

MAP
OF
BETHESDA DISTRICT
MONTGOMERY COUNTY
MARYLAND

Compiled by S.D. Caldwell

Scale ⊢———┼———┼———┼———┦ 1 Mile

1915

- LEGEND -
MACADAMIZED ROADS
BRADLEY HILLS CO
CABIN JOHN PARK

One of the largest of Edgemoor's elegant houses was the home a Colonel Philips built at 7500 Hampden Lane about 1919. It is one of the five original Edgemoor homes of several different styles all said to have been designed by the same architect, perhaps Theodore D. Boal. The Italian-French structure with its pink tile roof, wrought iron balcony, fifteen French doors and elaborate carvings originally stood on three landscaped acres.

The Philips-New house, "kissin' cousin" to "Tuxeden"

When Colonel Phillips died, the estate was broken up, and President Harding's postmaster, Senator Harry S. New of Indiana, purchased the home and a one-acre lot. He hosted many diplomatic and political parties at the house, and both Harding and President Coolidge were regular visitors. Mrs. New cultivated rare irises and filled the driveway area with roses, and the News took an active role in community affairs. As Coolidge's Postmaster General, New participated in the opening of the post office in Tuckerman's three-story store on Wisconsin Avenue in 1926 and was also involved in the dedication of the Madonna of the Trail in 1929.

Another home where there was a great deal of gracious entertaining was the fifteen-room mansion built by J. Maury Dove, which was modeled on Tudor Place in Georgetown. The huge estate occupied a whole block at Beverly and Edgemoor and included a guest house across Beverley. Dove was born in Washington in 1855, but his family moved to the County when he was a youngster. By 1883 he owned Stover and Company, the coal business where he had started as a clerk. After becoming one of the largest coal suppliers in the metropolitan area, Dove diversified his interests and holdings. He organized the Lanston Monotype Company of Philadelphia and England, and then he bought the Shoreham Hotel from Levi Morton in 1912. His other hotel interests included part ownership of the Raleigh and the Willard. After Dove's death in 1924 the American Ice Company purchased and operated the coal enterprise.

J. Maury Dove's Edgemoor estate became the home of Pierce-Arrow distributor Frederick Parkhurst and still later of Reece Sewell's Longfellow School. Other homeowners of note in the late `20's included the Hathaways on Moorland; the Davisons just past the Tuckermans on Edgemoor; the Fredericks, the Pughs and the Warrens at Glenbrook and Montgomery, and the Novak place at Glenbrook and Hampden. On the east side of Arlington at Edgemoor, E. Taylor Chewning of United Clay built one of the best looking brick houses in the area. Edgemoor, mostly open spaces and weedy fields, was off to a stately start. On the west side of Arlington at 5000 Edgemoor Lane, the Orienta Coffee Company's number one saleman, Oscar W. Shumate, made his home. His sons enjoyed the Chewning's tennis court and raced the Chewning's bobsled down the hill toward Hampden Lane. The empty lot beside the Shumate house was long a neighborhood playground when the Parkhursts chased football games off their front lawn.

Edgemoor, mostly open spaces and weedy fields, was off to a busy if not stately start. If the coming of the first electric streetcar in 1891 was the most important event in the early history of Bethesda, then the arrival of Walter, Edith and Laura Tuckerman in 1913 ranks a close second.[41]

At about the same time that the Hamptons and the Tuckermans moved to Bethesda and started building Bradley Hills and Edgemoor, draftsman John Imirie, whose F Street office dealt mainly with patent applications, moved to Chevy Chase with his large family. On Bradley Lane, he built a solid brick home with white pillars out front for his wife Mary and their children, Scott F., G. Wady, John Fred, Mary B., Helen, Donald, and Paul. The Imiries soon had an impact on their new community.

According to Wady Imirie:

In 1916 my brother Fred wanted to get into the gasoline business. Will Counselman ran the feed store where Mazor is now, on Willow Lane. Next to that was where Will lived. Counselman had an alcohol problem and decided to get out of the feed business. So in 1916 he rented the feed store to me and my brother. We got a gas pump in there and had a garage.

Fred brought along a friend of his, Earl Groverman, to help tend the store. Wady Imirie had planned to be a patent attorney like his father and worked at his father's office while he was in school, but his health broke down and on doctor's advice he decided to find a career that was not all office work.[42]

By then Mr. Counselman, Doree Holman's step-father, was a recognized Bethesda character who sometimes closed his store for days, made himself a bed of grain sacks in the back, fixed a piece of tubing to a keg of wine, and drank himself into temporary oblivion. In addition to his drinking problem, "Uncle Billy" had accumulated a number of pets over the years, and one was a big peacock that he called Jimmy.

Mr. Wilson's store had a peculiar fascination for Jimmy. About eight in the morning when everyone was hurrying into town to work, or to training camp, Jimmy would spread his gorgeous tail and strut slowly and proudly across the pike, with irate people shouting and brakes grinding. Most people laughed, for in a war-torn world such nonchalance, even on the part of peafowls was a welcome relief.[43]

G. Wady Imirie, who had attended both business college and Georgetown law school, pumped Gulf gasoline, fixed flats, sold a few spark plugs and repaired cars on the east side of the Pike for about a year, and then his father bought a lot from Charlie Miller, which was diagonally across the street. The Imiries purchased an old, portable elementary school classroom, probably one of the four that had been placed on Rosemary Street in 1912 and was no longer needed, had it placed in front of an old barn on Bethesda Avenue and turned it into a service station while still working at Counselman's store. Wady Imirie, by his own admission, did not know much about fixing cars, and Fred Imirie and Earl Groverman, according to Wady's wife, "were rich men's sons who were running-around minded."

In 1918 Imirie Brothers moved across the street, and established a profitable business that would last at that location for forty years. The brothers were not without competition. At Old Georgetown and Cedar Lane, Bernard Wine, who advertised tinning, guttering, roof painting and stove repairing among his skills, also did "automobile repairing in all its branches." Francis Day was renting cars and offering "free air" at his Bethesda Garage near the railroad bridge, and Alfred Wilson had been

The garage at Wisconsin and Bethesda Avenue

selling tires, gasoline and motor oil next to his hay scale for some time.

One of Wady Imirie's favorite stories was about a fellow who brought him a truck to repair early in his career. When the customer drove into his barn-garage, the front end broke through the floor and fell into the cellar while the back end stayed in the doorway. While the Imiries were wondering how they were going to get the truck out of the basement, a trolley approached on Wisconsin Avenue. Fred ran out and asked the conductor if he could help pull the truck out of the hole. The trainman said he could not stop then because he had a schedule to keep, but that if they would have a heavy rope ready when he came back he would try to help. An hour of so later the trolley's gong sounded; a stout rope attached to the truck's back axle and passed around a tree was hooked onto the coupler, and the truck was slowly extracted. The trolley car went on its way toward the District Line, and Wady Imirie set to work learning to be a mechanic.[44]

Will Counselman went back to storekeeping and, along with the Wilson brothers and the Imiries, watched Bethesda change. More houses edged Wisconsin Avenue, still just a dirt road east of the streetcar tracks. The new homes were often white clapboard or shingle pseudo-Victorians with fancy trim and narrow porches. Several were "twins" and many had chamfered corners, gables and turrets and gambreled roofs in what some thought of as a Bethesda "style."

William Van Ness started Chevy Chase Transfer and Storage in 1917 just off Leland Street about three blocks east of Wisconsin near the Gummels' place. On the "main drag," houses and businesses all mixed together along with gardens and barns, weedy empty lots and fields full of fruit trees. "Zoning" was not to be found in dictionaries much less in Bethesda

The original directors included most of the Bethesda businessmen of time. (Left to right): Millard E Peake, Claude H Woodward, Robert Wilson, Lewis Keiser, Charles Miller, H Latane Lewis, B Peyton Whalen, Walter E Perry, Walter R Tuckerman, Edward L Stock, S Walter Bogley, Francis C Wallace, M Willson Offutt, Dr. E. C. Schroeder

where many of the barns now held a flivver rather than a horse. The Model-T and all its multitude of cousins were changing the suburbs that the electric railways had created. Bethesda's growth shifted into second.[45]

In 1919 Walter Tuckerman and George Sacks established the Bank of Bethesda. The first depositors were mailman Charlie Hurley, who also opened a savings account for his young daughter Christine, and businessman G. Wady Imirie who moved his account from Riggs.

According to Ed Stock Sr., the bank was really his idea. He thought it would help him teach his three sons thrift. His story was that one day he walked into Tuckerman's real estate office and said, "Walter, we're going to start a bank here." And Tuckerman asked, "You and who else?" Stock said that he went to see Milton Ailes at Riggs who thought it was a good idea and was willing to put $3,000 of "pig money" from his West Virginia farm into it. Then he got Judge Robert Peter interested. The Peter family had been running the County off

and on since the War of 1812 and had owned Bethesda property even longer. Stock had Ailes talk to George Sacks, who did not favor the idea, but Sacks hosted the first organizational meeting with Tuckerman, Stock, Judge Peter, Frank Wallace and M. Willson Offutt Sr., in attendance. They picked the name for the bank and decided to hire Walter Bogley as cashier.[46]

When negotiations with the Masons over locating the bank on their property foundered, Sacks offered the use of the small, stone building at Bradley and Wisconsin, which had been the Bradley Hills sales office and trolley station, but the founders decided to quarter the bank in the "Gate House" of the Edgemoor subdivision. The bank was capitalized at $25,000 with a surplus of $5,000. A thousand shares of capital stock with a par value of $25 were sold at $30 to produce the surplus.

The *Sentinel* reported that the "management of the bank will be in the hands of well-known and conservative business men, nearly all residents of Bethesda or Chevy Chase" and that

"Mr. Walter R. Tuckerman has been asked to serve as first President. He has been interested in Bethesda since 1910, and a resident since 1913, and is the President of the Corporation which has developed Edgemoor." The vice-presidents were Edward L. Stock of Bradley Hills, vice-president of Hart and Crouse, and George P. Sacks of the Chapin-Sacks Manufacturing Company. Walter Bogley, of the Potomac Savings Bank in Georgetown and a "member of a well-known Montgomery County family" accepted the post of cashier. Walter Perry later recalled that when he was invited to become a stockholder for $300, "I had a heck of a time scraping that much money together." [47]

The new bank did business in such a small room, about 350 square feet in Tuckerman's office-gate house, that jokesters predicted some night it would be carried off in toto. Tuckerman had gratings put on the window and bought an old counter and a secondhand customers' window from Western Union for $14 and had them installed about six feet inside the door. He acquired a small, fireproof safe, purchased some stationary, and hired Mary Cunningham as the bank's first secretary.

When money was transported, the bank engaged deputy sheriff E. V. Caywood to escort Mr. Bogley downtown. On one such trip the Park Police arrested the sheriff for carrying a gun in Rock Creek Park. Another of Mr. Bogley's duties was to keep the coal stove fueled in cold weather. In the first year deposits totaled $49,000.

During that first year of business, the bank's directors again talked with the leaders of the Bethesda Lodge of the A. F. and A. M. about locating their permanent building on Masonic

Tuckerman in his Bethesda office

Temple's point of land at Old Georgetown Road and the Pike where they planned to build a meeting hall and library. The Hall Committee of the Bethesda Lodge No. 204 had purchased the property in 1910 for $3,000 with five members signing a $500 note for the first payment.

Roy Lochte moved his family's blacksmith operation from that long-rented land to a space behind Walter Perry's store. The Masons then bought a tent and "got up" a fete and raised enough to meet the note. According to William Chitty, the Fair's success "was due entirely to these ladies, for we men just did what they told us to do, and the work was, indeed, immense." From then on the Masons held an annual bazaar on that point of land and were not eager to lose their prime location.

According to the local Mason's history:

On a cold day in November, 1922 the Washington Alexandria Lodge brought to the Bethesda ceremony the trowel used by George Washington in the laying of the cornerstone of the Capitol. Following true Masonic form, the Most Worshipful Grand Master of Masons in Maryland used this trowel in the laying of the cornerstone for Bethesda Lodge No. 204, our present location.[48]

Meanwhile, the little bank in Tuckerman's building added bulletproof glass to its counter and bought a burglar alarm, a huge sign to hang out front advertising it and a larger, manganese safe. Walter Tuckerman built a small, frame ell on the back for his office so Mr. Bogley's space could be increased. His oldest daughter, Laura, remembered visiting her father there and how proud she was that he had his own office.

He rode there every day on his bicycle because mother needed the car. He had clamps he put on his trousers. Once I was playing in the bushes looking at our dog cemetery and he couldn't see me, and something had gone wrong at the bank. It's the only time I ever heard him swear, and I think he was saying "Darn, darn,darn," as he pedaled past. I was absolutely astonished. I told him afterward and he roared.

In the early-`20s George Sacks purchased the Mason's surplus property for $3,000 and held it for a year until the Bank took up its option in 1923. It contracted for the construction of its $53,000 building two years later. The bank proudly opened for business on September 26, 1926, behind its eighteen-inch-thick stone walls and its ten-ton, steel vault door. Seven employees moved into the new building, one of the most modern in the area.

The bank was built of the same Stoneyhurst Quarry mica schist used in C&P's building and in the rows of stores both Walter Tuckerman and George Sacks put up within the next two years. They were evidently trying to establish a different Bethesda style. By the end of 1926 deposits reached $250,000 and the capitalization was increased to $100,000. The bank was the chief landmark and symbol of the town for the next half century. Bethesdans gave directions and measured distances in relation to the Bank, and its solid, stolid presence exuded the hopes of its founders.

In 1928 while Walter Tuckerman was out of the country, George Sacks became president, and the next year deposits reached the one million dollar mark. The bank weathered the crash and Depression, reopening on March 15, 1933, after the frightening bank "holiday." By 1939 the deposits topped $2 million and few argued with Walter Tuckerman's belief that the bank's "success was largely responsible for the rapidity of growth here." By then the Bank of Bethesda had made more than $1.5 million in FHA loans.[49]

In 1920 when Wady Imirie's brother married and his new wife decided he should go into the booming real estate business or become a car dealer, he offered to sell out his interest in the garage for $6,000. "Well, to make a long story short," Imirie told an interviewer, "I went up to Walter Tuckerman and said, 'I need $6,000.' He said, 'All right, when do you need it?' That was that."

Imirie ran his business on a cash basis often carrying a wad of bills containing five or six hundred dollars. He paid for his gas deliveries in cash and paid his workers that way, too. When the pile of bills got too big to carry, he made a deposit but generally used the bank more for loans than anything else. Within ten years he was pumping 100,000 gallons of gas a month and had fourteen people working for him. By then Imirie's garage was the largest building in town and was sometimes used for public meetings, and Imirie had been chosen president of the County auto dealers' association. In those ten years Bethesda's population jumped from about 4,800 in 1920 to over 12,000 in 1930.[50]

Back in 1915 Bethesda was in competition with Chevy Chase and Kensington for a high school. The Bethesda District Federation of Home and School Associations suggested a consolidated school to house about 400 students near Bradley and Wisconsin, but nothing came of it. Most Bethesda youngsters went into Washington for high school. A few took the trolley up to Rockville. Many did not even finish the seven grades at the Bethesda-area schools. It would be more than ten years before a down-county high school opened.

For Bethesda children, other than lessons at the yellow, frame school on Wilson Lane or organized activities at churches or those offered by groups such as Scouts, there was lots of country to roam and all sorts of things to do. Most youngsters had some chickens or animals to care for and many had daily chores. Creeks were there to splash in, trolleys and trains to wave at and sneak rides on, and many old, empty houses such as the Loughborough place to explore.

The "old road," Georgetown Road, or Old Georgetown Road–the three names were used about equally then–followed the broad crest of a ridge and was a watershed between the streams that flowed to Rock Creek, where several swimming holes catered to boys only, and those that ran to the Cabin John Creek and the Potomac River, where the youngsters who called themselves "river rats" played. When Horace Hampton was young, he rose before daybreak and walked his trapline along Willett Creek, which ran down beside the stables where his father kept the scores of horses and mules used to build Bradley Boulevard.

I'd come back home, skin the muskrats, board the skins and go to school and come home at night time and hang them up to dry. When they dried, we'd ship them out to Chicago, and I got four dollars a skin for them. I must have smelled when I went to school.

One of the boys who sometimes went trapping with Horace was his neighbor Ed Stock who recalled a different adventure.

Gil Dorsey was my main partner in trapping muskrats. We used to ride over on our bikes with a little flashlight in front. One dark morning in December we went down under the bridge there, the railroad bridge, and we saw something in front of us. We couldn't quite figure out what it was. Finally we hit it. It was a skunk. When we got home my mother took one smell of us and said, "You take off all your clothes and leave them out there before you get in the house." It was bitter cold but she made us do it.

Back then, that was World War I, we used to sell these pelts in St. Louis and built a little

trappers' house up in the woods. After we trapped the animals, we'd put them on dryers, board dryers, hang them up around our trappers' cabin, and sell the pelts in St. Louis, muskrats, possums, squirrels. We got $5 a piece, not too bad way back then.[51]

Horace Hampton shot at the rats at the experiment station "just for fun," played ball on several fields in Bethesda, and on some Sunday afternoons he and his friends would go over to watch a ballgame at Crow Hill. Hampton also remembered another activity:

On the hillside of the railroad track some of the men in Bethesda wanted to do trap shooting, and my friend and I would load the clay pigeons for them where Arlington Road is now, across from the shopping center. And then we had dogs, and when the men wanted to go hunting, we knew where every covey of quail was, and we'd take them in the great big field where the shopping center is. There were always birds in there.

Even before Edgemoor was begun with its promise of tennis courts and a swimming pool, numerous early Bethesdans founded clubs, both formal and informal, and devised many ways to have fun and to serve civic needs. Literary guilds, women's clubs and citizens' associations of various types blossomed just as they had in other pioneer suburbs. Mrs. Warren Gingell wrote:

In the long winter months there were very few amusements for the young people of Bethesda. Sometimes we ventured into the city to attend some of the theaters such as Poli's or Cosmos or the Belasco.

The young people of the community got together and organized old-fashioned square dances in their homes. The ladies made cakes and sandwiches which would be served with coffee after the dance. All we had for our music was a fiddle and a banjo. Eugene Fling called the figures for the dances. Each dance was held in a different person's house and everyone got a chance to entertain the crowd.

Young Miss Holman and her friends such as Blanche Braddock, Rosalie and Arthur Mace, and Vincent Magruder formed the Hayseed Club for people who lived along the old road as far out as Montrose. They held lively weekly "meetings" with recitations, quartet singing, charades and refreshments.

The first formal women's club, and surely the most influential in the early days, was the Newcomb Club, which began in 1906 with Mrs. Harry T. Newcomb of Alta Vista as its first president. The inside joke still repeated by older club members was that when they were seeking a name someone suggested the "newcomers club" and Mrs. Newcomb said she would be honored to have her family name used. Since no one could figure out how to tell her she had misheard, the name stuck.

The club limited itself to fifty members, but they tended to be the fifty that could get things done. The membership included Mrs. Gittings and her daughter Mrs. Whalen as well as both the first and second Mrs. Walter Perry. The Newcomb Club promoted the establishment of a kindergarten at the Bethesda School and worked long and hard for the creation of a public library in Bethesda.

Five years later, in 1911 at the home of Mrs. Franklin Getzendanner, the Woman's Club of Bethesda was formed, "an earnest club for earnest women." Because meetings were held in members' homes, it also tried to limit its membership to fifty. Its first big project was getting the Old Road repaved and having sidewalks built for the children at the Bethesda School. By 1924 there were ninety-four members, and in 1927 the Woman's Club of Bethesda moved into its handsome home in Sonoma, the first woman's club in the County to have its own clubhouse.[52]

Home of the Woman's Club of Bethesda

Numerous other clubs developed and disappeared such as the Bradley Hills Community League and the Clara Barton Club of Glen Echo. The W.C.T.U. was very powerful during Prohibition and at one time was headed by Mrs. Jed Gittings. Chapters of the D.A.R, the Eastern Star and Job's Daughters came a bit later.

The Bethesda team in the Montgomery County Baseball League of which Busey Howard of Bethesda was president in the mid-20s, came in second to Rockville in 1924 and won the pennant in `25. Other teams represented Dickerson, Washington Grove, and

Boyds. There were double headers most weekends, and admission was a quarter, season tickets two dollars.

In Edgemoor residents organized a tennis club in the summer of 1920, and laid out two courts in the midst of open fields while discussion continued with Mr. Tuckerman about the lease or purchase of the property. The members voted down a plan to get an old street car to use as a club house. The club picked green and white as its colors and set the initiation fee at $25 and dues at $15 a year.

The minutes reflect that :

Everyone turned out one Saturday to arrange a grandstand. Mr. Tuckerman supplied an old bench, which, after much scrubbing, was pronounced fit to sit upon. Some of the men constructed a sturdy framework over which was stretched an awning, also donated by Mr. Tuckerman, which did excellent service in giving shade to spectators until destroyed by the violent winds and rains of the summer.[53]

They held several tournaments that first year and "refreshments were served at the courts by the ladies of the club every Saturday afternoon." The Club was incorporated in 1922 with twenty resident members and a budget of $11,000 to purchase land and build a seventy-five-by-twenty-five-foot swimming pool and some dressing rooms. Eventually they scaled down the plans and built a white, frame clubhouse. Two more courts, a practice board, bowling green and putting green were added later.

In the mid-1920s when some city tennis clubs lost their property, Edgemoor Club made "tennis memberships" available to several of Washington's leading players and raised membership to one hundred. But during the Depression the club fell on hard times, all but two of the courts became weedy and just about unplayable, and most meetings ended with a "discussion of the indebtedness due Mr. Walter R. Tuckerman." Minerva Bassett, whose husband Bill started playing tennis there in 1941, remembered Mr. Tuckerman coming to the meetings year after year and saying, "I don't want the property back, but couldn't you just pay the interest on the loan?"

The property north of the clubhouse was sold, and in 1932 the $17,530.34 debt was refinanced and the initiation fee suspended. Most older members gave R. Strand Johnsen, masseur to the rich and famous, credit for saving the Club during the war years. Many residents be-

lieve that the Club, even more than the active citizens' association, has kept the neighborhood together and made it a special place.[54]

Across Wilson Lane twenty-two housewives led by Mrs. George Pariseau decided they had to do something about the treeless, red-clay fields where they lived. They started the Battery Park Garden Club in November 1923 and went to Dr. David Lumsden of the USDA, husband of a member, for advice. Honorary President Lumsden encouraged the club members to plant roses in the "parking areas" between their sidewalks and the street. The club grew to more than a hundred members and in 1930 changed its name to the Bethesda Community Garden Club. Its annual shows and projects along with Mrs. Chase Donaldson's notes became anticipated traditions.

In June 1928 the Montgomery Suburban Garden Club was organized at Somerset School for the five communities down Wisconsin; Kenwood joined a few years later. The first president was Aubrey B. Carter of Chevy Chase Terrace. Three months later this organization was one of the first to urge that the USDA experiment station be converted to park use as part of the proposed Willett Brook Parkway to River Road. But its biggest project in the first few years was the beautification of Wisconsin Avenue, mainly by planting flowering cherry and other trees along the road. Its annual shows featured roses and peonies, and by the time James C. Dulin Jr., became its second president in 1931, Kenwood had joined and a Christmas lighting award had been added. Dr. Whitman Cross of Chevy Chase won a blue ribbon for his display of forty-eight varieties of roses that June.[55]

The Montgomery Country Club with its high aspirations, had been shaken by the Bradley Hills debacle. In November 1924 it bought the John Thompson estate in Sligo, had architect Henry de Sibour remodel the farmhouse, and moved what little it had left from Bradley Hills. By the early 1930s it was down to thirty-five regular and fifteen associate members and had six vacancies on the board headed by Donald A. DeLashmutt.

The Congressional Women's Country Club, organized in 1929, took over the Bradley Boulevard site and later changed its name to the National Women's Country Club. Fred Finlay modeled its nine-hole course on St. Andrews and gave it the first traps filled with white sand. Its membership list included Mrs.

Wilson, Mrs. Coolidge, Mrs. Taft, as well as Mrs. Tuckerman, whose husband played an active role in its creation.

In 1931 the women undertook the restoration of the old clubhouse and the construction of a "harmonious," two-story addition measuring 82 by 27 feet with a green-shingled roof. The annex would contain a large lobby or lounge with a beamed ceiling, walls of tapestry brick and a large fireplace. The new building also housed two locker rooms, a beauty parlor, and quarters for the manager. Members who did not care to golf enjoyed knitting and card games on the porch. Jocko Miller, a starter for Wiffy Cox as well as a prize fighter with something of a local reputation, served as club pro for several years.

The club was noted for its lane of fifty-five elm trees, planted in 1932, each honoring a woman from a different nation and for its manager, Captain Illarion Vikenty Mishtowt, who had been the Russian government's naval attache at the time of the revolution. Mishtowt, a survivor of the Russian debacle at Tsushima, married a lady-in-waiting to the Czarina, the widow of his predecessor in Washington, and became an American citizen. He had several business interests in addition to the club and worked for the Army as a specialist in port facilities.

The "International Memorial Lane" and a book with a brief history of each woman represented were the gift of Gertrude Helm Remey. Among the women honored, who ranged from Clara Barton to Queen Isabella, were poets, patriots, and feminists from all over the world. Then the Depression took its toll, and by the late `30s the leased facilities served as a public course.

According to Walter Tuckerman, one of its founders, the Burning Tree Club grew out of the impatience of a foursome at the Chevy Chase Club. One of those four, Marshall Whitlatch, found a pair of hundred-acre farms near River Road for about $300 an acre, and Tuckerman added thirty acres of his own. Under a 1922 agreement each member subscribed $10,000.

The Founders' (always capitalized) contributions mounted steadily as work gangs and horse teams cleared the heavily forested land for the links designed by Colt, Mackenzie and Alison of London and raised the stone clubhouse, mostly the work of architect Harry F. Cunningham. Otho Swain and Herman Jackson, two of the men who helped build the course for $3.20 a day, were still club employees forty years later. By the time work was finished, the Founders had advanced their club $242,000 and accrued $300,000 in mortgages. By far the largest monetary contributions were by club president Isaac T. Mann who also held the second mortgage and gave the Club the gate posts, driveway and parking area.

From the first day of play in May 1924 experts praised the course for its fine greens and challenging holes "laid out for the accurate hitter, not the long ball." Traditions, such as the Sunday foursomes, marked this male sanctuary known for its golf and gin rummy. Another tradition stated that "there's an easy way to tell members from guests: guests relieve themselves behind a tree, members don't bother." At the end of 1924 the club had seventy-seven members and by 1930 148 resident members and thirty-three non-residents.

Some order was brought to the anarchy that characterized the club's early years and finances by James K. McClintock, Secretary and manager for twenty-five years. Tom Fisher, a Scot, stayed for more than twenty years as greens keeper. Supervision of the course became the "hobby" of Dr. Walter S. Harban, first president of the D.C. Golf Association.

Laura Tuckerman Triest recalled:

It was built on part of our farm. I've been in it several times. One reason they haven't had women members, you'd have to blame my mother and me. They were going to vote them in during the Depression, and we told Daddy that they were insane if they did. They were going to be allowed to come in twice a week. And I said, "I guarantee if you let us in twice a week, at the end of three months we'll be there seven days a week." And I said, "You will ruin your club." That's the gospel truth. For Daddy it was an escape from his household of women, which he needed immensely, and I can't imagine the wives getting along anyway. It is not the right membership for a family club; it's so mixed.

Walter Tuckerman, first head of the house committee and author of the club's first history, wrote down his version of the legend behind the club's name.[56]

Ten miles or so Northwest of the Capital City, a pleasant hilltop rises above a wooded, rolling plain. It is genial land. Dogwood blossoms brighten the woods in springtime and lavender-colored Judas trees beckon the shad to spawn in the streams. Through a gorge beyond, a great river hurries over the rocks to reach this place, then

leisurely pursues its way to the Chesapeake. Across the river, a line of hills tells a tale of mountains, yet to see.

Upon the summit of this eminence there once stood a noble tree. This was long ago, before there was a Capitol or a White House, before Lord Baltimore and the Virginians named these lands for their Queens.

On occasion, the great tree smoked: Whether from the embers of old camp fires, or from phosphorescence, or just because the Great Spirit willed it so, we do not know. But the native Indians saw and understood the signal. Silently through the wood and along the trails, down the river in canoes, across the blue hills and up from the shore came the Algonquin tribes. The Powtowmack and the Occoquan, the Analostan and the Accotink, the Powhatan, Nacostine and Piscataway. They brought provisions for a feast, and a dance, and a game of ball; they potlatched their goods, paid tribute to the Chief, smoked a pipe of peace, and had a great pow-wow.

They called it Potomac, the Place of the Burning Tree.

The Congressional Country Club, born in the minds of two Indiana congressmen in 1921, and promoted nationwide with $1,000 life memberships as a place to meet the high and mighty, opened with one of the greatest traffic jams in Bethesda history. It began with Herbert Hoover as president, par-six holes at the start of each nine, and a promise by member E. Brooke Lee to get River Road extended and paved. By 1927 the board of directors had spent $100,000 for land and $625,000 for buildings and was carrying $20,000 in members' unpaid bills. It was refinanced by Acacia Mutual Life and reorganized in 1928 on a less grand scale and staggered through the Thirties on bar profits until it went broke for the second time in 1940.

Meanwhile the Town and Country Club, founded by German Jews in Petworth in 1916, purchased 116 acres north of Battery Lane from three members of the Peter family, moved out of the growing city and converted Dr. Armistead

Peter's summer house, the stone and brick, mansard-roofed "Winona," into its white frame, Georgian "country" clubhouse in 1922. The members all bought $1,200 shares to finance the move. Since almost everyone called it "Woodmont," the club's name was officially changed in 1930.

The 250 members enjoyed meals on the screened back porch near the last green. The thirty-by-fifty-foot ballroom, bar, and dining room occupied the other side of the expanded clubhouse. Locker rooms and card rooms, where some games seemed to go on for years, were on the second floor. The "shack" used by pro A. B. Thorn really was a shack, but it housed a slot machine that paid off in golf balls. Prizes for Sunday morning tournaments included locally purchased honey and eggs. Many years would pass before any of this old club's members lived in Bethesda, and most Bethesdans knew it only for the best sleigh-riding hills around rather than for its challenging golf course of eighteen played on nine fairways.

Flourishing Kenwood, struggling Bannockburn, homey Woodmont, pretentious Congressional, salvaged Burning Tree, the "tradesmen's" Columbia, "the Club," plus Georgetown Prep and White Flint just to the north, provided the acres of fairways, roughs, greens, ballrooms and shady verandas that made the "Country Club community" label an easy one for Bethesda's boosters to apply in the Roaring Twenties' boom and through the New Deal revival. But,

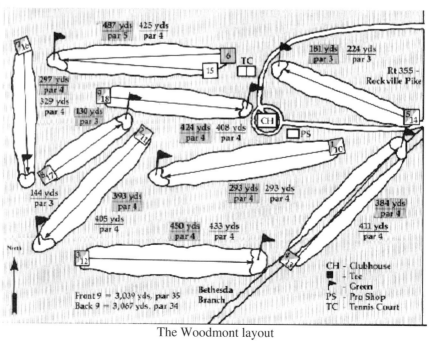

The Woodmont layout

Winona converted into the Woodmont clubhouse

except at Kenwood, and at Woodmont during WWII, there was little evidence that the country clubs were directly involved in the affairs of the community.[57]

Of course, there were many less formal, neighborhood get-togethers. Every year the churches and clubs staged a cycle of "lawn fetes" to raise funds as well as to have fun. The Masonic Hall and Library held an annual bazaar in the middle of Bethesda for several years; later the firemen's carnivals marked each summer, and nearly everyone looked forward to taking the open streetcars out to the fairgrounds in Rockville and perhaps even risking a dollar or two on a horse race. Many Bethesda churches and clubs held "days" at Glen Echo or went down the river to Marshall Hall for an excursion. One of the longest remembered 4th of July celebrations was held in 1921 at the Bethesda School. An estimated 2,500 attended this giant party, and Walter Tuckerman set up a five-hole golf course along Edgemoor Lane as part of the entertainment.

While the establishment of the Bank surely marked another turning point, the growth of Bethesda into a recognizable suburban community rested on six other major events or developments. These were the improvements in transportation, the founding of the Washington Suburban Sanitary Commission, the creation of suburban taxing districts, the acceptance of regional planning and zoning, the coming of the New Deal, and the building of the National Institutes of Health and National Naval Medical Center. Each was important in isolation but can only be understood fully in conjunction with the others. Each had immediate as well as very long range impact. The creation of modern Bethesda rested on these forces in combination.

But even they were not the whole story, for example, it is very difficult to make sense of the Charter movement of the 1940s without some knowledge of the conflicts between the Eastern and Western Suburban Districts and between the newcomers brought in by the expansion of government service and the entrenched, Rockville-centered, good-old-boy bureaucracy, which existed long before FDR's time. And although some west of Rock Creek are loath to admit it, there was a seventh factor, which was an important influence, a dynamic man from Silver Spring named E. Brooke Lee.

Surely the coming of the electric railway must be listed as the initiating event in Bethesda's growth just as Miss Holman wrote, but the development of the motorcar as reasonably cheap and relatively reliable transportation actually had more to do with the expansion of the town. Many homes built in the Washington suburbs before the Great War were tied to the trolley tracks, although the largest of them, like those built away from the railways, had coach houses or sheds as well as other outbuildings such as pump houses and privies, or if you prefer, necessaries. Numerous paved streets in the older suburbs were, and some still are, too narrow for both parked cars and through traffic, not to mention fire engines or moving vans. Pressure to widen the main streets and improve the neighborhood roads was constant through the time of Bethesda's development.

In the 1920s almost every Bethesda neighborhood grew with the automobile in mind although it might have been hard to convince some car owners in the tangled lanes of Battery Park and all those in the Woodmont Triangle who lived on a single, narrow lot beside deep, stone gutters along rutted, bluestone streets. Soon garages were the only standard outbuildings, which stood on the back lines of a multitude of home sites. It was the rare new house that did not have a gravel driveway or twin strips of concrete leading to a ten-by-twenty, corrugated metal or shingle-roofed wooden shed usually featuring a window or two and a double door, often clapboard and usually white or green. Built-in garages became increasingly popular in larger homes, even though Kenwood insisted that they be invisible from the street. Into the 1940s only a few houses were built without off-street parking, and several featured driveways shared by a pair of neighbors. The multiplication of Fords and Chevys, Chryslers and Studebakers, Packards and Terraplanes

freed subdivisions from the trolley lines and made home owners independently mobile if not permanently peripatetic.

Of course, they created other problems having to do with street maintenance and traffic control, but modern Bethesda grew up with the flivver, the roadster, and the sedan trying to cope with various "bottlenecks" and changes in parking regulations all through the `30s and `40s. Complaints about street conditions in new subdivisions were endemic, and news stories about the post office refusing to deliver mail in certain neighborhoods until the roads solidified were common.

Automobiles also meant business for Bethesda. Not only did the number of gasoline service stations and garages rapidly multiply, but dealerships for various marques soon appeared, and rows of used cars replaced the weeds and sheds on Wisconsin Avenue lots while hopeful entrepreneurs built showrooms and service facilities on Bethesda Avenue and Hampden Lane down in Miller's Flats.

Providing sufficient parking for shoppers soon became a major concern for Bethesda businessmen, and the need for sidewalks, traffic lights and crossing guards closely followed. By 1930, 4,137 or twenty-nine percent of the 14,338 cars in the County were located in the Seventh Election District.[58]

At the turn of the century more than $30,000 had been spent on the Rockville Pike, but most of the roads were still impassable at times. A "good roads" movement began in farm communities, and after a State Geological Survey study, the legislature appropriated $200,000 a year on a matching basis for improving roads. In the Bethesda area, Old Georgetown Road was improved out to Beane with this funding. In 1908 State Senator Blair Lee ramrodded a bill creating the State Roads

Lack of curbs and gutters was a common problem

Commission through the General Assembly, and Maryland became the first state to create a real system of highways.

Between 1910 and 1915 the State built 1,305 miles of roads connecting Baltimore and the county seats. After 1912 the standard surface was concrete rather than stone and asphalt, and in 1914 the standard width was set at fourteen and a half feet, which was generally achieved by adding concrete shoulders to existing humpbacked roads. Soon dairy farms became common in all parts of the County and land along the hard surfaced roads greatly increased in value. Suburbs now spread away from the trolley lines, but in 1920 eighty percent of all County land was still devoted to farming.

Montgomery County's rate of population growth since 1900 had been below the national average, but while many up-county areas now had fewer people, the population of the Bethesda and Wheaton-Silver Spring regions had doubled and redoubled. Between 1910 and 1920 every district in the County lost population except Wheaton, which increased from about five thousand to almost eight thousand. Bethesda went from 3,217 to 4,757. And the boom was just beginning.[59]

In percentage terms, Bethesda was also becoming "whiter," a trend that would accelerate. At the turn of the century about fifty black families, including several who farmed their own land, lived in the Seventh Election District. By the 1920 census no African-American households were left in Chevy Chase although there were quite a few in the rest of the area. A small cluster of homes remained in Cabin John, and about fifteen black families with some seventy-five members lived in the Glen Echo area. "Crow Hill" was a fairly stable community, and a few blacks made homes in the Beane-Alta Vista area while Walter and Catherine Brown and their nine children and Oscar and Gara Brown and their seven lived near the Pike. Some fifteen African-American families with more than sixty children lived in "unincorporated" Bethesda .[60]

The second major event that produced modern Bethesda and its sister suburbs in Prince George's as well as Montgomery County was the creation of the Washington Suburban Sanitary Commission. The Siamese twin problems of providing potable water and sewage disposal had haunted the start and limited the growth of most subdivisions. Each semi-self-governing special taxing area in Chevy Chase

had a health officer even though the Chevy Chase Land Company provided excellent water and disposed of sewerage in a generally acceptable manner in bordering "farms" or drainage fields. The first problem engaging the attention of the town fathers of Somerset was the failure of the sewer system, and their health officer was concerned with the condition of neighboring streams as well as the local dairy farms.

Typhoid had been a recurring problem, which ravaged the Middle Atlantic area at the time of the Spanish-American War. Both Montgomery County and the District of Columbia reported many cases. No one could stop all the children from playing in the creeks or building their swimming holes and dams in the polluted streams that ran through numerous communities. In the summer when water flow in many of the small runs lessened to a trickle, the threat was exacerbated. The Citizens' Committee of Friendship Heights was among the first to call for action.

By 1910 Bethesda's Willett Creek and Little Falls Branch and Chevy Chase's Rock Creek and all its feeders were so dangerously polluted that the District government protested. Superintendent of Sewers Asa E. Phillips suggested the creation of a suburban sewer system that fed into the Capital's treatment plant. [61]

Walter Tuckerman led the Bethesdans calling for action. The Chevy Chase sewer field, he said, "stank to high heaven as you drove from here to Washington, and had a very depressing effect on property values." He thought the solution might be a pipeline to the Potomac and led a hike from Edgemoor to "see what would be involved." Across the fields he went, followed by portly M. Willson Offutt, lean Emory H. Bogley, and William T. S. Curtis, the nominal mayor of Chevy Chase. Long before they reached the Potomac, it was obvious that such a sewer line would not only be very expensive but would require an Act of Congress to condemn the right-of-way. "We concluded," Tuckerman said, "that nothing could be accomplished without a public service corporation to deal with the owners, and especially the U.S. Government."[62]

Curtis hosted the next important meeting with Phillips and representatives of the State Board of Health, and it led to an appeal to the Maryland General Assembly for legislative relief. A 1912 commission reported two years later with a recommendation for a regional effort. Governor Goldsborough supported the

proposed bill, but it failed in the final days of the session. Instead, the State gave the Board of Commissioners in Montgomery County the power to act as a Board of Health while the Governor's unpaid commissioners, three from each county, continued their work. By 1916 when they reported again, the County Commissioners were quite willing to admit that the sewage problem was too big and too "delicate" and that acting as a Board of Health took up too much of their time.

The State lawmakers disregarded much of the report made by Chairman T. Howard Duckett but agreed to appropriate $10,000 for further study and chose another commission. Finally in 1918 the legislature accepted the exhaustive report along with conclusions and plans drawn by Robert B. Morse, and passed legislation drafted by Duckett to create the bi-county Washington Suburban Sanitary Commission.

Mr. Duckett admitted that he had more trouble with the delegation from his native Prince George's County than he did with the delegates and senators from Montgomery. He credited the work of recently returned war-hero Maj. E. Brooke Lee of the 29th Division for the bill's smooth passage through the General Assembly. May 1, 1918, marks the beginning of the WSSC. Like most successes it had many fathers although attorney-banker Duckett was generally recognized as the founder.[63]

The "charter" WSSC Commissioners were Mr. Duckett, representing PG County; attorney Emory Bogley, chosen by the Montgomery County Commissioners, plus William T. S. Curtis, the governor's appointee. They started with nothing but a mandate, met on May 15, 1918, chose Mr. Curtis chairman, hired a secretary, ordered a telephone, "borrowed" engineer Robert B. Morse from the health department, and established offices in Hyattsville and at 611 F Street where Duckett had his office.

By mid-June they were meeting three times a week, had been authorized to issue $50,000 in bonds, and initiated a survey of Piney Branch as a water supply and of the Little Falls Branch for a major trunk sewer project to connect with the D.C. system. Plans for taking over the water and sewer companies in Chevy Chase, Edgemoor, Friendship Heights, Glen Echo and Somerset were soon in the works. In less than a year the WSSC had a rate schedule and a method for assessments and tax levies patterned on that of Elizabeth, N. J. Real estate

taxes paid for the trunk lines, special assessments including front-foot benefits for lateral lines, and metered service rates for operations.

They began hiring "bright young" Hopkins grads away from the State Health Department and started digging ditches, laying pipe, and cleaning up urban pollution problems in an area containing some 30,000 people. Because East West Highway did not exist, many of the engineers and work crews camped out on the Bethesda-area jobs in order to avoid long trips through D.C.

When the District showed no interest in sharing its water supply, Morse found an idle World War I filter plant in Culpeper, Virginia, bought it, packed it up, and had it hauled to Burnt Mills on the Northwest Branch where the native New Englander designed a processing basin the size and shape of a regulation hockey rink. By 1920, Burnt Mills produced drinking water for Bethesda homes.

The "norm" for Washington's suburbs in the period of World War I included sewer drains that led to cesspools, neighbors sharing wells often windmill powered, and refuse burned, buried or fed to pigs. The WSSC's first survey found fifty miles of water mains and sixty miles of sewer pipes in seventeen public systems, all of which were labeled "inadequate." Nine systems had pipes too small to support fire hydrants, and many had very low pressure. In most towns, the engineers reported, "the only good derived from fire hydrants was that they offered an excuse for having an annual carnival." Only seven of the seventeen systems produced acceptably pure water, and forty-seven of the eighty-five wells tested failed to meet health department standards.

So while Morse delegated a few men to rebuild and maintain old systems, he had five times as many creating a whole new network. Within four years the WSSC had purchased most of the private and public systems for about $350,000. Some like Edgemoor's became the basis of the new water supply system, but most had to be replaced completely. Although many in Chevy Chase mourned the loss of their delicious water, the change benefited the whole Bethesda area.[64]

In 1922 the Maryland General Assembly codified what had become obvious as well as generally accepted by giving the WSSC the right to approve or demand changes in subdivision plats and to plan the highways and streets in the area under its jurisdiction. This act not only diminished the power of the County Commissioners, but it also introduced the concept of rational, staged growth. Future development "down county" was, for a time, in the hands of the three commissioners of the WSSC. In the 1930s the creation of the Eastern and Western Suburban taxing areas and of the Maryland-National Capital Park and Planning Commission along with the yeasty turmoil of the New Deal accelerated more changes in the suburbs.

By the early Twenties, Dr. Benjamin Perry had replaced the late Dr. Lewis as the most popular physician in Bethesda. Perry was also one of the most powerful political leaders of his time. Twice he was elected County Commissioner and served as president of the Board. He became a valued if independent-minded member of the Lee machine, which ran the County with few, brief interruptions in the period between the wars. If Bethesda had had a mayor in the `20s and `30s, Perry would probably have won every election even if all his patients had not voted for him.[65]

Dr. Benjamin Perry

When a Bethesdan wanted a job with the County government, Dr. Perry was the man to see. Feared by some and considered cold and aloof by others, Dr. Perry was loved and admired by most. Folks smiled and waved hello when the doctor made his daily round of house visits, driven by Milton Smith, one of whose brothers ran the Sugarbowl tavern over on River Road. Young Horace Hampton admired Dr. Perry greatly. Hampton came home from the University of Maryland one summer feeling kind of poorly and went to see the doctor, was examined and received a prescription to go find a nice girl and enjoy himself.

Laura Tuckerman Triest remembered Dr. Perry.

He was quite a character. He came to our house on the average of three nights a week when there was an emergency. He always had on the same navy-blue suit; he was always plump; he always had the same fedora and the same chauffeur who drove him 24 hours-a-day. I recall his driver got into a bad fight one night with a curious little

character who wasn't improved by the fight and came to do odd jobs for us for several years afterwards."[66]

Alfred Wilson, by then Bethesda's justice of the peace and called "Judge," sold his store to George Bradley in 1922 and left the area after his wife's death. He returned in 1929 to take up his duties in the County Building and live with his daughter and son-in-law, Stanley Everhart, on Montgomery Avenue.

Walter Perry was still there selling feed and seed as well as gaining some notoriety for the flock of sheep he kept on Old Georgetown Road. After his first wife, the second female member of the County school board and a leader of the League of Women Voters, died of appendicitis in November 1931, he married one of the few women in Bethesda society known by her given name, Willie Green Day, a social worker from Georgia who soon rivaled Mrs. B. Payton Whalen for civic leadership. "A real catbird," Sumpter Embrey labeled her. Some thought Walter kept the sheep just to annoy his wife and her society friends although he claimed they saved a lot of lawn mowing. His big lot backed up to his doctor-brother's property, but he was not interested in politics. "I tend to business," said Mr. Perry, "and let the women folks look after civic activities."[67]

Willie Green Day Perry

The number of gas pumps in front of Imirie's kept growing in the 1920s, and he married Sue Magruder and built a house on Old Georgetown Road in 1923 on part of what had been his wife's family-farm. At first it was just a bungalow, but he added the second floor in `36. A number of new businesses appeared and some disappeared almost as rapidly. W. G. Price was the proprietor of the Edgewood Market that offered "home dressed meats," and U. S. Grant Osborne operated The Home Bakery in Wilson's Bethesda Market before World War I. F. N. Loria came to Bethesda just after that war, drove for the Tuckermans and then went into the plumbing and heating business. He married,

made his home on Walsh Street, and watched his business on Miller Avenue grow.

In Woodmont several small stores including Mrs. Morris's up on the Pike became very popular with Woodmont folks. The widow Lane, according to Mrs. Gingell, had the second general store in Bethesda on Melrose (Cordell) Avenue. This was the shop later run by Sophia Shackleford who added variety to the stock. John, her husband, who worked at the Chevy Chase Club caddy shop, made deliveries, a service that came to be expected of nearly every market and shop in the 1920s.

Groceries, Provisions,
Fresh Meats and
Feed of all Kinds

S. E. SHACKLEFORD

WOODMONT,

Phone, Bethesda 57K   BETHESDA P. O., MD.

The Shackleford's moved to Bethesda in 1891 with their young daughter Myrtle and lived in a small house behind Wilson's store. Myrtle soon learned that she could take an egg from their chicken's nest and trade for a piece of candy at the store. Her granddaughter Winifred Krueger (B-CC `40) said:

In 1909 Grandmother bought the property that was the store on Melrose from a Mr. Steel and moved into that. They lived on one side, and the store was the other side of the house. She had always had the desire to operate a store. My grandmother lived there until she died.

Mrs. Grace Nash was the first of several proprietors of a store on Old Georgetown Road near Del Ray. Mrs. Gingell wrote that Mrs. Nash did her best to please her customers.

Regardless of your order, if she could not fill it she would offer a substitute, which in most cases was impossible to use. One day she was unable to supply me with a lamp chimney and suggested a lantern globe. Another time she suggested pancake flour when I wanted oatmeal. A sale was the thing with Mrs. Nash!

When Evan and Stella Condon took over, they called it the Bethesda Variety Store and added to its popularity by stocking ice cream in addition to the dry goods, notions, cigars, and candy. After several more changes in ownership, just after World War I, Leslie W. Beall, "a born storekeeper" from the city, purchased the store and added meats and vegetables. His market was so successful that he finally had the

Morrison brothers build him a new and larger store on the other side of Old Georgetown. Beall's Market was remembered as one of the best places in town to shop even if Mr. Beall was not always recalled as the most pleasant man in Bethesda to deal with.[68]

Sometime in the mid-Twenties, with Bethesda's growth firmly in second gear, the builders stomped on the gas. In 1922 Maddux, Marshall and Company entered the Bethesda building boom by purchasing a large, triangular chunk of the old fields and scrub land between Wilson's lane and the Georgetown road. The blacksmith Lochtes had tenant farmed from a house surrounded by willows on the hill where Del Ray later curved. The last member of the family to raise corn and potatoes on the land was "Dinks" Rodgers, whose mother was Roy Lochte's sister. This fifty-two acre subdivision was the first in Bethesda to benefit from the birth of the WSSC.

The developers of Battery Park divided the land into three sections with over two hundred lots. They drew the streets in a manner both idiosyncratic and confusing and included Bethesda's first traffic circle and one street that used another as an alley. The builders placed ads in journals read by military officers, both active and retired, laid water and sewer lines and began building houses in various styles of architecture and types of construction. The Bethesda and Chevy Chase areas have a number of "Spanish-style" houses, but Battery Park probably has more than all the other subdivisions put together including electrical contractor Bancroft Foley's white stucco home on four building lots at the corner of Battery Lane and Old Georgetown Road. Some called Maddux and Marshall's development the "jealous younger brother of Edgemoor," but by the mid-Twenties their enterprise was selling lots and building homes in both communities.[69]

The company became the "four M's" with the addition of Colonel James A. Moss and Lt. Commander C. K. Mallory and rapidly developed the subdivision. The brains behind Battery Park were retired Brigadier General Richard C. Marshall Jr. and former Army medical corps administrator Henry Cabell Maddux, Virginians and cousins.

Maddux, born in 1886, lettered in both football and baseball at the University of Virginia. He was the organizer and president of the company. He commanded three large

Maddux   Marshall   Moss   Mallory

hospitals in France in the First World War. Maddux retired from the Army as a light colonel after thirteen years of service and went into real estate.

As his partner, he signed up General Marshall, seven years his senior and supervisor of more than 500 huge projects as chief of the Army's construction division at the end of World War I. A direct descendant of the great Chief Justice, Marshall was a graduate of VMI who had seen Spanish-American War service before joining the regular army, first in artillery and later in the Quartermaster Corps.[70]

Maddux, Marshall and Co., at 1108 16th Street, NW, issued its first prospectus in October 1922. It ran twenty-three well-printed pages and included excellent drawings and breathless descriptions of eight types of homes plus a stamped-in afterthought, which stated that "homes can be built from any plans or specifications submitted." The houses ranged from the bungalow which, the builders stated, helped solve "the problem of keeping a house without a servant" to the Italian Villa with the servant's room on the third floor and included several versions of the popular colonial. Four types of construction were offered: frame, frame-stucco, hollow tile-stucco, or brick. House prices ranged from $5,900 to $18,000 and lot prices from $1,500 to $4,200. According to the builders, a $12,000 home could be carried for about $90 a month with a $2,400 down payment.

One of those who saw an early Maddux and Marshall ad in the *Army and Navy Journal* was Grace Pariseau, then living in Florida with her physician husband. She wanted to move back north, but his health would not allow that, so Battery Park was a compromise. Entirely by correspondence they purchased a lot and contracted for a house at what became 7814 Maple Ridge Road. The very petite Mrs. Pariseau, remembered by Bethesda old-timers for the tiny Austin coupe she drove, wrote out her memories of moving in.[71]

We didn't know where Bethesda was and didn't care. We arrived the first week of April 1923, only to find nothing had been started on our house. No hotel rooms, no houses and no boarding facilities were available, so we ended up at the tourist camp in Potomac Park. During the night a blizzard arrived bringing 8 inches of snow and a temperature reading of 11°.

Doctor had active TB and was not an acceptable tenant anywhere. Major Maddux suggested putting up our garage with temporary flooring, running water and a single electric light. They also put up an outbuilding across the road — primitive to say the least. Our children and my mother bunked in the garage and Doctor and I had a tent in the yard.

Edgemoor residents were very unhappy with the development with its "cheesy houses at their very doors" and our living arrangements didn't help much. The children from Edgemoor daily rode horseback past us and around us. At a much later date we were accepted and joined their club.

When we moved here five houses were completed and occupied—three on Fairfax road and two on Wilson Lane. Several more on Glenbrook, Battery Lane and Wilson Lane were near completion and their streets were paved. Our house was completed and we moved in on July 5, 1923. We discovered that ticks and fleas moved in with us.

A short time later the firm presented the clubhouse to the residents and the Citizens Association was formed. A bridge club was set up and in November the Garden Club was organized. Trees and rosebushes were planted along each street under the guidance of Professor David Lumsden. The landscaping was backbreaking work - the builders had scraped off the top soil leaving only red clay.

Maddux, Marshall, Moss and Mallory had money difficulties and we nearly lost the clubhouse for taxes. The Citizens Association took action, and we all chipped in and saved the Clubhouse.

The point of land that is now commercial was hardly suitable for a house and soon a gas station (by an underhanded deed) had been built on the west side of Melrose and Georgetown Road, we voted to make the whole point of land commercial.

During my 54 years in Battery Park, I felt that it was a good friendly place to be. There were tense and uneasy times due to differences of opinion about what should or should not be done at times, but in the long run we remained good neighbors and friendly.

Mrs. Pariseau, born in 1887, studied for three years at Tufts Medical School before she married her doctor husband who, despite his ill health, lived until 1956. She was widely active in civic and church activities, once president of the Women's Club of Bethesda, member of the DAR, one of the founders of the Girls' Friendly Society at St. John's Episcopal Church and a member of the Juvenile Court board. She started a dancing class in her home and later moved it to the clubhouse. Mrs. Pariseau took in many girls in need of help, generally had a boarder or two, and her little car and huge hemlock hedge were local landmarks for years.

Another very early family in Battery Park was that of attorney R. Granville Curry. He had brought his wife and infant daughter from Staunton, Virginia, to 17th and K, NW, in 1918 and taken a position with the Interstate Commerce Commission. He could walk home for lunch. After the birth of their second daughter, the Currys moved up the hill to Clifton Terrace, and then Maddox and Marshall persuaded him and his friend and fellow University of Virginia graduate, T. Hardy Todd, to invest in their real estate enterprise. The Curry's older daughter, Tempe, recalled:

In 1924 on the first of January we moved into 405 Battery Lane; it's 5207 now. The house was finished, but the street wasn't. I was five, but I remember because it was all so new. We had moved from the town to the county, and the taxi let us off at the corner of Exeter which wasn't in at all. I remember carrying my doll around the corner and going into the house. It was heated by a coal furnace. They did have oil furnaces in some of those houses; the one on the corner, the Hartnett's house, did. We had coal and it took a long time to warm up and no rugs on the floor.

There was nobody next door. Wilson Lane was behind us and across the street was land owned by a gardener; Daugherty's and then the Smalls that used to be down on Connecticut Avenue grew everything right there. There was no road in front of the house, just cinders and that was where my father use to dump the ashes.

When we went out to play with the Todds, we put on boots. We'd get stuck in the mud and couldn't pull our feet out. We'd get out in our stocking feet,

Judge Curry

pull our boots out and run into the house. We crawled through every one of those pipes that was underneath the ground. When we moved in, they took a horse and plow and plowed up our lawn and put a strip of sod next to the sidewalk. My father explained it was to keep the dirt from washing away.

The sawmill was around on the other side of Battery Lane; you could see it from the trolley line. It wasn't that far away, and I can still see those tracks in the mud from the tractors that pulled the lumber around and the sawdust. There was nothing across from us, but up on Del Ray there was a wonderful tree we climbed, and an excavation, sort of a dump, that was the original old house.

The sawmill at Battery Park

Over on the other side of Old Georgetown was a hedge, and we walked along there up to the Bank of Bethesda to get an ice cream cone. And on the way people would say, "Go home. You're too little to be walking the streetcar tracks." We didn't talk to the people in Woodmont. They scared the hell out of us. We didn't go behind the hedge.

The next year Maddux and Marshall put in the streets, and Tempe Curry could clamp on her skates and skate around the block. She and her friends dug a cave in one of the vacant lots, covered it over with wooden signs taken from the vacant houses, and had a clubhouse to rival the adults' although they also played at the real clubhouse. One day when her father was coming home on the streetcar, the motorman said, "Some people in Battery Park sure don't look after their kids." Mr. Curry agreed and then looked where the trolleyman pointed and saw his daughter walking up the roof of the community clubhouse.

Tempe Curry Grant recalled that their trashman was "Mason," the minister of the Baptist church that later moved to River Road, "so you never worried when he went down in the basement to get your trash." The Curry's maid, Amelia Robinson, who had come from Virginia with them, married their ice man, Booker, and went to live in an apartment on Bethesda Avenue in the "flats." She was replaced in the Curry household by her sister Bernice, and since Mrs. Curry did not cook, Thursday and Sunday nights meant going out to dinner, a problem in Bethesda, or eating cereal. The Curry's neighbors in the 1920s included many active and retired military officers.[72]

Tempe Curry Grant remembered most of them:

Colonel Hartnett was on one side, and Captain Sears was next to us. Mr. Todd had been in the service, then there was Colonel Blumberg, and right across the street was Colonel Strong who had six children and Colonel Murphy had twelve. Mr. Pariseau was a major. Next to the Hartnetts was the red brick of General Marshall then Colonel Coleman, who rented out his house, and at Fairfax, Major Lawrence had two daughters, one a diving champion. Around the corner was Colonel Bennett, then Colonel Gilbreath, who won the prizes for his garden by going out and buying new plants while everybody else pruned and mulched, and at the end of Fairfax was Captain Richmond, who became a general.

Battery Park grew steadily and, as the real estate market boomed in the 1920s, rapidly. By the time the New Deal began, most of the lots had been sold, and more than three-quarters of the houses built. Mr. and Mrs. Parks C. Steed moved there in 1931, first renting and then buying a house at 7816 Maple Ridge. "It was a good location," Mrs. Steed recalled. "Battery Park was almost always reserved from other parts of the area. In those days you could just leave your car outside with the keys in it, and it would never disappear." They had a number of neighbors, including the Pariseaus, when they moved in, but Custer Road was not cut through, and there was a lot of forest behind them. Mrs. Steed said that there was an unwritten rule that

children had to be home by six and that when kids came over to play with her son, "They would keep asking, 'What time is it now?'"

Mrs. Steed also remembered the "Stew Club" that Cary and Florence Quinn organized. When some of the older residents objected to drinking, "We called it the Shakespeare Club. The requirement for new members was that they had to recite one line of poetry from Shakespeare." The "club" met only three or four times a year, and a committee would buy food, sometimes cold cuts, sometimes a roast, sometimes a real dinner. "One year the cost was $4.50 a couple. You had to bring your own bottle. This was after Prohibition so it was all legal. They rented an orchestra for Christmas and Halloween and maybe after Lent at Easter." The Steeds seldom went to the clubhouse at other times but did have a bridge group that included Chevrolet dealer Art Bowis, the Montedonicos and the Delaneys.[73]

Battery Park, like most other communities of the period, developed a very active citizens' association. As Mrs. Pariseau noted, they saved their little clubhouse at 7908 Glenbrook Road, and they finished it with a Bank of Bethesda loan. It had been presented to the community in September 1926 with Maj. R. B. Lawrence accepting for the community and Maddux claiming that it was the "culmination of a dream."

In 1927 Frederic P. Lee drafted a charter that the State Legislature passed, and the area became a special taxing district mainly to keep the clubhouse operating. The assessed value of Battery Park was established at $630,970 that year, and the tax rate set to raise $1,000 a year. In 1932 the civic association asked each household to contribute five dollars for the purchase of trees. The State Department of Forestry had maple, ash, locust, and other varieties available at 35¢ for 5-7 footers and $1.15 for trees 12 to 15 feet. Cmdr. William A. Porter told a meeting, "It takes a long time to grow a tree and as the Park is already 19 years behind, it doesn't seem logical that any tree smaller than 12 feet should be planted." The committee bought and planted 282 trees, all over twelve feet tall, for $507.60.[74]

The clubhouse became the center of Halloween, 4th of July and other celebrations and was used for the meetings of all sorts of clubs as well as for parties. Some years the Christmas parties drew more than two hundred members and guests. The association also fought against

Madam Vassileff's Battery Park dancing class. ID by Phyllis Michaux: that's me Phyllis Ann Mitchell in a red pongee dress, and Palmer Smith who came to our house for breakfast regularly, an unknown, then probably Nancy Robbins later Davis and then Reagan, and Mary Katherine Willis who hated the class. This is about 1928.

the intrusion of apartments and the granting of beer licenses and, with the mothers' prodding and the fathers' labor, built a fenced playground for their children.

Well-remembered community leaders of the early years include Capt. Frederick O. Smith, Joseph Montedonico, and attorney and Texan Carey Quinn. Mrs. Quinn said that when they moved into 5014 Del Ray, there were only three other houses on the street and one of those was Captain Smith's up on the corner of Wilson Lane. Newspaper publisher William Prescott Allen, activist Mrs. Louis Gravelle, the Centro Hobby Shop's Mrs. James Henry Taylor, and Mrs. Paul Ledig of the Campfire Girls all lived in Battery Park at one time as did "Emmy Lou" Thompson and her husband.[75]

Mrs. Raymond Kohin called it "the most fascinating, friendly place I ever lived." She and her SEC-employed husband came to the Washington area in early 1936, rented an apartment and started looking.

We lived in the apartment about a year, maybe, then moved up to Glenbrook in Battery Park, between Maple Ridge and Battery Lane, a little bungalow. And a German lived next door, and he had an American wife and a little blond child that ran around the neighborhood no matter what she had on, about two years old. It was a bed of intrigue. We'd see cars come down Fairfax Road and blink lights. They burned a lot of papers one day. Then they were interned later. Someone said he was Goering's right-hand man. He told my husband

one day that he regretted his wife was an American and that he would be fighting her people. This was in 1939, around then.

I joined the garden club, and they had meetings and talks at night. It was a nice place to live. We knew Mrs. Pariseau, who lived in a tent while her house was being built, and Mr. Barclay, who was the first one. My aunt rented a room in Mrs. Pariseau's house; she had an apartment upstairs that she rented out. It was a big house. And quilting, she had a big loom in her living room. She was very active, a little person, little bitty. A little, bitty person with a little car.

I spent all my time up at the school, every day. I was very active in the lunchroom there. They had this big, fat woman in the kitchen who was a terrific cook. I learned more things in that kitchen from that woman. She was smart. We made sandwiches in there. That was a good school.

I went to a little gift shop up there and Emmy Lou's. Emmy Lou had great cakes, the best food in town. And the farmer's market was at that corner for a while, I used it and the grocery store on Old Georgetown, Battery Park Market.

We loved Woodmont with all the trees, trees lined Battery Lane to Wisconsin. The street was like a roller coaster, and Arlington Road had big trees. I also used the shopping center at Leland Street. The drug store had everything, and the meat market had the best calves livers. And on hot summer days, we often went to the Hiser for the air conditioning.

In 1936 an observer wrote:

No other section in Bethesda has grown more rapidly than Battery Park. The building lumber used for this subdivision was prepared in a large mill located right on the job. Many army officers bought homes in this neighborhood and for a time it appeared that the subdivision was limited to just that class of people. However, with further development this movement did not persist. Battery Park is well planned and contains some very fine homes.

Not everyone agreed. As a young carpenter, Abe Morrison worked on some houses in Battery Park. "We went in there ten years later and built some nice houses. Most of the stuff the corporation built was what we call commercial building, cheap as you can do it. Ours cost more money." Morrison noted that some of the early Battery Park homes were made of terra cotta tile.

We didn't like them. A lot of people used them for foundations. It was the worst material you could possibly use. It cracked and leaked, and if

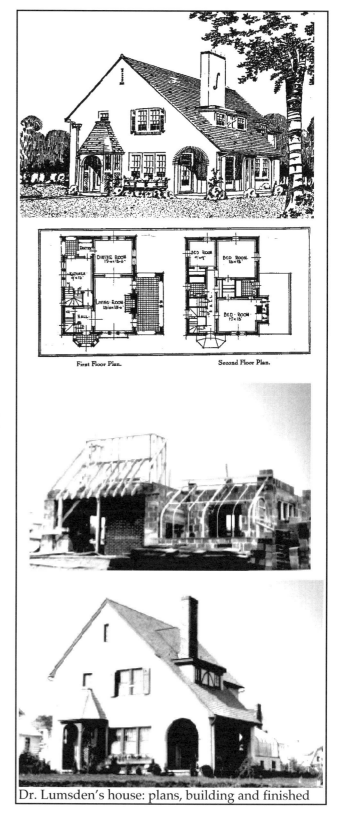

First Floor Plan.   Second Floor Plan.

Dr. Lumsden's house: plans, building and finished

you backfilled against it it, would fall in. If people wanted that, we'd build the house and finish it and put the roof on before we backfilled it. The weight was what you needed.

Despite the fact that the neighborhood was one of the first built in the age of the motor car and that most houses had detached garages and hard-surfaced driveways, Battery Park was also one of the first areas to have real automobile concerns as the following "news" item reveals.[76]

Battery Park seems to be having its own parking problems. "Why Shucks!" opines Capt. Fred Smith, perennial president of that area, "We have more crooked streets than a bar fly can make on a beer stained mahogany top in a week, and if something isn't done we'll need wings to get through."

"Boston has nothing on Battery Park. You have to head east to land on the north side," Uncle Jimmy King, chairman of the government affairs committee of that military sounding area says. "Our streets would make that collection of hind legs the old voodoos saved from their departed canines look like a pile of telephone poles, and with a few extra parked cars you have to sight to go round the corners."

Joe Montedonico, the genial secretary of Battery Park, confesses to going shopping with his Missus after he'd lived there six month and he drove around an hour trying to find his house, only to stumble upon it right in front.

What's it all about? Your reporter gathers that because they have the crookedest streets in Battery Park of any place in Montgomery County, including Takoma Park, the leading citizens in a board meeting Monday, December 4, decided that either the good people of this ex-army home center must park their cars on their own driveways or they're going to corral Carey Quinn and go chase Commissioner Earl Hampton and have him put up some more nice clean "No Parking At Any Time" signs.

A little farther out Wilson Lane, just past Battery Park and before one reaches Greenwich Forest, at the top of the hill stands the large, white, frame house built by Samuel Wheatley in 1893 as a summer home. District Commissioner Wheatley, whose year-round residence was in Georgetown, had a very successful lumber mill business in the city. The eighteen room, three-and-a-half story house, which occupies one of Bethesda's highest spots, originally stood on eighteen acres of farmland. The house has a wide, two-story veranda, a fine entrance-hall and fancy mantles and very high ceilings in its formal, first floor rooms. Sometimes the Wheatley's eight children

protested against being "buried alive" way out in the sticks, but the family enjoyed "Moreland," for many years. His widow turned it into a year-round home.

Roy Phillips, one-time Montgomery County policeman, was born on the Wheatley estate, delivered by Dr. Perry at 7824 Moreland in 1926. He grew up near the "big house" and recalled that the Wheatleys often went south for the winter. That was when he used to play in the house with the children of the servants.

Both his father and grandfather were Wheatley's farmers. There were two barns; the bigger one nearer Moreland Lane had a harness or tack room and housed ten two-horse teams. Into the mid-1930s these teams were used to dig house cellars with a scoop-skid, and they were under contract to the County to mow the areas between streets and sidewalks with a sickle bar. In the winter Roy used to wrap his feet in several burlap bags and ride with his grandfather, Andrew J. Philips, as the horses pulled a wedge-shaped snow plow through Bethesda's streets. Descendants of the Wheatley's lived there until 1944 although the farm had been subdivided and Marion Lane built in 1939.[77]

The boom of the 1920s swept across Chevy Chase, finally turning red ink black, eddied through the communities down Wisconsin, filling some of the gardens of double-lot homes, raced up the hill to the Hunts' property, and on into Kenwood where it may have crested. In Bethesda itself, builders staked long-platted property into building lots, and the local carpenters, plumbers, bricklayers, sheetmetal mechanics and house painters had all the work they could handle. Undeveloped land prices rose to $1,000 an acre and more.

From Rollingwood to Sonoma the ring of hammers and the smell of fresh-cut lumber drew curious children and ambitious speculators to Roosevelt Street and Wilson Lane, up Stanford Street and West Virginia Avenue, and down 44th and 45th Streets where E. Brooke Lee and company soon soured on Bethesda enterprises and decided to stay on their own side of the Creek. From Glenbrook Road to beyond Maple Ridge, the west side of narrow Old Georgetown Road came to look like a row of sample homes while trolley cars still rumbled by across the street atop a roadbed built on a narrow bank of dirt to level out the many hills and gullies.

Commercial building soon followed home construction, and in those pre-zoning days not always segregated from residential areas, especially in the Woodmont Triangle where small businesses, growing churches, and private homes lived side by side for many years. Out near Sonoma, two of the most disparate pieces of local architecture became neighbors. The Community Store opened on the Old Road at what was then Cedar Lane about 1924. John Moyer built it with lumber brought from an old country store at Cedar Grove on property owned by John Huffman. There may have even been an earlier establishment called Morgan's Store on the same site.

The little store was rented and run by a series of proprietors including the former contractor Tom Owens and his family, "Old Sweetie" Williams, the Fergusons, and the Ernest Browns. Emory Bogley bought it along with the Huffman's frame house behind it and just over an acre of ground in June 1937. He proposed building a Sanitary grocery store and a parking lot, but the neighbors petitioned to keep the old store and Bogley gave up the idea. Trade continued with the same counters and showcases that had always been there. The Community Store, the oldest continuing business in town, is not only a survivor but a real tie to the past as is its high walled-neighbor.[78]

Across Old Georgetown Road from the small, whitewashed store, and at about the same time it was built, the Sisters of the Visitation with the proceeds of the sale of their school on Connecticut Avenue, purchased sixty-four and a half acres of what had been Spates family property for $36,750. The contemplative order of nuns had A. B. Mullett & Company and Marsh and Peter, both prestigious local building firms, construct a walled convent based on plans from their 17th Century French manual. The resulting building was beautiful in its solidity and simplicity, and in 1923 the sisters retreated within its high brick walls to pray in their rooms off a long corridor around a central courtyard.

They maintained their own gardens and raised both cattle and poultry. They had a cottage for the visiting priest and a cemetery. Non-cloistered nuns, outsiders, lived, ate, and worshipped separately, and while the chapel was open to the public, a screened area kept the sisters apart.

Meanwhile, the mundane world continued to prosper. The Eisingers moved their lumber yard back to Bethesda and opened a milling operation in the Twenties. The company had been founded by Walter G. Eisinger and his brother Frank in 1902 on Georgia Avenue. Lured to Bethesda after hauling many loads of lumber by horse and wagon to what seemed a fast-growing area, they bought three and a half acres of Miller's land near the B&O spur, built some sheds and opened a branch office in 1912. When that boom ran out, they withdrew to D.C. and sometime later the yard burned. In 1925 Walter Eisinger formed a new company with his sons Roger and Constantine and moved back to Bethesda to stay. Other lumber dealers soon followed their lead.[79]

That was the year, 1925, when Bethesda's few businessmen began discussions that led to the formation of the Chamber of Commerce. According to Wady Imirie, the chief organizer was newspaperman Thomas Everett. He called a meeting at his wife's small restaurant just south of Imirie's garage where Joe Virga later opened his store. George Sacks, Walter Tuckerman, Lewis Keiser, Thomas Hampton, William Counselman, and Wady Imirie attended. After several get-togethers, they formed a permanent organization in February 1926 and chose Walter Tuckerman, president; George P. Sacks, vice-president; S. Walter Bogley, secretary; and G. Wady Imirie, treasurer, to serve one-year terms starting in April 1926. At that time, according to the *Chevy Chase Gazette*, the retail businesses in Bethesda included one bank, three garages, five coal yards, two feed stores, two barbers, three lunchrooms, a grocery store, a notion store, a drugstore, and the old hardware store.

The Chamber's first big project was encouraging the formation of the Bethesda Fire Department. Mr. Tuckerman was re-elected in 1927 and Col. Wallace M. Craigie, who was in charge of the D.C. schools' cadet program, was the reluctant president for 1928. In 1929, Brainard Parker of Woodward and Lothrop pulled the organization back together and through the efforts of Emory Bogley saw to its incorporation.[80]

The Chamber did not get going without a few false steps. In 1928, amid agitation to incorporate Bethesda, some of the real estate promoters decided that their land might sell better if the whole area were called "Chevy Chase." They persuaded the Chamber of Commerce to endorse the plan whereupon the Newcomb Club and the Woman's Club of

Bethesda vied to be first to tell the men that it was a stupid idea and to drop it. They did.

In the early `30s the Chamber worked to have the Board of Education secure a high school site on Watkins Avenue (East West Highway) and to have traffic lights installed. Its 1930 traffic study showed 8,000 cars coming through town on Rockville Pike in just ten hours. The Chamber also made a house-to-house survey about Bethesda businesses and discovered that most people shopped downtown because there was so little selection in Bethesda. The Chamber started a "Buy in Bethesda" campaign , urged new businesses to locate in town, and tried to get established merchants to stock a greater variety of products. In 1933 the Chamber acknowledged the Depression by reducing dues from $10 to $5 and by sponsoring Sunday morning movies to benefit various charities.[81]

Led by Oakmont's Oliver Owen Kuhn, managing editor of the *Star*, and prompted by two serious fires on Locust Avenue in Alta Vista, a movement for a volunteer fire department gathered momentum in the mid-1920s. The young Chamber of Commerce quickly backed the idea. Most of the up-county towns as well as Kensington and Silver Spring already had fire departments. The numerous citizens' associations and the year-old Civic Federation, in which Mr. Kuhn also had an active hand, were soon involved.[82]

Walter Tuckerman, recalling his experience in Edgemoor, was quick to join the effort. He told an interviewer asking about the early days of his subdivision:

> *There was no fire department, so we got ourselves a little contraption and a volunteer group, and we 'ran with the old machine' just like the song. There were mostly brush fires but one house burned to the ground, and we had to call in the Washington department. That led to a demand for a fire department in the Twenties.*[83]

The organizers developed a plan for the whole Bethesda District. They created a temporary fire board of three trustees and proposed a later, permanent one composed of a representative from each community contributing at least $1,000 to the effort. In May 1926 a mass meeting at the school approved plans and the collection of at least $25,000 for buildings and equipment. A Fourth of July fire in Alta Vista caused $12,000 damage and spurred both the fund raising and the recruitment of volunteers. The firemen from Kensington and Rockville were barely able to protect neighboring homes by the time they arrived.

The Fire Board was organized on July 23, 1926, with Mr. Kuhn as president; attorney William W. Bride of Edgemoor, vice-president; S. Walter Bogley of Friendship Heights, treasurer; and Hobart S. Langdon of Alta Vista as secretary. Emory Bogley headed the committee

Young Sumpter Embrey riding the old water wagon (the one Horace Hampton described) in a 1926 fund drive.

1)Andrew Pugh, 2)John Leahy, 3)John Smith, 4)Jess Barber, 5)George Pugh, 6)Dr. Thomas Armstrong, 7)John Sumner, 8)Harold Nichols, 9)Francis Gloyd, 10)Dudley Browne, 11)Asst. Chief Richard Kuster, 12)James Breeden, 13)John Magruder, 14)Hammal Compton, 15)Raymond Shoemaker, 16)James Spiller, 17)Eldon Ray, 18)Carrol Trail, 19)James McAuliffe in cap, 20)George Spangler, 21)William Pyles, 22)Chief G. Wady Imirie, 23)Albert Watkins, 24)John Pyles, 25)John L. Imirie, 26)Robert Lucas, 27)Ralph Ward, 28)William Hartley, 29)John Murdock, 30)Capt. Hiram Musgrove, 31)Frank Stone, 32)Roland Yarrington, 3)Sgt. Arthur Oldfield   (1928 photo)

on organization and wrote the constitution that was adopted. The equipment committee recommended the purchase of two triple-combination pumpers and one chemical truck. The committee on housing continued to seek a site, but its problem was soon solved when Walter Tuckerman offered to contribute a valuable piece of property on Old Georgetown Road about half way between Edgemoor and Wilson Lanes. By then "flying squadrons" of volunteers had raised more than $35,000.

Chevy Chase's special taxing areas declined to participate since plans for their own fire de-

partment were well advanced, and the Bethesdans returned contributions from Chevy Chase residents so they might be applied to those efforts. The Bethesda planners had originally hoped to create a unified department with two sub-stations, but Chevy Chase rejected this idea as it had the thought of the two areas becoming a single city.

Architect M. Willson Offutt Jr.–everyone knew him as "Rats"–donated his services to design the cupola-crowned fire house, and J. Frederick Imirie contracted to build it for $15,694.15.   The cornerstone was laid with

appropriate pomp on September 25, 1926, and the main speaker, Bernard Welsh, chief of the Rockville VFD, received derisive laughs when he said he "hoped to see a real community" in Bethesda some day. The building, complete with kitchen, sleeping quarters, and brass pole was finished and occupied three months later.

While the Fire Board was raising money, and Imirie was failing to stay within his budget, developer Thomas Hampton took over the training of the volunteers. Almost a hundred men signed up including the members of the fire board and most of the fund raisers. Unlike Chevy Chase, there was no differentiation between administrators and firemen in Bethesda; everyone was an amateur firefighter. The first meeting became an enthusiastic rally at the Edgemoor clubhouse, and then the group met every Monday at the Masonic temple. The would-be firemen heard experts from D.C., Rockville, the Red Cross and the Bureau of Standards. Captain William A. Dixon of the District of Columbia fire department was in overall command of the training. Finally the volunteers elected their own leaders and chose G. Wady Imirie as the first fire chief. They organized two companies of forty men each, and experts from the American LaFrance Engine Company trained them to use the new, triple-combination pumpers. The Board hired two men to man the station around the clock, Andrew Philips and George Gummel.[84]

The firehouse, No. 6 in the County, was dedicated on December 16, 1926, with speeches by local politicians and Walter Johnson. The firemen showed off their new uniforms and shining red pumpers. Citizens admired the brick firehouse, which held not only the gleaming equipment but a club room and sleeping quarters for ten men.

For many young men the volunteer fire department became the center of social life, and the annual carnivals, minstrel shows and ball games enlivened and united the fast growing town. The 1933 BVFD baseball team was one of its best, defeating the proud Gaithersburg Aces 7-3 in an early-season game. The firemen also participated in parades all over the area and in a series of "hook-up" contests with neighboring volunteer companies for trophies and bragging rights.

Sumpter Embrey, a charter BVFD member, remembered one competiton.[85]

We had this hookup contest, and an old chief from D.C. was the judge. And Bethesda had the best time so far. Man, Rockville came down there, and they hooked that thing up in nothing flat and beat our time. And this old chief, he chewed tobacco and had juice running down the sides you know, he went over and said, "Hey, son" to the boy putting the hose back on the truck. "Hey, son, break that coupling for me." So they broke the coupling, and they had chiseled all the threads out of it except one thread, and Rockville got disqualified. That was Chief Lanahan.

When the new fire department answered the first call during class hours at nearby Bethesda School, "the siren paralyzed everyone for a minute, then we rushed to the windows to watch the engines go by," teacher Dorothy Young recalled. It was considered another milestone in Bethesda history.[86]

The same year that the Chamber of Commerce and the Volunteer Fire Department were organized, the Archbishop of Baltimore and Washington decided that there were enough Catholics in Bethesda that they should not have go to Tenleytown or Chevy Chase Circle to attend Mass. The bishop dispatched Father James J. O'Connor to find a suitable home for a new parish, Our Lady of Lourdes. He decided on the Watkins' old, turreted home, which the Walkers had bought and sold and was then the Chinese ambassador's summer residence. Fr. O'Connor arranged to purchase the 40-year-old house, outbuildings, windmill and property for

John C. Walker, his son Curtis and a servant/friend, circa 1904, at the Watkins house that became Our Lady of Lourdes first church.

about $25,000 and turned the first floor into a church and the rooms upstairs into his rectory.

At the start, thirty families made up the parish, but by January 1927 nuns from Immaculata were conducting Sunday school at Lourdes. Leslie Bell's family joined the parish when they moved to Bethesda in 1928. "You parked at Hagner's farm and walked up a winding walk to the old farm house," Ellen Bell Touhy said. "We had Mass in the living room, and then we had Sunday school with the Sisters of Providence." In 1930, with more than 400 names in the parish register, Father O'Connor needed a real church. He found a small, frame one that St. Francis Xavier parish in D.C. had outgrown, bought it and had it moved to the corner of still-uncompleted East West Highway and Pearl Street, all for $9,000. Some parishioners remembered it as a "cardboard church" with bare lathing inside, which was assembled like a child's Christmas toy.

Our Lady of Lourdes' second church

Soon an active Sodality and a Holy Name Society began meeting, but when contributions fell by fifty percent, it became difficult for the congregation to meet its obligations. Father O'-Connor's health failed, and he was replaced by Father Joseph A. Little in 1933. For the growing parish with a sizable debt, the appointment of Father Little was a turning point. Soon Lourdes' carnivals were popular, annual, summer attractions, and the parish was paying down its debt. In 1937, when the parish rolls had reached a thousand, Father John Sweeney arrived as an assistant. The next year, Father Little finally paid off the old debt and purchased property on Pearl Street for a new building.

In 1938 the Rock Creek Council of the Knights of Columbus began meeting in the loft of the barn on the back of the Lourdes property. The Knights gave up their hopes of building a meeting place there when Father Little asked for the land for his planned school. Then for a while they met at Forest Glen, Kenwood, the Woman's Club of Bethesda, the American Legion home, and the "junior hall" in Cabin John. Joseph A. Cantrel was the first Grand Knight and John A. Overholt succeeded him.

The Protestant churches of Bethesda also tried to keep pace with the needs of the growing community. Dr. Parke Poindexter Flournoy had taken over the Presbyterian pulpits in Rockville and Bethesda in 1875 when the Elders were Greenbury Watkins, C. W. Landsdale, J. Lewis Bohrer and Henry Renshaw.

The white bearded minister finally retired in 1922 at the age of 83, became pastor emeritus and devoted more time to his poetry and other writings. His successor, the Rev. Stanley White, saw the need for another move as the membership of nearly a hundred had outgrown the old, frame church. The officers purchased the property just west of the Bethesda School on Wilson Lane and sold the meeting house and manse.[87]

The church's handsome, new, English-style building, designed by Reverend Flournoy's son Benjamin, was not finished until July of 1926. The Presbyterians rented and used John E. Beall's large house in the interim. They brought the walnut pulpit and pews with aisle doors from the old church and hung a painting of Dr. Flournoy in a place of honor. By the time Reverend White resigned and was replaced by John L. Parkes, the church had 160 members. Soon two services had to be held on some Sundays to accommodate the growing congregation, and while the brick home that became the church office was being built on Clarendon Road, a committee began planning to expand the steep-roofed, rectangular church.[88]

Across Wilson Lane from the Presbyterians rose the Bethesda First Baptist Church, which had its beginnings in worship services held in the late 1920s at the Masonic Hall. A minister from Kensington served for about a year, and then Mr. J. Wesley Loftis, pastor of the Silver Spring Baptist Church, began holding afternoon

services in the summer of 1931, and John J. Pool of the Wisconsin Avenue Baptist Church organized a Sunday school. The Rev. William Bort remembered:

Albert Scopin and I and Joe Schwartz went to that little Sunday school at three o'clock in the afternoon. And we got so excited about that we got more kids to come, and it wasn't long before we filled the place up with kids and a few adults. Then they sent Osgood out there, and we had a morning worship service and the Sunday school.

Bertram M. Osgood, the Bethesda mission's first full-time pastor, oversaw the church's formal organization on October 14, 1934, when there were twenty-eight members. Morning services were held at the Masonic Hall and the much better-attended evening services at the State Theater. Mr. Osgood, a pensioner from the Rockville Baptist Church, served without pay, but church finances were a serious problem. Osgood died in 1935 and was replaced by Rev. George W. Griffin. During his short tenure, the church's leaders requested affiliation with the Columbia Association of Baptist Churches instead of the Maryland group because of opposition by the Mt. Zion church.[89]

The Columbia Association proved generous and helped the church purchase the lot at the corner of Wilson and Melrose (Cordell) Avenue for $4,800 in the fall of 1936. In that year the church had twenty-four female and eighteen male members and sixty-one pupils in the Sunday school. The annual expenses totaled $1,087.19 of which the pastor's salary was $439.75.

In January 1937, Reverend Griffin resigned, and after two years without a regular pastor, Dr. J. Raymond Nelson, accepted the position in October 1938 and remained until the end of 1949. During his time in Bethesda the membership grew from about fifty to 350. A building program began in 1939 with help from the D.C. Baptist Convention, which contributed $5,000 and helped finance the purchase of a parsonage on Moreland Lane.[90]

St. John's Norwood Parish, which traced its history back to 1872 when it was a mission of the Labyrinth Parish, was served by seven clergymen between 1895, when it became an independent parish, and the summer of 1929 when the Rev. Joseph E. Williams assumed the rectorship. Membership had grown from sixty-three to 172 during those years, and by 1929 there were 182 Sunday school pupils.

After the 1914 fire, which started while the building was being painted, the vestry took the insurance money, sold the rectory on Old Georgetown Road, and built a faintly Gothic stone church, which would seat two hundred with a bit of crowding. Delos Smith was the architect, and the Owens brothers of Bethesda did the construction. The old Bethesda School bell, which had been blown out of the steeple of the frame church, was reinstalled and used to announce morning services and Sunday school classes. The congregation met in a Tuckerman-owned barn on the west side of Wisconsin near the railroad tracks until the new church was finished. Then they built a new rectory on the foundations of the old, frame church.

By 1920 the vestreymen had purchased three adjoining lots. Mrs. Stock and Mrs. Carr organized a Junior Guild, and Mrs. Pariseau and Virgie Offutt began the Girls' Friendly Society. With contributions from George P. Sacks and M. Willson Offutt, St. John's added a parish hall in 1923. In 1926, Mr. Offutt donated a pipe organ, but the church had to be enlarged to accommodate it. Both church membership and revenue declined rapidly in the late `20s. Volunteers cut the lawn and swept the building, and treasurer James L. Martin tended the furnace.

Walter Tuckerman's daughter, Laura, recalled:

Mother had a terrible time getting us all to church, and she used to get terribly embarrassed. One day we were a little bit late and one of us had a hat come off, and we had to take care of that. We had to sit in the front row, which mother hated to do, but that's all there was. And the sermon was on the subject of men playing golf on Sundays. And here was poor mother getting redder and redder because that's where Daddy was, playing golf.

Reverend Williams served St. John's for

St. John's Norwood Sunday School choir 1938

sixteen years, until December 1945. During his long tenure the number of communicants doubled, and Sunday school attendance overflowed the parish hall. Several choirs were vested and an Altar Guild was organized.[91]

The Women's Guild worked hard to raise money with dinners, card parties, and rummage sales. A fireworks sale brought in money each summer, but the church remained in debt and for many years had no vote in the Diocesan Convention since it failed to meet its quota of support. A Men's Club began in 1930 and sponsored several very popular father-son nights and dances. The club was reorganized in `36 as a chapter of the Laymen's League with William Tyler Page as the first president. It was not until 1942 that through hard work and Tuckerman generosity the mortgage was paid off and discussion of building plans could begin.[92]

Meanwhile George Bradley had slapped a coat of stucco on Wilson's old store and, as business improved, hired two of James Broadhurst's sons, Ralph and Henry, as his clerks. When the Depression drove Bradley out, the clerks took over the business in 1931. Henry Broadhurst later told a friend that he did not like the way Mr. Bradley treated some of the customers. He said he decided to do things differently the day he saw the owner refuse to help a lady carry a can of kerosene across muddy Wisconsin Avenue.

The Broadhursts worked twelve-hour days and six-day weeks and were able to buy the store and property in 1933. They survived the Depression while often taking in less than ten dollars a day. Ralph drove the truck and did most of the manual labor, and Henry kept the store and did most of the book work. As Bethesda began to grow again, they began buying adjoining lots and enlarging the store by building on to the back and by establishing their reputation as the most friendly, cooperative and knowledgeable of businessmen.

Mrs. Ralph Broadhurst started coming out to Bethesda on the streetcar to watch her husband and his brothers bowl. "All the Broadhursts bowled," she remembered. "When I was going with Ralph, he bowled down at Henry Hiser's alleys on Leland Street. From the back all the Broadhurst brothers looked alike, but I could tell which brother was which. I knew him. Women were there to watch the men bowl. There was another girl in Bethesda that was after my husband."

After they were married, she and Ralph made their home in the apartment over the store and began their family. "We'd take the baby out at night and walk up the street, sometimes to Whittlesey's or to Peoples and get an ice cream cone. On the way back we'd stop at the frozen custard with polar bears out front. Sometimes we would have three cones on one walk around Bethesda."

A number of other long-lived businesses such as Bob Wehrle's plumbing company and Gordon Burrows' gas station across from the old Offutt place also survived the Depression. And a few others began in the late `20s such as Bell Laundry, which was started on Hampden Lane by Leslie Bell. "The old Chevy Chase Laundry had gone bankrupt in the Depression," according to Leslie Bell Jr.

It was where the back end of the bank that used to be Suburban Trust is (between Elm and Hampton). They had gone bankrupt, and my dad had run a laundry for the Army over in France during the war and liked it. He came back and met my mother at a Red Cross dance. They married, and he ran a laundry up in McKeesport, Pennsylvania, for a while and then came back here.

When Chevy Chase Laundry went broke, it was full of new machinery, and my dad made American Laundry Machinery Company an offer, which was rather picayune, but it was a better deal for them than packing all that stuff up and shipping it back to Cincinnati.

So he got the laundry started, and he said he never lost money. He was a good businessman. Harry Wolfe had worked for the Chevy Chase Laundry, and he was out of a job, so my dad asked him if he would like to continue, and he was manager for about twenty-six years.

By then Wisconsin Avenue had been paved, widened and repaved. The old turnpike was resurfaced for the first time in response to the District government paving Connecticut, Wisconsin, and River roads out to the District Line. Including the widening of the B&O bridge in the middle of town, that first mile and three-fifths cost more than $75,000 in 1926 and only covered the macadam road west of the trolley tracks. In the middle of Bethesda the people living and working east of the tracks faced a sometimes dusty and often muddy lane about twenty-five feet wide. Some planted hedges to screen them from the highway.

At Dr. Perry's insistence and with the acquiescence of the other County Commissioners, they paved the east side from Bradley Lane to

the Bank in 1927 for about $50,000. This created several problems. First, the east side was, in most places, about eighteen inches lower than the west side, which had been the old macadam turnpike, and second, the trolley tracks and the wooden power poles now ran down the middle of the street in a shallow trench. These two features made it difficult for a horse and wagon to cross Wisconsin Avenue and dangerous for an automobile to try.

Politicians and the Chamber of Commerce began lobbying WRECo to move its tracks to the side of the street and the State Roads Commission to finance another repaving to level out the middle of town. They accomplished the second in 1929 for $32,000 but not the first. Dr. Perry even succeeded in having two miles of sidewalks laid. So when Wisconsin Avenue was finished, by the time of the stock market crash, it was reasonably level and had sidewalks four feet wide, but it also had a ten-foot wide, eighteen-inch-deep ditch down the center where the streetcars ran.

Col. James McAuliffe remembered those tracks from his time as a young policeman.

One day I was answering a fire call on my motorcycle, and the man in front of me pulled over very sharply. I had no place to go but in the car tracks. Fortunately I was able to lay it across the tracks and get out from under. I pulled myself up on the street across from Burrows' gas station, and a streetcar came along a few seconds later and hit my motorcycle, took it about a hundred and fifty feet. I ran up to see what the result was, and the motorman opened the doors and asked, "Has there been an accident?"

The paving of Wisconsin was finally finished in the fall of 1936, about a year after the last trolley whirred and sparked its way into D.C. After rejecting all earlier bids as too high, the State Roads Commission accepted the M. J. Grove Company's $43,700 offer to fill the trolley-line space from Bethesda to the District Line with concrete.

The third problem created by paving and widening Wisconsin in Bethesda was called the "bottleneck." From the Twenties into the Forties, at the Bank, Wisconsin Avenue for all practical purposes became "the Pike" and narrowed to the width of the old road with homes, businesses, and parking on both sides. On beyond Battery Lane the road to Rockville was a typical three-lane Maryland highway, and wise drivers avoided cresting its many hills in that middle lane.

In Bethesda, property would have to be condemned to widen the street, and some of the land on the east belonged to people with good political connections such as the Hagners and the Bradleys. On the west stood the bank, the property belonging to Sacks, Ailes, Perry, Peake, and to the people of Woodmont such as the Morris family. So, despite promises and annual predictions, the bottleneck at the Bank became a fact of Bethesda life. Old Georgetown Road was an even more narrow street with the trolley tracks on the east hedging it in, but it was widened long before the bottleneck problem was solved.

Starting in the early 1920s at his real estate office and bank, Walter Tuckerman's company put up a frame, orange-roofed tea house, and then three groups of stone and brick-fronted stores on Wisconsin at Edgemoor's eastern edge. Ground was broken for the third unit, which featured a movie theater and bowling alley, in the spring of 1928. The cost of that project was put at $150,000. One of the first tenants to sign a twenty-year lease was Harry Wolfson, proprietor of the Bethesda Fashion Shop that was part of the group of stores built in front of the theater's auditorium. Under his store Wolfson operated a small cleaning and tailor shop later taken over by Patsy Jones and her husband who also lived in the basement. Mrs. Jones worked for a dollar a day as a maid while her husband took care of the cleaning trade.

North of Wolfson's shop a narrow alley with cement steps led to a large parking lot and separated the theater group from the largest of Tuckerman's stores, which was rented by the post office and had two floors of apartments above it. Carpenter-builder Riley Evers and grocery clerk-fireman Lee Higgins were among the first to install their families there. The new post office opened on February 15, 1926, with Postmaster General New handing out the first piece of mail.

Warren Gingell's plumbing supply shop was in the oldest part of Tuckerman's row, which also contained a Piggly Wiggly grocery store. Gingell, who had been operating out of his big, stucco home in Woodmont, sold radio sets, the newest fad, as well as plumbing supplies. Beyond his store was the Orange Roof Tea Room, Mrs. E's, the town's first real restaurant where Austin Carlin (B-CC '33) had his first paying job. It burned to the ground in April 1931.

Peggy Evers in the field behind Tuckerman's row - note both bank buildings in background

Tuckerman rebuilt the northern set of stores as a single unit in the `30s with Peoples Drug Store on the corner taking over his remodeled real estate office and bank building. The post office was left free standing.

On the south side of the Wolfson's clothing store was Bill's Sandwich Shop, which had narrow steps that led down to the bowling alleys beneath the movie house and then came the flat front of the theater itself with two sharp stone peaks framing the apartment or office windows above the modest marquee. A set of cement steps led down to the bowling alleys.

John Henry Hiser came to Bethesda in 1928 to take over the bowling alleys beneath the theater, which had been struggling under a succession of inept operators. Hiser, born in D.C. in 1897 and reared in Prince George's County, attended trade school until he was thirteen and held a Navy Yard job before joining the National Guard at the time of the Mexican border troubles. Sent to France in World War I, he was felled by the "Spanish" flu while at the front.

After the war he gained a reputation as an athlete and ballroom dancer while he studied drafting and returned to his government job. He played on Washington's first professional football team in 1919-20, managed several semi-pro baseball teams, and always claimed that he had bowled more games than anyone. By 1924, when he took over the operation of the Arcade Alleys in Hyattsville, he was recognized as a champion bowler. In 1928, Hiser quit his job to move to Bethesda and run the bowling alleys under the movie house, which booked two-day runs of silent films accompanied by Pearl Hauer on the organ.

Hiser rigged up what he claimed were the first lights on Wisconsin Avenue when he put two spotlights in an elm tree to illuminate the steps down to his eight bowling alleys. His ads, signed John H. Hiser, stated "special attention given to ladies" and offered 10¢ games to women and children on weekday afternoons. It was not long before duckpin bowling became a very popular sport in Bethesda, and leagues formed among members of various clubs, churches and businesses.

In the middle of 1929, John Henry Hiser took over the nameless, floundering movie house that most folks called the "Bethesda," and soon Brooke Johns, a friend from his National Guard days, and other vaudeville acts were on his narrow stage. The next year he installed a first class, Western Electric sound system, and remodeled the interior but kept the wooden seats. He decided to call it the "State" theater and had that name painted on the stuccoed side of the building in black letters fifteen feet high. Also in 1930 he took a team to the national bowling championship in Connecticut and came back with the trophy and reams of free publicity.

John Henry Hiser

Hiser's movie house limped along, closing down in the summer months because of the heat and on Sundays because of the Blue Laws, but within five years he was making a profit and had a growing reputation as both a shrewd businessman and an inveterate, high-stakes gambler. Hiser made large bets on sporting events such as fights and football games and became a regular at a weekly poker game that involved several builders and businessmen. That game went on for years. But he also kept up his bowling skills, and in the summers he often sponsored and played outfield for Hiser's All-Stars, a team featuring several University of Maryland players.[93]

The film of the Louis-Schmeling bout in 1936 was the turning point for the "State." Hiser showed it from eleven in the morning until one the next day, sold 75,000 tickets in three weeks and often had to turn patrons away

State Theater and Bill's Place prior to the the new marquee

from packed houses. A Belasco billboard for Hedy Lamarr's sexy ("uncut and uncensored") art film "Ecstasy" titilated adolescents from the inside of the tall sandwich board in front of the theater for many years. His business grew with the area, and until 1938 his only nearby rival was Crandall's Chevy Chase Theater, later christened the Avalon after a well-publicized naming contest.

Hiser married a Hyattsville beauty queen in 1932 and settled down, first in Edgemoor and eventually in a large house in Alta Vista, to help raise seven daughters and a son. In 1934, Hiser added what he called the Boulevard Bowling Alley under the Northwest Ford corner of Sacks' row. The assistant manager's job, once Jim McAuliffe's, went to Lester "Fats" Robinson. In the mid-30's Hiser hired Warren Gingell's son Ray to run the movie house, but he kept a close eye on all the operations. Gingell, who had done odd jobs at the theater while still in high school in order to have practice time on the big organ, said, "He never trusted me."

Bethesda's Babbitt, Hiser was a "joiner" who became involved in every Chamber of Commerce activity. He was a leader of various civic and fraternal organizations and often lent his theater to good causes, including the Newcomb Club's library, for benefit shows. He served on innumerable committees and worked tirelessly to promote the town and his own businesses. He had grandiose plans and dreams, many of which were never realized, but

he became a Bethesda fixture who swept the sidewalk in front of his theater every morning.

It was a sheltered, adolescent, Bethesda male who did not set pins in Hiser's alleys in the `30s and `40s and then put back his four cents a line into the row of pinball machines that jangled by the dirty windows. There were no flippers in those days, and it took a deft touch to whack and bump a machine without tripping the tilt mechanism. Pinball skill was at least as admired as bowling ability among those who "hung out" at Hiser's. Many boys never bowled at all. A few girls also set pins for a club, class or social outing, rather than for money, but except on a dare or in a giggling group, girls "never" played the gaudy pinball machines.

Once in a while when a machine chonged too long on one note, Mr. Hiser would put aside his eyeshade, leave his desk and walk down the flickering line pushing the "tilt" button to wipe out ill-gotten free games if he caught a boy with a coat hanger under the glass or shims under the front legs. "Sandy" Astin recalled a time when his brother had a machine resting on his toes and was running up a huge score.

Hiser came up and started talking to us, and we had quite a long conversation before he suddenly realized that John had the machine up on his feet. Hiser punched him out, slugged him in the face. I guess he felt humiliated that we were cheating right there in front of him while he was talking to us.

Henry Hiser kept a pocket full of nickels and made change for those flashing machines all day and much of the evening when the bigger boys came in to set pins for the smoky league games. Hiser's ads for pin boys always specified "white and at least 14," but he never asked anyone his age, and often tried to pay off younger boys with movie tickets. He must have worried when youngsters went home with teeth loosened or fingers mashed from the hot and dangerous work. Some wiseguys liked to loft balls at the pins before the sweating setter had jumped behind the heavy curtain or down into the pit of the other alley.

Older boys who set for the leagues picked up good tips, two or three dollars a night rolled down the gutters, if they worked hard and showed they understood what they were about. Some pin boys became very good bowlers and were not above stirring up a challenge for a dollar or two with a visiting sailor or salesman. Hustling, they called it. Very few parents ever

knew that their sons set pins, which was probably a good thing.

Hiser's alleys were also the only place in town where boys had access to a condom machine. It was screwed to the wall of the wretched men's room dispensing Trojans for a quarter, surrounded by graffiti criticizing its products and graphically describing their use.[94]

Forty percent of the 647 building permits granted in the County in 1926 were in Bethesda. The boom accelerated.

By the late Twenties the acknowledged leader of Bethesda's businessmen was imperious George P. Sacks. He and his partner and fellow Mason, Arthur A. Chapin, had moved to Bethesda in the first flush of the Bradley Hills development and became neighbors in two of Hampton's large, stone houses.

Sacks and Chapin as up-and-coming young businessmen

George's father, German immigrant Eckart Sacks, had a flourishing butter and egg business operating out of Centre Market. Young George apprenticed in several similar Baltimore businesses, and in 1894 he became a partner in Chapin's butter wholesaling company. Chapin, six years older than Sacks, had been in business for himself since he was nineteen. Their partnership thrived, and around the turn of the century, they established the first cold storage plant in D.C. and became the largest butter and egg wholesaler south of New York.

After he moved to Bethesda, Sacks began investing heavily in local real estate and picked up a number of properties during the collapse of the Bradley Hills companies. He and Walter Tuckerman were involved in several ventures including the Bank of Bethesda. Different in many ways, those two "made" Bethesda. If Tuckerman was Bethesda's friendly "father," then Sacks was its rich "Dutch uncle."

Sacks told a local newspaper:

I established my residence and made my investments in this community because experience in business taught me that all large metropolitan cities develop toward the suburbs and generally toward the northwest – just as we are located with respect to the National Capital. I felt certain of residential development at the time and equally certain of enhancement in the value of all property, whether it be business or residential, and I have never lost confidence in that belief.[95]

South of Leland Street and across repaved Wisconsin Avenue from the Warren brothers' line of Tudor-style shops, George Sacks raised a stone-fronted row of stores and apartments on property purchased from M. Willson Offutt in November 1925. He paid $75,000 for a little over seventeen acres, about $4,365 per acre, to set a new local record.

He filled a creek-cut defile and built a row of eleven stores with Northwest Ford's showroom and shop holding a ten-year lease to the northern end. Sacks followed Tuckerman's lead and set his stores far enough back from the street to allow angle parking in front of them as well as providing for future road widening. He kept rents low on both the shops and the apartments above them hoping to attract businesses to Bethesda.

Sacks' row of stores (A Hugo Brooks photo)

One of the first tenants was Robert Eastham who brought his bride to Bethesda in 1929 when he came to town to run Standard Oil of New Jersey's service station at Miller and Wisconsin. The company told him that if he could get gasoline sales up to 10,000 gallons a month, they would let him wear a white coat.[96]

Two other early businessmen were Dennis and Marvin Simmons, who opened a barber shop under the Masonic Building behind the bank in 1925. These Carolina farm boys, who claimed to have gone into barbering because they enjoyed sheep shearing, soon moved across to Walter Bachrach's wedge of stores that backed up to Edgemoor Lane.

Marvin, who had been buying and selling cars as a sideline for some time, sold his share of the barber shop to his brother in 1928 and

opened a Dodge agency at Wisconsin and Miller in 1932. Dennis enlarged the barber shop and then added a beauty parlor and by the late 1930s had six busy chairs in each.

Marvin began building houses as rental properties and moved his young family down to the small apartment over the showroom while he had a home built at 5008 Hampden Lane in Edgemoor. His wife, Virginia, who was a Notary and sometimes assumed the agency's office work, recalled that her older daughter came home from Sears one day with a box of chicks and that they raised them in the apartment until her husband's mechanics built a small coop behind the shop. Dennis married one of his hairdressers and lived on Old Georgetown in Battery Park and became a stalwart member of the Bethesda Masonic lodge, its Master in 1936, and Deputy Grand Lecturer for the area.

Another pair of early entrepreneurs was a bit younger. Horace Hampton was one, but he refused to name his partner.

One summer we needed some money and decided to go in the fireworks business, so we went to Alexandria and bought our fireworks. We set up a stand right on the bridge on Wisconsin Avenue, with this other fellow, a week before.

The 4th came and this woman came tearing in there and grabbed my partner and said all prices should be reduced since it was the 4th. He said, "Lady, they're all on sale." She said, "What are the prices?" He said, "All ten cent items are two for a quarter and all the fifteen cent items are three for fifty cents," and she bought twelve dollars worth and went out of there with a smile on her face. We were still in high school.

Two more early businessmen were Herbert Hyatt and Bates Watkins from up-county who ran Bethesda Building Supply in front of the old ice house where the Keisers had also sold some lumber. They went to work for Ray Souder in 1926 and, like the Broadhursts diagonally across the bridge, bought the business. Hyatt ran the office and Watkins the yard, and they advertised "Everything to Build Anything." Until their side of Wisconsin was paved, a high hedge in front shielded them from the dusty street and trolley tracks. Prospering in the great building spree of the late '30s, they had twenty employees by the outbreak of war.

A number of early Bethesdans such as the Keisers and the Offutts got into the real estate

business itself although most of the salesmen in this period had Washington offices. By far the most successful of these agents was Henry Latane Lewis. Born in 1876 in Virginia, son of Dr. Warner Lewis, he earned a law degree from George Washington University in 1908. Lewis married James Heath Dodge's daughter Mary, and they reared a son and two daughters at their home on the Pike. Like his father-in-law, Lewis was an active Mason and headed the Bethesda lodge in 1913.

H. Latane Lewis negotiated sale after sale that set new records for the prices of Bethesda acreage. In 1925 when Francis Bennet Poe purchased the sixty-acre Shoemaker tract for $150,000, Lewis established a benchmark. When the 132-acre Charles Bohrer farm brought $80,000 the same year, it made Bethesda farmers look at their fields in a different way. Through Mr. Lewis, Miss Mary Freedman bought ninety-eight acres on Old Georgetown to be developed by Morris Cafritz, and the tax stamps showed the price to be more than $100,000. Lewis sold the Bethesda Presbyterian Church, manse and seven acres to Mrs. William Fitch Kelley for $19,000. Then Lewis handled the sale of the McTier's "handsome home" at Connecticut and Bradley for $45,000 and negotiated George P. Sacks' purchase of M. Willson Offutt's seventeen acres in the middle of Bethesda, another record. In 1928 H. Latane Lewis was the agent for the heirs of Dr. John L. Lewis when Mr. Sacks purchased the doctor's old house and two acres behind the bank for $48,000. The doctor had paid $1,800 for the land and $5,000 for the house in 1902. Lewis also handled the sale of the 264-acre Nailor tract west of Kenwood for $200,000.

In 1928 the whole County was reassessed, and the total value of all real estate was said to be $70 million. Of that, Bethesda's property, the 7th Election District, made up $28.9 million plus another million for the homes of Gilbert Grosvenor, Merle Thorpe, and Captain Chester Wells, the assessments of which were held up until 1929.[97]

Rockville Pike was becoming famous for its mansions. The elder Dr. Peter's "Winona" became the Woodmont clubhouse, but one rolling hill away George Freeland Peter owned a handsome Colonial Revival "Stone House," designed by his brother and built in 1930. Mr. and Mrs. Luke I. Wilson's "Tree Tops" graced a hilltop where the Moore's "plantation" had been in the

"Tree Tops"

Civil War. Some recall the Wilson's stone entrance gates with their flaming torches. Across the Pike stood the home of George E. Hamilton, chairman of Capital Traction, organizer of Union Trust, counsel for the B&O, and teacher and dean at the Georgetown Law School for twenty-seven years. Hamilton built his Colonial Revival mansion about 1904 and added to it several times. "Stone Ridge" was assessed at $10,000 in 1905 and, including all the additional land and outbuildings, at $40,000 in 1923.[98]

Diagonally across from it was the "Cedarcroft" estate, begun in 1892 and purchased in 1923 by Brainard W. Parker. His wife and Luke Wilson's were sisters, the daughters of Samuel Walter Woodward, founder of the department store. Past the church came the large home and farm of hydraulic engineer Charles W. Hawley, built at the boom's height.[99]

His neighbor was the publisher of *Business Week*, Merle Thorpe, who raised perhaps the best known of these huge homes, the stone, Tudor style "Pooks Hill," on more than a hundred rolling acres in 1927. Off Grosvenor Lane, previously Transformer Lane for the trolley line and before that Bangerter Road for the dairy farmer on the Pike, was "Wild Acres," the home of Gilbert Grosvenor of *National Geographic*. The Grosvenors, she the daughter of Alexander Graham Bell, purchased the 105-acre tract in 1912, and by the time they finished their home in 1929 it was already famous for the number and diversity of birds it attracted.

On beyond the Bethesda precincts were the Charles Corby estate on the east at the top of the hill and just past the Prep school on the west the home of mustachioed banker John Joy Edson. Out along River Road, there were also several large houses including Willard Kiplinger's "Ohio Hill" farm and the home of James W. Austin on part of what had been Erasmus Perry's farm. The 1890s stone and frame, classical-revival home was bought early in the 20th Century by Mary Cassells, who improved the house and lived there until 1938.[100]

Between M. Willson's Offutt's big, square home behind the horse chestnut trees near Bradley Boulevard to his brother Hilleary's equally big and equally square house on the wooded hill just past Georgetown Prep, lay a remarkable concentration of wealthy families and big houses on huge estates especially if one included the Parkhurst, Tuckerman, Wheatley, Hagner, Perry and Bradley houses, which were right in Bethesda.

In 1928 one millionaire came to Bethesda to build a farm instead of a mansion. John C. Letts, principal owner of the Sanitary grocery store chain, decided to show the County's gentlemen farmers what a real dairy operation could be. He purchased John Bohrer's place on Cedar Lane and established a small herd of dairy cattle there. Then a few years later he bought the neighboring farm from the late Mahlon Austin's daughter and combined the two to form the hundred-acre Ayrlawn Farms, which became famous for its Jersey cows and their rich milk.

Letts and his manager, H. George Thompson, designed and built a model dairy and poultry operation with gleaming white barns and shining stainless steel equipment of the highest quality. The Morrison Brothers were Letts' general contractor, and Abe Morrison recalled Mr. Letts and his instructions:

His farm was just a hobby. He went out and purchased cows in the Jersey islands, little old cows that looked like a mouse, and he paid thousands of dollars for those animals. He told me when we were building the mangers, "Now, I want that smooth and slick. I don't want to tear the tongue off these cattle on rough concrete." And we gave him a finish like the top of that table.

Ayrlawn Farms' ads usually featured pictures and descriptions of the Jersey cattle, prize winners with names such as Sybil's Successor, Poppy's You'll Do, and Watfern's Dreamer, and bragged of the butter-fat content of their milk. The farm grew most of its own feed on its acres of clover, alfalfa and bluegrass, and Letts bred, exhibited and sold his champion Jerseys as well as their milk. He also gave calves away to 4-H

and similar projects. Ayrlawn marketed about half of the ninety gallons produced each day as whole milk sold from the farm. The other half of the output was pasteurized and put up in half-pint bottles sealed with caps printed at Ayrlawn and delivered to a widespread list of customers including the Sanitarium in Takoma Park.

The herd grew to 150, and Ayrlawn became a tourist attraction visited by school children and diplomats as well as by experts in animal husbandry. The beautiful barns and

Ayrlawn Farms

sheds gleamed like modern kitchens with their tiled walls and enamel paint. Everything was top quality: slate roofs, copper guttering, oak floors, and well-designed plantings. Letts also raised medal winning hogs and kept about 2,000 laying hens on the farm.

Billy Lehr, "Zip" Lehr's son, grew up in Sonoma in what at that time was the last house on the street. He and his friends used the Ayrlawn Farms fields as their playground, and he remembered the prize jersey cows and the office walls covered with blue ribbons.

They had bullwalkers. They ran the hook through their nose and took them around and around. I really don't think they sold the milk or products to make money, but we got milk from them. They came around in a horsedrawn thing with rubber tires and little lights on the side, and I think they just did it to get rid of the products.

The kids from the Baptist Home also played on the farm fields. Once in a while they'd come over and chase us out. Our Sonoma Road-Greentree group was constantly in fear of the Oak Place gang, Dickie Latimer and his older brother Herk and some of those guys. They were a little older, and they'd come over and we'd run; they'd throw apples at us from an orchard on the hill where they kept the bulls. They scared the heck out of us.

We went sleigh riding at Ayrlawn. We could go down to almost where North Bethesda Junior High was built. There was a big hill there with oak trees on top that went down to a creek in hose days. The Baptist Home kids' hill was the other end of the field. Sometimes we went down Greentree Road and sneaked over the hill and down to Bowis Creek for crawfish and whatever, and we

always had to be looking up the hill 'cause that creek was their creek. The road was blacktop to the Home and stopped there. Then it was just rocks and gravel. The Home kids were a group to themselves when they went out.

We had chickens–in our house. We had a coop in the back and raised chicks in the basement. My father built a five-tier brooder. My job was to clean up after them. We raised chickens and ate them, sold a few, held back some layers, the others we ate. When he cut off their heads, my job was to hold the wing tips and the feet and he'd pull the head out and "whunk," and I'd stuff it in the leaf pile. Once in a while when he'd turn his back I'd let one go to see what it would do, to see it run. Ayrlawn Farms had white Leghorns; my father was partial to Rhode Island Reds.

Richard Latimer freely admits to chucking apples at Billy Lehr and his buddies. "We felt it was our duty to keep them out of our field," he said. Dick Latimer grew up in his family's new house near Ayrlawn. His father was a good friend of Walter Johnson, who was a neighbor when they moved to Oakmont in 1926.

"He loved Walter," Latimer said.

Dad had hunting dogs and some chickens, and one morning he heard a terrible ruckus, and there was a damned fox out there. He shot it and went out there and looked, and it was Walter Johnson's pet fox with a collar and chain. It just about tore him up when he had to take it up and talk to Walter.

Ford dealer Raphael Sabine lived across the street from the Latimers and built several houses in the Oakmont.

Dick Latimer remembered him, too:

> He was short and extremely stout. He put a handkerchief on his stomach when he drove so the steering wheel wouldn't soil his suit. His house and lawn were immaculate. He'd bring down a load of manure from the farm spread it on his gardens. Our front yard had a pitcher's mound and home plate, and we kicked field goals over phone wires. It was mostly mud but our parents knew where we were. His lawn was beautiful and, of course, we couldn't play over there. One time he came to Dad about the lawn, and he said "Well, right now I'm raising children and not grass."

At the Community Store, "Brownie's," Latimer and his buddies would trade in empty gingerale bottles for pennies to buy candy, but if they wanted B-Bs or a new baseball because the one with tar tape on it was getting odd shaped, they would pool their money and ride up to Bethesda. The tar tape usually came from the telephone linemen who would give some to the kids or "donate" it when their backs were turned.

"Some folks still had ice delivered," Dick Latimer recalled, "and we got slivers off the truck in summer, splinters of ice." In the winter they took their sleds to Ayrlawn Farms, or:

> We could go all the way down Oak Place belly flopping, and a parent would take turns hauling you back up with a car. One guy would grab the bumper and the rest would follow along behind him. And we'd go up to Cedar Lane and start at the water tower. You could go all the way across Rockville Pike and get a parent to haul us back up. There was no traffic, you know.

One of the parents the local children often called on was John L. Imirie. His daughter Millie recalled the knocks on the door and the hopeful, "Can Mr. Imirie come out tonight?"

As a little kid, Dick Latimer spent a lot of time looking over his shoulder when he was playing in the woods near Ayrlawn. The older boys always said a bull was going to get loose.

> We made big snowballs to put on trolley tracks and put pennies on to see how they'd get mashed. I used the tracks to go to school, Alta Vista, went there when it opened in `35. It was a great little school. Everybody knew everybody else, even knew what you were eating for lunch. It was a three-room school for a while, then four.

> My sister is seven years younger, and I went to her elementary school graduation when I was in college. When I was at Alta Vista, the big sport was softball at recess or lunchtime or whatever, any time. I remembered that there were some

> pine trees way out in left field, and if you could hit a ball and launch it over those pine trees you had a sure home run. Now I was a big time college kid watching these sixth graders get graduated, and I walked down the hall and opened the door and looked at my past glories, and I wished I had never done it because those pine trees are directly behind third base. I mean you didn't have to hit it anywhere to get over those damn pine trees, and I had been thinking I was Babe Ruth and Ted Williams.

> We had the farm there and played an awful lot of sports in the Ayrlawn farm fields. Every once in a while they chased us out. But we got to feeling the farm was ours, and we had to protect it. We usually played in the calf field adjacent to our house. The Estes lived next to the farm; we were one house back.

> The fences were out of bounds, and we played football and baseball there using cow pies as bases. Other kids could not believe we would play football out there. It got so cow manure was insignificant. I mean sometimes we'd get mad and sling it at each other. You'd have to take time out to wipe the ball off once in a while. I remember coming home one night, and my mother made me undress out on the stoop.

> If you wanted to play ball, when some kid had to cut the lawn everybody would help so he could play. Sometimes four or five guys were cutting a lawn going around in circles.

> There were no secrets about life, or birth, or death because of the farm. It was just a matter of fact. You'd go down there and help milk, or deliver pigs, or candle eggs. And we walked all around the garden and blacksmith shop.

> Sometimes we'd go down to the farm and get some milk and come back to eat cookies. We knew where everything was in the creamery and the cooler. We got a quart milk bottle and opened up the cooler and stuck the bottle in, glug glug glug, filled it up. I remember thinking I can't drink all this milk and then I realized I'd just drunk a quart of cream cause I hadn't stirred it up. The cream on the bottle was three-quarters the way down and so thick - it was orange it was so thick. During the war they delivered with a horse and buggy. I remember the clop clop clop.

> We went everywhere on bicycles. Once after dinner we took our bicycles and, riding as fast as we could, went out Old Georgetown to Congressional Airport and turned around and came back as fast as we could, and we saw three cars.

> Halloween. I'm glad the kids aren't like we were. It was just tricks, no treats involved. Our next door neighbor was an Ivy League grad. When

we'd play ball, it would go over his fence, and when we'd go over his fence, it infuriated the hell out of him. One Halloween we went down to the farm and got two or three ears of corn and shucked it, and we went around and punched holes in his lawn with our fingers and stuck corn in all over his front yard. The next summer, all that corn came up and that guy could not understand what was happening to his lawn.

We had lots of time to think. I guess the worst thing we did was take the cow manure in a big, old, five-gallon can or something and pour it on some poor guy's front porch and cover it with leaves and set it on fire, ring the doorbell and go hide in the bushes and watch people try to stomp it out and then take off their shoes to go back in the house.

Sleigh riding on the farm, that was great fun. They had a hill with trees on it and some big flint-like rocks. It went down to the creek. We'd put bales of hay out there and build bonfires and come home sopping wet and sit in front of the fireplace steaming.

Of course, girls played there, too. One of Billy Lehr's friends was Janie Bradley whose folks built a home on what came to be called Greentree Road. She remembered:

We lived there, and we crawled through all those sewers. I get claustrophobic at night thinking about it. When I was ten, most of the kids were younger. I took three little girls and two little boys out under the big cedar tree in that field with a pack of cigarettes that I had gone up to Mr. Brown's store and told him they were for my father, and we smoked the whole pack. And the little boys got so sick, the little girls were fine. The little boys turned green, and their mothers called my mother and said I was leading them astray. "What kind of child do you have?" they asked.

Millie Imirie and her older sister, Peggy, also grew up and played all over that area. Margaret sometimes conducted a play-school for Kay Kelly, Janie Bradley and some of the other, younger children. They all went to Brown's regularly, and one of their favorite baseball fields was on the other side of Old Georgetown near the caretaker's house and barn at the Visitation Convent.

Fred Strunk and his handyman, Lafayette who was called Lafe, were there "forever," Millie Imirie recalled. She also remembered annoying the nuns by riding her bike up their walks and roadways and by occasionally standing on her bicycle seat and peaking over the wall at the sisters. One of the "outside" nuns saved

postage stamps for Millie who sometimes checked twice a day for anything new since there were two mail deliveries then.

John Letts died in 1937, and the California based Safeway chain took over the Sanitary Stores. His widow and Mr. Johnson operated the farm until the war, and then Letts' daughter Catherine and her husband F. Henry Jones kept the place going using horsedrawn delivery wagons during the days of gas rationing. After the war the farm was sold and subdivided, and a fire destroyed the main barn and one silo. Park and Planning salvaged eighteen acres and used it for a recreation center and an elementary school. The school preserved one silo, capped by a cow weathervane, as an incinerator and turned the pasteurization barn into a library. At one time there were several other outbuildings on the school and rec center property along with an alley of sheds and garages.

Two houses also survived. Farmer Mahlon Austin's home, built about 1900 and much changed, is at 9104 Hempstead Avenue. The owners have kept an Ayrlawn Farms corner and other memorabilia and worked to preserve the memory of the farm. The other house was once the "palace" of Letts's prize bulls. It was moved about 200 feet to its present location at 6005 Johnson Avenue after the war.[101]

As the building boom continued, some skilled craftsmen such as Warren Gingell and Bob Wehrle went into business for themselves while others remained scrabbling day laborers. Lawrence "Bootsie" Lochte grew up in the Triangle in a Rugby Street house with a dirt cellar. He left school after the fifth grade knowing he could not follow in the smithy footsteps of his grandfather and father. He apprenticed with a steam fitter and then became a plumber's helper and learned both of those trades.

Woodmont seemed to attract plumbers. Among the earliest were L. Earle Donaldson and partners Ellis Fuller and E. C. Musgrove. Bootsie Lochte worked for his brother-in-law A. R. Lucas on Del Ray and then for A. C. Ketchem, one of the first to rent a store in Sacks' row. Lochte recalled working beside metal mechanic Jim McAuliffe on the Kenwood clubhouse job. It was the last one he did for Ketchem who was paying him twenty-five cents an hour as a helper.

Lochte tried the electrician's trade briefly and then went to work for Walter Gingell, became a journeyman plumber, and stayed with

him for twenty years with time out for the Seabees. Gingell lost heavily when the Hunts failed in the Depression, gave up his store and moved his business back to his house in Woodmont across from the Bealls. He enclosed the big, wrap-around porch and worked from there for the rest of the 1930s.

Earl Hill was also born and raised in Woodmont. His father owned a home there and worked at the USDA experimental station. In the Depression Earl Hill fed his young family on what he could earn with his dump truck. He spent long days landscaping until he became a full-time, paid fireman at Chevy Chase.

It was pretty hard to get a steady job. Taxes were $56 a year on our lots, which we were trying to save. We had two kids and were living on three dollars a week for food, usually a pot of beans. We had to live on what we made. I don't ever want to see those days again. I heard Chevy Chase had this opening because some guys were going to work in D.C. It was for a houseman, answering the phone for $50 a month, but it was regular, and I brought in some more with the truck. I worked five to seven, seven to five shifts, and later as a fireman made $100 a month.

Bill Austin, the Chevy Chase policeman, became the Hill's neighbor in Woodmont.

Earl Hill lived behind me on Rugby, my lot went through. One time he and I had a brilliant idea. He had the truck and knew somebody that was cutting down a sycamore tree. And I didn't know a damn thing about wood, but I got him to get the old tree and dump it on the lot next to him, and we were going to cut up that big sycamore and sell it for wood. Impossible. If you drive a wedge in a sycamore it goes in like in hard dough. That damn old tree lay on that lot for about two years.

Mary, his wife (looking out our kitchen looked into her front door), when he was a fireman she turned her whole household around when he changed shifts. The kids, when he was working over there, would be out in the street at midnight. My wife and I said those kids will never figure out which way is up, but they all turned out fine.[102]

In 1926, when he was barely old enough to make a contract, Abraham Morrison and his older brother, auto mechanic Ralph, formed a general contracting partnership with their brother-in-law Calvin Owens, a grocery clerk whose father had been a builder for a long time. No other construction firm had more to do with the building of modern Bethesda.

The Morrisons had grown up on a 140-acre farm on Cedar Lane (now Greentree Road). Neighbors included the Austins and the Bohrers, later combined for the model Ayrlawn Farms operation. On the north, the Morrison farm touched the Stellwagen place where the children's Uncle Chester was in charge. "Edland" was stocked with beautiful milch cows about which Stellwagen could brag to his fellow "gentleman farmers" John Joy Edson, George E. Hamilton, and Charles I. Corby, all of whom claimed their cows were the best in the County.[103]

James Morrison was no gentleman farmer. He and his wife, the former Annie Bogley, reared five sons and three daughters at their big home with its red barn and stables. The Morrisons sowed fields of wheat and corn and also raised a wide variety of vegetables. They kept a herd of dairy cows and a large flock of chickens. James Sr. bought a Dayton wagon and soon had a profitable route of customers for his milk, eggs, chickens and vegetables.

Abe was the youngest of the children and was not allowed to go with his brothers on the teams his father hired out to the builders of Bradley Hills Boulevard. But he milked cows, chopped firewood for the kitchen stove, and at threshing time had an important job.

Farmers would harvest their wheat and put it in the barn until they got time to thrash it, had to take care of hay first, then they could thrash the wheat close to September. They didn't all do it at the same time, since there was only one machine in the neighborhood, steam powered; it pulled the thresher and bailer.

My job was to go down to the branch, five or six hundred feet from the barn; they had a sled and the water horse, and on the sled they fastened four barrels covered with canvas with a hoop on it to keep the water from sloshing out. I went down there where there was a place where you could pull the sled into the stream. Then I had to stand on the front and take a bucket and fill the barrels, and put the hoop on and go up there where the steam engine would suck the water out of the barrels and then go back and get some more. Sometimes if you didn't quite make it, he'd blow the whistle, or else they had to shut it down if you didn't get the water there. The Huffmans kept machinery at the corner of Cedar and Old Georgetown where that little store was built.

Cedar Lane went all the way to the Potomac; it was the only road back there. The

County Commissioners hired farmers to maintain a mile or so of road, and my father maintained from the creek to Old Georgetown Road. When you'd get a mud hole, you'd take a wagon load of stone out and fill it up and pack it down. He had a horse-drawn scraper that belonged to the county. You always knew where it was; it moved back and forth between the people on the road. And he cleaned out the ditches along the road at certain times of the year.[104]

The Morrison children walked across the fields to the old, one-room Beane School at the top of the hill on Bells Mill Road where one teacher taught seven classes. It was built on an acre of Bohrer land purchased for $50 in 1882. Some of their fellow students, including a few of the girls, rode horses to school and tied them in the pines when the shed was full.

When that school was closed in 1915, the Morrisons walked out to Old Georgetown and took the trolley past the school at Woodmont and down to Bradley Boulevard and walked over to the Rosemary school in Chevy Chase with the Stock boys and other children from the communities down Wisconsin. Later the County provided a school bus on Bradley Boulevard. Then they walked through the Hall farm next to the Galligher place where James Jr. was superintendent. Mr. Morrison also remembered that farm for its gooseberry bushes. He smiled seventy years later, "Lord, they were good."

Although he did not attend school in Bethesda, Abe Morrison followed his brothers Ralph and Roy into the Bethesda Band, which practiced at the school on Wilson Lane. They put on a "big lawn fete" every year to raise money and played for churches and clubs. Morrison, born in 1904, joined in his teens and remembered it as a very successful country band.

There was a fellow name of Smoot, a railroad motorman, he started it. They had brass instruments. Smoot would write the music instead of buying real band music. My brother played the baritone horn, and I took it over when I was about fourteen.

Some of the boys were musicians like Roy Allison. He played violin and the trombone and was employed by the Fox theater full time. He could play anything. A damn good musician. He played right along side of me and helped me a lot. His family lived on Leland Street. I had a little bit of piano, could read music. Miss Holman used to

come by the farm on Cedar Lane, and she taught me and my sisters. She was a nice person.

Some others came in later that were musicians. Originally there were no musicians. We were playing something that sounded pretty good from a distance. And then we hired Mr. Schaefer, director of the Marine Band, and he brought his two sons out. We had sixty-four members at that time, played in two inaugural parades.

When Mr. Case came in, he lived over on Chevy Chase Circle, a wealthy man, he bought all the band silver-plated instruments, Conn and Kings; that's when they hired Schaefer. I got a big, new baritone horn. Fay Wilkinson was in the band and he got a big tuba, a big silver bass horn that circled around. Alan Luckter and his brother, Alan played coronet and his brother played the bass horn, they were musicians. Luckter couldn't read music, but he was right in there. Mr. Schaefer, he liked that boy, wished he had him in the Marines. We marched in parades; we played at all the church lawn fetes over on River Road at Concord and everywhere.

Abe Morrison's father was a successful farmer feeding his family of ten and saving enough money to make loans to other farmers, and his grandfather had plowed the land that became Georgetown Prep as well as operating the toll gate at Garrett Park. But Abrom took up building and went to Tech high school at night. When he was fifteen, he joined a Geodetic Survey team mapping part of the Oregon mountains and learned surveying the hard way as a rod boy. Then he returned to Tech part-time and took up the carpenter's trade. His older brother Leonard was a union carpenter, and young Abe learned from him.

In the Twenties carpenters started at 20¢ an hour as an apprentice, then worked up fifty cents, seventy-five cents, a dollar was about it for a journeyman. Once when I was making seventy-five out here, I went down to an apartment job in D.C. where most of the workers were Virginians. The superintendent asked if I could do roof framing. His fellows had used successive cuts as a pattern, and it opened up on them. I had to take the roof down, four floors up, and build a new one, had to make new hip rafters, too. At the end of the week when they paid me off, they paid me a dollar an hour. I would have been happy with seventy-five.

Most of the partnership's early projects were in Chevy Chase, and they built some of the early houses in Kenwood including the Somerville's. The Morrison Brothers first big job

was for society architect Jules Henri de Sibour, designer of the Chevy Chase clubhouse and Keith's Theater, and some English investors.

They bought property on Turner and Taylor on the other side of Brookville Road, and they had a planner design the buildings, and we contracted to build them. We put up twenty-seven houses in about eight months. They were in a big rush. Hilleary Burroughs did the basements, and we did the carpentry.

The small shopping strip on Brookeville Road was another of the Morrisons' early projects. It was done for dentist and friend, Dr. Wilbur E. Evans, whose son Jebbie operated the gas station there for a long time. Then they built some Spanish-style houses near Rosemary Circle for Reginald W. Geare. Morrison Brothers did the whole job from clearing the land to handing over the keys. One of the houses even had a putting green in the basement. Shortly after they were finished, Geare committed suicide. He had been the architect of the Knickerbocker Theater at 18th and Columbia Road where ninety-eight people were killed when the roof collapsed under twenty-eight inches of snow on January 28, 1922.

The Morrisons also built the new hall for the Village of Chevy Chase and later added the post office. Then they did a lot of work for the school system and for Charlie Miller "down in the flats." Morrison said,

I liked him. You know he had been a Texas Ranger as a youngster. There was a lot of people couldn't get along with him, but it wasn't Charlie's fault. He was a nice person, really. He used to take me down to his house. He had a range in his basement, and he'd give me a .45 and say, "Hit that." I said, "That damn thing would jump out of my hand," but he could shoot that thing.

I introduced him to Jim Miller after the war, he was a lawyer who had handled settlements for us, badly wounded in the war. Charlie's thing had got so big it was interfering with our general contracting work. Charlie would come up with an idea and you'd have to take it and have the plans drawn and build it. We built almost all of those things, those warehouses, in the flats.

The Morrison firm opened an office in the Bank of Bethesda building and eventually occupied the whole top floor. In 1927 they won the bids for several frame "colored schools." In those days the school board had decided that all the white schools would be brick and the "black" schools frame. In 1928 the Board of Education gave them a contract to maintain, repair, and renovate all the public schools.[105]

And then they were awarded the contract for the County Building in Bethesda and about two years later put up Dr. Perry's office building almost next door to it. Shook and James from Frederick did a great deal of their masonry and added to their reputation for quality workmanship. Soon the Morrisons were building houses all over the Bethesda area with the partners handling hammers and saws themselves on a number of jobs.

They built Burrow's gas station and garage for Charlie Miller and Burrell Marsh's showroom and shop on lots one of the Morrisons' sisters owned. The highly successful firm also constructed the Farm Women's Market, the two big Baptist Home dormitories, and in 1935 they erected the first buildings of both Blair and Bethesda-Chevy Chase High Schools. Of all the Bethesda workmen who went into business for themselves in the Twenties, Abe Morrison was by far the most successful.

He built Bethesda.

[1] Nudged a bit farther south and set atop a steel framework, it became the only survivor of Bethesda's 19th century business district.

[2] "Early Whitehall — An Historical Account" by Mrs. O. G. Whitlow in May 1959 *News Carrier* of the Western Bethesda Community Planning Association. Mrs. Whitlow, a Wilson granddaughter, lived at 5605 Wilson Lane where the family's well had been, and she also recalled the land being sold to the Bradley Hills syndicate in 1914.
It is possible that the Wilson's Lane name is older than the Canadian family's appearance since there was a mill and tavern on River Road known as Wilson's in the mid-19th century. In the early 20th Century, the western part of Wilson Lane was generally called "New Cut Road."

[3] See Bethesda *Journal*, July 17, 1942. Warren "Jingle" was very likely the motorman on that famous Georgetown coal car crash in `99.

[4] Almost all of the above from "Old Bethesda" by Doree Germaine Holman in the Bethesda *Journal*, April 28 and July 7, 1939, and Feb. 16 and 23, 1940. Obviously Miss Holman was right up to 1940, and the second coming of the electric train has had as big an impact as the first.

[5] See Rambler articles in *Star*, June 3, 1917, and June 22, 1919. The writer can no more explain the spelling of Beane/Bean than can he explain the missing "e" in Brookville Road.

[6] Her father's farm became the site of St. Jane Frances de Chantal church and school.

[7] Warner also donated $20 gold pieces as prizes in the school system's oratorical contest as well as scholarships to a "commercial college in Washington." *From One Room to Open Space*, p. 154.

[8] See Maryland Historic Sites Inventory by Anne Cissel and Eileen McGuckian, 1979, and the plat maps at the County Courthouse.

[9] The Hospital was established in the 1880's. In 1911 the name became the Washington Home for Foundlings, and in 1929 moved from 15th Street to 42nd and Brandywine in Tenleytown. In the 1950s it became an adoption agency, the Pierce-Warwick Trust, now part of Family and Child Services of Washington, D.C. The Bethesda location was probably used mainly as a summer retreat and home for older children.

[10] His son and name-sake, attorney "Bud" Keiser, established his office within a block of his father's and in his grandfather's subdivision near the site of the old, family ice house.
Roger Eisinger destroyed the last vestiges of the ice house as he developed property north of the tracks. "If people had known that ice plant was there, I might have been confronted with the same problem I had with Community Paint and Hardware. I certainly didn't tell anybody."

[11] See U. S. census report on unincorporated areas (1890 - 1,143, 1900 - 2,027, 1910 - 3,217 people and about 700 families) and for a list of 1915 Bethesdans see the directory in appendix D

[12] "Town Government" by Anne Bushart in *The Town of Chevy Chase*.

[13] Later the site of the Beth El synagogue. During the Civil War, the County established a school (#3) at Darcy's Store which was damaged, probably in Early's 1864 "raid." There may also have been a school at Locust Grove/Beane and there was another at Concord (#4) in that period.

[14] Again, mainly from Holman's "Old Bethesda" articles. Mt. Zion, Nov. 11 and 24, 1939, and school July 7, 1939, and the Gingell essay of July 31, 1942, in the Bethesda *Journal*. It is likely that an earlier school stood on the same site; see the 1879 map.
Chitty quotes from "In the Beginning...The formative years of the Bethesda Lodge No. 204 A.F. & A.M. at its Seventy-fifth Anniversary" (1981).

[15] Collection of MCHS, donated by Hilma Morris.

[16] *Journal*, July 31, 1942.

[17] *Annual Report and Public Schools of Montgomery County Maryland, Calendar 1916-17*   MCHS.

[18] Leslie Bell Jr. located the church on "the Elm Street side."

[19] *Record*, May 24, 1946. Among those who started Lodge No. 204 were J. Heath Dodge, Dr. John Latane Lewis, H. Latane Lewis, Jedidiah Gittings (first Senior Warden), Edward R. Magie (first Junior Warden), Cyrus Keiser, Evan A. Condon and Frank Sharp.

[20]Herbert H. Harwood, *Impossible Challenge: The Baltimore and Ohio Railroad in Maryland*, 1979, p. 324. Harwood states that during the Korean War a troop train was backed through Bethesda and into Georgetown at night providing the only passenger service ever on the line.

[21]See the plat maps in the land records at the courthouse. Little is known about either speculator John E. Beall or H Street physician Ralph Walsh, both important in early Bethesda land deals.

[22]Mrs J. Reed Bradley's "Vignette" in *Journal*, Oct. 4, 1940. On the Moores, an interview with Mrs. Angel who was a friend of their daughter, Arelia.
Keplinger put up a cup as first prize, which was "retired" if the same player won it three times. By the end of the war that had happened four times: by Mr. Bopst in 1925, Mr. Hiatt in `30, Mr. Schmitter in `41 when Robert Chichester, winner in `35 and `36 and runner-up in `40, collapsed and defaulted, and by Mr. Morell in 1944.

[23]Minutes of the Citizen's Committee of Northwest Park in the collection of the MCHS.

[24]Plat book 1, folio 49. "The Tiniest Town" by Morris Fraden, *Star* Sunday Magazine, Sept. 25, 1966, and "Growth Bypasses Oakmont" by Ray Py, *Sentinel*, Sept. 28, 1989.
In 1925, Walter Johnson purchased the large parcel of land assembled by Ralph E. Burgess in 1908 and built the lane that became Johnson Avenue and a house that is still there..

[25]Walking four blocks west from Old Georgetown on Roosevelt is time travel at a block a decade.

[26]*Star*, June 22, 1919.

[27]*Star*, Feb. 1, 1898. Chapter 29 of *Bethesda Not So Old* by Mrs. Bradley.

[28]*Record*, Jan. 5, 1945, at the time of Perry's retirement. Perry's store lasted until Metro arrived.

[29]*Journal*, July 17, 1942.

[30]Dr. Morris's 1911 journal was given to the MCHS by his daughter, Hilma.

[31]*Star*, Aug. 21, 1908.

[32]*Brill's Magazine*, Sept. 15, 1908, and "The Headway Recorder," Feb. 1960 and April 1960.

[33]See *Star* April 5 and *Sentinel*, April 6, 1917. The injured included Eugene Lochte, who required Dr. Lewis's attention, F. C. Getzendanner, Mrs. Robert Warfield, and the Misses Bessie Beckwith, May Smith, Noma Thompson and Amie Robertson

[34]Mrs. Gingell in the *Journal*, July 24, 1942.

[35]"But all the mail started going out to a government arsenal by that name. It was a blamed nuisance. So we tried Edgewood Park, and nobody liked that," said Tuckerman. Since Moorland Lane existed, they called it Edgemoor.

[36]Architect Theodore Boal and his partner Ward Brown had offices at 1712 H St., NW. The carraige house is 5506 Exeter.

[37]Except for W. E. Perry's sheep and Hagner's guinea fowl, that probably marked the end of farming in downtown Bethesda.

[38]Armentrout, in his 1936 U. of Md. thesis, among others, called Edgemoor the "prettiest." All the Tuckerman quotes, including the one above, are from an article by Elizabeth Hillenbrand in the March 1959 *News Carrier* of the Western Bethesda Community Planning Association.

[39]"We lived on stories of Alaska," said daughter Laura. "He was at the Chevy Chase Club having a drink with Tom Riggs, who had just been appointed to the survey. Daddy said it sounded great, and Tom said, 'Well, Walter, why don't you come with us?' Daddy said, 'I don't know anything about surveying.' 'You can shoot, can't you?' Daddy said, 'Yes.' So that's how he got it."

[40]All five of the Tuckerman daughters made their debuts at the house, the last, Peggy, in the spring of 1940. Neighbors said he sold off a piece of property for each, but daughter Laura said they were actually very modest affairs.

[41]Article in the March 1960 WBCPA *News Carrier* by Millicent Paulding Eifler, who lived at 7500 Hampden at that time.

[42]This and later Imirie quotes from an interview by Alan Hall in July 1981. Mr. Imirie's name was often rendered "Wade" or "Wadie". His wife called him "Wade" for seventy-two years. Earl

Groverman played for the Bearcats.   Robert Stevens recalled a homemade "Imirie and Groverman" sign out front at one time.

[43]Bethesda *Journal*, Feb. 16, 1940.

[44]This was one of the stories told at G. Wady Imirie's funeral.

[45]The first car dealer in town may have been Stewart Wirgman, a one-time driver for Henry Ford, whose agency antedated Northwest Ford at Leland and Wisconsin.

[46]*Record*, Dec. 1, 1944.   According to the Bank's history those in attendance at the Sept. 25, 1919, meeting at Sacks' home also included Edwin H. Etz, James R. Ellis, Busey, H. Howard, Vernon M. Dorsey, H. Latane Lewis, Edward J. Stellwagan, Dr. Benjamin C. Perry, and Dr. Ernest C. Schroeder.   There may, in fact, have been two meetings.

[47]Milton A. Ailes, Arthur A. Chapin, Vernon M. Dorsey, William H. Gottlieb, Thomas Hampton, John Fred Imirie, Lewis Keiser, H. Latane Lewis, Charles F. Miller, M. Willson Offutt, Millard E. Peake, Dr. Benjamin C. Perry, Walter E. Perry, Dr. E. C. Schroeder, Francis C. Wallace, Robert Wilson, Claude H. Woodward, and B. Peyton Whalen.

[48]"In the Beginning..." ob.cit.   The Masons are still there but in a modern building.

[49]*Sentinel*, Nov. 28, 1919; *Journal*, Dec. 15, 1939, *Tribune* , Dec. 8, 1939, *News Carrier*, March 1959 and the 25th Anniversary banquet program of Dec. 1, 1944.   "I went to school one year in Europe with some friends," said Laura Triest, "and somebody was going to take us over and at the last minute they couldn't, so Daddy took us all over, three of us.   And while he was gone, he was superseded by Mr. Sacks.   They wanted a change and took that opportunity.   Someone, perhaps Mr. Dove, came and told Mother and Daddy about it afterwards.   He had not liked what had happened.   There was a little behind-the-scenes business there."

[50]Alan Hall 1981 interview and June 2, 1939, Bethesda *Tribune*.   Wade's widow remembered the amount as $2,000 and recalled a time when her husband brought his receipts to their place on Chesapeake Bay, got caught in a rain squall, and they had to dry checks and money on the stove. He was better about making deposits after that.
Between 1920 and 1930 the County's population grew from 35,000 to 49,000.   The D.C. metropolitan area had about 700,000 inhabitants in 1930 and about three-fourths of the jobs and people were in the District.

[51]CCHS oral history.   Ed Stock's mother, Mollie, was a Republican candidate for the State Senate in 1924, the first woman to win a primary in the U.S. and probably the first woman to make a political radio broadcast.   A non-swimmer, she lifeguarded the Stocks' pool by counting heads.

[52]Among the founders of the Bethesda Women's Club were Mrs. Evelyn C. Condon, Mrs. Eleanor T. Cronin, Mrs. Morris L. Croxall, Mrs. Charles Dickens, Mrs. Daniel Morgan, and Mrs. E. Winsor Offutt.   The Morrison brothers built the clubhouse, and Roy Morrison, whose home was just across Sonoma Road fell on the job, broke his back, and was paralyzed.

[53]The original officers were J. Garvin Peters, president; C. R. Lindsay, Jr., vice-president; Mrs Helen Scudder, secretary; Charles G. Randle, treasurer; and board of directors members Evans Browne, J. Maury Dove, Jr., and Walter R. Tuckerman, who held the mortgage.

[54]Mostly from "Brief History of the Edgemoor Club" by Minerva Bassett, 1962.   Early presidents of the club: 1922-24 Charles S. Robb, `25 W. R. Tuckerman, `26 William W. Bride, 1927-29 D. D. L. McGrew, 1930-31 Harrison R. Hathaway, 1932-35 Robert F. Fleming, `36 E. J. Gray, 1937-38 W. R. Tuckerman again, 1939-41 D. L. Mitchell, `42 Frank Shore, 1943-46 Strand Johnsen.

[55]*Sentinel*, June 7 and September 13, 1929;   Jan. 30 and June 12, 1931. Other original officers: Dr W. L. Kline of Friendship Heights was 1st vice-president, Miss Helen Stohlman of Somerset 2nd vice-president, Miss Rose Royce of Chevy Chase Gardens secretary-treasurer, and Mrs. Lulu Richardson of Drummond was chosen librarian.

[56]The writer assumes that Mr. Tuckerman's tongue was pretty far in his cheek when he wrote this although he likely knew that there is a suggested meaning of "Potomac" as "the burning pine, resembling a council fire."   See Chapter 1.

[57]Most of the clubs, except for Columbia, have produced their own histories.

[58] The Wheaton district had a few more cars, but Bethesda's were more valuable - worth $1,024,675 or almost $250 apiece. *Sentinel*, Nov. 6, 1931.

[59] See Chapter 13, "Clinging to a Rural America" in *A Grateful Remembrance*.

[60] County-wide between 1910 and 1920, the white population grew about 4,000 and the black population declined about 1,000 and fell from 29% to 24%. By 1930 African-Americans were only 17% of the County population and in 1940 just 10.6%. There were fewer blacks in the County in 1940 than there had been in 1910 (8,885 to 9,235) while the white population grew from 22,846 to 75,986.

[61] Little Falls Branch was the most serious problem. Not only did Chevy Chase use it, but Somerset's 12-inch pipe carried sewage, toilet and bathroom, from forty houses into the stream. See *History of the Washington Suburban Sanitary Commission* by Arthur P. Bingham, 1988.

[62] Elizabeth Hillenbrand in the *News Carrier*, March 1959.

[63] *A Brief History of the Washington Suburban Sanitary Commission* by Arthur P. Bingham, WSSC 1979, and in *The Montgomery County Story*, August 1978.

[64] See MacMaster's and Hiebert's *A Grateful Remembrance*, Chapter 14, and Wade Elgin Jr.'s thesis "The Early History of the Washington Suburban Sanitary Commission" at the U. of Md.

[65] According to his daughter, Leslie Bell would have been the first mayor if Bethesda had become a town or city. "He and Dr. Perry had it all worked out," she said.

[66] Milton Smith, according to many sources, held the record for the eight-mile, bank-to-the-courthouse "run."

[67] Wilson's JP replacement, Upton Perrell, was tried for embezzlement and convicted of "misconduct in office" in 1925. Perry quotes from Nov. 2, 1945, *Record*.

[68] Imirie's home is now #9515. In the mid-1990s, Beall's home, surrounded by new office buildings, remained on the southwest side of the Old Road. *Journal*, July 17, 1942.

[69] See the special section of the Washington *Post* for Sunday, Sept. 19, 1926, celebrating the firm's fourth anniversary. In '26 Edgemoor lots went for $3-7,000, Battery Park' $2,000-3,500.

[70] Mostly from *Prominent Personages of the Nation's Capital* published by the Washington Times Company, no date - circa 1925.

[71] From an unpublished and undated one-page manuscript, MCHS.

[72] See Armentrout's "History of Land Subdivision . . ." *op.cit.*, the land records, and Gertrude Bradley's "Bethesda Not So Old." The actual number of active or retired military who settled here is difficult to ascertain, but there were many.

[73] Interview by Alan Hall in January 1984. *Tribune*, Jan 14, 1938.

[74] One source suggests that the clubhouse was actually sold to cover back taxes, and then after three years of litigation and negotiation, the new owner resold it to the residents who scraped together $591.28 and borrowed $4,000 for the purchase. See the Battery Park "Five Star General" Vol. 3 No.1, June 1967.

[75] As did the writer for a couple of years.

[76] *Journal*, Dec. 8, 1939.

[77] Roy Philips interview by Alan Hall, December 1990. See the article by Mrs. Verla P. Richtmyer in the May 1959 *News Carrier* of the WBCPA.

[78] The Bank of Bethesda is older, but the building is two years younger. Eastham's gas station is the oldest business still run by the same family. Except for the 1919 Sycamore Store, "Brown's" wins. Many local people insist on calling the store "Brown's" out of long-rooted habit seemingly passed through generations of children like jump rope rhymes. Suburban Hospital now owns the property. Roland Custer: "Brown wasn't there long; he was a big drinker, used to sit back and when people would come in, he'd say, 'Well, help yourself.' He liked the kids, he'd give them a popsicle now and then."

[79] A long-term disagreement between Eisinger and Miller over building a railroad spur kept several lawyers busy for twenty years.

80 At that time the officers, in addition to Mr. Parker, were Mr. Sacks, 1st v-p; publisher Merle Thorpe, 2nd v-p; builder Thomas E. Hampton, secretary; and Mr. Imirie, still treasurer.   The first Board of Directors included both Emory and Walter Bogley, Wady Imirie's father, John, Col. Hampton, Capt. Chester Wells, and Luke I. Wilson.

81 Based almost entirely on G. W. Imirie's 1963 "Early History of the Bethesda-Chevy Chase Chamber of Commerce," the name adopted in 1956.   Other early presidents: 1930 John J. Miller, 1931 Capt. Chester Wells, 1932 Thomas E. Hampton, 1933 J. Harry Welch, `34 Samuel E. Shoemaker, `35 William Buckley, `36 Adlai S. Magee, `37 Harry Golladay, `38 John A. Overholt, `39 Burrell H. Marsh Jr., 1940 J. Henry Hiser, `41 John L. Imirie, `42 Clarence C. Keiser, `43 Edmond E. Bass, `44 Carl A. Bachschmid, 1945 Henry J. Connor.
The first printed examples of the "Buy in Bethesda" slogan that the writer has found are in the *Kenwood* magazines of the early 1930s.
The other officers chosen for 1933 were Dr. Washington Waters, 1st vp; Ralph Sabine, 2nd vp; and as usual John Overholt, secretary, and S. Walter Bogley, treasurer.

82 The Civic Federation, established in 1924-25, drew delegates from various citizen groups, worked through committees, and generally favored the modernization of County government.

83 "Walter Tuckerman, Edgemoor Founder, Recalls Early Days" *News Carrier*, Mar. 1959. Like Chevy Chase, Bethesda did have a very informal volunteer company with its equipment kept behind Wilson's store, but it did not have fire hydrants until the coming of the WSSC.

84 Later there were three paid men, Jesse Barber, James Breeden, and Gummel.
The two fire engines were delivered on Dec. 3, 1926, and No. 1, now lovingly restored, is back in Bethesda thanks to Henry Latimer, Sumpter Embrey and a lot of other folks.

85 The 1933 Bethesda firemen: outfielders Lucas, Kyder, Murdock, Royer, and Gucklon; the infielders Higgins, Hargett, Oldfield, Velinneza, and Fuller, and Nichols was the pitcher.

86 *Sentinel*, July 9, July 30, Dec. 10, 1926; Chevy Chase *Gazette*, special issue Dec. 18, 1926.   Young quote from the *Tattler*, April 23, 1976.   Miss Young was the first B-CC counselor.

87 The White Fathers of Africa acquired the property as a missionary home in 1944, and more recently it has become the Temple Hills Baptist Church.

88 Mostly from *Bethesda Presbyterian Church*, published by the Celebration 360 Committee in 1984.   For more detail see Eugene and Edythe Clarke's *The Spirit of Captain John*, 1970.

89 The first deacons were James E. Ainley, the treasurer, and Wilbur A. Bouic, the clerk.   Mrs. Hugh G. Myers was the first deaconess.

90 *Bethesda First Baptist 1934-1984*, booklet prepared by anniversary committee, 1984.

91 The Reverend Mr. Williams was widely known among the young set as "Holy Joe."

92 *St. John's Norwood* by Richard Hanson Weightman (1968), warden, registar, and in 1937 renovator of the parish hall kitchen.

93 Leslie Bell Jr. said, "Henry was a gambler, He lost his ass off on Dewey. My dad used to say if you want to get rich, bet against Henry Hiser."   Roland Custer: "He'd bet on anything. He and Wolfson next door used to bet on elections."

94 *Journal*, Sept. 22, 1939.   One of the few Bethesdans interviewed who did <u>not</u> set pins at Hiser's was Bob Eastham Jr. whose father thought bowling alleys were like pool halls and no place for his son. Eastham married Nancy Hiser, one of John Henry's daughters, and became his father-in-law's friend. For a contemporary view of Hiser see the *Record*, Oct. 26, 1945.
"Condom" was not a familiar word to most pinboys; "rubbers" was, or "prophylactic" for those who liked to show off. For more on pinsetting, see the appendix F.

95 *Tribune*, May 27, 1937.

96 When Sabine gave up the dealership and went into real estate, Bell Laundry moved into part of that building using its trucks to haul equipment down from Hampden Lane over a weekend.

97 *Sentinel*, Feb. 6 and July 10, 1925, Jan. 14, 1927, Jan. 6 and June 29, 1928, Feb. 8, 1929.
Wheaton-Silver Spring was second with property assessed at $17.3 million.

98 Both the Stone House and Tree Tops, which the Wilsons tried to give to Thomas W. Sidwell for a school, still stand on the NIH campus along with some of the Wilson cottages. Since becoming the Stone Ridge school, Hamilton's house has been even more heavily modified.

99 Renovated if not restored, the Parker house is the headquarters of Goodwill Industries.

100 Edson refused to become a D.C. commissioner but for thirty years headed the Board of Charities and spearheaded penal reform. The Austin-Cassells home became Holton Arms School.

101 Morris Fradin, "Still Called Ayrlawn" in the *Star Sunday Magazine*, Dec. 4, 1966, and "When Ayrlawn Was in Clover" ms and photos at MCHS.

102 Thirty years later, Earl Hill became the chief of the Chevy Chase Fire Department.

103 See the Rambler in the *Star*, June 22, 1919. Morrison is "Abrom" in the census.

104 See the Rambler's report on Cedar Lane in the *Star*, May 13, 1917.

105 *Sentinel* July 1, 1927. The "colored" school bids: Rockville $4,395, Scotland $2,195, Cabin John (River Road) $4,695, and Ken-Gar $2,195.

The middle of Bethesda about 1925 - Wisconsin Avenue runs from lower left to upper right and the B&O from mid-left to lower right. The "sign lot" near the center is where the Farm Women's Market was built, and Leland Street and a few bungalows are clearly evident, but the Warren's row of stores is yet to be built. The Chevy Chase water tower may be seen at the top center of this photo. The houses at lower left are on Montgomery Avenue in Highland Park.

CHAPTER 8

Bethesda Not So Old

Bethesda had finally gotten a high school of sorts ten years before the Morrisons built the cupola-topped, three-story one on East West Highway. At the end of 1924 Superintendent of Schools Edwin Broome had his teachers conduct a census of all children under nineteen. At that time the Bethesda school had six teachers plus principal Ella Umbeck; the Chevy Chase school also had six teachers and principal Myrtle Anderson, and the Glen Echo school two teachers in addition to principal Anna McKay.

By then the number of County high school graduates had grown from 34 in 1920 to 95 in 1925, and the school board had received numerous petitions for down-county schools. "Professor" Broome's survey revealed that there were "6,057 white boys, 5,621 white girls, 1,744 colored boys and 1,722 colored girls" in the County and that nearly half of all the children lived in the Bethesda and Wheaton-Silver Spring districts. Bethesda had 2,005 white and 116 African-American children according to the teachers' count.

The County had eight high schools in 1924-25 : Rockville, Gaithersburg, Poolesville, Germantown, Sandy Spring, Dickerson, Damascus, and Fairland. Super-intendent Broome announced that he was planning high schools on both sides of Rock Creek in the near future.[1]

The superintendent convinced the school board, and by the spring thaw, work was well underway on a large, two-story brick school behind the old frame building on Wilson Lane. The April 10 *Sentinel* rhapsodized:

One of the busiest spots in Montgomery county just now is the Bethesda school site. As the new school house ceases to be a house of dreams, and begins to loom up in substantial brick and masonry, teachers and pupils alike are finding the unavoidable confusion and noise incident to building operations only the difficulties that inspire to increased effort, and all are striving to make this a year of preparation for the broader school and community life, which the new structure will make possible.

The $80,000 building with fourteen classrooms, a gym and an assembly room was finished by September 1925 and opened to 388 pupils in grades one through eight with Mrs. Anna McKay, former Cabin John principal, in charge of a staff of nine women. The PTA, under the leadership of its president, Mrs. H. Latane Lewis, held a housewarming. They had purchased most of the gym equipment with funds raised at a card party to go with Dr. Perry's $50 gift.[2]

Then there was the formal dedication on September 25th with speeches by Governor Albert Ritchie, music by the Bethesda Band and

The Bethesda School on Wilson Lane about 1926

prayers from Reverend White of Bethesda Presbyterian and Reverend Kirkpatrick of St. John's. Mrs. O. O. Kuhn led the tour of the building; Mrs. Walter Perry, a member of the school board, had the governor to dinner.

Tempe Curry went to both the old school and the new one. She entered first grade in the fall of 1924.

In the old wooden school, you went right in front, past the principal's office, and there were rooms on each side, four rooms, two up and two down. We went in the morning and the third grade came in afternoon because it was crowded.

When we went straight through, that was to the outside, the playground. And when it was time to come in, the principal rang a hand bell.

But the next year, after they built the addition, they had doors to the rooms and we had to line up to go in. I think they covered the old school with brick when they put on the addition.

I had first and second grades with Miss Nell Cashell. She was from Frederick, and we learned a lot of Maryland history. In third grade I had Mrs. Bricker, who later was principal at Somerset. In 4th we sat two in a desk and had four teachers that year. By then they had the high school there in the auditorium.

Tempe (3rd from right) in Mrs. Bricker's 3rd grade class

In June 1926, Thomas W. Pyle was named to replace Mrs. McKay. Pyle became, over the next twenty years, the most respected man in Bethesda. In September, at a reception to meet with parents, Pyle announced that enrollment was up to 550 and that Bethesda was the County's second largest school. The school added the ninth grade, and the staff grew to fifteen, with one male, Franklin Lehr. Within a month Broome assigned extra teachers to Bethesda, and the school board began considering the need for a separate school like the one built for Takoma Park-Silver Spring in 1925.

H. Franklin Lehr grew up in Frostburg where his father laid track in the coal mines and was a leader of the UMWA. Lehr graduated from the Normal School in 1925, and after looking into jobs in several counties, signed on with Dr. Broome as the principal-teacher at the Ednor school. "I didn't ask to move," he said.

Broome called me to come to his office and said, "We're opening up a junior high in Bethesda." He said, "We're going to have six, seven, eight, nine this year." He said, "You'll teach PE; you'll teach shop; you'll have a home room and be dean of boys."

The all-grade school in Bethesda was generally called the "high school," but it also housed the County's first kindergarten, a paid program promoted by the Newcomb Club and the Federation of Women's Clubs. The kindergartners "with their little chairs" and their teacher, Miss Brandt, attended the Newcomb Club's planting of a ten-foot Austrian pine in November and were visited by members of the Federation of Women's Clubs in January 1926. Meanwhile, the upper grade students tried to behave like high schoolers initiating athletic teams, a dramatics club and the school newspaper, *The Tattler*, under editor John Adair. [3]

It was Ludelle Hinaman who decided that the school needed a newspaper, and music teacher Geneve Bourdeaux became its cosponsor. Hinaman was an English and history teacher who also coached the girls' teams and hauled them to games in her yellow roadster. "I was young and silly then and it didn't matter how much work I did."

She described editor Adair as "always full of pep and into everything that was going on in school." Coach Lehr remembered him as a black-haired boy with thick glasses who was "a different guy, very outspoken and a hard worker who got off wisecracks sometimes." The first issue of the school paper carried news of the new bank building and firehouse as well as ads from nine Bethesda businesses. Adair thanked the advertisers in a front page note.

Lehr became the athletic director and boys' coach. His first team was in soccer. Thirteen boys turned out, but they did not all stick with it so the coach recruited six or seven girls. He recalled:

Poolesville called one day and said they heard that the city kids were playing soccer, and they wanted to give us a lesson. I said, "Sure, we're ready to learn," and we went up there, and when they saw there was five or six girls in there,

they went in and got the principal out, and they said weren't going to play girls. We didn't have but nine boys and one had asthma so bad he couldn't play, so I had to have some substitutes. Anyhow the girls played, but they beat us two to nothing. Some of those girls could outplay the boys; they were bigger, too.

Bethesda lost every soccer game. Only nine boys were on the first basketball team so they had to scrimmage the girls now and then. The gym, called "spacious and well-planned" by the *Sentinel*, was so small that players could shoot baskets from one end to the other according to Coach Lehr. The Bethesda school's teams came to be known as the "City Slickers" or sometimes just Slickers.

Franklin Lehr also wrote the school's first fight song, to the tune of the popular "Washington and Lee Swing."[4]

> It's for Bethesda,
> It's for Bethesda,
> The pride of blue and gold so dear.
> Come on you old lads,
> Join with the new lads,
> It's for Bethesda now we cheer,
> Rah, Rah, Rah!

That was also the school year that a Latin Club and a Footlight Club were started and a three-act play, "Daddy Long-Legs," was presented. The school held its first "junior high school" graduation in June of 1927 for the eighteen boys and twenty-three girls who had finished the ninth grade. The County schools under Superintendent Broome's firm hand were in the process of changing from the old 7-4 pattern to a 6-3-3 grade arrangement, the first in the State to do so.

In late June 1927 the school board gave Alfred Warthen of Kensington the $52,475 contract to build eight classrooms at 44th and Willow in the Warrens' Leland community for the "Chevy Chase-Bethesda high school." The

Back of the Bethesda school showing the gym

rooms were not ready by the fall when the Wilson Lane school started classes with twenty-two teachers including three males.

In January the boys' basketball team, wearing its new orange trunks and blue jerseys, defeated Rockville in a shocking upset; the girls' team, unfortunately, lost. That was the year that Beatrice Crocker, the girls' coach, ordered the new tunic-style uniforms and discarded the black pantaloons. Some parents were shocked.

It was also the year that young H. Franklin Lehr became "Zip."

After that first year, I went to Carnegie in `27. I took cabinet making, mechanical drawing, and wood turning. I was there six weeks. Wood turning was an extra credit, and I had to see Professor Smith to get permission to take it. I introduced myself, and he said "Oh, Free Stater, huh." Anyway, the professor let me take it without anything on my schedule. He said, "You just do what I ask you, and it'll be all right."

Three weeks came on, so he asked, "Lehr, what have you got for your wood turning?" I said, "Mr. Smith, you never told me to get started." He said, "Didn't I tell you to make one project by today?" I said, "You didn't tell me."

So he told me to skip my next class, and to get on the lathe and do something. In about an hour from 12 o'clock to a few minutes after one, I made a set of candlesticks and put them on his desk. He wasn't in there. When he got back, he said, "By gawd, who put these on my desk?" I said, "You asked me to have a project." He looked at the clock and said, "That's a damn good looking pair of sticks. If you want to get rid of them, I know somebody'd like to have 'em."

So next morning when he called the roll, there were eighteen in the class, he went, "Lanceford, Zip, Lyons..." I said, "What's this zip?" He said, "After what you did yesterday in an hour and three minutes, from now on you'll be known as Zip."

The second year, two Keene boys from Butler, Pennsylvania, came in. Their father got work in the government and decided to live in Bethesda. The first day in school, I met them. One was rough and the other kind of quiet. They asked if I was the shop teacher and what we had. So I told them about wood turning, making a sewing cabinet or a bench, about seven things.

The next morning they came in, I had them in homeroom, "Morning, Zip," they said. I said, "What did you say?" They said, "Morning, Zip. Why, aren't you called 'zip'?" I said, "Yes, I am

Zip Lehr

but how did you know about it?" "My uncle," one said, "was sitting next to you for six weeks at Carnegie Tech." So then we only had 19 or 20 shop students, and half of them said "Goodnight, Zip" by the end of the day.

Next day Mr. Pyle came down and said, "Mr. Lehr, what's this zip business?" "Well," I said, "it's a long story." "Why did you tell them about it?" he asked. I told him I didn't and I explained. He said, "Well now, I think we should keep our students and faculty to their own. I'm not in favor of too much conviviality." I said I agreed with him. He said, "It isn't professional for a student to call a teacher 'Zip'" I said, "Well, when we have an assembly, why don't you say something to them about it."

So when we did, he got up and said, "Boys and girls, I told you that if we had anything that concerned us all I would come to you and talk to you about it. And there's one thing; I don't think it's professionally right to use nicknames. Let us get to know each other better before we start giving people nicknames." He says, "So I don't want you to call him Mr. Lehr now. I want you to call him Zip." And he sat down next to me and asked, "What are they laughing at?" I said, "Think back on what you just said." So he got up, said, "Dismissed" and walked out.

About five minutes later the secretary came down and said, "Mr. Pyle would like to see you in the office." Well, you never saw such a look, and he says, "Did I really say that?"

I tried to stop it for a while but gave up. So it's followed me all my life.[5]

One of Zip's Bethesda School shop classes

The next summer "Zip" Lehr of Frostburg married Miss Emily Evelyn Castle of Williamsport where she had taught for two years. He had met her at a dance at the Normal School in 1924. Lehr brought his bride to Bethesda and to a job at the Bethesda school where she taught first grade and third grade for forty-seven years with two short breaks to bear a son and daughter.

"They didn't like two married people teaching in the same school," Mr. Lehr said, "but the school was growing fast and they needed teachers." At first they rented a room on Sonoma Road, and by the end of the month, they had worn holes in their shoes walking down to Wilson Lane. "Zip" remembered their first house.

After we got married, we got a house on Georgetown Road at Wilson back of the tracks, across from the Piggly Wiggly. We rented for forty-five dollars a month. And when the streetcar came down from the bank to that crossing at Del Ray Avenue, the street car would rock up and down because the road was bumpy, and at night, 11 o'clock was the last one, when it came down from Battery Lane, the last stop, I would be shaking in bed. Many a time it woke me from sleep thinking I'd find a streetcar in my lap.

Billy Lehr was told that when he was small, he played along and between the tracks. "It was my private sandbox," he said, and his mother would have to come running from behind their hedge to get him when she heard the trolley car coming.

It was nearly spring in 1928 when grades seven through ten from Bethesda and the 6th graders from overcrowded Chevy Chase Elementary moved into the new, dark-red brick building facing 44th Street that some were calling Leland high school. It was just a solid rectangle of tall-windowed classrooms, most on the first floor with doors leading directly outside. Miss Bourdeaux recalled, "In March we moved over to the Leland grounds, and they literally built the building around us." Mr. Pyle continued as principal of both buildings into the next year.

Shortly after settling into their new building, the high school faced its first crisis. When "Zip" Lehr heard that the gym planned for the new school might be cut by the State legislature, with the PTA's help he organized a trip to Annapolis for the whole student body and with Brooke Lee's approval packed the gallery of the State House. Lehr recalled:

Chevy Chase-Bethesda Junior-Senior High School in 1928

We took two hundred and twenty-five kids. We went by bus and a lot of parents went, too. Brooke Lee was the 'shin-dig' lawyer then, and when we got to the State House, he was out on the porch and lined them up for a talk and said, "Now, I want you to get in there and convince those people to pay for your new gym. Can you yell loud?" and two or three cheered, and he said, "Well, you'll have to do better than that," and they really yelled, and he said, "Come on, let's go in. Now when you get in the building, be quiet or you'll be ushered out, but when I give you the hand drop, go into your cheer."

We'd been rehearsing for two days. We went upstairs, and he got up and dropped his hand and said, 'Now!' and they almost took the roof off with "Yea, Bethesda!" And he came out and slapped me on the back and about knotted my shoulders. He says, "You couldn't have done a better thing. I bet you get your gym." And he called up the next week and said, "The appropriation's already okayed."

In April, a track and field day for all white students in the area took place on the new school grounds. It had been scheduled but rained out the previous year. Mr. Pyle headed up the officials; Mr. Lehr was the chief starter, and Mrs. Crocker and Miss Young acted as chief timers and clerks. Students from the high school, Bethesda

Thomas W. Pyle

Grammar as it was now being called, Glen Echo-Cabin John, and Chevy Chase took part. For the first time in the County, there were several races for girls as well as volleyball and dodge ball games and the standing broad jump. Both boys' and girls' events were divided by grade and weight classes.

Among the more notable participants were Lillian Lee, who won the 50-yard dash for 6th graders, and a new student, Bill Guckeyson, who finished second in the 70-yard dash (115 pound class) and running broad jump. In a special event Beatrice Crocker won the 60 yard dash for teachers with Miss Loar second and Miss Stover third. A press report suggested that "this race will go down in Bethesda-Chevy Chase history with falling significance." The crowd was estimated at over a thousand.[6]

The principal was everywhere. Miss Young recalled, "When class attendance looked meager, Mr. Pyle got in his old, high coupe and went to Rock Creek to bring back some sheepish looking boys." Mrs. J. William Mohler, later known as "Ma" Mohler, had been the principal of the K-7 Woodside school for two years when Dr. Broome sent her to B-CC to take over a class of eighteen boys "so obstreperous they were making teaching impossible in regular classrooms." Mrs. Mohler said Broome thought from "my size and voice and the fact that I had taken Woodside out of a rather chaotic situation, that I could handle them. And I did. We had a really good year." "Zip" Lehr remembered that the boys "were giving people the devil–sitting on people's porches and lawns across from school. She stopped all that."

In July 1928 the contracts were let for a gym, assembly hall, and six classrooms, again to Alfred C.

Mary B. Mohler

Warthen and Sons, for a total of $145,000. The "assembly hall" turned out to be the biggest and best auditorium in the area, complete with proscenium arch, raked floor, theater-type seats and broad balcony. And because there was a big, folding wall, it was theoretically possible to watch games in the gym behind the stage from seats in the auditorium. "Zip" Lehr said that they tried it a couple of times but quit for fear the students would tear up the seats. The gymnasium with its end-on, parquet, hardwood floor and two-story high ceiling had a huge folding door to divide it for PE classes.[7]

Bethesda's two-campus school continued through 1928-29, and, as Bethesda continued to grow, Dr. Broome asked for almost $150,000 worth of additional labs, shops, and class-rooms. He only got the classrooms then with another contract to Warthen. In the spring, the school census showed Bethesda by far the fastest growing area of the County with an increase since 1924 of 1,596 white students out of the total County increase of 2,464 for the five years. And by then Bethesda had what was easily the largest school in Montgomery County with an auditorium that would hold 1,500. With later additions, it housed more than 2,000 students for several years as a junior high.[8]

The PTA had been organized before the building was occupied and worked hard on creating a cafeteria program, improving the barren school grounds and laying out safe paths from various neighborhoods. Mrs. Douglas Griessmer was the first president.[9]

South entrance to auditorium in the addition

In school year 1928-29, Principal Pyle combined two rooms to produce a library. Dorothy Young, later to become B-CC's first guidance counselor, began the cheering club and Mrs. Beebe's dog, Hugo, often visited her ground-level classroom. Zip's soccer team won the County championship that year.

When it came time for the first graduation, the Prom for the fourteen Seniors was held in the library with music provided by a radio. The Juniors paid for the Senior banquet at the Patty-Kitch-Inn under the Bank on the Old Georgetown Road side. The equally small Class of 1930 was the first twelve-year class to graduate. By then the world was quite different in many ways.[10]

These may or may not be the first graduates

A by-product of the new Leland building and its first-class auditorium was the creation of the Montgomery Players in 1929. In part, it grew out of an informal, basically faculty group and "The Players," a mainly Bethesda Methodist amateur acting company. "Zip" Lehr credited Dorothy Young, Mr. Pyle, Judge Prettyman and Clitus Musgrove as well as himself among the founders of the Bethesda Players and said he thought Stella Werner was also a member. Lehr said he was among the "weak-kneed" actors and that he directed several plays and helped build and paint the sets until his teams' basketball games on Friday night made him give it up .

Judge E. Barrett Prettyman was the first president of the Montgomery Players, but Mr. and Mrs. Irving Day of Somerset are usually credited as the founding family. The first play, "A Successful Calamity," was directed by Arthur B. White of the D.C. Arts Club. Four plays a year became expected of them, and the Montgomery Players developed a loyal following and a membership of thirty to forty regulars.

A very early dramatic group at the high school

Mr. Day and Jane Plummer Rice appeared in or directed a play during each season of the Players' first decade.[11]

One of the Montgomery Players most active and interesting members was Harrison R. Hathaway who lived on Moorland Lane in Edgemoor and whose brother was married to the hereditary ruler of the Isle of Sark. A trophy-winning tennis player, good golfer and avid bridge player, Hathaway directed several plays, acted in an average of one a year and wrote a few one-acters. One of his hobbies was making miniature sets and characters to work out the "business" in the plays he directed. He was proud of the roses around his big, frame home, which he called "Four Winds," but even prouder of his woodworking projects. In his well-equipped basement shop, he made several pieces of furniture for his home including beds and bookcases for one of his three daughters. The Yale grad and life insurance man obviously did not find the lack of a left arm a handicap.[12]

Other organizations took advantage of the stage at 44th and Willow to put on plays and shows as fund raisers. In February of 1929, the Federation of Women's Clubs, the Newcomb Club, and the Woman's Club of Bethesda presented three one-act plays. The Newcomb Club's play was an original written by Maj. R. B. Lawrence of Battery Park and directed by E. Barrett Prettyman. The County finals of the Statewide oratorical contest were held on

the stage, and Lucy Franks of B-CC won the gold medal in April 1931. The Scouts held their "courts" and presented their awards in the auditorium; the fire department staged money-making minstrel shows there for many years, and, of course, the Footlight Club had annual presentations.[13]

The faculty regularly had fun and raised money with romantic melodramas on the wide stage. One of their first efforts was "Seven Chances," starring Miss Bourdeaux and F. J. Carmody, a D.C. drama critic. "Jake Carmody was the brother-in-law of Ludelle Hinaman,"

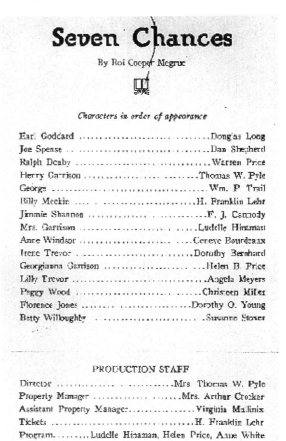

Mrs. Hoyle recalled. "He was very funny." By the time they gave the play for the third time in February 1929, they had raised enough money to buy a clock and bell system for the school and some supplies for themselves as well as for the library. "Zip" Lehr remembered that they "took the play up to New Market one night and had them hanging from the rafters of the Grange Hall."

In the theoretically "dry" Twenties, the local constables and deputy sheriffs, who had been adequate for rural Montgomery County before the automobile era, were finally replaced by

policemen. In April 1922 the Commissioners, through an act of the General Assembly, gained the power to name constables-at-large or policemen, and five officers and a chief were given two-year, political appointments. They established an office at the Rockville courthouse and provided the department with five motorcycles and a Ford coupe for Chief Charles T. Cooley. The chief was paid $1,800 a year, the men $1,500, and all received $300 to cover the cost of their uniforms, equipment, and motorcycle maintenance.

LeRoy Rodgers, known generally as "Dinks," covered the Bethesda and Chevy Chase areas, and Guy Jones patrolled Silver Spring-Wheaton. The police force met daily at 2 pm on the Courthouse steps and spent a great deal of its time chasing rum runners and trying to apprehend bootleggers and still operators. Enforcing the traffic laws became increasingly onerous, especially for Rodgers and Jones, but trying to catch chicken thieves may have taken up more police time. William Aud, a former sheriff, replaced Cooley as chief in 1924, and he was succeeded by Alvie Moxley, another former sheriff, in 1926. Chief Moxley served for the next nine years, a period of great change.[14]

In 1927 the legislature authorized the expansion of the force to twenty men including three sergeants and three patrolmen first-class and circumscribed the power of the County sheriff. The only job protection an officer had was being a member of the proper faction of the political party in power, which usually meant being a Lee Democrat.

Feeding this period of rapid growth and giving it structure as well as sustenance were two more important developments, both from the fertile mind of politico E. Brooke Lee: the creation of suburban taxing areas and of the bi-county Park and Planning Commission. In his 1926 campaign for the House of Delegates, a race he made as a favor to Governor Ritchie, Lee proposed making the whole Bethesda election district a special taxing area since that was where most of the small, self-taxing towns were located and seemed to be the region making the most noise about the need for better schools, police protection, and other expensive services. After the election and in response to pressures from civic groups east of Rock Creek, Lee expanded his proposal to cover about the same area as the WSSC and to include control of parks, garbage collection, and zoning.

Brooke Lee, who was immediately chosen Speaker of the House, feared loss of his political power in Montgomery County and hoped to defuse the growing split between the agricultural upper county, which opposed tax increases and more bonded indebtedness, and the burgeoning suburbs, which wanted more government involvement in their rapid growth as well as more services. In early 1920, Major Lee made an uneasy peace with Robert Peter, who controlled the upper county and the courthouse gang, by putting together the United Democratic Clubs. Now the suburban boom from which he and his family were profiting was threatening this shaky coalition.[15]

Led by Sacks and Tuckerman, Bethesda's leaders saw in Lee's initiative an opportunity to split from both up-county and Silver Spring by incorporating their town as a city and absorbing the rich tax base of Chevy Chase while they were at it. Chevy Chase quickly declined the honor, with some expressions of horror that a tawdry upstart had proposed such a union.

From a Civic Federation meeting in the Battery Park clubhouse on December 13, 1926, went up a call for a new form of government. While President O. O. Kuhn tried to keep order, Emory Bogley presented the report of his committee on by-laws only to be immediately upstaged by George Sacks's resolution calling for a municipal government for the whole election district. Sacks and his followers had concluded that Bethesda had "outgrown" the county government of its rural past. The idea was referred to the committee on legislation and legal action chaired by Walter R. Tuckerman, but Lee's concept had precedence and, in several ways, made the whole 7th Election District into a town, complete with a mayor, no matter what dowagerish Chevy Chase thought.[16]

The plan Lee finally hammered into shape greatly increased the power of the County Commissioners while creating two suburban districts divided by Rock Creek. It called for opening County office buildings in Silver Spring and in Bethesda, and for taxing suburban residents to build and maintain their streets, sidewalks and street lighting. Each of the suburban districts would have its own executive (a whole new commissioner district was created for Bethesda), and its own revenues and budget. The State legislature passed Lee's proposal in 1927.

In the same session, the General Assembly authorized an $800,000 bond issue for County

road construction making possible the widening and paving of Wisconsin Avenue, which along with Massachusetts and Connecticut Avenues, had been improved some three miles out from the District Line just the year before. Lee thus separated the expensive suburbs near the District from the rural up-county, which seemed satisfied with high-crowned and graveled two-lane roads, two-room schools, and short walks to the "facilities," although indoor plumbing was becoming more popular and was an advertised feature of most new homes in Rockville.

While this major restructuring of the County government was in progress, E. Brooke Lee, in another burst of enlightened self-interest, introduced the concept of professional land planning and the idea of a regional planning agency into the political bouillabaisse. In 1926 Congress established, as an advisory body, the National Capital Park and Planning Commission, which began a regional study of the Potomac and Rock Creek valleys.

Governor Ritchie, who generally opposed the growth of Federal power, appointed his own commission; then Brooke Lee invited in his own expert. Lee discussed his plans with his friend and attorney, the WSSC's Howard Duckett, and after a series of meetings, staged a dinner for some two hundred influential men from both Montgomery and Prince George's County at the City Club in the District. Lee laid out his plan for a bi-county planning body that would take over control of highways and subdivision zoning from the Sanitary Commission. The response was so enthusiastic that Lee forgot to collect the price of the meal from his guests, each of whom was expected to pay for his own, and accepted the whole $630 tab himself.

Despite opposition from counsel J. Bond Smith and engineer Robert B. Morse of the WSSC, Lee won Duckett's grudging support and brought the bill they drafted to the House floor two months after being elected Speaker and then steered it to passage. The law created the Maryland-National Capital Park and Planning Commission composed of six commissioners, three from each county, named, in theory, by the Governor.

The Commission had the power to tax, to issue bonds, to acquire park land, and to create a master plan for zoning and subdivision control. On Sunday night, April 17, 1927, the leaders of the County Democratic party met in Silver Spring and decided to have the Governor

name banker Robert Hilton of Rockville, who chaired the State Central Committee, attorney George P. Hoover of Chevy Chase, and E. Brooke Lee's younger brother, Blair, as Montgomery County's commissioners. Blair Lee resigned a year later and was replaced by his partner in the real estate and building supply businesses, James H. Cissell.

Builders and real estate men dominated the M-NCP&PC in the early years. J. Bond Smith resigned from the WSSC to become the Commission's first counsel, and builder Thomas E. Hampton of Bethesda was chosen as secretary-treasurer. The Commission then hired planner Irving Root from Flint, Michigan, and went to work. Within a year he had produced a preliminary master plan, and in 1932, the Commission began building the local park system with the help of the Federal Capper-Crampton Act, which paid a third of the cost. By the time Root left in 1941 to become head of the District's parks, the agency had acquired more than 1,400 acres for park land.

The tax rate was established at ten cents per $100 (3¢ for planning, 7¢ for parks) and did not increase for thirty years, but it did add another fee to suburbanites' tax bills. In 1927, in addition to the WSSC levy, home owners in the Western Suburban District also paid ten cents per assessed $100 plus ten cents more in Bethesda and twelve cents in Chevy Chase as a fire district tax. [17]

The creation of the Eastern and Western Suburban Districts and the establishment of a master plan for parks and highways by the M-NCP&PC occurred just before the Roaring Twenties' building boom blew a head gasket and then threw a rod. But when banks failed, businesses collapsed and land values plummeted, the WSSC, the Suburban District structure and the Park and Planning operations helped provide stability and hope for the future of Bethesda.

While the Silver Spring to Bethesda highway was grinding its tortuous way over and around the hills west of 16th Street and engendering humorous canards about its wandering path being designed to touch as much Brooke Lee land as possible, Bethesda got its County Building. The Morrison Brothers were the prime contractors for the $30,000, two-story, native stone structure at the southeast corner of Wisconsin and Montgomery Avenues. The Tenley-town firm of Louis Perna and Sons, Italian

The County Building at Wisconsin and Montgomery Avenue

masons who had their own quarry in Maryland, did the stone work, but much of the granite came from the Stoneyhurst quarries. The walls spanned eighteen inches above grade and were even thicker in the basement with its steel-barred jail cells. The building contained nine, well-finished offices and a large, handsome hearing room. Impressive woodwork and gleaming hardware embellished the high quality project.

Abe Morrison was as proud of the County Building as of anything he built.

It was a beautiful stone building, solid stone, furred and plastered. It had concrete steps up and a veranda and four big pillars that went all the way up to the second story. Why the hell they tore it down and built this thing they got now I never could understand. It even had an auditorium in it and four cells in the basement. It was a beautiful job.

The police established a 24-hour presence in Bethesda, and the building inspectors and Park and Planning officials opened offices in the County Building. Judge Alfred Wilson resumed his duties as justice of the peace, and James C. Christopher became the County Clerk as Dr. Perry staffed his office as County Commissioner for the Western Suburban District.

For all practical and political purposes, Dr. Perry was Bethesda's first mayor. When William Van Ness of Chevy Chase raised a question about Perry's accepting extra pay for what was supposed to be a full-time job, the good doctor, who still made his chauffeur-

driven rounds and kept regular office hours, grudgingly refunded the fifty dollars a month to the County treasury.[18]

By the summer of 1928, with Bethesda's government ensconced in its new quarters, two other finishing touches were in the wings. The contract was let for a $30,000, three-span, steel bridge over the B&O tracks between Connecticut and Wisconsin Avenues to complete what would be called East West Highway, and in March of `29 ground was broken for the Madonna of the Trail monument diagonally across from the County Building.

On Friday afternoon, April 19th, Bethesdans gathered to dedicate the statue honoring pioneer mothers before some 5,000 spectators. Walter Tuckerman presented the deed to the property he had donated; Postmaster New accepted the statue for the people of Bethesda

Bethesda's Madonna

and Mrs. Getzendanner accepted for the DAR. Judge Harry S Truman, president of the National Old Trails Road Association, spoke, and Mrs. William Talbott, assisted by young Winsor and Willson Offutt dressed in their new white outfits, unveiled the cast concrete Madonna, last of a series of twelve. William Tyler Page then recited The American Creed.

Soon after the creation of the suburban taxing districts, the State began issuing driving permits in Bethesda, at the fire house until the stone County Building was finished. By then Sgt. "Dinks" Rodgers and patrolmen Joseph Oldfield, Oscar T. Gaither, G. Dean Wilkinson and Joseph A. Case operated a round-the-clock patrol in the Bethesda district. The day men worked ten hours, and the two night men had a fourteen-hour shift and took turns napping by the phone. Since they had no radios, the men on patrol called in from time to time. Later they used a red light on the top of the County Building to signal the man on the motorcycle to check in.

This was the police force James S. McAuliffe joined in 1929. Charles Federline, the historian of the Montgomery County police force, concluded: "It was a truly important appointment for the department. No other single person had a greater impact on the direction, professionalism, and image of the department than James McAuliffe."[19]

Jim McAuliffe, "Rix," grew up in Friendship Heights. He had the usual chores around home such as pumping water and cleaning out the chicken coop, and he also had a paper route. Other than those jobs, one of the first he recalled getting paid for was chipping ice out of the trolley tracks at the time of the Knickerbocker snow. After graduating from St. Ann's school in Tenleytown, McAuliffe entered junior high school at McKinley Tech, but he did not stay there long. "It was a rough school, junior Tech at 7th and O," he explained.

Some boys were fighting, and the teacher put me out in the hall although I wasn't involved. My daddy was working in that school as an engineer at that time, so I thought , "This is going to be bad for me" so I went on down the fire escape and came home. I was finished at that school. I was 16 or so, 10th grade.

He apprenticed in the plumbing, heating, and sheet metal trades downtown and soon was skilled enough to seek jobs on his own out in the County. McAuliffe also played a lot of baseball as well as other sports. He was a very fast fielder and a good hitter.

When the volunteer fire department organized in Bethesda, 19-year-old Jim McAuliffe joined and for a while slept at the firehouse.

The first one down the pole got to drive the engine, and one day when the big bell, as we used to call it, went off, I was upstairs and slid down the pole and jumped up into the driver's seat, and Dick Custer, who was a fireman in Washington, climbed up alongside me. And they opened the doors, and we went out and got up to where East West Highway joins, and he said, "Where's the fire?" I said. "I thought you knew," he said. But I was driving, that's what was important.

The fire department helped me get the police job. It was an important part of the neighborhood, and I was a good fireman for quite a while. I spent a lot of time there and did a lot of work for them. I was on the hook-up drill team, and we competed with other fire departments. I was a pumper man like John Adair.

I didn't play ball with the Fire Department. I played with the Chevy Chase Bearcats. We had a pretty good team. We wound up as champions in this area for a while when I was twenty-two or so. They played serious. We were in the County league for a while.

Later in the County League, I played for Glen Echo. They gave me a pair of spiked shoes and a glove and tickets to Glen Echo Park to come over and play for them. You could hire a couple of baseball players in those days. We had a couple from downtown. One of the boys that played for us, Bobby Stevens, he went up to the majors and got beaned or something up there. He was playing, I think, with Philadelphia. We had some good players.[20]

We played at a place called Trimont, one of the places, on Wisconsin Avenue, a half-mile or mile north of the District Line. Counselman used to ride a horse down and watch the games. It was quite a sight to see him coming in on that horse, right through the ball diamond. There was another field we played on out Georgetown Road where the Broadhursts lived, all through there.

McAuliffe established himself in Bethesda at an early age as a good worker, an excellent athlete, and a nice guy to be with down at the firehouse. One of his fellow firemen and coworkers was Red Spiller, a plasterer and sometime bootlegger who lived in Woodmont. Spiller was working on a job in Bethesda one day when the fire siren went off. He jumped into his new, red Ford roadster, roared down Old

Georgetown Road and turned sharply onto the high banked bed of the trolley tracks and yanked at the brake. The car shuddered, the front wheels slewed, and the roadster rolled over on its side. Red clambered out as firemen ran to help him. "Let it lay," he yelled. "Let's go." And he sprinted for the fire engine leaving his car draining water and gasoline into the street.

McAuliffe remembered him:

> He was a wild one. He had that reputation. For a while he worked for me in the sheet-metal business. We were doing some work on the Kenwood Club. I hope the work is still there. He was helping me, and he made some comments to some of the golfers there, and they reported it and it came back to me. I was working for Ketchem, plumbing and heating, he was taking on a little sheet metal work. He called me in about it. And I called Spiller in. I always liked him, he was a little wild, but I liked the guy.[21]

When he was twenty, McAuliffe married and went to live in the house his father built at 320 High Street in Friendship Heights. His son, Circuit Court Judge James McAuliffe, recalled his mother and her family.

> Mom was a Morningstar. Her parents established their home in Barnesville. Mom was a very good student in school and went as far as the family means would allow. She came down to Bethesda as a young girl, fifteen or sixteen years old, and worked for the telephone company. She was a very good operator and became a supervisor.

So McAuliffe had a profitable trade, a new wife, and a good bunch of friends at the firehouse. Then in one game as he was running across the outfield reaching for a line drive, he felt something inside his ribs pull loose.

> I had started to make a business of my own, and I was doing pretty good too, till I fell one day playing ball. I ruptured a blood vessel or something in there. I started upchucking blood that night, but it healed. I had to take it easy for a while. I went in as an assistant manager of a bowling alley, not Hiser's, down on Leland Street under the Ford dealer. But we were going to have a baby so I needed a better job.

> I was not much of a politician, but Dr. Perry was a leader at that time, and "Dinks" Rodgers was sergeant at the police station, and I knew him. He was instrumental in getting me on. He was also a fireman. I had recommended him for captain of one of the squads before I got on the police force; I guess this was a way of returning the favor. Dr. Perry was the one that got me the ap-pointment. I was the eleventh man on the force.

> Harleys was about all we had to ride when I first went on the force. Joe Oldfield was my instructor, and he didn't tell me about the clutch on that motorcycle. So I came out of the garage and went straight over into the bank and bent the handlebars all up, hurt my elbow. I was kind of a little bit wild myself. So even with the handlebars all bent up, I jumped on the darn thing and rode it all around Bethesda. I wanted to conquer it anyhow.

> Later we had a roadster, and we could ride in that from 2 o'clock to 8 o'clock in the morning if we were working the night shift. The night shift was kind of long, fourteen hours. We got two days off every other week, during the daytime. We had seven straight nights.

> They gave you a revolver and didn't tell you which end the bullet comes out. We were making our own bullets. We'd get the lead from some of the telephone people. We couldn't afford to buy them. They also gave us a blackjack, which I never liked. And a full uniform including a reefer, and a pair of handcuffs.

> I used to ride home sometimes for my lunch, and take my boys, John and Jim, for a little ride around the neighborhood. They got a kick out of that. Jim was not much for getting on a motorcycle, but John was.[22]

> My older brother John was a Metropolitan policeman who got killed down there, No. 7, in Georgetown, shortly before I went on the police force. My mother wasn't in favor of it. But I took it. I don't know whether it was meant to be a permanent job or temporary. I thought it would just be temporary, but it ended up forty-two years of it.

Crime was not a serious concern for Bethesda during this time of rapid growth although increasing reports of house robberies in Chevy Chase began to appear in the newspapers. Punch cards were a problem off and on as were slot machines, claw machines, and pinball machines that paid off in more than free games. Down in Miller's Flats, Willie Smith was building a bad reputation; someone was usually selling home-brew on weekends, and there were places in the Triangle where one could buy a pint or find a prostitute at almost any time.

One of Bethesda's few violent crimes of the period took place in the "Flats" in 1931 when Fred Oldfield went looking for beer and got into some sort of dispute with Maynard Miles who hit him in the head with a stone and killed him. Miles, a black man, was sentenced to three years, which suggested that some doubt existed as to who was to blame for the violence.

The police discovered stills in the basement of a home on Maple Avenue and in an old house in Woodmont and found another out in the grove near the old Beane school. Moonshining and bootlegging were constant problems when McAuliffe became Bethesda's rookie policeman. "We worked on prohibition by looking for stills in the woods," McAuliffe recalled. "Chief Moxley was the greatest one for calling you to tell you he thought he knew where there was a still. That man was twice my age but he could walk you to death, and he was delighted to find a still to bust."

One of the problems the police tried to stay out of was the "war on spooners" declared by the Newcomb Club and residents of several dark neighborhoods, especially out Alta Vista way. Young couples, mostly in cars with D.C. tags, were causing the problems. "They park in your lanes, in your driveway, in the wheat fields, and anywhere they can get until 4 o'clock in the morning," said Mrs. Cora Potter. Better street lighting and more police cooperation were requested.[23]

Once in a while there was some excitement when a still was found or a rum runner was caught, but that was rare. When arrests were made, the miscreant had to be taken to the station on the back of the motorcycle or in the car of a cooperative citizen. In the rural upper-county, there was talk of reviving the whipping post for chicken thieves, and some farmers started "branding" their hens by clipping off a particular toe. But except for an occasional weekend shooting or knifing and some awful automobile accidents and train-car collisions at grade-level crossings, there was not much violence. McAuliffe had trouble recalling an incident in which a gun was used.[24]

I knew the constable up there in Bethesda, a fellow named Caywood. He was a wild bird. I remember one time, the "Run" used to be down there, that was a black settlement, we went down there one time to raid a crap game. They were shooting out in the middle of the street, and we were sneaking up on them, and they started running. I was chasing one and there was Caywood with his guns out shooting overtop of my head. Nobody thought much of it at the time except me; I didn't like the idea.

He had a car with the top down, and he'd usually be riding around town with a couple of ladies with him. And he wasn't any spring chicken then.

Edward Caywood with his wife, Julia Har-

low, had operated a canal lock from 1893 until 1911 when they moved to Bethesda and built a house in the "flats." Deputy Sheriff Caywood worked as a guard at Chevy Chase Lake from time to time. Mrs. Caywood was storekeeper Sophia Shackleford's sister.

Bethesda did not stop growing after the stock market crash and the beginning of the great Depression, but it slowed perceptibly until the New Deal brought an eager horde of government workers to town and created programs that encouraged home building. Applications for building permits, which had begun slipping in 1927, dropped rapidly. Some developments stood unfinished for years; a few completed houses sat empty for many months, and the number of properties sold for failure to pay taxes increased rapidly.

Several grand projects disappeared altogether. For eighteen months prior to the Crash, the Great Falls Bridge Company, Harry A. Seay, President, had been gathering permits and investors for its planned 1,740-foot, steel, toll bridge over the Potomac at Great Falls. The bridge would connect Conduit Road to the new George Washington Parkway on the Virginia side and have spotlights to illuminate the Falls at night. Preliminary work began in February 1930, but then the plan and its backers vanished as quickly and thoroughly as unwise swimmers at Great Falls.

Another plan that disappeared in the cascade of sell orders, bank failures, worthless notes and bankruptcies was the proposed Bethesda public library. The women's clubs had been promoting the library idea for some time when, in May 1927, Mr. and Mrs. Frederick A. Parkhurst appeared at a meeting at the Bethesda school and offered to donate a large lot they owned on Edgemoor Lane under certain conditions. The lot cost the Parkhursts $16,800 and the planned library-auditorium was budgeted at $30,000. The Parkhursts would pay half, but the community would have to raise $23,400 to match their contribution.

O. O. Kuhn urged Bethesda to meet the challenge and, of course, a committee was formed. Colonel Wallace Craigie chaired the meeting at which William Tyler Page, Dr. Edwin Etz, Thomas Pyle and others including Adeline Pratt of Baltimore spoke enthusiastically for the project. Miss Fannie Fogleman was elected secretary of the library and auditorium fund and an account was opened at the Bank of

Bethesda. Children began saving pennies to buy library books, and every civic-minded organization in town supported the project. But it evaporated like cotton candy at a carnival as Parkhurst's Pierce Arrow distributorship died in the collapse of the luxury-car market. The Newcomb Club took up the task of creating a public library.

Some government projects went down the same drain. In late 1928 the M-NCP&PC approved the construction of a hundred-foot-wide parkway to Great Falls following the route of the old Bradley Hills trolley line. George Sacks, Colonel Hampton, Dr. Perry and Mr. Root were all involved, but nothing happened except that the right-of-way was maintained as well as another bottleneck where Bradley (Hills) Boulevard burrowed under the B&O.

On the other hand, some projects not only survived but actually prospered. The Chevy Chase Building and Loan Association, Incorporated, started life in 1929 in a rented room at the District Line. Shortly, it moved to more spacious quarters, and then in 1933, purchased a 50-by-150-foot lot and put up a brick, Georgian-style home in Bethesda. Within a few years the savings and loan was a sturdy fixture behind a white picket fence on the west side of Wisconsin Avenue at Stanford Street.

Lumber dealer Roger Eisinger was president of the corporation and of the board of directors, and J. Horace Smithey was the executive vice-president and secretary who managed the savings and loan. Smithey, a singer of some experience, also led the large, male choral group known as the Chevy Chase Chanters, which was founded in 1925. They sang everything from Bach to boogie woogie in concerts throughout the Capital area and were without local competition until the Newcomb Club's Bethesda Community Singers decided to start giving public performances in 1934 under the leadership of Mrs. Ruth L. Morgan.

Other sizable projects survived. One of these was the construction of the Baptist Home for Children on Greentree Road. The Columbia Association of Churches (D.C. Baptist Convention) started the Home in 1915 in a house donated by John B. Lord. The house was enlarged from nine to twenty-one

rooms, but the operation rapidly outgrew its Northeast home, and in 1924 the trustees purchased James Morrison's 140-acre farm for about $42,000 as a summer home and began collecting money for planned buildings on the Cedar Lane (Greentree Road) site.

Fund raising proceeded slowly until robber baron Jay Gould's son Edwin, a pious Baptist, volunteered to lend $84,000, the projected cost of the furnished building for twenty-five girls, if the Home's trustees would match it. The Columbia Association raised $90,000 for the other dormitory to house twenty-eight boys. Ground was broken in 1930 with John B. Lord IV, age 2, turning the first spade of earth.[25]

The Baptists hired Morrison Brothers to build the two large "cottages" of native stone, stucco and timber construction. Abe Morrison said it made him feel sad and kind of odd to tear down the house he grew up in as he cleared the land for the new structures. Edwin Gould laid the cornerstone of the girls' building in October 1930 before a crowd of some five hundred, and a little over a year later, the facility was dedicated with Mrs. Hoover in attendance. The reporters described the First Lady's costume down to her hat pin, and she surprised and pleased the sponsors by speaking briefly to the children. "We all hope that you'll have a very happy life in the home, and that the home will have a long life after you have gone into the world from it." The County helped by rebuilding the road out to Old Georgetown and by authorizing the WSSC to provide free water and sewerage for the Home.

The new Home had actually opened in June 1931 with two main buildings, Gould Hall for girls and Lord Memorial Hall for boys. Mary N. Talmadge, hired as supervisor of boys in 1922 and made superintendent in 1924, was in charge. Above her were a Board of Trustees and a Board of Lady Managers chosen by the local churches. The home admitted children

The main "cottages" of the Baptist Home for Children

from three to twelve years of age who could stay until they were sixteen.

Each of the new buildings had quarters for about thirty children plus a dining hall, play room, music rooms, nurseries and bedrooms for staff members. A kitchen, laundry, and workshop were also built. There was a large playground as well as plans for tennis courts and a real athletic field. At the rear, the hill down toward the creek was one of the best sledding areas for miles, and the creek soon boasted a fine swimming hole. A supervisor hired by the board of trustees farmed most of the 130 acres. The boys and girls worked in the gardens, and the Home used much of the produce. They sold the surplus, and although the farm did not make a profit, it provided good food and important learning experiences.

The children rose at 6:15 and, after bathing and taking care of their rooms, had breakfast at seven and worked at various chores until the school bus came at 8:30. The rule was "each child must do his share," and all had tasks and were expected to perform them satisfactorily. They cleared the tables and washed and dried the dishes while the littlest ones swept up the crumbs from under the tables. An observer noted that there "was very little grumbling and the children seem to enjoy working together." The tasks were rotated weekly.

When the school bus arrived, the children were each given a bag lunch prepared by Miss Talmadge and some of the older girls. Within a short time there were Baptist Home children in every grade at Bethesda Elementary and later at Alta Vista and at the junior high and high schools. The school buses returned about 4 pm, and most children had an hour of work and an hour of play before supper. Mrs. J. Reed Bradley visited the Home in 1939 and reported on a well organized and happy operation.

All the cooking is done by the older girls. The meals are planned by a staff dietician and as the girls grow old enough to work in the kitchen they are taught the proper way to prepare and serve foods. The girls are also taught sewing, mending and laundering.

The boys' interest is centered in the farm and general upkeep of the Home. There are chickens to be fed, eggs to be gathered, garden work to be done and their own rooms to be tidied and kept clean.

Mrs. Bradley noted the twelve-acre garden and the several hundred chickens as well as the apple and peach orchards, flower beds and rock gardens. She was told that when the Home moved to Bethesda, some of the children objected saying they did not want to become "hicks." Now, she wrote, most of them seemed to enjoy the farm and "go about their work with smiles and songs."

Dinner time was six, and at the average meal, the forty-eight children quartered there in 1939 consumed a half bushel of potatoes, sixteen quarts of milk, a half bushel of vegetables, sixteen pounds of meat, six loaves of bread, and more than a pound of butter. After they cleared away and washed the dishes, it was study hall for the school-age children and story time for the younger ones with their dormitory mothers. Bedtime varied but usually was about 9:30 for the older children.

On weekends there were movies at the local theaters or in their own auditorium. In the summer, they had picnics and days at Glen Echo and at the beach sponsored by various organizations. Two doctors and one dentist supplied free care, and the children were taken to church services on Sundays.

One by-product of the establishment of the Home in Bethesda was the revival of the Mt. Zion Baptist Church and of its Sunday school under the leadership of James Morrison Jr., oldest son of the owner of the farm where the Home now stood. Morrison staged band concerts and other fund raisers and supported the program with his own resources. The Rev. Ford Barker, a missionary returned from Armenia, took over the pulpit, and soon picnics were being held under the trees, a new, hundred-feet-deep artesian well was dug, and the ladies were helping out at the Home for Children.

The annual Donation Day Tea began in 1940 and soon became the Baptist Home's chief fund-raising event. At first the Home's constitution required children to leave at age eighteen, but in 1938, the by-laws were changed and no one left without a place to live and a way to support himself or herself. By 1940 nearly 200 children had been cared for and about $250,000 expended.

Mildred Carleton Johnson came to the Home in 1922 when she was six and her sister only four. She stayed until 1936 when she graduated from the University of Maryland and married. "It was just like growing up in a big family," she recalled. "Miss Talmadge's door was always open to us. She was truly just like a mother." Thanksgiving, when the alumni returned, and Christmas with its tree and

presents were special times. "Mom" Talmadge retired in 1943, but the Home's work went on.[26]

Despite the Depression, in 1930, the Chamber of Commerce decided to beautify Wisconsin Avenue. Washington Waters, who ran the campaign, asked Park and Planning to advise, and nurseryman M. G. Coplan offered to donate Japanese cherry trees to the cause. By March George Sacks announced that the plan was to plant elms sixty feet apart along the highway with dogwoods and cherry trees between them. The design included a circle at Wisconsin and Western and the widening of the avenue if the electric railway could be convinced to replace its old, ugly, wooden poles and move its tracks from the middle of the street. The project was to be a memorial to those who died in the Great War, and all the local garden clubs and thirteen civic associations quickly endorsed the idea.

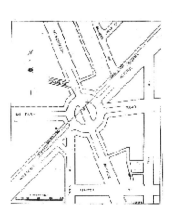

That was also the year when the County installed a "mechanical policeman" at Five Points. The first traffic light in Bethesda was controlled through rubber strips in the road and kept the traffic moving on Wisconsin while giving only short delays to cars on Old Georgetown-Edgemoor Lane and on Watkins/East West Highway. It did not take children long to figure out that they could change the lights by jumping on the treadles.

B-CC, at the time abbreviated B. C. C. H. S., became a junior-senior high school in 1930, and established "senior privileges" for the first group of 12th graders, all fifteen of them. Two cafeteria tables were set aside for their use. On "junior day" they were waited on by the 11th graders, and on senior day there were no classes for them. The girls' volleyball team won the championship that year, B-CC's first sport's title. Ten academic and five commercial diplomas were awarded to B-CC grads in the class of 1930.

In 1930, forty-four percent of the 8,460 telephones in Montgomery County were in Bethesda, 2,816 phones with a WIsconsin number and 920 subscribers on the BRadley exchange who had to pay fifty cents more a month to make calls into the city. That year the Bethesda PTA was asking for more teachers and for a school at Alta Vista.

At a Civic Federation meeting, George H. Lamar, a leading "dry" and streetcar supporter, introduced a resolution calling for a home-rule "charter" for the County under the provisions of the Maryland constitution. Lamar noted the need for both a County executive and for a local legislature. The suggestion was referred to committee. The Woman's Club of Bethesda adopted a resolution supporting jury service for women and the creation of juvenile courts. [27]

Millard Peake, who had sold his milk business to Chevy Chase Dairy and taken a job as a supervisor, was still selling ice on Rockville Pike in Woodmont and gaining fame as the County's best horseshoe pitcher. Bethesda Elementary won the County field day championship, and Bethesda-Chevy Chase High School with 92 points came in second to Rockville High's 127. Miss Holman's piano students, including seven-year-old Gilbert Gude, gave their usual recital at the Battery Park Community Club.

Dr. Perry suffered a slight stroke, ruled out another run for County Commissioner, and watched big Bob Hagner beat Republican Louis Keiser for his job, 9,351 to 8,603, in the 1930 off-year election and become Bethesda's second "mayor." The result was much closer than the experts had expected, but the portly doctor's political influence was far from over.[28]

The Hagner family had been among Georgetown's founders, and Peter's son, Bob, was proud of being one of Bethesda's early promoters. Robert Hagner acquired the property on the northeast corner of Rockville Pike and Watkins Lane in 1898 through his mother's family, the Dodges, but friends could not understand why he wanted to move to the "sticks." Hagner was an early member of St. John's vestry, built on Dodge-donated land, and some remembered him counting the collection money at his dining-room table with a shotgun beside him.

After working as an accountant for the IRS, Hagner received his real estate license in 1916 and actively encouraged Bethesda's growth. Horses were his special interest, and he kept several on the property and built a small riding ring beside his home. He was well over six feet tall, and some of his buddies called him "high-tops" because all his trousers seemed to end about eight inches above his shoes.

His wife died in the flu epidemic of 1918

leaving him with an infant daughter, Anne, who became well known as a rider and newspaper reporter. In high school she worked on both the yearbook and the newspaper and was editor of the *Tattler* as a senior. By then she was also a stringer for the *Star* calling in the blotter from the police desk in the County Building when there was anything to report and getting paid by the inch. One of Anne's friends remembered that the first year they were in the new high school they could see Hagner's house and barn from the second story windows, and when someone forget to close a gate and the horses galloped across the field the yell would go up "the horses are out," and Anne and her pals ran and corralled them.

Anne had passes to the swimming pools at the Lake and Glen Echo, and while getting to the Chevy Chase Lake pool was simply a stroll down the railroad tracks, the Crystal Pool was a different problem. Patsy Royster Lozupone recalled that she and Anne often went to the police station and asked the hunchbacked desk officer, Jimmy Nichols, when the next car was going to Glen Echo. "So we rode with the police everywhere," she said.

When the counting in census year 1930 was done, the area of the County with the largest population increase since 1920 was found to be Bethesda. Montgomery County had grown by 14,152 people in ten years to over 40,000, and Bethesda's population had jumped from 4,757 to 12,018.

The big story in 1930 was the drought. Not since Jubal Early and a few thousand of his friends came to town in 1864 had there been such a hot, dry, dusty summer. There were eleven days of 100° or more, and by the time the $90,000 Chevy Chase sewer line was finished, even Rock Creek was reduced to a trickle. Rainfall for 1930 measured 21.7 inches, about fifty percent of normal and the lowest total since measurements began. Streams dried up, wells failed and many up-county families had to haul water long distances in order to survive.[29]

As the Depression deepened, the drought compounded the disaster for County farmers. Many families could no longer meet their mortgage obligations and some could not even pay their taxes. In 1930 more than three hundred and fifty pieces of land were sold at auction owing over $100,000 in taxes. Most were bought in by the County.

Just as land developers such as the Hunts saw their plans turn to ashes, so the people of the upper county faced hard times, watched their fields become dust, put off improvements and repairs and raised loud complaints about the bond issues, schools and road building planned by the Commissioners in Rockville.

While the house painters, plasterers, plumbers and carpenters such as the Touheys of Cabin John, Oldfields of Bethesda, and Simpsons of Chevy Chase scrambled for work, most government employees were reasonably secure in their Civil Service jobs. The bad economic times hit various parts of the area unequally, and the division between the up-county and the suburbs festered, turned septic and then, for a generation, became a wound that would not heal.

Farm leaders organized the Non-Partisan Taxpayers League and fought the Lee machine demanding lower taxes and an end to programs such as the WSSC water and sewer projects, which, as they saw it, benefited only the suburbs. The County's debt had risen from about a half million dollars in 1920 to almost nine million in 1932, the year FDR swept Montgomery County. The bonded indebtedness of the County ate a third of its revenues, and in 1933, the County Commissioners abandoned their proposed $300,000 bond issue in the face of nearly unanimous rural opposition.

Retrenchment was in the air and to farmers' eyes the suburbs were not the solution, they and their constantly growing needs were the problem. One group of women disagreed.[30]

The Extension Service of the University of Maryland had sponsored Home Demonstration Clubs for a number of years with the help of both the County government and the USDA. The "agent" for Montgomery County was Blanche Corwin, who, by 1932, had been on the job for a decade. She was admired, respected, and even loved from Cabin John to Poolesville for her classes in cooking, sewing, and baby care. After a series of meetings with a number of up-county farm women over a period of months (sources and human memories disagree about the numbers of meetings, women and months), a decision was made to sell farm produce and products in the Washington suburbs.

At their club meetings, the women, with the help of specialists in nutrition, poultry, dairy products, and animal husbandry, worked to standardize their products. Potential products were brought to

meetings to be checked and graded. This process went on until the women fully understood the required standards for top quality.[31]

Among the early participants and leaders, from both Bethesda and the farm areas, were Mrs. James D. King, Mrs. Windsor Hodges, the A. A. Potters, Mrs. John Darby, Mrs. George W. Stone, Mrs. Julian Waters, Mrs. Walter R. Tuckerman and Mrs. B. Payton Whalen. Both the Federation of Women's Clubs and the Montgomery County Farm Bureau expressed interest and support. In the spring of 1931, the countryside was strangely silent, no frogs croaked as the drought continued. "The supposition is," the *Sentinel* reported on April 3rd, referring to amphibians, "that the entire family has become extinct." More land was sold for taxes. But the farm women continued with their plans. Mollie Gladhill, one of the pioneer members, recalled that "we worked on it for a year, almost a year at least, before we had the first sales day." By March of `31, the women had chosen Bethesda as the site.[32]

On the 2nd of February 1932, nineteen women brought their tables, their baked goods, their fryers and their eggs, their jellies, jams, pickle relish and canned beets, beans, peaches, and hopes to a small, vacant store between Leland and Walsh Streets; just a "hole in the wall" one called it. They had distributed handbills in the neighborhoods and run ads in the papers. Mrs. Whalen had promised to encourage club women to be patrons. But they did not know what to expect.

Monday had been the coldest day of the winter so far, and on Tuesday, the 2nd, the groundhog got snow on his whiskers. The lunchtime temperature was 32°. Had it been worth all the preparation and the effort to produce first-quality goods? Some of their menfolk were supportive, but others made fun of their plans. They helped the women unpack and then went off to Imirie's garage or on down to Georgetown, some smiling and shaking their heads, others hopeful.

The aproned women sold almost everything. The news spread on the party lines, and two weeks later, joined by a few friends, they came back and tried again. Maybe it had been a fluke as some of the men said. But the customers flocked to their tables and smiled and bought, and that night there were two dozen farm houses with more than just butter and egg money to count on oilcloth-covered kitchen tables. The sales became weekly events for both the sellers and the buyers, and both groups steadily increased in number.

Miss Corwin leased a small store at 4606 Leland Street, and they established the Wednesday and Saturday schedule. In those early days, according to Mrs. Gladhill, "Mrs. James King was on one side of the door and I was on the other, and then the rest of the ladies were all around us.... I was known as the chocolate cake lady." By that spring, more sellers had joined, and they raised a tent in front of the store to cover the crowd. By August, sixty women were regularly involved and taking in more than a $1,000 a week. The need for a more formal organization became obvious.

Then things got rather hectic. The lease would soon expire. The Extension Service decided that Miss Corwin was taking up too much of her time with the enterprise. The women had been looking at a Five Points site where a Piggy Wiggly had done good business, but the Edgemoor citizenry were opposed to the market locating in their neighborhood. The idea of a cooperative had been broached and opposition was developing to what some considered a "radical" idea. By September, when the whole operation moved to a large tent on Wisconsin Avenue just north of Leland Street where the firemen usually staged their carnival.

The husbands put up the tent just south of the Market's permanent site on land that had been assembled by Amanda Counselman in the 1890s and passed on to her heirs. Big outdoor advertising billboards outlined the area. The women spread sawdust on the ground under the big tent, which one participant estimated was about forty-five feet wide and ninety feet long. Then they purchased a large ice box; it held 600 pounds of ice, and on through the summer met their customers twice a week despite the controversies and dissension.

From across the street at his Esso pumps, Robert Eastham watched all this and saw the horses, which may well have included Gummel's ponies, grazing around the tent when the ladies were not there and the hordes of flies they attracted. He told his wife not to shop there, but she was one of the few who avoided the market where prices were often lower and quality better than in the local grocery stores.[33]

That hot August, several conflicts came to a boil all at once. The search for a permanent site for the market came to center on the intersection of Wisconsin and Old Georgetown between the new and imposing Bank of Bethesda building and the row of stone fronted stores on the front of Tuckerman's Edgemoor development. The Bachrach property, on the point there, seemed ideally suited to the leaders of the market. The affluent burghers of Edgemoor disagreed. They approved of the market, but not in their upscale front yard, which they labeled "one of the most beautiful and highly desirable residential sections of the metropolitan area."

Looking south from Woodmont in the early `30s - Note Bachrach's stores between the bank and Edgemoor and the trolley line in the middle of Wisconsin Avenue.

The *Sentinel* reported that County officials approved of the idea of a market but not of the proposed location. The newspaper also revealed that Blanche Corwin had been reprimanded for her stand favoring the site and told that continued agitation on her part might bring about the withholding of her pay. Meanwhile the women hired Albert Bouic as their attorney and moved toward incorporation while factions developed within their ranks.[34]

On Saturday, August 20, Dr. T. B. Symons of the University of Maryland, director of the agricultural extension service, "summarily dismissed" Blanche M. Corwin by telegram. He scheduled a Monday meeting in Rockville to explain the action and make future plans. Phone lines vibrated all weekend. Dr. Symons told reporters that "extension workers are not permitted to enter into activities such as those undertaken by Miss Corwin in connection with the market." He also said she had been dismissed for the "good of the service" because of the ill-feeling generated by the choice of the Edgemoor site. He emphasized that it was the duty of extension workers to cooperate with all the County's citizens and not just with the farmers. Dr. Symons named Miss Edyth Turner to replace Miss Corwin.[35]

Miss Turner never forgot the first day on her new job. The fact that there was a solar eclipse on August 22, 1932, helped her remember.

That evening there were two meetings. The smaller but perhaps louder group protested the firing of Miss Corwin. Those women hired her as the manager of their proposed market, without deciding about salary, and stated their intention of continuing much as they had since February. The leaders of this group included Mrs. A. A. Potter, Mrs. Lee Englehart, Mrs. Beulah Dill, and Mrs. John N. Darby.

The other, somewhat larger group assembled at the courthouse to hear from Dr. Symons, Miss Turner, and Otis W. Anderson who had been the County's farm agent since 1926. Dr. Symons stated that Miss Corwin had "repeatedly disobeyed instructions in regard to the farm market" and that while he approved of the idea, he opposed both the site in Edgemoor and the idea of the women going into debt. The officials called another meeting for the next Monday and said that they hoped to bring the two groups back together and "provide for sound operations."

In an editorial on August 26 the *Sentinel* concluded that "If the residents of the suburban

sections disapprove of the market being placed (in Edgemoor), the women of the county who furnish the produce should view the matter in the light of 'the goose that lays the golden egg.'"

The stormy meeting on the 29th failed to heal the wounds, and two separate organizations went their diverse ways toward similar goals. The group opposed to the University of Maryland's co-op plan, basically the supporters of Miss Corwin, stated that they had rented a site and would open their own market. The others followed the lead of State and County officials and moved toward incorporation and took steps to prevent equipment from being taken from the tent at Leland and Wisconsin. That night twenty-nine farm women decided to create a producer owned, controlled and operated cooperative.

The legal founders of the Farm Women's Cooperative Market, Incorporated chose Mrs. James D. King as their first president. Any woman who lived on a farm where the majority of the family's income came from the land and who was a member of one of the extension service clubs could become a member.[36]

Somewhat reduced in numbers, the market continued under the tent while seventy-five feet back from Wisconsin Avenue, Leon Arnold had the Morrison Brothers begin construction of a large frame building on a concrete block foundation. The women had agreed to rent it for $125 a month if he would build it. With Macie King in the chair, the organization changed its name to the "Women's Farm-to-Home Market," a name that they used in their ads but just about everyone else ignored.[37]

J. T. Hoyle had a special reason for remembering the Market.

At Jenifer Street was a large gas station owned by Ralph Bohrer who lived on Battery Lane . He also had a construction company. I was looking for a summer job and happend to run into him, and he thought I was a qualified engineer because one had just called him about a job. So he hired me, and he sent me up to Bethesda, told me where the place was and said, "My man, Gene Higgins, will meet you there with a steam shovel. Here are the plans" and so on, and he left.

So I went up there and found it and waiting for me was a County inspector. Well, I didn't know beans about how to start the thing but before the day was through we got finished laying the floor for the Market; we'd poured it. The County inspector didn't realize what he was

doing, but he was running the job and I just left him alone.

So I went back and Mr. Bohrer said, "How are you doing?" and I said, "You better go up there and look; I think it's finished."

While the 105-by-45-foot building took shape, Miss Turner brought extra overshoes and mittens for sale-days under the tent where the best means of keeping warm was to keep moving. By Thanksgiving, the simple frame structure was almost completed. The story-and-a-half market had gleaming white siding, big double doors at the front and back, and twelve-light windows under its asbestos shingled, hipped roof. Inside, the one big room was covered with vertical tongue and groove siding. There was nothing fancy about it, but now they could advertise "electric refrigeration."

A cabinetmaker in Rockville–Mildred Watkins remembered his name as Mr. Brown–made and installed the golden oak display cases. On Friday night, December 2, they had the grand opening with entertainment for visitors to the market. The sellers all wore their new, long, white uniforms.[38]

Meanwhile, up on Old Georgetown Road at Melrose, now Cordell, in an old Piggly Wiggly store, Miss Corwin and her loyalists had begun their own market and soon opened another on Carroll Avenue in Takoma Park. After about a year, the Bethesda operation moved to the east end of the same block and took up residence in what Mrs. Potter called the flat-iron building at the corner of Wilson Lane and Old Georgetown where the Sanitary Store had been. Under Miss Corwin's imperious rule and a sign that named it the Women's Farm Market without the words "incorporated" or "cooperative," this store operated well into the Thirties. The ladies who sold eggs and cakes there brought with them a group of loyal customers and hired a male butcher.

In the late 1930s, they moved to a small shop two doors from Dellinger's store on Wisconsin Avenue in Friendship Heights. Lloyd (Buzzy) Potter remembered Miss Corwin showing him how to attract customers to his pickup truck full of sweet corn across from that store. In the fall and winter he sold firewood, $21 a cord for the best and bundles of split kindling or surplus white pine, three for two dollars, beside his mother's dried flowers and house plants.

The co-op's board of directors hired Mrs. J. E. Shillinger of Somerset as their first manager

and proudly boasted that it was a market run entirely by women. Lillian Shillinger, graduate of the Carnegie Institute in home economics, was paid $70 a month, and Miss Turner and the extension service retreated to an advisory role. The board also began enforcing a strict dress code with all of the sellers wearing white dresses or uniforms. By Christmas, the membership had increased to forty-two and a waiting list was begun. Total sales for the first month in the new home were about $5000. By the next Christmas, the average had nearly doubled, and all through the rest of the Thirties, it was a slow month when the gross was less that $10,000.

Mrs. Mindeleff succeeded Mrs. Shillinger as manager in the fall of `33, and she was followed by Miss Wadsworth in the spring of `35. Then Katie Shaw, a power in Democratic political circles, became the manager in April 1937 and held the job for the next fifteen years. The co-op kept five percent of the sales as well as a monthly two dollar fee for each counter and began paying off its debts and building up a savings account. All co-op members owned capital stock in the corporation and shared in the surplus at the end of each year in proportion to their sales. Members of the co-op met occasionally at the new Milo theater in Rockville to see films and hear extension service talks on farm-to-market topics.[39]

Next door to the Market, Mrs. Shillinger opened the Farm Women's Exchange in the winter of 1933 where she offered tea and sandwiches and sold needlework, smocking, handmade dolls, quilts, and other craft work produced by some fifty County farm women who could not get down to the Market twice a week. This operation, called the Tea Room and open daily, continued for several years adding woven rugs and bags as well as wood work to its inventory and advertising "waffles, country sausage and coffee 35¢" in 1934.[40]

Despite the continuing Depression, the Market was an immediate success. Mrs. Gladhill recalled leaving her farm one morning with sixty cakes in the car. In those days a seven-inch, two-layer cake sold for a dollar. She baked all day on Thursday and Friday and seldom had to bring anything home. "What we

didn't sell, we ate," she said. One of her customers had her chauffeur come in every Saturday morning to buy an orange loaf cake. "When summertime came, we sold corn and beans and just everything out of the garden. . . . And dairy products, we had one woman who took a five-gallon can of milk every Saturday."[41]

Sometime late in 1934, the builder-owner of the market was approached with a good offer to purchase the structure and lot for another commercial enterprise, and by the next summer, he was about to sell. By then the market had become something of an institution claiming patronage from the White House and diplomatic corps as well as being an important source of income to scores of farm families. The ladies did not want to have to move again so the board of directors decided to borrow the money needed to buy the building and the land it stood on. They secured an option to purchase the property, which gave them a little time.

Mrs. Julian Waters of Germantown, who specialized in sausage, scrapple, chickens and eggs at her stand just a few steps to the right of the front door and who had just been elected the third president of the association, looked for a source of a lot of money while others investigated alternate sites.[42]

Someone suggested the Baltimore Bank for Cooperatives. Mrs. Waters described her visit:

When I went over to the Cooperative Bank in Baltimore and asked to borrow $50,000; the bank officials thought I was crazy. They told me that was a lot of money. They didn't believe a group of farm women could make that amount in a market. The president said he would take it up with his Board and I would hear from him. This was in September, 1935. Two weeks went by and we didn't hear anything. I spoke to the president again. This time it was another excuse, and more time slipped by. I contacted him once more. Finally a man was sent out to look the place over. I

had previously told the president that all I wanted him to do was pay us a visit himself some Saturday and see the business we were doing. I was beginning to be a mite discouraged when one Saturday just before Christmas, I looked up and there he was in person. After a cheery greeting, he said, "You may have the money." By Christmas the property was ours.[43]

Almost every account notes the event with amusement.

When the bank representative arrived at the market that Saturday morning, he got the shock of his life. The place was teeming with life. Cars were packed in the parking areas on three sides of the little frame building. Inside, the place was jammed with eager buyers. Flowers decorated every one of the 80 glass-covered counters. Behind each stood a farm woman seller, dressed in a fresh white smock, and busily engaged with customers.

To enlarge their parking lot, the ladies bought a 5,886 square foot lot on the corner of Willow and Wisconsin at the same time. That brought their property up to a total of 30,000 square feet.[44]

By 1940, much of the $17,000 second mortgage had been repaid and the first trust of $30,000 was being whittled down. Before the end of the war the competing market disappeared, and many of the women who had followed Miss Corwin's dissent from the co-op rejoined their old friends. Some like Charlotte Potter became long-time fixtures. According to her neighbor and fellow Homemakers' Club member, Mrs. C. R. Smith, "Mrs. Potter sold flowers there, and peculiar thing — When she sold a bunch of flowers the expression on her face looked like she was parting with a friend."[45]

The newspapers and the radio stations did stories about the market. Groups of farm women from all over the country and from other nations came to see, study, and admire the operation. Even popular national journals such as the *Readers' Digest* and the *Woman's Home Companion* took note, calling the Market "an institution as distinctively American as the Lincoln Memorial and the Washington Monument."

You stop before a showcase which contains the following items: One dressed chicken as golden yellow as a spectator's blouse at a tennis match, one shoulder of fresh pork in a delectable shade of blush pink, one mold of fresh sausage with sage, one without, one coil of fresh sausage links, one smoked, one mold of scrapple, one roll of head cheese, one pound of golden butter, one dozen per-

fectly matched white eggs, one pound cake, one sunshine cake. And in the center glistens a cake of ice in a glass bowl.

You wait impatiently while a Korean who is marketing for a foreign minister makes his deliberate selections. His purchases are then taken not from the showcase but from an electrical refrigerator behind the saleswoman. Before you can place your order, an eager young matron inquires:

"Did you bring any of that special sausage today?"

"Oh yes, Mrs. J—. One or two pounds?"

Later you learn that this specialist in pork products makes not less than six types of sausage to please patrons who like it mild, highly seasoned, especially peppered, or even flavored with celery seed. An average of one hundred hogs a year are raised and butchered on her farm to supply the needs of her customers.

Across the aisle is a farmer's wife who specializes in poultry. . .One woman is known throughout the Washington area for her piccalilli, another for her sauerkraut, a third for her baked beans and still a fourth for her noodles made with fresh eggs!

At one counter I learned that orders for firewood would be taken and at another orders for rabbits. I bought rich sweet pickled peaches at seventy-five cents a half-gallon, and delicious corn relish at twenty-five cents a pint. Deviled eggs that melted in the mouth cost three halves for ten cents and honey was offered at two thirds of what I pay in town.[46]

Within a few years many of the women had developed specialities. Reporters noted the following: salt-rising bread, ice-box rolls, Maryland beaten biscuits, peach and apple butter, hominy and baked beans, hams and bacon, pickled pears and peaches, ducks and guineas dressed for cooking or ready to serve, sweet and salted butter, buttermilk and cottage cheese, and flowers. In season, flowers and fruit decorated every counter. Tessie Lee Moxley became popular for her hollowed gourds, cut flowers and cleaned chickens. She also operated an inn in Claggetsville where she served chicken dinners.[47]

By 1940, Mrs. Waters' family was raising two thousand chickens and four hundred turkeys a year to meet the Market's demands. Except in the hottest summer months, the Waters butchered one hog every Tuesday and two on Fridays for the Market, and they had acres of corn and a huge garden full of tomatoes, cucumbers and cabbages.

The women and their daughters and husbands, brothers and sons, worked long and hard. Customers remembered Mrs. Burdette, one of the originals, and her hard working daughters. They recalled Mrs. Shorb's rolls, Mrs. Purdum's cakes and Mrs. Barnsley's jellies, cookies and pies. For many farm families Wednesdays and Saturdays were the easiest days of the long week. Hours of plucking chickens, of baking cakes, snapping beans, kneading dough and getting ready filled the other days and nights. One woman told the *Companion*'s reporter, "I may dress as high as fifty frying chickens for one market day and for the Christmas Eve market I dressed turkeys from 7 am to midnight. At 2:30 am we packed them into our truck."

On many farms, long-established practices changed and much of the production was re-designed for the sale days. The market undoubtedly was also a social institution of some influence at which rural women saw each other and exchanged news and gossip and at which city housewives met their country counterparts. Otis Weaver concluded:

This market has no doubt contributed to a better understanding between the rural and urban women who meet there. Compliments which the farm women frequently receive on their products are evidence of the appreciation of customers. Both groups are mutually benefited by the services of the market.[48]

And it paid. Farms were saved and children went to college. Barns were painted and people smiled again.

It has given us all a sense of security which even drought and depression cannot shake. We have helped out husbands to pay off mortgages and pay back taxes. Our homes are now equipped with electricity, running water and other labor-saving devices. We have been able to give our children a higher type of education and our social life is brighter because we have cash in hand. Few of us would be willing to return to the old plan of accepting what our husbands can afford to give us. We women have established an almost sure cash market. We are a cheerful group.[49]

Bethesda was still in transition. Barns, sheds and privies dotted backyards all over town although most of windmills had disappeared. Betty Milne, whose family came to a new house on Curtis Street in Chevy Chase in 1927, recalled the middle of Bethesda when she was a youngster in the Thirties.

The Gummels, they were good friends, and they kept ponies. We played up where the Ford Building is now at Leland and Wisconsin, grazed the ponies and played baseball there. Built our own sandlot field.

The Gummels had four ponies. They had Little Red, which was my pony since I was the youngest in the neighborhood. He was a little Shetland. And Matchless, he was a Shetland but he was black and white, and he was a little mean. The boys usually rode him, and Moonie who had one eye, she had an accident, and Princess. My brother usually rode Princess. But Princess killed herself coming out of their barn, hit her head. We used to muck out the stalls. Kenneth and Mildred and I rode the ponies, and she had a cart.

The Royers lived across the street. Then two Offutt families lived up the street. I knew the Fred Offutts, Billy, and Dougie, and Tommy, and Catherine was the mother. The Allisons were good friends with the Gummels, Roy and Horatio.

The Gummel kids and I sometimes went to Hiser's. Somebody would buy a fifteen cent ticket and go in, and the rest of us would go up the fire escape on the back, and the person with the ticket would let us in. I'd get nickels from my mother's gingerale bottles to raise the fifteen cents.

Even before the election of Franklin Roosevelt, Bethesda inched back toward what had been its accustomed rate of growth. Not all the important projects died in the crash although it was a disaster for Walter Tuckerman and others caught holding numerous second trusts.

In 1931, B. Francis Saul, M. Willson Offutt, Mrs. Walter E. Perry, and James C. Christopher 2nd died. James C. Christopher 3rd replaced his late father as clerk of the Western Suburban District. R. Granville Curry was named the first County Juvenile Court Judge, and Miss Willie Green Day, executive secretary of the Social Service League, became probation officer of the Juvenile Court. J. Fred Imirie was the new chief of the Bethesda Volunteer Fire Department. George P. Sacks joined the Board of Education to finish the late Mrs. Perry's term. Mrs. Calvin Milans took the blue ribbon for her "Lady Alice Stanley" rose, and Mr. H. D. Scantlin of Drummond won the peony-blossom prize at Somerset's annual garden show.[50]

And businesses bloomed in Bethesda. Early in the Depression, Mrs. Mazie Perham filled her front room with old furniture and three cats and presided over P&P Antiques in an old house just across Montgomery Avenue from the

County Building. Sarah Randall opened her cleaning shop, and Randall's became a Bethesda landmark later run by her cousin Nathan Kellner with tailor Nathan Cohen and presser-delivery truck driver George Rhodes.

Ed Stock, who told a friend that he planned to be a "gentleman farmer" when asked why he was studying agriculture at Cornell, started his nursery in an old shack his father owned on the ballfield across Wisconsin Avenue from the County Building. He and his brother Steve used their father's tools and Model-T and created a business "devoted to the principal that suburban life should give us fun." When Steve went off to college, Ed and Charley Rudd became partners and bought a four-acre tract on Bradley Boulevard, "just up from the viaduct," they advertised. They moved the shed there and soon had contracts to maintain more than a hundred gardens and the Quaint Acres development.

The nursery and shop on Bradley Boulevard

For a while they called themselves "hortitians." One of Stock Brothers' mottoes for their employees was "If you don't do any more than you're paid for doing then you're not earning what you do get." The business grew as the area recovered, and Ed Stock became locally famous for having grown up in Bethesda's best-known haunted house, having one of the best singing voices in town and heading the wartime Victory Garden campaign.

In late 1931, the Newcomb Club took up the challenge of establishing a public library. They were not the first, however. Seven years earlier, the Woman's Club of Bethesda had secured some space in George Bradley's hardware store and begun a circulating library. The Maryland Public Library Commission stocked the "traveling book shelf," and the ladies changed the collection every three months. They lent books

for two weeks and collected a fine of two cents a day on those overdue. This system lasted for several years in the mid-20s. But by 1931, those shelves were filled with hardware, and the Parkhursts' grand scheme had been abandoned. So the Newcomb Club under its president, Mrs. Benjamin C. Potter, took on the library as a major project. The club had maintained a small, circulating library for some time, and its store of books had grown to the point where it could be more widely shared.

The club's president headed the committee, which included, no surprise, Mrs. B. Peyton Whalen, along with Mrs. A. Brookhouse Foster, Mrs. J. K. O'Shaughnessy, Mrs. Charles W. Bouvet, Mrs. William Ross Dellett, and Mrs. J. A. Bell. They began collecting more books, and Mrs. Walter Tuckerman was the hostess at a bridge party fund-raiser at the National Women's Country Club.

Henry Hiser let the ladies show movies on Sunday when his theater was closed by the blue laws. Mrs. Royster sold tickets and her daughter, Patsy, took them. By the time the club had collected some three hundred books, Walter Tuckerman had been convinced to let them use two rooms in the old bank building on Edgemoor Lane.[51]

In October 1931, the ladies were busy cleaning up the small building in hope of opening by Thanksgiving with about 1,000 books on the shelves. Businessmen, prodded by their club-women wives, donated building supplies, heating equipment, and fuel. The library opened on December 8, 1931, and more than a hundred people signed up for library cards the first day. That winter the library, staffed by Newcomb Club volunteers led by Mrs. Foster, was a going concern with regular hours. Patsy Royster, a 7th grader whose mother signed a letter so she could read adult books, was one of those volunteers, and she remembered the library as a busy place.

In 1932 to have more space for its 4,000 volumes and growing clientele, the library moved to the basement of the Masonic Building

Second library faced Old Georgetown under the Masonic Temple (former Patty-Kitch-Inn) Mrs.Foster in doorway[53]

behind the Bank where the Imirie's Patty-Kitch-Inn had been located. That year the effort was incorporated as the Newcomb-Bethesda Public Library, Inc. with Mrs. George P. Sacks as president and an advisory board of ministers, business leaders and high school principal. When the effort to secure a special tax failed, the committee decided to charge three dollars per family for library use. The number of card holders dropped from 2,032 to about fifty.

After five years, the time, effort, and cost were too much for the Club, and the little library closed in 1936. Local schools were given first choice of the books for their own libraries, and the remainder were sold or sent to schools without libraries. Mrs. Foster, president of the Newcomb Club from 1934 to 1938, told Gertrude Bradley that "she and her coworkers never attended a funeral that was any sadder." She then began working to secure a tax supported and professionally staffed library for Bethesda.[52]

Mrs. Foster struggled for two years before having any real success and then for two years more to see the library finally open in 1940. The second Mrs. W. E. Perry, John Henry Hiser, Maj. Samuel Syme, Mrs. William H. Winkler, and B-CC English teacher Mary Mohler enlisted or were drafted into Mrs. Foster's army. The first sign of progress came in November 1938 when seventy-five citizens including Carey Quinn, John Overholt, Frederic Lee and Stella Werner attended a meeting chaired by hard-working Delegate Ruth Shoemaker at the County Building. A steering committee dragooned a community advisory group of about forty members and sent out questionnaires.

Their survey showed a lot more support in Bethesda than in Chevy Chase as well as a broad interest in reading and in the project. Mrs. Foster plowed on.

Tony Kupka became the boys' coach and athletic director at the high school in 1931 and finding himself with a $25 budget, staged a very successful alumni game as a fund-raiser. It became traditional. His basketball team won the County championship and the first baseball team went 11-1. In May 1932, B-CC boys and girls won both the junior and senior high school divisions of the annual County field day. Led by forward Lillian Lee who also lettered in soccer, the girls' basketball team took both the County championship and the sportsmanship trophy that year. Redheaded Lillian and her sisters Margaret and Rae were among the best athletes at the high school in those early years. The B-CC graduating class of 1932 numbered forty, second only to Rockville High's seventy-two.

Bethesda was recovering, but the up-county story was not as bright, and the relative prosperity of the suburbs did little to ameliorate the growing schism between the rural and urbanized areas. By the end of 1931, the price of wheat had dropped more than fifty percent and some 350 pieces of land went to auction for failure to pay taxes. In 1932 ,the venerable but impecunious Montgomery County Agricultural Society held its 79th and last Fair and sold its land to the school board. The fair grounds became the site of the school system's annual field days, the Rockville firemen's carnival, and later the new high school.

That year the Social Service League budget grew by $10,000 and grumbling increased about the cost of government and expensive luxuries such as new schools with fancy auditoriums. Almost one-third of the County tax levy for 1932 went to debt service and another third to the school budget. The County Commissioners pledged to lower the tax rate and then reduced their employees' salaries, including those of the teachers and police, by ten percent.[54]

Franklin Roosevelt swept the County as well as the country in the election of 1932. The County vote was FDR 11,804 and Hoover 8,257. In Bethesda, the Democratic ticket had 1,253 votes, Hoover 1,027; in Chevy Chase Hoover won 1,201 to 804, but Roosevelt was the overwhelming choice in the Glen Echo precinct 423 to 206. For the whole Western

Suburban area, the vote was very close, but Hoover carried the Bethesda Election District 2,434 to 2,408. The rest of the County noticed.

At one time, it had not been "respectable" to be a white Republican in Montgomery County, and more than one newcomer heard that it was a waste of time to register as Republican since the Democratic primary was the election that really mattered. Obviously, things political were changing in the 7th District.

In 1933, the banks reorganized and re-opened, and 3.2 beer returned. Hope returned, too, as Emergency Relief funds helped the Social Service League meet the needs of its growing clientele, and the Blue Eagle spread its wings over County businesses. More than a thousand Civil Works Administration projects made jobs for County workmen, who, among other tasks, built pairs of sanitary privies at forty-one schools. That was the year the Bethesda fire department bought its first ambulance, a Buick modified by the Flexible Company. It cost $2,385.[55]

When the Harold Ickes' Public Works Administration began "pump priming," Brooke Lee and Bethesda's Frederic Lee, no relation, were high in the ranks of local decision makers. They funneled school, road, and park projects to those New Deal programs, and the white CCC boys from their camp in Garrett Park cleaned up Rock Creek Park, while the African-American CCCers from Carderock worked along the canal. The Agriculture Adjustment Act helped local farmers, and the controls placed on wheat acreage raised prices to $1.20 a bushel.

In September, the long awaited vote on the repeal of Prohibition took place. In Bethesda, 750 voted for the repeal delegates and 197 for those opposed, in Chevy Chase it was 725 to 195 for repeal, in Glen Echo 245 to 30, and County-wide 6,199 to 2,891. Only Damascus and Takoma Park voted against repeal. The "drys," led by Mrs. Jesse W. Nicholson and George H. Lamar, "viewed with alarm" the return of hard liquor, but in the Western Suburban District, the vote was an overwhelming 1,859 for repeal to 440 against with eleven votes for unpledged delegates to the State convention called to ratify the 21st Amendment.

The end of Prohibition also marked the start of the County Liquor Control Board and the "dispensary" system as the County government became the sole legal distributor of spirits. Bethesdans were deeply involved in this process from the start. The Commissioners chose

Dr. Benjamin C. Perry to head the new and controversial board, and appointed John C. Walker of Chevy Chase to the Board and put him in charge of the dispensaries. For the Bethesda area, they named George A. Sacks manager.[56]

Neighborhood objections delayed the licenses for the Congressional and Columbia country clubs and for the Rossdhu Castle Club and Bondareff's and Isidor Suser's stores on Brookeville Road, but soon beer was flowing freely at a nickel a glass and ten cents a bottle from more than a hundred establishments willing to pay fifty dollars for an "on" license and twenty-five for an "off" license, which allowed the sale of beer "to go," minimum order twelve bottles.[57]

By school year `32-`33, the junior-senior high school library had accumulated about 2,300 books, and Takoma Park-Silver Spring high school had become Bethesda's "traditional" sports rival. The "Demons," as the Bethesdans now chose to be called, won the County basketball championship again that year.

The Class of `32 had the first printed yearbook thanks to hard work by Neal Potter, *Tattler* editor Haylette Shaw, and editor-in-chief Ray Gingell. All the photography was by Malcom Walter of Kensington. In `33 the students, led by senior class president and *Pine Tree* editor Haylett Shaw, published the first full-sized yearbook with five pages of ads.

Neal Potter was president of the student council for both of those school years. In the class of `33, only one girl and seven boys at B-CC earned "general" diplomas; all the rest were taking the "academic" program, by far the highest proportion in the County. Bethesda-area students, who wanted to take commercial courses, such as Loretta Tuohey from Cabin John, had to transfer to the Rockville high school and provide their own transport. The PTA sponsored high school band, in its third year, played a Newcomb Club Library benefit and at a University of Maryland football game as well as for school assemblies.[58]

The boys' team featured 6'2" Walter Johnson, speedy Bill Guckeyson, and high-scoring Dick Nichols. "Our offense was basically fast break," said Coach Kupka. "We generally got a basket if we controlled the tap." In those low-scoring days of center-jumps after every basket, B-CC whipped Sherwood 52-10, Rockville 60-23, and Gaithersburg 60-10. In six games they outscored their County opponents 323 to 69.

The girls' basketball team led by juniors Elsie Winkler and Lillian Lee, who were both about 5'10", won the County championship and then went on to take the District AAU title and like the boys rolled up big scores. Lillian Lee Phillips recalled her coach's rules: "We had to eat right and go to bed and get plenty of sleep. She told us and we did it. We loved to play. She was never hard on you; we never got bawled out."

Coach Kupka and his `33 team

Beatrice Crocker and her `33 team

At the annual field day in May 1933, B-CC won the junior high division led by the girls' relay and volleyball teams and Howard Mizell's victory in the 50-yard dash and record-setting 7'11" in the standing broad jump. Rockville beat B-CC in the senior high division, but the Bethesda girls won the title in volleyball and Lillian Lee set a new record in the running broad jump of 15' 11". The boys did not do as well, but Bill Guckeyson won both the shot and hundred yard dash. At the State meet in College Park two weeks later, the girls' volleyball team smashed its way through teams from Baltimore, Howard, Caroline and Kent counties to win the championship.[59]

Bill Guckeyson, John W. actually, lived with his grandmother, Mrs. F. W. Council, in Chevy Chase where he was reputed to be the biggest shredded-wheat eater in the neighborhood. Guckeyson was by far the best athlete in the class of 1933, and perhaps the best athlete ever at a school with a tradition of sports and sportsmanship. He was captain of the high school soccer team for three years and of the basketball team for two. His parents were circus acrobats, and his grandmother was said to have had a horse act at one time. Guckeyson excelled in soccer, baseball, and basketball, but track was his forte. At the State track meet in June `33, he broke the high school shot put record with a toss of fifty feet, the old record was 46'7", and then won the 100-yard dash with a time of 10.2 seconds.

Guckeyson went to the University of Maryland on a football scholarship, and then, after some prepping at Bullis, entered West Point in 1938 where he played soccer and became a world class javelin thrower. Those who played with and against him at the high school level have never forgotten him. The stadium at B-CC was named for him as was "Zip" Lehr's son.

1933 was quite a year and a very interesting senior class. The high school kept growing, and the teachers survived a long period without paychecks. Austin Carlin, business manager of *The Tattler* and circulation manager of the yearbook, worked from a small office in the front hall. Class president Haylette Shaw won the County oratorical contest, and Steve Fuller, class president as a freshman and junior, was chosen the "most representative boy." Jane Heineken won that honor among the girls. Voted most popular were Bob Althaus and Hariette Hartnett; best looking, Walter Johnson Jr. and Jean Duvall; most athletic Bill Guckeyson and Lillian Lee, and most studious, Isabella Counselman and Neal Potter.[60]

Economically, the next year was not much better. Dorothy Plitt, a member of the class of `34, recalled that they were asked to bring

Lillian Lee   Bill Guckeyson

electric fans to their graduation ceremonies but that people fainted anyhow.

I graduated on a Wednesday night, and on Thursday morning my mother took me down to the phone company with one of my father's C&P business cards, and on Monday I was sitting at a switchboard. They paid us $13.33 for a six-day week and sometimes we had to work a split shift. I wore out shoes walking to work.

I gave my mother five dollars, put twenty-five cents into the Bank of Bethesda for a Christmas fund and had eight dollars to spend. And all my friends said, "A job! How did you find a job?"

I remember when the bonus marchers came by; we could hear them, and the supervisor would go look and say, "They're still coming." We were tied to that switchboard. It was like working for Hitler, but the chief operator wanted to keep her good record.

We used to send down to Gellman's drug store for lunch. A Coke and a tuna fish sandwich was about twenty cents and they would deliver. Nobody even thought of giving Skinny Pugh a tip. Nobody had any money.

Art Gellman worked in his father's store after school, on weekends and all summer.

The girls from the phone company would call and order Coca-Colas every day, and one would like a chocolate Coke, another a cherry Coke, a lemon Coke, and I got to know who liked which one. Sometimes I'd carry six, eight, ten Cokes up there. Sometimes for a nickel coke they'd give me a dime. Wow, in those days, a nickel tip sometimes, if the girls had it.

Harry Gellman came down from Brooklyn, rented a house near the Soldiers' Home for his wife, Pearl, and their two sons, and bought the

Art and Doc Gellman behind their soda fountain

Leland Pharmacy business in the mid-1930s. A Russian immigrant, he had grown up in Washington, attended pharmacy school in New York and opened a neighborhood store during Prohibition where, along with the prescriptions and patent medicines, he dispensed small bottles of grain alcohol with a little caramel coloring. His son recalled that a policeman came in almost every day to ask, "My medicine ready, Doc?" and received a neatly labeled bottle of brownish liquid. Arthur Gellman also remembered telling his father that the policeman must be awful sick to need medicine every day.

The Gellman family soon grew with the addition of two daughters. Father and son rode the trolleys and buses and sometimes trudged through deep snow to keep the business open seven-days-a-week, even on the high holy days much to Art's grandfather's disgust. At the end of the lunch counter, where big Lawrence "Skinny" Pugh manned the sandwich board, two pin ball machines jangled away helping to pay the rent. Art Gellman said that his father also sold punch board chances from time to time to help pay the bills, especially after Whittlesey's bigger and newer store opened just up the street.

Slowly "Doc" Gellman built up a loyal clientele by making deliveries and extending credit. The soda fountain helped, too, and umpire Bill McGowan, for one, was a dedicated fan of Skinny's milkshakes. Calvin "Sonny" Baldwin enjoyed using his parents' charge account to get Skinny's, thick, fifteen-cent shakes. Art Gellman got to know most of the regulars so that when Fred Offutt, for example, came through the door, he opened the box of five-cent White Owls without being asked.

In 1933, while Ed Stock was trying to make a go of it as a "hortitian," some businessmen organized the Bethesda-Chevy Chase Rotary Club, and its charter members included nearly every well known man in town: Leslie W. Beall, Leslie B. Bell, Dr. George Clendenin, Walter Eisinger, State Senator T. E. Hampton, Henry Hiser, Wady Imirie, Baptist minister the Rev. Bertram Osgood, T. W., W. E., and Dr. Benjamin Perry, Tom Pyle, excavator F. Irwin Ray, R. P. Sabine, George Sacks, real estate appraiser Curtis Walker, and Donal Chamberlin. Sacks was the first president and Osgood, of course, the Sky Pilot. They met at Mrs. Imirie's lunch room and the Columbia Dining Room and then at Kenwood and were at least as active as the Chamber of Commerce in promoting Bethesda.

Somehow they missed Joe Virga, probably because he was just getting his own furniture business started. It was the Rotary's loss and later the Lions Club's gain. Virga was a baritone horn virtuoso who came to the U.S. first in 1913 on a Chautauqua tour. He stayed and played his baritone in the Army band in World War I and then learned upholstery at the Studebaker plant where he was also a member of the company band. Virga and his wife moved to Washington, and he worked for twelve years for W & J Sloan saving his money to purchase small pieces of property in Bethesda. In 1933 Joe Virga started his business in one tiny storeroom and expanded into three buildings. Among his regular clients were C&P, the Raleigh Hotel, the Westchester Apartments, and Jelleffs. In 1937 he was joined by Roger Bearse who had studied interior design in New York and Paris and also worked for Sloan.

Joseph Virga

Joe Virga built a reputation as a careful businessman, a natty dresser, a lover of big cars and a terrific spaghetti maker. Each year he cooked up a batch to feed the hungry Lions. His recipe: 18 pounds of meat, 3 pounds of roasted almonds, 6 pounds of Italian cheese, one dozen eggs, 13 pounds of spaghetti, a basket of mushrooms, a lot of tomato paste and a pint of whiskey, which he mixed with the meat before he fried the meatballs in olive oil.[61]

The Quota Club, composed of women who were business executives or who made their living from their profession, organized in 1932, and the Soroptomist Club of Montgomery County began in 1934 with a meeting at the Woman's Club of Bethesda at which thirty women including Anna Rose, principal of the Chevy Chase Elementary School, enrolled as charter members. They elected Blanche Corwin as their first president and, in 1939, launched the Venture Club.

Despite all the growth in the business community, one did not have to travel far from the Bank of Bethesda to find corn or cows. Frank Hall, who was born "right where Washington National Airport is today," remembered his family's farm.

> My father was a detective on RF&P railroad, which was the Potomac Yards. They were looking for a place to farm since the railroad couldn't support the family even though they paid good money. There were eight boys and three girls. He wanted a place where he could work a farm, but he couldn't afford to buy. He rented from W. T. Galligher lumber company. It was out on Bradley Boulevard right where Huntington Parkway comes out. What is Rayburn Street today was the driveway up to the farm. The land ran all the way to Greentree Road and went out to the end of Roosevelt Street which stopped at Jefferson.

> We moved out there about '33. We raised grain and hay and corn and had a dairy herd. We shipped the milk downtown. A lot of the grain was used for the dairy herd and some of it was sold. The fields that went out towards Greentree Road were quite extensive; we had pretty close to 50 acres. The house set back a ways but it overlooked Bradley. There was nothing in front of it but open ground.

> The Baptist Home for Children was a neighbor. The children went to the public schools, and we knew some of them. A guy by the name of Tyler lived over on Greentree at Ewing. He was like the caretaker, and they had two girls that my sisters knew.

The Broadhursts and W. E. Perry were still doing a brisk business in animal feed in the 1930s. Up in Sonoma, "Zip" Lehr was incubating chicks in his basement, and the Hagners kept several horses as well as some chickens and guinea hens at East West and Wisconsin. Bethesda was becoming citified, but many still liked to squish mud between their toes and inhale the smell of fresh manure.

At the high school, enrollment continued to grow. Dr. Broome hired Robert H. Best, graduate of the Williamson Trade School, paid his train fare from Philadelphia, met him at Union Station and offered him $1,100 a year to be a shop teacher. Best recalled:

> They were hurting. School had started. So I said, "I am a teacher under the Smith-Hughes Act; if you teach a trade in a public school they will pay half so I should get $2,200." I had no idea of teaching kids to be a carpenter. I was making broom holders and bird houses and what every other manual trade teacher was, and I was getting $2,200.

Bob Best was by far the best paid teacher at the school for many years, and he was so young

that teachers were always telling him to get in line when they saw him in the halls. He recalled,

We had a big room, which grew into three rooms with Al Bender. I hired him with the principal. He taught metal work, and Petrie, he taught auto. But he didn't fix any. He took them apart, but then they couldn't find the parts to put them back together. I had to take my Studebaker to the dealer where I bought it to get it put back together.

Best roomed with "Zip" Lehr and his wife up in Sonoma for a while and started a constant search for outside work that finally led to his leaving teaching after the war. One of his first big summer jobs was building Tom Pyle's new house on Highland Avenue after he convinced his principal that he really was more of a carpenter than he was. Another summer he did renovations at the school, and Rod Day recalled making a little money by chipping holes in the concrete so they could install stair railings.[62]

Milkman Roland Custer had been so successful in building up his route in fast-growing Bethesda that he decided to leave his rented house on Rugby Avenue in Woodmont for a place of his own in Sonoma.

I went up to Chevy Chase Building and Loan and gave Horace Smithey the plans for my house and told him I wanted $4,000. He said I could build it for $3,300. It cost $3,600 and I paid $600 for the lot. I worked on it, and Dick Pugh did the brick work. My two brothers did the carpenter work, and George Schaefer did the plaster.

In the mid-Thirties, Lillian Lee gave up on her ambition to become a physical education teacher. Her family could not afford to send anyone to college, but she had won a scholarship to the Washington School for Physical Education. "I could never have made it," she said ruefully. "All that anatomy and stuff. I never heard of so many bones."

She applied for a job with the telephone company and convinced her mother to move from the little house near the new high school and rent a bungalow between the Keisers and Miss Birdy Flack on recently completed East West Highway so she could have a telephone installed. Having a phone was a prerequisite to employment, and her family would have had to pay for putting up two poles to get a phone down to her old home.

Ludwell L. Lee, from near Upperville, Virginia, married young Goldie Caton of Alexandria after his first wife died leaving him with two young children. He brought his rapidly growing family to Woodmont about 1910 and found a small house near the Coplin's old home and orchard. Lillian was born there in 1915 and remembered playing in the deep ditches along the narrow streets and peering through the fence at the soldiers marching by after the war. When she was four, the family moved to a small, two-story frame house near the end of Watkins Lane. Lillian Lee Phillips remembered it as "being down a little lane with a tall hedge near where the high school gym is now."

Dad bought the house and about a half-acre of land. We had a barn with a cow and horse or two, pigs, and chickens. Until the school came, he used other land we didn't own and planted corn and potatoes. On our small farm he had peas and beans and lima beans and all that stuff, and we had a garden and lots of chickens. We had water pumped from Miss Golumbuski's, otherwise we had to carry it from the spring. When she went up on him, we carried it. It just went to the kitchen sink. We had an outhouse.

Mom had eight children. The last one died because no one told her how to care for a premature baby, and the poor thing starved to death. Her doctor was away at the time; she just had a midwife. It was a girl. She only had one boy, and he was killed in an accident. I don't think Dad ever recovered from that. When my sister Rae Wilson was born, he named her that 'cause he wanted another boy so bad.

At the end of Watkin's lane was a circle and a big house. We called it the "castle" and it scared us. We didn't go near it. There was another one like up where the Catholic church went in. Some nice people lived there. When we went to school we sometimes got a ride with Mr. Hagner. He took his daughter Anne and us to school. He had a little place out back for his wife who had TB.

Lillian Lee and her sisters sat around the dinner table under a shiny kerosene lamp to do their homework. In a drafty house heated by a iron stove that burned both wood and coal, children did not stay upstairs very long. They had an ice box with a pan that had to be emptied regularly, and Mrs. Lee, and later the girls, pressed their clothes with heavy irons heated on the stove. The privy was only a short walk from their back door.

When the girls got home after dark, Lillian recalled, they would stand on East West Highway at the top of their narrow, dark lane and then:

We'd close our eyes, hold hands and run straight down past the hole in the hedge that led to

the apple orchard. One night a cow was lying right across the path–scared us to death. We didn't know it was a cow till we jumped over it. Another time my brother-in-law was sitting on the front porch with a white shirt on and just as we got there, he stood up–waaa! That was John Buell, I tell you, we were scared.

When it snowed, the Lee's little house became a popular gathering place for chilled sleigh riders. Starting in the Lee's backyard was one of the best sledding hills in town on which a daring rider could reach Colquin Creek near the back end of Columbia Club if he or she could make all the turns and miss all the trees.

Mr. Lee worked as a farmhand on the Wilkerson place when he first came to Bethesda and then found employment at the Experimental Farm and stayed there until the operation moved to Beltsville. "The last Depression," his daughter Lillian said, "it didn't hit us because Dad worked and made the same, and we had a garden and milk. It didn't bother us."

By school year 1933-34, Bethesda elementary school led by principal Ruth B. Clapp had fifteen teachers; Chevy Chase under Anna P. Rose had fourteen teachers; J. E. Thornton, principal of Glen Echo-Cabin John, who was soon to take a Justice Department job, supervised eight teachers; Mrs. Bricker at Somerset had seven teachers on her staff, and at the River Road "colored school," Maud Howard was the principal-teacher and Margaret Wood was her assistant. Tom Pyle at the junior-senior high school now had thirty teachers on his staff.[63]

One of the members of the class of `34 was George Mishtowt. He was fairly typical of a class that graduated at a time when, for many, there was no money. Dr. Mishtowt remembered that his father bought a used Ford from Northwest Motors just before the bank "holiday" and then received a call the next Monday asking for cash or the car back because his check did not clear. His father, the last naval attache of the Imperial Russian government as well as administrator of the Czar's naval procurement funds, doled out grants to stranded Russian naval officers and even established a scholarship fund for their children, but after the embassy closed, he supported his wife and family with a succession of ill-fitting jobs. In 1921, he bought a large house on Stanford Street for $6,000.

When we moved in, it was a dirt road. The house didn't have running water; we had a well with an electric pump, but I think it had sewage. On Stanford Street, there was a house just west of us that Mr. Dunning owned, on the east side were the Balls, and there was a house diagonally across from us, but the whole front from the Walsh house down to Wisconsin Avenue was a wheat field, and there was a tenant farmer's house down at East Street.

The neighborhood included the Episcopal church on the corner and the big stone houses across from it. And downtown Bethesda, as I recall it, had a grocery store, two hardware stores, Imirie's garage, and the Bank of Bethesda, which consisted of a house about the size of our garage with two rooms. There was a house by the church that was lifted up and moved back a block and the big Offutt house was diagonally across there for a long time. The rest was empty lots.

George went to E. V. Brown for a year and then to the "Rosemary School" where he and some of his buddies climbed the water tower at lunchtime with great regularity. He recalled taking the open trolley out Bradley Boulevard to Great Falls for weekend picnics and how fascinating the old gold mine was.

By the time George Mishtowt was in high school his father's hotel supply business had collapsed after his partner absconded with most of the funds. The elder Mishtowt then managed Walter Tuckerman's Point Lookout Hotel for several summers in the late Twenties and early 1930s, and the family spent the hot months down there watching Tuckerman's investment fail. "The Depression was terrible," Dr. Mishtowt recalled.

Our house had four bedrooms on the second floor and two more on the third, and we had Russian naval officers staying with us months at a time. Father would give them two dimes in the morning. They would walk to the District Line, take the trolley and look for a job, no lunch, take the trolley back and walk home.

Young George shined shoes at Mancini's shop "for nickels and dimes," ushered for Henry Hiser on the weekends and occasional evenings, and was "a part-time janitor at school. At 3:30 I started sweeping out classrooms and halls. We were paid 30¢ an hour." He also had a paper route that took in most of the "Leland" community east of Wisconsin from Bradley to the railroad tracks and found time to become an Eagle Scout. When he was sixteen, he got his driver's license and bought a four-cylinder Stutz touring car "that we never did really get running. It had pistons eight or

ten inches in diameter." And he then purchased one of "Buzzy" Potter's motorcycles "for ten bucks."

> *It had been in the barn, a Harley Davidson with a sidecar bracket; it had a reverse, which was most unusual. It took us about a month to get it so it would run, and I took it out Rockville Pike, which had just been put in concrete, three lanes to Garrett Park. I wanted to see how fast I could go, of course.*
>
> *I came back through Edgemoor and was going around the corner by the club and ran head on into Mrs. Adams, Tinsley Adams's mother. I flew over her car and landed on the concrete and spent the next three weeks at Georgetown Hospital trying to get my wrist fixed up. It was badly fractured, and Dr. Perry couldn't do it in his office. It was the last time I've been on a motorcycle.*

Manicini's shoe repair shop was in the row that included Walter Perry's feed store and Frick's lunchroom. Buck Plitt smiled and remembered:

> *North of the Pughs and Perry's was the shoe store, that was Mike Mancini. Joe Fortuna used to sell O'Sullivan rubber heels and other shoe supplies to him, and when Mike went out of business, Joe bought it from him. Mike was a character, an old Italian shoe man, and he used to like to run the numbers. He didn't pay off once, and somebody threw him right through his damn glass window out into the street. His wife used to drive a big, tan Studebaker. She was real blonde, one of the Pugh's I think, and she'd sit up and drive that thing around. They were characters. Everybody knew Mike ran the numbers there; you could go in there and play the numbers and get your shoes fixed."*

In the spring of 1934, the school board began accepting bids for the construction of two big, three-story, brick high schools in Silver Spring and Bethesda and submitted architect Howard Cutler's plans to the PWA for approval. The design for the "Western high school" included the usual offices and classrooms plus two large science labs and an English room with a small stage. On the second floor would be extra-large library, music, and domestic science rooms and a teachers' room measuring eleven and a half by sixteen feet. A big dining hall, 118-by-56 feet, plus a kitchen took up the third floor. Plans for the gym were pending, and the basement was left unfinished.

The Morrison Brothers won the contract for both the eastern and western high schools and

learned to deal with all the Federal paperwork and the workers hired through the government programs as they cleared the Watkins' land for the new building along the unfinished highway to Silver Spring. When Tempe Curry and her friends heard about the proposed high school and then saw the land being cleared, they went to see Mr. Pyle.

> *Mr. Pyle was our friend, and we were the ones that told him, Look, the county wants to build this new high school and call it Western Suburban High School. We said, "You can't do that."*
>
> *Patsy, Anne, me, John Dodge, about six of us. We said we have been here since the first grade, and it can't be anything but "Bethesda." We want you to know that we want the name. And he went to Rockville and got it.*

Despite the excitement generated by plans for a big, new school, the real story in 1934 was political. In January, Brooke Lee resigned as leader of the United Democrats. Mired in debts of about $1.5 million, he faced bankruptcy. More than one hundred families had given him back the keys to the homes they had bought from him because they could not meet their mortgage payments. In February, F. Bernard Welsh began what became the Fusion Party, which was organized at a meeting in March on the model Fiorello LaGuardia had used to become New York's mayor. The Democratic *Sentinel* described attorney Welch as a Republican tycoon who wanted to become judge of the circuit court.

The Republicans numbered about one-third of the County's registered voters, but with the help of anti-Lee Democrats, who called themselves Progressives, they saw in the discontent of the up-County farmers a chance to win. The Fusion Party ignored the State-wide races for Governor and U.S. Senator and concentrated on gaining control of the County Board of Commissioners and the delegation to the State House. Their publicity harped on the County government's purchase of Lee-owned property.

Charles Benson, Mrs. Eugene Stevens, Thomas Robertson, and Joseph and Vivian Simpson were among the well-known and respected early leaders of the uprising. Other Bethesda Fusionists included Walter Bachrach, Louis Keiser, Lex Morris, Leonard Morrison, Millard Peake, and A. M. Ferry of Kenwood. E. Brooke Lee himself, active or not, and the administration of the County over the previous dozen or so years were the issues. The

Bethesda "regulars" followed the lead of Dr. Perry, Emory Bogley, George P. Sacks, Bob Hagner, T. E. Hampton, Ruth Shoemaker, Judge Curry, and young Jim Christopher.

Both sides used radio in the campaign's last days, and fiery Joseph Cantrel of Bethesda spoke for the Fusionists on WJSV on election eve. Robert V. Bray, the *Tribune*'s phantom political pundit, later concluded that Cantrel "more than any other person" was responsible for the Fusion Party's victory. On election day, Democratic party workers collected twenty dollar bills at Dr. Perry's office so they would use their cars to bring voters to the polls. Stella Werner, who took one of those twenties, stayed with the party that year even though she learned that Lavinia Engle was being "cut" by some Bethesda leaders.[64]

The vote was close, and the results were not final until Thursday morning, and then they were shocking. The Fusionists won control of the County government. The aching rural areas swamped the divided down-county as seventy-five percent of the voters went to the polls. It was, announced the *Star*, the end of E. Brooke Lee's fifteen-year reign as County boss. In the most lopsided result, Lee's long-time lieutenant, the respected League of Women Voters leader Lavinia Engle, lost by more than a thousand votes for the Silver Spring Commission district seat although she carried both Wheaton-Silver Spring and Bethesda. She had spoken out forcefully for more and better schools and of the need for recreation facilities.

In the Bethesda district, Dr. Perry's hand-picked successor, Bob Hagner, barely defeated "Progressive Democrat" Samuel E. Stonebraker, 2,627 to 2,237 in the Bethesda precincts and 10,276 to 10,181 Countywide. But the Fusionists controlled the County Commission, which returned from seven to five members, three to two, and that meant they controlled all the patronage jobs from chief of police to Courthouse phone operator. Immediate cries of fraud and demands for recounts made no difference.

Charles W. Woodward held on to his job as Circuit Court judge by narrowly defeating Welsh who ran as a Republican not as a Fusionist. On the State level, Republican Harry Nice had stopped Governor Ritchie's bid for a fifth term, so the Fusionists had even more power than they expected in Annapolis. However the Democrats still controlled the County delegation to which Cantrel and Walter M. Magruder were chosen as Fusionists but in which Friend-

ship Heights' Ruth Shoemaker and two more Democrats held seats. In addition, Stedman "Nippy" Prescott, the nominal leader of the regular Democrats since Lee's resignation, beat Fusion leader John Oxley for the State Senate.

Because of the way the Maryland legislature worked in those days and, in fact, still does, local laws were generally passed without opposition if the local delegation favored them. This "courtesy" made it possible for the Democratic delegation from Montgomery County to limit the Fusionists' power by some very quick, legal maneuvering, which put about three hundred County jobs under a jerry-built merit system.[65]

Ruth Shoemaker was surely one of the most interesting of Bethesda's political leaders to emerge for the 1934 election. Descendant of the family that had owned farms along the District Line for more than a century, Miss Shoemaker worked at several jobs including a stint as a market research reporter before returning to her grandfather's farm on River Road to raise red raspberries and other fancy fruits and vegetables. In the legislature she was among the first to propose laws controlling the use of firearms in the County and the sale of fireworks in Bethesda as well as the bill requiring signs on State roads explaining the school bus law. She also worked tirelessly to make it possible for women to serve on juries in Maryland. In the `30s she was elected and reelected president of the Women's Democratic Club. Miss Shoemaker, who admitted that she had wanted to be a boy when she was growing up, was a familiar figure driving her tractor on the farm near River Road where she lived with her father.

The unashamedly Democratic *Sentinel*'s first editorial after the election supported a merit system for the police department. The most positive, long-term effect of the revolution of 1934 was a serious look at who held County jobs and how they were chosen, at who made County laws and how they were made. The Fusion era lasted only four years, and then the Lee machine was able to compromise and co-opt itself back into power as the rural Democrats and the down-county Republicans found they really did not have many shared interests. The next big political fight, the Charter battle, which led to another reported death of the old regime, was only ten years down the road, and the leaders of that fight-to-come learned in the Thirties that the Lee machine could be defeated but was awfully hard to kill.

Meanwhile, the newly elected Commissioners went to work cleaning house and rewarding their friends. Ralph Fowler of Chevy Chase took over the Liquor Control Board and, despite protests, P. Ray Souder replaced the new Mrs. Perry, Willie Green Day, on the welfare board. Edward Peter, some called him the Fusion Party boss, received a $5,000-a-year plum as the Commissioners' attorney. Then the new Board turned its attention to the police force. Despite pressures from Bethesda Fusionists, who claimed they had been "virtually assured of the job," the Commissioners passed over former sheriff B. Peyton Whalen, and chose up-county Republican J. William Garrett as chief of police. Within weeks the Commissioners had fired seventeen of the twenty-seven men on the force and replaced them with their supporters.

The pogrom wiped out the entire Bethesda detail except for Jim McAuliffe who came to be thought of as somewhat of a Fusionists' pet. He and officer Joseph Nolte won promotion to sergeant mainly for their work on the sensational Lydanne murder-conspiracy case. Within weeks Prescott and Shoemaker pushed a bill through the General Assembly, and put the police under a merit system. Fifteen "old" men and fifteen newly hired officers went on the force. McAuliffe and Nolte lost their stripes.

When the dust settled, the Bethesda station was manned by sergeants LeRoy Snyder and Earl Burdine and patrolmen Nolte, McAuliffe, William Crawford, Marion Dayoff, Ernest Thompson, John Barrie, Leo Day, Joseph Ward, and James Shoemaker. Stella Werner worked hard to help James Nichols salvage his job as Bethesda's police clerk. Then a special bill sailed through the State House, and McAuliffe and Nolte were sergeants again.

Chief Garrett became McAuliffe's mentor, sent him to FBI school, made him part of the first detective bureau, put him in charge of the long-needed training program, and named him as his executive assistant. Through much of the Thirties, McAuliffe was the acting chief when Garrett was unavailable and came to be considered a Fusionist in some political circles. He also played shortstop for the police team in their annual game against the Rockville firemen in which everyone was given a nickname. The speedy McAuliffe was usually called "Rabbit" or "G-man."

The police officer's older son remembered his father taking him and his brother John for rides in a motorcycle sidecar, and he also re-called that his mother's parents moved to Bethesda during that period.

My mother's father and mother came down from Barnesville and lived in the Woodmont triangle. My grandmother was the most pleasant person I think I've ever met with wonderful, wonderful stories to tell. I could hear about tippy toes and shiny eyes for a long time. She had a way of telling stories. They would baby sit.

My grandmother's name was Florine, they called her Flo, we called her Grandma. They lived on Del Ray. My aunt married Earl Hill and also lived in Woodmont. I remember when he drove a truck and lived off his truck.

My grandfather's name was Edgar, and he maintained the County building in Bethesda. I think he kept some chickens in Woodmont, and I know he made ice cream. He outlived my grandmother, and when he became too elderly, he came to live with my mom and dad on High Street.

Capital Traction and the Washington Railway and Electric Company (WRECo) had merged to form Capital Transit in 1933 and unified all street railway operations. It was not long before the new company was looking with a jaundiced eye at both its Chevy Chase and Bethesda-Rockville lines where patronage was declining, criticism increasing, and requested improvements depressing. In mid-June 1934, the County Commissioners and representatives of Capital Transit met at the County Building in Bethesda to discuss the trolley's fate especially in light of the planned widening of Wisconsin Avenue to seventy-five feet. To move the tracks and the poles would be very expensive, so a decision was delayed. In 1928-29, WRECo had moved the poles to the sides of the road from Georgetown to Massachusetts Avenue. Under pressure, Capital Transit extended that project out to Gloria Point in Tenleytown by the summer of '35.

Robert Rickey remembered the trolley line very well even though his family moved to Bethesda only two years before it died, but he recalled riding out to Rockville only once, for the school system's annual field day. "It was quite an adventure for me, through open fields and right through the middle of some farms. You could see the cattle in the fields and the crops. The old car would swing from side to side, and those straps you hang onto, they were slapping back and forth." WRECo was running some of the new Brill "blue stripe" one-man cars with their plush seating, whistles, and Golden

Glow headlamps on the Alta Vista-Rockville line. By the time of the Capital Transit merger, the company had installed new leather seats in all of its cars.

Rockville's politicians and Chamber of Commerce favored a modern bus system with certain qualifications. Capital Transit did not want to invest an estimated $75,000 to modernize the line, but it did make some changes. It started selling $1.25 weekly passes to its Maryland customers and, in September 1934, began terminating its Alta Vista-Rockville cars at Wisconsin and M. In June 1935, the District Line became the transfer point for the trolleys that ran through Bethesda, and August 3rd, a Saturday, saw the last trolley run. Bus service began to the District Line with an old streetcar as a temporary waiting station. The end came quietly. The city newspapers barely noted it.

Most Bethesdans saw the demise of the forty-five-year-old, single-track streetcar line as a move toward modernization, and everyone was happy to get the tracks out of the middle of Wisconsin Avenue. Unlike Connecticut Avenue, where trolley operation ended six weeks later but the fight over the right-of-way went on for years, the repaving of Wisconsin was almost immediate, and for a short time the middle of the street became a diagonal parking area. Georgetown Road, unfortunately, was another story, and by the time the State and local road builders got around to widening it, some land owners including the Bank had become very attached to the abandoned right-of-way, which by law and tradition reverted to their use.

While Joseph Cantrel, Fusion delegate to Annapolis from Bethesda, ranted about the cost of County government and introduced regressive legislation to strip away functions and powers, the Civic Federation spoke out again in favor of "home rule." But most folks had heard enough about politics and enjoyed the return of relative prosperity in 1935.

The New Deal refueled the building boom with FHA loans and repaired it with eager buyers, and in the mid-30s the town was ready to shift into high gear. By the end of June 1934, construction was back to the 1926-27 level with 310 permits for $1,244,000 worth of building in the Western Suburban District. In all of 1934 only 332 permits for just under a million and a half in construction had been requested.

By the fall of 1934, the Lutheran Ministerial Association of Washington, D.C., decided that enough Lutherans lived in the Bethesda area that a "mission" might succeed. They sent Henry Whiting to investigate. He was a local boy fresh out of the Philadelphia seminary who had graduated from the University of Maryland in 1931 as president of the student government. After a few weeks of walking the streets and ringing doorbells, Whiting found fifty-four adults and thirty-three children who expressed interest in the "project."

John Henry Hiser, a Lutheran, offered the use of the State Theater, and after distributing handbills and show window placards and placing notices in all the papers, Whiting held the first service of the Lutheran Mission of Bethesda at 11 am on December 2, 1934, in the 500-seat theater. His father and two other men built and installed the altar and pulpit in front of Hiser's stage. William Von Bernewitz donated a white marble cross and Dr. S. T. Nichols a lectern. The Grace Lutheran Church contributed the hymnals. Other contributions included Bibles, altar candlesticks, and some cash. Louise Mantz and Frank Perley mimeographed a blue covered booklet with the order of the first service, and 163 people participated and contributed $90.50 to the "mission."

The congregation formed a church council with Herbert Ehrman as president, Claude Stanton secretary, and Albert Klaas treasurer. Warren S. Schantz became superintendent of the church school; Guy Campbell, choir director and supervisor of worship, and Mrs. Dorothy Iffert Lakin, organist. In January 1935, attendance was in the twenties and thirties at Sunday services and the offering was often less than five dollars. On February 10, twenty-seven worshippers contributed $3.07.

The Depression was real, but the Sunday school still began at 9:45 on Sunday mornings.

Ready for Lutheran services at the State Theater

By mid-1935, the church had adopted the name of Christ Lutheran, held its first picnic out at Wash-ington Grove, and applied for membership in the Eastern District. Its Sunday bulletin carried the slogan "The Little Church with the Big Welcome," and by the third anniversary at the State Theater it had 147 baptized members, ninety-nine confirmed, seventy-five communicants and was ready to start talking about a building program. Guy Watkins accepted the chairmanship of the building committee.

Christ Lutheran Church

In March 1938, for $9,000, the trustees purchased the "Garrett place," John E. Beall's fine Victorian home with its turreted front. The church then financed its renovation with a "$7,000 in Seven Days" campaign in mid-May 1938. They replaced the old house's offset turret with a square, clapboard steeple and converted the first floor into a space for 200 worshippers plus two Sunday school rooms. The upper floors became the home of the minister. On December 11, 1938, the Lutheran congregation marched from the movie theater to their new church on the hill singing "Onward Christian Soldiers." The Woman's Club announced that it was planning to present an organ and the Men's Club the drapes for the chapel. Reverend Whiting resigned in August 1939 to accept a position with the Inner Mission Society and was replaced by the Rev. Raymond A. Vogeley who initiated an evangelical program to increase attendance at both church and Sunday school.[66]

The Presbyterian, Methodist, Baptist, and Lutheran churches of Bethesda held a joint Thanksgiving Day service at the Presbyterian church on Wilson Lane in 1938. The Rev. J. Raymond Nelson, First Baptist's new pastor, preached the sermon; a combined young people's choir sang, and a layman from each church made a short Thanksgiving talk. This was one of the first steps that led to the formation of the Bethesda Council of Churches.

The annual school survey showed that the Seventh Election District had 4,401 white and 193 African-American children in 1935. That spring, Rockville won the high school division at the field day with Bethesda second and newly named Montgomery Blair High School third. B-CC won the junior high title with 116 points to Sherwood's 100 as more than 6,400 youngsters participated.

That summer many Bethesdans enjoyed rousing melodramas such as "Murder in the Red Barn" at the Roadside Theater built in the hayloft of the Offutt's barn on Rockville Pike. With three revolving platforms on the stage and canvas seats for the audience, Edith Allen's young actors played to mostly full houses. At intermission, Marjorie Hendricks sold small sandwiches and cold drinks from the corn crib.

The Bay beaches were becoming popular weekend or even week-long resorts, and Southern Maryland's slot machines, unlike the more covert local ones, were in full swing. By fall, the PWA had approved plans for a gym and another classroom unit at the new "Western" high school.[67]

The Class of 1935, the last one in the "old" school, tried replacing soccer with football, but Kupka's twenty-man squad only played one game, against Landon, and under pressure from Rockville and because of the difficulty of getting the players insured, the school dropped the sport after another year. According to the 1935 *Pine Tree*, that first team's backfield was composed of Bob Harris, voted best male athlete of the year, Al Diffenback, Oliver Zoernor, and Moir Fulks at quarterback. The first-string linemen were Atkinson, Amiss, Weaver, Mason, Hicks, and Woody Putnam.

B-CC's first football team

The boy's basketball team, which Coach Kupka thought was his best in the old school, beat all its County opponents and participated in both the *Star* and Washington and Lee tourneys while the girls' team made it to the finals of the AAU championship under Mrs. Crocker who wrote a poem about the only game they lost in the whole season, the last one. The stanzas ended "in spite of our loss–it was fun."

Shop teacher Al Bender helped Coach Kupka by refereeing scrimmages and practice games. "He gave us a hard time," said Frank Lozupone, who was on the basketball team all four years and a member of the baseball and football teams as well.

We were practicing one night at the Leland school, and he drove an Austin. Eddie Johnson and Tom Finlayson, myself, Woodrow Putnam, and two or three others walked out, and there was Mr. Bender's car parked in front of school. So we picked the damn thing up and carried it inside and parked it by Mr. Pyle's office and left. I don't know how he got the thing out, down those steps.

Sororities and fraternities had been a part of school life at B-CC since the early 1930s when they were established by students who had been exposed to them in the D.C. schools where they had gone through a turbulent existence. Louis Lozupone was never asked to join a fraternity when he was at B-CC, but in his 1934 yearbook, numerous autographs of both seniors and juniors had Greek letters under the signatures. For example, Joe Parks, Ray Stone, Harvey "Moo Moo" Johnson Jr. and William "Woozy" Moore wrote Pi Phi under their names, and Helen "Sister" Smith and Martha "Baby" Thomas inscribed "Beta Sigma" under theirs. "Buck" Plitt (B-CC `35) and many of his friends were fraternity members well before the school moved over to East West Highway.

I was a member of Alpha Delta Sigma.

They were illegal, but the school didn't do anything about it. Everybody used to wear their fraternity pins, and they didn't bother you. We used to have a dance a couple of times a year, and we'd make up advertisements, called them floaters, and hand them out to the students. We had them at the Bethesda Woman's Club or the National Women's Club, sometimes at Kenwood. You could rent those places for $25 or $35 a night. We used to get bands from Washington. We tried to outdo the other fraternities. They had a band called Pete Moss one time, so we got one and called them Black Rasputin and His Fourteen Mad Monks. We just put some name on it.

And they would come and dance their heads off. We'd charge a dollar or something to get in, and it would be enough to pay for the band and the hall if we got a hundred people there. The band would be about $35 if they had seven. Sometimes they played free 'cause they'd shoot craps with the guys when we'd pay them off at intermission.

Once when they were putting an addition on Kenwood, we went over there. Of course, it was always a big thing to crash the school dances. And we went there and Mr. Pyle was there and Miss Young, and they were downstairs at the bottom of the steps greeting everybody. And one or two of the guys found a ladder and put it up, and my gosh, it must have been fifty kids got in by that ladder. We hid in a little room and then went out and mixed. All the teachers wondered where all these people came from since they didn't come through the door

It did get kind of wild. Curtis Walker was in our fraternity. And they got to thinking that all you did is drink and have a good time. They had a beer bust somewhere, and he got killed in an automobile accident.

Girls had their sororities. There must have been seven or eight groups. You had to be asked to go in. They had initiations and held a meeting every week and kept minutes and charged like fifteen cents a week dues or something like that. It was something to do.

Patsy Lozupone, neé Royster, along with her friend Tempe Grant, neé Curry, was an active member of Beta Sigma, one of the two large sororities of that time.

They were a wonderful social outlet, and drinking wasn't very common. The girls weren't drinking. We met on Friday nights in peoples' homes, and boys came over afterwards and took the girls home. They were giving dances once a month at $1.50 a couple. Sometimes a policeman chaperoned. At the National Woman's Country Club, he stood in the john and didn't let anybody come in the window.

I had evening dresses that the bottoms of them wore off. We dressed up and went to dances all the time.

But her now-husband and then-boyfriend, Frank Lozupone, did not belong to a fraternity. "I couldn't afford it," he said. He and his wife, both class of '36, agreed that the fraternities and sororities were "tolerated" during their high school years.

Another member of the class of '36, Jane Dunbar Tedeschi, a good student-athlete and friend of Tempe Curry and Patsy Royster, had been a member of a girls' club that met above a garage in Somerset even before she entered the junior-senior high school. The oath members of the "Jacel Club" took ended with a promise to "do no evil or try to anyway." While at B. C. C. H. S., she and many of her friends had "a lunch group in the summer time. We'd go to each other's houses. Tempe and Doris, Patsy, Hulga, Anne and Nancy, eight or twelve of us. We'd play crazy games. This began in junior high."

Later, I belonged to a sorority and then it was co-opted by an older girls' sorority. Lambda Tau, that's what we were. Beta Sigma began rushing girls from our sorority, and I didn't think

that was a very nice thing to do. I refused my invitation, and there was another sorority and they invited me to join, and I decided not to belong to any of them. Most of the others did. That broke up our group, and I think that's when the lunches ended.

Donald MacLeod, president of his class as a freshman, sophomore and as a senior in 1936-37, said that he never joined "since I felt it would restrict my class activities" and that he had many friends both in and out of fraternities and sororities. He concluded that they were "generally small units with little other than social activity for cement" and that while he never felt left out, he was sure that some people did. The administration would have preferred they did not exist, he was sure. Tempe Curry Grant recalled that teachers, including Mrs. Mohler, told them sororities were illegal, but "we thought they were nuts. They made high school fun."

Edmund Bennett took a different tack.

I was the organizer of the Cavaliers. We were above the Greek-letters men. They were the conformists. Joe Doyle was in the Cavaliers, Arthur Eisele, Jack Moran, Allan Stimpson, Ben Pace; we were all "intellectuals." These other guys were beer drinkers. We met at kids' houses and had parties, beer and otherwise. It only lasted a couple of years.

Band and orchestra member Rod Day, also class of '37, remembered being a Cavalier.

A bunch of us didn't go along with the fraternities' philosophies and initiation stuff, paddling and all that crap, and they didn't ask us to join, so we formed our own, a nice group of fellows.

We had blanket parties while the other guys were up running around and chasing women. We'd go down to Rock Creek Park, and we'd sit around the blanket, open the chips, drink beer and discuss things, very high type, high tech things.

The highlight was in our senior year when we decided to have a ball at the Kennedy-Warren. We rented the hall, had dinner and dancing, and we invited our best girls or the ones we wanted to be best girls, and it was black tie, which was unusual. We had a beautiful evening.

Tempe Curry   Donald MacLeod

There was undoubtedly a class structure at the high school from its very early days. Girls came to school wearing dresses, stockings and "sensible" shoes, and most boys wore a shirt, tie and jacket or a sweater. The poorer kids from Glen Echo-Cabin John and the Woodmont Triangle had to struggle to keep up. Many of the "in-group" girls dropped out of athletics as juniors and seniors, but for some boys prowess on the basketball court or baseball diamond was a ticket to fraternity membership.

Jane Tedeschi said she did not think neighborhood or class status really counted and mentioned the Willetts as an example, but she admitted that the distinctions "may have mattered to them" and said, "We'd walk three miles before we'd ride a school bus. The bus was for people from those areas."

Winifred Krueger née Donaldson grew up in Woodmont where her grandfather tried to keep her out of the Shackleford store's penny candy with a mousetrap. Her first job was at the high school where Kenneth Petrie asked her and a classmate to work an hour after school in the office for nine dollars a month when she was in the 9th grade. She and her friends were never asked to join a sorority, but she did become a member of Job's Daughters. "The clothes you wore to school and having more spending money separated the kids," she said. Later, during the end-of-the-day activity period while other students went to club meetings, Winifred worked at the "dime store" and at Della's Bakery both on the counter and as bookkeeper.

In September 1935, the 10th, 11th, and 12th grade students moved into their new building and decided to keep their old name as Tempe Curry, Patsy Royster and their friends had insisted they must. The high school teams would now be the "Highwaymen," and the trees inside the old Watkins' hedge on the side lawn became the "grove" where smoking was at first tolerated and then condoned. It was not long before teachers were assigned "duty" there before and after school and at lunch.[68]

Senior Jane Dunbar, the perennial class secretary, recalled the rows of lockers in the bare halls and her

Jane Dunbar

The new school on East West Highway

performances in one-act plays at Footlight Club assemblies. She also remembered that her classmates gave new history teacher Kenneth Frisbie a hard time. "The music teacher was our history teacher, and on our tests we opened our books and he never did anything about it. We didn't give him any rude behavior; we just weren't cooperative. It was his first year, and he just threw himself on our mercy I guess." She claims to still profit from Mrs. Crocker's dictum "Don't stand like a tree-keep your feet moving" in tennis and other sports and recalled the only time she skipped school was to go hear Guy Lombardo's orchestra at the Earle Theater.

Edmund Bennett, a member of the first sophomore class in the new school, remembered it as "a pretty barren place, just one big building with a wooden boardwalk across muddy fields and a gravel parking lot."

Mrs. Gertrude Bouvet, the cafeteria manager, led a crew that prepared lunches from "scratch" each day after hauling food up to the third floor kitchen. Christine Schneider neé Hurley, class of `37 and long-time B-CC secretary, remembered fondly the apple brown betty her mother made when she was one of those early cafeteria workers.

The students formed a committee to plan the activity or "social personality" period, and the number of clubs multiplied. Since the gym was not finished, the PE classes used the muddy fields around the school as well as the unfinished basement and sometimes the "attic" where Patty Popp taught her fellow students fencing. The drama club went back to the big stage at what was now the junior high for its production. The girls had field hockey and soccer games on the flats west of the school, but the boys played their baseball games up at Garrett Park. The basketball teams practiced and

played at their old school, and the boys' again won the County championship. No matter who was playing, spectators at Leland's gym were in the action.

A high school game in Leland's gym

After the boys lost to Eastern in the city tourney, Mr. Pyle received a letter for O. O. Kuhn, the *Star*'s managing editor, praising the "splendid spirit" of B-CC's students.

The courageous perseverance of the players and the unswerving loyalty of the Bethesda-Chevy Chase boys and girls in the stands were inspiring and I believe this was the reaction of all present.

The PTA worked hard to try to get sidewalks laid on East West Highway. The first parents' school night included a schedule of ten-minute classes. Mr. Pyle planted his third pine tree, a symbol of growth he said, and everyone looked forward to the next year when there would be a gym, more classrooms, a baseball field and a lot less mud.

Angela Darby, long-time B-CC teacher and oft-times senior advisor, believed that "Tom Pyle was the best principal that we ever had. He had a faculty meeting every single Monday, and let everybody talk. He was a Quaker and it showed." Mrs. Darby grew up in Baltimore and first taught at Poolesville where she met her husband who had been reared on the farm where she later lived. She recalled that she was paid $1,200 the first year she taught "but the second year I only got $1,100 because it was the Depression. Mr. Pyle was president of the

teachers' organization, and he had us all stand up and vote that we would cut our salaries."

When her husband took a job in the city, they moved to Bethesda in 1934, and she went to work at the junior-senior high where she taught "everything, even 8th grade science. Mr. Pyle had a habit of going around the classrooms," she said.

He could cover ten classrooms in an hour and know what was going on, in one door and then out the back door, and he knew what was going on. I remember we were giving mice alcohol one time when Tom Pyle came in, and he stayed and watched. The kids were so interested and he was, too.

The first year on East West Highway was also the year when the administration finally caught up with Patricia Ann Royster and some of her friends. Patsy, who had been elected to the Honor Society as a junior, remembered that event in her own, arch style.

In our era money was hard to come by. Down at the Earle and the Fox theaters, they had stage shows. Things you needed to attend for your cultural education. It was necessary to go on a Friday because it only cost twenty-five cents, and it cost a dollar and half to go at other times. You had to go on Saturday morning to see the other show.

So it was necessary for people to leave school on Fridays. We upstanding citizens didn't think it was necessary to leave before and not go to early classes, but we had to get downtown by eleven o'clock.

In the senior year we had Joe Parks, the president of our class who had a car, and he dated Helen Hathaway. So we would leave school, and I would go into the office where Helen Hendricks was Mr. Pyle's secretary. I signed out everybody else with doublewriting, like doubletalk; it looked like writing but it wasn't saying anything. We had been doing this thing and going downtown regularly.

I had been smart enough from the very beginning never to let my parents' signatures enter the school system and wrote all notes excusing things. This had gone on, and nobody's grades were suffering; nobody even missed us. Until somebody went to look

Patsy Royster

for one of us one day. We had the president of the class, the captain of the basketball team and the president of the honor society, who had been skipping school every Friday for a couple of years. I thought they wouldn't say anything since we had been doing it for so long. It was a comment on them that they hadn't noticed. They kept us in after school for the last six weeks.

In school year 1936-37 at a cost of $200,000, B-CC added a square block of classrooms called "B" building and a gym which also served as an auditorium. Mary Mohler, who had come over to the new building with the upper grades, recalled that she had "lived through trying to teach with all the construction going on when they added the north side and auditorium" at Leland, and now "we had been there just a year when they began to build again... I said my life was made up of construction." Many people thought Leland had the better gym, and some basketball players claimed they had to relearn their two-handed set shots because of the lower rafters and lights at the high school.

School clubs and activities multiplied; a student court was instituted, and Dorothy O. Young, of the Fussell-Young ice cream Youngs, began her long career as a counselor. Among the most popular activities were the microscope, science, footlight, art metal, photography, commercial, knitting, tap dancing, and "find 'em out" clubs. Mr. Frisbie's opera club presented Gilbert and Sullivan's *Patience* in April starring sophomore Eleanor Reid, junior Kenneth Kinsella and senior Bruce Hall. Edmund Bennett and some other survivors of the octet formed at Leland several years before sang in the chorus. And the faculty put on a show that was long remembered, especially by the seniors who were the butt of most of the jokes.

There were, for the first time, more than one hundred seniors that year. Playing in their new gym, both the boys' and girls' basketball teams were County champs, and bowling teams got started up at Hiser's alleys. Both B-CC and Leland triumphed at the annual field day in May of 1936. In school athletics, Bethesda had become dominant in the County.

The building the high school students and Tom Pyle left behind was renamed Leland Junior High School since that was the name of the subdivision where it was located. Robert Rickey recalled that the school's hallways were a lot less crowded after the bigger kids had moved over to the new school. He remembered Leland as a good place to go to school, but said he only "woke up" academically in the 9th grade. Among the teachers he recalled were his art teacher Miss Rowe; Mrs. Sasscer, who introduced him to essay questions, and sisters Virginia and Helen Mullinix and his shop teacher, Al Bender, who shared time between the two schools for a while and who married Helen Mullinix.

Mrs. Bender, Leland's smiling librarian for some thirty years, was the staff member nearly all older Leland graduates recalled. Helen Price Bready was the principal of the junior high school for its first eight years and built a reputation as a no-nonsense administrator and educational innovator.

"Zip" Lehr returned to Leland from Sherwood H. S. when Tony Kupka went to B-CC with the upper classes. For a few years his teams were the "Pirates," but that did not sit well with some of the female gym teachers, and after the brown and gold colors were adopted, they became the "Yellowjackets." The intramural program was

The gym, "B" building, and a lot of local trees at the new school on East West

One of Zip's "Pirate" teams–champs as usual

part of the "social personality" or activity period instead of the lunchtime recess starting in 1937, and in the spring, softball games often took place before classes began.

It did not take long for Leland to become crowded once more, and soon the school was "graduating" classes of 300 students with most of them going on to B-CC. Some Leland grads or their parents still chose D.C. high schools or one of the many private schools in the Washington area for college bound students.

Bethesda was home to a number of private schools ranging from Lady Isabel's primary school on shady Edgemoor Lane to the college preparatory Landon School on winding Wilson Lane. There were several cooperative nursery schools, some sponsored by churches or community organizations, and later one at the Recreation Center. Mrs. Helen Sutch operated a K-6 school at her home on Battery Lane beginning in 1937, and the Green Acres progressive day school on Old Georgetown Road was a model for several non-profit operations. At Green Acres, Ruth Egerton Hoge and her staff offered a program of "learning by doing" on two and one-half wooded acres. Activities including numerous field trips for children from two to eight.

In Edgemoor, Isabel McGee and her assistant, Mrs. Eldridge Johnson, taught their young charges dancing and art as well as reading and writing and how to tie their shoes and take care of their clothes. The children played tirelessly inside a wooden fence, but unruly scholars spent time in the misery chair. A simple party at which children took turns serving each other ended every school day at Lady Isabel's. For older children there were several choices and

philosophies of education. The Slade School on Old Georgetown gave way to Thomas Walton's co-ed school in 1939, and that was also about the time the Longfellow School for boys and the primary school at Whitehall were getting organized.

The oldest private school in the Bethesda area, the Georgetown Preparatory School, moved out of the city in 1919. In 1915, Hilleary and Kate Offutt sold the tenant-farmed ninety-two acres south of their home to the Jesuits for $32,000. Thanks to a $130,000 gift from Henry Walters, Georgetown University class of 1869, the Georgian structures Marsh and Peter designed were ready for occupancy in 1918 but were leased to the YWCA to house female government workers until after the Armistice. The Prep school's first graduation at Garrett Park, a class of twenty-seven, took place in 1923.[69]

Of all of Bethesda's private schools, Landon became the best known and eventually rivaled the older Prep School in both prestige and facilities. Paul Landon Banfield and his wife started the school in a rented mansion on Massachusetts Avenue in 1929 with fourteen day-students, eight boarders, eight faculty members and Earnest Brock, who stayed for thirty-five years as general factotum, bus driver, custodian, and waiter at school dances. He was the man who knew where everything was.

The young school survived the immediate effects of the stock market crash, a fire, and the lack of a playing field. Steady growth in enrollment led Banfield to incorporate his venture as a non-profit operation with Mrs. Banfield on salary as secretary and treasurer and to seek a new and larger site.

In 1934, the school moved to the unfinished estate Evelyn McLean had built for her mother, Mrs. Thomas Walsh, on thirty-four acres south of Wilson Lane along Bradley Boulevard. The house had never been occupied but had become famous as the place where Mrs. McLean and her agents gave Gaston Means $100,000 to ransom the Lindbergh baby. Mr. Brock used the school's stationwagon to make the move, but the work was unfinished when school began in the fall. Students and masters earned seven cents a square yard sodding the football field before and after classes.

Traditions, like the June Ball and the Rose Tea, and a waiting list soon developed, and two years later, when Banfield had the opportunity to purchase the sprawling Andrews' estate, owned by the father of a former student

who was willing to make generous terms, he took it despite the dim view of the trustees. Frantic fund raising still left Banfield $6,000 short when his 30-day option ran out, but H. L. Rust rescued him with a personal loan. The upper school moved to the new location while the lower forms under William Triplett stayed at Whitehall for four more years.

The caretaker's house, Tumblestone, became the Banfields' home, and architect Horace Peaslee designed the school. A big, barn-like gym was added in 1939 in honor of a student killed in a Montana train wreck. Most of its $60,000 cost and much of the labor to build it were donated. The honorary Hat Club and the Press Club, which produced the school's monthly newspaper and annual yearbook, also began in '39. In 1940 the lower school was finished, and the students moved from the Walsh estate, which became the Whitehall Country School for girls under Mrs. Henry H. Pitts.[70]

Bethesda was obviously growing again. The Federline brothers, who had been reared in Tenleytown and set up in the Centre Market with the help of their grandfather, A. J. Riley, acquired a DGS franchise, rented a store in Tuckerman's row right at the head of East West Highway, and opened Meadowbrook Market in 1935 in direct competition with several nearby Piggly Wiggly, A&P and Sanitary stores. James handled the meats and Marion, who was called "Hots," took care of the fruits and vegetables.

Marion Federline moved to a house on Middleton Lane, and James rented and then bought a big, old house at St. Elmo and Old Georgetown from Clarence Keiser. Policeman-historian Charles Federline grew up there and remembered the house as one of the originals, a white clapboard of two-and-a-half stories on a quartz foundation with a dirt basement. Every room had a fireplace that had been plastered up, and,

Federline said, the place was haunted. His cat could "see" whatever it was, and he could hear it; one room "breathed."

Up on Old Georgetown Road, Frank Riley opened his Battery Park Market in 1936 and moved his family to a house on Montgomery Avenue. He was soon joined by Karl Lehman who brought some Chevy Chase customers with him from the Pure Foods store on Connecticut at McKinley. Lehman was an expert bowler who later helped to mange the new bowling center in Bethesda. Battery Park Market had a very large delivery business and kept four or five trucks on the road much of the time.

Ray Shoemaker, B-CC '39, drove a delivery truck for both the Battery Park Market and the Federline brothers when he was in high school. His house-painter father had moved to Maple Avenue about 1920 and then after some time in D.C. moved back again in the '30s. Like many Bethesda youngsters, Ray had several jobs before he finished high school. At one time in the mid-30s, he and a cousin had the *Daily News* route for almost all of Bethesda, about a hundred papers, at the same time the Bort boys in Woodmont had most of the *Star* routes pretty well wrapped up. When he could, Ray caddied at the Woodmont Club. "I got more money

Mid-town in the mid-'30s-note the horse ring between Hagner's and the Bradley house that became the funeral home, the Bank at the intersection of Wisconsin and Old Georgetown with the Masonic library behind it, the State Theater at the south end of Tuckerman's "row" with the post office building just north of it and an empty lot to the south where the new post office would go with angle parking out front and, at lower right, the County Building with its tall pillars.

caddying one day than I did delivering newspapers for a month. The caddy master was Dick Barnsley, Bill Barnsley's brother. We usually got seventy-five cents for nine holes; sometimes we carried two bags and got a tip or two. Some of those caddies were kind of rough though." He shook his head, remembering.

Those newspaper routes were a "sore point" with the Rev. William Bort as he recalled his young days in Woodmont.

Dad took over that newspaper route with sixty-five papers, the Star, and when he gave it up in 1942, we had something like 6,000 customers. He had everything from Wisconsin Avenue to Battery Lane and down to River Road and Kenwood, Battery Park, Woodmont, all of that. I started with a wagon and, in wintertime, a sled. I went down Arlington Road and did all of Edgemoor and then swung across to do Battery Park, every day from the time I was ten years old until I was sixteen.

Then Dad was very sick so when I was sixteen, he had my mother teach me how to drive. Then he turned over the truck to me, and my job on Sunday morning was to make all the drop-offs for the kids and then do all the boxes on River Road

William Bort in `38

and on Bradley Boulevard and down Wilson Lane and then bring the truck back to him and do my route in Edgemoor and Battery Park. Everybody did it; even my sister served his papers. My mother used to drive an old Model-T Ford up to Alta Vista and on up where Georgetown Roads hits Wisconsin Avenue, and my sister used to jump papers off that Ford.

Dad had all these boys serving newspapers, but we had to go out and do all the collecting. I was out to nine or ten every night after serving my routes. Dad didn't care about the weather; you had to go.

"Buck" Plitt remembered Willie Bort's older brother Harry.

He hauled papers in this high-sided wagon with great big wheels, like bicycle wheels. And he stayed out in the street. I used to watch him "box" those papers and sail them up toward the porches. He never missed. The paper would hit the front edge of the porch, whop, and slide up to the door.

Soon the little Piggly Wiggly and Sanitary stores would be giving way to the big, rectangular Safeways. The Piggly Wigglys were the first self-service stores in the area with a turnstile at the entrance and a cash register at the exit. They started with an explosion, opening twenty-five stores in one day in 1920 and soon had more than forty markets in the D.C. area. Their motto was "help yourself." ("How about a kiss?" asked he. "Piggly Wiggly," answered she.)

There were several in Bethesda including one on the corner of Edgemoor and Wisconsin. "The day that opened," Laura Triest recalled, "I went up there with my father. We were fascinated. You had to go through a turnstile to get out. It was the latest thing." Lett's Sanitary Store chain bought them out in 1935 and was in turn sold to the Safeway Stores company in 1938. They were tough competition for the old markets like Beall's and the new DGS, but Federline's store did well even though the brothers extended credit to their delivery customers.

Bethesda Paint and Hardware, a W. R. Winslow store, opened in Tuckerman's row before they built a big, new store behind the bank with entrances on both Old Georgetown and Wisconsin. The beautiful Weathered Oak Herb Farm at Bradley and Seven Locks began selling boxwood and flowers at Bethesda Floral Gardens at Wisconsin at Bradley to give Ed Stock a bit of competition.

Designed to look old, the Weathered Oak buildings between Seven Locks Road and Bradley Boulevard included a harvest house, the plow shed, the herb house and a blacksmith shop, which displayed a forge and old tools including some from Lochte's smithy in Bethesda. Many of the heavy beams came from the Valley Mill in Colesville, the framework from old barns, and the floors were made of bricks from Frederick and Georgetown streets.

They grew more than a hundred different herbs, dried them on racks in the attic of the harvest house and then took them to the herb house, an old Pennsylvania grist mill Charles H. Merryman had dismantled and shipped to the site. He had the roof watered daily to keep the moss a healthy green. There the workers, as Dorothy Schultz recalled, "stripped them from the stems and made up mixes for salads, soups, fish, etc. and also for jars of individual herbs. The labels had a picture of the Herb House . . . (which) looked like a woodcut. Then I handprinted the contents at the bottoms of the

label." Landscape architect Merryman and Mrs. G. C. F. Bratenahl, who were behind the Weathered Oak business, also designed the Bishop's Garden at the National Cathedral.[71]

Not all of the plans and projects turned out as well as the Farm Women's Market. In the fall of 1935, for example, the FHA and the owners of the old Shoemaker farm at the District Line, Donald Woodward and Mrs. Parker, came very close to creating a 300-home project worth about $3.5 million on that sixty-acre property. For some reason, like the circle for Wisconsin and Western, it never happened, and hitting buckets of balls at the driving range continued to be the only use made of that land except for the short-lived Hot Shoppe.

In Bethesda, hydro-engineer Charles W. Hawley was looking for a real estate investment. His talents had taken him all over the world and made him rich, but he decided not to fight the Corps of Engineers in this country. So he moved to the Washington area for "contacts," first to Virginia and then to 16 W. Lenox Street in Chevy Chase. He opened an office in the Muncie Building and began building and investing in commercial properties in the Washington region.

Just before the stock market crash, he built a beautiful house for his family on fifty-seven acres near Pooks Hill on Rockville Pike, and his wife became one of the Bell Laundry's best customers for hand-finished tablecloths and the like. Hawley saw Shannon and Luchs's first shopping center on Connecticut Avenue at Ordway Street in 1930 and was impressed. According to his son and namesake, "Dad decided it was a good idea for Bethesda, but everybody said, No, you'll lose your shirt. So he kept asking until he found somebody that agreed with him, and then he built it."

Hawley constructed the L-shaped "Stop and Shop" group of stores at Leland and Wisconsin in late 1936 and opened it in early 1937. Excavating, he found, according to his son, "a big lake in there." He went down two and half stories below grade for basements and storage rooms and "encountered all kinds of water so he had to put in all kinds of sump pumps."

The original tenants of the fireproof, limestone-faced stores included

"Whittlesey's Drug Stores, Inc., Sanitary Grocery Co. Inc., American Stores, Peoples Hardware Stores, Leon Bondareff trading as Lakeview Market, Mrs. Josephine Warner trading as Rosalind Beauty Salon, Clover Crest Dairy Stores Inc., for use for the sale of dairy products and as a dairy lunch, and Mrs. Agnes R. Waesche trading as Florence Ann Shop, for use as a ladies dress and millinery shop." The Streamline National Acceptance Corporation leased the big unit on the north end for another grocery store.

Hawley provided living space under the stores for an attendant-janitor who also helped direct traffic at crowded hours in the big parking area out front. Shannon and Luchs, which copyrighted the "Park and Shop" name and formed a corporation to manage its developments, assisted in the rental of stores at the new shopping center.[72]

The *American City* magazine in October 1937 described Bethesda's big, new shopping center as:

> . . . *particularly attractive and well-built, the limestone front presenting a very pleasing appearance. The shopping in this territory of detached homes is almost all done by the use of automobiles, and the parking area is not only a convenience but also a necessity.*

The tenants were on a percentage rental, and as business in Bethesda increased so did Hawley's profits. It was, obviously, a good investment, and soon when one said "shopping center" in Bethesda, everyone knew what was meant. Not all of the stores were successful,

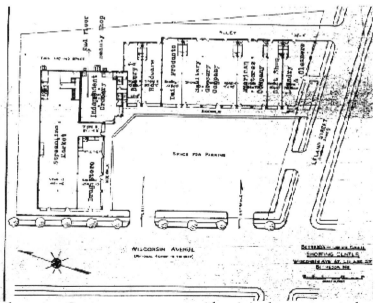

Shopping Center arrangement with original tenants noted.

but Whittlesey's and Bondareff's businesses prospered from the start and became a part of the Bethesda landscape.

W. H. Whittlesey reached his goal in Bethesda, he told a reporter. He had a high class business in a high class town. He had started in drug stores as a soda jerk and then graduated from the GW school of pharmacy before serving in the medical corps in France in World War I. Before he came to Bethesda and put his name on the store, he had owned drug stores in Virginia, Georgetown, and in the Park and Shop on Connecticut Avenue, which he kept for several years after moving to Bethesda.

"Doc" Whittlesey, with his neatly buttoned,

long-sleeved white shirts and quiet manner became an institution as did his store, which, not always to his delight, became the gathering place for the junior high school kids who crowded his long fountain after school. He eventually had to institute an unpopular "curfew."

W. H. Whittlesey

Young Bob Eastham impressed some of his buddies by charging Cokes and strawberry sodas with an airy, "Put it on the bill, Doris." His father, whose gas station was right across the street, had a charge account at Whittelsey's. Eastham also recalled that when a five-gallon can of Breyer's ice cream got down near the bottom, "some of the guys who lived down on Leland Street near where I lived would go in there and keep an eye on it, and when it got real low, they'd let you take it and scrape out what was left. That was a treat."

A number of businesses came and went in the shopping center, and in the end, the only one that stayed as long as Doc's drug store was the Lakeview Market, the "Magruder's of the suburbs." The Bondareffs, he a native Washingtonian, long remembered for his sense of humor, and she a Polish immigrant and as hard a worker as her husband, started their first store on Brookeville Road in 1931. "In old man Sonneman's house,"

Mrs. Bondareff recalled:

He had a garden store. We rented the store and built an addition on the back and lived there, had a kitchen and a bedroom and a living room and a little porch. He cleaned it out and let us in. They lived in a lovely house next to the store. Then we built up a good business with a really wealthy clientele, but they wouldn't allow us to build on the lot next to us, and they wouldn't let us expand.

In those days it was easy, for instance, White Rose was a very well-known brand in those days, and they would come out and fill your shelves and then come back in a month, and what you'd sold you'd pay them for. Canada Dry, Cliquot Club, they would stock your shelves the same way. And the faster you paid your bills the better. We never had a credit problem.

We built up a big business, mostly deliveries, and our customers became friends. I remember Dr. William Mercer Sprigg, lived on Primrose Street, right on the corner. He started Doctors' Hospital. They had one daughter. All around there, they became friends. Then the Depression came and people were in bad shape. My husband didn't turn anyone down for credit as long as he could possibly pay, to keep it going. Of all the people that he carried, there wasn't but one didn't pay him back.

When our child was born, we knew we had to do something even though we didn't have two nickels to rub together. When we opened this store here, we were told by everyone, "Mr. Bondareff, you don't want to go in there; you'll never make it. They will not accept a Jew." When my kid graduated from high school, he was the only Jewish child at B-CC; when my daughter graduated three years later, there were a few, and when she and a friend went to the beach together there was a sign, "No Jews Allowed," and they came back.

3. BETHESDA CHEVY CHASE SHOPPING CENTER

Anyhow, they said they won't deal with you, when we came to Bethesda. We never heard it in Chevy Chase. I have never felt any anti-Semitism. At least I wasn't aware of it. My children felt it, but I didn't.

When we first opened up, I'm not sure of the dates, that was the first Shopping Center. Across was all woods, and there was the big Offutt estate that went down Bradley from Wisconsin Avenue. I think Sacks owned it. Just a lot of wild rabbits and so forth. We beat a path through the woods from the house we rented on Norwood Drive to the store. When we first opened, I was bookkeeper, then I took the telephone orders, and later I was at the cash register.

At that time S. S. Pierce was the fanciest goods, and we had it for this area. The next was Magruders in Georgetown. We had frozen food as soon as it came out. The Farm Women's Market was no competition. They brought people. My husband believed that the more places there were that sold the same thing you did, that would bring more people into the area and then it was up to you to make a go of it. I bought corn from the Farm Women's Market. I told everybody that wanted to know; they picked it so fresh.

We had a butcher, Kirk Fleming, the one before him was Mr. Monaghan, and two clerks and a deliveryman. Lee did his own butchering when we started; he learned from his brother at the store on Broad Branch. Meat was our big business. A man called Joe Mazer later brought us choice meat.

The Parkers were good customers. The chauffeur would come and get the garbage from our store for their animals. Their estate once ran all the way to Grosvenor Lane. Mrs. Parker on one side and Mrs. Luke Wilson on the other, and they were sisters. The Parkers owned Woodward and Lothrop; Guy Wilson was the Arrow collar man. The Woodward girl married B. W. Parker and her sister married Luke I. Wilson. Luke Wilson died of cancer, and she left the property to NIH.

They were nice people, Mrs. Parker was wonderful. She left hers to Goodwill. After Parker died, they had a home in Jamestown, R. I., she called me and said come take anything you want from this house. I didn't want to but Mrs. Parker insisted and gave me a ormolu clock, a lamp, and a Chinese plate.

When she ordered lima beans, she wanted them all the same size. She had more money than she could spend in two lifetimes. We bought a bushel, and maybe she wanted a pint or quart, so we sat the driver down and he shelled the lima beans to get her a pint or quart. She knew she was

Leon Bondareff at the cash register

paying for the bushel, ten times the cost, but she got what she wanted.

We used to bring the bills home here at the end of the month and figure them out and mail them. When the order was delivered, the customer got the carbon and you kept the original, and at the end of the month you added up the originals and sent them the bill.

Mrs. Bondareff and her husband bought a house on Wellington Drive to be closer to the store. Cafritz tried to sell them the house on Norwood for $8,000, but they thought the Recreation Center would make too much traffic.

A large number of automobile dealerships came and went in Bethesda in the 1920s and `30s such as J. Milton Rowe's short lived Packard agency after Imirie-Rowe Chevrolet called it quits and Scott Imirie opened a small restaurant and bar. Vernon Motors, a DeSoto dealer, lasted for quite a while, and was replaced by the Hammond Motor Company, which took over the store used by the Women's Farm Market at 7300 Old Georgetown in 1937 and then moved up to the Star Service Station on Wisconsin the next year. Covington Motor Co. sold Pontiacs "at the sign of the airplane wind sock" near the railroad bridge. One that stayed was Merson and Thompson, the

Chrysler-Plymouth dealer on Hampden Lane that opened in 1937 as Bethesda Merson Chrysler. Blake Merson, a County native, had a number of business interests in addition to both a beef and a dairy farm up-county. He had been involved with automobiles mainly as a Nash distributor when he joined up with Massachusetts-born Lyle Thompson who ended up more or less running the business.

Merson's trash collecting company was always having problems when trucks parked in residential neighborhoods back on East Lane began leaking noisome liquids into the gutters, and he had his other heated irons to check on. But the car business did well, and Merson and Thompson developed a reputation for good mechanical work and fair dealing. It was not long before big, shiny Chryslers became the cars of choice for Bethesda businessmen who had made it. Some of their friends and competitors called Merson and Thompson the "gold dust twins."

At about the same time Merson and Thompson got rolling, a number of other businesses opened in Bethesda. Near Dr. Perry's building, Dr. L. A. Sordo took over the Bethesda Animal Hospital which had begun as a branch of a D.C. vet's business. Dr. Sordo treated dogs and cats almost exclusively and probably would have been surprised at the mix of Dr. Morris's clientele thirty years before. Sordo was a dog lover who said he was not sure that cats were really domesticated. Rowena Holdren's store called The Band Box, on Leland Street across from the new Shopping Center, was probably Bethesda's first gift shop with its large greeting card department and unusual ceramics. In the shopping center, Arnold Hurt was a newcomer, and his fabric and upholstery business grew slowly, but Hurt and Horney soon included the Mayflower Hotel and Congressional Country Club as clients. New businesses were starting in Bethesda at a rate of about one a week in the late Thirties.

As home construction rebounded, whole new neighborhoods and subdivisions opened up. Morris Cafritz bought the land bordered by Wilson's farm on the west and the Wheatley place on the east and called his development Greenwich Forest. Alvin Aubinoe designed and built most of the first homes taking care to preserve as many trees as possible. It soon became a popular, up-scale neighborhood.

The "English farm style" home built for Mr. and Mrs. Robert Slaughter at the entrance to Greenwich Forest was a prize winner. It took years of work to get grass to grow on the foundation lines of the old smokehouse that had stood on that site. Dr. and Mrs. G. B. Clendenin were among the other early residents of the new community, which soon developed its own traditions of bridge and dinner parties, carol singing around the Christmas tree at the entrance, and picnics on the big Aubinoe lawn next to their home at 8000 Overhill.

Starting in 1930, the Aubinoes held an "at home" party at Alandotte, which grew until they were entertaining some five hundred friends and neighbors on New Year's Eves. By the late Thirties, Greenwich Foresters were holding dinner-dances at Congressional and talking of building a clubhouse. As in many other neighborhoods, women got together to hook rugs and men to play poker, and soon there was an active community association.

Other neighborhoods were not doing as well. Woodmont had been considered the "wrong side of the tracks" long before the tracks disappeared. At a time when each new development tried to out-snob its neighbors, the Triangle was déclassé and gaining a reputation for gangs of tough young men and for houses where beer, booze, betting, and sometimes other pleasures, were easily available at almost any hour. Lex Morris's store and beer joint and both Peake's Red Fox and Phillips' Whippet Tavern up on the Pike were reasonably well-run restaurants and beer halls, which advertised good meals of Maryland fried chicken or Smithfield ham for less than a dollar. But they were avoided by the "better" types in Bethesda. Between them was the greying American Ice Company, the old dairy, with the compressors in the back and loading dock on the north side. In the middle of the next block was the Ailes' big house and then Dr. Perry's.

When Bill Austin first came to Bethesda about 1937 he rented one of the "shotgun" houses next to the Whippet for himself and his wife who was soon to bear their first child. His wife was making $10 a week as a seamstress down at the Tolman Laundry near the carbarn, and he found a job with Gordon Burrows at $14.50 for a sixty-hour week. Austin recalled, "Doc Perry had two little houses right across the street from the driving range that Leo Wolper ran. It wasn't a bad house, but it had a swing on the front porch, and the drunks used to come out of the Whippet Tavern and end up

on my porch swing. I'm trying to go to sleep, and I'd hear that swing swinging." It was not long before Austin moved his family down to Del Ray Avenue and rented another house.

The large Bort family was one of the best remembered clans in Woodmont. The Rev. William Bort, who claimed he was sure his teachers would be surprised that he ended up as a minister, explained his family.

Most of us were born on Cedar Lane (now Greentree Road) in a little log cabin that's still there renovated into a show place. I think there's still part of the old logs left in a corner. When my dad was discharged from the Navy, he was not supposed to live. He came back and stayed in the log cabin with us. There was a ladder up to a loft where the children slept.[73]

My father was an intern in the Navy. He was interning at Walter Reed Hospital, and he came down with some kind of pancreas problem so they discharged him from the Navy and sent him home to die. He was all messed up. And he lay in bed up in that log cabin, and Uncle Mack used to come dress him and take care of him and build a fire to keep the place warm. He was a black man that worked in that convent across the road. He didn't die, but he was a very sick man and bled constantly from this pancreas. He would pass out and lie on the floor, and we would think we was dead, but he would recuperate and keep going.

My mother walked down to the Chevy Chase Club where she worked for fifty cents a day. She didn't take the trolley so she could save a nickel. Artie, Harry and Ralph, the three boys older than I am, they were all raised in the Foundling Home. It was just a "poor house." There was no food in the house and no clothes, so they stayed there until we moved into Bethesda. The old Foundling Home used to be out there on Cedar Lane on the other side of Old Georgetown by that big water tank where those office buildings are now. It was a big, wooden, green house.

When I was two years old, we moved to Woodmont. That was about 1920 or `21. The house we moved to in Bethesda was owned, I think, by the guy in Edgemoor that had the horses, Tuckerman. He sold that house to my dad; he gave it to him at an unbelievable price. It was on Melrose Avenue. Across the street was a big open field, and Parker used to have his cattle out there. Old man Parker, he was blind in one eye.

Melrose Avenue, there was trees all up and down there. There was a place up on Melrose where Arlington Road came around that had an old, deserted house on it. We called it the spook house. It

had an orchard in there. Joe Scopin, the father, lived in an old house, and he was an Italian, and he had Joe and Raymond and Alfred. And Mrs. Scopin was very close to my mother. I used to go over there and work in the shop for Joe Scopin. As a neighborhood it was pretty close.

Our neighbors were the Burrows, the Shacklefords who had that little store, the Armentrouts lived in the middle of that place, and the Spillers. Of course, "Red" Spiller was the brute of that community. Somebody stabbed him in the heart down on Robertson's porch one day, but his heart was on the wrong side. He didn't like black people, you know. When he went down the street, if a black man was there, he would tell him to get on the other side or get killed. So one of them stabbed him one day.

We were as poor as green grass when I was a kid, and when Red Spiller would see me, he'd pull in his pocket and give me a penny or two. That was a lot of money in those days. He was always nice to me.

We played in Parker's field and used the dung out there for bases. We didn't slide very much. Up at the elementary school, we used to play golf up there. From Norfolk Avenue halfway down to Melrose was an open field. It went down to the Grays; he was with the Chevy Chase dairy.

We used to call it "Mudmont" because when it rained there was nothing but mud down there. There wasn't any such thing as sewers, but they had these V-shaped drains going under the roads that we sometimes played in. Tawley Ricketts was out there when one of these flash floods came, and he fell in that stream and got underneath the drainpipe and drowned before he came out the other side. He was only thirteen or fourteen years old. His family lived up on Georgetown Road next to Robertson's store.

When they started putting the sewers in, they dug deep trenches. And the Bensons lived up on St. Elmo, Jack Benson, and Warner. The little girl that was raised in that family was about twelve when she was out riding her bicycle and it slipped and she went into that ditch they dug. And I went down and pulled her out. And when people asked where I met my wife, I always said I got her out of a ditch. I married her when she was sixteen years old. When the Lee girls heard she was going to marry me, they said they weren't going to have any more to do with her if she did.

There was plenty of places to play. And fight. Old man Peake that had the dairy out there, he used to be a horseshoe pitcher, and the only one he couldn't beat was my brother Harry. They used

to have real fistfights. Harry would fight anybody that crossed him. He used to beat me up every day for practice. Joe Usuda called him "Hairless Harry" one time, and he threw Joe and his bicycle across the street and into a field.

Dick Peake was a legend too. He ran around with Calvin Owens and a bunch of reprobate kids. There was a guy down the street named Turpin Brown, he and Billy Lee were dreadnaughts. If you got in their way you were in trouble. They called my father Andy Gump, and they came down and shot at him with a .22 rifle one time. They got killed in an automobile accident.

My father was a disciplinarian. He had a baseball bat, and if you didn't do what he told you to do, he was a sick man, but he'd rap you with that baseball bat. When we had that newspaper route, he'd tell you if you don't put that paper up on the porch, you _will_ go put it up on the porch.

My dad built a little shack next door to the house, a little bakery and got a Dutch oven, and he got to making donuts and pies and cakes. He was a real baker. People used to buy up his pies and apple tarts and stuff, and he made Ralph and Arty go out and sell them. And if they brought some back, he really got angry. Ralph got to a point where he used to throw his over in the woods. That didn't last too long, but I remember cutting the donuts.

He took that shack and joined it to the garage and made a house out of it and rented it. Every time he had another kid in the family, he built another room. He took a little two-bedroom house and built that thing into fourteen rooms. Joe Scopin used to help him. He put an apartment upstairs and a balcony on the back porch.

The Scopin brothers grew up in Woodmont right where their business was still located in the 1990s. Their father, Joe Scopin, Senior, was an Italian-speaking Austrian who, as a ship's carpenter, came to America at about the time of the First World War and settled in Norfolk where he found work with DuPont. Joe Scopin Jr. remembered,

While he was working there he met my mother's brother, who was also working in the shipyards at Hampton Roads. My mother was a true North Carolinian, and her family went back to the Indians. She was a Rivenbark. They got married when she was only thirteen right after the war. My older brother was born down around Norfolk, and then they moved up to Bethesda around 1923, and I was born in `24 in an apartment over the blacksmith's shop at Wisconsin and Elm. We lived there a year or so and then he bought the property where we are now, four lots. My brother was born there in

Scopin's workshop in Woodmont

`25. It used to be called Melrose Avenue before it was Cordell.

First he built the house we lived in, and then he built a little shed. He helped build houses in Edgemoor and Battery Park as a carpenter, a cabinetmaker. Then he started bringing chairs in to glue and repair, and that's the way he started the business. He worked in the shed at night, and when he got enough business going, he didn't work as a carpenter any more. And it's right where we are today.

We never had a Depression in my family. My father said, and I agree with him, "If you can work with your hands, you'll always eat." We always had something to eat. It might have been fatback, but we had some meat.

It was swampy back there. They had narrow streets with deep ditches along them and lots of trees, big trees, and when the rain came it all came down our way. Every block had a ditch around it.

Woodmont Avenue did not reach Old Georgetown then and Norfolk stopped where Woodmont crossed. The grade of Woodmont was different too; from Norfolk and St. Elmo, it was easy to sled down to Cordell and beyond, although most kids went over to the Woodmont Club to sleigh ride.

Raymond Scopin, Joe Jr. and their father

Beyond the streets and the Perrys' properties was the "Patch," a woody and weedy area where kids played "guns" or "war" after school and practiced shooting each other from ambush with cap pistols and home-made wooden weapons. Other youngsters, as "Bud" Keiser recalled, would not venture into the patch where boys built tree forts and dug caves and tried smoking whatever they could find: cadged cigarettes, old cigar butts, corn silk in wild grape leaves, Indian cigars that grew on trees and poke weed. Charlie Federline recalled cutting a poke weed stem, lighting it and inhaling a mouthful of ants. That was when he started swiping Herbert Tarletons from his father's store.

At times, Woodmont's reputation, like Tenleytown's, was both earned and deserved. The Woodmont gang did exist, a group of rough young men in the Depression, some of whom ended up doing time in prison. Charlie Federline said, "The tough parts were Cordell Avenue from Old Georgetown all the way over to Rugby, that was one tough, fricking zone. Those kids would beat you up if they didn't know you. It was their territory." Both Joe Scopin and "Willie" Bort remembered getting beat up, and they lived there.

Rodney Day, whose business address for his Bethesda Refrigeration Service was the home where he grew up at 4831 Del Ray, disagreed. His cornice plasterer father moved his young family to what was then 212 Del Ray in 1921 when Rodney was about one-and-a-half.

I didn't think it was a tough neighborhood. Nobody ever picked on me, and there were no bullies

I couldn't handle. There was a big house at the corner of Norfolk and Del Ray, a big Victorian, and up the street another big one. Right back of us was the Hills. They had a kind of a farm and back of them the ground went up and that's where we used to sleigh ride. It was just a pasture. We'd hunt over there too, squirrel and rabbit. We had cinder streets, and the foundation of my house is cinder, mixed up and poured in a form. You can knock a piece out any place, but its never cracked.

There were also churches and businesses and families that called the Triangle home and never thought about which side of the tracks they were on. Joe Scopin recalled where the Woodmont children played in his day.

We used to play up on the roof of all those stores at Wilson and Old Georgetown. Sometimes we'd have forty or fifty kids up there playing cops and robbers or hide and seek. We used to go skating over there, that was the thing, and when we got tired of that we'd sneak up on the roofs. And there was a big apple orchard on Woodmont at Cordell, lots of apples, and we used to play up there. The Usudas lived up there. We made a ball field right across from our building and put up a basket. We played baseball and basketball over there. When my father went out in the delivery truck, we'd get out and play ball and keep a lookout up on the hill so we'd know when he was coming back.

In the summer, we hung out at the swimming pool at Chevy Chase Lake. Then we had the swimming hole off Cedar Lane where all the boys in Woodmont went. We never wore anything; this was a private boys' swimming place. We used to go up to the church where old man Albritton was the Scoutmaster. We used to go in that church on St. Elmo and play at night, all these kids just playing around, not damaging anything.

There was never a Hallowe'en went by that guys a little older than me would go out, and the next morning you'd look at the telephone poles and somebody's chair or sofa off the front porch was up there. We always went over to Chevy Chase, and they would put a penny or nickel in your bag and wouldn't just run you off. In Woodmont you didn't get anything.

Not everyone in Bethesda lived in a "nice" home in a "good" neighborhood. One family in Alta Vista lived in an old trolley car for years and, when they became a bit

Boy Scout Troop 204 started at the Methodist church in Woodmont in 1933

more prosperous, used their former home as a chicken coop. The houses beside Columbia Country Club built for trolley car operators all shared a single pump. There were several forgotten areas of sub-standard homes without sewer or water connections where life was not much different from the squatters along the river or up the hills of Glen Echo.

And three trailer camps operated right in Bethesda and several others on the northern fringes. One was on Wisconsin Avenue across from Burrows's service station and next to the old Offutt house and the miniature golf course. Up behind the bank and north of where We Cab set up an office, was another Sacks's trailer park facing a path that became Commerce Lane, a street Sacks built and then dedicated to the County. A third was in Woodmont just off Old Georgetown at Fairmont near Warren Gingell's house and office.

Trailers next to the Offutt house - apartments on Strathmore in back

The election of 1936 was held using the old paper ballots after the County Commissioners voted five to one, Hagner dissented, to defer the purchase of voting machines. In Bethesda, voters went along with the rest of the County and nation in supporting Franklin Roosevelt, but Chevy Chase stuck with the Republican candidate from Kansas. In the County, the vote was FDR 12,730 and Landon 9,882, but in the Bethesda precincts, the Democrat only edged out his Republican challenger 2,880 to 2,821. In Bethesda itself, Roosevelt beat Landon 1,486 to 1,205; in Chevy Chase, Landon garnered 1,306 votes to the Democrat's 874, and if it had not been for the votes cast by residents of Glen Echo and Cabin John, who went for FDR 520-310, Landon would have carried the Western Suburban District. Obviously the New Deal was attracting Republicans as well as Democrats to the suburbs.

By the time Roosevelt started his second term, Bethesda had over 5,700 listed telephone subscribers, a thousand more than Silver Spring and four thousand more than Rockville. Roads were still a problem, and narrow, poorly maintained Old Georgetown, a particular pain. After two motorists died in a collision with a bus in early December 1936, citizens' associations began to circulate petitions deploring the condition of what one leader called "a paved cow trail." Samuel Stonebraker of the Chamber of Commerce promised support, but the State Roads officials pled poverty and only promised to put the old road high on their list.[74]

Area developers and citizens' associations held the line against more apartment projects, but the production of single-family homes had accelerated. Then the Federal government announced its plan to build a facility for the purpose of raising experimental animals for research by the Hygienic Laboratory of the Public Health Service's National Institute of Health. The mice, rats, guinea pigs and rabbits raised on the proposed $100,000 Bethesda farm were to be used in ongoing studies of Rocky Mountain spotted tick fever, encephalitis, polio, psittacosis, typhus, tularemia, and other deadly diseases. The resulting howl was certainly heard in Beltsville, which is where the NIH might have been located had it not been for the generosity of Mr. and Mrs. Luke I. Wilson.[75]

In January 1933, after talking with Harold Ickes, Luke I. Wilson had written to Marvin McIntyre asking him to come out and see "Tree Tops" and suggest how the government might use the property. The Wilsons had in mind donating ninety acres for public use after giving up plans for establishing an "International Center."

Bethesda's leaders had only recently, after a long and seemingly endless struggle, seen the last of the sickly cows at USDA experimental farm on the end of Norwood Drive. With the help of the CCC boys, that land was now being turned into a recreation center to be operated by Park and Planning and the County's fledgling recreation department. The Commissioners, led by Bethesda "mayor" Robert Hagner, came out loudly against the PHS proposal, which they labeled "outrageous." The Bethesda Chamber of Commerce joined the hue and cry and the M-NCP&PC was not far behind. They all pointed to the homes of Merle Thorpe,

Canon Freeland Peter, C. B. Hawley, and George Hamilton as well as to "Cedarcroft," the home of Helen Wilson's sister. "It would destroy the residential character of the neighborhood," the businessmen and public officials maintained.

But Wilson and his equally wealthy wife met with Dr. Lewis Thompson, the Assistant Surgeon general and later director of the NIH, and became convinced that what the Public Health people intended would do no such thing, and so they stuck with the offer they had made to the Secretary of the Interior and in a follow-up letter to President Roosevelt. In August 1935, for ten dollars, the Wilsons deeded nearly half their land, forty-five acres, to the U.S. Government and then sailed for Europe on the *Bremen*.[76]

The first newspaper story about the new facility, headlined "Where U.S. Will Raise Laboratory Animals," featured photos of the rolling land and one of the Wilson's cottages. The accompanying story told of the government's plans to raise white mice, rabbits and guinea pigs to aid fifty scientists in their "search for life-saving serums." Soon other stories emphasized objections to the "guinea pig farm" from Bethesda residents and showed pictures of the planned three-story $100,000 laboratory.[77]

With added impetus from the public health research provisions of the Social Security Act, which provided $2 million a year, the new Surgeon General, Dr. Thomas Parran, moved the whole building program of the NIH to Bethesda. Protests continued that the project would "smash real estate values along the Pike where many of Maryland's richest estates are located."[78]

In 1937, Luke I. Wilson's doctors diagnosed cancer. He died just a few days before the adoption of the bill establishing the National Cancer Institute in July 1937, and his widow offered ten more acres for the building of the Cancer Institute and later gave the NIH almost all of her land as well as her home and moved into the "Lodge," her guesthouse.[79]

What had started as a $100,000 appropriation for a experimental animal farm was now a $1,463,000 project and the cancer institute added $750,000 to that. Landscaping and road building began in the summer of `37; the groundbreaking took place on the first day of 1938, and by December, scientists and administrators occupied three red-brick, Georgian buildings on the NIH campus, and two more

Mrs. Wilson on the construction site

buildings had been authorized. Building Six, the Cancer Institute, was completed in the fall of 1939.

Across the Pike, negotiations for acquiring the land for FDR's naval hospital were nearly complete. The government had purchased all but forty-two of the needed two hundred-plus acres by the end of 1938, and the Commissioners had agreed to relocate Jones Bridge Road on the huge reservation's southern border.[80]

No event since the coming of the electric trolley had such an effect on the town as the building of the two, huge, medical institutions. The NIH not only created hundreds of jobs for Bethesdans, it brought many well-educated scientists and their families to the area. The fears of the County Commissioners and Chamber of Commerce proved groundless, and the neighborhoods that sprang up around the NIH came to be some of the most popular developments of the `30s building boom. The desires of new residents for a pleasant and safe place to live and for good schools and playgrounds coincided with the hopes of Bethesda's long-time promoters such as Tuckerman and Sacks.[81]

Places to play were seldom a problem for Bethesda youngsters. Some ballfields disappeared in rapid development, but almost every neighborhood had a vacant lot or two, and except for the main roads, the streets were safe for games of all kinds. "Bud" Keiser played hockey on Arlington Road in the `30s,

and there was a good baseball field on the west side of Arlington where it ended at Bethesda Avenue in a series of red clay hills that were a challenge to climb and tunnel in. Dr. Perry let kids play on part of his big lot, and, of course, the school fields always had room for games of work-up, two-knocker, hot-box or pitcher's hand.

The construction boom provided the raw materials for innumerable shacks, tree houses, and underground hideaways all over Bethesda. A big one hid near the railroad tracks where the Imiries were developing Montgomery Avenue, and one of the more elaborate structures was in Kenwood where newly hired salesman S. H. Mumford almost fell into an underground hut made of store boxes with hammered out tin cans for roofing.

Going to the movies on Saturday afternoon became a regular part of the life of many Bethesda children. Often there was a double feature of Westerns or adventure films and always a serial with a cliff-hanging ending to every one of its dozen or more episodes. (When that cabin exploded with our hero in it, we had to get back the next Saturday even though we knew from experience that salvation would be by a trap door, which suddenly appeared in the middle of what had been a bare floor.) Usually there was a cartoon or two and sometimes a newsreel and a trailer, a "preview of coming attractions."

Lots of kids stopped by the Gulf station just across Montgomery Lane from Hiser's State theater for a free comic book and in Peoples or the little store next to the movie house for a box of Good and Plentys, Nibs, bubble gum or some other kind of candy. Tickets cost a dime plus tax, and often there was some excitement even before the lights dimmed and the show started when the exit doors near the stage quietly opened to let in a stream of dazzling sunlight and a few friends without the price of a ticket. The ushers trotted down, but they knew that kids could crawl up the aisles and along the rows faster than they could run.

Boys and girls left their bikes lying on the steep bank beside the theater where the post office was later built, and when they came out of the matinee and got their eyes readjusted, they always found them right where they put them. Nobody locked a bike. Sometimes the theater managers would make wondrous mistakes. Once the Bethesda ushers gave away small boxes of dog biscuits, which, as soon as

the lights went down, became mortar shells arcing through the projector's beam to fall on unsuspecting victims who could only fire back blindly with their own supply of biscuits.

The Recreation Center, of course, became a favorite place for young Bethesdans who lived in that neighborhood or had bicycles, and nearly everyone had a bike. Robert Rickey, who moved into 4621 Langdrum Lane with his family in June 1933, delivered the *Daily News* on his bike. His big route stretched from the bank, where he got his papers by the trolley car switch, all the way down to Bradley Lane and covered everything between Wisconsin and Connecticut. He had a speedometer on his bicycle and could get it up to 40 mph going down the Dorset hill in Somerset before zooming across the creek into Kenwood where he later lived in Charlie Ross's old stone house on Kennedy Drive. Rickey went to schol at Somerset for a year and joined Scout Troop 237, which met there. He recalled that money raised for his troop by selling tickets to a benefit at the State Theater disappeared along with one of the Scoutmasters.[82]

For a while it was fun playing in the remains of the old experimental farm, but as the sheds and cattle pens disappeared, tennis courts and ball fields took their place. Carroll Grenfell, who lived on Chevy Chase Boulevard, and Robert Rickey and their friends explored the old buildings, many of them roofless, and had BB gun battles all through the deserted farm using watering troughs for foxholes. Rickey remembered another game.

There was an old water tower down there, out in an open field. We loved to climb up on that thing. Then another damn-fool thing, we got a box, I guess we found it up there, an old wooden packing box. And we cut windows in it and pulled that thing up on that water tower with a big rope and played airplane. Two guys on the ground with ropes would pull it back and forth, and that thing would swing out there in space about thirty feet up. And all the while this big rope was fraying, chafing away on the edge of the platform. Fortunately it held until we got tired of doing it.

Eventually, the recreation department pulled down most of the derelict buildings or renovated them for other uses, and built a stone-fronted, grass-floored outdoor stage facing the rough amphitheater at the far end of the old farm. Real backstops and goal posts appeared on the playing fields. The "Rec Center" became the best place in town for pickup games

of all kinds as well as for the much more organized summer camps and numerous teams sponsored by the recreation department.

Bob Eastham remembers pondering the name long before he tagged along with some older kids; he thought that "rec" was "wreck" and the place was full of old, junked cars, and that was why his folks had told him not to go there. "But it was wonderful," he recalled.

Washington's Leading Suburban Home Section
BETHESDA CHEVY CHASE TRIBUNE

Bethesda got its first newspaper, a bi-weekly tabloid called the *Bethesda Chevy-Chase Tribune* in April 1937. The editor-publisher was William Prescott Allen of Battery Park. It sold for five cents; a one-year subscription was a dollar. The "flag" at the top of page one featured a drawing of the Madonna of the Trail on her pedestal and promised "5000 distribution certified guaranteed." The front page photo showed the unfinished gym and "B" building at the high school, and the lead story in the first edition was the building boom, "twice as great as that of 1936 when Montgomery County set an all-time record with $7,500,000 in construction . . . ." Allen quoted Inspector E. J. Gray as saying that it "represents the greatest display of building activity in the Western Suburban District."

Bill Allen was a Georgia native who had graduated from Mercer University and worked on his father's Florida daily before moving to D.C. and taking a job with the Hearst papers. The first issue of his paper had a feature story on Thomas W. Pyle and on the Kenwood cherry trees, which were then in bloom. Dorothy Sheiry Hilland offered a column of "Garden Tips" and praised the Elm Street homeowners for their beautiful lawns and shrubs.

T. W. Perry's ad listed ten types of coal from $8.25 to $11.00 per 2,240-pound ton while at the Lakeview Market fancy rib roasts went for twenty-seven cents a pound. Other local advertisers in that first edition included the Home Confectionary, which preceded Emmy Lou's, Simmons Barber & Beauty Shop, Loria Plumbing, Bethesda Motor Sales, R. B. Sadler's Bethesda Printing Co. whose ad asked "How Do You Like the 'Tribune'?", Glen Echo, Magee Radio, Bethesda Paint & Hardware, the Pat-A-Cake Bake Shop in the new shopping center,

Pumphrey's funeral home, and The Montgomery Farm Women's Cooperative Market Incorporated. Whittlesey's only took a small ad for Bisma-Rex but soon became a full-back-page advertiser. A full-page ad in that first issue cost Parkway Ford ninety dollars. It was not long before Bill Allen's little paper was sponsoring track meets at the Rec Center, a cooking school at the State Theater and editorializing on the need for more variety in Bethesda businesses.[83]

Early issues of the *Tribune* featured short "Why I Live Here" essays from such luminaries as J. Harry Welsh, Gilbert Grosvenor, and Joseph Cantrel. Allen's editorials urged fair reassessment, widening of Old Georgetown Road, cleaning up Bethesda, and a summer parks program for children. In general, the *Tribune* supported the County Commissioners but viewed with alarm the Fusion members' refusal to approve bond issues to support school construction. Allen's paper soon became a recognized mouthpiece of the regular Democrats and an all-out supporter of the E. Brooke Lee.

The big news in Bethesda in the spring of 1937 was the strength of the building boom, the preliminary work on the N.I.H. campus, the high school baseball team, which went undefeated, and the creation of a new park on the experimental farm property. Emory Bogley received much praise for that accomplishment as well as the Kuhn Cup given by the Chamber of Commerce for his contributions to Bethesda. At B-CC High School Tom Pyle was predicting the enrollment of 725 students in the fall and citing the need for six more teachers. He staged a housewarming for the new gym, PE, art, and

From the April 28, 1937, *Tribune*

home ec classrooms for the parents and incoming 10th graders.

Mrs. Daniel Walser of Chevy Chase, a Board of Education member, presented diplomas to the B-CC students in the auditorium at Leland, and Mrs. Roosevelt was the main speaker at graduation on June 15, 1937, to top off a busy and memorable year. Senior Elizabeth Wilson broke the tradition of having only seniors on the graduation program and persuaded the First Lady to take part.

Class president Donald MacLeod had the job of introducing Mrs. Roosevelt who seemed to him "the tallest and most unassuming female I ever met. I was afraid people could hear my knees shaking, but she spoke quietly to me and calmed my fears." Eleanor Roosevelt echoed her husband's first speech as president when she told the graduates that "To be afraid is to be beaten." She urged them to help their communities and said that "young people who think are needed today to help solve the problems of the nation."

Fireworks were legal in most of Bethesda, but the 4th of July 1937 was a fairly quiet one. Battery Park canceled its usual celebration, and at the Edgemoor Club, no fireworks followed the swimming, diving and tennis contests. The Chamber of Commerce, backing a public hospital for the Western Suburban District, was eyeing the new park at the end of Norwood Drive as a possible site. The *Tribune's* swimming meet at Glen Echo and track meet at Leland attracted hundreds of Bethesda youngsters in August. High school principal Tom Pyle headed the Rotary Club's Youth Service Committee, which organized temporary summer jobs for many high school students.

By the time schools reopened, the political pot was starting to bubble, but problems with bus service and the election of a "Xmas Lane" queen distracted many from the issue of school bonds and the usual Democratic Party internecine bloodletting.

In November of 1937, the Bethesda-Chevy Chase Lions Club organized with twenty-four charter members. The first officers chosen were Paul Imirie, president; "Doc" Whittlesey, vice-president; James R. Enright, who had recently moved his electrical appliance business from Rockville to Sacks' row of stores, secretary; William K. Brecht, treasurer, and printer Ralph B. Sadler, tail-twister. Among the original members were Esso's Robert J. Eastham,

Doctors Bashore and Bauersfeld, former B-CC coach Anthony Kupka and his replacement, Alan Vogt, and the Simmons brothers. The regular meetings were at the Kenwood Club.

Rumblings emerged from some Bethesda business circles about the semi-political activities of the Chamber of Commerce, but almost everyone joined in the second annual Christmas Lane celebration in 1937, which included the coronation of a queen just after the parade of forty floats, numerous marching organizations and ten bands including one from the Chestnut Farms-Chevy Chase Dairy. The organizers closed Old Georgetown Road and Wisconsin Avenue for two hours and built the reviewing stand at the shopping center. Burrell Marsh chaired the proceedings for the Chamber of Commerce, and Joseph Cantrel crowned Mrs. Margaret Sartwell Perrell "Miss Bethesda-Chevy Chase." Unfortunately, not all the anticipated sponsors came through, and the Chamber ended up with a lot of red ink and scaled-down plans for future celebrations.

B-CC students lighted the first community Christmas Tree on the front lawn of the high school to start a tradition, and in the spring, the big production was *The Pirates of Penzance* with Rex Minckler, president of the Activity Council and member of the Honor Society, as the "modern major general." The PTA grew to over 450 members by '38, and the school began offering adult education classes in art, crafts and homemaking in the evenings.[84]

In the fall of 1937, Kay Greaney arrived at B-CC after graduating from Colby and teaching for seven years in Maine. Dr. Broome promised her the top salary in the County, $1,800 a year, if she would take a job at Bethesda rather than the one she had been offered at Western in D.C. In those days the superintendent made individual deals with his teachers and generally paid men more than women. Miss Greaney taught a world history and a Latin class in addition to her English classes and became sponsor of the yearbook, the knitting club, and the movie club. Her room was in the unfinished basement.

It was just a bare room with a concrete floor, and I wore my sister-in-law's short fur coat to classes because it was so cold; the only heat was in some pipes that ran across the top. I can remember storming up to T. W. Pyle; I had been told by an older teacher that I wasn't going to get anywhere if I didn't speak up, speak my mind, so I had that damnable room down in the basement, unheated, and I went up to him with my class and held them

outside and went in and said, "Mr. Pyle, I either quit today, or I get a room that is warm enough for me to live in." It was September, and I had on a fur coat. And so he took half of a room. There's a big room there that had a stage in it; this woman high on his list had the whole thing. I was teaching three subjects, so I got the part with the stage in it, but in my free period I had to get out so she could have the whole thing.[85]

In a few years Miss Greaney had a room of her own on the second floor and was part of what students sometimes called "murderers' row." By then Tom Pyle was surely the most respected and best liked member of the Bethesda community. He was active in the Chamber of Commerce, the Civic Federation, the teachers' association and the Rotary Club and seemed to have time for any project to improve the town or B-CC. When he came to the school on Wilson Lane, all five hundred of Bethesda's students fit in that one building. By the end of 1937 there were six schools housing about 2,000 students, and the graduating senior class had grown from fourteen to 112. Pyle believed that no man was educated who could not work with his hands and as a hobby made his own furniture and carved the symbol and gavel of B-CC's Honor Society.

"He taught by example respect for the dignity of people: the unsuccessful as well as the successful, the laborer as well as the intellectual, the poor as well as the prosperous," said teacher Margaret Casey. Patsy Lozupone remembered that "at assemblies Mr. Pyle taught you how to behave. You faced forward no matter what happened. I still stand at weddings facing forward when everyone else turns and looks. He had a profound influence on us."

Robert Rickey, class of 1940, struggled at Leland, but:

I enjoyed high school and my academics improved. I figured I'd reached the peak when old Thomas Pyle, I was in the 10th grade, and he named me delegate-at-large. I got a nice letter from him. He was wonderful. He said "decisions" as "deeceesions" and used the word frequently. "You all will have to make some hard deeceesions," he would say.

Pyle credited the community, the student body and the faculty for the school's success, but Miss Casey insisted that "those who worked with him knew it was the spirit of excellence he engendered that gave the school the incentive to excel." He saw to it that the high school was accredited soon after it moved to

East West Highway, the first in the County to be so evaluated. And he established the first guidance services and college bureau in a County high school and probably staged the first college and career nights.

English teacher Kay Greaney remembered something else about Pyle.

Late one afternoon as I was leaving a seemingly deserted building, I met Mr. Pyle near a side exit. I took the opportunity to seek his help about a yearbook publication problem. As we talked a group of boys came along the corridor who presumably had no business being there at that hour and were surely up to no good. Instead of acting suspicious or accusing them of infringement of rules, he engaged them in conversation in a friendly manner, learning in doing so that their presence there was for a legitimate and worthy purpose. He offered to stay with them until they had completed their task..

Front: Morell, Kimmel, Vannais, Fuller, Hayden

School year 1937-38 featured what many thought was B-CC's best boys' basketball team, coached by Tony Kupka and Alan Vogt, who transferred from Rockville High in January 1938 when Kupka followed "Zip" Lehr's lead and took a coaching job at Woodrow Wilson High School in the District. It featured Leon Vannais, "Fuzzy" Morell , "Ace" Fuller, Pete Kimmel and high-point man Carroll Hayden. "They combined a powerful offense with a very aggressive defense," said Kupka, and Vogt agreed saying they were the best team he had in ten years at B-CC. They lost to Joe Gallagher and St. John's in the Star Tourney and to Bones McKinney and Durham High at Lexington in the South Atlantic Tournament.[86]

For Bethesda, 1938 was the best year yet. Not only had home construction reached an all-time high, but contractors completed three of

the town's basic buildings that year. The Boro Theater, soon to be renamed the Bethesda, opened in mid-May with a special issue of the *Tribune* to celebrate the event. Originally designed by John Eberson as the centerpiece of a much larger shopping center, the art deco theater was an immediate success. Eberson, who also designed the Silver Theater, produced a tall and distinctive marquee and a structure with a blond brick facade banded near the top with courses of black bricks.

The theater was part of the growing Sidney Lust chain and boasted comfortable, upholstered chairs and a 500-space parking lot. William Jobes was the first manager, and the theater was staffed mainly by Bethesdans. Within a week, Henry Hiser advertised that he and Roger Eisinger were planning a thousand-seat, air-conditioned theater and shopping center in the 6800 block of Wisconsin Avenue. De-

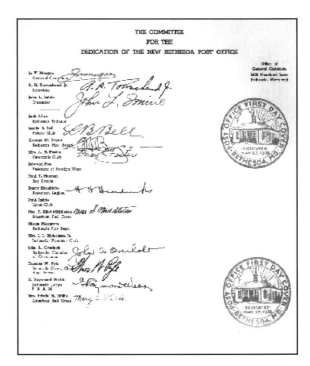

spite having John Zink, the Uptown's architect, as designer and hiring T. Calvin Owens as general contractor, the project never materialized.

After an April that ended with a thunderstorm and golfball-sized hail, local and Federal officials dedicated the new WPA-financed post office on the first of June with suitable pomp. Sofarelli Brothers of Jamaica, New York, built it of local stone after bidding $54,112 on the 270-day project and promising not to move or disturb the Madonna. In ceremonies led by John Overholt, executive secretary of the Chamber of Commerce, leaders of Lodge 204 of the F.A.& A.M. inserted the cornerstone, containing a copy of the *Tribune*, some stamps, and the day's program.

The building reflected the style of the stolid bank and County Building but in a more graceful manner. Everyone liked the cupola, hipped roof, and rounded windows of the big, new post office. In his speech, Assistant Postmaster Smith W. Purdum, a native of Damascus, mentioned that in ten years, post office receipts in Bethesda had risen about 300 percent, from $7,993 in 1927 to $31,419 in 1937.

With the new post office, Bethesda was get-

ting a few more tons of Stoneyhurst mica schist, and there was more to come with Peoples Drug Store's new façade on the other corner of Tuckerman's row and the telephone company's big addition down at Stanford Street. By Christmas, Bethesda had another piece of public art. D.C. artist Robert Gates finished his mural of the Farm Women's Market in the new post office. Gates earned $1,000 for his painting in the Grant Wood-ish, WPA style.[87]

The third important new building was what most local folks called the "ten-cent store." In late September, with banana splits for a dime as the big attraction, the F. W. Woolworth Company opened its "new and modern store" on Wisconsin Avenue near what had been Darcy's store. Soon a Sears and Roebuck would go on the corner between Woolworth's and the Farm Women's Market, but north of the ten-cent store a gas station, several old houses being used for various businesses and some used-car lots crowded the sidewalk. No one could argue about the signs of progress, but the jumble of run-down, shabby, weed-filled lots and new construction still left plenty of room for improvement. With all this building it was no surprise when Maloney Concrete bought a lot at the end of Bethesda Avenue and put up a cement batch plant with a forty-foot, corrugated metal tower and a long conveyor belt.

Up behind Pumphrey's Funeral Home, Bowling and Gardiner started building four-unit apartments on Avondale for Dr. William Ba-

shore in mid-1937. The dentist had an office in the first building at 5434-36, and by 1940, there were eleven square, red brick, colonial-revival structures in Bethesda's first big, garden apartment project. Riley Evers had put up the first separate apartment buildings on Hampden Lane in the mid-30s. Before his three-unit development and the two, big brick buildings on Edgemoor Lane, the only apartments had been over individual stores and in the rows of shops built on Wisconsin Avenue.

One of Riley Ever's Hampden Lane apartments

Most Bethesda neighborhoods continued to oppose apartments in a reflexive manner, and the Morrison Brothers and other builders found themselves fighting Carey Quinn, Frederic Lee and the representatives of various citizens' associations every time they asked for an apartment building permit. In 1937-38, County builders put up almost 3,000 single-family homes but only about 600 multi-family units and just a handful of those in Bethesda.[88]

Thirty-eight was also the year that F. Meade Bell's father, later president of B. F. Saul, had Bolling and Gardiner build a big, white Sonneman designed house on the curve of Wilson Lane next to Landon school on three acres of what had been the Galligher land near the Hall's farm.

Meade Bell said:

When we came there were corn fields all around us and a big barn at Bradley and Bradmoor where a creek ran and two, tenant farm houses where black families lived. I saw a pig slaughtered there and learned I never had to see that again.

Paul Stone had two big, Belgian work horses, draft horses with big feet like the ones Budweiser uses and a Clyde McCoy circus pinto and a couple of others, and we used to go and ride them. You could put five on one of those Belgian horses; they were really powerful. It wasn't an operating farm, but it ran from Bradley to Greentree.

Banfield had just started Landon. So we'd hide in the woods with the horses, and when we saw him coming, we'd gallop across his driveway. Paul was sort of a pain as far as kids were concerned. He'd try to chase us as we galloped around his house. He was still mad at me when he got into the Rotary Club.

Farther out Wilson Lane past the older farm houses in what was later called Cohasset, Helen and Charles Baldwin built a large Art Deco house designed by Francis Palms Jr. on eleven acres. It featured large overhangs, lots of glass and glass brick, several porches and was labeled an "imposing modern design" by *Architectural Forum* in November 1941. It looked as if the trend of building large houses on impressive estates was also being reborn.

Baldwin's house-About 80,000 cu.ft. for about $35,000

Of course, there was also an off-year election in 1938 highlighted by FDR's attempt to purge U. S. Senator Millard Tydings and by the quiet comeback of the Lee machine in slightly different dress. The failure of the Fusion-dominated County Commissioners to issue more school bonds seemed to be the issue of interest to most Bethesdans especially when the local elementary bulged with nearly 700 students. The campaign had started on the 4th of July in `37 when Joseph A. Cantrel announced that he would seek the State Senate seat in the Democratic primary. Then came the formation of the Democratic Party Tax Reduction Committee headed by Steven B. Fuller, candidate for County Commissioner, J. Sumner Wood, running for the State Senate, both of whom lived in Chevy Chase, and Dulaney Hunter of Kenwood, who declared for the House of Delegates.

In early 1938, Bob Hagner, Bethesda's County Commissioner, announced that he was retiring from politics to spend more time on his

real estate business. He had recently offered his big lot on the corner of Wisconsin and East West to Abe Morrison before selling it to Charles Hawley for $75,000. Hawley, who often went duck hunting with Hagner, told him that the property would be a "gold mine," but Hagner said he had to sell it.

Hagner's number one assistant, Andrew Newman, with American Legion and Chevy Chase backing, and Thomas Earle Hampton, active in the Civic Federation, Chamber and real estate circles, elbowed each other for the job. Hampton, whose father was secretary-treasurer of the M-NCP&PC, won the backing of Hagner and what was left of Dr. Perry's organization, while T. W. Perry and Curtis Walker headed the faction that supported Newman. It was no real surprise when the party regulars led by their newly chosen leader, Robert Peter, endorsed T. Earle Hampton.[89]

The second hint of another split in Democratic ranks came when New Dealer Eugene Casey tried to derail the endorsement of Senator Tydings's re-election. In April, attorney-general Herbert O'Conor began his campaign for governor at Congressional Country Club with Willie Green Day crying "the worm has turned." The Party regulars supported Mayor Jackson of Baltimore for governor, but Mrs. Werner convinced Dr. Perry to ask his people to split their ticket and vote for her first cousin John Goutrum who was running for attorney general with O'Conor. The United Democrats' banner was in tatters with only nine incumbents seeking reelection to the twenty-one County posts.

Meanwhile, the Republicans split over another Fusion coalition. The Fusion cause was not helped when two of its appointees were indicted for embezzling County funds and the supervisor of relief was convicted of forgery.

Fusionist Joseph Cantrel decided to run for the House of Representatives instead of the State Senate and changed his support to O'Conor for governor. Cantrel, a Georgetown-educated lawyer, had built a home next to the Imirie's on Bradley Lane in 1927 and moved there with his second wife and three-year-old twin sons whose mother had died in childbirth. Now his teen-aged sons were actively involved.

"I remember campaigning for him up in Cumberland in '38 when he ran for Congress," Joseph Jr. said:

They gave him a car with loud speakers on the top, and we ran through all these little towns up in Western Maryland. Lex Morris drove, and

Frank and I were passing out literature. We ran our legs off; we were spindly little guys at the time."

Frank Cantrel added:

Able, honest and fearless, he campaigned as. He was an excellent public speaker, the best I've heard in my whole life, and I've heard a lot of them. He was something

By July, Lee had co-opted the Fusion group's Democratic leaders, and it looked like smooth sailing for the old machine until Eugene B. Casey, supported by Jim Pugh, Walter Magruder and the president of the Democratic Women's Clubs, Marguerite Fischer, announced the formation of the Independent Democrats and sent Charles T. Crockett, Edgemoor contractor, into the primary against T. E. Hampton and fielded an almost full slate of other candidates.

The United Democratic Organization crunched through the primary like a bulldozer, winning most races by more than 3,000 votes, while the Republicans, who had few fights, boasted of Walter Johnson as one of their winners. For the Bethesda area Commissioner seat, Thomas Earle Hampton with 8,678 votes swamped both Crockett's 3,174 and Stephen Fuller's 1,322 to run against the Republican, Captain Chester Wells, who was unopposed in the primary. "Bill" Byron of Washington County defeated Cantrel for the nomination to run for Congress, and Tydings easily beat Representative David J. Lewis despite FDR's and Gene Casey's best efforts.

The *Tribune* reported that "a prominent citizen of Edgemoor" lost $1,500 in two bets on the outcome, but few observers were surprised by the Lee machine's comeback. W. Prescott Allen's paper concluded post-primary coverage with "It is the staunch belief of The Tribune that if Montgomery County is to enjoy lower tax rates, good roads, proper school facilities, adequate police protection and other highly desirable improvements they must come from within the Democratic party."[90]

Nationwide, the '38 election was bad news for the New Deal. The Democrats lost eight Senate seats and sixty votes in the House. But in Maryland, Tydings buried his Republican challenger and O'Conor beat Nice. In Montgomery County only Walter Johnson survived the Democratic tsunami. Johnson, who had moved from Alta Vista to a farm in Germantown, made a nationwide radio broadcast for the GOP on election eve in which he urged a return to the "American way of life." "Barney"

became the lone Republican on the Board of Commissioners by whipping Clay Plummer.

Hampton defeated Captain Wells by 4,000 votes although the race was closer in the Bethesda precincts. When the new County Commissioners met for the first time in January, T. Earle Hampton, Bethesda's third "mayor," was chosen as president of the Board. Reluctantly, the Commissioners agreed to a promised study of the County's government. Despite a lot of foot dragging, they eventually contacted the Brookings Institution and the fateful examination began.[91]

With things political back to what was considered normal, that is, with Brooke Lee and his friends once more running the Court House, Bethesda went back to the business of growth. A solid foundation had been laid for a high quality residential area, and the business community was beginning to look much better. In fact it already contained most of the enterprises and many of the business owners who would build Bethesda's reputation as a good place to shop as well as to live. The economic health of the whole capital area showed in the start of work on the new airport at Gravelly Point and the ground breaking for the Jefferson Memorial.

There is no doubt that among adults, the Broadhursts were far and away the favorite storekeepers in Bethesda history. Carbert's, Leon's, and Gretchen Cole's had many friends and fans, but they never touched the old hardware store for admiration bordering on love. C. W. Hawley, who had been around the world and was a businessman not given to wasted words, said it was the best run hardware store anywhere.

Whittlesey's had its young fans, lots of them, and so did Peoples once it got established on the corner (where else would you go for Evening in Paris perfume as a Christmas present for your mother?). The "dime store" was great with its counters divided by pieces of heavy glass. The Centro Hobby Shop was quiet fun, the kind of place where aunts and grandmothers could buy birthday presents. Later, Gifford's and the Hot Shoppe were very popular with teenagers who had enough money.

But it is probable that among children the best loved storekeeper in the whole history of Bethesda was Mrs. Emma C. Thompson of Battery Park, but none of them would have known her as "Mrs. Thompson." Her style was described as "stern, brisk cheerfulness" and her

store was a grocery, more or less, called Emmy Lou's.

Among Bethesda children with a penny or two and the ability to reach the counter and see the marvels in the case and glass jars, there was no place else. And the thing that made Mrs. Thompson, and her helper Robert Harding, special to children was that they were patient and treated them like customers. Oh, if you spent more than ten minutes or so reading a comic book, someone might clear his or her throat or ask if you were planning to buy it, but that was expected. (It was probably only at Doc Gellman's Leland Pharmacy that you could bring a funny book to the soda fountain and read it while you nursed a lemon phosphate and not be bothered.)

But attitude was not all that Emmy Lou's had–it had candy, all kinds of candy, cheap candy, exciting candy, wonderful candy. Jaw breakers of all kinds and degrees of hotness and both red and black licorice whips, wax lips and little wax toys with colored sugar water in them, lemon drops and butterscotches, jujubes and nonpareils, hot cinnamon drops, lollipops, twisted sticks of lemon and peppermint, every candy bar ever made and boxes of Good and Plenty, Nibs and candied peanuts, everything. Penny candy and two-for-a-nicklel, and five-cent candy. Sometimes you got them in a little, brown paper sack, but often the jawbreakers went from her hand to your hand to your mouth as your coin went the other way.

The kids crowded in after school, hollering and pushing. One learned to wait his turn despite urgent whispers of "Hurry up will ya, I gotta go" from the back. Grubby hands placed hoarded dimes and nickels on the counter or pennies unspent on warm lunchroom milk, and she asked, "What would you like?" and "How many?" while you pointed "Some of those" or asked "Don't you got some of those marshmallow things?" She told a reporter that the children were "some of my best customers."

Emmy Lou, who had been called that since she was a child in Iowa, soon knew everyone in the neighborhood. Four businesses had failed on that corner of Wilson Lane and Cordell before she arrived in 1938 to go in competition with the Safeway and the Battery Park Market.

She brought with her eleven years of experience on Georgia Avenue and four years at the Argonne Market on Columbia Road when she and her government-employee husband moved to Battery Park. She stocked Wonder Bread

and Wilkins coffee, some staples like cigarettes, chewing tobacco and a few cans of beans and corn and had a delicatessen case and a small soda fountain with magazine racks stuffed in wherever there was space. Overlapping cards held bottle openers, corn-cob pipes, and fingernail clippers. Space she did not have.

Most of the children probably did not know it, but Emmy Lou's specialty was cakes and pies. Production was limited because her oven would only do four at a time, but she took special orders and seldom had any leftovers. Some of the club women, she said, sneaked her cakes in as their own at bake sales and club meetings. In ads she called it the "Sweet Shoppe," but no one else did.[92]

To generations of young Bethesdans in the Thirties and Forties, Emmy Lou's was the most important place in town, and a visit there with some money was at least as much fun as the Saturday matinee at the Hiser. A lot of grandparents around Montgomery County can enter a dark, old store and hear that bell above the door tinkle and know the candy counter should be on the right, its glass front covered with small, smudged hand prints.

Despite Chairman Burrell Marsh's misgivings, the third annual Christmas Lane celebration opened on Friday night, December 2, with a parade up Wisconsin Avenue from Bradley and out Old Georgetown to Arlington Road. The 1937 event had cost the Chamber dearly, but Marsh had been unable to persuade the leadership to stage a scaled-down celebration. So they took the lights and decorations out of storage and installed them on the telephone poles along both sides of the main street and then the rain, hail and heavy snowstorm on Thanksgiving almost destroyed them.

Police Chief Garrett and Chamber President Overholt led the parade followed by Miss Bethesda-Chevy Chase, Ruth Estelle Parks, Queen of the Christmas Lane. Then came the American Legion drum and bugle corps, Warner Pumphrey's ambulance and the State Theater float with Santa Claus. Marchers from Chevy

Chase Elementary School and the Farm Women's Market preceded the Bethesda Fire Department, the Rock Creek ginger ale float and G. W. Imirie's comedy skit, which had become a regular attraction. Leland's band was next and then floats sponsored by Chestnut Farms-Chevy Chase Dairy, Frank Loria, Chevy Chase Transfer and Storage, Artcraft Cleaners, Parkway Cleaners, Emil Critchfield and Pi Phi fraternity. The high school had both a band and float in the parade, and C&P sent its mobile telephone service truck. The Elks' Boys Band marched, and the Glen Echo Volunteer Fire Department took part. Trucks representing the Loughborough Oil, J. R. Enright, Virga and Co., Powell's Auto Service and Bowling and Gardner took part, and there were units from Job's Daughters and Simmon's Barber Shop.

In front of the bank, J. Horace Smithey led a

Chevy Chase Elementary's marching band

choir and his Chevy Chase Chanters. The Christmas lights went on at 7:30 pm, and at the Park and Shop Center, the queen was crowned and presented with a silver cup donated by the *Tribune*. A party and block dance at the Shopping Center ended the festivities. On Christmas Day, a light snow fell.

Bethesda had enjoyed a year of growth and progress and looked forward to a bigger and even better 1939.

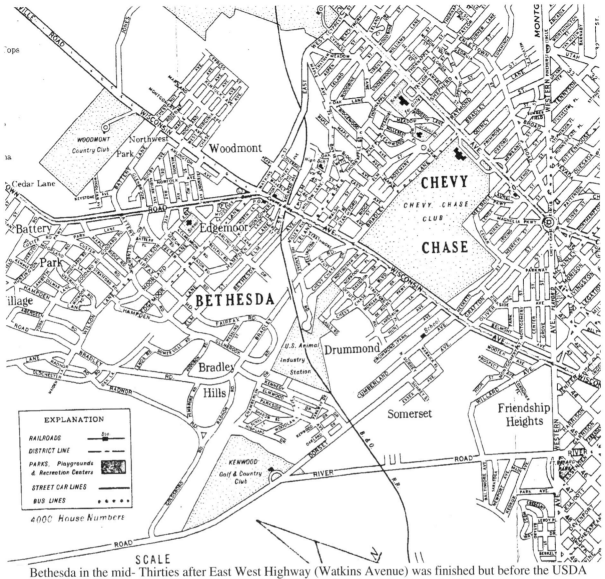

Bethesda in the mid- Thirties after East West Highway (Watkins Avenue) was finished but before the USDA experimental farm (Animal Industry Station) was closed and the high school was moved

[1] *Sentinel*, Feb. 6, 1925.   Residents of Battery Park, Bradley Hills and other neighborhoods had asked the D.C. PUC for a bus line to Western High School in `25.

[2] *Sentinel*, April 10, 1925.

[3] In 1926, kindergarten teachers were assigned to Chevy Chase, Takoma Park, Woodside, Kensington, and Bethesda. BOE minutes cited in Jewell's *From One Room . . . .*

Miss Holman: "The four room frame school on Wilson land has grown like Mr. Finney's turnip."

[4] Thanks to Tempe Curry Grant who sang it several times, could not quite recall the bridge, but remembered that it was sung sitting down so everyone could stand up at the end and cheer.

[5] When interviewed, Mr. Lehr had the maple candlesticks on oak bases that he made that summer.

[6] From an unattributed and undated story in "Zip" Lehr's scrapbook, probably the Chevy Chase *Gazette*. The Guckeyson result is notable because he did not win.

[7] *Sentinel*, July 1, 1927; March 2, 1928; May 18, 1928; July 20, 1928 and *Tattler*, May 25, 1951 and April 23, 1976. Mohler quote from oral history at Rockville Public Library.

The addition cost $123,500, plus heating $17,778, and plumbing $3,900.

[8]*Sentinel*, Jan. 4, March 8, and Sept. 13, 1929. Broome requested $35,850 for laboratory rooms, shops and a commercial department; $47,200 for six more classrooms and ten domestic science classrooms for $65,000.

Pyle took on additional duties in 1930 as the first MCPS high school supervisor, a job that took him out of his building four half-days most weeks.

[9] The other original officers were Mrs. Elmont Hazard, vice-president; Mrs. E. H. Hartnett, treasurer; and Mrs. Marshall, secretary.

[10]The first graduating class (1929) was composed of John Adair Jr., Carrie Estelle Allen, Catherine L. Beane, Margaret Irene Benson, Lloyd F. Cunningham, Barbara Stock Daskin, Kenneth Davis, Curtis M. Dellinger, Elizabeth Litchfield Drown, John E. King, Virginia Alene Lawrence, Mary Margaret Niemeyer, Eugene Purvis O'Neal, and Margaret Post. Note that only about a third of those who "graduated" from the ninth grade finished high school at Bethesda (14 of 41). This trend continued through the period with Leland JHS bigger than B-CC year after year. Some, of course, quit school, but many still went to D.C. public schools or enrolled in private schools. The photo is from the *Tattler*, May 9, 1986.

[11]Other early members and players included Mr. and Mrs. Raymond Sanford, Mrs. William J. Peters, Ralph Fowler, and Maybelle Jennings.

[12]Walter Tuckerman's oldest daugher recalled that Mr. Hathaway was also an agent for Scottish-made clothing and that as a neighborly gesture her mother ordered a $40 blue jacket for her which arrived a bright red. Laura and her four sisters in turn wore it and then she reclaimed it, let the sleeves down ("the color had not faded in the least") and with a red and black hat a friend made, wore it again as a three-quarter length coat when she worked in the city and looked "snappy as the devil."

[13]This work uses "B-CC" as the abbreviation for the high school, but "B.C.C.H.S." was the contemporary mode.

[14]The other police appointed for two-year terms in 1922 were Earl Burdine, Lawrence Clagett and Oscar Gaither.

[15]For more on E. Brooke Lee and his father, Blair Lee, and on the tangled knot of County politics in the early 20th century, see Chapter 14 of *A Grateful Remembrance*.

[16]See *Sentinel*, Dec. 10, 1926. Some find in this era the genesis of the Charter movement which did modernize County government and break both Rockville's and Lee's grip on the area. Lee's friends later called him "Colonel," a National Guard title, others called him "boss." All agreed he was handsome and powerful. Bethesda and Chevy Chase have shared a high school but little else, and this was mostly by Chevy Chase's choice, cf. fire departments and public libraries.

[17]See Chapter 15 "Citizens Push for Modernization" in MacMaster and Hiebert. The Capper-Cramton (Congressman Lewis Cramton of Md.) Act allowed Maryland to borrow Federal money to extend D.C. parks into Maryland.

[18]See *Sentinel* April 25, 1930. Dr. Perry attached a long letter to his $1,050 check defending his actions as both doctor and Commissioner and describing his long office hours and frequent evening hearings for the County.

[19]*A Worthy Innovation: A History of the Montgomery County Police* by Donald Brooks and Charles A. Federline, 1988.

[20]From the *Baseball Encyclopedia*: "Robert Jordan Stevens, born Apr. 17, 1907. 1931. Philadelphia Phillies, shortstop, in 12 games hit .353 (35 ab, 12 hits, 3 runs, 4 RBI)". See Chevy Chase chapter.

[21]Spiller, shot while gambling and stabbed in an argument, was seriously wounded when an Edgemoor homeowner shot him while he was picking peaches without permission. Some said there was a fight every time Red visited the firemen's carnival.

[22]Son Jim said, "It seems to me that I enjoyed it."

[23]*Sentinel*, June 15, 1928.

[24]*Sentinel*, Feb. 6, 1931. The Fort Reno section of Tenleytown was famous for its bootleggers, and Brookeville Road was one of their main routes.

[25]The Home's*Touch* called Gould's donation a "gift" on the part of his foundation in its 75th anniversary history, July 1991, but other sources say that Gould's loan was to bear an interest rate of one-half percent if a woman were superintendent and one percent if a man was hired.

[26]Mrs. Bradley's article is in the Bethesda *Journal*, Aug. 11, 1939. See also the *Record* Nov. 1, 1946, and the *Sentinel* June 26, 1925; Oct. 17, 1930; Nov. 20, 1931. *Touch*, July and September 1991. At the time of Mrs. Bradley's visit, the staff in addition to Miss Talmadge included Barbara Hackett, girls' house mother; Mary Strange, house mother for the younger boys; Mr. and Mrs. R. S. Wilson, house parents for older boys (Mr. Wilson took care of the shop and recreation programs); Agnes Stephens, practical nurse; Mrs. Guy Guthridge, dietitian; and Mrs. Daisy O'Brien was in charge of the laundry. The manager of the farm was C. E. Arnold.

[27]MacMaster and Heibert, citing Dorothy Himstead and John Muncaster, credit Sandy Spring's delegates to the Civic Federation for the County manager idea in 1935, pp. 313-4. The Alta Vista school was not built for five more years.

[28]Mr. Gude did not recall the recital but did say that the piano lessons did not "take."
The number of Commissioners increased from five to seven from 1930 to 1934 and then went back to five.

[29]Between 1920-30 housing units increased from 7,500 to 11,000 and by 1940 to 23,555.

[30]For more on these hard times, see chapters 16 and 17 of *A Grateful Remembrance*.

[31] See *Sentinel*, Jan 30, 1931. "The Montgomery Farm Women's Cooperative Market" by Mary Charlotte Crook in *The Montgomery County Story*, August 1982.
The Home Demonstration movement had begun in Rockville in 1914. Mrs. O. W. H. Talbott and Supt. of Schools Willis Burdette are usually credited with its organization.

[32]*Sentinel*, Jan. 30 and March 9, 1931 and May 31, 1956. Gladhill oral history by Janet Dager, MCHS 1974. Under the old numbering 6710 Wisconsin was the first site.

[33]*Sentinel*, May 31, 1956, in "Hits for Mrs" column by Dorothy Waleski, which includes an interview with Miss Turner.

[34]*Sentinel*, Aug.12 and Aug 19, 1932.

[35]*Sunday Star*, Aug. 21, 1932.

[36]*Sentinel* Aug. 26 and Sept 2, 1932, and Miss Crook's essay for the MCHS, Aug. 1982.
Founders: Mrs. Chester Clagget, Mrs. Elizabeth Graybill, Mrs. Rosa C. Jones, Mrs. Forest King, and Miss Pearl E. Marlow. The directors chosen to act until the first annual meeting in January 1933 were the five women named above plus Mrs. Albert J. Cissel, Mrs. Augustus D. Oursler, Mrs. Edwin M. West, and President King.

[37]See ad on page 275 and also note ad for "tea room" on same page

[38]See Miss Crook's MCHS essay, the Waleski article, the Mildred Watkins oral history by the CCHS, and the *Sentinel* Oct. 21, 1932. Mrs. Watkins, who has been coming to the Market since 1942, also noted that they did not have the little tables out in front originally.

[39]See the Crook essay for the MCHS, August 1982.

[40]Also see *Sentinel* Dec. 21, 1933, and *Kenwood* magazine 1933-34 where the Market advertised regularly. The Exchange was at 6803 Wisconsin in the old numbering system.

[41]MCHS oral history.

[42]This may have been a Sears offer. They also tried to buy Imirie's across the street at about that time. See "Farm Women Operate a Cooperative" by Otis T. Weaver in *News for Farmer Cooperatives*, December 1937.
In `34 the Market reincorporated with capital stock of $12,000 (400 $25 shares and 1000 $2 shares), see *Sentinel* March 29, 1934.

[43]"The Drought of 1930 Was Responsible For Farm Women's Market" by Myrtle B. Rowe in the *Record*, Jan. 31, 1945. A slightly different version is in Otis Weaver's article cited above.

See Liber 612 Folio 360 of the County land records. There were two lots totaling about 30,000 square feet, they added the one at Willow and Wisconsin of 5,886 sq. ft. for additional parking. See *Sentinel* Jan. 2, 1936.

[44]"The Co-op That Farm Women Built" by Mabel Hebel in *The American Agriculturalist*, May 1940.

[45]From Elizabeth Kytle's *Time Was*, p. 40. Miss Corwin, who had become Mrs. Wilcox in 1936, made her home on the road to Potomac behind Chestnut Lodge where her husband worked. She was, according to Lloyd Potter, a "late bloomer."

[46]"Gourmets Gather Here" by Anna Steese Richardson in *Woman's Home Companion*, October 1939.

[47]Hebel, *op. cit.* and Weaver, *op. cit.*

[48]Weaver, p. 21.

[49] Mrs. J. Reed Bradley on Mrs. Waters in the Bethesda *Journal*, Sept. 27, 1940. Richardson, *op. cit.*

[50]The LWV sponsored an act creating the Juvenile Court intending it to be a model for the State.

[51]This space later became the back of Peoples Drug Store, mainly a storeroom.

[52]*Journal*, October 27, 1939, "Vignette."

[53]Frame of 16 mm movie film made by Leslie Bell Sr. - photo by Bill Mills, MCPS.

[54]County farmland in '31 was 238,728 acres of which 95,678 were producing crops. Teachers, through their association, had volunteered to contribute one day's pay for three months unemployment relief.

[55]Brain Truster Raymond Moley claimed that American capitalism was saved in the eight days at the beginning of the New Deal which included the first "fireside chat." CWA, a part of emergency relief, became WPA in 1935.

[56]Walker Sr., who lived at 1 East Lennox, had suffered severe reverses in the Depression. "Bobo," as the family knew him, had done well as a Dupont Circle grocer and LaSalle dealer–the car of choice for cabinet officers and bootleggers.

[57]See *A Grateful Remembrance*, Chapter 16, for more. *Sentinel* March 18 and Dec. 7, 1933.

[58]The first B-CC yearbook, the *Pine Tree*, had come out in '31 as a four-page supplement, including one picture, in the last issue of the *Tattler*.
Nancy Wheeler Diamond ('36) drove herself down from her Gaithersburg farm to attend B.C.C.H.S. and was envied because she had her own car.

[59]The team members were Captain Claire Boekhoff, Joan Daskan, Rosemary Hazard, Lillian Lee, Lois Molyneaux, Doris Ryon, Helen Sterling, Norma Curtis, Elsie Winkler, Margaret Snow, Joan Daskam, Anita Britton, Betty Jane Oswald, Alison Chaflin, Lois Bestor, and Manager Margaret Courtney.

[60]In the *Pine Tree* A. Neal Potter was listed as the most studious "girl," but since he and Haylett Shaw were co-editors of the yearbook it was likely just an editing error or a joke.

[61]*Record*, April 22, 1944. Almost all of the above on businessman from *Record, Tribune*, and *Journal* stories.

[62]Best was successful at selling encyclopedias and cemetery lots and eventually became an area home builder. The kids called the auto shop teacher "Gumshoe" Petrie because he wore soft-soled shoes and they seldom heard him coming.

[63]Just about the only non-segregated activity for children in the D.C. area was the annual Easter egg roll on the White House lawn.

[64]Bray, a long-time enigma in Bethesda-area politics, was probably a creation of William Prescott Allen, and the columns were written by Brooke Lee himself, Blair Lee, and Byron Wick among others. Wick ("Wick Byron") said, "Allen couldn't write" and that he and the others did them off and on, sometimes for a month at a time. Hugo Brooks, who worked for Allen as well as for the editors of the other Bethesda weeklies, knew this, but the secret was well kept and the search for the elusive "Bray" continued during the period. Even the astute Stella Werner, according to her oral biography, did not know who he was.

[65]*A Grateful Remembrance*, p. 306.

66Mostly from the archives of Christ Lutheran Church and its publications. Other early leaders of the church included Dr. John G. Ball, Dr. William C. Bashore, Clinton Dowling, Arthur Hilland, Grover Brake, George Smith, DeWitt Hyde and J. Forrest Krumm.

67The Offutts, including the writer, enjoyed the excitement created by the young actors, the rows of cars parked out in the field, and the gunshots every night. Lillian Offutt sometimes helped Mrs. Hendricks at the corn crib during intermission.

68The "fast" crowd hung out in the grove, at least as members of the non-fast crowd perceived it. Suggestions of sexual promiscuity were often attached to girls who frequented the smoking area. Some newspaper sports writers continued to call the high school teams "Lelanders."

69*Fifty Years at Garrett Park 1919-1969* by William S. Abell (1970) is a good history of the school's early years and Stephen J. Ochs *Academy on the Potowmack* (1989) has an excellent section on the history of the land.

70*The Landon Story* by Clyde Wilson, 1968. *Journal*, Jan. 19, 1940.

71Quote from letter to M-NCP&P from Dorothy R. Schultz who earned $15 a week there. See *Star*, Nov. 9, 1941, and *Tribune*, Nov. 25, 1959. The two main houses survived, one in the present development and the other as a school.

72*Star*, Feb. 20, 1937.

73It is likely that there were two log cabins in this area, and that the one remaining on Garfield Street is not the one the Borts rented but a house used as an inn, roadhouse or tearoom during and after the Bethesda Park era. The name "Blue Iris" has stuck to it.

74*Star*, Dec. 9, 1936.

75Mr. Wilson, for some reason, was almost always referred to as "Luke I. Wilson" complete with middle initial. George Sacks was sometimes called "George P." in his later life to distinguish him from his son, and Mrs. B. Payton Whalen seldom was written about without the full name or as Edith. Women's names are a special problem because of the common practice of using only the husband's name in public.

76There was actually a series of nine or ten letters and memos between 1933 and 1935 before the Wilson's land was accepted by the Secretary of the Treasury.

77*Star*, August 13, 1935 and *News*, August 21, 1935.

78*Star*, June 25, 1936.

79Helen Woodward Wilson donated 10.65 acres in May `38, 14.4 acres in September `38, 11.6 acres in September `40, and 10.87 acres in March `42 for a total of 92.5 acres valued then at $154,000 (including the houses and cottages on them).

80See "History of Site and Construction of Buildings for the National Institutes of Health at Bethesda, Maryland" by Thomas W. May, n.d. (in NIH historian's files).

81See "The National Institutes of Health: A Bethesda Landmark Celebrates Its Centennial" by Dorothy Pugh in the MCHS "Story" of February 1987.

82By the late-1930s, all the Washington daily newspapers were doing well, but the *Evening Star*, which set a record with a 90-page daily edition, was by far the healthiest.

83The first edition, preserved at the MCHS and on microfilm at the Rockville public library, contains Allen's penciled figuring on ad costs, including discounts, as well as his accounting in the worn margin.

84D.C. paid coaches for coaching; Montgomery County did not. Much of the above from the *Tattler* and from issues of the *Pine Tree*. Mohler quote from 1972 oral history at Rockville Public Library. *Tribune*, Feb. 11, 1938.

Jay Fitzgerald (B-CC `40) agreed that the `37-`38 team was the best in his summing up of B-CC athletics in the *Tribune* (Jan. 3, 1947). His all-time best team had All-Met Johnny Shumate at forward along with Eddie Johnson, who later starred at the U. of Md.; Leon Vannais at center and Bob Althaus and Bill Guckeyson at guards. Second team: forwards Carroll Hayden and Bob Cremins, Bill Barnsley at center and Bob Brewer and Bill Fuller at guards.

[85] *Vistas*, MC Retired Teachers Assn., 1976 and *Tattler*, Apr. 23, 1976. Mohler *op cit.*

[86] Jim Kinsman (B-CC `40) recalled that the coach's wife, English teacher Anna Kupka, would scrimmage against the JV when he was a sophomore and "she played like the boys."

[87] A short-lived minature golf course had occupied the post office site in the 1930s.

[88] Most of the above from the *Tribune* and the *Sentinel*. See also *A Grateful Remembrance* for more on the building boom in Chapter 16, "Surviving the Depression."

[89] American Legion Post 105 began in 1932 and received a permanent charter in 1934.

[90] Most of the above from *Sentinel* and *Tribune* stories, quote from Sept. 30, 1938. See Bray note at #63 above.

Hallowe'en 1938 is remembered for the broadcast of Orson Welles' *The War of the Worlds*, but the Martians barely caused a stir in the Bethesda area.

[91] The original impetus for this study may have come from Roger B. Farquhar in 1935. See *Old Homes and History*, p. 41.

[92] The writer thought his mother had baked all those cherry pies we had at home.

Roland Custer: "Emmy Lou, she was a wonderful women. That was a worker. She loved kids, but she didn't want any, 'I wouldn't have one of those brats for nothing,' she'd say."

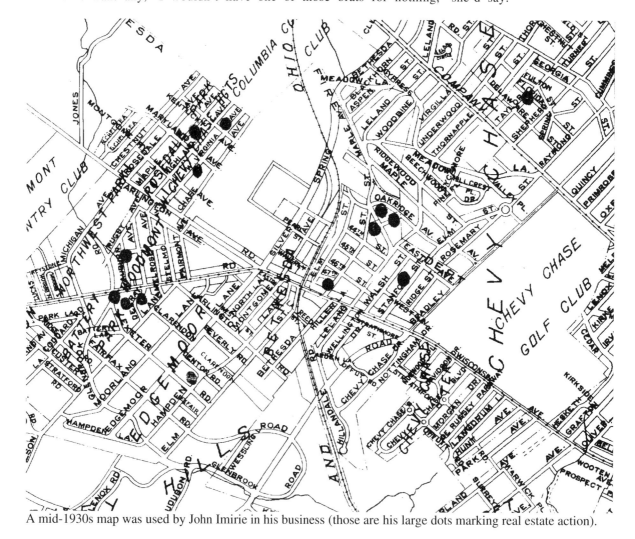

A mid-1930s map was used by John Imirie in his business (those are his large dots marking real estate action).

CHAPTER 9

Prewar Boom

When they were over, most folks agreed that the years just before the war had been the best yet for Bethesda. The building boom in single-family houses hammered along without a letup, and new businesses confidently opened at the rate of nearly one a week. The already-busy NIH and the planned U.S. Navy hospital promised to bring in many more families and jobs as well as filling the cash registers, schools and churches.

In the town's multiplying auto dealerships, lights gleamed on some of the sleekest and best-built cars ever. Imirie, Eastham and Burrows soon had plenty of competition as a new gas station seemed to start pumping every month somewhere along Wisconsin or Old Georgetown. Bob Guillot's Sunoco service station at East West and Wisconsin was on its way to becoming a Bethesda landmark. He advertised "A to Z" lubrication in thirty minutes for seventy-five cents and offered to call for and deliver your car at "no extra charge." The Coke box in front of his office was always filled with icy water and soft drinks, and it soon became a popular place to grab a Nehi Orange or Cherry Smash. Coca Cola drinkers always checked the bottom of their bottle to see how far away it had come from.

Both of Bethesda's movie theaters printed weekly programs (left), usually showed a movie for only two or three days and screened first-run films a few weeks after they closed downtown. The Bethesda showed "Gone With the Wind" in May 1940 on a reserved seat basis for seventy-five cents at matinees and $1.10 in the evenings. The renovated Hiser capitalized by reviving "Birth of a Nation" with added music and sound effects. On Saturdays the theaters competed for the bubble gum trade with stage shows and double features plus adventure serials and cartoons. One Saturday the Hiser offered free candy with cash prizes, an hour of comedies, two new serials: "Mandrake the Magician" and "Oregon Trail," plus Gene Autry and Jane Withers in "Shooting High," and on another Saturday afternoon Lust's Bethesda theater countered with a real magician on stage before the cartoons and the double feature.

"The community is bound to grow," said a "prominent" Bethesdan. "As a matter of fact there is nothing we can do to stop its growth if we wanted to. The important thing is to join together in a teamwork that will direct its growth so that we'll all enjoy the quality of the community life as well as the quantity."

Bethesda soon supported a second weekly newspaper. Day Thorpe's *Bethesda Journal* established its offices in Hagner's small, white frame, real estate office on the northeast corner of East West and Wisconsin and forced William Prescott Allen to

Day Thorpe

Tribune. Printed on heavy, white stock, the new paper featured Doree Germaine Holman's long series on "Old Bethesda," profiles of business leaders, a garden column by an eponymous "Papagena," almost endless "Vignettes of Bethesda Women" by Mrs. J. Reed Bradley who soon became women's editor and a short-lived, humorous letter about River Road "society" happenings from Willard Kiplinger.

In his self-introductory editorial, Thorpe claimed to have been raised on the smell of printer's ink and to have written for the papers at Friends, St. Albans, Lawrenceville and Yale. "I have no political ax to grind," he disingenuously wrote.

The *Journal*'s first edition on April 28, 1939, headlined the size and importance of the Naval Medical Center and predicted that Bethesda "should grow to be a town of nearly 40,000 in the next five years." Stories included news of an apartment zoning fight, the installation of V.F.W. officers and the decision of the Woman's Club of Chevy Chase to limit its membership to eight hundred. There were also articles on the history of Georgetown Prep and the im-

portance of the Grosvenor's "Wild Acres" as a bird sanctuary where Bethesda's most famous family had counted forty species and 189 nesting pairs.

The *Journal* also had a story on the Bethesda baseball team sponsored by local businessmen and coached by Howard Duvall, manager of the Sears-Roebuck store. It was the first team in five years, entirely of local high school and college players, no ringers, and planned to use the field at Arlington Road and Bethesda Avenue "through the kindness of C. E. Miller." The I. S. Turover Lumber Company contributed and erected the backstop.

Advertisers in the first issue included the Chevy Chase Land Company, Whittlesey's drug stores, Bell Laundry and Washington-Maryland Motors, the new Nash and Willys Overland dealer on Hampden Lane. It took a few months for most Bethesdans to categorize the *Journal* as the town's Republican paper, but well before the Willkie-FDR, third-term election campaign, many suspected that Merle Thorpe, the squire of Pook's Hill and publisher of *Nation's Business*, was pulling the strings if not writing the new paper's editorials and that his son's claim of impartiality was bunkum.[1]

Clifford Berryman cartoon for the *Journal* in 1939

The high school graduated 199 seniors in June 1939 with Postmaster James Farley as the main speaker, while 302 finished at Leland JHS where the students staged their own graduation with Marvin Rowe as emcee and Betty Lou Trowbridge as soloist of the Girls' Glee Club. The school solved the promotion problem presented by the twenty Chevy Chase sixth graders transferred there to relieve overcrowding by having them all repeat the seventh grade. Not everyone agreed with that decision.[2]

Cabin John-Glen Echo promoted thirty-eight students to ninth grade. At Chevy Chase Elementary, where budding cartoonists Pete Clapper and Art Wood had produced a school paper and made money at it, ninety-six pupils finished the sixth grade. From Bethesda Elementary eighty-seven moved on to junior high; Somerset graduated forty-five and twenty-one graduated from Alta Vista after hearing Birch E. Bayh, president of the school association, praise the work of their principal, Mrs. Walker.

An automobile accident quickly overshadowed the joy of the graduation season. On Friday night, June 24, Curtis Walker Jr. and Harper Roberts Jr., both eighteen, died after the car Walker was driving on Beach Drive near Kensington skidded more than a hundred feet and wrapped itself around a tree. Roberts was killed instantly. It took rescue workers more than an hour to extricate Walker. He died the next day. The three other young men including graduating B-CC senior Roy "Fox" Gilfix, who crawled out to Connecticut Avenue to get help, were injured. The police suspected that both alcohol and high speed contributed to the accident.

The handsome, popular, 6'2" Curtis and some of the other boys were members of Alpha Delta Sigma, a national high school fraternity, and were on their way home from a party at the Kensington Cabin. The police had the wreck hauled up to Burrows' gas station, and it sat out in the back lot for a while. Jack Sullivan recalled that "the entire inside of the car was filled with blood and covered with flies." Curtis's grandmother had given him her car as a graduation present only a few days before the accident.[3]

Frank Cantrel, a good friend of both Curtis and "Clackie" Walker, remembered:

The death was a very sad occasion. I used to spend a lot of time down at their house, and Mrs. Walker was a gracious and lovely lady. Curtis was

going to a military school. He was a handsome guy. After that their house was a lifeless place.

Where a dozen or so subdivisions competed before the Depression, now more than a hundred flourished. Newbold Development had "triple insulated" houses in Glenbrook Village under $7,000 while Permanent Homes advertised six-room, two-bath models for $6,000 in Wyngate. Columbia Construction began building square, brick colonials on Cheltenham Drive near the high school, and Bowling and Gardiner offered dozens of new brick models with attached garages just off Old Georgetown Road. For planning purposes, the zoning authorities of the M-NCP&PC recognized forty-six distinct residential sections in the Seventh Election District from Alta Vista to Westmoreland Hills. That year the O. O. Kuhn Trophy went to Kennedy-Chamberlin for the beauty brought to Bethesda by its Kenwood cherry trees.

The public utility companies estimated the area's population to be almost 25,000, up fifty percent in five years and seven times what it had been twenty years before. At the end of the year, an old idea re-emerged when editor Bill Allen suggested that Bethesda had what Chevy Chase lacked, and that "The time, then, has arrived when this area should function as a city." Chevy Chase, where civic leaders were still mired in Connecticut Avenue repaving, responded with silence.[4]

The enormous growth of Bethesda's population, especially of families with young children, could be gauged by the expansion and success of scouting groups. By `39, more than a score of Girl Scout troops met regularly and Brownie groups multiplied like eager fifth graders. The Girl Scouts participated in many charitable activities, particularly at Christmas time, and took dozens of field trips and outings. One of their favorite destinations was the Kiplinger cabin at Great Falls, and Mrs. Vernon M. Pierce of Chevy Chase lent a cabin and some land for use by all District Three Scouts especially for nature study. The visit of the British king and queen made for some special projects, and later the Bundles for Britain campaign involved nearly all the Scouts.[5]

The Campfire Girls also had several Bethesda-area clubs. Mrs. Paul Ledig, president of the local guardians' association, led the older groups. In the spring, they trekked to Lurelake Farm in a truck supplied by Simmons' Dodge. Mrs. Ralph Simmons, the newest

guardian, kindled the fire, and Mrs. Marvin Simmons recalled:

> We slept on the ground on a blanket, and you would be surprised how many little rocks and acorns you found. That was the last time we did that. We also took them up to Great Falls and then didn't do that anymore. All those kids going around on those rocks scared me to death."[6]

Among the Boy Scouts, Dr. John Ball's Troop 211 led by Eagle Scout Scott Brewer won the 1939 inspection, and Troop 240 took on the job of cleaning up and roofing an old building at the former experimental farm for a meeting place. Harry Callaghan later became their leader. Troop 204, founded in 1933, was still going strong at the Methodist church. The annual Camporee took place at Burnt Mills in June 1939 and involved more than 300 Scouts from the County's twenty-eight troops.[7]

All the groups had the usual meetings, hikes, ceremonies and activities. The local papers recorded a few. In a model of acute observation and careful reportage, Frank Fallowfield produced the following account of one group's activities on Saturday, May 27, 1939.

> Troop 255 went on its first overnight hike. The boys left about 3 o'clock and started for the Dunlap farm. We finally got there about 7:30 after a long trudge of ten and one-half miles. Some of the boys had hitch-hiked and got here early, and they won the job of pitching tents.
>
> When we all got there we started cooking supper and didn't finish until about 10 o'clock. During the night we went down to the spring and filled our canteens. Coming back we bumped into a cow and we were nearly scared out of our wits.
>
> Many of the boys stayed up all night sitting around a fire which we kept going. The rest got up at dawn for breakfast and we started back about 6 am. Some of the boys rode home with the Scoutmaster, while others walked so they could pass their first-class regulation 14-mile hike test.[8]

Old Georgetown Road at about Glenbrook in the 1930s

The Bradley Boulevard viaduct

A few worrisome clouds darkened the generally sunny landscape. The older stores and converted houses sandwiched between the newer commercial buildings were deteriorating, and the business district included many weedy yards, tired fences and noisome piles of trash. In fact, trash removal itself was a growing problem, and a few neighborhoods such as Fairway Hills were still pouring raw sewage into the streams. Old Georgetown Road remained a very narrow, two-lane street, much of it without sidewalks or curbs, and the bottlenecks at the Bank and at the narrow B&O viaduct continued to be an annoyances

But the biggest storm of 1939 arose out of an institution most Bethesdans had long regarded as a problem well solved–the fire department. The tall, red brick firehouse in the hollow on Old Georgetown had become almost as much of a landmark as the bank, and the siren calling the volunteers to duty was an accepted part of the town's life. In his fourth year as chief, Hiram Musgrove, his red Ford coupe usually bristling with lengths of pipe and his plumber's tools, was nearly as well known as Henry Hiser or T. W. Pyle. When that siren went off, men all over Bethesda put down their hammers or paint brushes, their pencils or shovels and came on the run.

One Saturday, J. Fred Imirie was up at the Patty-Kitch-Inn under the Bank helping his wife fix sandwiches when the siren went off. He tossed down his knife, tore off his apron, and ran down the middle of Old Georgetown to the firehouse. The boys were sitting out front gabbing with some kids when Fred ran up, puffing, and gasped, "Where's the fire?"

"It's Saturday, Fred," one of the firemen reminded him, and he walked back up the street, redfaced. The siren sounded every Saturday at noon. It was part of Bethesda's pulse.

Grocery clerk Lee Higgins, a volunteer in Glen Echo before they even had a fire engine, was often left alone to run the Sanitary store at the corner of Wilson and Old Georgetown when the manager, Jesse Barber, ran to answer the fire alarm. Those who saw Barber running down Old Georgetown Road still wearing his bloody apron retained the memory.

And riding the fire engines could be dangerous as Sumpter Embrey recalled.

We had this Cadillac that Mrs. Woods over in Edgemoor donated to the firehouse. They had a body put on it and these ladders on top of it because they didn't have any ladder truck. This thing was top heavy, and when you went around a curve, it leaned way over.

Dr. Armstrong, that was the druggist up at the corner behind the Bank of Bethesda, he'd run down to the firehouse every time the whistle'd blow. He was on the back of this thing when Red Spiller was driving; he was crazy with that foot. He was drivin' and Doc Armstrong was on the back, hangin' on, and when they got over by Landon School on that curve, he abandoned ship cause he thought it was going over. Broke his collarbone.

The fire department added a rescue squad in the Thirties, and John Imirie went out to Ohio to fetch the Buick ambulance. The firemen put a horn up in the cupola with the siren and for rescue work blew this shrill air whistle. A lot of volunteers did not bother to answer the rescue squad signal; everyone reacted to the fire siren.

In 1938 the volunteers had made some equipment demands that were ignored, and the Fire Board's Liaison Committee had concluded that "the morale of these men was very low and it was difficult to determine the exact cause of this condition." In early 1939, the Fire Board decided that it was time for the town to have more, full-time, paid firemen. A committee headed by Commissioner Thomas E. Hampton produced the reorganization plan. To supervise the paid men, the Board resolved to hire a professional as chief. The Bethesda VFD would then be much the same as the Chevy Chase Fire Department with whom it often competed and sometimes cooperated.[9]

After some discussion, the Fire Board voted to hire six additional paid men, to give them a total of nine, and a paid chief. Salary for the full-time firemen, to be recruited from the ranks of the volunteers, was set at $100 per month with a ceiling in five years of $1,800 annually. Like their brethren near the Lake, the Bethesdans looked to the D.C. fire department for an

officer. Lieutenant Angelo J. Bargagni, due to retire from the DCFD at the age of sixty, accepted the post at a salary of $2,500.[10]

While this was quietly going on, the volunteers presented their eighth annual charity minstrel show in Leland's auditorium with help from the University of Maryland "Cotton Pickers Minstrels." Paul L. "Doc" Oldfield was in charge of the popular event, and the show involved a number of volunteers including Chief Musgrove and Secretary Sumpter Embrey.

By 1939, the roster of volunteers listed fifty men including ten charter members and thirty who had served at least eight years. The volunteers had answered 423 calls in 1938, 221 with fire trucks and 202 by the ambulance. An average of sixteen men responded to each fire alarm, and the firemen claimed that an engine with at least four members rolled out in less than two minutes. The firemen had also given twenty-seven blood transfusions during that same period.

When George W. Bryan, president of the Fire Board, announced the proposed changes in early June, he elicited an immediate, loud, and angry response from Chief Musgrove and most of the volunteers. Their eventual consensus was that they had been insulted and would not serve under A. J. Bargagni or any other "outsider." They would respond to the alarm, they said, but they would ignore Bargagni.

The Fire Board tried to mollify Hiram Musgrove by offering him the position of captain and the title of "fire marshal" at $600 a year, but he declined. The volunteers dug in their heels and demanded that Musgrove be made chief. They sent a letter to civic organizations asking support for the volunteers and laying out his experience and credentials. In June the Board received a petiton for Musgrove as chief signed by 138 local citizens. The Fire Board praised Musgrove's loyalty and bravery but concluded that he lacked the training and experience needed to lead a semi-paid department. They then hired Arthur and Paul Oldfield, Harry Sumner, James Breeden Jr., Hugh Poates, and Richard Pugh to go along with George Gummel, Jesse Barber, and James Breeden Sr., who had been serving as paid men. The Fire Board asked the six new men to leave the volunteers and not attend their meetings, which at that time were still going on in the firehouse.

By the summer of 1939 both of the local papers had weighed in with editorials, and the

Journal carried several caustic cartoons on the situation. In the *Tribune* Bill Allen wrote that "the attitude of some of the volunteers in protesting the appointment of a paid chief from outside their own organization is quite understandable and not unnatural." Day Thorpe concluded in August that "it is high time that higher officials step in and settle the matter."

Before they were barred from the firehouse, the volunteers choose builder-insurance man Sam Robertson as their president and spokesmen and Hiram Musgrove as fire chief. The volunteers stated that they planned to claim the $500 per year per unit of equipment provided by the County.[11]

Sumpter Embrey became deeply involved in this brouhaha and, long after the events, ruminated on what had happened.

Things were going along pretty good between the volunteers and the Fire Board. When they started, everyone was a fire fighter, and the firehouse was the center of attraction. Everybody wanted to ride the fire truck. But then the white collars had to separate from the workers, and finally only one or two people, including J. L. Imirie, were both on the Fire Board and volunteers, he and the chief. They had an election every year for chief.

Hiram Musgrove, unbeknownst to me and the rest of the volunteers, figured that there was going to be a paid-chief job. And Hiram goes to Mr. George Bryan, under the table, and tells him that the fellows are not responding to the fire calls. It was true to a point. In the springtime we got a lot of brush fires, and then the guys that were taking off, per diem workers, lost that time, and the boss gets mad, too. Musgrove was putting a needle in that we need some paid personnel. I found this

out later, or I wouldn't have gone all the way for him at the time.

Some members of the Fire Board, like J. L. Imirie, a first cousin to Wady, and Wady Imirie and a few others got together and held a secret meeting - I don't think it was held in the firehouse - and decided they would get a hired chief. And Musgrove didn't have a great education. He wasn't a very good speaker, a good plumber though and a real likeable fellow, but he wasn't polished; let's say it that way. And Bargagni was trying to look polished.

When we needed some training in Bethesda, for years I'd take the fire chief's car and go down and pick up Bargagni. He was a training officer. So I'd go over to Decatur Street, and he'd come and do his demonstrations and his training exercises, and then he decided to start a training school in Montgomery County, that had no training in '37. (See John Imirie's certificate below, signed by Bargagni.) Held it at Kensington and Bethesda. It was all volunteer including Bargagni's time, and he was doing this in Virginia, too. He also initiated the firemen's parade in D.C.

So these people in Bethesda decided this is the guy we want for chief. They knew he was close to retirement in D.C. They underhandedly solicited the D.C. Commissioners for Bargagni as chief - all under the table. So, on July 1, 1939, it was decided he would retire and come out as chief, and they would hire three men on each shift. They would drive the apparatus, bring it back, wash it, and put the new hose on and hang the wet hose in the tower, and the volunteers could go back to their jobs.

So then they told us, "We are going to have a paid fire chief and these hired men so you can get back to your jobs, and they'll do the driving and so forth." And that took the fire out of the volunteer

---

Montgomery County Association
of
Volunteer Firemen
Montgomery County, Maryland

Fire Training School

This certifies that *John Lewis Imirie* has completed the First Year Course of Modern and Practical Fire Fighting, conducted by this association at Kensington, Maryland, January and February, 1937.

A.J. Bargagni
Instructor

J. F. Kennedy
President, Montgomery County Association
Volunteer Firemen

John Imirie's certificate signed by Angelo Bargagni

fire department. Here I'm going to be a fireman, and I won't ever get to drive this apparatus? Went over like somebody dumped the upstairs down on the bottom. There was no yelling; it wasn't a rowdy meeting. They just told us that Bargagni had been hired. This turned Musgrove upside down because he thought it was his idea.

Then the volunteers had a meeting, and one of these guys, a rabble-rouser named Sam Robertson, a dissenter and not a real, regular member, decided we'd separate, that we wouldn't respond. And we had volunteers that lived in the firehouse; I was one of them before I got married in '34. Anyhow, we said we wouldn't answer any calls.

On July 1st we had a rescue call, a child was drowned at Chevy Chase Swimming Pool, and I responded. I came that day and here was one of the hirees in the seat of the rescue wagon, Jim Breeden Jr. I grabbed him by the collar and pulled him out and said, "Get the hell out of there," and I took the rescue truck and answered the call. When we got back to the firehouse, Bargagni said, "Sumpter, you ought not to have done that."

From that time the fight really started. I had to write my boss, G. W. Imirie, I was secretary of volunteers. So I wrote a letter, some of it is in the paper. We didn't say it had to be Musgrove, just some member of the present volunteer fire department. And we cited all of Hiram Musgrove's achievements and what we had done and so on. But it boiled down to I wrote the letter to my boss. He was chairman of this committee. So I went in to him and said, "Boss, I must have a talk with you." And I told him this thing was going to a head, and the volunteers were going to separate if they didn't appoint somebody else - this was before July 1st.

So he said, "Sumpter, whatever you do after you leave here at night is your business." And he was a fair man to say that. "As long as you give me a day's work for a day's pay." I really was relieved. This thing went on and the newspapers got hold of it, and it made a big, nasty smell.

Then Bargagni was hired, and nobody was going to answer fire calls in Bethesda, so they had to hire enough men real quick to make up a company with. I don't know the number, fifteen or so. So they hired some volunteers who needed a job. One of them was Pap Oldfield, and he got to be an officer.

Bargagni never intended to fight a fire; Musgrove would go in and "waller in it," you know. This was a white collar man. He had a chief's car, and he'd come down and direct it from outside. He did his time in D.C., and he wasn't about to get hurt out here.

We volunteers decided to start our own fire department. So we bought a piece of property up on Fairmont Avenue. Will Flack, a real regular at the firehouse, he was a carpenter, lived with his sister Miss Birdy. Flack put up around five or six thousand, and we signed a note for it. And Millard Broadhurst, who was a brick contractor, and the volunteers put that house together. There was one big tree out in front that had roots that went to China, and we worked on that thing every evening and chopped on that root and put jacks on it and finally got that tree out. There was hardly anything back there then except houses.

So we built this firehouse and ordered a brand new fire engine from the Hahn Company in Hamburg, Pennsylvania. It was a sleek little thing, and it would really run. And they threw in a Stutz ladder truck, four cylinders; you could almost see them move when it started up - pop, pop, pop. Must have had a six-inch bore. Only paid around $4,000 for the two of them.

All the labor was by the volunteers, but we needed some steel beams for it, and there was a bunch down by the railroad tracks that had been there for a long time. So we found out who owned them, and we needed at least three, maybe four, to make this thing with no poles in it. I took Imirie's tow truck over and a Model A rear end we were working on and put the beams on that and lashed it up and towed it up the road, going the back way around, with a red flag on it. Then one of these men, maybe Irving Ray, brought his shovel up there and put the beams into place on the brick pillars we built. There was a stage area in front where you could talk and have bingo or whatever, and underneath was a used heating plant, and we were in business. We had our own siren and the works.

Here comes the killer. We had the telephone number Wisconsin 1000, a quick number. And Bethesda had Bradley 217, a different number. Ours was a better number, and we were getting all the calls. Here were these people on Old Georgetown Road, and they'd hear our sirens going and they're not getting any calls. It was embarrassing to a lot of folks and the big businessmen, one belonged to C&P and the Chamber of Commerce. So they had the number fixed so it would ring at the old firehouse for the paid firemen. Our lawyer said we could sue as long as we paid our bill for that number, but that would make another heavy stink so we didn't do it.

In October the *Tribune* editorialized, "There is no room for competing fire companies. Chaotic conditions would develop in a situation where two bitterly opposing factions

Hiram Musgrove   Angelo Bargagni

would be in constant battle for the business of fighting fires." Lee Higgins, William Hall, and Edward R. Barber joined the list of paid men, and Bargagni organized two platoons with Clinton Quigley as the "swing man." The Fire Board severed its connections with the volunteers and stated that it wanted no volunteer help after October 10. It demanded, without effect, that volunteers return the uniforms and equipment they had taken with them.

The siren on the roof stayed silent. An era had ended.

Bethesda came to accept the existence of two fire departments. Bargagni staged drills and spectacular demonstrations, began inspections of businesses and schools, and the firemen built a float with 5,000 crepe paper American Beauty roses for the Christmas Lane parade.

Led by Sam Robertson, the volunteers plodded on, held their own carnival in May, and in July 1940 dedicated their firehouse at 4800 Fairmont with help from Representative Byron and Commissioner Walter Johnson. Judge Charles Woodward laid the cornerstone, and Judge Stedman Prescott made a short speech praising the volunteers.

Frank Hall, a rookie fireman during the war when his brother and many other firemen went into the service, remembered Bargagni well. Fifty years after he trained, he could still walk through the paces the old chief taught him.[12]

He went in the D.C. fire department in 1901 at twenty and half, lied about his age and told them he was 21. Came out in `39 and stayed at Bethesda for seventeen years. He set up the department just like the District. He had a captain riding the front seat when they pulled up on the fire ground.

They trained. I don't care if it was 95 degrees in the summer of '39; they got out there, and they ran down that street, and they hooked up to that hydrant, and they charged that line.

He had a couple or three guys that were carpenters, one of them was Poates, and they built a training tower. And they had to take that ladder out there, and he stood right out there himself and did all the training himself, and they had to take that line up that ladder in a certain way. Under your right arm and over your left shoulder. You had to take that line like that when you went in because you stepped off the ladder to the right of the window and the hose came over the ladder and you got in, turned around and started pulling and then stuck that nozzle back out the window and said, "Charge the line."

And you didn't pull any tricks on him either. He knew them all. He made the firefighters set up and notice. Doc Oldfield, Pap Oldfield, and guys like that, they knew how to fight fires before he came there. What he did was sharpen them up and make them better. There were some crackerjack volunteers, but, well . . . .

Sumpter Embrey later left Imirie's garage, where he ran the parts department, and went into D.C. to become a professional fire fighter. He kept his ties with the volunteers, calling the bingo games and leading Civil Defense classes, but before he left he had one parting shot at the new chief.

Joyce, Jean and John Schaefer, left front, Edwina and Diane Cummings in seat next to Arthur Oldfield, and rookie fireman Frank Hall at right in 1944

Bargagni, every time they did a good job, he'd come down to G. W. Imirie's and report, tell the boss. And there I was out front on the counter. He told the boss they were going to have this civilian defense class up there and a demonstration on bombs, gases and things. Even things that would burn under water. So he's making a big play with the boss.

So I got one of these little things you attach to your car that goes whooooo and makes a little smoke and a loud bang, and I wired his car. He's parked out in front right by the gas pumps. I said, "Chief, could you move your car. We've got a truck coming in here wants gas out of that first pump."

Old man got behind the wheel and turned it on, and it went WHOOooo-oo, and he held on to it for dear life, on to the steering wheel, and she went BOOM and the hood shook like a leaf and smoke poured out. I thought he was going to have a heart attack and was so ashamed of myself, so sorry; I didn't realize it was going to be as loud as it was. And he was still sitting there holding on to that wheel, didn't even move it.

He never knew it was me, and they haven't caught me yet.

Bethesdans turned their attention to other concerns. Some wondered about the length of time the Brookings Institution was taking with the report on the County government, but a more immediate worry was reassessment. Because of the Depression, the County had not been reassessed since 1927, and the work had to be finished by 1940 for the tax levy. The Commissioners put Wilton T. Allen of Chevy Chase, a Republican, in charge and hired William P. Richards, who had held a similar job in D.C., to oversee the work. A fifteen-man crew began in the sparsely settled northwest part of the County, and the number of assessors grew to fifty as the work moved into the Washington suburbs.

In July, Richards talked to a reporter:

The job's coming along pretty well, better than I expected. The great difficulty is that there was a great deal of inequality in the previous assessment of the various real estate subdivisions here in Bethesda. Settlements right side by side show a wide discrepancy in their rate. It makes it hard to arrive at a just figure, but the men that are working the Bethesda area are among the best in the business and we'll manage it all right.

My estimate is that farm lands will show an increase in assessment of about three percent over the last valuation, while other property may be up from 20 to 30 percent.[13]

New assessments were to be based on the record of sales and construction, the opinions of landowners and neighbors about their property and the last reassessment in `27, an admittedly high-priced year. House assessments at "full market value" were reckoned by the cubic foot from about 40¢ per at the high end for a "first-class stone house" to 20¢ for a moderately priced frame home. The assessors usually figured the lots at one-fifth the value of the house. Commercial property values depended, in part, on potential earning capacity. Although it was actually a State matter, complaints were to be addressed to the County Commissioners who had the final say on assessments.[14]

By November, when the County sent reassessment notices to upcounty residents, Mr. Richards was estimating that the County's tax base would increase to about $115 million, a good bit lower than the $150 million guessed by some "experts." In the Bethesda region, assessors were finding homes without water or sewer service in "buried" communities. One such area was in the "hollow" at the rear of Brookdale between Western Avenue and River Road.

The reassessment notices to the downcounty areas went out early in December, and under the law, appeals and requests for hearings had to be made before December 31. Protests became everyday occurrences and hundreds requested hearings. Taxpayers noted variations in evaluations on the same street as well as much larger discrepancies between values in adjoining neighborhoods. Sonoma residents howled when assessments in their area doubled, and soon Battery Park and Chevy Chase neighborhoods raised the decibel level of the complaints. Reports circulated of home buyers forfeiting their down payments because of the expected rise in taxes. In general,

Hugo Brooks found these rundown Bethesda houses.

Bethesda and Chevy Chase properties were re-assessed upward from ten to twenty-five percent, which, in most cases, accurately reflected the change in values, but when neighbors compared their notices, the trouble started. Mr. Richards asked to retire because of his health and headed to Florida for the winter.

With Curtis J. Ireland of Friendship Heights as president and women's club leader Mrs. Franklin Getzendanner of Chevy Chase as secretary, an Emergency Taxpayers Association quickly organized early in 1940. The group's first action was to ask the Commissioners for an extension of the time to file appeals. Mr. Ireland told the *Journal*, "We are not crusaders, nor seeking the limelight of publicity." He said his group came together spontaneously, and if the people "are aroused and feel something should be done about it, well, here is the opportunity."

Within a week, the Association claimed five  hundred members and was in heated, open-letter correspondence with the Commissioners and the supervisor of assessment, Wilton Allen. Despite the outcry from the Bethesda area, the assessment office reported that only one in twenty property owners had requested a hearing and that the Commissioners would have every protested evaluation reassessed. Obviously this was going to be an important political issue in the 1940 campaign. While Allen's *Tribune* tended to play down the story, the *Journal* ran it on the front page week after week and kept the controversy bubbling.[15]

Mrs. Getzendanner

In the middle of one of the coldest and snowiest Januarys anyone could remember, Wilton Allen met with Bethesda's business owners to explain the new assessments as the protests continued. By the end of January, the Emergency Taxpayers Association, looking more and more like a permanent body, opened offices at 4711 Hampden Lane and promulgated a four-point program much broader than protesting reassessments. The Association retained Arthur Hilland of Battery Park as its counsel, and Curtis Ireland warned that the tax rate might not go down just because the assessments had gone up.

In a February marked by two, fierce almost-blizzards, the Association began studying the County's bonded indebtedness and then things quieted down until Frederic P. Lee, chairman of the Civic Federation's committee on finance and budget, proposed a fifteen cent increase in the County tax rate to reduce the debt. Merle Thorpe's name came to be publicly connected with the Taxpayers Association, and the auto club's Washington I. Cleveland stood as the spokesman of its last-minute Citizens' Emergency Committee, which staged a hastily called mass meeting at the end of March. In the end, despite all the noise and telegrams, the Commissioners decided to keep the now-almost-sacred $1.50 tax rate and to retire more than a half-million dollars of bonded indebtedness.

The Taxpayers Association regrouped in April with a broader based board of directors including W. F. Bullis, Marquis Childs, Washington Cleveland, A. Montague Ferry, and Joseph Montedonico and produced a booklet of "Tax Facts" asking questions about the cost of local government. With the *Journal*'s help, the Association continued to harass the County Commissioners until the election and then almost disappeared as the Brookings Report took center stage. Curtis Ireland's last shot at the County government was a suit over the length and dates of the tax year. In June 1940, the Civic Federation presented the Evening Star Cup for public service to Frederic P. Lee, mainly for his work and reports during the reassessment period. Lee had been a calm voice during a stormy time.

But many homeowners in Bethesda suffered from the long-overdue reassessment and from the changes taking place in their neighborhoods. One of the most plaintive cries came from Henry S. Frisbie who had lived at 5523 Wisconsin Avenue in Friendship Heights for thirty-five years and had seen his County tax bill rise from $60 to $334.64 while his home deteriorated and the regraded highway depressed the value of his land. In his long letter to the *Journal* he claimed he could not afford to pay his tax bill and accused the local government of  Frederic Lee

waste and excess. Many who lived in the areas shared his pain.[16]

Despite reassessments, higher taxes and dire predictions, Bethesda's rate of growth went into overdrive. In the spring of 1939, Luke I. Wilson's widow helped lay the cornerstone at the National Cancer Institute, and across the Pike the Navy broke ground for its $4,850,000 medical center. At the Cancer Institute, Dr. Thomas Parran presided, and Senator Homer T. Bone applied the mortar and made the main speech. Rear Admiral Ben Morell, chief of Bureau of Yards and Docks, was in charge of the Navy's ceremony, and White House physician Admiral Ross T. McIntire spoke and brought FDR's regrets that he could not be present. Admiral Percival S. Rossiter, retired, turned the first spade of dirt. But Roosevelt was there in spirit because the tower, perhaps modeled on the Nebraska Capitol where he had spoken in the `36 campaign, was his idea, and the site, chosen from a field of eighty, was his choice.

The President had dabbled in Capital-area architecture before, particularly in the design of the Archives building and the Jefferson Memorial, but this time Roosevelt "himself led the action, determining not only the site and materials, but designing the basic elevation as well. So it was at Bethesda that FDR came closest to actually assuming the role of architect of a building in the Washington area." When Congress authorized a new naval medical center in 1937, the President made a sketch of a fifteen-story tower with two low wings and then went looking for a place to put it.

On July 5, 1938, FDR, McIntyre and Adm. Rossiter plus a car full of Secret Service men and a couple of motorcycle policemen toured the Bladen's Fairmont Farms Dairy on Rockville Pike. Tom Bladen and his large family had been raising cows and corn on the old Bohrer "plantation" since 1924, and their youngest, Aubrey, held the gate and shook FDR's hand that summer day. The President had his open car stopped on a gentle rise, reached over the side and stuck his cane in the ground. "We will build it here," he said. The government purchased three parcels of rolling farmland and dense woods totaling 264.7 acres with a 2,300-foot frontage on Rockville Pike.

Influenced by the President's 1937 sketch, the Bureau of Yards and Docks with the advice of architect Paul Cret, professor emeritus at the University of Pennsylvania, prepared preliminary drawings, which showed a sixteen-story

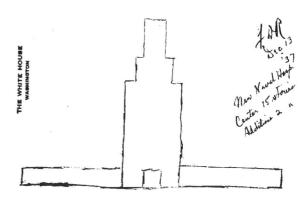

FDR's sketch on White House stationery

tower of Indiana limestone with three-story wings. The Park and Planning Commission and the Fine Arts Commission immediately disapproved of the design. Gilmore Clarke, chairman of the Fine Arts Commission, urged Roosevelt to look at the "simple" colonial buildings of the NIH. Frederic Delano, chairman of Park and Planning, objected to the height, which violated the 130-foot ceiling of the city that the suburbs had, until now, followed.[17]

New plans showed an even higher tower, and Delano asked the President to "restrain" the naval architects and received a "Dear Uncle Fred " letter in which FDR promised to remove "two whole stories" and stated his belief that the tower in the suburbs "will be a landmark for generations to come." It would be, the obdurate President suggested, like those church towers that add beauty to the English countryside. Delano renewed his objections, but got nowhere.

Cret and William H. Livingston delivered the final drawings in 1939 and, against their advice, the President ordered exterior walls of exposed aggregate, precast concrete panels that he had seen at the model basin at Carderock. This decision added weight and made a redesign of the steel work necessary. The tower, approved over the protest of M-NCP&PC as well as the D.C. authorities, would provide "healthful conditions for the treatment of certain types of pulmonary and bronchial ailments" according to the Navy. The grounds, suggested FDR, should be treated "romantically" like a pasture, and he ordered the site enclosed by an "old English sheep fence."[18]

John McShain Inc. won the contract to build the foundations for $98,000, and work started on the bluff 558 feet above sea level. For the main contract the Navy printed and mailed out two hundred sets of blueprints of 327 pages

each. The weight of the mailing was five tons. McShain won again with a $4,360,000 bid.

The very public medical center on the Pike overshadowed the other major Navy project in the Bethesda area. North of Cabin John at Carderock, $3,500,000 worth of construction and $1 million in equipment were going into the David W. Taylor Ship Model Basin. By the spring of `39, the contractors had completed the major construction on the 1,300-foot basin and the 900-foot-long office and lab complex of light-colored, precast concrete.

The basin at the TMB under construction

Under the long, curved, silver roof of the basin were concrete barrel arches and a thick layer of insulation. Beneath lay the deep water basin, 963 feet long, 51 feet wide and 22 feet deep, a shallow water basin, 303-by-51-by-10 feet, in which the depth could be raised, and parallel to it, the even longer high-speed basin where model speeds up to sixty-two knots were possible. It measured 1,168 by 21 by 10 feet. The rails along the sides of the basin were of flame treated, carbon manganese steel and bent three-eighths of an inch to follow the earth's curvature and eliminate gravity from the tests. At the western end of the shallow basin was a J-shaped turning basin in a space measuring 112 by 150 by 44 feet with cameras in the ceiling.

Capt. Harold Eugene Saunders USN, who acted as liaison with the Bureau of Construction and insisted on perfection and accuracy, designed the facility. One admiring observer remarked, "This place is being constructed as if the Hamilton Watch Company were doing a building job for the Pennsylvania Railroad."[19]

Construction, under the supervision of George F. Ferris of the Turner Construction Company and Cmdr. Hugo C. Fischer, finished ahead of schedule, and Fischer moved over to Bethesda as officer in charge of the building of the National Naval Medical Center (NNMC).

The government took over the TMB complex without fanfare or ceremony in July 1939.

Retired and ailing, Rear Admiral David W. Taylor himself came to the station in an ambulance and watched the dedication from a wheelchair on November 4, 1939. A year later, the small freight station in Bethesda received the thirty-three ton, precision-built, steel towing carriage, which was transported to the model basin in sections. It was likely both the largest and the most valuable item ever shipped to Bethesda, and the Navy had to reinforce the intersection of Conduit and Persimmon Tree Roads before it could be moved. Once it was installed, the Navy transferred almost all its testing work from the basin Naval Constructor Taylor had designed and built at the Washington Navy Yard in 1898.

About the time the model basin at Carderock was completed, the Navy ordered the construction of a hundred homes for white workers on the twenty-two-acre Bobinger-Cabin John Hotel site and another twenty houses off Persimmon Tree for its African-American employees. The government purchased what had been Henry Brown's four-and-a-half acres from Lena Brown and her half-brothers for what became the Carver Road project.

Cabin John Gardens consisted of seventy-five two-bedroom and twenty-five three-bedroom houses, all with coal furnaces, the first private sewer system in the County, a community office with a small workshop and a network of private roads all built by the Federal Works Agency. Club and Scout meetings, social events and other community get-togethers regularly filled the Community House.

The Federal government, in lieu of taxes on the low-cost housing built at Cabin John and a 70-unit project for noncommisioned officers at

Saturday at Cabin John Gardens

Walter Reed's Forest Glen annex, agreed to pay the County fourteen percent of the rent, an estimated $7,000 annually. The County agreed not to charge the Government for services provided in conjunction with the construction or administration of the government-owned houses.[20]

Barely noticed in the development of the NIH and the NNMC, the Federal government purchased the C&O Canal from the Chesapeake and Ohio Railroad for $2,800,000 and began buying up land between Conduit Road and the Potomac River from Georgetown to Great Falls for the George Washington Memorial Parkway (later renamed for Clara Barton). For the next three years, the park service with the help of the CCC worked to replace lock gates, clean up the towpath, dredge out the waterway and repair the masonry. After all this park work and the extension of River Road to Seneca, the desire for a bridge at Great Falls re-emerged, but again the plans evaporated.NP-2 at Carderock did much of the work along

The young, African-American Civilian Conservation Corps enrollees at camps NP-1 and the canal. Housed in coal-heated, temporary buildings and fed for thirty-nine cents a day ($0.3890), the 160 to 180 men who lived and worked in this area from the fall of 1938 until the spring of 1942 repaired the tow path, rebuilt bridges, cleared and landscaped picnic areas and performed many other valuable services including fire suppression.

They had a library and an educational program, weekly movies, occasional dances, regular trips to D.C. and several basketball teams in a league that included the Prince George's black CCC camp. The residents of Crow Hill on River Road always knew when the CCCers were paid because Bill Smith's beer joint was the nearest place for them to spend their money and blow off steam.

Camp "Tow Path" had a doctor and a chaplain plus weekly visits from volunteer clergymen including Cleveland Clipper. But the CCC inspectors sometimes found the camp unclean, the lights inadequate and the meals not properly balanced. In the early years some young men "deserted" or were discharged as "unfit," but many others stayed, conquered illiteracy and developed useful skills. One evaluation noted that "a great number of enrollees have entered camp with no objective in life and with a spirit of defeatism" but had profited

from courses ranging from reading and penmanship to excavation and truck driving.[21]

In the first two weeks of May 1939, according to the *Journal*, seventy-seven new families moved into Bethesda homes. By the end of the month 145 families had arrived, and in the first five months of 1939, building permits authorized $2,500,000 in private construction, almost all of it single-family homes although nine apartment projects costing $90,000 had also been approved.

By August 1939, new private building in the Western Suburban District reached $4 million, and permit applications were averaging well over $100,000 per week. Schools opened in September with enrollments at all-time highs, and some elementaries were overcrowded since the new Massachusetts Avenue school was still unfinished. The phone company planned a $160,000 addition to keep up with the demand, which had grown 220 percent since its building at Wisconsin and Stanford opened in 1928.

Drawing of the phone company addition in Bethesda

When he totaled up the construction splurge of 1939, Jack S. Eaton, building inspector for the Western Suburban Area, announced that his office had issued 917 permits for single-family dwellings ranging in cost from $2,740 to $40,000 with the average about $6,500. Sixty-six apartment units had also been authorized. The total for the year was $5,726,865, which was $1.5 million higher than the previous year when two hundred fewer permits had been approved.

On Wisconsin next to Community Hardware, Henry Hiser's new archery range, managed by Carroll Mullikan, (twenty arrows for 25¢) competed with B. L. William's nine-hole, miniature golf course down near the Offutt house (two games for two bits), while over at the "Lake," the swimming pool offered books of twenty-one swim tickets, $6.00 for adults and $3.00 for children under twelve (usually 25¢ and 15¢ per swim). The Ice Palace on Connecticut Avenue competed with rows of bowling

Peoples' mica schist facade at Edgemoor and Wisconsin

alleys and an archery range in addition to the skating rink and a popular Hot Shoppe across the street. Corr's, a 9th Street institution, opened a sporting goods and hobby store in Sacks' row. Peoples Service Drug Store doubled its space by annexing the old bank near the corner of Edgemoor and Wisconsin, and landlord Tuckerman built a stone front with big show windows for the enlarged store.

Twenty-six-year-old Leon Sherman took over the old post office, employed B-CC grads Bill Barnsley and George Heffner, and soon had the most popular men's store in town, Leon's.

I opened on April first, 1939. It was a Saturday. I put half of my last week's salary in the register and gave the other half to my wife. And we did a couple of hundred dollars worth of business that day, and I thought I had it made. But then it just about stopped for a while. One day we took in $5.96.

Both Leon Sherman and his wife, Frances, were native-born Washingtonians. His immigrant father had a tailor shop at 35th and N in Georgetown and later a men's shop on M Street in what had been a shooting gallery. Leon Sherman was working for his father and going to GW when he fell in love and married in 1938.

I was a collector for my father. Two dollars here and two dollars there, and finally I saw this place when I was out in Bethesda collecting from Ray Parks and ran back to my father. The old post office was for rent. In there you walked through the door and then down some steps. We put a level floor in and changed one of the bathrooms, they were

Leon Sherman

marked "white" and "colored," changed one into a dressing room. A guy named Frischman rebuilt the store, and his son was my first employee.

I borrowed merchandise from my father to fill up the shelves, and my father-in-law had a shoe store down in Southeast. He guaranteed me some credit with a shoe firm, and I ordered some children's shoes.

I hired high school kids right away. Barnsely, Duke Hashagen, Lebling, Jimmy Wallace. How was I going to attract their business? I slanted everything toward young guys. We used to chaperone all the dances. I lent them clothes. One boy I lent my beautiful plaid suit to go to graduation in, and I never got it back.

I paid Barnsley and the other high school boys twenty-five cents an hour. I remember one day he was waiting on a customer, and the customer finally walked out so I asked, "What did he want, Billy?"

"He wanted three of these underwear shorts for a dollar. And I told him, No indeed, they cost thirty-five cents apiece."

One guy, I kept telling him, when you get on the phone and you don't know what it's about, repeat what's said and look at me, and I'll give you a signal. So I heard this young fellow talking to somebody, and he's saying, "No, nope, uh-uh, no." So when he hung up I said, "What did he want?"

"He wanted a naval officer's outfit with a sword, and I knew we didn't have any." That was about a four or five hundred dollar sale.

My wife was only twenty-one and Barnsley was eighteen when we opened, and some people thought she was his sister. One day a boy came in and asked me if I thought it was okay to ask Billy's sister out. I said I didn't think her husband would appreciate that.

The building was owned by the then-president of Peoples Drug Stores, Gibbs. It was the only piece of property sold to settle the estate.

So I went to my father and said, "I've got to buy this building." He said, "No, I'll buy it and you'll pay me rent." He paid $59,500. It is a good thing he was our landlord in the lean times, especially during the war. He moved in upstairs later.

We rented an apartment from Burton Foster in the hollow of Hampden Lane, down below Riley Evers, 4905 Hampden Lane. We were not really accepted when we came to Bethesda. It never occurred to me that I wouldn't be.

Mrs. Sherman picked up the story.

We tried to rent an apartment. I hate to mention his name, he was a dentist; we tried to rent an apartment on Avondale, and they kept

putting us off. Finally Malora Christman called me and said forget it. She said, "Let's try to find a house." So she took us out to Greenwich Forest to see a house, and I loved the house, but they wouldn't accept a contract there.

Malora Christman told the Shermans that if they wanted one of the apartments on Avondale they could get it if they fought for it and publicized what they were doing. Leon Sherman and his wife decided that would not "pay" and they would rather not have it.

Leon Sherman continued:

I went to the Bank of Bethesda to borrow $5,000. Bogley said, "Sorry." I said, "What the hell kind of a place is this? Is this the United States of America? I can't rent an apartment, can't borrow money." I went to my father-in-law's bank down in Southeast and borrowed $10,000. And I always let Sacks know.

I was never asked to join the Lions or the Kiwanis or the Rotary, but I was active in the Chamber and that Board of Trade that wasn't much of a deal. And I was a founder of the Optimist Club later.

Bargains? One could golf at the National Woman's Country Club for fifty cents on weekdays and a dollar on weekends or drive to Silver Spring to get a gallon of Gifford's ice cream for $1.30. An all-expense trip to see the Redskins play the Brooklyn Dodgers including railroad fare, a room at the Gov. Clinton Hotel, and a reserved seat ticket cost $11.15. Prosperity and confidence were in the air.

In the fall of `39, Columbia Specialty moved into its new, brick, Bowling and Gardiner-built headquarters on Bradley Boulevard. The company's business had grown from $10,000 in 1925 to over $1 million and the employee rolls from three to 140 under the leadership of founder Joseph Richards. Fuel oil had been the company's main business since 1930, and it now could store 200,000 gallons and in `38 delivered more than five million gallons.

Chestnut Farms-Chevy Chase Dairy offered the cream-top bottle; Harvey Dairy's ads featured local children who had flourished on their products, and Thompson's made a virtue of the butter-fat content of its Golden Guernsey. The Adams' Bethesda Gardens at the District Line provided some more competition for the Stock Brothers' nursery on Bradley Boulevard as had Small's Rock Creek Valley Garden Shop over on Jones Mill Road. Charles Merryman's Bethesda Floral Gardens brightened the Bradley corner.

Columbia Specialty's new headquarters, 1939

Powell's Auto Service built a new shop on Hampden Lane and claimed "no matter what is wrong with your car - we can fix it." In December 1939, the first big, modern Sanitary Store opened at 7011 Old Georgetown Road, but many local women preferred to shop at or phone their orders to one of the D.G.S. stores or the many private markets such as L. J. Peterson's Kenwood Market, which delivered beer and wine as well as groceries.[22]

By the end of September, Henry Hiser's name glowed atop his big, new, triangular marquee. After installing cushioned seats and air conditioning, he reopened his modernized and renamed theater with a stage show. In addition to several new barber shops, Neilson's Beauty Salon opened next to the Bethesda Theater featuring the "Croquinole wave." Various "schools" offered dance lessons at the Columbia Dining Room and the Masonic Hall.

Howard's "kash and karry" Odorless Cleaners had cut-rate prices, while the Artcraft Cleaners had pick-up and delivery service from their office and plant at Wilson and Old Georgetown. The new branch of Elite Laundry opened in the glass-walled wedge with the half-timbered facade on the point of Old Georgetown and Edgemoor where the Piggly Wiggly and A&P had been. Manager Beulah Bledsoe, the former postmistress of Barnesville, was known by her maiden name, Miss Morningstar. She encouraged churches and clubs to hold craft

Tuckerman's row with the new theater marquee

and bake sales and charity bazaars in her store and always welcomed in people waiting for a bus on rainy days. Normandy Farms advertised its French onion soup and hot popovers, and the Little Tavern by the railroad bridge promoted those greasy, onion-covered, five-cent hamburgers with the slogan "Buy 'em by the Bag." Teenagers called them deathburgers but gobbled them up.

In November 1939, Dr. Bashore moved his dental office from the State/Hiser Theater building where he had been for seven years to one of his new apartments on Avondale, and Dr. William Kress set up his office "for the practice of orthodontia," a Bethesda first, in Dr. Ball's home and office on Old Georgetown Road. Zim's Sign Service, Poole's Printing and the Budget Finance Company all came to Bethesda that winter of `39. Even Adlai Magee's radio and record store, where "Victor" the big RCA papier maché dog stood by the door broadcasting the ball games to pedestrians, would soon have competition.

A visiting "expert" on community planning found the "business section as it stands is quite large enough to supply the needs of the area" even though some residents had to travel more than a half-mile to shop. He urged cooperation in planning and enforcing zoning regulations and preparing for future growth by designating areas for business development. A survey by the *Journal* showed that most of those opposed to business growth were very recent residents. Older Bethesdans favored more and better stores and an expanded shopping area. The *Journal* editorialized:

The merchants of Bethesda know better than any other group that there is still much to be desired in the stores on and near Wisconsin Avenue. They feel that they can improve and grow, that the few gaps in merchandise, notably both men's and women's clothing, can be filled in only if they are supported by the residents.[23]

And just as a reminder of the town's not-so-distant rural past, a minor incident on Bladen's farm, where the big naval hospital was to be built, caught the public's attention. When a Corps of Engineers crew making test borings went off to Gravelly Point for some airport work, they left a drill and its rig stuck in the mud. Not wanting to risk a truck, the workers persuaded Tommy Bladen to hitch up his team of horses to extricate the drill carriage and haul it out to the road.

The horses heaved, but the rig would not budge, and the government foreman struck one horse with a length of rope to urge it on. The horse pulled, sighed, collapsed and died. The foreman promised to send someone to certify the horse's death and pay Bladen the hundred dollars he claimed it was worth.

After a few days and a few complaints from his neighbors, the health department ordered Bladen to bury the dead horse, which he claimed he needed in order to get his money. He phoned the War Department. The files contained no record of Bladen or his horse. He called the Navy, and they referred him to the Judge Advocate General while the County health officer threatened to have him jailed. The JAG officer told him to bury the horse and get three written statements from reputable citizens as to its value. At the JAG office with his certificates, Bladen learned that the engineer in charge of the drill gang had presented a statement saying that Bladen volunteered his labor and that the horse in question was old and sick. The government would not pay, but of course Bladen could sue and in five or six years might get his money.

When he returned to Bethesda, Bladen told his story to a young engineer who promised that when the drill team returned he would have the farmer put on their payroll for a couple of weeks.[24]

Leaders of the on-going drive to produce a public library decided to limit themselves to the Bethesda Fire Board area after a survey showed little Chevy Chase interest. They wrote up a constitution, developed a proposed budget, and in January 1939 incorporated the Bethesda Public Library Association. Its board of directors included Emory Bogley, president; James Fieser, vice-president; Willie Green Day Perry, secretary; and Mrs. A. B. Foster, treasurer. She had been hard at work on the project since the Newcomb Club's library closed three years earlier. The library's trustees had the assistance of a forty-person Advisory

Council headed by Anthony Gould of *U.S. News & World Report* with George Bryan as vice-chairman and every civic leader in the area lending at least his or her name. Frederic P. Lee, who had been on the original steering committee, drafted a bill, which Delegate Ruth Shoemaker introduced and guided through the State legislature, and by May 1939, the library had its special taxing area.[25]

Now the Library Board went to work writing by-laws while Mrs. Winkler's committee collected books at 4707 Hampden Lane. The directors asked for and received a levy of five cents per $100 valuation for the first year to meet their start-up budget of $11,500. The board allowed $1,800 a year for a full-time librarian and $900 for an assistant. It budgeted about $3,000 for the purchase of circulating books and another $3,000 for heat, light, janitor services and supplies.

Mr. Hiser headed the committee seeking a suitable home, but its work ended abruptly when the Board of Education offered an unused and unfinished space in the basement of the new high school on East West Highway. The high ceilinged room on the east side of the school measured thirty-two by eighty-four feet, had a wall of large windows and a separate entrance. It provided room for the stacks and several, rather narrow reading spaces plus a children's alcove, a lavatory and a work room. Best of all it was rent-free. Mrs. J. William "Ma" Mohler chaired the committee in charge of decorating and furnishing the library with the assistance of Catherine Cutler from the school architect's office.

More than forty-five librarians applied for the Bethesda job, and after a very long series of

The Library Board: Mrs. A. B. Foster, Mrs. W. E. Perry, Mrs. Wm. Mohler, Mrs. Wm. Winkler and Rev. Francis Cockrell, Samuel Syme, Emory Bogley, J. Henry Hiser, James S. Fieser

interviews, the Library Board hired Dorothy Annable of Salem, Massachusetts. Miss Annable was a graduate of the Simmons School of Library Science and the Library School of the University of the Chicago. She had worked in Indiana, Iowa, New Hampshire, and most recently in the office of the regional librarian at Rutland, Vermont. As her assistant, the Board chose a County native, Ruth Carter Coplen, a graduate of Goucher and Simmons College. Miss Coplen, who lived with her parents near Halpine, took charge of the children's books. In mid-December Mrs. Walter E. Perry announced that the library would open by the end of January,

Librarian Annable

Librarian Coplen

delayed about two months due to a strike at the radiator factory.[26]

Over 3,000 books were catalogued including over one thousand donated volumes; heavy and highly finished Gaylord furniture was purchased and installed, and the library was opened on February 13, 1940. Mr. Hiser took charge of the arrangements for the grand opening. Reverend Cockrell, whose committee had prepared the budget, gave the invocation and Mr. Bogley, Miss Shoemaker, and Mrs. Mohler spoke briefly. Then Mrs. Foster unveiled a brass plaque with the dates of organization, incorporation and opening and the names of the Board of Trustees.[27]

Several hundred Bethesdans came out that cold Tuesday night to inspect their new library and sign up for cards. Library users from outside the taxing area had to pay one dollar for borrowing privileges. The library was open from 2 pm until 9 pm Monday through Friday and from 9 am to 6 pm on Saturday. The children's collection was immediately popular,

The new public library in the high school basement

former D.C. librarians, Mrs. Julian Branch and Mrs. Arthur Palmer, directed the work over a period of two years. They collected books and magazines; enlisted high school boys to build bookcases under the windows; cut down and refinished old, round dining room tables, and raised money to create a "sunny room full of children and books."

The library opened in the spring of 1941, and teacher Agnes Kain's Creative Club was one happy result. Its members dramatized stories, Monroe Leaf's *Ferdinand* was a favorite. They put on shows in the auditorium next to the cafeteria and raised money to buy more books. The PTA also operated the cooperative cafeteria on the ground floor of the west wing under the supervision of Mrs. Russell Sowers and with the help of many apron-clad mothers. The volunteer help of parents had become a tradition at Chevy Chase and at most other Bethesda-area schools.[28]

In 1939, Room 6 at Chevy Chase Elementary produced an ambitious, mimeographed history entitled "Chevy Chase: Yesterday and Today," which sold for ten cents. It had sections on the early schools, the delivery of groceries, public utilities, the fire department, housing, and economics, which included the cost of raising children, an estimated $1,000 a year, and the fact that "almost every child has about 25¢ allowance." It also included an interview with Mrs. J. H. Werner on local customs and reached the general conclusion that "Chevy Chase is quiet."[29]

Schools had become a very high priority item for most Bethesda-area groups by 1939. The level of teacher pay and the cost of educa-

and older students soon found a large collection of magazines such as *Popular Science*, *Popular Mechanics*, and *National Geographic* with which to fill rainy afternoons. Business grew steadily and contributions continued to supplement purchases. Mrs. Luke I. Wilson donated twenty-three books in mid-February, and library patrons checked out 750 books in the first two weeks. Most books could be borrowed for two weeks and magazines for seven days.

Classes of students from Somerset and Leland visited the library, and the librarians soon began writing items for the local papers on new acquisitions and special events. By spring, more than 2,000 new books were circulating, and a story-telling program began on Saturdays for the younger patrons. The library also established a rental shelf of popular new titles, which put it in competition with several local businesses. Later that year the library opened a branch at the "colored school" on River Road with teacher Margaret Wood in charge.

In June 1940, Mrs. A. Brookhouse Foster became the first woman to receive the premier local award for public service, the Star Cup created in memory of O. O. Kuhn. The Chamber of Commerce thus recognized the long effort that brought Bethesda a public library.

Unplugging the fire siren and opening the public library were both rites of passage as Bethesda matured.

Library development seemed to be in the air. In 1939 under the leadership of Chevy Chase Eleementary PTA president Edith Dinwoodey and with the support of Principal Anna P. Rose, parents began planning the County's first elementary school library. Two

Mrs. Rose by the windows in the new school library

tion were commonly debated topics. In 1938 the County had expended $126 per high school student, a state high, and $71 a year for elementary pupils, third highest in Maryland. The cost of County public education was approaching $1.5 million per year, but not only were some classrooms still overcrowded, many students attended D.C. schools because parents believed they were better. When schools opened for the 1939-40 school year, the total Seventh District enrollment was 3,811, up 228 over the previous year.

At the Glen Echo-Cabin John school, principal David Trumble installed a new schedule with longer periods, and the school offered shop work and home arts courses to seventh and eighth grade students for the first time. Ruth B. Clapp at Bethesda Elementary, she of the plaited hair and no-nonsense mien, had to schedule two classes in the auditorium, start a new first grade class, combine a fourth and fifth grade and hire two more teachers in the first week of school as enrollment in her 625-capacity building approached 800. The PTA hired Marie Kromas to run its cafeteria while Mrs. Scott Brewer arranged for volunteer help. That year Bethesda's sixth graders painted murals in the auditorium, and the 5th grade students decorated the cafeteria.

Chevy Chase and Somerset enrollments were down slightly, but both opened with large groups of Massachusetts Avenue kids who were eager for their new school to be finished. Chevy Chase Elementary suffered a great deal of vandalism over the summer with 139 broken windows and the kindergarten playhouse destroyed. Local boys were blamed and parents were asked to cooperate as they had two years previously during a similar outbreak.[30]

Early in the year, the County health department began its physicals of kindergarteners and new first graders plus 4th, 7th, and 10th grade students. Dr. John G. Ball and Dr. Leo I. Donovan were among the physicians selected to make the exams.

Muddy paths led to the still unfinished school building out Massachusetts Avenue extended when its PTA organized in October at the Somerset School. They elected Mrs W. W. Rubey of Westmoreland Hills their first president and Mrs. Donald Adams of Brookdale, vice-president. In January 1940, 200 parents and civic association members attended the first meeting at the new school at Baltimore Avenue and Allen Road. Superintendent

Broome and Major Howard Cutler, the architect who designed the Williamsburgish-Georgian-colonial school, spoke and then introduced Mrs. Thomas H. McNamara, the principal. The students, who were being taught by their own teachers at Chevy Chase and Somerset, arrived in early February.

The teachers and their 150 pupils moved into an air-conditioned, two-story building with room for twice that number of children. Each corner room had a fireplace and a bay window. Two PTA mothers, Mrs. Ames and Mrs. Golibart, operated the kitchen on the second floor. Within a month the students were producing a six-page newspaper, "The Babbling Brook," and selling ads to raise money to buy their own mimeograph machine. The sixth grade safety patrols with Billy Sutton as captain manned the street corners and produced a map for each student. By the time of the PTA's fund-raising dance at Kenwood in April, the new school in Westhaven had everything but a name. That did not come until June.[31]

Meanwhile, after turning down an offer from Newbold for a lot on Jones Bridge Road, the school board's planners met with the Chevy Chase Land Company about a site for a new school in East Bethesda. In the first week of March 1940, the Board advertised its intention to buy three acres on the east side of Cypress between Maple and Chase Avenues at $3,500 per acre and take an option on seven additional acres at a slightly higher price. The land was in the area where a small, red plane had crashed the previous spring as the pilot dipped his wings to friends on Highland Avenue.

In June, the school board accepted the Morrison Brothers bid of $37,100 for the first unit of the school and work began almost immediately on a one-story brick building containing five classroom with removable partitions. The PTA for the unnamed school serving the area north of East West Highway and east of Wisconsin Avenue organized even before the excavation began. The parents elected Ray H. Smith of Middleton Lane president, Mrs. R. C. Hardy vice-president. George Condron headed the committee that helped plan the layout of playgrounds and athletic fields.

One of the big Chevy Chase Elementary projects that year was the production of "Pinocchio" as an operetta. Almost the whole school became involved in making scenery and costumes and practicing for the performances at school and for a paying audience at the

Leland auditorium in February 1940. Large choruses and two forty-five member bands, one of just harmonica players, involved almost five hundred students. The production, directed by Mrs. Catherine Lavin, raised money for a mimeograph machine and school supplies.[32]

Dick Hudgens, Edward Burnap, Stephen Falk as Pinocchio, Ann Belser and Woodlief Thomas on stage

At Leland the school paper, the safety patrol and other activities had their annual rebirth, and the band staged a benefit movie at the Hiser to raise money for new uniforms. Mrs. Bender's library, with 8th and 9th grade assistants, now boasted 2,700 volumes, about half of them fiction, plus thirty magazine subscriptions and a bulging vertical file of clippings. About 200 students used the library every day, many in the morning when it opened at 8:40. The County provided $100 each year for the library, and the PTA added funds from its book sale at the Shopping Center.

That fall 797 students, a record ninety-five percent, bought Leland budget cards. "Zip" Lehr soon had twenty-three teams and some 300 boys involved in basketball intramurals. And the school used its community. Mrs. Arthur Hilland talked to 7th grade classes about flower arrangement, and girls from Leland skated weekly at the Chevy Chase Ice Palace with Miss Ferry while others bowled at Hiser's alleys. The PTA sponsored a series of teas for parents and teachers in January.

Both Joe and Frank Cantrel went to Leland after finishing at Blessed Sacrament a year apart, and both recalled Coach Lehr. "He'd get you out on that damn floor of that damn gym and he'd get a lock, at the end of a damn rope, and swing it around for you to jump. If that

lock hit you," Frank winced. "I played basketball at Leland, and Zip had a pair of black, platform basketball shoes. I wanted shoes like that, but I never could find them."

"He'd get us under his arm and rub our heads," Joe Cantrel said. "He called Loring Appleby, Applewoman, things like that. I think everybody liked him."

Isabel Gaither Lynch (B-CC `44) remembered her junior high days fondly.

I was in 7-C, seventh grade was by alphabet, 8th and 9th were by the track system. I was in 8B. If I had been in 8-G I wouldn't have told you. I remember that we thought a couple of teachers were having a romance. I played basketball on those beautiful hardwood floors. They let us roller-skate in there at lunchtime for a while. I was on a winning volleyball team. Miss Ferry was our coach, and I had her for English. I had been a C student, but after I got on the team I became an A and B student. She got to know me better.

The fast crowd at Leland not only smoked, they French kissed, too. I can remember the first time I learned that a good friend of mine French kissed some boy. I couldn't believe it.

At the high school, a few rooms were being renovated and, in addition to the public library, the other areas left unfinished in the original construction were being completed. Joseph C. Gardner of Edgemoor drew up plans for athletic fields on the sixteen acres behind the school while the PE classes played touch football out on the front lawn. Mr. Frisbie organized an orchestra in the fall of 1939, and the Izaac Walton League sponsored a rifle team that soon had sixty members.

The "Greeks" and the other secret societies were very active at the high school. Pi Phi, which was affiliated with a national organization, put on a dinner dance at the Congressional Country Club and sponsored a hay ride to Great Falls and then a father-son banquet. Chi Alpha, which had a summer cottage at Tall Timbers on the way to Piney Point, also staged a party at Congressional with "popular favors" for the boys' dates, and a somewhat subdued Alpha Delta Sigma ended the `39 season with a stag party at the Kensington Cabin while Kappa Phi Sigma organized a picnic for members and their guests.

Mr. Pyle himself sponsored the Hi-Y club for boys, which served as a school-sanctioned alternative to fraternities. In the late Thirties it attracted some student leaders and athletes and even took on some of the more colorful

traditions of the Greeks. Robert Rickey recalled that the first time he tasted beer was at his Hi-Y initiation.

It always wound up with dropping you off someplace, and you walking home. They left me at the big stone water towers in Tenleytown. We'd gone to the Hot Shoppe on Connecticut Avenue and had to do all sorts of things like suck raw eggs and make fools of ourselves. Then they blindfolded us and dropped us off in different places. When I took off the blindfold and saw those big towers, I knew where I was; I was about two miles from Lang-drum Lane and had no trouble walking home.

As a senior, Rickey was president of Hi-Y and on the other side of the initiation fun.

John Shumate, president of his class all three years, pledged Chi Alpha and ended up "lost in Rock Creek with slop all over me" during his initiation. "They were important then," he said, "and almost all the school leaders, the Student Council, the Honor Society, were in one." John Henry Sullivan Jr. (B-CC `43) thought that most athletes and popular kids were in fraternities when he was in high school. "The socially active," he labeled them, and he also remembered his induction.

They initiated us down where the Meadow-brook stables are now. They took you down there and blindfolded you and drove you all around all sorts of circuitous routes to get you lost, and then they got you out in the field late at night, and you're sitting there just in your shorts, that's all, and they are cracking eggs over your head, making all kinds of marks on your body with lipstick, and they're hitting you with these paddles. They broke three paddles on my rear end.

They would have parties at people's houses with a lot of drinking, mostly beer, but there was a drink called moose milk, grapefruit juice and gin. They'd make a big hopper of it, and people would sit there with straws. Cremins and Haven Rettew were both in ADS. That was a drinking fraternity.[33]

Thomas (Loring) Appleby (B-CC `42) disagreed about where the popular and socially active congregated. He pledged Pi Phi and "went through all the goat business and decided it was a lot of crap." Appleby, Tom Kirby and Bob Brewer of the class of `43 were among the leaders of the non-fraternity students. Appleby admitted that having a car helped. He bought a `36 Chevrolet for $250 when he was a sophomore.

I had wanted a convertible, but all I could find were Fords. Finally I found this Chevy with a

Appleby and his Chevy at Burrows

rumble seat. When I drove through the Rock Creek fords, a sheet of water went up over me and drowned the rumble seat passengers. They learned to close that lid in a hurry. I drove kids to all the games for three years when I was on the JV and varsity, and I once raced Doug Williams in reverse up Wisconsin Avenue, my Chevy losing to his `34 Ford. He'd already beat me going forward.

In school year 1939-40, for a variety of reasons, probably including the Curtis Walker accident of the previous spring, the school administration cracked down on fraternities, and some students loudly stated they would transfer to D.C. high schools if the organizations were banned.

Bob Lebling (B-CC `41), president of his class all four years and an active Pi Phi member, said most people knew who the fraternity and sorority members were, but nobody bothered them. A compromise resulted in the Greeks becoming less blatant with their hazing and in advertising their activities, but the issue was not resolved.

When Leonard Williams moved on from Leland to B-CC in the fall of 1940, Mr. Pyle greeted the incoming freshmen with a lecture emphasizing that secret societies were illegal, and he threatened that members of fraternities and sororities would not be allowed to be in clubs or on teams or in the student government. Since Williams wanted to play basketball "more than anything," he decided not to join a fraternity although his older brother had belonged to Southern Society, and he had been ready to follow his lead.

Bob Brewer, a student leader and outstanding athlete, said, "My folks didn't want me to get involved with fraternities and I didn't." Jay Fitzgerald, *Tattler* sports editor in 1940-41 who later covered sports for the

Journal, and Doug Berry, who was on the JV basketball team with Williams and Brewer, were both members of Southern Society. Williams' class was the first to feel the wrath of the administration when some seniors known to be fraternity or sorority members were not allowed to participate in the formal graduation ceremony in June 1943.[34]

At B-CC in the 1939-40 school year, at least forty different clubs from auto maintenance to Shakespeare and from chess and checkers to consumer education competed for students' time twice each week during the last period of the day, 2:45 to 3:30 pm. A new organization, the Bachelors' Club, attracted two dozen members who made aprons for themselves and then turned their attention to fried doughnuts, brownies, and pigs in the blanket. The Footlight Club's big production was "The Red Lamp," its thirteenth annual spring play and the first staged in B-CC's own gym-auditorium.

Dorothy Young, the school counselor who was in charge of activities, operated an employment bureau with the help of the PTA. She tried to match students with part-time jobs during the school year and to find permanent employment for graduating seniors. She also did college counseling and met with incoming students from Leland and Kensington junior highs. Miss Young lived with her parents in Alta Vista and became known for her flower gardening and her work with the Methodist church where she taught Sunday school and was secretary of the board of stewards.[35]

As the B-CC boys' basketball team prepared for another season under coach Alan Vogt, the cheerleading squad led by captain Carmen "Chooky" Ornelas donned their white flannel skirts and bulky sweaters. Their sponsor was PE teacher Kate Terhune. The girls led the afternoon pep rallies before the games and stirred up the crowd with their "Susie Q" after each Blue and Gold score. Even their huge megaphone, Arabella, became well-known, and Carmen Ornelas was later elected the "most popular" and the "best all around" girl in school. Basketball star and class president John Shumate won those honors among the boys.

Early in the season, B-CC beat Blair 19-18 before 2,000 screaming fans at the University of Maryland gym when a Silver Spring player's last second layup rolled off the rim. By 1939, the rivalry with the Silver Spring school had become intense as well as traditional.

John Shumate, at 6'0" the tallest regular on the team, led B-CC in scoring that season. In an era of center-jumps and low scores, he averaged in double figures with his two-handed set-shot and was a unanimous choice to the all-area teams. He called being chosen as B-CC's first All-Metro "the highlight of my life."[36]

Shumate had grown up in Edgemoor playing baseball on the firemen's lot in Miller's Flats, but because of a heart murmer, he had not played basketball competitively until his junior year. By then, his family lived in a new house in Greenwich Forest, and he had given up his *Herald* route in Woodmont because of the problems he had trying to collect each month. He recalled that his brother's *Daily News* route in Edgemoor was much more successful because so many maids subscribed to get the day's winning number.

Johnny Shumate and his older brother Oscar shared a `34 Plymouth two-door, and JV player Tom Appleby recalled racing back from a game and leading cars driven by Bobby Cremins and Shumate as they headed down East West Highway from Connecticut. Cremins tried to pass him on the hill up to the railroad bridge only to be stymied by a car coming the other way, but Shumate won by cutting across the front lawn of the high school to reach the parking lot first.

Even before the end of the season, B-CC was invited to the South Atlantic Tournament at Durham and to the Star Tourney, if they beat Blair again. In a tune-up for the county championship game, B-CC crushed Landon 36-13 although the Bears had the city's leading scorer in Paul Baker and were playing in their big, new gym.

The second Blair game in late February 1940, like the first, took place in the University of Maryland fieldhouse. Bethesda routed Blair 51-30 with Shumate, Bobby Cremins and Bill Barnsley in double figures, but the game was long remembered because of the massive brawl that broke out after a B-CC rooter snatched a Blair banner near the game's end.[37]

There had been some quickly quelled trouble at the half, but this time the fighting swept through the stands and across the gym floor and went on for at least twenty minutes. Ninth grader "Sonny" Baldwin, a rabid fan, watched from the stands as more than 200 youngsters battled. "I stayed as far away from that as I could," he said. State troopers slowly got the melee stopped. With 1:15 left on the game

clock Cres Bride, the Blair coach, called the game and had the lights turned out.

Team captain John Shumate said, "The players stayed out of it. Jim Kinsman was standing on the foul line when the lights went out, and the ref said, "Go ahead and shoot it."" Kinsman himself recalled that there was "some trouble up in the stands," and remembered making the foul shot in the semi-dark. The next day B-CC played its third game in three days and beat St. Albans 41-34 to raise its record to 18-5.[38]

The girls' team led by senior Margaret Lee, voted outstanding player in the Star Tournament, also had a fine season and defeated Mt. Rainier in the tourney but lost to Hyattsville 31-28 for the city title. Both B-CC teams plus the cheerleaders joined for a banquet at the Brook Farm Tea Room in mid-March to receive their letters and emblems. The B-CC JV team under young coach Pete Smith won twelve in a row and then lost to Eastern's JV for the local title. At Leland Zip Lehr's teams had won the County championship for three years in a row but lost to Sherwood 22-19 in the annual County tournament that winter.

The basketball season was almost over when a disastrous fire at Rockville's high school destroyed not only most of the building but the Board of Education offices as well. Dr. Broome, who was restrained by firemen when he tried to save his budget work, moved his records and staff to the public library. The Rockville 7th graders, all 115 of them, came to Chevy Chase Elementary on March 12 to finish their school year while the 225 8th and 9th graders attended Kensington Junior High. The "commercial" juniors and seniors resumed their work in rooms at B-CC, and the academic students, after a ten-day break, went back to school in a partitioned gym and the annex, all that was left of their school.

Meanwhile, at the old experimental farm in March 1939, Mrs. John Werner and Mrs. George Bryan staged a dedication of the new recreation center honoring Emory Bogley's nine years of hard work. The main speaker, Frederic P. Lee, said:

Projects for the public good do not come about without effort. Behind each project that takes life and matures, there usually stands a key man. He is the man who, despite disappointment on the way, sees a fight through. He brings to the cause not only vision but also tenacity of purpose and

tact, patience and perseverance, painstaking industry and energy. We had such a man in one of our neighbors, Emory Bogley.

It was one of the few times during Bogley's long service to his community that he received public thanks and applause.[39]

Then, while local banks purchased the $30,000 in bonds authorized for its completion, M-NCP&PC planners proposed building tennis courts, a swimming pool, an amphitheater, basketball courts plus football and baseball fields and, of course, parking lots. The Boy Scouts started working on two buildings toward the back of the center beside an extension of Davidson Drive and soon had them ready for roofing and chimney construction.

The tennis courts were finished first, and after a spate of complaints from neighbors about how close they had been built to their houses, play began in the summer. In charge at the "Rec Center" was its neighbor Rene Beard whose family had been the first to buy in the Davidson

Emory H. Bogley

subdivision at 4708 Chevy Chase Boulevard. Miss Beard, a junior majoring in art at The American University and a graduate of B-CC (class of `36), was the first woman ever put in charge of a playground by the Park and Planning Commission. The only other employees were a caretaker and a janitor. Summer programs, which used the Glen Echo pool weekly, were also offered in 1939 at Somerset under James Cross and at Bethesda Elementary under Victor Purse.[40]

When Dorothy Young organized the Youth Research Council composed of school principals, PTA presidents and church leaders, Stella Werner became chairman of its recreation committee in addition to her work with the Methodist church, the Bethesda Elementary PTA and the Democratic Party organization. Once the dedication ceremonies ended, her recreation committee accepted the task of finishing the main building and hiring a director. They collected furniture from various sources and help from all their friends.

The Chevy Chase Fire Department donated a ping pong table, and the Bethesda Woman's Club made the drapes. Mrs. Werner "passed the hat" at the Chevy Chase PTA and raised money to buy a second-hand piano. Then came more formal structure.

"Emory Bogley came to my house to work up an advisory board," Mrs. Werner said. "Dr. Perry sent him to see me. We picked the members in my living room and later got out a formal letter of appointment. The first meeting was March 29, 1939." She listed and described the board she chaired: T. E. Hampton, Dr. Perry, Reverend Whiting of the Lutheran church, Wilton T. Allen the assessor, Joseph Gardner of the Civic Federation, John Imirie and John Overholt of the Chamber of Commerce, T. W. Pyle, Somerset's mayor William Horne, Mrs. Curtis Walker of the school board, Mrs. F. Elliot Middleton of the Democratic Club, active Republican Mrs. Arthur Hilland, Mrs. Preston Carter Alexander of the Bethesda PTA, and clubwomen Mrs. George Farrell, Mrs. Louis Gravelle, and Mrs. William Morell.[41]

The committee adopted rules, which included no alcohol at the center and no roller skating in the buildings, and then set out to find a director. It was not long before the "Rec Center" became the favorite place for local organizations to meet. Christ Lutheran, Bethesda Methodist and the nearby schools held outings at the Recreation Center in the spring. The

Newcomb Club, Red Cross, Girl Scouts and D.A.R chapters met there, and the women clubs helped furnish the kitchen.

Stella B. Werner moved to the Leland subdivision of Chevy Chase with her government-employee husband in 1929 while she was expecting their first child. They bought a house on 45th Street for $500 down. She described as "a little place with a nice kitchen and fireplace, a big back yard and small trees." She immediately became involved in her neighborhood, and both she and her husband were very active in the Methodist church in Woodmont.

Mrs. Werner said that Judge Van Court, a JP at the County Building who lived with his daughter on Elm Street, was very influential in her political life. By 1933, she had organized the Western Democratic Club, which began in her living room, and worked hard to get new residents registered and informed. She became a minor adjunct of the Lee machine. At the end of the Fusion campaign of 1934, she recalled:

On election day at Dr. Perry's office I accepted $20 for using my car to bring in voters. Everybody did. County employees checked on who had not voted and took cars out to get them. The County Building was empty.[42]

"Little" Stella, Mrs. Leroy Allison:

I remember being pulled in the wagon up the street. Mother would say we are going for our vaccination, up to Dr. Perry. The first didn't take so we had to have another ride in the little wagon. After I got my shot, I was shunted aside while this long conversation went on at the old office on Wisconsin.

Mrs. Allison also said that there were "always" meetings going on in their living room when she was a child.

In the fall of 1939, Montgomery County's Federation of Women's Clubs, with Mrs. B. Payton Whalen in her fourth term as president, initiated a "Know Your County" program. It was another of those "clouds no bigger than a fist" as far as the County Commissioners and the Lee machine were concerned. "Only by making citizenship a part of our daily lives will we have a trained group capable of meeting the problems that face us," said

Stella Werner

Edith Whalen

thje indominable, 4' 10"'" Mrs. Whalen. "Women must learn to demand that offices be filled by men without trickery and without price."

Mrs. Joseph Travers Maguire, former president of the Woman's Club of Chevy Chase, chaired the activity using a booklet from the League of Women Voters as a guide. Several "study groups" began to look very carefully at how the County Commissioners were spending tax dollars and especially at the County Aid office, which the Democrats had pledged to abolish after a fight led by Mrs. Walter E. Perry. Other study areas included the police, bonded indebtedness, fire departments, and the judiciary.

Almost all of the local women's clubs participated in the program. The Chevy Chase club's group, led by Mrs. Harold DeCourcey, held classes open to all on the first and third Fridays at lunchtime. The Newcomb Club's study group, chaired by Mrs. Clyde DeBinder, also met twice a month. In October, delegate Ruth Shoemaker told Newcomb members that what the County needed was a modern bookkeeping system that would reveal true expenses to both the taxpayers and the Commissioners. She said she doubted, for example, that the Commissioners even knew what they were paying to have coal ashes hauled away. The next month Miss Young talked about the cost of education in a meeting at the County Building. Soon Commissioners' phones started ringing with questions from women who had attended these meetings.

In general, the women's clubs, civic associations, businessmen's groups, scouting groups, and even church activities followed the school calendar and usually closed down for the summer months. The schedule of the Woman's Club of Bethesda was fairly typical. It had its executive board and international relations study group meetings on the first Tuesday of each month. The second Tuesday was for business meetings and a luncheon, the third for book reviews and the fourth for special speakers. The club president, Mrs. Louis Gravelle, appointed

Mrs. Gravelle

a committee to institute a "Know Your County" study. The Bethesda club also sponsored a series of Monday afternoon dessert bridge parties, several seasonal activities and, in the spring, four diet and cooking forums attended by more than a thousand women.

Cartoonists and social critics poked a lot of fun and criticism at "club women" during the New Deal era, but in Bethesda very little progress was made without them. Mrs. Gravelle was reasonably typical of the "class." She and her lawyer-husband bought a house in Battery Park in 1928 and by 1936 had moved to a new and larger home, which they called "The Oaks," on three wooded acres out Bradley Boulevard. She organized the first supervised summer playground program at Bethesda Elementary when she was PTA president in 1936-37, and the popular activity continued for more than ten years. She was also a member of the Public Health Lay Committee, the Bethesda Garden Club, the League of Women Voters and the Presbyterian church. When the Gravelles moved away, their absence was noted.

In the snowy winter of 1939-40, other signs of Bethesda's continuing growth appeared. The telephone company enlarged its office at Stanford Street with a two-story stone addition and prepared to switch Bethesda's more than 10,000 phones to dial service. The post office reported that it was handling an average of 1,500 pieces of mail each day, and Sgt. James McAuliffe stated that the police station received about twenty-five calls a day.

The State Roads Commission and the County Commissioners approved and contracted for the installation of five new traffic lights on Wisconsin Avenue including an improved system at East West and Old Georgetown. A light for the Old Georgetown-Wilson Lane intersection was also being discussed. A 24-hour survey of Wisconsin Avenue showed that of the 19,500 vehicles that crossed the District Line heading north, 18,000 reached Bradley Boulevard and 15,000 came to the in-

The Light That Failed

tersection at East West Highway and about half of those continued on north on the Pike. During the same period 5,700 cars came into the Bank of Bethesda intersection on Old Georgetown Road and 9,500 reached "five points" on East West Highway.

In 1939, the Chevy Chase Section Two "board" decided they needed a new policeman. Edward S. Northrup had been Superintendent of Public Service, the town manager of the "Village," for five years. The 28-year-old GW Law School graduate supervised a staff of fifteen and oversaw trash removal, street repair including preservation of the old cobblestone curbs, street lighting and police protection.

"Old Man" Springirth, he discovered, instead of doing his job of checking on vacant houses and patrolling the neighborhood until midnight, had been checking in, saying hello to a few people and then going to the movies down past the Circle, coming back to the town hall and going to bed.

According to his successor, the breaking point came when:

Right across from the post office a woman that was on the board caught a burglar in her house. The husband called Springirth who was in that little room where he could sleep. He said, "I've got a man here; I caught a

Edward Northrup

burglar." Old Man Springirth said, "What'd you want me to do?"

"I want you to come over here and take him," the man said. *"To hell with that," said Springirth, and he hung up.*

So they woke up, but they felt a little bit guilty themselves; it wasn't all his fault, so they decided to make a job for him and called it the night watchman for the building.

At age 22, Bill Austin left the Navy after serving for five years and married Mildred Warfield from Sugarloaf Mountain six weeks after he met her. "Her father had fourteen children," he smiled, "and I always said when you married into that family you took one away, you didn't move in." One of Austin's sisters lived in Bethesda, so he landed there looking for a job.

I went to work first for Gordon Burrows. He was awful. If you did something, if we didn't clear your windshield, say, and he had seven people in the office there, he never said a word until after the car left, and then he would call you in, in front of these people, and he would raise hell, cuss you out. I worked for him for $14.50 a week, ten-hour days, pumping gas and greasing cars. I was there six months or so.

A fellow there had been a slater's helper, and we talked, and he said I ain't gonna take this crap. I'm going down to the man I used to work for, and he says, if you want I'll see if I can get you a job with him. So I went and got a job carrying slate for a mechanic, and if you get ahead good, you can tack some slate on, and he'll watch you and make sure you do it right and that's how you get to be a slater. Thompson, I think, was the boss, he was always in debt. I did stay there enough to learn a little bit, and then I went to work for a guy named Bill Griffin.

Lightbaum was building on Western Avenue. He was a very good builder, and we worked on some of his houses.

One day Griffin come along and said, "Get your tools. I want you to start a house down here." I had never done anything but work with another mechanic, but I went down on Western Avenue to one of these, we called them, broken-back houses, Dutch type. Klinepeter was the contractor. He said you start this off and gave me a black fellow as my helper. So I got up there and done the best I could to line it off and start a little bit. A guy came along that I knew and looked at what I had done and changed some of the lines so that is was better. I'd never worked on a house like that, but I plugged off on it. It seemed like forever getting that roof on.

Later he told me, "I put you down there and if you had said, no, I can't do that, I wasn't even going to keep you on as a helper." He lost money on that because I was there a couple of weeks, but I only got forty cents an hour at that time.

Then I heard that Chevy Chase Village was looking from a friend of my sister's who was a desk clerk at the Bethesda police station. So I went over and talked to Mr. Northrop. He was going to law school and lived there in the Village. It was kind of a part-time job. He asked me to come and meet the board, and it got down to me and another fellow. They talked to us both, and a couple of days later he called me in and said, "You've got the job." It was $125 a month and furnish your own car. They'd pay the gas and tires, and I had this old Oldsmobile I'd bought from Burrell Marsh, a 1930 I think, a two-door.

The Park and Planning Commission announced its intention to revamp the street numbering in the suburban areas to conform to the Washington, D.C., system and to rename dozens of streets. The Commission's survey showed thirteen Montgomery streets, eleven Maples, eight Parks, and seven Cedar and Ridge streets. It also found that some roads were known by several different names. For example, East West Highway was called Watkins Avenue in Bethesda and Bethesda-Silver Spring Highway on many maps and Cypress Street in other areas while in Chevy Chase, Stanford, Elm, Rosemary and Raymond were all the same street.

Numbering also posed many problems with adjacent and parallel streets often having completely different numbers and some streets, such as Old Georgetown Road, having numbers that suddenly dropped from thousands to hundreds. In the middle of Bethesda the 6800 and 6900 blocks of Wisconsin Avenue ran from Leland Street to the bank with Critchfield's service station numbered 6800 and Peoples Drug Store, 6998. Another difficulty was that many suburban streets did not run east and west or north and south but wandered and circled in what developers believed was a more artful and saleable manner.

The changes had been State-authorized since 1937, and Charles M. Jones was the M-NCP&P man in charge. The target was to get it done by the end of 1940. The work started in the Silver Spring-Takoma Park area, and it took a while before Park and Planning abandoned the idea of alphabetically renaming the streets starting at the District Line and using Connecticut Avenue as a model. By the fall, the County was ordering metal signs for the Silver Spring area and admitting Bethesda would have to wait.

Other signs of growth included the revitalization of the country club that had been the National Women's CC. The Bradley Hills Country Club announced a membership drive along with plans for building a full 18-hole course. The new owner, Eddie Adams, reported that they were "now hitting on all six with the club's new pro, Al Jamison, proving increasingly popular with links enthusiasts." Bad weather slowed Adams's plans. He told reporters that he hoped to have the new nine ready for `41, "But you can't do much with a snow-covered landscape." Jamison, who grubbed new fairways out of scrubby woodland that spring, remembered:[43]

Adams was a Dodge dealer in Silver Spring and a member of Indian Springs. He took the lease on Bradley Hills with an option to buy for $175,000 that included the Burning Tree Estates land. And he knew Indian Springs where I worked was sold, so he asked me to go over there with him.

I drew the design and hired the bulldozers and the men. Got a topo map and laid it out. You can't change nature. When you lay out a golf course, drainage is number one. You can't have greens sitting down in a hole. Water seeks its own level so you better not stop it. You put swales in the fairways to get the water moving. You can cut a swale you wouldn't even notice if you do it right.

At the Rec Center, the Community Cooperative Nursery School had morning sessions for thirty children between the ages of two and five in the big room on the right side of the old administration building. Tuition was $4.50 per month; Mrs. Alfred Davidson was in charge, and the mothers took turns transporting and helping to care for the youngsters. The program was a popular success, but in June it had to seek a new home when the County Red Cross occupied its space after being burned out of offices in Rockville's high school. Through the summer, the nursery school used the decrepit Bolton Building at the Rec Center, and in the fall of 1940, found room at Chevy Chase Elementary and continued there with Anna Rose's blessings.[44]

In Battery Park, the citizens' association dedicated their playground with a parade and flag raising. Captain F. O. Smith, in his fifth

term as president of the association, presided, and Joseph D. Montedonico received much praise for his hard work and donated equipment. Mrs. Frank Bennett's committee drew up the rules and provided volunteer supervision.

The Huntington Terrace Citizens' Association finally convinced the post office to make deliveries to the door instead at the curb. It was a significant victory in a neighborhood where the mailmen had refused service altogether a few years before because the roads were so bad. Unfortunately, Garfield Street was still a muddy mess especially in the winter.

Garfield Street after a rain

And new businesses kept coming to Bethesda. In the spring, Art Bowis, with R. B. Suddith as vice-president and service manager, opened the Chevy Chase Motor Company just north of the Bethesda Theater. According to his grandson, Bowis and his partner drove out and looked over that end of town. "I think this would be a great place for an auto dealership," Bowis said. "There hasn't been a single car drive by in 30 minutes!" his partner pointed out.

Saul and Tanya Bendit started the Ladies Specialty Shoppe on Wisconsin Avenue between Peoples and the DGS with a line of "accessories," drapes, curtains, and linens. The Baby Mode, later Lane's Tots to Teens, arrived in the Shopping Center. Evelyn and Clyde L. Steadman brought their wholesale Mexican food business from Anacostia to 4717 Miller Avenue where they produced and canned hundreds of gallons of chili for Peoples Drug Stores and other restaurant customers as well as making tamales and tortillas. They added a new and interesting smell to the

neighborhood. Sam Harvey's dairy established a third milk route in Bethesda, and the town even got another newspaper although it did not last very long. Ralph B. Sadler, who started the Bethesda Printing Company in 1930, produced a local weekly, the Bethesda-Chevy Chase *Leader,* in the spring, but it did not survive the summer. City Motors, headed by Arthur Eisele, replaced Dibb as the town's Studebaker dealer.

The Bethesda Junior Chamber of Commerce held its first meeting in March 1940 at Ed Warner's new, air conditioned restaurant and chose builder George W. DeFranceaux president. Day Thorpe weighed in with an editorial headlined "Shopkeepers and Merchants" that offended some of the older businessmen. It concluded:

Bethesda will never develop into the community it is destined to become until more of its storekeepers become merchants, or until the passing of time brings about the natural passing out of the storekeepers to make place for real merchants.[45]

In the spring, the Chamber of Commerce planned its first Cherry Blossom Festival. G. Wady Imirie fathered the idea and received cooperation from Donal Chamberlin of Kenwood and Fire Chief Bargagni who had been involved in the D.C. festival. The committee "elected" Bob Hagner's daughter Anne queen of the pageant.

Henry Hiser, newly elected president of the Chamber, along with Miss Hagner, her maids of honor, Tempe Curry and Charlotte Eisele, and several local big-wigs visited Annapolis and convinced Governor O'Conor to crown the queen and take part in the festival. FDR expressed regrets after a similar invitation, but his office assured the planners that he would tour Kenwood when the blossoms were at their height. A few letters-to-the-editor viewed with

Mr. Oldfield of We Cab takes delivery from Mr. Suddith

Tempe Curry plants a tree as Earle Hampton, Margaret McDonald, Patsy Royster and the princesses watch.

alarm the Chamber's implied support of a particular real estate development and all the free advertising Kenwood received.

To get ready for the festival, the Chamber of Commerce and the new Junior Chamber sponsored a Clean Up and Paint Up Campaign with Harry Danilson as chairman and a lot of Boy Scout participation. As G. W. Imirie and the politicians watched, Miss Curry planted a cherry tree in front of the post office at the end of March, and in his short speech, Commissioner Hampton praised M. G. Coplen for the other trees he planted on Wisconsin Avenue. Then on April 20, 1940, Miss Hagner rode to her coronation in Kenwood in Grover Cleveland's horse drawn carriage, renovated by Chief Bargagni. The queen sat on the same throne used at the Tidal Basin the week before. Children from all the elementary schools and the hundred-member band led by Raymond Hart performed. Twenty-eight County policemen and twenty-five young men from the CCC camp helped with traffic control as thousands of sightseers toured the blossom-filled area.[46]

At the end of April, the police began enforcing new parking regulations in Bethesda including, for the first time, rush-hour restrictions. No parking was allowed on the west side of Wisconsin in the morning nor on the east side in the late afternoon, and new restrictions were placed on parking in the Bank bottleneck. The 45-degree angle-parking in front of the post office and Hiser theater was limited to twenty minutes during the day.

In Edgemoor, the first one-way street signs went up on East, North, West, and Middlesex

Lanes and No Parking signs appeared in several busy areas along Arlington, Fairfax and a few other streets. The police report for the first half of 1940 showed twenty-one automobile accidents on Wisconsin Avenue between Bradley and Old Georgetown. Agitation for building a safety island in the middle of Bethesda's main street increased.

Over in Section Two, new policeman Bill Austin was getting used to his job. For the first couple of weeks he rode with police from the Bethesda station to get to know the local routines, and then he had begun his regular 6 pm to 6 am shift.

I started in March '39. They gave me a gun and a uniform. My job was to go around to all the vacant houses. They called in, and I had a list of them. The old man, Springirth, hated my guts. He blamed me. All he had to do was keep the coal furnace fired. He wouldn't even take messages for me.[47]

After two in the morning they had a place where I could go to sleep. If I wasn't sleepy, I'd ride around with the Bethesda guys. Les Thompson, I was with him a couple of times. He was a character. One time I stopped this guy on Connecticut Avenue for driving drunk, and he had his hands down through the steering wheel, and I couldn't get him out of the car. So I didn't want to hit him in the face. He was turned toward me, so I took my blackjack and put it out toward the windshield and hit up along the side of his head. I just tapped him a couple of times, and he calmed down and got out the car, and I put him in my police car and took him over to Bethesda.

William Austin

And old Les was in there while I was explaining to the sergeant about putting the guy in jail, and I said, "He isn't hurt; I just tapped him a little there." After I come upstairs from putting the guy in the cells, Les said, "Austin, gawdamnit, when you're going to hit a guy with a blackjack, hit him, none of this damn pissy footing." He gave me a hell of a lecture.

One of my duties was, and Springirth used to do this too, there's room under that circle about ten by twelve and machinery down there to pump

that water. The reason those willow oaks did so well is that thing leaked out every day, and they grew like crazy. Nothing else could have been better for a willow oak. But this manhole, I had to go down it and it had an iron ladder, every night I had to turn on the water, turn off the pump and fill the fountain and go off somewhere for an hour or so and then go down then turn it off. I was in a clean uniform climbing up and down that thing in rain and snow, and I used to cuss out that thing.

I patrolled around, and they decided that hiring me was a success. They decided they wanted a police car. They bought a demonstrator, a blue Plymouth, off the floor over in Silver Spring somewhere and had a sign put on the side and a siren and all that business. It was a doozy, robin's-egg blue.

Ed Northrop, I didn't know he was in ONI, Naval Intelligence, that's the spy end of it. He was still going to school. Before the war ever broke out, he said to me he was in this thing. He said, "I expect to be called whether we get in this war or not, and we're going to get in this war." He said, "I'm going to recommend you for my job."[48]

By far the biggest political question in 1940 was, of course, the propriety of a "third term." The first local balloting was in Chevy Chase Section Four where William DeLashmutt was reelected for the thirteenth time and J. Slater Davidson replaced the "Hatched" Loren G. Polhamus as secretary-treasurer. Down in Sections One and Two, Arthur W. Defenderfer headed the Citizens' Committee for 1940-41 with George M. Ferris vice-chairman and building inspector.[49]

In Glen Echo, Beulah McCuen announced that she would stand for reelection but would turn the job back to her husband if the Hatch Act were modified. She and councilmen Donald Canada and Barry Kirn ran unopposed. According to the new census, Glen Echo's population had grown from 222 to 395 in the previous ten years.

In the larger pond, one of the first to get involved surprised most observers. The popular but notoriously taciturn Walter Johnson, only Republican survivor of the '38 landslide, allowed that he intended to run for Congress. Relieved of his duties as Senators' play-by-play man with the return of Arch McDonald from New York, where his country style failed to enthuse, the Big Train announced for William Byron's 6th District seat. Soon Johnson-For-Congress Clubs sprang up with headquarters in the old Northwest Ford showroom. Johnson's volunteers contacted all 2,500 Republicans in the 7th Election District and asked for their support. Two labor-endorsed men from Allegany County and Frank Long of Kensington entered the race against Johnson while Democratic Congressman Byron stood unopposed.

For the Senate seat, businessman Howard Bruce, with Brooke Lee's support, ran against the incumbent George Radcliffe who was backed by Senator Tydings from his Eastern Shore power base. It was one of the shortest primary ballots ever. Among the unopposed County delegates to the State party conventions were African-American Republican Robert Carter of Glen Echo and Democrat Irene Christopher of Bethesda.

May 6 was primary and local election day. Somerset chose Irving M. Day mayor to replace the "Hatched" William Horne. Day had sixty votes and his three opponents had a total of thirty-one. Mrs. Marquis Childs became the second woman elected to the town's council, and Somersetters amended their charter to prohibit keeping horses or cattle within town boundaries. The 1940 census showed that Somerset's population had grown from 298 to 397 in ten years. Drummond chose Clyde Miller, James Carry, and Dr. John A. Fleming who was the top vote getter with twenty-two supporters.

Walter Johnson was an easy winner, and the Republicans picked former Governor Nice to run against the Democratic winner, Senator Radcliffe. As expected, Bruce carried Montgomery County but only by 700 votes in the election's only surprise. Some suggested that the Lee machine was still not what it had been.

And Bethesda grew some more. Well back from Wisconsin between the Broadhursts' hardware store and Herbert Wilson's old grocery, just where Potter's Plumbing Supply had spead its wares, the Eisinger Mill and Lumber Company built a new, frame office building called the Housing Guild. It opened during the first week of April 1940 with seven tenants, all businesses related to home building. Contractor O. F. Smith, architect George Brocht and Frederick Berens' mortgage and loan business. Paperhangers, house painters and Roger Eisinger had desks in thirteen-by-nine-foot rooms displaying various types of building materials and techniques.

Eisinger's Housing Guild office building

In August, when workmen jacked up Bob Hagner's house, with him in it, and put it on rollers as preliminary work for the new Hot Shoppe began, Day Thorpe moved his *Journal* office down to the Housing Guild Building. The office building was so successful that Roger Eisinger added a three-story, brick addition on the back about a year later with space for twenty more offices and big garages underneath. Next door, the Broadhursts began work on a two-story, white brick building for the Wayside Shop and other stores.

The Bank of Bethesda built a $50,000 addition on the Old Georgetown Road side and modernized its lobby and counters, all, it emphasized, with "local labor" and sub-contractors. Sanitary Stores opened their third, big, self-service grocery in Bethesda on Wisconsin at Chase Avenue. The other two, at that time, were in the "Park and Shop" and on Old Georgetown at Commerce Lane. John Young, for a generation one of the best-known and best-liked grocers in town, managed the store in the shopping center.

That spring M. Willson Offutt Jr. designed

Hugo Brooks by Hugo

and, with his brother Winsor, built the row of Bradley Terrace Apartments on the east side of Strathmore Street. Dressed in the colonial-revival style, the apartments featured corner entrances, wooden cupolas and formal plantings. Riley Evers opened his twenty-unit "Hampden Hall"

apartment house on Hampden Lane with young photographer Hugo Brooks' studio on the ground floor and Hugo's wife, Emily, as resident manager. Van Tiel H. Bien, better known for his Kenwood homes, designed the big building with its two-story Palladian windows.

Hugo Brooks' father came to D.C. in 1907 with a new bride and ten years of photographic experience. He established his studio on Pennsylvania Avenue and by the 1930s had a successful business in addition to three daughters and two sons who were apprenticing in his trade. In 1937 Hugo Brooks went out on his own, married S. Walter Bogley's daughter and took a job in Hecht's advertising department.

A year or so later he had his own makeshift studio and darkroom in the recreation room of Evers' apartment building and was doing work for Bethesda's weeklies. After a few months, with a loan from the Bank of Bethesda, Brooks set up his first real studio in Walter Tuckerman's building next to the firehouse. Within a year he had paid off the loan.

Other Bethesda businesses were also doing well. Bell Laundry announced a "new airconditioned, moth-proof storage vault" and like its D.C. competitor, Tolman's, offered to pick up and deliver "your fine furs, woolens, and rugs." Samuel E. Bogley, Emory's son, established his real estate office in a building he designed and built at the south end of Sacks row, 6698 Wisconsin in the old, yet-to-be-changed numbering system. Across the street the Lincoln Loan Service occupied the one-time market at 6722 Wisconsin on the Leland corner.

Sidney Weinberg and his wife became the local Hotpoint dealers at their new Bethesda Appliance Company, which replaced the Louise Lingerie Shop and six months later moved to a bigger store at Wisconsin and Hampden Lane. By then J. R. Enright, the Fridgidaire and fuel oil dealer in Sachs' row, was well established and had Bethesda's biggest and least reliable clock on the big black sign above his door. Texas-born Enright had run a successful store in Rockville since 1929 and moved to Bethesda in `37 closing his upcounty operation two years later.

Bethesda-area churches were also busy with building programs to meet the constant influx of new parishioners. Brookmont's Baptists established their new church in a rented building in 1939 and in the spring of 1940 bought a home at the corner of Virginia Place and Ridge Circle.

The Self Realization Fellowship began meeting on Western Avenue at 49th Street under the leadership of Brahmachari Jotin of Calcutta. In addition to the regular Sunday morning services, classes in philosophy and yoga took place on Wednesday evenings.

Riley Evers at center and John Werner at right

The Methodists built a much needed parsonage for their minister. They raised more than $2,000 and successfully solicited donations of building materials from seventeen local firms and contractors, and then under Riley Evers' supervision, they put up the modest home at 130 St. Elmo. Stella Allison recalled being her father's "gofer" and hauling lumber, nails and other supplies to the men doing the work.

On the last Sunday in November 1939, A. B. Foster, president of the board of trustees, presented Reverend Cockrell with the key, and Mrs. John H. Werner, the president of the Woman's Missionary Society and leader of the financial drive, kindled the logs in the fireplace saying, "I light the flames of loyalty to God, home and fellow man."[50]

By far the biggest church building project was at Our Lady of Lourdes where Calvin Owens' firm began construction on Pearl Street of the T-shaped, $154,000 complex designed by A. Hamilton Wilson. The final price was closer to $200,000, but Father Little won praise for putting his church, school, and convent under one roof so economically. Lourdes' fourth annual carnival in the summer of 1940 was bigger than ever with band concerts added and a Packard as the main raffle prize. In the fall, Gordon Burrows, treasurer of the Holy Name Society, chaired the committee that put on the annual card party at the Wardman Park, and Fred Genau and John Overholt as chairman and treasurer of the parish finance committee sought other means of fund raising.

The Chevy Chase Methodist Church installed a new pipe organ in the spring of 1940.

Riley A. Gwynn, Bishop of the Chevy Chase Ward of the Church of Jesus Christ of the Latter Day Saints held services at the Woman's Club of Chevy Chase where Earl B. Snell was in charge of the Mormon's Sunday school. On the first Sunday of April, the Rev. J. S. Albertson officially became the pastor of the Bethesda Presbyterian Church, and about two months later Rev. Hartwell F. Chandler replaced the Reverend Cockrell at the Methodist church.

In Glen Echo, the Episcopal Bishop of Washington laid the cornerstone of the new, brick Chapel of the Redemeer, and in September, Bishop Freeman, Rector Perkins and lay reader Thomas G. Spence took part in the dedication ceremonies. The Chapel, designed by Elmer Cappellmann and built by O. T. and W. A. Carr, was the first part of a planned three-unit building. At the first regular Sunday service on September 22, the Rev. Clyde Brown, who helped plan the building, was the guest preacher.

The new Chapel of the Redeemer in Glen Echo

In June 1940, the Bethesda Baptists broke ground for their church in Battery Park. Designed by E. Burton Corning and built by congregation members Guy Marlow and Hugh G. Myers, the first unit contained a chapel seating 200, a small fellowship hall and six rooms for

Drawing of the new Baptist Church

both adult and children's Sunday school. By December 1940, the congregation was worshipping in their new building with its big rose window donated in memory of John Pool. The organ, purchased as a bunch of parts spread across a garage floor, provided fine accompaniment for Gertrude Price's young choir.

That summer, All Saints Episcopal, St. Paul's Lutheran, Wesley Methodist, Chevy Chase Methodist and Chevy Chase Presbyterian jointly sponsored the 14th annual Vacation Bible School in the Presbyterian church on the Circle. In Bethesda, the Methodists and Baptists joined for a summer school at the Methodist church while the Lutherans and Presbyterians each had their own vacation-school classes.

Judge Alfred Wilson

The Rev. William G. Oram established the Christ Memorial Christian Church in his home at 4416 East West Highway in late July. It was the first branch of this denomination in the down-county area, and Judge Alfred Wilson acted as treasurer and advisor. By year's end, twenty members had enrolled. In the fall the Christ Lutheran Church started building an addition for its fast-growing membership.

In the spring of 1940, the State Roads Commission made a firm commitment to repave Connecticut Avenue where the trolley tracks had been and to widen Old Georgetown Road by using the trolley right-of-way. Unfortunately, no one had checked to see if there were claims on the abandoned railway's land.

After a great deal of prodding, the State placed 35 mph speed limit signs on Wisconsin Avenue but kept its big sign at the District Line stating that 55 mph was the Maryland speed limit. There was talk, again, of building safety islands in the middle of Wisconsin in Bethesda and of painting lane lines on that street to "channelize" the traffic. The four new sets of traffic lights, despite some complaints about their overhead positioning, seemed to be working well, and pedestrians praised the push-button controls at Highland, Leland, Dorset and Bradley. By fall, Chevy Chase Village had persuaded the State Roads people to hang a light at Bradley and Connecticut. Some drivers always called it a "nuisance light."

In what was now called Meadowbrook Village, the builders paved Chelton Street just east of the high school, which made the library a bit easier to get to. On Cheltenham, it was neighbor against neighbor over the question of installing curbs. Over in The Hamlet, George B. Hatley created a lot of newspaper publicity for the "Consensus Home" he was building by making modifications based on suggestions from hundreds of potential buyers.

And in May, fourteen local businessmen organized Bethesda's Civitan Club and chose real estate dealer Paul M. Ludt as their first president with Dr. Ball 1st vp, Dennis Simmons 2nd vp and Arnold Hurt secretary-treasurer. There were now enough service clubs in town for them to have their own bowling league.

In the 26th annual field day at Rockville, the last one for "white" schools, B-CC's 440 relay team of Jay Fitzgerald, Bill Barnsley, George Sorrell and Eddie Leahy set a new record of 46.01. Eddie, nicknamed "Screwball," was famous for his mustache, his typing speed and his rabid behavior at Blair games. The high school girls' volleyball team won the championship, and younger athletes from Chevy Chase, Bethesda and Somerset elementaries also came home with medals and blue ribbons.

In June 1940, B-CC graduated 209 seniors, another record, and 250 completed the ninth grade at Leland, which held Class Day and a big dance on June 7 with the gym decorated to look like a cruise ship. Then on the 13th, after a student-written drama and several songs by the Glee Club, Principal Bready presented diplomas to the ninth graders. The boys wore white trousers and blue coats and the girls, white dresses and white pumps.

Meanwhile, a committee composed of Mrs. Werner, Mrs. Hilland, Mr. Pyle and John L. Imirie interviewed sixteen applicants to find the first director for the new community recreation center. Working mainly in the Werner living room, they whittled the list down to three, and in April the M-NCP&PC chose Harry C. Callaghan for the job. Mr. Callaghan and his wife moved into an apartment in the main building replacing the janitor-custodian, and Callaghan went to work on May 1. He was a graduate of Western Maryland and the Ithaca College of Physical Education and had been a life guard instructor, Scout leader, PE director at Cape May, coach of various sports and summer camp operator. The

summer of 1940 was the first big, busy one at the Rec Center, and Callaghan's first job was to plan the activities.

In August, the Commissioners chose Andrew Newman of Chevy Chase as the new police chief. He had been deputy clerk for Commissioners Hagner and Hampton at the County Building in Bethesda for four years, and he also had Justice Department experience as well as previous service as superintendent of County roads. Ralph H. Chase, like Newman active in Martin's Additions and with the fire department, took over the duties of Clerk of the Western Suburban District.

With that out of the way, vacations and playgrounds were the order of the day. The political campaign could wait until the fall even if a Willkie-Nice-Johnson Club made Bethesda its home, and Leonard Williams started a Willkie-for-President club for Chevy Chase youngsters and went back in the newspaper business with "The Independent." The Chevy Chase Wildcats, winners of the D.C. Boys Club peewee championship the previous summer, moved up to the "insect" class and sought new sponsors. The library ran a popular Vacation Reading Club for young people.

And while the CCC boys were putting finishing touches on the playing fields and then starting work on the $7,000 fieldhouse-shower room, Harry Callaghan announced that there would be organized programs at the new Rec Center each weekday morning, rain or shine, for children up to fifteen years of age. The basement of the main building and two large sheds were ready for rainy days. High school students and adults would have use of the fields in the afternoons and early evenings.

Harry Callaghan demonstrates bunting technique

As volunteer leader for the younger children, Callaghan recruited Joan Beveridge. Joyce Snodgrass and Norman McDonald assisted with tennis and folk dancing, and Andy Gottschall oversaw the archery groups. All lived in the immediate neighborhood. The Somerset PTA hired Catherine Winchell to assist Mr. Callaghan and shut down its own recreation program. Many people down Wisconsin called the Rec Center "Somerset" for a while. By July, it was serving 700 youngster a week, had initiated a point system of awards and was seeking opponents for its baseball and softball teams.

In the middle of a very hot July, thirty-five boys, with the main goal of creating a football team, organized the Bethesda - Chevy Chase Athletic Association at the Rec Center. Harry Callaghan acted as advisor, and the boys elected John Beveridge president and set about promoting a minstrel show to raise money for equipment. The show committee, chaired by Frank Seward, included Arthur Dunsmore, Carroll Grenfell and Faris Mirhage.

Dick Daly and his younger brother Phil, two of the Daly's seven children, were among the "regulars" at the Rec Center. They were often winners in races and other contests, and eleven-year-old Phil gained some fame in the summer of 1940 for his prowess as a magazine salesman. While Dick stuck with the newspaper route near his East West Highway home, Phil sold an average of 400 *Liberty* magazines a week plus sixty *Saturday Evening Post*s, forty *Ladies Home Journal*s and a few monthlies, mostly movie magazines. Some weeks he made as much as $10. In the second week of August 1940, Phil set a local record by selling a thousand *Liberty*s and won himself a radio

Phil Daly

and a trip to the World's Fair in New York. Leslie and Elsie Marie Daly had moved to Bethesda in 1935 and struggled through some difficult times even after he found a job with the Treasury Department.[51]

Glen Echo opened with a new airplane ride, the Flying Scooter, and a modernized cafeteria and roof garden. But that summer, persistent

rumors that a girl was bitten by a snake on the World Cruise, the amusement park's "tunnel of love," cut down the crowds. Manager Leonard B. Schloss denied the report and explained that water for the ride was pumped up through a strainer from the stream below and that the attraction was inspected every day. But the water-moccasin story became entrenched in juvenile folklore much as the tales of malaria had been a generation or two earlier.[52]

THE POLICE

AND PRIVATE INVESTIGATORS ARE RUNNING DOWN EVERY POSSIBLE CLUE TO APPREHEND THE PERSON OR PERSONS WHO HAVE MALICIOUSLY SPREAD THE REPORT THAT A GIRL WAS BITTEN BY A SNAKE AT GLEN ECHO PARK AND DIED. THAT SERIOUS ACCIDENTS HAVE OCCURRED. THAT SNAKES WERE IN THE SWIMMING POOL AND THAT THE PARK IS CLOSED.

THESE RUMORS ARE UNTRUE

WHEN THE PERSON OR PERSONS WHO HAVE SPREAD THESE DASTARDLY REPORTS ARE CAUGHT THEY WILL BE PROSECUTED TO THE FULLEST EXTENT OF THE LAW.
GLEN ECHO PARK CO.
By LEONARD B. SCHLOSS,
Vice President & General Manager

July 19, 1940

Down in Friendship Heights, Charlie Hughes tried to deliver a hundred-paper *Post* route that took in all of Brookdale, but gave it up after a couple of weeks, and Jim McAuliffe, the policeman's son, had a *Daily News*, a shopper, a *Post* route and helped out on a *Star* route from time to time.

My recollection was that I delivered the shopper to 108 homes, which went all the way from Wisconsin Avenue back through High Street and down Willard out to River Road. Back in that area, across Willard, and up in that general area, a young man and his family lived back there, Hardy Sorrell. He tolerated me as a little fellow. I really thought he was tremendous and one of the finest athletes I ever saw. They lived back in the woods.

We still had ice delivered to our home. We had electricity but we still had an ice box. My grandfather had just about everything; he had a farm. Well, it wasn't large enough to be called a farm or small enough to be called a garden. When my brother and I got the job of going over to plow the rows for the potatoes, we thought it was too

large to be called a garden. He had cherries and pears, all sorts of fruit trees, a large grape arbor, and he raised chickens. It was amazing all the things he was able to do and do well. He worked hard around the place and built it up from nothing.

There were a lot of kids in the neighborhood, and we had a field to play on right across Wisconsin Avenue. There was an open field there where we played football. We did play some baseball and at one time put up a basketball goal, made our own rough court, but it was mostly football.

I went to Somerset Elementary for kindergarten and first grade and then transferred to St. Ann's. I think the reasoning was that all of my family had attended and graduated from St. Ann's, and it would be nice if we went there, John and I. Mom, sometimes Dad, mostly Mom, drove us in the mornings, and we would catch the streetcar in the afternoon with those little tickets. Very often I walked home past the carbarns.

When we were in our coin collecting phase, the carbarns were our prime source. You could go in there with the coins you had gone through and exchange them for rolls of their coins. Then you'd have a fresh supply to go through. You could make some mighty fine finds.

Bill Austin, the Chevy Chase policeman remembered Sergeant McAuliffe and his boys.

McAuliffe and I got along fine. His father lived next door. The old man was always sitting in the swing early in the evening, and I loved to hear an Irishman talk, the bigger the brogue the better. So we had a poker group, penny-ante, all officers, and it really was penny-ante. We used to play in Rix McAuliffe's house. In the summertime coming down there it was still light, and I'd talk with his old man until everybody got there.

We had some real poker games there. One time somebody brought in a guest who wasn't a policeman. There was a mantle there, and we were all out on the porch, and somebody said let's get started, so we go in and a guy puts his pistol up there and another guy pulls out a pistol and first thing you know there's five pistols on the mantle. This new guy said, "What kind of game am I in?"

We'd be sitting there playing cards, and in would come these boys of Rix's. They'd been playing football over there where Saks is now. Jim, he'd come in and he'd hardly be dirty, but the younger one would have his pants tore and dirt on his face and everything. And Rix would be sitting there, and they'd be going down the hall, and he'd say. "I don't know what the hell I'm ever going to do with them boys." But they turned out pretty good.

Before the summer was over Bethesda acquired two more landmarks on opposite ends of the business district. One was rather short-lived. Delayed by a vicious thunderstorm, the American Legion installed the barrel of a French 75 artillery piece on a concrete base in the middle of Wisconsin Avenue at Bradley Boulevard on Tuesday, July 23.

Jack Irwin presided for the Legion, but Paul Ludt of the Civitan Club was the only dignitary to wait out the storm with him. It was not until Sunday that Dr. Floyd J. Carter of the VFW placed his wreath at the monument to the County's dead in the First World War.

Later in 1940, when Scott Brewer Sr. established his Allied Realty Corporation in the little stone house that had been the Bradley Hills trolley and real estate office, he took on the job of raising the memorial's American flag. Long

The war memorial cannon at Wisconsin and Bradley

after the cannon barrel had disappeared in a scrap drive, Brewer performed his self-imposed duty. An Indiana banker, businessman and Republican, Brewer had come to town with his family in 1934 to take a New Deal job with the Federal Housing Administration only to be struck down by a heart attack. After a long fight back to relatively good health, he went into business with his wife, Eda, and rental agent Malora Christman.

The other and much longer-lived landmark was Gifford's, which opened near the Bethesda Theater, in early July. The successful Silver Spring company built a big, airy, white brick building with a large parking lot along Middleton Lane. The bright interior spread with pastel colors featured a large area with plenty of tables and chairs, big display counters full of "homemade" candy, and gallons and gallons of

The Bradley Hills office as Brewer's Allied Realty

great ice cream behind a long, high counter. George Milroy kept the place wonderfully clean and managed a staff of mostly high school girls.

By the end of the first summer, Gifford's had become a favorite place for family treats and movie dates. Huge banana splits with three flavors of ice cream, gobs of sauce, and real whipped cream, rivaled wonderful hot fudge sundaes and foamy ice cream sodas. Having a job at Giffords could make one almost instantly popular as well as envied, and there were arguments among both young customers and employees about whether a pre-packed pint of coffee ice cream or chocolate chip made a better lunch. Ads featured ice cream rolls for 50¢, "butter krunch" candy at 49¢ a pound and dry-ice packing for a nickel.[53]

At summer's end, Carl A. Bachschmid, long-time buyer for R. Harris, became the co-proprietor of Carbert's on Wisconsin between Magee's Radio and the Building Supply Company. Carbert's featured fine china, high quality glassware, good jewelry, diamonds, watches, and a repair department manned by partner Robert W. Mitchell. Carbert's became the place for buying engagement rings, wedding presents and graduation gifts. Like Leon Sherman's, the Lakeview Market and Gifford's, Carbert's was recognized almost immediately as a store with class. Bachschmid's decision to locate in Bethesda was another indication of the way the town was changing.

The summer was not without problems. The Japanese beetles seemed worse than ever. Rose bushes were among their favorite targets. By mid-July 30,000 beetles had been killed in the metal traps scattered around the County. While the Japanese beetles were annoying, ticks were frightening.[54]

Since the early-1930s, Rocky Mountain spotted tick fever was a regular summer visitor

and a killer almost as frightening as polio. In 1938, three of the seven County cases resulted in fatalities, and in `39 two of the nine people diagnosed with the disease died. While the number of deaths was small, ticks were prevalent; dogs often were carriers; no cure was known, and the danger frightened many parents. Each spring newspapers carried advice about tick inspection and removal. Locally the Federal government supplied the tick fever vaccines without cost to doctors and public health services and provided the series of two shots free at the NIH.[55]

The war in Europe, which had started the previous September, accelerated during the summer of 1940, and in rapid succession Norway, the Netherlands, Belgium and France fell to the Nazi blitzkrieg. Dunkirk was the only hopeful scene in this long, tragic opera. The newsreels showed American factory workers making tanks, warplanes and anti-aircraft guns and convoys carrying supplies from U.S. ports to England where London was burning and people were sleeping in subway stations.

A few Bethesdans ran off to Canada to join the fight, and Mrs. Walter Tuckerman headed the local British-American Ambulance Corps. Bundles for Britain became a common activity of both women's clubs and scouting groups in 1940. Comic books and bubble gum cards began to feature war scenes in China and Europe, and Corr's and the Centro Hobby Shop stocked models of Stukas and Hurricanes. Lois Hall said *Mein Kampf* was the best seller and most popular rental book at the gift shop that summer.[56]

As the Battle of Britain began in August and Ed Murrow became a familiar voice, the debate in Bethesda and much of the nation centered on American neutrality and the question of conscription. Locally, the *Tribune* endorsed the proposed selective service program, but the *Journal* editorialized that "we are attempting to build national defense through hysteria" and found only one young Bethesdan who supported a year's compulsory service.[57]

The Selective Training and Service Act, calling for the first peacetime draft, passed in September, and in mid-October 16,400,000 men registered including about 12,000 in Montgomery County. Both the police department and the school system granted employees absences for military duty without loss of tenure or benefits. Registration took place at the

Chevy Chase firehouse, the Community House in Glen Echo, and the County Building. Draft Board No. 3 covered the Seventh Election District from the old USDA building at the Recreation Center. The other two County draft boards were in Silver Spring and Rockville.

Frederic P. Lee served as first chairman of the Bethesda board. James B. Fitzgerald and Francis W. Hill of Kenwood were the other members with Mrs. Elizabeth C. Stratton as chief clerk. Mrs. P. C. Alexander of Battery Park coordinated volunteer helpers as 2,843 young men registered. At the draft board, workers shuffled and stamped their cards with serial numbers and then everyone waited.[58]

While the Junior Chamber fumbled the planned "Buy in Bethesda" campaign, the Chamber of Commerce again raised the issue of creating a city government for the down-county area. The 1940 census showed that while the number of Americans had increased only seven percent in a decade, the County's population grew sixty percent in those ten years and that about three-fourths of the 81,444 people who lived in Montgomery County were in the Washington suburbs and about one-third of them in Bethesda. The Seventh Election District's population increased from 12,018 to 26,114 between 1930 and 1940. For the metropolitan area the Census Bureau reported a forty-three percent growth in population to 962,752 with D.C. itself up to 663,153 from 496,869 in 1930. The metro area had grown only seventeen percent in the previous decade.[59]

Watched by a couple of horses in Bob Hagner's barn, the long awaited Hot Shoppe at East West and Wisconsin was taking shape, while the smaller Hubbard House, halfway

The new "fast food" franchise across from Leon's

between East West and the County Building, would soon be ready to compete for the town's hamburger and coffee business along with the Little Tavern at the railroad bridge. And just across the District Line Fred Johannsen was putting the finishing touches on his new cocktail lounge-supper club, the Silver Fox.

By the time people were ready to start thinking about school again, the steel framework of the naval hospital with its red beacon light was a familiar sight. [60]

Dr. Broome announced that Rockville high school students would attend B-CC again in September. The new athletic association staged a benefit show at the Hiser and on September 2 held the first football practice at the Rec Center. Sixty boys showed up. At about the same time, Dr. Lewis Meriam, head of the department of political research of the Brookings Institute, stated that his long-awaited report and recommendations on County government should be completed soon. Both of the Bethesda newspapers grumbled about the delay.

For reasons unstated, the library board accepted Dorothy Annable's resignation at the end of her first year of service and named Miss Coplen acting librarian with Helen Shedd as her assistant. Miss Coplen served as Bethesda's librarian until the spring of 1942. In its first financial report the Library Board reported that as of June 30 the library had collected $70 in gifts, $22 for non-residents' cards, $65 in overdue book fines, and $5 from book rentals plus the $11,910 received from County taxes and after paying all the bills had $1,300 on hand.

On August 23, Day Thorpe's *Journal* announced that although the editor was a registered Democrat, the paper supported Willkie for President and Walter Johnson for Congress. "We fear Mr. Roosevelt sees war as inevitable.

NNMC tower

He has courted war for three years with artfully created alarms," wrote the editor who also concluded that "the New Deal has failed." Allen's *Tribune* praised FDR's "trade" of fifty reconditioned destroyers for British naval bases and wholeheartedly endorsed the Democratic ticket.

As election day neared, the rhetoric of the two local weeklies intensified. Thorpe called Democrats "the War Party" and said the President "was using the great powers acquired by eight years in office to force himself on the people for another term or terms." Bill Allen poked at the *Journal's* inconsistencies and emphasized Willkie's general endorsement of Roosevelt's policies. The Democrats were tardy getting organized but settled into the usual pattern. They chose Thomas Earle Hampton president of the Roosevelt-Wallace-Byron-Radcliffe Club with Dr. Benjamin Perry as leader in Bethesda and mercurial Joseph Cantrel in Chevy Chase.

When school did open, neither the parochial school at Our Lady of Lourdes nor the new East Bethesda Elementary was ready. The new public school's two hundred students were bused to Chevy Chase Elementary for about a month. Some thirty sixth graders from the East Bethesda area who had been scheduled to attend Chevy Chase had to return to Bethesda Elementary. Dr. Broome chose Mrs. Elsie D. Bosley as principal of the new school, and on Monday, October 14, classes began in the building with novel, folding walls between several classrooms. That Wednesday evening the PTA put on a reception and house warming party.

Other area schools were also growing. The Lady Isabel School for Children added a first and second grade and a new teacher, Mrs. Francis Johnson. Landon's new $50,000 building, constructed by Morrison Brothers, featured

octagonal classrooms and administrative offices. It was ready when Paul Banfield, his twenty teachers and 175 boys from grade three on up went back to work. Boys and girls in the lower grades went to the Whitehall School where Mrs. Henry Pitts was in charge.

The Walton School on Old Georgetown Road, after a successful summer camp program, increased its faculty by adding Thomas W. Walton Jr. and a crafts teacher, and at Georgetown Prep the staff of eighteen was ready to start the 157th year for about a hundred students including sixty-five boarders. The National Park College at Forest Glen enrolled some 350, and at Chevy Chase Junior College, where Kendric Nichols Marshall was temporary president, more than eighty-five young ladies started classes. Miss Holman announced "a new season of pianoforte instruction."

The women's clubs and civic associations started meeting again. The 1941 models began to arrive in local auto showrooms: the Hydra-Matic Olds, the Fluid Drive Chrysler, the Pontiac Torpedo, and the Dodge Luxury Liner. Bethesda got back to the business of growing.

After years of waiting, the contract for promised repaving of Connecticut Avenue from the Circle to the Lake as a dual lane highway was let for $166,000, and the work finally started in October. The low bid for widening and resurfacing Old Georgetown Road for almost two miles starting at the Bank was $61,600. And starting at the Bank, a problem emerged when the work crews showed up. Some businesses had exercised what they called "reversionary rights" since 1935 and made use of the old trolley right-of-way for sidewalks, parking places, and display space.

The Bank of Bethesda did not want the street improved on what it considered its property, and all work stopped while the Chamber

and Bill Allen's *Tribune* fumed. Commissioner Hampton, acting as Bethesda's "mayor," stepped in and proposed a simple waiver form in early October. It took several meetings and more than two weeks, but the Bank and the Masonic Library finally agreed to a new property line, and the work began again.[61]

At Leland JHS, the big news in the fall was that "Zip" Lehr, the well-liked coach, intramural director and activity sponsor, took a job at a D.C. high school. "Then we got a fellow named Jimmy Cross as our gym teacher and basketball coach," Charlie Hughes remembered.

He was great and everybody loved him. He had leather thongs on his whistle and he had a habit, if you were out of line the least bit, he would come around with that and, whap! It would really sting so you made sure you stayed in line.

The big news at the high school was the *Tattler* contest to choose a new nickname for the school's teams and the formation of the A Cappela Choir directed by Mrs. Dwight Shaw, which made its first public appearance at an assembly on Armistice Day. Faye Finlay Shaw's choir and her music appreciation classes were often listed by B-CC grads as among their fondest recollections. Fellow teacher Angela Darby recalled that Mrs. Shaw "took in any kid that couldn't make it in any other class, kids that were thrown out of other classes. It was amazing."

Joe Cantrel, class of '42, remembered Mrs. Darby and many other teachers.

Kay Greaney was excellent. Those who were hard on you, you remember. We read The Virginian, "Smile when you say that." Leland John Rogers Williams was my favorite. He got old Joe up there to recite the prologue to the Canterbury Tales in Old English He called me "Slick." "Come on, Slick," he'd say, "you can do it." So,
     When that Aprille with his shoures sote
     The droughte of March has perced to the rote.
And I did it. The yearbook called me the class clown; I'll tell you how that came about. I put a patomine on in Mrs. Black's public speaking class that brought the house down. I got up there, and I was imitating a juggler, behind me and then I missed a ball and around the back. That's exactly how I got that.[62]

Enrollments were up at almost all local schools. The high school had 795 students, an increase of 108; Leland 859, up fifty from the year before. More than seventy-five students crowded into the River Road Colored School's

two classrooms. Chevy Chase found room for 562 on the first day, Somerset 225 and Alta Vista 126 for an increase of about two dozen at each school. Bethesda Elementary counted 705 for a 172 increase, and the new East Bethesda school enrolled 211, far above the anticipated number. There the PTA's first order of business was to request that the second unit of the school be built immediately.

More war refugees began showing up in Bethesda-area classrooms. Bethesda Elementary had at least four in September 1940. Fourth grader John Sheperd and his seven-year-old sister, Mary, and their mother were living with friends in Edgemoor "for the duration" while their father stayed in England. Beverly Snyder, who was London-born, entered Bethesda's kindergarten. She was living with her refugee parents on Park Lane in Battery Park. Nine-year-old Ralph Reisner and his parents escaped the Jewish persecutions in Germany and made their way through Italy and Cuba to Battery Park where they stayed with the Shereshefsky family on Maple Ridge Road.

Crown Princess Martha of Norway, with her three children and retinue, arrived in October, leased and then purchased Pook's Hill from the Thorpes, added a bomb shelter and a whole new wing for servants with, it was rumored with knowing nods, FDR's help. Her children and those of some of her servants also attended local schools.[63]

The Bethesda-Chevy Chase Co-operative Nursery School reopened in mid-October at the "Rosemary" school. Dr. Broome had approved the use of space at Chevy Chase, and principal Rose met with the thirty mothers to arrange for the little children to arrive after classes began, to use the playground when the older children were inside and to talk about parking spaces. Mrs. Davidson continued as director, and Mrs. Gustave Burmeister was elected president of the first session.

In addition to the dozens of brush fires that kept all the local fire companies busy, a common fall phenomenon, Bethesda suffered some big blazes that autumn. On what had been Galliher's farm on Bradley Boulevard, where some sub-division home building had begun, the big old barn burned to the ground, and in Edgemoor a family was fortunate to escape with their lives when fire engulfed their home. But by far the season's biggest and most dangerous fire began early in the morning of

Simmons' showroom later used by the OSS

Wednesday, October 16, at Marvin Simmons' recently remodeled Dodge dealership.

William Reed, a mechanic who lived in an apartment above the shop with his wife and two young children, discovered and reported the fire at 3:42 am. Both the Bethesda and Chevy Chase fire departments responded, but by the time they arrived, shop supplies, paint thinner and anti-freeze had fed the flames. The fire destroyed the showroom, two new cars, and the shop in back, but the firemen saved the new garage next door. Robert Eastham praised the firemen for not letting the blaze spread to his adjacent Esso station. Chief Bargagni said that if that had happened they would have lost the whole block.

At the end of October, President Roosevelt drove to Bethesda and participated in the dedication of the six-building campus of the National Institute of Health. By then the administrative offices and library had been operating in Building 1 for almost two years as had the Divisions of Industrial Hygiene and Public Health Methods. The National Cancer Institute's Building 6 and the officers' quarters rose on the twenty-five acres Luke I. Wilson's widow donated and were occupied a year before the dedication. The Divisions of Chemistry, Pharmacology and Zoology moved into Building 4 and Biologics Control and Infectious Diseases into Building 5 in the summer of 1940. By the time of the dedication, the NIH had 1,137 employees and was expending $707,000 for research and operations.

Less than two weeks later, the Presidential Packard and a small group of notables returned to Bethesda, and Roosevelt laid the cornerstone of the Naval Medical Center, his building in many ways. Captain Robert D. Workman of Chevy Chase, a Navy chaplain, gave the invocation. Strikes against some suppliers and sub-contractors caused delays, but the builders

NNMC in the winter of 1940-41

hoped to have the hospital finished in about a year.[64]

The election for President, Senator and Congressman and deciding State constitutional questions went off smoothly on November 5 despite the fact that voting machines were used for the first time. Since September, machines had been available for demonstration and practice at the County Building and at the firehouse in Chevy Chase, and all election officials had attended instructional classes. The list of eligible voters in the 7th Election District in 1940 showed 6,991 Democrats, 2,460 Republicans and 453 "declines," and Countywide the registration was almost three to one Democratic.

On election day, Walter Johnson and Wendell Willkie carried Bethesda but lost the County as 29,000 voters, the heaviest turnout ever, went to the polls. Because of the short ballot and the new machines, the supervisors had the tally ready in two hours. Roosevelt beat Willkie 15,100 to 13,700 but lost in the 7th District 4,739 to 3,368 in the unofficial returns. Representative Byron barely defeated Walter Johnson in the County, 14,696 to 14,168, but carried Washington, Garrett and Allegany counties to win by 7,000 votes. In the Bethesda area, Johnson beat Byron 4,418 to 3,371. Eighty-two percent of Bethesda's voters went to the polls.

The *Tribune*'s nom-de-plumed political columnist, Robert Bray, viewed the two-to-one Willkie victory in Chevy Chase and some parts of Bethesda with dismay, while the *Journal* trumpeted the "closest race in history" and quoted Republican leader Meredith Daubin's claim that the "Republican party has found its strength in this county and we aren't going to

lose it in the future." Carey Quinn, voluble Civic Federation, Battery Park and Democratic leader, had said, "What Montgomery County needs more than anything else at the present time to insure good government by the Democratic party is a live Republican organization which can furnish opposition." Now the 7th District Republicans rubbed the overconfident Democrats' noses in the local results.[65]

precinct/area/polling place		
	FDR	Willkie
1/Eastern Bethesda/ B-CC high school		
	884	796
2/Chevy Chase south of Bradley/CC library		
	183	510
3/Gl. Echo & Cbn. John/GE Community House		
	602	308
4/Bethesda W. of Wisc/Bethesda ES		
	921	1379
5/CC N.of Bradley & E. of Conn/CC firehouse		
	338	732
6/CC N.of Bradley & W.of Conn/CC elem.		
	205	617
7/Mass. Ave. extended/Westbrook ES		
	235	397

In its lead post-election editorial, Thorpe's *Journal* criticized Harry Callaghan and through him the way the County government operated. Schools were closed on election day, the *Journal*'s editor wrote, but "the children were disappointed when they trooped into the Recreation Center. Mr. Callaghan was not there to greet them. Some waited for him in vain, some went away discouraged." It was, the paper noted, a paid holiday for him and for other County employees. Callaghan was at Bethesda polling places handing out Democratic sample ballots and urging people to "vote right," the editorial claimed.

A week later the *Tribune* observed that to "single Mr. Callaghan out for editorial rebuke is further evidence of the bad temper and poor sportsmanship displayed so regularly in the editorial columns of the Bethesda Journal." The acrimonious chasm between Bethesda's two papers grew deeper and wider over the next twelve months.[66]

Meanwhile, the local draft board sent out questionnaires and then began classifying the nearly 3,000 registrants. Blindfolded, the Secretary of War drew the first numbers from a big fishbowl on October 29, 1940, with the news-

reel cameras and radio microphones clustered about. Joseph Owen Devlin, who worked at Gordon Burrows' Esso station, was one of the 6,175 who held number 158, the first number drawn. Devlin was 29, married and living in an apartment on Old Georgetown Road. He was quoted as saying he would not mind the training and the year of service. He thought that working seven years for Burrows in all kinds of weather had hardened him and that military training "would be a snap." Soon the form letter, which began: "Greeting, Having submitted yourself to the local draft board composed of your neighbors . . ." became nationally well-known.[67]

But the first draft call for the County in November was only seven and for Board No. 3 just two, and five men volunteered for service before the Board had even processed the questionnaires. Doctors Huff, Dunn and Bauersfeld conducted the physical examinations, which included venereal disease screening. The first two volunteers to pass their physicals and be inducted were Warner Wilson Connell of Bethesda and Edmund Ignatius Oakes Jr. of Chevy Chase. Early on November 28, they arrived at the Recreation Center where they received fountain pens from Larry Coe of the American Legion and sat through short talks by T. E. Hampton, Dr. Carter of the VFW, Mr. Hiser of the Chamber of Commerce, Robert Owens of the Rotary Club and Charles Schlichter of the Lions Club. They were driven to Silver Spring, put on the B&O's Capital Limited and from the induction center on Indiana Avenue were sent on to Fort Meade.

By mid-December, the Board had twenty men classified as 1-A and had granted student deferments until July 1 to seven others. At the end of January 1940, 169 men between 21 and 35 had undergone their physicals, and 47 had been disqualified as unfit for duty. This twenty-eight percent failure rate was much better than the national average of forty percent. Eye defects and hernias led the list of problems. Thirteen men had syphilis and ten tuberculosis. The monthly calls were no longer news, and the speeches and fountain pens stopped, but the American Legion did present billfolds to the dozen "selectees" in January.

Harry Callaghan's football team at the Rec Center had a good first season despite the request by Alan Vogt that his high school basketball players not get involved. Bob Lebling and a few others withdrew, but enough boys remained to field a varsity and a lightweight or JV team. On September 27, the varsity scrimmaged a St. Albans' team led by Earl Elliot and Jimmy Trimble to a 6-6 tie in the afternoon and then took on Landon the next morning and did not do as well. The junior varsity practiced against the Leland Wildcats at Meadowbrook.[68]

The next Saturday, the big team opened its season by beating Glen Echo 25-6 with Bill Lowe scoring once and passing to set up the other touchdowns. A week later, the high school inter-fraternity All Stars defeated the B-CC AA 12-7 by scoring two touchdowns against the second team in what amounted to another scrimmage.

On Sunday, the Bethesda team with Larry Eaton quarterbacking their single-wing offense surprised Sacred Heart and ended its two-year winning streak 15-0. The JV's six-man team tied the Somerset Bulldogs 13-13 and then the 11-man team defeated Leland and the Woodmont Terriers. Among the JV's outstanding players were Billy Cremins, Fitzgerald, Mudd, Bayer, Benson, Lenhart, Shoemaker and Humphries.

Twelve-year-old Roger Mudd was the smallest lineman on the jayvee team. He repainted his older brother John's leather helmet and wore a dark blue sweatshirt with a hood over his size-too-large shoulder pads. After being dragged down by the hood several times, he finally tore it off. "He was a hard-nosed competitor," teammate Charlie Hughes recalled.

The Mudds had built a home on Leland Street in Rollingwood in 1937, and Roger went to "Rosemary" and Leland where he played lacrosse for Mr. Albertson's team and basketball for "Zip" Lehr before following his brother's trail to Wilson High School. He remembered getting the wind knocked out of him during a football game at Meadowbrook in the fall of 1940, and Billy Cremins lifting him by his belt until he could breathe again. "Leave him in," Cremins said. "He's a brave little kid." Roger Mudd said he lived on that accolade for many years.

The varsity scraped out a win over St. Martin's in the mud by blocking six kicks and recovering one for the only score. On the last weekend of October, they gained some prestige by beating Woodward Prep 19-7 and then lost to the Cardinal AC.

The Rec Center's 1940 team with Grenfell over the ball

First-string center Carroll Grenfell remembered the next game better than most:

Then we played at the old place called Ballston. They had old wooden seats over there with some lockers underneath, not the best field in the world. We went over there and it was raining, and it was one of the sloppiest games you've ever seen. When we got through, there wasn't one of us that wasn't caked with mud from head to toe.

But they beat the Gibson Grays 20-0 after Duvall returned the opening kickoff for a touchdown. Grenfell smiled

Bing Duvall, heck of a running back, a little guy. When he ran his butt and legs were right on the ground. He could really move. And Beefy Manchester, that's what we used to call him, he could block. And that guy Eaton, what a helluva running back he was.

Under the watery lights at Ballston, Larry Eaton closed out the scoring of that Friday night game. Two days later at Meadowbrook and before the biggest crowd yet, the B-CC AA defeated the Maryland Aces from Prince George's County.

That fall, Callaghan's team played a home-and-home series with Chestertown High of Kent County, a team with a statewide reputation for good football. Bethesda won both games. Grenfell recalled that "Sammy Miller drove those guys crazy down at Chestertown" with his passing. On Sunday, November 17, the team traveled to Queens

Carroll Grenfell

Chapel Road to play the Mount Rainier Ramblers. It was another game Carroll Grenfell never forgot.

I was center on offense and linebacker on defense. It was sixty-minute ball. And this guy with a rubber cap on, did not have a helmet on, he beat me to death. You know when you're down at center, you're helpless. McGowan played beside me; he and I used to try to hit 'em high and low, trap 'em. That guy in the rubber cap slapped my head, I mean really slapped it, boy! He was rough as a cob. I got back at him though when I was line backing. I liked that better than playing center.

Bethesda lost 15-7, but came back on Thanksgiving to beat Lanham 7-6. In the final game, "Bing" Duvall scored twice as the Rec Center beat the Silver Spring Merchants 13-0, outgaining them 223 yards to forty-five. Callaghan's boys ended up with a 12-2 record, outscored their opponents 247 to 41 and claimed the County championship.[69]

By the time the football season ended, the bowling leagues were all in action. Bank of Bethesda cashier S. Walter Bogley of the Eldbrooke Methodist team got his name in the paper by bowling a record 183 at the Ice Palace, and Mack Segretti tied the league record with a 442 set at Hiser's. The teams from Martin's Delicatessen and Simmons' Barbershop led the Bethesda Duckpin League while the Rotary team topped the Civic League, and the Chevy Chase Methodists and Bethesda Presbyterians were tied for the lead of the Church League where the Broadhursts and the Troths were among the best bowlers. Martin's team also led the women's league as winter began.

Henry Hiser sponsored a team in the County "unlimited" basketball league that was made up mainly of Rockville boys, and the Rec Center organized four teams that played at the high school and at Leland's gym. The Athletic Association, generally called the "boys' club," now with support from the Junior Chamber of Commerce welfare committee headed by Hugo Brooks, organized a wrestling program and a ping pong tourney as well as basketball teams. It put an "unlimited" team on the court featuring Bob Harris, Bill Morell, Grayo Dawson, Carroll Hayden, Elliot Young, Frank Althouse, Bob Finlayson and Frank Lozupone who had to lower the high arching shots he used at Leland

to fit in the high school gym. The Rec Center also had a 135-pound squad and a midget and pee-wee team.

At B-CC, a sophomore five coached by Loris Williams won the high school intramural championship by defeating Kay Greaney's seniors 17-13 and then Sue Boyer's juniors 18-17. At Leland JHS, the varsity had a nine-game schedule, and James G. Cross, the new PE instructor, organized weight-level teams to play D.C. Boys Club, Rec Center and AAU teams.[70]

The high school varsity started its season with a win over Roosevelt, the previous year's Interhigh champion, and with a new nickname, "Barons." The new moniker, suggested by senior Carolyn "Kaky" Martin, won approval by a vote of 266 to 220 over the old appellation, "Highwaymen." The team led by juniors Dick Poerstel and Bob Cremins, when he was out of the doghouse, and seniors "Duke" Hashagen, Elton McClure and Central transfer Al Gaist ended the regular season with a 19 and 5 record, beat Blair twice, and made it to the second round of the Star Tourney and again went to the Duke-Durham tournament. The junior varsity team, coached by Bill Morell and featuring Loring Appleby, Tom Kirby and Al Sherline, also had a very good season.

Compared to previous years, the Blair games were relatively calm affairs. But at half-time of the second game, Leonard Williams and a buddy, both junior varsity players, made their way under the stands and behind the Blair rooting section and began pulling down the big, brown paper banners the Silver Spring school's cheerleaders had taped to the gym walls. When they were spotted, they ran for it trailing the last, tattered poster and the brawl was on. Leonard Williams said he never knew what happened after that because he was on the bottom of the pile. This time the teachers and police were ready and quickly restored order.[71]

At the end of November, Bethesda reached another milestone when Commissioner Thomas Earle Hampton placed the first dial call to Mrs. Gilbert Grosvenor, daughter of Alexander Graham Bell, as C&P manager Raymond B. Leavitt looked on. The phone company placed ads thanking Bethesdans for putting up with changes in their phones and phone numbers and urged them to throw away their old phone books and to use the newly issued one. Later newspaper ads reminded patrons to stop using the suffixes, such as "M" and "J," that had followed some old numbers and to dial only the first two letters of the exchanges. About 12,500 phones operated with the WIsconsin, BRadley and new OLiver exchanges.

Irving Root resigned after thirteen years of service as chief engineer of the M-NCP&PC with praise from all corners of the County. The *Journal* editorial stated that "There is probably no man who has done more for Montgomery County during the past decade in its time of coming of age than Root." During his tenure, the basic zoning ordinance was adopted; subdivision regulations were established; more than a thousand acres of parkland was acquired; and a preliminary master plan was developed. On January 2, 1941, Mr. Root became superintendent of the National Capital Parks.[72]

The Chevy Chase Fire Board could not know that suspending Don Dunnington would have such long-range effects. After several warnings, they forced Dunnington out for regularly following fire engines too closely. Reuben "Smokey" Stivers, one of the few volunteers to actually live at the firehouse, recalled being on the rear step of an engine doing 50 mph and looking back and seeing Dunnington ten feet away. "I could have spit on him," he said. Dunnington's departure was rather raucous. "He was furious, screaming and hollering," Stivers said.

But within months Dunnington organized a "first aid corps" and purchased a used ambulance for $75 and announced that he and his friends, mostly volunteer firemen and all with Red Cross first aid training, would support the Bethesda Fire Department ambulance. Other original members included Leslie Shaw, John Ferrari, Edgar Tuller, John Graham, Bill Harnesburger, Bill Robey and Bernie Doyle. Dunnington and his fellow college and high school students collected money door-to-door on both sides of the District Line and sold Christmas trees at Chevy Chase Circle. Since the local volunteer fire departments raised money the same way, conflicts were inevitable and strained relations, especially with the volunteer companies along the river, were a continuing problem.

By the end of the year, Dunnington's Corps bought a $1,500 Packard ambulance and relegated the old Nash to canteen status to carry coffee and sandwiches donated by the Hot Shoppes or Peoples. The boys showed up at almost every multiple-alarm fire. They installed big, chrome headlights from a old Chevrolet on the roof of the Packard and talked Woodward

and Lothrop's into donating the linens and Peoples, the first-aid supplies. The equipment usually stayed in the side yard of Bernie Doyle's home at 3939 McKinley Street, N.W. Doyle's father drew up the incorporation papers, and in the early days the emergency phones were in Bernie's bedroom and at "Duck" Dunnington's out on Ridge Street in Chevy Chase. When the phone rang, Doyle jumped into his boots and got the ambulance rolling, and the first man there rode with him to the scene. In the first three months, they had almost a hundred "runs" and a growing reputation as very fast drivers.

Lt. John Ferrari and the new Packard

In the spring, the Chevy Chase First Aid Corps organized an auxiliary composed of pretty girls in white uniforms and began winning trophies in the Apple Blossom, Cherry Blossom and similar festivals and at local fire department parades. They produced their own license plates and hat badges with a red cross in the center. The Red Cross threatened to sue until the squad pointed out they had no copyright on a cross in a gold circle like theirs. The original officer list showed Dunnington as captain, John Ferrari as lieutenant and John Graham, sergeant.[73]

The *Journal* continued to slash away at the County government and ran front page cartoons poking not-so-gentle fun at Commissioner Hampton as the symbol of "petty politics, favoritism and graft," while the *Tribune* generally defended the status quo and accused its rival of repeatedly falling to new lows of unsupported claims and untrue charges. The delay in issuing the Brookings report and the convoluted appointment of E. Brooke Lee back to the State legislature fueled the feud.

Meanwhile, the evangelical Protestant churches were becoming more friendly and cooperative. In 1940, five churches united for a Thanksgiving service at the old Mt. Zion Church with the Presbyterian minister, Reverend Albertson, doing the preaching and Bethesda Methodist, Christ Memorial Christian and First Baptist members involved. The same five congregations also joined at Christmas-time at the Presbyterian church with Reverend Chandler as the main preacher.

J. Phillip Schaefer headed the Chamber of Commerce committee that planned a very different Christmas program for 1940. The long delayed "Buy in Bethesda" campaign combined with Xmas Lane began on December 2 with fireworks at Wisconsin and Elm. That month, Bethesda merchants gave out tickets with each purchase for prize drawings on Monday evenings at the Farm Women's Market. The Treasure Barrel crowds grew from a thousand to 2,500 and watched dozens of prizes from appliances to puppies being awarded while they enjoyed the carols that rang out from an electric carillon. St. Nick and his reindeer stood at Bradley and Wisconsin with decorated trees near the cannon. New "Xmas Lane" lights and big candles, ten feet high, glowed at the primary intersections.

At the high school, Irene Tilly, a good athlete as well as president of the student council, threw the switch at the fourth annual tree lighting ceremony, and there was decorated tree in the public library thanks to the Girl Scouts and Campfire Girls. Chevy Chase Girl Scouts, led by Mrs. Harold F. Stimpson, tied bundles of grain to trees in Fort DeRussey Park as a treat for the birds.

John H. Bayless of 4311 East West Highway won the *Tribune*'s outdoor lighting contest as well as the grand prize gas range in the Treasure Barrel drawing. The Stock Brothers life-size outdoor crèche on Bradley Boulevard had many admirers. Ed Stock and Charlie Rudd built the display and lit it with an old automobile headlight hooked to a car battery. Area firemen raised funds and collected food and toys for the "needy," and both the Hiser and the Bethesda theaters held matinees where they collected clothing and toys in lieu of tickets.

A few more milestones marked the year's end. Kensington Parkway opened on December 7 with all the usual dignitaries in attendance. Newly elected Lions Club president Joseph Cantrel became counsel for the Board of Com-

missioners at $3,000 a year, a major political plum. The Brookings Institute announced that its report would be published as an 800-page book and an 85-page summary—soon.

The Hot Shoppe in Bethesda and the River Road Market at the B&O tracks both won beer licenses despite local opposition. The Morrison Brothers began construction of an eight-room medical office building for Sam Bogley. In late October, the Commissioners had rezoned his Wisconsin Avenue property between Chase and Chestnut from residential to commercial with a fifty-foot set back, an indication that Rockville was at least conscious that a bottleneck existed. The Presbyterian church building committee headed by Albert C. Rose began plans to expand their auditorium to seat 750 and the school to house 900. The Smiling Buddha restaurant in Sacks' row announced that the price of the "businessman's lunch" was still thirty-five cents.

The war in Europe and the draft in America did not slow County or Bethesda-area building in 1940. In July, Eaton's office issued 131 single-family permits for homes totaling $784,000 and in August, authorized 102 houses worth $576,000. Eaton noted several new estates in the Bradley Boulevard-River Road area and a record number of permits issued for homes valued at over $20,000. Along the Potomac River and the George Washington Memorial Parkway, telephone, electric and gas lines were soon followed by white fences and horse crossing signs. County-wide, $12 million worth of private building began in 1940, and more than half of it was in the Bethesda area.

America placed an embargo on trade with Japan; fighting broke out in the Balkans and North Africa; President Roosevelt called for America to become the "arsenal of democracy," and James Blaine Fitzgerald headed the Maryland Home Defense Committee, which planned to train auxiliary firemen and policemen. The Lions closed out the holiday season with their traditional party at Kenwood for the fifty-one residents of the Baptist Home for Children.

In 1941 as the Battle of the Atlantic raged and FDR urged Congress to approve the Lend Lease program, a fight over beer distracted Bethesdans. A State law had ended the Liquor Control Board's monopoly over the County beer business in 1939, and for more than a year readers of local newspapers had noticed a series of unusually large, well-illustrated and obviously expensive ads for Maryland and na-

tional brewers and associations of beer distributors. The advertisements stressed not only the qualities of the "beverage of moderation" but also the thousands of citizens who worked in the industry and the millions in taxes it contributed each year.

In January, as the bock beer ads appeared and the State legislature began a 90-day session, the reason for all the support provided to local papers became clear when County politicians proposed that beer be put back under the dispensary system's control. The wholesalers, led by Kensington's Eugene J. C. Raney, president of the Maryland Beer Distributors' Association, howled. Their first ad on the topic, "An Appeal to Reason," pointed out that the County dispensary business barely broke even and suggested that political patronage was the politicians' only goal.

In the *Tribune*'s first and only editorial on the topic on January 17, editor Allen concluded that "the county government should stay out of the beer business." An ad that asked "What is wrong with the beer business in Montgomery County?" and answered "nothing" filled his back page. The *Journal* supported the wholesalers in editorials that decried the "injustice" of the plan.

The dispute involved a number of Bethesdans. Ruth Shoemaker, a loyal Brooke Lee ally, supported the change and asked that the lawmakers give the County the control it requested. James H. Pugh, attorney for the beer distributors, told the legislators that the matter was more than local and could lead to other counties seeking exemption from the State act of 1939. He also pointed out that under that act the dispensaries may sell beer if they wish. Harry Welsh also spoke for the beer dealers and asked that good citizens not be put out of work. Petitions signed by 1,400 people and eighty dealers were presented. Adlai Magee represented the Bethesda Chamber, which unanimously opposed the legislation. Marjorie Hendricks and other local business people spoke against the proposed bill.

But the bill passed, and despite petitions signed by 5,000 residents and the appearance of some 200 representatives of civic organizations, business and women's groups and the ministry at a special hearing, the governor signed it into law. On May 1, the County went back into the wholesale beer business and sought a warehouse to rent. In many Rockville bars and restaurants, the price of a bottle of

beer jumped from a dime to fifteen cents, which Mr. Gill immediately labeled "profiteering." Ten cent beer lived on at Bethesda's many "watering holes."[74]

In downtown Bethesda, which counted forty new businesses in 1940, the pace of growth and change continued to accelerate. The Hot Shoppe opened early in January and quickly became the lunchtime meeting place of local business leaders and the site of a Sunday dinner treat for many families. The thirteenth full-sized restaurant in J. W. Marriott's chain featured curb service, a long soda fountain, a retail ice cream counter, uniformly good food and a well-trained staff.

Although the Connecticut Avenue Hot Shoppe across from the Ice Palace had been the gathering place for B-CCers with cars since the winter of `38, the Bethesda restaurant soon rivaled it for weekend dates. In fact, on activity days, high school customers began showing up before three o'clock. Only Giffords had milk shakes that were as rich, and nobody had anything that rivaled the hot fudge ice cream cake. Bill Marriott had come a long way from his 1928 A&W hot dog stand, and it had only been thirty years since Walter Tuckerman said you couldn't buy a cup of coffee in Bethesda. Within a month, Howard Johnsons announced its intention to build a $50,000 restaurant on the northeast corner of Wisconsin and Western next to the bus-streetcar station..

Sherwin-Williams arrived to anchor the south end of the Shopping Center with E. E. Bass as manager, and Burrell Marsh moved his Oldsmobile dealership down to his new showroom at 4800 Hampden Lane after six years on Wisconsin Avenue. Sanitary opened a big, new store on Wisconsin Avenue just north of St. John's Church and closed its Shopping Center market. Clerk Wilson Frazier moved to the new store along with manager John Young. Frazier had come up to Washington from Luray in the Depression and found a part-time grocery clerk job that paid him $18 for a sixty-hour week. He went to work in Bethesda for Sanitary and manager Young in 1937 and was involved along with several other Bethesda grocery clerks in organizing what eventually became Local 400.[75]

Wiggington's dry goods and dress shop on Leland Street was the first to advertise a January clearance sale closely followed by the Holbrook Bargain Store near the firehouse. Young, white-haired Charles Holbrook's little store at 7542 Old Georgetown was the place to go if "you can't find it anyplace else." Out on Cedar Lane, not far from the skeet club, WMAL's new, $200,000 transmitter went into operation. The Rock Creek Riding Club received permission from the County Commissioners to use the old carbarn at Chevy Chase Lake as a stable.

And Henry Hiser announced plans to build a 32-alley bowling center between the Housing Guild and the Broadhursts' stores. In mid-February, he said that the old tourist home there would be torn down and work by Charles H. Tomkins Construction Company would begin immediately on the $100,000 project. It never did. Early in the spring George W. Huguely and E. P. Knollman announced their plans to build a large, two-story, air-conditioned, brick and concrete structure across from the firehouse on Old Georgetown Road to house four stores, twelve offices and forty bowling alleys. Construction began almost immediately on the 120-by-132-foot foundations.

Also in early 1941, parking was prohibited on Brookville Road and around Chevy Chase Circle except on Sundays. New traffic lights were authorized at Wisconsin and Montgomery and in front of the firehouse, and Sam Stonebraker suggested that 600 parking meters be installed in Bethesda. His suggestion was referred to a Chamber of Commerce committee.

At the end of March, building inspector and permit issuer Eaton announced another record-breaking three months of building in the

Bethesda-Chevy Chase area. His office authorized construction of 208 single-family dwellings, all for homes in the "higher than average range," compared to 148 in the same period of 1940. So many new residents were arriving that both Bethesda papers ran "welcome to the community" columns in almost every edition.

At Our Lady of Lourdes, where the number of parishioners had reached almost two thousand, Father Little said the first Mass in the new church on the last Sunday in January. It seated more than 600 and could be converted into a gym when a separate church was built. The large auditorium cum lunchroom beneath the chapel was put to immediate use by various church groups. The pastor announced that the eight-classroom school and the convent would be ready for the next school year. And on that same Sunday, January 26, Dr. J. Raymond Nelson held the first services in the new First Baptist Church on Wilson Lane for a membership grown to 121.

In the spring, the Lutherans, with Princess Martha in attendance, dedicated their beautiful, new, white sanctuary with its blue carpeting, which they had started planning in 1939. And the Rev. Clifford Homer Richmond became the pastor of Chevy Chase Methodist when the Rev. Edward G. Latch, after serving nine years, transferred to Metropolitan Memorial in D.C.

The public library celebrated its first birthday while its board still sought a new head librarian. The first annual report showed that there were 2,180 card-holding borrowers including forty-five non-residents and that 32,940 books including 8,436 non-fiction works had circulated during the first year. Over 2,500 books had been added to the collection during the year, and the library now subscribed to thirty-nine periodicals.

The Board of Education proposed another new elementary school somewhere in the west Bethesda-Bradley Boulevard area and included additional classrooms for Leland and East Bethesda in its budget. After rejecting a Greenwich Forest site, the school board purchased part of the old Galliher farm in Bradmoor for the new school. The second term of adult evening classes began at the high school with offerings ranging from lip reading to blueprint reading and from conversational Spanish to clay modeling. Sponsored by the National Defense Program, a course in airplane mechanics met five nights a week.

David Trumble, principal of the Glen Echo-Cabin John school, held a low draft number and volunteered for service. Cathryn Wilson served as acting principal until the end of the school year when Dorothy Nichols took over as principal of what then became a K-6 school. After much debate and some delay, the Morrison Brothers won the contract to build the new $250,000 high school in Rockville, which was to be called Richard Montgomery.

The paid and volunteer fire departments cooperated to fight a fire in the basement of the Bethesda Paint and Hardware store, and later, after putting out a fire at Bethesda Building Supply, fire chiefs Bargagni and Musgrove shook hands, and Bargagni congratulated the volunteers for their good work in battling a difficult blaze. Both fires were considered somewhat "suspicious."

In mid-February, legal advertisements appeared for a zoning hearing in March on George P. Sacks' request to rezone the old Offutt-Bradley Hills land between the Rec Center and the B&O tracks south of Bradley Boulevard for apartments. Nearby citizens' associations immediately moved to oppose the request.

And after roping off the sidewalk around his triangle of shops at Old Georgetown and Edgemoor, Walter K. Bachrach won his fight with the County tax office. The taxes he paid on the sidewalks were refunded, and the area was removed from the tax books. Dr. Walter G. Eisinger proposed building a general hospital in Bethesda and announced that his group was seeking an appropriate site.

Late on the cold, still evening of February 28, a Wednesday night with the threat of snow in the air, Judge Alfred Wilson's grandson, B-CC senior Wilson Everhart, broke into the high school. He entered through an open window, made his way down the empty, echoing hallways and up the flights of enclosed stairs to the cafeteria on the third floor of the main building. There Everhart found some old newspapers and in the faint moonlight stuffed them under the eaves and put a match to them.

"Willie" Everhart, a slight young man about six feet tall whose hobbies were hunting and gun collecting, had been in the glee club as a sophomore, but his only senior year school activity was the Isaac Walton League. He told a yearbook reporter that he wanted to be a

veterinarian. He spent most of his extra time at the small, square firehouse on Fairmont Avenue.

Wilson Everhart, volunteer fireman, had already started several fires in the area, including the one at Bethesda Paint and Hardware, most of them within a few blocks of his home on Montgomery Avenue. When he set fires, he was almost always among the first to reach the firehouse and ride the pumper to the blaze. And when he came to school late with his knuckles blackened and his clothes still smelling of smoke, he attracted attention. There was one girl in particular that Willie wanted to impress.

Setting fires was not entirely unusual behavior among young volunteer firemen. The habits of a few in Cabin John had caused several shake ups in that fire department, and some of the young members of the Glen Echo VFD came to be called the "touch-off crew." One had embarrassed himself by giving the driver directions to a fire even though he had not been at the station when the call came in. Abandoned houses and overgrown fields were the usual targets, but this night young Everhart started his fire near the partition in the cafeteria, almost under the cupola in the center of the steep, dormered roof of "A" building.

By the time he made his way out of the building, across East West Highway and past the Hurleys' barn, the fire glow danced in the small, semi-circular, third floor windows. Everhart went home and waited. An off-duty Secret Service man, saw the flames as he drove past and reported the fire to the Bethesda police station shortly before midnight. The volunteers' siren cried out, and Wilson Everhart resisted the urge to run toward Pearl Street. His parents had forced him to quit the fire department and return his uniform and equipment.

Both Bargagni's and Musgrove's men quickly responded and a call went in to Chevy Chase. By the time the firemen arrived and began laying hose to every hydrant in the area, the flames had broken through the roof and were feeding on the rafters at both sides of the cupola, which seemed to be acting as a chimney. None of the companies had ladders or equipment to bring water to the roof ridge more than fifty feet above them so hoses had to be snaked up the stairwells at each end of the building and the fire attacked from inside. The blaze was visible all over Bethesda. Leroy Allison recalled seeing it from the back rooms of his home on Leland Street, and Ken Muir watched the roof burn from the side porch of his home at Chatham and East West.

Despite the below-freezing temperatures, a large crowd began to gather on the south side of the highway. Christine Hurley Schneider (B-CC `37), the school secretary, stood on the curb worrying about the records and was tempted to try to rescue them. The police closed East West Highway to traffic and established lines with sputtering flares. Mrs. Schneider and her husband, Larry (also `37), huddled deeper into their coats and watched the firemen pour water into their school. "Sonny" Baldwin called his long-time friend Loring Appleby and yelled, "It's burning. It's burning!" and then hung up and ran outside. "We were all celebrating," said Baldwin, whose family had rented the Imirie's house right across from the school. "Bill Plitt picked me up over there in the grove and yelled, 'We're not gonna have to go to school tomorrow!' The gawdamn flames, you could have seen them down at Chevy Chase Circle."

Chief Bargagni called for more help, and Takoma Park, Kensington, Glen Echo, Cabin John, and Silver Spring sent units to support the local pumpers and their men. District Companies 9 and 20 also responded. The firemen laid about 10,000 feet of hose and placed sandbags and sawdust in front of the stairwell doors to keep the water flowing down instead of spreading along the classroom corridors.

When the doorways filled with hoses, the Chevy Chase firemen put one of their 35-foot ladders up to a window on the East West Highway side of the building and brought another hose in that way. The fire crawled under the eaves, and despite the extra pumpers and manpower, it took more than an hour to control. Over in the grove, half filled with high school students blowing on their hands and stamping their feet, the mood was one of joy mixed with awe as the flames roared through the roof.

While the firemen were still pouring water into the attic cafeteria, English teacher and senior class advisor Leland J. R. Williams made his way into the building and gathered up as much of the *Tattler*'s records as he could carry. He slipped on the wet floor under his heavy load, heard something snap, and thought he had broken his leg. History teacher Raymond Dugan helped carry Williams out and load him into the Bethesda FD ambulance for a ride to Georgetown Hospital where a dislocation was diagnosed.

Earl Hill was one of the Chevy Chase fire-fighters manning the heavy hose on the third floor as the fire was brought under control. "I was in there and told the chief we had too much pressure for the fire we had," he said.

Before I got down to the pumper, the line went slack. I couldn't believe it. The water went to nothing. I went down to check on it, and they told me John Adair was hit. Some doctor hit John and broke the hose off and drove him up against the fender of that piece of heavy apparatus.

John Adair, 28, called a pumper man or an engineer, had been a paid employee at the Chevy Chase Fire Department for more than three years and a volunteer before that. He lived in Silver Spring with his wife, Ann, and their two-year-old daughter. His job was to stay at the side of the big Seagraves pumper and control the pressure to the hoses. His fire engine stood on East West Highway near the fireplug just east of the school. The police were detouring traffic down Montgomery Avenue.

Dr. Mark O. Davis, 60, labeled by the newspapers "a prominent Washington dentist," spent that evening at Columbia Country Club playing cards, drinking, and kibitzing. He left at about one-thirty on the morning of February 27 and turned toward Bethesda on East West Highway. He picked up speed going down the hill, and when he got to the top and the railroad bridge, he was still traveling fast. He saw the glare of lights and the row of flares, and perhaps he was confused. He roared past the policeman flagging him to go down Montgomery, ignored the flashlights being waved at him, and his car smashed into John Adair and sheared off the heavy brass hose couplings on the fire engine. Adair's broken body glanced off the fender of his engine and tumbled seventy-five feet past the front of the high school. He was impaled on a telephone pole.

The Bethesda ambulance, just returned from taking teacher Williams to Georgetown, rushed the mangled fireman down to Georgetown where he was pronounced dead on arrival. The police kept Dr. Davis in jail overnight, charged him with manslaughter, and then released him on a $2,500 bond the next morning.

Meanwhile, County road crews, on alert because of expected snow, starting arriving about 2 am to help prevent further water damage to the school and public library and to help pump out the lower levels of the building including the

John Adair

boilerroom. School was cancelled for two days, and downtown at the Capital Theater, emcee Art Brown asked the Friday crowd, "How do you like skipping legally?" and got a roared response. Water damage was minimal, even in the library, and crews organized by shop teacher Al Bender got the classrooms cleaned and ready for school to resume on Monday under a temporary roof minus the cupola, which survived the fire but not the repairs. Some of "Buck" Bender's students earned fifty cents an hour repairing cafeteria furniture after school, and students ate lunch in their homerooms for the next few days.

The police investigation of the fire began, and Superintendent Broome said he "hadn't the remotest idea" how the fire began but that "it seemed uncanny" for there to have been three major high school fires in a year. The Rockville fire had been almost exactly a year before and a month previously the "colored" high school, Lincoln Park, suffered a great deal of damage. Bargagni stated that no wiring, paper, or trash

Officials examine the damage from the cafeteria

was found where the fire began. A month later, another night-time fire of suspicious origin roared through Mr. Bender's machine shop destroying tools and supplies.

On March 20, the grand jury indicted Dr. Davis on charges of manslaughter. His trial was set for April 9. Davis hired F. Bernard Welsh as his chief defense counsel. He was considered the best in the County. Welsh added Robert B. Peter, a mainstay of Democratic politics, and Joseph T. Sherier of Washington, D.C., to the defense team. State's Attorney Ben G. Wilkinson prosecuted the Circuit Court jury trial before Judges Charles Woodward and Stedman Prescott.

The first witness in the one-day trial was policeman James Shoemaker who estimated that Dr. Davis drove past him as he was standing with a red flare directing traffic at "60 to 70 miles an hour" and that after the accident he "detected the odor of alcohol" on the doctor's breath. Five policemen testified that in their opinion the dentist was "under the influ-

ence of alcohol" at the time of the accident and estimated his speed as at least 50 mph.

The State's "star" witness, Dr. Emil Bauersfeld, called by the police to examine the doctor after his arrest, said that in his opinion Dr. Davis was "in a state of alcoholic stupor" that night. Under cross-examination by Mr. Welsh, Dr. Bauersfeld said he had "inspected" and "observed" the defendant but had not given him a complete physical examination because the police came in and took him away. Welsh then asked, "Did you examine his eyes?"

"I was close enough to observe his eyes," Bauersfeld replied.

"Has Dr. Davis a glass eye?" Welsh asked.

"I don't know" was the answer.

On the stand, Dr. Davis testified that he had been at Columbia Country Club from about 9:30 pm until 1:30 am watching friends play cards and that he had drunk only one scotch and soda. His friends later swore that he was "perfectly" sober when he left the club. Davis stated that had never been speeding, in fact, had driven no faster than 40 mph. He said he was blinded by the lights at the top of the hill and slowed down and that "While still blinded, I felt the collision." He said he was not going more than 30 mph when the accident occurred.

Eight character witnesses came forth for Dr. Davis, whose practice included many prominent Washingtonians. Two justices of the D.C. District Court testified that the doctor had a very good reputation for sobriety and good order. They were both his patients and said they knew him personally. His other character witnesses were three doctors, two officers of the H. L. Rust Company and a Bethesda realtor, Thomas D. Lewis.

At 9:30 pm, the jury returned, and Judge Woodward warned the spectators against a demonstration when the verdict was read. Those in the courtroom received the decision quietly. The jury found Dr. Davis "not guilty." His friends rushed to congratulate him.[76]

In early April, Paul Voight, who had joined the Bethesda VFD only a few hours earlier, was arrested for setting fire to the brush on the Bergdoll tract. He never even got to ride a fire engine because the paid men put out the fire before the volunteers could get rolling. On April 20, shortly after the night watchman had made his rounds, an unfinished home in the 5200 block of East Roosevelt Street caught fire. Before the Bethesda and Chevy Chase firemen could extinguish the blaze, it had done more

than $1,000 worth of damage. It was added to a growing list of suspicious fires.

Shortly after Easter, Sgt. James McAuliffe completed his investigation and called Wilson Everhart on the phone. He asked him to walk up Montgomery Avenue to the police station. After a short conversation about the evidence, Everhart admitted his guilt, and McAuliffe placed him under arrest.

The ruined roof and charred cupola.

The next day, Wilson and his mother sat in the living room of their small home and talked to reporters. "When I was a little kid, I used to build oil fires in the basement of our home," he told them. "I guess I've just had a mania for fires all my life, but I think I'm over it now." His mother could not understand it. "It's simply a case of going haywire, I guess," she said. "But he's over it now."

Young Everhart described how he started the fires. He set a piles of papers ablaze in a vacant house and threw a cigarette into a box of excelsior at the hardware store where he had an after-school job. "I get a thrill out of seeing fire engines racing to a fire," he said. "I didn't have anything against the school. I don't have a grudge against anyone." Both he and his mother thought it would be a good thing if he would join the army. "I sincerely think he's over it now. In other words, he's had his last fire thrill," his mother said. The possibility of going to jail was not discussed.

M. L. Broadhurst, president of the volunteers, told a reporter, "Why, he was one of the nicest boys in Bethesda. None of us around here can believe it. He's a bright boy. Well up in his studies. The quiet kind." Broadhurst said Wilson's parents had returned his equipment about a month before and that the boy had been "a probational volunteer. He would probably have been voted in sometime this month." Wilson said he quit because "it just seemed this mania was getting the best of me." His parents had told Mr. Broadhurst that the firefighting was hurting their son's studies.[77]

Mildred Plitt Swank remembered the day Wilson Everhart's picture and the story were on the morning paper's front page.

His sister and I were going to go downtown, then it was in the paper, the morning paper, the Post *or* Times Herald, *right on the front page. Jane was crying, everybody was upset.*

His grandfather was Judge Wilson with the white hair and mustache. They lived on Montgomery Avenue right next to the Milans. It was a new house on an empty lot, a Cape Cod. He had two younger sisters, Jane and Maudell. I remember Jane crying and saying he had ruined everything.

Isabel Gaither Lynch, who was "Maudie" Everhart's friend, recalled:

Judge Wilson was devastated by it. Those of us who knew Wilson were pretty surprised. He was just a nice looking chap who was always around and no real particular presence. Mrs. Everhart was dying of cancer at that time. It was really hard on that family.

On May 21, the grand jury handed up indictments of Paul J. Voight, 22, and Wilson E. Everhart, 19, both volunteer firemen. Voight was charged with setting a brush fire in Somerset. Everhart was indicted on a charge of arson for setting fire to an unoccupied dwelling on Montgomery Avenue in mid-March, attempting to burn the Bethesda Paint and Hardware store, and burning and attempting to burn a public building, namely the high school. Trials were set for June 9.

Everhart, represented by State Senator Robert Peter, pleaded guilty and stated that he had joined the volunteer fire department to take his mind off a girl friend who no longer would see him. He said he set the fires to "make himself appear a hero to his former sweetheart."

Peter called Dr. John E. Lind of St. Elizabeth's Hospital who testified that young Everhart was not insane but seemed to have an abnormal interest in fires. Under questioning, Dr. Lind could not assure the court that the boy would not set any more fires, but urged that Everhart be placed in an institution under a psychiatrist's care.

Judge Woodward stated that he did not wish to have the defendant at large and also wanted to discourage others from similar actions. He sentenced Wilson Everhart to four years in the Maryland House of Correction. Paul Voight also pleaded guilty and was given a six-month sentence. During the summer, Calvin Owens' workmen restored the roof to its original appearance, cupola and all, but the cafeteria smelled like smoke for most of the first semester.[78]

On March 15, 1941, a week after the heaviest snow since the Knickerbocker disaster, the long-awaited Brookings report finally appeared, and as many expected, it was very critical of some aspects of County government and recommended home rule and other basic changes. The *Journal* welcomed the Report with a double-column, front-page story praising itself and headlining "Patronage, Inefficiency, Waste Hit By Investigator." Allen's *Tribune*, because of its biweekly schedule, did not feature the story until March 28 and then simply stated that the report's findings would be election issues and that response so far had been "cautious." For six months, William Prescott Allen ignored the report editorially.[79]

The *Tribune* sold copies of the report at cost, $2.50 for the 740-page book and fifteen cents for the 85-page summary. Brookings, which had added more than $30,000 of its own to the $5,000 authorized by the Commissioners for the study, sold the report for $3.50 and the summary for a quarter. The *Journal* gave the report to those who purchased a $3.50, two-year subscription

The Washington *Post* published the whole summary report and concluded that the "most essential change to be recommended is the selection of county employees solely on the basis of their ability to perform the duties of the position to which they are appointed and the continuing of such employees in office so long as they obey the rules of the government and render efficient service." The *Star*'s story, headlined "Broad Changes in Montgomery Setup Urged," credited the Civic Federation with instigating the Report and emphasized the fiscal recommendations. *Star* reporters interviewed County leaders and

found most noncommittal but urging study. Carey Quinn told a reporter that he found the report a "trifle Utopian" and wondered why it suggested doing away with political parties.[80]

O. Morton Kile of Mohican Hills, president of the Civic Federation, appointed a special committee to "promote the widespread distribution and study" of the report. Kile chose Allen H. Gardner of Silver Spring to head the committee. Other members of the seven-man group included Emory Bogley, Washington Cleveland, Frederic Lee and Richard B. Barker of Westmoreland Hills. The Federation's fourteen committees began a careful study of the aspects of the report which fell within their purview. E. Brooke Lee believed that the County had been cheated by Brookings; "shortchanged" was the word he used.[81]

They agreed to recommend an improved form of commissioner government . . . . In other words, they took the authorization of the Commissioners, a very moderate fee for participating in the work -- they may have paid them 10 or 15¢ on the dollar for what they spent -- and they failed to produce an outline of county commissioner government. Now they might tell you that that was because it was impossible. It wasn't that. It was really because they were against it.

Among the Brookings Institute's recommended changes were the establishment of a civil service board and merit system for all County employees including the police; the creation of the offices of County administrator or manager, County attorney and County comptroller; the reorganization of the County engineer's office; the abolition of the Liquor Control Board; the reduction of the bonded debt, and the transfer of the M-NCP&PC's planning functions to the new County Council.

Don Quixote — 1906 Model
That is T. E. Hampton as Sancho in this cartoon

By far, the report's most controversial suggestion was the creation of a nine-member, legislative County Council to be elected on a non-partisan basis and to serve without pay. The obvious reason for suggesting non-partisan elections was to avoid the effects of the Hatch Act and make it possible for Federal employees to be involved in local politics and serve on the new council. The report also dealt with shortcomings in the school system, the fire departments, the welfare services and problems with road building and maintenance. Brookings praised Bethesda's paid firemen as the "only fire department, which assumes responsibility for fire prevention" with regular inspections of public buildings such as schools and theaters.[82]

Since the State legislature, where the County's laws were made, was still in session, the Brookings report resulted in the filing of a number of last-minute bills including several that went diametrically against its recommendations. The Commissioners, however, adopted some of the report's suggestions in the following months including the appointment of a full-time County attorney and a purchasing agent.

But the basic question was "home rule" or the creation of a charter for the County. Blair Lee's Progressives had amended the Maryland Constitution in 1914 to allow a referendum by petition of twenty percent of the voters to select a "charter board" to draw up a constitution for a County (or city) that would provide for a body to make local laws. The voters would then approve or disapprove the charter at the next election. The amendment had been on the books twenty-seven years without being used.

Within a few months, the Civic Federation's special committee headed by Allen Gardner became the foundation of a Charter study committee involving most County organizations including the PTAs, the Federation of Women's Clubs, the Farm Bureau and the League of Women Voters. Mrs. Ralph Himstead of Chevy Chase and the LWV was chosen secretary.[83]

The *Journal*'s March 28 editorial, headlined "Complete the Job," urged that the Brookings Institution be hired to draft a model charter and set up a merit system. Curtis Ireland's languishing Taxpayers' Association sprang to life with a study committee headed by Aldo Raffa of Georgetown University. Dr. Lewis Meriam, the report's editor-in-chief, began a round of talks to civic associations and woman's clubs. Mrs. Himstead and the League in-

stituted a series of weekly study classes on Thursday mornings at the public library. Since she was only a five-year County resident, Mrs. Himstead said that she felt herself neutral in regard to the personalities involved, but although she did not say it, she certainly knew that for all purposes, practical and otherwise, only one personality was involved, and he was not happy.

Carey Quinn

In the middle of the waves kicked up by the Brookings report, two other political stories briefly distracted both voters and politicians, and Carey Quinn "put his foot in it." At the very end of the General Assembly session, on the afternoon of Saturday, March 29, after suspension of the rules, Delegate E. Brooke Lee introduced a bill endorsed by three other County delegates including Ruth Shoemaker, which legalized pari-mutuel betting on jai alai in Montgomery County. Despite the bitter opposition of Del. Charles C. Jones of Kensington who called the bill "one of the most crooked pieces of legislation I ever saw introduced in the House," the bill passed in less than fifteen minutes, was printed and sent to the Senate where Sen. Robert Peter gave it a quick, favorable report. The bill was amended, passed by the Senate and accepted by the House on Monday, the last day of the session, as the citizens' associations screamed their protests and as the Sunpapers labeled the handling of the bill "an exhibition of irresponsibility."

The fight then shifted to the governor's mansion with demands for a veto. Even Bob Hagner stood up to the Lee machine. "I personally think it is one of the greatest mistakes that could possibly be made," he said. "The decent people of the county certainly are not in favor of anything like that. In the first place they don't like the way it was shoved down their throats at the last minute and they would not be in favor of such a bill anyway."

Ruth Shoemaker explained her support as purely fiscal; jai alai could bring in a half-million dollars a year in taxes and fees. She said that if the people did not want it, then the governor could veto it. And even Walter

Johnson, who seldom said anything, spoke out against it saying he thought "the big-wig politicians are at the breaking point." Within a week the opposition was so strong and so widespread that the County delegation disowned the bill, and even Brooke Lee joined in a request for the Governor O'Conor to veto the measure, which he did.

Looking back at those events with some thirty-five years of hindsight and experience, Stella Werner concluded, "I think the introduction of jai alai in Annapolis sparked home rule." At the time Mrs. Werner, in perhaps her first public political utterance, wrote a letter to the editor of the *Journal* urging readers to write the Governor in support of a veto and stating that legalized gambling put the state "in a partnership with criminals . . . ."

The fight certainly presaged a break with many of Lee's Bethesda-area supporters and was a long-remembered blot on his legislative record. Lee blamed his defeat on "organized publicity" and a small minority of church people. At least one cleric jumped into the fray. Dr. J. Hillman Hollister, pastor of Chevy Chase Presbyterian Church, in his sermon on the first Sunday of May said he was thrilled that the gambling bill had been defeated and urged his congregation "to vote out of office at the first opportunity those unrepresentative of us and utterly unfit to legislate and rule." Of course, "Colonel" Lee had his defenders and chief among them was Judge Henry Jackson Hunt III who produced a five-column paean to his benefactor in May.[84]

Usually sure-footed Carey Quinn, in the midst of the jai alai imbroglio, sent a letter to James Gill, chairman of the County delegation, in the name of the executive committee of the Civic Federation, commending the delegation's work and endorsing all the bills it proposed. O. M. Kile quickly called a meeting of the Executive and Advisory Committee, which reprimanded Mr. Quinn, who was chairman of the Legislative and Legal Action Committee, for writing the laudatory letter without authority. Quinn apologized for causing Kile so much trouble, but a month later his committee's report was referred back on the grounds that it represented the "observations of Mr. Quinn and not the conclusions of the committee as a whole." Other Bethesdans might waver, but few doubted Carey Quinn's unswerving loyalty to Boss Lee.[85]

The second political distraction was more serious. On February 27, Representative William D. Byron of the Sixth Congressional District, which included Montgomery County and Western Maryland, died in an airplane crash near Atlanta. There was some talk of E. Brooke Lee making a run for the seat in the special election, and Joseph Cantrel's name was mentioned several times while William Preston Lane seemed the favorite as the Democrats had their usual spate of loud caucuses. The Republicans quickly settled on A. Charles Stewart of Frostburg who had lost to Byron in 1938 by only 1,400 votes.[86]

Sentiment was strong to nominate Byron's widow to finish his term, but Montgomery County's organization Democrats did not seem to think she could win. Barely a month before the May 27 special election, the Democrats met in Hagerstown and settled on Mrs. Byron as their candidate. She opened her campaign at Bethesda Elementary School before a meeting of the United Democratic Organization, which had opposed her nomination, and was greeted with cheers and a Brooke Lee endorsement. Local supporters organized a Byron-for-Congress Club at Dorothy Nicholson's home on Newlands Street in Chevy Chase, and Mrs. Byron spoke at the Chevy Chase Library on the evening of April 28 and to the Bethesda Women's Democratic Club at the Rec Center in mid-May.

The *Journal* supported Republican Stewart as did Walter Johnson, and their candidate rallied his female supporters in a meeting at the Galen Tait home at 4900 Western Avenue in early May and operated locally out of an office in the Housing Guild building. In his election-week editorial, Day Thorpe made it simple: "A vote for Byron is a vote for Brooke Lee. A vote for Stewart is a vote for good government–in general the government outlined and recommended in the Brookings Report."

The *Tribune* came out four square for Mrs. Byron in a front page editorial that praised her youth and courage. Editor Allen concluded that the voters had an "obligation" to support "a Candidate whose membership in Congress will be an assurance of the continuance of sound, representative government plus the creation of an impregnable national defense." Without real issues, the campaign had been quiet and relatively mild, but because of the Republican showing in 1940, the outcome was in doubt. The prognosticators almost all said "Byron" but hedged the margin on the turnout.

Mrs. Byron became Maryland's first Congresswoman by 1,200 votes as only 50,000 went to the polls compared to 112,000 in the previous election. Stewart carried only Garrett and his home county, Allegany. In the seven Bethesda-area precincts Mrs. Byron had 1,646 votes compared to Stewart's 1,531 and carried Montgomery County by 2,471 losing in only the three Chevy Chase precincts.

Bethesda continued to grow and to attract new businesses in the last spring before the war. The Sanitary stores became Safeways in 1941 but still advertised themselves as "Your Sanitary Store." The big, yellow-brick Acme on Old Georgetown and the A&P across from the phone company on Wisconsin had brought supermarket competition to town.

The big, new supermarket at 7500 Old Georgetown

The House of Fashion, featuring sports dresses as well as daytime and evening wear, arrived in the Shopping Center in March with William A. Curtin Jr. as owner-manager. Peoples Hardware opened a branch in the space the Sanitary had vacated in the Shopping Center, and Montgomery Ward started a catalog order office in May.

And later in the spring, Phil Banfield and plumbing contractor W. J. Wolfarth founded Edgemoor Ford, began receiving some new cars at a temporary building, and started constructing their modern stone and brick one-story showroom and shop at 7411 Wisconsin. Their dealership with its ramp to a parking lot on the roof became the northern marker of the Bethesda business district. Out at Carderock the government began construction of a half-million dollar wind tunnel, and the steel framework of the Navy hospital disappeared in sheets of concrete and stone.[87]

The Glen Echo volunteer fire department purchased a new $6,200 pumper and had it painted white trimmed with gold. At the amusement park, 69-year-old general manager Leonard B. Schloss was getting ready for his thirty-first year by trying out all the rides except the "flying scooters" that wobbled and dove through the budding trees. He was back with what he called his "family": Tom Mulligan who had been taking tickets at the Midway for as long as Schloss had been there, superintendent Joe Hart in his twenty-eighth year, Tom Much and Mike Prather with a combined thirty-six years on the Coaster Dips, Emory Crouch at the former Old Mill, now the World Cruise, Ira Pope who ran the merry-go-round and Steve Maroney who had overseen the penny arcade for sixteen years.[88]

The Cantrels had twin girls on the 17th anniversary of the birth of twin sons, Frank and Joseph. Eckert Sacks died at age ninety-three; the German immigrant, who started with a Centre Market stall and helped found the Washington Permanent Building Association, had lived at 105 Chevy Chase Drive for twenty-five years. Kirke Hopper declared bankruptcy. His Shell station behind Bachrach's stores at Edgemoor and Old Georgetown closed after nine years, a victim of the gasoline price war between D.C. and suburban dealers. Radio stations changed their positions on the dial; WJSV, for example, moved to 1500, and all push-button radios had to be readjusted. In May, WWDC made its debut at 1450 with a transmitter near the Meadowbrook Saddle Club on zig-zag East West Highway. At Griffith Stadium, Walter Johnson threw out the first ball on May 28 for the Senators' first night game at the old ball park.[89]

The Chamber of Commerce awarded the O. O. Kuhn Cup to the Offutt brothers, M. Willson and the late Winsor, for their Bradley Terrace apartment development on Strathmore Street. George P. Sacks displayed architect Harvey Warwick's drawings of his planned apartment development on Bradley Boulevard. His designs called for 544 units east of the railroad costing about $1,250,000. The buildings, said Mr. Warwick, would be garden-type and "scattered among large land spaces and playgrounds." The rezoning hearing was set for May 8. "I feel that it is a necessary project to meet the demands of this community," said Sacks.

And as E. Brooke Lee extolled the merits of apartments in the Sligo Creek area, Scott Appelby proposed a second, and even larger, apartment project for Bethesda, this one just west of Massachusetts Avenue extended at the

B&O tracks. Within a week six citizens' associations met at Westbrook Elementary School to plan their fight against the $5,000,000 project.

The *Tribune* came out editorially in support of apartments asking "Should our population growth be restricted only to those individuals now receiving sufficient wages that allow them to purchase homes at the beginning?" and concluded that "Everyone will benefit if residential zones gradually merge into commercial areas through the use of apartments." The *Journal* derided Brooke Lee's love of apartments and generally opposed rezoning.

In mid-May, the Civic Federation, after some soul searching, internal debate and two votes, took a stand against any and all apartment zoning. At the hearing on the Sacks' request, Carey Quinn spoke for the fifteen civic groups that opposed the building of apartments. James C. Christopher represented the property owners and, ignoring nearby Kenwood, said the railroad made the land unsuitable for single-family homes and that apartments would act as a buffer between existing neighborhoods and commercial development.

The County Commissioners took the question under advisement and after a month voted 2-2 with Mr. Hampton abstaining because his family owned adjoining property. A week later, without explanation, Walter Johnson changed his vote and the Sacks' plan was approved For the first time the single-family-home forces had been defeated. The *Journal* attacked and the *Tribune* defended Johnson's vote.[90]

Charles Jones, of Park and Planning announced, again, that the renumbering and renaming of streets would start soon, and he offered the public an opportunity to suggest new street names. Park Commissioner Lacy Shaw said the job should be finished in time for the fall/winter phone books.

By May, Lawrence Troth ran out of patience. In his letter to the *Tribune* he stated that he built his home at 6617 Summit Avenue four years ago and then found out that there

Proposed New Street Names

OLD NAME AND LOCATION	NEW NAME
Arlington Avenue, Woodmont	Arliss Ave.
Arlington Road, Edgemoor	Audley Road
Aberdeen Road, running North from Wilson Lane	Garfield St.
Brown's Lane, Alta Vista	Oakmont Ave.
Cedar Lane, West from Old Georgetown Road	Green Tree Road
Chestnut Ave., West Chevy Chase Hgts.	Shirley Ave.
Curtis Road, Leland St. to Oakridge Ave.	Oakridge Place
Cypress Ave., Alta Vista	Carlton Ave.
Cypress St., Meadow Lane to East West Highway	Meadow Lane
Cypress St., Meadow Lane to Conn. Ave.	East-West Highway
Cypress St., East-West Highway to Dunlop St.	Dudley St.
Chevy Chase Blvd., North	Davidson Drive
Delmar Place, Greenwich Forest	Westover Road
Elm St., Chevy Chase	Stanford St.
Elm St., Wisconsin Ave. to Oakridge Ave.	Elmridge Ave.
Elm St., North of Leland St.	Oakridge Ave.
Elm St. and Montgomery Lane, Glenbrook Rd. to Wisconsin Ave.	Fayette St.
Hampden Lane, that portion running North	Jefferson St.
High St., Friendship Hgts.	Friendship Ave.
Highland Ave., Moorland La. to Custer Road	Harwood Ave.
Harrison St., Huntington Terrace	Hoover St.
Lenox Road, Bradley Blvd. to Somerville Rd.	Cardiff Road
Montgomery Ave., Kenilworth	Lafayette Ave.
Montgomery Ave., Rosedale	Tilbury St.
Montgomery St., Friendship Hgts.	Friendship Ave.
Montgomery Drive, Alta Vista	Northfield Drive
Moorland Lane, Greenwich Forest	Grant St.
Montrose Dr., Kenilworth	Corinth Drive
Maple Ave., Alta Vista	Crothers Ave.
Maple Ave., Bradley Lane to East-West Highway	Kingwood Drive
Maple Terrace, Chevy Chase	Kingwood Terrace
Maple Ave., Rosedale Park	Monterey Ave.
Maryland Ave., Rosedale Park	Pearl St.
Michigan Ave. and Battery Lane, Batery Park	Rosedale Ave.
Midwood Road, Huntington Terrace	Overhill Place
Melrose St., Thornapple St. to Underwood St.	Thornapple Place
Melrose St., Woodmont	Cordell St.
Oakridge Lane, Elm St. to Leland St.	Elmridge Ave.
Oak Lane, Meadow Lane to Leland St.	Vale St.
Oak Lane, Radnor Rd. to Bradley Blvd.	Durbin Road
Radnor Road, Bradley Blvd. to Goldsboro Rd.	Goldsboro Road
Ridge St., Chevy Chase	Rosemary St.
Stratford Road	Sumner Road
Saul Rd., Chevy Chase Terrace	Sherrill Road
Watkins Ave., Bethesda	East-West Highway

was another house with the same address. He wrote that he complained to Park and Planning at least once a year, and that even though the changes were authorized in 1937 by the State legislature, nothing had been done. "Why has it taken so long?" he asked.[91]

The draft calls rose from forty-seven in March, when Frank Lozupone was inducted, to seventy-six in April when both of the Ahrendts brothers were called.

At the Recreation Center the long-promised "sylvan theater" neared completion with a stone-fronted stage seventy-five feet wide raised four feet above the "orchestra pit" and

backed by evergreens. Two church baseball leagues began playing at the Rec Center, one for eleven- to fifteen-year-olds and the other for younger boys. Both used equipment purchased with the $500 raised by the Junior Chamber of Commerce and about 200 youngsters participated. Harry Callaghan also entered a team in the County baseball league where Bethesda had not been represented the previous year, but the league collapsed and the team played as an independent.

"Duck" Dunnington, who played in the outfield for that team, announced that his squad would serve iced tea, lemonade and sandwiches to fire fighters during the summer months. In a meeting at Nancy Reutlinger's home on Chesapeake Street, Dunnington was reelected captain.[92]

As usual, Dr. Ellicott, the County health officer, was warning about ticks again. In early May the new Bethesda-Chevy Chase Health Center opened at 4713 Hampden Lane, and the Scouts and Campfire Girls sold green tags to support the Public Health Lay Council project, which included the child health and maternity clinic. The public health nurse for the Bethesda area, Martha Keys Fry, had been working out of a tiny office on the second floor of the County Building just over the front door and conducting her clinics in the hearing room when Jim Christopher was not using it.

A small but significant dispute arose on April 11, Good Friday in 1941. On that legal holiday Eugene Casey's crews began cutting down trees behind Oakmont. The day before Casey received a permit to build a road between Johnson Avenue and Oak Street, through the Walter Johnson tract to Ayrlawn Farms, but ten feet of its thirty-foot width would be in the Oakmont special taxing area. Dozens of large trees fell before attorney E. Austin Carlin and the local citizens could get Mr. Casey to stop and postpone excavation until the County Commissioners reviewed the case. Casey had tried to build the same street in 1936 only to be stymied by Oakmont protests. The legal question involved the conflicting rights of the special taxing areas and of the County government. The *Journal* leapt into the fight with an editorial deploring Gene Casey's political power. Citing the Brookings report's recommendations, Day Thorpe supported the local taxing authorities.[93]

On May 13, on advice of their counsel, Mr. Cantrel, the County Commissioners denied the appeal of the Oakmont Citizens' Committee for reversal of the permit claiming they had concurrent authority with respect to streets. Oakmont then sought an injunction, and Judge Woodward ordered Casey and the Commissioners to appear in his court June 4. Casey could not be served with a summons and said he would not appear. Cantrel filed a demurrer, saying that the Circuit Court lacked jurisdiction.

William Daley of 27 Oak Place, longtime leader of the special taxing area, roared, "The Board is like a tyrant. It can brook no authority but its own." A hearing on both the complaint and the demurrer took place before Judge Charles W. Woodward on June 25. Road building was delayed, briefs on the question of jurisdiction were requested, and at the judge's suggestion the Commissioners and the citizens' association met to discuss the proposed road.

Trade association executive Daley, Department of Labor attorney Harold C. Nystrom, and Catholic University English professor Dr. James Kerby Neill, the unpaid leaders of the tiny taxing area, stood firm against powerful New Dealer Casey and his silent partner, Harry Hoskinson, and reached an out-of-court settlement, which added a third to the taxing area's population but relieved it of any responsibility for maintaining the new road one-third of which was built on its land.[94]

As spring moved toward summer, the local country clubs began staging the usual variety of tourneys and championships. Amateur Bobby Brownell won the best-ball tournament at Bannockburn and then won the Middle Atlantic championship. A reorganization committee led by Myron Davy worked with Acacia as the Congressional Country Club defaulted on its first trust of $270,000 and second trust of about $143,000. The deal hung up on the unhappiness of the second trust bondholders who were to receive the eighty disputed acres north of River Road, but the District Court allowed the foreclosure sale to proceed in April 1940. The new corporation with a $300,000 loan from Acacia was the only bidder at $270,000. Led by Gen. Frank T. Hines, the new board wiped out the non-dues-paying life memberships, converted the ornate Pompeian Room into a cocktail lounge and set out to attract new members. The war and the OSS saved it.[95]

The Washington Horse Show at Meadowbrook drew a record 1,019 entries, and tennis whites came out of storage for another season in the sun as Edgemoor hosted the City of Washington tournament. Barney Welsh won

the men's singles and then teamed with Hugh Lynch to win the doubles title. Paul Baker and John Sager pitched Landon to the Interstate Academic Conference championship over St. Albans. B-CC junior Alton Willett of the River Road Willetts won the Metropolitan Schoolboy Golf Championship with a 12-foot putt on the 18th at Congressional. And out at the new Bradley Hills Country Club, Al Jamison used seven of the nine holes in the old Women's National links and laid out one of the longest 18-hole courses in the area. He planned to have the whole layout ready by the next spring.

At the high school and at Leland JHS, students organized junior committees of the Bundles for Britain campaign. While the junior high kids collected money and clothes, junior Mary Bradley led the group of B-CC girls assembling make-up kits, including bars of soap, for British women. High school boys including senior Jack MacLeod cleaned up an abandoned real estate office on West Leland Street, found some furniture, and replaced thirty broken windows. It became the headquarters of the local committees. The Chevy Chase branch of Bundles for Britain staged a benefit, children's theater performance of "Little Women" at the Woman's Club of Chevy Chase, and the Huntington Terrace group put on bridge parties at the Columbia Tea Room and at Mrs. B. Payton Whalen's home.

The high school graduation took place at Leland again, and a record 215 students, the girls in long white dresses and boys in white or tan suits with maroon ties and handkerchiefs, listened to Dr. Peter Marshall of the New York Avenue Presbyterian Church and then enjoyed the alumni–PTA dance at the Woman's Club of Chevy Chase. Leland Junior High graduated 300 ninth graders. At Glen Echo-Cabin John three grades graduated as the school's 7th and 8th grade classes moved to Leland for the next school year, and 275 sixth grade students were promoted by the elementary schools.

In June the call went out for men who had recently become twenty-one to register. The draft calls, always divided by race, increased, but 28-year-olds were deferred under the new rules. Judge Granville Curry of Battery Park replaced James B. Fitzgerald on Draft Board 3 when Fitzgerald was called to service in the National Guard. President Roosevelt declared an "unlimited national emergency," and as the American government agreed to defend Greenland and Iceland, the German army

plunged deeply into Russia, and the Japanese occupied French Indo-China.[96]

A new recreation center opened at Rock Creek with a broad playground, stone field house, ford across the creek and four tennis courts under the supervision of Blair Smith. The ford immediately became the most popular car washing place around. The Park and Planning recreation director lived in the new shelter built behind the Meadowbrook Saddle Club. Over on Conduit Road, David Clothier was the director at the playground and tennis courts near the Cabin John Bridge, and families in the area staged an equipment "shower" to help their recreation program get off to a good start.

At the "old" Rec Center on Norwood Drive, Harry Callaghan hired three female and two male assistants for the summer. Craft work filled one of the shelters while the other housed ping-pong tables. Three more tennis courts opened, and almost two hundred boys were on baseball teams and an equal number of girls played softball that summer. The center's Junior American Legion team won the County championship over Cissel-Saxon of Silver Spring with a 13-4 record, and the unlimited team had eighteen wins and eight losses in "pick-up" games with some of the County's better clubs. Callaghan complained about the small number of spectators at the games and wondered aloud if Bethesda really wanted a team. A total of 1,185 Bethesdans of all ages participated in summer programs.

At the Whitehall School, physical education teacher Elizabeth Loomis conducted a camp for girls, and the Walton School had an eleven-week summer camp for fifty-two boys and girls that included the formation of a rifle team. Bible schools operated at many churches, as usual. The largest of these was the Community Vacation School at the Presbyterian church at the Circle under the direction of Rev. Edward O. Clark, pastor of Chevy Chase Baptist.

The Chamber of Commerce played the American Legion in softball three times that summer, and while the Legionnaires claimed no one was able to figure out who won, catcher and Chamber president John L. Imirie said the Chamber did, 20-13 and 16-14, but he was not sure of the last game's score either. The public library tripled the business it had done the previous summer, added 75 to 100 new books each month and saw circulation rise to 125 a day. And Irving Root, now head of the D.C.

parks, started horse-drawn barge trips up the C&O Canal from Chain Bridge to Cabin John.

The Bethesda branch of the Red Cross, headed by Mrs. Alvin Aubinoe, had its headquarters at the sewing room of the high school for the summer. Mrs. Aubinoe, who claimed to have been dragged away from a bridge table to take the job, convinced the Masons to "lend" their hall as the local headquarters. With the help of her builder-husband and $85 worth of donated paint and venetian blinds, she renovated the old banquet hall, moved in work tables, chairs, sewing machines, an old Norge refrigerator and enough canteen equipment to serve a hundred people in an emergency. The Masons learned to at least "tolerate" all the women who sewed and folded bandages for the clinic and the war effort and used the hall as headquarters of their fund raising until space was made available elsewhere. During Dorothy Aubinoe's three years as head of the local Red Cross, contributions increased from about $1,000 yearly to nearly $20,000.

With the cooperation of the American Legion, Bethesda acquired two aircraft observation posts. At the caddy house of the Bradley Hills Country Club, the head of the local Legion post, Carroll M. Murnane, along with H. L. Shrader and Lowry Coe led twenty-five other Legionnaires and at the Brueninger real estate office at Yorketown Village, J. Coleman Denton, Jim Costello, and Dr. Floyd Cater were in charge. The volunteers took turns in 12-hour watches and phoned reports of flights of two or more planes to Mitchell Field in New York.

As Hitler's armies encircled Leningrad and threatened Moscow and American-Japanese relations worsened, high school girls began collecting money for the USO at the local theaters, and more young men went north to join the Royal Canadian armed forces. And as the threat of German U-boat attacks increased along the Atlantic coast, there was talk of a gasoline shortage, and filling stations started closing at 7 pm. Bethesda's main streets were a lot darker. Chief Bargagni urged drivers not to hoard gas in their garages, and businesses started to advertise that Bethesdans could save gas by shopping locally.

One of the big County events during the summer of `41 was an aluminum drive, part of a national defense aluminum collection campaign. Fire Chief A. J. Bargagni headed the local effort, and his lieutenants were Mrs. Jesse Nicholson in Chevy Chase, Laura Gilland in

North Chevy Chase, Royal Carlock for Brookmont, H. T. McCuen, of course, in Glen Echo and P. T. Hannen in Cabin John. Receiving stations went up at the fire stations in Bethesda and Chevy Chase, and Bargagni enlisted both Boy Scouts and service club members. July 24 and 25 became "special collection" days as trucks toured the neighborhoods.

Bargagni found the remains of an old biplane in a barn at Landon and towed it to the firehouse where he collected pots and pans. Woman's clubs staged aluminum "showers," and the Bethesda theater collected 700 pieces at an aluminum matinee. The old utensils poured in. Bargagni estimated that 20,000 items were received in Bethesda, and Mrs. Nicholson put the Chevy Chase total at about 12,000 pieces. Bethesda's 17,000 pounds of pots, pans and other aluminum ended up in a Philadelphia smelter under supervision of the Office of Production Management with the profits going to defense production.

In another kind of war effort, the County installed 6,000 Japanese beetle traps, two-thirds of them in the Bethesda and Silver Spring areas. Jack Stevens maintained the Bethesda traps, and Jack Wolfe took care of the ones in Somerset. Gardeners who wanted extra green, metal traps could rent them at the County Building, twenty cents for two years. It was a bad season for tick fever, too. In August a seven-year-old girl, a student at Alta Vista Elementary, died of the disease, the year's second fatal case.

On Sunday night, July 6, two fires of very suspicious origin broke out in the Huntington Terrace area. At about 11 pm, a homeowner discovered a small blaze in the basement of his home on Roosevelt Street. The Bethesda firemen put out the fire and estimated the damages at about $1,000. Less than a half-hour later John Imirie saw smoke billowing from under the front porch of Brown's store as he drove home. Imirie stopped and pulled out a bundle of papers and rags which burst into flames. After he stamped out the fire, Imirie called the police who were already investigating several fires in the same general area.

A charred Harrisburg newspaper found at the store on Old Georgetown led to the arrest of a 16-year-old B-CC high school student who had been noticed by police at several recent blazes. Col. McAuliffe remembered, "I worked on that case. The boy that set fire to that store left behind a piece of paper. It had a city name

on it, and I asked him where he was from. He said this town and solved his own case." The young man admitted setting twenty-five fires in the Bethesda area over the past two years including the two on Sunday night, one of which was at his own home. He said that he had started a number of brush fires, burned down several garages, tried to set fire to at least one automobile, and started a major fire at a house under construction. He said he "liked the excitement" and had been stimulated by reading about Wilson Everhart.[97]

Commissioner Earle Hampton, after meeting with the State Roads Commission, predicted an end to the bottleneck and an early widening of Wisconsin Avenue from the Bank to the Naval Hospital with the State paying the entire cost. Only a few more rights-of-way were needed, he said. Almost no one in Bethesda seemed to expect any action soon although the long awaited street renumbering did begin in August. That process brought some cries of anguish from the "Village" and especially from those on the cross streets designed "east" and "west" who were attached to their old, low numbers and who, in the end, managed to hold on to them.

The *Tribune* spent much of the summer defending the County Council and E. Brooke Lee while the *Journal* enjoyed criticizing "Boss" Lee, his "Organization" and his mouthpiece, the *Maryland News*, and prodding the County government for its inaction on the Brookings report. It was almost the end of August before the Commissioners reluctantly appointed their own study committee. About the only thing the two papers agreed on was the need to get rid of the bottleneck at the Bank.

The Protestant churches in town conducted "union" evening services and planned a Community Church Campaign for the fall after a survey of neighborhoods. As the new bowling center on Old Georgetown moved toward completion, manager Roger Peacock began signing up leagues for the fall. And despite a suit by R. E. Lee and Virginia N. H. W. Wiltberger of 102 Chevy Chase Drive, ground was broken for the first 160 units of the Sacks' apartments on Bradley Boulevard. In October, Judge Woodward upheld the zoning and dismissed the injunction suit.

And new businesses kept arriving. W. L. Lebling opened his real estate office in the Housing Guild, and Mike Hare started Hare Brothers auto parts and repair shop on Hampden Lane in what was becoming "automobile row." Gretchen Cole, a one-time buyer for Lansburgh's, took over the ground floor of the Broadhurst's new building and offered several lines of stylish women's clothes while upstairs Virginia Head and Charles Wallace had the walls painted peach and blue and set up a branch of their beauty parlor, Heads of Connecticut Avenue.

The B&O, after operating out of the back of Griffith Consumers and two empty box cars for some time, built a twenty by seventy foot, brick freight station down in the "flats" at Bethesda and Reed. Carl Frankenfield succeeded J. R. Davis as agent. The Eisingers and others had been seeking a station for years. In the Shopping Center, the House of Fashion doubled its space and added a "college shop," and Tom Elward from Wilkes-Barre opened his men's store, which offered six-day delivery on made-to-measure garments.

John M. Smith of Oakmont started his House of Furniture on Hampden Lane before moving down to the old Offutt house on Wisconsin Avenue. Just across from the phone company, a new, big A&P grocery store opened, and youngsters in that end of town soon found that they could earn a few nickels and dimes carrying bags of groceries out to ladies' cars.

During the summer, the Archbishop of Baltimore and

The southern end of town in the 1940s

Washington, Michael J. Curley, came out to Bethesda, complimented Father Little and Father Sweeney on their work and blessed the new school, church and convent at Our Lady of Lourdes. Mother Generosa, Provincial of the Franciscan Sisters from Glen Riddle, Pennsylvania, was there with the nuns who were to teach in the new school. The Rev. Neil Gargan, S.J., of Georgetown Prep and Charles Corcoran of the Knights of Columbus also took part in the ceremony. The next Sunday the sisters started registering children for the new school with its eight classrooms, library, offices, large auditorium and stage. Public school officials were happy to see the parochial school open that fall since the Morrison Brothers still had a long way to go on the four additional rooms at East Bethesda and Keller and Sons had barely begun work on the Bradley Boulevard elementary school when classes began.[98]In September, the County schools welcomed another record enrollment. At East Bethesda more than a hundred children showed up for the first three grades, and half-day sessions began immediately for first and second graders. At Westbrook, kindergarten and first graders also went into split classes and half-days. Two Bethesda Elementary classes met in the old gym where new windows had been installed and another in the auditorium. The additional rooms at East Bethesda and the new school in Bradmoor were scheduled to be finished in January, unless a shortage of steel beams caused delay.

At Lourdes, the parish school began with some 240 students and their teachers attending a Mass celebrated by the pastor. Father Sweeney, he of the wonderfully broken nose, led the pledge to the flag, and the new assistant, Fr. John Palm, whose aesthetic good looks had some feminine hearts aflutter, conducted a program of patriotic songs. Classes met for only a half-day the first week, but after that, the sisters and their charges got down to work, and the mothers began operating the cafeteria. One of the teachers at the new school was a 24-year-old Irish woman named Ellen Glynn who was called Sister Emmanuel Mary. She had taught in Klamath Falls, Oregon, for a year and at Little Flower in Baltimore for three years before coming to Bethesda in 1941.[99]

When we arrived at that convent, food was in the refrigerator, towels in the bathroom, and the beds were made. We were loved the moment we went there. The youngsters, we took them in, and it was school as if it had gone on forever.

I had combined fifth and sixth. In those days we were accustomed to teaching seventy students in a class. One teacher in Baltimore had a hundred in the first grade, and those kids learned to read and learned their numbers. Seventy was no problem. They had to become independent because they couldn't depend on the teacher to do everything. But when I came back West to Takoma, it was a real pleasure to only have forty-five.

The school was brand new, but we had to make do without books for a little while. They were ordered but hadn't arrived. We went to the public library and got a basket of books for the youngsters. That school had blowers under the windows and those children never got cold. There was no such thing as PE, but after their lunch they played hard, and we were in charge of that. I was right in with them. Jump rope and I played ball. I remember hitting one girl and breaking her tooth. Oh my word, I died. Sister Helen Regina would pick up her habits and pin them up and play baseball. I didn't know much about baseball, but I was all right at throwing the ball.

There were some younger than I was, but Sister Emma was much older, about forty. To me she seemed seventy at the time, and we were careful of her. She was the principal, 8th grade teacher, and superior, but that wasn't much since we seven nuns were so good. We didn't think of disobeying. We didn't get out much in those days, but all the sisters liked being in a new school and being close to D.C.

Father Little was the pastor and there was Father Sweeney and Father Palm, who was very young I would say. He later became a Jesuit. He had a gorgeous singing voice. Fr. Sweeney was wonderful. He was a boy's man. He set up their games and played with them. He was down there after school in his shirt playing ball. He was a great guy. Father Little was interesting. The first time I ever tasted champagne in my life, he brought us a basket with a huge bottle of champagne and the glasses. I think it must have been for New Year's Day. It was on ice, and he opened it up and poured out our little glasses. And I couldn't stand it, it was so bitter. He was really like a father to us, at our beck and call. He was no good at doing anything for us like repairing anything. Fr. Sweeney was that kind of guy. But Fr. Little was very wonderful.

My reputation was tough; I was a tough teacher. I was demanding, and I'm sure I gave a lot of homework. All the teachers were demanding

and insisted that the work was done right. It went with the large classes. In those days parents knew what their children were doing in school. I don't remember any big incident of misbehaving.

It took a while for Bethesda's Catholic youngsters to get used to these hard-working women in their long, black habits cinched with rosaries; broad, starched, white collars and concealing headdresses. They took no nonsense and sometimes were quick with a ruler. But soon all the teachers' tempers had been tested and evaluated and most of the students learned the limits of their new school world. Boldness might have been admired in some circles, but it was not an attribute the nuns tolerated in their pupils.[100]

Of course, the other schools also started their new years. William N. Morell, president of the high school PTA, suggested that B-CC organize a cadet corps like the ones in most D.C. high schools. He appointed a committee composed almost entirely of military officers to explore his proposal. At Leland Junior High the playground had been completely rehabilitated, and a student committee headed by Richard Ream began planning its use.

At Landon, the boys welcomed Walter Boyson of New Jersey as the new coach. He replaced headmaster Paul Banfield who had been filling in since Bob McCartee went on active duty with the Army. Miss Libbey's in Chevy Chase, Lady Isabel's in Edgemoor, The Walton School, and the others were joined by Reese Sewell who brought his Longfellow School for boys to Bethesda. Thomas Jefferson Barlow of Drummond, a teacher at St. Albans and later assistant headmaster at Longfellow, remembered Sewell.

Reece Sewell was from Snow Hill down in Eastern Maryland. The Sewells came over right after Lord Baltimore, but they weren't Catholic. He grew up down there, and went to the University of Maryland and got a degree in agriculture. That was an agriculture school until old Coach Byrd came along. That degree in agriculture was all he ever got. Reese was not an educator; he was a real estate man. He sold that property out there for $160,000. He never taught, not a day in his life. Oh, he tried to teach some 8th grade boys. He went to all the auctions, and that's how we furnished that place.

Now it was Parkhurst's. He was with the Pierce Arrow automobile company. He had a place here and a place in Florida. He was never up here

in the winter. You know, it's a copy of the Peter home down on R Street. Back of it, that was a garage and above it was where the children stayed. It was a six-car garage. Later Reese bought a house across Beverly. He had three lots. We used to have commencement exercises over there in the garden.[101]

Parkhurst lost it in the Depression, and the Corcoran art gallery bought it, their foundation, and Riggs handled it. I think he bought it for less than $45,000, six acres. The Parkhurst house had been empty for three or four years. And he bought the house on the corner from R. Harris. Reese offered it to me, a three-story house, and Dell bought it. Donald Dell that went to Landon, all the boys became tennis players, and they came over to Longfellow and played on our courts.

He started the school in `34 over in Calverton and had a boys' camp down on the Severn River called Camp Longfellow. He came over to Bethesda in `41. The school fed the camp on the Bay. Teachers picked up kids on their way in to school, and later they had three buses: Chevy Chase, Kensington, and Georgetown. The chef, Harold Russell, who lived on R Street drove that bus out.

I don't think he had over a dozen boys when he opened that school. He took in boys that couldn't get into St. Albans or Landon; then they would come to Longfellow.

Down at the Norwood Drive Rec Center, Harry Callaghan was getting ready for another football season. At first, he tried to have a team of just B-CC High School boys, but after drills began a number of players decided they would rather stick to basketball. So Callaghan opened the roster and put his team in the South Atlantic Semi-Pro Football League, which played games on Tuesdays and Fridays. Fifteen players returned including Billy Cremins and Carroll Grenfell. Hardy Sorrell and Bob Cremins were among the newcomers. The team opened with a 2-0 win over the Richmond Optomists on Tommy O'Hanlon's blocked punt in the end zone, and went on to have another winning season. In addition to the "varsity," Callaghan organized a 120-pound team, and an eight-team league of six-man football teams for boys under fifteen.[102]

At the high school the girls began with field hockey and the boys with touch football. The new athletic field had been graded, but the sod had not arrived when school began. When woodshop teacher and senior class advisor Edward Hayes left to do missionary teaching in

Kentucky and metal shop instructor Austin Gisreil became an inspector with Glenn L. Martin, seniors Joe Scopin and Bill Hannon and a couple of juniors became assistant teachers in woodworking. The senior class elected Georges Edelen, who was in only his second year at B-CC, as their president.

"I didn't want the bloody job," Edelen said. "Everybody liked Loring Appleby, who had been president for two years, but were tired of the way he ran meetings." Some of Edelen's friends from Kenwood nominated him and in a three-way race, he won. He had been active in student government in New York and New Jersey before his father was tranferred to Washington by Westinghouse and his family found a foreclosed home on North Chelsea. The tall, thin youngster soon joined a circle that enjoyed bridge and music, and during the summer, he worked on what was likely the first B-CC student handbook. After Mr. Pyle approved, the volunteers mimeographed it themselves.[103]

At Leland, after a three-party campaign, the ninth-graders elected George Van Wagner class president over newcomer Chet McCall and Morris Fetrow whose running mates Sally Baldwin, Bill Mizell and Charles "Herbie" Benson won their races for vice-president, parliamentarian and sergeant-at-arms. Benson, section 9-A's president and basketball captain, who broke his leg in a bike accident early in the year, was by far the biggest vote getter. He received 200 votes, Hardy Sorrell, 74 and Dan Toll, 26 in their race. The big surprise was that Van Wagner only defeated McCall 144 to 121 and that student council president Fetrow received just 32 votes.

The elder Chester McCall with his wife and sons had returned to the area in the fall of 1941. He had grown up in the Pacific Northwest, boxed a bit, married young and become an Assistant Secretary of Commerce during the first FDR term at the age of 27. Then McCall started a career in advertising in New York.

In Bethesda, he dabbled in real estate and found some success as a Dale Carnegie teacher. His wife held the family together through a time when dandelion greens were a regular part of the diet, and his sons, Chet and Kendrick, then called Mickey, found Leland easy going after the Horace Mann School in New York City. All four of the personable McCalls were constantly active in school and community organizations.

Leland's mimeographed *Pine Cone* appeared just about every two weeks under editor Tom

Gittings. The papers averaged six pages with a construction-paper cover and featured cartoons by Bob McNinch and Art Wood, articles about new students and teachers, stories on student behavior during fire drills and on the playground, descriptions of assembly programs and dances, and lots of sports and club news. In the fashion column Patsy Pugh reported that plaid skirts, Western shirts, fancy anklets and saddle shoes were all in style and that some "smartly dressed" girls were wearing skull caps.

At Leland's weekly assemblies, the whole student body stood and saluted the flag before each program. After the form of the salute changed, the *Pine Cone* ran a story.

BILL MIZELL BELIEVES SALUTE SHOULD BE FROM THE HEART

Bill Mizell, who leads the school in the salute to the flag in assembly every Thursday, had a real reason for changing the form of the salute from the head to the heart. He believes that a salute from the heart shows more feeling for the flag because of one's love for the flag; that an American's salute to the National Emblem just naturally begins with the heart and ends with the hands outstretched toward the flag.

When asked what he thought of the argument concerning the similarity of the American salute, with outstretched hand, to the Nazi salute, he said he could see no reason why Americans should change their salute of allegiance to their flag just because the Nazis happened to choose a similar sign of loyalty to their flag.

Bill believes that the important thing is to look straight ahead at the Flag while giving the Salute, and to really mean every word that is spoken.

Following the Latin Club's assembly, the *Pine Cone* reminded its readers of Mrs. Bready's dictum, "It has become a tradition at Leland not to whistle or boo at any gatherings in school." Among the biggest school problems that fall, judging from letters to the editor, were the crowded halls, the sunlight in the auditorium when movies were shown, the new fence around part of the resurfaced playground and the fact that few boys participated when there was dancing the gym on rainy days.

The basketball season started early with the selection of the cheering squad led by Betty Reed and Peggy Babcock. The newspaper wondered why the girls "have to wear boys' coats when they are leading a cheer? Is it a bet, a ritual, a custom, a fad, or just plain 'boy and

girl'?" The Varsity itself opened its season on November 28 by defeating the faculty 27-11. Male teachers Cross, Alderton, Kruzburg, Burke and Mumford got their revenge by defeating the JV team of 8th graders a week later with considerable help of Varsity member Birch Bayh at center.[104]

The six pastors of Bethesda's Protestant churches met at the end of September and launched their Community Church Campaign with a Sunday evening service at Leland Junior High. The survey made by Elmond Bass's committee showed that Bethesda was not a very church-going town. More than 120 volunteers from the Presbyterian, Methodist, Baptist, Lutheran, Episcopalian and Christian churches surveyed 3,268 residents. Of those 805 belonged to other churches, 22 refused to answer and 147 said they belonged to no church. Of the Episcopalians who responded only 27 percent of the 557 surveyed said they regularly attended services. For the Presbyterians it was 11 percent of 549, of the Methodists 11 percent of 476, the Baptists showed 17 percent of 264, Lutheran 18 percent of 187 and of the Christian 41 percent of 61 who said that was their religion actually belonged and attended their church. The ministers concluded that there was plenty of room for improvement and much work to be done.

In September, the Lutherans honored their first pastor by dedicating a portion of the original church as the Henry Whiting Chapel. George Whiting, the minister's father, had made the altar and other furniture in what was now the children's chapel. Also in September, Rev. Oram constructed a baptistry and made the basement of his house into a space for Christian Church services. Later Bethesda Presbyterian began a 30-month, $49,500 fund drive to finance enlargement of its sanctuary.

In Cabin John, the Rev. John A. Grose resigned and went to Florida for the winter. He had been holding morning services at the Cabin John Methodist Church and afternoon services at the old Concord Church for about two years. His replacement was Rev. Ulysses S. A. Heavener, 75, of Kensington who had retired three years previously after having preached for more than fifty years.

After meeting at members' homes and at the Chevy Chase Village Library for about a year, the First Church of Christ, Scientist of Chevy Chase was organized. A reading room was established on Wilson Lane, and Sunday school was conducted at Chevy Chase Elementary when the classes outgrew a large, private home.

In the more mundane world, the Howard Johnson restaurant at the District line opened with Arch Butler as its first manager, and former W. & J. Sloan employees Clarence E. Whitmore and Vern M. Smith started the Whitmore Furniture Store in the Shopping Center. Bell Laundry signed a twenty-year lease on the Sacks building on Leland Street and after thirteen years on Hampden Lane used their big trucks to move all the heavy equipment over a weekend and were back in operation on Monday morning. The parts department under the front of the store became a highly profitable, cold-storage vault. Some folks never forgave the laundry for plastering over the stone front of the old Ford service department.

Ellen Bell Tuohey remembered when her father's laundry got the contract for Glen Echo's Crystal Pool.

That was a great day for us. Many Sunday mornings I stood there and folded towels. Everybody in the family folded towels."

On his way home every night, my father put the laundry money in the Bank of Bethesda night depository, but they were forever trying to blow up the safe. They would break in and steal clothes, and the police would always know where to go. The clothes would be back the next morning, and he'd clean them again. It was always so and so or his cousin.

Almost all the business was done through trucks. He would send the drivers home with the trucks, and at six in the morning they would go around and collect the people who worked in the plant and bring them in. They would be finished by 2:30. They all were farm people, and it was set up so they could get the cows milked. I think in the winter they worked a little later. As soon as somebody hit sixteen, they signed up.

H. Seren Gulian, a Russian Armenian, opened his small, mid-town jewelry and watch repair store in October. The Montgomery County Credit Bureau began operations in Bethesda with Parker Badger as manager. Local businesses were offered free, trial memberships.

Home building and home sales continued at about the 1940 pace. Captain Charles W. O. Bunker, commanding officer of the medical school at the soon-to-be-opened naval hospital, bought a home at 5312 Moorland Lane and

"Doc" Everitt and the Bradmoor bunch having fun.

moved in with his wife and daughter. In Brad-moor new neighbors "chipped in" for refreshments and got to know each other at a wiener roast. William E. Yost's development, which began in 1940, now had fifty houses occupied, twenty-four more under construction, regular station wagon service to Chevy Chase Circle and a school promised in January.

James T. Hoyle, who had been in the area earlier as an engineering student, was one of the original purchasers of a Yost house.

Mr. Bell, a real estate agent, says, "Give me a call, I'd like you to ride around a little bit." There wasn't much to see. Thockmorton had some houses on Huntington, and we wound up in Bradmoor. It was kind of naked, no trees or anything like that. Just one block of Hempstead, Irvington and Bradmoor had been finished between McKinley and Roosevelt. No sidewalks, just gravel streets with curbs and fire plugs. The houses on Irvington had a few more square feet than the ones on Hempstead, and there were bungalows on Bradmoor. My wife said, "Lets make up our minds; this it it," so we did.

I looked around for some advice from somebody so I went to the bank, and it was then I

learned how extensive NIH was to be. Mr. Sacks suggested that we buy two houses, that Yost was eager to sell. He needed the cash. We, at his suggestion, bought two houses on two different contracts, for $7,500 each.

We lived at 8506 Hempstead and rented the house across the street. It worked out very nicely. We had a very very good tenant, an NIH scientist. I'd see him the end of every month go down to mail the rent check to me. We had a lot of friends who worked at NIH. The average person doesn't realize what an economic impact NIH has on the community.

In Oakmont, home owners protested Mrs. Ola Powell Malcolm's plan to build a small, wood and cotton composition house on the back of her property with material developed by the Department of Agriculture where she worked. Malcolm received a building permit from the County Commissioners to erect the "cotton house" to be used as a "garage, study, winter storage of ferns and plants" but not "as a separate housekeeping unit." The quarrel again raised the issue of the power of local taxing areas, and disturbed the hornets' nest of zoning disputes.[105]

To end another argument, the State Attorney General ruled that Crown Princess Martha would have to pay State income tax, the real estate tax on Pook's Hill and purchase her car tags. The former Thorpe estate was assessed at $136,000 and the tax amounted to $2,779.

As wells and streams dried up that fall, old residents recalled the drought of 1930. Newer ones wondered if there was any "normal" for local weather.

Spread across these two pages are, left to right, Messrs Williams, Simmons, Dellinger, Suddith, Thompson, Banfield and Marsh with their new Buick, Dodge, Studebaker, Chevrolet, Chrysler, Ford and Oldsmobile cars for 1942.

Hugo Brooks made the montage for the *Journal.*

While the 1942 model cars began arriving and theaters swung into the fall season with amateur shows and Sammy Baugh himself at the Bethesda for the first episode of "King of the Texas Rangers," some more serious events were taking place. The American Legion along with the Lions and Rotary clubs planned Armistice Day ceremonies on the grounds of St. John's, Norwood Parish, with the Rev. Joseph Williams offering a prayer and Ray Leavitt Jr. sounding taps. They placed a wreath on the Memorial Gun at Wisconsin and Bradley. Attorney Albert E. Brault of Bethesda became Defense Director of Montgomery County and began to recruit air raid wardens and organize a control center. He named Wilton T. Allen and Judge Woodward assistant chief air-raid wardens with Allen supervising the Bethesda area.

Mrs. Ernest L. Smith of Rollingwood, head of the Red Cross motor corps, organized a course in car repair for twenty women at Burrows' service station, and Mrs. B. Payton Whalen, who headed the Women's Division of Montgomery County Council of Defense, urged women to volunteer and sign up with the Central Volunteer Bureau headed by Mrs. James Parker Nolan of Chevy Chase. Registration for air raid wardens, auxiliary firemen and police began in November.

"Ed Northrup was called before Pearl Harbor," Bill Austin recalled.

I'm sure it was, and they called me in, and said "Mr. Austin, you know we only have one job, and legally it's Mr. Northrup's job and if he wants it, it's his when he comes back." But he had told me, "I won't tell them this," he was a neighbor and friend who grew up with most of them; he told me, "You take the job. I'm not coming back here, win or lose." So they said, "We'll call this Assistant Superintendent of Public Safety." I said I don't care what kind of title this is, but I sure would like to have the salary. It was a boost to what I had. Then they wanted me to get another policeman.[106]

The Brookings report still topped the list of local civic and political interests. A speakers' bureau began operating, and Mrs. Joseph T. Maguire of Chevy Chase headed the study group under Allen Gardner. Willard Day, manager of Henrico County since 1934, took a federal job and moved to Langdrum Lane in Chevy Chase. Because of his experience and expertise, his opinions were sought in the Brookings debate.

In the first of a series of study group meetings, Frederic Lee labeled the County government obsolete; "like a 1906 car," he said. "The present set-up just isn't adequate for the solution of these problems," Lee concluded. Bill Allen's ghostly political pundit, labeled Fred Lee's remarks "so overdone as to be unrealistic" and called his speech "harmful and unprovoked descriptive fiction." Bray went on to categorize those at the meeting as mostly Civic Federation hotheads, Republican leaders, Democratic Antis, and a few disinterested citizens.[107]

In the second meeting, Mrs. Dean Dinwoodey of Chevy Chase, a PTA leader, told the audience that Brookings generally praised the County schools, and Mrs. Donald F. Roberts of Bethesda, president of the Social Welfare Council, discussed the report's call for centralized control of welfare services. Dr. Meriam spoke about the need for a merit system at the third meeting. He said the report showed too many "make work" jobs now existed and that even the current police system was not truly on a merit basis.

At the fourth study meeting, Dr. Paul William Walker, University of Maryland

economist, warned of the size of the bonded debt of the county and said the report showed the "amber light of caution." In the final meeting Daniel Selko of the Brookings staff said local taxpayers were not getting their money's worth and that this was especially true in the suburban taxing districts. The County Commissioners continued their silence in regard to the report, and the study group began a series of round table discussions.

After five years of financial struggle, the Chamber of Commerce gave up on the Christmas Lane celebration. Blame was placed about equally on national defense considerations and the cost. Chairman G. Wady Imirie announced a contest for the best decorated and illuminated Christmas store window with a first prize of $25. As usual, the firemen collected and repaired toys and asked contributions for the needy.

After a dress rehearsal for sections 9A and 9D, Leland Williams' high school Footlight Club put on a production of "Icebound" in the big, junior high auditorium and drew large and appreciative crowds. Mrs. Ralph Simmons' Okipa Campfire group decorated Whittlesey's front window to boost the sale of Christmas

The firemen and some of their toys - J. L. Imirie at right

Seals, and the Pa-wa-ten-ya Group took on the job of decorating the library and its large Christmas tree. S. Walter Bogley of the Bank of Bethesda announced that the Christmas savings this year amounted to $90,000, about $40,000 more than the year before.

An easy win over N.T.S., left Coach Alan Vogt's boys' basketball team eager to take on the previous year's city champion, Roosevelt. The game was scheduled for the high school on Tuesday, December 9th.

---

[1] Quotes, including the one from the "prominent" resident, from Bethesda *Journal*, Apr. 28, 1939, which estimated 6,620 families in town. Mrs. Bradley became assistant editor on October 27.

[2] A previous group of Chevy Chase 6th graders had "skipped" a year of school when they moved at mid-year to the 7th grade in 1936.

[3] Thomas Lohn and John "Billy" Mann were the other passengers. Claxton Walker, Curtis's next younger brother, recalled the funeral, which was held from the home, and believes that some law-suits resulted from the crash. The Walkers soon left Chevy Chase and moved to Bradmoor and then to Drummond.

[4] 9,000 phones were in service. Chevy Chase Section Two, with an OK from the CCLCo, annexed Section One following residents' petitons to add some $500,000 to its tax base but delayed taking in Section 1-A.

[5] Chevy Chase Senior Troop 11 led by Mrs. J. Roy Allgyer, Troop 122 by Mrs. Lucretia Blackman and Mrs. Frank Dow, and Miss Kemp's Brownie Troop 10 all met at Chevy Chase Elementary School. Troop 112 with Mrs. R. C. Hibbins as leader, Troop 93, Mrs. Donnell B. Young, and Troop 39, led by Mrs. James Baldwin, met at Leland. Mrs. L. E. Warren's Troop 29 met at Chevy Chase Methodist while Troop 45 assembled at Chevy Chase Baptist with Mrs. O. M. Johnson. Mrs. Carl (Marion C.) Aslakson's Troop 75 along with Troop 119 led by Mrs. E. D. (Laura H.) Ellis met at All Saints. Mrs. Aslakson had been a member of the first Girl Guide group in Savannah. Other Girl Scout troops and leaders included #84, Mrs. Kenneth Rouse; #56, a senior group; #43, Mrs. William D Appel; #42, Mrs. H. C. Bryant; #40, Mrs. Herman Byer; #5, Mr. Burton Marsh; #118 at Blessed Sacrament, and #30 in Bethesda. Brownies #146 led by Mrs. George Meleney met at the Battery Park clubhouse along with a new Brownie group led by Mrs. Richard Wilson and Mrs. Allen Laing.

[6]The Shatashi group, led by Mrs. Carroll (Pat) Murnane and then by Mrs. Ivan Andrews, met at the Recreation Center. Mrs. Ralph Simmons was guardian of the Wayncoza group, and there was a group called Owasakaska in Kensington and the Okia group in Battery Park with Mrs. Helen Schaefer as guardian. The Brookmont group met with Mrs. C. F. Wells. Mrs. Eleanor Hearn led one of the many Bluebird clubs. In Alta Vista, a new club, the Tanda group, had Mrs. Walter (Helen) Young with Mrs. Hazel Gough as leaders, and Mrs. Roscoe Broadhurst led Bluebirds called Welcome Robins at Alta Vista. More than 200 girls took part in the Grand Council Fire at the high school gym in the fall of 1939.

[7]Troop 204 at the Methodist Church was led by mailman Alex Britton for six years then by Louie Strosnider. The Mormon church sponsored Troop 241. Newer troops included 255 at the Methodist church in Chevy Chase led by C. W. Wahl followed by Fred Plitt and 210 of Alta Vista with George H. Richardson followed by A. E. McPherson as Scoutmaster. In Cabin John J. E. Lynch led Troop 205, and Thomas L. Walker was Scoutmaster of Troop 207 in Glen Echo. In Chevy Chase Serge Benson headed 244. Joseph Lemmo started the new Cub Pack 211, and by the time of Pearl Harbor, Cub Pack 255 had more than one hundred members.

[8]*Tribune*, June 9, 1939.

[9]Excerpts from minutes of the Bethesda Fire Board (at Station 20 and MCHS).

[10]Salaries are hard to compare. In 1941 half of those on the Federal payroll made $1,500 or less and the median urban family income was $1,463 in 1940.

[11]The volunteers' executive committee included Sumpter Embrey, William Flack, Alexander Britton, Lewis P. Stone and Robert Fremeau. There were three holdover engine captains, Gaither Musgrove, LeRoy Lochte and Frank Stone. James Peake replaced Richard Pugh on Engine 3.

[12]Frank Hall rose to become chief of the Bethesda fire department. Bargagni's men generally drilled two hours a day.

[13]*Journal*, July 21, 1939.

[14]*Journal*, June 23, 1939.

[15]*Journal*, Dec. 29, 1939 and *Tribune*, Jan. 4, 1940.

[16]*Journal*, Nov. 22, 1940.

[17]General order No. 70 (June 20, 1935) as amended on August 16, 1937, authorized the Secretary of the Navy to construct a hospital in D.C. or vicinity. The funding for land acquisition passed on April 21, 1938. There was strong and sometimes clandestine opposition to the Bethesda site with many in and out of the military proposing Walter Reed, the Soldier's Home or St. Elizabeth's as preferable. See "Naval Medical Center [1937 - 1984]," E. Caylor Bowen, editor (and for the most part, author). Some wiseguys called the tower "Franklin's erection" and named the lake after his peripatetic wife.

[18]Quotes from "Franklin D. Roosevelt and Washington Architecture" by Egon Verheyen in *Records of the Columbia Historical Society*, Vol. 52, 1989. See "Citadel of Navy Medicine" by Sidney Shallet in *New York Times Magazine*, April 18, 1943, reprinted by *Journal*, April 23, 1943. No one knew what a sheep fence looked like so the Bureau of Yards and Docks invented one, showed it to FDR, and received a "That's exactly it!" response. See Bowen.

[19]C. Lester Walker, "We Model Our Fighting Ships," *Harpers Magazine*, November 1943. Lateral tolerance for the rails was 5/1000 and level tolerance 15/10,000 of an inch. The original 107 acres purchased from Woodside Home Corp. cost $61,424 in 1937. The Navy acquired 52 more acres in 1943 and another 55 acres in 1945.

[20]In 1957, after a series of disputes, the Navy sold the property to Cabin John Gardens, Inc, a co-op of seventy-six occupant-purchasers who formed a Government Committee and paid off the mortgage in 1972.

[21]CCC records at the National Archives including annual inspection reports.

[22]All addresses are on the old scale, correct for the date given.

[23]*Journal*, Nov. 24, 1939 and Jan. 4, 1940.

---

[24] "Local Horse Unwinds Miles of Red Tape" by Theodora L. Johnson in *Journal*, May 12, 1939.

[25] Others on the board were the Rev. Francis I. Cockrell, Major Syme, Mrs. William H. Winkler, Mr. Hiser, and Mrs. Mohler. For the earlier part of this story see Chapter 8.

[26] *Tribune*, Sept 1, 1939, and *Journal*, Feb. 2, 1940. The County library system was created in 1950.

[27] Twice moved, the plaque survives in the Bethesda Regional Library on Arlington Road.

[28] Bill Duvall and his co-writers made coherent some of Pappy Jewel's history of the MCPS in the *The Town of Chevy Chase*. See also "The Rosemary PTA Library Story" by Marion Holland at the CCHS. Mrs. Bradley's article on the library is in the *Journal*, May 2, 1941.
Mrs. Kain's husband, Paul, was the well-known, long-time, Glen Echo band leader.

[29] In the collection of the CCHS and MCHS. Names not indexed in this work. The editors were Ralph Williams, Marjory Heilman, Lydia McAllister, June Heap, Anne Molander, Jean Chapman, William Bristow, Mary Jane Colton, Franklin Loving, Stella Werner, Carter Prescott and Jimmy Maddox. Contributing writers were Lee Carter, Woodlief Thomas, Rosalie Smith, Jean Webster, Brice Toole, Lowell Leake, Kendall Brooks, Dick Love, Ralph Howard, Penny Perkins, Mary Browning, Beverly Cook, Rieta Latch, Vivette Allen, Amelia Olson, Billy Wohlfarth, Donald Waite, Margaret Johnson, John Egbert, John Campbell, David Semmes, Arthur Hayes, Ralph Lee, Mary Helen Morrison, Jane Kinsman, Patty Marsh, Dorothy Smith and Dorothy Warren.

[30] Chevy Chase ES went through an epidemic of window breaking again in the summer of `42 and the spring of `43. Junior high-age boys were generally blamed.

[31] The original staff members were Mary McAndrew, Rachel Mitchell, Dorothy West and Betty Adler.

[32] Eda Schrader and most of the other 2nd graders were "chickies." Ed Burnap was the only rooster. Mary Day's dancers also participated.

[33] Moose milk has many recipes and seems to have been a generic term for fraternity punches. Farley Mowat reported the Canadian troops' WWII moose milk as a mix of "issue rum, maple syrup (when available), evaporated milk and/or chicken noodle soup. The last item is optional." *My Father's Son*, (1992).

[34] *Journal*, May 12, 1939.

[35] Based on interviews, more than half the B-CC grads of the late Thirties and early Forties were college bound. In the clas of `38, according to their yearbook, about seventy-fvie of the 160 intended to enter colleges or universities and another twenty prep schools or business schools.

[36] The *Post* All-District team, chosen by a poll of coaches and IABBO officials, included George West and Hymie Perlo of interhigh champ Roosevelt, Bob Custer of Eastern, Bob Mulvhill of Gonzaga and Shumate who had 256 points in twenty-five games.

[37] Shumate said, "Two of my fraternity brothers, Bill Hepner and Bud Montee, went to grab a banner and started that fight." But Hobart "Buddy" Montee, class of `41, denied it and said he does not recall even being at that game.

[38] In the Metro or Star tourney B-CC beat Tech but lost to Roosevelt 31-25, and the Raiders went on to defeat Eastern for the title.

[39] *Tribune*, March 31, 1939. Almost all of the above from stories in the *Journal* and *Tribune*.

[40] As early as 1937 the Edgemoor Citizens' Assoc. had asked the County to provide a playground supervisor and received permission to use school property but no help.

[41] Mrs. Morell, a native Washingtonian and Central High grad, was, during her long life in Bethesda, chairman of the Md. Federation of Women's Clubs, president of the Newcomb Club, the B-CC Public Health Lay Committee and the County YMCA, which she helped found, executive secretary of the County TB Association, a charter member of the Community Chest and an active member of the DAR, Ark and Dove, Magna Carta Dames and Jamestown Society as well an an organizer of the USO and the group that started Suburban Hospital plus the mother of five

children.   She had thirteen grandchildren and eighteen great-grandchildren at the time of her death in 1994.

[42] All Stella Werner quotes from the oral biography on deposit at the Rockville Library which was based on sixty interviews with Joseph H. Green between 1971 and 1975.

[43] *Star*, Feb. 9, 1940.   One-time prize fighter Jocko Miller, the Nat'l Women's Club pro, went over to Kenwood as Wiffy Cox's assistant.   It was a long, cold winter with six weeks of sub-freezing temperatures and snow-covered fairways, fields and lawns.

[44] As of 1992, the cooperative nursery school was back where it started in what is now called Norwood Park but is still the "Rec Center."

[45] Other Junior Chamber leaders included J. Walsh Richards, Dr. A. R. Tolley and V. M. Emory. *Journal*, Jan. 26, 1940.   The Adams quote from the *Tribune*,   March 8, 1940, and most of the above from those two papers, which raised subscription rates to $2.00 in 1940.
In another year Dellinger Motors would be the Studebaker dealer.   Bowis quotes from "Would You Buy a New Car From This Man-Please?" by Tim Larimer in *The Washington Post Magazine*, May 17, 1992.

[46] The cherry trees, which Dr. David Fairchild brought back to Bethesda in 1905 and "naturalized" in his Chevy Chase woods, led to a 1911 plan to ring the Tidal Basin.   The first batch from Japan was diseased and had to be replaced, but by 1915 the "Speedway" had springtime traffic jams. The D.C. Board of Trade sponsored the first "festival" in 1927.

[47] Springirth was paid $60 a month until 1945 when he received a $15 raise.

[48] On his first year on the job with a car, Austin made 172 arrests, 140 for traffic violations and 14 vagrants, 8 drunk and begging, 5 drunk and disorderly, 3 immoral conduct and 2 for illegal vending.   See CC Village annual reports.

[49] Historians are unsure when FDR made the decision to run.   The annual Gridiron dinner featured a huge papier-mache Sphinx with Roosevelt's face and cigarette holder, and there was some doubt even at the convention where the v-p nomination fight split the Party.

[50] *Journal*, Dec. 1, 1939.

[51] When it came time to sell the *Catholic Standard* at Lourdes, the Dalys outworked everyone and brought in scores of subscriptions when most kids were lucky to get five.   The children, in order, were Claire, Les, Hope, Dick, Frank, Phil and Jack.

[52] This myth is evidently an old and very widepread one with many permutations.

[53] The writer, who did work there, always favored plain chocolate chip, by the pre-packed pint.

[54] Jack Clark manned the Bethesda traps while Leo Day and Herbert Ehrman looked after those in Chevy Chase and Richard Cleveland had the responsibility in Somerset.

[55] *Rocky Mountain Spotted Fever* by Victoria A. Harden (NIH/Hopkins 1990).   See the long article in the *Tribune*, May 10, 1940.   The writer's father was one of the 1938 victims, transported to Georgetown Hospital by the Bethesda ambulance crew headed by Sumpter Embrey, and the writer and his brother got the shots at the NIH every summer.
In 1943, Dr. Spencer, one of the developers of the vaccine, became head of the NIH Cancer Insitute.   He lived on West Drive in Bethesda. See appendix

[56] The leaders of the Bethesda section of the campaign to knit and collect warm clothes for the British included Mrs. John A. Dickinson, Mrs. H. T. Thompson, Mrs. Alvin L. Aubinoe, Mrs. Donald F. Robert and Mrs. Scott Brewer with Mrs. Fredric P. Lee as chairman.

[57] *Journal*, Aug. 16, 1940 and *Tribune*, Aug. 23, 1940.

[58] In D.C., with 19 draft boards, 114,341 registered for the "So long dear, I'll be back in a year" draft sometimes called "OHIO" for "over the hill in October."

[59] By 1940 the Washington Aqueduct had 720,000 people in its service area.   Average summer daily consumption of water was 121.5 million gallons (MG) with maximum 152.6 MG.   By the end of the war those figures were 161.7 and 194.1 MG.   U.S. population   was 131.6 million in 1940 and 56% urban.   Federal jobs increased from 22% in the metro area in 1930 to 32% in 1940.

[60]John Henry Sullivan Jr. - "I climbed up the steel frame of the Naval Hospital. Joe Cantrel and I sneaked in and climbed up ladder by ladder, floor by floor, and when we got up to the top we had the most beautiful view of the whole area."

[61]On the other side of Old Georgetown Road, Bachrach was having a different kind of dispute with the County about the sidewalk, as shall be seen.

[62]There is also a photo of Joe doing a handstand on p. 107 of his yearbook.

[63]*Tribune*, September 27, 1940. The four Secret Service men assigned to guard the family were sworn in as deputy sheriffs.

[64]"Seventy Acres of Science" an exhibit on establishing the NIH campus at Bethesda by Dr. Richard Mandel at the DeWitt Stetten, Jr. Museum of Medical Research, 1991.

[65] Since it is impossible to ascertain who wrote which "Bray" columns, the by-line name is used. See Chapter 8, footnote 63. *Journal,* Sept. 27 and Nov. 8, 1940.

[66]See *Journal*, Nov. 8, and *Tribune*, Nov. 15, 1940. FDR, after hanging "Martin, Barton and Fish" around Willkie's neck, won 55% of the popular vote carrying 38 states with 449 electoral votes. Willkie won over perhaps six million new GOP voters including many first-time voters.

[67]*Journal*, Nov. 1, 1940.

[68]Some B-CC basketball players did keep playing for their fraternity teams. Al Sherline recalled getting hurt in one game and then having to face coach Vogt. A fraternity football league of sorts existed and saw some very rough games. Few players had pads or helmets.

[69]Regulars on that first team: Plitt, McNutt, Hillock, Lowe, Grenfell, Werner, B. Scott, McGowan, Seward, Williams, DeBinder, Bell, Miller, H. Scott, B. Duvall, W. Duvall, L. Jenkins and Eaton. Subs: Appel, Snyder, Manchester, McLeod, Gottschall, Boyer, Bill Cremins, Sorrell, Van Wagner, V. O'Brien, Garwood, Gauld, McCullough and Keyser. See both local papers. Careful readers should note that football was being played by public schools on the Eastern Shore in 1940-see later discussion regarding 1944 team. Football in high school was endorsed by various groups. One of the earliest was the Young Men's Democratic Club of Chevy Chase in May 1940.

[70]The winning sophs: captain Don Swenson, Al Sherline, Buddy Stevens, Carter Squire and Don Simmons, a Baptist Home resident.

[71]The JV team, led by Al Sherline and Loring Appleby, also beat Blair twice.

[72]*Journal*, Dec. 6, 1940.

[73]The connections between this organization and the post-war rescue squad are Dunnington and the money held by Doyle's father from the sale of the Packard. See *Journal*, Dec. 27, 1940.

[74]Beer continued to wholesale for $1.60 a case, but the County discontinued the private wholesalers' practice of giving discounts for quantity purchases.

[75]Local 639A, chartered 12-6-37, and #1501, chartered 10-1-41, merged in 1958 to form Local 400 of the Retail Clerks International, which joined with the Amalgamated Meat Cutters and Butcher Workmen of North America in 1979.

[76]The foreman of the jury was J. Russell Allnutt. The other jurors were John A. Wrightman, James H. Nolan, George H. Jones, Earl L. Holland, Clarence C. Offutt, Edward A. Henderson, Ronald L. Banks Sr., John L. King, Harold A. Pierce, J. Vinson Peter and Joseph B. Pyles.

[77]Mostly from the *Evening Star*, Apr. 16, 1941. Also see *Post* and *Times-Herald* on April 17. The Broadhurst quotes from the *News*, Apr. 16, 1941. Neither Bethesda paper ran the story - probably because it was news everyone knew by that Friday and possibly out of sensitivity for Judge Wilson's family.
At the time the volunteers claimed ninety-eight members including fifteen charter members and twenty-five with at least eight years experience.

[78]From contemporary newspaper accounts. Cross examination quotes from the *Evening Star*, April 10, 1941. Everhart was pardoned by Gov. O'Conor in October 1942 after serving about sixteen months of his four-year term. He completed Army paratroop training in 1944.

[79]See Chapter 17 of *A Grateful Remembrance* by MacMaster and Heibert for a full discussion of the report and the eight-year Charter fight that followed.

[80]*Star* and *Post* stories, March 16 and 17, 1945.

[81]Oral history of E. B. Lee by James Scull, 1977, MCHS, made thirty-five years after the event.

[82]See *Government of Montgomery County Maryland: A Survey Made at the Request of the Board of County Commissioners*, The Brookings Institution (1941), in the collection of the MCHS and at the Rockville Public Library.

[83]The League of Women Voters, founded in 1921, was revitalized in the mid-1930s under its President, Mrs. James V. Bennett. No group worked harder in the Charter fight. In 1948 Mrs. Himstead became the first woman member of the County Council.

[84]From contemporary newspaper reports. The *Post* quote from March 16. The Hagner quote and Werner letter from the *Journal* of April 4. The Werner quote is from her oral autobiography by Joseph H. Green at the Rockville Library. Hollister's sermon is in May 9 *Journal*. The Hunt letter is in the *Tribune* of May 23, 1945.

[85]See *Journal*, April 11 and May 16, 1941.

[86]Eddie Rickenbacker was injured in this crash of an Eastern "sleeper" caused by an altimeter and pilot error.

[87]The spring `41 roster of the Shopping Center: Clover Crest, House of Fashion, Baby Mode, Corrine's Hats, Mrs. Erk's Gift Shop, Horney and Hurt, Lakeview Market, Montgomery Ward, Peoples Hardware, Rosalind Beauty Salon, Sherwin Williams, Thornton Studios (photographer) and Whittlesey's.

[88]Sunday *Star*, April 13, 1941.

[89]The Cantrel boys' mother, Catherine Kelly, had died when they were born. The new twins' mother was Esther Kelly, Cantrel's first wife's cousin.

[90]See *Journal*, March 14 and 21, July 25; *Tribune,* April 25, and Aug. 1, 1941. Sacks and Warwick quotes in *Tribune*, April 11. The Civic Federation had to vote twice on the issue.

[91]*Tribune*, May 9, 1941.

[92]The new CCFAC officers were Bernard Doyle, 1st lieutenant; Edger Tuller, sergeant; Jean Fontaine, secretary and Jean Roundtree, treasurer.

[93]See Oakmont records for more on both Casey disputes.

[94]See Equity case #9953. The Oakmont Citizens' Association's annual meeting usually took place in the log cabin behind Mr. Daley's home.

[95]*Congressional Country Club 1924-1984* edited by Anne Riley Dolan, the history by Neil Strawser, gives a good picture of the collapse of the original grand plan.

[96]Among the African-American men from Bethesda inducted in late June were Cleveland Clipper, Charles Swann, Sylvester High, Clarence Bates, Ralph Windear and Judge Lee Snapp. The local papers often carried the names of only the whites drafted.

[97]*Star*, July 8 and 9, *Journal*, July 11, 1941. The case evidently ended up in Juvenile Court, and no press reports have been found.

[98] The Chamber of Commerce awarded Father Little the Kuhn Cup in 1942 for his "contributions to Bethesda." The cost of the church-school-convent including furnishings was $225,000. Corcoran was the third Grand Knight of the Rock Creek Council and was succeeded by John Heister, James Shannon and Sylvester Mittenberg.

[99]Many teachers are forgotten over the years, but the writer found not one of Sister Ellen Glynn's students who did not remember her very clearly. (See Jim Quinn.) The other members of the original staff were Sister Emma, principal; Sister Charles Louise, the housekeeper; and Sisters Caroline, Helen Regina, Elaine Francis and Elizabeth Joseph. The convent contained twelve bedrooms, four baths, a large community room, dining room, kitchen and two reception rooms.

[100]Survivors were those who accurately assessed what could be done for fun in a crowded classroom and who also learned not to duck Father Sweeney's quickly thrown erasers. They always

wondered if the sisters ever figured out how all those paper wads got into the light fixtures or what caused the noises in the heating system and how "brazen" and "brass" were related.

[101] Tudor Place is the old Peter home in Georgetown.

[102] Fifteen players returned including backs George Keyser, Sam Miller, Spek Fitzgerald and Harvey Bloomberg and linemen Gordon Manchester, Donald Shoemaker, Bill McGowan and Tommy Gauld. Among the new boys trying out were Hubert Carlock, Bus Myrstik, Jack Sullivan, Bill Humphries and Bob Watkins.

[103] Thomas (Loring) Appleby, student council president at Leland as well as president of the sophomore and junior classes at B-CC, only recalled that the senior class president "had to make a speech," and he was not very interested in doing that. When his father found out he had been chosen "best looking" by his classmates, he said, "I can't think of anything less important you could have won," and the son agreed.

[104] *Pine Cone*, Oct 22, 1941 et seq. - from Chet McCall's collection now at the MCHS.

[105] See Oakmont correspondence on cotton house from 1939 to 1948. Other experimental houses in Bethesda included a large copper house on Edgemoor Lane (torn down in 1994) and four smaller ones on Montgomery Avenue and several steel houses with real Pullman kitchens in Huntington Terrace.

[106] Austin did the job for the next forty years and finally convinced the Village elders to call it "town manager" after he tired of explaining the title. Northrup kept the title and did much of the town's legal work during the war while he was stationed in D.C. Austin was promoted at the war's end while Northrup still served the Village in "an advisory capacity."

[107] *Journal, Tribune*, Oct. 24, 1941.

CHAPTER 10

Everybody's life was going to change

Dawn, faintly pink, led to a cold, cloudy, winter Sunday. The paper boys puffed steam as they dragged their clattering wagons through the neighborhoods and slid fat Sunday *Star*s and Washington *Post*s or *Times-Herald*s under welcome mats or inside storm doors. In the early Masses at Our Lady of Lourdes, fasting altar boys hurried through their Latin responses hoping to get home for the first crack at the funnies, especially this week's "Spirit" comic book, while their mothers stirred up pancakes or fried scrapple and French toast.

All over Bethesda youngsters lay on living room rugs or slumped in easy chairs to read about Joe Palooka, now in uniform, talking Knobby into investing in Defense Bonds instead of betting on a sure thing. Prince Valiant and his beautiful princess were still in danger on that island, and the Katzenjammer Kids and Smokey Stover were up to their usual, dumb tricks. Some kids pointed out the Lansburgh's ad to their parents; two Lionel trains were on sale Monday only, $6.99 for the regular set and $10.99 for the one with the whistling locomotive. On the sports pages they saw that it looked like both Sid Hudson and Cecil Travis were going to be drafted, as if the Senators did not have enough troubles.

On that first Sunday of December in 1941, the newspapers were full of wedding announcements, and almost everyone who was anyone was planning a Christmas party according to the society columns. The Hiser was showing "A Yank in the R.A.F." with Tyronne Power and Betty Grable, and the Bethesda had Dorothy Lamour in a sarong saga.

Christ Lutheran marked its seventh anniversary with a special Sunday school assembly and Reverend Vogeley's sermon, "I Love My Church." The Presbyterians heard their minister speak at some length on "The Romance of the Bible." At First Baptist, Pastor Nelson's sermon was about "Christian Ties." The young people at the Methodist Church planned a "Shipwreck Party" while the Ladies Guild at St. John's prepared for a Christmas Gift Sale and Dessert-Bridge.

The local fire fighters scheduled a morning meeting at the Chevy Chase station house to form a chiefs' organization under the Civilian Defense Council. And sixty-four Bethesda-area teams were getting warmed up for the *Star* duckpin tourney, which was to begin the next week. Many Bethesdans bundled up to go down to Griffith Stadium for the last game of the pro football season, but most fans would just listen to it on the radio. The Redskins hoped to break a four-game losing streak and end with a 6-5 record, their worst since 1935. Except for the drug stores, movie theaters and a few eating places, Bethesda was closed.

At three minutes after seven that morning just outside Pearl Harbor, the destroyer *Ward* dropped depth charges on the Japanese submarine it had fired at fifteen minutes previously. Lookouts spotted black, oily bubbles in the destroyer's wake. At about the same time the radar station on Oahu's northern coast reported a large group of incoming aircraft. Probably B-17s from the Mainland, the authorities decided. The attack on Pearl Harbor

began at 7:49 am, Hawaii time. At Griffith Stadium it was about ten minutes until kickoff, and late arriving fans were fumbling for quarters to pay local children to "watch" their cars or were stepping from streetcars and hurrying toward the turnstiles and their seats. The general talk was that they sure hoped this season ended better than the last one had when the Bears had destroyed Sammy Baugh and company 73-0. By kickoff the sun appeared, and the temperature slowly rose to 41°.

At the White House, Mrs. Roosevelt entertained thirty guests at lunch, but the President begged off, ate with Harry Hopkins and then worked on his stamp collection. Secretary of the Navy Frank Knox informed the President of the attack almost immediately. At 2:05 FDR called Secretary of State Hull, who was awaiting the Japanese emissaries, and then had Steve Early contact the news services. At 2:25 pm bells clanged on the teletype machines as the wire services ran the bulletin: "White House Says Japs Attack Pearl Harbor."

Reporters at the Stadium first suspected something when the AP man was told, "Keep it short." At the end of the first quarter, the word came: "The Japanese have kicked off. War now." Ray Michaels began paging high-ranking military officers on the PA system. By half-time only one photographer walked the sidelines as the favored Skins went to the locker room trailing. Rumors stuttered through the stands as more announcements boomed out calling diplomats, newspaper circulation managers, admirals and generals. The game went on. Except for the few who had successfully eavesdropped on the press box, the crowd cheered in confused suspense. Local radio stations broadcast the news just before three that afternoon, but in those days very few fans took their bulky portable radios to the games. A thermos or flask was much more important.[1]

"Little" Stella Werner was one of the first young Bethesdans to hear the news.

Daddy was in the basement working and mother was upstairs, and I can remember Daddy had the radio on. I can hear him holler to this day, "We're going to war!" and mother came to the top of the steps and said, "What?" He said, "Come here," and we both went downstairs and became kind of paralyzed as we listened to the radio.

The man Stella later married, Leroy Allison, was working at the skeet club out near Locust Grove.

It was a bitter cold day, and my brother and cousins heard it on a car radio. I had read about Pearl Harbor in Reader's Digest *and started telling them about it, and one member said, "Leroy, don't you know that's secret information.'"*

Charlie Hughes also heard the news on the radio.

Right after Thanksgiving when I was in the ninth grade, we beat the Georgetown Boys Club and the next day we played Cleveland Park at the Rec Center, and on the first play I hurt my hip, knocked it right out of the socket. It was cold as hell, and I guess I hadn't warmed up. I was in a cast for about four weeks, and on that Sunday I was lying in bed with that cast on, and I didn't think much of the announcement. I wanted them to get back to the game; they were playing the Eagles. My father explained it to me.

Billy Miles and her sons were at the Presbyterian church on Chevy Chase Circle. "I heard about it while the kids were in Sunday school. We were not surprised," she said. "We had been expecting it." Her son Murray recalled thinking "It was the end of the world." Thomas Walton Jr. was getting ready for church when he and his family heard the news at their school on Old Georgetown Road. "After we got home, one of the teachers came over, and we talked about it. We were shocked." On Stanford Street, George Mishtowt and his brother listened to the Redskin game and, when they heard the news, got in their car and drove down Massachusetts Avenue to stand with a quiet crowd in front of the Japanese Embassy and watch men burn documents in the yard. Mr. and Mrs. Marvin Simmons were over in Virginia inspecting some tools a man had for sale. "He was looking at what the man was selling, and we were sitting out in the automobile with the radio on, and they announced it. Of course," Virginia Simmons said, "I didn't know where it was. I had never heard of Pearl Harbor."

Tempe Curry Grant, a bride of less than a year, was playing bridge when the news broke up the game. Joseph Devereux's eight-year-old daughter Ann was sitting on the wall between the two houses her family had long owned on Bradley Lane when someone ran out with the news. She wondered what would happen to her Uncle Jim out on Wake Island. Major James Devereux's seven-year-old son Patrick was at his mother's home in New York. Farther up Bradley, 17-year-old Joe Cantrel heard the news on the radio and was soon out selling *Daily News* "extras" on the streets of Bethesda.

Carroll Grenfell and some of his buddies had "snuck" into Landon, played some basketball and then went down to a beer joint and heard the report in the car going home. John Troth was at Reuben "Smokey" Stiver's house.

It came over the radio on my first date with my wife. She was my cousin and had come up here from Kentucky to work for the FBI. We were having a party. It was a shock, a real shock.

Buzzy Potter also remembered exactly where he was and who he was with. He nodding twaord his wife:

It was her birthday. We were on a Sunday date in that `36 Ford, up on Jones Mill Road near the end where the beltway is now, sitting there listening to Sammy Kaye's program enjoying each other's company out near kissing rock in Rock Creek Park. It was cut off with the announcement that the Japanese had bombed Pearl Harbor. We went home. We knew everybody's life was going to change.[2]

Loretta Wilson drove to Union Station to pick up her boyfriend who was arriving from Ft. Bragg.

We came up Massachusetts Avenue past the Japanese Embassy, and there was all this excitement, and we didn't know what was going on. I didn't have a radio in my car. And when we got home, his buddy told him. I didn't even know what Pearl Harbor was.

Hazel O'Neal was at home.

My brother Gene had been drafted, but he was one of the older ones. He was stationed at Ft. Meade hoping he would be discharged, and he was home lying on the couch and listening to the radio. When they announced that Pearl Harbor had been hit, he jumped up and said, "Now I'll never get out of this army." He didn't like it for anything.

Milkman Roland Custer had been out for a Sunday drive, visiting relatives.

We were over to my brother-in-law's and coming home with all the kids. Coming through town, up Pennsylvania Avenue, we saw all these soldiers up on government buildings with guns. They were guarding everything. I said, "What the hell's going on?" So we get home and turned the radio on and found out.

Hartley Day cried when he heard the news. "It didn't really sink in except, God, we're at war. I delivered papers that morning and crashed out on the couch, listening to the radio. I felt bad." High school junior Al Sherline was at his girlfriend's house listening to the radio when they heard the news. "I had no idea what it meant," he said.

Young Jim McAuliffe had been hanging around Miller's golf range that Sunday picking up some dimes for gathering up buckets of balls.

I was walking from there on the parking area, the Hot Shoppe parking lot backed up to Miller's parking area, I was in that general vicinity when someone said that Pearl Harbor had been bombed. I was aware that something very significant had happened, and we were going to war.

Frank Lozupone was on maneuvers with a topographic company.at Fort Jackson, Mississippi. Some of the older men had their orders to go home and others over twenty-eight were expecting to get out when they heard the news. His wife-to-be, Patsy Royster, was visiting in New York and had been listening to a Shostakovich symphony when the music was interrupted. For some reason she went to Times Square. It was empty.

Cleveland Clipper had been in the Army seven months and was an acting buck sergeant helping build Egland Field near Pensacola.

I thought I was only going to be in a year, and I was in fifty-five months. That was a long year. It had been raining for two weeks, and one boy had just gotten his ring back in the mail, and we all went out and got drunk. Alongside the road a man sold him a whole case, twenty-four pints, of Ancient Age, and he got crazy drunk.

One boy had a radio and hollered, "Did you hear that? Listen to the radio!" And then they asked me since I was the oldest man down there, I was 33, what was this Pearl Harbor and where was it at. I said it must be near the water, but I didn't know where it was, and I still don't. But I knew what it meant.

Many other Bethesdans were also out of town. Edmund Bennett was at Stanford and heard the news in the morning. "That night they turned off the power all over the Bay area. Everybody was frightened. It was a complete blackout." Robert Rickey was studying in his room at Dartmouth when he heard a commotion in the hall and learned that the Japanese had bombed Pearl Harbor. Austin Carlin was pushing a car up Canal Street in New Orleans, and Bernie Doyle was coming home from a Bryn Mawr junior prom weekend when they heard the news. Al Jamison was getting ready to play in the Miami Open, and he "heard it all over. The tournament went on." Bill Metzel was a freshman at Staunton Military Academy, and he watched the cadets celebrating in the

quadrangle. His father was a naval officer on convoy duty; he did not join them.

Laura Tuckerman was staying with some Swedish friends in Philadelphia.

We were going to have cocktails with some other old friends from Washington. And it was snowing slightly. My host and hostess were out in the car, and I came running out and started saying "I didn't mean to keep you waiting" or something, and they said, "Shut up and listen" They had the car radio on. And that was it. Pearl Harbor. I'll never forget it.

I had a number of things planned, and I didn't know what to do, so I went on to New York where I had a luncheon date with some young man. And he said, "What would you like to do?'" It was a very overcast day. I said, "I want to go up in the Statue of Liberty," which I'd never done in all the times I had been to New York. So that's what we did.

Edward R. Murrow, recently returned from London, was playing a second round at Burning Tree when someone brought word of the attack. Murrow asked what the source was, and when he was told it was Reuters, decided that it was not good enough and finished his round. Later after the news was confirmed, "Murrow sat down, deep in a locker alley, put his hands to his face, and quietly wept."[3]

Horace Hampton was with the telephone company, and he was called in to work.

FDR called and said disconnect all the German and Japanese phone lines. I said I'll disconnect them, but I think it's the wrong thing to do. I called the FBI and my friends called Hoover who told Roosevelt that we were listening in on all those lines to find who their contacts are, so within an hour we had those lines hooked back up.

Presley Wedding, then teaching architecture at Catholic University, recalled:

I was at a gas station on Rockville Pike on my way to Urbana, Maryland, to talk with my cousin, who was a Methodist minister, about making arrangements to marry my girlfriend and me. She was with me. We stopped at a gas station to get filled up, and they had the radio on and we heard about it. Unbelief! I hadn't kept up with things. I was occupied with other concerns. I couldn't believe it. We went up there and talked to my cousin and got married on Christmas Day. The world had changed.

A. D. "Mickey" Harris got the news a different way.

We were going roller skating and heard about someplace called Pearl Harbor being bombed.

We didn't know what Pearl Harbor was so when we came home that evening there were soldiers at every place you could get to the water supply on Conduit Road, and the Army had taken over the upper level of the firehouse, had trucks pulled into there. Then we knew.

Gordon Tuohey heard the news at his mother's house and then watched the soldiers arrive.

There's natural drainage ditches that go under those tunnels on Conduit Road. Twenty-four hours after Pearl Harbor there was a tent pitched by every one of those culverts and a soldier from Fort Myer with a rifle. And they stayed there 24-hours-a-day, all the way from Great Falls to the District Line. If you walked the road at night, you walked the middle of the road. There was a lot of dogs and cats killed. And the Women's Auxiliary had a Christmas party for 200 of those men that year.

Loretta Tuohey was working as switchboard operator on Sundays at the Governor Shepherd Apartments, one of her several jobs, when she heard the news on the radio. Both Tuoheys recalled that the first question most people asked was "Where's Pearl Harbor?"[4]

Grace Sims, Mrs. Lewis Sims, was at home in Rollingwood and awfully busy.

I was giving a tea for Radcliffe alums. I was chosen or volunteered. I was working hard fixing those sandwiches and so forth, and my husband was abolished to the den where there was no radio. I didn't know what had happened until ladies started arriving and talked about not be able to get through Massachusetts Avenue. They were delayed getting here, and near the end I realized that something serious had happened

As the ladies were leaving, I heard Mrs. Marvin, wife of the president of G.W., saying she hoped it wasn't too serious, but Pearl Harbor had been bombed, and then we turned on the radio.

The next day Mr. Sims sat in his DeSoto and listened to FDR's speech instead of going to a University of Chicago luncheon meeting.

"Sonny" Baldwin, who had attended the 73-0 debacle with his father the year before, was listening to the game in his living room.

My father was reading the newspaper, and they interrupted the ball game to make this announcement, and I was complaining about the interruption, and my father, ordinarily very tolerant of me, said, "Be quiet. This may be the most important thing that happened in your life."

Chet McCall was shooting baskets in the driveway of his home at 44th and Leland Streets when he heard the news, and Kenny

Poerstel was listening to the Redskin game and watching his sister, Shirley, play catch with her Marine date in the field across from their Wisconsin Avenue home. The Marine tossed him the football, buttoned up his uniform jacket and disappeared in a hurry.

Willie Bort and some of his friends from Woodmont played football down at the Whitehall school that afternoon.

We came to Emmy Lou's store, and stopped in there and heard all this going on about the attack. And Joe Usuda said, "Well, I feel sorry for the United States. The Japanese are going to wipe them out." And we like-to've killed him. We beat the hell out of him.

Alton Cleveland, as he often did, rode the trolley all the way down to the 7th Street wharfs and then took it back out to Takoma Park to go to work at his family's restaurant on 4th Street. When he got off the streetcar, a kid was standing on the corner with a bunch of papers yelling about war. "That's how I found out," he said. "But I didn't understand what it meant until I saw my father's face." Cleveland had one brother in the service already and two others who were draft age.

Jack Sullivan was pumping gas at Gordon Burrow's station when he heard. He was not sure where Pearl Harbor was, but he did understand what an attack on the Pacific fleet meant. Lois Copenhaver's mother, Helen Too, was addressing Christmas cards while listening to the symphony on the radio. She called her daughter down to listen to the news. In Battery Park, the Kohins heard about the attack while listening to the Redskin game. It was "shattering," Mrs. Kohin recalled.

Sixth-grader Jane Bradley and a group of neighborhood friends had gone to the matinee at the Hiser. She said, "When my father picked us up in front of the post office, he told us, 'The Japs have bombed Pearl Harbor,' but none of us knew where that was." Ken Muir, who was eight, recalled how angry he was that his favorite radio shows were not on that afternoon; "There was just all this news."

Meanwhile at Griffith Stadium, the Redskins were making a comeback, and the crowd roared early in the fourth quarter as "Slinging Sammy" Baugh connected with rookie Joe Aguirre for a touchdown to tie the game. Somewhere up in the stands, now almost emptied of flag-rank officers, a young ensign named John Fitzgerald Kennedy joined in the cheers.

Bill Duvall and his father had season tickets, and "during the ballgame, we knew something had happened because they started this business on the public address system, will Admiral so-and-so please report to his office. We watched the game, but we knew something had happened." Leslie Bell was in the box seats he had bought from George Preston Marshall when the Redskins came to town. He thought people were leaving because they were disgusted with the Skins' efforts and did not find out what was going on until he got back to Edgemoor.

Ed Gauvreau went to the game with a buddy, a salesman who peddled things to his office. He said, "Sure, we heard the announcements, but we didn't know what was going on." Leon Sherman, who had season tickets, sat in the field stands with his friend Dr. Raymond Fields and noticed the growing hub-bub. Bill Austin, by then Section Two's assistant town manager, remembered the constant PA calls for captains and admirals. English teacher Kay Greaney was there with her brother-in-law's group of about thirty people in the construction and millwork businesses. "Charlie Malone was my favorite on the team," she said. "We had more fun, but every once in a while an announcement would come out for Rear Admiral so-and-so or General so-and-so."

Robert Stevens had season tickets until Sammy Baugh retired.

I was going to fight the draft until the Japs dropped that thing on Pearl Harbor. I was out watching the Redskins beat the Eagles. Time that game was over the stadium was half empty; all the uniforms were gone.

Sonny Marsh was at that game, too, and so was Jim Quinn who started using his mother's ticket when his sister was born in 1939. He remembered his father discussing the PA announcements with their neighbor Mr. Tobin. Leslie Bell Jr. and his friend Harry Lee watched the game from bleacher seats as did B-CC senior Loring Appleby and junior Bob Brewer who rode the streetcar to the stadium. College students Bell and Lee knew the draft would soon be after them when they turned on the car radio after the game, but Bob Brewer did not understand all the calls for generals and admirals until he got home that evening.

Near the end of the game, short runs by Andy Farkus set up Baugh's third touchdown pass, again to Aguirre, and the Redskins won 21-14. As some fans rushed to tear down the

goalposts, others hurried toward the exits to find out what was going on. Those with car radios, like the Quinns, got the news on the way home. Ed Gauvreau and Bill Austin recalled seeing boys selling extras with the war headlines as they left the stadium. Bill Duvall's mother met him and his father two blocks from the stadium and told them the news. The next day when Duvall went to work at the new War Department building at 23rd and Virginia Avenue, soldiers with fixed bayonets stood in front of every entrance.

Nine-year-old Donald Robertson was also at the game as was his father, but they did not sit together.

A fellow on Leland Street in a house just completed then, 124 East Leland, Bill Bonneville, and I pulled his mother's crab grass at ten cents an hour to buy one Redskins season ticket for $9.90, that was the season price. His parents, I think, had tickets and knew somebody in the office. We got one ticket and shared the seat. Both of us sat in it, one would sit forward one half and back the next half. They had an arrangement with the guy at the turnstile to let us in on one ticket.

We had heard all these public address announcements. That day we rode with my father and Ted Rogers' father, I think, and heard about Pearl Harbor riding up Meridian Hill at 15th or 16th. My mother had tried to have my father paged because his paper, PM, wanted to get in touch with him.

I remember standing by the mantelpiece at 6 East Melrose Street with two other kids from the neighborhood, and we were talking about how easy this war was going to be because Japan was a small country, and it would be over in three weeks."

That night many Bethesdans polished brass and brushed uniforms they seldom had worn while on duty in the District of Columbia. On that cold, grey Monday the city was full of Navy blue and olive drab. Some people started hoarding food. Sumpter Embrey did not have a radio in his car and spent Sunday visiting his wife's people down in Warrenton. He came to work on Monday, turned on the radio and was shocked to hear that America was at war. Like many others, he recalled FDR's "Day of Infamy" speech.[5]

In several ways December 7th marked the end of the first part of Bethesda's story just as it was a turning point for the United States and the rest of the world. Isolation was as dead as Prohibition, but Jim Crow lived on. Women were about to put aside their aprons and go to work in government and industry; many would find they liked it. The day when a middle class woman could easily afford a maid was almost over. The Naval Hospital joined the NIH as a major employer, and the town that once had, at most, two doctors at a time soon had more per acre than any place on earth. The building boom, except for apartments, just about stopped, but the local population grew explosively. Soon there were no spare rooms in town. Everybody really did sleep here.

For Bethesda the war was busy, stimulating, heart breaking. Nothing was ever the same.

---

[1] Hawaii was five and a half hours behind D. C. in 1941; when it was noon in Washington it was 6:30 am at Pearl Harbor. This work uses Gordon Prange's times. Povich column, Dec. 8 *Post*.

[2] Potter's lovely Ford phaeton was one of the stars of the TV mini-series "War and Rememberance."

[3] *Burning Tree Club: A History 1922-62*.

[4] The original guard unit was probably from the 12th Infantry Regiment of the 16th Brigade later replaced by men of the 176th Infantry and still later by the 804th MPs.
The Corps of Engineers, concerned about the security of the aqueduct since the Spanish-American War, had produced plans including chain link fencing, but little had been done.

[5] See David Brinkley's *Washington Goes to War* (1988), Chapter IV, for more on that day in town and Prange's *At Dawn We Slept*, (1981) Chapters 62 and 63, for the event itself.

CHAPTER 11

B-town Goes to War

When the young corpsmen at the Naval Hospital tired of hanging around the Ship's Service soda fountain or wanted to avoid the Saturday night hot dogs and beans down in the mess hall, they headed for B-town. It was just a short walk down one hill and up the next. When the off-duty soldiers who guarded the aqueduct had enough of playing pool or shooting the breeze with the firemen in Glen Echo, somebody would suggest, "Let's go over to B-town where the action is," and they would promote a ride from one of the loungers or start hitch-hiking up Conduit Road to Wilson Lane. It was not long before "B-town" became part of the slang of Bethesda's adolescents as well as of the visitors in uniform who crowded the bars and sidewalks on weekends.

Of course, many servicemen headed downtown to the dingy joys of 9th Street's burlesque, peep shows and tattoo parlors, plus the big band stage shows and all those government girls, but some never got south of the District Line. B-town's activities and at-tractions were manifold. Most of the ser-vicemen had never seen duckpins, but they flocked to the alleys and even sat and ap-plauded the league action when they could not find a lane to bowl on. Pinboys hustled sailors shamelessly, challenging them to games by spotting them a few pins or conning them out of bigger tips to impress their dates.

If the young sailors and Marines could put together a team, they almost always found some high school boys willing to play them in any sport. Some rough sandlot football resulted, but skinned elbows and bloody noses mended around gas station soft drink boxes or dark tables at D.C. beer joints.

The movie theaters established special rates for servicemen in uniform, and from time to time Gifford's, the Hot Shoppe, the Tastee Diner, the Hubbard House, even the Little Tavern all had their counters filled by young men in summer whites or dusty green. The Red Fox became a favorite and some-times loud hangout, generally more crowded than the "under new management" Whippet. The juke boxes played six records for a quarter and wore out "Don't Fence Me In" and "You Are My Sunshine." No one asked a sailor or Marine how old he was when he ordered a beer. Bar bets were common, and bare hands crushed many a beer glass. One local regularly paid his tab by taking a bite out of a glass. Martin's had a reputation for more sedate behavior where table hopping was discouraged and the juke box was turned down low, but a serviceman could usually find a warm companion there, too.

And Bethesda meant girls to look at, at least. You might even find one you could talk into going down to Hains Point to watch the sub-marine races, or go roller skating or just have a Coke. Maybe she would take you home for dinner or hold your hand or neck with you in the

back row of the dim movie theater. Some girls even had cars and knew where they could buy gas without a ration card.

Happy, long-legged, high school girls with their text-books clasped across their chests looked awfully good. Their younger sisters, traveling in pairs or packs, with too much make-up and too many giggles, obviously were jail bait.

Bobby soxers with brothers in the Marines or the Army. Girls who were pleased if you gave them a brass insignia or an extra set of stripes. Bright red smiles, that soft sweater and those strings of pearls. Busy girls behind the soda counters dipping ice cream or cranking a cash register at the ten-cent store. And older girls alone for the duration; grass widows who seldom passed a hitchhiker in uniform.

The schools, Scouts, the Red Cross, civic and women's clubs all did their part to make life easier for the young men far from home. Church socials, Rec Center picnics, parties, dances, carnivals and later the U.S.O. were all great. But the girls did the most.

The first year of the war brought frantic Civil Defense activity and vituperative political conflict. Blackouts and rationing became a part of everyone's life as did buying War Bonds and learning the names of remote places in North Africa and the South Pacific. But even the war did not deter local politics. The growing conflict over the conclusions in the Brookings report built steadily until it crowded out almost all other issues in the next election. Of course, E. Brooke Lee was the real issue, but the old and bitter divisions between up- and down-county reappeared as did a growing antipathy between Bethesda and Silver Spring.

In every school, most homes and many places of business, Bethesdans listened to President Roosevelt's short speech to a joint session of Congress asking for a declaration of war. Some people remembered his ringing "day of infamy" declamation better than they did the news of the attack on Pearl Harbor. In the *Pine Cone*, seventh grader Betsy Hartshorn reported that it "was a very solemn group of boys and girls that gathered in the auditorium of Leland Junior High on Monday, December 8, to hear President Roosevelt deliver his War Message to Congress." Her essay ended:

"It is up to us to do our part in helping to win this war. Just at the moment, the only thing we can do is study and work with all our might in order to be ready for whatever may come."[1]

Tuesday, December 9, the bright day some patriot with a hatchet attacked the cherry trees around the Tidal Basin, many Bethesdans felt the first frightening thrill of war. A bogus alarm caused by an "unidentified" aircraft led to an air raid alarm in New York City, which many Manhattanites simply ignored. Somehow news of the scream of sirens and the false reports of enemy planes reached the Baltimore area in a garbled form. At 1:15 pm Maryland civil defense authorities announced an air raid, whether it was practice or not was unclear. It sounded real. The authorities ordered schools closed, and many Bethesda-area students hurried home carrying the confused reports with them. When the sirens sounded, the police stopped all traffic. Everyone waited and listened.[2]

Small rumors grew in size and strength, and soon neighbors were exchanging stories about German bombers hitting New York, or

was it Philadelphia, maybe both, and other planes heading south toward the Capital. The attackers came from submarines, some claimed with a knowing look. Devotees of *Popular Science* suggested that they might have been launched from Zeppelins.

After Sunday's shock, many found the rumors easy to believe, but boys who had made models of Junkers and Stukas since the blitzkrieg in '39 wondered how they could possibly fly so far. B-CC sophomore Hartley Day and his friend John Bryan started walking back toward their homes in Somerset. They had ridden bikes to Leland for three years, but high school students did not ride bicycles. Hartley Day recalled, "I said, 'Let's go down Wisconsin Avenue,' and John said, 'No, that's where they are going to bomb. Lets go down the railroad tracks,' and I replied, 'No, they'll hit the railroad first.'" Somehow they made it home safely and waited.

"Reds" Auerbach and his Roosevelt basketball team, D.C. champs in both '40 and '41, had to turn around and go back to 13th Street because the air raid canceled the game with B-CC. The warning reached the city about 2:30 pm, but D.C. officials waited for confirmation and then ordered a partial blackout that night. They turned off the spotlights illuminating the Capitol dome for the duration.[3]

No explanation of the sirens or of the school closings was forthcoming. By the time Bethesda's head warden, Jim Christopher, received word that the alarm should be canceled, it was too late. Most of the rest of the County had ignored the signal. Nervous smiles were the order of the day. The high schools rescheduled the basketball game for Thursday, and Dr. Broome decided not to send students home again. Instead he told each school to work out its own plans, have practice drills and investigate the possible dispersal of students.[4]

Leland Junior High, by far the largest school in the area with over a thousand students, created and tested a dispersal and air-raid-shelter program before Christmas. Shortly after the war began, the school staged a few drills with all the students crowding into basement rooms and corridors and still planned to use that system in case of a "red" alert to take immediate cover. Then with the

help of the PTA and local air raid wardens, teachers identified a hundred homes in the neighborhood where a Leland student lived and a responsible adult was willing to take in and shelter ten of his or her classmates. Principal Helen Bready prepared and distributed rules, and then invited in the press and staged a rehearsal. The drill even impressed the *Pine Cone,* and the student-editor noted, "While confusion usually reigns in the locker rooms at 3:30, the drills have shown that wraps <u>can</u> be taken from lockers without noise."

The *Star's* reporter praised the effort:

It might have been the end of the school day. The children were streaming out of Leland Junior High School in Chevy Chase, Md. Yet there was something peculiar about the way they left.

This was the strange part of it. They walked in silence. It was an extraordinary contrast to the laughing, chattering groups that leave school every afternoon.

But this, it developed, was an air raid drill. And what to do in such an event had been worked out with precision at Leland. Silence is part of the training, for the school authorities figure that talk might lead to confusion and even panic if the students were following the evacuation plan in an actual enemy attack. . . .

The adjacent streets were emptied of children in a surprisingly short time. They'd simply melted into adjacent homes.

At school, a map showed the location of all the shelter-homes and a board with a

Keeping track of the classes during a drill

series of discs told when each section was "out" or back "in." The school paper reported:

> There is already a rivalry among the sections to see, which one can be the first to have all members in their seats after a drill so that their representatives can turn the "in" disc for the section first.

The editor reminded Lelanders of the praise they had gained from their air raid drills and urged, "Let's keep up the good work and help protect our new reputation."[5]

Newcomer Larry Jennings, placed in Mr. Steinert's 8-S homeroom after some test taking, recalled that the kids enjoyed practicing both the sneak attacks and the dispersal to homes. Of course, it was not long before some adolescents with typewriters and carbon paper were circulating their own directions on "What To Do In Case Of An Air Raid." A few sample "rules":

1. As soon as the bombs start dropping, run like hell. (It doesn't matter where, as long as you run like hell.)

2. Take advantage of opportunities offered you when air raid sirens sound the warning of attack; for example:

   A. If in a bakery, grab some pies or cake, etc.

   B. If in a tavern, grab a few beers.

   C. If in a movie or taxi, grab a blonde.

3. If you find an unexploded bomb, always pick it up and shake it like hell. (Maybe the firing pin is stuck.)

4. Always get excited and holler bloody murder. (It will add to the fun and confusion, and scare the hell outa the kids!)

5. If you should be a victim of a direct bomb hit, don't go to pieces. (Lie still and you won't be noticed)[6]

The Chamber's window-decorating contest became the war's first local victim, canceled immediately with the prize money given to civil defense. The Chevy Chase firemen called off their Christmas dance. The 7th Battalion of the State Guard, Lt. Col. E. Brooke Lee commanding, went on full alert. Harry Callaghan, in charge of first aid for the Red Cross, asked for donations of blankets, flashlights, tools and rope, especially rope. Under the direction of Mrs. Edward Boothby, the Red Cross began a door-to-door canvass

to raise $25,000 as part of the nationwide war relief fund drive.

Tuesday night, after the jitters of the air raid "drill" had passed, Chief Bargagni showed a crowd of some two hundred how to fight fires caused by incendiary bombs. Bargagni urged homeowners to leave their set tubs full when they were not washing clothes and to keep a garden hose hooked up even in the winter. Eager tyros flooded the rolls of the old volunteer fire department and the new Bethesda Auxiliary Fire Department where Chief E. C. Forsythe soon named district fire wardens and their assistants, organized the unassigned into teams of five, created a headquarters squad and appointed dozens of block supervisors.

One of the shortest volunteer-fireman careers was that of clothier Leon Sherman. The first time he heard the siren sound, he rushed out of his shop and ran four blocks up Wisconsin, jumped into his canvas coat and grabbed a stanchion on the back of the truck as it headed out.

> We went down Wisconsin to Western and turned right and then went out River Road where there was a shack on fire near the railroad tracks. That thing was bouncing along, and I was flying, hanging on for dear life. When we got back to Fairmont Avenue, I quit. I signed up to be an air raid warden.

The Commissioners voted $1,000 for emergency expenses and asked for contributions as hundreds of citizens volunteered for Civil Defense positions. The V.F.W., led by chiropractor Floyd J. Carter of Chevy Chase, offered the services of its membership, and the American Legion began recruiting more airplane spotters. The radio voice of the Washington Senators, natty Arch McDonald, became the area's chief air raid warden. Civil Defense scheduled the first blackout for 8:45 Monday night, December 15.[7]

Both the local weeklies and the D.C. daily newspapers labeled that first, fifteen-minute blackout, which extended from the District Line through Rockville, a "complete success." Nearly 1,500 wardens patrolled the streets, and they turned in only a few reports of uncooperative citizens.

Because D.C. authorities had opposed the original plan for a total blackout, the streetlights remained on and traffic continued to flow on Wisconsin and Connecticut

Avenues. Police at the District Line asked motorists coming into Maryland to dim their lights. In the middle of Bethesda, a forgotten neon sign glowed briefly, and the lights in the office of the gas station across from the County Building had been left on. Other than those gaffes, the only real problem noted was that many people could not hear the warning sirens. The only horn judged adequate was the one at the college in Forest Glen, which also had the best shelters in the area in the third-of-a-mile, fifty-year-old tunnels that carried steam pipes under the buildings.

MONTGOMERY COUNTY "BLACKOUT" BEFORE AND AFTER—The "gay white way" of Bethesda before last night's blackout is shown above in a view taken from the Bank of Bethesda Building. The streaks of light are made by the headlights of moving automobiles.

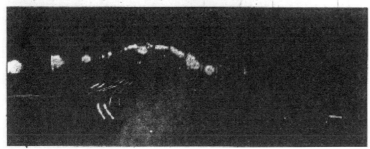

The first blackout hits Bethesda's main drag

Before the month was out the Commissioners appropriated $10,500 to buy thirty-eight two-horsepower sirens, two larger sirens, and thirty car sirens to use in rural areas. The local Lions Club immediately donated $100 and pledged to raise enough in thirty days to pay for Bethesda's siren. The County Commissioners passed the first Washington-area blackout ordinance, which included a $50 fine or thirty days in jail for failure to comply with the regulations and cooperate with the wardens. The Commissioners also allocated $300 for the construction of a plane spotter's lookout tower at the Bradley Hills Country Club.

The Bethesda area's original air raid wardens included a number of very familiar names. Trial magistrate James C. Christopher

was district warden and Billy Prescott his assistant. The precinct wardens included Frederick Berens, Harry McCuen, Hunter Davidson, Millard Peake, William Prescott Allen, and James R. Enright.[8]

Mrs. B. Peyton Whalen, chairman of the Civil Defense Women's Division, announced the appointment of area captains who were to select street leaders to organize women to disseminate information and work with air raid wardens. Despite the first false alarm, it took the men some time to realize that air raids and other emergencies might take place while the sun was shining and most of them were downtown. It was not until the end of January that Army Interceptor Command asked women to sign up as daytime aircraft spotters. The Women's Division opened a volunteer-staffed headquarters at 4713 Hampden Lane, which soon became the center for several salvage drives and other war-related activities.

The city and metropolitan area, burgeoned to more than a million, prepared for the first drill at the end of the month. In preparation, on December 21 the District of Columbia conducted a practice exercise. Almost no one could hear the sirens, and it was a complete and embarrassing failure. The metropolitan area blackout went off as scheduled on December 30, and in the city, police cars and fire stations hit their sirens, churches rang their bells and most of the town darkened.

Bethesda did not do so well. The seldom-used siren on top of the firehouse on Old Georgetown Road stuck when, as planned, they tried to sound it briefly to decentralize the fire equipment. Its continuous wail led most Bethesdans to turn off their lights twenty minutes before the drill began. When the real air raid alarm sounded, they turned their lights back on. Block wardens began shouting and running from home to home pounding on doors, trying to explain the mistake and telling confused homeowners to turn their lights off again. Most did. Two wardens who had been secretly told to report fires to the message center called the Chevy Chase Fire Department instead, and out roared the engines onto the darkened streets.

The Red Cross Motor Corps dispersed its equipment for the first time in this drill, stationing units at Bethesda and Chevy Chase elementaries and at the Glen Echo firehouse. The evaluation of this blackout led to a hurry-up call for more and better sirens and the regularization of the signals: five blasts at half-second intervals repeated three times for alarm and three long blasts for "all clear."

The next step in preparedness for the attacks that never came was the appearance of huge piles of sand beside the firehouse on Old Georgetown and at the Meadowbrook Saddle Club. Each householder had to get an invoice from his local warden, provide a large bag or bucket, and secure fifty pounds of sand, provided free by the Commissioners, for the purpose of dousing incendiary bombs. Homeowners were told not to turn off the pilot light on their gas appliances nor to turn off the gas main unless an explosion damaged their home. This talk of fire bombs and blackouts frightened some, and almost everyone took the preparations seriously.[9]

One Leland student reported on the airraid preparations at his house.

Our family, after looking at the civilian defense items, chose my room in the basement as our "Air raid shelter." It has far less window space than any other room in the house.

According to the papers, we must equip our shelter with a strong table. The only thing in our house which would suit is my work bench, which shall probably die of old age in the same place it is now. "Oh well, skip the table," say my family. "We'll get around to it some day."

Next comes a tub full of water, stacks of games to idle away the blackout, books, food and piles of it, radio, five or six flashlights, magazines, a football (to toss around), a first aid kit with aspirin, bandages, iodine and cough medicine. Add a blackout, air raid wardens, antiaircraft and the Luftwaffe and you get a hectic night!

God bless our home![10]

More organization developed. Landon's head master, Paul Banfield, became chief of transportation, emergency shelter and food services with Albert Walker as his Bethesda-area assistant. Police chief Andrew Newman organized auxiliary policemen in a meeting at Bethesda Elementary and swore in Arch McDonald and his top assistants as deputy sheriffs to bolster their police powers in enforcing blackout regulations. Some 1,300 air raid wardens began taking a first-aid course, and the Red Cross opened additional classes for ambulance drivers and started canteen-aide sessions at the Glen Echo Fire Hall.

One of those to sign-up early for Red Cross work was Mrs. Leon Sherman.

I wanted to do something to help so I went to the Red Cross. They needed somebody who could drive and was available any time. My main job was going into D.C. to get blood down on Virginia Avenue. I went out many a night, and many times took a Red Cross ambulance home. I learned how to repair engines; you had to take a course before you could drive. I used to take guys to the baseball game, too, and drove a bus. Sometimes Leon went with me, and I got him to drive the bus."

By the end of the first month after Pearl Harbor more than 4,000 volunteers were in some sort of civil defense training in Montgomery County. *Tribune* editor W. Prescott Allen praised the spirit of cooperation shown in local civil defense work and noted with seeming wonder that "there has been no public squabbling in Montgomery County about who's who or what's what or even about what to do." At the same time Robert V. Bray, Allen's political columnist, blasted the *Journal* again for its criticism of the Commissioners and wondered if the "bilious boys that write the bilge" have either "sand or sense."[11]

Two events brought the war home to many in the Bethesda area. Three days after the attack on Hawaii, the Federal Director of Priorities banned the sale of new automobile tires. An outcry and scramble immediately followed. Regulations required the inspection of old tires, banned hoarding and established an "A list" of essential users such as doctors, postmen and farmers and a "B list" for everyone else.

Governor O'Conor named J. Horace Smithey of Chevy Chase Building and Loan to head the local Commodities Rationing Board, then generally known as the Tire Rationing Board. In Bethesda, Burrows Service Station was the place to have tires inspected and to secure application blanks for new tires. For January 1942 the allocation for the whole County was eighty-one passenger car tires and sixty-eight tubes. Inner tubes that had gone to the beach and

old tires, which had been hung up as swings went back in the garage. Some tires and rims disappeared on dark nights including those on a car and a truck belonging to former sheriff Moxley. Sears advertised tire locks, five for $1.99. Drivers became much more careful about hitting curbs and avoiding potholes.[12]

The other event that made the war real to many younger people was the resignation of Harry Callaghan, Bethesda's first full-time recreation director, who enlisted in the Navy. In mid-February all men between 20 and 45, who had not previously registered with Selective Service, had to sign up. White public schools stayed open over the weekend for this registration, and the superintendent canceled Monday classes as school teachers assisted in the process. Red Cross volunteers at the registration points signed up men willing to donate blood, and in Bethesda, 217 young men agreed to become blood donors.

While the world was changing, some things, including local politics, went on as usual. It was an "off" election year, and the first local hat in the 1942 ring was Mrs. Jesse Nicholson's chapeau. In January she announced her intention to run for the Congressional seat held by Mrs. Byron. An ardent Prohibitionist, Mollie Nicholson had been on both sides of the Brooke Lee fence over the years and even left the party in `28 to support Herbert Hoover. The cognoscenti expected Colonel Lee himself to enter the Democratic primary against her when the time was right.[13]

But of more immediate interest was the continuing saga of the Brookings report. In the summer of 1941 the Commissioners, still headed by Bethesda's "mayor," Thomas Earle Hampton, had stated their intention to appoint a non-partisan committee to study the recommendations. Nothing had happened by the time the bombs fell on Battleship Row and Hickam Field. On Monday night, December 8, Allen H. Gardner of Silver Spring urged the Civic Federation to action. He criticized the Commissioners for their failure to study the long-awaited report and asked that petitions begin to be circulated to put the question of the election of a charter board on the ballot. The Federation delayed action so that delegates could ascertain the will of their constituencies.

The next week the Commissioners named a committee of thirty-six men and women headed by M-NCP&PC counsel J. Bond Smith to study the report. As the Bethesda *Journal* quickly noted, most of the committee members were either local government employees or Democratic party workers. Among the Bethesdans on the committee were S. Walter Bogley, Ruth Shoemaker, Joseph Cantrel, Royal Carlock, James Christopher, Carey Quinn and Albert Walker. It was hardly the promised "non-partisan" group.

At the January meeting of the Civic Federation, Gardner's resolution to start a petition drive was on the floor for debate. Allen Gardner, who had chaired the Federation's Brookings report study committee, emphasized that he did not intend to put the Federation on the record in support of change but only to let the voters decide whether or not to have a charter-writing board. Trial magistrate Hugh Frampton of Drummond opposed the motion, labeled the Brookings report "Utopian" and stood firmly against putting the issue before the voters. James Gill, attorney for the Liquor Control Board, called the Gardner proposal "outrageous" and stated his opinion that circulating petitions would violate the Hatch Act. Carey Quinn of Battery Park offered an amendment to put the Federation on record as opposed to circulating petitions. This ended debate on the original motion and led to adjournment.

Pseudonymous Bray in the *Tribune* suggested that the proponents did not have the votes that night, and in addition, that the charter leaders were mainly Republicans and malcontents. Editor Allen wrote that the "Civic shouters" were crying wolf and doing the County's reputation great harm, and he wondered why the Capital papers bothered to cover their meetings.

At the next Civic Federation meeting on Monday, February 9, J. Bond Smith made an impassioned, last minute appeal for delay and criticized the Brookings report's position on planning and zoning, but this time the proponents had the votes. The Federation voted 90 to 25 to begin circulating petitions to bring about a vote on whether or not to have a charter board and on the membership of that body. The seven-year charter fight had begun.

The *Tribune* headlined the pro-charter leadership's movement away from Brookings

and noted that all of the delegates from the agricultural up-county voted against the resolution. Bray saw it all as a "Civic-Republican" plot to get more Republicans to the polls in the fall. Day Thorpe in the *Journal* gave "round one" to the anti-machine forces, assumed that collecting the 8,000 signatures would be no problem but foresaw a long, hard fight when round two began.[14]

Guam fell and Wake fought on. The Japanese destroyed MacArthur's air force on the ground and invaded the Philippines. U-boats torpedoed tankers just off the Ocean City beaches. Maryland decided to issue small steel tabs instead of new auto license plates for 1942. The government asked people to stop hoarding pennies. The new phone book for Bethesda had 300 pages, twenty more than the previous edition; C&P distributed 13,500 copies. The phone company office in Bethesda blacked out all its windows and doors "for the duration." Overnight "for the duration" became part of everyday vocabulary along with "Don't you know there's a war on?" as an excuse for shortages, delays or almost anything else.

Despite restrictions and shortages of copper and steel, the building boom had rolled on through 1941 as the federal government added almost 50,000 new employees. In the Western Suburban area, construction totaled almost $7 million, a million more than the previous year. Harry J. Connor, for example, was showing a whole row of new, $10,000, three-bedroom houses on Harwood Road when the war began, and Edson Briggs had just opened his Locust Hill Estates with the *Post* display home priced at $14,950.

New businesses kept arriving, too. The Bethesda Bowling Center began operating in January `42. It was the largest private

The new Bowling Center on Old Georgetown

Forty Alleys gave bowling a new, clean look

building in the County with almost 40,000 square feet on two floors. Paneled in red gum trimmed with maple, the forty alleys were high ceilinged, well lit, air conditioned and featured lounges of blue and beige leather.

The contrast between the Bowling Center and both of Henry Hiser's cramped, smoky, fifteen-year-old alleys could not have been greater. There was even a separate room for pinball machines and a real soda fountain at the new place. Within six months manager George Peacock, a champion golfer and former manager of the Indian Spring Country Club, was greeting up to 500 bowlers a day, most of them women. A lawyer, two lumber companies, a contractor, Sanitary Grocery Stores, W. Prescott Allen's newspaper, and later the Charter Committee, rented second-floor office space, and Aristo Cleaners and Nancy's Beauty Parlor were among the first tenants in the four street-level stores. "Forty Alleys," as most Bethesdans called it, drew enough business away from Hiser that he could advertise open bowling two nights a week. The building's thick, steel-reinforced, concrete ceiling and floors made it Bethesda's biggest and best bomb shelter.

Edgemoor Ford finished its modern shop and showroom with parking on the roof and celebrated by offering a ring job and front end alignment for $49.95. E. O. Likens, a distributor of coin-operated machines, opened a gift shop near Emmy Lou's on Wilson Lane. At first he featured party supplies, magic tricks and used records from his juke boxes. He soon added model airplanes, boats and railroading equipment, and made it more of a toy store. Likens' was also a source of peas for pea shooters when grocers discouraged boys from buying their ammuntion at the markets.

When Battery Park organized for civil defense, Likens became the chief air raid warden and Robert Guthen the chief fire warden.

Christmas approached. The Hiser had the usual toy matinee to collect toys, food and clothing for needy children. The Bethesda started offering Defense Saving Stamps as change at the ticket booth, and at the Tastee Diner Ed Warner's employees agreed to accept two dollars of their weekly pay in Savings Stamps. Paper boys began selling defense stamps on their routes, and Leland ninth-grader Mickey Weaver (B-CC `45) of the Conduit Road area was among the first to win the pins and other awards offered by the Treasury Department. Well-meaning aunts, uncles and grandparents soon made Defense Stamps and War Bonds the most common and least appreciated birthday, graduation and Christmas gifts of the war years.

At Leland the usual, religious Christmas assembly featured the glee clubs and the drama club plus impressive "cathedral" windows produced by the art department. Lighted Christmas trees glowed in front of the high school and in Greenwich Forest and many other communities. At the White House, Winston Churchill joined FDR to light the national tree.

In Cabin John the women's auxiliary of the volunteer fire department threw a Christmas party for 200 of the Ft. Myer soldiers who guarded sinuous Conduit Road carrying bayonet-tipped Springfield rifles and wearing World War I helmets and canvas puttees. These soldiers, who stood lonely and boring watches at all the culverts and at the valves and access points, bivouacked on both sides of Conduit Road at Sangamore. The Army built a small PX for them, but when it was closed, the Hill Top Inn across the street got much of their business. It was not long before local children were visiting with the soldiers, sharing their sandwiches and challenging them to pinball games.

A bit later there was more neighborhood excitement when light tanks appeared on Sangamore Road and clanked up into the woods behind the reservoir to practice firing their cannon. "They fired those things up there for hours at a time," Marvin Shoemaker recalled.

At the high school, the basketball team returned to its interrupted season. The rescheduled game against Roosevelt proved to be one of the best of the year. With fifteen seconds left Al Sherline tied the game with a long set-shot, and the Barons won 33-31 in triple overtime when Bobby Cremins took a pass from Sherline and scored on a "snowbird."

The B-CC Activity Council sold defense stamps from a booth in the office and sponsored Red Cross activities as did the Girl Reserves. The shop classes began turning out incendiary bomb snuffers, and many students joined the Volunteer Messenger Corps. Principal Pyle discouraged talk of shortening vacations and graduating students in three years but participated in the active consideration of establishing a cadet corps. The students burned out of Richard Montgomery High in the spring of 1940 returned to their rebuilt school after the Christmas holidays.

Near year's end the government admitted that the battleship *Arizona* and five lesser ships had been sunk at Pearl Harbor and claimed that B-17 pilot Colin Kelly had died a hero after sinking a Japanese battleship. When Wake Island fell, pictures of Chevy Chase's Col. James P. S. Devereux, who commanded the Marines there, were in all the papers. His name led the first list of prisoners.

"Friendship," the McLean estate sold for a housing project, had its last Christmas party. Cecil Travis received his draft notice. His .359 batting average had been second in the `41 season to Ted Williams's remarkable .406. On New Year's Eve revelers jammed F Street and crowded the night clubs (cover charge at the Shoreham's Blue Room $8.50, the Mayflower $6.60, the Willard $3.50), but "restraint" marked most of the celebrations according to the society columns. The announcements of weddings multiplied rapidly in both the local and city papers, and many of the young grooms appeared in dress uniforms. On New Year's Day the OPA ended the sale of new automobiles with the dealers' existing stock held to be rationed.[15]

Friday, January 9, three, young, Navy pilots from Anacostia NAS flying, bright yellow, bi-wing Stearman PT-12's stunted and roared over Bethesda, dove at the high school several times, zoomed past Leland level with the second floor windows and brought

Bethesdans running from their homes. Sophomore "Willie" Snape was in Miss Greaney's English class in the B-CC basement, and he recalled "they really buzzed the school. You could see them from down there and hear them, too."

Leroy Allison saw them even better.

These Yellow Perils came up and bounced on the football field. We were in Lenora Aiken's French class. They flew down and touched on the field and flew over the gym and bounced down on the softball lot and came up over the main building and did that three or four times.

The *Pine Cone* reported that the "exhibition was enjoyed by the students at Leland, but was extremely dangerous." The Navy apologized, labeled the pilots' behavior "overenthusiastic" and said they would be disciplined.[16]

Washington settled in for a cold winter. By the second Sunday in January, the temperature had fallen to 6° and hundreds skated on the Reflecting Pool. On February 9 Americans went on "war time" and moved their clocks ahead one hour "for the duration." By then all aliens had been required to report to their neighborhood post office bringing with them three photos and their 1940 registration. They were asked fourteen questions and sent home to worry. More than 2,300 foreign nationals were taken into custody, the Usuda family disappeared from Woodmont, and the round up of Japanese-Americans on the West Coast began.

Albert Brault

The leaders of the Manor Hunt, the Potomac Hunt and the Redland Hunt volunteered their horses and riders to Albert Brault, executive director of the County Civil Defense Council, to carry messages and spread the alarm should the phone system break down in an emergency. Brault accepted their offer.

In Bethesda, the six evangelical Protestant churches, which had long cooperated with each other in various activities, formalized their relationship. In January at Christ Lutheran Church, after a series of preliminary meetings, they formed the Bethesda Council of Churches and established a board of directors composed of the pastor and two laymen from each church with a hundred members or less and an additional representative for each additional hundred members. Rev. Raymond A. Vogeley became the first president with Rev. J. Raymond Nelson vice-president, Mrs. Walter B. Zerbe secretary and Calvin Yowell treasurer. The organization's first projects included preparing for Lenten services at lunch time on Thursdays at the Hiser Theater and planning an Easter sunrise service in the new amphitheater at the Recreation Center. With the cooperation of the phone company, the Council welcomed newcomers to Bethesda and provided them with information about the local churches and the community.

Chevy Chase Elementary's defense activities were typical of those in local grade schools. Money was collected for the Red Cross; savings stamps were sold; afghan squares were knitted; scrapbooks were created, and air raid drills became a part of school life as fire drills had been. All elementary school PTAs had defense planning meetings that winter and developed various emergency procedures. At East Bethesda the Victory Club organized by teacher John Mahan raised money to send a carton of cigarettes a week to a selected serviceman or military base. To raise money, the club sold firewood and then put on a minstrel show.

Somerset's activities were a bit different. There a group of parents led by retired naval officer Charles Parsons decided to build a bomb shelter. They surveyed the neighborhood and, with permission, chopped down a large number of trees and hauled them to the school. They cut the logs to the proper length, split them and built barricades in front of the school's nine basement windows. With the help of the school janitor, they installed burlap-covered screens inside the windows. Then the parents stocked the basement with canned milk, fruit juice and crackers and had a shelter big enough for all 230 of the students. The PTA under president W. J. Duiker also provided each classroom with a bucket of sand and a shovel and the shelter with a garden hose, stirrup pump and first-aid supplies. Completing the project took the whole winter.[17]

At Leland Junior High School, national defense activities involved nearly everyone. Students organized two Red Cross clubs, and all the teachers enrolled in a first-aid course. Art teacher Rose Hranac's students filled the halls with "Help Uncle Sam" posters, and Vincent Imirie's committee set up tables in the main hall and sold more than a $100 of savings stamps a week. The posters also urged support of the salvage campaigns, and Lelanders piled up a thousand pounds of newspapers each week in the front hall.

The student council gave each ninth grade homeroom a specific area of salvage. Bill Humphries of 9B was in charge of rubber, and Roger Mudd was chairman of 9F, which was collecting all kinds of scrap metal. Other sections had different kinds of tasks. Jean Moore's 9C section collected jigsaw puzzles, games and books for the Army hospital, and Chet McCall had his 9D workers gathering wire coat hangers, then much in demand.[18]

Mr. Kreuzburg, one of the shop teachers, was also a second lieutenant in the Air Corps Reserve; he left in January. Rapid and continuous teacher turnover disrupted school life at Leland more than at any other local school.

Over on the highway, while some boys considered leaving high school and joining the Army or Navy, classes and social activities went on much as usual. As the first basketball game with Blair neared, the cross-creek rivalry intensified. On Monday of game week, January 26, Blair students discovered that person or persons unknown had smashed out fifty-eight windows in their school and splashed "BETHESDA" in letters two-feet high on the side of their new addition. The painters had added "Beat Blair" and some supplementary and scatological remarks. Three carloads of Blair students roared off toward Bethesda, but someone saw them leave, and when the fifteen boys arrived, they found the police waiting. The Blairites spent some time at the County Building before being turned over to their principal and sent back to Silver Spring with a warning. On Thursday Superintendent Broome canceled the game.[19]

Meanwhile the B-CC girls' basketball team captained by Marcia Boteler breezed through its schedule, avenged an early season loss to Hyattsville, beat Blair twice and then took the County championship with a two-point win over Rockville's now revitalized Richard Montgomery High School.

The boys did better in the second half of their season. Bob Cremins missed several games, but seniors Dick Poerstel and Carll Jullien, who lived with the Poerstels for a semester, improved steadily. Jullien, although new to the school, was chosen "Baron of the Year," and the Poerstels made the season a family show with sister Shirley captaining the cheerleaders and brother Kenny running the scoreboard. Coach Al Vogt had let Dickie Latimer and young Poerstel shoot baskets at halftime since they were in elementary school.

After promises by leaders of both student bodies to keep school spirit under control, on February 19 Bethesda played Blair at Ritchie Coliseum in College Park before 2,500 fans and, after a close first half, put the Blazers away in the third quarter to lead 34-17 and then installed the second team to coast to a 46-22 victory. The JV team, having an even better season than the varsity, defeated Blair 41-22 in the preliminary game. The news stories noted that it was the first game in several years without a fight. Then the varsity beat Prep, the private school champ they had lost to earlier, Coolidge and Landon and again entered the Star tourney for the city championship.

In the first round the Barons rolled over Blair again and then scraped by St. John's "iron men," who had beaten them twice in the regular season. In the final, Washington and Lee came from ten points behind to defeat B-CC 24-23 on a last-second shot. Al Sherline recalled:

I broke my foot so I was sitting on the bench with crutches. WL had a hotshot named Bobby Phillips. Seconds were left; we had two guys hanging on this guy, and he threw that thing up lopsided and it swished.

The Bethesda girls won the city championship by downing Fairfax 22-20. The girls' team had an easy time with St. Cecelia's in the first round, winning 38-14. In the title game at Roosevelt's gym, Bethesda built a 14-9 halftime lead behind Carter Dawson's shooting, but led by series MVP Peggy Mathers, Fairfax went ahead with two minutes left. Stadtler's basket tied the game at 20-20, and Betty Milne won it with a shot from the side. It was the second city title for the girls.

At Leland the first girls' varsity basketball team had an up and down season, which

began with a loss to Rockville and included two games against the faculty. Most junior high girls seemed more interested and involved with the intramural volleyball and basketball contests between the homeroom sections. The boys' team led by George Van Wagner and captain Hardy Sorrell swept through its twelve-game season undefeated and then faced Sherwood, champion the previous two years, in the first round of the tournament, a game that packed the sidelines and balcony of Leland's gym with a record crowd. Leland shut out Sherwood from the floor, won 38-5 and then took the title with a 40-11 victory over Kensington. Mr. Cross's 1941-42 team, despite having both Herbie Benson and Charlie Hughes out for most of the season, was the first in school history to finish undefeated.[20]

In the adult world, Ola Malcolm delayed her attempt to erect the plywood and cotton-board house she had purchased at a Department of Agriculture exhibit after a hearing at which twelve of her Oakmont neighbors opposed her plan and presented a petition to the Commissioners with the names of thirty more in opposition. After a month of consid-

eration, the Commissioners rescinded building permit #6081. Mrs. Malcolm, however, citing the national emergency and need for housing, finished and moved into her "garage" and rented her large, stone home.

Five months after his second wife divorced him, Bob Hagner married Mary Reed Rodgers, the policeman's former wife, at Christ Lutheran Church and took her on a Florida honeymoon. When they returned, he began a campaign to win back his Commissioner seat as an "independent" Democrat.[21]

Schoolmaster Thomas W. Walton died of a heart attack after fighting a brush fire that began on the Hiser property next door to his school on Old Georgetown Road. He had begun his career as an educator with the YMCA in Detroit and then in D.C., founded the Woodward School for Boys and worked for many years as a comptroller before returning to the area and starting the Walton School in 1939. The *Journal* editorial called him a "true teacher." His widow and son continued his work.

In February 1942, the U.S. Naval Hospital under the command of Rear Admiral Charles M. Oman moved its 200 patients and their doctors and nurses from 23rd and E Streets into the new Bethesda center. By then the hospital's twenty-story tower was a landmark that proud Bethesdans showed visiting relatives. Folks were seldom sure what to call it. Some said "Navy Hospital" or "Naval Hospital" while others adopted the term "Medical Center" or later "NNMC" for National Naval Medical Center since it included a medical school, a dental school and a dispensary in addition to the 450-bed hospital and out-patient department.

The administration building and tower with its gleaming 362-foot front and art deco flourishes boasted a lobby two stories high sheathed in curved slabs of green Vermont marble and piers of dark green serpentine. The trim was white bronze and the mezzanine rail stainless steel. Set in the floor was a brass compass face six feet in diameter while above hung an egg-shaped, white glass lamp decorated with a steel ring and capped by lotus leaves. It was a beautiful and impressive space, unmatched in the suburbs.

Originally, in an emergency, the hospital could take care of 1,200 patients, but during the war this increased to 2,000 beds and by

late 1945 to 2,464. The center housed the latest in equipment, two ward buildings, a medical library and a small "crew's" library, quarters for 250 corpsmen and seventy nurses, a garage, a laundry, a power and refrigeration building, and a theater that seated 600. Five sets of officers quarters were the only structures not built of steel and pre-cast concrete-aggregate panels.[22]

Officers' Quarters at the Naval Medical Center

The Medical School specialized in post-graduate training in such areas as field and submarine hygiene, aviation medicine and tropical diseases and in turning out class after class of corpsmen. The Dental School in the north wing trained doctors and served both the hospital and the area's naval community.

The landscaping of the site profited from the work of Marshall Finnan of the Park Service who laid out a nine-hole golf course, sculpted spring-fed Lake Eleanor and transplanted many large trees from Gravelly Point where National Airport was taking shape. The Navy planned a recreation area and an artificial lake for the dense woods in the back.

Through the winter new air raid sirens arrived; defense films were common fare at club meetings; D.C. Commissioner Russell Young became the metro-area civil defense coordinator. Men's stores began selling cuffless "Victory suits," and ad's explained how much material was being saved for uniforms. The Hecht Co. showed an $8.99 rayon gabardine Victory dress for "girls on the job."

Hardware stores advertised flashlights, pumps, blackout paint and curtain material. The Berkeley Springs Mineral Water Company took advantage of the prediction of D.C.'s chief air raid warden that the Capital "would be bombed mercilessly" by publicizing his words to sell its bottled water. The Post quoted the same warden as saying, "I believe we are going to die by the thousands on these streets within six months." And early on the morning of February 26, D.C. police dispatchers overheard an Army equipment check announcing a "yellow alert," and the sirens screamed at 1:31 am. It took thirteen minutes to trace this "real thing" warning and sound the "all-clear." Washingtonians sheepishly came out from under their beds.[23]

The next, big, planned drill was a ten-hour blackout on March 3 from 8 pm until 6 am. It was almost flawless. A Takoma Park warden suffered a dog bite that rainy evening, and the police visited a River Road home where residents were reluctant to douse their lights. During the drill, 150 auxiliary firemen went through graduation exercises in the blacked out Leland auditorium. Chief Warden Arch McDonald warned his men not to become overconfident. He said that Fifth Columnists might try to infiltrate the warden service and create dissension. Then he headed for Florida to check on the progress of Stan Spence and Mickey Vernon.

By the time of the next drill on March 13, when the authorities doused streetlights and halted traffic, gas stations were back on their 7 am to 7 pm schedule. Gasoline supplies shrank twenty percent, and talk of rationing was in the air with prices "frozen" at 17.8¢ a gallon for regular and 19.8¢ for premium. The authorities warned motorists to save their anti-freeze when they drained their radiators because a shortage was likely the next winter.

On Palm Sunday, March 29, with the newspapers filled with stories of the "amazing" Nats and of Glen Echo getting ready to open, a wet, eighteen-inch snow crushed the Washington area. As usual, it reminded old-timers of the Knickerbocker disaster of 1922. Power lines fell, trees split, and falling limbs crushed automobiles. Porches collapsed, daffodils disappeared, and weathermen looked for a place to hide.

The surprise snow started Saturday night and fell all day Sunday. It was too deep and too wet for sledding, but quite a few snow forts, snow ball fights, and short-lived snowmen resulted. Firemen shoveled off the roof of Normandy Farm and enjoyed a free meal for their work. Routemen were late with their newspaper deliveries, but most paperboys did their jobs even if some subscribers did not get their Sunday paper before supper time. It took until Tuesday for State police to rescue a group of Chevy Chase youngsters camping near the Appalachian Trail, but by then the snow was just a muddy memory in Bethesda.

The next Sunday the sunrise service at the Rec Center went on as scheduled with the A Cappella Choir, a brass quartet from the Army Band, readings by Dr. Nelson and Reverend Vogeley's sermon. Easter egg rolling moved to the Capitol lawn and to the Zoo instead of the now security-conscious White House acres, and more than 130,000 children took part as the temperature climbed to 91°.

That first wartime spring, the government canceled the cherry blossom festival since tourists were not wanted in the Capital. What were being called "Oriental" or Korean cherry trees were left to bud in silence. By then bus and trolley ridership had risen to eight million a month, up two million from the first of the year, and the old, wooden trolley-cars with their wicker seats were out of storage and back on the streets. That was the spring when the OPA announced the first big group of price ceilings on canned goods; the WPB halted the manufacture of radios and phonographs, and federal agencies multiplied at an unprecedented rate with the OWM, OWI, NHA, WMC and OSS among those added to the area's alphabet soup.[24]

By Congressional action, which began in Jennings Randolph's District Committee, Conduit Road in D.C. became MacArthur Boulevard in March, shortly before "Dugout Mac" left Corregidor and flew to Australia. The name change extended all the way to Great Falls by May, but the Conduit Road Fire Board retained its name. By then the prices on almost everything had been frozen at March levels.[25]

In May the Army Map Service of the Corps of Engineers moved from the Engineering Reproduction Plant in Southwest, D.C., out to its brand new building in Brookmont. Employees were told to empty out their desks, gather up their equipment and head for Glen Echo since most of them knew where that was and almost none of them had ever heard of Brookmont.

Bill Stickel, then a 17-year-old apprentice who had been working at ERP for six months, recalled the move:[26]

We all departed at about 10 am and arrived at the new facility about a half hour later. There was no parking lot, only a bulldozed red clay area across the street. What a mess that was, especially on rainy days. Some bluestone was added later.... The new building was really

unique. The roof was flat, no windows, steel sides and just the main entrance and loading dock for entering and exiting. The structure, we were informed, was bomb proof, except for a direct hit. In case of an indirect hit, the cement columns, centered every 20 feet, would support the roof and floors while the walls fell out, keeping the people from being buried alive. Without windows the building required air-conditioning. The air-conditioning would help stabilize film, acetate and other materials for better plotting and registration.

The only problem was we moved in before all the components to operate the air-conditioning system arrived. We also beat the furniture, leaving us ample time to tour the facility (on our own) from the main floor to the basement and sub-basement.

By noon there was little left to explore so the tour moved on to the Hill Top Inn, or the "Greasy Spoon." It was just an old, run-down house converted into a restaurant. Rustic would hardly describe its condition. I will just say that the best tables were outside on the porch. (Another restaurant just past Bonfield's gas station was nicknamed Ptomaine Tavern.) That day may have been the all time noon beer sales day for the Greasy Spoon. I settled for cokes.

Map Service draftsmen in their new building

Through that summer they worked without air-conditioning. The fans installed as a temporary measure caused map makers many problems, and the men down in the press room worked shirtless in their shorts. When the electricity went out, Perry Gilbert recalled, "It was like being inside an inkwell," and pretty hard on those who were a bit claustrophobic. Workers emerged to some surprises from both the weather and the Corps of Engineers. "Camouflage paint had been applied to the outside of the building one day," Bill Stickel said.

Then fake trees were placed on the roof. On another day it looked like small bombs had hit between the sidewalk and roadway. The next day small trees were in the holes. Still another day we emerged to find tar spread over the beautiful roadway with wood chips scattered over the tar.

The name soon changed from ERP to Army Map Service. Perry Gilbert recalled that early in the war they sent "boatloads" of maps to North Africa. In the draft, he said:

The apprentice boys went first. Later they got to journeymen and the married, and we found ourselves in the same units. The trouble was when we got there the apprentices were staff and tech sergeants, and we were privates.

AMS produced 500 million topographic maps during World War II, and when its employees returned from the service they found that the Ruth Building, which they had thought so large when they moved in, was the small building of the still-growing complex.[27]

At both Leland and B-CC, shop students began producing wooden model airplanes from government plans to be used by the Navy in aircraft spotting drills. An inspection committee evaluated the work and created an elaborate system of awards. Mr. Bender at the high school and Mr. Steigner at the junior high supervised the project.

With the help of the PTA, speech class students, and the A Capella Choir, Florence Massey Black bought a $350 recording machine, which allowed students to hear themselves on records. Her speech classes also produced fourteen radio programs, which WWDC aired with the Chamber of Commerce as sponsor. The war did not seem to interfere with most social activities although the ban on pleasure driving got a few B-CCers in trouble and increased the popularity of the Bethesda Hot Shoppe over the one across from the Ice Palace.[28]

Several months before the traditional Junior-Senior Prom, the junior class took on the job of providing decorations. Carter Dawson, vice-president of her class all three years, told president Leonard Williams that her father's neighbor up in Rockville had a row of apple trees in his side yard, and she was sure he would let them gather some apple blossoms to decorate the gym. On the Friday before the dance, several cars and sta-

Not exactly car-pooling at the high school

tion wagons full of junior- and senior-class officers drove out to the place Carter showed them and began breaking off the lower limbs of apple trees heavy with blooms. They stuffed their cars full and drove back to the high school where a police car followed them into the parking lot.

Williams and several other students ("Almost the whole student council," he said) ended up in the police station and spent several hours trying to explain what happened

Leonard Williams

before they convinced the authorities that it was all an honest mistake. The land, unbeknownst to the young lady who made the arrangements, had been sold, and the new owner knew nothing about a school dance and, seeing vandals in his yard, called the law. Under Leonard Williams's yearbook picture the editors put "Allergic to: Apple blossoms."

One group of high school girls, widely known as the "Dirty Dozen," dominated certain school activities. As juniors in 1941-42, they formed the Sub-Deb Club, which lasted only that one year but amounted to a school-sanctioned sorority. Helen Almy and Marian Brackett were among the leaders of the group, which produced two senior-class officers, Carter Dawson and Betty Broaddus, and the president of the Activities Council,

Bob Brewer with Sub-Debs Broaddus and Dawson

Dorothy Mathews, a survivor of the apple blossomed junior-senior prom.

Teacher Angela Darby recalled:

Dr. Broome came down and spoke to the faculty and said that fraternities and sororities were outlawed. Well, I wasn't going to get myself in a mess with the students, so when Betty Broaddus told me, "Mrs. Darby, I'm in a sorority, but don't you tell anybody," I said, "I didn't hear it."[29]

The ten-cent store started selling small, rectangular banners with one or more stars on them for the families of servicemen to hang in their windows. By spring the Columbia Specialty Company on Bradley Boulevard near the railroad bridge had a red bordered service banner with thirty-five blue stars for the five officers, nineteen "selectees" and eleven of its employees who had enlisted. Before summer they added six more stars.

By the end of the year some windows would show gold stars instead of blue ones. The first Bethesda-area war casualties were Navy Lt. Harold Halvorsen, 36, killed in a plane crash near Bel Air, Maryland, and Noble Dowling, 48, first officer of a missing merchant ship presumed sunk in the Atlantic. Halvorsen's widow and three young children lived on Del Ray Avenue. Dowling's parents and one of his brothers and a sister also lived in Bethesda.[30]

In March the Civil Service Commission ruled that federal employees could be active participants in the charter referendum. Specifically, the ruling allowed government workers to circulate petitions, become candidates for election to the charter writing board, campaign for the candidates of their choice and work for or against the adoption of a charter in a future election. The process of collecting signatures did not begin immediately, and no one expected much in the way of action until after the dog days of summer.

Following an informational "broadside" by Mrs. Aldo Raffa's government operations committee, the League of Women Voters endorsed the circulation of petitions to put the charter question on the ballot. The decision brought Delegate Ruth Shoemaker to a later LWV meeting to defend Brooke Lee as a "benevolent politician" and to sugest that the County would be better off if he had more power. Robert Bray, reporting civic association meetings for Bill Allen's *Tribune*, found "no enthusiasm among the people of Montgomery County for the much shouted about charter changes or for the Brookings recommendations."[31]

The Bethesda papers kept up the fight even if the public's interest seemed elsewhere. At the end of March the *Journal* attacked "Boss" Lee directly for his attitude toward reform, and the next week the *Tribune* savaged Day Thorpe with, "The bitter boy-editor never wrote a more naive or more impertinent column." In April a small storm resulted from criticsm by the *Maryland News* of the Somerset PTA's endorsement of circulating charter petitions. Lee suggested what would become a central theme of many who opposed the Charter, the charge that the Brookings report smelled of totalitarianism.[32]

Arch McDonald and Clark Griffith in a pre-season pose

In April as Arch McDonald was dusting off his theme-song record of "They Chopped Down the Old Pine Tree" and getting his chimes tuned up for another season of re-creating out-of-town baseball games with the help of a summary fed him by Shirley Povich, the Washington *Post* labeled Bethesda-Chevy Chase High School "probably the most sports-minded institution in this vicinity."[33]

That spring when the janitors disappeared in the draft or into better-paying jobs downtown, the Student Council took over the task of cleaning up the high school, and volunteers washed blackboards, swept the floors and tidied up the building for the rest of the year. That was also the spring when Al Sherline "won five bucks off a guy. We used to go out there and toss a ball around when the girls were playing. On a bet, I threw a softball from in front of the gym over the A building roof. I had an arm."

Spring began with a parade up Wisconsin Avenue on Army Day, Easter Monday, that featured a fire department display of magnesium incendiary bombs exploding on a truck bed. More than a thousand Civil Defense workers took part. Three hundred and eighty auxiliary firemen and one firewoman, Mrs. W. H. Blair, marched carrying shovels, pails, pumps and other fire fighting equipment. The parade started at Bradley Lane and ended just past a reviewing stand at the fire house on Old Georgetown Road. "Duck" Dunnington's First Aid Corps auxiliary paraded in their white uniforms and new, white overseas caps, and it was no surprise that the young ladies saw their picture in the *Post* the next day sitting on the running board of the

ambulance. Leland's band marched even though that Monday was one of the two spring holidays in 1942 as the school board decided to shorten the semester.

That night Sgt. Carl E. Plitt of Bethesda sat with the generals for a dinner at the Mayflower where he was honored as the "typical citizen soldier." His mother agreed that "Buck" was typical.

The Army drafted him after he had five years experience with the telephone company. Did they put him to work in communications?

Sgt. "Buck" Plitt

No! They made him a mess sergeant. We just took it as a joke.[34]

Bethesda welcomed two new employees that spring. After a diligent search and many interviews by Stella Werner's Advisory Board, the M-NCP&PC appointed Louis G. Mitchell to replace Harry Callaghan as Recreation Director at the Rec Center. Mitchell, from Prince George's County, brought twelve years of experience in playground supervision, the last three as an area supervisor in the District.

Mrs. Werner, chair of the Civil Defense Women's Activities Committee, mapped out a comprehensive recreation program. She said:

Profiting from England's experience, we must see that our young people have some wholesome recreation during the months when there is no school to keep them busy and interested.

The PTA at Bethesda ES continued to maintain its pioneering program. The committee created morning activities for pre-school children at each center.[35]

The second new leader of a Bethesda institution took much longer to find. After more than a year of trying to secure a suitable, local applicant for the librarian position, the Board of Trustees of the Bethesda Public Library hired Marjorie B. Robinson, and she went to work on April 1. Mrs. Robinson was a graduate of Wellesley, Harvard and the Drexel library science program who came to Bethesda from the library in New Rochelle, N.Y. Acting librarian Ruth Coplen was soon replaced by Mrs. Thomas C. Bagg who then became the high school's librarian and was, in early 1943, superceded by Eleanor Titsworth, an Eastern Shore native.

Librarian Robinson

That spring also saw the first steps that led to the creation of Suburban Hospital. The Bethesda-area branch of the Montgomery County Lay Health Council, chaired by Mrs. Randolph G. Bishop, called a meeting at the County Building on April 10 to discuss steps

needed to secure funds for a 100-bed hospital under the Community Facilities (Lanham) Act. Officials of the Public Health Service, then in the process of moving to its temporary, frame building on the NIH campus, were present as were Dr. John G. Ball and the County health officer, Dr. V. L. Ellicott.

From that meeting came a "temporary committee" headed by Randolph G. Bishop, which, after a meeting at the Bishops' Bradley Boulevard home, filed for incorporation of the Suburban Hospital Association, and "Bill" Perry launched a campaign to secure 2,000 members. Mr. Butler's sub-committee began seeking a two-to-five-acre site and applied for a $500,000 grant to build and equip the hospital and nurses' home.[36]

By May, Mrs. Perry had signed up 2,300 Bethesdans who pledged to "aid in every way possible the establishment and operation of the hospital," and the committee staged a rally at Leland. Paul Banfield chaired the Hospital Day meeting, and speakers included Surgeon General Thomas Parran and Baird Snyder of the Federal Works Agency, which controlled the funds for hospital construction. Snyder told the crowd that hospital construction "as usual" was a victim of the war effort and that communities would have to give up "monumental" building plans and be satisfied with one-and-a-half-story, frame structures under Lanham Act grants. Dr. Parran said that his office had certified the need for a hospital in the Bethesda area to the FWA and commended the Association's efforts.

Randolph Bishop, now president of the Suburban Hospital Association, said that they planned to ask the public to contribute to a fund to purchase a site for the hospital. A low hospital in the suburbs was just what they had in mind, he said. The meeting was adjourned at 9:30 pm so that everyone could get home in time for the blackout. The need for a Bethesda hospital was one of the few issues on which the Bethesda's weekly newspapers agreed. Bill Allen called it "vital" and urged all citizens to support the effort, and Thorpe's *Tribune* concluded that "no wiser way to spend our tax money, or more necessary addition to our community can be thought of." The *Star* and the Woman's Club of Bethesda were not far behind in endorsement and praise, and the Hospital soon became a unifying effort.

The first, half-hour air raid drill of the spring took place on Tuesday, April 14, the first day of the baseball season. OCD Director Albert Brault wanted a full-blown dress rehearsal with all Civil Defense workers reporting to their posts and other emergency services functioning as if a real raid were in progress. He stated:

This practice is not being staged for fun. It is a deadly earnest business intended to prepare our people for the grim spectre of actual air raids that we have no reason to believe will fail to arrive when the enemy feels the time appropriate for his benefit

He planned a total blackout with all traffic stopped. Emergency vehicles had their lights hooded and were limited to 20 mph. People were asked not to use their phones during the blackout. All thirty-eight of the new sirens were ready to howl.[37]

The blackout at 10:27 pm was a great success everywhere except in Bethesda. Washington vanished for fifteen minutes. But in Bethesda confusion reigned. The night before the drill, the chief of the Bethesda Volunteer Fire Department promised John Oden, chief of the Auxiliary Fire Service, that the volunteers would not sound their siren. The local air raid wardens were notified of his promise. Tuesday night as the minutes crept past nine and on towards ten, many of the men at the little firehouse on Fairmont Avenue tired of waiting and straggled home. The only way the chief could think of to get them back was to turn on the siren. He did.

All over Bethesda tense homeowners and businessmen doused their lights and pulled their blackout curtains. The *Journal* said that downtown Bethesda looked like it did before Henry Hiser moved here. Almost two thousand auxiliary firemen, policemen and air raid wardens hurried to their posts. When the actual alarm blew about a half hour later, Bethesdans began turning on their lights, and the 1,500 local block wardens took the brunt of their abuse when they were told a mistake had been made, again, and they should turn off all their lights, again.

John Oden, who thought he had made sure this sort of thing would not happen, was furious. Albert Brault impatiently listened to the Bethesda volunteers' explanation, and then said publicly that more than 7,000 civil defense workers had gone to their posts at 9

Volunteers' ladder truck and pumpers at their firehouse on Fairmont

o'clock and they had "waited for the alarm without getting tired."

Brault directed a letter to all County fire chiefs instructing them not to sound their sirens during announced drills. He stated that he meant no criticism of other fire companies and hoped "this action will settle the difficulty." Brault pointed out that one of the purposes of the drills was to "establish possible errors and failures."

One result of the confusion caused by the Bethesda volunteers was that the "alert" signal was changed to a long, three or four minute, sounding of sirens or horns with a rising and falling tone. Another result was that the volunteer company, already embarrassed by harboring firebugs, began to fade from the Bethesda scene.[38]

The drill showed that the new sirens could be heard in most parts of the County. Civil Defense then began the process of hooking them all to a central control point so they could be sounded simultaneously. OCD also announced the appointment of Virginia Coleman of Friendship Heights as head of its messenger service with Mrs. Perry T. Burton of Bethesda as deputy chief. Volunteers in this group furnished their own cars, received more than twenty hours of training and provided backup to telephone service from the report and casualty centers. The County Civil Defense Office also created a Committee on Child Care and began a search for volunteers to operate neighborhood day-care centers.[39]

Over in Glen Echo, the amusement park opened a week early. At Bradley Hills Country Club Al Jamison and Eddie Adams parted company, and Al, much to his "for the

duration" regret, cleaned out his pro shop and sent hundreds of golf balls back to the manufacturers. Tommy Doerer, hired as pro and course manager, said that the nine new fairways should be ready for play under winter rules by early summer, but that the whole, redesigned 18-hole layout would not be ready for another year. Bradley Hills, still claiming 200 members, planned to operate as a semi-public course.

Also at Bradley Hills, carpenters completed the airplane observation post. Adams donated the land; the Maloney Concrete Company, the cement; Eisinger and Turover, the lumber; and Doyle and Ecklund supervised the construction without cost. The Commissioners, the American Legion, Leslie Bell and a number of other individuals contributed to the project, which resulted in a single room topped by a glass cupola atop ten-foot piers. The Legion paid the maintenance and phone bills. Most of the daytime shifts were "manned" by women from the volunteer bureau, and Legionnaires covered the evening hours. It was not unknown, on long, cold winter nights, for a few of the aircraft spotters to bring some high-proof freeze inhibitor to their duties, which made for a more convivial atmosphere if not more accurate airplane identification.[40]

Bannockburn's spring was not as happy. The former Capital Golf and Country Club, which had started on the Kirkwood links, had fallen on hard times since the Depression. Although it claimed to have 200 members, the club was unable to pay its bills or even the interest on its loans. Harry Gray, a government official, was president of the club whose members were responsible for about $75,000 in first-trust notes. The big clubhouse, the golf shop, outbuildings and 125-acre, 18-hole golf course went on the block at a foreclosure auction on Saturday morning, April 25. Two bidders challenged John J. Shinners Jr. of Eaglesville, Pa., who had owned the property and leased it to the club since November 1940. The bidding started at $45,000, moved along swiftly and resulted in Shinners' purchasing Bannockburn for $92,000. He said his intention was to modernize the clubhouse and the golf course and to continue the operation under the same name.[41]

The news continued to be a mixture of utter surprises, mundane occurrences and trivial annoyances. Now one had to take back the old, rolled-up toothpaste tube in order to buy another. Lansburgh's delivery trucks had become ambulances. Coffee and bananas disappeared from grocery stores, and toilet paper shortages traumatized many households. Safety pins vanished. Some odd brands of cigarettes appeared in drug stores (Wings were probably the worst); a lot of people learned to roll their own. Newcomers wondered if the Camels, Chesterfields and Luckies were being saved for the "regulars." (In many cases, they were.) Lew Worsham of Burning Tree won the pro-am at Kenwood with a 72. Doolittle's Tokyo raiders, said FDR, came from "Shangri-La." In late April, men 45 to 64 signed up for the draft at public schools.

B-CC coach Al Vogt resigned to become a lieutenant junior grade in the Navy reserves. He was assigned to Annapolis to train air cadets. Harry Bertschy from Gaithersburg HS finished the year for him. Trial magistrate James Christopher followed Vogt into the Navy as a jaygee. Albert Brault, the Civil Defense chief, replaced him as Bethesda's judge. Clarence C. Keiser, newly elected president of the Chamber of Commerce, became deputy district air raid warden for the Bethesda business and industrial area, and his basement soon filled up with buckets of sand and rows of stirrup pumps.

Sugar rationing began in late April with all dealers, restaurant owners, bakers and other institutional and industrial users signing up at the high school and at Leland JHS. The next week at all elementary schools, the heads of households registered with teacher "volunteers" for War Ration Book One. They had to sign up and carefully describe every man, woman and child in the family and declare, to the pound, how much sugar was in the house. Stamps were to be removed for all sugar over two pounds per person. No one was really surprised how few people admitted that they had even close to that much. All the newspapers printed the blank forms prior to the registration dates, and the process went reasonably smoothly at the primary schools where classes ended at noon for those four days in early May.[42]

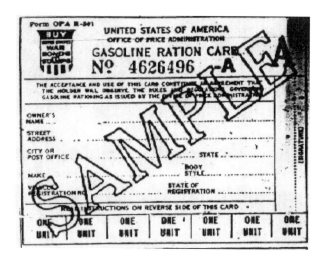

No sooner had Bethesdans gotten used to having sugar rationing books than the government mandated gas rationing for the East Coast mainly to save rubber but also because of the U-boats' successes in sinking tankers. "Normally," the OPA's Leon Henderson noted, "more than 90 percent of the 1,500,000 barrels of the petroleum products we consume daily in the East is brought in by tanker."

The owners of all autos, motorcycles and inboard motorboats had to register and be issued a card allowing them to purchase gasoline. The "A" card entitled registrants to seven units of three gallons each between May 15 and July 1, but if drivers needed more for war-related activities or travel to work there were various levels of "B" cards (B-1 eleven units, B-2 fifteen, B-3 nineteen) and even an "X" card, which allowed unlimited purchases and was intended for doctors and those with similar needs.[43]

The newspaper photos showed a smiling Eleanor Roosevelt with her A card and Henderson with his, but over half of the D.C.-area registrants received B-3 or X cards. Obviously it was very difficult for the overworked teachers to say no to the high-powered drivers they faced across a folding table. And the next week requests for supplemental allotments swamped the Commodity Rationing Boards. Henderson, who also had his photo in the papers riding a bike to work with his secretary on the handlebars, was so angry he made the X-list public. To no one's surprise almost all Congressmen had X cards. The system lasted

NINETEEN FORTY-TWO   517

only two months and then had to be done all over again.[44]

The next air raid drill and blackout took place on May 12 at 10:55 pm for thirty minutes. The D.C. wardens sported their recently issued helmets, and the suburban wardens had new armbands to replace the highly flammable plastic ones they had been wearing. With more than 7,500 volunteers participating, Montgomery County officials pronounced it the best drill yet.

The only major error took place in Bethesda, again, when the local report center forgot to notify the doctors of the drill and many were late in reaching their stations. Up in Alta Vista, a warden was "horrified" to see a bunch of people with flashlights scurrying about. When he yelled at them to get inside, they answered, "We can't. We're wardens." A few homes and stores were slow in responding to the sirens, and some businesses had closed with their lights left burning.

Judge Brault praised the volunteer firemen for refraining from blowing their sirens in this drill, but warned:

The general public has been given an opportunity to become accustomed to the routine and to learn the requirements, and we feel that the safety of the community requires that we discontinue leniency to violators in the future...the police will be instructed to make arrests for violations in future blackouts.[45]

The metropolitan area held its first daylight air raid drill on the morning of Tuesday, June 2, and to the relief of many, Bethesda came through with a flawless performance. For the first time female air raid wardens patrolled many of the neighborhoods as emergency volunteers. Male wardens working more than ten minutes from their posts were instructed to stay at work and seek shelter. Traffic was halted, and drivers were led or directed to shelters, but bus and streetcar riders were allowed to stay on the vehicles.

Some schools, including Leland, tried out their dispersal plans, sending groups of children to nearby homes, but most sheltered pupils in their basements. One class of Bethesda Elementary children "dispersed" to the basement of Emmy Lou's and became the target of envy from the rest of the school. "Bud" Keiser was one of those lucky kids, and he recalled that he and his friends were not always sure which were "real" and which were just "pretend" air raids.

By the time of this practice raid, more than 10,000 County residents had signed up in one or another of the civil defense organizations, and soon after it, older Boy Scouts began working as aides at casualty stations and as messengers in the report centers. With the school board's approval, the FBI initiated a program to fingerprint all children. The never-completed project began with a class at Bethesda Elementary.

By June 7, news of the great American victory at Midway, now recognized as the turning point of the war in the Pacific, spread across the Sunday papers. They heralded the victory as revenge for Pearl Harbor. It was probably coincidental that the local branch of the League of Women Voters had to divide its Post-War Planning group into two sections by the end of the month.

The high school held a rather subdued graduation. The senior class, led by tall, studious Georges Edelen, Clayton Rogers of the A Cappella Choir, *Tattler* editor Carolyn "Moots" Moody and Tom Kerby, Mary Jane Gott, Eddie Jacobsen and a number of others, staged their senior banquet and dance at the Woman's Club of Chevy Chase instead of the usual downtown hotel. The seniors presented the school with a trophy case made in the school shop to hold all the awards won by the Class of `42. The president of The American University, Dr. Paul Douglas, spoke to the 220 graduates in the blue-and-gold decorated Leland auditorium after class president Edelen reminded his fellow seniors that they were "not going out to set the world on fire, but to stop a conflagration already started."

Admittance was free for alumni in uniform at the annual alumni-senior class dance following graduation. The fee was $1.10, stag or drag, for everyone else.[46]

Among the non-graduates was Al Sherline, probably the only B-CCer pictured as a senior in two yearbooks.

My class was `42. I was sixteen-years-old in June; I skipped 2nd grade and was born in July. When basketball season ended, I was in love with a younger girl, and I was a pretty damn good athlete, and I loved it. So I decided to quit going to school and come back and be with my girl and play ball and be a big shot. I left home every morning and hung around out in the grove, made it to class occasionally, and, of course, I failed.

Al Vogt was drafted, and Ray Fehrman came, and somewhere along the line I started smoking. I didn't smoke the previous year. Vogt was my god, and Fehrman caught me smoking and threw me off the team the second year I was a senior. I was standing around after practice like an idiot with another guy from Garrett Park, standing across the street from school, hitchhiking. He threw us both off, but he let me back on, and I played a game or two, and I got caught again, absolute stupidity, and then I had measles and didn't play any baseball. I went ahead and graduated. I turned 18 in July and joined the Marines. The Marines saved me.

Al Sherline

Summer school classes began at Bethesda-Chevy Chase High School on June 22 under the direction of Mary Roeming, the no-nonsense math and physics teacher. Students could earn a full semester of credit in six weeks of two-and-one-half-hour classes and take two subjects if they were willing to work from 8 am until 1 pm. Tuition was $6.00 per course, and almost two hundred students signed up. Other students registered to grow vegetables in the large field behind the grove, now plowed up for what people were starting to call Victory Gardens. Mr. Pyle and several of his teachers also staked out their plots in the school yard that spring.

Politics did not even wait for the end of the school year to get rolling again. By mid-May, Mrs. Byron had changed her mind and decided to stand for re-election to her late husband's 6th District Congressional seat. Her announcement left Montgomery County Democratic leaders both surprised and decidedly cool. The reason for their lack of enthusiasm became clear a week later when County "boss" E. Brooke Lee let it be known that the "experts" were right and that he would run for Congress. Lee's entry into the campaign may not have surprised the contemporary politicos, but in retrospect it was probably an almost fatal mistake. It divided Lee's energies in the fight against the charter and gave his enemies, and they were numerous, a target with which to bring out the vote. Perhaps the old boss forgot the price of pride.[47]

In early June, "Bill" Perry, as storekeeper Walter E. Perry's active and vocal second wife was sometimes known to her confreres, invited Stella Werner to lunch at the Cosmos Club. Willie Green Day Perry had broken with her doctor brother-in-law's political faction long before Mrs. Werner did. At lunch Allen Gardner, Stephen James, and Fred Lee talked with Mrs. Werner about the job of executive director of the pro-charter campaign, and after about two hours, she accepted the position at $50 a week. Her first task was forming an operating committee, and Mrs. Perry and Mrs. Werner called about fifty people before they could get eighteen from various parts of the County to agree to serve.[48]

At the end of June, the County Charter Committee headed by Allen Gardner pulled itself together in a meeting at the Woman's Club of Bethesda. Its executive committee included men and women of varying political stripes from all over the County. Captain Charles E. Parsons of Somerset was treasurer, and other Bethesdans in positions of influence in this early stage of the charter fight included publicity chairman Marquis Childs, speakers' bureau head Marie Bennett, field division chairman Roy C. Corderman and finance chairman James A. Cosgrove.[49]

Mrs. Minier Hostetler, state president of the LWV, headed the board of directors. The hundred or so in attendance adopted a twelve-page constitution, which stated their goal as "working for the election of a non-partisan charter board and the drafting of a charter of government for submission to the vote of the people."[50]

Despite recent voter registration figures, which encouraged Brooke Lee loyalists because they showed huge majorities for the Democrats, the County continued to change. The suburbs, especially west of Rock Creek, were becoming the home of a lot of second-phase New Dealers, Republicans caught up in the national defense frenzy and what some called "goo goos," reformers or "good government" people. Shut out of local politics by a combination of the Hatch Act and a solidly entrenched old-boy network, which ran tile-tight from Doc Perry to Bob Hagner to Earle Hampton to Billy Prescott in the Western Suburban District, they sought other ways to bring their new home's rural relic of a government into the 20th Century. To the Demo-

cratic regulars, the "goo goos" and other new-comers were just a small bunch of sore losers.[51]

Brooke Lee and his minions, the "court-house gang," disdainfully called the leaders of the reform movement the "civics" and under that title lumped together most members of the League of Women Voters, the neighborhood associations, the women's clubs' study groups, the old Fusionists, the Willkie Republicans and the Civic Federation leadership as well as miscellaneous Charterites. To some, such as J. Bond Smith and those who wanted to build apartments along the County's creeks, the fight was over zoning and the power of M-NCP&PC, which was certainly controlled by Lee's friends. The Brookings report proposed giving most zoning authority to the elected, non-partisan County Council. To others, such as Joe Cantrel, it appeared a struggle between absolute good and shining American values against the forces of foul evil and alien darkness.

Most observers saw the basic battle then being joined as pitting the party-politics-as-usual bunch, backed by rural interests who feared something like one-man-one-vote, against activist immigrants to the suburbs and defenders of single-family homes, backed by Republicans and anti-Lee Democrats tired of being out of power. There were, undoubtedly, noble-minded people who viewed the two-party system as the sturdy backbone of our way of life as well as clear-headed political scientists who espoused local lawmaking and the county-manager system as the cleansing wave of progress. But the fight, in the end, came down to turf and power, and the victory, finally, went to neither the swift nor to the strong but to the patient.

In mid-July Mrs. Werner opened the Mont-gomery County Charter Committee headquar-ters on the second floor of the Bethesda Bowling Center and hired Miss DeCoursey, "a pretty girl from Somerset," as secretary. The purpose of Stella Werner's office was mainly to collect signatures on petitions and disseminate information about the Commit-tee's goals. Their guide, according to Mrs. Werner, was "City Management, the Cincin-nati Experiment" by Charles Taft, but, she said, "Allen Gardner was really our guide." Stella Werner organized the petition drive as she had numerous political campaigns and

Stella Werner, "Bill" Perry, Adlai Magee, Allen Gardner

Methodist fund-raisings, from field divisions down to block workers responsible for fifty voters. John Willmott put together a manual for the volunteers, mostly LWV or Civic Fed-eration women, and Mrs. Werner encouraged them to talk about home rule and the jai alai bill. "They made a big mistake over introduc-ing that," she insisted. Their slogan was "Don't let the cat take care of the canary."

She recalled that "we got most of our sig-natures in Bethesda," where Eleanor Vaughan was chairman, and that there was only one African-American volunteer, Mrs. Geneva Mason of Seven Locks Road.

Marquis Childs, as publicity chairmen, put together a committee of novelists, news-papermen and columnists, which turned out a number of pamphlets, handouts and broadsides. Among his fellow writers were William Kiplinger, Robert McCormick of *Colliers*, Merlo Pusey of the *Post*, Frederick Barkley of the N.Y.*Times*, Paul Ward of the Baltimore *Sun*, Charles Ross of the St. Louis *Post-Dispatch*, Mrs. Frank Garfield from the LWV and McClure columnist Ray Tucker, who was also on the Charter Committee's board of directors. It looked like a Who's Who in journalism, wrote Mrs. Werner.[52]

Tireless Stella Werner, with two young daughters to care for, brought with her a great deal of political savvy and the admiration of hundreds of workers from her church, recre-ation and civic activities. She was a native born Maryland Democrat with two state sen-ators in her family. The Goucher graduate had worked in Hutzler's personnel depart-ment for seven years before moving to Bethesda and becoming active in the Demo-cratic organization. She usually told inter-viewers that her work in social relations for

the Women's Society of Christian Service of the Methodist Church came first on her priority list. She was well known in Bethesda for her contributions to the recreation program with the Youth Research Council and then the Women's Defense Council. Her most recent project had been planning entertainment for the men stationed at the Naval Hospital.

The United Democratic Organization, 800 delegates strong, met in mid-July and endorsed the candidacy of E. Brooke Lee for Congress and voted unanimous opposition to the charter proposal. They passed a resolution urging County voters not to sign the petitions and authorized the printing and distribution of 10,000 pamphlets asking why the County should be made a "guinea pig" for experimenters and why people should work to overthrow majority rule and establish a permanent, unelected administrator. Among the Bethesdans speaking out against the Charter were James Blaine Fitzgerald, Roger J. Whiteford, Joseph A. Cantrel, Carey Quinn, and Hugh Frampton. In time, attorneys Cantrel and Whiteford became the most vociferous of the anti-charter spokesmen.

Joseph Cantrel   Roger Whiteford

One of the oddities about the charter fight was that neither side could take the summer off as was the generally accepted behavior. The Charterites' need to get twenty percent of the voters to sign petitions by September precluded that. In its annual banquet at the Brooke Farm Tea House, the Civic Federation awarded Allen Gardner the Star Trophy for "outstanding contributions" to the County and listened to re-elected president Joseph B. Matre uphold the right of a free people to

have whatever kind of government they choose and to "change it whenever they please, in peace or war."

Bill Allen attended the banquet, picked up the gauntlet and mused in his long editorial the next week about why good people criticized what he considered a good government. "Why are Civic Leaders the way they are in Montgomery County?" he asked. He answered:

Educated, cultured, professional, technical and prosperous people frequently produce, cling to and strive to perpetuate ideals, ideas or prejudices that are unwise both for themselves and the world.

He urged the Charterites to examine their reasoning and put "first things first in 1942." Among the critics of the charter forces, Allen seemed a moderate willing to say now is not the time.[53]

E. Brooke Lee's campaign for the Democratic Congressional nomination began in June with the first of a series of thirty rallies. Maj. James B. Fitzgerald headed Lee's veterans' committee and Joe Cantrel was his political agent and another link between the primary campaign and the charter fight. In a meeting at the home of Thomas W. Perry with Curtis Walker presiding, Lee stated his basic message that unity on the homefront was needed during a time of war.

All strife between Americans must be put in cold storage for the period of the emergency. Contests and disagreements between Americans help the Axis.

Before the summer ended Mrs. Byron, unable to find funds or workers, withdrew from the race and left "Colonel" Lee unopposed.[54]

In July, J. Glenn Beall, a Western Maryland realtor and insurance man who had been a state senator and chairman of the State Roads Commission, announced his candidacy for the Republican nomination for the 6th District's Congressional seat. While Montgomery County Republicans seemed to be having trouble finding candidates for some of the local positions, Beall began to gather support out in the Western hills.

In late July, Joseph Cantrel in a long open letter to Allen Gardner accused the charter forces of not only Republican leanings but also of un-American tendencies. It was, by far, the meanest salvo of the long campaign. Cantrel, the County Commissioner's chief le-

gal advisor, began by asking Gardner "is it not true that you have recently stated there is little reason for people to be so worked up over the general question of winning the war because when Hitler has taken what he wants a negotiated peace will be arranged?" He asked if Gardner had said he did not have time for civilian defense activities because he was "so busy leading the movement to change the government of Montgomery County to something called 'charter'?" He inquired if any members of the charter committee had voted for FDR in 1936 or `40 and why "you and your small group of republican associates refuse to tell the people of Montgomery County what your program under charter would be?" The Brookings report's recommendations, Cantrel concluded, are "based on a profound underlying distrust of the American voters."

William Prescott Allen echoed part of Cantrel's theme in an editorial, which condemned the Brookings "professors" for suggesting that the County be divided into nine council districts and that voters choose only their own council members instead of voting for all nine. In a later editorial Allen joined those calling the Charterites "Utopians" and urged his readers not to sign the petitions. Obviously the attempts of the charter forces to disassociate themselves from the Brookings report had failed.[55]

Edgemoor's Frederic P. Lee answered part of Cantrel's and Allen's charges by pointing out that no charter board had been elected and no charter written so opponents were attacking an imaginary charter they had created. "This is all silly," he said, "the building of a straw man for the sake of tearing him down." The critics were the same people who tried to foist jai alai on us, he noted. If Cantrel was going to hang Brookings around charter's neck, he would pin a gambler label on the boss's chest. Fred Lee emphasized the non-partisan nature of the charter campaign and tried to disassociate it from the on-going Congressional race.

Obviously referring to Cantrel's diatribe, he said:

I am confident no amount of personal abuse or false charges or flights of fancy will lead any of us to make similar unbecoming spectacles of ourselves. We can't waste time in replying to horseplay and nonsense and other insults to the voters' intelligence. The facts are with us and we rest on them.

Gardner issued an unqualified denial of Cantrel's charges that almost accused him of Nazi leanings. "His technique of personal abuse is the old familiar answer of little politicians – leave governmental improvement alone or be smeared." The charter idea was "the essence of American democracy," he wrote: let the voters decide. "It is an effort to break through the tight little ring of bossism and give the people greater powers."[56]

Into this bubbling, political ragout plopped an Independent Party. Republicans and anti-Lee Democrats, many of them Bethesdans, formed a new bipartisan group, which stated loudly from its birth in mid-August that its goal was to capture control of the County Commission as the Fusion Party had in `34 and that it had "absolutely no connection with the Charter Movement or any other movement in the county." Lee's spokesmen decided almost immediately that the newcomer "doth protest too much." The new group pointedly avoided the Fusion Party tag because of the sad record of that group in the 1934-38 period.

Bethesda lawyer John R. Reeves, who had filed as a Republican for state's attorney, withdrew his name from that ballot and refiled as an Independent. Robert P. Dunlop of Chevy Chase stood as the Independent candidate for the Bethesda County Commission seat on a ticket headed by incumbent Republican Commissioner Walter Perry Johnson. Among the new coalition's candidates for the state legislature were Bethesdan Claude V. Hyson and Chevy Chasers Muriel B. Adams and William A. King. Paul Imirie was the new party's man for County treasurer and John D. Sadler of Edgemoor their choice for the Orphans' Court.

The new candidates immediately began circulating petitions to gather the necessary five hundred signatures to put them on the ballot. The United Democratic Organization's spokesman, J. Bond Smith, welcomed this additional petition drive, assumed it would just annoy the voters more and hurt the Charter Committee as well as showing the Republicans' weakness.

Toward the end of the summer, with the Charter petitions still circulating, the Independents filed almost a full slate with

about 700 names on each petition. Joseph Cantrel and J. Bond Smith tried to tie the two efforts together by saying both aimed to destroy the two-party system. "Both are Republican-anti-Roosevelt inspired," said Smith in a press release.

The Fusion group, however, is a little more frank than Mr. Gardner. They openly admit that their objective is the defeat of the candidates of the Democratic Party in November. Mr. Gardner's group does not possess that much courage.

Willie Green Day Perry took on both Cantrel and Smith. She asked why the only opposition to the Charter drive had come from professional politicians and job holders. She reminded people that Cantrel was the same "Jumping Joe" who had urged reforms in the `30s until he "was awarded the nice fat plum of counsel to the County Commissioners at a good salary of $4,600 a year. Now he takes back all he said." And, Mrs. Perry continued, "Mr. Smith, counsel to the Park and Planning Commission, has been a good boy all along undoubtedly because he is the holder of an appointive job."

Cantrel and Smith responded that, while they did not want to attack a "lady," they doubted Mrs. Perry's sincerity. They pointed out that she had been a County office holder and wondered if perhaps she simply had an "itch for office." They concluded that Democrats associated with the Charter movement were either uninformed or had some ulterior motive and stated that the effort to change the local government was "an all time high not only in stupidity but in its callous indifference to the war effort itself." Just before the primary, the new Independent Party jumped on the accelerating Charter wagon thus confirming what the Organization Democrats had believed all along–it was all a Republican plot.[57]

While the politicians were more than usually busy during the summer of `42, Bethesda kept right on growing. The lack of tar slowed road building, but the Pearl Street bypass parallel to the Pike, which County road superintendent George McCeney deemed "essential" and hoped would relieve the East West-Wisconsin intersection, grew several blocks north to Sleaford Street. Many of the local merchants joined a hot-weather "Buy in Bethesda" campaign emphasizing how tires

and gas could be saved by patronizing the town's businesses. An early summer gasoline shortage that made hoses wrapped around empty pumps a common sight helped the effort. The promoters, operating outside the Chamber of Commerce, instituted a "Why I like to shop in Bethesda" contest and began advertising their bargains in a two-page spread in the *Journal*.

This new businessmen's club picked Carl Bachschmid of Carbert's as its temporary chairman and began a discussion of mutual problems. Within a month the informal group had become the Bethesda Board of Trade with sixty dues-paying members devoted to encouraging Bethesdans to shop at home. After awarding prizes in their letter writing contest, the new Board of Trade started planning a "Victory Day" to sell bonds and inaugurate Thursday evening shopping hours. Businessmen pledged to buy War Stamps

Carl Bachschmid

A couple of phramacist mates help Ann Carmody

equal to their employees' earnings on that day, and chairman and *Journal* business manager Nelson Smith planned a Bargagni-firebomb demonstration and a Horace Smithey-led community sing. The committee erected a Victory Thermometer on Hiser's lot next to the Housing Guild showing the names of the companies participating, and by September 10, thirty businesses had pledged more than $6,000. After the festivities the member-stores staged a fifteen-minute "whiteout" when nothing but War Bonds and Stamps were sold in most of Bethesda. Arch McDonald emceed the event, Bethesdans purchased $30,000 in War Bonds, and those buying a $25 bond had a chance to autograph a real torpedo on display at Hampden and Wisconsin.

After the success of its Victory Day promotion, the Board of Trade organized its committees. President Bachschmid named Mr. Nelson to head the "Booster" group with Mrs. Jay and Mr. Smithey. Parker Badger became the chairman of the membership committee, and Mrs. Taylor of the Centro Hobby Shop headed the education committee. Furniture store owner John Smith led the business protection committee and Leon Sherman, the program group, while Ed Stock headed up the

finance committee and Mrs. Bradley agreed to take charge of publicity. Early in the fall, Board of Trade members decided to stay open late on Friday instead of Thursday after being informed that Thursday was the usual "maid's night off" when many women went downtown to dine with their husbands. The Booster Committee began planning the Christmas celebration as the Chamber of Commerce slipped further into the background.

In early August, Frank R. Jelleff's opened its Bethesda Shop in the Chevy Chase Building and Loan's new, modern structure at 6936 Wisconsin Avenue. The store with its big show window and heavy-glass front doors had high ceilings, air conditioning, eight fitting rooms and 3,800 square feet of selling space. A steep driveway led to a parking lot beneath and behind the 50-by-124-foot building. Jelleff's formal opening featured two fashion shows with local young women and "matrons" as models. Lillian Jay, the new store's manager, said the shows demonstrated what she called "war time trends of fashion" under the WPB restrictions and insisted that there was really nothing wrong with rayon stockings.

Next door, the building and loan celebrated its thirteenth birthday by moving into its new, modern office building with its concrete and glass-brick front, sixteen-foot ceiling and mezzanine floor for meetings and offices. The small brick building behind the white picket fence, the bank's office since 1933, had been razed to make way for the big, new structure. Executive secretary J. Horace Smithey announced that while savings accounts and home loans were still the Association's only business, they would be selling War Bonds and Stamps "for the duration."[58]

About a month later the Palais Royal department store took a ten-year lease on the store Sears had been using and brought another first-class retail operation to town. Staffed almost entirely by Bethesdans, the redecorated store opened on September 30. J. J. Halsey, vice-president and general manager of the sixty-five-year-old Washington institution, said it was a "patriotic duty and also good business" to bring their store closer to their customers.

Palais Royal's assistant treasurer, William F. Hisey, was the first manager of the new store, which concentrated on women's and

The refurbished store at Wisconsin and Willow

children's apparel but had a small, men's department. Just up the street from the Palais Royal, the eighty-year-old, two-story, frame building that had been Darcey's old store, Bethesda's first, was torn down. The store, which had given Bethesda its name from 1862 to 1871, had been Pearce's and then Counselman's before being remodeled and divided up into several small offices. Once cleared, the space emerged as a much-needed parking lot.[59]

Out on River Road next to the railroad tracks, the Briggs Clarifier Company had been growing steadily since January 1942 in the old stone-cutting area near Crow Hill's ballfield. By summer the plant had about two hundred employees, operated on a round-the-clock basis and planned expansion in a new building and the hiring of another hundred workers. The basic product was a Fullers Earth filter used on large diesel engines by Navy ships and on generating plants and some tanks and trucks. The company's officers were mainly local men. Southwick Briggs, the inventor, was vice president and general manager; Chase Donaldson of Bethesda, president and sales manager; and Landra Platt of Chevy Chase, chairman of the board.

Smaller defense-related businesses, such as Bowen Engineering, began to grow and multiply in the flats along the railroad tracks west of Wisconsin Avenue. Ads appeared regularly in the local papers for skilled workers, and the U.S. Employment Service accepted applications at the County Building on Thursday evenings.

The ground breaking had been March 23, and by mid-summer builders completed the first two 48-unit sections of the Bradley Boulevard Apartments and began renting to defense workers, a broadly defined term. Albert Walker, president of the corporation,

which built and now owned the development, said he was pleased with the rate of construction, and work on the next 134-apartment set of buildings began before the summer was over. The building of single-family housing quickly dried up under wartime restrictions, but as the Washington area's population continued to grow, Bethesda's basements, garages and spare rooms soon filled with government girls, sailors' families and all the others who worked at the Navy hospital or downtown in the old government offices or the tempos on the Mall.

Several small milestones marked the passage of the long summer of '42. Economy Auto Supply went out of business and sold off its stock including all its tricycles, wagons and scooters. Ralph B. Sadler sold his Bethesda Printing Company to J. A. Wilkerson and joined the OSS. Adlai Magee offered Savings Stamps, cash or trade-in value, at six cents a pound, for old records in any condition at his radio and record store. Blake Merson stopped parking his smelly garbage trucks on East, Hampden and Montgomery Lanes after receiving a petition signed by eighty-two of his neighbors, but claimed trash in the alley between Elm and Hampden was the source of the rats and not his trucks.

Taylor Auto Upholstering on Hampden Lane did a good business making blackout curtains to order. The Bank of Bethesda instituted banking by mail to save gasoline, and the public library began allowing borrowers to renew books by phone. Hugo Brooks offered six 5x7 inch "platinum finish" portraits for $12 at his Old Georgetown Road studio. Joseph Crivella took over the old Quality Shop on the railroad bridge and turned it into the Bridge Market offering fresh fruit and vegetables, Takoma Park honey and "chickens dressed while you wait."

Mrs. William J. Norfleet of Battery Park won the sweepstakes prize, a garden rake, at the annual spring show of the Bethesda Community Garden Club in addition to nine blue ribbons and a pair of gold ribbons

for two of her tea roses. Mrs. Norfleet and the club's Defense Committee chairman, Mrs. John D. Fox, started a Victory Garden on a small plot at Bethesda Elementary School and then visited all of the lower grade classes to show the children how they prepared the soil and chose their seeds. Soon several class-sponsored gardens, which the children patriotically promised to care for during the summer, surrounded the ladies' neat furrows.

The high school baseball team plus coach Loris Williams and a few college boys entered the County league and had a break-even season. In bowling Hare Brothers and Martin's topped the Bethesda Major League. The Edgemoor Club advertised that it had room for "a few selected members" and that its tennis courts were "ready to play with a professional in attendance."

The Soroptomists entertained the Quota Club and the Business and Professional Women's Club at a dinner meeting. The Rotary Club elected William L. Orem president, Thomas Pyle vice-president, and Paul Banfield treasurer. The Lions picked Dr. Bashore as their president and to conserve gasoline, abandoned their annual rural Stag Day.

Mrs. Curtis Walker

Gov. O'Conor named Helen Claxton Walker of Chevy Chase to a six-year term on the school board. Mrs. Walker had been president of both the Chevy Chase Elementary and the Leland PTAs. Another Chevy Chase woman, who had also served in both of those PTAs, Mrs. Dean Dinwoodey, was elected president of the Montgomery County League of Women Voters. Beulah McCuen of Glen Echo, Maryland's only woman mayor, gained another honor when she became the County's only female Justice of the Peace. The Community Baptist Church of Glen Echo, which had been meeting in the Community House for more than a year, acquired the old church building at Harvard and University Avenues and held a "formal opening" celebration on the first Sunday of August.

On June 30, all eighteen- and nineteen-year-old men registered for the draft. By the 4th of July, 6,305 men under the age of 45 had registered with Draft Board No. 3, which had sent 360 for induction while another 356 had enlisted or accepted commissions. Soon the draft calls grew to thirty or forty a week, and Judge Curry stayed busy making his short farewell speech.

The Joseph Kuhn family of Friendship Heights was probably the first to hang a banner with three stars on it in their front window when youngest son Daniel joined the Marines. One of his older brothers was a captain in the Army Medical Corps and the other a lieutenant in the Engineers. By the end of the year the E. E. Shannons of Glen Echo Heights topped them with five sons, all B-CC graduates, in the service. Ellsworth was in the Signal Corp, Kenneth in the Field Artillery, James in the Army, Howard in the Coast Guard and the youngest, Harold, who had been one of Mr. Bender's right-hand men at the high school, at the Navy Radio School.

In July, the County began testing all its air raid sirens at noon on Saturdays with the long alarm signal followed three minutes later by the "all clear." Just like the good old days, remarked a number of old-timers. Bank of Bethesda employees practiced until they could stow their money and bookkeeping records in the fireproof vault in less than two minutes and then roll two large containers of sand in front of the door. At "Doc" Everitt's Bradmoor neighborhood picnic, Chief Bargagni gave his now-famous incendiary bomb demonstration. The dances for Navy hospital sailors, which Stella Werner had begun at Leland's gym early in the summer, became much more popular when they moved to the Corpsmen's Quarters on the hospital grounds. Mrs. Arthur Hilland was in charge of the one sponsored by the Woman's Club of Bethesda in June. The ladies planned picnics for the corpsmen later in the summer.

Four Bethesda cab drivers were convicted of stealing tires; three got a year in prison and the other 90 days of road labor. Judge Brault was particularly incensed since taxi drivers were entitled to purchase tires under the rationing restrictions, but those whose tires had been stolen could not get new ones.[60]

One of the real struggles of the summer was the effort on the part of a number of people to have a rationing board branch office established in Bethesda. The original board, of course, met up in Rockville and for

several months its chairman, Julius P. Stadler, tried to get permission from the State Board to have branch offices in Silver Spring and in Bethesda to save gasoline, tires and time.

Early in July a three-man Commodity Rationing Board opened an office in the Silver Spring County Building to handle gasoline and sugar rationing. It was four miles closer for most Bethesdans, but as *Tribune* editor Allen wrote, it was not enough, and in some ways seeing Silver Spring get its own rationing board just made Bethesda's situation seem worse. Allen concluded:

Perhaps some of the energy that has been expended by our civic leaders in chasing will-o-the-wisp charter dreams might be utilized in convincing the State Board that Bethesda-Chevy Chase is also an important community in Montgomery County.[61]

On July 9, 10 and 11 at Leland JHS and most area elementary schools, teachers and other volunteers issued the second gas ration books. This time everyone received an "A" book with six pages of eight coupons each. Those who thought they needed more gas were given an application for a supplementary ration. While waiting for the State to act, the County rationing authority set up a temporary office at the high school staffed by volunteer teachers to issue supplemental gasoline applications and ration books.[62]

At the end of July, building inspector Jack S. Eaton was named to head a rationing board for Bethesda. The other board members, all of whom served without pay, were Austin B. Rohrbaugh of Wellington Drive and Dr. W. C. Killinger of Rosedale Avenue. Ed Warner and James Enright joined the Board later. Mrs. Charles E. Roach of Friendship Heights accepted the administrative assistant position and began several weeks of training at the OPA office in Baltimore.

Gas rationers: Davies, Eaton, Rohrbaugh, Killinger

Finally, on Thursday August 6, the new board closed the B-CC room and scheduled the grand opening of its Bethesda office for Friday morning in what had been Northwest Ford's showroom. For a variety of reasons, the office was not ready, but after another week of confusion and unhappy drivers waving their empty coupon books, the Ration Board was in business. It kept its doors open daily from 9 to 4:30, on Saturdays from 9 until noon, and planned Friday evening hours when more volunteer workers could be found. One of the new board's most popular activities that summer was authorizing additional sugar for home canning. The rules allowed an additional pound for every four quarts of fruit housewives put up plus a pound per family member for jams and jellies.[63]

Dottie McAuliffe in the foreground. One of her jobs was going with "Gran'ma" Roach to check food and drink ceiling prices, even at Burning Tree Club.

Somewhat larger milestones marked the first summer of the war. Day Thorpe moved to Fairfax and took a government censorship job after his father sold Pooks Hill, and Mrs. J. Reed Bradley, managing editor of his paper for more than two years, became the *Bethesda Tribune*'s editor and publisher as of the first issue of June 1942. The Thorpes offered to sell the paper to Mrs. Bradley, but she had no funds, and a New York advertising man, Mel Hickerson, bought it and asked her to stay. According to Mrs. Bradley, "He said he intended to make me part owner." The new owner urged neutrality on the Charter "for business reasons."

Within a few weeks, Gertrude Bradley's mark was on a much healthier paper. In her first editorial comment on her new position, she introduced herself as a child growing up in her father's newspaper office and learning

from him that the first rule was "stick to the news." Then she got right down to the question many had asked, was she going to continue the paper's antagonistic attitude toward the present County government? Her answer, "I could not do so and still be consistent with my ideal of service to the community."

While Allen's *Tribune* was lucky to fill four tabloid pages, the rejuvenated *Journal* was soon up to eight full-size pages with three times the advertising. Allen probably missed Day Thorpe and his sniping at Boss Lee, but that did not last long. Gertrude Bradley played the first charter fight on the front page and right down the middle giving equal exposure to statements from opponents and proponents, and when it got down to election day, she urged people to make up their own minds and vote.[64]

Certainly the most surprising social event of the summer was the marriage of County Commissioner Thomas Earle Hampton to Helen Branham of Brunswick, Georgia. Mr. Hampton, Bethesda's third "mayor" as commissioner for the Western Suburban District, met Miss Branham, a nurse, during the First World War when he worked for his father building cargo ships in Georgia.

Hampton, who had been in the real estate and insurance business in Bethesda for more than thirty years, returned during his honeymoon for a meeting of the County Commissioners since he was president of the Board. The Bethesda Rotary Club feted the newlyweds, and the new Mrs. Hampton received an orchid and a rolling pin, the housewife's

Mr. and Mrs. Thomas Earle Hampton

traditional weapon in all the comic strips. Hampton had announced his candidacy for Robert Peter's State Senate seat shortly before he left on a "vacation" and returned with a wife. Judge Stedman Prescott's brother William, a building-business partner of J. Curtis Walker, was the organization's choice for Hampton's Commission seat.[65]

On June 17, several Maryland counties and the Washington area staged an all-night blackout combined with an air raid drill early in the evening. For the first time aircraft from First Interceptor Command flew over the area during the drill, and "incidents" phoned or carried to the report and control centers resulted in the dispatch of emergency equipment. The only real accident during the drill happened in Cabin John where Fire Chief Kenneth Tuohey was struck in the head by a fire plug cover as a hose was being hooked up. He had his head cut treated at the Glen Echo casualty station. This was also the first drill using messengers and the first in which local ministers, enlisted in the Morale Service, took part wearing their new armbands.

Some problems occurred when the all-clear sounded and homeowners turned their lights on in what was intended to be a blackout until dawn. But the biggest complaints about this drill came from the Civil Defense workers themselves after they found the Red Cross canteens set up at the firehouses were charging for the sandwiches and coffee. Judge Brault said he would look into it. This drill also resulted in the first arrest and trial of a blackout violator–a Silver Spring businessman who paid a $15 fine for leaving a 40-watt bulb burning in the back of his store.

Another daylight drill passed without incident on Saturday, June 27, and the whole State of Maryland took part in a 9 pm Wednesday to 5 am Thursday blackout on July 15-16, which included a half-hour air raid drill. On Monday, July 20, the first unannounced blackout and air raid drill took place in the metropolitan area, and Montgomery County did very well with only two arrests for blackout violations reported. In D.C. almost 150 light burners, mostly business establishment owners, faced prosecution. Chief Warden Arch McDonald warned home owners to get out of the habit of leaving a light on when they were away from the house at night and said "no leniency" will be shown to those who leave lights unattended during a drill.

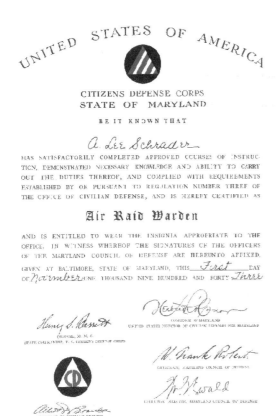

One of the arrests from the July 15 blackout was of Leslie Daly Sr. of 4402 East West Highway, who had gotten home late from work and was eating his supper when Warden Hood Marshall told him to turn the lights out. He complied but then turned a light back on to finish his meal. Warden Joseph Webb knocked on his door. In the loud discussion that followed, Mr. Daly said he had not heard the alarm and that he was not going to turn his lights out until he finished eating. Sometime during this second warning, Les Daly swung at his neighbor Joe Webb. In the first jury trial ever for a Maryland blackout violation, Mr. Daly was found guilty and Judge Woodward fined him ten dollars and costs.[66]

Before the summer was over the Civil Defense authorities issued white, steel, WWI-style helmets to all members of the Citizens Defense Corps who had finished their training and taken the oath of office. By then unannounced or "surprise" air raid drills were the norm.

It was a summer of Ladies Night ball games and scrap drives, of larger draft calls and war bond sales, of the execution of six German saboteurs in the D.C. electric chair and of intensified political name-calling. For some it was a "Buy in Bethesda" campaign and, for others, vacations as usual. Teacher Florence Massey Black described life in Ocean City, where she and her friend and fellow teacher Lillian Moore owned property and rented out apartments.[67]

So many people from Bethesda and Chevy Chase have written to me asking about Ocean City, the dimout, the oil in the water, and the fishing, not to mention the gas situation, that I wondered if you wouldn't run an article in the Journal telling something about it here.

The beaches and water at Ocean City are free from oil. The sand is clean and white and dotted with gay umbrellas beneath which lounge lazy vacationists whose only pastime is gazing out at the equally lazy ocean. The water is exceptionally warm this season and seems bound to make people forget that there is such a thing as a war. When the sun sets into Sinepuxent Bay and the stars and moon come out, a gentle glamour settles upon the city. The dim boardwalk and street lights only heighten the effect. The darkness makes the ocean seem mysterious with the ghost-like effect of the white and breaking waves. The shadows of the soldiers and coast guards patrolling the beach lend an added sense of security.

Today the calm ocean was speckled with boats, some of them pleasure craft, some of them the daily fishing trawlers, two of them sailing yachts. Then there were the air mattresses, and even a silly rubber raft, and of course the proverbial fat men on inner tubes which the rubber administration hasn't found yet!

Although there can be no marlin fishing this year (they were always caught about 35 miles out) the surf and bay fishermen have come into their own. The other day a party of three, one of them a woman, cast their lines from the beach and in a few hours had a catch of 64 kingfish. A man went past our house yesterday loaded down with a two-hour catch. These are only two examples of surf fishing. Last Thursday two men stopped traffic with an express wagon load of trout all of which were over two feet long. They got theirs in the inlet. They said that if we thought these were big we should have seen the ones they got the day before. Of course that may have been another fish story, but they were doing all right!

Last year Ocean City was a madhouse. Everybody and his brother seemed determined to keep us from having our annual peaceful

vacation. This summer is different. There are plenty of people, but there is also plenty of room. We don't feel like a package of sardines. We can stretch, mentally and physically. And we can feel sorry for the people in the crowded and hot cities. When that good old Southern breeze ruffles our already ruined hair-do we say, "Don't you feel sorry for the folks at home?"

We swim until we are almost starved, then we go in to eat those delicious fish, caught that morning. Of course we also have to eat the fried chicken, hot rolls, and all the fresh vegetables the Eastern Sho' grows. And then we remember our girlish figures! That's a blow, but a good brisk walk the length of the boardwalk or a bicycle ride soon remedies that.

And oh yes, the gas shortage. Well, here's one for Bob Ripley: Ocean City doesn't know there is one. Believe it or not, everyone seems to have plenty of gasoline. A "No Gas" sign is unheard of. But gasoline down here goes farther. That may be because everyone enjoys walking and just parks his car.

If you don't believe that Ocean City is the place to come for a vacation, come down and see for yourself. Perhaps I should send you a picture postcard with only the message, "Having a wonderful time. Wish you were here."

When Mrs. Donald Roberts and her family returned from a long weekend in Rehoboth, she described the "dim-out" there. At sundown, she said, "Rehoboth is a ghost town with the street lights blackened on the ocean side, buses shuttered to the east and shades pulled down on every lighted room." Servicemen strolling the darkened boardwalk have to take their dates into a hamburger joint to get a good look at them, she claimed. Cars must use parking lights at night, and sentries walked a path along the beach, and even if night bathers answer "friend" to their challenge, they are told, "Friend or foe, get off the beach." She reported on gun emplacements and searchlights and said planes "zoom all day long along the coast." But she saw many of her friends from Bethesda and Chevy Chase vacationing there including Maybelle and Henry Muir and their sons.[68]

The Muirs were Washington natives who often rented a cottage for a month at the shore. Ken recalled the Coast Guard men who patrolled the beach with their dogs and the "racket" made by the artillery practice down toward Dewey Beach. The Muirs had moved to the corner of East West and Chatham Road shortly after they were married in 1931, and that is where Ken and his brother, Gordon, grew up.

Ken Muir went to the E. V. Brown School for kindergarten and first grade and then attended Chevy Chase Elementary. He had a *Daily News* route along Connecticut Avenue that included one customer at the Club, "a pretty impressive place to deliver a paper," and then he got a *Post* route closer to home. "That included the houses on the East West Highway hill, which was a bear to ride on a bicycle." He played games on the lot behind the Chevy Chase post office with Don Robertson and a lot of other kids and explored the woods and creek across from his home on the highway. Later he and a friend took a .22 over to the Columbia Country Club dump in those woods and set up empty liquor bottles to plink at.

Don Robertson probably held some sort of record for wartime paper routes. He started on the day after Pearl Harbor with a *Daily News* route spread all across the east side of Connecticut and then delivered, seriatim, the *Star* on Grafton, Hesketh and Oliver Streets, the *Post* in his Shepherd Street neighborhood and the *Times-Herald* in a spotty route like the one he started with. He remembered himself as a procrastinator about collecting whose mother pushed him out to do that job toward the end of every month.

Emory Bogley's advisory board for the Recreation Center started the season by raising $500 from the business community for summer activities. Louis Mitchell used the money to hire several part-time aides and began his ambitious program in mid-June with organized games, arts and crafts, several tournaments in different sports and a few special events. Lucille Johnson, the public school music supervisor, came down on Tuesday afternoons and led a program of singing, folk dancing and instrumental music and held community sings for the parents on one evening each week.

Selma Baernstein and Scott Brewer Jr., college sophomores, hired on as assistants to Mr. Mitchell; Joseph Gardiner, Bert Cleveland and George Van Wagner organized a tennis lessons and a tournament. Loris Williams was there part-time for baseball instruction, and Henry Hiser donated prizes for the ping

pong tourney, won by Nelson Embrey. Bob Poch won the horseshoe crown over thirty-two entrants by defeating the favorite, George Van Wagner, and then Art Baker. A Pee Wee baseball league ran all summer, and the Rec Center's team led by Herbie Benson and Dick and Phil Daly beat Jessup Blair for the County recreation department title.

Recreation Center Daily Program Schedule
9 am to noon-elementary school age children-ring and quiet games, arts and crafts, nature study and physical activities, low organized games.
1 to 5 pm-junior hs age group-clubs and classes and tournament play. Also art and crafts groups. League games in physical activities.
5 to 9 pm-free and running games for all ages, tournaments, picnic and family activities, open for adults to relax and rest.

special programs

Mon	10 to noon - tennis instruction, boys
	1 to 3 pm - tennis instruction, girls
	2 pm - hunt club for boys with air rifles
	1 to 3 pm - badminton, boys and girls
Tues	1 to 3 pm - baseball school, boys
	1 to 3 pm - music, singing, folk dancing
	2 to 3 pm - archery, boys and girls
	7 to 9 pm - family community singing
Wed	10 am to noon - art club, boys and girls
	1 to 3 pm - badminton, boys and girls
	3 to 5 pm - wood craft, boys and girls
Thurs	1 to 3 pm - baseball school
	2 to 4 pm - archery, boys and girls
	2 to 5 pm- nature walk, boys
Frid	1 to 3 pm - tennis instruction
	2 to 4 pm - model craft club
Sat	2 to 4 pm - camera club
	4 to 6 pm - archery

A junior high-age girls' club met regularly, and square dancing proved to be very popular. In mid-August "Sue" Baernstein (B-CC `41), who had been in charge of most of the activities for younger children, drew a big crowd when she staged a "dress-up" day with prizes awarded for the best costumes. A field day involving Rock Creek and Jessup Blair recreation centers ended the season. By then more than 8,000 young people had taken part in Rec Center activities during the summer.

As the Bradley Boulevard elementary school neared completion, the superintendent asked Mrs. Lendell A. Connor of Huntington Terrace to head a committee to take a census of the children who would attend the new school and to help get a PTA organized. Dr. Broome chose Martha White, a teacher at Bethesda Elementary, to be the principal-teacher at the new school. The Superintendent met with Mrs. Connor and her committee at the school, which, he noted, was badly in need of landscaping. He hoped the community would take on this job after the lot was graded and seeded, and he also asked for volunteers for the school's cafeteria.

The new school featured large windows, brightly painted walls, and, much like East Bethesda, sliding doors that allowed rooms to be connected for assemblies. Dr. Broome assured the parents that one street from Bradley Boulevard would be graded and graveled before September and a walk built from Garfield Street to the school.

Meanwhile, parents at East Bethesda Elementary started a cooperative nursery school, and soon Mrs. Herman Silverman had eighteen two- to five-year-olds registered and hard at play. The fourth grade room-mother, Mrs. George R. Kinzie of Maple Avenue, sponsored a new group of Blue Birds who named themselves the "Morning Glories." When school reopened, a serious competition developed between the numerous Blue Bird, Brownie and Cub Scout groups to see who could bring the most paper to school.

The East Bethesda Victory Club met almost every Thursday and quickly involved women who lived on Cheltenham and neighboring streets in Westboro and within a few weeks had branches in Glenbrook and Rosedale. Mrs. William H. Winkler was the "sergeant major and mother superior" of this neighborhood. She had been a physiotherapist at Walter Reed and Children's Hospital for several years and very active with the Camp Fire Girls when she accepted appointment to the Women's Activities Division of civil defense and began organizing Victory Clubs with a "speak to your neighbor" campaign.

She urged the women, many of them young wives of officers at the Naval Hospital, to bring their babies with them to meetings, and this led to the development of a recreation center for children in the wooded

area behind the elementary school. The women helped the school develop an evacuation plan, supervised area scrap drives and acted as daytime air raid wardens. "Individually, our activities may seem small," Mrs. Winkler said. "Collectively they add up to a sizeable program. We are standing ready to do the particular thing that needs to be done in the community of which we are a part."[69]

The Bethesda-Chevy Chase Branch of the Montgomery County Public Health Lay Clinic led by Mrs. Louis Gravelle enlarged the clinic at 4713 Hampden Lane and reconditioned it with contributions from local hardware stores. The District Dental Society donated long-needed

The salvage from Chevy Chase Terrace included one rubber bunny

dental equipment, installed, gratis, by E. M. Fry and Kenneth W. Trunnell. Two public health nurses, Mrs. Mable Sibley Clark and Miss Clare Campbell, stayed busy making home visits and holding maternal and child welfare clinics.[70]

The clinic served mothers-to-be and twenty-five to forty children each month and provided diphtheria toxoids, vitamins and gave out over 30,000 cod liver oil capsules in less than a year. The committee members also furnished canned milk for the nurses to distribute as needed and made dressings for midwife kits and layettes for mothers in need.

By the summer of `42, salvage drives were a part of the everyday life of most Bethesdans. The Women's Activities Division of the Council of Defense headed by Mrs. Walter A. Brown Jr. collected tons of tin cans, iron and steel in bins at the firehouses, at the Chevy Chase post office and in front of the Farm Women's Market. In June, rubber salvage got underway through filling stations, which, for the first month, were authorized to pay one cent a pound for old galoshes, garden hoses, and worn out tires. Old girdles were not wanted. By the end of the first week Gordon Burrows had accumulated 5,000 pounds of rubber in a bin labeled "Rubber Scrap to Beat the Jap." A group of kids in Chevy Chase Terrace, led by Betty Gottschall, scoured their neighborhood for scrap rubber and metal and got their picture in the paper.

In late August, George Menke, the County salvage chairman, with the cooooperation of Sidney Lust, staged a big junk rally in the parking lot of the Bethesda Theater. More than 500 people attended and brought almost fifteen tons of scrap with them. In September, all the Civilian Defense groups

JUNK RALLY
For Bethesda-Chevy Chase
and vicinity

August 24th
at
Bethesda Theatre
7:30 to 9:00 P. M.

Junk helps make guns, tanks, ships for our fighting men . . . .
Bring in anything made of metal or rubber . . . .
Proceeds to Go to the Bethesda Women's Defense Council
Bring your family
Meet your friends
Throw YOUR scrap into the fight!

JUNK MAKES FIGHTING WEAPONS

Let's Jolt them with Junk from Bethesda-Chevy Chase
This Message Paid For By Sidney Lust

mobilized under the leadership of senior air raid wardens for an emergency scrap drive, which brought in over 350 tons County-wide.

Members of the Women's Activities group had been saving oils and fats and giving them to the Girl Scouts and farm women to make soap, but in mid-summer the Government began asking butchers to purchase salvaged cooking grease from housewives at three cents a pound, and another drive was on. Soon there was an empty coffee can on the back of most Bethesda stoves that slowly filled with congealed and speckled grease from frying eggs or hamburgers.

Every school became involved in the salvage drives. "Sandy" Astin, then a sixth grader, recalled dragging his wagon through Woodmont and Battery Park, knocking on doors and collecting scrap metal to take to Bethesda Elementary. The Boy Scouts purchased a truck to help their campaign and, operating from the old market at Wisconsin and Walsh, collected twenty tons of heavy metal, seven tons of newspapers, three tons of brass and 3,000 pounds of copper by early fall.

And despite some regrets, the American Legion donated the gun barrel it had installed as a memorial at Bradley and Wisconsin and replaced it with a flag pole. That old cannon added 2,660 pounds to the scrap drive.

The summer ended with two surprise air-raid drills in August, and while there was some confusion partly because of a thunderstorm during the first one, the main problem continued to be with businessmen and homeowners who left lights burning when they closed their shops or were away from home. After the first drill, Clarence Keiser issued a stern warning to store owners in the business district that warrants would be sworn out if violations continued, and after the second drill two of the twenty citations handed out were to Bethesda establishments. Keiser also installed some new wardens including the first female precinct warden in the County, Mrs. Kurtz Hanson of 9319 Old Georgetown Road, who was chosen after wardens in her area "insisted that she was the most efficient and conscientious worker in the precinct and fully capable of handling the job."

On Monday afternoon, August 31, President Franklin Roosevelt drove through Bethesda in his big, open Packard and then delivered a short talk dedicating the Naval Hospital "in the green, peaceful Maryland countryside." It was a fighting speech in which he warned that carelessness hampered the war effort. He said that during the first months of the war, the enemy had asked "Where is the United States Navy?" Now, he said they know. "They learned in the Atlantic, they learned in the Coral Sea, they learned off Midway . . . ." The Navy, he went on is "where it has always been. It is in there fighting."

On this hundredth anniversary of the naval medical service, doctors at several foreign stations joined the President in the radio broadcast of the dedication. Captain Charles

FDR at NNMC

W. O. Bunker, who had headed the medical school, took command of what was now being called the National Naval Medical Center as of the first of September with a promotion to rear admiral. Bunker, a native of Iowa, entered the Navy in 1907 and graduated from Cornell's medical school. He had served in the Atlantic Transport Service in the First World War. In the fall, Ann A. Bernatitus, head nurse at NNMC, was presented with the Legion of Merit for her service on Bataan and Corregidor. She was one of the few evacuated by submarine and was the first person in naval service to receive the medal.[71]

Even before the new school year began, Bethesda-Chevy Chase High School offered free bench metal classes, which met four nights a week for twelve weeks. The course,

which included instruction in aircraft, sheet metal, acetylene welding and small parts assembly, attracted dozens of Bethesdans and extra sessions were quickly created. Jobs were available right in Bethesda for the graduates. One of the five Bethesda defense plants, which gobbled up graduates of the B-CC classes, was the Falge Engineering Company on Hampden Lane that turned out signal lights for the Navy and Coast Guard and rescue lights for the Army engineers.

The first woman worker at Falge was Mrs. Lewis Eisele, who said she took the metal work class and the job to help her flyer-son win the war. By the end of 1942, twenty-six women worked on Falge's assembly line benches, under the direction of shop foreman Henry Latterner, assembling products from parts produced by some sixty sub-contractors. Two of the women in the paint shop were University

Mrs. Eisele drilling

of Chicago classmates who had not seen each other for years, and many other college-educated women worked at the plant six days a week. The general attitude of the employees, who proudly displayed their "Victory Banner" flag for 100 percent war bond enrollment, was that they were making a real contribution to the war effort.

Raymond Falge himself had been a manufacturer's representative selling products, including signaling lights, to the military. When

Raymond Falge Jr. with his father's signal lamp.

he could not convince one of his companies to modify its lamps to meet the Navy's specifications, he decided to design a new battery-powered lamp himself. Working with Navy men who were concerned about submarines detecting light spillage from existing equipment, he came up with a triggered lamp with a long tubular shield, and when that still did not meet specifications, he filled the shield with large soda straws spray-painted flat black. The Navy placed a small order for testing, and then after some modifications, a much larger order. That was when Falge moved his family from Virginia and came to Bethesda to find the workers he needed.

Out at Carderock, the David Taylor Model Basin hired and trained forty women in milling operations, instrument production and model making. The Chapel of the Redeemer at Fairway Hills established a day care center for their children, and their foreman said they were performing like "old hands" and could soon take over most of the machine work. Some of their male coworkers disagreed.[72]

Several new businesses arrived in Bethesda that fall, and there were some significant personnel changes in other operations. Despite opposition from Lady Isabel, the fire department and the churches, "Beanie" Brown's Raw Bar at 7546 Old Georgetown Road, officially the Georgetown Road Grill, received a beer and wine license and soon became well known for its spiced shrimp, fresh clams and crab cakes. The NorBud Shop opened next to the "10¢ store" with racks of lingerie, blouses and women's clothing, while the Ladies Specialty Shop added a fur department. George Teunis, already active in the Junior Chamber of Commerce, moved his optician's office to 7004 Wisconsin Avenue but six months later moved back to 1800 Eye Street.

Small's Rock Creek Valley Garden Shop north of Chevy Chase Lake increased its business, but the Rock Creek Riding Academy in the old carbarn lost its permit much to the relief of its neighbors who had complained about the flies, odors and wandering horses. The stable's manager disappeared leaving unpaid bills and unfed horses. The abandoned animals, many in very bad shape, were taken to a farm near Norbeck and then auctioned off in the spring to pay some of the operation's debts. The Bethesda Theater had

a new manager, Doug Smiley, as did Peoples Hardware Store in Ray Kidwell at its new location, 7000 Wisconsin Avenue, where Margaret Costello was proving that a woman could be knowledgeable and helpful in that business. The Montgomery Ward mail order store also hired a new manager, Mrs. J. E. Prescott. Charles Neyman came down from Brooklyn to become the butcher in his brother-in-law Herman Horowitz's Woodmont DGS, the Bethesda Economy Market at Chase and Wisconsin.

Marvin Simmons went into the real estate business and advertised his own 6,600 square foot "Dodge Building" for rent. The OSS took it, let down the venetian blinds and spent the war there assembling and testing radios and other communications equipment, but Simmons kept his paint shop farther down Miller and bought, sold and repaired cars all during the war. Somewhat less mysteriously, up at 7812 Old Georgetown Road, Madame Carroll hung out her shingle and offered advice on "business affairs, love affairs, wills, deeds, lost and stolen articles, will give the names of enemies and friends and who and when you will marry." She offered readings to "Colored and White" and guaranteed her work.[73]

Chevy Chase Junior College, its non-profit, tax-exempt status established, opened for its forty-first year under a new president, Carrie Sutherland who had been academic dean and then president of Arlington Hall Junior College. Mrs. Alexander Fromhold signed on as director of extracurricular activities, and the administration promised that schedules would allow students plenty of time for volunteer, war-effort activities.

Our Lady of Lourdes school, which had a first graduating class of fifteen, grew by almost a third and enrolled 325 students in the fall. A science museum and a first-aid course for 8th graders were planned. Lady Isabel's, Miss Libbey's, Landon, Longfellow, the Walton School, Green Acres and Mrs. Helen D. Sutch's school in her Battery Lane home also were back in business.

Public schools opened on September 14 with the superintendent decrying the shortage of male teachers and promising Westbrook Elementary that two temporary, wooden classrooms would be built as soon as materials were available. Bradley Elementary, as it was now being called, welcomed its first students. Bradmoor Street was graveled from Bradley Boulevard, but the path from the corner of Madison and Garfield was not finished when school began. Children from Irvington and Hempstead soon made their own path through the piney woods. The PTA, led by Mrs. Lawrence M. Vaughan, sponsored a series of square dances to help parents get acquainted and to raise some money.[75]

Jane Bradley, who lived in Sonoma, was in the new school's first sixth grade class.

I went to Bradley school for a year when it opened. It was a neat school, little after Bethesda Elementary where we had three classes of each grade. I thought I'd gone to heaven. I could walk to school, come home for lunch, didn't have to ride a bus. We named it, and I was sure they named it for me. There was one of each grade and maybe a duo. Our teacher was a Mrs. Miller, who was probably the best teacher I ever had. I think she had been at Rosemary.

The kids did the landscaping. We cut a path to Greentree Road. We built a footbridge over a ditch, and I wrote a poem about that bridge. We did a unit in social studies about the stuff we did. There wasn't any playground

Father Little with the first graduates of his school[74]

equipment, but there was a cafeteria where you could just get milk and sometimes soup.

The second building at East Bethesda opened in the fall, and the playground was finally completely equipped but still unsurfaced. Mrs. Bosley said that many of the school programs would deal with the war effort and the need to conserve resources. The school had three new teachers and was developing a music program. The PTA staged a bingo, 500 rummy and bridge party to raise money to finish the playground.

At Chevy Chase Elementary, Principal Anna Rose announced that all 680 students were one big Victory Committee. "Children can no longer be ministered to," she said, "but must perform a definite service to society." Upper grade children reconditioned desks and chairs, and in the first week the scrap drive produced 2,000 pounds including an old coal stove, which several youngsters hauled out of a neighbor's cellar. Much smaller Alta Vista school with only 148 students also brought in a ton of scrap metal in the first week of school. Principal Louise Walker was proud of her program and planned a series of "scrap Fridays."

Bethesda Elementary was finally back down to its 600 capacity with the opening of Bradley Elementary, and Ruth Clapp had her upper-grade classes taking over janitor duties four days a week in addition to organizing a number of service clubs and Victory groups. Because of the increase in food prices, cafeteria manager Marie Kromas had to raise the price of nickel items to six cents and the plate lunch from a dime to twelve cents.[76]

At Leland Junior High, where the enrollment was well over one thousand and still growing, three lunch shifts were needed, and there were so many applicants for service clubs that membership was put on a "civil service" basis. Each homeroom took care of its own janitorial tasks, and a "voluntary" Clean Up Squad looked after the halls and grounds. The faculty had fourteen new teachers and a new, work-experience program for some ninth graders.

At the high school the enrollment stayed about the same, 800, but the incoming sophomore class was the largest ever, 305. The total staff was cut by five, but Angela Darby, who took on the job of senior-class advisor, and home ec teacher Kayte Womac returned;

shop teacher Robert Best and boys' PE instructor-coach Ray Fehrman were the new staff members.

The curriculum included courses in "The Science of Aeronautics" and "Aircraft Metal Training." Seventeen boys, including Leroy Allison, were chosen from hundreds of applicants for the "aeronautics" course taught by R. Victor Cooney with the aim of producing air cadets. Unfortunately, Cooney left in October to take a pilot-instructor position with the Air Transport Command, and physics and math teacher Mary Roeming took over the aeronautics course.[77]

Paper shortages doomed the school newspaper, *The Tattler*, that year and almost deprived the Class of `43 of a yearbook. But after hearing Principal Tom Pyle declare that paper and metal shortages would mean no annual, senior class president Leonard Williams did some checking on his own through contacts he had developed in his political and skeet shooting activities and found a printer. He did not want his class to become the only one not to leave a written record behind. At the first class meeting, Williams arranged for a delegate to move that the *Pine Tree* be printed, and the motion carried by acclamation before Mr. Pyle could say "wait" or anything else. Marilyn Snyder and Rita Laws, under the sponsorship of English teacher Jane Williams and with the help of a large staff, produced a first-class yearbook on an early deadline.

Leonard Williams was missing from the senior-officer group photo at the front of the book because he left B-CC during the Christmas holidays and enrolled in a college program at Mount St. Marys. Carter "Lambie" Dawson took over as class president. After the Blair game riot, apple blossom affair and yearbook incident, Williams did not have any problem getting Mr. Pyle to sign the needed papers to leave school early.

Despite missing the last half of his senior year and chance to play more basketball, Leonard Williams was voted the boy who did the most for his school as well as "Most Ambitious." Among the girls, the seniors chose Marilyn Snyder as the person who "did most for school" and labeled Carter Dawson "Most Versatile."

The fraternities, although battered by "Ma" Mohler, were still in vogue, as Houston Swink remembered:

I was in a fraternity. We went through the hazing, got our butts beat with a paddle and all that, Southern Society. There were only two main ones I think. We'd meet in different people's houses and paid dues and all that. We were pledged then, in `42. A lot of good athletes were. Most all the

The B-CC student body exercises in front of the school

jocks were in fraternities. Harry Andrews, he was a great organizer.

Charlie Hughes and a number of his friends attended a "rush" meeting to hear about all the advantages of belonging, but since he had been told they were illegal, he did not join. Hardy Sorrell, George Van Wagner and some of the other good athletes did however, and when they signed Hughes' yearbook put "XA" under their names for Chi Alpha. Sophomore Lois Copenhaver, a regular on the basketball team and a class leader, went to one sorority party but, like Hughes, did not join. She knew the organizations were outlawed. The mood was changing.[78]

In November the Victory Corps became an important part of high school life. The program's purpose was "to train students for war service, which will come after they leave school and for active participation in the community's war effort."[79]

As part of the Victory Corps regimen the whole school, both student body and faculty, exercised together for fifteen minutes almost

every day, and juniors and seniors could join one of five specialized divisions: air, land, sea, production, or community service. There were requirements and expectations for each program. Mr. Bender's shop programs became an important part of the Victory Corps program. With the help of several student instructors such as senior Les Dame in electricity, juniors Dan Baernstein in radio, Bill Boyer in model planes, Fred Garlock in auto and aircraft mechanics, and Jim Whitmore in the machine shop, teachers Best and Bender stretched their offerings. Other students studied Morse code, aircraft identification and map making.

The Community Service division provided substitute teachers and office help, supported the Red Cross production unit and even had a drill squad and a chorus. One of the unexpected benefits of the Victory Corps exercise program was the pleasure it gave students watching some of their overweight or superannuated teachers trying to bend their knees or perform "jumping jacks." Crude drawings of "Ma" Mohler trying to touch her toes became prized locker art.[80]

A short-lived, mimeographed substitute for the *Tattler* first appeared in late November. The *Echo*, produced with the help of Commercial Department students, featured Bill Jenning's cartoons, an occasional poem and all the usual school news including the word that a path through the grove was about to be paved thanks to the student council's efforts and Mr. Bender's students. The *Tattler* would return, mimeographed, in 1943.[81]

Al Bender also became a kind of unofficial truant officer for the high school and

occasionally checked out the Hot Shoppe, bowling alleys and nearby homes for absent scholars. Al Sherline recalled one of Mr. Bender's victories:

In the big band era, they all came to the Capital Theater, and we would cut class and go down there. I saw Sinatra, Glenn Miller, all of them. We were in line one time, and the line went around the block, and when we got to the damn ticket window, Al Bender was standing there pulling them out of line. As you got there he'd say, "Go back to school, go back to school." He was a tough guy.

After a lackluster primary election, which barely served to help voters get used to new precinct assignments, politics moved back on the boil as the charter forces filed a petition list of 8,953 names in mid-September, more than enough to put the question on the ballot. Allen Gardner and Stella Werner said that there could have been many more names, and that they would file some supplementary petitions, but that some areas had not been thoroughly canvassed especially in the upper County where gas and tire rationing made it difficult. The 7th Election District (Bethesda) contributed 4,414 signers, and most were Democrats.

Mr. Gardner notified the Commissioners that the petition had been filed and reminded them that they had until September 24 to nominate candidates for the charter-writing board. When asked if the charter committee would now begin to collect 2,000 signers on petitions to name candidates for the charter board, Mr. Gardner responded, "We prefer to wait for the County Commissioners to nominate candidates."[82]

He did not have to wait long. The next day the Commissioners met in special session and picked their five choices for the charter board, should the referendum succeed, which they loudly doubted. President Thomas Earle Hampton issued a statement on behalf of the three "organization" Democrats who had chosen the slate. Lone Republican Walter Johnson missed the meeting and "fusion" Democrat John Oxley voted against those named saying "people don't hire house wreckers to build their homes."

In their statement, the Commissioners said that they "believed Allen H. Gardner of 1515 Dale Drive, Woodside Park, has done as much work as any other citizen in the county in producing charter petitions," and so they nominated him but noted that they "continue greatly concerned about what might be the results if an unusual and untested form of County government were adopted." So they chose as the four others County Farm Agent O. W. Anderson and three lawyers with ties to the Lee "machine": Joseph A. Cantrel, J. Bond Smith, and Roger J. Whiteford, the three most vocal and consistent critics of the charter idea.

Earle Hampton defended the three attorneys as men who "have first hand knowledge of governmental practices and problems." Oxley said that if he had voted for the Commissioners' list he would have felt "like a lawyer hired to defend a man and at the same time doing everything possible to help the prosecution." The *Tribune*'s Bray, sounding much like Colonel Lee, wrote that there "are no brighter legal lights resident in Montgomery County than" Cantrel, Whiteford and Smith and then predicted that the referendum would be "overwhelmed" in the up-County areas, badly beaten in Silver Spring and do no better than a tie in the 7th District.[83]

Whiteford accepted the nomination although he stated that he continued to be opposed to the idea of a new charter. Allen Gardner declined the Commissioners' appointment, to almost no one's surprise, with a statement that he could not serve with three men who "had previously attempted to destroy the charter movement with misleading statements." He called the Commissioners' action "hypocrisy true to the best traditions of professional politicians." The Commissioners named Judge Albert Brault, Bethesda trial magistrate and director of the Civilian Defense Council, to replace Gardner, and the Democratic organization issued a statement in which it expressed "surprise" that Gardner did not want minority opinion represented. Queried by the League of Women Voters all five of the Commissioners' candidates responded, "No, I do not favor the election of a Charter Board."

In less than a week the charter committee put forth its own slate and began collecting the petition signatures due October 13. The charter forces named five of what Brooke Lee's people called "civics": Alice Hostetler, Judge Thomas Anderson, Stephen James, Tarlton Brooke and Frederic P. Lee, and by

the end of the month Mrs. Werner presented 163 pages of petitions with 2,842 signatures to put them on the ballot.

Ex-law professor Fred Lee, chairman of the Bethesda draft board and one-time legislative counsel to the U.S. Senate, became the leading spokesman of the charter forces in the drive toward the November 3 election. Lee was Gardner's number one lieutenant and a "perfect complement" to Gardner since he came from West of Rock Creek and had a good reputation in the suburbs and in the city. *His prose was both eloquent and precise; he was a spell-binding advocate in court. He served the cause, as probably no one else could have done, as tribune, legal adviser and charter-framer; his reputation and his brilliance made him a hard man to beat.*[84]

Probably the trend that annoyed the organization Democrats, anti-charter forces and Brooke Lee loyalists the most was the general attitude of the Washington newspapers toward the County and the reform movement. Columnist Robert Bray expressed outrage on several occasions that Civic Federation and local association meetings were reported no matter how few were in attendance, and Bill Allen echoed the general view of Lee's *Maryland News* and the long-loyal *Sentinel* when he asked why Washington papers thought the County government was so bad when it had done so many good things. It was, he wrote, "entirely unfair and completely unjustified."

The best city-paper coverage was by Washington *Post* reporter Chester Vanemann who seemed to be one of the few able to separate the Brookings report from the move toward writing a home rule charter for Montgomery County. The often vicious fight, Vanemann concluded, was not really about "charter" but because the County had been ruled "by a Democratic Party organization, which has, with a few minor interruptions, been in power for generations" and had operated a very successful spoils system and did not want that to change. The Washington *Daily News* generally supported the Charter idea and in August boosted the movement with a series of six articles by Martha Strayer. She summarized the fight as "Who's Who vs. The Montgomery County politicians."[85]

This journalistic aspect of the charter fight came to a head during the late in September when the *Post* printed an editorial captioned "Democracy in Action" and Commissioner Hampton responded. The *Post* held that:

This fight for better local government is a good example of democracy in action. Thousands of voteless Washingtonians must be watching it with the greatest of interest and envy.

(The County has) *outgrown the loosely organized, patronage-dominated, rural government, which it inherited. The efforts of these citizens to obtain better service from their government, without impairing democracy, deserve a better response than the cynical action taken by the county commissioners.*[86]

Hampton's response, printed in some papers as a paid, full-page ad, attacked the Brookings report as well as the *Post* while praising the County's progress in schools, police protection, highways, parks, water and sewer systems and tax rate. The charterites, wrote Hampton, far from seeking democracy in action, wanted to do away with the two-party system and majority rule. Hampton defended his nominees as lawyers of ability and integrity wronged by the Capital press. Commissioner Hampton repeated many of Joseph Cantrel's and J. Bond Smith's favorite shibboleths and expressed shock that the *Post* had been so unfair.[87]

While the charter battle took center stage for many Bethesdans, the Republicans sent out the mellifluous Theodore Roosevelt McKeldin to challenge Governor O'Conor, and the battle between J. Glenn Beall and Brooke Lee for the House seat grew bitter. Arthur Hilland headed the Republican forces in Montgomery County and opened his party's headquarters in the Housing Guild Building on Wisconsin Avenue. Judge Henry J. Hunt III, the "Plain Poet of Western Maryland," dashed into the fight with a long letter extolling Colonel Lee's virtues and a verse in minstrel-show dialect supporting the Democratic ticket. The campaign descended from there and included an odd dispute over who did or did not support the Townsend Plan and a more serious conflict over the conduct of the war, which most people knew was not going at all well that fall.[88]

While the parties wheeled their champions from rally to rally and Major James B. Fitzgerald endorsed Lee for Congress and called on the veterans of the 29th Division for their support, the pro- and anti-charter forces debated zoning law. The Civic Federation ducked endorsing a charter slate at its first

fall meeting to the surprise of many, but the League of Women Voters went on record in unanimous support of the charter movement despite some Democratic women's pleas. The LWV circulated a flier called "Let the People Decide" in support of the petition drive and in its "Voter's Guide" made clear its support for both home rule and pro-Charter candidates.

Clarence Small's Independent Party also backed the charter slate and issued an anti-Lee campaign tabloid. Their slogan was "Kill One-Man Rule/Vote Independent November 3." In a polite debate on radio station WRC, Stephen James tried to explain to J. Bond Smith that home rule was the issue, but Smith insisted that he was not against home rule but opposed to the radical Brookings charter. This discussion led to a less polite debate with Dr. Meriam of Brookings, who accused J. Bond Smith of a series of misstatements. Smith responded that Brookings entry in the campaign showed "how desperately they need assistance."

With little more than a week to go, the pro-charter candidates all appeared at a rally and roundtable discussion at Bethesda Elementary School, and the anti-charter forces brought back Alfred Bettman, Cincinnati zoning authority, who expressed serious doubts about the legal status of the proposed County law-making authority. The antis even took out an ad in the D.C. dailies to spread his views.

The *Journal* summed up the arguments for and against the charter in a long article starting on the front page, but both Editor Allen and columnist Bray of the *Tribune* ignored the charter fight in the last edition before the election to trumpet various endorsements of Lee's candidacy for Congress. In a spread of multi-page ads paid for by the Democratic State Central Committee, the Commissioners' slate of charter board nominees was listed as part of the "United Democratic Organization" ticket.

The election resulted in a surprisingly easy victory for the charter referendum by a fifty-six percent plurality and for all five of the charter-board-endorsed candidates who won by an average vote of 8,800 to 4,800. Even more surprising

was the defeat of E. Brooke Lee by J. Glenn Beall. The *Sentinel* called it "one of the greatest upsets in recent years." Lee lost by 21,000 votes and was defeated in Montgomery by 1,500 while Democrats won almost all other local races except for Lawson King's losing to Republican Commissioner Walter Johnson by 1,300 votes. Thomas E. Hampton crushed the leader of the Independent Party, Charles H. Small, 11,500 to 8,500 to become the County's State Senator.[89]

The stunning defeat of Lee, especially in his home county, was almost certainly the result of the charter fight. Robert V. Bray called Lee's defeat a "terrible beating" and analyzed it carefully if not impartially. Lee won in only two Bethesda-area precincts, but in even those the charter-board candidates generally defeated the commissioners' choices. Almost 3,200 of the 7,800 voting for the charter, more than forty percent, were from Bethesda precincts. The antis noted, however, that a lot fewer people voted for the charter than signed the petitions.[90]

Analysts pointed out that, in the precincts where the charter did best, Lee did worst and that the voters who came to the polls to support the charter question may well have made the difference. Lee blamed the Charter fight for his defeat. He said the Charter was "murder for me" because it "simply lined up the Charter people with the Republican Party all down the line. But they were there anyhow," he added, concluding oddly, "It didn't make much difference."[91]

Bray also noted that fewer than 8,000 voted for the Charter while the average Democratic winner garnered 11,000 votes and Lee in losing had 10,400 votes. "This," he concluded, "leaves the charter leaders something to think about" as they look toward submitting their yet-to-be-written plan to the voters in 1944. The Charter Committee also faced a debt of almost a thousand dollars. It spent $4,186.98, about a third of what the Democratic organization expended to try to

Voting machine line-up in 1942 election

defeat the charter, but collected only about $3,200 from fewer than 200 individuals. [92]

The Bethesda *Journal* headlined the election coverage "Charter Board Endorsed by Voters" while the *Tribune* banner read "County Democrats Score Sweep" and said the voters balloted "to fasten the charter effort on the County" while the *Journal* concluded that "an aroused electorate approved the Charter movement." Both papers quoted J. Bond Smith as saying charter government would not work and "we await with confidence the ultimate verdict two years hence."[93]

Tribune editor Allen viewed the results soberly. He summed up the enterprise ahead of the newly elected charter board and concluded:

The supporters of charter are now faced with the task of producing a definite plan for the operation of the county government. Hitherto they have been supporting an undefined utopia, something better than it is now. They will now have to outline to the voters and taxpayers of the county the details of their plan for charter government.

The Brookings report would soon re-emerge as an issue, but this was the first time an anti-charter leader publicly recognized a potentially clean slate. As he had before when he wrote that this was not the time, W. Prescott Allen showed much more tolerance for the possibility of a charter government than most of his good-old-boy peers.[94]

According to the *Journal*, Stella Werner said, "I'm going home to give my house a thorough cleaning after neglecting it for months."

Stella Werner and her daughters

With only six months to produce a draft of their plan for revamping the County government, the unpaid Charter Board quickly found office space in the Teachers Conference Room of the Social Agencies Building in Rockville, chose Frederic P. Lee as their chairman and Thomas Robertson as secretary and got down to work and planned a series of public meetings to hear suggestions. The Board members paid their own expenses, relied on the two attorney-members for legal advice and were able to persuade a series of consultants to meet with them without compensation. Marjorie Garfield, the Charter committee's unofficial historian, told Marie Garber, "Actually, Fred Lee and his personal office staff contributed enormously to the cost of drawing up the charter."[95]

Among their first experts were Dr. Lewis Meriam of Brookings, Joseph P. Chamberlin of the Legislative Drafting Research Bureau of Columbia University, Greenbelt City Manager Roy S. Braden who was president of the International City Managers Association, and Willard F. Day, FHA supervisor and former county manager in Henrico County, Virginia. Chairman Lee solicited written statements from individuals and groups, and shortly after Christmas the Charter Board was ready for a series of public hearings.

Lee, Stephen James and Mrs. Hostetler resigned from the County Charter Committee, and Adlai Magee's nominating committee picked three, up-county leaders to replace them. In the first Charter Committee meeting after their victory Stella Werner praised her

precinct workers "who stuck to their jobs until they were sure of victory." Allen Gardner continued as president of the Committee and urged all the citizens of the County, if they wanted "the Charter to be what it should be," to "give their most thoughtful suggestions to the Charter Board."

When the newly elected Board of County Commissioners got down to work, they elected Lacy Shaw of the Eastern Suburban District president. William Prescott, the newly chosen Commissioner from the Bethesda District, set up his office in the County Building and agreed to represent the Commissioners on the Welfare Board. Prescott, 42, a graduate of St. Albans and Johns Hopkins, had been active in area real estate for eighteen years and served as a member of the County Board of Assessors. He got off to a good start by having Bethesda's main streets swept thoroughly and then having the trash-filled banks of the railroad tracks cleaned up on both sides of busy Wisconsin Avenue.

The Commissioners retained Joseph A. Cantrel as their counsel and made some big news by confirming the Governor's appointment of Lt. Col. E. Brooke Lee to the Maryland-National Capital Park and Planning Commission to replace Lacy Shaw. Arthur Hilland was first in line to denounce the appointment as more politics and "bossism" as usual.

While this political tumult continued, the war and everyday life in Bethesda proceeded. The government introduced V-Mail, and Admiral Nimitz urged those writing to men overseas to use the microfilm service. Naval battles in the Solomons and fighting in the streets of Stalingrad held the headlines until the long Guadalcanal campaign grew increasingly bloody.

That fight came home to many Bethesdans with the death of Marine Pvt. Frank Lewis Fahrenwald, who had attended Leland and graduated from Western High School. "Dutch" was remembered by many as the popular assistant golf pro at Kenwood where he spent much of his time. The 20-year-old was killed in action on Guadalcanal in mid-September, the first from the County to die in combat in World War II. His mother worked at Bell Laundry and his older brother, Henry, was an Army sergeant stationed at Fort Bliss.

Later Lt. Edward B. Gibbons, a 28-year-old Navy flyer who was wounded when the cruiser *Quincy* was sunk while his plane was on the catapult, told his story of the Guadalcanal fight as a patient at the Naval Hospital. His wife, who was expecting their first child, was living with her father, Col. C. M. Trammell, on Oliver Street in Chevy Chase.[96]

The draft began to take married men without children and then, by October, 20-year-olds. Company Ten of the Maryland Minuteman Militia Reserve organized with Capt. Joseph A. Cantrel in charge. They drilled at Leland JHS and practiced on the new rifle range just north of Rock Creek off East West Highway. Both of Cantrel's twin sons joined up. "We were shooting against the hill at Meadowbrook, and I remember marching out on the playground at Leland," Frank said. "We had khaki uniforms."

Joe smiled:

These old guys couldn't shoot worth a damn. My old man would get up there, and they'd be all over the target. We'd laugh, and say, "Good God, if they're going to defend us, we're in trouble."

The first group of WAACs headed for Fort Des Moines with Margaret M. Hartnett of Battery Park in charge. By the end of the year, teacher Catherine Cockburn of Glenwood Road became an ensign in the SPARS, and B-CC librarian-English teacher Arila McGinniss enrolled in a WAVE officer training course.[97]

The Suburban Hospital planners, assured of $665,000 in Federal Works money for a hundred-bed facility, announced that they would hire married nurses and establish a play school to help care for their children. They continued to seek a suitable ten-acre site.

The Army Medical Corps took over the fifty-year-old National Park College at Forest Glen as a convalescent facility much to the chagrin of Dr. Roy Tascoe Davis, his faculty, 400 students and the horses and riding master the girls' school had acquired the previous year when the government confiscated Arlington Hall in Virginia. Down south of Tenleytown behind the stone wall with its lion-head water trough, the McLean estate was being cleared for a huge garden apartment project, and its fancy iron gate went into a scrap drive.

Father Henry Collins purchased the original chapel of Our Lady of Lourdes, had it taken apart and packed up in October and moved it into D.C. where it was reassembled and used as a meeting hall by the Knights of Columbus and other parish groups at Annunciation parish. At Lourdes a Debt Fund Drive led by John Overholt helped Father Little pay off $38,000 of the parish mortgage.

That fall, gas rationing spread nationwide, and fuel oil rationing began with a temperature limit of 65°. F. Eliot Middleton Sr., a Bethesda realtor, was named chairman of the fuel oil rationing panel, which included Wilton Allen and William J. Rowan, a Chevy Chase attorney. After recruiting a few math teachers and "some of the brighter math students" as volunteers to process the applications, they issued coupons good for sixty-five percent of the oil used the previous year. Ration Board Chairman Jack Eaton warned that poorly insulated houses would never get enough heating oil. Some homeowners who had recently converted from coal to oil seriously considered changing back. Gas rationing convinced Eddie Adams to give up trying to operate Bradley Hills as a country club, and he began renting rooms with golf privileges to defense workers. It did not take him long to have twenty happy tenants and a long waiting list.

The first of the streamlined PCC streetcars, which Capital Transit had ordered just before Pearl Harbor, went into service, but both trolleys and buses were packed during rush hours. In Washington in 1942 , the only slogan heard more often than "Remember Pearl Harbor" and "Don'cha know there's a war on" was "Move to the rear."

Maryland began enforcing its 35 mph speed limit and forwarding the names of violators to their rationing boards. Car owners had to register their tires and have the serial numbers recorded that winter, and after November 22, no one was allowed to own more than five tires. "Idle" tires had to be sold to the Government. In the Bethesda area ten gas stations, Chevy Chase, Edgemoor and Community Motors, the Community Store in Cabin John and the new tire repair shop Lester Carroll and Charles Downs opened at 7029 Wisconsin were authorized to perform inspections.

The Montgomery Players, under new president George N. Mathews, planned four productions at Leland's auditorium including Lillian Hellman's *Watch on the Rhine* and *Arsenic and Old Lace* in which young Hartley Day played one of the policemen. After staying downtown for more than two months, *Mrs. Miniver* finally made it to the Bethesda Theater at the end of October, and frog-voiced Smiley Burdette was there "in person" at a Saturday matinee in November. Three members of the Stock family, Edward L. as the "modern" Major General, his brother J. Stephen as the Pirate King and Angela as one of the general's wards, starred in the Montgomery County Savoyard's production of *Pirates of Penzance*, which played benefits in Rockville and at the Naval Hospital before coming to Leland's auditorium under Board of Trade sponsorship. Mrs. Bradley wrote that hearing Ed Stock sing was well worth the price of admission.

Professor Wesley Gewehr of the University of Maryland history department was a favorite speaker to business and civic groups on "The Coming Peace" and postwar plans. Wilma (Billy) Miles showed her Burma Road pictures to the Leland student body in an assembly and to the Soroptimists during their meeting at Kenwood Club, and Marquis Childs spoke on the problems of reporting Washington in wartime as a feature of National Book Week at the public library.

Jelleff's advertised the answer to the nylon shortage, Elizabeth Arden's leg film, for $1 plus ten percent tax. And the Hot Shoppe would deliver its supper special-two hot dogs with relish on grilled buns, a pint of potato salad and a pint of ice cream, "a real meal for two," for 75¢. In one of his ads G. W. Imirie said that he still had lots of Model T and Model A parts in stock. Merle Travis went in business for herself and opened a beauty shop in the Professional Building at 7942 Wisconsin. Thanksgiving dinner at the Gates' Columbia Dining Room at 7011 Wisconsin, with all the trimmings, was $1.75 for adults and 85¢ for children.

Air raid drills and blackouts seemed to go much smoother after the installation of a synchronized alarm system. Civil Defense organized a War Emergency Radio Service in November and put PEPCO technician William H. Blair of Bethesda in charge. He asked for skilled volunteers and for old radios and parts to be converted into sending and receiving units. Albert Brault appointed

Joseph Giammatteo of the GEVFD head of the County's auxiliary firemen.

Horace Ward of 405 Rosemary Street in Chevy Chase testified before a Congressional committee that he had made $431,463 in the previous six months as a manufacturers' representative who specialized in entertaining Army and Navy officers. "I'm socially inclined," he said although he admitted that he charged his parties off as business expenses. "Everybody knows you can't influence a government contract," said Mr. Ward.

In December 18-year-old men began registering for the draft. B-CC grad Hubert "Skilly" Carlock of Brookmont was first and Landon student "Clackie" Walker second in line. Walker, who had been trying to volunteer for the Air Corps, eventually joined the Marine Corps–without telling his mother.

In September at its Recreation Center headquarters, the local branch of the Red Cross led by Mrs. Alvin Aubinoe welcomed the first visit of the mobile unit of the blood bank. One hundred donors showed up on a schedule established by Mrs. J. Robert Corry through the cooperation of local businesses. Mrs. B. Payton Whalen gave up her post on the Welfare Board because of the pressure of war work, and Mrs. Albert W. Walker of Westmoreland Hills replaced her. Irving W. Johnson of the Glen Echo Volunteer Fire Department was elected president of the Montgomery County Firemen's Association and replaced John Oden as head of fire services for Civilian Defense. Paul Banfield resigned his Civil Defense jobs and left Landon to enter the service. In October, the mobile blood donor unit returned to Bethesda and set up in the hall of Lourdes' school with NNMC doctors and corpsmen in attendance.

Bethesdans mourned the death of two valued citizens in the same week that fall. William Tyler Page died quietly in his sleep at his home in Friendship Heights. He was 74. John E. Buell died violently in the flood waters of the Cabin John Run. He was 31.

Page, well-known author of "The American's Creed," had worked in the House of Representative since 1881 and had been minority clerk since 1931. Mrs. Bradley of the *Journal* saluted him with an editorial titled "A Landmark Passes" in which she summarized his long career and wrote that this area "felt highly honored that he chose to make his home here." Friendship Heights remembered

him as a good neighbor. Those who recalled him most fondly and perhaps the longest were the many for whom he was a diligent and patient Sunday school teacher when they were children. For years he had remembered their birthdays with silver dollars.

The American's Creed

I believe in the United States of America as a Government of the people, by the people, for the people; whose just powers are derived from the consent of the governed; a democracy in a republic, a sovereign Nation of many sovereign States; a perfect Union one and inseparable; established upon those principles of freedom, equality, justice and humanity for which American patriots sacrificed their lives and fortunes. I therefore believe it is my duty to my country to love it, to support its Constitution, to obey its laws, to respect its flag, and to defend it against all enemies.

John Buell was a native of Takoma Park who moved to Bethesda when he married Pauline Lee in 1931. He operated a small garage and towing service at 7810 Wisconsin Avenue near Moore's store in Woodmont, less than a block from the volunteers' firehouse. After several years of loyal service, he was elected chief of the Bethesda Volunteer Fire Department. The Bethesda police knew he would always turn out to help them with his tow truck or with a fire engine. On Friday night, October 16, heavy rains produced a flash flood in the Potomac River valley, and Buell had been kept busy all night helping stranded motorists. His last call came long after he had closed his garage, and despite his wife's urging that he stay home, he and Hammond Tressler went out River Road where they found a car almost covered with water. Buell attached a line to the car's bumper, but as his helper started the winch the automobile rolled over, and Buell and the car disappeared into the flooded creek. His body was found lodged against a rock 200 yards away. He was survived by his wife, Pauline; son, Robert Lee, 10, and daughter, Nancy, 5.

At the Rec Center, the football team began its season with a victory over the Chevy Chase D.C. Playground club. The third Rec Center eleven featured Frank, Phil and Dick Daly and played mostly Boys' Club teams. Bob Brewer, who played in the backfield, said it was a short season, only four or five

games. Jack Sullivan, like Brewer in the B-CC class of `43, played tackle and end on that team and remembered a game against the University of Maryland "B" team. "They really made us look like what we were, amateurs," he said.[98]

The second wartime Christmas approached in a spirit of cautious hopefulness. The naval battles near Guadalcanal had been costly but decisive. The Russians were counterattacking in the Stalingrad area and continued to hold Leningrad despite more than a year of siege. B-17s of the 8th Air Force had joined the British in bombing attacks on the Ruhr. In North Africa, Montgomery stopped Rommel at El Alamein. Eisenhower's Operation Torch drove Allied forces into Tunisia in November, and the French scuttled their fleet.

On the home front coffee rationing began on December 1, and holders of Ration Book No. 1 who were over fifteen could buy one pound every five weeks. Judge Brault complained to the OCD when the County was not allocated any stirrup pumps after D.C. received 21,000. Motorists could apply for new tires after December 1, but "A" book holders could only get recaps.

Homeowners were discouraged from putting up their outdoor lights, and the big tree at the high school stayed dark for the first time in many years. B-CC's shop classes did produce a ten-foot high wooden Santa Claus, which was installed at Bradley and Wisconsin, and the Board of Trade offered a prize for the best business display. Jelleff's won with a "White Christmas" window. The Junior Chamber of Commerce asked for a blood donation as a Christmas gift and sponsored the Mobile Blood Unit at Christ Lutheran Church in December.

M. S. Ginn and Company replaced Whitmore's in the shopping center but kept C. E. Whitmore as manager of their furniture and stationary store. Hugo Brooks, photographer for both Bethesda papers from time to time, closed his shop on Old Georgetown Road, sent his negatives downtown to his father's F Street studio and joined the Military Air Transport service and began navigator training at National Airport. At the high school, students were preparing a holiday letter to send to graduates in the service and asked the public for help in getting up-to-date addresses. The Bank of Bethesda sent out more than $100,000 in Christmas Club savings

checks, and the post office asked everyone to mail early.

In the month before Christmas the Federal Works Agency announced that it had approved the purchase of the Whalen tract for the planned Suburban Hospital. Randolph Bishop called a meeting of the trustees to plan the ground breaking ceremonies on the five-and-a-half acre site west of Old Georgetown Road between McKinley and Lincoln Streets and to hear committee reports.

With the first spade of dirt yet to be turned, Dr. Charles R. L. Halley of Chevy Chase was chosen as chief of the division of medicine; Dr. Walter W. Boyd of Bethesda was named chief of obstetrics, and Dr. Arch L. Riddick chief of surgery. Mrs. Page Hufty's committee had received forty applications for superintendent of the hospital. Mrs. Perry's women's auxiliary boasted more than a hundred members. The East Bethesda Victory Club raised money for the hospital's nursery with a Christmas bazaar.[99]

A surprise air raid drill in the first week of December put a lot of Bethesdans out of their homes on a cold, rainy night. Albert Brault was relaxing at Kenwood when the sirens sounded and the phones began to ring. When Brault totaled up his forces at the end of the war's first year, he found that he had 4,428 trained workers, including 2,148 air raid wardens, 1,350 volunteers still in training and another seventy on waiting lists. He paid particular praise to James Cummings Jr. of Bethesda for the work of his visual communication committee and to Mrs. B. Peyton Whalen whose women's activities committee had recently started day care centers.[100]

And, of course, many events, such as bowling, never seemed to change. As the end of 1942 neared, the Tastee Diner team led Covington Motors and Hare Brothers in the Bethesda Major League while the Whittlesey's team topped the women's league. Both the David Taylor Model Basin and the NIH had their own leagues as did the country clubs and several church groups. George Huguely sponsored a picked team he called the "Bethesdans" and challenged all comers. WINX covered their match against Baltimore's stars in what was probably the first local radio broadcast of bowling.[101]

The Camp Fire Girls of the East Bethesda area sent a package of toys, gifts and eighty-

five pairs of hand-knit mittens to poor children in Virginia. The usual toy matinee took place at both the Hiser and the Bethesda theaters; the Rotarians enjoyed their annual Christmas party with the children at the Baptist Home, and the PTA sponsored a Christmas Dance at the high school. Both Jelleff's "Little Store" and the Palais Royal hired real Santas children could talk to, and E. O. Likens had a large upstairs toy display despite the shortage of metal toys such as electric trains. Mrs. Thomas Pyle wrote and directed the Christmas pageant at B-CC, which was presented to the public at Leland's auditorium on the Sunday before Christmas. The Leland students' own Yuletide assembly featured the Glee Club and section 7H's presentation of "The Littlest Shepherd." Reverend Albertson preached at the Council of Churches' Christmas Eve service at the Baptist Church, and a combined choir from the local churches sang at the Naval Hospital.

The authorities suspended air raid drills and blackouts during the Christmas season, and the issues that seemed to have Bethesdans most excited as the first year of the war ended were the possibility of establishing a USO, trash collection, the anticipated "point" rationing of canned food and the possible rezoning of Bob Hagner's land behind the Hot Shoppe. Fuel oil rationing was a confusing mess, and a four-inch snow followed by zero temperatures just before Christmas made things worse. The Government campaign to get people to stop hoarding pennies failed, and the mint announced plans to produce steel cents. The first WAVES arrived at NNMC, and the post office began hiring woman to deliver the mail. Down in Texas at Randolph Field, Bill Guckeyson graduated from fighter school and received his wings.

At the end of the year, for some incomprehensible reason, the U.S. Government ordered bakeries to stop slicing bread.

---

[1] *Pine Cone*, Dec. 23, 1941.

[2] Laura Tuckerman Triest, in NYC at the time, recalled being taken to a shelter and seeing people pour back onto the strangely empty streets when the "all clear" sounded. Times Square was cleared, but many passengers stayed on their buses, and most pedestrians ignored the sirens. The Army sent out interceptors and actually signalled two raids, at 1:30 and at 2:04 pm. N. Y. *Times*, Dec. 10, 1941.

[3] He became "Red" Auerbach sometime later.

[4] The order to evacuate the schools had come from the Baltimore "filter center" and was carried out by Judge Christopher who notified the fire department and the police. See *Star*, Dec. 10, 1941.

[5] *Pine Cone*, Dec. 23, 1941, *Star*, Jan. 21 and March 18, 1942. Leland's neighbors had learned to tolerate a fair amount of rowdyism and casual vandalism.

[6] From Chet McCall's collection now at MCHS.

[7] WJSV paid $25,000 to air the Nats baseball games with Arch McDonald and then signed up Lifebuoy and Wheaties as sponsors. McDonald had broadcast the Senators' games every year since 1934 except in '40 when he went to New York. He lived on Rosemary Street and was always generous with the cases of TruAde and Dr. Pepper his sponsors delivered to his back porch.

[8] First precinct, Frederick Berens, 324 East West Highway; second, Paul A. Davis; third, which was Glen Echo-Cabin John, Harry T. McCuen, 105 Harvard Avenue and then George E. Graham; fourth, E. J. Gray, 6915 Fairfax Road; fifth, Hunter Davidson, 11 W. Inverness; sixth, A. W. Palmer, 100 Rosemary; seventh, Oliver Walker, 30 Dalecarlia; eighth, Millard E. Peake, 7125 Arlington; ninth, Robert F. Carter, 4501 W. Virginia Avenue; tenth, Kurt Hanson, 9318 Old Georgetown; eleventh, Ellis B. Harrison, 4714 Chevy Chase Boulevard; twelfth, Lendell Connor, W. P. Allen and then Woodruff Clark; and in Chevy Chase, twentieth, J. R. Enright, 1 Primrose Street; twenty-first, John S. Easton, 14 E. Underwood; and twenty-second, Raymond Fisher, 8514 Maple Avenue and then Wendell Schuh. Later R. A. Fisher became sector warden for Chevy

Chase, W. Prescott Allen and Frederick Berens divided Bethesda's precincts, and Harry McCuen supervised the whole Conduit Road area.

[9]Instructions for extinguishing an incendiary bomb: 1)preferred method, drop a 25-pound bag of sand on it; 2)alternate method, pour out a pile of sand, carry the bomb in a long-handled shovel onto the sand, pour the rest of the sand in the bucket on the bomb.

[10]George Carrington in the *Pine Cone*, Dec. 23, 1941.

[11]*Tribune*, Jan. 2, 1942.

[12]Normal national tire consumption had been about four million tires per month. OPA authorized 35,000 per month. By '43 A-ration-book holders got no tires; B-book folks could buy recaps or regrooved tires, and C-book owners could buy new tires if they were available.

[13]Patsy Royster Lozupone recalled Mrs. Nicholson as chaperone of her sorority's beach house. It was Patsy's job to kept Mrs. N. supplied with cocktails so the girls could enjoy their sloe gins.

[14]*Journal*, Jan. 16 and Feb. 12, 1942. *Tribune*, Jan. 23 and Feb. 13, 1942.

[15]For a brief description of the fight for Wake Island see *Eagle Against the Sun* by Ronald H. Spector (1985), which also contains an analysis of revistionists' handiwork and of the role of code breaking. The "Send More Japs" message was a product of the propaganda machine.
In February the OPA released, to their hopeful owners, the cars that had been paid for before Pearl Harbor. The government set maximum prices on the existing stocks: Chevrolet sedan $800, Ford $850, Packard $1,275, Studebaker $809, Hudson 6 $945, Nash $873.

[16]This was only the first of numerous war-time buzzings Bethesda and Chevy Chase received from boys revisiting their old stomping grounds or fliers waggling wings at their girlfriends. See *Journal*, Jan. 16, 1942.

[17]*Journal*, March 6, 1942. See also "Somerset School 1928-1988" prepared by the PTA. Fathers involved in the project included Orr, Kingsbury, Riley, Bainbridge, Genau, Simon, Riggleman, Steuart, Onslow, Turlington, Pugh, and Burmeister. The story says 300 trees were cut down.

[18]Leland was also having a sprinkler system installed that winter. Teachers and students learned to work to the sound of hammering as 16,200 feet of pipe went in.

[19]Senior class president Edelen along with seniors Mary Bradley and Mary Jane Gott had a long meeting with their peers at Blair, which helped defuse the situation, but as Edelen noted, "The people doing it weren't there." Only Al Sherline admitted, "I kind of think maybe I was involved in the group that went over there as were a couple of other guys on the team."

[20]Members of the first girls' varsity: Captain Betty Beard, Lois Coperhaver, Eleanor Latimer, Joy Anne Bowers, Miriam Bopp, Joan Schrader, the Taylor twins, Clare Okie, Martha Alexander, Joan Rice, Mary Thulman, Ann Schuman, and Delores Lilly was student manager. Varsity members who received letters were Hardy Sorrell, George Van Wagner, Chris Chappell, Andy "Pete" Smith, Chester McCall, Johnnie Harrison, Burrell Marsh, Birch Bayh, Jim Cupper, Dick Daly, Dan Toll, Morris Fetrow, Charlie Hughes, Herbie Benson, and manager Bill Mizell.

[21]The Mary Reed-Dinks Rodgers-Bob Hagner story was the major scandal of the time.

[22]The writer's mother, Lillian G. Offutt, a former Library of Congress clerk, ran the Crew's Library during the war with the help of a few sailors.

[23]See *Post*, Feb. 21, 1942, and *Journal*, Feb. 27, 1942.

[24]Between 1942 and 1945 the cost of living rose only nine percent. See acronym list, Appendix J.

[25]See H.R. 6536 of the 2nd Session of the 77th Congress.

[26]From "Surf 'n' Turf," the Defense Mapping Agency newsletter, April/May 1992, reprinted from interviews published by the Association of Mapping Seniors.

[27]*Ibid*. and taped interviews, "50 Years at Brookmont." Hydrographic/Topographic Center, DMA.

[28]The Bethesda Hot Shoppe served beer during this time, but the records are not clear about when it stopped. Charles Hughes recalled high school seniors buying beers there when he was a sophomore in 1942-43. Many others do not. Marriott is not sure.

[29] Other Sub-Debs: Gussie Arnold, Patricia Eldridge, Mary Murphy, Peggy Napier, Ruth Small, Kit Willoughby and senior Marion Cummins. That makes twelve.

[30] In October of `42 Congress authorized the Secretary of War to approve a design for service flags, which he did in February of `43 for the white rectangle with a red border and blue stars (or gold atop the blue for those who died while in service).

[31] *Tribune*, March 13, 1942. Over 300 delegates were certified by the Civic Federation.

[32] *Journal*, March 27, 1942. *Tribune*, March 27 and April 3, 1942. The *Journal* was the only County paper that carried the LWV series explaining the Brookings Report.

[33] Typical out-of-town broadcast segment: (dead air, then click, click, clack, click)"The ducks are on the pond, runners on first and third, two out." (clack, click, click) "Three and two, what's he gonna do?" (click, click, rustle, click) "Here's the pitch. Vernon swings, and it's way back there, a long fly, DiMaggio looks up (bong, bong, pause, bong, longer pause, bong) "Homerun! Mickey Vernon trots across the plate, and the Nats lead three to two."

[34] *Post,* April 3 and 8, 1942, and *Journal*, April 10, 1942.

[35] *Journal*, April 24, 1942. Dr. Irene Barrett chaired the Bethesda-area group and developed programs for the Rec Center. After Blair Smith went into the service, Lloyd Ambrosen became the Rock Creek Park leader; at Leland JHS Mrs. Omar Herrmann was in charge, and Mrs. William Winkler was the East Bethesda leader.

[36] Committee members included Paul Banfield, William N. Morell, Mrs. Walter E. Perry, Dr. Irene Barrett, Joseph D. Montedonico, Dr. Charles R. L. Halley, Lee D. Butler, Dr. John G. Ball, and Mrs. James Parker Nolan.

[37] *Tribune*, April 10, 1942. Many agreed with historian Cabell Phillips' (*The 1940s.*) conclusion "that OCD was an overelaborate response to a false alarm." But in those early days no one was sure we would not be attacked.

[38] The death of 61-year-old Will Flack, fatally injured when he was knocked off scaffolding at the Brookeville Reservoir on his last day of work, also hurt the volunteers. Flack had put up the money for the firehouse back in `39.

[39] From *Journal* and *Tribune*, April 10, 17, and 24, 1942. The *Journal* noted "Statistically speaking the population of Montgomery County is composed of air raid wardens and those who are not air raid wardens. There are somewhat fewer of the former than of the latter."
The OCD messenger service was one of the few ways new bicycles could be obtained during the war, and children with air raid warden fathers were known to use that method to get a new bike.

[40] Larry Jennings, who subbed for his father a time or two, recalled that spotters phoned in "planes heard in such-and-such a direction" as well as sightings.

[41] *Journal*, May 1, 1942.

[42] The early closings were much appreciated that May; it hit a record 94° on May 1.

[43] Motorcyclists received less gas per unit; non-commerical inboard motorboats got "A" cards, and other non-highway users such as outboard motor boats and farm machinery were exempt.

[44] See David Brinkley's *Washington Goes to War* (1988) for a good overview of gas rationing problems especially with Congressmen. In Montgomery County only 20% accepted A cards, 55% received B-3 cards, and 10% X cards as almost 30,000 drivers signed up.

[45] *Tribune*, May 15, 1942.

[46] *Journal*, June 12, 1942, and *Pine Tree* 1942. Some fraternity members including Bill Duvall, president of Chi Alpha, were not allowed to participate in the exercises.

[47] *Journal*, May 29, 1942.

[48] See Mrs. Werner's oral biography at the Rockville library. The Cosmos Club, she said, "was a sort of second meeting place for Charter people." Stella Werner, early in this crusade, went to see Dr. Perry seeking support for the Brookings' findings and home rule. She failed.

---

[49] Other Bethesda charter leaders: the Rev. Oscar F. Blackwelder of Westmoreland Hills, Donal Chamberlin, Mrs. Dean Dinwoodey, Frederic P. Lee, George E. Hamilton, Sr., Adlai S. Magee, and Capt. Chester Wells.

[50] For a good summary of the charter fight, see Chapter 17, "The Charter Movement Succeeds" in *A Grateful Remembrance* by MacMaster and Hiebert (1976). County-wide in `42 there were 40,186 registered voters: 29,751 Democrats and 9,281 Republicans. In Bethesda 8,197 Dems, 2,523 GOP, 542 unaffiliated "declines," 1 Prohibitionist, total–11,181.

[51] New voters signed up for the 1942 election were more than three to one Democratic (3,187 to 253 between November `41 and April `42), 9-1 in Bethesda and 16-1 in Cabin John-Glen Echo.

[52] Oral biography, *op. cit.* and April 1943 article in *National Municipal Review*.

[53] *Tribune*, June 12, 1942, with a picture of the Civic Federation leaders on page 1.

[54] *Tribune*, July 10, 1942.

[55] *Tribune*, July 31, 1942.

[56] *Journal*, August 7, 1942.

[57] See local weeklies, especially *Journal*, August 28, 1942 and *Star*, Aug. 21, 1942.

[58] Miss or Mrs. Jay's name was Mrs. M. L. Jelliffe. She adopted the business name when she went to work for Jelleff's in the `30s to avoid answering oft-asked questions.

[59] Darcey's store was about where Lowen's later located. Woodward and Lothrop bought Palais Royal in 1946, and the Bethesda store became Woodies' very popular Budget Store.

[60] Ralph Breedon served two months, was released, retried and found not guilty in March 1943.

[61] *Tribune*, July 10, 1942.

[62] Leland ninth grader Ronnie Ingraham of Acacia Avenue received his own gasoline rationing "E" book for his model planes. A gallon generally lasted him about six months, an ounce at a time.

[63] The paid staff included Charles K. Davis Jr. of Chevy Chase as assistant to Mrs. Roach, and the clerks were Katherine Orme of Chevy Chase, Carol Walker of Gaithersburg, Esther Darrow of Bethesda, and Ruth Berry of Somerset.

[64] *Journal*, June 19, 1942. One feature of Mrs. Bradley's stewardship was the series of articles by Mrs. Warren W. Gingell of South Chelsea Lane cited earlier. See Bradley oral history by LWV.

[65] In Bethesda, Prescott and Walker built many houses in the area behind the Bethesda Theater.

[66] *Journal* and *Tribune*, Nov. 27, 1942. Daly's eldest daughter, Mary Claire, testified that she had turned off all the lights. She still believes there was "a miscarriage of justice."

[67] *Journal*, July 24, 1942.

[68] *Journal*, July 10, 1942. "Ginny" Roberts sons were also Kenneth and Gordon.

[69] *Journal*, May 28, 1943. Other leaders: Rosedale club, Mrs. R. G. Carlsen; Westboro, Mrs. Richard J. Powers; Glenbrook, Mrs. Charles L. Poor.

[70] The examining physician was Dr. Katherine Chapman, president of the County Medical Society and Dr. Roy Bridger was the Health Department's dentist. Among the volunteers were two trained nurses, Mrs. Donald Thompson and Mrs. John Wells.

[71] Bunker served as C.O. of the Naval Hospital until July 1944.

[72] *Journal*, Dec. 31, 1942, and Jan. 15, 1943.

[73] Mrs. Marvin Simmons said the OSS paid enough rent to "buy the family groceries." *Journal*, May 15, 1942.

[74] (l-r) Jerome Zeutzius, Robert Sigwald, James Dwyer, Francis Daly, Janet Whalen, Helen McKee, Charlotte White, Rosalie Courtney, Mary Ann Gathof, Margaret Wolter, Mary Ann Haley, James Fitzgerald, James Swain, John Maher, Gene Estes.

[75] The original Bradley ES staff: teachers Dorothy Brethouwer, Frances Mitchell, Jeanette Mae Miller, and Marguerite Henderson plus principal-teacher Martha White. Naomi Fisher was added to the staff soon after school began.

[76] *Journal*, Sept. 25, 1942.

[77]Georges Edelen called Cooney "a brilliant teacher" with a "flashy reputation" who was known for his convertibles and his blondes, and Thomas Appleby recalled that Cooney was a part-time Ford salesman. Dr. Gretchen Rudnick took over his math and science classes and taught photography in the Victory Corps period. The new courses were part of the Civilian Pre-Induction Training Program of the War Department. See *The Wartime History of the Military District of Washington 1942-1945.*

[78]Evidently some frats pledged students in the ninth grade. "Clackie" Walker joined ADS at Leland before going to Augusta Military Academy and Landon.

[79]*The Echo*, Nov. 25, 1942.

[80]*The Pine Tree 1943*.

[81]The work was done by juniors Harry Donoghue and Bruce Drake, who pushed the idea, along with Eddie Callahan and Joe Gardner.

[82] See *Star* Sept. 16 and *Tribune* and *Journal*, Sept 18. 1942. Because of population growth precincts had been added and boundaries redrawn: 1st-B-CC H.S., 2nd-CC Library, 3rd-Glen Echo firehouse, 4th-Bethesda ES, 5th-CC firehouse, 6th-Chevy Chase ES, 7th-Westbrook ES, 8th-Christ Lutheran Church, 9th-Lynnbrook ES (East Bethesda), 10th-Alta Vista ES, 11th-Rec Center Norwood drive, 12th-Battery Park clubhouse, 20th-Sonnemann's store, 21st-CC Methodist Church, 22nd-real estate office, SE corner Leland and Oak Lane. About 35% of the Democrats and 10% of the Republicans voted in the primary.
Of the charter petition signers in Bethesda, the top five areas were the 4th precinct with 621, 12th-454, 11th-449, 7th-416, and 21st-324. The Board of Election Supervisors certified 8,750 of the signatures. Gardner stirred up a small controversy when he suggested that there might be 10,000 more voters on the rolls than in the County.

[83]*Star,* Sept. 17 and *Tribune* and *Journal*, September 18, 1942. Full text of Commissioners' statement in the *Journal*.

[84]Marie Garber's assessment in her 1964 GW MA thesis, "E. Brooke Lee vs. Charter: The Fight to Modernize Montgomery County Government, 1938-1950."
Mrs. Minier Hostetler, graduate of DePauw and the University of Maryland, had served on the Welfare Board and as president of the County LWV and was president of the State League of Women Voters and a director of the Central Volunteer Board. Anderson, a Republican, had been a member of the County bar since 1927 and had served as a juvenile court judge. He lived on a farm near Rockville and was a County native. James, who lived in the Linden section of Silver Spring, was chairman of the Highway Education Board and the Pan American Highway Confederation. He was a past president of the Civic Federation and a member of the Silver Spring draft board. Brooke, a Norbeck-area farmer who could trace his family back 200 years in the County, was a director of the Savings Institution of Sandy Spring.

[85]*Tribune* and *Journal*, Sept. 4, 1942, and *Post*, Sept. 31, 1942, where Vanemann wrote that the Lee machine "functions with the tight-knit smoothness that would put to shame Boss Hague" and suggested that the area "probably has more brains per capita than any other county in the United States."
Phil Austenson, who covered the County for the *Post*, was almost undoubtedly in Brooke Lee's pocket, See Garber thesis, footnotes 63 and 87. *News* articles Aug. 24-29, 1942.

[86]*Post*, Sept. 22, 1942.

[87]*Tribune* (full text on back page), Sept. 25, 1942.

[88]Ad in *Tribune* of Oct. 2, 1942, and response in *Journal* and as a paid ad in *Tribune* of Oct. 9, 1942. Harry Hunt had made it his habit to show up late at politcal rallies and then to be carried in on the elder Cleveland Clipper's back and helped into his seat. The act always drew a hush and then applause. Hunt's letter is in Oct. 23 *Tribune* and his poem, titled "To a Friend" in the next week's issue. It began:

> What de dickens is de matter,
> Wid all dis chin and chatter,
> Bout de Democratic ticket we will play.
> De Publicans done had a fit
> 'Taint not a darn thing wrong wid it
> 'Cept whoop it up and carry it,
> To victory on de day.

[89]County-wide, the five charter supporters had between 8,250 to 9,000 votes while their opponents received 4,600 to 5,400.

[90]The only two Bethesda-area precincts that the old boss carried were the third in Glen Echo-Cabin John, which he won 373-279 and charter referendum lost 219-194, and the 22nd in Chevy Chase, which Lee took 196-115 and the charter lost 138 to 72.

[91]In the U.S. Congress, the Republicans gained 46 House seats and 9 in the Senate, but the Democrats retained control of both. E. B. Lee oral history, MCHS.

[92]*Tribune*, Nov. 6, 1942. and *Journal*, Nov. 27, 1942. The Democrats spent $15,990 and the Republicans $1,720. Only 155 service men returned absentee ballots (about 200 of the 4,000 in the military requested them), and in the soldier vote, Lee defeated Beall 106 to 67 and the charter lost 67 to 55. Someone in the Lee camp noted this.

[93] William H. Prescott replaced Hampton on the Board of Commissioners as Bethesda's third "mayor" after defeating Robert P. Dunlop 11,600 to 8,200.

[94]*Journal* and *Tribune*, Nov. 6, 1942. Nelly Baines (Mrs. Sullivan J.) Ross, 64, Republican election judge and first female member of the Friendship Heights council, died of a heart attack at Somerset ES polling place during vote tabulation.

[95]Garber thesis, footnote 45.

[96]Cmdr. Malcolm P. Hanson of Langdrum Lane died in a war operation in August but was not "killed-in-action." Gibson's story is in the Nov. 13, 1942, *Journal*.

[97]Among the early WAVE recruits were Hulda Pifer of Brookmont, Sybil Batchelor and Marjorie Lincoln of Chevy Chase, and Carolyn Elizabeth Schmidt of Westmoreland Hills.

[98]BCC Rec Center '42 football team: Jack Poulter, Dick Latham, Frank, Phil, and Dick Daly, Howard Morris, Bill Thomas, Warren Barrett, Burt Muffett, Bill Shaub, Billy Pogge, Marion Davis, Charlie Harrison, Bill Eiseman, Burt Mahinney, Hugh Shoemaker, John Eisele, Houston Swink, Bill Marsh, L. Allison, C. Chappell, Marrion and Swain.

[99]The government set the price for the Whalen property at $20,000. The Whalens appealed. In December '43, a District Court condemnation jury gave them $29,500

[100]Nationwide, eight to ten million volunteers enrolled in various OCD activities under the nominal leadership of the "Little Flower," NYC Mayor Fiorello H. LaGuardia.

[101] Bowling Center team: Ed Blakeney, El Geib, Karl Gochenour, Bill King, Tony Santini, and Hokie Smith.

CHAPTER 12

Another Year of Change

By the second year of the war, almost everyone in Bethesda was sure that the Allies were going to win, and the major differences of opinion were about how long it would take and whether we should defeat Hitler or Tojo first. Kilroy had visited B-town as had his big-nosed buddy Chad. Most classrooms and many youngsters' bedrooms displayed world maps decorated with flags and pins to show areas of combat. New words entered the vocabularies of young and old alike; GI and jeep, Zero and flattop, 4-Fs and WACs, Sad Sack and zoot suit, gizmo and gremlin, flak and CINCPAC, "in like Flynn" and "snafu," which in the civilian version meant "situation normal, all <u>fouled</u> up."[1]

Mothers who had never considered using margarine now gave the nearest child the job of breaking the capsule of coloring and kneading the bag of vegetable lard and then tried to shape the yellowish mass into a block that no one thought was much like butter. Boys who used to be able to tell a LaSalle from a Cadillac at a hundred yards, now claimed they could spot the differences between a TBF and a TBM at a glance, and, when a "Mitchell" thundered over, did not even look up before saying, "B-25." Girls who once learned all about Frank Sinatra and Dick Haymes now knew that Army colonels and Navy captains were about the same ranks and talked knowingly of jaygees and shavetails, Gyrenes and swabjockies, PT boats and Liberty ships.

The year of "Praise the Lord and Pass the Ammunition" had ended with Irving Berlin's "White Christmas" on every radio, and the big songs of `43 would be equally sentimental;

"You'll Never Know," "My Heart Tells Me," "People Will Say We're in Love," and the other wonderful *Oklahoma!* tunes. Glenn Miller and his Army Air Force Band made the blues march while the separated Dorsey brothers and Harry James were still swinging. The juke boxes featured "Deep in the Heart of Texas," and the school children learned "Off We Go Into the Wild Blue Yonder," and "The Volga Boatman." Big brothers or sailors on the town taught youngsters lyrics to other tunes such as "Into the Air, Junior Birdmen," and "Bell-Bottom Trousers." One of the most-repeated jokes of the day was about the girl who slapped a sailor for whistling dirty songs.

Like the movies, radio was a shared experience for Bethesdans. From Pearl Harbor until V-J Day, young and old turned to the big box in the living room for the news and for escape. The radio tied us to both FDR and great entertainers. The day started with Arthur Godfrey, Bill Herson or another of the cheerful morning men such as WINX's Jerry Strong who lived on Windsor Lane. Then came the soap operas, which all seemed to be sponsored by Rinso or Oxydol, and after school *Jack Armstrong, the All-American Boy* and the other adventure serials sold Wheaties and Ovaltine. (Have you sent in for your secret decoder ring?) The news was at supper time and then the really good shows came on.

Sunday night meant laughing with Jack Benny, Charlie McCarthy, and Fred Allen although some listeners entered the *Inner Sanctum.* Monday featured good music from the *Voice of Firestone* and *The Telephone Hour* plus *Dr. I. Q.* and his silver dollars ("I have a lady in the balcony, Doctor."), and Tuesday was

one of the best nights because *Fibber McGee and Molly* ("Don't open that closet, McGee."), George Burns and Gracie Allen, Bob Hope and Red Skelton followed each other in rapid succession ("We're a little late, so good night folks."). Wednesday's music came from Sammy Kaye and *Kay Kayser's Kollege of Musical Knowledge* ("That's right, you're wrong"). On Thursday Fanny Brice and Bing Crosby always had wonderful guests, and Friday night featured Kate Smith. Her booming "God Bless America" seemed as much a war song as "Remember Pearl Harbor" and "I Left My Heart at the Stage Door Canteen." Saturday night, in many homes, meant the *National Barn Dance* and *Your Hit Parade*.

In the summer, kids playing kick the can or capture the flag out on the street kept track of time by the radio shows, and as they walked home past lawns sparkling with fireflies, they could hear Arch McDonald calling an out-of-town night game or follow the jokes down Fred Allen's alley from porch radios or through open windows. One of curmudgeon Russ Edwards' favorite gripes in his Bethesda *Journal* columns was about the neighbor whose loud radio inflicted his choice of programs on your yard.[2]

Just as tire rationing had started the previous year with a jolt for automobile drivers, Leon Henderson's successor at OPA gave them another shock in early January of `43 when he ordered a ban on all pleasure driving. Local police and ration boards were to enforce the regulation, and violators could lose their gasoline ration card. Theaters, night clubs, sports events and teen-age joy riding all felt the pinch although some Bethesda youngsters still enjoyed taking out the family car and doing a little clandestine racing. For the duration, the Sunday driver stayed home and Simonized old Bessie, and some parents found that gas ration stamps were great motivators for diligence by their high school-age children.[3]

The shaken boards of governors at the local country clubs met to consider their future, if any. Bannockburn simply closed for the winter. Chevy Chase and Columbia, closer to town and on a good bus line, saw no need for change. Isolated Congressional knew it was in trouble and started looking for help, government help, as it shut down most operations. The remortgaged and reorganized club saw

membership rapidly declining and put all plans for improvements and expansion on "hold." Kenwood carried on since many patrons could walk to the club. Woodmont saw play decline to a rare weekday twosome and the new president, Arthur J. Sundlun, and his board met to consider the future. Members gradually adjusted to getting there by streetcar and "Naval Hospital" bus. Burning Tree sometimes went for a week with no golfers but decided to cope rather than close, and manager Joseph Langer, especially on Sunday mornings, provided a kind of bus service as he drove to work. Sometimes a member with business in the Bethesda area "would find it conscionable to drop by the Club for a game. When this happened his car was often parked off in the woods lest some prying eye misunderstand."[4]

Burning Tree extended special war memberships to some thirty-five men "on emergency duty in connection with the National Defense," and Chevy Chase did the same for officers of flag rank. Woodmont accepted Naval Hospital and NIH officers as temporary members for $5.55 a month and invited all male and female military personnel stationed in Bethesda to play on weekdays. Patients at NNMC also toured the golf course as part of their therapy, and occasionally the Army, OCD, and later the USO, used Woodmont's facilities.

The war made holding Club championships difficult, but a Woodmont member recalled one in particular:[5]

One year there was an officer named Murphy over at the Naval Hospital. Hell of a swell gentleman and a good golfer. He played so much golf at the Club, we allowed him to play in the Club Handicap Championship. He got to the finals. Everybody in Woodmont with a sense of humor was dying for him to win, so the papers would carry "Murphy-New Golf Champion at Woodmont." Unfortunately somebody beat him.

Nationally, it was the year of John L. Lewis and Ernie Pyle, of plane crashes and train wrecks, and of race riots in Detroit and Los Angeles. For Bethesda, 1943 was Victory Gardens, despite a very dry summer; the year of the USO, although it took forever to get organized; and just barely, the year of Suburban Hospital. It was the year when gold stars appeared on the high school honor roll, and map study turned from Stalingrad and dusty Tunisia to Sicily and muddy Italy and from

Guadalcanal and mountainous Burma to Kiska and bloody Tarawa. It was a big year for the recreation department, the OSS, the Jeep House and the collection of flattened tin cans and a bad year for dogs, Greeks, Willie Smith and pleasure drivers. It was the year that the Conduit Road Fire Board proudly announced the conversion of the Glen Echo fire house from oil to coal heat and the installation of an automatic stoker.

The four-man-one-woman Charter Board began receiving advice from civic groups and citizens' associations as soon as it sat down in the new year. Kensington urged the adoption of a county-manager form of government. The Civic Federation emphasized the merit system, non-partisan election at-large, and the right of referendum. Chevy Chase Section Four suggested a county manager chosen by competitive exam with a fixed term and a broad civil service system. The Edgemoor Citizens' Association urged a referendum clause to replace the governor's veto.

During January, the Charter Board held hearings in Silver Spring, at the Recreation Center in Bethesda, and then in Sandy Spring and Gaithersburg. While these were going on, in Annapolis the County Commissioners asked the General Assembly for a bill giving them "broadly enumerated," war-emergency powers to issue bonds and expend funds to provide needed public facilities. This brought an immediate, negative reaction from several civic groups, which the bill's proponents countered by saying they were only giving the Commissioners what the charter people wanted, local authority.

Despite the opposition of the Civic Federation and many other organizations, House Bill 115 passed the House of Delegates as "emergency" legislation and then, after the uproar that followed, was withdrawn. The County's delegation, all "organization" Democrats, said they were testing the sincerity of charter proponents.

We expected to conclusively demonstrate to all the people of the County just how inconsistent and partisan these Civic politicians are in their fight for a complete home rule Charter."[6]

The actions of James W. Gill and the other three delegates who proposed and then withdrew Bill 115 were too much for Gertrude Bradley. After firmly maintaining her neutral stance on the charter question since June 1942,

she was finally taxed "beyond endurance." She accused the County delegation of "an insult to the intelligence of the people of Montgomery County" and wrote that their behavior was "nothing more than horseplay designed to confuse and confound the voters." In the long charter struggle, Bill 115 may have been a turning point. Gertrude Bradley was not one to be trifled with or taken for granted.

By the end of March, the Charter Board completed a preliminary draft of its proposed constitution and, after some revisions, sent copies to interested groups. Some local papers, but not the *Tribune*, published the putative charter in mid-April. With the final draft due on May 3, the Charter Board asked for "frank and candid criticism" and received it, but neither William Prescott Allen nor his columnist alter ego, Robert V. Bray, commented. Allen printed the final draft as a three-page, government-paid ad.[7]

The first charter relied heavily on the Brookings report's recommendations and the suggestions of most major civic associations. It created an unpaid, nine member, non-partisan council with legislative and executive powers plus a county manager and a merit system. The *Post* found "little or nothing novel" in the draft and editorialized that the plan, if approved, "should give Montgomery County more efficient and responsive government than it has had in the past."[8]

The Charter Board made some changes, including several proposed by the Civic Federation, and presented the completed draft of the document to Lacy Shaw, president of the Board of County Commissioners, on May 3. The charter writers received praise from many quarters, but only silence from the County government. For more than a year, Brooke Lee's partisans laid low and planned their strategy.

The League of Women Voters commended the writing committee "for drawing up a charter worded simply enough so that the layman may know its meaning and so full of social philosophy." Alfred Willoughby of the National Municipal League wrote, "This draft impresses us as being outstandingly excellent and in line with the best standards of thought." The Civic Federation praised the Charter Board for "the skillful formation" of the document. And Dr. Lewis Meriam, the document's godfather if not grandfather, offered "congratulations on general excellence of

the charter" and said that if the people adopted it in the 1944 election, "they will have the foundation for a democratic and efficient local government well adapted to presentday conditions."[9]

The Charter Board, its work finished, disbanded, but the Charter Committee stayed alive and wary. Soon Stella Werner and Fred Lee were out talking to various clubs and associations and preparing for what they knew would be a difficult battle in the fall of `44. The Charter Committee also did some fund raising. Treasurer Charles E. Parsons said Allen Gardner himself had paid off most of the earlier deficit but that it "takes money to make the mare go."

In Bethesda the first big fight of the year was over former-commissioner Hagner's request to rezone his East West Highway property behind the Hot Shoppe for stores and offices on the front 150 feet and for apartments on the back of his lot nearest Our Lady of Lourdes Church and convent. At the hearing, Mr. Hagner, as part owner and current tenant of the property, testified that his neighbors had filed many complaints about his chicken house and horse stable, that most of the nearby buildings were now used by doctors or businesses and that the property was no longer suitable for a residence.

Representatives of Our Lady of Lourdes parish testified that there was plenty of unused commercial property in the neighborhood, that rezoning Hagner's land would damage the value of theirs and that commercial establishments there would threaten the safety of their school children and be against M-NCP&PC policy. They presented a petition signed by 650 parishioners and a letter from Archbishop Curley, the nominal owner of the church property. The Commissioners took the matter under advisement and, after hearing a negative report from Park and Planning, denied Hagner's request for commercial zoning on the front footage but said he and his partners could build apartments on the back.

The deaths of three long-time Bethesdans marked the early months of 1943. Dr. Benjamin C. Perry died at Georgetown Hospital in January at the age of 62. E. Brooke Lee's lieutenant west of Rock Creek, Dr. Perry had been a generally benevolent boss, source of employment and distributor of spoils as well as the family doctor for hundreds of Bethesdans.

He had been Bethesda's first "mayor" and raised the town's first office building, now rented to the County to provide more space for his successors.[10]

Two weeks later Dora Counselman died at 80. Her father, Franklin Mace, was a descendant of William Viers and her mother was Fanny Riley. Dora grew up on what was left of the old Riley plantation near Lux Manor where "Uncle Tom" Henson had been a slave. She married attorney James Holman who died young leaving her with two small children, Doree Germaine and James Davie Jr. Several years later she married storekeeper Will Counselman and moved down to Bethesda to live over the store until he died in 1936, and then she moved to Montgomery Avenue. Mrs. Counselman enjoyed telling stories of Bethesda when the toll-gate keeper still collected a nickel, and she clearly recalled Garfield's inauguration and Coxey's Army. She was buried at her church, Mt. Zion on Georgetown Road.

A month later 70-year-old George P. Sacks died at home of a coronary thrombosis. Sacks had been as much a leader of the business interests of Bethesda as Dr. Perry had been of its political life. Sacks helped found the Bank, the Chamber of Commerce and the Rotary Club. Much of the town's development west of Wisconsin and south of Leland Street, including the huge apartment complex still growing along Hillandale, had been his idea. As president of the Bank of Bethesda since 1928, he oversaw the financing of much of the area's growth, and by the time of his death, the Bank's assets had grown to $3 million.

The trash collection problem came to a head when the draft caught up with the owner of the company that collected garbage in Silver Spring and left homes there without service until Blake Merson's crews could take over. In December of 1942, the Civic Federation urged the County to assume the "collection and disposal of garbage, trash and ashes" under the current suburban tax rate. By mid-January the Commissioners recommended not only a unified trash collection system but the construction of storm sewers for the suburban areas.

Mrs. Bradley of the *Journal* was delighted. She had purchased her home in Sonoma, in part, because it had "a picturesque stream on the back of the lot." It was not until later that she discovered that her brook drained the

whole area and sometimes became a tumbling, brown river that left her backyard a "sea of mud and leaves and ash cans and garbage pails." Her unusually personal editorial ended:

There's real gratitude in my heart when I say the present board of county commissioners is to be congratulated for taking a definite step to solve the problem of storm drainage.[11]

In a late February public hearing on the proposed WSSC bill, Bethesda's support for the trash collection plan was almost unanimous. The enabling legislation breezed through the legislature as locally endorsed bills almost always did, and by April, J. Donald Clagett, Montgomery County's representative on the WSSC, announced that trash, ash and garbage collection from kitchen or cellar doors would begin as soon as equipment and personnel could be acquired. Special taxing areas, commercial buildings and apartments were not covered in the original plan.

The Sanitary Commission opened negotiations with Blake Merson and other private trash collectors for their people and trucks. The Commission also began looking for sites for sanitary land fills and started discussing the possibility of constructing an incinerator. June 1 passed, the date WSSC was authorized to take over the collection service, but Commissioner Clagett announced that they still had not been able to acquire the priorities needed for trucks and other equipment. Julius Stadler offered a piece of swampland as landfill, and finally, on October 1, WSSC began refuse collection in Silver Spring. Bethesda would have to wait until 1944.[12]

Meanwhile, school life went on. Public health nurse Anne Dunay, who had twenty-five girls at the high school taking a home nursing course, said she wished students would dress more sensibly. She blamed a lot of the colds and absenteeism on girls wearing short socks and flimsy moccasins instead of sensible, knee high stockings and good, sturdy shoes.

At B-CC a couple of young males were reported to be sporting "zoot suits" from time to time, but the style conscious still went to Leon's. Mr. Sherman recalled that cuffs and pleats had both been outlawed, but, "If a kid came in and wanted pleats and he was size 30, I would sell him a size 34 and pinch them in and sew them."

Mr. Bender's shop class students volunteered to repair household gadgets free of charge "for the duration," and Mr. Best started a new and very popular class for girls called Home Mechanics. The students learned to fix leaky faucets, repair sash cords, install window glass, adjust door locks and perform dozens of other tasks usually done by the "man of the house."

At Leland, with help from the well-established organization at the high school, students organized a Victory Corps and soon had 172 members enrolled and a semi-military organization operating. "Colonel" Laurence Jennings, treasurer of the ninth-grade class, led the group but called it a "completely paper organization" led by "untroublesome kids who did the mimeographing and, when necessary, swept the floors while the privates and corporals laughed at them." The school's Red Cross Club collected and distributed games, puzzles and books to the patients at the Navy Hospital, and the Defense Club, sponsored by gym teacher Harold Alderton, collected five tons of tin cans in February alone. On January 12, Lelanders went home early because the school ran out of oil. They happily contributed their lunch money to the Red Cross as they left.

The schools signed up new students almost every week that winter. At just opened Bradley Elementary, enrollment climbed steadily, and by the end of the first semester 264 students were crowding every available space, and the school board was asking for two additional rooms, quickly. Westbrook, with two portables in operation, had 348 students, put grades K-1-2 on double sessions and needed at least four more classrooms. The other Bethesda-area elementaries soon were equally overfull.

Wartime Washington burst at the seams with at least a quarter of a million new residents since Pearl Harbor, and the widespread housing shortage became a subject for jokes, plays and movies as well as a real hardship for many servicemen and their families. Despite very little new building, Bethesda's population grew to about 37,000 by 1943. The *Record* based its estimate on ration book applications by 11,744 heads of households applying for 33,937 ration books (see chart on next page) plus about a thousand late applications for three or four thousand individuals who were not classified by neighborhood.[13]

Ration Book Applications schools	
applicants	ration books
Alta Vista	
421	1,219
Bethesda	
2,164	6,208
B-CC	
1,287	3,333
Bradley	
515	1,736
Glen Echo-Cabin John	
1,211	3,710
Leland JHS	
2,967	8,181
Lynnbrook	
726	2,477
River Road Colored	
84	228
Somerset	
1,161	3,257
Westbrook	
1,217	3,588
total	
11, 744	33,937

Tin can salvage started early in the year with Merson's trash men collecting cans at the curb after they were washed, had the labels removed, the ends cut off and inserted, and then were flattened. The trash collectors proved erratic and caused complaints, so elementary school children began collecting from their homes and neighborhoods. County liquor trucks came around regularly to pick up the tin cans from the big boxes at each school. Unfortunately, these depots became community trash bins, eyesores and rodent breeders.[14]

Louis Mitchell at the Rec Center put together a church-sponsored league, and teams from Chevy Chase Methodist, Bethesda Presbyterian, Chevy Chase Presbyterian, Bethesda Methodist, Chevy Chase Baptist, Blessed Sacrament, and Our Lady of Lourdes competed in basketball games at the high school and at Alice Deal's gym and then in a round-robin tourney after the Chevy Chase Methodists finished the regular season undefeated. Although there had been plenty of games between rival Boy Scout troops from the churches down on Chevy Chase Circle, this was probably the first time that Catholics and Protestants played against each other in an organized league in the Bethesda area.

At B-CC new coach Ray Fehrman's first basketball team had a very rocky season. Several players quit or became academically ineligible, and he suspended Al Sherline and another first stringer for rule breaking. Big Bob Brewer kept the team going although soph George Van Wagner did well when he earned some playing time. By the day of the first Blair game the varsity had a 4-4 record. Because of gas rationing and the ban on pleasure driving, the Blair-Bethesda games returned to the school gyms.

Ferry, Slaughter and Seitz scramble in Blair's gym

In the first game before 500 screaming Blairites, the Barons fought and scrambled to a 20-17 win by holding the Blazers to four field goals. With Harry Phillips back on the floor, they beat Rockville, rolled over Landon after the Bears' top scorer, "Clackie" Walker, enlisted in the Marine Corps, and then crushed Blair at home 49-35. But with their big center ineligible, B-CC lost to Eastern in the first round of the Star tourney for the city championship A lot of B-CCers were disappointed when Bob Brewer only received "honorable mention" on the All-Met team.

The girls' team, city champs the year before, had an even worse time. Captained by center Betty Milne and featuring several other experienced players including Ruth Small, Pat Eldridge, and the wild-shooting Carter Dawson, the team and student manager Dorothy Miller looked forward to another winning season. Then at the semester break, Coach Alice Morgan resigned to take a job with the D.C. public schools and left the team without a sponsor. Betty Milne had her Pentagon-employee-mother's car and gasoline ration book, and a few teachers and parents drove once in a while, but no teacher-sponsor came forward so many of the games were canceled.

The girls did have home-and-home series with Richard Montgomery and Sherwood and lost only one game that shortened season; unfortunately it was to Blair.

Leland's boys' basketball team again won the County title by defeating Montgomery Hills 34-4 and then Takoma 29-16 in the championship game of the post-season tournament. The girls also had a good team and finished off their season by defeating the faculty 16 to 9. High school athlete Betty Milne refereed, and the teachers' team featured Misses Rice, Baker, Bowen, White, Sargeant, Stanford, and Johnson.[15]

Air raid drills continued, the first one of `43 on Wednesday, January 6, at 10:28 am. The authorities called the results "excellent," but no one explained why planes wrote a large "J" in the sky. In Bethesda the practice raid showed the need for more daytime wardens. It had been a real surprise drill, and the few Civil Defense volunteers available had difficulty halting traffic and getting people to shelters.[16]

January was a wild month of slushy snow followed by mild days with temperatures in the sixties; 72° on Saturday the 16th, which had girls running about in shorts, was followed by 70 mph winds and a temperature drop to 18° on the 18th. Then while Roosevelt and Churchill discussed unconditional surrender in Casablanca and Errol Flynn denied everything in Hollywood, a heavy snowfall followed by a record two and a half inches of sleet closed the Capital on the 29th.

In Bethesda, Commissioner Prescott took personal command of the cleanup and had ten County trucks, twelve State plows, and a crew of twenty shovelers working two days and nights to clear the streets. When they finished, Bill Allen crowed that the County's "obsolete government" had won another victory for the "spoils system" by getting the streets cleaned while the D.C.'s merit system workers were still looking for alibis. It was another example, he wrote, "that loose charges about the inefficiency of the present government are given the lie by the actual facts."[17]

February's extra cold weather depressed Bethesdans' spirits as rationing spread to cover much more of American life. Tires had been the first item rationed in January of `42 and then cars in March, sugar and gasoline in May, bicycles in July, fuel oil in October, and

coffee in November. Early in February a rumor of shoe rationing led to a rush of buying, and then the fact of shoe rationing limited almost everyone to three pairs a year.

On Sunday, February 21, the government halted the sale of canned, frozen, and dried food and put a price freeze on fresh vegetables such as tomatoes, beans, carrots, cabbage and peas in preparation for "point rationing." All Bethesda-area schools canceled classes from Tuesday through Friday during the last week of February, and one representative of each family, usually the housewife, took all the family's No. 1 ration books to the nearest school and registered with teacher-volunteers for Book No. 2. The schools stayed open from 9:30 am until 7:30 pm, and Rationing Administrator Julius P. Stadler said, "When the roll of honor for self-sacrifice in the war effort is written, school teachers will be high on the list."[18]

Once housewives sat down and looked at the point values, they had to make changes. Rationing would provide each person with about thirty-three pounds of canned food a year, a cut of almost thirty percent. Point values varied from time to time depending on needs and shortages, but in general a family of four had 192 ration points a month for canned or frozen food or about an average of four cans per week. A few women, especially those who had never cooked, turned the job over to their maids and an even smaller number took the books to their grocer and let him take care of the problem. For grocery store owners, it was a bookkeeping nightmare.

March started with an announcement that pleased almost everybody: the government rescinded the prohibition on slicing bread with the lame explanation that it had been imposed to save waxed paper. Next the OPA began fixing meat prices starting with pork. And, at about the same time, butter, like Lucky Strike green, went to war. It disappeared even before the government announced that it would start rationing cheese, oil, butter and meat, at two pounds a week, starting in April. By the end of March, the butchers' tall, white counters were empty.

In Bethesda, the ration board expanded by taking over the space next door. William A. Royal, who lived behind his business, moved his barber shop down one store to make room for them. The dispensary just down the street

shortened its hours in the hope that liquor rationing could be avoided.

Mrs. Bondareff of the Lakeview Market recalled the days of rationing and shortages:

During the war my husband went once a week to Frederick where he knew some private slaughterers and got meat every week. I don't think any of our accounts did without meat. If he'd been in the black market, we would have been very wealthy people. We saved our extra meat points and stamps for the nuns at the Visitation Convent on Georgetown Road. One sister did the ordering, she insisted I take her orders, and they got a little more. We lived on ours exactly, but he let them have a little more.

Soon lost and damaged ration books became a problem. Children played with them; dogs chewed on them, or they just disappeared. A lost book had to be advertised in a daily paper for three days and then reported. The wait for a new book was thirty days. Ann Johnson of Ridge Street, Chevy Chase, put her lament in a verse that she gave to Alice Berry, the local Ration Board's registrar, better known as the "Sugar Lady."[19]

I've Lost M' Ration

The store was just closing, I'd made a wild
       dash
To the meat man I panted, "Please give me
       some hash,
Some bacon, baloney, and a lamb chop or
       two."
"Twill be 50 points," he said; that was my cue.
With gusto I opened my tightly held purse
And I searched and I hunted and discovered
       the worst:
Lip stick and powder, gas coupons and paint,
I cluttered the counter-but nope, they just ain't!
I looked on the floor, I went through the
       sawdust
Determined to find them if there or bust
But the truth was something nobody could bear
I've looked and I've hunted-the darn things
       weren't there.
We tore up the house and we tore up our car,
We looked in the chimney, high, low, and far;
I wept and I cried in true Hollywood fashion,
Only to realize, too late. that I'd lost m' ration.
That's why, Mrs. Berry, I'm writing to you
To ask what in thunder a body's to do,
I've spent two-o-seven to put in the ad
But nary a word from the thing have I had.

A small number of Bethesdans started Victory Gardens in their side or back yards in the first summer of the war, and the high school plowed up a large plot near the gym, but the rationing of canned food accelerated the movement until no empty lot was safe. "Buzzy" Potter made a fair profit by hauling his small Ford tractor around the suburbs to plow and harrow gardeners' plots. He did so well that he was able to marry Colonel and Mrs. George P. Bush's daughter, Virginia, among the beautiful iris at their home on Beech Avenue in Alta Vista. Neal Potter acted as his brother's best man.[20]

Mrs. Chase Donaldson, local chairperson of the American Volunteer Services, started a Victory Garden course at Bethesda Elementary on Wednesday evenings. Chester McCall of Chevy Chase had a 1942 garden that was the envy of many of his neighbors, and he shared some of the valuable lessons he had learned. "The most important thing about the Victory garden," he said, 'is the plan that you make." He urged would-be gardeners to stick to things that grew well in the area. "My three staple plantings last year were tomatoes, string beans, and lettuce. I will concentrate on these and turnip greens this year."

He also noted what failed:

I did not have much success with carrots, beets, and radishes last year but am going to try one row of each this year, after giving the ground a deeper preparation and adding some extra humus and sand to the rows as they are planted.

Mr. McCall promised that "No vegetables ever taste quite so good as those you grow yourself."[21]

Mrs. Bouvet, the B-CC cafeteria manager, promised students that she would "can every little tomato and string bean we can grow and have it ready for us next winter." And the *Echo* reporter noted that the garden "would be next to the grove (very convenient for the hoers)." Mr. Pyle led a group of boys who cultivated the vegetables as their Victory Corps project.[22]

In early February the Commissioners voted to furnish plowed plots, rent free, to gardeners in the suburban areas if there was enough demand. In Bethesda those interested were asked to call Commissioner Prescott's office in the County Building. Within a week "Billy" Prescott learned that there was plenty of interest and stated that in neighborhoods where at least fifteen people signed up to tend

gardens, land would be secured and plowed. He said the plan was to provide at least 1,000-square-foot plots.

Some landowners offered vacant ground free of charge, and the Western Suburban Area rented other land with tax funds. By the end of February more than 500 Bethesdans had expressed interest in having the County provide and prepare plots for their gardens including twenty-five in Bradmoor and twenty in both Huntington Terrace and Sonoma. Philip Milestone donated enough land near the new Bradley school for a hundred of these neighbors to have gardens.

Editor William Prescott Allen asked, "Are Victory Gardens Feasible?" even before frigid February left the area. He suggested that a real working committee was important "to educate and aid our people in the rudiments of Victory Gardening." His fear was that "Much seed is going to be wasted unless intelligent direction is provided for the patriotic sweat of our residents." He could not resist suggesting that garden clubs and civic groups "forget delphiniums and mayhap even charter for a few short hours to study this problem."[23]

Mrs. Bradley was not far behind but somewhat more positive. She commended the County Commissioners and urged everyone who could spare the time and effort to register for a plot if their own yard was too small or too shady. "You're not going to be patriotically fashionable this summer," she noted, "unless you have a Victory Garden to work in and talk about." Then she signed up nurseryman Ed Stock for a weekly gardening column.

Stock began by echoing Allen that the need was great but only serious people should begin. He suggested that would-be gardeners ask themselves if they were willing to work in the garden three or four times a week in the really hot weather and if they had a fairly level spot in full sun to work in and if their soil was a "fair clay loam" and not subsoil dug out of the basement. If they answered yes, Stock said, then they "can probably have a satisfactory vegetable garden."[24]

In his first column Stock discussed the need for getting fertilizer, sand and limestone into the soil. Stock Brothers' ad that week offered stable manure at $10 a cubic yard, twenty-two bushels of it. The next week Edward L. Stock Jr. was named chairman of the Victory Garden program of the Montgomery County Citizens Service Corps. He appointed

Mrs. Chase Donaldson, a skilled landscape gardener, chair for the Bethesda-Chevy Chase area and set her up in an office in the County Building annex with a stack of USDA bulletins and the job of getting experienced gardeners to volunteer to help the many novices, having soil tests made and trying to keep track of who was planning to plant where.

On Lincoln Street, where Mrs. Whalen had donated four acres for gardening, the "farmers" formed a club with each member contributing for plowing, fertilizer and prizes. George Teunis, elected president, recruited Walter Johnson to come judge the gardens in the summer in what was likely the first local move toward competitive agriculture. The Lincoln Street men also laid out a horseshoe pitch nearby and often rested in the shade of Mrs. Whalen's ancient oaks while their wives worked in the "fields."

By the time spring arrived with a wet, five-inch snow on March 21, more than 2,000 Victory Gardens were taking shape on twenty-seven communal tracts in the Bethesda area. Hundreds more were being spaded up without County help or formal registration. By then Ed Stock and Commissioner Prescott had fought back a rumor that every Victory Gardener was going to be given a free pressure cooker and were busy trying to find more vacant land.

Out near the WMAL radio towers off Bradley Boulevard, thirty families signed up with Mrs. Robert Ash to start gardening on a 25-acre tract cut into 50-by-100-foot plots. They had already planned a midsummer show of their produce. After the County plowed and harrowed the land in Bradmoor, some sixty families began work on their gardens. Two Beltsville scientists, Dr. Mark Haller and Dr. Cam LeFebvre were co-chairmen of this project, which was where John L. Imirie and his daughter Millie and J. Reed Bradley and his daughter Jane had their Victory Gardens. The Huntington-Sonoma folks posted a "no dogs allowed-except on leash" sign on their acreage while next door the fifty-eight Bradmoor families, led by Mrs. Duncan Brooks, planned to use dogs to guard their crops.

Another Bradmoor gardener, J. T. Hoyle, recalled:

Irvington and Hempstead stopped at McKinley Street, and the gardens started there and extended from Hempstead to Bradmoor. Some were cleared off neater than others, of course.

On the north side toward Hempstead is where Yost built a fireplace and chimney for cookouts; we used it heavily. They cleared the place out up there, and we had a flag pole; supposedly it was the first organized Victory Garden in the country with a flag pole and a committee.

One lady was planting peas, and I asked what she was doing with a ruler, and she said the package says six inches apart. She was planting peas with a ruler. Somebody asked my son Jimmy, "What are you going to plant?" And he thought a while, and said, "I'm going to plant raisins and potato chips."

Russ Hodges was interested in our Victory Gardens, and he was there for the so-called dedication. It was announced on the radio that morning, and he read all the officers and chairmen. They've always kidded me about it, that I was chairman of the compost committee. We got a farmer out on Georgetown Road to bring us a truckload of manure, and when he found out what it was for, he didn't make us any charge.

Everybody worked six days a week, but on Sundays we'd work in the gardens and then have a ballgame at the corner of Bradmoor and Bradley; there were two vacant lots down there. If you hit a ball good and strong it went out into Bradley Boulevard.

It was a real treat when somebody could get his hands on a case of beer. Duncan Brooks had a steel wheelbarrow, and we'd go up to the ice house and get a hunk of ice to put in the wheelbarrow with the beer and go play ball and then have a cookout.

Larry Jennings (B-CC `46), who lived with his family on McKinley Street at Irvington, recalled going to a lecture about Victory Gardening and dumping his notes in his father's lap. "The gardens across the street seemed to stretch on to infinity," he said, "but I only remember pulling up a few turnips."

Over on the Luke I. Wilson property along Cedar Lane more than a hundred NIH employees signed up with chairman Clarence May and nearly as many registered with T. Ritchie Edmondston to plant on the Dunlop tract on East West Highway. Ruth Shoemaker and her sister, Mrs. Rudolph Bopp, donated twenty acres of their land for a group of Westmoreland Hills folks to garden. Their chairman was Raymond B. Leavitt. Dozens of other groups formed, and the Bethesda Civitans, led by Dennis Simmons, got into the act by volunteering to garden a tract in Wyngate. His brother, Marvin, had a big Victory Garden in his yard that backed up on Elm Street, and there were hundreds more like it, never counted or added to the "official" total.

Victory Gardeners cultivated other large tracts in Alta Vista, near the new apartments on Bradley Boulevard, at the Whitehall School, in Brookmont, in Cabin John, on the Wheatley property, at the Recreation Center and right in the middle of Kenwood. Dr. Mordecai Ezekiel plowed up a quarter-acre near "Milton" at the western end of Allandale Road and shared it with his neighbors. At Columbia Country Club more than thirty members had garden plots near the 8th hole, and the club itself put in a big garden between the 8th, 9th and 10th fairways. According to the *Star*'s George Kennedy, Mr. and Mrs. Milo Perkins tended one of the best looking gardens at Landon School. He was the director of the Board of Economic Warfare until it was abolished, and she worked in the school office. Their son, George, who had recently received his wings, was killed in a training accident that spring.[25]

The County provided signs warning that stealing from Victory Gardens was against the law and specifying the penalties, up to a $1,000 fine or five years in jail, and each community garden had a covered bulletin board for posting information and announcements. Pilfering from gardens became a more or less serious problem in some areas later that summer, and some gardeners created elaborate, noise-making traps and alarms from string and tins cans to keep tomato thieves out of their well-tended plots while others took turns watching over their rows of vegetables on moonless nights.

Mary Ellen Whitcomb neé Taft, who grew up in Brookdale near River Road, was only four or five when she found the community gardens near the back of the driving range on Western Avenue.

My friend and I were just walking around the neighborhood when we discovered them. We decided that since nobody lived there, this stuff just grew. So we played farmer and filled baskets, and we weren't a bit secretive about it. We came home swinging these baskets and brought all these things to our parents.

And they said, "Where'd you get `em?" And we said, "We found it," and they didn't really connect until they got this phone call from some people who were not too pleased that we were stealing their vegetables.

To provide cheap and reliable summer labor, Mrs. John D. Fox organized a Victory Garden Corps at the Rec Center. Thirty boys from 12 to 16 learned to hoe, rake, weed and perform other tasks before being sent out on jobs. Pay started at 25¢ an hour and went up to 45¢ for hard workers. Cash prizes lay at the end of the season for those who were the most consistent gardeners. Requests for services of Corps members came through the Rec Center, and Mrs. Fox immediately began receiving thank-you letters from overworked women.

We know lots of patriotic housewives in this region who were getting permanently warped from the back-breaking work that has to be done before you pat the seeds into place. Things came to such a pass with a friend of mine that she said she didn't care if her family starved next summer, she was going to take an aspirin, burn her Victory garden pamphlets, and go to bed for two days.[26]

By June, with the public library full of books and pamphlets on Victory Gardens and every newspaper featuring at least one column of gardening advice, Ed Stock pronounced Victory Gardening our "national recreation." He said he had:

heard men (mostly men, for they seem to like to brag about their accomplishments more than women) standing at the ration board counter or waiting for the "checker" in the grocery store telling that they had tomatoes in bloom or have corn 18 inches high, or have harvested their first peas. The story grows with the telling, of course. But haven't you heard fishermen and golfers go on in the same way. It is part of recreation to boast, mildly, about one's ability.

The dour Russ Edwards feared that a pest as awful as the porch-radio demon would soon "sweep the land," the amateur gardener. "We will have to listen to how he did it. We will have to gaze in awe at his prize tomato like the vote-seeking politician gazes in rapture at the child of a voter."[27]

Both local, weekly newspapers began to carry columns of stories about the men and women from the Bethesda area who were in the service. For information they relied on releases from military public information officers and items phoned in or written by local families. In the early part of '43 most of the news was pretty good.

B-CC graduate Eddie Leahy, class of 1940, remembered for his mustache and school spirit, ran into his old chemistry teacher, now a sergeant, F. Hughes Evans, in northern Morocco. They both had been drafted at about the same time. Maude Currin of Middleton Lane had three stars on her service flag for her oldest son Clifton, an ROTC officer at the University of Maryland, and his two younger brothers, Robert and John, who left B-CC early to join the Navy. Mr. and Mrs. George H. Sweet of Meadow Lane also had three young men, all B-CC grads, in the service: Ensign George Jr. in the Med, William in Engineer OCS, and Donald in Naval Aviation training at Jacksonville. When the Baptist Home dedicated its service flag in the spring, it had twenty blue stars and one gold one.

Often when men were on leave, they went to the high school, and soon Dorothy Young's office became the unofficial clearing house for news and new addresses. When Navy Lt. Steve Fuller, better known as Lefty in the class of '33, came home to visit with his parents on Elm Street, he told about Japanese planes crashing into the *Hornet*, and how his watch stopped at five minutes of five, the time he abandoned the sinking ship and entered the Pacific.

By '43, married men without children had been reclassified, and by the end of the year those with children were being drafted. Draft calls continued high in the spring of 1943 with up to ninety men a week reporting for induction to Draft Board No. 3 although most musters were closer to thirty. In April the local draft board reported that twenty-two percent of the 9,000 men between 18 and 65 who had registered were in the service.

Mrs. John R. Devereux added an eleventh star to her service flag in the window on West Bradley when her grandson, Landon grad Joseph, who had starred in both football and basketball, joined the Navy. She had three sons in the service other than James, a prisoner of the Japanese since the fall of Wake Island, plus three sons-in-law, two other grandsons and a grandson-in-law.

Some activities went on pretty much as always, while others bent and changed to fit the times. The Montgomery Players took their production of *Watch on the Rhine* to the Naval Hospital and to the men at Camp Lewis and the Model Basin as well as before the usual audiences at Leland's auditorium. Palais

Royal broke with department-store tradition and initiated a Victory Room where customers, instead of being waited on, took articles from bins or shelves to the cashier. Mrs. Bessie White of Bethesda was on duty to answer questions, display fragile or easily soiled goods and handle the order book.

The Ration Board ruled Civic Federation meetings non-essential, much to the pleasure of some who said they were happy to have a break from so many meetings. Rotary Club members walked or took a bus to their meetings. At the Gates' Columbia Dining Room, the customers did not complain about so much fish and poultry on the menu or not getting a refill on their coffee, but they did, almost universally ask, "What, no butter!" Both large restaurants like the Gates's, which served 150 customers a day and twice as many on Sunday, and small ones like the Moore's, which did mainly a breakfast and lunch business, had ration-point accounts with the OPA and wrote "checks" against a balance, which was renewed monthly and based on the establishment's December 1942 business.

The Bethesda Fire Board chose Capt. F. O. Smith as their new president and gave retiring G. Wady Imirie a watch and thanks for his long service. Chief Bargagni, beginning to feel the loss of men to the draft, reported that calls had decreased thirty percent in 1942 to 317. There had been 457 alarms in 1941 and 467 in 1940. The chief credited increased inspections and the work of Civil Defense volunteers for the improvement in fire safety.

The First Aid Corps, through the draft and enlistment, dwindled and then disappeared. After Don Dunnington went into the service, Carroll "Bernie" Doyle became captain, and

Edgar Tuller, Donald Dunnington and Bernard Doyle

when he enlisted, it left only Austin Voorhees of Gladwin Drive. The Lions Club paid off the loan on the Packard ambulance and was willing to finance the operation, but there were no more volunteers. Since an accident had wiped out the Bethesda Fire Department's old red Buick, the nearest non-military ambulances available to folks along Wisconsin and Connecticut Avenues and out Old Georgetown Road were in Cabin John and Kensington. The Commissioners named Leslie Carlin police chief to succeed Andrew Newman of Martin's Additions who accepted a Navy commission.

The Health Center on Hampden Lane found that the venereal disease clinic it started in September of `42 at the River Road School was increasingly needed and moved it to the County Building. By the spring of 1943, it had almost eighty patients, and attendance at the weekly clinics held on Thursday evenings was about fifty. The Bethesda center, which provided many rejected draftees the treatment required by law, was part of the Public Health Service plan to control the spread of syphilis.

The Chamber of Commerce dunned the transit company for some larger buses to serve the Bethesda business district and received a "don't you know there's a war on" type of response, but by April there were bigger buses on the Alta Vista, Naval Medical Center, and Rockville lines. The Commissioners provided free parking on an acre and a half leased from the Chevy Chase Land Company at Wisconsin and Western. Car pooling was soon as popular and patriotic as Victory Gardening and buying bonds.

Capital Transit, which despite the FEPC refused to hire African-American men as drivers but had started training women, took over the routes of the Community Bus Lines, which had long served Rollingwood, Kenwood, Edgemoor, and Woodhaven. Among the women hired by Capital Transit was Edna Cobb of Bethesda who lived with her baby, mother and invalid husband in a trailer on Old Georgetown Road. She said the hardest part of the job was overcoming her fears of the seventeen-ton streetcar during her five-week training period. After her runs, she showered and sometimes did her laundry in the new rest rooms the transit company built for its twenty-two female bus and streetcar operators. She said that when the war was over she expected to give her job back to its "rightful owner."[28]

Fred Tuemmler, director of planning for M-NCP&PC, unveiled the underpass proposed for the busy Wisconsin-East West Highway intersection and displayed his model at Meadowbrook Market and at the County Building only to find most merchants and property owners opposed to the post-war project. Local businessmen called for Wisconsin Avenue to be widened from East West to the NNMC and for "channelization." Their chief objection was that the underpass would divert traffic from local businesses, and Edgemoor residents protested the suggestion of making Edgemoor Lane one-way east. Park and Planning went back to the drawing board.

The members of the Board of Trade re-elected Carl Bachschmid president and elected Lillian Jay vice-president, Ethel Taylor secretary-treasurer and added Ed Stock and John Smith to their board of directors. The Board of Trade voted to close most Bethesda stores on Washington's Birthday, and Bachschmid announced plans to produce a business directory with the cooperation of the Chamber of Commerce.

The Chamber, meanwhile, sponsored a Bethesda service-flag design contest for local school children, and in the spring, elected Elmond E. Bass, manager of the Sherwin-Williams store, president and Carl Bachschmid first vice-president. The flag contest drew sixty-four entries, and chairman Philip Schaefer announced Doris Severe, 16, a sophomore at B-CC, as the winner. She received $5 in War Savings Stamps. The Chamber gave the Kuhn Award to the Bowling Center for its contributions to the area.[29]

The war itself ground on in New Guinea, and the Japanese suffered a blow that brought on national mourning when P-38 pilots shot down Admiral Yamamoto's plane. After driving the enemy out of the Aleutians, American forces moved through the Solomons toward Rabaul as the Grumman Hellcats, more than a match for the Mitsubishi Zero, began reaching the fleet aircraft carriers. In Europe the Russians pushed the Germans out of the Ukraine; Patton and Montgomery competed for Sicily, and the Eighth Air Force attacked the ball-bearing works at Schweinfurt. After the loss of 108 merchant ships to U-boats in March, better defended convoys and improved anti-submarine techniques turned the tide in the crucial Battle of the Atlantic.

Despite rationing and shortages, Bethesda kept attracting new businesses. The Wayside Market opened in the old Warren brothers' store at Walsh Street that the Boy Scouts had used as a salvage headquarters. Benny Rotter and W. H. Bass offered fancy fruits and vegetables as well as deli service and "fresh-killed" chickens. Many markets, and the laundries, found that they had to cut back or eliminate deliveries during 1943, and Wayside Market never started such a service. Stock Brothers' nursery and several other businesses, including all of the drug stores, made as many deliveries as they could by bicycle.

At the Wayside Shop, 7242 Wisconsin in the Broadhursts' new building, L. K. Ruebsam offered extensive upholstering services and then before summer began, sold his store's name and location to M. S. Ginn and Company, which moved there from the shopping center. Ginn's manager, Clarence E. Whitmore, used the living space upstairs to display the "apartment of the month" and renamed the operation Ginn's Wayside Shop. One new, wartime product at Ginn's was a day bed with wooden springs.

Joe Crivella completely renovated the old Bridge Market and adopted a new motto: "If it grows, we have it!" Because of the shortage of tin cans, Steadmen's Mexican Food Products on Miller Avenue started a retail business selling chili for 25¢ a pint, plus three meat points, if you brought your own container. A couple of new radio repair stores opened, one on Wilson Lane near Emmy Lou's and the other was Roger W. Wing's People's Radio Service on Wisconsin across from Chase.

Two local men, J. R. Pugh and Bill Henney, started the Montgomery Cab Company at 7245 Wisconsin near Elm Street, and We Cab had more competition a month later when Community Cab opened up at 7320 Wisconsin. C. H. Gaines, who lived at Denton and Elm, took over as manager of the Esso station at 7701 Wisconsin between Gifford's and the Bethesda theater, and became an aggressive advertiser in the local papers. He even stayed open on Sundays.

At the Bank of Bethesda the Board of Directors elected S. Walter Bogley, cashier since 1919, to succeed the late George P. Sacks as president, and promoted W. Paul Stallsmith to cashier. Bogley, active in the Masons, the Rotary, the Chamber of Commerce and the

Eldbrooke Methodist Church, was also County chairman of the War Savings Bond campaigns, which exceeded their quota time after time.

Mrs. Everett J. Boothby's Red Cross Fund Drive got off to a slow start in the spring of `43. The Bethesda Branch led by Dr. George B. Clendenin and Mrs. Fred Berens was the first to top its quota and kept right on collecting through air raid wardens toward the County's $46,000 goal. Mrs. Edgar F. Fowler treated her volunteers to tea at the Woman's Club of Chevy Chase after they exceeded her area's goal by more than $1,000. By April the County chapter was pleased to announce that $57,469 had been collected. Of that total the Bethesda-Chevy Chase area contributed more than $28,000.

The Red Cross Blood Mobile continued to make its rounds, and when it appeared at the Bethesda Presbyterian Church that spring, Mrs. Alexandria R. Kalcy, an employee of Bowen Electronics, gave blood for the eighth time in seventeen months. "It's the only way I can help win the war," she said. By the end of the year, six other women had joined the Red Cross "Gallon Club."[30]

After all the necessary agencies approved the site selected for the Suburban Hospital, the War Production Board moved quickly, and by mid-February authorized construction along with priorities for all the needed materials and equipment. The Suburban Hospital Association established an office at 7653 Old Georgetown and released the specifications for bids by contractors. In mid-March the Board of Directors appointed J. Dewey Lutes superintendent of the hospital at a salary of $6,000 a year. He announced that ground would be broken about the first of April and that he hoped construction would be completed by August 15.

Lutes brought twenty years of hospital administrative experience with him to Bethesda. He organized and was director of the American College of Hospital Administrators and had supervised several expansion and construction programs. A Kentucky native and long-time Chicago resident, Lutes said he was sure everyone understood the need for the hospital. "It is my duty and the Board's responsibility," he said, "to make available to the citizens of Montgomery

Ground breaking at Suburban Hospital

County a hospital that will fulfill their highest expectations of hospital and medical service."

On Tuesday, April 9, with Martye Bishop at the controls of a bulldozer for the photographers, the usual phalanx of dignitaries took part in ground breaking ceremonies, and construction of Suburban Hospital began on the first anniversary of the Public Health Lay Committee meeting that had resulted in the creation of the hospital association. For the Board of Trustees, Randolph Bishop paid tribute to the lay health group for spearheading the effort that produced the hospital and thanked Dr. Ellicott, the County heath officer, and the Public Health Service for their support. By the end of April, Lutes was accepting applications for employment and saying that under Board of Trustees policies, County residents would be favored.[31]

C. M. H. (Chappelle, McCall, and Herring) Construction of Washington, D.C., under the supervision of the Public Buildings Administration, built Suburban Hospital. The plans by Waldron Faulkner of Faulkner and Kingsbury provided for a one-story, brick-faced structure with a partial basement, plaster walls, linoleum floors, and air-space above the ceilings. The flat-roofed design provided a two-foot overhang to shade the big windows. The exterior was to be painted white with grey trim and the interior silver grey and "colonial" yellow. The 400-foot main corridor paralleled Lincoln street and the four 150-foot wings reached toward McKinley Street and the planned two-story dormitory for fifty-six nurses. The contractors promised to save as many of the Whalen's fine, old trees as they could.

Soon women's clubs, churches, civic associations and business groups vied to donate rooms or equipment to the new hospital. The Battery Park Citizens' Association held a benefit card party and dance in May, and the Civitan Club was not far behind in pledging to furnish a room as did the Soroptomists. A line formed. The Rosedale Victory Club was the first organization to come up with $300 to sponsor a private room, and F. Irwin Ray was the first individual to do so. Mrs. John Imirie donated a room in memory of her daughter, Mary Imirie Rowe; Walter E. Perry sponsored one in memory of his doctor brother and many more donations followed. The Newcomb Club established a fund to carry on social service activities, and led by their president, Mrs. Gordon M. Kline, they soon made Suburban a permanent part of their organization's work.

Mrs. Walter E. Perry, chairman of women's activities for the new hospital, put Mrs. Samuel A. Syme in charge of sewing projects, and she soon had the Rosedale Victory Club hemming kitchen towels and making white flannel socks for operating-room use while the Somerset Woman's Club worked on layettes. In June a permanent Women's Auxiliary wrote by-laws and chose officers. Mrs. Perry led the temporary officers and set up nineteen committees for the 110 volunteers. Before the school year ended, elementary school children contributed enough flatware to equip eighty-two trays with a knife, fork, soup spoon, two teaspoons and a salad fork plus 135 extra pieces; all, according to Mrs. Elwyn J. Rowell, in excellent condition.[32]

That spring, Bannockburn Country Club, operated by Mr. and Mrs. Ernest Anderson, brought its golf course back into play although amenities consisted of little more than a Coke box in the clubhouse. If one joined the "club," the initiation fee was $12, and monthly dues were $6 plus tax. Bannockburn invited servicemen to come play a round of golf for 50¢ during the week and $1.00 on weekends; for civilian "visitors" it was 75¢ and $1.50.

Congressional Country Club closed down altogether in February, asked Wiffy Cox to put his affairs in order and ousted the twenty-five resident members who had been living in the spacious clubhouse. In April, General Frank T. Hines announced that the entire facility was to be used for "military training purposes." General "Wild Bill" Donovan's Office of Strategic Services took over the club for $4,000 a month plus a promise to pay for damages at the end of the war. OSS, the cloak-and-dagger, dirty-tricks progenitor of the CIA, established its headquarters in Que Building in Foggy Botton near the Heurich Brewery. (Almost every recruit recalled the smell of the place.) It then acquired a number of training sites and safe houses in the Washington metropolitan area and, later, in other parts of the country.[33]

The OSS moved into Congressional (Area F) on April 28, 1943, with Serge Obolensky as commander. John Swanson remained as a caretaker with the only full set of keys and watched as the trainers tore up the fairways and greens, pitched tents on the tennis courts and destroyed all the work that had gone into building the third nine. Obolensky, one-time manager of the Sherry Netherlands and the Savoy Plaza, had to replace all the stoves, ovens and dishwashing equipment. The heating plant needed work, and there were other difficulties resulting from the financial problems the club had long faced, but he soon had the place in first-class condition, and General Donovan could bring his society friends out for cocktails on the terrace so they could watch his men climb ropes hanging from the big trees along the drive and run through the obstacle course, which started at the swimming pool.[34]

Early on, OSS, known in some circles as the "Oh So Social," acquired a reputation for hiring society matrons, playboys, Ivy League dilettantes, and the prettiest girls in town, debutantes or not. Many of the young men who came to Congressional for operational group training were of a quite different type.[35]

Australian-born Lt. Col. Dan Fairbairn, one-time Shanghai police chief and a naturalized American, ran the training program with Hans Tofte, a Dane active in the underground and on the Burma Road, as his second in command. Their job was to teach mayhem and silent killing. Recruits carried pointed and double-edged Fairbairn knives and learned to use them. The ballroom became a huge classroom with blackboards and folding chairs, and they boarded over the indoor pool and used it as a workroom. The main dining room became the mess hall for enlisted men with a corner screened off for officers who also lounged in the bar with its overstuffed chairs and tired pool tables.

Machine guns placed on the 15th green fired over students crawling toward the lake,

and one trainee was killed there when he crawled over a snake and jumped up. They built a pill box and a range for firing Thompson submachine guns and pistols across River Road on the eighty disputed acres the club claimed there. The back end of a C-47 fuselage stood on the putting green for parachute jumping practice into a six-by-six-foot box of sawdust. Quonset huts and other temporary buildings sprouted about the grounds. Obolensky's station complement grew to about eighty men including the cooks and the perimeter security force.[36]

The first group to arrive at Area F for training was called Company A. Their target was Italy, and many of the enlisted men were Italian-Americans from New York City. Among the first officers in that group was Lt. Al Materazzi who reported to Que Building and then to Area C down near Triangle, Virginia, because Congressional was not ready. He had been recruited by Major, later Lt. Colonel, Russell Livermore, who became head of all Italian OGs and later of all operational groups, and Sicilian Max Corvo, who headed up secret intelligence in Italy.

Al Materazzi remembered:

Corvo was there to test our Italian. And my parents came from Tuscany and spoke perfect Italian; I had to laugh. I got a degree from the University of Rome. A description of the best Italian is Tuscan in the mouth of a Roman. . . .

I was teaching close order drill to a bunch of Mexican-Americans they had recruited out of Arizona. Then the filing system worked and kicked me out as a guy that speaks Italian and knows demolition.

So they called me in and asked if I would consider operating in Italy clandestinely or whatever, and I said I might think about it. Next thing you know, I had orders . . . . We lived in pyramidal tents, and we did most of our own training. Fairbairn was supposed to teach us dirty tricks, but I'm sure there were two or three of our guys that could have taught him. The engineer officers taught demolitions. They had no maps, so I went to the Geological Survey and picked up the four quadrangles covering the Congressional Country Club. I took them down to the Que Building reproduction plant, had them pasted together and blown up to 1 to 50,000, the scale European maps used. I used filters to get all the colors, especially the streams, and then had an atlas grid drawn up with numbers one way and letters the other way and had that put on in purple. It

came out to be a pretty good-sized map, and that's what we trained with and what I taught maps with.

We did dream up our own problems. In one we were supposed to attack about where Democracy Boulevard runs into Cabin John now. It was all wild country then, and there was an old barn there, and we planned an attack on it from two different directions. My group came up Cabin John Creek. I was back, and the enlisted men were doing this after I took them through on the map and showed them the trail and estimated the time it would take.

One of the places we thought might be a problem was a culvert. When they got there, a guard was on the bridge and our scouts were captured, so I sent three of them up to take care of the guard. There was woods right up to a parapet on the bridge. One guy came out of the woods, climbed up on the parapet, waited till the guard turned around and dropped behind him and said, "OK, you're dead, now we can come through." The guy, scared to death, station-complement type, we had a bad reputation; we were Mafia; he turned around and walked right into the knife. It must have caught him right in the heart.

I took over and sent the guy back under guard and finished the exercise and then came back.

Every day we would go on a ten-mile hike someplace or other. The favorite one was to go out River Road and down toward Normandy Farms or down MacArthur toward Glen Echo. We got some training on foreign weapons, and we learned how to make shaped charges, theory and practice.

When Aaron Bank arrived later in the spring of '43, he got a cab after checking in at Que Building, stowed his gear and said, "Congressional Country Club, please." The cabbie said "What! Not another one of those guerrillas!" At the club he found "the social rooms were still smartly decorated and the dining room, bar, and even the bedrooms were fully furnished. I was quartered in a room with twin beds and a private bath."

He recalled mostly commando-type training with practice ambushes, sentry elimination, simulated destruction of bridges, culverts, railroads, canal locks, electric transformers and pylons. The most frustrating incidents, according to Bank, would occur when, after painfully crawling through the underbrush to apply simulated plastic explosive to guarded bridges and culverts, the night silence would be shattered by a childish

yell of triumph: "There they are!" The local kids made a game out of harassing the trainees.[37]

Francis Coleman, whose friends call him "Fig," thought the war was going to pass him by when the Army canceled his OCS artillery training and sent him to the University of Maryland to learn about occupation government. He studied French and European history after the paratroops turned him down because he was too big. In May of 1943 after a dinner in D.C., he saw a very large colonel wearing paratrooper wings, followed him to his car at the Mayflower and stood with his foot on the running board and asked him how he got into the paratroops at his size.

In accented English, he questioned me about my skills and said he was in a group more interested in fighting than in size. Finally, he said, "Vell, you write me, Serge Obolensky, Post Office Box 26704, Washington, D.C."

My family knew him and his Astor connection, so I wrote, and in a week I got an answer on OSS letterhead and then got a call for an interview at Que Building followed by a transfer. My C. O. at Maryland asked me what kind of outfit OSS was when I left since they had sent a staff car and sergeant for me, and I was just a corporal. "Ask if they've got a job for me," he said.

They drove to me to Que Building and tore off my stripes and destroyed everything with my name on it. Then they loaded a bunch of us into an Army truck and took us to Congressional Country Club. They sorted us out, and we were assigned to winterized tents with wooden floors, four to a tent with a coal stove, but this was spring.

Then we were called to meet the C.O., and it turned out to be Obolensky, and he recognized me. He thought it was funny how I got there. His office was in back over the swimming pool; he often worked in a bathing suit and went to swim a lap or two sometimes.

We did compass training at night. They took us out to get back unobserved with the trainers trying to catch us. But the first lecture in the big ballroom was from Fairbairn on hand to hand combat. He didn't look very tough, but he called the biggest man up and floored him.

We tried out all sorts of gadgets, threw grenades into sand bunkers. One night I ran around trailing a string from my belt with a rag filled with some stuff that was supposed to keep dogs from tracking you while they chased me with

a bunch of dogs. Then they sent us to Area A, an old CCC camp near Hagerstown, which had the highest VD rate in the nation. We fired many different kinds of weapons up there. We did parachute training in Algiers and then went into Southern France and returned to Benning by Christmas of 1944.

According to Roger Hall, of *You're Stepping on My Cloak and Dagger* fame, "The men crawled over the golf course, blew up the caddy shack and ambushed the morning milk truck driver." But the training regime at Congressional became more and more regularized. The course for the Norwegian Contingent included about 120 hours of carefully scheduled hard work.

By the time W. C. "Bud" Dutton got to Area F as part of the cadre, the training routine was pretty well set. Dutton became part of the staff and trained operational group members in small arms and demolition, particularly the use of plastic explosives. He recalled a few exercises involving "roaming around the grounds at night and down to the canal for simulated blowing up of canal bridges." They had a curriculum to follow and a tight chedule, but:

Sometimes we skipped camp and walked down River Road to a bar, south toward D.C. Not often though, and we jumped off the road when cars came. We didn't want to be detected, but the place was neither fenced nor guarded.

They ate in the dining room, and he remembered "good chow, for Army chow."

A new issue, which stirred up quite a few Bethesdans and Chevy Chasers, arrived with the "Oriental" cherry blossoms, which drew big crowds to the Tidal Basin that spring. The issue was dogs. Mrs. Bradley raised it in an April 9 editorial in the *Journal* in reference to Victory Gardens. She estimated that some 2,000 dogs roamed the Bethesda area more or less freely. (Her supposition was based on 8,000 homes and one dog per four houses.) She noted that there were also about 2,000 people who had expressed a willingness to start a Victory Garden, which meant, she figured, one dog per garden. "Doesn't sound so bad considered individually," she wrote, "but just suppose a dozen dogs take it into their heads to make your victory garden their headquarters." We "love our dogs" and want them to be happy, "but for the period of victory gardening, we should see to it that they

are kept in their own back yards or their own cellars unless we have time to accompany them on their strolls."

The *Journal*, which ran a regular dog column by Mrs. Linden P. Oliver, received a basket of mail, much of it supportive but at least as much critical of the editor's stand. Mrs. Oliver asked for reasonable cooperation and understanding and reminded readers that dog-owners had some rights. "You hit a man in a vulnerable spot when you revile his dog," she concluded. Mrs. Bradley stuck to her unpopular position: "Dogs ought not to be allowed out except on leash for the duration."[38]

The dog problem became more complicated in May when the respected principal of Chevy Chase Elementary, Anna P. Rose, asked for help to rid her playground of a pack of two-dozen dogs that frightened children at recess, roamed the halls looking for food and water and even pushed their way into classrooms. Both the Chevy Chase PTA and the police seemed unable to find an answer, so Mrs. Bradley took a try. She printed the County law, which said that every dog owner had to pay an annual tax and that every dog had to wear a tag. Dogs without tags could be killed, and owners fined $25 plus costs or sent to jail for up to thirty days. A canine census by the police began June 1 to find owners of untaxed dogs, and there was such a sudden rush to the deputy treasurer's office that Bob Hagner ran out of tags.[39]

By mid-June Anna Rose and Gertrude Bradley were both "off the hook." On Friday, June 11, a stray dog wandered through Glen Echo behaving strangely. It attacked and bit at least ten other dogs before being captured and found to be rabid. Three days later the Maryland State Department of Agriculture imposed a ninety-day quarantine on all dogs in the 7th Election District. It required that dogs be confined and walked on a leash. Police were ordered to kill tagless strays and issue citations to the owners of wandering pets, which could be ordered destroyed.

The Commissioners revived a 1938 muzzle law, which subjected unmuzzled dogs to impoundment and set a fifteen dollar fine for owners of such dogs found running loose. This placed even tagged dogs at risk of being destroyed after being held five days. The police built an improvised pound behind the County Building in Bethesda. In the fall, health officials extended the quarantine period to the end of the year, and the Commissioners appointed a full-time dog catcher, and then built a pound at the Meadowbrook Saddle Club. All this activity led to a call for the formation of a humane society and Mrs. Oliver's conclusion that all strays should be removed from the streets and pets kept under reasonable control.[40]

Another "worthy cause," which engaged the energies of many Bethesdans in the spring of `43, was teacher pay. The real issue was teacher retention. Many County teachers, the best paid in Maryland, with an average annual salary of $1,672, found better paying defense jobs, accepted teaching posts in the District where extra duties such as coaching brought extra stipends or were drafted or offered commissions.

The League of Women Voters asked the General Assembly delegation for action but got nowhere mainly because the State had authorized a one-time, two hundred dollar bonus paid at $20 per month for the next fiscal year. Arthur Hilland caustically compared the scorn the teachers' request received to pay raises authorized for members of the "boss-controlled political machine." Dr. Broome reported that 145 teachers had resigned since the previous June, and the Civic Federation joined the call for action to hold on to the County's teachers. In 1943 the turnover rate for County teachers was twenty-three percent; the State figure was fifty percent. By then only fifty of the County 540 teachers were men and most of them were above draft age.

On March 24, representatives of nineteen suburban PTAs met at Leland JHS to discuss the problem. William N. Morell of the Leland PTA chaired the meeting, and Stella Werner told them that the situation should be expected when school janitors were paid more than teachers and rookie policemen earned more than teachers with fifteen years experience. Mrs. Curtis Walker, a school board member, said she felt teachers should be paid like other County employees and not just receive temporary bonuses. The assembly called upon the Commissioners to pay teachers an additional $20 per month until the State money came through and to continue those increases until the General Assembly met again in 1945. In mid-April, the Commissioners authorized a "wartime bonus" of $100 for teachers, and at the same time they gave the policemen a $300 raise.

First 161 units at Offutt Lane ready to rent.

Unit 2 on Hillandale nearing completion. Both designed by Schreirer and Patterson

That spring, H. L. Rust began renting the 134 units in the second section of the Bradley Boulevard Apartments built and owned by Albert Walker's corporations. The Second War Loan campaign, which sought thirteen billion dollars nationwide and two million in the County, began in April, while at the Navy Hospital, construction of a WAVES barracks and school neared completion. At the Woman's Club of Bethesda, members who wished to take part in the monthly bridge party had to meet the criteria of Mrs. John Miles Mader's Victory Program, which involved assisting the Red Cross surgical dressing group, purchasing war stamps or bonds with their own money, collecting books and magazines for servicemen and saving rayon or silk stockings.

The Bethesda Ration Board announced that it would issue supplemental gas stamps only to car poolers in the future. In Wood Acres, after developer Albert Walker discontinued his bus service, home owners joined together in a "Share the Ride" operation and received additional ration stamps for their efforts. Intermittent gas shortages plagued the area, and some motorists got in the habit of following tank trucks to their destination. The line to the pumps at Burrow's station sometimes threatened to block off Bradley Lane. For several months the transit company curtailed bus service during non-rush hours. The gas shortage also produced a Boy Scout camporee on the Edland Farm on Old Georgetown Road. Almost 130 Scouts participated al-

though they had a hard time believing they were really way "out in the country."

For Jack Sullivan and the other boys who worked for Gordon Burrows at twenty-five cents an hour, there was no gas shortage. Sullivan, owner of a well-known `34 Ford convertible with a broad-striped awning for a top, said:

When they started rationing gas, I pumped my own. I didn't need any ration book. We took the stamps and pumped the gas allowed, but as far as I'm concerned, the way that guy treated us, we were just getting even. We took care of ourselves.

Rationing did not stop drag racing either although most Bethesda-area boys used Viers Mill Road or Massachusetts Avenue extended for that activity. Jack Sullivan:

Bob Brewer came by one night while I was studying. He honked the horn. He had his father's car and wanted to race me. My father had a 1939 Buick Century, a powerful car. So we drove down Bradley Lane and made a U-turn on Connecticut Avenue and went north from Bradley when the light changed, and we went across East West Highway side-by-side at 90 mph.[41]

The Bethesda Public Library's annual report showed that it had circulated over 57,000 books in the past twelve months. The staff reorganized the deposit station at the River Road Colored School, installed new library furniture there and improved both its adult and juvenile collection. Volunteers under the

direction of teacher Margaret Wood operated the library room every Friday.

While the flowers in front of the Wayside Market and down at the Bethesda Floral Gardens brightened everyone's spring, Park Commissioner E. Brooke Lee announced a tree planting campaign directed by landscape architect William R. Hall. The first Bethesda areas to benefit were in Drummond, on Singleton Drive in Wyngate, on Moorland and Middlesex Lanes in Edgemoor, along Chestnut Avenue in Rosedale Park and on Elm Street near Leland JHS.

Air raid drills continued, about every two or three weeks and generally unannounced, and all defense corps members mobilized monthly. That spring they changed their meeting time from 8 to 9 pm for the benefit of the wardens and auxiliary police and firemen who were also Victory Gardeners. Arch McDonald resigned as chief air raid warden, and retired Coast Guard Rear Admiral Harry G. Hamlet, who lived on Beechwood Drive in Chevy Chase, took over the job.. The blackout drill on May 28 included a test of the new "all clear" signal, a 15-second blast.

Newly appointed deputy treasurer Robert D. Hagner, whose job existed to save taxpayers' gas, started a room registry in his office in the County Building annex to help servicemen

Clarence Keiser and Admiral Hamlet with a new pump

find housing and urged home owners with spare beds to make them available. Judge Albert Brault named Bethesdan Richard Schaefer, sales manager of a D.C. auto accessory company, County salvage director to replace the fatigued George Menke who resigned after his operation had accumulated more than a million pounds of paper, metal and rubber. When *Tribune* editor-publisher and Brooke Lee-loyalist Bill Allen became custodian of civil defense property at $125 a month, Mrs. Bradley produced a "sour grapes" editorial.[42]

Over near the river, Henry T. McCuen chaired a committee that planned to provide recreational and welfare services to the civilian and military personnel working or stationed in the area. One of their first events was a dance at the Cabin John fire house enjoyed by more than a hundred service men. McCuen put out a call for furniture, games and magazines and set up a lounge in the fire house at Cabin John several months before the USO in Bethesda opened. The men at Camp Lewis later asked Mrs. Aubinoe and the Red Cross to help them furnish their own recreation room. "Buzzy" Potter lent them a canoe to use in the canal, which they immediately took over to the river and lost.[43]

Camp Lewis, one of the first units of its kind, started as a Training Center for the Military District of Washington in July 1942 on the site of the Carderock CCC camp. "The commander of the Training Center was a former high school principal, and the instructors were selected on the basis of their training and teaching background." The camp was unofficially named for Maj. Gen. John T. Lewis, the first C. O. of the MDW.

Its establishment was prompted by the fact that various units within the District found that the prosecution of their mission was deterred by the presence among their enlisted men of several problem cases.

These men on "special duty" underwent basic, technical, and tactical instruction at Camp Lewis. The first group of enlisted men send out to Carderock for training were disciplinary or alcoholic cases, which led to the camp being looked on as a punitive area. However, the MDW viewed it as a substitute for the guardhouse and its goal as fitting "inapt" men to serve in their units.

Only in extreme instances was discharge recommended. The effectiveness of the Center can be seen in the fact that between August 1943 and

February 1944, some 580 enlisted men were processed, of whom all but eight were reassigned within the Military District or transferred to overseas theaters.

After the first group most of the trainees were "illiterate, lacking in education or slow in learning." The Training Center ran a thirteen-week program for them, and those "who mastered the necessary fundamentals" returned to their units in the MDW.

Raymond Frazier of Cabin John made a few dollars by running a bus service with his one-ton, flat-bed Chevrolet truck. He charged the soldiers a dime to haul them, standing and holding on to each other in the back, down to the Glen Echo trolley loop.

The Training Center ceased operation in July 1944, and, according to some locals, Camp Lewis became a prison for Army miscreants who were held within a double chain link fence topped by barbed wire, patrolled by Dobermans and watched by guards on two machine gun towers. Escapees usually turned up at Tuohey's, Canada's or one of the other nearby beer joints, which had also been the first places searched by MP's when trainees went AWOL. From February `43 to June `44 an MP company replaced the 176th Infantry encamped at Carderock.[44]

At the high school, evening, war industry-training classes continued including an extra session on electric arc welding. A new typing class offered twenty-four two-hour sessions for a dollar. Falge Engineering and other Bethesda defense contractors advertised that they would train new employees themselves and pay them 25¢ an hour while they learned.

Help was getting hard to find, and both Jelleff's and Palais Royal hired high school students as did the telephone company ($23 to $26.50 a week with rapid increases). The Hot Shoppe restaurant regularly advertised for new employees ($35 a week plus meals), and the laundries stopped accepting new customers. Draft deferred men had their pick of permanent jobs, and no teenager had to look long to find work. The high school scheduled tests for the Army's specialized training and the Navy V-12 program in April.

The B-CC Baron's young and inexperienced baseball team had a difficult year especially after power hitter Harry Phillips' name came up on the ineligible list for the first half of the season, but they ended up 11-5. The girls' softball team coached by Helen Randels,

the new PE teacher, enjoyed a more successful season shortened by transportation problems. Captained by first baseman Betty Milne, the team beat Leland 17-5, Sherwood 33-8, Blair 20-9, then lost to Sherwood before defeating Blair again. They also played the faculty women, but the score of that game stayed a tightly guarded secret.

That school year, coordinator Page Furth's Distributive Education Class provided work experience for twenty seniors who earned almost $7,500 for 16,850 hours of work. Fifteen of the twenty graduated, and the other five left school to enlist in the military. The students worked at diverse jobs for employers such as the Palais Royal, Army Map Service, Soper's Esso Station and Bell Laundry. Five high school seniors won competitive scholarships, and several others earned awards and "assigned" scholarships.

In May at its annual meeting, the Montgomery County Teachers' Association elected Lillian Moore, head of B-CC's commercial department, as its president. She was the first classroom teacher chosen for that post in the organization's thirteen-year history. A graduate of Goucher and Columbia, she lived on South Chelsea Street with Mrs. Massey Black.

The graduating class was one of the smallest in several years as 200 juniors shrank to 176 seniors, 104 of them female. As graduation neared, a group of boys left school early under Mr. Bender's supervision to do some pea picking on County farms. But most of the class stayed and took part in the senior day activities led by "Herky" Latimer and the Senior Banquet and Prom their mothers staged at the Woman's Club of Chevy Chase after hotels and caterers refused because of food and labor shortages.

Dr. Peter Marshall preached the baccalaureate sermon at Chevy Chase Presbyterian on June 13, and on the evening of the 15th the farm workers were back, and most, but not all, of the graduates crossed the stage and accepted their diplomas from Mrs. Curtis Walker. Among the better known graduates were Jango and *Life* cover-girl Helen "Lambie" Almy, athletes Betty Milne and Bob Brewer, table tennis champ Carolyn Wilson, winner of every local title in sight, and 6'3" Alton Willett, Metro area schoolboy golf champion in both his sophomore and senior years who signed yearbooks, "Pro."[45]

Class president Leonard Williams, now in the Navy V-12 program at Harvard, sat in the audience and listened to Carter Dawson make the traditional greeting. Speech class choices Lester Dame and Richard Greaves followed with talks asking "What Are We Fighting For?" and "What Are We Working For?", and refugee Dr. Sigmund Skard told the graduates and their guests why Norway would never give in to the Nazis. After the distribution of diplomas, Principal Thomas W. Pyle, in a short talk about "The Secret Weapon," made a case for values beyond the physical and political. The fact that the high school had recently put two gold stars on its service flag was an unstated part of the ceremony.[46]

The reason some seniors did not graduate in the Leland-auditorium festivities and receive their diplomas in public was that, for the first time, the school administration decided to make an example of a few fraternity and sorority members. Some secret societies had been less than subtle. Southern Society had advertised a spring dance that featured Rae Scott's all-girl band, a raffle and a prize for the most beautiful girl in attendance. John Henry Sullivan Jr., active in Alpha Delta Sigma, was one of those called down to the office, given his diploma and told not to participate in the ceremonies. It bothered Jack that Harry Andrews and others in fraternities lied about their membership and marched across the stage, but his parents were not upset. However, Mr. Pyle's decision outraged several parents who complained bitterly to the Superintendent and to the local newspapers.[47]

The administrators remained quiet, but in the fall Mrs. J. Reed Bradley responded in a series of *Journal* editorials, which brought forth several letters from students whose names were withheld at their request. Mrs. Bradley called high school secret societies undemocratic and harmful to both students and the school. She urged parents to cooperate with the school in getting rid of them and in replacing fraternities with other clubs and activities. The anonymous students defended their right to join and pointed to the open acceptance of fraternities and sororities in D.C. high schools. They criticized the state law that forced them to be "secret" and said that organizations such as the Rotary, of which their principal was president, selected their members.[48]

Just before the end of the school year, popular Leland gym teacher Harold L. Alder-

ton left to become a chief petty officer in the Navy. By June the school system had lost sixty more teachers to war-related moves.[49]

Henrietta Baker of the music department planned Leland's graduation, which featured a Latin American fiesta. No special clothes or shoes were required, and in fact, the directions to parents urged that they not waste shoe coupon #17. The girls wore white blouses and dirndl skirts; many of them had made their own. At East Bethesda end-of-year events included the formal renaming of the school as Lynnbrook and the completion of six fireplaces in the park area for community use. Both Bethesda Elementary and Glen Echo-Cabin John students celebrated the end of school by christening the jeeps they "bought" by purchasing savings stamps and bonds. At Chevy Chase ES, many fifth and sixth graders signed up with the Community Helpers Agency to do jobs such as running errands, cutting lawns and weeding gardens at prices from 5¢ to 25¢ an hour.

Cub Scout John Skilling christens Bethesda's jeep.

Prodded by the advisory board of Emory Bogley, Stella Werner, William Horn and Dorothy Hilland and following a survey of 2,000 parents and children, Bethesda went into the summer of '43 with a bigger-than-ever, 12-week recreation and child-care program. Louis Mitchell became head of the whole County summer effort sponsored jointly by the

Commissioners, Park and Planning and the school board. Lynnbrook's principal, Elsie Bosley, was program director for the Western Suburban Area, and day-care centers opened at the high school, the Rec Center, Bethesda Elementary, Leland JHS and Glen Echo-Cabin John Elementary. Encouraged by Commissioner Lee's statement on the value of competitive athletics, "Zip" Lehr at Leland, Fred Mulvey at Cabin John and Loris Williams at the Rec Center headed team-sport programs.

A Board of Trade committee headed by the Centro Hobby Shop's Ethel Taylor, in co-operation with the Junior Red Cross under Mrs. R. J. Powers, created a very successful "defense" center for kids, which they named the Jeep House. George A. Sacks donated an empty store at 7014 Wisconsin Avenue, which Victory Corps boys cleaned and volunteers painted a light green. Bernadette Sheehan's B-CC art class then decorated the walls with pictographs of the center's activities. Eisinger's built three large tables, and Jelleff's lent forty folding chairs. Mrs. Jay visited the schools to explain the program while Ed Stock furnished the room with donated materials and borrowed sewing machines.

The Junior Red Cross included home nursing, production units, sewing, first aid and a bicycle errand corps among the choices for students nine and up. Older boys and girls, mostly girls, had courses in staff assistance and canteen work. On Saturday, June 5, 160 children signed up, and by the time the Jeep House opened on Monday morning, June 21, more than 300 had registered, and there were waiting lists for several classes. In the first two weeks, the youngsters turned out 1,200

surgical dressings, and only had to refold a few, and a month later, they had produced 5,400 two-by-two dressings. The woodworkers under the direction of Ed Stock's partner, Charlie Rudd, made hundreds of small bowls and dozens of cribbage and checker boards for hospital patients and put out a request for mayonnaise jar lids, which they planned to fashion into ashtrays. Mr. Rudd volunteered his time and supplied most of the hand tools. The home nursing course drew eighty-five girls from ten to fifteen who made their own uniforms and then learned to care for and change the bed linen of a sick person and how to bathe a baby. As more kids arrived, Jeep House expanded into the basement and installed the woodworkers there.

Some things seemed not to change. Tom Elward became head of the Civitan Club, J. R. Enright president of the Lions and Tom Pyle leader of the Rotary Club and later president of the Maryland State Teachers' Association. When Mrs. Arthur Hilland became head of the Woodland Citizens' Association, she was only the second woman in the County to hold such a post.

In Drummond Dr. John R. Fleming, who had been on the Citizens' Committee for as long as anyone could remember, was re-elected. The new head of County LWV was Mrs. Frank Garfield of Somerset. She was a Connecticut native, a graduate of Mt. Holyoke College and the University of North Carolina and a local resident for eight years. She said she looked forward to a busy and interesting year.

The Farm Women's Market continued to be "a madhouse" on Saturday mornings. Russ Edwards wondered "how do those charming customers get up that early and all get there at once?" The white-aproned ladies did have a run-in with the OPA over ceiling prices in late spring. A customer reported the market for violating the rolled-back price on fresh chickens. Mrs. Julian Waters responded that they had been trying for some time to get OPA to say exactly what their price should be since they sold "above-average chickens, thoroughly cleaned and ready for the pot." The farm women lowered their price from sixty-three to sixty cents a

Signing up for Jeep House

pound and refiled their appeal. In July Jack Eaton and the local board ruled they could raise the price back to 63¢ since their chickens were "special."

By spring, rationing had become rather complex, and most housewives juggled several different books every time they went shopping.

The regulations for a typical week of rationing, the first week of June 1943:

In Book 1, stamps 15 and 16 were each good for 5 lbs. of sugar for home canning, and coupon 13 was good for 5 lbs. for the next six weeks; stamp 24 made it possible to buy one pound of coffee that month; shoe stamp 17 was OK for one pair through June 15, then #18 become good. In Book 2, blue coupons G, H, J, K, L, and M were acceptable for rationed canned goods (G,H,J expired June 7, K,L,M July 7); red coupons for meat, butter, fats, and oil included J and K through June, L on June 6, M on June 13, and N on June 20. Forms for book three had to be filled out and mailed back at once. (Once it was issued, housewives would have brown stamps to deal with as well as the white, red, and blue of the first two books.) Shoppers were asked to note posted ceiling price lists in the stores and report violators.

All pleasure driving was still forbidden, and A coupon #5 was valid for three gallons through July 21; B and C coupons were good for 2 1/2 gallons each at the dates on the books. Fuel oil coupon No 5 could be used for 10 gallons through September.

No one explained what to do when a shopper had the stamps and the money but no one had the goods. People trailed meat trucks around to see where they were going to make a

delivery. Dorothy Plitt Brown, then a young wife and mother, said:

Rationing really was not a problem because we didn't have a lot of money. But we did have trouble getting meat. We'd take a number and wait and wait, and then the butcher would appear like the star of the show. When it was your turn, everybody was making comments so you were even afraid to ask for a half-a-pound of hot dogs. It made you feel awful.

Chet McCall remembered that his mother and deli-owner Benny Rotter became good friends and that they could always get meat for special occasions.

Some days all the gas stations were closed, and for weeks the only potatoes in the metropolitan area were for sale at two or three times the ceiling price at black markets operating from the back of trucks. Leon Sherman was offered men's clothes from a Baltimore wholesaler only if he would pay one dollar a piece under the table. He refused but was sure others did not.

Historian Cabell Phillips concluded:

Unquestionably, rationing was the most common social irritant to afflict the home front during the war, and it fostered a kind of low-caliber lawlessness even in the very best circles that was widely tolerated if not always condoned.[50]

It was a very hot and extremely dry summer that reminded many of the drought year of 1930. Early in the spring the WSSC warned that there would be a water shortage because they had been unable to secure the pipes and equipment to put a new pumping station into operation and the demand for water had greatly increased. The agency asked for voluntary restraint in lawn sprinkling and car washing.

It was the summer when Marine ace Joe Foss, credited with twenty-six kills, had his picture on the cover of *Life* and came home from the Guadalcanal campaign. It was the summer when everyone was reading Richard Tregaskis's *Guadalcanal Diary* and Wendell Willkie's *One World*, or at least saying they were. It was the summer when folks started putting postal zone numbers in addresses: Bethesda 14, Chevy Chase 15, Mass. Ave. 16. Some liquor dealers downtown tried to force people to buy a bottle of wine when they purchased a fifth of whiskey. Some drug stores attempted to tie sherbet and ice

cream together the same way. Kids sitting on the rose-covered bridges in Delaware yelled, "Pleasure driver!" at cars headed toward the shore.

Meanwhile in Chevy Chase at Miss Byrd Belt's home on Meadow Lane, the Chevy Chase Chapter of the Daughters of the American Revolution organized early in 1943. By the end of the year the chapter had twenty-one members and had donated more than a thousand books to the Merchant Marine libraries. Previously, most local DAR members belonged to either the Janet Montgomery Chapter, which boasted of Lily Stone as one of its best-known members and often met at the Columbia Dining Room, or to the Colonel Tench Tilghman Chapter, which included the Loughborough sisters and a number of cave dwellers among it members and generally met at members' homes.[51]

Workers at the David Taylor Model Basin, led by Rear Admiral Herbert S. Howard, set a local record by giving 205 pints of blood in two days. The Model Basin, which had started in 1940 with eight officers and 209 civilians, now had three times that number on round-the-clock shifts and was attempting to find billets for its first three WAVE officers. When mosquitoes became a problem, the administrators purchased 200 large goldfish and released them into the deep water tank to eat the larvae. The fish disappeared.

The TMB started turning out a monthly newsletter, "Basin Chatter," in `43. It regularly reported on the softball and bowling leagues, the marriages and babies, former employees now in the service and the steady growth of the facility. Various divisions held picnics at Glen Echo Park, and the Machine Shop team defeated the soldiers from Camp Carderock 9-1 in a softball season abbreviated by the gasoline shortage.[52]

Work continued on the Wind Tunnel Building, which included a small movie theater, and began on a large test pond, which held 3.5 million gallons of water and on a gun range where cannon up to 5" were fired to test blast effects. In the pentagon-shaped test pond, 125 feet on each side and 25 feet deep, the Navy studied the effects of blasts on plate steel. The Beebe bathyscape, on loan for the duration from the N. Y. Zoological Society, became an underwater photographic chamber. Using ultra high-speed cameras, the TMB

technicians were the first to get a picture of a shock wave on film. At the wind tunnels, the six-bladed props failed and were replaced with four-blade models. The basin's administrators liked the Lieb Construction Company's shed so much that they kept it after the wind tunnel work and used it for several purposes before it became the headquarters of the apprentice school.

Down at Cabin John Gardens, "that satellite of TMB" as the newsletter called it, residents elected Ken Wilcoxon chairman of the Citizens' Committee, which began staging various recreation activities, including movies on weekends, in the Community House at the foot of Webb Street. As the number of stars on the Basin's service banner passed a hundred, more women came aboard, and the MacArthur Boulevard Child Day Care Center moved to the Church of the Redeemer and became the Fairway Hills Child Care Center under the direction of Elizabeth Terwilliger. War workers' children between ages two to five were kept, fed and entertained from 7:15 am to 6:30 pm for a small weekly charge.

For Kenwood and Green Acres it was a somewhat quieter summer. Five years of almost constant opposition to Willie Smith's Sugar Bowl finally paid off. After listening to the complaints of neighbors and hearing the Briggs Clarifier supervisors tell stories of workers coming back from lunch full of beer, the liquor control board denied William E. Smith a renewal of his class D, on-sale license. Almost eighty residents had signed petitions, and more than a hundred showed up at the hearing.to say the Sugar Bowl "disrupted the peace, quiet and safety of the neighborhood."

This was the second time Willie Smith had lost his license under pressure from the encroaching all-white suburbs, but three years previously the State board had restored his right to sell beer. This time it stuck. Dr. Perry was dead.

With great pleasure, Cleveland Clipper smiled remembering the end of Willie Smith in Crow Hill and Milton in Bethesda. "When Dr. Perry was so big," he said, "they would give the police a whole lot of lip, but when Dr. Perry died, they didn't even allow them in the liquor store in Bethesda. That's the truth. They wouldn't let `em in the coffee spot by the railroad bridge to get nothing to eat." He laughed and clapped his hands.

For many Bethesda women, no matter what else it was, 1943 was the year of the USO. It began with a meeting in January at the County Building. A representative from the Naval Hospital explained the need for additional recreation for some 900 enlisted men, as well as the twenty officers, ninety nurses and a hundred WAVES on the base. The next Monday, fifty community representatives attended a meeting called by Albert Brault as director of Civil Defense.

Mrs. Sholar (center) signs up Mary Helen Davidson, Caroline Morell, Helen Papps, and Cynthia Donnelly as USO Junior Hostesses

He named George N. Mathews chairman of the War Recreation and Hospitality Committee for Bethesda, and the group agreed to make application to the national United Service Organization and to begin planning for a "drop-in" center.

Mathews, president of the Montgomery Players, veteran of the RAF in World War I, Cunard Line representative and a County resident for ten years, named to his committee Mrs. William N. Morell as vice-chair, Stella Werner, both Mrs. J. Reed Bradley of the *Journal* and William Prescott Allen of the *Tribune*, plus a pharmacist's mate and the welfare and recreation officer at NNMC. During the week of January 20, the committee applied for a USO center and filed a list of suitable Bethesda properties.

Mrs. Morell took over the project with Mrs. Werner heading the hospitality committee and acting as a clearing house for entertainment. Editors Bradley and Allen co-chaired publicity and fund raising of start-up money. From that point on the USO in Bethesda became an almost entirely female operation and, for many women, the most tiring, exciting and rewarding work of the war.

By mid-February, USO headquarters had approved the use of the old Sanitary store at 7808 Old Georgetown that had stood vacant for two years and appropriated $6,000 to convert it by, among other things, improving the bathrooms and installing a wooden floor. The site was considered excellent because of the nearby school playground and church halls, which could be used for various events and the generously low rent. Mrs. Daniel Walser donated a grand piano, and Mrs. Luke I. Wilson offered furniture for the lounge.

These were just the first of many who contributed goods, services and time.

The YWCA of Washington, D.C., which supervised several United Service Organization sites in the Capital, appointed Mrs. William J. Sholar director of the local center, and she and Mrs. Maurice Davidson began signing up hostesses in April. Within two weeks, 126 junior (ages 18 to 30) and 116 senior hostesses registered and then attended lectures at Bethesda Elementary on USO history and on wartime psychology. In May, fifty of the junior hostesses went to a charm school at the National Theater, which featured tennis star Alice Marble and *Harpers Bazaar* editor Carmel Snow.

Although there had been a cookout for two-dozen NNMC men and junior hostesses at the Rec Center on May 30, the first, real, local-USO social event took place at Woodmont Country Club on Friday evening, June 4. It was an informal dance for WAVES, corpsmen and junior hostesses with music by the Navy School of Music band. Shortly after that, Mrs. Sholar and her two new assistants, Mrs. Raymond Brooks and Leland teacher Mary Fisher, moved their office from the County Building to the unfinished center on Old Georgetown Road. From then on there were picnics almost every Sunday with tennis, softball and other games and on the last Friday of June, a dance in B-CC's gym.

On Saturday night, April 10, the Civil Defense Council held a reception and dance at Woodmont Country Club for area naval officers and their wives. It was the first of a planned series with expenses borne by twenty-four patron couples and fifty hostesses. In late May, the Kenwood Golf and Country

Club sponsored a reception and dance for officer WAVES and nurses. On the 4th of July, the USO sponsored a picnic for all servicemen and women in uniform from 4 until 9 pm at the Recreation Center. It was a tough Fourth for many pleasure drivers as OPA inspectors and Park Police took the tag numbers of more than 600 cars parked near swimming pools, carnivals and amusement centers.

The dry, plus-90° days that had started in June burned on, and the streetcars to Glen Echo and its Crystal Pool were more crowded than ever. Service men and women could swim there for 28¢ (.25 + .03 tax), and of course, the locals used the pool, too. Bill Lehr remembered when he and his friends from Cabin John went swimming.

The Cabin John boys had a reputation. There would be times in the summer when we'd go over to Glen Echo, the pool, and we'd go in at 7 o'clock, and I'd stay with Bubby Worsham or Joe Sullivan, with a group of their friends, and there might be a hundred people in the pool and in a half hour we were the only people in that pool— suddenly. They would harass these people until they left. I watched in awe, bumping people, dunking them. They were bad asses sometimes, tough kids.

County health officials closed the Chevy Chase Pool in July because of unsanitary conditions and lack of a competent operator. It stayed padlocked for almost three weeks and then reopened advertising "swimming water as pure as water can be—tested by State and County Health Depts."

The County's planned canning program grounded on a WPB snafu that delayed the fifty needed pressure cookers. When the canning centers finally opened in August, they proved very popular. Mrs. R. Vance Johnson supervised the Leland center; Mrs. Claude Norton ran the centers at Westbrook in the mornings and at Glen Echo-Cabin John in the afternoons, and Mrs. Gerald L. Wallace was in charge of the Chevy Chase canning project at the Woman's Club and the Rosemary School.

Except that they bought all the produce they canned, the Chevy Chase group was typical. Mrs. Wallace split up some seventy canners into groups of ten and instructed them in both purchasing and canning. They worked cooperatively, but bought their own jars and lids. The marketers got up early and made their buys at the farmers' markets on Florida

Avenue, and after six or eight hours of canning, the products were divided among the ten canners. By mid-August the Chevy Chase groups had canned 5,291 quarts of food and were not finished yet.

At Leland the hundred canners included two Russian women, one English refugee, and six men, who, Mrs. Johnson said, "brought their aprons along and settled down to work immediately." They processed more than 10,000 jars of food, about one-third of which came from Victory Gardens and, when school started again, worked out a system of circulating the pressure cookers to continue canning.[53]

The sultry, overcast evening of July 8 was one some Bethesdans remembered for a long time. Shortly after dark, while the children were still chasing lightning bugs, a single-engine airplane started circling over the town. The silvery BT-12 went away but then returned to fly low over the tree tops with its landing lights on and then rise and circle again. Some people thought the pilot was trying to land at the high school or the Rec Center; most concluded that he was lost. He was.

The plane was part of a group from the 86th Basic Flying Training Squadron based at Gunter Field in Alabama flying cross-country from Charlotte, N. C., on an "individual navigation training flight" to Bolling Field. The pilot, 2nd Lt. James G. Thames Jr. had logged over 200 hours in trainers but only seven and a half in BT-12s and had only ten hours of instrument flying experience.[54]

Thames flew north on his captain's wing, theoretically doing his own navigation, and followed the flight leader down through the overcast above Washington. Visibility was four miles, and the other trainers in the flight landed safely at Bolling.

According to the accident report: *Lt. Thames lost sight of Capt. Kirsch in the overcast, but continued descending until he broke out of the overcast at about 2000'. Lateral visibility was very poor and he was unable to orient himself."*

Ashby Chamberlin recalled hearing the plane low over his Kenwood house and wondering if the Japs had finally come. On Leland Street, Leroy Allison could see the plane's landing lights and thought the pilot was trying to land on the golf course at the Chevy Chase Club.

The BT-12

The plane continued to drone over Bethesda for more than a half-hour before the pilot and his headquarters-command passenger decided to jump and take their chances on their parachutes. According to the AAF accident report:

His fuel supply was very low, so he climbed to about 2500' and ordered Sgt. Ciorrocco to bail out. After the Sgt. jumped, Lt. Thames also jumped, using his parachute successfully.

The abandoned airplane spiraled down as scores of people looked up trying to see it against the grey overcast, many sure it was going to crash right on their home. From his front porch on Chevy Chase Drive, Ed Gauvreau heard the plane swoosh past just over the Recreation Center's trees. His neighbor Charles Carr ran out in the back yard and looked up. "It scared the hell out of us," he said. They both heard the sounds of the plane breaking up and then silence.

The two-ton BT-12 with its forty-foot wingspan had fluttered past the new apartments on Hillandale, zoomed down toward the big, old bungalows and Stock's nursery on Bradley and then turned, struck a tree, began to fold up and smashed into the bank of Willett Creek on the edge of the Victory Gardens between Kenwood and the Rec Center. There was no fire although the craft was not out of fuel.

Gauvreau saw the pilot hanging from his parachute and silently coming down toward the old, red brick, USDA building where the draft board now operated. The chute caught in a tree just past the Recreation Center, and Lt. Thames landed safely in the front lawn of 4605 Davidson Drive. His passenger, Sgt. Dominic Ciorrocco, who had jumped first, floated down across the District Line until his parachute became entangled in a tree in front

of 4209 Warren Street, NW, near Tenley Circle. D.C. firemen were able to get the chute out of the tree and return it to him. Neither man was injured.

Meanwhile, Bethesda police and firemen aided by air raid wardens and curious neighbors searched for the wreck in the black night. It took them about fifteen minutes to discover the plane with its wings crumpled and its engine driven six feet into the plowed earth near the creek that paralleled Glenwood Road. The airplane had caused very little damage to the Victory Gardens, but the lights and noise attracted a crowd that trampled dozens of carefully tended plots and ruined many tomato vines, stalks of sweet corn and bean bushes. Ashby Chamberlin's folks would not let him out to look at the crash, but some of his friends in Kenwood came away with shiny pieces of the plane.[55]

The USO signed up more junior hostesses and continued with its dances at Woodmont and weekend picnics in the park while the summer heat seared lawns and Victory Gardens. Using hoses to water gardens, as well as lawns, was soon forbidden. Gardeners hauled buckets of water to their plots in newspaper wagons, baby carriages and car trunks, sure that what they were doing could not be called "pleasure" driving. By August the weather bureau had recorded more than forty days of 90° or above and only one good rain since summer began.

Ed Stock told his readers how to get seeds to germinate in hot, dry weather by planting deeper and mulching and then told them how to prepare their gardens for the rains he was sure were coming. He wrote several columns on the importance of mulching. It was the end of August before the drought broke and then only after Stock and Judge Brault had asked all the local ministers to pray for rain. It was too late for about 1,200 County gardens.

Despite the drought the first garden prizes began to be awarded in August. John Werner was one of the first winners; he received a $25 War Bond for the best garden among those of his twenty-two fellow Federal Works Administration employees. When the Chevy Chase Garden Club had its Victory Garden show at the Hayes Mansion, their hostess, Mrs. G. Thomas Dunlop, won the prize for the best collection of vegetables; she had eighteen varieties. Fire departments and Civil Defense au-

Albert Brault and Ed Stock with Chevy Chase firemen

or how much it would cost them on payday. When the withholding tax law went into effect in July, Bethesda had its first two strikes. The women who worked at the Blue Ribbon Laundry on Hampden Lane stopped work when their pay-checks showed twenty percent of their earnings missing. They thought owner Samuel F. Boorstein was trying to put something over on them and refused to work until a Department of Labor conciliator and a representative of the War Manpower Commission convinced them they were not being cheated. The laundry workers claimed they had never heard of a pay-as-you-go tax plan. The Montgomery County Refuse Company also had a strike. Following a Saturday payday, twenty drivers showed up on Monday but refused to work until the tax withheld was given back. Blake Merson convinced ten of them to go back to work and fired the others.

Other than Walker's apartments on Hillandale, one of the biggest wartime construction projects right in Bethesda proceeded on such a secret basis that the builder never learned what his building was used for. In the spring of 1943, General Donovan of the fast growing OSS contacted Abe Morrison, and as Mr. Morrison remembered:

He said he wanted quarters, but he didn't tell me what for. I said, "Sure we can give you anything you want." So we built that little building; it really wasn't so little. It was 20,000 square feet right where the railroad curves at Bethesda Avenue and on back. He was in a big hurry, and I think we put that thing up in about six weeks. We built the damn thing so it was tucked back there where nobody could get to it. It had a little front on Bethesda Avenue. Nobody ever told me what they used it for, but they paid their bills on time, monthly.

In July 1943, OSS consolidated its communications warehouse operations into the new Bethesda facility. During the high point of this project, the new warehouse contained more than 5,000 separate items. All of the equipment received from manufacturers was inspected at the new warehouse before being packed in Bethesda and shipped all over the world on the orders of the various theater commanders.[56]

thorities helped in late summer, providing artificial rain for gardens near streams where they could sink their hoses, but soon most of the creeks ran dry. The national OCD gave Judge Brault a citation for the idea and praised the program on its *Not For Glory* radio series.

Warren Gingell, whose family once owned much of central Bethesda, was one of the year's best individual Victory Gardeners. He "farmed" a 50-by-75-foot garden beside his home and plumbing business in Woodmont and raised lettuce, onions, beets, beans, squash, lima beans, cucumbers, cabbage, greens, swiss chard, corn, potatoes and cantaloupe. His Kentucky Wonder beans were taller than he was, and his tomato plants were almost that big. By the middle of July the Gingells had canned fifty quarts of beans, twenty-five quarts of beets, a good supply of kale and had put down a bushel of onions for the winter. Of course, they were able to get water to their garden easily while many other Victory Gardeners had to haul it to the community lots. Murray Miles recalled his grandmother trucking water to their Kenwood garden in trashcans in the trunk of their car. Their garden was odd shaped and up in one corner, but the program organizers, he remembered, had nice, rectangular gardens down in the front.

Most people were anxious to get their first envelope or paycheck with the "pay-as-you-go" tax withheld. Newspapers had been running articles for weeks about it, but many employees still were not sure how it would work

Late that summer, all holders of B and C gas-ration-books had to apply for new books with a different style of stamp. The black market had become a serious problem by then, and gasoline stamps could be purchased in several Bethesda-area locations including the Recreation Centers and bowling alleys. The Ration Board called for volunteers to help issue 12,000 new books with the same number of stamps in them as people turned in. That was also the summer when rumors of soap being rationed cleaned off grocers' shelves and forced them to restrict buyers to one box of soap powder or cake of soap at a time. For a few weeks, the County limited whisky sales to Tuesday, Thursday, and Saturday because of shortages. Returning beer and soft drink deposit bottles and getting copper pennies into circulation also were considered "patriotic." It was the one and only year of the zinc-clad, "steel" penny.

The Rev. Henry Teller Cocke, because of ill health, retired from All Saints Episcopal Church at Chevy Chase Circle after almost twenty years of service. His replacement was Rev. Dr. Charles W. Lowrey, a professor at Virginia Theological Seminary. After serving for eight years as principal of Leland Junior High School, Helen Bready resigned to join her captain-husband in Cumberland. Esthelene Morgan, principal of Montgomery Hills JHS, took her place as head of the 1,150 student school and its fast-changing staff. On August 6, with Marquis Childs making the baccalaureate address, forty students graduated from summer school at B-CC. Half the class was from the Bethesda area and three-fourths of the graduates expected to enter the service almost immediately.

During that summer, Ray Parks of Covington Motors offered "top dollar" for 1939 to 1942 cars and advertised that he was willing to come to your home to make the deal. Since they were among the few, large air-conditioned spaces in town, both the Hiser and the Bethesda theaters had very profitable summers, changing features every two or three days and showing lots of double bills. Like radio, movies were a regular part of the life of most families. Among the most popular films that summer were *Bambi*, *Frankenstein Meets the Wolf Man*, *My Friend Flicka*, *Dive Bomber*, *Strawberry Blonde*, and *Stage Door Canteen*, a "tear-jerker" which the Bethesda showed for five days at "no increase in admissions."

The USO held six dances at Woodmont Country Club that summer, several picnics at the Rec Center and one as guests of the Sycamore Island Club, and some of the junior hostess helped show servicemen around the Smithsonian museums on weekends. Many servicemen were home with sharply presed unifroms and new stripes or officers' bars. Ensign Adlai S. Magee Jr. was among those who came home on leave that summer. Although he was barely twenty, he had been chosen as a pilot instructor at Pensacola.

The summer ended with a circus and a family picnic at the Recreation Center and with a parade of the Jeep House kids down Wisconsin Avenue. More than 250 children rode or marched from the bank to the Rec Center for a picnic. Behind the police escort came forty boys of the bike corps and thirty boys of the wood-working class. Then in their blue seersucker pinafores marched the Red Cross girls including the sixty-five surgical-dressing makers. They wore white veils. As their last activity, the Jeep House participants, there had been more than 300, made toys, dolls and scrap books for the children's ward at Suburban Hospital.

Fall brought not only a break in the weather following a heavy rain in early September, but a return to the routines of work, school, club meetings and bowl-ing leagues. With Ration Book 3 completely distributed, the first brown stamps for meats and oils went into use, and housewives had to manage three separate books for each member of their family. Both the Lions and the American Legion staged carnivals in September, one right after the other, on the east side of Wisconsin in the 7800 block. The Commissioners announced that the County would charge for fall plowing of Victory Gardens, plowing and harrowing a 30-by-50 plot in groups of ten or more, $1.50, in groups of less that ten, $3.00.

The Washington Senators, in unaccus-

Book I for sugar

Book II for processed foods (blue stamps)

Book III (after Sept. 12) for meats, fats and oils, and other foods previously rationed by red stamps in Book II.

tomed second place, ten games behind the Yankees, acquired Louis "Buck" Newsome for the third time. Bobo Newsome added color to the end of a strange season. Many Bethesdans enjoyed the huge show of military equipment on the Monument grounds, part of the "Back the Attack" War Bond drive. Even though the ban on pleasure driving ended, most folks took a bus or streetcar downtown to climb over the guns and tanks and gawk at the captured German and Japanese aircraft.

The air-raid drill early on the morning of September 6 resulted in a court appearance for Allen Simonds of Ridgewood Avenue who had barely arrived home from his night club job when the sirens sounded. He told the wardens, "To hell with the lights! I'm not going to turn them off." His was the only violation for which a warrant was issued.

Ed Stock talked T. Ritchie Edmonston into becoming chairman of the big Harvest Show planned for the high school gym in early October and convinced Tom Pyle that B-CC should choose the Harvest Queen. The Montgomery Players decided to open their fifteenth season with Bernard Shaw's *Pygmalion*. The director, William Jarvis, cast himself as Higgins, Angela MacDougal as Eliza and Jane Plummer Rice as Mrs. Higgins. And Briggs Clarifier at River Road and the railroad, Bethesda's biggest defense contractor, won the Army-Navy "E" award and was the first County enterprise to fly the flag symbolizing productive excellence.

The Methodist Church in Cabin John organized a Sunday school and began planning to build more rooms while Mrs. Ruth Strother and Rev. Elgar Soper selected the teachers. Reverend Heavener had secured some pew ends from an old Baltimore church the previous year. He and Judge Benson with the help of W. D. Hannon and some other parishioners built sixteen pews. Then they learned of a church being torn down in Southern Maryland, and lumber from that church plus numerous donations including $65 from each committee member, a pledge of $1,000 from the Ladies Aid Society, now the Woman's Society of Christian Service, and a loan of $750 from the Methodist Union allowed them to build a fifteen-foot ell on the sanctuary for Sunday school classes. At the Chapel of the Redeemer in Fairway Hills, Rev. Robert Evans Browning dedicated two stained glass windows donated by members of the parish.

The public schools opened still looking for a few teachers and with additions at Bradley and Westbrook Elementaries under construction. At Chevy Chase Elementary, Ocie Dodd organized a school store, which older students operated, and the PTA supervised after-school play programs for 4th, 5th, and 6th graders. New director Richard Schaefer recruited students as the primary salvage gatherers and asked them to collect all the newspapers, magazines and tin cans possible as he began developing a system of rewards.

Principal Pyle said he expected greater emphasis on technical subjects and physical education for both boys and girls, and soon after school opened, Mr. Bender's shop classes started building a sprawling "commando" obstacle course, which included ditches, fences, a tunnel and overhead ladders. The high school took in eighty students from crowded Leland, divided them into two sections and housed them in unfinished rooms behind the public library. Math and science teacher Rosa Moss and English-social studies teacher Winifred Sherwood came with them.

The Victory Corps added a Fire Fighter group and twenty-two boys, with Chief Bargagni's help, learned to climb ladders and fight fires. Eleven B-CC students worked out a program to graduate in February, a first, and the seniors elected a girl, Mary Dow, president, another first.

With a lot of help, Bob Roth revived the *Tattler* in mimeographed form. Volume 1, No. 1 of the "Duration" *Tattler*, produced by the Victory Corps journalism class, appeared on December 20, 1943, featuring stories about the varsity basketball team, current fashions and the almost-completed obstacle course. The

On the obstacle course at the high school

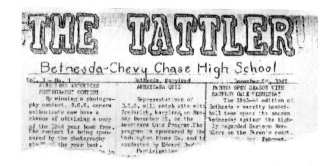

school paper reported that cafeteria manager Gertrude Bouvet had "nearly 600 quarts of home-processed foods representing long hours of labor on the half acre of school land plowed last spring for a Victory Garden."[57]

Isabel Gaither edited one of the most imaginative *Pine Tree*'s ever, complete with a spoof of *Life* magazine. Her *Tattler* profile said that "Izzie has many nicknames, some of which are "Isa" Dizzie, Bizzie and Toddy" and that in her childhood she climbed more trees "and beat up more boys than Maud Eberhart." She remembered:[58]

In the 1944 *Pine Tree*

Miss Williams, the sponsor, I had her for English in 10th grade, and we enjoyed a mutual wit. I just felt that the other yearbooks if not boring were constantly the same. I have no idea why I did it. I hadn't worked for the school newspaper, but I had helped a teacher where my mother worked put together a book for the Glen Echo-Cabin John kids.

I gave a marvelous speech, a very good speech on how the yearbook must be changed, it must be something we would be proud of. And I got the job. I delegated responsibility, and we all worked very hard. I didn't like the favorite teacher idea. The dedication is to our town, to "Main Street." In writing the dedication, I wrote it to walking on the streets of our town, and Miss Williams changed it to get away from street walking. I'm sure I didn't know what that meant.

I saw the Life idea in a college yearbook, so I wrote to Life to ask for permission, and they said

they would like to see the page beforehand. But by the time the page was available there was no way we were going to change it so we just ignored their request. It cost; in fact, Shirley Rowe who did the next yearbook was angry with me because we passed on a debt. 'We had to pay for that color in your yearbook,' she said.

It was exciting because it was so different. It was my idea that the advertisers should not be put out in left field. We set up a very elaborate sales campaign and included pictures of the 9th graders for the first time to get more sales.

The *Tattler*, mimeographed for the rest of the war, still managed to publish some cartoons and cover the high school social scene. It also ran a regular "servicemen's corner" with news of alumni in uniform. It was the school year of "little moron" jokes, intramural sports, "L.S./M.F.T.," more arguments about sororities and fraternities and the constant refrain of "Pistol Packin' Mama." The high school's first bond drive started with the dedication of a "duck," an amphibious truck bought with the $7,000 raised the previous April. Then with a goal of buying five jeeps, the Activity Council collected $5,853 in two weeks. Bethesda's other high school, Landon, kept its staff together but, with Paul Banfield in the service, had a new headmaster, Albert E. Rogers.[59]

Leland Junior High School not only had a new principal and assistant principal but a new look. Fluorescent lighting had been added to every classroom, and the cafeteria had new stoves, refrigerators and a $750 dishwasher. The County enlarged the playground and installed drainage tile and a hard sub-surface to make the area more usable in bad weather. A PTA-faculty reception welcomed Principal Esthelene Morgan and her new assistant, Elwood Mason, the former principal of Ocean City's high school. Mrs. Morgan set up fourteen student committees to advise her and to carry out tasks such as assisting in the library, room cleaning and planning social and war activities. That fall there were assemblies almost every Wednesday with a variety of programs and speakers.

One of the seventh graders, Jane Bradley, daughter of the *Journal* editor, recalled:

Leland was really different. We had a homeroom for the first time, moved around, ev-

Jane Bradley

erybody got lost and scared to death, and gym. You had to take showers.

I remember walking up from Leland to the dime store and buying a ten-cent tube of Tangee lipstick that was orange, and my mother said, "What have you done to your face?" After that I was smart enough to keep it in my pocketbook and put it on in school.

I rode the school bus for a while but that became very bourgeois. The neat kids rode the big bus. That's where I met Vink. There were twenty or thirty kids in our circle, the "elite." We grew up too fast. I think it was the war. We were a lot more sophisticated than kids twenty years later. We were pretty much on our own.

Draft Board No. 3, along with all the other draft boards, closed down for a two week inventory and report in early September, but all indications were that fathers would be drafted soon, probably by Thanksgiving. Frederic Lee, chairman of the local board said it clearly:

If we have to fill a quota in October, we will not be able to complete it without calling fathers. We do not have any other men available except an occasional man whose occupational deferment expires and an occasional young man becoming 18 years old.

The Selective Service Board called the first ten "pre-Pearl Harbor" fathers in November.[60]

Up on Old Georgetown Road, Virginia Sholar and her secretary, Mary Brooks, struggled all summer to get the USO center finished while the hostesses enjoyed picnics and dances. Wartime shortages and the slow process of having priorities approved delayed the work planned by architect Maurice May and local builder Henry Connor.

President Sundlun and the board of directors of the Woodmont Country Club gave their facilities to the USO for five dances during the summer and even contributed food and refreshments at one of them. Picnics took place not only at the Rec Center but at Mrs. Luke I. Wilson's estate, at the Kensington Cabin, and at Fort Kemble Park. The junior

hostesses had several get-togethers at Bethesda Elementary, and service wives enjoyed a picnic at Weathered Oak Farm. The senior hostesses and the Red Cross Canteen Corps provided food and transportation for all these activities.

When materials finally arrived in early September, the contractor and his associates quickly installed two bathrooms, a new heating plant, a kitchen and a bar and built a checkroom and office in the old grocery store. They patched and cleaned the terrazzo floor, built a small wooden stage, put two coats of paint on the interior and produced a usable space of 612 square feet with a thirteen foot ceiling.

The sub-contractors included plumber Seymour H. Wentz, electrician W. K. Trunnell, and painter B. H. Mohler. Eisinger's supplied the mill work and Arthur Farber, the signs. John Werner made the window valances, and Carroll Murnane built the bookcases and window seat. Mrs. R. G. Carlsen and Mrs. Irwin Snyder led the group that made the curtains, pillows and chair covers to add color to the green, brick, and yellow color scheme. The women's auxiliary of the American Institute of Mining Engineers contributed a free lending library of 800 volumes, and the Woman's Club of Chevy Chase donated a record player. The American Legion gave a radio and subscriptions to eight magazines, and Adlai Magee contributed an old-fashioned organ from the VFW. Corpsmen and WAVES from the Naval Hospital helped junior hostesses uncrate furniture and get the place ready.

Finally on the evening of Saturday, September 25, with the regional USO brass and Admiral Bunker of the NNMC in the receiving line, the Bethesda USO formally opened and then held an open house for the public the next afternoon. Hundreds attended. Thanks and congratulations went to Virginia Sholar and Mrs. Morell, who started it all; to Mrs. Maurice Davidson, who headed the senior hostesses, to Mrs. John Alsever, in charge of 150 junior hostesses and to Stella Werner, the recreation chairman of the OCD who greeted guests at the door during the grand opening and then took over as room-registry chairman.

Once the hoopla was over, Bethesda's USO club operated every day from 10 am to 11 pm and featured dancing on Monday, Thursday, and Saturday and table tennis,

bridge and other games every day. Two or three senior hostesses were always there, and junior hostesses worked 5 to 7 or 7 to 11 shifts. By October the USO was staging supper parties for groups of convalescing patients brought to the center by bus.[61]

A couple of early signs of politics appeared during the fall of 1943 as five supplemental registration boards, including one at the Bethesda County Building, started signing up new voters and receiving the "declarations of intention" from would-be Maryland citizens. Newly arrived residents who wanted to vote in `44 had to declare their intention to do so before November 1943 under the law then in effect.

The Republicans led by Arthur Hilland established their headquarters at 7649 Old Georgetown Road and instituted a membership drive. Their chairman concluded that while we fought one-party governments around the world, it was "high time that we restore the two-party system throughout America. It is our job to do it in Montgomery County." The League of Women Voters, which had tried to get the "intention" law repealed by the General Assembly, joined in urging new residents to register as did Allen Gardner, who reminded potential voters that the Charter would be on the next ballot. It would, he said, be "a practical test of democracy, which like charity, begins at home."[62]

Phil Austensen of the Washington *Post* sounded the second political note in an article that quoted Democrat Organization leaders as saying they planned to "lay off" the proposed Charter and concentrate on the national and State races. The reporter quoted a "leader" as saying it would not cost the Party much in patronage if the Charter won and concluding:

> *We would be better off if Charter is passed and takes over the headaches we have been assuming. We feel we have given the people of this county one of the best governments in the country. If they wish to try something else, that is their business.*

Robert V. Bray followed with a column quoting Austensen at length and pointing out that this did not mean that the Democratic leadership endorsed the Charter but only that they had "more important things to worry about at present." In retrospect the Austensen story seemed a journalistic Trojan Horse cobbled up by Brooke Lee and friends.[63]

At the end of September, for the first time, the Bethesda-Chevy Chase Jewish Community Group held what the local newspapers called "Hebrew" religious services. The temporary officers of the newly formed organization were Dr. Murray J. Shear, David G. Berger, Mrs. Raymond Fields, and Abe Bloomberg, "a salesman in the 'rag trade,' from the factories," according to Leon Sherman. They made arrangements with the secretary of the Masonic Hall and Library Association to use the lower hall for New Year's and Day of Atonement services. The committee in charge of the religious observances included Mr. Berger, Louis Epstein, owner of Lane's, the children's store in the shopping center, Leon Sherman's father, Samuel Joseph Sherman, and Joel D. Wolfsohn who lived in Chevy Chase.

The committee informed men and women of the armed forces, especially those at the Naval Hospital, of their plans and invited them to participate, and Washington synagogues cooperated by lending sacred scrolls and prayer books. The first evening service celebrating Rosh Hashanah began at 8:30 pm on Wednesday, September 29. The Yom Kippur ceremonies started with the Kol Nidre service on Friday, October 8. As part of the Day of Atonement, the members donated $300 to Suburban Hospital as their initial civic gift.

While the High Holy Days were being observed, another committee began planning for a Sunday school. This group included Dr. Achinstein, Mr. Epstein, Mrs. Millstein, Mrs. Schiff, Mrs. Weinberg, and Mrs. Zinder. In a November meeting at the Woodmont Country Club, they launched their adult education program with a talk by Zionist leader Simon Shetzer. The Jewish Community Group elected Mr. Wolfsohn as its first president, Mr. Berger vice-president, Mr. Bloomberg treasurer, and Mrs. Fields and Irving Posner secretaries. They also expressed their gratitude to Dr. Shear of Children's Hospital and the Public Health Service who was instrumental in getting the organization started.

The most spectacular local fire of 1943 broke out at noon in the Hot Shoppe at Wisconsin and Western. The lunchtime crowd fled the smoky building carrying their sandwiches and iced tea with them and stood across the street and watched the excitement while they finished their meals. The manager

Smoky fire at the Wisconsin and Western Hot Shoppe

had detected smoke in the basement and emptied three fire extinguishers on a smouldering wall panel before sounding the alarm. Fire companies from Bethesda, Chevy Chase, Rockville and the District responded, and firemen donned masks to fight the blaze through dense smoke.

Young Jim McAuliffe from Friendship Heights recalled, "I stood there on the corner watching the flames come up through the roof. It was one of the first big fires I ever saw, sort of a frightening experience." Mary Ellen Taft agreed. Her mother and a neighbor had driven their children over to see the excitement. "I remember crouching down in the back seat and peeking out between my fingers and watching the sheets of flames. It's a very vivid memory." She was four. The fire destroyed the building, causing, J. W. Marriott estimated, $80,000 in damages, and because of the short-term lease, the restaurant was not rebuilt. The charred, boarded-up hulk decorated the corner at the District Line for the next half-dozen years.

What had started out being called the "Victory Shop," planned for the sale or exchange of used clothing, furniture, household goods and toys by women of the defense, health and welfare agencies, became the Thrift Shop. The indefatigable Edith Whalen headed the project, postponed by the spring gasoline shortage. After some restructuring, Mrs. Donald Roberts, in charge of publicity, explained that agencies would share profits in proportion to donations by their members. Suburban Hospital, Montgomery County General Hospital, the Public Health Lay Committee, and the Mater-

nal Welfare Association agreed to participate, and the Womens Activities Committee of the OCD paid the rent and expenses from funds earned from salvage.

The ladies found a small store at 4713 Hampden Lane, and W. J. Gates and his workmen built the furnishings at nominal cost. On September 27, Mrs. Robert Huse, chairman of volunteers, began accepting donations of clothes, toys, furniture and brick-a-brack, which volunteers sorted and priced.[64]

The Thrift Shop opened on Monday, October 4, with Mrs. George Neuhaus as manager (she took her pay in War Bonds) and Mrs. J. Hamilton Vance as treasurer. Mrs. Clifford Rodlun, who helped get the interior organized, became the receiving chair, and Mrs. C. M. Louitt was first leader of the pricing committee. The shop displayed more than a thousand items including a large supply of outgrown fall and winter clothing, children's shoes and mounds of second-hand galoshes. It also had everything from "bunny jackets" to amethyst vases and Halloween costumes, and soon enjoyed a crowd of customers between 10 am and 4 pm. After the first month, Mrs. Neuhaus had some remodeling done to get ready for a brisk Christmas season.[65]

At Suburban Hospital, Mrs. Edward M. Willis, chairman of the Patients' Library Committee of the Women's Auxiliary, began accepting gifts of books. The library set up in the Assembly Room, and the Woman's Club of Bethesda donated a cart so volunteers could make daily rounds of the wards. B-CC principal Tom Pyle designed the cornices for the reception room and other public areas and a Dutch cupboard for the dining room. Albert Bender and his woodworking class made these items from materials donated by Walter Eisinger.

Al "Buck" Bender

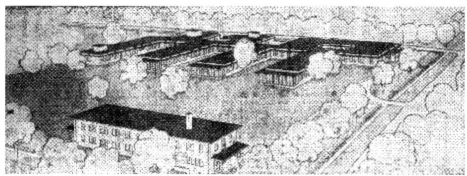

Architect's drawing of Suburban Hospital buildings with nurses' quarters in the foreground

Almost every business in Bethesda contributed to the decorating committee. In late October, Randolph Bishop announced that the hospital would be open, for medical and obstetrical cases at least, on December 1, and in November, Superintendent Lutes and Director of Nurses Dorothy Glynn said that the nursing staff was ready and that they were seeking nurse's aides.

With Suburban Hospital's basic construction nearing completion, Superintendent Lutes began naming his staff and planning for the month of clean up and testing. His secretary, Phyllis A. Goodall, who had been at work for months, was from Chicago and the author of several books on nursing, but many of the other original staff were local people. Bookkeeper Virginia Sinnot, lab technician Mrs. H. B. Sommer, seamstress Mary Goodlin, and engineer Benjamin G. Potter were all from Bethesda.[66]

Mrs. Frederic P. Lee planned the open house celebration as gifts continued to pour in. The Lions Club donated its $1,200 carnival profit to the hospital for physiotherapy equipment. The Macedonia Baptist Church led by Rev. William Mason contributed $300 for a room in the "colored wing" of the hospital. Reverend Mason said it was a privilege for his people to be part of the community but that "supporting the hospital for this community cannot be a healthful one unless the health needs of the colored people are cared for, too." The Wheatley's daughters donated a room in memory of their parents, and Ralph Morrison donated one in memory of his mother. James Tibbitts of Somerset gave the hospital six boxwoods for its front walk.[67]

After twenty-one years of service, Miss Mary N. Talmadge retired as head of the Baptist Home for Children. Edwin Bowen presented her with a bouquet on behalf of the children; she had been "mother" to 177 of

them. By then the Home's service banner had twenty-six blue stars and one gold star.

William K. Hodges replaced Raymond B. Leavitt as manager of the Bethesda C&P office after he accepted a naval commission. Carolyn Hagner Shaw took over her late mother's editorship of the Washington Social List, a daunting task fraught with dangers because of the multitude of military and foreign titles in town. Subscribers could call Callie Shaw with questions on protocol or the social niceties. The Shaws, he was with Gates Contracting, lived on Battery Lane.

The Red Cross informed the family of Lt. Dorsey Adams (B-CC `40), an 8th Air Force bombardier who had been reported "missing," that he was a prisoner of war. His parents lived on West Virginia Avenue and his wife, Kathleen Molohon (B-CC `40), was at the University of Utah. Sgt. Margaret Hartnett, after nine months in North Africa, entered WAC OCS at Fort Oglethorpe and emerged a second lieutenant by Christmas.

At the end of the Victory Garden season, Gertrude Bradley praised Mrs. Donaldson and Ed Stock, whose doubts about the usefulness of his newspaper column were put to rest by many letters of thanks and baskets of vegetables. Mrs. Donaldson said she thought that gardening brought out the best in people. "People who work in the soil are naturally nice folks," she insisted. "They have gone all out for charm as well as for Victory."

The grand culmination was a huge Harvest Show in the Bethesda Chevy Chase High School gym on Sunday, Oct. 3. Every gardener in the area was urged to enter at least one exhibit, and many did. Bethesda businesses donated dozens of prizes. All eight garden clubs participated, and there was even a separate rose judging with its own prizes. The Chevy Chase Garden Club took care of artistic arrangements, and the Bethesda Garden Club sponsored an exhibit of specimen flowers. The school band, the A Cappella Choir, and W. H. Hochbaum, the national Victory Garden chairman, took part.

Marine Pvt. T. H. Cunningham, wounded and decorated on Guadalcanal, and Commissioner William Prescott awarded the prizes. The fifty boys in the Victory Garden Corps received a J. Edgar Hoover letter of praise, and the OCD showed off its commendation and equipment. Jane Bradley, 11, the *Journal* editor's daughter, displayed what forty cents worth of seed and fertilizer could produce with her fourteen-dozen gourds.

That's where I learn to garden. And I'm still at it We grew beans, pole beans, tomatoes, and we canned beans and tomatoes. We grew peas, onions, maybe a little corn. My job was hoeing, and we all had to haul water in big buckets in a wheelbarrow.

I'd pick my gourds and shellac `em, and my mother would take them up to the office and sell them for a dollar a dozen and bring me this money. I thought it was the greatest thing that ever happened.

We always took things to the Harvest Shows, but I don't think we ever won a prize. The Victory Gardens were wonderful because the community was all there in the evening. There was a nice camaraderie, and it was a great outlet for getting rid of a lot of stress.

The sweepstakes winners included the Richard Akers of Hampden Lane who won blue ribbons for their red tomatoes, corn, sweet potatoes and eggplant and red ribbons for their white potatoes and yellow tomatoes. Mrs. R. L. Jarnigan and Mrs. Harry W. Farmer, both of Chevy Chase, won most of the canning prizes, and Mrs. William Cross of Chevy Chase tied Mrs. Arthur Hilland of Bethesda for the flower arranging prize.

The $100 bond first prize for Victory Gardens went to Dr. C. M. Lefevre, which was a little embarrassing since he headed the judging committee and had already won the $25 Evening Star prize for the best garden in the Western Suburban area. A plant pathologist at Beltsville, Dr. Lefevre had sixteen crops producing in his two plots near Bradley Elementary despite the drought. Second prize, a $50 bond, went to the joint Jarnigan-Farmer garden, and Mrs. Lillian M. Essex of Summit Street in Chevy Chase won the $25 bond third prize. Special prizes for community gardens went to Dr. Fred Coe for the group at York Lane and Marion Street, Dr. LeFevre for the Sonoma group, and to the show's chairman, T.

Ritchie Edmonston, for the gardens on the Dunlop property at Beach Drive.[68]

Young Paul Magee was sitting on the curb in front of his uncle's house on Leland Street when the grey car with the white star on its door drove up and stopped. He watched two men, Navy officers, get out and walk up to the front door. A week later there was a requiem Mass at Our Lady of Lourdes, and then the Adlai Magees buried their oldest son, Ensign Adlai Magee Jr., at Arlington Cemetery. He died in a plane crash at Pensacola. A picture of a skinny boy wearing dress whites and a big smile was on the front page of the *Tribune*.

In 1943 the deaths of Bethesda boys all came as shocks. In `44 they seldom made the front page.

Registration for Ration Book Number 4 took place at the public schools on Thursday and Friday, October 21 and 22, with teachers again manning the tables. School children carried home the registration forms, and applicants had to bring in Book 3 to receive Book 4. In Montgomery County 34,453 families signed up for 103,122 ration books and about one-third of those were in the Bethesda area.

Registration by schools:

households	books issued
	Alta Vista ES
421	1,219
	Bethesda ES
2,164	6,208
	B-CC HS
1,278	3,333
	Bradley ES
515	1,736
	Chevy Chase/Leland
2,967	8,181
	Glen Echo-Cabin John
1,211	3,710
	Lynnbrook ES
726	2,477
	River Road Colored
84	228
	Somerset ES
1,161	3,257
	Westbrook ES
1,217	3,588
total	
11,744	33,937

That fall two more rezoning requests stirred up loud protests and organized resistance. The first was for the establishment of a "used car and junk lot" at the corner of

Chestnut Street and Wisconsin Avenue. The East Bethesda Citizens' Association quickly fired off letters of protest to Park and Planning and to the Commissioners. They reminded the Commissioners that when the north end of Wisconsin was rezoned commercial, they were promised that nothing but "the finest type of commercial buildings would be erected." The lot owners abandoned their plans before that request was disapproved.

The second was for the construction of apartment houses on the 132-acre Bergdoll tract between Friendship Heights and Somerset. The trustees of the estate made the request in the name of Gerta Bergdoll, the famous draft-dodger's wife, whose name had been on the title since 1938. Before opponents could even swing into full cry, that request was postponed for consideration in 1944 after engineers drew a street plan.

On Tuesday morning November 23, the air raid sirens began screaming at 11:30 am and went on for a long time; it sounded like the "blue" signal, which meant an attack was imminent. The only two people in Bethesda who were sure it was not a drill were Judge Brault and Jimmy Nichols who were working at the County Building. They hurried out to see what was going on as the police switchboard lit up. Parents began calling the schools as that frisson of fear felt two days after Pearl Harbor tingled again. A telephone lineman had shorted the circuits, figured out what he had done and stopped it, but then caused another short and the sirens wailed again. By lunchtime everyone had calmed down, a bit embarrassed by the confused response.

There had been talk of Nazi secret weapons, but the war seemed to be going well on all fronts. The Russians had recaptured Kiev. The Italian government had surrendered although Mussolini escaped and the Germans fought on in Northern Italy. Admiral Chester Nimitz's forces began island hopping toward Japan by capturing Tarawa and Makin in the Gilbert Islands. It was over Tarawa in November that the humpbacked, thick-winged F6F-3 Hellcats proved to be the Zero killers Grumman and the Navy hoped they would be. In two days Navy pilots shot down thirty "Zekes," had ten more "probables," and lost only one of their own. All through that fall and winter the NNMC's grey Pontiac and Packard ambulances regularly went to the railroad station in Silver Spring to pick up wounded men returning from the Pacific.[69]

By then the USO had become part of Bethesda's everyday life. "I was there one day a week," said Virginia Simmons, wife of the Dodge dealer, who seemed to feel that what she did was the norm.

I went up there like all the other women. And we had snacks and things for them and a radio. We listened to their stories. It was nothing fancy, just like a big store. We wore a little nametag. It was interesting. During that war everybody jumped in and helped the other person. Most of them were from the Naval Hospital, but they came from all over the country. And once in a while the families of the sailors in the hospital would come, and, of course, there was no place for them to stay, so we had an extra bedroom, and I'd take them home and keep them overnight."

As assistant superintendent of public safety for Chevy Chase Village, Bill Austin received a request from ten-year-old Bobby Greene of Grafton Street to keep a "nanny goat." Bobby assured the village manager that the goat "would eat weeds and poison ivy and furnish fertilizer for our Victory garden" and that she "would not be as noisy as barking dogs in our neighborhood and far safer than these mad dogs." Austin had to turn Bobby down because of Village regulations.

He wrote Bobby:

As a boy I also owned a goat and know the disappointment of having to give up my goat due to rules and regulations, which at that time I did not understand; however as you grow older you will find that the game should always be played by the rules, whether it be life or sports, and the closer we stay to the rules the more we enjoy the game, and our part in it.

As organizations began winding up the year's activities, Ed Stock recommended a bigger and better, County-sponsored Victory Garden program with three paid administrators and an organization modeled on the air raid wardens'. At Carl Bachschmid's suggestion the very active, two-year-old Board of Trade became a committee of the Chamber of Commerce. The Chamber decided that in lieu of its usual Christmas Lane celebration it would sponsor a holiday party for servicemen and women at the USO. The VFW, headed by Adlai Magee, planned shelters at the Naval Hospital and at the District Line for hitchhiking servicemen. And the USO itself

planned a big, formal Christmas dance at Woodmont.

The Liquor Control Board, expecting the usual holiday rush, instituted strict rules, which limited the sale of liquor to County residents only. Buyers had to present Ration Book 3 or 4 and have the date of purchase stamped on the back. It was not rationing exactly, but adults could buy only one bottle of whisky every two weeks that winter. Store windows in Bethesda became a project for Mrs. Furth's retail merchandising classes, and almost every big store in town and many of the small ones participated. The Palais Royal "Home for Christmas" window, designed and decorated by Hope Daly, won the first prize.

At the high school, the big winter project was a letter writing campaign to all the school's graduates in the service. Late in November, English classes began drafting appropriate "greetings," which were edited, criticized and turned over to a committee of seniors who "wrote" the final letter under the direction of English teachers Kay Greaney and Jane Williams. Meanwhile, business teacher Lorraine Hatfield and her Community Service group from the Victory Corps, with help from counselor Dorothy Young, gathered names, updated addresses and made a card file from which Lillian Moore's students addressed envelopes that Alice Weinberg's group checked and stuffed. The project resulted in letters for 689 former students, 280 of them overseas.

Mrs. Karl Plitt of Delaware Street in Chevy Chase undertook a similar effort on a somewhat smaller scale. "Mom" Plitt, whose kitchen had long been a gathering place for neighborhood children, wrote fifty-five young people far from home, most in the military, and solicited letters from them. Forty-five responded, and Mrs. Plitt added letters from two local ministers and "Ma" Mohler and then mimeographed them all with the help of Mrs. W. Harold Snape whose minister husband had finished his chaplain training at Great Lakes and, according to his letters, was "somewhere in the Pacific." Each person who wrote Mrs. Plitt received a bulky package of all the other letters under a Christmas cover and learned where his or her friends were and what they had been doing.[70]

Suburban Hospital scheduled its grand opening for December 1, and both the *Tribune* and the *Journal* issued special editions complete with front page drawings of the hospital

The new hospital's first snow

and nurses' dormitory and numerous stories about the facility, the staff and the gift-givers. More than 2,500 Bethesdans toured the hospital, which was beautifully decorated for the occasion despite "Ma" Mohler spraining both ankles while she was out picking up some last-minute art work.

Unfortunately, the long-ordered laboratory equipment did not arrive, the sterilizers were stuck in Frederick, and the hospital could not open. The Public Health clinic for tuberculosis, venereal diseases, maternity cases and child care did move from Hampden Lane and began operating. All the baskets of flowers went to the Naval Hospital. Finally, with the sterilizers in place and the lab equipment on the premises but still not installed, the hospital began accepting medical patients on December 13.

One of those visiting the new hospital on opening day was retired chef William C. Powell who had been running a boarding house on Fairmont Avenue for about fifteen years. The large, well-equipped kitchen impressed him since he had worked at the Congressional and Columbia clubs before going into business for himself. On December 2, 1943, he answered the hospital's ad for a chef and stayed throughout the war.[71]

Another early employee was the Rev. Charles Smallwood, an operating suite orderly six days a week, who served his congregations at the Germantown, Boyds, Clarksburg and Hyattstown Methodist-Episcopal churches on Sundays. The stocky, grey-haired

Reverend Smallwood

Reverend Smallwood was a 1918 graduate of Morgan State with a degree from Howard's school of religion. At Suburban he wheeled patients to and from the operating room with a "steady hand and kind, cheerful voice" and kept the surgical suite clean and waxed. He soon was a familiar figure as he distributed newspapers with a smile and a good word for all the patients. Reverend Smallwood took the job, he said, to fill a wartime need and to "cheer the weary traveler."[72]

Leland put on a Christmas pageant, "The Shrine of the Star," produced by Helen Deveraux (Mrs. Thomas W.) Pyle, and the *Tribune* sponsored the "first annual" songfest at the high school in cooperation with the Council of Churches. Arch McDonald emceed, and J. Horace Smithey led the singing with George Gummell as Santa Claus, and at the conclusion, just before Mr. Hiser's cartoons, Father John Baptist Palm of Our Lady of Lourdes gave the benediction, which made it the most ecumenical event of the period.

At Christ Lutheran, Reverend Vogeley arranged for the whole Christmas service including his sermon to be mimeographed and mailed to all the local men and women serving overseas. The Camp Fire Girls and Blue Birds had their vespers service at the Christ Lutheran Church. And on Christmas Eve groups of carolers from the USO strolled through the streets of Bethesda.

It had been a difficult year for women. Sons, fathers, brothers, husbands and boyfriends were far from Bethesda. Many women had to work and then come home, feed the kids, care for the house, pay the bills and figure out the ration books. Tanya Bendit, mother of a four-month-old son, became the manager of the Ladies Specialty Shop when her husband Saul answered his draft call. Women ran the nursery schools and the Cub Scouts, as usual. They also made the draft board and the ration board work as well as getting the Thrift Shop, the USO, and Suburban Hospital started.

A mother on Northfield whose children and pets had been bothered by a wandering Spitz called the police, and when they could not find the stray, took down her husband's 20 gauge, found the dog and killed it. Walter E. Perry's old observation that women ran everything was righter than ever.

One woman wrote her own declaration of independence. On December 17 in a signed, front page box, Mrs. J. Reed Bradley printed her "Swan Song." She had built the *Journal* into an alert and readable publication with a circulation of 5,000. She wrote that for a year and a half she had believed she was a partner with the New York publisher Mel Hickerson, but now found she was not and probably could never become one. So she resigned. Her daughter recalled, "Hickerson became a bad word around our house."

In the next issue on December 24, her last, in the same space but headlined "Excelsior!" she wrote that she had received so much encouragement that she would try to acquire the *Journal* and, if she failed, would start a new paper. She also printed a column of letters from readers praising her work and regretting her decision, and a short. laudatory editorial by competitor William Prescott Allen in which he expressed the hope that she would be back. The *Journal* would struggle on under quirky leadership for a number of years, but when Mrs. Bradley left, it lost both head and heart.

[1] And variations such as "tarfu" and "fubar." See Paul Fussell's *Wartime* (Oxford, 1989).

[2] On July 16, 1943, about the "porch radio fiends," he wrote that it was "Curious how little consideration is given the other fellow. Maybe that's the reason we have wars." Edwards' annual spring topic was "Don't take 'em off yet. We'll tell you when."
In 1943 WJSV became WTOP "at the top of your dial." The writer's favorite was the *The Lone Ranger* on WMAL.

[3] Henderson was succeeded briefly by Sen. Chester Brown and then by Chester Bowles.
Bob Brewer (B-CC `43): "My father got extra stamps because he was in the real estate business, but I could only drive if I brought home a report card with all B's or better."

[4] *Burning Tree Club, A History 1922-1962*, by Col. Benjamin Castle.

[5] Henry J. Kaufman's *Woodmont County Club; A History* (1988), used with permission.

[6] *Journal*, Feb. 26, 1943.

[7] See *Journal* April 16, 1943, for draft, and *Journal* and *Tribune* May 21, 1943, for revised draft.

[8] *Post*, April 17, 1943.

[9] *Journal* and *Tribune*, April 30 and May 7, 1943.

[10] According to some sources, Dr. Perry's last wishes included that his driver, Milton Smith, be buried next to him in the Rockville Cemetery. When Smith, who was almost as well known as Dr. Perry, died, the executors considered the problem, debated a secret, nighttime burial, but decided to buy Smith a plot in the "colored" burying ground nearby.

[11] Jan. 22, 1943.

[12] As the U-boat inflicted gasoline shortage deepened in the spring of 1943, Blake Merson had to cut his twenty-two trucks back to one trash pick-up a week.

[13] *Record*, March 2, 1945. See also David Brinkley's *Washington Goes to War*, Chapter IX. Brinkley has some good photos and repeats the standard wartime housing joke as well as revealing, on the same page, 231, a bit of local scandal.

[14] Just getting the cans ready for collection was not an easy job in those days before electric can openers. Most children liked the flattening part best.

[15] The 1943 Leland boys' varsity featured Leon Utterback at center, Frank Daly and George Wallace at forward, and Lefty Schaub and team captain Alan Fitch at guard.

[16] Again the Army changed the air raid signals. Now there was a blue signal, a long, steady blast, which meant planes were headed our way. It called for a blackout, but traffic continued to move. The red alert, a series of short blasts or a wavering tone, announced enemy planes almost overhead. It stopped traffic. Then the "blue" signal again, but no "all clear." That was announced on the radio or by the street lights being turned back on. The new signals were first used in an announced drill on February 17 and then in a blackout on Monday, February 22, throughout the Military District of Washington.

[17] *Tribune*, Feb. 5, 1943.

[18] *Journal*, Feb. 19, 1943. When two cars and a delivery truck were destroyed in a Bradley Boulevard garage fire, the news story emphasized that one of the cars had four new tires. During full-scale rationing some three billion small squares of gummed paper changed hands monthly. Store owners passed them on to wholesalers and jobbers who "cashed" them with the producers who accounted to OPA.

[19] *Journal*, July 9, 1943.

[20] Mrs. Bush was a widely exhibited artist best known for her paintings of orchids. The trapezes and swings Miss Bush and her three brothers had played on were put away for the day, and Baby Snooks, Mrs. Bush's friendly gray squirrel, was generally ignored for a change.

[21] *Journal*, Jan. 29, 1943. Chet McCall remembered the Victory Garden by the garage but said his mother did most of the work as well as a lot of canning.

[22] *The Echo*, Vol. 1, No. 1, November 25, 1942. (The writer doubts that there is an intentional pun in there.) *Tattler*, Dec. 20, 1943. Thanks to Doris Severe Bruffey (B-CC `45) who saved them and almost all the wartime Tattlers along with a great deal more.

[23] *Tribune*, Feb. 26, 1943.

[24] *Journal*, Feb. 19, 1943. Ed Stock's series continued well into the fall, see Appendix G.

[25] See *Journal*, April 16, 1943, for list of community gardens and chairmen.
The Perkins' story (the activities building at Landon was named for their son who had died in a train wreck five years before) was in the *Star* of June 21, 1943.

[26] *Journal*, April 23, 1943. The pay rate may sound low, but during the war years, cutting a lawn with a push mower seldom earned a boy more than fifty cents and a glass of Kool Aid. The letter was from Catherine Turlington.

[27] *Journal*, June 18, 1943, and for Edwards, March 28, 1943. Nationwide 20.5 million garden plots produced about a third of the nation's fresh vegetables.

[28] For more on race relations at Capital Transit see David Brinkley's *Washington Goes to War* near the end of Chapter IX. *Journal*, August 9, 1943. The Community Bus Line, which used "stretch" limos, was often so crowded that government "girls" sat on male passengers' laps on the way home. No one complained; there was a war on.

[29] Doris Bruffey's design was not used because the War Dept. had standardized service banners.

[30] Bowen was spreading out in the "flats" after winning the contract to produce, on a pilot basis, the radio proximity fuse, the war's second-most-secret weapon.

[31] *Journal*, March 12, 1943 and *Tribune*, April 9, 1943.

[32] Somerset provided enough silver for 19 complete trays, Bradley 13, Bethesda 23, Lynnbrook 12, Alta Vista 15.

[33] The major training areas included:
A - 5,000 acres of wooded terrain five miles west of Quantico at Chopawamsic, special operations
B - 9,000 acres of mountain terrain in the Catoctin area, 20 miles north of Frederick, Camp David (Deerfield), operational groups
C - 4,000 acres woodland adjacent to A, communications
D - 1,400 acres of wooded terrain at Smith's Point across the Potomac from Quantico, special operations
F - Congressional Country Club for military operations..

[34] For more on the OSS see *Wild Bill Donovan The Last Hero* by Anthony Cave Brown, (Times Books, 1982), and *The War Report of the OSS*, (Walker and Co, 1976).

[35] One of the best known Bethesdans in OSS was Walter Tuckerman's oldest daughter, Laura, who worked downtown and in North Africa and Italy in the research branch.

[36] Obolensky, who started WW II as a National Guard private, had been an officer in the Russian army in WW I. He and a small OG parachuted into Sardinia in September 1943.
See *Congressional Country Club 1924-1984* for more on this era.

[37] *From OSS to Green Berets* by Col. Aaron Bank, (Pocket Books, 1986).

[38] *Journal*, April 9, April 23, and May 28, 1943.

[39] James Nichols, who actually collected the dog tax, mailed out tags to about 300 owners that spring. The majority of the 2,000+ tags sold that year went in May and June.

[40] *Tribune*, June 18, 1943, and *Journal*, June 23 and Nov. 12, 1943.

[41] Sullivan also recalled that he and his fellow pump-jockeys had occasional grease-gun fights and that all the boys enjoyed seeing how fast customers' cars would go when they delivered them. Senior-again Al Sherline's `31 Olds convertible with the wheel wells and yellow, shower-curtain top was another B-town regular.

[42] See *Tribune* and *Journal* August 13, 1943, for Allen appointment and reaction. The County Commissioners also named Emory Bogley to the Board of Assessments to replace William Prescott and chose Samuel Stonebraker to the Board of Zoning Appeals to replace Mr. Bogley.

[43] The MDW records do not use the name Camp Lewis. The TMB newsletter usually called it Camp Carderock, but that name was also used for the bivouac of soldiers who guarded the aqueduct.

[44] All quotes from *The Military District of Washington in the War Years 1941-45* by William H. Cartwright Jr. and WAC Major Louise E. Goeden, 1946, on deposit at the Old Guard Museum at Fort Myer. No written evidence of the prison camp operation has been found.

[45] It was likely the least expensive prom in the high school's history on the highway. A dollar for the dinner and another dollar for the dance. See *Tribune*, June 4, 1943. Note "Dirty Dozen" story in `42 chapter. Sub-deb Helen Almy's story was in the April 26, 1943, *Life*.

[46] All three speeches are printed in the *Journal* for June 18, 1943.

[47] The 1943 B-CC yearbooks the writer has examined, including the one owned by sophomore Chet McCall, are full of autographs followed by Greek letters or "S.S." Al Sherline, among others, said that there was a lot of drinking in the class of `43, both beer and "moose milk."

[48] See *Tribune*, Nov. 12, 1943, *et seq.* Chet McCall, who was not a fraternity member, wrote one of the anonymous letters, which asked, among other things, what right the school had to regulate what students did outside of school.

[49] The number of n's in "Lynnbrook" was an immediate and continuing problem to the school, neighborhood and newspapers.

[50] Cabell Phillips, *The 1940s: Decade of Triumph and Troubles*, (NY Times, 1975).

[51] Mrs. Harriet Belt Ingersoll was chosen as the first regent and Mrs. Jesse Nicholson first vice-regent; Mrs. Roger Whiteford, 2nd vice-regent, and Mrs. Robert K. Winters chaplain. In June Miss Belt succeeded her sister as regent.

[52] The names Camp Lewis and Camp Carderock were both informal. The latter may have referred to the camp of the 804th Military Police Battalion, which was assigned to the Mobile Force of the MDW and stationed at Carderock. In June 1944, the 804th was transferred to Fort Devens, Mass..

[53] *Journal*, September 17, 1943.

[54] The BT-12 was an all stainless steel, spot welded, low wing, two-place trainer with a 450-hp Pratt and Whitney nine-cylinder radial engine. It was similar to the much more common Vultee Valiant, the BT-13A known derisively as the Vibrator, but had a higher canopy. The Fleetwings factory in Bristol, Pa., delivered only twenty-five planes before the order was cancelled.

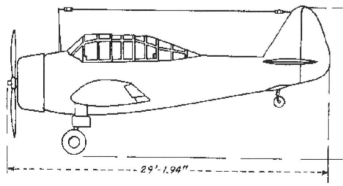

[55]The crash site was between Kennedy, Glenwood and Bradley. See *Journal* on July 16 and July 30, 1943. The accident report filed on 22 July 1943 is held at Norton Air Force Base in California, but only half of it (see below) was made available after a FOI Act request and appeal.

[56]It is possible that the Dodge dealership was used as an office for this warehouse, but there is no mention of it in the documents at Archives. Mrs. Marvin (Virginia) Simmons found out what they did there when she met one of the enlisted men at the USO where she volunteered. He told her they unpacked and assembled radios "and then read the directions." For more on the growth of the OSS see *Donovan and the CIA* by Thomas F. Troy (Aletheia Books, 1981), Chapter 5.

[57]Francis Moran is listed as Editor in Vol. 1, No. 2, but after that it is Bob Roth with Martha Alexander as Assistant Editor.

[58]That is Marine Al Sherline at the school's front door in the Life spoof.

[59]In November 1943 the County school board asked the State superintendent of schools for an "interpretation" of the rules regarding secret societies, and after receiving it, adopted strict regulations in January 1944.

[60]*Journal*, September 17, 1943.

[61]See *Tribune*, Sept. 17 and Oct. 1 and *Journal*, Sept. 24, 1943, which contains a list of the all the original hostesses and contributors.

[62]*Journal*, Sept. 24 and Oct. 8, 1943.

[63] Lee and company, of course, also spoke through Bray. *Journal* and *Tribune*, Oct. 8, 1943.

[64]The original chairwomen were Mrs. Percy Royster representing Suburban Hospital, Mrs. E. A. Merritt for Montgomery General, Mrs. Earl Breeding of the Lay Health Committee and Mrs. John B. Ecker for Maternal Welfare.

[65]For a list of the original pricing and selling volunteers see the *Journal* of Oct. 29, 1943.

[66]Pharmacist Alice Odlan from Massachusetts, record librarian Virginia Lee from St. Paul, Minn., dietitian Katherine Spencer from Cook County, Ill., and auditor Ejnar Christensen of Takoma Park were also among the original supervisory employees.

[67]*Journal*, Dec. 10, 1943.

[68]For more prize winners see the *Tribune* of October 8, 1943.

[69]The 2nd Marine Division lost 913 killed or missing and 2,037 wounded in taking Tarawa in November 1943. The Japanese lost about 4,000 killed in action; very few surrendered.

[70]*Record*, Feb. 5, 1944. Bill Snape recalled receiving that package of letters, including one from his father, when he was in the Navy in `44.

[71]*Record*, Sept. 15, 1944.

[72]*Record*, December 1, 1944. The first patient was Mrs. S. P. Wagner of Rockville.

CHAPTER 13

Victories and Defeats

As the third year of the war began, Bethesdans followed the slow Allied advance up the boot of Italy. On the dreaded Eastern Front, the Red Army's winter campaign ground relentlessly on, devouring villages, tanks and men. With sandpaper and powdered glue, youngsters made solid-wood Strombecker models of the B-17s and the B-24s that carried Jimmy Doolittle's bomber crews deeper into Germany. Everyone admired the handsome pilots who flew the "Jugs," Mustangs and heavy bombers. In the newsreels they grinned beside planes decorated with pin-up art and neat rows of bombs or swastikas. The second front, the invasion, was an omnipresent topic.

In the Pacific, American forces moved toward the Marshalls and the Admiralties where Captain Arleigh (31 Knot) Burke of Langdrum Lane earned fame leading a destroyer task force in the attack on Rabaul. Out in the China-Burma-India theater, forgotten warriors slogged over ridge after nameless ridge. Stories of Japanese atrocities began to filter back, and civilians learned of the beheading of some of Doolittle's Tokyo raiders and of the brutality of the Bataan "death march."

On the home front surprise snows, continued rationing, the housing shortage, a lengthy dog quarantine and the debate over whether or not *Esquire* was too racy to go through the mails dominated conversations. Bethesdans waited dubiously while the WSSC tried to organize the garbage and ash collection service it had promised. The D.C. area's population had grown twenty-eight percent since the 1940 census, from 958,000 to an estimated 1,229,000 excluding service personnel, and there were thousands of them. Car pools had become the norm.

Suburban Hospital shook off its opening-day embarrassment and, by the end of the first week of 1944, had admitted forty-five patients and was well into its first nurse's aide training program. Out at Carderock, workers completed two subsonic wind tunnels, and Captain Holden C. Richardson, one of the designers of the NC-4, moved his staff to the Model Basin. The Fourth War Loan Drive began.

The VFW finished the shelter for servicemen and women waiting for rides at the District Line. They painted it white with a red and a blue stripe and installed maps and a mirror. Then they started working on another one at the Naval Hospital. Phil Schaefer designed the Chamber of Commerce shelter near the Hot Shoppe, and a committee headed by Stanley Everhart built it with lumber donated by Eisinger's and paint from Sherwin Williams. The high school shop classes

John Imirie stops to pick up some hitchhikers

equipped it with forty long, white "paddles" with the names of cities on them to help uniformed hitchhikers flag down rides.

Chief Bargagni began advertising for firemen "with draft-exempt status." Chester McCall, president of the high school PTA, called the "appalling loss of teachers" the "most serious problem on the Maryland home front," but others were equally concerned about the drafting of police officers and firemen. At the high school, happy and grateful replies to the 700 Christmas letters started to arrive.[1]

One of the petty annoyances of 1944 was milk bottle caps without staples on their pull-tabs, which led to the "jab and pray" method of opening except on those cold days when milk left on the porch froze and put up a column of slushy cream. And just as the inevitability of the cross-channel invasion seemed to loom behind all the war news, the coming vote on the proposed charter permeated local political events.

The war's third year brought very bad news to many Bethesda-area homes. Dozens of young men were reported killed, wounded, missing-in-action or prisoners of the enemy. As the pace and intensity of the war increased, the death toll also accelerated. The first local military fatality of 1944 was not a young man, by most standards, and was not in action, by the usual definition, but it brought forth a tribute, which expressed attitudes shared by many in the community.

The War Comes to 45th Street

Sam Syme was the only man from our block in the armed forces. The Dawsons, McCloskeys, Gessfords, Gerards, and Werners had a pride and a security in the knowledge that Sam was defending us and would win the war for us. Because he was in the invasion of Africa at Casablanca, took Sicily, and went up into Italy, and was working with General Patton on his staff, America would win the war.

When he was here with us he had been a good neighbor and friend. He had remembered all of us during the 15 months he had been away. Every child on the street had received some little gift. My Mary and Stella each received a pin made by a native of North Africa.

Sam had kept the bombs from 45th Street. He had protected the children there that loved him. However no bomb could have fallen that would have been a bigger shock to all of us than the telegram the boy handed to Martha Syme late Friday night. "Major Samuel Syme died on January 2 in Algiers. A letter will follow."

I'm writing this because little 9-year-old Sam has been with me some part of every day since last Friday and this question has gone through my mind. "He has given so much for us. What can we do for him?"

We on 45th Street have promised him that we would give our lives in making life here at home happy for all, as his father had tried to make it so when he lived here. As individuals we will practice the principles of love in daily living with our neighbors; give of our energy to make our community a place wherein God may dwell, and help to spread through the world understanding of other peoples and brotherly kindness that we may not know war any more.

Sam Syme gave his life. Martha gave her husband; Sam gave his father, so we can surely live to bring about in this world the way of life for which they have given so much.

Stella Werner
(Mrs. John H. Werner)

Gertrude Bradley printed Mrs. Werner's eulogy on the front page of the second issue of her new, weekly newspaper, *The Record*, which first appeared with the NNMC tower in the middle of its title "flag" on January 8, 1944. The paper was an obvious success from the beginning with as much display advertising and local news as its two competitors combined, and within six months, the editor and owner could crow over almost 3,000 paid subscriptions at $2.00 each.

Meanwhile, Bill Allen sometimes had trouble filling his four-page, single-sheet *Tribune*, and the *Journal*, with its 5,000 circulation and popular classified section, stumbled on editorless for several weeks until owner J. M. Hickerson found Craddock Goins to take over. Georgian Goins brought Southern charm, a folksy manner, long newspaper experience and a broad promotional background with him. The new editor and his wife found a home on Garfield Street and immersed themselves in local activities and organizations. Goins and H. R. Daniel, now listed as publisher, moved the paper's office to the first floor of the Bowling Center on Old Georgetown and invited everyone to stop by and visit.

Clarence "Bud" Keiser's was a "go-fer" at the *Journal*. He recalled that Craddock Goins had some "country" habits, such as blowing his nose in the waste baskets.

His wife ran the office, and one of my jobs was to pedal up to the Bethesda post office and pick up the mail and stacks of newspapers from the printer. I also punched out addressograph plates from the Bethesda telephone book and ran the machine to make the labels.

Mrs. Goins occasionally covered social events and women's political meetings, and when she got a by-line, it was "Mable Marie."

From the start *The Record* was, at least in public, an all-woman operation and as such soon gained a certain amount of attention from the D.C. dailies and radio commentators as well as a few articles in business and journalism magazines. The original staff consisted of the owner-editor, Mrs. Bradley; office and circulation manager Mrs. N. F. Rabner; and advertising manager Mrs. John Miles Mader, who by her own admission had never sold a line of advertising or drawn up an ad before she took the job. In little more than a week, the three of them got the paper started. Pearl McPherson soon took on the job of subscription solicitor, and Jane Russell Snyder joined to cover the society "beat" early in the paper's second year. All worked "at their own convenience."

The end product was a five-column, twelve-page tabloid filled with church and club news, USO doings, library announcements, high school sports, Camp Fire and Scouting columns, lots of items on men and women in the service and, by fall, the return of columnist Russ Edwards. Almost all the

Journal's columns moved over to the *Record* including Mrs. Oliver's about dogs and dog owners and "Blue and Gold" sports by "The Four Barons," which was really just B-CC junior Chet McCall. Senior Julie Carrington reported on girls' sports at the high school.[2]

Jane Bradley Lowe recalled the start of her mother's paper:

Henry Hiser, Carl Bachschmid and some others felt like there wasn't a real newspaper. Bill Allen's was awful. They encouraged her and probably gave her some backing.

They were all friends, all in their forties. Margaret Rabner did the bookkeeping, and Joyce Mader, who was something else, an Englishwoman, decided she was going to sell the advertisements. My father accused her of vamping all the businessmen up and down the Avenue. She had black hair and pretty skin and a line of patter like you've never heard.

There was a hall in the professional building, and Mother's office was out in the hall to start with, for at least a month. The telephone company came in and hooked up phones in that hall. Henry Connor got her desks, and there she sat in this hall until a couple of offices opened up. She found a printer, Mr Burton down on 5th and G Streets. He had an old web press and employed deaf mutes to run the Linotypes.[3]

The first five weeks were throwaways, no charge, and my friends and I, she never paid us much, carried them around. I never covered so much of Montgomery County on foot in my life. We delivered papers all weekend, put them on peoples' front steps.

According to Mrs. Mader, Gertrude Bradley believed that "advertising should take care of all the overhead and that advertising profits should go back into the paper when circumstances permit." Mader, whose only business experience had been as a secretary twelve years earlier, claimed that her first call was on

. . . the advertising manager of a large department store in Washington. He asked me what a 3 x 10 ad would cost him. I couldn't tell him. All I knew was that The Record was charging $1.00 an inch for its advertising. He did his own calculating. But I got the ad.

She sold 5,000 lines at seven cents a line and soon was calling two hundred businesses and selling over 7,000 lines almost every week. Mrs. Bradley took the subscription money as her pay on the theory that if "the paper is good from a reader angle, she makes

Editor Bradley

money." Henry Hiser hosted a luncheon to launch the new paper. Many of the town's business leaders attended including Art Bowis of Chevy Chase Motors, William Hodges of C&P, Walter Bogley and about forty others. Women's clubs sent out circulars about the newspaper, and "Ma" Mohler joined with Mrs. Black and Miss Moore, leaders of the Quota Club, to get subscriptions.[4]

In her first editorial, Bradley claimed that the decision to produce a paper occurred only ten days before the first issue appeared. A local paper, she wrote, lives on good will, which she claimed to have reason to believe she had earned in her five-year tenure at the *Journal*. She announced her editorial independence and stated that her columns were open to all points of view. As for the name, she admitted its choice was sentimental and based on her father's first, country paper, "The Gauley Record," in West Virginia. Her *Record*, she wrote "will not propagate or simulate. It will record."

After graduating from West Virginia University, Gertrude Bradley came to Washington to work in a Congressman's office and met her husband-to-be who was earning his way through law school as a Capitol guard. They married; he passed the bar exam and took a job with Travelers Insurance, and they rented a house in Bethesda in 1932. In 1934 they built their house at the corner of Cedar (Greentree) and Oneida Lanes as their daughter recalled:

A man named Bien, an architect, designed our house, and two more down at the end of the street, as an English cottage, designed it with a sag in the roof. People would come and knock on the door and say do you know that your roof is sagging. It was a neat house with hand-hewn beams that workers chopped on the premises. [5]

I was four when we moved in, and I met Bill Lehr. I fell off the back of his tricycle, and he dragged me up the sidewalk on my knees.

For start-up capital, the publisher borrowed on her husband's life insurance, and he and her daughter, in Mrs. Bradley's words, "trudged the streets handing out the first issue." Her husband also oversaw the paper's bookkeeper, and he and daughter Jane were involved in mailing out the paper right from the start. Their neighbor, "Zip" Lehr's son Bill, recalled the process:

Jane and I used to go downtown on the bus and streetcar, and we'd meet her father at the printer, and he would stamp the labels on with the address machine, a portable one, down around 5th and something. We'd load these things in mail sacks and put them in the back seat, and Janie and I would be sitting up there all bent over. We'd go down to the main post office and mail them and come home at 9, 10 o'clock. Reed Bradley around six would ask what we wanted. We'd get french fries and Cokes and sit on the papers and eat.

The *Record* started with guest columnists such as Ray Tucker and Marquis Childs, but Mrs. Bradley quickly dropped that idea to rely on her own legwork and on the scores of items phoned and mailed in each week by readers who became part-time "bird-dogs" and fulltime publicists for their neighborhoods and clubs. The paper soon was something of a women's cause, and a number of the editor's friends volunteered to work for nothing.

Leaders of the Republican Party offered support if she would make the *Record* a Republican paper. "I didn't consider it," she said. Within six weeks she had more news than she could print under wartime paper restrictions. She tried some fancy typography and lay-outs including an attempt to separate items of interest to men and women, but soon settled into a clean format with most stories finished on the page where they began. Editing to fit the space available became her forte.

Somehow Bethesda managed to support three weekly newspapers for a half-dozen years, each claiming a circulation of some 5,000. The *Record* soon overshadowed the other two in coverage and lines of advertising, but all three contributed a different "voice" to the mercantile and political dialogue, and as the election of 1944 neared, each staked out its own bailiwick.

Suburban Hospital opened a second patient pavilion early in January but was still waiting for the equipment needed to finish the

surgical and obstetrical departments. For several weeks similar problems prevented the hospital from providing emergency care or even first aid. Doctors Robert S. Smith and Herbert Martyn, both George Washington graduates, became full-time residents at Suburban, the quota allowed the hospital under wartime manpower regulations. Dr. Richard Bauersfeld, a senior medical student at GW, signed on to assist the residents in providing night service.

Meanwhile more gifts appeared in the form of both money and goods such as shrubbery and crutches. I. S. Turover contributed the lumber for library shelves, and local artists continued to donate or lend their work. Lona Miller Keplinger, a member of Mrs. Mohler's committee, donated two of her own paintings as did several other committee members. Soon the doctor's lounge, the children's ward and the main hall glowed with the works of local painters. Will Towles of South Chelsea Lane gave the hospital a picture of the Clarysville, Maryland, hospital which his father had acquired when he worked there as a nurse during the Civil War, and it soon hung on a corridor wall.

At the end of January at the Woman's Club of Bethesda, Dorothy E. Glynn, Suburban's director of nursing, presented caps to her first class of nineteen nurse's aides and started a second session of two-hour evening classes, three nights each week. Because of the wartime nurse shortage, "We couldn't possibly do without their help," said Miss Glynn. This group of not-so-young women, the first nurse's aides in Montgomery County, included a number of Army and Navy wives and retired professionals. Among the graduates were Mrs. Parker Dodge, a trustee of Somerset elementary; Mrs. Floyd McClure of Friendship Heights, who had spent many years in China; Mrs. William Johnson Howard, active in British War Relief and the Lay Health Council; Mrs. Thomas W. Pyle, and Mrs. Alvin Aubinoe, who had "retired" as head of the local Red Cross chapter after three years of active service.[6]

The patients' library began operating before January was over. Staffed by fifteen volunteers, survivors of a training program and a written exam, the library served both patients and staff on Tuesday and Friday afternoons. The Woman's Club of Bethesda started the project under the aegis of the Women's Auxil-

iary with a $250 contribution. Mrs. Edward Willis chaired the effort with the help of librarian Marjorie Robinson and a committee, which included Mrs. George Pariseau. The public library served as a center for the donation of books, circulated some of its collection through the hospital library and offered to fill patients' requests for specific titles. Suburban's library opened with more than 200 volumes on its shelves and numerous gift subscriptions to popular periodicals.

On Monday, January 24, 1944, Suburban proudly announced that its surgical and obstetrical departments and emergency-care facility were ready. The X-ray department and pathological laboratory were staffed and fully equipped, but Miss Glynn was still looking for more graduate nurses for all shifts.

The hospital's first baby, however, did not wait for the official opening but used insider influence to make his appearance at 9:34 am on Sunday morning, January 23. He was the eight-and-a-half-pound son of Captain and Mrs. Charles P. Olson, and his uncle-with-the-influence was Resident Dr. Robert Shaw Smith. Within the next two weeks eleven other babies, six girls and five boys, joined young Charles Paul Olson Jr. as the obstetrical unit swung into almost daily action.

In February, the hospital inaugurated its Physical Therapy Department with Scottish-trained Miss Ray Carrie in charge and some $1,200 in equipment donated by the Lions Club. And in late March the Out-Patient Department and Clinic opened its separate entrance on Lincoln Street from one to three in the afternoon on Mondays, Wednesdays, and Fridays with Dr. Felipe A. Martinez in charge. At the same time the Public Health Lay Committee sponsored a program to train volunteers for the clinics in its wing of the hospital. About the only complaint patients had that first year was the early morning squawking of the guinea hens roosting in what was left of the Whelan's orchard

Mrs. Walter Perry, head of the hospital's busy Women's Auxiliary, asked for increased donations to the Thrift Shop, especially after Mrs. Percy Royster announced that the Auxiliary would receive more than $500 as the first quarterly dividend from the Shop's operation. Mrs. Perry proudly claimed that more than three-fourths of all the donations to the Hospital came "from people who had some personal contact with members of the Women's

Auxiliary." As of February, gifts to the Hospital totaled $14,795 including $8,100 for sponsored rooms.

The Auxiliary then turned its attention to the nurses' quarters, voted $200 to provide glass curtains for their plainly furnished, government-issue rooms, and urged donations of comfortable chairs, rugs, lamps and other furnishings. The Rosedale Victory Club was the first to respond with a donation for fireplace equipment and a mirror, and by April $3,000 had been contributed for the nurses' residence.

Early in the year, Mrs. Donald Roberts joined the Board of Trustees of Suburban Hospital to replace Mrs. Luke I. Wilson. A Wellesley graduate and an active member of St. John's, Norwood Parish, Mrs. Roberts was one of Bethesda's busier matrons as the mother of two young sons, president of Bradley's PTA, president of the County Homemaker Clubs, and vice-chairman of the Women's Activities Committee of the OCD. She also served on the Thrift Shop board, as a trustee of the Community Chest, as chairman for schools of the Public Health Lay Committee and on the board of the Maryland League for Planned Parenthood.[7]

In April, the Chamber of Commerce awarded its prestigious Oliver Owen Kuhn memorial cup to Randolph G. Bishop and Willie Green Day Perry. The Evening Star award recognized not only the physical improvement of the community brought about by the creation of the hospital but also the thousands of hours of volunteer work contributed by local citizens. The Chamber's committee on awards, chaired by Henry Hiser, felt that through Mr. Bishop and Mrs. Perry "it was paying tribute to the entire community's spirit of cooperation."[8]

The big Fourth War Loan Drive and the renewal of the Charter fight both began early in 1944. Walter Bogley, Mrs. B. Payton Whalen, and Clarence Keiser headed the bond-sale campaign for the Western Suburban Area. Soon every business, club, school and church had some sort of war bond rally or "buy-a-bond" activity. Before January was over, members of Leonora Aiken's speech class were visiting other classrooms at the high school to promote bond sales, and one high school fraternities invested half its funds in war bonds. A wrecked German fighter, an

ME-109, toured schools and business areas on a flatbed truck to promote bond sales, and the Falge Engineering Service, still advertising for help on its night shift, purchased $7,475 worth of bonds at one rally. The Civitan Club put on a show and sale at the Leland auditorium, which netted $36,000 for Uncle Sam. Their rally featured the A Cappella Choir from the high school, the Camp Fire Girls glee club, a contingent from the Military District of Washington, which put on a twenty-minute demonstration that included the capture of an "intruder" by a trained war dog and the technicolor "Back the Attack" film. Brooke Johns and insurance salesman King Mularkey shared the emcee duties.

Every school staged its own bond drive and most had a rally featuring a "Quiz Kids" contest. Chevy Chase Elementary raised $20,350 including over $8,000 at a rally and quiz program for 4th, 5th, and 6th graders. Fifth grader Donald Kurth won $5.00 worth of war stamps, the first prize, and 4th grader Walter Schiff was second while, as her father bragged for months, 6th grader Eda Schrader was the only girl in the contest. At Bethesda Elementary, families bought $22,000 in bonds before their rally with Russ Hodges as emcee. Bradley Elementary netted $8,400 with Kenneth Evans of WOL as quiz master, and Lynnbrook sold $6,000 worth of bonds and stamps with the help of Jerry Strong while Bill Herson did the honors at the Clara Barton school. At the high school, an auction of scarce goods including a smoked ham brought in more than $4,000.

The Montgomery County Charter Committee held its second annual meeting at the Woman's Club of Chevy Chase in mid-January and heard from Charles P. Taft of Cincinnati who called the draft charter before the voters ""workmanlike"" and supported the idea of non-partisan elections and a merit system. Among those elected as directors of the Charter Committee were O. M. Kile of Mohican Hills and Adlai S. Magee of Bethesda.

In Mrs. Bradley's first *Record* editorial on the subject, she summarized the history of the movement and praised the backers for trying to keep the public informed. The Charter front remained quiet until spring when the League of Women Voters, after a luncheon meeting attended by about a hundred delegates at the Chevy Chase Methodist Church,

voted unanimous endorsement of the Charter and pledged active support in the campaign. Mrs. Minier Hostetler told the group, "The charter is as nearly what the people of Montgomery County asked for as it was possible to make it under State constitutional restrictions." The Lee forces kept their peace adding credence to the earlier story that they did not plan to make a fight.[9]

Meanwhile, Judge Albert Brault received a ribbon denoting five-thousand hours of volunteer service to the Civil Defense program, and the Victory Garden Committee sponsored the first of a series of lectures at Bethesda Elementary School. At the high school, the two girls and nine boys of the January graduating class heard Dr. Ben Wood of Columbia University speak on "Aviation and Youth." The Activity Council staged a special Blue and Gold Prom to honor the early graduates, most of whom planned to enter military service.

The Bethesda Fire Department re-elected Capt. F. O. Smith as president; Capt. Chester Wells was elected president of the National Capital Area Council of the Boy Scouts for the twelfth consecutive year, and J. Harry Welch was named to head the County Community Chest. The Bethesda Council of Churches chose the Rev. C. A. Brubaker of Mt. Zion Baptist president, and Mrs. Richard J. Powers succeeded Mrs. Aubinoe as head of the local branch of the Red Cross.

Air raid drills and blackouts declined to one every three months and then on a Sunday night so war work would not be disrupted. During the war, most people worked a five-and-a-half or six-day week and several of Bethesda's war industries operated three shifts. The first drill of 1944 took place on the first Sunday of February and led to a widespread search for misplaced helmets, wrinkled brassards, and flashlight batteries.

Northwest Park had almost been forgotten as a "town" within Bethesda when it gave a boost to the WSSC by asking it to take over the taxing area's trash collection. It was still electing its council annually, dealing with street maintenance and drainage problems, especially from Soper's Esso station on the corner of Battery and Wisconsin, and working to improve its system of culverts. The "village" had produced Keplinger's now-famous tennis tournament and Philip A. Rosendorn, a citizen with unequaled years of service to his community and the local Masonic lodge.

Rosendorn had been one of the original incorporators of Northwest Park and the first chairman of its town council. All through the 1920s and `30s, his service continued with few interruptions, most often as the special taxing area's secretary-treasurer. In 1943 when a council member resigned, Rosendorn accepted appointment as secretary-treasurer again, but when he was elected chairman in 1944, he declined to serve. By 1944, he had retired as chief cartographic draftsman in the Interior Department's Bureau of Reclamation after thirty-nine years, but he was still secretary of Masonic Lodge 204.[10]

G. Wady Imirie led the Chamber of Commerce committee considering changes and improvements in post-war Bethesda. He sent out more than 4,000 questionnaires asking businessmen and residents about their plans for repairs, remodeling and expansion. Imirie's group suggested enlargement of the County Building, changing the law on business signs, zoning for apartments between business and residential areas, better street lighting, improved public transportation, two new fire stations and the removal of most trees along Wisconsin Avenue in the business district. The final recommendation brought an immediate outcry from the local garden clubs.

The Chamber also endorsed the idea of building a large hotel in the Bethesda area. Conrad Eisinger announced that he had the plans for an eight-floor, 168-room hotel with a roof garden as well as the land at Wisconsin and Elm and just needed the priorities to be approved. He said had been planning the project for five years. Within months another hotel, this one to be located north of the Naval Hospital and costing $15 million, was also in the publicity stage. Randolph Bishop quickly endorsed the idea and labeled the proposed hotel a "vital necessity" in his developing view of Bethesda as a World Health Center.[11]

The County Commissioners named Park and Planning Commissioner E. Brooke Lee and 224 other County leaders to an advisory committee on post-war planning. One of the first suggestions this large group heard came from Randolph Bishop. Mr. Bishop, retiring as president of Suburban Hospital's board of directors, suggested the development of the

County as a national health center and thereby promoted a discussion that lasted the rest of the year.

Bishop, secretary of the National Dental Hygiene Association, produced a series of articles, which the *Record* published starting in mid-February. His long range plan called for the forty to fifty "scientific and educational institu-tions" and the expansion of the NIH and NNMC to "many times their present size and facilities." He saw this development attracting "research laboratories of great industrial and pharma-ceutical corporations" that would line the railroad to "Rockville and beyond."

He called his plan a "Health Center," saw research as the basic factor and modeled his ideas on existing NIH programs. Bishop suggested that 400 acres would be needed to accommodate additional research facilities, clinical hospitals and other scientific buildings with half of that for Federal Government activities.

Bishop's proposals drew support from such divergent sources as Dr. Thomas Parran, Surgeon General of the U.S. Public Health Service, and "Merry Go-Round" columnist Drew Pearson, who praised Bishop's work for Suburban Hospital, lauded his second "pipe dream" and suggested that he might run for Congress.

As his idea germinated, Bishop began calling the proposal a health center "for the world." The articles and discussion continued on into the spring, and in June, Bishop produced his grand plan of the "Medical Research Community," at the Chamber meeting in the County Building. Bishop concluded his presentation:

Regardless of political administrations, our nation is headed toward a tremendous expansion of health benefits and facilities for all people in the post-war years. In the past, we as a people have depended in too large measure upon diagnosis and treatment and in too small measure upon seeking the cause of human ills. The scientist and research worker no longer has to justify his value to society. That has been amply demonstrated in this war. It is up to us as a people to make available to him the necessary facilities and working tools that he may serve us in even greater measure in the years to come.[12]

Several types of "canteens" served various Bethesda constituencies in 1944. The USO on Old Georgetown Road welcomed servicemen and women every afternoon and evening, and a church group or women's club served a special supper every Sunday night. The Women's Guild of St. John's Church and members of the Girls Friendly Society supported the canteen at the Parish Hall of Epiphany Church in D.C. The Canteen Corps of the Red Cross continued to supply food for the production groups and blood donor activities. The Red Cross also operated a mobile canteen donated by Woodmont Country Club. The Clubmobile made the rounds of the smaller, local military installations such as Camp Lewis on a regular schedule dispensing coffee, home-made sandwiches, pies, donuts, magazines, records and friendship.

Col. Kester Hastings, Mrs. Hastings, Mrs. Theodore Peyser and the Woodmont mobile canteen

At the end of February, the high school Activity Council, with the help of newly appointed recreation director Virginia Poole, organized and promoted a highly successful School Door Canteen, which staged parties two Fridays a month with games, ping pong, dancing, refreshments and a "live band" almost every month. It was such a success that the students and PTA held a fund-raising canteen night for parents in May, which featured bingo, square dancing, bridge, and entertainment including several numbers by young Stella Werner. a B-CC sophomore, on her big accordion.

"Little" Stella's musical career started in grade school and blossomed during the war.

I played the bass drum in the band at Chevy Chase. Dr. Hart was the director. We had hats like officers' hats and white pants and blue and gold capes. We were in a Constitution Avenue parade and one on Wisconsin Avenue, too. It was Poppa's drum; he was in a little band. They fashioned a baby carriage to haul the drum, and another girl pushed it.

My first performance with the accordion was at Leland where I played "12th Street Rag." Then was I busy. I had taken piano from Miss Holman on Montgomery Lane. She was very sweet. At one recital I played the lullaby, and my mother sang it. I got tired of piano. I would always choose doing-dishes-time to practice, so I could get away with not drying. Horatio Allison played the accordion, so Roy's (her husband) mother, Bessie, took my mother and father over to meet Sylvia Kaplowitz. She was well known and had played piano for Kate Smith and silent movies. I took lessons and had a nice, little, white accordion. My first solo was at Kitt's music store where she taught. I played "Two Guitars" and did very well although I forget the whole center part, but I never stopped

Stella and her big accordion

smiling and everybody said it was wonderful.

Sylvia had a whole troop that went from the Navy Hospital to Forest Glen to Quantico to play for servicemen. We played three or four times a week. Most of my high school days were taken up. Dates sat on the front steps waiting for me to get back home in my evening dress. That was the best part. We bought three dresses and a pair of shoes every September. I tried on a zillion and Lansburgh's delivered them. I got a 120 bass Excelsior (which she still has) *and gave my parents a lot of joy with that. Mother always looked so worried, afraid it was going to pinch me.*

Sometimes we went where we were locked in with men who were fairly well gone, and Sylvia kept a close tie on us. At Walter Reed once the guard at the gate said, "Oh, you're the

boogie woogie soloist aren't you." We played for amputees at Forest Glen, and one wasn't walking, for no reason. When I played my Tommy Dorsey's "Boogie Woogie," which was my thing, this boy got up and danced. At Quantico we gave many shows to boys being shipped out, a whole stage of girls in pretty dresses. They would stomp and cheer. I've had my share of applause.

The canteen craze had one more manifestation. From the Woodland Citizens Association came the idea for a teen-age "canteen club." Mrs. Arthur Hilland, president of the association, put Joseph Guandolo in charge but admitted, "I got it organized." In February, Guandolo explained his attempts to find room for the activity in the business district and reported Brooke Lee's offer of the old USDA building at the Rec Center.

Park and Planning named Louis Mitchell to head the commission's participation in the project, and before the winter was over, more than a thousand youngsters had responded positively to a survey made at Leland JHS, Our Lady of Lourdes School, and B-CC. The students chose representatives to participate in the planning and organization of the canteen and added Woodrow Wilson High School to the roster. The senior high advisory group was headed by B-CC senior Barbara Hanby and Joyce Snodgrass of Wilson while Harvey McClure and Joel Guandolo of Leland led the junior high group.[13]

With chaperones from the Woodland and the schools' PTAs, the "Canteen Club" opened with a junior-high dance on Friday, March 17, and a party for senior-high students the next night. Almost two hundred Leland and Lourdes kids showed up to dance to a juke box and mob the nickel snack bar and the game room in the basement. Over a hundred B-CCers and Wilsonites enjoyed the band on Saturday night despite a heavy rain. Dozens of students signed up. From then on the lounge and snack bar were open every day after school and on Saturdays from noon. Mrs. Hilland sought furniture and decorations for the building while Park and Planning lent some chairs and tables to get started.

With the help of a student committee, Dorothy Hilland wrote up some rules for the Canteen, and Louis Mitchell added to them and posted them in the lounge. They included the following: General good behavior will be maintained at all times. Smoking will be

confined to the lounge and eating to the lounge and game rooms–and not on the dance floor. Good care of game equipment will be appreciated. Servicemen who are alumni of the represented schools and holders of guest cards will be admitted as well as members.

By May, when the membership cards were ready, some shuffling of student leadership had taken place; membership was opened to all students of junior or senior high age in the area no matter what school they attended, and the canteen's name was changed to "Swing Grove" although few ever called it that. An adult "steering committee" headed by Chester McCall organized and submitted its by-laws to Emory Bogley and the Advisory Board of the Recreation Center.

Mrs. Val Sherman, chair of the committee on furnishing, planned red, white, and blue leather furniture for the lounge as the finance committee tried to raise the needed funds. WMAL featured the canteen on a Saturday show, and Mrs. Scott Brewer sought volunteer chaperones, but, according to "Butch" Hanby, "It never really caught on," and in May, Park and Planning decided to close the dance floor and game rooms in the afternoon to encourage children to play outdoors.

For Dorothy Hilland, that was the last step of what she saw as a long trail of unco-operative meddling.

So I put on my little hat, and trotted over to Brooke Lee's office. We had been having a good time, and it wasn't costing Park and Planning anything. I asked for more cooperation, especially with chaperones for the dances. And he said, "Mrs. Hilland, you can stay in or get out." I said, "I'm out. You run it."

Virginia Sholar, recently retired as director of the local USO, became the new chairman of the adult steering committee as Swing Grove went on a summer schedule.

At the high school, while some students were mourning the demise of the hedge around the grove, which made skipping school a good bit more difficult, the girls' basketball team got off to a much better start than the boys' team did. Senior guard Mary Williams captained the girls' team, which beat Blair twice, 18-12 and 19-10. Forwards Lois Copenhaver, JV grad Claire Ockey, and Betty Beard were the high scorers, "Butch" Hanby the manager and Helen Randels the coach. The girls even managed to beat the faculty despite the teacher forwards shooting at all

three baskets on their end of the court, Mrs. Randels using a ladder to "dunk" one shot and the cheerleading of Miss Greaney and Miss Boyer.

Herbie Benson

The boys, led by juniors Chris Chappell, Charlie Hughes, and Herbie Benson, got off to a terrible start. They lost to Eastern, Western, Roosevelt, and Mount Rainier before the first Blair game. On the Thursday night before playing Blair at home, cheerleaders Al Pettit and Chet McCall and team manager Bill Snape put together the biggest pep rally and bonfire in the school's history. Several hundred students assembled at 44th and Leland at sundown and snake danced up Wisconsin Avenue with a police escort to the baseball field where senior "Willie" Snape pulled together a pile of Christmas trees and scrap wood at the last minute.

Following a Friday afternoon pep assembly, more than five hundred spectators packed the gym. The JV team did its part, whipping Blair 14-9. The varsity came out flat, trailed 13-7 in the first half but made it close at the end, losing 31-30 to the "Red Blazers." It was the first time Blair had defeated B-CC at home.

After Danny "Nails" O'Brien and Charlie Johnson left at early graduation, Coach Ray Fehrman gave up on his man-to-man defense and switched to a zone. The team did better, beat Blair 20-15 in the second game and ended up nine and nine. As Charlie Hughes remembered it, playing a zone in that low-ceilinged gym at B-CC made a lot of sense since there was not much room to shoot when you faced five guys with their hands up. At the end of the season, as usual, Mr. and Mrs. Pyle hosted a buffet supper for the varisty teams and the cheerleaders.

The JV squad, led by Jack Peterson and Dick Pogue, lost its only game to Gonzaga in their old swimming pool-gym but then beat the Purple Eagles at home to end up 13-1.

At the junior high level, Leland swept through its long and difficult schedule and won the County tournament again by downing Montgomery Hills 7-4, with Harvey

McClure getting six points, and then defeating Takoma Park 37-13 to win the title. Bigger and older than most of the other boys, Mc-Clure ran the team. The varsity included eighth graders (Dick Latimer, Kenny Poerstel, and Dick Smith) for the first time, and for the first time, much to the annoyance of some ninth grade girls, eighth grade cheerleaders took the floor.

The Recreation Department followed a Christmas Tournament with a six-team league at the high school gym. Bill Snape kept the gym open and made $5 for seven hours work. His title was "assistant director of recreation;" it looked good on his permanent record card. Snape was one of the busiest and best liked young men in the class of `44. His fellow seniors voted him runner-up to Barbara Hanby as "Best All Around Person" and second to Francis "Turk" Moran as "Most Popular Boy." Snape's Methodist-minister father moved his family to Williams Lane in Chevy Chase in 1936 to become executive director of Washington's young Goodwill Industries program.

Bill grew up playing with the kids from Rollingwood and Martin's Additions in the pastures that became the Hamlet, in Tom Perry's side yard and on the big lot behind "Uncle Frank" Simpson's sawmill where they sometimes dammed up a stream. "They had a huge grape arbor back there," Snape recalled. "Jimmy Varela and I learned how to smoke down there; grape leaves, sawdust, Indian cigars, anything." They skated on the pond at Rossdhu Castle, and in Rollingwood "we could start at the top where Summit is and make it to the creek on our sleds. If it wasn't frozen, we could go over that small bridge."

Snape went to Chevy Chase Elementary for two years.

Ocie Dodd, my 5th grade teacher, she was great, and Mrs. Singles taught us in 6th grade. The patrol was the big thing; we got the belt and got out of class early, and then we got to march in a parade down Constitution Avenue. I remember the Maypole dance. Between the two buildings they set up a whole pageant.

Bill Snape also recalled that "field day was big deal. We spent a lot of time practicing for a little medal." And he remembered summer ball games on the playground that sometimes ended with a broken window in the east building of the school or a ball lost up on the roof.

Bill had a *Saturday Evening Post* and *Ladies Home Journal* route when he lived on Williams Lane, and then in 1941 his family moved to the house on Stanford Street; it was Elm then.

I had a Post route here. I took over from another boy at mid-term. At Christmas he beat me to some houses with calendars; that son of a gun had gotten there ahead of me.

At Leland, Bill Snape and his Chevy Chase friends finally met Bethesda kids who seemed a little tougher than the ones they walked to school with. He remembered a couple of boys from Woodmont fighting over Mary Dow down in the pine grove, and he recalled Zip Lehr as "a feisty little guy" who during one basketball game had to break up a fight by "picking up Bobby Cremins and carrying him to the office in the back and locking him in."

He also remembered teacher Edmund Burke:

I had him for math. He could look at you and throw a piece of chalk at somebody else and usually hit 'em. He was innovative in that when we did math or science problems, he incorporated current or practical things. We designed a town, called it Tuxedo Junction, using the math.

"I may have had too good a time at high school," said Snape who ranked 114th in a class of 179. He chose not to join a fraternity. "I was not much of a socialite. They did a lot of partying and dancing. I was never a dancer. "Junie" Andrews pushed me to get into Southern Society, but I never did." But Snape was active in many school organizations including the Student Council and as manager of the boys' basket-ball team.

To become manager, you ingratiated yourself with the coach. Managers at that time were responsible for contacting other schools, writing letters, setting up schedules. It was a long-term thing. You were responsible for equipment, uniforms, balls and all the necessary stuff.

Al Vogt was the first one I worked with, but I only knew him for a year. He went into the military. He was really and truly a great guy, and I liked him very much. And he had some damn good ball teams. We used to play McKinley, Central. Red Auerbach was coaching at Roosevelt, and Tony Kupka was down at Wilson. Dallas Shirley was the big ref in the area; he

Manager Snape

worked a lot of our games. The big rivalry, of course was Blair. That was serious business.

As for the faculty, I got along with Mr. Pyle all right. We used to call him "Tom Cat." Dorothy Young was pretty much running things, and Mary Roeming was a person I looked on

with real terror. I didn't want to get crosswise with her. She was a redhead. I avoided her. Kay

Mary Roeming

Greaney was the greatest. She put the fear of God in me; she and Mary Mohler were perhaps the best teachers I ever had at Bethesda. Mrs. Black was good. I never had any trouble with Al Bender. The "Indian gauntlet" where you ran through a line of people with belts, that happened a few times. You accepted it as part of school life. It

happened to me a time or two.

I was always sorry we didn't have a football team when I was there, but we played a lot of pickup games at Meadowbrook or the Rec Center. One game, we didn't have any equipment, of course; Danny O'Brien who lived up on Stanford Street and Dick Latham who lived on Strathmore were in it. I went down first. I cut my lip badly and went down the street to a local doctor who put three or four stitches in it. Danny O'Brien was next. He broke a collarbone, and then Dick Latham broke a leg. We didn't have a rescue squad, and they had to load Dick into his dad's car and drive him down to Georgetown.

Mary Zimmerli was the reason I got thrown out of school one time. Mary and I dated off and on. She was the love of my life, let's put it that way. We had an English class with Mrs. Mohler, and for some reason Mary got chastised

for something; we had been talking or something. "Ma" Mohler blew up; she looked like a pouter pigeon.

After class I went up and said it really wasn't Mary's fault, it was mine. And she said, "Why didn't you say something at the time?" And I said, "I figured you always had something against Mary, so I decided to let you get it off your chest." And she looked at me, and she said, "Ahh, that's it! You don't come back to this school `till your folks come and have a conference." I was expelled, and my poor mother had to come over; my father was out in the Pacific.

The number of gold stars adorning the service banner at the high school increased steadily. At each special assembly the Choir sang and, in most cases, students who knew the dead serviceman spoke about him and attached the star to the big pennant. Angela Darby, Kay Greaney and several other teachers stopped going to those assemblies. Miss Greaney said they were "just too hard to take," and Mrs. Darby added, "You didn't want to cry in front of the kids."

At the February assembly, the gold stars represented Sgt. Frank Coleman, class of `41, a radioman-gunner on a B-17 that crashed

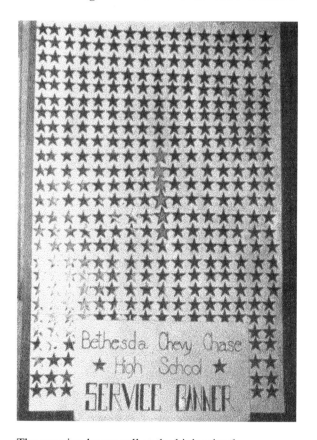

The growing honor roll at the high school

near Sioux City, Iowa; Lt. Robert Ruebsam, class of `36, whose parents had run the Wayside Shop, also died in a bomber training accident; and Ned Kemeys, who would have graduated in 1942 if he had not left school early and joined the Marine Corps. Senior Mary Rogers remembered him as a good-looking, good-natured, happy-go-lucky young man from Garrett Park. Private Kemeys had been wounded in the invasion of Tulagi and then was killed in action on January 28 "somewhere in the South Pacific." He was the first B-CC student to die in combat.[14]

Early in 1944 the County Health Officer, Dr. Ellicott, asked the Commissioners for stricter enforcement of the quarantine on dogs, which by then had been extended into the northern reaches of the County. After some debate, the Commissioners gave the police the power to shoot untagged dogs in some areas and stated that they would have owners of straying pets prosecuted for the first offense.

Following a preliminary meeting in October of `43, several Bethesdans created the Montgomery County Animal Rescue League on February 18, 1944. Its purposes were to care for strays and suffering animals and to prevent cruelty to all animals. Lt. Col. Stanford Chester (USAAF) of Bethesda, became the first president and H. Mortimer Barley of Bannockburn Heights, who had been active in the D.C. League, vice-president. The secretary was Mrs. W. Nelson Oliver of Mohican Hills, writer of the Record's dog column, and the treasurer W. S. Keenholts of Kenwood. Edward L. Stock Jr. was among those named to the board of directors.

In March, the County Commissioners extended the quarantine for three more months and then turned the stray-dog problem over to the Animal Rescue League, approved its four recommendations, and appropriated $1,000 to help it get started. The League had urged the construction of a suitable kennel and runways for sixty animals and intended to use most of the money to rehabilitate the one at the Meadowbrook stables. Second, they wanted to secure competent personnel to operate the pound, and third, provide suitable quarters for a kennel master. They hoped to find a couple and house them in a trailer on the site. The fourth recommendation was to improve record keeping so that

owners would have a better chance of getting their pets back and so multiple offenders could be discovered.[15]

One day that winter Sgt. "Dinks" Rodgers performed a very unpleasant duty, a duty he assigned himself. He knocked on the door of an apartment on Avondale Street and told Isabel Gaither that one of his men, new to the area, had seen Buddy, the dog she had grown up with, on the Catholic school playground and had shot and killed him.

In February, the Bethesda Lions Club embarked on its biggest wartime project, the erection of a permanent "Roll of Honor" to display the names of all those serving in the military from the area covered by Draft Board Number Three. Bethesda's fourth "mayor," Commissioner William H. Prescott, an active Lion, chaired the committee that took on the project, and the Record, Tribune and Journal quickly and eagerly endorsed the idea.

A local architect designed the big signboard with a wood frame, an ornate top and a metal face and estimated that it would cost about $1,700 to build it and then paint some 2,800 names on it. The plan was to list all those then in the service alphabetically and leave space at the bottom to add the names of those who joined or were drafted later.

Selective Service agreed to cooperate, and Mrs. Mader of the Record became treasurer of a fund-raising drive . "Sixty cents will put your own boy's name on the service Roll of Honor" read the front page box on the Record, and soon cash and checks came pouring in. Prescott said any money raised over the cost of the billboard would be used for landscaping. He announced that the planned location was a lot owned by St. John's Church near the intersection of Bradley and Wisconsin.

By spring about half the money was in the bank, but the estimated cost was up to $2,000. Commissioner Prescott manned a post-hole digger and Lions Club president J. R. Enright a long-handled shovel to break ground on the west side of Wisconsin on what had been Willson and Dixie Offutt's front lawn. With the cooperation of manager John M. Plank, the Lions opened a small booth in Peoples Drug Store and signed up the wives of men in the service to man it in the hope of increasing donations.

Jack Eaton watches "Billy" Prescott and J. R. Enright start work on the Roll of Honor

Every week the local papers published lists of the names of those who had been "sponsored." Dr. and Mrs. Emil Bauersfeld listed their four sons. The Frank Magnanellis of Cheltenham Drive also had four sons in the fight, three in Europe and one in the South Pacific. Mr. and Mrs. George Stevens of West Virginia Avenue added the names of their four sons and a son-in-law as did the S. Walter Bogleys of Friendship Heights, and Mrs. Reuel G. Phelps of Spring Street in Chevy Chase had the names of four sons and a WAVE daughter to put on the Roll of Honor. Mrs. Samuel Syme added her husband's name.

The local churches and their women's societies, men's clubs, and young people's groups continued on their usual calendar of liturgical-year observances. Most also participated actively in support of the USO, Red Cross, scouting groups and various wartime charities and activities such as making small homemaker kits for Russian relief, a favorite '44 cause. At the high school, voluntary devotional services took place at lunchtime on Wednesdays with Faye Finley Shaw's A Cappella Choir or the Victory Corps singing group and one of the local Protestant pastors. In February, the *Tattler* noted that these

"devotionals" were poorly attended and that the Choir was a bit embarrassed to be asking ministers to speak to so few.

At the end of March, Chevy Chase Methodist Church suffered $15,000 in damage from a fast-moving fire, which began in the furnace room of the old section of the building. Six fire departments fought the blaze, and hundreds of spectators watched the flames spread to the five-year-old church. Dr. Richmond held Sunday services in the sanctuary as usual, but the young people and junior departments moved across the street to the girls' school until repairs could be made. The organ was not damaged, but Scout Troop 255 lost most of its tents, hatchets and first aid equipment.

Mary Warren donated an illuminated cross to Bethesda Methodist Church in honor of Mary Fulford Foster who died that spring. The Arthur Brookhouse Fosters had come to Bethesda in 1926. Small, plain Mrs. Foster served on the church board and taught Sunday school for a number of years. She joined the Newcomb Club in 1928, set up its scholarship fund and was best remembered for her long and tireless effort to establish a public library in Bethesda. Shortly before she died, Mary Jane Foster held her own funeral and wake. She said that she wanted to see everybody while she was still alive. "It was a great party!" remembered Patsy Lozupone.

The Jewish Community Group under president Joel Wolfsohn began holding regular Friday evening services, often with a guest speaker. David Garrison Berger, the group's vice-president, arranged for the Passover seder and invited servicemen from the Naval Hospital and Walter Reed to attend. Mr. Berger, as vice-president of the local B'nai B'rith, began a campaign for members in the suburbs.

The Bethesda Council of Churches again sponsored Easter sunrise services at the Recreation Center and was rewarded with a beautiful morning. Dr. Gaye L. McGlothlen of Brookmont Baptist Church preached the sermon, and the A Cappella Choir plus a few alumnae provided the music and won praise from Mrs. Bradley for their "dignity and composure" as well as for music as natural as "that of the birds in the nearby trees." Representatives of all the local, evangelical, Protestant congregations took part in the services.

Typical newspaper ad explaining point rationing

The OPA eased restrictions on beef and pork in early 1944 and, except for steaks and roasts, made meat point-free in the spring. A new complication was the introduction of small blue and red ration tokens used as change for the ten-point stamps. The housewives and the grocers now had four different colors of stamps plus light, dime-sized, fiber tokens to deal with. Grocers also collected coffee cans filled with kitchen fat for which the housewife now received four cents a pound plus two brown points.

The salvage drives for fats, cardboard, tin cans and the like continued under the local leadership of Richard Schaefer. In the first three months of the year, he shipped 75,000 pounds of properly flattened tins cans. The

Richard Schaefer encouragesd by the WAVES

Salvation Army collected a ton of newspapers a day after it took over that job, and in March, Cub Pack 211 won the *Post* contest by collecting 24,000 pounds of newspapers. They received tickets to the "Water Follies" at Uline's and got to meet Buster "Tarzan" Crabbe. Meanwhile, Blake Merson's trucks picked up almost seven tons of cardboard and about seventeen tons of scrap metal including a lot of improperly flattened tin cans.[16]

Bethesda's USO found a new leader early in 1944 and continued to be one of the busiest and liveliest places in town. Mrs. J. William Sholar retired as director hoping to have more time to spend with her husband and son, and Marjorie Trayes replaced her. In a *Record* editorial, Mrs. Bradley praised Virginia Sholar for doing "a swell job" in creating a "friendly home-like atmosphere." With a luncheon at the USO clubhouse on Old Georgetown Road, Commissioner Prescott, OCD director Brault, War Recreation Director George Mathews and the Operating Committee welcomed Miss Trayes, a graduate of Ursinis with USO experience in Florida and North Carolina.

The *Record* carried a chatty column under the title "Scuttlebutt of the USO," and the other papers also ran news items and press releases of activities such as the Sadie Hawkins leap-year dance on February 29 and weekly bingo sessions on Thursday nights with a long-distance call as the big prize. In mid-March, the USO sponsored another dance at Woodmont Country Club with music by Jack Morton's orchestra, Stella Werner and her boogie-woogie accordion and Mary Davis's songs, which included "Elmer's Tune," "Three Little Fishes," and "Cow Cow Boogie." Ph.M.1/c Harry Gunnison was the emcee and introduced parts of the popular New Year's revue which had been requested by those who missed it the first time around.

In April, the Rock Creek Council of the Knights of Columbus sponsored the dance at Woodmont with the country club providing refreshments. Mrs. Bradley recognized

refreshments. Mrs. Bradley recognized Woodmont's generosity in an editorial, which concluded:

> Not many clubs have been so generous during the war emergency. The community should be proud to have in its midst a club that takes such an active interest in servicemen.[17]

Almost every Sunday night a church group or woman's club served a supper and presented a program. Mrs. Morell brought Marquis Childs as the guest speaker when she was the hostess, and on another evening Mrs. Milton Miles showed slides of her family's escape through Burma. Rationing limited the menu, but K. O. Lehman of the neighboring DGS donated the food for one extra-good supper. On March 19 despite a wet and unexpected snow, seventy servicemen and women assembled for a dinner served by the Civic Section of the Woman's Club of Chevy Chase. The women left behind four-dozen cups and saucers as a donation to the USO.

When the Advisory Committee served supper, Mrs. Werner and Mrs. Geyser were the hostesses with baked ham and Anna Gingell's potato salad on the menu. Then a quartet composed of sailor Bill Riggins on guitar, Greta Kaylor at the piano, "Little Stella" with her accordion and her father on drums entertained. Stella was there at least once a month, and her mother much more regularly. Mrs. Werner's contribution to entertainment was a palm reading act. "Boy, I would pair them off," she said. "I would describe to the boy the girl over there and . . . ." But her older daughter said that sometimes her mother would not tell a young man what she "saw" in his hand, especially if his life line seemed rather short.[18]

Donations came in regularly. Layer cakes, cookies made by the Camp Fire Girls or Girl Scouts, and Mrs. Luke I. Wilson's big boxes of candies were among the favorites. Just inside the door on the left was a quiet place to write letters and on the right a small library filled with mysteries and piles of magazines. Tickets to plays, ball games and dances were often available and sometimes became prizes in various games and contests. The snack bar was always open.

The hostesses invited visitors to stick a pin in their home town on a big U.S. map in the lounge and sign up in a notebook arranged by states. Soon almost every state had at least one pin in it. In a feature article head-

lined "A Peak Behind the Orange Curtains of the Local USO," Mrs. Bradley urged her readers to visit the club and to contribute. "While the club is for enlisted service folks," she wrote, "it cannot possibly be 'a home away from home' unless the people of the community cooperate in making it such."[19]

> How? First by dropping in occasionally at the club and finding out just what the routine is there. You'll probably see a uniformed lad or so playing badminton with a junior hostess or drinking a cup of coffee at the snack bar, or shining their shoes, wrapping a package, listening to the radio, reading a book, frying an egg if their wishes run in that direction or airing their views with a senior hostess who looks and talks like their Aunt Jane.

Betty Hynes of the *Time Herald* enthused, "Of all the excellent servicemen's clubs we had visited, none has so completely fulfilled the boys' ever present wish for 'something like home.'" She found it serving 3,000 enlisted men and women a month with twenty-two junior and three senior hostesses on duty every night. "The huge living room which extends from street to street, airy with wide open windows, doors and spinning fans, is full of flowers brought in by the neighbors." She wrote that the "habitués" called Marjorie Trayes "Buddy" and that the servicemen bragged about having the "prettiest girls of any canteen in the country."[20]

In 1944, the USO advisory committee met at the home of Mrs. William Morell, its chairman. That meeting was followed by one for all senior hostess at the County Building and then a retraining session for the junior hostesses. Some problems had developed as the number of badly burned and wounded men recuperating at the Naval Hospital increased. Mrs. Hilland, a senior hostess, recalled:[21]

> Two boys brought in a friend who had been terribly burned. It was his first time out, and he still had a long way to go. One side of his face was livid with scar tissue, but the junior hostesses smiled, talked with him, and he had a wonderful time.
>
> Then when we closed, a group of them decided to take him up to the Hot Shoppe. I tried to talk them out of it. He really wasn't ready for that, I told them, but off they went. Well, they went in and sat down, but when a waitress saw him, she dropped a whole tray of dishes right at his feet.

Mary Zimmerli Brown (B-CC `44) said that some of the junior hostesses, especially girls recruited for the dances, had no training at all. "They would just call on you."

It was just kind of to have some females around. I think it would have been nice if they had given us some indoctrination. The boys were a bit older than we were. I didn't find it great fun necessarily, but there were a couple of men from Dickinson College, in ROTC or something, they were quite nice, and Barbara and I did go to Dickinson to see them. I was always at the dances, but I was not on a schedule."

According to her yearbook, Barbara Macy (B-CC `43) was seen weekly "serving doughnuts to servicemen," and her friend Mary recalled that Barbara married a man she met at the USO.

Leslie Bell's daughter Ellen graduated from Immaculata in 1942 and went to college near Philadelphia. "I must have danced ten times around the world at that USO," she said.

I think they just pitched us in, and we fended for ourselves. It was great. They always had dances at Christmastime and Easter time and parties at Wilson's cabin. Our principal place in Bethesda, in that triangle, was nice, and they had dances, every once in a while with a combo. We got the sailors from the Naval Hospital, but also, what a lot of people didn't know, there were anti-aircraft batteries in a circle, well hidden around Bethesda.

USO rules said you didn't leave with a sailor; that didn't mean you didn't meet them later. They came in buses, and if they didn't go back on the bus, it was a fairly long hike.

The USO was a lot of fun. We danced, and that's where I learned to play bridge. All of the girls went. Everybody assumed you knew what to do with a boy. They would pick up a group of us and take us down to the Stage Door Canteen, and to the dances at Walter Reed and the annex at Forest Glen. We didn't always dance over there; we sat and talked with them. You never suggested dancing. We did get enough training not to ask what was wrong with them.

We were helping to win the war. That's how we felt.

In the spring, the sailors, Marines and junior hostesses built and painted window boxes and benches to put out on the sidewalk under a big awning and then painted the out-

side of the building. Anthony Gould of Battery Park let them use his tools and workshop, and Mrs. A. A. Potter donated an armful of plants. Mrs. George Mathews took over the job of planning the Sunday suppers; Mrs. Milton Harris was in charge of refreshments for the dances held every third week at the Woodmont Club, and Mrs. J. Philip Schaefer captained the snack bar operation. Mrs. Theodore Geyser, of the newly formed Hospitality Committee, oversaw all the special programs. Mrs. Sholar took charge of arranging dances for the officers.

As soon as the weather warmed, the junior hostesses organized a softball team and practiced on the Bethesda school's playground. In May, fifty-five girls signed up for the fifth Junior Hostess course taught at the County Building by new chairwoman Mrs. William H. Drum, Marjorie Trayes, and several NNMC doctors including Cmdr. William Gibb who talked to the girls about dealing with the returning wounded. In June, the weekend picnics began.

As the Navy hospital's patient list and staff increased in 1944, the hospital administration asked more and more corpsmen to find rooms "on shore." Wives and families arrived to visit injured relatives or those about to be shipped out, and some men stationed in Bethesda wanted to have their family with them. Mrs. John H. Werner took on the USO room registry and tried to meet a growing volume of requests. The USO set maximum rates ranging from $30 a month for a single bed with a shared bath to $50 for a double room with a private bath and urged those with rooms to list them.

But by the war's third year, there were very few vacant beds in Bethesda, and a lot of backyards had sailors' whites flying from their clotheslines. A few blue-noses and scandal-mongers sniffed and gossiped about the young men staying with widows or women whose husbands were overseas, but most of those providing sailors with rooms, and often breakfast, saw what they did as part of the war effort and ignored their nosy neighbors. Probably a majority of area homeowners gave or rented rooms to servicemen or government employees during the war, and in many cases relationships developed, which lasted, at least in the exchange of Christmas cards and baby pictures, long after V-J Day.

In some homes, servicemen filled the chairs left by absent fathers, sons, or uncles, and the extra money helped families meet the growing monthly bills. Sometimes there were other benefits, too. Sailors could usually get cartons of Camels, Chesterfields or Luckies and Hershey and Clark bars by the boxful.

Bill Snape recalled the Iowa couple, pharmacist mate Joe Shaner and his wife, who lived with his family in Chevy Chase while his father served as a Navy chaplain out in the Pacific. 'They came from Iowa," Snape said with a smile, "so there were chickens out by our Victory Garden in the back yard. You could do that in the war."

The public library reported circulation of 63,441 items, up ten percent for the year. It had 2,992 adults, 409 young people, and 2,443 children who were card holders and counted 11,220 volumes in its collection plus fifty-five periodicals. The library operated new deposit stations at Alta Vista, Bradley, and Somerset schools and at the patients' library in Suburban Hospital. The librarian said in her report that she hoped the library would be housed in its own building in the immediate post-war period.

Bethesda Elementary opened its new school library in mid-March. Sponsored by the PTA, which donated $300 worth of books, the reconditioned second-floor classroom featured a mural painted and donated by Buddy Manley. Mrs. Fred G. Warren chaired the project, and PTA members volunteered as librarians every day from ten until two-thirty. Principal Ruth Clapp praised the PTA and the faculty committee headed by Emily Lehr and Thelma Renfro for all their hard work.

The routines of life went on. A small fire caused some excitement but very little damage at the Chevy Chase Village town hall and post office. The outbreak of scarlet fever at the elementary school created a lot more concern. At Sammy Lee's hand laundry in Warren's old row of stores, they still collected change for refugee relief, but the cost of feeding a Chinese child for a day had risen from four to twenty-five cents. Pop Tate's pool hall in the same row of stores was still a hang-out for some of the high school boys, and for a while Houston Swink (B-CC `45) came in and brushed the tables and swept up

the place. "Eldridge Tate was his name," remembered Swink.

I used to go fishing with him. We got to be pretty good; of course, we shot for free. Everybody went to the pool hall. The regulars included Marshall Johnson and his brother, they lived on Walsh. We called Marshall "Mole' and then shortened it to "Mo," and Herbie Benson, Charlie Hughes. A lot of guys.

Hughes called it:

a social center. If you are going to go out at night, you'd go up there and meet to coordinate your plans. Mr. Tate ran an excellent establishment. I never saw anything going on in there that shouldn't have been. No drinking and no gambling, except on the games.

Roger "Rollo" Spencer, whose favorite pastime, according to the `45 yearbook, was "bumming weeds," had the reputation of being the best pool shot in Bethesda. Houston Swink was at Tate's when Bethesda received one of its fairly regular buzzings.

I can't think of the guy's name, who came down in his Wildcat, F4F; he'd always wanted to buzz Wisconsin Avenue. I thought that rascal was going to strafe us. It looked like you could reach up and touch him. It came down around Bradley and pulled up around East West, I was told. I couldn't see that. Then he peeled off and came around and did it again!

Leroy Allison recalled what he was pretty sure was a P-47 barrel rolling the length of Wisconsin and dipping lowest around Leland Street. Military aircraft flying over the town became an accepted part of wartime life, and it took a pretty loud and low plane to bring people out to have a look.[22]

The Red Cross moved its headquarters to the Jeep House across the street from the pool hall, laundryman Lee and Doc Gellman's drug store. Down across the District Line the

Jenifer Market opened, quickly became very popular and made deliveries to Bethesda on Tuesdays, Thursdays, and Fridays. Percy C. Grady changed the name of his body shop on Elm Street to Grady Motors, and William Bachschmid joined his brother Carl at Carbert's.

Isaac Ganim brought his twenty-four-year-old rug cleaning and repairing business to the Shopping Center and advertised that he employed "expert native weavers." Mr. and Mrs. F. Marion Clark opened a portrait photography studio in the Bowling Center. And in the best indication that Bethesda's business district was still healthy and growing, Malcolm Scates took over M. S. Ginn's Wayside Shop and brought his thirty years of furniture experience to town. A few months later the Julius Lansburgh Furniture Company opened a big store in the shopping center with Hugh B. Carper as manager and W. Earle Royer of Lincoln Street as his top assistant.[23]

Emory Bogley tried again to get the "non-conforming" Community Store, that folks insisted on calling "Brown's," and ramshackle house at Old Georgetown and Greentree rezoned and again gave it up as he had six years previously. He wanted to build a Safeway to serve the Huntington Terrace-Alta Vista area but found most of the area residents opposed the change. He decided to wait for the promised Master Plan.

The Rotary Club reluctantly left Columbia Country Club for the duration since getting help to serve the luncheons was becoming a problem. They presented a gift to Jim Whittingham, the seventy-five-year-old waiter who had served them for eleven years. The Chamber of Commerce installed twelve big trashcans on street corners and encouraged a spring clean up, and at the same time, the Commissioners warned against letting brush fires get out of control since there were a lot fewer fireman at most stations. Carl Bachschmid became president of the Chamber of Commerce with G. W. Imirie v-p and Phil Schaefer executive secretary.[24]

J. Phillip Schaefer

Louise Morell headed the first Early Diagnosis Clinics for the County TB Association, which provided free x-rays for teachers, food handlers and other County employees. Her almost equally active husband, William N. Morell, succeeded Randolph Bishop as head of the Suburban Hospital Association. They had been area residents since 1928, and Mr. Morell, a member of the Board of Veterans' Appeals, had served as president of both the Leland and B-CC PTAs and the Federal Bar Association. He was active in the American Legion and had been secretary of the hospital's board of trustees.

The forty delegates attending the annual meeting elected Mrs. B. Payton Whalen president of the Thrift Shop. In as unsurprising an election as the choice of Mrs. Whalen, Mrs. W. E. Perry, who had been acting chairman, was chosen head of busy Suburban Hospital's Women's Auxiliary.[25]

To help alleviate the nurse shortage Suburban accepted the volunteer help of more than forty high school girls that spring. These proto-Candy Stripers went through a brief

The first spring at Suburban Hospital

training regimen and then worked in the kitchen, labs and on all hospital services wearing brown and white seersucker jumpers over their white blouses. They signed up from 4 to 8 pm on school days, and many volunteered on both Saturday and Sunday. Among the leaders of the high school contingent were Mary Williams, Hope Anthony, and Carolyn Humphreys.[26]

Mrs. Bradley's daughter Jane was another of the early volunteers.

I was a candy striper up there since I lived close by. Barbara Scruggs and I were called one Sunday morning because the dietitian had walked out. We got a meal together, and I remember mashing potatoes with that huge machine. I worked up there three or four days a week; I had tremendous hours. I spent a lot of time walking up and down those corridors.

Before they built Suburban, it was Whalen's apple orchard, and I used to meet Vink there when we were grounded and weren't supposed to. He lived over on Lambeth Road and that was about the halfway point. I'd say, I'm going up to Mr. Brown's store, and that's where we met.

In the middle of the war with all the reports of local men killed, captured or wounded and the newsreel pictures of the fighting on Kwajalein and the bombing of Monte Cassino, the death of one, small boy shocked many Bethesdans. Alan Engle was eleven. Bright, very polite and well-liked by both his teachers and schoolmates, he was perhaps a bit smaller and a bit softer than some boys in the sixth grade, but he played hard at recess and went back to class pushing his shirttail into his trousers like all the rest. He had a *Star* paper route and worked hard at it, and he was a dutiful altar boy at Our Lady of Lourdes where he also went to school. He was a sixth grader.

Fifty years later Sister Ellen Glynn said:

I remember where he sat in the classroom. I had charge of the altar boys. Gad, it was rough, to think about even now. He was lovely fellow, a fine boy. He came to me and said, "I want to serve Mass all during Lent. I want to take the 6:30 Mass." And I said, "Alan, it's too hard." Well, he begged and I gave it to him. He was there on time every day.

And in Holy Week, he was waiting for his Dad to come home, and outside they had a

swing attached to a tree. And he went around this way, and it did him up. It was terrible."

His parents found him hanging from the rope, but neither they nor the firemen who arrived within minutes were able to revive him. Young Alan's death shocked the school, the parish and his Exeter Road neighborhood as no other wartime death had.[27]

At the high school Sgt. Eddie Leahy was back for a visit after nineteen months in North Africa, Sicily and Italy. He had gained fifty pounds on Army chow and once again sported the mustache he had worn all through high school but lost in boot camp. Students placed gold stars on the school's service banner for Lt. John Ligon, killed in a B-17 accident near McDill Field while his parents were on their way to visit him, and for young Bill Graham, one of the most popular boys of the class of `41, killed in Missouri while training to be a Navy pilot.

When Glen Echo opened that April, it had an exciting new ride, the Octopus. In a spring marked by a thunder snowstorm, the Victory Corps for boys from twelve to sixteen revived in the Victory Garden information center at 7353 Wisconsin Avenue and training sessions began at the Rec Center with the help of USDA's Dr. Lefebvre. The Victory Garden committee issued a "Manual" with sixty questions and answers, which it sold for ten cents, and the County once again provided spring plowing at nominal cost. The local newspapers began carrying weekly garden advice columns. When Mrs. Chase Donaldson retired as head of the local program, Ed Stock praised her as "a real dirt farmer." Mrs. Charles F. Baldwin, a volunteer at the Center since its inception, took her place.[28]

On its Farm and Home Hour radio program, the Department of Agriculture named four-year-old James Burgess of 300 Elm Street in Chevy Chase as the nation's youngest Victory Gardener. James, who said he grew tomatoes "because I love them," had a plot in a local community garden as did his eight-year-old brother and six-year-old sister.

As part of the continuing rabies control effort, in early April the County Commissioners ordered the vaccination of all of the County's 10,000 dogs and asked local veterinarians to vaccinate them free of charge. Col. Stanford Chester agreed to work out the

program for the Bethesda area. Soon long, barking lines assembled before the free clinics operating in the firehouses of Chevy Chase and Glen Echo and at the high school gym. The Civic Federation endorsed the strict enforcement of the quarantine and pointed out that despite it being in effect for almost a year, the number of rabies cases had risen from fifty-three in 1943 to sixty-two by April of `44.

A substitute mail carrier in Huntington Terrace must have agreed with the Federation's conclusion that the public was disregarding the law. He was treed by a pack led by a large bull dog and had to be rescued by a postal truck. George Corley, superintendent of the Bethesda post office, said the event was going to make it difficult to find "colored" substitutes for the Bethesda routes.

In an era when crimes were few and seldom serious, the robbery of Whittlesey's Drug Store on the night of April 3-4 created a small sensation. Police discovered the break-in before the store opened. Doc Whittlesey figured out that $1,600 in cash and about $160 worth of billfolds and fountain pens were missing. Sergeant McAuliffe and Cpl. John Leahy, who were the Bethesda Detective Bureau, went to work. McAuliffe recalled that "there was a piece of white paper out in front of the safe. We found out what he took, and he'd left his footprints there all right. We had a pretty solid case on him." In addition to the heel prints, the detectives found a sheet of hotel stationery with a room and phone number written on it in lipstick.

A few phone calls and a few questions produced the name of Mrs. Dale B. Haley, who lived at the nearby trailer camp and worked part-time at the drug store, and a description of her husband. Some more inquiries led to the arrest of the couple in Norfolk on Friday, four days after the robbery. Haley's shoes matched those marks on the wrapping paper, and he confessed. Doc Whittlesey got his gold-filled pen and pencil back, and the policemen received a lot of praise for their quick work including an editorial in the *Record* labeling them "Two Sherlock Holmes."[29]

On May 1, the primary election passed almost without notice. The Democrats' ballot had only the names of four hopefuls and the incumbent U.S. Senator whose job they wanted, Millard Tydings. The Republican ballot was a bit longer with eighteen office-seekers listed, mostly candidates to the State convention. Bethesda's fourteen polling places stayed empty most of the day.

More people showed interest in the first raising of the County flag on May 3 at the County buildings in Silver Spring and Bethesda and the courthouse in Rockville. Lilly C. Stone, who was generally credited with designing the flag based on Richard Montgomery's coat of arms, represented the Janet Montgomery Chapter of the D.A.R., which produced the silk banner. In Bethesda, troops of Boy and Girl Scouts formed the honor guard, and the bands from both Leland and the high school took part. Reverend Albertson gave the invocation; Commissioner Prescott accepted the flag for Bethesda, and State Sen. Thomas E. Hampton spoke.

While the Charter was not mentioned in the primary, it was far from forgotten, by supporters at least. Allen H. Gardner, re-elected president of the Charter Committee, named a number of Bethesdans to important jobs. Attorney James C. Rogers, who lived on Raymond Street, headed the Legal Committee; John H. Crider of the New York *Times*, who lived at Wilson and Broxburn, chaired the Education and Publicity Committee. The chairman of the Finance Committee was Adm. Adolphus Stanton of Chevy Chase, who was also president of the Silver Spring Board of Trade, and John Willmott of Greentree Road led the Research Committee while Randolph Bishop headed the Field Division and Mrs. James V. Bennett chaired the Speakers' Bureau.

Other Bethesda-area members of the board of directors included Adlai Magee, Dr. Oscar F. Blackwelder of Westmoreland Hills, Donal Chamberlin of Kenwood, Dean George E. Hamilton of Stone Ridge, Mrs. W. E. Perry, Ray Tucker, Mrs. Dean Dinwoodey, Capt. Chester Wells and O. M. Kile. J. Horace Smithey remained treasurer of the

Adlai S. Magee

organization. More than half of the leaders of the pro-Charter forces lived west of Rock Creek, and many of them such as Mr. Magee, of the Veterans of Foreign Wars Post 2598, and Mrs. Perry were known and respected County-wide.

In May, the Charter Committee headquarters in the Guild Building opened with Mrs. Werner in charge, and Mrs. Bradley published a history of the movement but continued her neutral stance. Allen Gardner laid out the basic issue: "We want our home rule to be truly representative, reflecting the will of the majority of the citizens rather than the decisions of some unelected political boss." With Stella Werner's help, John Willmott prepared two manuals for precinct workers, which tried to get them to operate in the spirit of door-to-door salesmen.[30]

A pair of local controversies reached critical mass in the spring of 1944. Off and on, for more than a dozen years, several Bethesda business leaders had promoted the idea of the town having its own, separate post office and identifying cancellation instead of being a sub-station of the D.C. post office. Proponents, including some of the leaders of the Chamber of Commerce, pointed to Silver Spring's independent status and argued that surely Bethesda deserved the same "honor." The *Tribune* supported the idea as being conducive to civic pride, and the *Journal* opened its columns to both sides, but in early May, Tom Elward's committee reported that Chevy Chase was not interested in joining such a move and that the $100,000 annual business and $60,000 payroll of the local branch would not leave enough income to maintain the current level of service. Elward also suggested that since most of the people served by the Bethesda Branch worked in the District, it was only fair that the Washington post office share the expenses.

Sam Stonebraker made an "impassioned" plea to "forget the whole thing" and reminded Phil Schaefer and the other Chamber members who supported the idea of the bitterness it had previously caused. Many original tub-thumpers for the plan decided that having the town classified as a "village" with a "third-class" post office would be somewhat embarrassing. They dropped the proposal.[31]

The other confrontation raised more hackles and temperatures and subsided very slowly. It involved the fire department's fifteen years of ambulance service. Annual reports showed that the ambulance made more than two-hundred runs a year, and Bethesdans were used to it and depended on it. For eleven years, ever since John Imirie drove it back from the factory, the same square ambulance, supported and manned by the Bethesda Fire Department, had traversed the community. When the volunteers withdrew their services in 1939, paid firemen began taking out the ambulance although it was common knowledge that Chief Bargagni frowned on this use of his manpower.

In December of 1943, the Fire Board announced that it was seeking the necessary priorities to purchase an aerial ladder truck and, almost as an afterthought, stated that the ambulance would be retired from service for thirty days because of the need for repairs and the lack of men to drive and maintain it. For that month "qualified local operators" would provide emergency service; for Bethesada that meant Pumphrey's Funeral Home.

Glen Echo and Cabin John still had ambulances operated by volunteers, but Dunnington's Chevy Chase First Aid Corps was completely out of business and had sold its Packard to the Kensington fire department. Eleven of its twelve members were in the service, and Judge Michael M. Doyle, Maj. Frank Dunnington, and George V. Graham, the fathers of three members, were trustees of the organization's funds.[32]

Bethesda's fire department was dangerously short of men. As Frank Hall recalled, they "didn't have anybody to take the jobs."

Bethesda Fire Department ambulance

I was only seventeen when I was appointed. I can hear Chief Bargagni right now. He walked out in front of the pumper and said, "Frank, Bill's being drafted into the army." That was my brother, "and he said you might be interested in the appointment." Now see, he saw me at the fire house and knew I didn't run around drinking, and I wasn't acting smart or cussing or carrying on. He said, "How old are you?"

"Almost eighteen," I told him.

In the spring Bill Allen's *Tribune* followed by Gertrude Bradley's *Record* editorially decried the absence of public ambulance service. The Civitan Club undertook an investigation, and then the Lions pounced when Capt. Frederick O. Smith, president of the Fire Board, admitted that the thirty-three-member board had voted unanimously to sell the old ambulance to Takoma Park. Said Smith with some heat:

We sold it, and I still think we did the right thing. Because of the lack of personnel, we were not prepared to operate the ambulance. We tried vainly to sell it to Suburban Hospital. We painted it up for that purpose.

Neither the Lions nor the Civitans were satisfied that "arrangements" had been made with Pumphrey's to have two ambulances at Bethesda's "disposal." There was additional unhappiness when it was revealed that the old ambulance, repainted and outfitted with new tires, only brought $150. Some thought that the tires alone were worth that much.

At the Lions Club meeting, OCD salvage chairman Richard Schaefer pointed out that the ambulance "saved my child's life three months ago, and I would gladly have taken money out of my pocket to keep it here." Judge Brault told the Lions that he was disappointed that the fire board acted "without giving the taxpayers a chance to arrange for ambulance protection." Both Civitans and Lions demanded a meeting with Captain Smith and Chief Bargagni. Indignant and stung by Brault's accusations, Smith agreed but pointed out that the function of the Fire Board was fire protection and that the local board's charter did not mention ambulance service.

William N. Morell, president of the Suburban Hospital Association, joined the "discussion" by stating that while the Association was sympathetic with efforts to improve and extend ambulance service, the

Hospital had no funds under its government grant to buy, maintain or operate an ambulance. The County Commissioners deftly fielded a request to intervene, suggested that the local fire departments should solve the ambulance problem and also noted that they had not agreed to pay Pumphrey's for ambulance runs as some had suggested. In Bethesda, an automobile accident, which left a seriously injured young girl lying in the street for almost a half an hour before an ambulance arrived, exacerbated the situation.

Dr. Bruce Benjamin led the Civitan's delegation which, along with Judge Brault and the Lions, met with the Fire Board. Out of that meeting came a compromise and a joint statement that the Bethesda Fire Department was "as completely equipped for First Aid service at the scene of an emergency as it has ever been and continues the policy of rendering this service whenever occasion demands." The announcement reminded Bethesdans that all fire fighters were trained in first aid and that one of the trucks, which responded to all calls, carried the necessary equipment, including the respirator donated by the Lions in 1941. Pumphrey's would continue to be asked to transport injured people, but the fire truck that carried the first aid equipment was now equipped with a stretcher and could carry a patient in "reasonable comfort."

Despite praise from the weeklies for the leadership shown by local officials, not everyone was satisfied. The volunteer firemen on Fairmont Avenue made it known that they were ready to man an ambulance; the Rotary Club tried to get a movement started to purchase one early that summer, and the Chamber of Commerce appointed a committee.[33]

Park Commissioner E. Brooke Lee called a meeting in early May for the advertised purpose of presenting the first part of the Master Plan for the Western Suburban area. Two hundred packed into the meeting room at the County Building and heard a 45-minute talk from Fred Tuemmler on planning principles and Commissioner Lee's prediction that the population of the area would probably double in the next fifteen years before being told that the plan was not ready. While most in the audience were interested in apartment zoning in the area between Western and Bradley, Lee steered the discussion to more general areas and asked for advice from

local citizens' associations. He passed out maps to the heads of civic groups and clubs, which Donal Chamberlin, among others, refused to accept. Chamberlin said, loudly, that it was the Commission's job to develop the plan for the people's reaction.

The audience went away disappointed, but Mrs. Bradley found the meeting useful and a sign that the Commission was interested in what the residents wanted. Of course, she wrote, "People who don't want apartments just don't want apartments and most of them are not willing to compromise regarding the matter."

Two weeks later, in an obvious attempt to provoke reaction, Lee proposed the development of the whole Woodmont Triangle for commercial use. He also announced that a meeting to discuss parks and roads was planned and that the Commission's decision on the Bergdoll tract zoning would be postponed until the master plan was completed.[34]

During that spring of worldwide anticipation, most of Bethesda went about its usual tasks. Park and Planning organized softball leagues for adults at the Recreation Center, Meadowbrook and Jessup Blair in Silver Spring. The Bethesda league, with 6 pm games, included teams from the Naval Medical Research Institute, NIH, Bowen & Co., and the X-ray unit at the Naval Hospital. The Commissioners found $300 to continue the canning center program and to circulate pressure cookers to those who could not come to Leland JHS, Chevy Chase Elementary, Westbrook Elementary, or the River Road School. Two classes at Leland made it to the Pathe newsreel because they were in sewing and cooking for boys. Attaching buttons, darning socks, frying eggs, and making spaghetti were among the curriculum's highlights.

That spring, B-CC's baseball team spent more time with hoes, shovels and rakes, attempting to get the field in good enough shape to play on, than it did with bats, balls, and gloves, trying to win games. A yearbook survey showed that the students' 1944 favorites included Tommy Dorsey and Harry James, Crosby and Sinatra, Dinah Shore and Helen O'Connell, Bob Hope, Terry and the Pirates, Slingin' Sammy Baugh, the Nat's speedy

George Case, and biology teacher Susan Boyer.

Mrs. Charles Lewis, already the mother of eight children, gave birth to the first twins at Suburban Hospital. *Star* boys took pride in the Pulitzer Prize that front-page, editorial cartoonist Clifford Berryman won although many liked Gib Crockett's sports-section cartoons better. On the first Monday of May, the spring blackout and air raid drill went smoothly with 106 of the 141 auxiliary firemen reporting for duty while at the USO they sang old songs around the piano in the dark. The police team won the Bethesda Bowling League crown by defeating Hare Brothers whose teams gained first place in two other leagues. The biggest movie in Bethesda that spring was *The Song of Bernadette*, which the Hiser showed "at advanced prices," $1.10 for adults, 60¢ for children and 76¢ for service men and women in uniform.

Mrs. Marquis Childs visited the wartime day-care nursery school at Bethesda Elementary. Eighteen two- to five-year-olds, the children of war-working mothers, were being cared for by three teachers in one big room from 6:30 am until 7:30 pm. She described how the youngsters would be brought in from play and fed at lunchtime with the "twos at one table, the threes at another and the four to fives at another."

As each child sits down, he is given a plate of hot food, perhaps spinach and potatoes escalloped with cheese. A teacher sits with each group. Mrs. Bowie has discovered that the youngsters eat better if given their food in courses. As soon as a child has finished his plate of solid food, he is given a glass of milk and some bread and butter. When that is eaten to the last crumb he is ready for chocolate pudding. Those making a rumpus are not served . . . . As they finish, they go down the hall again, then go to their respective cots, take off their suits or dress and shoes and lie down.

Mrs. Childs was surprised that most of the children actually slept despite the "din from the playground outside where the elementary school is having noon recess." She wrote that the staff looked forward to the summer in some ways but wondered "what it will be like out of doors in that blistering sun with no real shade anywhere and no grass." They glanced wistfully at the big trees and green lawns of Edgemoor.[35]

The usual spring elections saw Mrs. Joseph T. Maguire, a former president of the Woman's Club of Chevy Chase, become president of the Montgomery County Federation of Women's Clubs. Mrs. Maguire, admired for her "Know Your County" program, was considered an "ardent Charterite." The Woman's Club of Bethesda chose Mrs. George T. Condron president. She had only lived in Bethesda six years but had been active in the Red Cross and at the patients' library at Suburban Hospital. Job's Daughters crowned Peggy Ann Imirie "honored queen" of Bethel No. 4. County Soroptomists chose Mrs. Betty Tolson of Bethesda as their new president, and Mrs. Irving M. Day became president of the Montgomery Players in a meeting at the Edgemoor Club. Her son, Irving Jr., a B-24 bombardier with more than twenty-five missions, after having been listed as "missing" for six weeks, was a prisoner of the Germans.[36]

Richard B. Barker of Westmoreland Hills moved up to become president of the Civic Federation. He had been honored along with Allen Gardner and Scott Macgill for bringing about the Brookings study. The Civitan Club's new president was King Mularkey and the Rotary's Walter G. Kolb. The Washington Hebrew Congregation elected Theodore D. Peyser of Maple Avenue in Chevy Chase as its new president, and the B-CC Post of the American Legion made Joseph Cantrel commander.

At the high school, the "Fashioned for Fun" column in the *Tattler* stated that "Gathered skirts made out of bright flowered prints to complement those pretty spring blouses are B.C.C.'s favorite fashion these torrid days." And "both teachers and students have been taking advantage of the miracle of leg make up. It comes in many flattering shades but Oh the streaks when it rains!"[37]

And the deaths of young men continued. In March, Sgt. Harry Bort of Woodmont was killed in action in Italy. He was remembered for his years of newspaper delivery, his work at the Tastee Diner and the bad temper that got him thrown out of school. John W. Taylor, 19, died in Italy in May as a member of the Canadian Light Infantry. He left Woodrow Wilson HS after his junior year and went to Toronto to join up. His parents lived on Bradley Boulevard. Ensign James Lee

Oliver, 21, was killed when his Hellcat crashed in California. His family lived on Cumberland Avenue.

The draft call at the end of May was for eighteen white men including brothers Frank and John MacDonald of Williams Lane and one African-American, Gerald W. Hatton, who was among the many fathers called for induction that spring. He had been living in the District and working at the Gun Factory for some time and was enrolled at Howard, but the draft board would not let him change his registration. He remembered that at Draft Board No. 3 they were not listening to requests for delays. "We were told, 'All you boys are going away from here,' and we got a street car token and a one-way ticket from Union Station to boot camp."

Chevy Chase Village asked for and received an extension of the deferment of William Austin, which had been originally granted in December 1943. The request mentioned not only Austin's important service to the town but the fact that he had a wife and three young children. Chevy Chase had less luck with its policemen. Marshall K. Roberson of Del Ray Avenue had been hired in the spring of 1943 to replace Officer Moller when he joined the Coast Guard one step ahead of the draft board. Despite the pleas of the Village fathers, Officer Roberson was drafted in the spring.

The ending of deferments and the calling of older men and fathers led to special problems at the Model Basin and similar facilities. In the spring of '44, thirty-one officers, eight enlisted personnel and 649 civilians including 248 who were draft eligible staffed TMB. The response was the so-called "militarization plan." The idea was to have scientists and skilled technicians assigned back to their jobs after they were called. Those drafted received a "letter of direct assignment," and most went into the Naval Reserve as enlisted men, college graduates as officers.

Anticipated morale problems resulting from enlisted men giving directions to officers never materialized. The "militarized" personnel were a hundred percent in the payroll deduction War Bond program and invested an average of $28.88 each month, about ten dollars a month higher than the Navy average. A special indoctrination course on military customs and courtesy met twice a week for two hours followed by close-order drill

and calisthenics led by the drillmaster, Sgt. Francis Sullivan USMC.[38]

Machine shop technician Jack Widmayer and his brother Lincoln were both drafted back into their jobs in the wood shop at the Model Basin. They had helped build the facility and were charter employees. Jack, who lived "in one of those government houses with a cement floor" in Cabin John Gardens, recalled that the managers had tried "training women, housewives, to take over the men's jobs, but it didn't work out. It was just awful confusion." The only problem he had with militarization was that he had to "work around the clock" and did not get any of the overtime pay the civilians received.

The big news at Carderock in 1944 was the approval of the 1,820 foot extension of the basins for more model towing speed. The Navy allocated $6,432,000 plus another million dollars for the sixty knot towing carriage. The circulating water channel, the only facility of its type and size in the world, was built for about $500,000. The test section carried a stream of water around a fixed model at 11.3 knots. Photography in the superclear, filtered water proved very useful for evaluating submarines and other underwater shapes.

Sunday night June 4, while news of the fall of Rome was still spreading, men served the weekly supper at the USO. Under the leadership of Anthony Gould, they planned on having waffles and sausages with homemade jellies, jams and Maryland maple syrup, and they gathered up all the waffle irons they could find and even arranged to have additional electric circuits installed. The guest of honor was Eleanor Roosevelt who arrived wearing a print dress and a red hat. Mrs. Roosevelt visited all the tables, chatted with the servicemen and women, posed for snap-

shots and signed autographs before sitting down to her waffle and coffee.

Fifteen local "dignitaries" including T. W. Pyle, G. W. Imirie, Clarence Keiser, Dr. Fred Coe, William Morell, and Carey Quinn donned aprons and manned the waffle irons on each table. After supper, the President's well-traveled wife spoke briefly about post-war responsibilities and the exciting possibilities that lay ahead. She warned that all the world's problems would not be over at war's end. When asked, she claimed that her family's favorite Sunday evening supper was scrambled eggs, "a foolproof dish."[39]

Two days later, June 6, 1944, Bethes-dans

Cary Quinn and James Fieser serve the First Lady another waffle and some more coffee

awoke to the news of D-Day, as Allied troops stormed ashore on Normandy beaches in Operation Overlord. Since the "Blue and Grey" 29th Division was deeply involved in the invasion, many Bethesda-area families took special interest in the news. At the high school that Tuesday, Student Council president John "Chigger' Younger led a devotional program featuring a reading of the prayer for D-Day. Thousands went to church throughout the area.

During the week after the fall of Rome and excitement of D-Day, Bethesdans contributed $300 for the growing Roll of Honor, which now displayed the first several

rows of names. Some folks had immediately spotted misspellings and other errors. The Lions quickly promised corrections.

Many Bethesdans had established the habit of regularly giving blood when the mobile Red Cross unit visited one of the local churches. By the middle of 1944, Alexandrina Kalcy had donated fourteen times and persuaded a half-dozen people to join her in regular visits. Lelia Holman, who lived on Hampden Lane, saw it as "a simple way to help the war effort" and had given eleven times, and Raymond Peacock, chief clerk at the post office, had donated nine pints of blood, all of them on his lunch hour. In Chevy Chase the "Gallon Club" grew to thirty-three members.

By the end of the school year, the County had eighty-one teachers in the service, and the school board's banner included a gold star for Lynnbrook teacher Charles Gross, reported missing in action on Tarawa in February. Boy Scout Troop 204, sponsored by Bethesda Methodist Church, chipped in $27.60 to put the names of forty-six former members on the Honor Roll. The Lions had paid the $600 cost of the billboard, and the *Record* had collected $350, but as the names were being painted on panels and a 4th of July dedication was planned, the project was $1,200 short. The Lions set up a collection booth in front of the Roll of Honor, which their wives manned, and Judge Brault made a special plea for donations to honor "the men of this community who are sacrificing so much for us."

June, of course, meant graduations. At Chevy Chase Junior College an alumnae picnic preceded the Drama Club's "As You Like It," and Stringfellow Barr of St. John's College delivered the commencement address. A cable from Paul Banfield highlighted the Landon graduation. Our Lady of Lourdes school had an 8th grade graduating class of thirty-one, and the ninth graders from both B-CC and Leland watched a short play about the UN in the Leland auditorium before receiving their diplomas from Mrs. Morgan.

At Alta Vista elementary, part of the school closing celebration involved praise and presents for the outgoing principal, Louise Walker, who had led the school during its first nine years, and a welcome for first grade teacher Mary Z. Wirth, the new principal. At Bethesda Elementary they honored two long-time teachers, Mrs. Neil McGill and Mrs. Helen McIntyre, on their retirement. Chevy Chase Elementary staged its graduation exercises on the lawn with music by the school band, and at the Glen Echo-Cabin John school the students, parents and faculty celebrated the renaming of their school for Clara Barton.

At the high school, the revived Senior Day teaching had gone well, and now the school prepared to graduate 182 students, 117 of them young women. The administration had each student take home a card for a parent's response to a single question: Is your son/daughter a member of a fraternity, sorority or other secret society or organization? Yes or no. Two girls, Mary Zimmerli and her friend "Sis" Kennedy, checked the "yes" box and had the cards signed.

Mary Zimmerli had not been eager to join a sorority when she was a sophomore.

But they kept asking me, came up to me; Eleanor Woodson kept asking me from time to time. I spoke to my parents about it because I knew the school was not excited about you being in it. After I got into Sigma Theta Phi, I think that was it, I thought they would have meetings and that sort of thing, but we didn't have any of that. What we did was have a slumber party at somebody's house; we'd come after dinner. It seemed strictly social to me. I thought it would be more structured or organized. We didn't give any dances or anything like that. I think there were two and think the other was Beta Sigma, and I think there were two fraternities.

And then came graduation three years later. "I can see the little card," she said, "with one question."

My parents, they signed it and had to indicate yes or no, and I took it in. I was informed when we all began to get ready, I was told I was not going to graduate. No cap and gown, no rehearsals. Maybe they announced it. I don't recall feeling humiliated. I hadn't done anything. I really was more angry then anything. Do they think that Sis and I are the only ones in a sorority? Why punish the person who told the truth? It made me lose a great deal of respect for school.

I went to the prom at the woman's club, and Sis and I discussed what we should do that evening. We decided to go and watch.

Judging from the Greek letters beside autographs in yearbook editor Isabel Gaither's "Pine Tree," B-CC seniors in the class of `44 belonged to at least a half dozen different se-

cret societies. Sigma Theta Phi, in addition to admitted members Kennedy and Zimmerli, had early graduate Jeanne Andrews, beautiful Betty Heyser, B. A. Mauerman, and swimmer Maggie Wisda. Five senior girls including basketball starter Patricia Murphy belonged to Beta Sigma. Two early grads, Bill Sinclair and "Doc" Stringham, were among the members of Lamba Delta Phi. ADS, Chi Alpha and Kappa Phi Sigma also numbered seniors among their high school brothers.[40]

Then there were Job's Daughters. While their dates waited in the Hot Shoppe's parking lot making jokes about the red light burning over the small drug store next to the entrance to the Masonic Hall, the girls held their regular meetings. Isabel Lynch neé Gaither was one of the leaders.

Editor Gaither

They said sororities were out therefore a group of us started Job's Daughters, an offshoot of the Masons like the Rainbow Girls. We joined that and made it popular for a few years in lieu of a sorority.

We met in the Masonic Hall and the terrible rituals; they were absolutely awful, and we were only there to plan the annual Christmas dance or the spring picnic. You were supposed to memorize these things, all the tribulations of Job and so forth. What does that mean to blooming adolescents? And we wore these white robes with, I think, a purple tie around your neck and criss crossed and then around your waist. Being in Job's Daughters was a kind of camouflage.

President Dow   Editor Roth

Mrs. Chauncey B. Hanby and Mrs. Frank Dow, mothers of the class vice-president and president, saved the Senior Prom and Banquet. Mothers contributed the food, and fifteen junior girls volunteered to serve. Barbara Hanby offered the toast to the faculty, and there were several short speeches including one by Bill Snape. Then came the prom and the next Tuesday evening, graduation. Mary Dow made the address of welcome, and *Tattler* editor Bob Roth gave a tribute to "those who have gone before us" and listed the twenty-four members of the seniors' ninth-grade class who were then in the service. The Misses Kennedy and Zimmerli slumped in a back row and watched their classmates receive their diplomas on the well-lit stage.

In many ways the summer of `44 was a good one in Bethesda despite the long, hot, dry spell with 98∞ on June 18 and fifteen July days above ninety. Rome fell; Saipan followed, and the B-29s began to destroy Japanese cities with fire raids. The Nats were in the cellar by June, some defense industries began layoffs, and a horrible circus-tent fire in Hartford killed 167, but the Sunday newspapers were getting thicker and the yearlong rabies epidemic ended after more than 8,500 County dogs had been inoculated.

For some reason, the Ouija board made a big comeback; Borden's "Elsie" rivaled the teddy bear for popularity, and "Mairsey Doats" topped the Hit Parade despite the continuing popularity of hillbilly music and "Don't Fence Me In." A huge display of tanks, cannon, military aircraft and other equipment, both Allied and enemy, spread across the Mall, and an estimated 325,000 enjoyed the bond show and fireworks at the Monument on the 4th of July.

Girls adopted the "Sloppy Joe" look of loosefitting sweaters, pleated skirts and a string of pearls, and some boys insisted on leaving their shirt tails out. Everyone who could wore penny loafers. Silver ID bracelets, the bigger and heavier the better, were the mark of those going steady, a practice widely discussed at PTA meetings.

Eighth grader Jane Bradley, who went steady with Vink Guandolo through both junior and senior high, recalled:

My mother had an account at Jelleff's, and I would go in and Mrs. Jay'd say, "I've got something for you. I'll talk your mother into it."

I used to save up my lunch money, and I got a dollar a thousand for running the addressograph for my mother, and I'd go over to Gretchen Cole's and buy a sweater.

Senior "Isa" Gaither did most of her clothes shopping downtown. "I had Sloppy Joe sweaters, not a lot of them," she said. "It is better to have one good thing, and my nubby knits all came from Gretchen Cole's."

Many kids gathered milkweed late in the summer to replace kapok in life jackets, but spotted fever returned early that year. When an 18-month-old Chevy Chase girl was admitted to Suburban Hospital in late June, she was the fourth case of the week. The War Production Board made Suburban a "depot hospital" for the use, storage and distribution of Penicillin, and the hospital's pharmacist, Alice Odian, showed reporters the brownish, wonder-working crystals made from mold.

The Suburban Hospital pharmacy in 1944

The war ground on, but after the breakout from the Normandy invasion even the most diligent doubters admitted that now it was just a question of time, and "home alive in '45" became the slogan of the hour. Buzzbombs began falling on London. Warsaw burned, but Paris did not. The Japanese lost three carriers in the Battle of the Philippine Sea and in the "great Marianas turkeyshoot" had 345 planes destroyed while downing only sixteen Hellcats. A month later Premier Tojo and his cabinet resigned.[41]

Almost every day the city newspapers carried the pictures of a half-dozen or more local men killed in action, and Gen. Leslie McNair's name joined that list in late July. Pfc. Raymond Sanford Jr. of the 116th Infantry died of the wounds he received in the D-Day invasion. He had been Parliamentarian of the B-CC Class of '41 and a *Pine Tree* photographer. B-24 pilot Lt. John S. Fulks, 24, (B-CC '38) was killed in action over Austria. His wife gave birth to a daughter two months after his death. Lt. William C. Newbold, son of the developer of Glenbrook Village, was killed in a training accident. Pfc. Walter T. Shepard, (B-CC '42), who had lived on Cumberland Street, was killed in Italy early in the summer. His high school friends remembered him for his motorcycle and his love of horses. His neighbor, Marquis Childs, wrote a touching essay called "The Boy Next Door" that described him as "a grand boy, friendly and eager and gay."[42]

Capt. Edwin M. Schmitt, a 25-year-old Marine flier, was killed in action in June in the South Pacific. He was a Wilson graduate, and his family lived on Ridgewood Avenue. William A. Lumsden, a private in the 29th Infantry and the former manager of the Dupont Circle Flower Store, died near St. Lo five weeks after D-Day. His parents, Dr. and Mrs. David Lumsden, lived on West Glenbrook Road and were well known for their 200 varieties of orchids. Tech Sgt. Richard Kehoe died in action during his 45th bombing mission when his B-24 was shot down. Among the wounded was twenty-one-year-old Carroll Willett, a fine golfer at B-CC. He lost his right arm in Pacific combat.

Captain John W. "Bill" Guckeyson was shot down over Germany in June. Other pilots reported seeing a parachute, but his capture was not announced. His grandmother, his mother, Mrs. Mary G. Lynch; and his wife, the former Mary Petticrew of Texas, lived in the Chevy Chase house where he had grown up. Guckeyson, flying "Contrary Mary," his P-47 fighter-bomber, had scored seven kills including the Ju-88 he downed at the end of May to become an "ace." The women on 46th Street waited for reassurance that never came.

Captain Guckeyson

Two other fighter pilots, Lt. Richard Reid, whose family lived on East Thornapple Street, and Lt. Robert Comstock (B-CC `38), whose parents' home was on Montgomery Lane, were also reported as missing in action over France that summer. Reid escaped and made his way back to friendly lines, but Comstock became a prisoner of war.

The Methodists at the little church in Woodmont burned their mortgage, and for the first time were out of debt. Reverend Chandler announced that there was $2,000 in the building fund and that they would build a new church in the immediate postwar period on the property at Huntington Parkway. Volunteers staged several "clearing days" to prepare the lot. Christ Memorial Church, which met at the Bank of Bethesda building, changed its name to Bethesda Christian Church. The Jewish Community Group arranged to transport Bethesda-area children to a summer camp at 16th and Que.

The high school's third, seven-week, summer school session drew 250 students, seventy-five percent of them males, and the evening adult education program with courses in typing, slip cover making, and Spanish was also popular. Lynnbrook and Bradley cooperated to stage a summer day-camp on the Bradley school grounds, and the Glenbrook Cooperative Nursery School moved from the high school to Lynnbrook for its summer session. The Chevy Chase PTA sponsored a program for more than a hundred children at their school, which featured softball, archery and for a while, weekly swimming at Glen Echo. The biggest summer program, as usual, was at the Rec Center under Louis Mitchell's direction where more than 500 enrolled the first week. He hired Carolyn Throckmorton, Dick Latham, Mary Dow and Barbara Hanby as assistant instructors.

Swing Grove announced three summer band dances with the teenage canteen open every Tuesday and Friday night. One of the big Rec Center activities that summer was a newspaper salvage drive with squads of youngsters scouring their neighborhoods as the drought and heat continued into August.

Charlie Hughes helped run the summer program at Westbrook Elementary.

It was for anybody that wanted to come over. We had badminton and all sorts of games. I knew it was going to be the last summer I could

do anything so I decided it might as well be some-thing I enjoyed. I looked forward to taking the kids swimming at Glen Echo, but we couldn't go because of the polio epidemic that summer.[43]

Blue Birds and Camp Fire Girls began signing up for ten-day sessions at Camp Mawavi, tuition $17 plus $5 bus fare, and more than a hundred Boy Scouts enrolled for two weeks at Camp Theodore Roosevelt on the Chesapeake, $10 per week plus three red and two blue ration stamps. The Thrift Shop ended its year with a white elephant sale to benefit the Lay Health Committee and the Suburban Hospital Auxiliary and then closed down for July and August. Its profits since October `43 totaled $5,500. With support from the Chamber of Commerce, the Red Cross Jeep House opened again with the emphasis on classes and activities for girls. Its new home along with the Red Cross HQ was at 7508 Wisconsin Avenue where Peggy Evers was among the girls who made stuffed animals for Children's Hospital and Christmas decorations for men overseas.

Cleo Sullivan, who ran Jeep House that summer, was also a Girl Scout leader and a senior hostess at the USO. Once she complained to a reporter that she had "a brand new set of clubs and six prewar golf balls" but had not had a chance to play for two years. At the Woman's Club of Bethesda, Mrs. Arthur Hilland, War Service Chairman, planned an expanded program of activities and offered the club's facilities to the USO for dances and parties.[44]

On a Wednesday night at the end of June, the USO staged another Woodmont dance with Jack Morton's music and followed that with a barn dance on Saturday and a berry picking expedition on Sunday. The next Sunday, the Girls Friendly Society and the Women's Guild held a picnic supper for the USO on the St. John's Church lawn with Sen. George Radcliff as the guest of honor. The weekend after that featured a boat trip to Mount Vernon followed by a supper of fried chicken and homemade apple, chocolate and lemon pies sponsored by the Farm Women's Cooperative Market.

Bonnie Mason Throckmorton (B-CC `40) began coming to the USO every Friday evening and making portrait sketches, a service she had been performing at the D.C. Stage Door Canteen for some time. Table tennis champ Caroline Wilson put on an ex-

hibition and then played against all the servicemen and women willing to challenge her. Battery Park made its tennis courts available every Tuesday; the free bingo games took place out on the sidewalk "terrace" on Thursday nights, and Georgetown Prep opened its golf course to servicemen through the USO. The center also acquired a mascot, a red cocker spaniel called Butch, who became the focus of attention with a "work detail" list posted for those wishing to take him for walks.

One of the big changes for Bethesda during the summer of 1944 took place at the County Building where ailing Captain William LeRoy Rodgers finally retired on half pay, $125 a month, and Sgt. James S. McAuliffe was promoted to take his place. Corporal Jerry Hobbes, who had gone undercover investigating the carbarn murders, replaced McAuliffe as sergeant, and Corporals Leo Day and William Whalen took over the Bethesda detective bureau. Big Les Thompson became a corporal, and Charles E. Benson of Cabin John was the new desk clerk. The entire County police force went on three eight-hour shifts instead of the old ten and fourteen system.

Captain McAuliffe's appointment received universal praise. The general consensus was that "Rix" had earned it. The new commander, only 38, had been on the police force since July 1929, survived being labeled the Fusionists' boy, served in almost every possible capacity and had taken all the FBI training available. He now supervised twenty-seven officers and three clerks but remembered when Bethesda was patrolled by three policemen on Harley Davidsons. Now the Bethesda district was easily the busiest in the County, handling 600 calls a month.

Congratulations poured in, and the local papers added their praise. McAuliffe expressed his appreciation and said, "We have a good, clean community here, and I want to keep it that way."

His son Jim remembered:

The family was tremendously pleased. Dad had worked hard, and when they made him captain and put him in charge of the station that was our home, it was a great day for the McAuliffes.[45]

James S. "Rix" McAuliffe

Rear Admiral Charles W. O. Bunker, commanding officer of the National Naval Medical Center since it opened in September 1942, retired to his home in Edgemoor and his second-in-command, Captain John Harper, replaced him. One of Admiral Bunker's last duties was to preside at the graduation of a class of forty more Gray Ladies who received their veils and diplomas on July 6. A member of that class was Mrs. Lewis B. Sims who had lived in the D.C. area since the 1930s.

I came east from Chicago to live with my sister and her husband and to go to GW. We married only five months after we met and that changed things quite a bit. We both went to GW at night and worked during the day. Then we were up at Harvard and Radcliffe for roughly a year, and we lived on the stipend he was given, $1,500. We economized like crazy. This was `37, `38. I think we went to two concerts that year and one movie. It was mostly intensive work, but it was very stimulating.

In 1941 the Sims had George Hatley build them a house in Rollingwood. Lewis Sims recalled:

We moved in on February 7, 1941. Brennon Lane was a dead end up there, and the

Cummings farm was from there on, and there were some cows over there. We found out when we moved here that this had been the dump for the Cummings' farm. Mr. Hatley lived right across the street, and Brennon Lane came from his mother's maiden name; that's why it's spelled with an "o." We came from California, and I told him that what we would really like was a house all on one floor. "Oh Mr. Sims," he said, "you never could sell it.""

Grace Sims returned to her story:

When the war came, I decided I had to do some volunteer work, and I took courses in order to be a Grey Lady. There were many of us, and it was very interesting. Mrs. Gude was one of the great Grey Ladies. She was a dear, dear lady. She had the library carts.

They picked some of us out to work in locked wards, called NP wards. That was a great experience. The wards were F6 and C4 on the lower deck, and for the WAVES they were down below, wards 137 and 138. They were locked, and when you would go in, the nurse was always in a cubicle, well protected, and the corpsmen, it seemed to me, did all the work. I was doing some crafts, and at that time I played the piano a lot. They had a little piano, not a full keyboard by any means, and they would wheel it in. I happened to play by ear then, so if they could hum a tune, I could pretty much play the song, and some of them would sing. They were very receptive.

Eventually, the Red Cross let me bring a little recording machine. We had these little, tiny discs, and they all wanted to make a record and send it home. One boy said, "Mom, I'll be home this weekend." They wouldn't let me send that one out because he wouldn't be home. I was there a long time; Saipan, Tarawa, all those Pacific battlefields. The boys in those wards were in terrible shock. One Marine, Steve, was there eighteen months. He had a steel thing in his head. The Naval Hospital was known for that kind of work, neurosurgery.

It seemed to me I was there all day. I drove; Lew car pooled. Then I was there two or three days a week. We didn't go out much otherwise. Once we went in tuxedo and a long dress to the Shoreham Hotel on the bus. I had a bike with a basket on the front. I rode to Bethesda to the Farm Women's Market. I felt I was doing my patriotic duty to get a chicken and things.

Later someone came and asked some of us if we would be interested in doing this kind of work, not really the same, a different type work,

at an unexplained area. They didn't tell us where or anything. We would have a little more training for that. Mary Cahill and I volunteered. The Army would come here in a car to pick me up and then Mary Cahill in Spring Valley on the way to Congressional. Once they sent a jeep, that was fun. We were told that we could never go there on our own. We must wait for the car to pick us up and bring us home. We thought that was pure luxury.

The rules were very, very strict. We had to eat with the officers, but we mostly dealt with the enlisted men. The idea was that we should do what the boys wanted to do. They were there for R&R. If they wanted to play ping pong or cards or bridge, just be available. The training was mostly about rules, one thing was don't accept anything from the enlisted men. That was hard not to do. Keep your mouth shut, don't tell people where you were, you shouldn't say Congressional County Club if people asked you.

The boys loved when Mary Cahill and I came. She was older and a rather well-to-do person, and we always stopped at Wagshal's Delicatessen in Spring Valley, that wonderful place. They had a certain kind of candy that was very expensive. It just had everything in it, and she would buy a big box and take it to the boys and set it on the table. They looked forward to our coming. She was a very attractive lady, very blonde. There were no other young women there. They really thought, God, an American girl, and they made comments, but they saw my rings. They were thrilled to see us, that was kind of fun; we were clean and our hair was decent and so on.

We went out to OSS, it could have been two or three days a week, I don't remember. But the food was very good, things like roast beef that we weren't having at home. They were well served out there, elegant. One day I particularly remember, they had flown back from the CBI theater of war, all these people at one time. There must have been a hundred of them, and the place was overrun with men in battle fatigues, and they were being processed, their clothes were being taken to be burned, and they had to be deloused and everything. They were brought directly; I never did understand why they didn't let them be cleaned up before they got there.

Once they were dressed in clean clothes and things, that's when they would come out and talk to us. They wanted to give us all kinds of things. One guy showed me a pen that was some kind of knife and a lot of souvenirs, a wrist-

watch they had taken off somebody. But they especially wanted to give us home phone numbers and asked us to call home. We were not allowed to. One boy forced some foreign paper money on me. He said, "I have no use for it, take it." Japanese paper money, I think. It was a very interesting time. Complete bedlam.

One boy, most were gay and happy, but they couldn't call home for three days until they were debriefed, one boy was from Illinois, Oak Park, and he was in a real bad way, in shock. He had to be transferred to Walter Reed, ward 40B I think it was, which was locked, too. He had talked to me and when he found out I was from Chicago, he followed me around. He begged me not to let his mother come and see him there. He told me somebody had beheaded a Jap and brought it to his tent and showed him the Jap head on a bayonet.

They had sort of gutted Congressional at that time. That place didn't look like it does now. The boys weren't there very long, new faces all the time; the guy was gone next week, the one that wanted to play bridge.[46]

I was at the Naval Hospital on D-Day. We were called into the chapel for a service conducted by chaplains. We were just stunned. It was very sad. The other day that I recall so vividly was once between Silver Spring and the Naval Medical Center there were 118, I don't know why I remember that number, 118 ambulances that brought back patients, the wounded ones, I think from Europe. We hustled around getting toothbrushes and toothpaste for each one.

It was late on August first when 129 wounded men arrived at Bethesda's naval hospital. Up until that time it was the largest single intake of patients. They were part of the more than 600 returned from France aboard the hospital ship *Refuge*. It took about an hour to unload the train, which carried the fifty-four stretcher cases and other injured seamen dressed in an assortment of whites, khakis and fatigues. A few still wore their steel helmets. They loaded a long line of grey ambulances, trucks and busses for the trip across East West Highway. Many smiled and waved despite their wounds, and one casualty thanked the photographer for asking a nurse for her name and address after he took their picture. He had been trying to get that information since he boarded the train eight hours before.[47]

The summer of `44 was also the first for "Doc" Gellman's family at their new home in Edgemoor. After ten years of making the trip from Upshur Street and then Farragut Street and surviving the competition of Whittlesey's, Harry Gellman's little store was making enough that they could move. Now the pharmacist could walk to work, and his children, excited when they first saw the Edgemoor Club across the street, could sit on their front steps and watch the kids playing in the swimming pool and on the tennis courts. "We felt like outcasts," said younger daughter Ruth, who was seven when the family moved to Denton Road.

And our friends in D. C. had all said they guessed they'd never see us again once we moved to the country.

But we had nice neighbors. And later a committee came and told my father that they had decided Jewish people could join the club. He refused. . . . Well, we were disappointed.

Skinny Pugh still made shakes and sandwiches, and the pin ball machines still helped with the overhead, but son Arthur, a February graduate of Roosevelt High School, was in the combat engineers instead of working on the soda fountain and oiling the floor every week. The Gellmans hung a star in the window of their new home. Horace Smithey was one of Doc's regulars, and they often lunched together over at the Tastee Diner. Fred Offutt still came in every day for a White Owl cigar, and youngsters like Jim Quinn nursed a cherry Coke as long as they could while they read the newest *Batman* or *Captain America*. If he had made a quarter or so carrying out bags of groceries at the A&P, Jimmy might even buy the comic book.

C&P delivered the new phone book, streamlined for war use with four columns per page, to 15,600 subscribers and collected the old books for salvage. The Bethesda Hot Shoppe advertised for waitresses and offered "$35 per week guaranteed plus meals," and the Tastee Diner had jobs for white countermen, waitresses, dishwashers and short order cooks while the "Ship's Service" ad for similar jobs at the NNMC did not specify race. Harvey Dairy's ad was for "mature" milk route salesmen, and Bowen and Co. had jobs for those who could do "wire assembly work on radio devices."

As the drought continued, the fire departments once more came to the rescue of

Chief Sackett and the CCFD pumping water from Rock Creek onto the Victory Gardens at Meadowbrook

Victory gardeners with thousands of gallons of artificial rain. It was not until late August that the area received any heavy downpours.

Grady Motors became Bethesda's Hudson dealer, and Simmon's Bethesda Motors changed to a DeSoto dealership. Marvin Simmons believed that Dodge would specialize in trucks after the war and that there would be a bigger market for the upscale DeSoto. The dispensary increased the whiskey "ration," except for Scotch, to a fifth every fifteen days instead of one each month.

As many of the normal summertime activities occupied Bethesdans, the town continued to grow and prosper. A co-op store began with a meeting at the home of Mr. and Mrs. Francis Goodell and the support of the Washington-area Rochdale Cooperative. The co-op decided to rent the store next to Whittlesey's, most recently the House of Fashion. A deepfreeze operation announced that it also would soon open in the Shopping Center.

The midsummer dance at the Rec Center was a success with the proceeds going to the furnishing fund. Vink Guandolo won the door prize, a three-pound box of Gifford's candy, and his girlfriend, Jane Bradley, recalled the dances as "awful, just packed" but said that the kids "really danced" and did not just stand around talking.

In mid-July Suburban Hospital admitted its 1,000th patient. That month the Emergency Room treated a hundred accident cases.

With War Bond sales lagging, the Civitan Club staged a bond bingo and auction on the 4th of July on the parking lot in front of the unfinished Roll of Honor. Haberdasher Tom Elward and John Smith of the House of Furniture chaired the event and radio "personalities" Russ Hodges and Art Brown ran the auction. The Civitans sold over $10,000 worth of bonds.

The Red Cross honored Mrs. Joseph E. Bishop, 87, of East Woodbine Street for her years of hard work. She had started by picking lint during the Civil War and then had knitted for the Red Cross during the Spanish-American War and World War I. So far in the Second World War, she had made 114 articles including afghans, sweaters and scarves.

Charles Hurley, who had lived at 4401 Montgomery Avenue since he brought his bride there in 1916 and had worked for the post office since 1907, became superintendent of the Friendship Branch for the second time. Hurley had been Chevy Chase's first and only mail carrier in 1913 and recalled serving the 125 houses from the District Line to Bradley Lane with a horse and buggy. From 1920 until 1925 he headed the two-man Friendship office and then returned to Chevy Chase as superintendent from 1925 to 1936. In his new post Mr. Hurley supervised the work of eighty-four employees.

Another era passed when William S. Bowling purchased the Wheatley's "Moreland," the family's year-round, eighteen-room home since the turn of the century. One of the Wheatley daughters, Francis Borden, wrote a poem about her old home. She and her sister, Mrs. A. B. Veazey, lived in the house they built on Marion Street when the property was subdivided six years previously.[48]

During the summer, a small group of high school boys led by Bill Metzel began the final phase of a two-year campaign to create high school football team. For as long as any one could remember, uncorroborated rumors circulated that a governor's son had died playing football or that some boy up in Western Maryland had been killed in a game. Whatever the reasons, there was very little public high school football in Maryland and none in the County. Soccer had been a popular substitute for many years.[49]

Many young Bethesdans played for D.C. public or private schools. Landon and

Georgetown Prep had teams, and Devitt Prep had recently become a popular refuge for Bethesda's would-be gridiron stars. Both the State and local school boards were believed to be opposed to the sport, and B-CC's longtime principal, Thomas W. Pyle, was also known to be against the school having a football team. Mr. Pyle was, undoubtedly, one of the most respected men in town, and it took some courage to go against his recognized position.[50]

Bill Metzel

Tall, lean, and hard working, Bill Metzel became president of Hi-Y as a junior and made adding football to the school's athletic program the revived club's top priority. Hi-Y, which Mr. Pyle did support, successfully recruited a number of athletes such as Al Pettit, Jim Rehlander, Herbie Benson and other student leaders. "It was a very active group," member Art Wood recalled.

Bill Ray was a big athlete there and Chet McCall and Charlie Hughes, he was great. We were very anxious to get B-CC in the limelight. It was a combination of efforts by the teams and the Hi-Y group to get football. We knew it was going to be a very difficult job because of the political situation.

Chet McCall

Crewcut Hi-Y member Chet McCall solicited the support of his father, then president of the PTA, and the boys found in him an important ally. Little Bill Mizell, voted "best natured" by his peers, talked up football in his many activities, and respected younger athletes such as sophomores Roger Parkinson and Glenn Ferguson drummed up enthusiasm among their classmates.

In the spring, the YMCA sponsored a two-day model legislature in Annapolis. B-

Art Wood

CC sent junior Arthur Wood as its senator and senior Prentiss Childs, Marquis Child's son, along with juniors Harold Sutton and Thomas Gittings as its delegates. In the Senate, Art Wood introduced a bill "providing for tackle football in those high schools which do not have it," and Hank Childs did the same in the House. More than a hundred bills were introduced and referred to committee, and few made it to the floor for a vote. The Wood-Childs proposal was changed to a resolution, approved by the committee and then unanimously adopted by both houses. B-CC's delegation came home in triumph, and in the *Record* Mrs. Bradley predicted a bright political career for cartoonist Art Wood.[51]

The next week the *Journal* jumped on the football bandwagon and became the boys' most consistent booster. Editor Goins allowed that football "is a fine institution. It makes for manliness, discipline and self-reliance." He noted the Boys' Government endorsement and added that a team would be an asset which "advertises the community." At a Rec Center meeting, the youthful leaders organized field and finance committees.

For Bill Metzel and his friends, the next step was seeking support and funds from the business community since Mr. Pyle had made it clear that cost was part of the problem. Over the years this had become a common manner of raising funds to support athletics at the Recreation Center, and Leland teams had used it from time to time for extras such as warmup jackets.[52]

Art Wood was one of those soliciting the help of Bethesda merchants:

We went to Carbert's, and Eastham's Esso, and Leon's, Peoples, the Fire Department, all the business people. We went to parents, raised it from the kids, and even from the school, members of the faculty. Tom Pyle said we couldn't do that and made us give their money back. He gave us a very hard time during that whole period.

"It was a well-organized operation" Art Wood said. "It went very smoothly, and everybody worked their butt off. We spent all of our outside time on it." Bill Metzel remembered, still with a bit of surprise in his voice, that the boys even went to Mr. Pyle's home for a meeting, "something that was never done."

During the summer the would-be football players sold "booster tickets" totaling $1,200 worth of pledges, enough to cover the cost of very plain uniforms and basic equipment for about thirty players. Then, as Art Wood recalled, "We went over Tom Pyle's head to the superintendent of schools. And we got his support, and Pyle was sort of caught in the hole, and he backed down." Mr. Pyle agreed to establish an Athletic Board to consider the question as soon as school began in September, and Dr. Broome scheduled to a meeting at B-CC on September 15.

The long-simmering political struggle over the proposed Charter began to percolate early in the summer. The *Record* and then the *Journal* opened their columns to the League of Women Voters, which at first prepared both questions and answers about the document and later responded to readers' inquiries. Since the League was on record as endorsing home rule and since it was fairly well known that many of the Charter's most ardent signature gatherers and supporters were League members, many were surprised how long the other side held its peace.

Through the summer Bethesda's three newspapers provided Mrs. Bradley's generally sympathetic view, a seemingly neutral stance by newcomer Goins, and Bill Allen's consistent support for E. Brooke Lee and the status quo. In late June, the Washington *Post* rejoined the fray with an editorial which recognized Bethesda's role in producing a majority for reform and praised the Charter writers for "a good job" and the Charter Committee for "attempting to make certain that every voter in Montgomery County understands the issue." The *Post* essay concluded:

We wish the outlook for the modernization of the District government were half as bright as the outlook for setting up a modern charter in Montgomery County seems to be.

On into July the LWV columns ran, and Charterites made the circuit of clubs still meeting despite the heat. At the end of the month, the Civil Service Commission ruled that Federal employees could take an active part in the home-rule campaign without violating provisions of the Hatch Act. Mrs. Werner emphasized that this ruling demonstrated the non-partisan nature of the Charter effort, which, she said, "is sponsored by men and women of both political parties and has only the objective of modernizing Montgomery County's governmental system."[53]

On Friday night, August 18, Brooke Lee's attorney Roger J. Whiteford, a County resident since 1906 and the 1944 commencement speaker at the University of Maryland, fired the first salvo for the antis. He told a meeting of the Farmers' Association that he found it "inconceivable" that the voters "could possibly vote to turn the county's affairs over to a group of nonpaid theorists who would serve the county in their spare time." He said that his reasons for opposing the Charter included the fact that Silver Spring and Bethesda would control six of the nine seats on the new Council, the hiring of a powerful County Manager and the manner of lawmaking. Whiteford said it would kill the two-party system, slow road construction and double expenses. He labeled the pro-Charter forces "a minority group."

Alice Hostetler, who had helped draft the Charter, answered Whiteford at the meeting and pointed out what citizens had recently accomplished without pay such as conducting the War Loan drives and serving on the Selective Service Boards. She emphasized the importance of home rule and suggested that the Charter would end the "Annapolis mysteries" of unwanted legislation.[54]

On Monday night, August 21, a small group of influential citizens met at the Kenwood Club and organized the Citizens' Committee to Defeat the Charter (CCDC). They chose a temporary chairman, named Mrs. Jesse Nicholson, Arthur "Dutch" Bergman, and Richard C. Musser to a nominating committee, and announced that they would open their headquarters at 8001 Old Georgetown Road and have OLiver 8001 as their telephone number. The committee's executive secretary, treasurer and spokesman was Albert E. Brault. In his first public statement, Judge Brault, known and resepcted as leader of the local Civil Defense organiza-

tion, emphasized that the committee was strictly nonpartisan and would welcome contributions from all those "who wish to save their homes and their pocketbooks from the imposition of the Charter." He said that the proposed home rule framework was the brainchild of a group of professors with "no practical experience in the problems of local government," people who were bent on the abolition of the two-party system.

Among the Bethesdans listed as founding members of the Citizens' Committee were Craddock Goins, Jo Morgan, W. L. Lebling, H. King Mularkey, George Price, Albert Walker and Thomas Lewis. Chevy Chase residents on the Committee in addition to Mrs. Nicholson and Dutch Bergman included Lew Mohler, Wendell Combs and Robert Dunlop. Joseph Giammatteo and Norman Davis of Glen Echo were also Committee members.[55]

At the end of August, Roger Whiteford, one of the most diligent antis, told the Bethesda Civitan Club, which had heard Mrs. Werner the previous month, that "If you ever vote in this outrageous bureaucracy, you can never vote them out." Whiteford claimed that County taxpayers were getting more for their money than any place he knew and said that it was no time "to put in a bunch of professors and theorists."

Allen Gardner, leader of the pro-Charter forces, concluded that the "political bosses" were becoming "more than a little worried." He labeled the Citizens' Committee a "masquerade" and Judge Brault a tool of the machine that employed him. Gardner pointed out that the Charter ideas were "far from being untried" and emphasized that home rule would mean laws being made in Rockville and that a County manager "would give the county more efficient, economical management just as it has in many other places."

Brault responded to what he characterized as "a slur and smear" by citing his thousands of hours of local Civil Defense work. The long-anticipated Charter battle was finally joined.[56]

As summer ended, FDR surprised few by announcing that he would accept nomination for a fourth term, but he did allow the party to change vice-presidential horses in midstream and added Harry S Truman to the Democratic ticket in place of abrasive Henry Wallace. The Republicans countered with

Governor Dewey of N. Y. and Governor Bricker of Ohio. Newspaper headlines told of school children leaving London to escape the buzz bombs and of the death of Theodore Roosevelt Jr. shortly after he participated in the Normandy invasion. In Bill Mauldin's "Up Front" cartoons in the *Daily News*, Willy and Joe slogged into France while Roy Crane's Buz Sawyer and Roscoe Sweeney fought the Japanese from a carrier deck on the comic pages of the *Star*. Crockett Johnson's quirky "Barnaby" comic strip in the *Post*, which featured a fairy godfather named O'Malley, rivaled Jerry Kluttz's "Federal Diary" but not Milt Caniff's "Terry and the Pirates" for popularity.[57]

Forty young men and ten young women were graduated from the high school's summer program including ten boys and three girls from B-CC. Landon also graduated three classes in 1944: seventeen in February, eleven in June and four more boys in August. The Montgomery Players planned for a new season with shows at the Naval Hospital before each of their four plays opened on the big Leland stage. Working three nights a week, the men and women led by Mrs. Vance Johnson, wife of the Chicago *Sun* Washington correspondent, canned 19,000 pints of food at Leland in two months, an average of 130 pints per family.

Robert Eastham lost a finger when his hand was crushed at his service station. His neighbor and competitor, Sinclair dealer Emil Critchfield, rushed him to Suburban Hospital. Across the street Lois Hall Roberts moved her lending library, best sellers and children's books into a small store of her own in the Shopping Center. The bowling leagues got their seasons rolling as the town moved into another fall.

At the high school, true to his word, Principal Pyle created an Athletic Board to deal with the football problem Bill Metzel and his buddies had created. The faculty representatives were coaches Ray Fehrman and Helen Randels plus shop teacher "Buck" Bender and history teacher Watson Phillips, the Student Council sponsor. Charles Hughes and Chester McCall represented the parents and new PTA president Bushrod Allen attended all the meetings. The student members were senior Chris Chappell and junior class president Glenn Ferguson. The committee endorsed going ahead with the

sport and then sought Superintendent Broome's support. It also approved additional fund raising, and PTA treasurer Eda Brewer of Custer Road took charge of that. In mid-September Dr. Broome approved petitions from B-CC and Sherwood and forwarded them on to the State BOE where rubber-stamping took another six weeks.[58]

Late in August, led by Chet McCall and Glenn Ferguson, some boys had started practicing, and more than sixty candidates showed up for the first official practice. Their coach had to find equipment in the midst of wartime shortages. Fehrman told the *Star*'s Dick Slay that he scoured the sports stores of Baltimore:

I picked up a pair of shoes here, a helmet there. I found thirty jerseys all of one kind, and they were cotton. Grab 'em by the shoulder and they'd stretch all the way to the elbow and never go back. All the pants were too large, and the mothers did a wonderful job of making them fit. One of the teams we played had blue jerseys like ours so we bought some white ones like baseball undershirts and the art department stenciled on the numbers.[59]

Alton Cleveland from Garrett Park, a 137-pound linebacker, played enough to win his letter. As he recalled it, no one was "cut," but a few were injured or quit as practice grew more intense. Cleveland also played some quarterback on offense but could not remember ever handling the ball. His main job was to block for the tailback. Smiling, he said:

I could fold up my helmet and take it home. I had one Dad bought for my oldest brother. I painted it black and white to look like the rest of them. Most guys had hard helmets, mine wasn't. I buried my head in a lot of stomachs wearing that thing.

Cleveland, also a relief pitcher on the baseball team, said that Houston Swink, the senior he sometimes subbed for, did run the ball a lot.

Houston Swink grew up on Rosedale Avenue but had a lot of trouble getting to school on time. "I've never been punctual," he admitted. "Had it not been for Mrs. Shaw overlooking that and a gal named Shirley Stillwell and Barbara Simpson, who used to mark me present, I would never have made it." He had played for Mitchell's teams at the Rec Center where he worked rolling the tennis courts. While he was down at Fork Union for a year, he kept in contact and knew there was going to be a school team. With a grin, he remembered painting numbers on the sweatshirts:

We ran from singlewing then. The tail back was Chris Chappell or Leon Utterback. I was called quarterback. We always ran from an unbalanced line. On the line we had Kenny Parkinson, an end; Tommy March was a guard; Mark Raymond was a center; Charlie Huber was either an end or tackle; Dave Knight was a tackle; Hurley was an end. Chappell did everything; a tailback was the "Sammy Baugh" then; he passed, kicked, did everything.

Kenneth Parkinson had attended Leland

The 1944 B-CC football team in their "home" jerseys

Kenny Parkinson

Junior High School but then his family moved to Utah in 1942. He and his mother and brother returned to Bethesda in late September of 1944 after his father had gone to war.

I went to East High in Salt Lake City, a big school with a tremendous plant, like Wilson High School was then compared to B-CC, which was a real farm place. I was sort of a new boy on the block when I returned, but I knew a lot of these guys, nevertheless a fresh breeze from the West. In those days all the styles started on the West Coast and then came sweeping in. These kids here were way out of touch with what was really going on, in men's clothes, a lot of stuff.

The football team, it was mostly little guys, there weren't many big people on that team. It was pretty much basketball players, baseball players. They had all gotten together in junior high, good athletes and a nice crowd.

I went right out for football. They had already started, but I went out and got to be a left end, as I recall. Everything was going along just fine until we had a scrimmage among ourselves, and I dislocated Chris Chappell's shoulder. He came around the end, and I tackled him in some fashion and that was a disaster as far as I was concerned because here I was the new guy on the team. He was the real star, he was a terrific tailback. I just screwed up the best player, the star. I felt very uncomfortable about that.

But it was a great year I enjoyed being back. We played on the north side of school, just a grass slope that went down, and people sat on the grass to watch the game. I enjoyed playing football. It was a good smell, you go out there and smell the grass. I remember that even to this day. I guess anybody that's played football sometime around Labor Day smells cut grass and that reminds you.

Charlie Hughes saw the team's size a bit differently. "We came up with some big guys," he said. Houston Swink also recalled that the fledgling football team acquired a team doctor:

Dr. Kantor had just come into town and volunteered to be the physician, Paul E. Kantor, hell of a nice guy. He used to have his office up by the Sunoco station, a couple of houses from the corner. Anybody got hurt, you just ran up to Bethesda.

The team had a few scrimmages and student manager, Bill Mizell, tried to line up games. "Transportation for all sports," Charlie Hughes recalled, "was a problem and got to be more of a problem. A few people seemed to be able to come up with a car. Bill Mizell was one. He had an old Ford, and we piled in there."

In the week before the first game linebacker Bill Metzel won election as both class president and captain of the football team. He maintained that he never would have been class president if it had not been for getting football started, and many of his classmates agreed.

Cheerleaders were also named, eight females and three males, junior Wilmer Dodson, and seniors Al Pettit and Art Wood. "We had a great cheering squad in those days," Art Wood recalled.

Al Pettit and I did the vocals because we didn't have any mikes, and we both were loud. Our voices could be heard for about three blocks. And we had a bevy of really beautiful girls. A couple of them went on to be Powers models."

Halfback Hughes and quarterback Swink disagreed about Coach Fehrman. Swink said:

Ray Fehrman was a joke. We only had three plays essentially, and he got those out of 'Coach's Scholastic Journal,' and if anybody was open, you'd pass the ball. He was a good old boy, but he wasn't a football coach."

Houston Swink

The coach had a higher opinion of Houston Swink and called him "one of the best ball carriers ever to play for the Barons."

Charlie Hughes said:

Ray Fehrman was not a basketball coach, but he was a good football man. He was from the University of Kentucky and played football there. He did a good job of getting a team on the field that year. Some had never played football. He came up with a terrific line. These guys were 230, 240; Charlie Tabler, "Monster" March, and Dave Knight were big guys. Bill Metzel was big, too."

The first game was at Landon on Friday afternoon, October 20, at 3:30. The Bears under coach Bo Richards had lost to Friends but defeated St. James. The Barons gave up a safety in the first four minutes when Chappell stepped into the end zone on a quick kick. On the next series Chris Chappell intercepted a pass and ran 72 yards up the sideline for a score. End Buddy Lowell scrambled in with the missed kick for the extra point. Neither offense showed much power despite some good runs by Swink. With five minutes left to play, junior Leon Utterback returned a punt 40 yards for a touchdown. B-CC won 13-2 and never let Landon inside its twenty. Triple-threat Chappell and first string lineman Tom "Monster' March were injured in the game and unable to play the next week.[60]

The second game was at home on Hallowe'en, Tuesday, October 31, against Sherwood High School, also making its football debut in 1944. It took a lot of work to get the "bowl" behind the school ready, and many thought the game should have been played at the Rec Center. In the Sherwood game, quarterback Houston Swink was "all over the field blocking, tackling, and making many a spectacular run." Swink carried

the "snake hips" and "swivel hips" nicknames the news reports gave him for the rest of his time at B-CC and many years afterwards.

Leon Utterback passed for two scores. Junior Roger Parkinson caught an eight yard pass for a touchdown early in the game, and in the second half speedy Karl Hurley took a short throw over the middle and outran the Sherwood secon-dary for a TD. Then quarterback Swink scored on a 45-yard, broken field run; Alton Cleveland did some good running, and junior "Pete" Peterson caught a short pass to make it 24-0 Bethesda.

Charlie Hughes remembered the game "because I got in it. The coach put me in at quarterback, and I completed two passes. I was on top of the world. I was small, and they didn't have a big team. I only weighed about 135." Because Sherwood also had blue jerseys with white shoulders, the boys wore their new white sweatshirts after getting the team picture taken for the yearbook.[61]

Second string end Chet McCall's football

Utterback punts to Sherwood

The high school's first home game

career was briefer than most. "I played two games and then in practice a chunky kid came over, clipped me and knocked me out, and I stopped playing football. He really blasted me." McCall went back to sports writing and cheerleading.

For the final game of the abbreviated season, on Saturday, November 11, the team traveled to Fairfax County, Virginia, in a caravan of parents' cars. (The permission slip suggested it would take two hours and three different buses to get there.) A cold rain fell, but the Bethesda boys slid by Mount Vernon High School 13-6. A Ferguson to Hurley pass got the ball to eight, and Houston Swink crashed in from there. Bill Metzel took a pass for the PAT. In the third quarter Karl Hurley scored on a long pass from Glenn Ferguson. It was the toughest game of the short season. The hooded blue parkas that Leon Sherman had donated were warm, but they were not waterproof.

That was the one game Houston Swink remembered. "It was the worst thing we ever had to do," he said. "We came back in cars, cold and wet, and I thought we'd never get home." Sherwood cancelled their scheduled second game, and the B-CC students celebrated their unbeaten team with a "Pigskin Prom" in a gym decorated with goalposts. For several years after the Class of `45 graduated, the field where the football games were played was called the Metzel Bowl.[62]

In Bethesda that fall, the Thrift Shop added furniture to its inventory and reopened with a new manager, Mrs. Edward Marks. Terminal Ice installed a shiny, square structure in a corner of the Farm Women's Market parking lot where one could get ice at any time by inserting fifteen cents. Dorothy Mathews' Kitchen added the pleasant smells of plum puddings and fruit cakes from under Lebling's real estate office.

The long awaited Bethesda-Chevy Chase Cooperative Store held an open house on the evening of October 3, and then opened for business the next day and was mobbed. Manager John Crosby, an A&P veteran, and head butcher Edward Monohan, known as the Frank Sinatra of local meat cutters, tried to keep the crowd happy, but some customers waited twenty minutes to be checked out. Mrs. Francis Goodell reported

that Bethesdans had purchased $8,600 in co-op stock.

The Deepfreeze store owned by Donald F. Hipskind opened later in October as "an experiment in educating the public to the use of a new product." His brother John was the manager and Mary Snow the "food consultant." "Pop" Long, retired booker of vaudeville acts, and his wife, who, of course, was called "Mom," soon gained a wide local reputation for their frozen pies, biscuits and blueberry muffins. The novel store was featured in *Collier's* in January 1945.

The ten year old American Legion post, tired of meeting in the County Building, announced plans to raise a two-story, $25,000 home across Montgomery Lane from the post office. Designed by past-commander A. Hamilton Wilson, the new building would honor the veterans of World War II. Leslie Bell headed the building committee.

Mail carrier Alex Britton won a war bond for collecting the most "Roosevelt" steel pennies, which a local businessman hoped to take out of circulation. Lt. William Morell, USN, won Fred Keplinger's 28th tennis tournament for the third time in a row and retired the trophy. It was the first time Mr. Keplinger missed his own tourney; he was at Suburban Hospital recovering from an operation. Charles Merryman donated plans and plantings for a Court Garden at Suburban Hospital, and the Bethesda Community Garden Club added $100 from a plant sale. James Tibbitts of Somerset donated 2,000 narcissus bulbs to the project.

Bethesda acquired new stop signs at eleven more intersections, mostly in Woodmont and Edgemoor, and parking was banned in front of the County Building to make room for police cars. A new sidewalk with an iron handrail went in along the steep Georgetown Road side of the Bank.

The second annual Harvest Show took place on Sunday, October 1, in the high school gymnasium under the sponsorship of the area garden clubs, rose and dahlia societies and the Victory Garden Committee. The grand prizes went to Earl Carlin, leader of the Edgemoor gardens, and to J. Francis Moore of Kirkside for the best community garden plot. Mrs. L. M. Essex of Chevy Chase won the prize for the best back yard garden. Men carried away most of the blue ribbons for their canning efforts, and after the show

Editor Allen

ended, the Grey Ladies took all the flower displays out to the Naval Hospital.

In the *Tribune*, publisher Allen began a campaign to make every Friday evening "family night," and the Council of Churches promised sermons on the topic. The Commissioners endorsed his idea, and Dr. Broome allowed school children to carry home 5,000 enrollment blanks for families to sign up to spend a night together.

Christ Lutheran Church resumed its popular "Sunday at Eight" discussion program., At Our Lady of Lourdes, the parishioners held a farewell party for Father Palm who left to become a missionary. The First Baptist Church celebrated its tenth anniversary with special services during which charter member James E. Ainley reviewed its history.

The Bethesda Presbyterians began a campaign to pay off the $35,000 debt remaining from remodeling their church. At Cabin John Methodist Elgar C. Soper was the new minister. On the first Sunday in November the remodeled church dedicated its enlarged sanctuary, new chancel, three Sunday School rooms and social hall at a special service. Membership had grown to eighty and the Sunday School to almost a hundred.

The White Fathers of Africa purchased the old Presbyterian Church from Mary Kelly and converted it into the Seminary of Our Lady of Africa, a training center for English-speaking missionaries. Promoted by Randolph Bishop, plans for a Bethesda YMCA moved forward under the leadership of Frederick M. Nettleship.

In its second meeting at the Recreation Center that fall, the Jewish Community Group had thirty-two members sign its first charter and accepted I. S. Turover's offer to use his office for services. Frances Sherman recalled Turover's office filled with chairs and decorated for various celebrations. "The kids

were always involved," she said. "That was the real reason we started a synagogue." For the High Holy Days, Dr. Joshua Bernhart presided. "A very learned man, about my size with a white beard," Leon Sherman recalled. Mrs. Sylvia Garber headed the Sunday School program for about fifty youngsters. Abe Olshen led the choral group, and servicemen were invited to the harvest dance in November.

I. S. Turover

Turover's busy lumber and millwork yard had been in Bethesda for about seven years by 1944 after relocating from the Maine Avenue waterfront. A Polish immigrant and grand master chess player, Turover learned the lumber business as Wimsatt's bookkeeper before starting his own D.C. yard in 1923.

Draft calls continued at the rate of a dozen or more men each week, but discussions and preparation for victory were under way. Fire Chief Bargagni had a hundred American flags in storage and announced plans to lead a parade with the Bethesda fire equipment. The Bethesda Council of Churches planned a service at the Presbyterian Church one hour after the announcement of the end of hostilities, and local businesses said they would close for the day. The Liquor Board decided to close all three of the County dispensaries on VE-Day. Capital officials urged a "sane observance" of the end of the war in Europe, which many expected before Christmas.

Early in the fall, ill health forced Frederic P. Lee to resign as chairman of Draft Board No. 3. Mr. Lee stayed on the Board, but Francis W. Hill Jr. of Kenwood took over the duties of chairman. Hill was the former president of the District Bar Association and chairman of the County Republican Committee. He had been secretary of the local draft board; R. Granville Curry took over that post.

The USO celebrated its first birthday with Arthur Godfrey honoring it on his WTOP morning radio show and playing requests from NNMC patients. The USO room registry, which was handling more than a hundred requests each month, had a parttime paid secretary assigned to it after Mrs. Morell stressed the growing need for the service.

In his crystal ball, E. Brooke Lee saw a new community building for Bethesda with an auditorium and a swimming pool. He proposed that the County acquire land for public parking lots in the immediate future, and the County purchased Mrs. Thomas Armstrong's big lot at 4640 Montgomery Avenue for an addition to the County Building. Among Bethesda businessmen much of the talk was about postwar plans.

As the Browns and the Cardinals battled in the World Series and American and British bombers pounded Berlin, the Washington area was distracted from both the homefront problems and the momentum of the war by a crime, a terrible crime that had been long anticipated: the brutal rape and murder of a young government girl. It was not the first crime of its type nor would it be that last, but the victim and the rapist attracted special attention and sent a chill through many homes.

The criminal was a twenty-four-year-old Marine who was identified by a cab driver and arrested the day after the murder. The victim was eighteen, a tiny girl from Chippewa Falls, Wisconsin, who was identified by her high school ring. Dorothy Berrum was only four-foot-five and weighed ninety-two pounds. Her friends called her "Shorty" and worried about her because she was "too friendly." She did not drink or smoke and had not dated in Wisconsin. She came to Washington, found a job as a clerk-typist at the Pentagon and a room at Maine Hall in Arlington. She soon was a regular visitor to the USO clubs and went out with a number of servicemen she met on the street or the bus. Except for her size, she seemed a fairly typical and reasonably happy G-girl.

Miss Berrum's body was found, face up and fully clothed, near the sixth green of the East Potomac golf course on the morning of October 6. She had been, as the *Star* always put it, "criminally assaulted." The *Times-Herald* used more graphic language. Her face was bruised and scratched, and she had been strangled with her white snood. There were bloodstains near the roadway and evidence of a struggle in the trampled grass. Police found a new, black, Marine belt nearby, and a cabbie recalled taking a Marine and a small woman to Hains Point about 11 pm.

Their mothers demanded that two of the dead girl's friends from Chippewa Falls come home, and the crime sent a shock wave of fear through the whole area. "I told you so" and "I knew it would happen" and "It could have been you" echoed in many homes in the Bethesda area. High school girls who had enjoyed going to watch the "submarine races" at Hains Point or visiting downtown bars with sailors and Marines had second thoughts. For many young women, Dorothy Berrum's violent death ended what had been a very enjoyable war.[63]

Meanwhile the Presidential election of 1944 almost disappeared from the pages of the County's newspapers as the Charter fight warmed up. Many Bethesdans did take time to chuckle at Roosevelt's masterful Fala speech, but the local Democratic organization, despite the urging of Eugene Casey and Mrs. Luke I. Wilson, all but ignored the Presidential, Senatorial and Congressional races and poured its considerable resources into defeating the Charter.

The Citizens Committee to Defeat the Charter (CCDC) chose H. King Mularkey chairman and Mrs. Nicholson vice-chairman at a Rockville meeting where it claimed a membership of seventy including several more from the Western Suburban area. Dutch Bergman chaired the Bethesda branch of the anti-Charter forces, but both he and Mularkey were little more than window dressing. Friends said King Mularkey was just there for "sex appeal." Judge Brault and Roger Whiteford attacked the proposed Charter for creating a merit system, which, as they saw it, would make it all but impossible to remove a huge bureaucracy. Whiteford told the Civitans, "I don't believe in Civil Service for anybody beyond the rank of a clerk." Brault, who condemned the County Manager idea in general and its application to Montgomery County in particular, ran the campaign, but the longtime leader of what some called "Montgomery Democracy," E. Brooke Lee, was the brains as well as the issue.

Journal editor Craddock Goins, a founding member of the Committee to Defeat the Charter, came part of the way out of the editorial closet in his "Talk of the Town' column on September 8. The Charter question, he wrote, "has baffled me," but "I frankly can't figure out how this plan could provide any better government than is provided now." He reminded his readers that he had not been in Bethesda very long but wrote he found life "delightful" and "if there is anything wrong with Montgomery County, I haven't found it."

Brault authored a four-page letter mailed to all Montgomery County residents in the armed services along with the antis' analysis of the document. Brault compared the Charter supporters to the Prohibitionists who acted while men were away during the First World War and said that the plan to abolish the two-party system would produce chaos. The letter signed by Brault, former Legion head James B. Fitzgerald and the `43 Redskin's coach, Dutch Bergman concluded:

You can see that Charter not only changes the entire form of government while you are away, but fills all the county offices, locks them up under permanent civil service and throws the key away, while you are away from home fighting to keep America as it was when you went away. We do not think that anybody should have thought of doing this to you at this time.

When the "soldier vote" was counted in the week after the election, it showed 1,212 votes against the Charter and 778 in support of the proposal. Not enough to make a difference either way but an indication that Judge Brault's letter had an impact.[64]

Speakers pro and con toured the County conducting seventy-three debates, and it was a small civic association or neighborhood club that escaped. The two-party system was upheld as coming from the "founding fathers," and Brooke Lee was damned for "usurpation of executive powers." Roger Whiteford and his wife were injured in an automobile accident, but he kept his schedule of speaking engagements, and Mrs. James V. Bennett sent out letters to more than 150 organizations offering speakers from the Charter Committee's stable of experts.

The Rollingwood Citizens Association staged its debate at the Field House in Rock Creek Park. Lewis B. Sims added to the procharter side his report that the Commissioners had rejected the Civic Federation's advice that they retire more of the County's bonded indebtedness. Sims recalled that when he moved to Rollingwood in `41, he heard about the citizens' association, and "I wondered how you got in."

I thought you had to be sort of invited. I suppose it was in connection with the 1942 charter fight that I went down to my first meeting at Meadowbrook and heard a lady speaking, and, man, was she well informed about local government. That's where my heart was in college and graduate school, and by then I was assistant chief of the state and local government division of the Census Bureau. Well, it was Mrs. Dorothy Himstead of the League of Women Voters. Her husband was executive secretary of the American Association of University Professors. She was a live wire.

So we joined the citizens' association, and almost immediately I was elected a delegate to the Civic Federation. We always met at Bethesda Elementary in the auditorium, and we would come back and report. I don't think I ever missed a meeting. And I went on the public finance and budget committee and followed Fred Lee as chairman. That was a powerful committee.

I was active in the campaign, but I hadn't been here long enough to debate yet. I did make one speech, to the Edgemoor Citizens' Association at the tennis clubhouse. It was well attended, and I explained what the charter was about, and I said, "Let's carry on this campaign," which I thought surely we would win; "let's conduct the campaign at a high level." I said, "Two reasons: one, it's more fun

to win that way, as good sports, and secondly, after we win, we are going have to live with all these Brooke Lee people and it will be a lot better than if we are nasty."

In the next week, debates took place before the citizens' associations of Glencoe, Kenwood, Cabin John, Huntington Park Terrace, Chevy Chase View, Battery Park and at the Christ Lutheran Church. D.C. radio stations and Frederick's WFMD carried fourteen charter debates. The Bethesda Public Library set up a Charter shelf with a copy of the Brookings report, clippings of many newspaper articles, copies of the full text of the charter and publications of both the Charter Committee and the Committee to Defeat the Charter. As Lewis Sims recalled it, "In October of 1944, you didn't go to the movies or a party, you went to the debates. That's where the fun was."

On Monday night, October 9, the Montgomery County Civic Federation representing fifty-five organizations endorsed the Charter proposal by a vote of 79-4 after turning down Royal Carlock's resolution to repudiate the Charter as unconstitutional. The CCDC found the most receptive voters in the upper part of the County where the threat of downcounty domination was easy to sell. They circulated a document called the "Proposed Charter with Comments" that was mailed to every voter a month before the election. In his Maryland *News,* Brooke Lee urged readers to "withhold judgment until you have read this analysis" since "you cannot understand the charter" unless you are "a lawyer or a government expert."

The Charter forces' Field Division was very ineffective in the rural areas. Mrs. Werner admitted:[65]

We took the strategy of doing the campaign where we had the largest number of voters. There wasn't any use of covering too much ground and seeing very few people. However, I travelled all over the county and took stuff with me in the car. I took my two girls, Stella was in high school and Mary was seven years old.

Stella Werner Allison recalled that during the campaign:

We came up to the old Damascus High School for a Charter meeting. I brought my accordion and played in the old, wooden, school house, and all the farmers were looking in the

windows but nobody would come in. Nobody came in.

In what amounted to an anti-Charter rally at the Chevy Chase library, Mrs. Jesse Nicholson ridiculed the idea of the County making its own laws, and Mr. Whiteford rhetorically asked his audience if they wanted a government run at night, when they had nothing else to do, by nice people who did not get paid for it. One CCDC pamphlet implied that special taxing districts would lose their status if the Charter were approved.

The CCDC organized the Colored Committee to Defeat the Charter and sent a letter to all the County's African-American voters stating that Charter approval would give political control to the down-County area and deprive them of representation. The letter warned that white people had tried before "to take our vote away, and they always try through what they call a constitutional amendment" and that this year "a lot of smart outside folks from Bethesda and Chevy Chase" were trying to do just that. Seven well known African-American men including three ministers signed the letter.

Several members of the "Colored Committee" were County employees, one was a Farm Bureau agent and others had temporary jobs as school janitors after the election. Mrs. Werner said she found the letter "heartbreaking" because she had visited with two of the Methodist ministers and "secured support and leadership of a group for Charter. One told me later he had signed the letter in the Park and Planning Commission office."[66]

The pro-Charter forces howled about both this racial appeal and the letter to service men and women who applied for absentee ballots. The Lee-Brault forces responded with an innocent smile and the statement that, "We have never heard of anybody in Montgomery County before objecting to a general or form letter being addressed to voters on any issue upon which they were being asked to vote."

Charter forces marshaled a group of longtime up-County residents including an Allnutt, a Canby, a Bowman, and a Fulks in support of the Charter. They also produced a letter to servicemen signed by retired officers and veterans saying they were supporting the Charter so that when the servicemen came home there would be "... a modern,

businesslike, economical government free from the spoils system and based on democracy, the very thing they are fighting to preserve."

Another special letter went to teachers and yet another to both volunteer and paid firemen after the anti-charter forces suggested that the Charter would destroy local autonomy. Finally, the Charter Committee also responded to the CCDC broadsides with a leaflet called the "The Lie Detector," which listed twenty-nine "whoppers" and then the truth about each.[67]

Two weeks before the election, as Louis A. Gravelle tried to interest Republicans in trying out the new voting machine at Dewey-Bricker-Randall-Beall headquarters on Wisconsin Avenue and the Democrats did the same from their trailer office, Craddock Goins's *Journal* seconded Bill Allen's *Tribune* in editorial opposition to the Charter. He concluded that the Charterites had not made a convincing case "to substitute for a long-established system of government a proposition known in very few counties over the country" nor had they shown that E. Brooke Lee was a villain. He accused many Charter supporters of trying to avenge themselves on the "Cunnel," and wrote that the "Journal has a lot of respect for many people supporting the charter movement, but it has utterly no sympathy for the spirit of vengeance."[68]

In the last week before the election the antis played an ace. Following full page ads in the *Star* and *Post* on October 22, they trumpeted the statement of Dr. Gilbert Grosvenor, president of the National Geographic Society. He applauded the progress made by the County under its existing government and urged voters "to reject the pending Charter on November 7th." Dr. Grosvenor said that he had read the proposed Charter, and "I regard its provisions as experimental, dangerous and burdensome."

Grosvenor and his wife, Alexander Graham Bell's elder daughter, Elsie May, had been lauded by Mrs. Bradley in a front page profile the previous week and were generally considered Bethesda's "first family." Now Grosvenor paid to have the full-page, anti-charter ad printed in Mrs. Bradley's weekly newspaper, and the antis gleefully ran Grosvenor's statement in their next, big ad. The pro-Charter forces attempted to counter

with the endorsement of Elisha Hanson, counsel to the National Geographic Society and a resident of Alta Vista for over two dozen years, but Grosvenor's name and reputation were hard to top.

On October 29, the *Star* began a series of six pro and con articles on the front page of the local section, and the *Post* closely followed the election as did the *News* and to a lesser extent the *Times Herald*. In early November one supporting or opposing statement rapidly followed another in a storm of press releases. Real estate man Eugene M. Fry denounced the Charter as "an untried experiment," but storekeeper Walter E. Perry, who seldom dabbled in politics, said, "I have come to the conclusion that the citizens of the County who wish to protect their property rights must take the government out of the hands of the machine and place it in the hands of the citizens. Charter with home rule will do this."

George E. Hamilton Sr., Dean Emeritus of the Georgetown Law school and president of the Corcoran Gallery, was as close as the Charter forces came to trumping the antis' Grosvenor ace. He had lived in Bethesda for forty years, eight more than the Grosvenors, and was as well respected if not as well-known. Hamilton said that he believed that the County's "sound development has been hampered and impeded by personal aims, selfish ambitions, and partisan direction

Dean Hamilton

under the existing form of government."[69]

And Gertrude Bradley and the *Record* came out foursquare for the Charter "as nothing more than good, sound, common sense in government. It will let the citizens, the taxpayers run their own government. It will get the control back where it belongs — with the people, away from the politicians. Vote for it!" The *Record* was the only County paper to support the Charter in an age when governmental and legal advertising could pay a weekly's printing bill and the delinquent tax

list could put the whole operation in the black. The old, grey *Star* straddled the fence, and after summarizing the arguments of both sides, concluded that no matter how the vote came out the taxpayer stood to win because of the interest in government that had been generated. The *Post*, *Daily News* and Baltimore *Sun* supported the Charter.[70]

On election day both sides had their workers out at the polls. Lewis Sims covered his precinct which voted at the Chevy Chase fire house.

A guy by the name of Bob Dunlop was against the Charter, and I was out here handing out literature for the Charter. He and I got along fine, and once he said, "See this old guy coming along there, you know who that is? That's old man Martin." Who's that? "Of Martin's Addition," he said. "He's eighty-four."

So I thought I'll jolly him along–that's how you get along in politics, and he could see I had a Vote for the Charter badge on. He was mad right away at me and said, "What have you done for the County?"

Well, I said, I built a house and increased the assessed valuation. I thought that would be a little humorous, but that didn't strike him the way I thought it would. I was there all day long with Dunlop."

Although Maryland stayed in FDR's column, Montgomery County, along with Fairfax and Arlington counties in Virginia, went for the Republican in the Presidential race, and the vote in Prince George's County was very close. But despite the big majority for Dewey and for incumbent Congressman J. Glenn Beall, who won by 3,500 votes in the County, the leader of Montgomery Democracy, E. Brooke Lee, had one more, highly satisfying victory. The Charter lost.

By far the heaviest vote for home rule came from the Bethesda precincts, the least from the up-County where only 2,142 voted for and 5,444 cast ballots against the proposal, less than thirty percent approval. The tally in Rockville was 1,115 against to 522 for and in Gaithersburg 765 to 264. Silver Spring, Takoma Park, and Kensington were almost evenly divided. The Bethesda vote was 5,850 for and 3,415 against, a sixty-three percent plurality. Countywide about 5,800 voters did not cast ballots on the Charter referendum, which lost by 1,635, but the fact that four out of five voters did vote on the Charter showed very high interest in a ballot question.[71]

Mrs. Bradley, a stringer for the *Star* as well as editor of her own paper, accepted the assignment to cover E. Brooke Lee's office at Park and Planning on election evening. She reported at seven and "was greeted affably by the gentleman, whose charm is second only to that now displayed in the White House." In her own paper, reporter Bradley described her experience in the third person.

She felt like a dove in the eagle's nest when the party workers started drifting in from all parts of the county – one lone Charterite in a room full of antis. One look at her was enough to cause consternation. "What the h—— is she doing here?" their glances all seemed to say. Even her good friend, Lacy Shaw, who always had time to pat a girl on the shoulder, edged away with a cool look in his eye. He's a Record subscriber and had been reading the paper.

Soon the returns started coming so fast that she didn't have time for introspection. As the returns grew, so did the crowd until at last her "private" office was packed with anxious people. The returns were from Bethesda and the picture wasn't any too rosy.

Gradually the precincts from upcounty began to report and as they did the spirits of the crowd soared. They became a noisy, laughing, adoring mass of people – assembled to do homage to their boss. Each time the Colonel announced a piece of good news there was thunderous applause – as much for him as for the report he bore.

Gradually, too, the feeling toward the reporter changed. People she knew slightly began to grin when they looked at her; those she knew well patted her consolingly on the back. One man wrote a note and slipped it under the Star telephone reminding her he would be around to collect a bet the next morning.

At 11 it was all over. The Colonel had retired to his private office and closed the door. Only the elite could enter from now on.

The tumult and the shouting died. The crowd began to chatter good naturedly. She called in her last report to the Star.

Picking up her coat and pocketbook she slipped out the side door and headed for her side

of the railroad tracks where it's no sin to be a Charterite.

Mrs. Werner's post that evening was her small office in the Guild Building, which soon became crowded with volunteers. Her husband and daughters sat beside her at the old secondhand desk and helped with the tally. She later said:

The returns came in rapidly from the voting machines. We knew we had lost. Very little was said by anyone. My Stella and I were crying and I would cry now. My husband said, "You must do it again."

"I remember being on the basement steps weeping as if it were the end of the world because we had worked very, very hard," Stella Allison said. "I was handing out things at the polls since I was old to enough to hold them." Stella's mother insisted that she was not at all downcast. "The road of the reformer isn't an easy one," she said, "and we have to be prepared for these set backs."

The next day, Lewis Sims, who had been among the mourners at the Guild Building and recalled young Stella weeping, wrote Allen Gardner, "Count me as one who is willing to start all over again." Sims said, "And I thought, 'Well, I'll be the only squirrel in the County to do this,' but right away there was all sorts of support to start all over again."

In her postmortem of the campaign, Mrs. Werner pointed out one of Mr. Sims's speeches as typical of the logic and mild manner of most Charter proponents. A week later, when "Little" Stella read a congratulatory letter her mother had received from Mrs. Perry, it hit her. "Good Heavens, Mother," she said, "do we have to go through the whole mess of getting signatures on petitions?"

In precinct 7-5, which covered from Martins' Additions and Rollingwood to North Chevy Chase, George W. Stone, the precinct captain, called a meeting at Lewis Sims's home. Mr. Sims acted as secretary and reported some twenty suggestions to Allen Gardner. They ranged from recanvassing precincts for donations and investigating why people voted against the Charter to working up a "catalogue of atrocity stories" of the other side's dirty tricks and informing soldier voters and "colored voters now of the lies told to them."

Judge Brault, credited by many observers for the victory, feigned surprise over the news that the Charter folks were not finished.

It was amazing to read in both afternoon papers Wednesday and to hear of announcements over local broadcasting stations the same day that pro-charter supporters, after the recent campaign, were now proposing to continue their fight... (they) must love fighting just for the sake of fighting.

Brault analyzed Dewey's victory in the County and compared it to the Charter's defeat as showing the voters saw less wrong in Rockville than they did in Washington. He also concluded that this election had been the Charter force's best chance because they would soon lose the votes of "temporary residents" brought here by the war.

Brault concluded:

A study of the returns will establish that over 80 per cent of the precincts that were carried for charter are the locations of large groups of new homes that have been built during the past three to six years. The people living in these communities obviously are newcomers to the county, and since they lack firsthand information of the true conditions that really prevail in the county, they have during the past three years been the most fruitful subjects for the false political charges that the charter spokesmen have so industriously circulated.

Brault labeled the Charter leaders who wanted to continue the fight as "insatiably politically ambitious." E. Brooke Lee's retrospective assessment was that "We beat the first charter because of half a dozen extreme positions that many people thought impossible to live under."[72]

On the Friday evening after the election, the leaders of the Montgomery County Charter Committee decided to keep their office in the Housing Guild Building open and to initiate a fund-raising campaign to continue the fight. Mrs. Walter E. Perry and her nominating committee went to work to name candidates for the Board of Directors. The Charter Committee held its annual meeting on November 29 at the Woman's Club of Chevy Chase. Members heard reports from various committees and then the treasurer's report, which showed $5,736 collected but $7,313 expended on the campaign. They discussed their failures and the campaign's weaknesses especially in the rural areas.

Some thought their defeat was a product of overconfidence. John Willmott, the research director, blamed "lack of funds and shortage of ammunition," and Mrs. James V. Bennett reflected that Charterites were "unwittingly delivered into the hands of the enemy by their own friends, who asked for pro-and-con debates." In the end, Mrs. Marquis Childs summed up the attitude of the 300 in attendance when she said, "We're all ready to start in again and work tooth and toenail for the next election." Martha Strayer of the *News* concluded that these "earnest political amateurs" had learned some valuable lessons.[73]

Research chairman Willmott in a summary history titled "Machine Beats County Charter" for the *National Municipal Review* concluded that so many falsehoods were circulated and they were "repeated so insistently that it was no easy task to catch up with them" although his committee put out a final mailing to 25,000 voters "carrying quotations from newspaper editorials and a list of 200 prominent citizens who had endorsed the charter."

He summarized the vote as follows:

	For	Against
Suburban area	11,128	9,027
UpCounty	2,142	5,444
Soldier vote	778	1,212
Total	14,048	15,683

Willmott ended his essay with the statement that the Committee: *was determined to try again. And it has the support of a substantial group of citizens who know what they want and will not stop until they get it.*[74]

Von Braun's V-2's fell on London and Antwerp; Saipan's B-29's incinerated Japanese cities one after another, and MacArthur returned to the Philippines with the cameras rolling. Bethesda moved into another wartime winter and prepared to celebrate another Thanksgiving and another Christmas with many more of its young men far from home. The casualty list grew longer, and the Red Cross held a well-attended meeting at the Woman's Club of Chevy Chase to explain its prisoner-of-war services.

Battery Park dedicated its own roll of honor at the clubhouse with a speech by Carey Quinn, and high school students began drafting their third Christmas letter. "Ma" Mohler had posted signs at all the Bethesda-area polling places asking for the names and addresses of servicemen and women.[75]

In November, the high school added nine gold stars to its banner for pilot Johnny Fulks of the class of `38; Marine flier Billy Duvall of the class of `40 , whose plane exploded over the Gulf of Mexico; Ray Sanford, class of `41, who had played two years of varsity basketball; Sherman Taylor, who would have graduated in `42 if he had not left school early to join the Canadian army; Dick Kehoe, also of the class of `42; Lee Benjamin, an only child who graduated in 1942 at age 16 and was killed on Pelielu in September; Walt Shepard, class of `42, killed in Italy in July; Collier Carpenter, Mr. Bender's right hand man as a sophomore who left school to join the Marines instead of graduating in 1944, and then the shock, Hardy Sorrell, who would have been a senior.

A few students knew some of the others, most of whom were older than they were, but James Hardy Sorrell was one of them. He had been the best athlete in his class at Leland junior high, captain of the JV and varsity basketball teams there and a class officer. His picture appeared in the rows of sophomores in the 1943 *Pine Tree*, a dark, handsome young face, perhaps more mature than most. Hardy joined the Marines during the summer of `43.

Charlie Hughes, a classmate who had known him since they went to Somerset Elementary together, recalled, "I got a long letter from him and it was a sad letter. It wasn't like him. It was almost like he was expecting to get it." He wrote his mother that he had been baptized out on a South Pacific island and was finding God. He was killed on the sixth day of the fight for Guam. He was 19.

Hardy Sorrell

Another Bethesda war casualty died at the Naval Hospital in October. Dr. Richard G. Henderson of the Public Health Service lived on Cedar Lane with his wife and two small children. At the request of the military, he had been working at the NIH with Dr. Norman Topping, developer of the spotted fever serum, on a vaccine for scrub typhus. Somehow Dr. Henderson contracted the disease he was studying .

At David Taylor Model Basin, three gold stars joined the 182 blue ones on the service banner for apprentice George King, a B-17 tailgunner killed on his first mission; draftsman Mike Carlin, shot down over the Adriatic, and Pvt. Henry Glynn, formerly of the Machine Shop, who was killed in France.

Longfellow School had added a 9th grade that fall and moved the lower school into the old dorm and the upper into renovated classrooms. At Leland the 9th graders elected Richard Latimer class president. The boys in home ec studied the effects of feeding a guinea pig on cookies and candy, and straight-A student Tipton Stringer was one of the stars of the Dramatic Club's first one-act play.

The Leland band, twenty-five boys and 7th grader Barbara Hobelman, was a regularly scheduled class under Jacquelyn Rusen and made its debut at the school year's first bond rally, but the strings still met before and after school as an "activity."

One band member was 8th grader Alexander "Sandy" Astin:[76]

What I was most known for was music. I was active in the glee club and also played the trumpet and think I played for assemblies on different occasions and played in the band and was very active musically.

Sometimes I felt on the outside. There were cliques of boys and girls, the fast crowd or the pop crowd. I wasn't a member, but I wasn't a loner either, an outcast The fast crowd included the athletes and cheer leaders and so forth.

One day our algebra teacher went one-by-one around the class asking each student, quote, What is your father doing for the war effort? Most of the fathers were, of course, in the military and many were overseas. But I remember how humiliating and embarrassing it was to kids whose fathers were not in the service.

I remember a lot of characters when we were in junior high school. One was Bill Rice, a very smart guy, good student, but also a joker, kind of chubby. He was a very funny guy. The teacher asked him to do something at the board, asked him to erase something, and the class started laughing, and she turned around and hit him flush in the face. The eraser had written on it in bold letters "Noiseless Eraser," and as he erased, he was putting his ear up to the eraser.

When we would have standardized tests, Bill and I would get the highest math scores, we competed. It bothered me because the results were fed back. I wondered about people who got scores in the 15th percentile.

An experiment with tracking was a devastating experience for some students. They did it in 8th grade only and tried to disguise it. The brightest was 8Z, dumbest in 8P and 8Q, with the others in between. Kids in 8P and 8Q were unruly, mostly economically poor, behavior problems, probably hurt by the stigma. That happened when I was in the 7th grade.

I was a pretty good student in courses where it wasn't necessary to work hard. I goofed off, never did homework. My mother was a substitute teacher at Leland during World War II.

The Leland Band poses on the school's front steps (Astin with trumpet at left)

She taught everything from Latin to ballroom dancing in conjunction with gym classes and was well-known to a number of students as a tough but fair teacher. I had her in my Latin class for a semester, and believe me, I made sure that I got an A! I got sent to the principal's office a lot for joking and kidding around. I was trying to get approval and attention by being funny.

We had a population of relatively poor kids who lived in Woodmont. I even had a paper route in that section, a working class, blue collar neighborhood. Several families had kids, usually not good students, sometimes tough kids, some athletes, basically poor kids, relatively speaking, a little out of the whirl.

I remember our 8th grade gym class where the teacher paired the boys off according to their weight, put boxing gloves on them and forced them to go a few rounds with each other. I found this extremely distasteful, and I think a lot of other kids did.

I and many of my friends started smoking in 8th grade, and I remember several of us every day would sneak down on the "bank," a grassy slope at the extreme east end of the school grounds, where we would smoke cigarettes during recess.

Up on Wisconsin Avenue was Tate's pool hall. He was a little, thin guy, a chain smoker. He sat on a high stool in the corner by the entrance and chain smoked and watched the action. He was an excellent pool player himself. That was the hangout. My brother, a 9th grader, was a bigger aficionado of pool than I was, and he became somewhat of a hustler. John would challenge strangers to a pool match. There were some parents who weren't sure of that place, but nothing nefarious went on in Tate's Pool Hall, no drugs, no prostitution, no nothing.

There was the requisite amount of macho swearing and macho challenges to games and occasional threats over betting but basically a peaceful haven for young kids to act macho and learn an exacting, high skill sport.

One pool player I remember was a little short guy who wore leather leggings up to his knees and always had cigar in his mouth. He was known as Joe the Treeclimber, and once in a big match, Joe bit through his cigar and it fell on the table. It was an interesting mixing of kids with adults, and Tate didn't tolerate any misbehavior. It was a smoky, dingy pool hall, with four tables in the place, maybe five. We used to go over after school and play for an hour or so.

The bowling alleys were a gathering place for young kids, the equivalent of today's computer game places. The game of choice was pinball. Many people never bowled at all, just went to play the pinball machines. It was a highly competitive activity, and the occasion for the starting of a number of fights. One was under the Hiser. It was a particular hangout for junior high kids. I used to go in there a lot. I was a pretty good bowler and made money setting up pins. The big bowling alley was down on across from the firehouse called Forty Alleys. I used to hang out, play pin ball machines, set pins. We had all sorts of ways of cheating the pinball machines. That was part of the social milieu.

Leland went through dozens of teacher changes during the war, but one of those wartime appointments, Thomas Conlon Jr., soon became one of the most popular and active men at school despite being crippled by polio. Bill Herson emceed the bond rally at the junior high school, which featured band solos by John Astin on violin, Richard Curtis on the French horn, and James Morrison, Sandy Astin, Harry Chadduck and John Leister on trumpets. They sold $4,000 worth of war bonds, but the high school topped that with an auction which raised $14,000.

At B-CC, Walter G. Kolb crowned the War Bond evening by selling off King Mularkey's suit strip by strip while he was still wearing it. Kolb, whose hobby was emceeing and entertaining, had conducted dozens of bond rallies often using the "truth or consequences" format and depending on planted stooges. He also headed Kolb Electrical Company, was president of the Rotary Club, and a director of Chevy Chase Building and Loan Association. Led by Mrs. Black and Miss Aiken, the high school sold $33,125 in bonds and $1,000 worth of stamp in the November drive.

B-CC's revived but still mimeographed newspaper, *The Tattler*, now produced by Melva Hon's journalism class, celebrated its birthday with a staff party at editor Jeanne Curtiss's home, which featured a spaghetti dinner and four birthday cakes. Overcrowded Leland sent two sections of 9th graders to the high school as a small freshman class. The sixty students were, for the most part, those who had chosen non-academic programs and were scheduled for a "general" diploma. In the group were several good ath-

letes including Kenny Poerstel who played three sports that school year.

"Swing Grove" at the Rec Center held its first dance of the season on November 18 and required everyone to re-register. The Teen Age Canteen Club, as it was more formally called asked for payment of the pledges made the previous year. Only $175 had been collected, and Mrs. Sholar's committee expressed surprise that no civic group had stepped forward to sponsor the canteen. Mrs. Val Sherman, chairman of the lounge committee, discussed fabrics with the student group and then went shopping with Joyce Snodgrass and Hunter Creech while Mrs. Curtis Walker agreed to be in charge of making curtains for the clubhouse.

By the time the USO celebrated its first birthday with an open house, it had served 35,000 servicemen and women and had seventy-five senior and 160 junior hostesses on regular shifts. Mrs. Lewis E. Dixon, who handled up to three hundred requests each week, had 250 rooms in her registry. Her naval officer husband had been missing and presumed lost since his minesweeper was sunk off the coast of France.

The lounge had acquired musical instruments, a lending library, art materials, and "Jiving Jenny," the seldom quiet juke box. The snack bar was always open for a sailor or Marine who wanted to make his own breakfast or lunch, and the Bethesda women's club had started serving Wave Brunches on Sunday mornings. After a summer hiatus, a new Scuttlebutt column appeared in local papers, edited by Janice Huffman and John DeMarco with junior hostesses including Mildred Plitt reporters of daily activities.

Bethesda's volunteer firemen, all but ignored since the debacle with the air raid drills, sold off two of their three trucks and attempted to stimulate interest in starting a rescue squad by offering a first aid course. Hiram Musgrove, president of the group, denied rumors that they were planning to sell their firehouse on Fairmont Avenue. He claimed that the paid men had violated the agreement to call on them first when assistance was needed. Chief Bargagni denied that, and said, "The fact that the volunteer department has received only about five calls in the last two years just goes to prove that

two fire departments aren't needed in the Bethesda area."

Chief Bargagni

The volunteers, still claiming about twenty-five members, exercised their truck by running it around the block two or three times a week. In September the paid men received a ten percent raise, and at Chief Bargagni's request the B&O sent work crews to clear the right of way of weeds and trash from Reed Street to East West Highway.[77]

Over on the river, the Cabin John fire department struggled along with twenty-three men in the service but took delivery on a new 500 gpm Mack combination pumper in 1944. The Glen Echo VFD had twenty-five members serving in various branches of the military.

Howard Brubach, who worked in the respiratory physiology department at NIH, joined the Cabin John volunteers in 1941 and soon became a lieutenant and the leader of a Civil Defense unit shortly after the war began. He remembered, smiling:

I went to Brookmont with my crew during the drills, to a house and called in. Sometimes they would call that a practice bomb had been dropped. Once we came up there and saw a gang just standing around. The bomb hadn't arrived yet.

During the war, Mr. Brubach recalled, the firemen had "a cat named Meatball and a dog that ate cigarette butts" and an elderly house man named Smith, "paid as a janitor and to answer the phone.

When the call came in before that, the siren would go off and the first man in would take the phone and get directions. We had a rig on the wall with "house, auto, brush, rescue" and the five areas, and he'd code that up. Then the first qualified driver took the first piece out. Of course, the daytime was roughest for volunteers with just the Canadas' store and few others around.

He also recalled that during the war relations with the Cabin John firemen improved, and they even had joint classes. "But," he said, "every now and then we'd get a River Road call and go through Cabin John, and

Some of the Glen Echo Civil Defense volunteers

they resented that like hell." In the fall of `44, the Glen Echo firemen received permission to use the air raid siren on Massachusetts Avenue at Osceola for fire alarms so that more men could hear the call.

Starting in September 1944, Howard Brubach's friend and Wood Acres neighbor Charles Kocher wrote and produced the "T. O. Report," a monthly newsletter to "our T. O. Gang with Uncle Sam." Kocher, who signed himself "Plugwrench Pete," said the paper was Brubach's idea. News of the fires and other activities in Glen Echo filled the chatty letter and Plugwrench even predicted the defeat of the Charter, which evidently had provoked some heated discussions at the firehouse.

In November `44 he reported:

There is one product that seems to be plentiful, war or no war. That is the baby crop. And the odd thing is that they are mostly born late at night much to the discomfiture of the citizens of Glen Echo whose peaceful slumbers have been disturbed by the raucous voice of the siren calling the midwife detail. That's all changed now. No, they're still having babies, but we have a regular ambo crew for such cases that is on duty

for one week at a time, from 10:00 P.M. to 6:00 A.M. and is summoned by phone. The boys alternate at this job, working three at a time. You've got something to look forward to when you get back. Plugwrench's turn comes up on November 12 so if somebody else writes to you next month you will know that he has become a Godfather and the strain was too much for him.

About the title, Kocher said:

"T. O. Report," it was a joke. Some young fellows they always suspected of setting brush fires, so we called them the touchoff crew. It was just given to me. I was also writing the company newsletter at the same time, and they had many more men in the service. It's funny, I enjoyed writing, and I hated it in school.

The newsletter with its drawing of Leapin' Lena on the front ended in October 1945 with a painful report of a donkey baseball game against Cabin John during which Kocher was thrown by his mount and kicked in the ribs.[78]

The "Basin Chatter" news-letter at TMB featured the cartoons and personality-profile drawings of Joe Chizanskos. It reported on the fourteen-team bowling league's progress, the problems of the basketball team, the blood donation and bond drives and the arrival of the two 35,000 pound brass impellers for the 1,250 hp motors in the water tunnels.

At the Model Basin, construction began on an $8 million, 1,800 foot extension, which would lengthen the main building to over three thousand feet. In December the Navy staged the first, full-dress inspection for the men who had been "militarized." Admiral Howard, Captain Saunders and the C.O. of the Marine guard company, Captain Bell, observed, as "our boys" marched from the Wind Tunnel to the flagpole green before a big

Glen Echo Volunteer Fire Dept.
MONTHLY to our "T. O. Gang" with Uncle Sam

audience of Basinites. Admiral Howard praised the men for their hard work and had kind words for Marine Lt. Wade Schaefer and "Sully," the platoon leader and drill instructor. The inspection marked the end of drills and training for the winter.[79]

Life in Bethesda went on pretty much as usual despite the war. At Suburban Hospital, the number of patients admitted leveled off at about 200 each month plus about forty births, 120 outpatients, and a hundred or so emergency cases. Sixteen junior volunteers, including Miriam Bopp, Mary Dow and Barbara Hanby, received certificates of appreciation from the hospital.[80]

Carl Bachschmid, president of the Chamber of Commerce, accepted the job of heading up the Christmas Seal campaign. The Chevy Chase Chanters, led by J. Horace Smithey for the ninth season and featuring the solos of their treasurer, Ed Stock, swung back into action, and one of their first big concerts was at Leland JHS for Christmas Seals.

Francis Simons of Maple Ridge Road asked the OPA to investigate the "tie in" charge for garbage and water services by WSSC since he did not desire trash collection but had to pay for it. Dr. William Blum, active in affairs of Section Four and the Chevy Chase Presbyterian Church, won the Acheson Medal and $1,000 from the Electro-chemical Society for his work in electroplating, which helped produce both zinc-coated pennies and cartridge cases. Two doctors at the NNMC developed an artificial plastic eye made of acrylic resin.

Ed Stock resigned as head of the local Victory Garden program, and the Commissioners cut back on their support and closed the Bethesda office. Jack S. Eaton resigned as head of Rationing Board #3. He had been chairman since August 1942 and given over 10,000 hours of unpaid service. Mr. Eaton gave ill health as the reason for his decision and recommended Austin Rohrbaugh, his assistant, as his replacement. Eaton continued as County building inspector.

The cigarette shortage worsened, and many smokers resorted to rolling their own rather than trying to get used to the strange brands then available. Russ Edwards noted that very few cigarette butts were to be seen in Bethesda's gutters. Grady, Community, Bethesda Motors, Edgemoor, and the Chevy Chase Motor Company jointly sponsored an ad urging Bethesdans to sell their cars to a local dealer rather than to any of those downtown.

On Sunday afternoon, November 19, the Roll of Honor promoted by the Lions and *The Record* was dedicated at 6800 Wisconsin Avenue. The billboard bore the names of 3,000 men and women including forty-two dead, who had gold stars beside their names, and six missing-in-action. Father Sweeney of Our Lady of Lourdes gave the invocation and the benediction was offered by Reverend Williams of St. John's. Captain Clark Marshall, USA, and Francis Hill of the draft board spoke briefly in a program organized by Joseph Cantrel. The Army Air Force band played, and the Maryland Guard fired a rifle salute. The *Record* issued a special edition that week with stories and photos of most of the dead, wounded and missing. The campaign to pay for the honor roll was still $300 short.[81]

A spitting contest broke out between E. Brooke Lee and the Civic Federation. Lee, flushed with the victory over the Charterites, excoriated the "Civics" and the Federation in a 1,700 word editorial in mid-November. He accused the organization of being a bunch of frustrated politicians dominated by Bethesda-Chevy Chase groups, and as Mrs. Bradley put it, "tore this august body limb from limb and left the remains bleeding all over the front and back pages of the Maryland News."

Gertrude Bradley leapt into the fight, countering with her own editorial, "In Defense of the Watchdog." She had been a silent observer of the Civic Federation as a reporter for the *Star* and her own paper for five years and a delegate of the Bethesda Chamber in 1944. She stated that there was "no foundation" for Lee's charge of politics and pointed out that the Colonel did not start his criticism until after the Brookings report was issued. She concluded that the Federation had been "fair, responsible, wise and constructive" and urged the County administration to stop "its unsportsmanlike attacks on the defeated opposition. "Methinks the (Colonel) doth protest too much."

Richard B. Barker, president of the Civic Federation, followed with a challenge to Lee "to point out a single act of the Montgomery

County Civic Federation in recent years, which has not been motivated by constructive rather than destructive principles." Barker reminded Lee of the Federation's support of the Master Plan, zoning regulations and the postwar planning committee, and said:

The truth of the matter is, Mr. Lee, that the Federation ipso facto becomes destructive and disruptive to the welfare of Montgomery County only when they make a suggestion, which is contrary to your own personal desires of how the county should be run.

Barker offered to continue to work with Lee in the post-war group and with other County officials but made it plain that "I will never be blackjacked into subservient submission."[82]

Good news mixed with bad that fall. Lt. Irving Day (B-CC `40) met fellow pilots and Bethesdans Lt. Robert Dannemiller and Lt. Robert Comstock (B-CC `38) in the German's Stalag Luft 1 prison camp and managed through some clever writing to get word of that to his parents. That year's polio epidemic claimed forty-four County victims, mostly young, and the American Legion picked up $3,000 of their doctor's bills and the cost of transporting them to Baltimore for treatment. Christ Lutheran Church celebrated its tenth anniversary and its first full year of independence from the Mission Board.

The VFW, led by Adlai Magee, installed a large paper-salvage bin at Leland and Wisconsin on the corner of Critchfield's service station, a popular and appreciated addition. The Montgomery County Historical Society began to receive gifts, and Mrs. Stone appointed Judge Stedman Prescott, Phil Schaefer, Ed Stock and Walter Perry as a committee to find a home for them. Deer occasionally wandered through Bethesda, and a full grown doe was seen one November morning trying to jump the fence into the Chevy Chase Club at Bradley and Wisconsin.

When the Bergdoll tract rezoning for apartments came up again, Rufus Lusk led opponents organized by Edward Stohlman of Somerset. Lusk told the County Commissioners, sitting as District Zoning Council in Bethesda, of the gentlemen's agreement not to build apartments west of Rock Creek in the Metropolitan area and encouraged them to respect it. Then Donal Chamberlin and Montague Ferry of Kenwood and Arthur Lambert

of Chevy Chase Village also spoke against the proposed use. James Gill was the only pleader for the tract owners.

The petition to rezone land on Wisconsin north of Chestnut for apartments also produced opposition. Fifty home owners appeared with a petition against the zoning change signed by 200 residents of Glenbrook Village . Gill, representing the owners, read letters from NNMC and the Public Health Service on the need for rental housing. Sam Eig, one of the big contributors to the CCDC, announced his plans to build 1,000 homes on East West Highway in Rock Creek Forest when he requested rezoning for a small shopping center on Grubb Road.[83]

The Commissioners and the school board accepted $8,500 from FWA to build a nursery school at the Rec Center as well as $118,220 to maintain wartime child-care facilities between July 1943 and June 1945. The Bethesda public library asked the Board of Education for a new building as part of the high school. The Board approved that idea in principle. The County contracted for a service building at the Recreation Center and the remodeling of a Meadowbrook stable for use as a dog kennel. John J. Fee hired on to supervise the dog pound at $175 a month.[84]

Commander Jack Dempsey visited the USO for a cup of coffee and some hand shaking one Sunday in mid-November and stirred up some excitement. During its annual meeting at Mrs. Morell's home, the USO elected Mrs. Maurice Davidson of 45th Street as chairman of the operating committee for 1945 The regular Thursday hostesses, Mrs. Arthur Hilland, Mrs. William Sullivan, Mrs. DeWitt Hyde and Mrs. Warren Gingell, served Thanksgiving dinner buffet style. The Hot Shoppe cooked the turkeys, and there were candles on the tables. Reverend Vogeley asked the blessing, and Craddock Goins told Southern stories after the meal.[85]

Every week the Red Cross Motor Corps transported groups of thirty-five convalescing patients from the Naval Hospital to the White House for a visit and tea on Tuesday afternoon and another group for a movie on Wednesday evening. When Mrs. Roosevelt was home, she greeted the visitors and showed them around.

At a meeting of the 300-member Post War Planning Committee, James W. Gill, leader of the County delegation for the upcoming Gen-

eral Assembly session, suggested ten changes in County government, which could be made through legislative action in Annapolis. They incorporated many aspects of Charter plan including appointment of a county manager, broader civil service, hiring a purchasing agent, and, perhaps most surpisingly, bond payment from current revenue.

Allen Gardner responded:

It is a sign of some progress when a political machine which has long dominated a county government admits, however tardily, that it is willing to study proposals for improvement of that government.[86]

But, he warned, as far as he could tell, the machine still opposed reform.

Mrs. Beall's window display, which showed a fireplace behind a carpet of fruit, won the Chamber's Christmas contest with Jelleff's second and then Gifford's, Malcolm Scates, and Deep-freeze. The Bethesda Garden Club and Chevy Chase Garden Club cooperated to decorate Suburban Hospital for Christmas, and children at Bethesda Elementary and Lynnbrook made presents and decorations for the hospital.

Led by Carroll Murnane, the American Legion set up depots in most of the bigger stores, the fire department, Briggs Clarifier and the Hiser to collect Christmas gifts for the men at the Naval Hospital. The Glenwood Road Garden Club sent thirty wreaths to the Naval Hospital along with thirty-five pounds of homemade candy, and the war recreation board staged an officers' dance at Woodmont. The A Capella Choir made its usual round of appearances with a program of carols including a Sunday evening visit to the USO, and the high school sent out more than a thousand Christmas letters to former students in the service. At the Woman's Club of Bethesda, Dorothy Hilland and most of Bette Doyle's young pupils were looking forward to a "Christmas Cotillion," the first long-dress formal for most of the 11- to 14-year-olds.

The outbreak of the Battle of the Bulge in the Ardennes dampened many celebrations that Christmas season, but the electric trains in the front window of the USO and the big, flickering tree in back of the lounge helped some men and women forget the war for a while. Mrs. Hilland led a mob of cookie bakers on the Thursday before Christmas while servicemen and women decorated the tree

and built a big snowman. On Christmas Eve members of the Junior Woman's Club of Chevy Chase, several of whom were regular USO hostesses, served a candlelight supper of ham and sweet potatoes, and on Christmas Day Santa gave out presents at an open house, which started with waffles and was crowned by Mrs. George Mathews' huge, blazing plum pudding.

The Astin boys staged a special, surprise Christmas for their mother because their father was still in England demonstrating the proximity fuses he had helped to develop and Bowen and Company had helped to build. For many it was the wartime Christmas remembered for the greatest shortages. Gasoline was very scare, and many stations closed before sunset. Pork, beef, turkey, and chicken were unobtainable by Christmas week. Most home were cold due to fuel rationing. And even the venerable *Evening Star* ran into a paper shortage and did not publish on either December 23 or December 30th, which gave paper-boys two days off but led to some fancy juggling with their collecting.

One Bethesda institution passed with the end of the year. K. S. Veirs bought W. E. Perry's store. Mr. Veirs and his family returned to Bethesda after many years in South America and found a home just across the street from the Floyd Davis farm where Mr. Veirs's grandfather Samuel Clark Veirs had lived many years before. Walter E. Perry, who had been in business in Bethesda for thirty-five years, said he was planning to "just go around and annoy my family. If I get bored with that I own country land and I've always wanted to do a bit of wood sawing. I'll find things to keep me busy."

Mr. Veirs stated that he planned to continue carrying the wide range of products available at Perry's store, and also said he would keep secret the names of the customers in Chevy Chase who still were buying chicken feed.[87]

Storekeeper Perry

The third year of the war had added Kwajalein, Eniwetok, Saipan, Pelilu and Hollandia to Bethesdans' vocabularies. The great carrier battles of the Philippine Sea and the greatest naval battles of the war in Leyte Gulf all but destroyed the Japanese fleet. And in the fall MacArthur returned, getting his pants wet for the newsreel cameras. Few civilians had seen a Supefortress, and almost none knew about jet fighters.

The Allies had invaded Germany from both east and west. Aachen had fallen; the Russians took Budapest. Nazi industry moved underground as the cities burned, but the closed trains rumbled toward the death camps of Hitler's final solution.

At Dumbarton Oaks in Georgetown the Allies discussed a draft of the UN's charter and agreed on most points except for the veto provisions.

Downtown Bethesda in the war years

[1] Total enrollment in the County schools rose to 16,259, and cost per pupil for 1943-44 was $99.44 for white and $81.87 for "colored" children.

[2] For a short time McCall wrote about high school sports for both Allen and Bradley.

[3] Robert M. Burton, 707 6th Street NW.

[4] *Record*, Jan. 26, 1945.   Gertrude B. Dalrumple's 1971 LWV oral history in the County Archives.

[5] Architect V. T. H. Bien, whose office was on Vermont Avenue, lived across Cedar/Greentree in the old log house which may have served as an inn at the time of Bethesda Park.

[6] For a complete list see the *Record*, Jan. 22, 1944.

[7] Some of her more prudish neighbors found scandalous Mrs. Robert's habit of having her children run about unclothed during the summer.

[8] *Record*, April 9, 1944.

[9] *Star*, March 25, 1944.

[10] *Record*, April 15, 1944, and Northwest Park records at MCHS.

[11] *Star,* March 7, *Journal*, March 31 and June 9 and *Record* March 11 and April 8, 1944.

[12] *Record*, Feb. 19, 1944 through June 10, 1944. Also *Journal* April 28, 1944.

[13] See Feb. 18, 1944, *Journal* for Joseph Guandolo article. For original participants see *Record*, March 25, 1944. The vote: 1,152 in favor and only 62 against the idea, *Star*, Feb. 12, 1944.

[14] *Record*, Feb. 26, 1944.

[15] *Record*, March 11, 1944.

[16] "Stomping on Japs" was what some kids called the process of flattening tin cans.

[17] *Record*, April 29, 1944. Woodmont was, as far as the writer can discover, unique. Other country clubs staged war bond golf tournaments and charity affairs, or let flag rank officers play, but Woodmont opened its doors and treasury in unparalleled hospitality.

[18] Quote from Stella's Werner's oral biography in the Rockville Library.

[19] *Record*, April 22, 1944.

[20] *Journal*, July 21, 1944 reprinted from the *Times Herald*.

[21] The committee included Mrs. Maurice Davidson, Mrs. Theodore Peyser, Mrs. John H. Werner, Randolph Bishop, Carroll Murnane, Jo Morgan, and Mrs. George N. Matthews.

[22] These events, almost never reported in the newspapers, are very difficult to date. In fact, these two may have been the same one seen from different perspectives.

[23] Editor Goins crowed over the addition of Scates' and Lansburgh's stores to the Bethesda business community in a July 28 editorial in the *Journal*.

[24] Mr. Whittingham is one of the very few African-American workers of this period whose family name is known. Most domestics and blue collar workers were known only by their given name and not a few by an invented moniker.
   When "Your Crew at Kenwood" was featured in the Club's magazine, the all-black dining room staff was listed as "Sam, Jefferson, Moore, Eva, Columbus, Leonard, Shorty and Squirrel."

[25]B. Payton Whalen died in mid-March, age 67.

[26] Arthur G. Lambert remained vice-president, Joseph D. Montedonico, secretary, and S. Walter Bogley, treasurer of the Suburban Hospital Association. Many high school girls had been Jangos at other hospitals earlier - see *Life*, April 6, 1943.

[27]The writer knew and liked Alan and served Mass with him a few times but never at 6:30 in the morning. Alan always liked the "bell side." See *Star*, April 4, 1944.

[28]*Record*, April 15, 1944.

[29]*Record*, April 22, 1944. Both Dale Haley, 22, and Norma Viola Stutts, 27, pled guilty and were sentenced to two years.
In March in another case, which the local press did not cover, a 19-year-old Chevy Chase man shot and wounded a 14-year-old girl who lived on Brookeville Road because she refused to go out with him.

[30]*Record*, May 20, 1944. See materials on deposit at the County Archives.

[31]*Journal*, May 5, 1944.

[32]*Tribune*, Dec. 17, 1943. The 1944 *Tribune* is neither in the Pratt microfilm nor in the MCHS collection so references to its positions during that year are inferences from other sources, usually the other two papers.
Don Dunnington, Eddie Holloway, John Ferrari, Bernie Doyle, Thomas Carroll, and Frank Quinn were in the Army Air Corps. Edgar Tuller in the Merchant Marine, J. F. Graham, the Signal Corps; Raffe Mesrobian, the Marines; Billy Murphy, the Coast Guard; and Tony Miller, V-12 at Duke - *Record*, May 20, 1944.

[33]*Record*, May 13, 1944 et seq. and *Journal*, May 19, 1944 et seq.

[34]*Record*, May 6, 1944. Several rezonings for apartments on Bradley Blvd. were made without opposition that spring.
Grover Cleveland Bergdoll, WW I draft dodger, was released from prison in February. He had returned to the U.S. in 1939 with a wife and six children after living in Germany for years.

[35]*Journal*, June 9 and *Record*, June 10, 1944. Mrs. Bowie's assistants were Mrs. T. E. Larrimore and Mrs. James Birren.

[36]Day, left his nose position and buckled on his chute after the "bail out" command, and was the last one to leave his burning Liberator. He knocked himself out on the edge of the hatch. After falling several thousand feet, he came to and pulled the parachute handle and held on to it. When he was captured, he still had it, and the interrogator at the prison camp let him keep it. He stuck it in a knee pocket, brought it home, and still has his D-ring to show his grandchildren.

[37]*Tattler*, Vol. 1, No. 11, n.d., circa May 24, 1944.

[38]From a report in the archives of the DTRD. At the war's end the Model Basin had 12 officers and 79 enlisted men who had been "militarized." Plans for a drum and bugle corps were abandoned.

[39]*Star*, June 5, *Journal*, June 9 and *Record*, June 10 and 17, 1944.

[40]In January 1955 the Board of Education adopted regulations limiting the right of members of secret societies to participate in school and interscholastic activities.

[41]In one of the war's most memorable filmed scenes, Ensign Black of "Fighting Five" (VF-5) returned to the *Yorktown* in his F6F during the Battle of the Philippine Sea, grazed a turret, roared up the deck shedding wings and tail assembly, hit the island, broke the fuselage off behind the cockpit and climbed out with scratch on his forehead. One of Mitscher's pilots named that battle the "turkey shoot."
See Chapter 14 of *Eagle Against the Sun* on the Saipan campaign. Capt. Arleigh Burke, among others, was disappointed that some of the enemy escaped.

---

[42]The Childs' piece on Walter Shepard in the *Post* on July 28 and the *Record* on August 4, 1944, included a quote from his last letter: "If I live I will come home knowing life is a very unstable thing, and that it really pays to lead the best life you know how while you are here."

[43]In July, August and September there were 232 polio cases in the Metropolitan area, 94 of them in the suburbs.

[44]See *Journal*, July 7, and *Record*, July 8, 1944.

[45]*Record*, July 8, 1944.

[46]Another group of Gray Ladies headed by Congressional Club members Lillian Payne and Geraldine Keilty served doughnuts, coffee, and companionship in the evenings. According to the Club history, they produced 700 wrapped presents for the returned Chinese OGs at Christmas `45 "which were driven through the front door right into the Ballroom by a snow covered Santa in a jeep. . . ."

[47]*Star*, Aug. 2 and *Record*, Aug. 4, 1944. This was probably not the event Mrs. Sims recalled, however, since only twenty-seven ambulances were involved. Corpsman Dave Schrader remembered serving as a "janitor" on the women's ward and having thirteen-hour shifts of night duty at NNMC. He agreed with Mrs. Sims: "I do remember the distinct feeling that all of the 'nursing work' was done by the corpsmen and that the nurses, who held officer rank, simply supervised except when helping doctors."

[48]The poem is in the *Record*, July 28, 1944.

[49]In September the *Tattler* printed as gospel that "back in 1920 a boy was killed on a Baltimore (County) grid and his death blamed on poor equipment and coaching."

[50]Art Woods, for one, still believes it: "A former governor, I don't know if it was Millard Tydings or who it was, one of the former governor's sons was killed playing football. It's true, and so as a consequence they banned football in the state." George Van Wagner, who would have been in the class of `45, left to play for Devitt Prep. Some suggested that others left unhappy with new coach Fehrman. Bill Hahn, former Flint Hill and MCPS coach, said the reason for lack of football was the attitude of school administrators, period. Evidently no one recalled Tony Kupka's 1934-35 teams although one early *Star* story that the school "was returning to the football wars after an absence of ten years."

[51]*Tattler*, May 10, 1944. Bob Roth and Harold Sutton also attended the Boys' State session. *Record*, May 20, 1944. Art Wood recalled that after student lobbying, the Maryland General Assembly also passed a resolution supporting interscholastic tackle football.

[52]Leonard Williams remembered wearing a jacket with "Fortuna Luggage" on the back during his last year of junior high basketball.

[53]*Record*, June 3 et seq. and *Journal*, June 9 et seq. on LWV Q. and A. *Post*, June 24, 1944. Werner quote from *Record*, July 28, 1944.

[54]*Journal*, August 18 and *Record*, August 25, 1944.

[55]*Record*, August 25, 1944.

[56]*Journal*, and *Record*, September 1, 1944.

[57]From 1942-1946 Caniff also produced the "Male Call" strip, which featured Miss Lace, for service newspapers.

[58]There is nothing in the minutes of the Board of Education to indicate that this decision was more than an administrative act.

The *Tattler* reported that by Sept. 15, $1,009.15 had been pledged, $807.15 by 405 families and $202 by 41 Bethesda merchants, Sept. 28, 1944. Art Wood's memory is that they eventually raised a total of between $2,000 to $2,500.

[59]*Star*, Nov. 16, 1956, with thanks to Houston Swink who saved the clipping.

[60]The starting lineup for B-CC was reported as LE Hurley, LT Huber, LG Meixell, C Raymond, RG Knight, RT March, RE McCall, QB Chappell, LH Swink, RH Lowell, and FB Metzel, but it is

probably incorrect in several respects.   Glenn Ferguson missed the first game after spraining his ankle on the way to school.

Landon's yearbook credits the second score to Swink, and the *Star* reported that "Donnie Swink" scored both TDs.   No one can recall Herbie Benson playing football although he was issued uniform number 44.   Freshman Kenny Poerstel made the team but did not play.   "Jay-Dee" Olds was also a cheerleader and young Doug Hutton was the cheerleaders' "mascot."

61*Record*, Nov. 3 and *Journal*, Nov. 17, 1944. *The Pine Tree*, 1945 has the score of the Mt. Vernon game wrong.

62The first lettermen in football at B-CC HS were Chappell, Cleveland, Huber, Hughes, Hurley, Ferguson, Johnson, Knight, Lowell, March, Meixell, Metzel, R. Parkinson, Peterson, Raymond, Reese, Sabine, Swink, Tabler, Utterback, and manager Bill Mizell.

63By July 1945 the Marine, Earl McFarland, had been tried, convicted, and had his conviction upheld on appeal.

64*Record* and *Journal*, Sept. 8, 1944 and *Star*, Oct. 22, 1944. Only 2,000 of the 8,000 voting age men and women away from home in the service voted.

65Cited by Garber as from Mrs. Garfield's collection. *Md. News*, Sept. 29, 1944. Werner oral history.

66Biography of Stella Biddison Werner, 3 vol., in Rockville library.

67See Garber paper "E. Brooke Lee vs. the Charter" which cites the Garfield collection and Mrs. Garfield's comments on Mrs. Garber's thesis.

68*Journal*, Oct. 20, 1944 and *Star*, Oct. 21 and 29, 1944.

69In the battle to line up supporters for their cause, the antis listed several Charter supporters as being against home rule. Judge Brault admitted one of these, Mrs. George E. Hamilton Sr., really was a mistake.

70*Journal* and *Record*, Nov. 3, 1944 and *Star* Nov. 5 and 6, 1944.

71The "unofficial count" before the absentee ballots were read showed the vote was 14,610 against and 13,426 for the Charter. See Garber analysis in "E. Brooke Lee vs. Charter." The final total in the Bethesda precincts was 3,276 - 2,016, in Chevy Chase 1,829 - 1,000, and in Cabin John-Mass. Ave 1,107 - 846 so for 7th District a total of 6,212 for and 3,862 against or 61.6% favorable.

72See Chapter 17 of *A Grateful Remembrance* for more on the Charter fight. *Journal* and *Record*, Nov. 3 and 10, 1944. *Star*, Nov. 7, 1944. Werner oral biography. E. B. Lee oral history, MCHS.

73*Daily News*, Nov. 30 and *Record*, Dec. 1, 1944. See the Garber paper for a breakdown of campaign finances. The Lee "Organization" spent over $20,000 to defeat the Charter. Complete reports in *Record*, Dec. 8, 1944. In 1946 the Charter forces elected another charter board, and in 1948 the voters approved home rule 17,360 to 10,003, a Maryland first.

74*National Municipal Review*, December 1944.

75*Record*, Nov. 17, 1944. She wrote the *Record* that she was appalled that some voters were swayed by misstatements and appeals to prejudice and, in her opinion, were casting ballots without the facts. She saw it as an "indictment of public education."

764th row: Joseph, Andrews, Bonneville, Stewart, Curtis; 3rd row: Setser, Kellan, Forthman, Gilbert, Brown, Kochler 2nd row: Hobelman, Chadduck, Leister, Hoeck, Flood, Newbold, Willmott, Morrison, Miss Rusen 1st row: Astin, Carter, Machtman, Myers, Ong, Brewster, Beers.

77*Record*, Oct. 6, 1944.

78Thanks to Mr. Brubach and Mr. Kocker a complete collection of the "T. O. Report" is now in the files of the MCHS. These men also manned the Glen Echo VFD river rescue boat for many years.

79"Basin Chatter," January 1945.

80 For 1944 Suburban's admissions: total-2,489; babies-480; clinic-1,463; emergency room-1,274; operations-939. Operating budget: $273,000.

[81]The gold stars, much to the annoyance of the Lions and local editorial writers, disappeared almost as fast as they were put up to reappear on youngsters' bicycles, jackets and hats.

[82]*Maryland News*, Nov. 17; *Record*, Nov. 24. and Dec. 8, 1944.

[83]Both the Bergdoll and Glenbrook rezonings were denied.

[84]Board of Education minutes, September and October 1944.

[85] B-CC counselor Dorothy Young was elected vice-chairman; *U. S. News* vice-president Anthony Gould was chosen secretary, and attorney Jo V. Morgan treasurer. The other committee members were Carroll Murnane and Mrs. Morell, Mrs. Werner, Mrs. Mathews, and Mrs. Grosvenor.

[86]See *Record*, Dec. 22 and 29, 1944. Bethesdans in the delegation included State Senator Thomas Earle Hampton and Delegates Royal Carlock, 55, a photographer from Cabin John, and Thomas H. Hunter, 37, a lawyer who lived in Green Acres.

[87]*Record*, Jan. 5, 1945. "Veirs" is another of those County names spelled two ways regularly.

"We dedicate our book to those things which will remain as always, the familiar scenes of "our town." *Pine Tree* 1944

CHAPTER 14

Endings and Beginnings

The last year of the war began with a shortage of underwear and a run on shoe stores brought about by rumors of a ration stamp cancellation. Washington traffic moved much more freely since an estimated 1,500 cars abandoned the highways each month for lack of tires and parts, and the buses and streetcars were always crowded. Shortages, as well as the persistent mudhole on Wisconsin at Leland and the bottleneck at the bank, had become more a fact of life than an annoyance.

Smokers noted that when Lucky Strike green went to war, it took Camels and Chesterfields with it and left them to cope with odd brands, strange tastes and long lines. Several times when Tempe Curry Grant shopped in Bethesda with her two young children by the hand, Milton Smith would call out to her, "Miz Curry, you better get in line over at Peoples. The cigarettes just come in."

Whisky rationing, except for scotch, did end in the County, and few suggested doing away with the busy diagonal parking slots in front of the dispensary. Some very frigid weather closely followed by a coal shortage led to a lot more sweater wearing, a ban on display lighting and a "brown out." Judge Brault and the OCD took on the job of providing emergency coal supplies and handled some 400 calls for help from homeowners with empty bins, more than twenty percent of them in the Bethesda area.

Then another gasoline shortage resulted in long lines, hose-wrapped pumps and more frayed nerves. The ration board established Critchfield's station, which could be seen from the Board's Leland Street windows, as the place for doctors, nurses, fire fighters and policemen to purchase emergency supplies of fuel. The draft had made it almost impossible for most teenagers to avoid a paying job, and Mickey Johnston's father was able to get him a driver's license when he was only fourteen so he could make the grocery deliveries for the family's Sycamore Store.

Despite a six-day work week for most adults and a longer work day for many, the war produced a spirit of excited cooperation and practically universal participation in payroll-deduction bond buying and after-hours volunteering. Even the Thrift Shop started staying open one night a week so working housewives could look for bargains. Hundreds of servicemen, many with their families, found rooms with almost adoptive households in the Bethesda area, and their $30-a-month living allowance helped balance many family budgets.

Drivers generally picked up hitch-hiking servicemen and were editorially encouraged to do the same for civilians. One Bethesdan wrote the *Record* that during the war she and her husband had "rarely passed anyone at a bus stop if we had a seat in our car," but many drivers ignored her while she waited for a bus. "I regret to say that women are the worse offenders. I counted thirty-five in a few minutes one very rainy, windy day." Of course, not everyone had that "for the duration" spirit, and during 1945's meat shortage, black markets and under-the-counter dealing were widespread.[1]

Lee Higgins, who had clerked at the A&P until it closed in 1939, admitted that there was a black market "to some extent."

I used to get butter, and I never had trouble getting sugar. We kept some in the attic. My son Eddy liked cereal before he went to bed and once when the poker club was at my house, one of the fellows was a U.S. Marshal and another was a Montgomery County policeman. We was just having a good time. I came to the conclusion that nobody played except Methodists and Catholics, never had a Presbyterian playing. We were sitting there, and Eddy said he wanted some cereal. And he was putting that sugar on, and I said, "Take it easy on that sugar. That's all we got." And he said, "What about that seventy pounds up in the attic?" And the Marshal said, "What, what?" but nothing else was said, and I dealt the cards.

Down at the Frozen Food Mart, as the deepfreeze store was now known, Ann Long prepared 250 fish pies every week. Her recipe: filet of mackerel, mushrooms, peas, a dash of Worcestershire, pimento and a rich cream sauce in a pastry shell baked at 450° for about twenty minutes. The fish-every-Friday crowd grew larger in early `45; the once-patriotic meatless Tuesdays multiplied, and more cooks found different ways to serve Spam; hash and goulash were common.

Trash collection continued to exasperate many homeowners. During the cold, rainy weather, ten or twelve days often passed between visits by WSSC trucks. J. Donald Clagett blamed most of the problems on wartime labor conditions and continued to advertise for "colored men to report ready to work."

One Bethesdan reminisced about the good old days when for a dollar a month:

Mr. Willett and his merry men came three times a week to collect garbage and trash and, in winter time, twice a week for ashes. Mr. Willett's men came down to our basement and lugged the heavy ash cans out into the street into the truck. They made no mess in the performance of their duties and the whole business was a highly satisfactory arrangement.

But now, the writer complained, for a higher fee, "We have trash and garbage collections once a week or once every ten days" and the men do not come to work on cold days or when the weather is forbidding.The moral of the story, said the anonymous author, was that:

If trash and garbage were collected by an individual for a fee, that individual will work hard to make a living and keep satisfied custo-mers. But if he is on the County payroll, he may not feel like working on a cold or rainy day.[2]

The USO staged a very successful taffy pull early in the year, and Suburban Hospital proudly swaddled the region's first baby of 1945 as well as the first twins. At the high school both the boys' and the girls' basketball teams dribbled off to a good start as did the varsity at Leland, and downtown the OSS team led by high-scoring George Glamack was a real threat in the Heurich Basketball League. No one seemed to think it odd that the names of some of Gen. Donovan's hush-hush boys regularly appeared in box scores.[3]

In Bethesda, Gertrude Bradley celebrated the *Record*'s first birthday in her neat, pine-paneled office with a look back at the progress her all-woman staff had made and a thank-you to her husband for getting the papers mailed. She introduced a "Know Your Community" feature with some of Miss Holman's "Old Bethesda" essays and Thomas E. Robertson's history of Chevy Chase and by mid-year had hired her first male reporter.

For *Tribune* publisher-editor William Prescott Allen, 1945 was going to be the year in which he would become a recognized leader of many civic and religious activities and a thorn in the side of the Chamber of Commerce. He even began to consider a run for elective office if he had not thought about it before. And for Craddock Goins, who had tripled the *Journal*'s ad lineage and doubled its circulation, this would be the year he changed his mind about "Cunnel" Lee and made his paper the semi-official mouthpiece of the area's Republicans. He later found himself in a bit of hot water at the National Aviation Country Club in a dispute over slot machines and liquor licenses.

The so-called Gill Plan became the first big political issue of the year. E. Brooke Lee, chairman of the huge postwar planning committee, appointed a "well rounded," 120-member subcommittee to study the proposals to "modernize" the County government through legislative action. Park Commissioner Lee named former Civic Federation president Richard H. Akers of Edgemoor to chair the effort without asking him, and when Mr. Akers, a Charter supporter, declined because of his heavy work load, Lee turned to loyalist Jo V. Morgan who called the first meeting in mid-January at Bethesda Elementary and created four study groups to examine the ten

Gill proposals and James V. Bennett's suggestion for the non-partisan election of County Commissioners.

When it was called to Lee's attention that there were only a half-dozen women on the subcommittee, he quickly added thirty more. In committees, Lee believed the bigger the better. "Judge" Morgan set up an office in Room 200 of the Bethesda County Building, had stationery printed and asked for committee reports by the end of the month.[4]

Bennett's non-partisan election proposal, modified by Frederic P. Lee to have Commissioners elected on the same basis as Maryland judges, narrowly failed in the drafting committee where the Colonel himself had the decisive vote, but the Gill proposal to give the Commissioners more "home rule" legislative power won approval. The county-manager question became a raw point of contention even after Colonel Lee and Dean James J. Hayden, a leading Charter proponent, seemed to have reached a compromise.

Eventually Gill, as chairman of the County delegation, was able to take to the General Assembly in Annapolis just what E. Brooke Lee desired with the general support of the post-war planning group and the applause of the Democratic County Congress. Mrs. Werner, who chaired one of Morgan's subgroups, later described how those big meetings went in the auditorium at Bethesda Elementary School.[5]

The room was packed with the familiar faces of the hourly paid road workers seated in chairs lining the walls. Lacy Shaw, for years front man for the Democratic Party, was the floor leader. His resolutions or those to which he spoke favorably were always carried. The men lining the wall voted unanimously for them.

Although Stella Werner and many others worked doggedly, it was, as Marie Garber put it, an exercise in futility, and in the end Lee got what he wanted, external changes. The County manager, for example, ended up as an "agent and routine administrator of the county commissioners," a job which John Willmott later called "nothing but a $10,000 clerk and errand boy."

The home-rule proposal died after, and perhaps because, Frederic Lee praised it, and his letter to State Senator T. E. Hampton summed up the opinion of many Bethesdans.

To have imposed in this fashion on the time and energy of many citizens is unfortunate.

A majority of down county voters believe our county government is inefficient, fails to give full value in service for each tax dollar, and should be reorganized along modern lines. The net result of the maneuvering since December is that no genuine attempt has been made to meet even part way the views of these voters as to what legislation is necessary to such a reorganization.[6]

Meanwhile, the Advisory Committee on Post-War and County Planning made recommendations regarding new roads, such as Little Falls Branch Parkway, and off-street parking in the Silver Spring and Bethesda business districts. It was the latter question that provoked the year's second controversy. In early February the Committee suggested establishing tax-supported parking facilities in the commercial areas and changing zoning regulations regarding parking.

Banker S. Walter Bogley spoke for Bethesda merchants and commercial-property owners faced with a twenty percent tax increase if Lee's proposal became law. "There does not appear to be any justification for the plan, principles or methods of taxation," said Bogley, but he also stated that Bethesda businessmen would continue to study "this all-important subject."

The Board of Directors of the Bethesda Chamber of Commerce volleyed off a resolution opposing the parking plan and suggested that should off-street parking be needed at some future time, all property owners served by the business district should be asked to pay. They labeled the proposal "class legislation," the tax "unfair, inequitable and unjust," and the project "unique and practically untried as a public improvement service."[7]

The Civic Federation at first endorsed the parking-lot proposal and then wavered and approved a move to reconsider. The *Tribune*'s Bill Allen leapt to the defense of parking lots in a March 9 editorial headlined "Bethesda's Future Must Be Considered." He labeled the Chamber's opposition strictly financial and the Federation's equivocation utterly political and then took a reasonably prescient stand.

The Tribune feels that the entire future of Bethesda as a shopping center is related to the proper solution of this problem. Failure to realize that the shopper of the future is going to do his or her shopping where parking facilities are best is going to occasion many headaches for the merchants in any area but in Bethesda the provision of adequate parking

practically is a matter of bread and butter to the merchant.

If the customer cannot obtain the advantage of reasonable parking facilities in Bethesda, there is little reason for his or her continuing patronage of our stores. When gasoline and tires are once more just commonplace things purchased upon practically any corner, the customer might just as well drive downtown or over to Silver Spring where it would appear the merchants are going to insist upon having adequate parking space.

The Chamber of Commerce, as part of its opposition to tax-financed parking areas, authorized a study by G. Wady Imirie. His report, which excluded schools, churches and most smaller lots away from the main roads, showed almost 2,400 spaces used daily by about 750 employees and gave a reasonable picture of the business district at that time. The listing (at right) went from Bradley Lane northward along Wisconsin Avenue to Fairmont and then over to Old Georgetown.[8]

A third area of political dispute early in the year developed over the question of financing public improvements in the post-war era. Rollingwood's Lewis B. Sims, chairman of the Civic Federation's Committee on Public Finance and Budget, became the chief spokesman for planning and reform, and Lacy Shaw, president of the Board of County Commissioners, was the major defender of the status quo and of authority for $5 million in new bond issues. One of the problems, as Sims and others saw it, was that for a number of years re-funding of at least part of the County's growing bonded indebtedness had become an annual practice. The Commissioners had never developed a system to budget activities nor undertaken anything resembling long-term financial planning.

Before the General Assembly convened and while Colonel Lee's Brobdingnagian subcommittee was considering Gill's proposed bills, Sims laid out the issues in the *Record*. For the Civic Federation, he urged "a comprehensive plan for public improvements with individual projects ranged in order of urgency." He pointed out that Federal loans were dependent on such planning. Sims argued for a capital budget covering at least five years and for the continuing involvement of the public in decision making.[9]

Sims urged:

business	parking spaces
Safeway Wisc. & Bradley	40
Burrow's/Call Carl	80
Smith's Furniture and A&P	50
C&P Telephone Co.	4
Critchfield's & Eastham's	10
Park and Shop	50
Bethesda Motor Sales	35
Virga & Co.	12
Guild Building	30
Farm Women's Market	200
Comm'ty P&H & M. Scates	30
Eisinger's on Elm Street	16
Covington Motor Co.	10
Blue Ribbon Laundry	30
Little Tavern	6
Bethesda Building Supply	30
Sunoco at East West and Wisc.	8
Hot Shoppe	120
Hot Shoppe 2nd lot	100
Pumphrey's funeral home	20
Columbia Bakery	16
Gifford's Ice Cream Co.	45
Sack's tourist-Commerce St.	40
Dunne's service station	30
Caithness Buick	25
Bethesda Theater	250
Chevy Chase Motors	40
Red Fox and American Ice	25
Safeway Store at Chase	32
Whippet Tavern	16
Safeway Store Old Gtn	40
Bethesda Bowling Alley	250
Gulf, Esso, Sunoco, & Beall's	35
Shell station	20
Acme Market	150
behind stores from Peoples to Hiser	500

In our discussion of desirable projects and their planning we need to keep asking ourselves these questions: What will these improvements cost, both to construct and to operate and maintain? How are we going to get the money? How much will this increase our taxes?

With no such planning process in sight, the Civic Federation stood opposed to the $5 million bond issue authorized during the legislative session and urged the governor to veto the measure. Lacy Shaw defended the bill which included funding maturing bonds rather than raising taxes to pay them off. He expressed surprise at the Charterites opposition and labeled it purely political.[10]

The Briggs Clarifier Company, Bethesda's largest war industry with a workforce grown

Briggs Clarifier on River Road at the B&O

from GE, Zenith, Philco, Emerson and Wurlitzer came to Hampden Lane to learn how to build the devices in quantity. "The assembly operations were divided, with groups working in separate rooms," according to Bowen, "and the workers in these rooms were not aware of how the final device functioned." The U.S. produced over eight million proximity fuses in 1944, and their production occupied a fourth of the capacity of the American electronic industry and three-fourths of the plastic molding facilities.

Bethesda's most curious juveniles never found out what went on beyond those well-guarded doors, and the operation was even a problem for Fire Chief Bargagni. "Sometimes the fire department wasn't even allowed in," Frank Hall, a rookie fireman at the time, said.

A federal fire marshal would have to let you in there. In fact, there were houses right across the street from them. My wife's sister lived right across the street, and you couldn't go in there under any conditions. They had a small fire in there, and they wouldn't open the door until they cleared the area.

A lot of those women who worked there were housewives, and there were some jokes about what was going on in there. It was right behind Imirie's garage with the entrance on Bethesda Avenue.[12]

Allen Astin was educated and married in Utah and came to Johns Hopkins on a post-doctoral fellowship in 1930. John, the young

to over a thousand, continued to advertise for welders, spray painters and assemblers. Its ads promised a "bright post-war future" and bragged of the third star added to its Army-Navy "E" award. R. L. Falge stirred up some Edgemoor opposition when he asked to re-zone several lots to expand his defense business, while at Bowen and Co. almost three hundred women worked nine hours a day, six days a week assembling electronic devices without ever learning what they did. "When they need it the most, we give to them," said owner Edgar Bowen, praising the production levels achieved by his employees. The women worked behind paint-covered windows in old garages to assemble the super-secret proximity fuses developed by physicist Merle A. Tuve of the Carnegie Institute and a team at the National Bureau of Standards.

During the war, Tuve and his wife, Dr. Winifred Whitman, lived on Hesketh Street with their two children. He and Lawrence A. Hafstad of the Department of Terrestial Magnetism worked on the radio fuse for non-rotating projectiles, which was then developed at the Johns Hopkins Applied Physics Laboratory. Two other Bethesdans deeply involved with the fuses were Dr. Allen V. Astin of Battery Lane and Theodore H. Godfrey of Chester Road. The first tests took place in early 1941, but it took two more years before an operational item, the radio fuse, could be produced.[11]

Bowen & Co., which began work on the project in 1943, operated a pilot plant for assembling various parts of the fuses. Representatives

Workers at Bowen's Bethesda plant assemble the secret weapon

Allen Astin

couple's first son, was born there. Astin then moved to the Bureau of Standards and worked on a project funded by the Insull enterprises until that empire collapsed in the Depression. He recalled, "Well, I had another scramble for a job. . . . If I sent out in 1930 a couple of dozen inquires, I must have sent out fifty inquiries in 1932." That year his second son, Alexander William, "Sandy," arrived.

After working on a Navy death-ray project and ways to send telemetry from weather balloons for the study of cosmic rays, in 1935 the 31-year old Astin found a position at the Bureau in the Electricity Division devising means of measuring losses in capacitors. With job security the Astin family left their rented rowhouse for a home at 5008 Battery Lane in Bethesda's Northwest Park. By then gardening was Astin's hobby, and he began test growing hybrid roses for Jackson and Perkins. During the war a Victory garden filled most of the yard.

"Sandy" Astin recalled:

Our garden took up the whole backyard; my father didn't get into rose growing big-time until after the war. We had everything. They had created a hybrid vegetable that was supposed to be more efficient because it was supposed to have the stalk of celery and the leaves of lettuce. It was called celtus. I'll never forget this. I think what they ended up with was getting the stalk of the lettuce and the leaves of the celery. You were supposed to be able to eat the whole thing, and I recollect you couldn't eat anything. It was an awful vegetable. We had corn, beans, peas; we had a big asparagus patch. We had cucumbers, squash, potatoes, and it was a big chore working in the Victory Garden.

During the war years, Astin worked seven-days-a-week, mainly on the proximity fuses, and in 1944 went to England and visited various air bases to stage demonstrations of the fuses, which were so successful that:

The generals would not permit their use for fear that we would compromise our air superiority. Their general philosophy was that this was a much more valuable weapon to the enemy than it was to us. If we were to use it the enemy might get it and copy it and use it against us, and it would be disastrous.

On his return from Europe, Astin became Assistant Chief of the Ordnance Development Division and moved into the management track at the Bureau.[13]

Early in the year, the Chamber of Commerce endorsed G. Wady Imirie's report on the commercialization of the Woodmont area as recommended by the M-NCP&PC. Imirie's committee, which had been working on the Bethesda Master Plan, also suggested the commercial development of the south side of Old Georgetown to Auburn Avenue with apartments to Glenwood Road.

The Chamber itself, led by executive secretary J. Philip Schaefer, a PEPCO engineer, changed its by-laws and raised its dues in anticipation of establishing a permanent office with a paid secretary. During the year, a Chamber committee, led by Dr. J. Raymond Nelson, investigated several possibilities for permanent war memorials including various types of buildings, a swimming pool and a town clock.

In January, a dozen or so "old timers" organized the Bethesda Kiwanis Club during a meeting at the Columbia Dining Room. They elected editor William Prescott Allen as their first president and Dr. Leo Donovan and Emory Bogley as first and second vice-presidents. Chester McCall was chosen secretary-treasurer and Malcolm Scates and Wilton Wallace were elected to the board. Sixteen charter members signed up, and at the first regular meeting, they honored Mrs. Allen as "Queen of the Day," sang "Let Me Call You Sweetheart" and gave her a bouquet.

The new service club decided to meet at the Cape Cod Inn on Mondays, and the Rev. Hartwell Chandler became their first sky-pilot. Within a month there was a Kiwanettes group, with the wives serving in the same posts as their husbands. For a USO supper that winter the Kiwanis Club had the Hot Shoppe roast a 175-pound pig from Malcolm Scates' farm and then put on a talent show emceed by Art Brown at the piano and featuring solos by servicemen and women and "Little" Stella Werner's boogie woogie. In early spring, the Kiwanians pledged $1,300 to purchase an iron lung for Suburban Hospital as soon as one could be procured.

On Monday, January 22, at their annual meeting, the members of the Farm Women's Cooperative Market burned their $50,000 mortgage and announced that the market was debt free. Under the leadership of Mrs. J. B. Waters, it had taken them only nine years. By the time of the mortgage burning the cooperative had eighty-six sellers, most of whom were stockholders in the corporation, and had become not only a Bethesda institution but a nationally famous success.

Suburban Hospital with an annual budget of $272,000 went through several changes in 1945. At the end of January, it opened its fifth wing. The new wards in a renovated part of the original building were for African-American patients and included both private and semi-private rooms, a nursery and a diet kitchen. George M. Hawkins headed the program committee for the dedication featuring a talk by Dr. Ethel L. Nixon of Freedman's Hospital. The medical staff elected Dr. Edward J. Stieglitz to succeed Dr. Charles R. L. Halley as president. Dr. Stieglitz, a member of the hospital's Department of Medicine, had moved to the County in 1939 and made his home in Garrett Park.

In March, Superintendent J. Dewey Lutes, after serving for Suburban's first fifteen months, resigned to take a similar position at the Yonkers General Hospital. As one of his final acts, Mr. Lutes, chairman of the Sixth War Loan Drive, announced that the County had oversubscribed its $2,500,000 quota by 171 percent. While Mrs. Morell and the Board of Trustees sought a successor, RN Phyllis Goodman, Mr. Lutes' assistant, served as interim superintendent. Arthur B. Solon accepted the appointment and took over after moving down from Mt. Vernon, N. Y., in mid-April with his wife and two young children. Mr. Solon brought nineteen years of experience, mostly in large teaching hospitals in Wisconsin and New York, to the young, community hospital.

Bethesda's religious community was also active and changing. The Rev. Claude A. Brubaker's spontaneous peace-prayer movement spread rapidly until there were seventeen groups of various denominations praying regularly for the men and women overseas and for peace. The Mt. Zion minister hoped to interest the schools in the program.

The Bethesda Council of Churches elected the Rev. Hartwell F. Chandler, pastor of the Methodist Church, to succeed Reverend Brubaker as president and then met with Joseph Bunker, the newly hired executive-secretary of the County YMCA, and enthusiastically endorsed that program. The Y, newest member of the local Community Chest, hired Bunker under the leadership of Frederic Nettleship, chairman of the Committee on Management, and was in the process of planning activities for adolescent boys as its initial project. The Council of Churches also promoted the World Day of Prayer on February 16 and planned another union Easter service.

Bishop Abram H. Cannon of the 475-member Chevy Chase Ward of the Washington Mormon Stake announced plans to build a $200,000 church on Western Avenue at Kirkside. J. Willard Marriott headed the finance committee for that project. In February, the Jewish Community Group sponsored a chess exhibition and tournament at the Naval Hospital and, before the High Holy Days, presented a scroll of the Torah to the NNMC chaplains.

The USO started the New Year with more than just Lucille Culver's taffy pull. Skylights helped brighten the interior of the old Safeway, and a new storm door was very popular with the senior hostesses who staffed the desk by the front entrance. The service personnel and junior hostesses elected a planning committee composed of chairman PhM1/c Harry Gunnison, vice-chairman PhM 3/c Glenn A. Lee, secretary Martha Graham and "Scuttlebutt" editor Janice Hoffman. The recently married Gunnison, a bespectacled pipe smoker from Girard, Pennsylvania, was a graduate of Lehigh University and a senior

Gunnison, Graham, Hoffman and Lee at the USO

operating-room Corpsman. "Red" Lee, of Indian-Irish ancestry, grew up in Oklahoma and worked for Phillips Petroleum before enlisting in the Navy.[14]

Mrs. Scott Brewer, the Tuesday night senior hostess, took over the chairmanship of the Sunday night suppers, and a committee of the Jewish Community Group, headed by Mrs. Albert Lyman, served one of the first dinners of the year–fruit cup, chop suey, tossed salad and homemade pies. It was followed by Gershwin songs from Mrs. Charles Baum and her daughter Betty, and then Abe Lerner and his accordion had everyone singing along while Joel Wolfsohn, furrier Gad Jacobson, Abe Olshen and Fred Simon washed the dishes.

Another of the popular dances at Woodmont Country Club, a square dance at the clubhouse and a Saturday night birthday party for all those born in January were topped by a big open house to celebrate the fourth anniversary of the founding of the USO. The War Recreation Committee also staged dances for officers stationed or living in the Bethesda area, and, again, Woodmont provided the setting.

At the high school, Dr. Oscar Blackwelder of the Church of the Reformation addressed the nine-member, mid-year graduating class of which "Hob" Simons was president. After the ceremony, there was a tea for the parents and then a dance that evening. Senior Betty Reed reported the events in her gossipy *Tribune* column, "Between Hamburgers."

Friday the third accelerated class graduated. There were eight boys and one girl: George Betzold, who goes into the Army Airborne; Steve Edson, Navy; Ed Cowan, Army; Al Pettit, paratroopers; Jimmy Rehlander, Hobart Simons, Army; Nick Sinder, who goes to ASTRP at V.M.I.; George Sullivan, claimed by the Marines; and Anne Sherman who is going to college in Colorado. Everyone had a slight "lump in the throat" feeling as the graduates filed out . . . .

The Blue and Gold Prom Friday night in honor of the graduates was perfect! – many advocate it because the gym was illuminated only by one top light. All of Bethesda made their way through the snow to attend. AND the boys even induced Nick Sinder to come. Iris and Iris took a large picture of the dance and will post it in their window . . . .

At the end of January, the March of Dimes campaign involved many Bethesdans.

Henry Hiser donated one day's receipts from his bowling alleys, and George Huguely matched him with the Sunday proceeds, less pinboy costs, from his Forty Alleys. Mrs. William Sholar chaired the American Legion-sponsored President's Birthday Ball at Kenwood and sold the $5-a-couple tickets at Lebling's real estate office.

Out in Glen Echo, the Civic League of Brookmont and Vicinity sponsored a country dance at the social hall of the Chapel of the Redeemer to benefit the Fairway Hills Child Care Center. The sponsors credited the event's success to caller Howard Bakerman of Cabin John and the tunes of the Riverside Ramblers: fiddler Oscar Pearl, guitarist Harold Mansfield and banjoist Paul Connelly.

At both Leland and B-CC, the PTAs discussed Universal Military Training, a hot topic that winter. The Chamber of Commerce tabled a report from Reece Sewell and J. Philip Schaefer supporting UMT after some spirited discussion. The local weeklies generally supported the idea, Craddock Goins vociferously, but Principal Tom Pyle questioned both the need and cost of such a program. Meanwhile, the draft board was wiping out occupational deferments for men under thirty and reclassifying most of them 1-A.

At the high school, where the obstacle course was now seldom used, student interests, as usual, focused on sports and the opposite sex. Red-headed cheerleader Katy Bart had thought some of the girls rather "fast" when she arrived at B-CC as a junior from a small town school in Ohio, and she wondered why so many of them carried pocketbooks. Now she realized these were just the smokers who needed their cigarettes for gab sessions in the grove.

Kenny Parkinson, who had quickly become one of the top three "heartbreakers," had "Ma" Mohler for a homeroom teacher.

She took me aside and told me that I'd better straighten out, that I was getting myself mixed up with the wrong crowd of people. She said I should join Hi-Y and that I'd better do it right away 'cause other-wise things were going to look kind of dismal. She had perceived that I was hanging around with some people that were smoking cigarettes out in the pine trees, and I was going straight to hell if I started doing things like that. I listened to her carefully but didn't do what she recommended.

NINETEEN FORTY-FIVE   665

Smokers and others in the Grove

Parkinson remembered the students as being divided into many different groups with different interests, and Katy Bart Mizell recalled that she and her friends pretty much took over Job's Daughters, giggled through the meetings and operated it as a sub-rosa sorority. She also admitted that the high school was dominated by cliques of various sorts even if the Greeks no longer met openly.[15]

The fire board elected Charles S. Embrey of Edgemoor as president and went on record supporting a central fire alarm system for the whole County. Chief Bargagni reported that his men had responded to 203 fire and thirty-three rescue calls during the previous year, about a hundred fewer than the year before. The total fire loss for 1944 was only $6,055. Bargagni again urged Bethesdans to refrain from burning off their lawns and weedy lots and laid down strict rules for those who insisted on doing so. The State Department of Forests and Parks helped with a regulation prohibiting open burning before 4 pm. Agitation for an ambulance continued to simmer.

In February, the Victory Garden centers reopened with the chairperson dividing her time between Bethesda and Silver Spring. Ayrlawn Farms' two-year-old Jersey, Trixie Sybl Lily, became the State champion for both milk and butterfat with 9,057 pounds of milk and 6.22 percent, 563 pounds of fat, in 305 days. Letts's son-in-law, F. Henry Jones, was keeping the big farm operating and the fine herd prize winning, but he was willing to consider turning the huge barn into a shopping center someday and moving the dairy cows out to Laytonsville. After a visit, Craddock Goins called the barn "about the biggest business

establishment in Bethesda" and rhapsodized over the "beautiful little kingdom" with its honeysuckle hedges and acres of bluegrass.[16]

New businesses in Bethesda included the Hudson Supply Company branch store at 7341 Wisconsin, which sold kitchen appliances, storm windows and asphalt tile; Charles E. Gray's Little Shop at 8025 Wisconsin where he repaired, restored and reproduced antique furniture; and C. J. "Chet" Caithness' Buick dealership, which opened in early spring near the Bethesda Theater. Chuck Cashdan, owner of the year-old Universal Contracting Company on Hampden Lane, now had fifty employees and was using up a boxcar of roofing shingles every month.

The Rochdale Co-op declared a three percent refund for members on purchases made in 1944 and began sponsoring a series of luncheons to discuss ways of improving their store. Manager John B. Crosby, an old A&P man, coped with a constant turnover in personnel, a series of shortages and a growth in membership to 535 with about one thousand regular customers. The Ladies Speciality Shop solved the brown-out prohibitions by lighting its big front window with two large candles.

In February, Craddock Goins announced his intentions to make the *Journal* the County's Republican newspaper with a signed editorial urging more Republicans to register and declaring that a "new type of leadership" was needed on both the national and local levels. Party Chairman Francis Hill wrote his precinct leaders:

It is of the utmost importance to the Republican party that we have a strong partisan paper in our county. Any help you can give to the Bethesda Journal by way of either yourself subscribing or getting other precinct workers to subscribe will certainly be of aid to the Republican party in our County. Your cooperation will be greatly appreciated.

The *Record* noted that Goins's paper had been the "mouthpiece" of the Republicans when Merle and Day Thorpe ran it and that it was owned by a Republican, J. M. Hickerson of New York. Mrs. Bradley then weighed in with an editorial headlined "Declaration of Independence" in which she stated that she had been approached by County Republicans and told them she was not interested. She wrote,

Although the editor is a Republican by birth and conviction and has been registered as such

in Montgomery County for 12 years, she is a journalist first and a party member second. Her conception of a community newspaper is not that of a party organ.

Crime made the news in Bethesda that winter. Someone stole $75 and the cash box from the Iris and Iris studio in the Shopping Center in the middle of the day, and early on a February evening, two young women were attacked while walking up Wilson Lane just west of Emmy Lou's. A man struck them both on the head with a club or stick and then ran away when they screamed. One woman was treated for a concussion while the other was released from Suburban Hospital with slight injuries. Captain McAuliffe asked neighbors in the Battery Park area for information, but none was forthcoming. Thieves broke into Chevy Chase Motors twice, and the second time made off with forty tires. A. H. Bowis offered a reward for information about the robbery.

In mid-February auto painter Henry Corens reported that his wife, Pearl, was missing from their home on Gladwyne Drive near the Naval Medical Center. Two weeks later his wife's head was found in a ditch near Dranesville, Virginia. It had evidently been brought there in a half-bushel basket. After a neighbor reported that she had seen Corens changing the seat covers in his car, the police began questioning him and sifting the ashes in his furnace. In the spring he was indicted, tried in Anne Arundel County and convicted of her murder.

Despite this grisly act and except for housebreakings, the Bethesda and Chevy Chase areas were relatively free of major crimes. The "knights of the yellow triangle," as some adolescents labeled the police, spent most of their time trying to enforce parking restrictions and controling the flow of traffic.

The military casualty list kept mounting. On February 2, for example, the *Record* reported two local men killed in action and one who died of injuries received on maneuvers plus one missing in action in Belgium and Lt. DeWitt Smith's (B-CC '38) third Purple Heart for being shot in the knee at Bastogne. All three papers carried several columns of news of servicemen and women throughout the war, some supplied by relatives and some by military public information offices.

In February, readers of those stories could find out that "Sonny" Marsh, who had been drafted after graduating from high school at the end of the summer session at B-CC, had earned a second high school diploma by going back to Augusta Military Academy and finishing his work there before reporting to the Navy and that LeRoy Allison, who entered the Navy at 17 in 1943, had visited his parents briefly after completing his radar training at Corpus Christie and was now headed for California.[17]

At the high school, the second semester saw the addition of a course called Current History taught by Patricia Lozupone.[18]

Thomas W. Pyle called me up one day and said, "Patsy, I have a proposition for you." Dorothy Young had become a counselor during the war, and they had children up there that nobody would have in a class. He said, "Will you come up here and deal with them? We don't give a damn what you do with them. Just keep 'em in the classroom, and you can do whatever you want. Dorothy Young says you can do anything you want," and I was hired as her assistant.

So that's what I did during the war. We started out learning to fill out income tax forms because they were all working and making more money that I was. I had one boy whose mother let him drive the car, and he was only fifteen. And they would arrest him as soon as he would drive off at lunchtime so I would have to circle over there to the station and say, "Give me my student."

I had them all afternoon, from lunch to three o'clock. Dorothy had the idea I was going to do interest tests with them, but they didn't have enough interest to stick the pin in them. So, I said, "We'll take up things you are interested in. You all have to file income tax so let's sit down and learn income tax." Then I said, "Let's learn to read the newspaper." I had about twelve kids, both girls and boys.

I would show up at lunchtime, but sometimes I would get up and come substitute for Latin when they were really desperate because I could read Latin. I would come busting into the cafeteria up there on the third floor, and Mary Mohler, all the old teachers, would say, "Hi Patsy, Hi Patsy." Nobody else knew who the hell I was. They gave me the room and said do your best. Dorothy Young and I got along fine, and anything I could create was good enough for her.

Cheerleaders and Doug Hutton at the bonfire

The boys' varsity won six of their first seven games, losing only to the alumni, before facing Blair at Ritchie Coliseum. Herbie Benson and Charlie Hughes led the early season scoring, and sub Chet McCall, writing for the *Tribune*, agreed with the *Star*'s assessment that the team was "surprisingly strong." But Blair's Red Blazers overcame an early Baron lead and won 23-18 as Bethesda made only six of eighteen foul shots. Betty Reed noted that "it was a rather dejected group of Bethesdans who gathered at the A&W after the Blair game."

Bethesda won the next two including a 70-8 romp over Richard Montgomery but then lost to Jim "Big Boy" O'Donnell and Georgetown Prep. O'Donnell had been getting twenty points a game regularly that season, and no one at B-CC had done that for three years. On the Thursday night before the second Blair game, a snake dance with much cheering and singing started at the McCalls' house on 44th Street and wound up Wisconsin Avenue and down East West Highway to the Metzel Bowl where the varsity ignited the bonfire.

In the game, Bethesda led by twelve at halftime. "We were hot," guard Charlie Hughes remembered,

And we were playing a zone. One guy beat us, Johnny Klippstein. And Herbie Benson felt terrible because Klippstein would dribble up the court, sight the basket and fire. And he did not miss. Herbie and I were out front in the zone, and thank God, he liked Herbie's side. He must have hit ten straight. Then we got rattled.

Despite Chris Chappell's sixteen points, Blair won again, 43-38. Led by high-scoring freshman Kenny Poerstel, the B-CC JV team salvaged some honor by taking its ninth straight, 14-13, over the Blair Junior Varsity.[19]

The Barons only won one of their last four games, losing even to N.T.S. in the war years' greatest upset and perhaps roughest game, but the Star Tourney invited both Blair and B-CC as well as B-CC girls' team, which was led by Lois Copenhaver, who scored 108 points in twelve games, and team captain Betty Beard, who had seventy points for the season. St. John's did not have much trouble defeating the boys in the tournament's first round, and the heavily favored Fairfax girls pulled out a 16-15 win in the last seconds in the closest game of that year's first round.[20]

Leland's varsity led by Dick Latimer, David Parkinson, and high-scoring Johnny Ruggles raced through its season with a 13 and 4 record, but then tripped over Kensington in the first round of the championship tourney, a first, losing 23-19 to the eventual champions. In the recreation league Phil Daly led his Bethesda Eagles to an undefeated season, and they beat the Canteen Club 17-13 for the championship.

Lois Copenhaver grew up in Chevy Chase, D.C., and attended E. V. Brown before moving to Glenbrook Road at the far end of the Woodmont Triangle halfway through her fifth grade. She played baseball in the street, rode her bicycle over into Edgemoor where some people still were stabling horses, and bought penny candy at Emmy Lou's. "The stuff I ate at Emmy Lou's, I don't know why I'm alive today," she said. "Wax whistles with some kind of green and red juice, even when you ate it and drank it, you still had this white stuff. It was terrible." She also became a fan of the hot fudge sundaes at the Clover Crest store in the Shopping Center. She recalled the pebbly bottom of the swimming pool at Chevy Chase Lake and the riding lessons she took at the old carbarn across the street.

B-CCers enjoying swirled cones and sundaes

In the spring of 1939, Lois had been in the crowd that gathered around the small plane that crashed near the back of Columbia Country Club and recalled seeing the dead pilot in the crumpled wreckage. She practiced shooting baskets for "hours and hours" at a hoop on her garage, played basketball at Leland in the 8th and 9th grades and won the school badminton title one year. [21]

Although she was a bit shorter than most girls in her class, Lois played varsity basketball all three years at B-CC and was the leading scorer as both a junior and senior, proud of the swishes she could put in from the side. Almost every winter morning, she rode her bike over to Betty Beard's home on West Virginia Avenue and then walked to school with her friend to practice at 7 am. She was also a member of the Activity Council every year and president as a senior. About the School Door Canteen, she said:

It was just one of those spontaneous ideas that somebody had, not so much a war effort as a way to get people together. We wanted to provide activities for everybody, to have someplace to go and dance.

Now, Blue and Gold Day, I think that was my idea, related to generating enthusiasm in terms of people coming to the prom. I can almost hear me saying, "Suppose everybody wears blue and gold." It was surprising how many yellow sweaters showed up.

I didn't go to the Rec Center. I was so busy with study, athletics, activities. I went to St. Ann's Orphanage to wash orphans on weekends and joined the JANGOs and went down to Doctors' Hospital and worked as an aide. I dated all the time, not a lot of different boys, Steven Edson was one, on weekends, and I went to all the dances. There was not a lot of calling back and forth. We weren't allowed to hang on the phone. You went to the dance in a boy's father's car and better be sure you were back by the curfew hour.

She remembered her classmates as rather "homogeneous."

Lois Copenhaver

We had some parties, but everything was so serious. We were in a serious frame of mind. I guess it was the war that changed things. I don't remember having a lot of fun even playing basketball. I remember it more as a job, something you did. I liked to do it, and I was good, that helps, but everybody went home after school and studied. No cars was part of it.

She admitted that not everyone was as serious about school.

Oh, people skipped school once in a while, and there was a "fast crowd," that's what we called them, that wore lipstick and tight sweaters. But they were very nice, too. I went all over the place by myself. I was in a play at CU the summer before I was a senior, Jean and Walter Kerr's "Song of Bernadette." I used to come home after midnight, rode the bus to Tenley Circle, stood there.

That was the hallmark of our whole class. We did things. The idea that defines my high school days is good citizenship. We were always doing things like trying to get crossing lights on the corner at East West. I remember Ann Kline standing up and talking about how you could never cross the street at the bank because the lights were so bad.

We had a sense that we should vote, that we shouldn't litter. "Optimistic self assurance" somebody called it. It characterized our whole class. We didn't have these doubts. I don't know that our class was super accomplished, but they all did something.

That winter the high school PTA put on a talent show featuring a number of students and parents including Bob Tabler and his father and Stella Allison and her dad. The school's Activity Council pushed the war bond drives, started Blue and Gold days, and celebrated the first anniversary of the School Door Canteen with a big party that highlighted a four-tier birthday cake. Another party at the Meadowbrook Cabin that same mild, mid-February night ended with some B-CCers wading in Rock Creek. The next day it snowed.

Of course, in addition to all the wartime volunteer activities and sports, many students worked after school and on weekends, some out of choice to support their cars and clothes but many out of need with fathers away and most wages frozen at low levels. The twenty members of the retailing class in the Distributive Education program made $11,070.43 for their combined 21,000 hours of work and even purchased a half-page ad in the yearbook. Most of teacher-coordinator

Page Furth's boys were headed for the Navy right after jobs at Soper's Esso, Sherwin-Williams and Lowdermilk's. The girls had worked at department stores, banks, Carbert's and C&P, and most of them moved right into full-time positions when school was over. Many others held part-time jobs like Kenneth Parkinson's at Peoples.

"We went to the Hot Shoppe a lot," he said, trying to recall how he spent his money.

There was a lot of action on Friday and Saturday night, people milling around all over the place. We used to skate down at the Ice Palace, and in 12th grade we'd go down to Georgetown and visit the bars, the Silver Dollar on the corner of Wisconsin and M Street, and there was a place just below the District Line on the left-hand side that sold a glass of beer for ten cents. If you could afford a dollar's worth of beer, you were absolutely crocked.[22]

I had a job at Peoples Drug Store right there at East West Highway. Jack Plank's father was the manager. I worked on the soda fountain with this little, short black lady, lovely lady. In the back was a place you had to wash all the dishes, and then you would make up sandwiches, tuna fish on white toast. The black people went down to the end of the counter and got theirs in a paper bag. Later I went down to the District Line, Howard Johnson's, and worked on the side counter there.

The Activity Council at B-CC was also in charge of the honor roll assemblies, and at the first one of 1945 it added seven gold stars to the service banner for Ed Porter, class of `42, a B-17 co-pilot who died in England; Bob Barton, voted most personable in the class of `41, killed when a bomb exploded on his carrier; and bashful Robert Garvin, class of `43, killed in a bomber crash.

The students recited the 23rd Psalm together, and Lois Copenhaver read "High Flight" before the gold stars were placed on the new service banner. In his sports column Chet McCall noted that "Two years ago a boy named Bob "Killer' Garvin played ball on Bethesda's Varsity. At the first Blair game Bob was out in his lieutenant's bars and Air Corps wings rooting the team on."

The others honored were Bill Jennings, also of `43, winner of the 1940 D.C. soapbox derby and cartoonist for the high school newspaper, a B-17 gunner who died of polio; George Dorroh, class of `43, remembered for his pipes and his clothes, he died of meningi-

tis as a sergeant in the Signal Corps; Coast Guardsman Boyce Guthridge, `41, who had lived at the Baptist Home where his mother worked, was killed in an ammunition explosion at sea; and Sgt. Dick Bell, class of 1940, whose high school interests included football, woodshop, the Opera Club, and sub-debs, died in action in Europe after surviving the invasion of France and an earlier wound. The service banner in the main hall then had 1,200 blue stars and twenty-four gold ones.[23]

Leland Junior High School and its thousand students seemed to be in an almost constant state of fermentation during the war. The teacher turnover was very high, and in 1944-45 section, 8P, went through so many teachers that it was finally disbanded while 8U's numerous faculty changes led to "near riots" and 8R wore out a succession of math instructors. The school experimented with "tracking," but it did not take long for 8Z to figure out they were the smartest, and the other 8th graders to know where they stood.

Ruth Weld

Through it all "Weld's Willing Workers," as art teacher Ruth Weld called her succession of homerooms, 9VIII in the class of `45, toed the line, contributed to every collection and even won the intramural football cham-pionship and came in second in basketball. Each section expected to collect at least 150 pounds of paper per week, and in the War Bond Drive Mrs. Parkinson's 7B homeroom alone "purchased" five jeeps and $674 in medical supplies. Mr. Conlon and Mr. Schumaker began working out a point system so that students could win letters for service to the school as well as for athletics.

Leland adjusted to Elwood P. Mason, its third wartime principal, as well as to a new assistant principal in Alice Rawson and even a new secretary, Miss Meyers. Mason, a graduate of Washington College and Duke, had been the Ocean City, Md., high school principal before coming to Montgomery County. He was an experimenter who believed in providing opportunities for early

Principal Mason

Helen Bender

Milton L. McCullough

adolescents to explore many subjects. Willard Schumaker took over the boys' PE department, and at mid-year Mrs. D'Ambrosia replaced Mrs. Madden in the girls' physical education program. There was even a new cafeteria manager, Frances Lattie, who had help from four volunteer mothers and a few students in serving lunch every day.

A capable and loyal cadre of teachers kept Leland running reasonably smoothly amid the confusion of multiple faculty changes and wartime restrictions. Helen Bender, sponsor of the class of `45, coped with a library uprooted by construction and renovation. Stalwart Minette Gunderson and math teachers Alice Comer and her sister, Helen Dempsey, kept their senses of humor and their high standards. Ina Parkinson and Ruth Weld, equally creative and hard working, were always up to something new and interesting, and Milton L. McCullough, sponsor of the "grounds committee" was by far the most popular and feared teacher of the time.

Mr. Mac, a no-nonsense math teacher, was a ruddy, bluff, older man who immersed himself in the school and was loved by many; although some of the girls admitted they had been frightened of him when they were 7th graders. Millie Imirie said he had no patience with girls who had trouble in algebra class, and she admitted that the glee club pianist, Peggy Hudson, helped her survive. "Sandy" Astin labeled McCullough a martinet.

His willingness to participate in plays and assemblies became legend as did his sense of the ridiculous. When one of his students produced an owner-less pair of gym shorts, Mr.

Mac asked if there was any name in them. The boy read the label. "It says Julius Garfinckel." Mr. Mac sent him to the office to find out which section Julius was in, and by lunchtime the story had circled the building twice. On his classroom wall hung a fish and the warning, "Even a fish would not get in trouble if he kept his mouth shut."

Mr. Mac flew model airplanes with some of his students and enjoyed taking photographs of them and their pets. He attended most of the ball games and dances. His classes celebrated his November birthday, and it was he who gave section 9III its motto: "Hold your paper so I can see." [24]

In February the girls in Elizabeth Reid's sewing class showed off the dresses they made including Carol Benson's gold colored wool gabardine and Tipton Stringer's green cotton with the draw string neckline. Then in March all the ninth grade girls in Home Arts "paraded the almost 300 school, street and date dresses and play suits which they have made in the clothing classes" at an assembly. And Miss Reid surprised some boys that winter when she took over several shop courses. The coal shortage canceled all the Leland dances and parties, and Doc Whittlesey instituted a 3 pm "curfew," but there were still plenty of activities including the first after school YMCA programs.[25]

The war's pace accelerated in Europe. A huge Russian offensive smashed the Germans back through Poland while American forces reached the Rhine by March. In the Pacific the Philippines fell and B-29s intensified their raids on Japan. On February 19, the Marines landed on volcanic Iwo Jima to start a month-long campaign that would cost them 20,000 casualties including several that hit Bethesda extra hard. The famous flag-raising picture was on page A-3 of the February 24 *Star* .

On the home front, War Mobilization Director James F. Byrnes announced a midnight curfew on places of amusement, and the County Commissioners backed him up with an enforcement order to the local police. The OPA began to crack down on violators of its

price controls and several local businesses paid embarrassing fines. Grossman's Market on Western Avenue reached a settlement for overcharging one cent on 30,912 bottles of beer and paid $463.68, one-and-a-half times the overcharges, a Maryland record at the time. The Howard Johnson's at the District line paid a $25 fine for several overcharges on its menu, and the DGS on Brookeville Road was fined $25 for charging too much for B&B baked beans. Kenwood Golf and Country Club had to refund $831.10 to the Treasury for five and ten cent overcharges on whiskey and gin drinks. Karl Lehman of the Battery Park Market paid a $25 fine for small overcharges on canned peas, molasses and peanut butter.

As Bethesdans began to think of spring, the Canteen Club at the Rec Center attempted to get unredeemed pledges fulfilled, and elected a new steering committee headed by Leslie W. Orr with Capt. James S. McAuliffe as vice-chairman. The student committee reported membership of 342 with average attendance of sixty-five on canteen nights.

The Naval Medical Center asked Congress for $60,558 to build athletic fields and tennis courts, justified as important for rehabilitation, and Bill Allen started a campaign to urge people not to call the Medical Center the Navy Hospital or Naval Hospital. At the hospital a small but real newspaper, the National Naval Medical Center *News*, replaced the mimeographed weekly bulletin. Printed on the base, it featured profiles of military and civilian personnel, local gossip and cartoons by PhM3/c Andy Coleman whose "H. A. Deuce" strip was a favorite.

Bethesda's librarian, Marjorie B. Robinson, resigned that spring with praise from the Board of Directors and the *Tribune* for her three years of service and "friendly, helpful spirit." Her assistant, Eleanor Titsworth, took over as acting librarian for the next six months. The library then had 12,800 books, 6,000 regular borrowers, and an annual circulation of about 60,000.

In what became one of the most successful wartime efforts, George N. Mathews headed the local United Nations Relief and Rehabilitation Association's clothing drive. He put the collection for wartorn Europe in the hands of the service clubs and appointed Henry Hiser of Rotary, Malcolm Scates of the Kiwanis, Robert Best of the Lions and King Mularkey of the Civitans to help him. Mularkey passed the job on to E. O. Likens.

The Cabin John Citizens' Association stirred up opposition to the Army Engineers' proposed dams on the Potomac. Three of the fourteen dams would have been at Chain Bridge, just below Great Falls and above the falls at River Bend. Gen. U. S. Grant III of the NCP&PC led the chorus raised against inundating the river valley and the canal.

Meanwhile, the General Assembly convened in Annapolis with Albert W. Walker replacing Delegate Robert H. Hunter who resigned. Walker was a former Board of Education member as well as the developer of Westmoreland Hills, Green Acres, Woodacres and the apartments on Bradley Boulevard. He also owned and operated several commercial ventures along River Road.

The so-called Gill proposals went into the legislative hopper with the complete endorsement of the County delegation for a civil service system, a county supervisor and a purchasing agent, more "home rule" powers for the commissioners, taxicab regulation and a public utilities agent. It also authorized $5 million in bonds for post-war construction and contained a couple of surprises which extended the powers of the M-NCP&PC, giving it the right to hire its own police and to issue its own bonds, and provided healthy raises for the park commissioners. James Gill announced a public hearing on the proposed County bills at the Silver Spring Armory on Saturday, March 17.

When asked, E. Brooke Lee said that he did not think it necessary to present the Park Commission legislation to the Post War Planning Committee or to hold public hearings because he took the lack of criticism as a "positive endorsement of the record of this commission as well as my work as a member of the Commission." Lee and Dean Hayden exchanged barbed open letters on Lee's conduct and attitude which resulted in the rebirth of *Tribune* columnist Robert V. Bray, missing since the election. He returned in the March 23 edition, his vision undimmed:[26]

If the Charterites are determined to continue their senseless attacks upon the conduct of our county government and its officials, I guess I'll just have to come back from retirement and get to work again. . . .

The one good factor is that the very vehemence and violence of their attacks stultify the effect because the good voters of the county are of an intelligent type – as witness their defeat of the Charter last November.

During the dispute over proposed changes, Brooke Lee blasted the League of Women Voters for their criticism of the pending legislation. Mrs. Bradley and the *Record* sprang to the League's defense in an editorial that concluded, "

After running Montgomery County for 25 years the Colonel's skin ought to be impregnable to the remarks of a handful of harmless women. We are surprised he would take the time and space to recognize them in his paper. The Colonel must be feeling his years.

Craddock Goins was even more blunt. He responded to Lee's request for publicity and space to reply to the "attacks" by the Charter Committee with a short essay in which he claimed to have high personal regard for Lee but felt "that many of the people surrounding your public endeavors are far from the noblest Romans of all." He then suggested that State Sen. Thomas Earle Hampton "has the self-respect of a ring-tailed monkey." In his editorial on the legislative hearing, "Shadow Without Substance," Goins savaged James Gill and suggested that Gill "must know that without the blessings of Col. Lee, he'd be just another little boy rattling around in big britches."[27]

The reaction of the delegates was expressed in the attitude of that stocky, cocky, self-satisfied little fellow called James W. Gill, head of the Montgomery County delegation, who presided. From the outset, Mr. Gill's face, manner and speech took on the attitude of a fellow who feels extremely well pleased with himself and who has little concern for thoughts of the common citizen. He frowned, twitted, smirked, growled, heckled, admonished, interrupted, rebuked and at times gave off that subtle little smile of secret amusement characteristic of bullies, screwballs, stage villains and little children who know a good joke they don't intend to tell. . . .

We've never seen a Nazi gaulieter. We have seen Mr. James W. Gill in action.

As was usual at the time, all of the local bills supported by the County delegation passed the General Assembly quickly and quietly, and at the very end of the session, as a favor to his friend E. Brooke Lee who had been his roommate during four legislative sessions, Senate President James J. Lindsay of Baltimore City introduced Bill 580, which came to be called the Lindsay Law. Entered on March 26 and passed the next day without hearings, the bill was signed into law without comment or protest and then lay dormant, unrecognized for more than a year. It simply stated that, in counties with home rule charters, the county council must be elected on the same basis as the state legislators. In other words, it prevented charter counties from electing their lawmakers on a non-partisan basis. Lee had won an important battle by stealth.[28]

On April 20 at the State House, Governor O'Conor heard the requests of members of the Charter Board of Directors and the Civic Federation to veto five bills as well as Park Commissioner Lee's and Delegate James Gill's defense of the legislation. By far the most heated testimony came from James J. Hayden on the parks measure that he called a "salary, patronage and power grab" that not only gave E. Brooke Lee the right to give himself a $3,100 raise but also the power to create his own police force and appoint all the personnel in the recreation program. Dean Hayden also suggested that Lee might be guilty of malfeasance for failing to issue an annual financial accounting for three years.

Then, speaking for the Civic Federation, Lewis Sims called the park and planning legislation a "disreputable omnibus bill."[29]

I recall clearly when it came my turn. I was not too far from the Governor but not right down front. I remember standing. I did not write out my testimony; I did not memorize it, but I knew pretty well what I wanted to say, and I remember speaking vigorously. I stood right where I was so that everyone could hear me, and I spoke slowly and vigorously and with gestures and at the end I pleaded so: Please Governor O'Conor, save us from this law. Please veto it.

When the meeting was over, Allen Gardner, half a generation older than I, came back to me and put his right hand out and said, "Call me Allen." I was thrilled.

Because the bills in question had been supported unanimously by the County delegation, in early May, Governor O'Conor signed them all into law.

In what amounted to a side issue, at their annual meeting, the leaders of Chevy Chase Sections One and Two howled that the

County delegation led by James W. Gill had ignored their requests for legislation to clarify the status of incorporated areas in general and theirs in particular. Led by Arthur W. Defenderfer, the oldest part of Chevy Chase had drawn up a bill to change its name to Chevy Chase Village and the governing committee's name to the Board of Managers as well as redefining its boundaries and modifying some of its powers. Defenderfer said that it was the possible effect of the Charter on special taxing areas that brought about the need for clarification.

Delegate Albert Walker called for a hearing on the bill, and Defenderfer asked E. Brooke Lee, who had just dined with the delegation, to attend. Lee refused saying he knew the purpose of the meeting and opposed the legislation.[30]

Even after the legislature had adjourned, Defenderfer, whom Lee dismissed as "an active Republican," tried to get the delegation to "reconsider" its action. E. Brooke Lee pointed out that since most residents of Chevy Chase had supported the Charter movement and many were still working for it, it "does not seem very sporting to want to build a local protective wall around any section of Montgomery County and at the same time urge and vote for different treatment for those residents of the County who live beyond the wall."

Defenderfer concluded it was all political, partisan and biased and that the delegation took orders from Gill and that "Mr. Gill gets his orders from that well meaning, public spirited citizen, Mr. Brooke Lee. There is no one on this side of the County to whom we can turn."[31]

With spring came a half-price sale at the Thrift Shop, a fifteen-minute Victory Gardening show on WRC sponsored by the Bethesda Jelleff's, and numerous elections of new officers for civic associations and clubs. Builder Henry Connor of Westmoreland Hills replaced Carl Bachschmid as president of the Chamber of Commerce, which decided not to award the Kuhn Memorial Cup in 1945 because there had been so little building in the area. Mrs. Ralph Himstead took the gavel as president of the County League of Women Voters.

Newcomer Florence Mason became chair of the Camp and Hospital Service section of the Bethesda Red Cross and announced a plan to provide "special services and help for men who are returning from the front lines." Mary Grace Warner, whose husband owned the Tastee Diners, became Red Cross Canteen Chairman and supervised the work of thirty-two volunteers supplying refreshments to servicemen and blood donors. In Chevy Chase, Mrs. T. Stanley Holland headed the canteen unit. Burrell Marsh became president of the Rotary Club, and the Soroptimist Club elected Bethesdans Ethel Anderson and Ethel Taylor president and vice-president.

Several high school girls who were in the JANGO guild gained their classmates' envy by working at the Ship's Service at the NNMC, and the Junior Volunteer Corps at Suburban Hospital celebrated its first birthday by adding sixteen new members to bring the total to seventy-one and by distributing red, white, and blue service stripes to those young women who had given 100, 150, and 200 hours. At Chevy Chase Junior College, thirty girls met every Monday morning in the biology lab to roll bandages and prepare surgical dressings, and by spring the seventy girls in the Jeep House program at Chevy Chase Elementary had made more than a thousand items for servicemen including afghans, washcloths, greeting cards and scrapbooks.

Celebrating their thirty-third anniversary, some 300 Bethesda-area Girl Scouts were Princess Martha's guests at the Norwegian Embassy. Their spokesperson, thirteen-year-old Ellen MacEwen of Montgomery Lane, pledged support in helping "our special sisters, the first Girl Scout troop to be reestablished in Norway after its liberation."

Brush fires burned over twenty-five acres near Chevy Chase Lake and threatened a dozen homes in late March. Companies from Bethesda, Silver Spring, Takoma Park and Rockville joined the Chevy Chase firemen fighting the wind-blown flames while the Kensington firemen battled their own brush fire near the junior high school. The Civitans appropriated $1,000 for a community ambulance which, they hoped, the fire department would operate, and Bill Allen and the *Tribune* quickly claimed credit for the idea and offered to collect contributions. On April 1, Boy Scouts acted as ushers and

Faye Finley Shaw's A Cappella Choir sang at the fourth annual Easter Sunrise Service sponsored by the Bethesda Council of Churches. Ernest Paland, newly elected president of the soon-to-be-sold Bradley Hills Golf and County Club, invited all local golfers to play at the club which, he announced, would operate on a semi-public basis that year. The Potomac River Naval Command leased the Bannockburn club for use as a recreational facility.[32]

Due to the shortage of "man"power, the Montgomery Players switched scripts for their final production and put on "Nine Till Six," an English comedy featuring fourteen women and girls and no men. Doris Dewey Day directed what proved to be a popular success. The Civic Federation turned its attention to ash, trash and garbage collection and disposal, and the Kiwanians started planning for a V-E Day celebration.

Assistant County treasurer Bob Hagner's wife, Mary, who had worked at the County Building in Bethesda for fourteen years, was promoted to deputy clerk in Commissioner Prescott's office. Battery Park rose against one of its own when the citizens' association went on record opposing Dr. Leo Donovan's request to rezone the corner of Del Ray and Old Georgetown for a doctors' office building. Dr. Donovan withdrew his petition but admitted that the opposition surprised him. And in two sure signs that spring was really here, Dr. Ellicott issued a warning to guard against tick bites, and Glen Echo Park opened but only until 11:45 pm due to the curfew. Russ Edwards waited until the May 25 *Record* to make his seasonal announcement: "OK – you can take `em off now!"

George Mathews, head of the UNRRA clothing drive, had the Commissioners proclaim April "clothing collection month" and soon involved not only the service clubs but also the school system, the Quota and Soroptimists clubs, the American Legion, the ministerial association, the Bethesda Council of Churches, B'nai B'rith and the B-CC Jewish Community Group, all of the women's clubs, the Scouts and the Camp Fire Girls, and both the Silver Spring Board of Trade and the Bethesda Chamber of Commerce.

Every Western Suburban public school, firehouse, service station and post office became a drop-off point for useable clothing,

and in Bethesda additional depositories were set up at Virga's, the Hiser, Malcolm Scates and the Methodist Church. In one week the high school collected 3,176 pounds of clothes. The Bethesda theater held a matinee with a bundle of clothes as the price of admission, and the Montgomery Players used the Sherwin-Williams paint store for their part of the drive. The Rotary printed and the Boy Scouts distributed 10,000 handbills, and the Lions erected large signs at the District Line.

County trucks made collections and soon the OCD/WSSC warehouse across from the B&O freight station overflowed with an estimated seventy tons of donated clothing. George Mathews named Wesley Sauter to recruit volunteer sorters and packers and asked merchants to save all their cardboard cartons for the project.

In the hope of preventing future misunderstandings and more fistfights, newspapers began a campaign to familiarize the public with the small, brass, honorable discharge button, which most servicemen called the "ruptured duck." The USO observed "Be Kind to Butch Week" in early April and invited everyone to come meet their pampered cocker spaniel. The Chevy Chase Chanters, still forty voices strong despite having fourteen members in the service, entertained at the USO after one of the usual Sunday suppers and included in their program two numbers by their accompanist, E. Earle Ferguson, "Fire" and "Didn't My Lord Deliver Daniel?"

Ferguson, a government attorney with a law degree from Drake and a JD from Yale, grew up in a musical family in Iowa and was playing in the town band by the time he was nine. He joined the Chanters as a bass shortly after coming to Washington in 1936 and by 1940 was the chief accompanist and arranger. Rehearsals took place once a week, on Mondays, and during the war usually at St. Paul's Lutheran Church or All Saints on Chevy Chase Circle. Gas rationing was a problem, and car pooling was common. Ferguson, who then lived in Alexandria, often got a ride with a singer who worked for the War Department "and was able to get a bit extra."

The Chanters always had a spring concert, first at the Interior Department auditorium and later at Wilson High School or Alice Deal

Chevy Chase Chanters. *Seated, left to right:* Lynn L. Gilichrest; Frank W. S. Evans; Carson P. Frailey; Irving M. Tullar; Sterling Boekoven; Jack C. Davis; W. Arthur McCoy; Earle Ferguson; Ross J. Rudd; A. Owen Penney; Frank H. Storms; Arthur J. Richards; W. C. Whittlesey; Robert E. Kline, jr. *Standing, left to right:* William A. Rogers; Bernard S. Lavins; Thomas F. Slattery; Ronald H. Allen; W. N. McCutcheon; Edward L. Simpson; Ellsworth E. Condron; J. Horace Smithey (director); J. Benton Webb; Francis P. Heartsill; Benjamin B. Sewall; Alfred B. Hastings; Arthur B. Ilsley; Russell E. Singer; William H. Waters; J. Russell Lowe; Thomas H. Claffy.

Junior High. "We did a Christmas concert at the Methodist Home on Connecticut Avenue," Ferguson remembered, "and then went to the Lisner Home, and did some lodge functions. There were quiet a few Masons in the group." The chorus was financed by the five dollars in dues each member paid annually.

J. Horace Smithy

Mr. Ferguson called J. Horace Smithey "charismatic" as well as "outgoing and friendly." As for the songs performed for the USO, the composer said, "'Daniel' was our favorite, a really jazzy one, and 'Fire,' well, we had a WWI German army veteran named Joe Pies. He had one of these really deep, Russian bass voices, and so I wrote this as sort of colloquy between a tenor and this bass. Generally, it's 'Fire, fire's gonna burn up my soul. I've been a hell of a guy.' It went over well." Smithey and his wife, Hester, who were the backbones of the Chevy Chase Methodist Church music program, later brought Earle Ferguson into that work as assistant choir director.

As the first crippled B-29s started landing on Iwo Jima, casualty reports began coming in. Private George McNish, who left B-CC in early `43 to join the Marines, was wounded on March 1, and the first local

Marine reported killed on the volcanic island was Captain Carl O. Bachman, whose widow and 18-month-old daughter lived on Chevy Chase Drive. Lieutenant Samuel T. Robertson died on Iwo a month short of his 24th birthday. He was a graduate of both B-CC and the University of Maryland and his father was a well-known, long-time builder in the area.

Then Mrs. Reece Sewell was notified that her son, Pfc. Jimmy Trimble of the 3rd Marine Division, had been killed in action on February 28. She had recently received a letter from him dated Feb. 26 and shared it with the *Record.* In it Trimble wrote, "Now that we are getting closer to the Jap homeland, these Nips are becoming tougher and tougher to crack."

Jimmy attended Chevy Chase Elementary and graduated from St. Albans in 1943. After a tryout, Clark Griffith offered him a contract with the Senators when he was only 17. Instead he enrolled at Duke and then, after several tries, joined the Marines with time off to act as best man at his mother's wedding to the Longfellow School headmaster. Sent to the Pacific in June 1944, he pitched for an all-star team and led the 3rd Marine Division to victory in the Little World Series on Guam. Frank Cantrel who knew him and played against him said, "He would have been a big leaguer for sure" and "Clackie" Walker, who caught him on games down on the Ellipse, agreed. According to Thomas Jefferson Barlow, associated with Longfellow for many years, Mrs. Sewell never fully recovered from her son's death.

Bethesdans felt they knew President Roosevelt, and some were fairly sure that he knew them. He always waved and smiled when he rode across East West Highway and along Wisconsin Avenue in his big Packard on the way to the Naval Hospital or Pook's Hill. For many Bethesdans, perhaps a third, he was the only President

they had ever known, and while he was "that man in the White House" whose name was never said in some homes, he was also that voice on the radio asking for sacrifice and promising victory. In many Bethesda homes, his picture hung in a place of honor.

When his death was announced just before supper time on Thursday, April 12, youngsters heard the news first in many homes because they were tuned to "Jack Armstrong" or one of the other radio serials. By sundown almost everyone knew. Even though he had looked wan and haggard in the newsreel pictures from Yalta, only the insiders had been expecting it, for everyone else, friend or foe, it was a visceral shock. W. Prescott Allen echoed a common refrain when he wrote, "I feel I have lost a member of my family."

The A Cappella Choir walked down to the WRC studios and sang on the radio Friday morning and then again during a special assembly at B-CC that afternoon, and as flags stood at half staff, children and teachers in all the schools honored the late President and prayed for Mr. Truman's success. On that muggy Saturday, Bethesdans listened to Arthur Godfrey choke back tears as he described the return of Roosevelt's body to the White House through streets lined with mourners. On Sunday, in every church, there were prayers for the country and the new President while the burial services took place at Hyde Park.

But by Monday the first Truman jokes was making the rounds: Lincoln proved a poor man could be President; Roosevelt showed that a rich man can be president, and Truman proves that anybody can be President.

By then the war had cost 197,000 American lives, and the casualty reports kept coming in. Two Bethesdans, radioman 3/c Byron Masincupp, whose family lived on East Avenue, and Lt. Cmdr. John D. Harper Jr., whose wife and baby son were staying with her mother on Greentree Road, were reported "missing" when the submarine *Shark* failed to return to its base. B-29 pilot Lt. Robert Ziegle, whose mother lived on Brookville Road, died when his plane crashed on Guam after a raid on Japan. Sgt. E. Chase Donaldson, 19, whose father was president of Briggs Clarifier, was killed in action in Germany. Seaman 2/c Vic Mobley,

a noted jitterbug in the B-CC class of `43, died in action in the Pacific. His mother lived on Glenbrook Parkway.

Some families received good news. Mr. and Mrs. Daniel Ring of Langdrum Lane learned that their son, Sgt. Daniel L. Ring, who had been captured at Anzio, escaped from a German prison camp on his third try and was on his way home. Sgt. Homer Barnes, 19, of Brookmont, who had been reported missing in action, was now known to be a prisoner of the Germans.

In mid-April, ten Bethesda-area men reported for induction at Draft Board No. 3, and a week later the call went out to another ten. Mr. and Mrs. Joseph Devereux's 20-year-old daughter, Helen, joined the Marines with the goal of becoming a "grease-monkey." The niece of the "hero of Wake Island" had three brothers, six uncles and a cousin already in the service.

Leon Sherman, whose wife was expecting their second child, reported for induction, and his father saw him off from the Silver Spring B&O station. After his physical at the Fifth Regiment Armory in Baltimore, Sherman was told, "Sorry, we can't use you. It would cost too must to rehabilitate you," and he and his bad feet were given train fare home. "If he had seen me running down that hill to catch that train, he'd've changed his mind. I was flying," laughed Leon Sherman.

At Leland, the Hi-Y program began that spring with softball and volleyball games after school while at the high school the students hired Tiny Meeker's seven-piece orchestra to play for the Junior-Senior Prom, $1.50 stag or drag, on Friday night, April 27. In a gym decorated with purple and white streamers and before the largest dance crowd yet, class presidents Metzel and Ferguson crowned queen Betty Dossett. Betty Reed noted that three boys even wore tuxedos. The next night Charlie Hughes celebrated his eighteenth birthday and was kidded about being Private Hughes in the immediate future. The first of several false reports of German surrender enlivened the party.[33]

The Barons' baseball team got off to a slow start but then beat St. Paul behind Al Cleveland's two-hit pitching and won the next three in a row over Prep, W&L and Wilson, a two-hitter for Herbie Benson. Outfielder Mark Raymond got his second pitch-

ing victory, but then Blair beat Benson 4-0, and by early May, B-CC's record stood at seven and six with several rainouts to make up.

Charlie Hughes, who lettered in three sports, was the starting third baseman and one of the most consistent hitters. After three years on the team, he remembered the B-CC baseball field well if not fondly.

If you had a foul pop fly, you had to run uphill to get it from third. Larry Williams was our coach. He was a dedicated guy and did everything on his own. He bought the material and built the backstop with the help of a couple of guys; it was like telephone poles and wire.

On the day of the games, after lunch, everybody on the baseball team had to report to the diamond. We just formed a skirmish line and walked across the whole field picking up rocks and trash. There were always more rocks. Boy, when you'd get a ball hit to you on that skinned diamond, it was through your legs before you knew it.

I think Herbie Benson was one of the most effective pitchers I've ever seen. He threw that overhand curveball, and he would fool them. Earlier we'd had another real good pitcher, George Myers, who pitched a no-hitter against Cotton Smith of St. Albans. Blair had some nice kids playing for them. Johnny

Chris Chappell and George Myer who had just pitched a no-hitter against St. Albans' Cotton Smith

Klippstein pitched for them and went on to pitch for thirteen or fourteen years in the National League. I liked to hit against him because, even though he was very fast, he had a lot of control.

While the high school boys were playing baseball and wondering which branch of the service to choose, the Red Army closed in on Berlin, and the Hiser and Bethesda began showing horrific films of Belsen, Buchenwald and the other liberated concentration camps. Americans and Russians met at the Elbe while the 10th Army invaded Okinawa in what Japanese suicide planes made the Navy's costliest campaign. President Truman opened the San Francisco Conference on April 25, and for as long as that meeting ran, editor Bill Allen urged Bethesdans to a silent "moment of prayer" for the free world's leaders. He had asked the Commissioners for the use of air raid sirens at 6 pm each day to signal a time for prayer, but the Army had quashed that idea.

Austin Rohrbaugh, chairman of the Bethesda-Chevy Chase War Price and Rationing Board, announced that there would be less sugar available this year. Bethesda merchants joined in the observance of a "paper holiday," and customers were expected to accept unwrapped packages and re-use their paper bags.

Suburban Hospital began a $50,000 capital fund drive under the leadership of Major Paul Banfield, recently returned to Landon from the 13th Army Air Force. Down at the Rec Center, they quickly added a fire escape to the second floor of the War Nursery School after an inspection by Dr. Broome and State Senator Hampton.

Junior high students, teachers and Leland's Girls' Glee Club began visiting elementary schools, and at the high school, tenth graders' parents met to discuss dating after a PTA survey showed that students were giving a lot more thought to sex than their parents thought they were. The Public Lay Health Committee sponsored a series of lectures by the school system's health education supervisor, Dr. Irene Barrett, on preparing sixth graders to cope with adolescence and junior high school.

And as the Bethesda Bowling League moved into its last month, teams representing F. N. Loria, the American Legion, Bethesda Printing, the police department

and Bill's Place battled for the lead while Henry Hiser himself carried the highest average, 117, and had the high set, 411. Harold Broadhurst had bowled the highest individual game, a 167.[34]

Louis A. Gravelle became president of the newly organized Republican Club of Montgomery County at about the same time that Francis W. Hill Jr. resigned as chairman of the county GOP. Hill, in his farewell remarks, urged Republicans to cooperate with others interested in good government and said he meant Charterites and independent Democrats in particular.

In a major shakeup, which probably proved Stella Werner's contention that "party people were always taken care of," the Governor named Lacy Shaw to the Washington Suburban Sanitary Commission to replace J. Donald Claggett, who retired after eighteen years of service to look after his real estate interests and get away from complaints about trash collection. Assistant State's Attorney Alfred D. Noyes of Kensington took Shaw's place and was immediately elected president of the Commissioners. To the surprise of none, E. Brooke Lee was reappointed to the Maryland-National Capital Park and Planning Commission for another six year term.

At the end of April, a fire broke out in Briggs Clarifier's big, paper-filled warehouse. It caused $25,000 in damages. The Bethesda Fire Department responded quickly, and because they had previously inspected the warehouse and planned for fighting a fire there, Bargagni and his men cooled the roof before ventilating the building and were able to prevent an explosion, control the blaze and win the thanks of the company's officers. Chairman of the board Landra B. Platt wrote Chief Bargagni,

As you know, all that material was destined for the armed forces and, had the fire not been put out so promptly and with so little damage to surrounding buildings, our work for the war effort would have been seriously affected. It is a source of great comfort to this company to know that it enjoys such excellent fire protection.

Two days later a boxcar full of filters burst into flame, a fairly regular event as fireman Frank Hall recalled.

We kept getting railroad cars on fire down on Bethesda Avenue. We must have had five to ten boxcars fires. They were sealed cars. We con-

cluded that the material in those filters at a certain temperature would just combust. We finally just sent the brush wagon with 200 gallons of water, cut the seal on the door, and flooded it. That was all we could do, and we did the same thing over and over again. We had a rule: You never run Bethesda Avenue except for something on Bethesda Avenue.

At the high school, the A Cappella Choir gave its spring recital, which featured the boys singing "Stout Hearted Men" and pianist Bobby Stevens playing "Claire de Lune." Senior Day was Friday, May 4, and the upperclassmen took over the administrative offices and all the classes. That evening the School Door Canteen sponsored a treasure hunt, and students with flashlights prowled around the buildings and through the grove. The seniors were planning on a final paper drive to raise money for a class gift and began preparations for the banquet and prom in June. The baseball team continued plugging, playing five games one week and winning three of them, and the *Tattler* produced "Splinters," edited by Jeanne Curtiss and Gloria Lozupone, the winning entries in its first literary and art contest.[35]

After seeing photographs of the mutilated bodies of Mussolini and his mistress hanging from a gas station fence and reading Newbold Noyes's description of that event in the *Star*, Bethesdans coped with a series of premature reports of Hitler's death and then of the war's end. Then on Monday morning, May 7, while the businessmen and women settled in for another work week and the high school students struggled with their standardized English tests, the regular B&O freight came under the East West Highway bridge and through town with its whistle screaming the V-for-victory (wha-wha-wha-whooooo) again and again. The war in Europe was over!

It was not the "official" V-E Day, but a lot of students and many others, both young and old, celebrated for the rest of that Monday. Lourdes eighth-grader Jimmy Quinn was one of those who did not come back after lunch. He skipped school and, as he recalled, "just walked around Bethesda." He got caught, of course.

Washington celebrated V-E Day rather quietly partly because of the rainy weather but mainly because it was not a holiday and all government employees were expected to report for work. President Truman asked

that no celebrations take place and said he hoped Americans would continue "in the job before them." The wild demonstrations in Paris, London and Moscow were not repeated in America, and when a half million gathered in Times Square, Mayor LaGuardia asked them to go home or to their jobs. "Repressed excitement" was the mood.

In Bethesda, the long-planned celebration took place at the Presbyterian Church. Almost all the local Protestant ministers participated in a service of "Praise, Remembrance, Penitence, and Dedication." Most of the stores and other businesses closed for the morning. Reverend Chandler, as president of the Council of Churches, spoke first and then Reverend Albertson, Dr. Nelson and Dr. Claude Brubaker, who issued a challenge to the large congregation to finish the job and not to forget that Pearl Harbor, Bataan and Corregidor left debts that must be paid. At Our Lady of Lourdes the school children attended a special Mass of Thanksgiving.

Lynnbrook students gathered at 9 am to hear the official proclamation made by Truman and Churchill, and then the upper grades took part in a program led by Rev. Robert T. Wilkinson. At Bethesda Elementary, the exercises began with a salute to the flag, the Lord's Prayer and a musical celebration of victory. William Prescott Allen made a short speech in which he mentioned that the Germans had surrendered in a "little red schoolhouse." He told the children, according to the report of his extemporaneous speech in his own newspaper, that "America won because her people believed in freedom, down to the last mud-soaked GI fighting desperately in the Bastogne Bulge or at Anzio" and reminded them to keep buying war savings stamps to help finish the job. And then the children sang the Star Spangled Banner and returned to their classrooms.

At Leland Junior High School the faculty and student body assembled in the auditorium to hear President Truman's announcement. Willard Schumaker then led the flag salute and Jacquelyn Rusen the singing of the national anthem. Principal Elwood Mason spoke on "What are we going to do tomorrow?" and he was followed by five student speakers. "Sandy" Astin was one of those.

I was taking a speech class and was selected to give one of the V-E Day speeches before the entire student body and faculty. I might

even have a copy somewhere, and I remember the closing line said "that a little sooner, all the men and women throughout the world can celebrate a complete and final victory."

The Leland band and both glee clubs contributed several songs, and the program ended, as some students recalled a half century later, with teacher Tom Conlon singing the "Ballad of Roger Young," and everyone joining in the chorus. The high school also had a special assembly on what would have been, some of his friends noted, Bob Garvin's 20th birthday.

Downtown, the lights around the Capitol blazed for the first time since December 1941, and the old Dome glowed over a tired, happy city. Theater marquees and store windows gleamed with light after many months of relative darkness. In Rockville, the Commissioners approved William Prescott's V-E Day resolution to recommend that the school system build a new school in the Western Suburban area where veterans could finish their high school education. Later, he suggested, the proposed school would become a new junior high which Bethesda badly needed.

In the midst of the victory euphoria the League of Women Voters came out strongly for continuing the OPA's rationing and price controls, which some congressmen had urged be scrapped immediately. The meat lines at the stores continued to be long, and some Bethesda matrons again began following delivery trucks. Grocers were almost forced into under-the-counter selling to their "regulars," and the Co-op instituted a system of numbered tickets good on various days.

Mrs. Bradley noted that "one woman brought along her knitting and did half a sock while waiting for her turn to buy frankfurters. Another got out her tatting and tatted away while she chatted with an old friend she hadn't seen for months. But the woman who made the most practical use of her waiting time was the busy housewife who bought three pounds of peas and shelled them into her lap as she slowly moved up in the meat line." Mrs. Bradley also reported that the women enjoyed a laugh over the butcher's sign: "Please don't bring your fat cans here on Saturday." [36]

At a time when relations between grocers and their customers were often strained, the Safeway at 6801 Wisconsin Avenue near St.

John's church earned a special encomium in its fourth year of wartime service. Mrs. Edward L. Burns wrote to the chain on behalf of a number of area housewives and praised the store's staff unreservedly.[37]

We feel gratefully appreciative of the cheerful cooperation we have always received of the store manager, Mr. Wm. Powers. The appreciation which we wish to express has grown from the constant cooperative spirit and cheerful attitude of Mr. Powers. His maintenance of a clean and orderly market has always made it a pleasure to shop.

It is our contention that the manager of the meat counter, Mr. D. M. Barron, and his assistant, Mr. George Neal, rightfully earned some sort of distinguished service medal for their patience and cooperation. They have always endeavored to be most helpful. Their constant friendly attitude has created an atmosphere which is seldom found in the stores of a large metropolitan city. Mr. Barron's efficient distribution of meat has been most satisfying. The quiet manner and sense of refinement which the checkers possess has also added to the congenial atmosphere.

Other than the multitude of Cub Scout efforts, the American Legion staged the first carnival of the year, a two-week affair in the 7800 block of Wisconsin with country hams and cartons of cigarettes among the big prizes. The Legionnaires hoped to raise $5,000 for their building fund. Another Family Night Canteen at the high school earned $250 for student activities with bridge, bingo, square dancing, fortune telling, and other entertainment. The Kiwanis Club honored Mrs. Mary Veihmeyer at their Mother's Day luncheon. She sent two sons to WWI and had three sons and three grandsons in the Second World War.

C. Fred Kelley was the first Bethesda WW II veteran to open his own business, a real estate office on Old Georgetown Road. His family had gained some notoriety the previous year when his premature son was Suburban Hospital's first incubator baby.

That May, 84-year-old R. L. Emory led the ground breaking ceremony for the Brookmont Baptist Church to be built at Broad Street and Virginia Place. And Mrs. Roberts reported that racy if not ribald *Forever Amber* was the most popular rental book in a long time.

The Commissioners surprised no one when they announced that the property tax rate for the County would again be $1.50 per assessed $100, the same as it had been for ten years. The State tax was twelve cents per $100, and the special taxing districts' rates are shown in the chart below.[38]

The first big controversy of the spring brewed up over the future of the Bradley Hills Country Club that a group called National Airways had quietly purchased for $250,000. The new owners stated their intention to create an airpark country club on the 157-acre site, and the State Aviation Commission

Special Taxing District Rates		
Area	assessed value	
	tax per $100	expected revenue
CC 1&2	5,582,730	
	.30	17,558
CC 3	1,906,350	
	.30	5,719
CC 4	4,820,260	
	.30	14,461
CC 5	1,344,300	
	.35	4,705
Martin's Add.	1,545,335	
	.32	4,945
Fr. Heights	570,650	
	.25	1,427
Drummond	297,320	
	.35	1,041
N'west Park	270,480	
	.15	406
Oakmont	149,950	
	.10	150
North CC	416,665	
	.35	1,458
CC View	1,121,475	
	.10	1,121
Battery Park	1,173,025	
	.11	1,290
fire area taxes		
Bethesda	40,017,855	
	.10	40,018
Conduit Road	9,806,355	
	.10	9,806
Cabin John	2,311,910	
	.10	2,312
Chevy Chase	24,236,420	
	.15	36,354
Beth library	40,017,855	
	.03	12,005

issued them a Class One airport license before anyone in Bethesda knew that the old club had been sold. E. Brooke Lee, speaking for the Maryland-National Capital Park and Planning Commission, protested first, and much of Bethesda, except for the Chamber of Commerce, set politics aside and lined up behind him.

Although the new owners, led by John Price Hoberman, said that they intended to begin work on the landing field in mid-May, the State authority assured Colonel Lee that there would be no permit issued without a public hearing. Evidently the property had been "conspicuously posted" for three weeks before anyone noticed the sign and became aware of the proposal.

Led by Lee, the M-NCP&PC adopted a resolution in opposition noting that the site was the location of several "expensive, and generally desirable detached homes" whose worth might be adversely affected. Further, Park and Planning's resolution stated that there was no need for an airport in the area and that the nearby WMAL towers would constitute a hazard to such a use. Finally, the Park Commission stated that the "prominent posting" for thirty days was on a seldom-traveled back road and attached photos showing the sign nailed to a tree near unpaved Greentree Road to prove its point.

The State Aviation Commission scheduled a public hearing on the matter at the Bethesda County Building at 2 pm on May 29. Mrs. Bradley's first editorial on the topic urged her readers not to make the "horse and buggy mistake of standing in the way of progress. Let's consider this proposition carefully before we decide what is best for our community." She wrote that her investigation showed that "92 persons living in the Bethesda-Chevy Chase-Glen Echo area" had contracted to purchase airplanes right after the war and that another hundred were planning to learn to fly and many airmen would soon be returning from the war. "It takes little imagination to place at least 700 planes in this community within the next five years," the editor concluded.[39]

National Airways Corporation took out a full-page ad in the May 25 edition of the *Record* to publish an open letter to the citizens of the area. Mr. Hoberman claimed he had met with former club members and residents of the neighborhood "to explain to these

groups our plan. Under no circumstances was there any cause or intent to try to hide the plans of the corporation from the people of this community. It is for the people of this community the club is being built." The ad stated,

The plans are for a fine club house, sun terrace and restaurant, swimming pool and private cabanas, hard top tennis courts, a stable of riding horses, an eighteen-hole golf course; all this to be had in connection with the recreational activity of flying. The landing strips will be landscaped into the golf course and when this section is finished around the perimeter of the entire project will be built private homes ranging in cost from $15,000 to $25,000 for use by and sale to the executives of the Corporation and members of the club.

Hoberman emphasized that his company had paid $1,700 an acre for the land and was investing $100,000 to improve the property and certainly would not undertake "any operation that would depreciate the area as a whole."

More than a hundred local residents, almost all opposed to the project, turned up for the meeting, which lasted more than three hours. Jack Hoberman explained his company's plans and emphasized that only members of the club would be allowed to use the flying facilities. He said the posting had been made on the first tree on the golf course on Greentree Road because he thought it should be done on the proposed airpark and not on the clubhouse grounds.

Brooke Lee restated Park and Planning's position and then introduced more than a dozen local residents who objected to the airpark because it would depress their property values. Hoberman presented a petition signed by 139 persons who favored the project, and attorney Louis A. Gravelle, representing the Bradley Hills Citizens Association, asked the Commission to note carefully the addresses on the petition since none lived on Bradley Boulevard. The Aero Club of Washington sent a letter urging the Commission to disregard the "nuisance" objections, and the Aero Club of Maryland urged "prompt development of adequate air facilities in the county."

Henry T. Adams, who sold the club to Hoberman's group, was the only witness to speak in favor of the project. The Bethesda Chamber and the Civitan Club presented

resolutions favoring more airports in the area but not directly endorsing the Bradley Hills project. Hoberman reminded the Commission that the CAA had approved the site despite the nearness of the radio transmission towers. He stated that the club would be an asset to the community and a place with "dignity and character" for the entire family. He emphasized that the 2,600-foot, grass landing strips would be landscaped into the golf course and that the proposed airpark would be closer to Washington, D.C., than any other suburban airport. The Commission asked for briefs from the opposing attorneys and adjourned. Afterward, Hoberman announced that if the license were denied he would appeal that decision in the courts.

Redecorated and refurnished, the Washington Aviation Country Club opened in mid-June with a ham supper for members, guests and interested neighbors. The club began holding dances every Saturday night and buffet suppers on Sunday afternoons. President Hoberman invited all interested in joining to come out and enjoy the club. The swimming pool, he said, should be ready for use by the 4th of July.

In July, the club was granted a provisional 90-day license subject to approval by the County Commissioners, and the Bethesda Chamber of Commerce went on record as supporting the development of airparks in the Western Suburban District. The Chamber, committee chairman Frank Loria announced, planned to hold its annual outing at the Aviation Country Club in August. After the pool opened, Hoberman made all of the club's facilities available to the Bethesda USO at very nominal fees, and the dispute continued in the columns of the local papers and the meetings of citizens' associations and service clubs.[40]

At the Victory Garden office on the second floor of the County Building in Bethesda, Mrs. John C. Harmon handled requests for community garden space and plowing services. The County chairman, Mrs. Klinge, came over from Silver Spring once a week by police car to check on her progress and help answer questions. Elva Harmon had helped out at Bradley Elementary's cafeteria where her son went to school, worked with the Red Cross and managed the Boys' Victory Garden Corps before taking over the Bethesda office

Elva Harmon and the Victory Garden map

and the care of forty, local, community gardens. Ninety new gardeners had applied for spaces by May, and Mrs. Harmon was still handing out Mrs. Donaldson's popular manual every day along with the names of six men with tractors and two with horses who would plow gardens for $3.50 to $4.00 an hour.

In the gardeners' plans, tomatoes were by far the favorite crop with string beans a distant second. Some planned to experiment with melons, but most had given up trying to grow cauliflower. The largest gardening areas in Bethesda were the 116 plots at NIH under Clarence May, C. L. Lefebvre in Sonoma and Edward L. Everitt in Bradmoor with sixty each, and three Recreation Center gardens totaling 113 plots with A. L. Robinson, Fred Zimmerman and F. J. Schwoerer as leaders. In Chevy Chase A. C. Foster oversaw thirty-one plots on East West Highway and T. Richie Edmonston had two areas with a total of forty gardens while by far the biggest acreage was at Columbia Country Club where M. B. Swanson managed 183 gardens.[41]

In the continuing fight against rabies, a "rigid quarantine" began on May 21, and all dogs were again ordered to be vaccinated. Free clinics operated at the high school, Bethesda Elementary, the Glen Echo firehouse, the Kensington Armory and the animal shelter behind Meadowbrook Stables. The

inoculated dogs were released to wander freely on June 16, but all unvaccinated dogs were under quarantine for ninety days, and strays were to be captured, if that could be done easily, or shot. The Commissioners also ordered all impounded dogs to be vaccinated and the owners charged for the cost of the anti-toxin.

The Health Department reported the first tick fever cases in mid-May including one in the Bethesda area. Another Western Suburban case was reported in June. Dr. V. L. Ellicott again warned parents and those whose work took them through underbrush or into wooded areas to check carefully for and remove ticks every day. The vaccine, he said, was available in limited quantity "for those persons who are unusually exposed."

The Health Department also announced that, on April 12, an 8-year-old Bethesda girl had died from an allergic reaction, probably to egg protein, ninety minutes after receiving the tick fever serum. While the Army had records of a number of fatalities in reaction to the yellow fever vaccine with a similar protein, this death was unique in the D.C. area.[42]

At the end of May, the Veterans Service Council opened its office at the Recreation Center to assist returning service personnel in finding work or resuming their old jobs and in filing claims under State and Federal laws. S. Walter Bogley, chairman, said that more than a hundred veterans had already been interviewed. Meanwhile, the draft board began reconsidering the classifications of registrants between thirty and thirty-seven and, in May, called nine young men for the Army and two for the Marine Corps while postponing the induction of eight older men.

The *Tribune* again called for a Veterans' Memorial Building, with the emphasis on "building." Publisher W. Prescott Allen wrote that some of the suggestions for a memorial reminded him "of the little boy who gave his mother a bag of marbles for her birthday." Meanwhile, the leaders of the 7th War Loan Drive scheduled special shows at the local theaters and all of the other, now expected, activities. At the high school the bond drive's goal was $25,000 for a Navy training plane to be called the "B-Town Buzzer."[43]

At the high school the students added nine more gold stars to their service flag in a Memorial Day assembly with tributes to Pfc. Benjamin Yon, class of '43 and Pfc. Jack Stevens, class of '42, both killed in Germany; 1st Lt. George H. Thompkins and his brother, Major William Thompkins, both killed in action in the ETO; Pvt. Don Hollander, only one year out of school and six months after induction, killed near Saarbough with the 100th Infantry; Howard Victor Mobley Jr., Pvt. William McChesney Huntt, killed near Leipzig with the 104th, Seaman John Donaldson, B-CC '43, killed near Okinawa; and 1st Lt. Sam Robertson. The junior class presented the school with a copy of Constable's painting "The White Horse" in memory of their classmate Carolyn Young, niece of guidance counselor Dorothy Young.

The military services began notifying families of most men listed as "missing" in Europe that they were either prisoners or killed in action. Lt. Kenneth Kinsella, a B-CC grad, amateur singer, and 8th Air Force navigator reported missing since March, was one of the latter as was John W. Johnson Jr., 19, of Glen Echo Heights who had been reported as missing in action since the fighting in Belgium in December '44. The local papers also carried stories of POWs such as Lt. Irving Day who were now on their way home.

One River Road house displayed two gold stars in its front window that spring. Staff Sgt. Harry Dean, a former employee of the Glen Echo Volunteer Fire Department, was killed on Okinawa. His mother lived with Mrs. Christine Fahrenwald whose son, Frank, was the first County man killed in action in World War II. Both women worked at Bell Laundry.[44]

Briggs Clarifier continued to advertise for craters, laborers, stock clerks, assemblers, mechanics, offset pressmen, secretaries, Ediphone operators and welders. It began hiring veterans and assured its employees that "when peace comes we will have no reconversion problems, as we are making the same products we made before the war, our backlog of civilian demand insures full employment after V-J Day."

During V-E Day ceremonies company president Chase Donaldson had stressed that the war was far from over and said, "It is our responsibility to produce more than our quota to help speed final victory." He said that millions of dollars in war orders remained to be filled and that more were coming in for the Pacific campaigns. Donaldson stated his wish for all employees to stay with the

company after the war and his belief that future business possibilities were favorable.[45]

The USO enjoyed another spring of picnics in the parks, bicycle tours to Hains Point and training sessions for new hostesses. Saturday Cabaret Nights with red-checked table cloths, candlelight, a cigarette girl and, on occasion, young Stella Werner's accordion drew big crowds as did the Wednesday waffle suppers. The May 15 dance at Woodmont featured the debut of the National Naval Medical Center orchestra. On the last Saturday of the month, Bethesda Elementary students entertained servicemen with a May Pole dance, and Jack Morton's band played for a "May Frolics" evening, which included the crowning of a king and queen and the usual grand prize of a free phone call home.

On Sunday afternoon, June 3, the USO celebrated the opening of the Wilson Cabin on Rockville Pike, a gift from Mrs. Luke I. Wilson. She had kept two acres for her Tree Tops home and a small guest house when she donated her land to the National Cancer Research Institute. Helen Woodward Wilson had held a number of receptions and parties for servicemen and women in her home during

Buddy Trayes serves at a cabin picnic

the war and now decided that the guest house would provide more opportunities for USO activities.

The "cabin," all on one floor, had a large main room furnished with arm chairs and couches plus a piano, a radio-phonograph and plenty of dancing room. Mrs. Wilson stocked the shelves with books from her own library saying, "Books are no good except to read." Behind the living room were a screened-in porch and a kitchen with a refrigerator that was always full of soft drinks. At one side was a room with windows on three sides and indirect lighting, which the USO furnished with art supplies, and behind the cottage were an outdoor grill and several tables and benches.

Mrs. Wilson came down to speak briefly at the dedication but did not stay for the baked bean supper, horseshoe pitching, softball game and dancing that followed. With the help of Elizabeth Herriot, music programs filled the cabin on Tuesdays and Thursdays, and there was an open house every Sunday. Parties and picnics for special groups were scheduled on the other days, and the Wilson Cabin was soon almost as popular as the old Safeway on Georgetown Road.[46]

The Chevy Chase Lake swimming pool again had problems. At a public hearing on a permit for George Heon's eighteen-year-old pool, Chevy Chase residents stated that the toilets and showers were in "deplorable" condition and that the flooring repairs had been made in a "slip shod" manner. Stella Werner testified that leaves and debris often littered the pool's deep end, that there was no proper distribution of chlorine and that the bad flooring had caused cuts on patrons' feet. The Commissioners withheld the permit pending an inspection, but by mid-June the pool was open and advertising itself as "completely modernized." The Health Department almost closed the pool again after a mid-July inspection, but some immediate changes kept it open for the rest of the summer.

At Kenwood's pool, 14-year-old Kenny Poerstel was a popular life guard although his bleached hair had turned rather green. He only charged his buddies a quarter to look the other way when they came out for a swim.

Other signs of warmer weather included Dr. Broome and Mr. Pyle asking for a law to prevent Good Humor trucks from parking

next to schools. A more serious indication of spring was a letter signed by the presidents of the PTAs of Chevy Chase, Bethesda, Somerset and Westbrook elementaries and sent to the parents of children in those schools. It deplored "the sporadic outbreaks of vandalism in these schools, taking the form for the most part of more or less wholesale breaking of windows." The letter also described the ransacking and egging of a cafeteria and theft of school supplies and radios. The problem, wrote the PTA presidents, was the attitude of parents who seemed to think that the stories were exaggerated or that "boys will be boys."

As to these odd reactions, (1) the stories are not exaggerated. One hundred and forty-five windows broken, by far the most with rocks, in one school in one year is an actual number, not an exaggeration. (2) Quite apart from the war shortages of labor and materials, boys have been boys too often and too much. . . (3) It is not clear what anti-criminal tendency is being built up in these boys when their irresponsibility and lack of respect for property, both public and private, is condoned, not occasionally, but repeatedly.

At the high school as the end of the year and graduation approached, the seniors, led by Dave Knight and John Shively, collected scrap paper to raise money for a class gift and then came back to clean up the buildings and grounds on their Memorial Day holiday. The all-female Pepper Club held a picnic, and Job's Daughters staged a dance, but rain wiped out the big senior picnic. Mrs. Massey Black's room became the center of activity for seniors practicing speeches and toasts, while out on the baseball field Herbie Benson and catcher Chris Chappell enlivened the game against Devitt Prep by switching positions.[47]

Air Corps Lt. Bob Brewer brought students jumping to the windows during one third period by making a low-level pass over the school in his B-26 (as well as buzzing Sally Baldwin's house). The senior class enjoyed a banquet and prom at the Woman's Club of Chevy Chase. Bill Mizell, a skillful ad libber, acted as toastmaster and introduced short speeches by Bob Rehlander and Dotti Storck and a shorter speech plus some songs in the Sinatra manner by Herbie Benson.[48]

Sunday was the baccalaureate at All Saints featuring the A Cappella Choir, and graduation exercises took place on Tuesday

evening in the Leland auditorium. Class chaplain Art Wood opened the program; president Bill Metzel, already sworn into the Navy, followed with a speech of welcome, and Hal Sutton read a tribute to the "vanguard" already in the war. After the 187 members of the class received their diplomas, Principal T. W. Pyle made a short speech of farewell, and Lois Copenhaver closed the ceremony with a prayer.

A noisy reception followed in the Leland gym and then several smaller parties grew in various parts of town. On Wednesday yearbooks finally arrived much to editor "Toddy" Rowe's relief and then there were more parties, a breakfast at Peggy Painter's Thursday morning and a party at Bill Metzel's that night. Friday most students went back to school for a final assembly and the distribution of report cards and spent the rest of the morning in the grove signing each other's yearbooks.[49]

At Leland Mrs. Hamilton and the *Pine Cone* staff led by editor Bruce Fleming published the school's first real yearbook with the help of Charlotte B. White and Mr. Mac. They called it the "Pine Log" and the Bethesda Printing Company produced it. The yellow-covered booklet contained group pictures of all the 9th grade homerooms with "noted for" and "always seen" comments about each person. John Astin, for example, was noted for "following 8th grade girls" and always seen "taking pictures"  while Tippy Stringer was noted for "straight A's" and was always seen with "Senta" (Bell). The book also had group pictures of the 7th and 8th graders out behind the new addition. The first yearbook featured a class history and will, pictures of the varsity, the cheerleaders, the band, the glee clubs plus several pages of ads including congratulations on the first *Pine Log* from the *Record*.

Dick Latimer and Phil Fleming led the graduation program and presented the school with a Maryland flag as a class gift. Then came a pageant on the theme of "My Country

Ina Parkinson

Tis of Thee" prepared by English teacher Ina Parkinson. She had a son in the ninth grade as did both Reverend Nelson and Reverend Blackwelder who gave the invocation and benediction. The sixty ninth graders at the high school had their own, separate graduation .

Chevy Chase Elementary, where Anna P. Rose was finishing her seventeenth year as principal, and Bethesda Elementary both had large graduating classes of eight-six students. At Lynnbrook, class president Millard Broadhurst won the DAR prize for his essay, and Mrs. Bosley and Miss Robertson, the 6th grade teacher, presented certificates to the twenty-four graduates.

Chevy Chase Junior College graduated twenty-nine, Georgetown Preparatory School twenty-five and Landon thirteen. The forty-four members of Sister Emma's eighth grade class at Our Lady of Lourdes School had a very subdued graduation, and the long class picture showed the front of the school and church draped in black.

The dean of Bethesda's pastors, Father Joseph A. Little, died of a heart attack on Friday, June 8, at age sixty-six. He had been in poor health for some time. During his tenure, the parish had grown to 2,500 members and the school enrollment had climbed to 500. A weekend of mourning followed with the small priest's body resting in the old rectory on Saturday and then, after the last Sunday Mass, in the church he built. Our Lady of Lourdes' church stayed open all night as hundreds came to pay their respects. A plain and simple man who became a very successful fund raiser and builder, Joseph Little left his church debt-free. The pastor based his favorite sermon on the Biblical admonition to consider the beauty of the lilies of the field who neither toiled nor spun, and his congregation looked forward to that annual homily. He had become a familiar figure to the children in the neighborhood as he walked about in his rusty cassock and squared biretta reading his breviary.

Sister Ellen Glynn, a teacher in the school he built, remembered him:

He was like a real father to us although he was no good for repairing anything. Father Sweeney was that kind of a guy. I remember I was up on a chair taking down something from the shelves, and Father Little asked me when I was born. I told him 1917, and he said, "My God, you're a child. I was long a priest at that time." Later on he got something wrong in the equilibrium area, and his doctor told him to bend down and do something. So he picked all the dandelions growing on the hill."

Monday, three priests from neighboring parishes celebrated a High Requiem Mass. The burial took place in Father Little's hometown in Pennsylvania. The *Journal* remembered him with an editorial:

Members of the Catholic faith parted with an old friend when the Rev. Joseph A. Little passed away. For 13 years he was the shepherd of the flock of Our Lady of Lourdes Catholic Church. He had been here longer than any other pastor. When the present church was built he was awarded the Oliver Owen Kuhn trophy for contributing the most in that year to the community's upbuilding. He will be mourned by many friends of other faiths as well as among those he served so long and loyally.

The Bethesda-Chevy Chase Jewish Community Group elected Philip Schiff of Woodside Place, director of the Jewish Welfare Board, as its new president. The other officers were Abe Lerner of Southwick Street, vice-president; Jonas Stein of McKinley Street, treasurer; Mrs. Albert Lyman who lived on Edgemoor Lane and Mrs. Louis Pinck whose home was on Bradley Boulevard, secretaries. The officers were installed at a party celebrating the Feast of the Tabernacles.

Father Little, center, at the dedication of his new church and school with Father Sweeney at far left.

The local ministers gave a farewell dinner for Rev. and Mrs. Raymond Vogeley, which ended with the singing of "Blest Be the Tie that Binds." Bethesda Presbyterian hired Ruth Isabel Hale, a recent graduate of the training school in Richmond, as Pastor's Assistant, and the Bethesda Methodists honored Rev. Hartwell Chandler who, during his five years of service, had paid off the church's debt, started a new building fund and added 281 members to the church rolls.

The Methodist Church of Cabin John, for two years part of the Potomac charge under Reverend Soper, became independent and acquired its own pastor, the Rev. Fred A. Tolden. And the local YMCA reported on the induction of new Hi-Y members and the preparation of a handbook for the high school. The after school program Mr. Bunker had started at Leland was beginning to spread to the elementary schools. The First Baptist Church planned a summer school for children ages four to twelve under the general direction of Reverend Nelson.

The Bethesda Rotary Club was honored when the new Secretary of Agriculture, Clinton P. Anderson, interrupted a busy schedule to attend its stag party at Kenwood. Mr. Anderson, a member of the local group for several years, had once been president of Rotary International. The Kiwanians staged their first annual, Hot Shoppes-catered, "Save-A-Wife" picnic, which included rolling pin throwing and husband-calling contests.

William F. Hisey, manager of the Palais Royal, was the new president of the Civitan Club, and the Bethesda Lions elected plumbing supplies executive Richard W. Fisher 3rd as their president. The Civic Federation chose William B. Horne of Somerset, their one-time treasurer and a member of the Federation since its founding, as their new president. The Chevy Chase DAR elected Mrs. Jesse Nicholson regent.

The Bethesda Chamber of Commerce rented Room 27 in the Housing Guild Building and opened its first permanent office with Grace H. McLean as executive secretary. The office, open from 11 am to 3 pm, provided information about Bethesda businesses and business space, handled complaints regarding services provided by local merchants and tradesmen, conducted research and fostered the Buy in Bethesda campaign. Mrs. McLean, a six-year resident with a home on Glenbrook

Parkway, had two sons in high school and was the gold star mother of seaman Vic Mobley. She had been working with the Red Cross staff at the Navy Hospital.

The Maryland-National Capital Park and Planning Commission re-elected E. Brooke Lee vice-chairman and park commissioner and then appointed attorney Alfred F. Schrider as its first park policeman. Brooke Lee announced that twenty-four County recreation centers and play sites would be operating during the summer. The Junior Red Cross Jeep House moved to the Scouts' new log cabin at the Rec Center but had a hard time attracting volunteers even after adding a cooking school and offering Junior Life Saving classes at Columbia County Club's pool. The high school's summer school program offered classes in both the morning and afternoon.

The draft board continued its work at the rate of about ten men a month, and the rationing board sent out forms for oil heating allotments and continued to enforce ceiling prices. Victory Gardens flourished, but the blood donor and E Bond campaigns had a harder time meeting their quotas. Before the end of June, the Office of Civil Defense closed down its protective service operations, and dozens of air raid wardens reluctantly put away their white helmets and tattered armbands. Most of the stirrup pumps were already being used in the Victory Gardens. Judge Brault presented certificates of appreciation to the chiefs and their deputies and paid special tribute to the volunteer firemen, police and Red Cross workers. He put Admiral Harry G. Hamlet, chief air raid warden, in charge of liquidation and salvage operations of Civil Defense materials.[50]

The Red Cross awarded forty-four special service bars to Bethesda branch workers, and the Public Health Lay Committee installed Mrs. Louis A. Gravelle as its new chairman and thanked the many volunteers who had staffed the Health Center at Suburban Hospital during the past year. Mrs. Ferndale Sherrill became Director of Nursing at Suburban in June after a long career in Texas, Alabama and Baltimore.

At the Woman's Club of Chevy Chase Mrs. William H. Wagner's surgical dressing unit toted up their wartime output and were amazed to find they had turned out over 40,000 dressings since June of 1941. Nine women had stuck with the group from the

start including Mrs. Thomas E. Robertson and Mrs. Eugene Stevens. They were then folding a special dressing for the main operating room at the NNMC.

Suburban Hospital's fund raising campaign continued. Superintendent Solon hoped it would provide funds to carry Suburban through slack periods. By 1945, the community hospital had eighty-six attending physicians and a staff of 116 including thirty-one nurses and was usually operating at about seventy-five percent occupancy. On Montgomery Avenue Nancy and Patsy Kemp, Carol and Anne Stuart and Frances Cronin dubbed themselves the "Salvage Sisters" and raised $25 for Suburban with a bingo game for adults only that featured prizes donated by Whittlesey's, Lois Roberts, Palais Royal and other Bethesda businesses. Kids on East Quincy Street raised $19.18 with two performances of their Great Smith & Connor Circus, and by the end of June neighborhood workers in an area-wide campaign had collected more than $20,000. Chairmen Paul Banfield and William L. Orem urged their volunteers on toward the $50,000 goal.

The East Bradley Lane neighborhood of Chevy Chase Section Two, led by Dr. Charles R. L. Halley, rose in indignant opposition to Mrs. Florence Rockenbaugh's application to operate a nursing home in her residence at 22 E. Bradley. Two years previously she had been found guilty of violating zoning regulations with her operation, but her appeal and two civil suits were still pending, and she was still housing some elderly women, some described by neighbors as "mentally disturbed." An investigation, including a report from the local post office, showed that Mrs. Rockenbaugh had nine or ten "boarders" much of the time. The court finally issued a restraining order, and Mrs. Rockenbaugh left Chevy Chase, slowly.

In Bethesda, home owners on Montgomery Avenue in Highland Park finally became fed up with the weeds, trash, and sheds sometimes used as outhouses along the B&O tracks, which their petition to the Commissioners stated "creates a situation embarrassing to the women of the community." It took some prodding from fire chief Bargagni before B&O crews cleaned up the right-of-way.

Wednesday evening, June 20, Woodmont Country Club hosted another USO dance with the NNMC band, and that Saturday night's dance at the clubhouse on Old Georgetown honored all the fathers serving in the Bethesda area. The father with the cutest baby picture won a phone call home. That same night the War Recreation and Hospitality Service staged the monthly dance for officers at Woodmont.

Then on Sunday night, June 24, the service people hosted an appreciation supper for some of the organizations that had supported the USO. Lack of space forced the planning committee to invite only one couple from each organization that had served a supper in recent months. After the tuna and noodle casserole and the ice cream and cookies for sixty-six representatives, there was a short talk by Lt. Ben Dixon, songs by Seaman 3/c Adele Sudnik and a color movie of local USO activities filmed, narrated and produced by members of the service community.

June's last Saturday warmed into a real summer day with a high, blue sky and a few fluffy clouds. Shorts, undershirts and bare feet were the uniform for most youngsters, and despite the six-day work week, the Farm Women's Market and the rest of Bethesda were crowded with shoppers by lunch time. At the Hiser the fourth in a series of morning matinees under the auspices of the Glenbrook Cooperative Nursery School featured Walt Disney's "Bambi" with shows at 10 and 11:30 am. Cars dropping off children lined up back to Peoples all morning.

Bell Laundry was so swamped with slip covers, curtains, blankets and other "seasonal laundry" that it stopped accepting both laundry and dry cleaning for a week, but Parkway Cleaners & Dyers over at Chevy Chase Lake started a Friday pickup and delivery service in Bethesda. The Sherwin-Williams store in the Shopping Center did a big business in screen enamel, 69¢ a quart, and Kem-Tone, $2.98 a gallon, while Peoples Hardware behind the bank featured Cello floor cleaners and waxes, Vigoro, garden tools and Firestone paints.

Reece Sewell spent the day signing up boys for the Longfellow summer camp on the Severn. The Safeway ads featured lemons and iced tea, Canterbury tea was 22¢ a quarter pound, Wilkins 25¢. J. R. Enright urged his customers to deposit their fuel oil coupons with him so that they could prevent corrosion.by keeping their tanks full.

As the temperature climbed toward 98°, the swimming pools at Glen Echo, Kenwood and Chevy Chase Lake began to fill despite the continuing talk of polio. At Gifford's and Howard Johnson's, young men bent deeply into five-gallon cans to scrape out the butter brickle and chocolate chip. Every ball field from Rock Creek to the River rang with "I-got-it" and arguments about who was safe or out. Slow-moving foursomes dotted the golf courses. Car and dog washing filled Bethesda's driveways, and children ran squealing in and out of sprinklers all over town.

At about two that afternoon a pair of dark blue, Navy Hellcats flew high over town. The pilots were running their throttles up and down and changing their manifold settings. The irregular sound of their engines caused some shoppers and ball players to look up and shade their eyes against the glare. Military planes circling and stunting over Bethesda were so common that most people, after a glance, went back to their games or chores. The pair of Grummans, flying in loose formation and weaving back and forth, stooged over the area for a few minutes and then disappeared to the north with the bright sun sparkling from their plexiglas canopies.

Grumman's Bethpage plants on Long Island delivered 4,403 F6F-3s and 7,870 F6F-5s in thirty months, and in their two years of action, the Hellcats accounted for 5,155 of the 6,477 Japanese planes destroyed by the U.S. Navy's carrier forces. It was the fighter that beat the Zero, that turned the tide, that dominated Pacific skies. The Hellcat weighed more than seven-and-a-half tons, was thirty-three feet and seven inches long and its strong, folding wing spanned almost forty-three feet. It was powered by Pratt and Whitney's 2,000 hp Double Wasp R2800-10, an eighteen-cylinder, air-cooled engine that swung a Hamilton Standard Hydromatic three-blade prop and gave the Hellcat a ceiling of 34,000 feet, a range of 1,000 miles and a maximum speed of 376 mph (later models could do over 400 mph).[51]

The pilots of this duo's planes were Lt.(jg) Charles W. Arnott and friend Ensign Robert J. Juhl. Both were members of Fighting Squadron VF-93 then assigned to the Naval Air Station at Norfolk after returning from the shakedown cruise of the *U.S.S. Boxer* (CV-21) in the Caribbean. They had received brand new F6F-5s, and as Arnott recalled:

We were assigned familiarization flights for the first week just to break in the engines. We varied power settings from low to high so it wouldn't run rough, so the cylinders are all equally smooth from low to high power.

Juhl and I were kind of avid acrobatic pilots and a little bit apart from the rest of the group in that respect. I was in seven groups during my time in the Navy, and it was my observation that only ten percent were acrobatic pilots. The rest just took off and landed and did the minimum. There weren't many "top gun" types. Most just did the job, like driving a car to work. Of the fifty guys in that carrier squadron, there were only five who were the wildies, and Bob and I were in that group.

The stunting over Bethesda in the early afternoon was not the pair's first flight of the day as Arnott recalled.

Bob and I take off from Norfolk and head up to Atlantic City on the morning of June 30, 1945. And the reason we are going to Atlantic City is I have a girlfriend who works in the Salt Water Taffy House on the Boardwalk, and I want to let her know that we're home and in the area. We're going to give them a big explosion breakup over the hotel.

We had done this hundreds of times before. We'd fly out to sea at ninety degrees from the beach at about 1,500 feet, the exact altitude you need to do a safe half roll. And we'd fly out about a mile and do a half roll in formation and get the attention of the crowd on the beach, and then we'd come in very tight, right off the water, at about like five feet, heading right at the Boardwalk. We're below the Boardwalk at five feet off the water. We come in until we're just at the end of the Steel Pier, and we'd pull up at about seventy degrees and roll out over the hotels in very close formation and thrill the crowd.

A pair of Hellcats

Lt. Charles Arnott

This was something we had done a lot of times, and it was exciting. It was against regulations, but the way we did it was the optimum way not to have any numbers taken. You start rotating and nobody can read it and you're out of sight before they know what hit 'em.

Then we flew to Norfolk and had our noonday meal and talked about our afternoon flight. Bob had a girlfriend at Bethesda, a nurse at Bethesda Hospital, in the Navy. He said, "Why don't we go up to Bethesda today, Charlie, and do the same sort of thing to let what's-her-name know we're back." And I said, "Fine, we'll go up there."

By mid-1945, both of the young pilots were reasonably experienced. Arnott had logged 811.8 hours in the air since entering the Navy in June 1942 including 375 in F6Fs, and Juhl had 650 hours in his book including 260 in Hellcats.

During recent carrier flights, Arnott had developed a somewhat unusual habit. He explained:

For the past six months or so I did not connect my parachute harness. I had a friend drown at sea. He made a water landing but couldn't get out. He was held back by the chute. So I decided I would never ever need to jump anyway, so I would just get out of the airplane in the event of a sea landing and reach back in and get the raft rather than being held up getting out.

So we took off about 1:15, 1:30 and flew up to the Washington, D.C., area, and there were no flights permitted over Washington at any altitude, they don't care how high you are. So we came in high enough that no one could read our numbers and circled around together kind'a trying to locate the target, so to speak.

Since it was Ensign Juhl's girlfriend they were going to "visit," he took the lead. "The location was no problem," he stated. "I picked up my lady friend Evelyn right in the lobby, so I knew exactly the location of the hospital. We made a very fast pass on the right side of the tower at around five hundred feet, or at least I did because I'm not watching Charlie. He could have been lower."

"We streaked across there about seventy-five feet in front of the tower at, I guess, 240 knots and even with the first floor there. And I pulled up into our usual, oh, seventy degree vertical roll," Arnott said. "We'd done it many times before, and no one 22-years-old ever figures disaster before success." As the fighters clumbed over Bethesda and started to roll in unison, (Juhl says it was at his suggestion) they came together - very briefly. Each pilot recalled the frightening incident differently.

"The moment I completed the roll," Juhl wrote, "there occurs a loud bang, and his plane swipes across my nose and leaves me behind very quickly, minus a tail."

"When I was about, almost three-quarters around," Arnott said, "I heard this fantastic noise. It was similar to the noise you'd have if you went off the freeway with a large car at a hundred miles an hour through the ravines and just listened to it till it stopped. There was a lot of tin can noise, and it was his propeller going through my fuselage and cutting the whole tail section off."

Juhl remembers them as "straight and level" but Arnott thought they were "in a steep climbing angle." He said, "I knew I'd had it. There was no control; both rudder pedals were loose, completely. We might have been at a thousand feet when I got hit."

It was about two-thirty, and both of Bethesda's theaters were packed with youngsters for the usual double features. Cars lined up at the traffic lights at Old Georgetown, Wisconsin, and East West Highway. The

Acme and the Safeways were crowded with shoppers trying to use up red and blue points at the end of the month. A half a dozen gas stations in middle of town were doing all the business they could handle, and the parking lot at the Hot Shoppe was almost filled with drive-in customers. Most of the convertibles had their tops down.

The fighter planes roared toward Bethesda. A young child playing in her front yard across from the high school ran screaming into her house, but many seemed to freeze in place and later described the event as happening in slow motion.[52]

Loretta Wilson worked in the Red Cross office at the Naval Hospital. "We had a lot of fun out there," she recalled.

Some of the ladies lived in Glenbrook; one was with me that afternoon. I don't remember why we were there, I guess we had been at the hospital, perhaps we worked a halfday. We were on Jones Bridge Road, and we could hear these two planes. So I stopped the car because I was always excited about airplanes. My brother was born and raised breathing airplanes. We got out and we looked at these fellows, and they came across and buzzed that tower, from northwest to southeast, towards Columbia's golf course, and all of a sudden one of them cut the tail off the other. It was the most frightening thing to see.

I knew they were Navy planes. I had been stationed at Mitchell Field, and I knew all of the Air Corps planes and the nearest thing to those was the P-47. They disappeared from our sight down toward Bethesda. I didn't see the pilot get out. I really didn't want to go down there and see it.

"Sandy" Astin was caddying at Woodmont Club, and his twosome had just teed off on the hole that paralleled Wisconsin Avenue.

It was a lovely sunny afternoon, and we were walking along when all of a sudden heading toward us from the north were a couple of Navy warplanes, Grummans, two planes flying in very close formation and very, very low. We were walking north with our players carrying our golf bags, and these two planes were flying right at us, couldn't have been more than 700, 800 feet up if that, and they collided right over our heads, just as we were looking up. One plane's propeller sheared off the entire tail section of the other plane.

The plane with no tail went out of control and disappeared behind us headed right into the center of Bethesda; the other plane flew away.

The tail section fluttered down and landed on Battery Lane. We were sure the pilot had been killed. These guys were stunting; they were playing. It was probably the most visually spectacular event of my life.

Horace Hampton and his wife were driving up Wisconsin just north of Bradley Boulevard when he saw "two little planes come together right over the bank. I saw them hit each other and watched the pilot climb out."

Juhl's Grumman twisted away from Arnott's plane with a bent prop, a tear in the leading edge of the right wing and its engine cowling deformed and flapping. The tail of Arnott's F6F fell in the general direction of the Woodmont Country Club tumbling over and over and trailing severed cables while the rest of the fighter turned on its back.

When I was hit I might have been going 150 knots, and the nose came down and I started losing altitude. The thing rotated, tumbled, like being pushed off the top of a large hotel in a bathtub, and I knew I had to get out of there. The first thing to enter my mind was "I'm jumping without a chute and I'm going to hit the ground like a tomato." But it didn't make any difference, I thought it would be better than hitting with the airplane and going out in a blast and fire and all that.

I think the only reason I was able to get out was that this F6F-5 had a crank that would open the canopy in four and a half turns, clockwise. It seemed like a half-hour as I was thinking about what to do, but it really was only microseconds. I just opened that thing, hit my seatbelt and was thrown out as the plane tumbled. I didn't even disconnect the radio jack from my helmet.

I thought, I don't want to jump. I hate jumping. That's scary and I don't want to do that. Besides I'm going to be killed. So I just did it.

When I went out of there I could have seen your eyes if you'd been down on the ground. I was that close. I could see details of grass and flowers and trees. I'd guess my altitude was six, seven hundred feet. The chute's not supposed to work under a thousand. There's not enough time to deploy. They were very large chutes. They always told you to count to ten in the little pamphlet we read, but we never had any training. I knew there was no time to count to nothing, so I hit the safety belt and pulled that rip cord ring and went out face down looking at the street and the trees.

Back at East Field the plane captain, as they always did, had come up and helped to hook us in, not like on a carrier where we did it ourselves, and I had just come from a carrier. So the thought that my parachute wasn't attached really didn't come until I jumped. The chute peeled out only because we were on a seventy degree angle, a diagonal rather than straight up.

When that thing opened and grabbed me, I couldn't believe it. It fell over a large tree on Wisconsin Avenue in the front yard of this home. It broke my fall, and immediately hundreds of people are coming over there, young dollies most of them, wanting my autograph, and I'm signing these things like a circus performer. "I did it. It's me."

I was limp as a sandbag. The only people that would really know the terror I felt are probably people that didn't make it, that are dead. There's no way to escape at the altitude I was. I know this had to be the lowest jump in history. For months afterward I dreamt of this thing almost every night, reliving it, and waking up in a panic.

Up above Bethesda's busiest intersection, Ensign Juhl throttled back and circled in his badly vibrating Hellcat. Long after the accident he wrote:

I immediately offered prayers to the Lord, over and over, during his descent, and I'm sure they helped save his life, and lives on the ground. You may not understand, but I've always felt very close to the Lord from my boyhood to the present. I firmly believe the Lord answered my prayers. It was a miracle all the way.

You would have to witness his plane without a tail tumbling end over end, and then his chute opening in the tree tops, probably 100 ft. above ground. He told me the tree branches allowed him to tip-toe onto a woman's front lawn. She came to the door, saw him and fainted.

Almost as soon as it fully opened, Arnott's billowing parachute caught in the big oak tree just across from Gifford's in front of what had been Dr. Perry's home. The empennage fluttered down in the front yard of photographer Walter Van Durand's home at 4811 Battery Lane narrowly missing the canvas pool where his children often played. He had seen the accident but was very surprised to find the tail section just outside his front door when he got home with neighborhood kids hauling away pieces of it for keepsakes.

The tail on Battery Lane

The Hellcat rolled over, somehow righted itself and roared back toward the middle of Bethesda, wings rocking erratically.

Lee Higgins, the former grocery store clerk and ex-Bethesda fireman, was then driving a delivery truck for Bell Laundry. He had just come out of the back entrance of People's Hardware and was about to get into his truck when the accident happened. He had perhaps the best view of the plane's descent.

Oh, hell, that damn thing. I'm standing there watching it come to me, that son of a bitch. The man bailed out. I seen the thing open up and some guy come out. I'm standing with one foot on the running board and door open on that Ford or Dodge laundry truck that I had parked right in back of that hardware store. I had stopped there for something and was standing there outside looking up Georgetown Road, and I see this plane coming at me with it wings waggling like this. And I'm standing there like a fool. And it come down over the firehouse and those other stores with the engine roaring.

I stayed there until that son of a bitch hit down in the ground. And as soon as it hit the ground, pshew, flames come up. Less than a hundred yards away, in that parking lot, the only empty spot there was. It broke some windows over there and on North Lane.

I beat it down to the firehouse, and by the time I got there, the engines were coming out. I didn't see any other plane. This one came down wobbling, and I saw his parachute opening up. He was way up there by the Methodist Church when he jumped out, not too high.

I had to leave, to go to Rockville on my route. People were lucky. If I'd had a ball in my hand, I could've hit the plane; it was that close.

By the time I got back, it was roped off, they wouldn't let anybody in there.

Frances Sherman, pregnant with her second child, was working at her husband's clothing store.

I was standing in front of the store, and this plane was coming towards me from up on Rockville Pike, and I yelled to Leon, "There's a plane coming and I think its going to crash." We had a back door, and I ran through the store. The plane crashed just as I got to the door. It was really a frightening thing. I saw the parachute come down up past Pumphrey's.

The big, thick-winged plane, still at full throttle, had screamed over the busy Acme, Simmon's barber shop and a line of trees with only a few feet to spare. Barber Louis Spruill, clipping at a customer's hair while the usual Saturday crowd waited, said, "I thought we all were going to die" as bottles on his back counter rattled and the light fixtures and mirrors shook. Customers with sheets still tied around their necks and barbers with scissors in their hands rushed out the Edgemoor Lane door. With a solid, window-rattling whunk, the Hellcat plowed nose down into the soft earth between the red brick apartment house and the parking lot behind the row of stores on Wisconsin.

One blade of the propeller spun off toward Montgomery Lane as the heavy engine buried itself. The front part of the fighter along with the inner parts of the wings and the cockpit disintegrated in an explosion of high octane fuel. The back third of the fuselage broke off behind the cockpit canopy and shuddered at the end of the crater showing the neat edge Juhl's prop had made and scorched white star insignias. The heavy landing gear struts and some wing ribs, hinges and pieces of red-painted flaps lay in the grass, but the outer panels of the wings flew into hundreds of fragments from the force of the crash and the explosion that followed. Clods of earth smashed onto the apartment walls and scattered across the parking lot toward the Hiser theater and the post office. Dozens of windows shattered. A huge ball of smoke, flame and dust followed by a column of black smoke climbed into the summer sky. But no one was injured, and except for the broken glass and the muddy hole and charred weeds in the empty lot, there was no damage.

Firemen and police, both only a block away, arrived quickly, controlled the fast-growing crowd as boys began pocketing shards of aluminum. Leon Sherman and his

Firemen spray the smouldering wreck

shaken wife watched from their store's back door as firemen hosed down the wreckage and then the area to keep brush fires from spreading. The engine smoked fiercely when water struck it, but within minutes the fire was out, and the firemen stopped spraying the wreckage because it only produced more clouds of billowing steam. After the burst of incredible noise it was strangely quiet as the cooling engine hissed beneath a curtain of white smoke. The crowd spoke in whispers for some reason, but soon more sirens announced that neighboring fire departments had heard Bethesda's call and that additional police were rushing to the scene. Most people moved back into whatever shade they could find from the shimmering heat.

Patsy Lozupone was living on East West Highway near Meadow Lane while her Army-officer husband was in China. She said,

I heard this plane and then the sound of the crash. It was hot as hell, so I went in and got a bamboo parasol and went trotting down East West and trudging up the hill and then ran to to Peoples where people were milling around. It was the neatest crash anybody could pull off. Bloodless. There was a crowd but no fire, and it seemed like a minor incident to most people.

Walter Birtles, who had just finished his freshman year at the high school was watching "Alaska," the first part of the Hiser's Saturday double feature, which was usually a Western. "It was summertime and just about every Saturday we'd go to the matinee," he recalled.

I met somebody I knew out in line, one of the kids at school, and we sat together. I didn't hear it hit or anything, and they didn't stop the show, but there was all this damn commotion,

After a bit, without saying anything to anyone although there were a lot of people asking me questions about different things, I walked over to where the aircraft had dug this hole from the impact and was on fire. Then I started thinking, "What happened to Bob? What happened to Bob?" and I couldn't see him anywhere.

Then I was informed by some Navy personnel there that I was in deep you-know-what. He was a lieutenant commander who was strictly an Eagle Scout, eager-beaver type that came from the Pentagon I suppose. He had seen it apparently, and he came over and said, "Your career is gone." I thought, Hey, buster, I don't care. And besides I was destined to go to Tokyo on the big push so if they don't want to use me, great.

Anyway it was a relief to see that the airplane didn't kill anybody. I didn't even think about the tail. But I didn't kill anyone. It was a very big relief to me. I was very lucky. I don't know how my personality would have dealt with that. I was the one that instigated the thing. It was my responsibility.

I managed to pick up a backing plate off one of the .50 calibre machine guns for a souvenir, and then I went with this lieutenant commander and a WAVE lieutenant who was there. They took me out to the hospital for a checkup. I was over there undergoing a blood pressure check and a little interrogation about how do I feel and all that. I felt like a bag of meal but so excited to be alive. They just gave me a general exam, and while this was going on an admiral that was in charge of the hospital came in and asked me if I was the young man that had just flown by his window. I said, "Yes, Sir." This admiral was a very, very amiable, regular-guy type.

Anyway, I was taken over to, I think it was, Anacostia, and that was where Bob Juhl, my wingman, had landed. He had suffered bad damage to his prop, of course, cutting my fuselage in half, and he also had the whole leading edge of his wing wiped out all the way back to the front spar. He probably limped back over

and we left the movie to see what was going on. Fire engines were running around so I went up to Peoples, and they said there was a plane crash out back. They had it all cordoned off, but we had to see what was going on. Hell, what it was was really a great big hole in the ground smoldering and carrying on. It was the only empty lot. I don't know how that happened.

I stood there for two hours, just watching, There were cops and firemen all around. We stood around trying to find out what happened. I was afraid I was going to miss something.

After seeing Arnott's plane crash, Ensign Juhl flew south and landed his damaged fighter at Bolling Field. He was asked to write up a detailed accident report immediately. Lieutenant Arnott meanwhile was recovering from the initial shock of his brief parachute jump.

I wasn't injured at all, just shook up.

A quiet and curious crowd watches the firemen.

there at full throttle just to hold it in the air anyway he could.

When Arnott found Juhl, he read the report that his friend had concocted. Juhl claimed they had been criss-crossing to keep each other in sight while breaking in new engines and that Juhl's Hellcat suddenly crossed under the other plane's tail while Juhl was looking down at his break-in instructions. Much relieved, Arnott praised his buddy for doing a great job of covering up the accident.

"And then the papers came out Sunday and had all this stuff about low level acrobatics," Arnott recalled. "So we said, 'They just don't understand about airplanes and can't judge altitudes. We were at altitude and did a slow weave and had an unavoidable accident.'"

I stayed overnight at the air station there and had a big time at the BOQ drinking and reliving it with a group there. And in the morning , I insisted on flying myself back. They wanted to fly me back in an SNB, a twin-engine utility aircraft, but I said no, I wanted to fly myself back in a Hellcat. So they let me have one, and I took off out of there and had to admit to myself that I was scared to death. I heard things that weren't there like the engine missing on takeoff.

Leland 8th grader Millie Imirie had been playing in her yard in Sonoma when she heard airplanes roaring toward her. She looked up toward town and saw them close together but then lost sight of them below the trees. She did not hear the planes come together or the explosion when the fighter impacted, but soon afterward heard on the radio that a plane had crashed in Bethesda. Millie got on her bike and rode up Old Georgetown Road toward Peoples.

A lot of firemen were still standing around, and the wreck was smoldering at the back of the parking lot. She marveled at how close the plane had come to hitting the apartment building and thought the "Man above" must have guided it down. Shards of aluminum littered the ground. She picked up a triangular piece about as big as a pie plate. It was braced on one side, and she was surprised at its weight. Millie got back on her bicycle and took her souvenir home.

By late Saturday afternoon, the Navy had heavy equipment at the scene, had carted off the broken back part of the fuselage, picked up the tail section on Battery Lane and detailed a crew to gather up all the scraps and pieces they could find including the prop blade, which was on the lawn at 4821 Montgomery behind the post office. MPs and SPs armed with "Garand rifles," as the newspapers put it, stood guard and kept everyone away from the plane. Cameramen, according to the *Post*, "were barred from taking pictures of the fuselage." Under flood-

Naval officers and SPs take over the wreck site.

lights, the dungareed workers dug down to the mangled engine and pulled it out of the clay with a truck-mounted hoist, and then began filling up the hole. By the time people went back to work on Monday, only the scarred earth, a few shards of aluminum and the clods of dirt high on the apartment house wall remained.

Sunday's *Star*, *Post* and *Times-Herald* all featured stories about the crash. All three carried eye-witness reports of the planes "stunting" over Bethesda and a policeman's description of them "barrel-rolling" before the crash. Then the military clamped censorship on the story, and no follow-up items appeared in the Washington dailies. The *Daily News*, with no Sunday edition, never reported the crash, and the stories in the town's three weeklies were mainly about local reactions.

Naval authorities assured local officials that "appropriate disciplinary action" would be taken, but the official, public Navy report on the accident seemed to accept Arnott's story that at the time of the accident the pilots "were checking the run-in operation sheets and failed to see each other in time to avoid the collision." However, under "percentage each cause" both Arnott's and Juhl's accident report cards state "100% PE (50% carelessness, 50% inattentiveness)."[53]

Meanwhile, Lieutenant Arnott and Ensign Juhl fully expected the ax to fall. Arnott finished the story.

When I got back to Norfolk, I found that both Bob and I had been restricted to quarters until further notice pending the investigation. So I went to see Bob and said, "Let's go home." We took my car, a yellow `36 Ford convertible that I was really proud of. We filled up with aircraft fuel and drove to Springfield, Illinois. We stuffed our beds with pillows and stuff like in the movies and just left. When we got to Bob's house, there was a telegram telling us we had better get back to Norfolk because we were in deep trouble. But we went on to my house in St. Louis, about another 200 miles. We just visited overnight and then went back as quickly as we could.

When we got back, it wasn't as bad as we thought. We had to stay in seclusion until time for sailing, about another week. Then we went on down through the Canal and up to San Francisco to reprovision. While we were there, we gave an air show, and Bob and I did all the showy, acrobatic stuff, . The accident didn't really bother

me as it should have. I was back at it in about a month.

Juhl recalled neither the "air show" nor the seclusion. After their home visits in Arnott's car, "The executive office, Lt. Bob Luker, authorized us to fly home in our Hellcats," Juhl wrote. "He was liked by all the pilots."

Screams of protest rose from every organization in the Bethesda area and from many irate individuals. J. Philip Schaefer, who lived on Middlesex Lane, just a long block from the crash site, was the first into public print with a request to the Chamber of Commerce that it "lodge a protest with our County Commissioners and with the proper governmental authorities against the life-and-property-endangering antics of low-flying pilots over the Bethesda area who are doing aviation a disservice." Schaefer reminded the Chamber that this was not the "first time that Army and Navy pilots have been found operating too close to the ground by Bethesda citizens and have been punished for it."

The former executive-secretary of the Chamber echoed what was in almost everyone's mind when he wrote that the "accident on Saturday could have been a tragedy had the plane fallen fifty feet from its landing place in any direction. Houses, including a large apartment house, surround the small field in which the plane fell and small children are numerous in the neighborhood." All three Bethesda papers printed Schaefer's request along with very brief, one-paragraph descriptions of the incident. The *Tribune* carried a picture from the *Post*, and the *Journal* used a *Star* photo. No eyewitness accounts appeared in any of the local newspapers.[54]

The *Journal* headlined its story "Action Waited In Air Terror Over Bethesda" and described the planes' maneuvers as "swooping over the business district" and then "barrel-rolling together" which was the same phrase used by volunteer fireman L. E. Lagerson of Windsor Lane. Bill Allen editorialized that the accident showed both the need to ban stunting over populated areas and the need for more modern rescue equipment "such as asbestos suits and fog mist fire facilities and equipment for moving people from houses that have been struck by airplanes."

All three papers agreed that Bethesda had a "miraculous escape" and that the plane falling into the only vacant lot in the area was "an act of God." The papers carried no

follow-up stories on the crash itself and no relevant letters-to-the-editor. The Navy's censorship was very effective, but few days passed that summer when the firemen sitting out in front of the station under the "Are You Lost? Ask Us" sign did not speculate about what might have happened if the Hellcat had hit the Acme or the crowded Hiser Theater.

X marks the spot where the fighter crashed

The Chamber of Commerce followed through with a protest to the War and Navy Departments asking for action. Both services responded with sympathy and concern. They pointed out that their regulations prohibited both stunting and low flying. The Navy assured the Chamber's Board of Directors that the accident in Bethesda had been "thoroughly investigated by the Navy department and the cognizant command and the pilots involved have been subjected to disciplinary action in accordance with Navy regulations." The State Aviation Commission wrote the Commissioners that it would use its powers to prevent stunt flying and to seek prosecution of offenders.[55]

At the same time the Chamber endorsed the construction of airports in the Western Suburban Area. King Mularkey's resolution called for a "county owned and developed airport to be leased to private operators" and the only debate was over the "county owned" provision. Meanwhile, the Washington Aviation Country Club received a provisional license from the State to establish an air park on its property if it could secure permission from the local zoning authority.

As both sides girded for a renewal of the fight, J. P. Hoberman opened his club to the USO for a day, allowed the Civitan Club to hold an evening meeting in the clubhouse with a guest speaker who lauded the airpark idea and then hosted the first annual Chamber of

Commerce outing. The Edgemoor Citizens' Association was the first to join the Bradley Hills Citizens' Association in opposition to the proposed zoning change. Unfortunately for Mularkey, Hoberman and other airport enthusiasts, the crash of a B-25 into the Empire State Building filled the newspapers, magazines and newsreels with pictures of death and destruction just before the next public hearing.

The Charter Committee re-energized itself at a Kenwood meeting attended by seventy-two members and adopted a budget of $11,500 for the 1946 campaign. They authorized John Willmott to hire a full-time aide to "conduct a continuous and thorough study of all country activities and financial transactions. . ." Mrs. James V. Bennett, chair of the Finance Committee, sponsored the meeting and O. M. Kile helped her raise $2,000 after the meal. Mrs. Hostetler announced that her field division was in the process of organizing in all fifty-one precincts to create a "respectable machine." Her group's motto, she said, was "Now Is the Time." Allen Gardner assured his followers that their defeat at the polls "means only a four-year delay in carrying out our program for good government." Stella Werner's daughter and namesake furnished the dinner music.

When H. King Mularkey, representing Connecticut Life, sold the Commissioners a group insurance policy for their employees, some of the Colonel Lee's enemies suggested loudly that the "Kingfisher," as Craddock Goins called Mularkey, was being rewarded for his anti-charter work. The Charter Committee quickly agreed and issued a statement saying that it "approves of an insurance plan for county employees. It does not approve of the way in which the contract was awarded."

This is the first obvious pay-off for last year's campaign. It is another piece of evidence that our county government is run on the "pork barrel" plan, not as an efficient business. The Charter Committee is determined to watch these maneuvers and we intend, whenever this kind of "pork-barrel deal" occurs, to call public attention to it.

Alfred Noyes, new president of the Board of County Commissioners, immediately responded that, as the *Journal*'s headline put it, "tain't so." Three companies offered very similar bids on the insurance, he wrote, and

Connecticut General was chosen because of "several advantages" in the contract they offered. The charges of a "pay-off," he maintained, were "inaccurate and unjustified."

Obviously the election victory had not ended the Charter fight, and no one seemed to be enjoying that more than editor Goins who labeled Mularkey "defender of the county's ruling regime" in his coverage. In the *Journal* the line between news and comment had completely dissolved.[56]

At Selective Service Board No. 3 Mrs. Elizabeth C. Stratton resigned as chief clerk, a post she had held since October 20, 1941. Elsie C. Harkins, assistant clerk since December 1942, took her place (a job she held through two more wars). S. Walter Bogley announced that the Bethesda area had exceeded its quota in the "Mighty Seventh" War Loan by fifty percent with a total purchase of $890,925.50 in bonds. Victory gardeners began registering for the canning classes in Leland's cafeteria. The Grey Ladies at Forest Glen, Walter Reed and the NNMC asked for donations of comic books for their patients.

The County Commissioners adopted a resolution expressing the "heartfelt thanks and appreciation of the county and all its people" to Judge Albert E. Brault for his work as director of Civil Defense since September 1941. The Commissioners also presented a framed commendation scroll to George Mathews for his leadership of the clothing drive, which collected 131,255 pounds of clothes, bedding and shoes.

No opposition appeared to the proposed off-street-parking zoning ordinance at the final public hearing, and on July 3 the Commissioners adopted the measure to require developers of commercial properties to provide adequate parking spaces. Bethesda's Commissioner, William Prescott, abstained saying he felt his area's business district was poorly defined and had been subject to spot zoning that created problems for property owners.

A Chamber of Commerce committee headed by Sam Stonebraker concluded that Wisconsin Avenue was too narrow and too busy with 17,000 cars a day for additional angle parking in Bethesda. The area by the post office and just south of Leland Street was ninety feet wide, which made such parking possible, but the rest of the road was only eighty feet across.

While Bill Allen and Craddock Goins argued about angle parking, Captain J. S. McAuliffe announced that his policemen were going to begin to strictly enforce parking regulations in Bethesda. People who double-parked or parked by yellow-painted curbs on Wisconsin Avenue would be ticketed, he said, and he urged motorists to find space on side streets. The *Tribune* carried this notice in a black bordered box on its front page.[57]

Joseph and Arthur Rein took over the Crefelle Body Works where they had been employed and moved the business from Hampden Lane to 4760 Elm Street. Charles G. Holbrook closed his notions store after nine years and gave all of his furnishings and materials to the Thrift Shop, which raised $400 for Suburban Hospital through their sale. Holbrook took a job at Woodies, and Raleigh Chinn installed his Hammaker Brothers monument and memorial business in the little store near the Acme and began displaying his tombstones on the tiny side yard.

K. S. Veirs, who had taken over Walter Perry's old store, acquired Harold N. Lagerson as a partner and changed the name of their business to the Farmers Feed & Hardware Company. Bell Laundry's labor problems finally forced it to take in laundry only one day a week. On the first day of this program they accepted 527 bundles of wash between 7 am and 11:30 am and then quit counting as customers lined up all the way to Wisconsin Avenue.[58]

The line at the laundry

As Burrell Marsh eagerly awaited the delivery of the 1946 Oldsmobiles with their big chrome grillwork, Rollin J. Martin built and opened a Studebaker agency with 10,000 square feet of floor space at 4904 Hampden Lane next to the Bowen company . Martin Motor Sales did not receive a new vehicle until the end of August and then it was a stake body truck. Construction on the Exfair Gardens apartments by L. E. Breuninger &

Sons began at Bradley, Fairfax and Clarenden. And the curb all but disappeared when the mudhole at Leland and Wisconsin was finally paved. A Pennsylvania court authorized the sale of the 160-acre Bergdoll tract at auction after the famous draft-dodger and his siblings agreed to the compromise.

The telephone company began distributing 15,600 new directories, but the Bethesda office announced that due to wartime restrictions no new phones were on the way. Four hundred potential customers in the Oliver-Wisconsin-Bradley exchange area were on a waiting list and more names were added every day.

The War Recreation and Hospitality Services reported that in the last year, beyond the USO activities, they had provided entertainment for almost 6,000 service people and found housing for more than 600. At the housing desk LuWanna Henley said that "we located close to 150 rooms last month for relatives, wives and sweethearts of the service men and women" and that she tried "to fit the right people in the right surroundings." That summer, in addition to its usual programs on Old Georgetown and dancing outdoors at the Wilson Cabin, the Bethesda USO offered Saturday night horseback rides and Sunday beach parties on the Bay in cooperation with the Annapolis USO. Reverend Nelson's War Memorial Committee revealed its plan for a community building to house the public library and meeting rooms and asked for further suggestions.[59]

Chief Bargagni found some old shower heads and installed them in the cement courtyard at the side of the firehouse and offered open-air showers in both morning and afternoons. He soon had a gaggle of happy, small, squealing customers on hot summer days. The Recreation Department staged volleyball and badminton tournaments, and the YMCA chose Wesley L. Sauter to head its committee on building plans. Joseph Bunker reported that 115 boys and girls were now members of Y clubs and that more than 300 boys had participated in afterschool activities. He planned on starting a Hi-Y club at Leland in the fall.

At the Rec Center tennis lessons were very popular that summer, and Donald Benson won the down-county horseshoe championship. At the end of the season the Bethesda Recreation Center won both the boys' and girls' track meets, and Bethesda defeated Jessup Blair 4-1 behind Herbie Benson to win the senior-boys baseball title.

Some businesses, such as the Battery Park Market, closed for a week to give their workers a vacation and others, including Jelleff's, closed on Saturdays. "Doc" Harry Gellman even locked his door early on Sundays during July and August. Wady Imirie closed his shop for the first time in twenty-nine years and gave everyone the last week of July off.

The Hiser showed *Fighting Lady*, one of the war's best documentaries, and then *National Velvet*, which made numerous, male adolescents forget Peggy Ann Garner. Sidney Lust's Bethesda Theater announced that it would start screening "first-run" movies only three weeks after they opened downtown and then featured an Abbott and Costello film followed by an Olsen and Johnson comedy. Guest ministers filled many Bethesda pulpits, and at the end of July the Christ Lutheran Church installed its new pastor, the Rev. Otto C. Schuetze, in a ceremony attended by the church's founder, Reverend Whiting.

A shortlived controversy erupted in midsummer when the D.C. Health Officer accused the County of "dumping" polio cases on Washington hospitals. In August, the long-awaited iron lung donated by the Kiwanis Club finally arrived at Suburban Hospital and was unveiled by 11-year-old Carolyn Allen with help from Dr. Donovan and Mr. Morell. By then, twenty-five polio cases had originated in D.C., twenty-six in the suburbs, and three were being treated at the Bethesda Naval Hospital.

In July the County Commissioners chose Willard F. Day of Langdrum Lane to become the first "County Supervisor," a post created at the recent legislative session. Mr. Day, who had gained a national reputation in a similar position in Henrico County, Virginia, was to take his post on August 1 at a salary of $10,000. The tall, bespectacled, Baltimore-born Day, 51, was a civil engineer by training who had served as the city manager of Staunton, Virginia, for eleven years before taking the Henrico County job. He did "war work" for various agencies including the UN Relief Administration, the National Housing Agency and the Navy.

The Charter Committee applauded Day's appointment and called him "an able

administrator," but Dean Hayden maintained that the Lee machine had only adopted a semblance of the charter program in an effort to fool the voters. "But you can't put a ghost in government and make it work," he said. William Prescott Allen wished Day well in an editorial and warned that he would find no "bed of roses." He wrote that his success depended on balancing the needs of the Commissioners and the demands of the Charter forces and on showing that his office could produce increased efficiency. Allen wrote:

In any event, his work in the new office will be watched with great interest by all factions to determine whether the trend of county government will continue toward the county manager setup or will swing back to the purely commissioner form.

Mrs. Bradley praised the Commissioners' choice and wrote that it "will be interesting to find out how far they will go in making Mr. Day a real supervisor and not a $10,000 figurehead." She concluded that Day "is being paid for doing a cracker-jack job. The Record hopes he will be allowed to do it."[60]

In an interview with the *Star* just before he started his new job, Day said, "If I can't justify my salary, I will recommend getting another man for the post or abolishing it entirely." He said he was starting with "an open mind" and would not be drawn into the Charter controversy. He also said he was looking

Willard Day

for a new home since the rented house he lived in had been sold.

Day took the oath on August 1, the morning after a violent wind and rainstorm swept through the lower county flooding basements, uprooting trees, destroying Victory Gardens, and drowning 200 lab animals in an NIH basement and thereby destroying months of work on tropical diseases. Within the first month, the Commissioners put Day in charge of the police civil service appointments and named him temporary purchasing agent, an act which the *Record* hailed as a step

toward making him a "real" supervisor. His first official road work report showed that Bradmoor Drive and Irvington Avenue were macadamized up to Roosevelt Street as well as Glenwood Road for 250 feet east of Irvington and that work was under way on Selkirk and Orkney Drive. At the end of the month, he was able to announce a million dollar storm sewer program in cooperation with the State Roads Commission and the WSSC.

By the end of July, the Washington Suburban Sanitary Commission added fifteen men and five trucks to its trash collection service. Lacy Shaw claimed that by July 28 all collections in both suburban areas were "current," and he promised twice-weekly collection at all homes. The residents of Cheltenham Drive in Bethesda responded to Shaw's report by advertising for a buzzard after no collection for almost two weeks, and Huntington Terrace homeowners went ten days without a collection and complained about paying in advance for service not rendered. When Sonoma, where Mrs. Bradley lived, went for two weeks with no garbage collection she put the story on the *Record*'s front page under a simple headline: "It Stinks."

The Park and Planning Commission reaffirmed its position against locating an airport on the former Bradley Hills Country Club property, and the local papers agreed to sponsor a "mass meeting" at Bethesda Elementary School on August 20. Bill Allen reminded his readers that the meeting was "entirely unofficial" and restated his belief that the proposed airpark was a menace. The other two Bethesda papers maintained a wait-and-see attitude. The Kenwood and Greenwich Forest Citizens' Associations joined the chorus of opposition to the airpark.

On August 6, an atomic bomb dropped from a B-29 named for the pilot's mother, and the world changed as four square miles of Hiroshima and many of its people disappeared. The front page of the August 7 *Post* carried the headline:

Single Atomic Bomb Rocks Japanese
Army Base
With Mightier Force Than 20,000
Tons of TNT
To Open new Era of Power for
Benefit of Man.

Three days later, after the Soviets had entered the war against Japan, another bomb of a different design missed its aiming point but still destroyed much of Nagasaki. After a painfully slow exchange of telegrams and a false report from United Press on Sunday, the Japanese agreed to the Allied terms on Tuesday, August 13, and the Emperor delivered the unbelievable message of surrender to his people, most of whom had never heard his voice and many of whom could not understand his language as he asked them to "endure the unendurable."

The crowd in front of the White House and in Lafayette Park grew day-by-day as delay followed delay. President Truman finally announced the end of the war at 7 pm on August 15 while masses of servicemen and nurses lined the White House fence. F Street soon filled with a happy mob. Three days of celebrations followed, which included a two-day holiday for most government workers and the end of gas rationing. The newspapers described the Capital's revelry as the wildest since 1918.

During the week between the dropping of the first bomb and the final surrender, the Bethesda Council of Churches planned a service at the Presbyterian church two hours after the official announcement. By 9 pm, the sounds of celebration in the streets of Bethesda were growing louder, but the service of praise and thanksgiving went on with five pastors taking part. The church was filled.

Outside, in various neighborhoods, happy homeowners shook their dinner bells and banged pot lids together. Long-hoarded fire crackers exploded and shotguns boomed. Auto horns and fire sirens sounded constantly, and soon the middle of Bethesda overflowed with cars and celebrants. Up on Old Georgetown Road Sandy Astin and Roger Martin set fire to the newspaper collection bin and added to the excitement. In the theaters, the projectors stopped while the news was announced, and then the audiences sang the national anthem. A company of the National Guard stood ready at the Silver Spring Armory but was never called as police spent most of their time trying to unsnarl the traffic. County offices, the dispensaries and most businesses closed Wednesday and Thursday, and for many the celebration lasted well into Saturday night.[61]

By Monday, as most food rationing ended except on meats, oils and fats, Bethesda settled back into its usual late summer routine, but the casualty reports kept coming in. Lt. Russell Willson, USN, was killed in a plane crash, and Lt. Cmdr. Charles David Hayes of Chevy Chase, Chief Radio Technician Robert T. Thielscher of Kenwood and Lt. James D. Spencer of Chevy Chase were among the 875 lost in the tragic sinking of the *Indianapolis*, the ship the Navy lost track of after it had carried the atomic bomb triggers to Guam. In August, the Bethesda draft board inducted seventeen young men, and in September as the calls decreased, Francis Hill resigned as chairman and Judge Granville Curry, a member of the Board since 1941, took his place.[62]

On Friday, August 17, forty-four students received diplomas at the high school. Most were boys and the majority were from the Bethesda area. Chaplain John Borneman, who had been captured on Corregidor, spoke on "Living in Great Times." The County Board of Education, whose newest member was Mrs. C. Jonathan Hauck of Bethesda, approved a four-room addition and some major renovation at Leland Junior High at a cost of $114,000 and began considering a new junior high in the Goldsboro-River Road area as well as one in northern Bethesda. With the budget approved, school board employees began replacing the scores of windows broken at Chevy Chase Elementary. The library board hired Sarah Rodes Graham as Bethesda's third librarian, and she joined the local search for a place to live while she roomed in a tourist home. And the Victory Garden Committee announced plans for the September Harvest Show.

During the week before the big public meeting on his proposed airpark, Jack Hoberman hosted a number of his Bradley Hills neighbors in an informal get-together. Charles Merryman and Alfred Paul who lived on nearby estates, labeled themselves "old fogies" who wanted undisturbed peace in their country homes. Mr. Merryman stressed that he had put a lot of money into the Weathered Oak Herb Farm, and Mr. Paul said he was opposed to "letting down the bars" so that "a number of people outside the community can go flying around over us." Leslie Bell and Henry Wolfe along with C. A. Weymouth, all of whom owned property near

the club, expressed their support for Hoberman's plans.[63]

In the meeting on August 21 at Bethesda Elementary, more than 300 citizens crowded the auditorium, and almost all of them came to voice their strong opposition to the airpark proposal. Mr. Hoberman and his plans had the support of Eddie Adams, the club's former owner; King Mularkey, representing the Chamber of Commerce; L. D. Wilkinson of Bradley Hills, representing the Aero Club of Maryland, and several others. Louis Gravelle represented the Bradley Hills Citizens' Association and said he had a petition with 500 signatures of those opposed not only to this airpark but to any airport in the Western Suburban Area. Charles Merryman upbraided the Bethesda Chamber for its position in a "matter which does not concern the business area of Bethesda." At the end of the meeting, Mr. Hoberman said he was undecided what he would do next.

When Bill Allen found out that the Chamber's Board of Directors had voted ten to six to approve Mularkey's resolution favoring the airpark, the *Tribune* loudly joined Merryman in being "shocked." In an open letter, Merryman called the Chamber's action "highly improper" and reminded the public that the Chamber had opposed the coming of the National Institutes of Health and had narrowly avoided opposition to the Naval Hospital. "The action taken last night by the Board," said Merryman, "indicates that astute judgement is not always used in reaching these decisions." The choice, said Allen, was between "500 homes and their potential customers for the Bethesda area and 500 airplanes that have no reason to be bothered with 'Buy in Bethesda.'" The editor asked for a full membership meeting and a representative vote.[64]

Chamber President Henry Connor declined to call a special meeting but instead decided to "let things go the way they are." Allen urged Bethesda's merchants to petition for a meeting while Goins of the *Journal* applauded Connor's decision and stated that the question "certainly will not be settled by a newspaper that never has spoken for this community." Meanwhile Hoberman opened up a whole new venue for dispute by applying for a permit to build a stable to house sixty horses on his club property.

After reading letters opposed to the airpark in the local papers, Eddie Adams, who lived in Greenwich Forest, crafted a long reply:

The opposition has obtained many false ideas, as originated by the few men who for some unknown reason have set out to stop this milestone of advancement. When these men are pinned down to actual facts their only real complaint is: "I object – period."

There was no intention to seek commercial zoning for the airpark, said Adams, who then pointed out that the most vocal opponent, Merryman, used his property for an herb farm, a money-making venture, and that there were several farms in the area. "In other words this property is not residential property. It was last used as a dairy farm and for the last twenty-five years has not been used at all."[65]

While this issue continued to simmer, the summer wound down. The Thrift Shop opened for its third season with its completely redecorated showroom painted light green. Lions Club president Richard Fisher appointed vice-president Albert Brault to head a committee to raise $1,000 to add another 1,200 names to the honor roll on Wisconsin Avenue. The Red Cross suspended its blood donor program and closed down the Jeep House at the end of the season, but the recreation department continued the day nurseries created under the Lanham Act with the fee increased to a maximum of $9.00 per week per child.

The Montgomery Players advertised tryouts for "Over 21" directed by Jane Plummer Rice, the first play of its seventeenth season and selected E. Barrett Prettyman Jr.

Mrs. Ray Tucker and Mrs. Edwin Merritt discuss a Thrift Shop bargain with Mrs. Percy Royster, at right

for one of the youthful leads. On the Keplinger court, medical student Lawrence Mosier of Chevy Chase defeated Billy Wimot to win the 29th annual tennis tournament on the first weekend in September. The Lynnbrook Indian camp closed with a picnic for the 175 Bradley and Lynnbrook elementary children. The six tribes appeared in all their finery for games and contests, and the Lynnbrook mothers defeated the Bradley mothers in the featured footrace. The Newcomb Club's Community Singers led by Mrs. Charles G. Morgan resumed their pre-war activities.[66]

The biggest business news for the Bethesda area in the immediate post-war period was Woodward and Lothrop's decision to build a branch department store at Wisconsin and Western on a six-acre tract where the burnt out hulk of a Hot Shoppes still moldered. William Prescott Allen welcomed Woodies with an overjoyed editorial which also pointed "with pride to the fact that through the years we have foreseen such development of Bethesda and its business district and have offered every encouragement to reputable firms like this to come to our community." Allen was entitled to a bit a braggadocio as a long-term promoter of the town's growth. Mrs. Bradley put the drawing of Woodies proposed store on the front page of the *Record* and also wrote an editorial of welcome from the housewives' point of view.

Original design for Woodies at the District Line

A survey of local employers by the Chamber of Commerce showed that not only were they ready to hire the men returning from the service but that they also expected to employ up to twice as many as they had before the war. Howard Johnson's revealed plans to build a new restaurant out on Rockville Pike, and Art Bowis at Chevy Chase Motor Company started work on a sixty by ninety foot building for more and improved service bays. Bowis said he planned to expand from twenty-five to sixty employees in the immedi-

ate future and hoped to have the first new Chevrolets by October.

Carbert's added forty feet to the back of its store and then did a complete facelift on the façade creating a center entrance and two, big display windows. The Bank of Bethesda discontinued its late opening hours and went back to nine till two daily and nine to noon on Saturday. Mrs. Bradley hired her first male, 22-year-old A. Barton Barber Jr., and sent him exploring Bethesda's businesses for the *Record*. Willard Day asked that returning veterans consider County employment and stated that he had some twenty-five jobs available as of the first of September.

Most of Bethesda's war industries converted fairly painlessly back to peace time hours, work and work forces, but unfortunately the largest one did not. Falge Engineering Service, which produced many types of signal lights and instruments, had employed mostly Bethesda housewives who left their work, practically without complaint, once the emergency was over. Ray Falge admitted that the cancellation of war contracts had "been staggering." He was waiting for some patents to be confirmed before swinging into peacetime production.

Bowen and Company cut its work force from 200 to fifty-five, but its reconversion "was carried out smoothly to the satisfaction of all concerned." It withdrew from the buildings scattered around the "flats" and returned to manufacturing soil-testing and cement-testing instruments which, like its wartime output, depended on accurate measurements.[67]

The painful exception was Briggs Clarifier, which lost contracts that used ninety percent of its productive capacity within a week of V-J Day. The company, which had grown from 135 employees in 1941 to more than 1,100 workers at war's end and which was still advertising for workers when the bomb dropped, cut its work force by fifty-five percent on one day, August 16, when the military contracts were terminated. Many of the fired workers were schoolboys, women, and temporaries hired for summer work, but about half were not.

Both the *Record* and the *Tribune* played the Briggs Clarifier story in much the same way as they had the changes at Falge and Bowen, but the *Journal* savaged Chase Donaldson for firing many veterans among the 515 he laid off

and then for failing to meet with the American Legion Post 161 members at the County Building as he had promised. Goins addressed an open letter to Donaldson in which he said,

We feel a deep responsibility in this matter since this paper published much of your advertising and publicity which led prospective employees to believe that a job with your firm would be permanent after the war.

Some of the riffed employees had been sent to Briggs by the U.S. Employment Service. One was quoted as saying,

When we got back from the fighting front our only thought was where could we find security. Employment service officials assured us that we would find it with Briggs which has no re-conversion problems.

Donaldson responded to Goins that the "tone and implications" of his letter were "unwarranted by the facts." Donaldson stated that ninety-five percent of the laid-off workers had been with the company less than a year and that many were part-time employees hired just for the summer. "Seniority, as is customary in the industry," he said, "strongly influences the order of layoffs." The Briggs official emphasized that 560 workers continued to be employed because of "prompt conversion." Donaldson admitted that a few veterans with short service time were among those let go, but he also pointed out that there were "296 Briggs men still in service to welcome back."

Unfortunately for the *Journal*'s case, one of the veterans cited as mistreated, Ramon Carazo, who had lost an arm at Hickam Field on December 7, 1941, and worked for Briggs Clarifier for three years, had not been fired as claimed but had left to attend school under the GI Bill. In his open letter to Goins, which both the *Tribune* and *Record* printed, Carazo defended Donaldson's firing of some vets. "You must realize," he wrote, "the termination of war came before the majority of us expected it." Bethesdans soon turned their attention to other concerns.[68]

Schools opened as usual but with some modifications. The high school de-emphasized shop courses and discontinued the program designed to accelerate the senior year for draft-eligible males. Mr. Pyle said that several young veterans were being helped to complete their high school work with corre-

spondence courses and other were re-registering as regular students. B-CC expected to enlarge both the Retail Selling and Diversified Work Experience programs in 1945-46. Principal Pyle believed in vocational education. "We have glorified the white collar all out of proportion," he said.

B-CC welcomed eleven new teachers that fall, but no former faculty members had returned from service yet. The football team had a seven games scheduled when it started practice a week before classes began and then added a Thanksgiving Day game with Blair at the end of the season. Incoming B-CC students received a 32-page handbook prepared by the Hi-Y club; Glenn Ferguson was elected class president for the third year in a row, and the *Tattler* was once again a real, printed newspaper. Well-organized Larry Jennings, an admirer of faculty-sponsor Melva Hon's tight skirts, was the first editor of the reborn paper and associate-editor Astrid "Andy" Nye took over at mid-year as was the well-established custom.[69]

Despite warning letters, the fraternities, all but eliminated by the end of the war, reinvented themselves and had a vigorous fall as did Mr. Bunker's Hi-Y Club and the new Tri-Hi-Y for girls. Small herds of young men assembled at the pool hall, down in Hiser's alleys or at Leon's store where senior Jimmy Wallace of Chi Alpha was new father Leon Sherman's right-hand man. The girls tended more toward potluck clubs, but one or two sororities also continued to meet. As one male participant saw it:

They were just a formalized clique. Potluck girls, the cheerleaders and like that, met every Friday. We attached ourselves to a potluck group. Every Friday these gals would get together, and at eight or nine we'd go over there and pick up dates.

For girls, the school uniform was sweaters, skirts and often a string of pearls, and while many boys tried to dress in Leon's latest, others preferred old Army jackets covered with badges and slogans, pegged pants and, for a few, strange hats of various designs.

That fall the high school held its last gold star assembly. More than a thousand persons including relatives of many of the former students killed and missing in the war attended as gold stars were placed on the service flag for Robert Thielscher, class of `38; Wilson Tyrell, class of `31; Kenneth Kinsella, class of

`38, Byron Massincup, class of `40; Richard Russell, class of `43, and John W. Guckeyson, class of `33. The A Cappella Choir sang through the muffled sobs from the quiet rows of chairs. The banner hung before them with forty gold stars and 915 blue ones for those who had served.[70]

At Leland, where construction would continue all year on home arts classrooms and a new library, thirteen new teachers started work under Principal Elwood Mason. For many wartime Leland students, teacher-turnover was what they remembered best. Quite a few of the boys had acquired strange colored hair over the summer. Some were now blondes while others were more orange-headed and a few had hair tinged with green. Peroxide sales in the Bethesda area reached all-time highs.

Among the most envied boys at school were the few who arrived on new, red, Cushman motorscooters, which could be operated legally by 14-year-olds. For most students the big news was that there were now two cafeteria lines, a much bigger kitchen and a longer lunch period. For girls there was finally a varsity basketball team with a ten-game schedule. The ninth grade class officers were Chuck Wilson, Tom Brown, Dick Beckwith, Roddy Ware, Peggy Evers and Barbara Christensen. The boys were all on the varsity basketball team and both of the girls were cheerleaders.[71]

That year section 9VII became Weld's Willing Workers and boasted of Bob Ehrman, editor of the school paper and yearbook. When the Hi-Y got started at Leland, Dick Beckwith headed the 9th grade club, and Ben

A Cushman!

Aiken presided over the 8th grade group. More than 400 students on thirty teams took part in the Y's after school softball program.

After two months of florid writing about Bethesda business-men and women in a column called "All Around the Town," Barton Barber, the *Record*'s new reporter, interviewed two "typical" Leland ninth-graders that fall, Billy Lehr and Virginia Andrews. The diminutive Lehr, Zip's son and a "well known Leland cat," managed to pull the reporter's leg well out of joint but still came off as a reasonable young man with bleached hair and "unintelligible" slang.

Barton reported that Billy helped mail the *Record* on Wednesday, delivered the *Post* every morning, swept out the Leland gym every day, and then jerked sodas at Whittlesey's on weekends. Billy convinced Barber that most "cats" said "yos" for "yes." "newt" for "no," and "narry" for "never." Billy talked a lot about people he called "fruitbowls" and said "fruits" were "drips," the opposite of "cats." He also told the reporter that "hoas on that noise" simply meant "shut up." Barton evidently had a bad ear or a sheltered upbringing.

Billy Lehr

The reporter quoted Billy as saying that only tough guys who liked to crash parties smoked, and he did not associate with them.

Their evening parties are, he says, as decorous as you could wish; they involved nothing stronger than dancing and gossip and fruit punch, save for an occasional game of Spoon, one pasttime not permitted at the Friday evening entertainments of the Junior Canteen. Parties break up early in Mr. Lehr's group; one is allowed out no later than one o'clock on weekends (and nine or nine-thirty school nights).

Lehr said he was a good student and enjoyed some of his courses but shared with his friends "an intense dislike of teachers who will not meet their pupils halfway and share their pleasures on the lighter side of life." The men who never smiled and the women who

Cheerleaders for 1945-46 at Leland Junior High School[74]

did not wear make-up or smile "drew from their students a rain of spitballs and abuse. Such pedagogues, no matter how diligent, remain 'fruit' and heaven help them."[72]

Cheerleader and *Pine Cone* gossip columnist Virginia Andrews arrived for her interview with Barber "clutching an immense comb which she passed through her hair from time to time in the course of her statement." She explained that big combs were a current junior high fad and were usually carried on the back of the head or in a purse. To be in style girls also needed an identification bracelet, "the bigger the better, and this must be the gift, though not necessarily the love-token, of some young man" plus a friendship ring from a girlfriend. "She must at all time appear with flaming mouth, and should invest in at least two lipsticks a month costing not less than a dollar apiece." Revlon's "Pink Lightning" was the favorite that season.

As for proper costume, Virginia said it was still "loafers and bobby sox, skirt and sweater. The sweater should be large and loose or in Miss Andrews' term, 'monstrous.' The tight fitting sweater is definitely out of style. Those wearing them are called 'bwangy,' and are not welcomed in the best circles." Girls who smoked or dated older men or kissed more boys than they were in love with were ostracized." "In every thing you do you have to look out for your reputation in Bethesda," she said and avoid "what tends to cheapen a girl."

She told Barber that the "smart young woman at Leland" is permitted to study but not overdo it and should be encouraged to engage in classroom note passing and spend at least an hour on the phone each evening. Weekend parties, with lots of food and cokes, and slumber parties were popular. "A couple of girls I know sat down in the living room and piled furniture on another girl all night, " she said. Virginia, who was a junior volunteer at Suburban Hospital, admitted that popularity seemed "the be-all and end-all of existence" and that girls were perhaps not as carefree nor as happy as boys at Leland. She also suggested that junior high girls tended to argue more with their parents than did boys.[73]

Billy Lehr recalled the interview and his time at Leland with a smile.

Vink Guandolo and I applied to Doc for jobs as soda jerks. We worked there part time, sometimes on weekends, for a while. Well, on the soda jerk job some kids from school got a few goodies at Whittlesey's for less than was on the board up there. That might have cost me my job. Doc was sort of a grump, but then he was dealing with a lot of teenagers. He always had his eyeball on you. He'd hired enough kids that he had to do that.

Whittlesey's was busy all the time. These guys used to come to Vink and me and say can you get us any, you know, rubbers, condoms. And in the back room the drawer they were kept in was right by the pharmacy. I think occasionally some were lifted out of there, but you'd get these orders, and you'd go back there and go back there, and there was no way you could get any of those dudes. It was the place for Leland, for B-CC it was the Hot Shoppe.

Willard Schumaker gave me the job of sweeping and cleaning the gym. On Wednesday and Saturday I had to clean the locker room and disinfect the showers. Sweep the gym every day and sweep the locker room every day, but on Saturdays I had to really give it a going over. So I went to Schumaker and asked if it was any

problem if I get some help in here, and he said you know we are not going to pay anybody else.

So I'd get these kids to come in, sort of like a Tom Sawyer job. So I'd scrub the locker room first because that was the real chore then we'd go upstairs and play basketball and even if only one or two stayed we could mop the gym in ten or fifteen minutes. So we'd be over there two or three hours. We had some good times, some good games. A couple of times I let more people in than I should have, that was a mistake. We usually let in six or seven or eight guys. It was a great gym, fir blocks, 4x4's, set on end and a big wooden door pulled by hand across the middle.

Mason was principal, but it was Bready before that. She knew me 'cause she was there when my dad taught there. A couple of times when I got in a jam, rather than make me stay after or suspend me, she used to have me clean the windows in that damn auditorium. My lord, there are hundreds of them. That was one of her favorite things with me. She said she didn't want to call my dad. None of it was malicious, my mouth got me in trouble.

I had an awful time with Miss Loar, she taught Latin. I had peroxided my hair, had white hair when I did that interview. I mentioned something about Miss Loar only having two dresses or not wearing makeup. I didn't realize all this stuff was going to be in the paper. She dropped the article on my desk. I wasn't a good student, but she said she would pass me if I swore not to take Latin 2

We used to hang out at Hiser's bowling alley, and I set pins to get money for a movie when you couldn't get somebody to let you in. We'd go down there and chip in and get one ticket, then that guy would go down, pull the curtains closed and then try to open the door and get in as many people as you can before the ushers

came. You know when you opened that door in a dark theater it was bright as anything, and they'd come down with a flashlight trying to find the people crawling along the aisles.

The private schools were also returning to normal. Paul Banfield was back at Landon after regaling the Rotary Club and others with tales of headhunters in New Guinea where his plane made a forced landing. He was adding a new wing to the north end of the gym to house more labs and classrooms and hoped to have it finished by Thanksgiving. At Whitehall, new owner Dwight Collins, a Landon instructor to whom the 1945 *Brown and White* was dedicated, planned on building a new kindergarten cottage and adding a science course stressing the "facts of life."

Longfellow School added a wing to enlarge the dining room and accomplished some major remodeling including a new office for headmaster Reece Sewell. Longfellow's opening was postponed so that the new showers and locker rooms could be completed. Georgetown Prep returned Greek to its curriculum, and at Lynn Womack's new Howell Academy for Boys, which met in an old farmhouse with a new fire escape near Montrose, the emphasis was on old-fashioned discipline. Headmistress Carrie Sutherlin planned a new Humanities program at the Chevy Chase Junior College, which was "overwhelmed" with applications that had to be turned down for lack of space.[75]

The local churches also returned to peacetime activities and, in some cases, long-delayed building plans. The Council of Churches welcomed St. John's Episcopal to its membership and planned a religious census during the last two weeks of September, the first effort of its kind since 1940. Chevy Chase Methodist staged a seven-week study of the problems of returning GIs which began with the chief of Army Air Force chaplains speaking on "The Reconversion of G. I. Joe." At Bethesda Methodist, the building committee led by Scott Moring and including Riley Evers and John H. Werner accelerated plans for the new church at Huntington Parkway.

The Jewish Community Group, in its third year, announced plans for celebrating the High Holy Days at the I. S. Turover Building on Bethesda Avenue. Sunday school for boys and girls from 5 to 14 was again held at the Lynnbrook school and included for the first

Miss Loar (at right) and section 9-IV (1944-45)

time a confirmation class. Dr. J. M. Shear chaired the Sunday school committee.

At Our Lady of Lourdes, the Holy Name Society honored past presidents John Overholt, Joe Cantrel and Albert Brault on its seventeenth anniversary in a meeting attended by two hundred men. Father Sweeney, the acting pastor, announced that the Rev. Elmer T. Fisher would be coming from St. Mary's at Bryantown at the end of October to replace Father Little. Christ Lutheran signed up Wilfred A. Briggs, discharged after three years with the Army medical corps, as its new choir director. At Glen Echo Baptist Church the pastor, Dr. Pryce E. Gatlin, held daily afternoon cottage prayer meetings and evening revival services throughout September.

On September 7 at the Masonic Hall, its temporary quarters, the Bethesda Christian Church received its charter. More than a hundred attended the ceremonies, which also marked the first anniversary of Reverend Wilkerson's pastorate. The charter was accepted by Claude A. Cook, trustee and chairman of the congregation. Rev. C. A. Brubaker, pastor of what was now most often called "The Little Church in the Wildwood," announced plans for a Youth for Christ rally in October at the high school's Metzel Bowl.

That same Sunday afternoon, the Woman's Club of Bethesda served a "thank you" supper for the USO at their clubhouse. Brooke Johns emceed the entertainment, and an all-girl orchestra provided the dance music. In response to many questions, Marjorie M. Trayes issued a statement from USO headquarters that said, "It is abundantly evident that our mission has not yet been wholly fulfilled." On the September 23-24-25, the local USO celebrated its second birthday with a supper on Sunday, open house on Monday and then a formal dance on the anniversary itself. Miss Trayes said the organization would continue its work for at least another eighteen months, and she estimated that 80,000 service personnel had been entertained over the last two years.

Trayes thanked the community for:

Hundreds of cakes and pies, thousands of cookies, baskets of homemade jellies and other goodies, Sunday night suppers, thousands of magazines, records, hundreds of books, sports equipment, afghans, lamps, pillows, musical instruments, sheet music, dozens of eggs, gallons

of milk, beautiful flowers, potted plants, and room registry service.

She added that even "Butch," the club mascot, was a community loan and that "Bones for Butch were, during the peak of rationing days, and even now are an important item in our gift list." She concluded with thanks to the "Many of you have extended the hospitality of your own homes to our service folk."[76]

When infantry lieutenant Don Dunnington was discharged, he did not waste any time in restarting the Chevy Chase First Aid Corps. By September, he had acquired a Cadillac ambulance and was back in business. For the first time in more than a year, Bethesda had 24-hour ambulance service by calling Wisconsin 5172 or the local police.

Dunnington convinced four local service stations to contribute gasoline and talked Bell's Laundry into washing the linen Sears supplied. He made an appeal through the local papers for both donations and volunteers for which the only qualification, he said, was an interest in the project.

Bill Blackwood Sr. of the Chevy Chase Fire Department remembered the rebirth.

In '45 we went to the Tick Tock and discussed the ambulance service, which then only the funeral home had. The Civitans donated an old ambulance to us. We called it the "green hornet" and kept it at each other's house. We set up night duties and whoever had the duty kept it at his house. The Bethesda Fire Department would call us, and we had a phone chain. We met `em on the corner. It took us forever, of course.

Bill Allen welcomed the ambulance:

The Tribune feels that the First Aid Corps

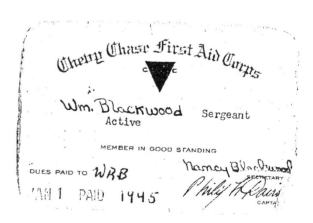

Blackwood's CCFAC membership card. His wife was the organization's secretary.

is a worthwhile addition to the community and that these young men are to be congratulated for their public spirited willingness to give their services in a cause which should have been provided by the officials of the county or the local suburban district.

The Civitan Club had agreed to fund the rescue squad's ambulance to the tune of $2,900. In September the squad answered twenty-five calls and won a prize from the County volunteer firemen for the best appearing and best equipped ambulance. Having the only uniformed women's auxiliary in the parade did not hurt their chances.

By winter the ambulance was paid for and was being housed in what came to be called the "mole hole" under Jelleff's while some people pressured the volunteer fire department to donate their little-used station house. By then "Duck" Dunnington's group had changed its name to the Bethesda-Chevy Chase First Aid Squad.

Blackwood recalled:

When we went to the mole hole, we got an old Nash and an old pie wagon. We wore old coats and white hats. We had that old Nash in D.C. one time, and it wouldn't come out of reverse so I had to back to Bethesda from Chevy Chase Circle.

Then, the rescue squad responded to the Bethesda Fire Department's big horn. You could

Civitan's Hisey presents Dunnington a check

hear it all over. People would come running. I would run from my house on Maple Avenue off Bradley Lane near the Chevy Chase Club all the way to the mole hole, and sometimes I wouldn't get there in time, and I'd be left behind.[77]

In Chevy Chase, an era ended with the retirement of mailman William J. Beron who had been coming to work before 5 am for more than twenty-three years. His departure was eased by the fact that Allison Blaine McQuin was still making his rounds. "Mac" knew most of the women and kids on his route by their first names and signalled a letter from a husband in the service by whistling the cardinal's mating call.

The citizens of Huntington Terrace began circulating a petition about their inadequate storm sewers, and at Lynnbrook Elementary more than fifty parents got together one Saturday and cleaned up the playground. Ed Stock was getting ready for the third Harvest Show, the biggest yet, while the Chamber of Commerce planned a clean-up-Bethesda campaign during Fire Prevention Week and started talking about reviving the Christmas Lane. Suburban Hospital signed up its hundredth junior volunteer, and newspaper collecting continued but tin can salvage ended.[78]

The American Legion displayed the final plans for its clubhouse, to be named for its former commander, James B. Fitzgerald. The Civitans led by Bill Austin finished a playground at the end of Norfolk Street in Woodmont, and Robert Bray wondered in print whatever had happened to the plans to widen Wisconsin Avenue and eliminate the bottleneck. That issue along with the appointment of Jo Morgan as Civil Service Commissioner and Al Brault as Public Utility Agent led to an east-west split in E. Brooke Lee's Democratic coalition.

Admiral Murray E. Miles was back home on Shadow Road in Kenwood with a couple of knife wound scars and many stories of his two years in China organizing guerrilla units behind Japanese lines. Every week, more were back: Ray Gingell, Sam Bogley, "Junie" Andrews, Bob Brewer. The Horton brothers, Sgt. DeValle and Corporal Everts, of Arlington Road both got out with 113 points.[79]

Chet Caithness was taking orders for new Buicks, and there were big crowds at Magee's store to see the first RCA Victor plastic records. Adlai Magee took the names of

those who wanted to buy radios or phonographs and put them on slips of paper in a big bowl, and then when some stock arrived, he drew out the names of "winning" customers. Henry Hiser started talking about building a new theater again, and humpbacked Jimmy Nichols, who had worked in the County Building since it opened, returned to his old post as police clerk.

On the last Sunday of September when the country went back on standard time after three-and-a-half years of daylight savings, it took awhile for all the clocks and people to readjust. Kids especially missed that extra hour of daylight to play after supper. Gifford's returned to eighteen percent butterfat in all its ice cream. Marvin Simmons reclaimed his showroom from the OSS and pledged his first 1946 Plymouth to an auction for the benefit of the Honor Roll, from which kids had taken all the gold stars by fall.[80]

At the volunteer firemen's convention, Captain George Arnold of the Glen Echo Volunteer Fire Department received an award for saving two boys from the river in May, and the volunteers elected David Tuohey of the Cabin John Volunteer Fire Department president of the association. The rationing board closed down with praise for all the volunteers and for three-year employee Anna Roach, one of Dr. Perry's last patronage-job nominees. Ruth Bondy of Willett Parkway was back home after two years overseas with a Red Cross clubmobile, which operated just behind the front lines in North Africa and Italy. She said she was looking forward to a barbeque and milk shake at the Hot Shoppe.[81]

During the week after V-J Day, ABC radio reported that Lt. Col. James P. S. Devereux, the hero of Wake Island and the purported "send more Japs" message, had been found alive in a Japanese prison camp. According to press reports, the colonel's eleven-year-old son, J. P. S. 2nd, who was called Paddy, greeted the news "with a shout of joy." Both Devereux's wife and mother had died during his long imprisonment.[82]

Bill Allen ran a front page editorial on August 24 calling for the celebration of Devereux Day when the colonel returned to Chevy Chase, and for a while it seemed as though the whole community would get behind the idea. Joseph A. Cantrel, State Commander of the American Legion, headed the planning

committee, and he soon involved the local Lions, Civitans, Kiwanis and Rotary Clubs. After some doubt and debate, the date was set as Saturday, September 29, and the Marines agreed to supply a band and 400 marchers for the proposed parade.

Craddock Goins, the *Journal*'s editor-publisher who had become an almost implacable enemy of W. Prescott Allen, wrote that it was the family's feelings which should concern "every person of good taste," and the clear implication was that Bill Allen would not be included in that group. Goins called for "nothing less than the simplest, most dignified reception" for Devereux.

While Mrs. Bradley stood aside and reported developments in the *Record* and Allen seemed to ignore Goins's jibes, Robert V. Bray scrambled to rescue his editor's honor. Bray insisted that the *Tribune* did not "try to capitalize on the idea" but put it where it belonged with the American Legion. "It would have been easy to carry the campaign as a Tribune feature but the gain of this paper would have been a loss to the celebration," and so the paper's management "stepped aside from the floodlights of glory."[83]

Goins responded that Bray "hee-haws strangely at times" and that editor Allen spent most of his time in promotions, mainly of himself. "I frankly never knew Ballyhoo Bill had a bandwagon. Some people think he has more brass than a Marine band, but it never was on wheels. At least it doesn't move anywhere." Goins concluded that he did not feel people of good taste had to be told how to greet a hero and he would just "stick to his knitting, in my small way, content with the thought that we don't have to leave our paper in public places to get it read."[84]

When Colonel Devereux arrived at Union Station, his son rushed to greet him with a grandmotherly present of handkerchiefs. Paddy threw his arms around his gaunt father and kissed him. It had been a separation of four years. A crowd of Devereuxs, in-laws, nieces and nephews filled the platform. The Colonel was driven to Marine headquarters where he met with General Vandegrift, received the Navy Cross and underwent a medical checkup while Paddy waited with his maternal grandparents, Colonel and Mrs. Welch. The boy had been staying with them in Butler, Pennsylvania, and was wearing the

Chinese officer's cap his grandfather had brought from the China-Burma-India theater of operations.

On Saturday morning, Chief Bargagni's firemen finished decorating the street with all of the bright flags he had been hoarding, dozens of colorful pennants and dull, leaky balloons, which were all he could find, and then strung a huge banner across Wisconsin Avenue near Bradley that proclaimed WELCOME HOME JIM. Almost every store had a big welcome sign in its window.

The threatened rain, which would have canceled the parade and put the ceremony in the Leland auditorium, held off as the temperature climbed past ninety. All of Bethesda's businesses closed at 3 pm, and the parade stepped off from the bank at 3:30. The police estimated that more than 20,000 people thronged the sidewalks, easily the biggest crowd in Bethesda's history. First came the police motorcycles and then Jimmy Devereux and son Patrick in the back of an open car toting two, big, olive-drab barrage balloons that carried the family name. The car's windshield still carried a tattered, black "A" ration sticker. The slight colonel wore his overseas cap and Paddy his Chinese hat, and they both waved and smiled.

They passed Peoples, the row of stores that Walter Tuckerman built and Hiser's marquee which read "Welcome Home Lt. Col. Devereux." The matinee had started at 12:30 and ended at three, and the ushers had quickly taken down "Eadie Was a Lady" to put up the more appropriate message. The new-made colonel and his son waved to the boys clinging to the Madonna of the Trail and the crowd under the big columns of the County Building. On across the bridge and past Crivella's market, people jumped, shouted and cheered while the first band began to play. They passed Judge Wilson's old store where the Broadhursts waved and the Western Union office in the Guild Building from which so many sad telegrams had come. The front of the growing parade reached the site of Darcy's Store, where the town's business district had begun, and then Woolworth's and Palais Royal.

Behind Devereux's car came one carrying Marine Corps commandant, Gen. Alexander A. Vandegrift, along with Major Barninger and Major Lewis who had served under Devereux's command. Then came cars with Billy Prescott, Joe Cantrel and other local politicians and dignitaries. Behind them the cheers rose again for three companies of Marines, the Marine Band from Quantico, and two platoons of Women Marines who drew both applause and whistles. "From the Halls of Montezuma" echoed down Wisconsin Avenue as Paddy waved to the ladies in white smocks and the mob of spectators at the Farm Women's Market, and his father saluted

Colonel Devereux and his son wave to the crowd

the folks in front of G. W. Imirie's and Joe Virga's. The Shopping Center and the gas stations across from it were packed with cars and people waving flags as the motorcade crossed Leland Street.

Anna Roach stood on a car bumper outside the ration board to watch them pass by and then hurried to the reviewing stand where she had a part in the ceremonies. Along Sacks' row, Yee Koon and his wife waved and bowed from the doorway of the Smiling Buddha, and Arvella Pugh and the crowd in front of Martin's applauded. Beanie Brown even stopped work at the former Red Cross store-front, which he was turning into the Sports Mart, to wave and hooray. Across the way in front of Lee's laundry, Tate's pool hall and Gellman's drug store, the trees were full

Bethesda's biggest crowd cheers the Devereuxs

of boys, and the crowd surged into the street after the motorcycles passed. Small children rode their fathers' shoulders and bigger ones chased along the curb keeping pace with the colonel's open car.

At the big, stone, phone company building and the A&P parking lot the crowd grew even bigger, and when the colonel's car turned in at the bunting-covered reviewing stand in front of the old Offutt place, dozens of children broke through the police lines and clambered over the convertible to gawk at his ribbons and shake his hand. With some help, he and Paddy extricated themselves and went up on the stand where they were joined by some forty-three other Devereux kin and twenty local notables who glanced from time to time at the gathering clouds.

From the platform, they watched as the Marines marched by followed by several Army units, a SPAR band, a hundred Maryland State Guardsmen, groups of Boy and Girl Scouts and some Cubs, a Navy band, units from the Veterans of Foreign Wars, Disabled American Veterans and Catholic War Veterans, Red Cross nurse's aides and Grey Ladies, and finally a contingent from the American Legion. It was Bethesda's biggest and best parade ever with about one thousand marchers.

The Marine Band stopped at the Honor Roll. As the other units reached Bradley Boulevard, most headed for their buses, but some went over to the Recreation Center where a picnic was planned, and others made their way back toward the reviewing stand and joined the crowd there.

Several boys climbed up the back of the big honor roll billboard and watched the ceremonies from its top while smaller children played in the shade under the platform. Many of the spectators had arrived early equipped with folding chairs, box lunches and camp stools, but most stood in a growing crowd that more than filled the street while boys ran back and forth towing the big balloons with Devereux's name on them.[85]

Msgr. Thomas Smyth of Blessed Sacrament gave the invocation, and then Joseph Cantrel took over as master of ceremonies. He talked about Devereux's youth on the streets of Bethesda and Chevy Chase when he attended "the little school by the water tower on Rosemary Street." Cantrel, a boyhood friend of the colonel, said, "In those days, little Jimmy Devereux could have no idea, as he studied his geography, that Wake Island was more than a remote speck beyond the Pacific horizon. He could have had no idea that one day his name was to glorify it in American history for all generations to come."

Cantrel introduced General Vandegrift who spoke of the heroic, sixteen-day defense of Wake and said its gallantry had encouraged the Marines on Guadalcanal, Tarawa, Saipan, Guam and Iwo Jima. "The Wake defenders have been a constant inspiration to the men of the Marine Corps," said their commandant. "While the slogan throughout the war for the whole nation has been 'Remember Pearl Harbor,' for the Marine

Corps it has been 'Remember Wake Island' as well."

Then the presentations began. Jack Batham gave Devereux a life membership in Post 105 of the American Legion, and Fred C. Byrne made him a life member in the James E. Brady Post No. 180 of the Catholic War Veterans. Cantrel presented him with a gold wrist watch inscribed as being the gift of "his fellow citizens." Mrs. Roach presented her framed copy of Devereux's Presidential citation, and Cantrel gave it to Paddy.

Mabel Marie Goins watched the younger Devereux as his father's merits were extolled. She wrote that "his fingers gripped a bayonet-studded memento of Wake Island" but he did not look at it. "He looked straight at his dad." The crowd "was lost" to him. "He had eyes only for the slender man who had inspired this mighty turnout." And when Lt. Col. Devereux stood to speak, his son "looked on with a face strangely grim for a child, with intensity that one would not expect of a little boy."

Devereux stood behind the microphone, a small man with a neat mustache, his shirt collar and uniform looking a bit too big for him. He waved as the crowd cheered on, and when it finally quieted, he said, "Even if I had the ability of our late commander-in-chief, I'd never possibly be able to express how I feel about this whole thing." He stopped and looked around. "I would simply like to say I thank you from the bottom of my heart. I thank you very much." There was a quiet pause and a few people clapped; then he nodded and turned back to his chair. The crowd cheered again.

Cantrel then introduced Zita McBride, and everyone stood and the many men in uniform saluted as she sang the "Star Spangled Banner" accompanied by the Marine Band. The crowd began to drift away, some toward the Rec Center, although it still looked like rain, and others to finish their Saturday shopping as the stores opened again. Devereux with his watch and framed citations led his son back to the car. He shook hands with dozens of people and told them it was good to be home.[86]

Atop the Roll of Honor billboard a curly-headed boy took one last shot at a pretty girl in the crowd with his pea shooter. Then he stuck it in his pocket and climbed down

It was over.

[1]Despite wartime wage and price controls, the commodity price index rose from 78.6 in 1940 to 105.8 in 1945. National income increased about 2 1/2 times during the war years.

[2]*Record*, April 20, 1945 by "B-J."

[3]George G. Glamack, 6'9", 230, UNC, the "Blind Bomber" played pro basketball before and after the war.

[4]*Tribune*, Jan. 5, and *Record*, Jan 5 and 19, 1945.

[5]Oral biography of Stella B. Werner, 3 vols. in Rockville Public Library. See editorial in *Record*, Feb. 9, 1945. For Hayden-Lee dispute see *Record*, Feb. 23, 1945. Garber reference from her cited thesis.

[6]Garber, op cit. Fred Lee letter in Gardner collection now in County Archives.

[7]*Tribune* and *Record* , Feb. 16 and 23, 1945.

[8]*Record*, April 6, 1945. At this writing twelve of the buildings listed still stand including all three of the Safeway stores and the oldest, the once-moved hardware store. A fourth old Safeway, site of the USO clubhouse, is at Wilson and Old Georgetown.
Mr. Imirie might have squeezed 500 cars in the hilly lot behind Tuckerman's row of stores, but it seldom held half that number. Some of his other estimates are also on the high side.

[9]*Record*, Jan. 12, 1945.

[10]*Record*, April 6, 1945. As Lewis Sims noted, the $1.50 tax rate seemed sacred and set in stone.

[11]For more on Dr. Astin and the proximity fuses see the commemorative biography prepared by the Department of Commerce for the Astin Memorial Symposium in 1985 (Science: Evidence, Truth & Integrity) and the history of the NBS by Rexmond C. Cochrane, *Measures for Progress*, 1966.

[12]Many consider the proximity fuse second only to the atomic bomb as a vital, secret weapon of WW II. The devices could explode shells within seventy feet of the target and were credited with helping turn back German tanks in the Battle of the Bulge, destroying many V-1 buzz bombs aimed at England and Belgium, and blunting the Kamikaze attacks made by the Japanese during the last year of the war. *Record*, March 23 and *Journal*, Sept. 28, 1945.
Bowen also made turbidimeters, compression cube molds, plasticimeters, autoclav bar molds, indentation testers, linear comparators and precision pantographs.

[13]All quotes from the commemorative biography by Elio Pasaglia, 1984. Alexander Astin said that his father tried to convince the high command that the Germans did not have the capacity to produce the fuses but failed. Astin was director of the Bureau of Standards, 1952-1969.

[14]After the war, Harry Gunnison returned to Bethesda as manager of Federal sales for a hospital equipment company and was active in the County Society for the Handicapped. He died in 1970.

[15]Chi Alpha, which Kenny Poerstel pledged as a freshman, may have been the only surviving fraternity.

[16]*Journal*, April 20, 1945.

[17]Future historians should be aware that not all the service items are equally trustworthy. The writer created the following entirely bogus story which the *Record* printed in 1945: *George Bragaw, Ph. M 1-c, son of Mr and Mrs Bragaw of 2773 McKinley Street, Bethesda, who has been on a destroyer escort in the Atlantic for the past couple of years, returned to the States recently and is now in New York. George expects to arrive in Bethesda on the 23rd for a 30-day furlough. A B-CC graduate, class of `41, George has a younger brother, Billy, who is a student at St John's in Washington.* In truth, George and I were both 13 at the time.

[18]See *Tattler*, March 6, 1945.

[19]Klippstein actually hit only five long shots in a row at the start of the second half, but it must have felt like twice that number.

[20]The National Training School for Boys (there was another for girls) was a "reform" school in D.C. that B-CC scheduled annually, often as a first game, N.T.S. *never* won.

[21]Thomas H. Latham, 33, of D. C. died as hundreds in Bethesda and on the golf course watched his red monoplane lose a wing and dive to the ground on April 22, 1939.

[22]John Shumate remembered that place as "Andre's," and said "they would sell anybody beer."

[23]Chet McCall may have been the first to use "B-CC" as the common abbreviation of the high school's name. The style of the `20s and `30s was "B.C.C.H.S." and in the `40s it was "Bethesda" or "B.C.C." but by `45 it was usually B-CC. See also *Tattler*, March 29, 1945.

[24]*Pine Log*s 1945 and 1946.

[25]*Record*, Feb. 23, and *Tribune,* March 30, 1945. Tired of having straw covers embedded in its ceiling and ten kids in a booth sharing two Cokes, the Hot Shoppe began closing at 3:30 pm to "wash the floor."

[26]*Record*, April 27, 1945, which also contains both Hayden's and Lee's statements. Again, the authorship of specific Bray columns is unknown, and this one may have been by Brooke Lee himself.

[27]*Record* and *Journal*, March 23, 1945.

[28]When the Charter proponents learned of this law (Lewis Sims said through Mrs. Dinwiddie reading of it in the *Sun*), they demanded its repeal without success. The Baltimore *Sun* revealed that the law was introduced at the request of E. Brooke Lee who admitted in his oral history that he and Lindsay were "quite close." See the Garber thesis, *op. cit.*
In the *Record,* 24 May 1946, E. B. Lee equated partisan elections with trial by jury and said that people don't always know what is good for them. He said that he believed that people have no rights except those given to them, and stated that he would not dare trust popular choice on some matters.

[29]*Record*, April 20 and 27, 1945, and *Tribune*, April 27, 1945.

[30]Lt. Commander Edward S. Northrup USNR evidently handled much of the work on this bill. The Village files contain a "Dear Earl and Albert" letter on Navy Department Office of Naval Operations letterhead transmitting the draft to T. E. Hampton and A. W. Walker in February 1945.

[31]*Tribune, Journal* and *Record*, April 20, 1945. The growing east-west spilt became wider with time.

[32]The Navy's lease expired in June 1946. On April 6, 1946, Bannockburn was sold for $196,000 ($50,000 in cash) to the Group Housing Cooperative.

[33]Hughes received his draft notice in May and went into the service six days after graduation. The writer was with his family at the Smiling Buddha the night of April 28 and recalls the extras proclaiming Hitler's death.
Dosset and Roger Parkinson headed the Jr.-Sr. prom committee, which planned the "Queen of 1945" program.

[34]Loria's team won the second half and then defeated the Bethesda police team for the title.

[35]Freshman Kenny Poerstel played some second base, and although he had been on the football team and the JV basketball squad, he missed all three pictures in the 1945 yearbook.

[36]*Record*, May 11, 1945.

[37]*Record*, Sept. 7, 1945.

[38]Report of the County Commissioners, May 29, 1945. The total value of the four fire districts which covered nearly all of the Western Suburban Area was $76,372,540.

[39]*Tribune* and *Record*, May 18 and 25, 1945. The belief in a post-war flying boom was widespread.

[40]Hoberman's club along with White Flint were caught operating slot machines in `46.

[41]For a full list see the *Record* of May 18, 1945.

[42]The child, Carol Ann, daughter of Mr. and Mrs. Robert E. Trullinger, died at Doctors Hospital April 12. Her parents had moved to Chicago by the time the story was released.

[43]*Tribune*, June 1, 1945. *Tattler*, May 10, 1945.

[44] Among the "missing" now known to have been killed were Marine combat correspondent T-Sgt. Richard Murphy whose family lived on Woodbine Street, Pfc. William G. Miller of Battery Lane who died in Italy with the 87th, Lt. Cmdr. Edward T. Grace whose parents lived on S. Chelsea died in the Okinawa campaign, and Lt. David Eiseman of Chevy Chase Parkway was killed in a B-17 collision over Germany.   Freed prisoners included P-51 pilots Robert Comstock and Richard Tracy, Lt. Dorsey Adams, who had been held since September of `43, and Pfc. Tom Morrison, captured during the Battle of the Bulge, both B-CC class of 1940.   Among the others freed were T-Sgt. James H. Wedding of Cabin John, Lt. Kenneth Wales of Chevy Chase, Sgt William New, a B-17 flight engineer whose family lived on Grafton Street;   Lt. Robert Dannemiller, a B-17 bombardier from Meadow Lane and Lt. Norman L. Stewart, whose wife and baby were waiting with her parents, Rev. and Mrs. Joseph E. Williams, on Bradley Lane.

[45] See ads in *Tribune* and *Record*, May 18, and story in *Record*, May 25, 1945.   In a June 29 ad Briggs sought several posting clerks and offered $45 a week "and up" with overtime.

[46] *Journal*, May 25, and *Tribune*, June 15, 1945.

[47] In a letter to the *Tattler* John "Chigger" Younger called Chappell "the best catcher Bethesda ever had." March 29, 1945.

[48] Brewer, a B-26 flight instructor in Texas, often flew cross-country to the Washington area and admitted that he may have buzzed Bethesda at night a time or two but does not recall doing so in the daytime that May.

[49] Betty Reed's "Between Hamburgers" column, which began in the Jan. 19 *Tribune,* ended with the June 22 edition. It made a unique contribution to the social history of the war years.

[50] For a list of those receiving awards for service see the *Tribune*, June 29, 1945.

[51] The output of Grumman F6F's included several night fighters and photo reconnaissance versions and almost 1,300 planes supplied to the British Fleet Air Arm, some of which were called Gannets.   See Bill Gunston's *Grumman, Sixty Years of Excellence* (Orion, 1988).

[52] The *Star* gave the time as 2:42; the accident reports said 2:20.

[53] PE = pilot error. Despite a request and appeal under the Freedom of Information Act, the "redacted" Aircraft Accident Card reproduced below is almost the only information the Navy is willing to provide about its investigation of this accident.

[54] In general, the American press exercised admirable voluntary censorship during the war, but in cases like this one, the military censorship was self-serving rather than preventing vital information from reaching the enemy, and the press's acquiescence was unfortunate as well as unnecessary.

[55] *Record*, August 10, 1945.   Phil Schaefer was also well known for his movies of colonial Maryland and his children, all JP's, Joan P., Jean P., Joyce P. and John P. Jr.
Arnott told the writer that there was no disciplinary action, almost no investigation and that the Navy's statement was "just bullshit."
Former Inspector Truscott of the Metropolitan Police was reported to be investigating the crash, but nothing more was heard of that either.

[56] *Record* and *Tribune,* July 6, 1945.   *Journal* (also *Tribune* and *Record*), August 3, 1945.

[57]*Record*, and *Tribune*, July 20, 1945. *Journal*, August 3, and *Tribune* , August 10, 1945. In the *Journal* Goins called Stonebraker "Screaming Sam" and suggested he favored Silver Spring's development rather than Bethesda's.

[58]Bell Laundry hired white workers. "My dad was a practicing bigot," Leslie Bell Jr. said. "He said the day they had the first black in his plant, he would close."

[59]*Tribune*, August 3, 1945.

[60]*Tribune* and *Record*, July 20, 1945.

[61]One arrest was made, of a car washer who took an automobile from the parking lot where he worked and then picked up nine of his friends for a Victory Day outing. Everything was going well until he ran into another car in front of the Bethesda police station. Convicted on seven counts, he was fined $81 and sentenced to seven months in the House of Correction. Other than that, V-J Day was almost crime free.

[62]The news of the sinking of the *Indianapolis* appeared in the same editions of the newspapers that carried "The War Is Over" headlines. It was some time before the gruesome details surfaced.

[63]Leslie Bell Jr.: Hoberman came along and gave a lot of business people in Bethesda free memberships. We belonged out there for years because membership was free.

[64]*Tribune*, August 24 and 31, 1945.

[65]*Tribune*, August 31 - September 28, 1945. *Journal*, Aug. 31 and Sept. 14, 1945.

[66]Dr. Paul Philippe Cret, designer of the NNMC tower, nurses' quarters, research institute, occupational therapy and recreation building, died in September 1945.

[67]*Record*, Sept. 14 and 21, 1945.

[68]See all three local papers, especially the Aug, 24, 1945 editions, Bray, *Tribune,* Sept. 14, 1945. Later in the year the company consolidated in Bethesda and reorganized as Briggs Filtration with cellulose and Fuller's earth filters its major product.

[69]Kenneth Frisbie returned early in the school year to teach history, and Allen Vogt was back as the basketball season began. The football team went 5-2-1 ending with a 6-6 tie with Blair on Thanksgiving Day in the mud at the University of Maryland.

[70]Sgt. Tyrell of the 106th Infantry died in Germany. John Johnson evidently attended B-CC so briefly that he was missed when the gold stars were awarded. His name has not been found in the yearbooks or school records although he was said to have been a student before enlisting in 1943.
In the spring of `46 when a big new pine tree was planted on the high school's front lawn to replace the one Blairites had cut down. It was dedicated to the forty-one B-CC grads who died in WWII.

[71]*Record*, Nov. 7, 1945. When Doc chased the junior high kids out, they sometimes assembled down at Della's Bakery near the pool hall.

[72]*Record*, Nov. 9, 1945.

[73]*Record*, Nov, 16, 1945.

[74]1st row: Evers, Bradley, Andrews, Jackson; 2nd: Gould, Christenson, Countryman, Shelby, Beedle; 3rd: Lehr, Cissel, Guandolo, Van Wagner; 4th row: Shoemaker, Mair, Miss White, Ware, Spain

[75]*Record*, September 14, 1945.

[76]In `45 the other two paid employees were Louise Meroney and Clare Arnold. Mrs. Maurice Davidson headed the Operating Committee, and there were a hundred senior hostesses and 250 junior hostesses who have given over 50,000 hours of volunteer work. *Tribune*, Sept. 21, 1945.

[77]Obviously, this was the start of what became the B-CC Rescue Squad.

[78]Donald Robertson, who admits to being rather frightened by McQuin at first, claims he can still do that whistle.
Among the winning backyard Victory Gardeners were Earl Carlin and Warren Gingell.

[79]Discharge after WWII was based on a complex point system no one claimed to really understand.

[80] During the last two years of the war, the County salvaged four million pounds of paper, 1,750,000 pounds of tin cans and 164,000 pounds of waste fat.
The Plymouth was won by John H. Wayne, known as "Bozo" to the patrons of Kenwood.

[81] Capt. Arnold Crons of the GEVFD aided in the rescue of the 10- and 12-year-old runaway brothers when the boat they had stolen went over the canal feeder dam below Glen Echo Park.

[82] Major Devereux, a Marine since 1923, took command of Wake Island's garrison in September 1941. The island was attacked by the Japanese on December 8. Cmdr. W. S. Cunningham along with Major Devereux and his men beat off the first attack but were overwhelmed by the second on Dec. 23. The Japanese shipped the surviving Marines and about 1,000 civilian workers to China in January 1942, and Devereux was reported to be a POW in February and promoted to lieutenant colonel three months later. He and his men were originally imprisoned at Shanghai and then moved to Honshu in the fall of `44 and then to Hokkaido where Devereux commanded Camp 3 in the Bibai area at the war's end.

[83] *Tribune*, Sept. 21, 1945.

[84] Goins writing about Allen, Brooke Lee and various religions became increasingly vituperative and became a community embarrassment. See Mrs. Bradley's *Record*, and Allen's *Tribune* Dec. 14, 1945. Note that Goins evidently did not know that Bray did not exist. Chapter 8, note 143.

[85] The *Post* reported that "it was certainly the biggest day the youngsters of Bethesda have ever seen" and that the local police "spent most of the afternoon chasing children all over town."

[86] *Star*, and *Post*, Sept. 30, 1945; *Journal, Tribune* and *Record*, Oct. 5, 1945.

Postwar Bethesda returns to normal

Appendix A:

Picture Credits: maps, photos and drawings not credited to a source are either the writer's or in the public domain. Most of the local newspaper photos are credited to the MCHS. Many were taken by Hugo Brooks and his conferes F. Marion Clark, Harry Marshack and Eddie Iris. Others came from microfilms and are separately credited. Obviously the copies of old halftones are of poor quality, especially those generated by microfilm printers, but they are the best available.

F3-*Pine Tree* (Sheila Young `44), F5-M-NCP&PC, Robert Truax, 6,7-Historical Society of Washington, D.C. (HSW), 23-Architect of the Capitol, 36-Archives, 37-Truax, 53-Library of Congress (LC), 61-MCHS, 70-Truax, 76-*Electrical World*, Leroy King Jr., 77,79-Truax, 80,81-*Post*, 82-MCHS, 83-HSW, 86-King, 87-88-Truax, 89-Fradin/MCHS, 90-Truax, 92-MLK Jr. Library, Truax, 97-Truax, 100-MLK, 102-Truax, 104-*Star*, 106-Clara Barton House, *Star*, 107,8-Truax, 112-Little Flower Parish, 113-Cabin John Methodist Church, 114-Millie Imirie, 116-Al Jamison, 118-Howard Brubach, 120-Fradin/MCHS,121,2,3-MCHS, 133-Truax, 139-*Post*, 140,41-Armes *Soldier*, 141-Nevada Historical Society, 149-*Electrical World*, Armes, 150-Armes, 151 Chevy Chase Land Co., 153-*Star*, HSW, 155-Harry Lerch, 156-Sonnemann family, 157-CCHS, 158-CCLCo., 159-MLK, 163,4-Robert Stevens, 169,70,71-Truax, 175-J.P. Devereux, 176-CCHS, 178-WSSC, 185-Dorothy Hilland, 190-HSW, 191,2-Celeste Lozupone Ridolfi, 193-CCFD, 198-Stevens, 201-MCHS, 202,3,6-Truax, 209-CCLCo., 219,20,21-Hilland, 224,27-Village of F.H., 229-Georgetown Univ., 231-Truax, 233-Marietta Andrews' *My Studio Window*, 234-MCHS, 238,9,41-Jane Dunbar Tedeschi, 242-Somerset ES, 243-Truax, *Post*, 246-MCHS, 247-Gerald Hatton, 250-*Kenwood Magazine*, 251-M. Imirie, 254-MC Land Records, 256-MCHS, 258-CCHS, 259-Lerch, 260-Ned Sacks/MCHS, 264-MCHS, 265-CCHS, 266-HSW, 267,8,9,70,71-*Kenwood*, 272,3-Truax, 274-M. Imirie, 275-*Kenwood*, 281-MCHS, 282-Winifred Krueger, 284-MCHS, 285-Clarence Keiser Jr., 286-Christ Lutheran Church, MCHS, 287-Masonic Lodge 204, Hilma Moore, 290-Bill Duvall/*Star*, 291-M.C. Land Records, 293-MCHS, 295-Laura Tuckerman Triest, H. Moore, 296-*Star*, 297-Truax, 298-301-Triest, 299 bottom-Ned Sacks/MCHS, 302,3-Truax, 304-Tempe Curry Grant/*Post*, 305-CCHS, 306,7-Triest, 309-MCHS, 312,13-Woodmont Club (with permission), 314,6,7-MCHS, 318-Grant/*Post*, 319-MCHS, 320-Battery Park Citizens' Assn., 321-Phyllis Michaux, 322-BPCA/MCHS, 325-Chevy Chase *Gazette*, 326-Bethesda Fire Dept., Inc. 327-John C. Walker III, 328-M. C. Daly, 329-MCHS, 332-Peggy Evers Marsh, MCHS, 333-MCHS, 334-HSW, Brooks, 336-National Medical Library, 337-*Pine Tree*, 348-Lerch, 349,50,51-Grant, 352-*Pine Log*, Lehr, 353-*Pine Tree*, 354-*Pine Tree*, *Tattler*, 355-Tedeschi, 358-James McAuliffe Sr., MCHS, 362-MCHS, 364-*Star*, 366-Bethesda FD, 367-*Star*, 369-MCHS, 372-CCHS, Tedeschi, 373-Ellen Bell Tuohy, 375-*Pine Tree*, 376-Arthur Gellman, 377-MCHS, 383,4-Christ Lutheran, Tedeschi, 385,6-*Pine Tree*, John Shumate, 387-*Pine Tree*, 388-Shumate, *Pine Tree*, 389-*Pine Tree*, 390-Lehr, 391-Lerch, 392-*Pine Tree*, 393-*National Real Estate Journal*, 394-MCHS, *The American City*, 395-MCHS, 398-Joseph Scopin, 399-Troop 204, 400-MCHS, 401-NMLibrary, 403-*Tribune*, 405-*Pine Tree*, 406-*Pine Tree*, M. Imirie, 407-Marsh, MCHS, 410-Marsh, 411-Univ. of Md. Library, 416-M. Imirie, 417-Tedeschi, MCHS418-*Journal*, 420-*Star*, MCHS, 422-*Journal*, M. Imirie, 424,5,6-MCHS, 427-NNMC, 428-David Taylor MB, 429,30,1,2,3-MCHS, 434-*Pine Tree*, MCHS, 437-*Pine Tree*, 439-*Star*, 440,1,2,4-MCHS, 445-Grant, MCHS, 447-MCHS, Hugo Brooks, 448,9,50-MCHS, 451-Clara Barton House, 452-MCHS, Scott Brewer Jr., 453-*Pine Tree*, 454-U.S.Navy, 455-MCHS, 456-*Pine Tree*, 457-U.S.Navy, 459-MCHS, *Pine Tree*, 461-Bernie Doyle, 463-MCHS, 466,7-*Star*, 469-*Pine Tree*, 469-Journal, 470-MCHS, 472-MCHS/Jane Sween, 473,7,82,83-MCHS/Brooks, 484-M.Imirie, 497,8-*Pine Tree*, 499,501-*Star*, 504-*Pine Tree*, 506-MCHS, 508-*Pine Cone*/Chet McCall (Art Wood), 509-U.S. Navy, 510-Defense Mapping Agency, 511,12-*Pine Tree*, MCHS, 513-MCHS, 515-Bethesda FD, 516-MCHS, 518-*Pine Tree*, 519,20,2,3,4,6,7, 31-MCHS, 532-U.S. Navy, 533,4-MCHS, 536-*Pine Tree*, *Star*/Doris Bruffey, 539,40, 56,62,64,69,70,2,3,4,6-MCHS, 578-Nat'l Air & Space Museum, 579,80, 81, 582- Bruffey/*Tattler*, *Pine Tree*, 583-*Pine Log*, 585-*Star*, *Pine Tree*, 586-MCHS, 589-Suburban Hospital, MCHS, 593-Air&Space, 594-U.S. Air Force, 595,7,8,602,3-MCHS, 604,6-*Pine Tree*, 608,9,12-MCHS, 613-MCHS, Sub.Hosp., 615-MCHS, 616-M. Imirie, 6320-MCHS, 622-*Pine Tree*, 623-Sub. Hosp., *Tattler*, 625,8-MCHS, 629,32-*Pine Tree*, 633-*Pine Tree*, Bruffey, 634-*Pine Tree*, 636,8,40-MCHS, 643-*Pine Tree*, 644-*Pine Log*, 646-MCHS, 647-Charles Kocher, David Taylor MB, 650-MCHS, 651-Lerch, 652-*Kenwood*, 656-*Pine Tree* (Barbara Hanby), 661-MCHS, 662-Dept. of Commerce, 663-MCHS, 665,7,8-*Pine Tree*, 669,70-*Pine Log*, 675-Earle Ferguson/ MCHS, 677-Bruffey, 682-*Record*, 684-MCHS, 685,6-*Pine Log*, MCHS, 689-Grumman, 690-Charles Arnott, 692-*Star*, 695 lower-*Star*(negative), 697-Lerch/Tom Bourdeaux Jr., 698,700,2,3-MCHS, 705,6,7-*Pine Log*, 708-Bill Blackwood Sr., 709-MCHS, 711,12-P.J. Devereux, 718-*Daily News*/MLK

Appendix B:
Selected Pre-war Subdivisions and Neighborhoods in Bethesda
(dates of home construction based on Lusk directories)

(note:`13 = 1913)

Alta Vista
Alta Vista Road
5420	`13
5432	`08
5435	`08
5443	`23
5505	`28
5509	`32
5511	`28
5515	`33

Charles Street
5500, 06, 33	`18
5501	`28
5507	`12
5512 &24	`13
5515 &21	`23
5525	`19

Beech Avenue
102	`38
5401	`25
5405	`39
5415	`14
5420	`11
5424	`23
5430	`33
5502	`14
5506	1898
5621	`03

Johnson Avenue
5500,06,20,22, 30,32,36	`40
5502 & 16	`44
5504	`39
5507,9,11,13,15	`39
5508,10,14,18, 28,34,38	`45
5512	`42
5521	`13
5523	`39
5524 & 26	`41
5601,3,5,7,11,13, 15,17,19	`41
5614	`45
5700	`17

Locust Avenue
5211 & 17	`23
5221	`08
5309	`26
5311	1898
5315	`08

Milroy Place
9302	`18

Montgomery Drive
9503	`39
9505	`36

Old Georgetown Road
9100	`03
9108 & 10	`39
9113 (20+ ac.)	`03
9114 (6.7 ac.)	1898
9200 (4+ ac.)	1898
9201	`18
9300	`08
9515	`22
9517	`33
9707	1888
10200(Mt.Zion)	1878

Ayrlawn
Hempstead Avenue
9038	`17

Oak Place
5628	`23

Bannockburn
Ayr Lane
6904, 08, 13	`38

Barr Road
66-6800	`38-41

Braeburn Pkwy.
3 houses in	`40-41

Broxburn Drive
6510	`31
6516	`42

Elgin Lane
6607 & 13	`40
6610 & 29	`39
6619 & 20	`36
6630	`37

Laverock Lane
7105	`41
7109	`42

Nevis Drive
7301	`39

Orkney Parkway
7000	`41
7105	`40

River Road
6120	1882
6220	`39
6415	`08
6508 & 10	`36
6509	`18
6609	`37
6624	`39
6625	`03
6701 (5 ac.)	`28
7001	`36
7105, 06, 16	`03
7301 (36 ac.)	`23
7309	1898
7310	`33
7315 (4 ac.)	1878

Selkirk Drive
6700, 08, 22	`40
6709	`36
6716, 26, 30	`39
6719	`38

6800 & 06	`39
6811	`37
6815	`38

Verne Street
6201,03,05,09	`36
6208	`41
6210	`39
6215 & 17	`40

Vorlich Lane
6200s	`39

Wilson Lane
6401	1898
6409	`23
6407	`38
6411	`43
6414	`13
6415	`38
6420	`03
6708	`13
6720	`03
6730	1878
6750	`23
6824, 28, 30	`40
6900	`37
6910	`36
6914	`40
6916 & 18	`38
7009	1898
7055	`31
7120	`34

Winston Drive
6206	`23
62,63,6400s	many `37-40

Battery Park
Cordell Avenue
5003	`30

Del Ray Avenue
5004	`38
5005	`33
5007	`38
5008	`30
5010	`23
5011	`25
5012	`28
5013	`43
5014	`23
5017	`42

Fairfax Road
7801 & 02	`33
7804 & 07	`23
7806	`21
7609	`24

Glenbrook Road
7800	`30
7801 & 18	`33
7804	`36
7805 & 07	`39
7806 & 26	`24

7812, 22, 24 `23
7814 `26
7816 `25
7820 `35
7902 `32
7903 `38
7905 `25
7907 `38
7909 `27
7914 `33
8000s mostly`30s
8100 & 02 `38
Maple Ridge Road
7801 `28
7802 & 14 `24
7803 `31
7804,8,12,13,16 `23
7805 `33
7806 `30
7809 `37
7810 `40
8000 `23
8004 & 06 `28
8005 `39
8007 `34
8009 & 11 `36
8010 `33
8012 `32
8013 `22
8014 `40
8028 `35
8101 & 02 `33
8104 `39
8105 `38
8106 `23
8707 `35
Marion Lane
7807 `40
7811 `36
7815 & 17 `39
7819 `40
Old Georgetown Road
7920 `32
7930 `23
7936 `40
8006 `43
8008 `21
8010 `27
8012 `26
8014 `30
8015 `23
8016 `39
8021 1878
(see North West Park)
Wilson Lane
5019 `35
5021 `38
5037 & 39 `28
5101, 03, 07 `28
5104 `33
5106 & 08 `30
5113 `26
5114 `31
5115 `35
5116 & 18 `28
5117 & 22 `38
5120 `27
5201 `22
5203 `28
5205 `36
5207 `33
5209 `28
5211 `36
5212 `42
5301 & 03 `23
5305 `28
5307 `29
5309 `36
5311 `40
5406 & 08 `37
5410 `24
(see Greenwich Village.)

Bethesda CBD
(includes **Sunnyside)**
Avondale Street
4500s most `40
4507&11 `38
4526 `35
East Avenue
6700 `26
6702 & 04 `28
6705 `33
6707 `31
6709 `06
6711 & 13 `23
6803 & 05 `36
6807 `35
6905 `27
6907 `13
6709 `25
Leland Street
4300, 04, 29 `27
4302 `25
4306 1897
4307 & 19 `13
4309 & 25 `23
4311 `18
5313 `32
4315 `34
4321 `08
4400 1897
4500 1897
4604 `31
4606 `26
(see Sack's Subdiv.)
Middleton Lane
4500s most `36-37
4537 `03
4538 `23
Old Georgetown Road
7500-10 `28-31
(also 4705-7 Edgemoor)
7532-34 `38
7542 `21
7545-48 `36
7601-11 `41
7649-59 `41
7624-30 `36
Ridge Street
4409 `18
4400s most `23-36
Stanford Street
4400 `28
4401,03, 05 `22
4402 & 16 `33
4404,12, 22 `23
4407,09, 11 `29
4413 1897
4415,17,19,21 `22
4420 `35
4423 & 25 `27
4424, 28 & 30`23
4500,1,2,3,7,9`22
4505 `25
Walsh Street
4400s most `22-25
4500s most `22-25
West Avenue
6801 `23
6803 `09
Wisconsin Avenue
6801 `40
6831 `40
6935 `28
6936 `44
7000 `42
7006-34 even`28
7007-29 odd `26
7126 `27
7136-40 `21
7200-06 `18
7210-18 `26
7301 `33
7327-35 `41
7337 `39
7345 `40
7347-49 `28
7434 `36
7438-40 `31
7557 `35
7500-06 `42
7508-10 `28
7514 `38
7613 `28
7615 `38
7619 `43
7701 `40
7758 `35
7801 `40
7845 `38
7800-02 `39
7816 `11
7824 `11
7828-30 `30
7832 `39
44th Street
7100s even `25
7100s odd `27
7200, 02, 04 `27
7206 `29

Bradmoor
Bradmoor Drive
  8500s most   `41
Glenwood Road
   5200s(Glenwood) `40-42
  5400s `38-39
  5500s `39-41
  5600s `40-42
  5700s 1st half`41-42
HazelwoodDr.(Glnw'd)
  8500s most `40-41
Hempstead Avenue
  8500-8600s `41
Irvington Avenue
  8401 & 03 `41
  8405,7,9,11 `42
  8500s `41
Old Georgetown Road
  8301 & 09 `38
  8305   `37
  8318(2 acres)1888
  8400(2 acres)1873
  8506   `33
  8700   `21
  8706(1.98 ac.)1878
  8712   `18
  8802   `23
  8906   `38
Rayburn Street
  8105,09,13 `40
  8108   `39
  8112   `38
  8116   `41
  8200   `40
  8201   `41
  8516   `42
Roosevelt Street
  5200s(Glnwd) `40-42
  5300s(Glnwd) `40-41
  5407, 27 & 28`23
  5411   `37
  5412 & 19 `18
  5415 & 24 `25
  5416, 20,23 `28
  5424   `25
  5500,2,4,6,8,
   10,12,14,16,23`37
  5501 & 05 `23
  5509,13,15,18,20 `38
  5517,19 , 21 `36
  5600,2,4,6 `40
  5603   `37
  5607,8,10,12,
   14,16,18 `38
  5609   `36
  5611   `39
  5615   `34
  5700   `39
  5702   `38
  5704   `36
  5800 t0 05 `41
Rosewood Street
  8500s(Glnwd) `40-41

Brookdale
Cooper Lane
  4600-05-7 `37
  4601   `33
  4602   `35
  4303   `42
  4604   `33
  4606-08 `34
Glen Cove Parkway
  4900s   `39
Montgomery Avenue
  4900s `38-39
Newport Avenue
  5201   `39
  5202   `37
  5203   `40
  5300   `39
River Road
  4600s `33-38
  4700 & 02 `38
  4701   `18
  4704   `08
  4720   `38
  4722   `41
  4724   `40
  4802 & 04 `39
  4900 to 12 even `39
  4901 (7.8 ac.)1868
  4915   `38
  4925   `13
  (see River Rd.)

Chevy Chase Terrace
Chevy Chase Gardens
Chevy Chase Blvd.
  4602-18 even #s`20s
  4600s others `30s
  4702-08-14 `20s
  4700s others `30s
  4805   `17
  4807   `40
  4824 & 60 `27
  4800s others `30s
  4900s `30s
Davidson Drive
  4602   `24
  4604, 06, 10 `29
  4605, 7, 9 ,11 `22
DeRussey Parkway
  4602   `29
  4604   `41
  4606 & 18 `35
  4608   `27
  4609,11,13,19,21 `29
  4614   `33
  4615   `27
  4616   `39
  4610,20,1,2 `37
  4702,8,10,12,13`27
  4703-07-11 `29
  4704-05-09 `31
  4706   `24
Hunt Avenue
  4605,20 & 22 `29

  4607,9,11,13,14,
   15,16,25 `27
  4612   `22
  4618   `32
  4623 & 24 `28
  4700,3,7,14,20 `27
  4702 & 04 `30
  4705,09,10,11,12 `29
  4706   `25
Langdrum Lane
  4600,15, 20 `27
  4603,4,8,10,14,
   18,22,24`29
  4606 & 16 `28
  4700,03,07,09`27
  4702,4,5,6,8,10`29
  4708   `28
  4711   `31
  4801   `22
  4803   `25
  4805   `29
  4822,23,24,25,
   26,27,29,31,
   32,33,34,35,
   36,37,38,39,
   41,43 `40
  4828 & 30 `41
Morgan Drive
  4600s `27-`37
  4700s `30's
Norwood Drive
  4602,4,5,6,8,
   10,14,16 `22
  4603, 07 & 12`27
  4609,11,13,
   15,19,21`29
Offutt Road
  6118   `29
  6120   `27
  6300   `22
  6401   `37
  6450   `33
Ruffin Road
  6414   `18
Stratford Road
  6200s mostly`36-38
  6200   `25
  6203   `29
  6300 & 02 `27
  6301   `29
  6400   `37
  6500   `39
  (see H'gton Terr.)
Wisconsin Avenue
  6208   `16
  6300   `24
  6302   `22
  6304   `33
  6500   `22
  6500   `22
  6510   `39
  6520   `23
  (see Bethesda)

Clean Drinking

Hawkins Lane

8807 & 15	`28
8823,5,7,9	`38
8822 & 24	`28

Crestview

Bayard Blvd.

4718	`27
others	`20s-30s
4841-4917	`35-6-7

Crescent Street

4700	`17
4704-06	`22
most others	late `30s
4800	`12

Earlston Drive

4800s	late `30s
4900s	`40-41
4923	`38
5000s	mostly`38-40
5004	`36
5008	`37

Westway Drive

4801, 03, 11	`37
4804 & 06	`39
4805,7,8,10,13,15	`35
4908,10,12,14, 16,18,20	`35
4919	`37
4922	`36
4924	`41
4926	`40

Edgemoor

Arlington Road

7425	'23
most others	`27-36

Beverly Road

7405	`35
7407 &09	`31
7411	`33
7415 (4 lots)	`22

Denton Road

5110	`31
7104-08-09	`40
7200 to 08	`37
7210	`38
7403	`39
7405	`41
7407	`37
7612 & 17	`39

East Lane

4801	`25
6902	`31

Edgemoor Lane

4710	`34
4801	`37
4805	`18
4820	`35
4824	`41
4828	`34
4900	`21

4901	`18
4905	`28
5000	`22
5001	`25
5005	`41
5009	`22
5010	`24
5025	`39
5029	`37
5033	`20
5101	`27
5108	`26
5110,12, 14	`28
5111 & 21	`38
5200 & 16	`22
5215	`12
5218	`17
5300, 01, 16	`22
5309	`07
5310	1897
5400	`37
5401	`17
5404	`41
5408	`32
5412	`22
5419	`28

Elm Street

4721	`36
4723	`38
4731	`42
4733	`36
4800-14	`18
4907	`41
4934-36	`38
5001,3,5,7	`38
5011	`40
5013	`30
5015	`38
5100, 04, 14	`40

Fairfax Road

6904, 04, 08	`38
6907 & 09	`41
6911, 19, 21, 23	`40
6913, 15, 17	`41
7101 &17	`40
7103,04,07,11	`42
7105 & 08	`41
7109	`44
7112	`38
7115	`39
7116	`15
7124 & 28	`38
7200	`39
7201 & 08	`35
7203 & 10	`32
7205	`31
7207, 09, 11	`33
7208	`35
7400	`32
7401 & 02	`25
7404	`37
7405	`35
7406	`26
7408	`35

7409	`17
7501	`12
7503	`22
7506	`24
7510	`27
7610	`12
7611	`14
(see Battery Park)	

Glenbrook Road

6800	`40
6801	`38
6803 & 05	`36
6835	`42
6844	`37
6845	`38
6846	`33
7000	`33
7001	`42
7005	`31
7009	`33
7010	`38
7101	`38
7116	`37
7117	`23
7118	`36
7201	`38
7204 & 10	`17
7401	`29
7402 & 05	`22
7404	`39
7406	`27
7407	`17
7601	`22
7604	`27

Middlesex Lane

4804,6,8,9,10,11,12	`28
4814,15,16,18	`30
4820	`31

Moorland Lane

4803	`39
4804,10, 11	`28
5000	`19
5004	`31
5016	`22
5100	`22
5103 & 07	`37
5104 & 12	`41
5108	`26
5111	`32
5113	`36
5115 & 20	`25
5116	`27
5119	`31
5215 (15,000#)	`17
5300 (30,000#)	`17
5303 & 05	`40
5310 (100x215)	`17
5314	`32
5316	`22
5406	`22
5408 & 10	`27
5409	`38
5425 (20,895#)	`17

5420   `22
5422   `27
7810 (Wh'ly Hills)1888
Montgomery Lane
4710   `24
4711   `23
4800s most mid`20s
4808   `34
4818 & 20   `33
4901   `26
4903 & 14   `23
4905   `36
4912, 16, 18   `28
North Lane
4800s early   `30s
West Lane
4831 & 33   `34

English Village
Aberdeen Road
7816&24   `37
7827   `40
Maiden Lane
5606   `34
5810   `21
Old Chester Road
5704   `20
7505,11,15,18   `32
7506 & 08   `22
7509   `37
7520   `29
7700   `39
7702   `35
7705   `37
7732   `36
7800s most   `39-40
Radnor Road
7500   `22
7508   `17
7514   `39
7515   `35
7516   `22
7520   `07
7702 & 04   `22
7705,7,9,11,13,15 `35
7710   `34
7802, 03 & 04`37
7807   `39
7900,2,4,6,8,10,12 `37
7901,05,11,15   `41
Wilson Lane
5701   `34
5702 to 20 even`35
5705   `32
5707   `36
5719   `37
5801 & 03   `37
5805, 09, 11   `39
5807   `40
5901,5,7,9   `40
6001   `36
6103   `33
6111   `38
6301 (6 ac.)   1863

(see Bannockburn)
Friendship (R. Rd.)
Dorsey Lane
5526-8   `28
Elmore Lane
7524,7600   `33
7602   `44
7604   `42

Drummond
Drummond Ave.

Address	Year
4501	1902
4510	1908
4514	1916
4515	1902
4518	1898
4521	1905
4522	1921
4600	1906
4604	1938
4605	1907
4608	1921
4609	1922
4612	1921
4613	1906
4616	1917
4617	1936
4620	1921
4621	1899
4700	1921
4704	1923
4705	1936
4708	1909
4709	1906
4712	1917
4713	1936
4716	1922
4717	1912
4720	1929
4721	1927
4724	1926
4725	1917
4801	1926
4804	1924
4809	1940
4811 to 21	1940
4822	1941
4825	1942
4828	1941
4829	1942
4832	1941

(thanks to T.J.Barlow)

Glenbrook Village
Brandt Place
8600s `40-42
Bywood Lane
4400s `40-41
4407   `43
North Chelsea Lane
4500s `38-40
4553   `43
4600s mostly`38
4621   `36
4600   `40
4700s `36-38
4700   `35
4704   `40
4708   `43
South Chelsea Lane
4500s `38-40
4512 &24   `36
4544   `43
4556   `41
4600s `36-38
4600 &08   `40
Fairfield Drive
4000s `38-41
4500s most   `38
4532   `37
4533   `35
4600s `37-38
Gladwyn Court
101 & 105   `42
Gladwyn Drive
4400-4500s   `40-42
4500   `43
Glenbrook Parkway
46-4700s most`40-42
4617   `38
4700   `39
Lancaster Road
8600s most   `40-41
Salem Way
8500s `37-40

Greenacres
Allandale Rd.
5300s most   `39
Greenway Drive
4900-5000s most `39
Little Falls Parkway
4934,36,38   `39
5200s `39
Malden Drive
5000s `39
Smallwood Drive
5000s `39
Ventnor Drive
52 & 5300s   `39
Wakefield Road
5300s   `38-41

Greenwich Forest
Charlcote Road
5505-19 odd#s`39

5502-24 even `41
Huntington Parkway
  5308   `35
  5400   `33
  5401,07,10,18`39
  5402   `38
  5403,4,5,6,9,12,
        14,16 `37
  5411 & 13   `40
  5801   `41
  7801   `34
Lambeth Road
  5402,6,8,10,12,
        14,16 `37
  5403   `34
  5405   `33
  55407 & 09   `40
  5411   `38
  5413,15,17,19`39
  5601   `39
  5620   `37
  5625,29,33   `39
Midwood Road
  5602   `33
  5605 & 15   `36
  5609   `37
Moorland Lane
  8203,5,7,8,10`37
  8202 & 04   `39
Northfield Road
  5505,7,9,11,12,13,
        14,15,16,17,
        18,19,21`39
  5510   `37
  5520   `41
  5523   `38
  5600s `39
Overhill Road
  7803,15,19,21,25,27
            `36
  7805   `26
  7818 & 20   `28
  7824 & 26   `38
  8000 + 2 lots`32
  8001   `37
  8003   `39
  8007   ?
Westover Road
  8000   `37
Wilson Lane
  5507   `34
  5605 & 09   `39
  5615   `32
  5617   `35
    (see English Village)

Highland   Park
East-West Highway
  4206-08   `39
  4210 & 24   `36
  4226   `41
  4300   `42
  4302-04   `36
  4306,28,30,2,4,6,8 `42

4309,11,13,15,17 `39
4340   `18
4344   `28
4400   `27
4401   `12
4402   `20
4404-06   `43
4407   `25
4414   `26
4416   `13
4419   `26
4420   `36
4421   `28
4422   `13
4500 & 02   `23
4617   `23
4648-52   `21
Montgomery Avenue
  4300,26,30,2,4`35
  4302,3,4,5,6,7,8,10 `37
  4312   `41
  4324 & 26   `35
  4325,7,9,31,3,5`33
  4328   `33
  4336,38,40,42 `34
  4339,41,43   `33
  4400 & 04   `34
  4401   `13
  4413   `38
  4414 & 18   `32
  4415   `30
  4419 & 23   `28
  4424   `38
  4425   `30
  4503   `32
  4539   `22
  4540,42,43, 47`23
  4550   `21
  4601   `20
  4602   `18
  4611   `18
  4612   `23
  4613   `13
  4616, 19, 20 `18
    (see Brookdale)
Pearl Street
  7202   `38
  8603   `38

Huntington   Terrace
Custer Road
  7803   `29
  7804   `31
  7805-07   `30
  7806   `28
  7809-11-13   `33
  7815-25 odd `36
  7808-24 even`36
  7823   `35
  7817   `39
  7828   `40
  7900   `28
  7901-02   `38
  7904   `39

7905   `23
7907-08   `40
8000-1-2-7   `38
8003   `40
8005-09   `41
8006-08   `39
8014   `37
8100 & 08   `37
  8100s others`35
  8200s mostly`37
8306-08   `39
Garfield Street
  8600s   late `30s-`40
  8604,6,8,10   `36
  8700s `38-40
  8702   `36
  8801   `40
  8804 + 3 lots`18
Grant Street
  8705   `39
  8707,9,10,11,18`38
  8802,04,08   `38
  8803   `36
  8805   `37
  8901   `38
  8903,05,15   `34
  8904,08,12   `36
  8909   `33
  8914   `35
  8916   `31
  9006   `36
  9007   `39
Greentree Road
  5506 to 22 even`36
  5601,03,07   `36
  5606   `18
  5608,10,12   `38
  5611 & 13   `34
  5615   `30
  5619   `34
  5620,22,24   `38
  5621   `32
  5701   `36
    (see Bradley Hills)
Jefferson Street
  8500s `37-38
  8600s `34-39
  8700s `39-40
Lincoln Street
  5415 - 19   `28
  5423   `26
  5427   `23
  5431   `35
  5506-10   `13
  5514   `33
  5516   `36
  5518 & 22   `38
  5520   `37
  5600 & 01   `38
  5602   `33
  5603 & 07   `36
  5606   `40
Madison Street
  5600s most   `40-42

4600s `38-41

Sleaford Drive
4302,04,06,08 `40
4313,15,17,19 `41
4321 `42
4523,25,27 `41
4600,2,4,6,8,
   10,12,14,16 `40
4601,3,5,7,9,
   11,13,15 `41

Tilbury Street
7711 `41
7803 & 13 `38
   (see Rosedale Park)

West Chevy Chase Heights

Chase Avenue
4400s `42
4401 `40
4500s `38-42
4600s `36-39
4603 `32
4704 &07 `26

Harling Lane
4500s `39-40
4600s `38-39

Highland Avenue
4400s mostly late `30s
4500s mostly mid `30s
4512,14,16 `27-28
4515 `26
4517 `23
4600,17 & 19`36
4601,3,5,7,10,11,
   12,13 `28
4509 `27
4602,4,6,8 `32
4614 `25
4615 `38
4616 `26
4618 `33
4700 `23
4701, 03, 06 `28
4702 `30
4704 `26
4705, 09, 11 `24
4707 `36

Kentbury Drive
4300s `45
4301 `40
4310 `44
7910,12,13,15`40

Kentbury Way
16 & 17 `40
20 `42

Kentucky Avenue
7900s `40-41

Lynnbrook Drive
4300s most `40-41
7900s mostly `41
8406,09,15 `38
8410 `40
8501,5,7,13,15 `40
8511 `38

8605,11,15 `41
8612 & 14 `42

West Virginia Avenue
4400 to14 even`40
4501,3,5,7,9 `35
4502,04,& 10 `36
4506 `33
4511,13,16,18`38
4514 `42
4515 `27
4517 `26
4519 `23
4601,7,9,11,14 `28
4602 `34
4605,08,15,17,19 `23
4610 `24
4612 `26
4700 & 07 `23
4701 `22
4702 `29
4703 & 05 `24
4704 `25
4706 `36

Westgate

Allan Road
5021-29 `38-41
5002-28 `40
5101-12 `36-38

Baltimore Avenue
5000s `36
5100s `40
5200s `39

Kentstone Drive
9402 `39
9500s `40-41

LeRoy Place
4900 `35

Linder Lane
5801,02,03,05`40
5804 `41

Newport Avenue
4900s `36-40
5000s `38-40
5100s most `38-40
5119 & 29 `23
5132 `30
5135 1897
5141 `30
5144 `36
   (see Brookdale)

Westmoreland Hills

Abington Road
5201-14 `32-35

Albemarle Street
5192-5209 `35-37
5213-16 `33-34
5302-17 `37-41

Blackistone Road
5307-18 `34-41

Carvel Circle
1-5 `35-6-7

Carvel Road

5300 block `35-41

Dalecarlia Drive
4520 `35
4522 `36

Duvall Drive
5100s most mid `30s
5116 `40
5200s mostly `37

Elliott Road
5217 `38
5224, 25, 29 `39
52228 `37
5230 `35

Jamestown Road
4715,16, 17 `40
4800,4,6,7,8,10,12 `40
4802 `39
4803 & 05 `37
4809 `41
4815 1887
4900,2,4,6,8,10 `40
4901 `37
4903,19,21,23,25 `41
4914 `38

Mass. Avenue (extended)
5129 & 49 `37
5138 `33
5200s most `37-41
5300 `40
   (see Woodacres)

Western Avenue
45, 46 & 4700`30s
4800s mostly`30s
4800 `22

Westwood Drive
5200s most `32-35

Wetherhill Drive
4500s most `32-37

Woodacres

Ardmore Court
2,3,4,5,6,7 `40

Avalon Drive
6316 `40

Cobalt Drive
5901,3,5,7,9,11`40
6001,3,5,7,9,11`40

Gloster Road
56-5700s most`40
5801 `40

Harwick Road
56-57-5900 `40

Mass. Avenue (extended)
6014 & 16 `38
6100 `40
6203,05,07 `40
6210 `42
6250 `41
6202,4,10,17`40
6302,4,10,17`40

Milo Drive
6000s `40

Welborn Drive
60, 61 & 6200s`40

Woodmont

Auburn   Avenue

4802	`19
4808	`28
4809 &13	`23
4812	`23
4907	`19
4915	`26
4827	1898
4930	1888

Cordell   Avenue

4829	`23
4842	`18
4843	`40
4861	`32
4865	`32
4905	`36
4910	`36
4918	`20
4922	`32
4923	`24
4927 &32	`28
4931	`26
5003	`30

Del Ray Avenue

4801, 11 & 27 `23	
4815,17,21,35 `28	
4818 to 28	`38
4832	`25
4838	`34
4842	1898
4900	`18
4905, 06, 35	`23
4913	`11
(see Battery Park)	

Fairmont   Avenue

4800	`43
4825	`32
4828	`06
4900 & 19	1875
4901	`28
4905	`30
4907 & 11	`20
4925	1900
4926	`31

Old Georgetown Road

7700	`41
7720	`40
7721-29	1896
7750	`41
7754	`37
7755	`20
7800	`35
7801	1898
7803	1898
7806	`35
7812	`33
7814	`35
7816-18	`35
7817	1898
7827	`11
7830	`43
7835	`25

7845	`38
7851	`31

Rugby   Avenue

4801	1873
4810, 35, 50	`38
4811	`21
4815	old
4819	`30
4823,25,42,55	`23
4845 & 49	`36
4911	`13
4926	old
5003	`36
5005, 14, 15	`38
5008	`37
5009	`33

St. Elmo Avenue

4808	1898
4809	`12
4818	`08
4826	`22
4831	`18
4833	`26
4839	`16
4906 & 26	`23
4910	`19
4914 & 18	`33
4928	`25
4938	`21

Wyngate

Flint Drive

4900s (5)	`38-`42

Singleton Drive

9500 & 02	`39
9508 & 10	`40
9512	`41

Yorktown   Village

Allan Rd.

4865-71	`41
4960	`22
4950	`35
4964	`34
4966	`42
4968	`43
5003-19	`40

Jamestown Court

4900s `37-38	

Appendix C:

A Chronological Index of Doree Germaine Holman's "Old Bethesda" and a list of Mrs. Bradley "Vignettes" of Bethesda women

Miss Holman's monumental series of essays ran for almost two years in Day Thorpe's Bethesda *Journal*. The weekly articles averaged about 600 to 800 words each and ranged widely even within a single, stated topic. In general, Miss Holman credited her sources in only the most broad terms, but she is, nevertheless, an important resource for anyone interested in the story of Bethesda and its neighboring towns.

The writer was introduced Vol. 1 No. 1 of the *Journal* on April 28, 1939:

Doree Germaine Holman first became interested in the fascinating history of Bethesda and the surrounding country at the knee of her grandfather, Franklin Mace, who lived for many decades in the Old Riley Home on the Old Georgetown Road. As she grew up, Miss Holman delved deeper into old archives, newspaper files, histories and memories, and gleaned from her friends and acquaintances many almost forgotten Bethesda tales and legends. She is now considered the best informed Bethesda historian in the community, and we believe the weekly column "Old Bethesda," which starts in this issue, will be of unusual interest to all Bethesdans.

Miss Holman was for two years editor of the *Maryland Club Woman*, and for three years local editor of the *Clear Creek Mining Journal*, in Idaho Springs, Colo. She is well known as a piano teacher.

4/28/39	#1	Beginnings - a church, a blacksmith, a tavern, a trolley line
5/5/39	#2	John Smith and Henry Fleete explore, hunting, Indian rocks
5/12/39	#3	The Potomac, the Piney Branch rock quarry, soapstone
5/19/39	#4	The Hayseed Club, young Bethesdans entertain each other
5/26/39	#5	Miss Counselman's haunted house on River Rd., a Civil War tale
6/2/39	#6	The Calverts and early Maryland pre-colonial history
6/9/39	#7	Calvert visits the Piscataways, early days and colonial trade.
6/16/39	#8	Margaret Brent and civil rights for women, the acting governor.
6/23/39	#9	Marylanders love to hunt and fish, "Miss Millie" a crack shot.
6/30/39	#10	Barter in the early days, tobacco and other media of exchange.
7/7/39	#11	Encouraging early settlement westward, Bethesda in 1879.
7/14/39	#12	Travel, especially on old roads, background of place names.
7/21/39	#13	Hundreds, the "rolling road" to Georgetown, the trip home
7/28/39	#14	Plantation life in early Bethesda, tobacco, amusements.
8/4/39	#15	Horses, racing, jousting, trotting races and other fun.
8/11/39	#16	James Hunt's Tusculum school, the court house, Renshaws.
8/18/39	#17	S.W. Magruder's house near Bell's Mill Rd., Wirt's account.
8/25/39	#18	Bethesda's first real school house and what happened to it.
9/1/39	#19	Rock Creek, Georgetown and its name, ads reflect the life.
9/8/39	#20	Georgetown houses and inns, F.S.Key described, Jenny Lind.
9/15/39	#21	A Baltimore riot, piked roads and MacAdam, the Act of 1805
9/22/39	#22	The Pike's condition, a Dickens comment, travel on the road.
9/29/39	#23	Naming Bethesda, the Presbyterian church, what it means.
10/6/39	#24	Dr. Flourney at Bethesda Presbyterian, later tenants there.
10/13/39	#25	Eyewitness to Jeb Stuart's 1863 raid, martial law, Ft. Reno.
10/20/39	#26	Sam Perry's `63 story, Early's `64 raid, death at Bohrer's farm.
10/27/39	#27	Ice house stories, Bethesda Park in 1891 and its small zoo.
11/3/39	#28	Bethesda Park activities, dancing, jousting, the phonograph.
11/10/39	#29	Howard Gingell's balloon ride at Bethesda Park, and a raid.
11/17/39	#30	Early history of Mt. Zion Baptist Church, established 1821.
11/24/39	#31	Growth of Mt. Zion church, pastors, and getting there.

A catalogue of Mrs. J. Reed Bradley's profiles of Bethesda women from the "Vignettes" in the Bethesda *Journal*

Dorothy Annable and Ruth Coplen - librarians 2/2/40
Mrs. W. B. Armstrong - Red Cross production leader, Cabin John 8/16/40
Mrs. Carl Aslakson - Girl Scout leader 11/22/40
Mrs. Jenny Ballou - author, Ella Wilcox biographer 1/26/40
Mrs. Frank Bennett - Bethesda ES PTA activities 5/10/40
Mrs. James V. Bennett - CC Community Forum leader 10/24/41
Mrs. Eugene Bollay - Red Cross, Campfire Girls 11/17/39
Mrs. Ralph Bonnett - WC of CC publicity chair, gardener 5/3/40
Mrs. Rudolph Bopp - writing Shoemaker history, Ruth's sister 8/22/41
Mrs. Philip Bradley - Public Health Lay Committee leader 3/1/40
Mrs. Berlin Brann - Cabin John Gray Lady, Aunt Pat, child welfare 8/4/39
Mrs. Anna K. Briefs - North CC linguist, teacher 6/20/41
Mrs. Ray Brown - chair Lay Health Committee, school health 12/1/39
Margaret Buckley - business woman, Mont. Players 12/29/39
Mrs. Jacob W. Bulger - WC of Beth., consumer ed teacher 7/26/40
Mrs. Bernard Chandler - Wellsley Club, free speech conference 11/21/41
Mrs. Elizabeth Chapin - Edgemoor Beauty Salon 3/8/40
Mrs. Ruth Clapp - principal Bethesda ES (9 yrs.) 2/21/41
Mrs. Morrison M. Clark - Lay Health Council leader, work of 5/9/41
Rose Robison Cohen - speech and drama teacher, Children's Studio 12/13/40
Mrs. Lew G. Coit - a family of craftsmen, weaver, Scout leader 4/19/40
Mrs. W. G. Counselman - former Mrs. Holman, native 1/24/41
Mrs. Eleanor Cronin - Women's Club of Bethesda founder 2/16/40
Isobel Dexter and sister, Mary D. Walton - prop. Chalet Nonpareil 9/22/39
Mrs. Anna B. Engle- proprietor The Handy Shop 7/12/40
Mrs. Ruth Farnham - Kennedy-Ch. interior decorator, accountant 1/19/40
Mrs. Harrison Fitts - "cutting" chair of MC Red Cross, club woman 7/11/41
Mrs. Esther Fleishell - Republican leader in Willkie campaign 10/11/40
Mrs. A. Brookhouse Foster - public library, FWC loan fund 10/27/39
Mrs. Martha Keys Fry - public health nurse for Bethesda area 3/7/41
Mrs. Della Furzer - baker, from FWM to bakery shop 8/18/39
Mrs. Franklin Getzendanner - public steno., women's club leader 8/9/40
Mrs. Louis A. Gravelle - PTA, pub. health, garden club 9/8/39
Mrs. I. F. Gravatt - musician, Scientist Cliffs 9/1/39
Mrs. Gilbert Grosvernor - traveler, Bell's daughter, club woman 12/27/40
Mrs. Norman F. Hearn - Campfire leader, Westmoreland Hills 2/28/41
Mrs. Edward H. Helmuth - CC Red Cross production chair, war relief 5/31/40
Marjory Hendricks - Normandy Farm, recipes 1/5/40
Mrs. Ralph Himstead - LWV Brookings Report study leader 4/25/41
Mrs. Frank M. Hoadley - speakers' bureau, clubwoman editor 10/6/39
Mrs. Hugh B. Johnson - art exhbiit at WC of Bethesda 4/26/40
Mrs. Fred Keplinger - artist on Battery Lane, kindergarten sponsor 10/4/40
Mrs. Frederick M. Kerby - Women's Club of CC leader, Hesketh St. 3/28/41
Mrs. Marie Kromas - Bethsda ES cafeteria manager 9/15/39
Mrs. Dorothy Kurtz - ex. sec. Welfare Board, agency summary 8/30/40
Mrs. Edward G. Latch - Dutch heritage, Methodist minister's wife 3/14/41
Mrs. Paul Ledig - Camp Fire and church leader, lecturer 2/14/41
Mrs. Joseph T. Maguire - WC of CC, Know Your County campaign 10/20/39
Mrs. Lawrence O. Manley - Woman's Club of CC forum leader 1/12/40

Mrs. Buelah H. McCuen - of Glen Echo, mayor, housewife, reformer 7/19/40
Alice Coe Mendham - Green Acres School (Mrs. Webster Powell) 2/23/40
Mary Virginia Merrick - Christ Child Society founder 11/15/40
Mrs. F. Eliot Middleton - direct County Red Cross, at rec center 6/21/40
Mrs. Milton E. Miles - Burma Road escape described, Navy wife 4/11/41
Mrs. Mary Barton Mohler - high school teacher, civic worker 4/12/40
Mrs. Lowell B. Moon - blood donor campaign leader 11/14/41
Mrs. William M. Morell - and family, Newcomb Club pres. 10/13/39
Newcomb-Bethesda Community Singers - history and activities 12/22/39
Mrs. Willis J. Nolan - wood carving, block printing, skiing 6/6/41
Mrs. Naomi G. Owens - Neddlework Guild leader, church work 11/1/40
Mrs. Roy M. Palmer - metal worker, artist 3/22/40
Mrs. George E. Pariseau - club woman, Girls Friendly Soc., gardener 7/28/39
Mrs. Carl Paulsen - missionary, travels, speaker 2/9/40
Mrs. Walter E. Perry - Willie Greene Day, social worker, activities 11/24/39
Mrs. Martha Roberts Pogge - Mont. Players leader, Somersetter 5/24/40
Mrs. Thomas W. Pyle - PTA, Mont.Players, club woman 6/14/40
Mrs. Jane Plummer Rice - Montgomery Players 12/8/39
Mrs. Donald Roberts - housing, birth control Maternal Welfare 9/26/41
Mrs. Thomas Robertson - CC pioneer, library and school supporter 4/4/41
Ruth Shoemaker - family bio., legislator, farmer 11/3/39
Vivian Simpson - active attorney, gardener 8/23/40
Helene Sinnott- public stenographer, actress, writer 5/17/40
Mrs. Ernest L. Smith - Red Cross Motor Corps leader, rider 10/10/41
Mrs. J. Horace Smithey - organist, choral music teacher 1/21/41
Mrs. Rebeccca Spitler - flower shop prop., Mariner Scout leader 8/2/40
Mrs. George Winchester Stone - Martin's Ad., her foreign students 5/30/41
Mrs. Lilly C. Stone - quarries, historical society, home: Glenmore 7/21/39
Mary N. Talmadge - Baptist Home superintendent 8/11/39
Mrs. James Henry Taylor - prop. Centro Hobby Shop 12/15/39
Mrs. Walter R. Tuckerman - and family at "Tuxeden," activities 7/5/40
Mrs. Julian B. Waters - Farm Women's Market leader at home 9/27/40
Mrs. C. Law Watkins - leads Red Cross knitters 3/29/40
Mrs. B. Payton Whalen - family, bio, club woman leader 8/25/39
Kathleen Wheeler - Somerset sculptress of horses and people 3/15/40
Mrs. Harry Dexter White - Anne Terry White, author 10/17/41
Mrs. Roger Whiteford - CC Red Cross war relief head 4/5/40
Mrs. Monica Williams - St. John's rector's wife, poet 12/20/40
Mrs. Edward M. Willis- local Red Cross chair 9/29/39
Dorothy Young - high school counselor, gardener 11/10/39

Appendix D:

Bethesda 1915

The following were some of the inhabitants of what was generally called Bethesda when Horace Hampton was a boy. Residents of Glen Echo, Cabin John, Somerset, Friendship Heights and The Hills, Chevy Chase and families such as Charles Corby's in the northern reaches near Garrett Park are not included in this list, which is based on Caldwell's 1915 *Directory* and, to a lesser extent, on the 1910 Census. The Thirteenth Census (1910) shows no addresses for Bethesdans but does have other information such as literacy.

For each family, the neighborhood, if known, is indicated in parenthesis and the names of children and other family members, if any, follow the semi-colon. African-American Bethesdans are marked with an asterisk (*) as they were by Caldwell. Sometimes only the head of the household is listed since that is all the information available. The spellings are Caldwell's (Wilhelminia, Katharine, Sirel), but the census taker, also made some imaginative attempts at names.

George L. Adams (Alta Vista)
James C. and Virginia Adkins; Elizabeth, Alvin (Oakmont)
Mrs. H. S. Ailes; Mis Lulu M. Ailes (Sunnyside, Rockville Pike)
Eugene and Sallie Ailes; Edna Jane, Stephen, John Cornwell (Sunnyside)
R. P. Allen (Old G'town Rd.)
H. C. Allison and his wife; Lawrence, Leroy, Horatio, Eugene, Dorothy(Norwood)
Frank G. and Susan Andrews (Rosedale Park)
Raymond G. Atwood
Mahlon H. and Mary L. Austin (Wilson Lane)
William H. H. and Margaret O. Austin (River Road)
Milton B. Austin (Wilson Lane)
James W. and Lucy B. Austin (River Road)
Joshua Thomas and Martha Austin; Mary Virginia, Laura Irene, Martha , Annie (Cedar)
Mary C. (Mrs. M. R.) Austin; Elsie G., Linwood (Bradley Hills)
Miss Mary Austin (Wilson Lane)
Miss Lena J. Austin (Alta Vista)

Ernest N. and Anne S. Bales; Gertrude Frances, Esther Lee, Ernest Rieneker (Oakmont)
John Edward and Martha Barbee; John, Charles, Mary (Woodmont)
Miss Mary A. and Mrs. O. H. Barnes (Woodmont)
J. Edward and Lucia Newcomb Bates; Lucia., George., Mary., J. E. jr., Evelyn (Drummond)
David H. and Annie L. Beall; Josephine, Florence (Wetzell Rd.)
Katie (Mrs.A.H.) Bean; Bessie, Fred, Ida (Alta Vista)
Benjamin A. and Mary F. Bean; John Leonard, E.V., M.G., M.C., Eunice, Clifford (Old G'tn)
Benjamin Everett and Stella Leola Bean; Catherine, —nn (NW Park)
James T. and Jane Bean (Northwest Park)
Murlin J. and Minnie E. Beardslee; John M. Albert N. (Woodmont)
Benjamin Harvey Beavers (Wetzell Rd.)
Charles H. and Emma A. Becker; William S., Wilhelmina H., Mabel E., Beulah, Emma, Ruth, Carl (NW
        Park)
Mrs. — Beckman (River Rd.)
Mrs. Margaret M. Berry ("West View" Bradley Hills)
George W. and Florence Best; Noah, John, Irene, Georgia May, Rebecca, Grover (R.Pike)
Leroy and Elsie M. Best; Elizabeth E. (River Rd.)
Charles C. and Annie R. Bohrer; Nannie H., Jay Louis, Ralph W., Eleanor C., and Mrs.
        Elizabeth, widow of John (Rockville Pike)
Henry B. Bohrer; Bradley, Mabel, Elizabeth, Benjamin (Cedar Lane)
Ronald C. and Maude E. Booth; Roland T. (River Rd.)
Mrs. Frances Borden; Samuel Wheatly (Huntington Terr., Moreland)
Mrs. Alice A. Bowdie; Charles E. (Woodmont)
Mrs. Cora Brabham; Vernon, Lillian, Mahlon, Ellen J. (Wilson Lane)
Henry F. Brewer; Zachariah, Salome, Alice, Guy Conrad, Mark D., Daniel M. (H'tn.Terr.)
Adolphus and Ida Brice; Roosevelt (Old G'town Rd.)*
J. Calvin and Kathryn Bright (Woodmont)
George A. and Valley Broadhurst; Earl, Millard, Viola, Emma Eileen (Woodmont)
Joshua Edward and Elizabeth Broadhurst; Bertrand, Eva (Woodmont)
William H. and Ollie B. Broadhurst; Lansing, Liston, Odessa (Woodmont)

William and Mary Brooks (River Road)*
William J. and Sarah Brown; Francis (River Road)
W. H. H. and Rachel Brown (River Road)*
Mr and Mrs. Walter Brown; 4 children (Rockville Pike)*
James Brown (Rockville Pike)*
Everett M. and Breta L. Bryant; Ruth L., Breta Page, Everett T. (Woodmont)
Martha Bundy (Alta Vista)*
Mrs. Mary E. Burdette (Wetzell Rd.)
George A. Burgess (Wilson Lane)
John E. Burgess (Wilson Lane)
Ralph E. and Eveline Newcomb Burgess; Ralph E. Jr. (Alta Vista)
John W. and Natoga Burley (River Rd.)*
Louis Burley jr. (River Rd.)*
John G. and Margaret E. Burroughs; Leo H. (River Rd.)
Edward E. and Amy A. Burroughs; Diamond, Alice Maude, Pearl May, Mary Belle, Amy Irene, Delia
        Victoria (Alta Vista)
William and Emma Butler; Joseph, Elizabeth (Rockville Pike)*
Benjamin F. and Julia Butterfield; Hart (Leland-Norwood)
Moseby O. and Ida Butts; Garner M., Raymond A. (River Rd.)

Samuel Dean and Jennie G. Caldwell (Old G'town-Colville)
Samuel D. jr and Hazel L.D. Caldwell; Samuel Dean 3d (Old G'town-Colville)
Mrs. J.C. and Miss Mary Logan Caldwell (Alta Vista)
Charles B. and Mary I. Cameron; W.Benson, Theodore E., Florence V., Walter S., Mildred E.
        (Woodmont)
Mrs. Alice J. Campbell, Mrs. Bayleff Campbell (Norwood)
Arthur Carey (Bangarter Rd.)*
Louise Cavanaugh (Rockville Pike)
Edward V. and Julia Caywood (Rockville Pike)
Nicholas Chaconas (Cedar Lane)
A.A. and Fannie Chapin; Raymond, Frances (Ch.Ch.Drive & Wisc Ave.)
Mrs. Georgiana V. Chase (Norwood)
Royden D. and Ivy G. Chase; Nancy Josephine (Norwood)
George M. and Mary Josephine Churchill; Elizabeth Sarah (River Rd.)
Isaac Clipper (River Rd.)*
William W. and Blanche Clipper; Cleveland (River Rd.)*
Cleveland and Susan Clipper (River Rd.)*
Richard and Janie Clubb; Laura (Woodmont)
Mrs. Amanda Coleman (Colville-Old G'town Rd.)*
George F. Coleman (River Rd.)*
Frank E. and Margaret Catherine Collins; Frances Catherine, James Alfred, Elmer Clifford, Preston
        Earl (Woodmont)
Joseph J. Collins (River Rd.)
James Edward Collins (River Rd.)
Thomas H. and Nannie L. Collins; Virginia, Rush Mitchell, Thomas H. jr, Dorsey R. (Huntington
        Terr.-Old G'town Rd.)
Evan A. and Stella Condon; James M., Genevieve, Ruth (Woodmont)
Miss Irene and Miss Pauline Connell (Norwood)
John S. and Rose M. Coombs; Elizabeth, Mrs. M.S. Coombs (Woodmont)
Miss Hester A. Counselman, Miss Jennie Counselman(Woodmont)
William G. and Dora Counselman (Rockville Pike)
Howard and Myrtle Crist; Howard Roger, Lewis Edgar (Woodmont)

Kirby and Lily Crist; Daisy (Norwood)
Prof. Edward E and Annie E. Crockett; Bessie, Louise (Wilson Lane)
Alfred and Ella Crockett (Rockville Pike)*
Hanson and Laura R. Cronise; George W., Susie M., Clyde H. (Woodmont)
Miss Annie Cryons (Rockville Pike)
Floyd Cunningham (Oakmont)
Richard and Ada E. Cunningham; Robert, Alms E., Mary E., Brooke (Woodmont)
George M. and Ora Earle Curtis; G. McLean jr. (Ch.Ch.Drive-Bradley Hills)
William J. and Ada Darcy (Huntington Terr.)
William Z. and May Darcy; Armisted, Nora, Goldie, Frank, Lewis (Htn. Terr.)
H.Bradley and M.Porter Davidson; H.Bradley jr, Richard (Wisc.Ave.)

Tobias A. Davis (Rockville Pike)
James W. and Edith A. Dean; Sarah E. (River Rd.)
John H. Dean (Alta Vista)
Peter L. and Winnie Decker (Northwest Park)
Charles C. and Mary A. Dodge; Abigail B. (Alta Vista)
James Heath and Dorothy S. Dodge (Rockville Pike)
William and Marie Donaldson (River Rd.)
L.Earle and Myrtle E. Donaldson (Woodmont)
Charles T.T. and Mary Dorsey; Joseph, Elizabeth (Woodmont)*
Mr and Mrs. Reuben Dove; 3 children (Bradley Hills)*
Reuben Doye (Old G'town Rd.)
Mr. and Mrs. George Doye; Frances Elizabeth,George, Madeline, Rosa (Old G'town)
Edward M. and Georgia Barnes Duncan (Alta Vista)

Mr. and Mrs. Robert Easton; 3 children (Old G'town Rd.)
Mr. and Mrs. Edward H. Edwards (Wilson Lane)
Mrs.C.A. (Alice L.) Edwards; Edna M., Annie E., —nn (Old G'town Rd.)
Norman T. Edwards (Rockville Pike)
Harry and Dora Ehrlick; Jacob, Samuel, Esau, Myer, Abram, Sarah (River Rd.)
Mrs. B. Eicholtz (River Rd.)
Edmund P. and Frances K. Ellis; Edmund K., Catherine P. (Wisc.Ave-Norwood)
Emmons K. and Floy J. Ellsworth; Lawrence (Northwest Park)
Mr. and Mrs. Elmo; —nn (River Rd.)
Edwin H. and Pearl Potter Etz; Constance (Bradley Hills)
Richard and Leanah Evans; Ethel May, Harry Leroy, Archie (River Rd.)

C.S. and Eva Fagan; Hamilton Lloyd (Oakmont)
Mr. and Mrs. Henry Fahrenwald (River Rd.)Orville N. and Martha R. Fansler; Mildred M. (Alta
        Vista)
William E. and Julia Fields; Artis, Golden, Doris (Woodmont)
Margaret Fields (Woodmont)
John A. and Henrietta Fleming; Margaret (Drummond)
James J. Florence (Old G'town Rd.)
Rev.P.Parke Flournoy; Benjamin C., Francis R., Richard W., Edward Stanhope,
        Addison H., Miss Nellie (Rockville Pike)
Paul D. and Berenice Foote; Jane (Norwood)
E.Norval Fortson (Rockville Pike)
Owen H. and Eliza M. Fowler; Elizabeth L., Grenville L. (Bradley Lane-Norwood)
Clarence and Martha Fox; Archie (Woodmont)
Mrs. Jennie J. Franklin; Lynn W., Neal Dow (Norwood)
Mrs. I. S. French (Drummond)
J.Walter and Barbara A, French; Albert, Walter, Arthur (Edgewood)
Ellis and Mary Fuller; Julia, Ellis jr, Ruth (Woodmont)

W. T. Galliher (Wilson Lane-Bradley Hills)
Richard and Cecelia Gannt (Old G'town Rd.)
Charles Garland (River Rd.)
Mrs. Amelia Gass (Rockville Pike)
Charles E. and Isabel Gingell; Nora, Estelle (Rockville Pike)
George J. and Annie R. Gingell; J.Elmer, Zenette H. (Huntington Terr.-Old G'tn)
Warren Wilfred and Belle Annie Gingell; Louise Helen, Raymond Warren (Wdmt)
Jed and Sookie S. Gittings (Huntington Terrace-Old G'town Rd.)
Dr.Larkin W. and Jane Cox Glazebrook; Larkin, Robinson (Sunnyside-Old G'tn)
Mrs. Lila Goldsborough; Heath, Phillips Lee (Woodmont)
H.C. and F.L. Gould; Miriam (Northwest Park)
Francis R. and Glennie Gray; Norman (Woodmont)
W. B. Gray (Woodmont)
Leonidas Layton and Eloise B. Green (Rockville Pike)
Mrs. Leora Green; Abbie S., Waldo M. (Norwood)
Mr. and Mrs. Gregory; Reginald (Rockville Pike)
Gilbert H. and Elsie May Grosvernor; Melville Bell, Gertrude Hubbard, Mabel, Lillian Waters, Carol
        (Bangarter Rd.-Rockville Pike "Stonycrest")
Robert D. Hagner (Rockville Pike)
W.A. and Vernia Haliday; Ethel, Ruth, Raymond, Clyde (Woodmont)

Mrs. Hall (Woodmont)

George E. Hamilton (Rockville Pike)

Mr. and Mrs. Thomas Hampton; Thomas E, Miss C.M., A.S., Edward M., Norman, Bertha,
    Winifred, Horace (Chevy Chase Drive)

George F. and Gertrude E. Hane; George C. (Oakmont)

E. K. (Mrs. W. M.) Haney (Northwest Park- Old G'town Rd.)

William H. and Mollie J. Haney; Stanley E., Miss Edith May (Drummond)

Clarence L. Harding (Edgewood)

Richard and Alice Hardy; Loree (Mrs. W.), Sherman D., Clifford (River Rd.)*

Sommers and Emma Hardy; Lillie May, Catherine Emily, Alice Stella Marie, Helen Frances, Mamie
    (River Rd.)*

John H. and Susan Harper; Joseph, Miss — (Wilson Lane)

Mrs. Sadie Hastings (Woodmont)

John C. and Emma B. Heald; Katherine B. (Old Georgetown Road)

Frank G. and Mary Heaton; Edgar J. and Elizabeth Heaton (Alta Vista)

Benjamin R. Heffner (River Rd.)

Francis E. and Janie Heffner; Miss Mamie (River Rd.)

William Columbus Heffner; Bessie, Emma, Blanche, Rosa, Edna, Leo (River Rd.)

Mrs. Euphemia Henderson (Drummond)

Herbert A. and Mary Henderson (Norwood)

Isaac S. and Annie Walton Hendry; Moses W., Miss Alma Lauck, Dr. Ernest Singleton, Morgan
    Leland (Old G'tn. Rd.)

William Washington Henry (Old G'tn. Rd.)*

Mr. and Mrs. William Edward Henson; 2 children (Bangarter Rd.)*

Clarence B. and Isabel B. Hight; Clarence jr, Annie I., Margaret (Highland Park)

George Washington and Mary Gertrude Hill; Earl Clifton (Woodmont)

Mrs. and Mrs. R. H. Hill (Drummond)

Miss Bessie Hodges (Rockville Pike)

William Thomas and Bessie Hollidge; Helen, Melvin (Highland Park)

James D. Holman (Rockville Pike)

Miss Dore Holman (Rockville Pike)

John William and Mary E. Huffman; Cornelia, Dora, Perry, Frank (H'tn Terr.)

Henry J. and Rosamund Aubrey Hunt; Henry J.4th, —nn (Drummond)

Richard C.D. and Evelyn C. Hunt; Richard jr (Drummond)

Leigh and Jessie Hunt; Henry, Helen (Rockville Pike)

Guy F. Hurt (Drummond)

John Henry and Cora Hutson; Ada, John H.jr (Woodmont)

John and Mary F.B. Imirie; Scott F., G. Wady, Fred J., Mary B., Helen, Donald, Paul
    (Bradley Lane, W. Ch.Ch-almost Bethesda.)

Reuben A. Ingalls (Cedar Lane)

Henry Edington and Edna Marie Inglass; Joseph, John (Wilson Lane)

Mr. and Mrs. Huntington Wolcott Jackson (Edgewood)

John Henry and Alice Jackson; Harry, Thomas (Rockville Pike)*

Sarah Elizabeth (Mrs. J.) Jacobsen; Jacob (Alta Vista)

Dora Johnson (Drummond)

Enoch G. and Grace Dean Johnson; Miriam E. (Alta Vista)

Hayden and Jeannette Johnson (River Rd.)

Mahalia Johnson (Alta Vista)*

Charles A. Johnson (Old G'town Rd.)

Annie Mary Jones (Huntington Terr.-Old G'tn. Rd.)*

J. Hampton Jones (Bradley Hills)

Mrs. L. N. Jones; Cyril, Leonard (Drummond)

Dennis Jordan (Wetzell Rd.)

Henry R. and Margaret Karr; Margaret, Neal (Norwood)

Frank B. and Martha M. Kaye; Alice L. (Ch.Ch.Drive-Bradley Hills)

Jacob L. and Mary Kefauver; Grace, William L., Joseph Leslie, Alexander Underwood, Edna, Mamie,
    Lena, Rebecca, Helen, Oscar (Bradley Hills)

Cyrus and Elizabeth Keiser; Cyrus jr (Alta Vista)

John P. and Ida Keiser (Alta Vista)

Lewis and Lois Keiser; Clarence (Alta Vista)

Miss Lucy C. Kellerhouse (Drummond)

Fred and Lona Miller Keplinger (Northwest Park)

Charles F. and Florence Kincheloe; Charles jr, Florence L. (Alta Vista)
John L. and May Elizabeth King; Elvira Elizabeth (Woodmont)
Wilson King (River Rd.)
Frank B. and Bessie Kinslow; James, Raymond, George, Gladys (River Rd.)*
George E. Kinslow; George L. and Lillie E. Kinslow, Ralph (River Rd.)*
Rev. James and May Dudley Kirkpatrick; James jr, Alice D. (Sunnyside-Old G'tn)
Henry B. and Mary E. Kisner (Alta Vista)
Ernest W. Kisner (Alta Vista)

William H. and Johanna C. Larman (Alta Vista)
Mr. and Mrs. Oscar W. Larman (Bangarter Rd.)
Lee D. and Augusta McC. Latimer; John McC., Ruth, Lee jr, Henry A.(Drummond)
Leonie St.Clair Le Fevre (River Rd.)
A. M. and Sallie U. Legg (Alta Vista)
William F. and Margaret Legg; Frank, Roland, Montgomery (Alta Vista)
Henry Latane and Mary Keith Lewis; Isabel, Margaret (Rockville Pike)
Dr. John L. and Mary E.C. Lewis; Thomas, Agnes, John (Old G'tn-R.Pike)
Mrs. Mary L. Lewis (Norwood-Bradley Lane)
Mrs. Grenville Lewis (Norwood-Bradley Lane)
Jacob Henry Link
Olof Alex and Milnor Ljungstedt (Alta Vista)
Emily Lockbuller (Highland Park)
William Lochte (Old Georgetown Road)
Lawrence Leroy and Lenna Lochte; Lawrence Andrew (Woodmont)
James Henry and Margaret Loughborough; David, Margaret, Ludwell Harrison, Nathan E., Carrie F.
    (River Rd.)
William and Julia Lowe; Daphine, Wm. Edward, Lillie, Nellie (Rockville Pike)
H. Newton and Grace Okie Lowry (River Rd.)
Samuel C. McCeney (Highland Park)
Edward B. McLean (Bradley Hills)
E. R. and Agnes Magie; Hazel (Alta Vista)
Martha V. (Mrs. T.L.) Magruder; Baruch O., William O., Albert, Harry Clinton and Cora W.(Mrs. H.C.)
    Magruder, Harry Thomas (River Rd.)
Lloyd Magruder (Old Georgetown Rd.)
Howard Magruder (River Rd.)
Eugene B. and Bertha Magruder; Bernard E., William T., Lila Spates (Old G'tn. Rd.)
Mr. and Mrs. Edward E. Magruder; John. Elsie, Leon, Grace Mae (Norwood)
Warren Vincent and Annie Magruder; Eliza, Susan, Annie, Henry, Warren, Arthur, Frances (Old
    Georgetown Rd.)
Clinton and Lola Mansfield (Woodmont)
Alfred Marlon (Rockville Pike)*
Miss S. E. Marlow (Drummond)
Mr. and Mrs. H. D. Marquard; Aususta (Woodmont)
Leonard C. Marsden (Wetzell Rd.)
William A. Mason (Old Georgetown Rd.)*
Albert T. Mason (Old Georgetown Rd.)*
Stephen Mason (Alta Vista)*
James Monroe Matthews, Lee D. Matthews (River Road)
Mrs. Lydia Matthews; Clarence, Alice (Wilson Lane)
Frank and Fannie Matthews (River Rd.)*
Charles W. and Annie Miller; Genevieve, Uranium (Wilson Lane)
Julian Hite and Fannie Miller; Lillian C, (Alta Vista)
Wharton and Emma Moore; Graham, John, Emma (Northwest Park)
David L. Morgal; Phares L. (Wetzell Rd.)
Daniel P. and Susan Morgan; E.W.Malcolm, J.Harold (Old G'town Rd.)
Dr. James F. and Hilma Louise Morris; Aldoph Frank, Hilma Maria, Lars James
        (Woodmont-Rockville Pike)
Alex H. and Dr. Mary E. Morrison; Alexis B. (Woodmont)
James L. and Annie E. Morrison (Cedar Lane)
James W. and Elsie Morrison; Lelure, Ralph, C.Leroy, Lily , C.Mildred, Abram (Br.Hills)
James A. Moxley (Oakmont)
Gilbert Thomas and Mamie Lee Mullican (Woodmont)
Charles D. Musgrove, Hiram D. Musgrove (Old Georgetown Rd.)
Charles F. and Ada P. Myers

Harry T. and Lucy Comstock Newcomb; Ellsworth, Winifred, Lucy lamson, Maryland, Holly, Josiah
        Turner, Simone, Janet, Harry Turner 2d. (Alta Vista)
Hon. Henry Martyn and Lucia Turner Newcomb (Alta Vista)
Benjamin F. Newman (Wetzell Rd.)
William and Elsie M. Niemeyer; Mary Margaret, William Price; Mrs. Mary C. Niemeyer
        (Northwest Park)
Mr. and Mrs. Chalres E. Norris, 4 children (Bangarter Rd.)
George W. Norris; Miss Emma A. (Beech Ave.-Alta Vista)
Augustus P. and Ivy B. Norton; Ivy L. (Northwest Park)

George W. and Susan A. O'Brien; George jr, Samuel F., Lewis M., Clara I., Mary Catherine,
        Clarence (Rockville Pike)
Mrs. Emma O'Bryhim; Shirley, James, Lee, Archie, Nelson (Woodmont)
Richard Henry and Mary Ellen Oden; Cleveland Ernest (Cedar Lane)
Joseph Henry and Valley Oden; Elizabeth, Raymond (Cedar Lane)
Joseph O'Donoghue (River Rd.)
Cornelius and Mary Ann O'Donoghue (River Rd.)
James O'Donoghue (River Rd.)
M. Willson and Dixie W. Offutt; M. Willson jr.
William Grendage and Bettie Offutt (Norwood-Leland St.)
Virginia Clotilda Offutt, Viola Offutt (Norwood-Leland St.)
Fred Jones and Lula Offutt; Julia Elizabeth, Brice Lyles(Norwood-Leland St.)
Robert W. and Mamie Offutt; Roland, Gladys, Leta (Wetzell Rd.)
Lewis P. and Lena Oldfield (Rockville Pike)
Fred A. Oldfield (Woodmont)
Benjamin W., Lewis P., John Walter, Fannie, Arthur Oldfield (Rockville Pike)
Mrs. H.M.D.Oliphant; T.G.Morgan, Margaret Coulter, M.Campbell (Drummond)
Eugene H. and Susie O'Neal; John William, Hester Eugene jr (Norwood)
William Ernest and Florence Onley (Rockville Pike)*
Mrs. E. S. Overby (Huntington Terr.-Cedar Lane)
Joseph W. and Mary Owen; Frank, Joseph jr, Bertie, Carrie, Eleanor, Irene (River Rd.)
W. Thomas and Nannie F.G. Owens; T.Calvin, Margaret G. (Highland Park)
Miss Martha F. Owings (Alta Vista)

John S. and Mary E. Park; John Marshall (Woodmont)
Cassius and Eliza Parker; Oilena, Harrison (River Rd.)*
Charles R. and Florence M. Parks; Charles Rusell jr, Frederick S., Pearl C., Lillian M.,
        Florence M., Raymond, Helen I. (River Rd.)
William A. and Fannie E. Pate; Ethel M., Wm. A.jr, Lester C., Doris (Alta Vista)
William T. and Mary Paxton; Joseph H. (River Rd.)
Millard Eldridge and Margaret Peake; Nellie, Joesph Millard (Highland Park)
Hezekiah Eugene and Emma May Perrell; Pauline (Woodmont)
Upton and Beatrice M. Perrell; Walter (Northwest Park-Old G'town Rd.)
Albert A. and Jane Perry (Wilson Lane)
Benjamine and Annie Perry; Cyrus Eli, J.Wilbert, Ethel, John B., Benj.jr (River Rd.)
Erasmus Perry; Thomas E., Virginia, Myrtle (Wilson Lane)
Stephen Boyd and Virginia Garland Perry; Charles, Robert, Frank, Louis, Walter (R.Rd)
Ninian M. and Mamie Perry (River Road)
John Ninian and Rose A. Perry (River Road)
Henry Clay and Vandelia Perry (River Road)
Bernard and Jennie Perry (River Road)
Noble F. and Myrtle E. Perry (River Road)
Thomas S. Perry (River Road)
James Henderson and Mary E. Peter (Old G'town Road)
John C. Peter (Rockville Pike)
Mrs. Lavinia R. Peter; Alton W., Reginald A., Ina F., David S. (Woodmont-R'ville Pike)
Eliza C. (Mrs. J.N.) Phillips (Woodmont-Rockville Pike)
Andrew J. and Cora Phillips; Andrew, Fannie, Robert, Ralph (Woodmont)
Maurice D. and Emily Elsie Phillips; Althea, Hilda, Francis, Andrew (Norwood-Leland)
Archibald and Catherine Phillips; Archibald Lawrence, Margaret (Rockville Pike)
Charles D. and Amanda M. Phillips; Charles E., Lillian, Myrtle, Leon, Emmett (H'land Pk.)
George W. Plummer; Geo. W. jr, Gertrude, Otho J., Mrs. Kate Plummer (Woodmont)
Mrs. Elizabeth Poole; Etta, John B., Wilbur (Old Georgetown Road)

William R. and Katherine Poole (Alta Vista)
George A. and Nellie Poore; Cyril Eldridge, Catherine (Woodmont)
Dr. Henry C. and Mary A.L. Porter; Henry Frederick (Huntington Terr.-Old G'tn. Rd.)
Hattie S. (wid. of Wm.S.) Powell; Rosa Mary, Harry Lee, Elizabeth (Mrs. H.L.), Edward Gorman, Lulu,
      Agnes (Woodmont)
Charles M. and Grace Powell; Anna, Savilla, John, Raymond, Helen, (Woodmont)
Grover William and Helen Powell (Moreland-Htn. Terr.)
Mr. and Mrs. Richard W. Pryor (River Rd.)*
Andrew D. and Mary Hilda Pugh; Mary, Helen, Audrey (Woodmont)
Lewis N. and Nannie Pugh; Bertie, Pearl (Rockville Pike)
Edward Richard Pyles; Hester (River Rd.)

Dr. Arthur T. Randall; Irene L. (Oakmont)
Mrs. Mary W. Rankin (Alta Vista)
J. M. Rankin (Rockville Pike)
Mrs. M. L. Ratjen (Drummond)
Joshua H. Rawlins (Wilson Lane)
Charles A. and Emilie Read (Oakmont)
George A. and Beulah Russell Randall Redhead (Oakmont)
Isiah Redrick (Rockville Pike)
Fred R. and Minnie Reid; G. B., Mary E., Cornelia Ellen (Highland Park)
Hugh Reilly (Wilson Lane)
Mr. and Mrs. John Willian Renshaw; Clara B, William M., Charles H. (Cedar Lane)
Mrs. Anna Renshaw (Old Georgetown Road)
Edwin C. and Julia V. Reynolds; Olive A., Edwin L., Hazel H. (River Rd.)
Samuel D. and Harriet L. Rhoads (Woodmont-Rockville Pike)
Mrs. Lulu C. Richardson; William W., Simeon (Drummond)
Mrs. Sarah E. Richardson (Drummond)
Mrs. Sarah Rivers, George W. Rivers jr (River Road)*
Dora Rivers, Henry C. Rivers (River Road)*
Walter Rivers (River Road)*
A.James and M.W. Robertson; A.J., M.A., J.A., A.P. (Alta Vista)
William Millard and Estelle A. Robery (Alta Vista)
Mrs. Catherine Rogers; Leroy, Anna May (Old Georgetown Road)
Philip A. and Carrie F. Rosendorn; Albert F. (Northwest Park-Old G'tn.Rd.)
James H. and Louise Catharine Royce; Arthur, Bethel, Gertrude, Lucy (River Rd.)
Benjamin L. Rucker
Adolph C. and I.V. Ruebsam; Miss Isabel E., Daisy (Moreland-Huntington Terr.)
Grace L. Ryan; Martin A. (Norwood-Bradley Lane)

George P. and Ida Sacks; George, Edwin (Ch.Ch.Drive & Wisc. Ave)
Goerge J. and Beatrice M. Sargent; Alfred Wm. George, Nina M. (Woodmont-Old G'tn. Rd.)
Charles E. and Annie E. Saul; Otlie Margaret, Wilhelmina, Charles Alvin, —nn (W'dmont)
David B. and Mabel B. Saunders (Northwest Park-Rockville Pike)
George W. and Maude Teresa Schaeffer; Guy (Woodmont)
Albert F. Schaub; Harvey E. (Woodmont)
Harvey E. Scherrer
Charles P. A. and Lela Madison Scherrer; Gladys Pauline (Jones Mill Rd.)
Frank C. Schneider (Rockville Pike)
Dr. Ernest C. and Florence R. Schroeder; Robert B. (Rockville Pike)
George and Nora Schumate (Huntington Terr.-Old G'tn-Cedar Lane)
Charles A. Schutz (Alta Vista)
Alphonsus W. Schwabel (Norwood)
Emil P. Secker (Alta Vista)
Richard E. and Margaret Seek; Margaret, Dorothy (Rockville Pike)
Robert J. and Laura R. Service; Ruth Marion (Alta Vista)
William H. and Martha Sewell (Highland Park)*
John S. and Sophia E. Shackleford (Woodmont)
W. R. and Laura Sheid (Oakmont)
Charles Edward and Elizabeth Shoemaker; Charles Wendell (River Road)
Isaac Webster and Florence E. Shoemaker; Hazel C., Carroll (Bangarter Rd.)
Samuel Shoemaker (River Rd.)
William D. and Margaret B. Shoemaker; W.Blair (Drummond)
Harvey and Isabella Simms; Alice, —nn, —nn (Rockville Pike)

Mrs. Sarah E. Slaymaker; Miss S. Elizabeth (Rockville Pike)
D. A. and Pearl Smith (Drummond)
Mrs. A. D. Smith (Drummond)
L. H. and Amelia Smith; Kenneth (Northwest Park)
W. A. Smith (Alta Vista)
Charles Henry and Dora V. Smoot (Woodmont)
Benjamin and Florence Smoot (Woodmont-Old G'town Rd.)
Pericles P. Smyrnas; Jennie, George, Carrie (Cedar Lane)
Herbert L. and Stella May Solyom; Judith Allen, Richard Lewis (River Road)
George L. and Annie D. Stabler; Herman and Bertha (Mrs.H.) Stabler (Bradley Hills)
Joseph Edward and Minnie Stacks; John, Elmer, Mrs. Sarah (River Road)
Thomas Jackson and Laura Stacks; Irene, Minnie, Sarah, Elizabeth (Wilson Lane)
William B. and Alice Stacks (River Rd.)
Mr. and Mrs. John Stacks (River Rd.)
Mrs. Maude Stallsmith, 3 children (Highland park)
William S. and Lynette Stamper; Martha, Mary F., Guy E. (Drummond)
Mrs. Nellie I. Steffey (Colville-Old G'tn. Rd.)
D. E. Stephen (Edgewood)
W. B. Stokes (River Road)
R. V. L. and Andrena Stratton (Bradley Hills)
Alfred C. and May Strother; Burrell, William, Leroy (Wilson Lane)
M. W. and Mary Lillian Strother (Wilson Lane)
Shirley H. and Marjorie Sudduth (Woodmont)
D. F. and Agnes Sullivan; Angelia, Patricia, Agnes, Gertrude, Edward, Frank, Ann (R.Rd.)

Mrs. Susie D. Tarr (Drummond)
Mr. and Mrs. Samuel L. Tetlow; Arthur R., Roger B., Samuel E., Marguerite, Louise   (Bangarter-Old
      G'town Rd.)
Augustus F. and Nola E. Thomsen (Alta Vista)
Charles A. Thompson (Huntington Terr.-Old G'town Rd.)
Charles W. and Martha Thompson (Alta Vista)*
Joseph M. and Blanche Thompson; Irvin William, Robert Henry, James S.M., John   Henry, Louisa
Ellen, Airy Elizabeth, Alice Roosevelt, Theodore Franklin, Clifton,   Kermit (Wilson Lane)*
Perry K. and Eva D. Thurston (Drummond)
Osmund Henry and Elizabeth Winship Tibbotts; Edward W., Lloyd (Alta Vista)
Harry and Matilda Timbers (River Rd.)*
George H. and Margaret V. Trail; Emma, Raymond B., Helen, Aaron L., Joseph C. (N'wood)
Mr. and Mrs. Zachary Taylor Trice; Jennie (Woodmont)
John Wilson and Rosa Evelina; Paul Wilson, Sadie Viola, Simon, Leo, Howard (Woodmont)
James Tucker (River Rd.)
R. E. Tucker (Rockville Pike)
Walter R. Tuckerman (Edgewood)
Edward and Annie Turner (River Rd.)*
William and Mollie Turner (Rockville Pike)*

Unger, Frederick W. (Bangarter Rd.)

Charles H. jr. and Era M. Viett; Lenor (Woodmont)
Mrs. Ella R. Walker (Huntington Terr.-Old G'tn. Rd.)
Francis C. and Alma F. Wallace; Brenta F., Mary C. (Drummond)
Julian C. and Brenta French Wallace; R.French, Irene E. (Drummond)
Edward and Nannie Warren (River Rd.)*
Henry Warren, Nelson Warren Sr.; Nelson jr. and Susan Warren; Stella, Anderson,   Blanche (River
      Road)*
Mrs. L. P. Wasem (Alta Vista)
George Washington (HuntingtonTerr.-Old G'tn. Rd.)*
Madison Washington (Wilson Lane)*
Peter and Laura Washington; Melvina, Leonia, William, Theodore (Wilson Lane)*
Frank and Maggie Waters; Charles, Catharine (Alta Vista)
James Watson (Woodmont)
Dr. Frederick C. and Alice L. Weber; Frederick T., Margaret C. (Alta Vista)
R. Hanson and Emma Jane Honey Weightman; Jane (Highland Park)
Benjamin Peyton and Edith K. Whalen; Horace K. (Bradley Hills)
Joseph F. and Elizabeth Whalen; Edna May (Bradley Hills)

Mrs. Virginia Wheatley; Miss Nellie, Dr. Charles (Moreland-Huntington Terr.)
M. F. White (Rockville Pike)
Jacob Wilbert (River Rd.)
Sirel E. and Pearl Emma Wilkinson; Fay Edwin, Gilbert D., Helen Viola (Rockville Pike)
Jehu Henry and Edith Willett; Charles W. Charles Edward, Elbert (River Rd.)
David Ellis and Jessie Willett; Clara, Edith, Harriet, Samuel J. Tilden (River Rd.)
Mrs. E. O. Williams; Miss E. O. Williams (Huntington Terrace-Cedar Lane)
E. L. and Pearl Estelle Williams; Frederick Henry, Martha Matilda Elizabeth, Marguerite
          (Highland Park)
Mrs. Ada Wilson (Sunnyside-Rockville Pike)
Alfred and Minnie Wilson; George Alfred, Ruth (Highland Park)
Miss Elizabeth Wilson (Sunnyside-Rockville Pike)
James and Elizabeth Wilson; William Wallace, James T., Leo Bruce, Charles F. (Woodmont)
James R. and Mary Wilson (Rockville Pike)*
J. Herbert and Mary W. Wilson; —nn (Rockville Pike)
Mr. and Mrs. Robert Wilson (Rockville Pike)
Miss Phoebe Wilson (Sunnyside-Rockville Pike)
James H. and Elizabeth Windsor (River Rd.)
Bernard and Rebecca F. Wine (Huntington Terr.-Old G'tn.-Cedar Lane)
William Winston (Huntington Terr.-Old G'tn. Rd.)*
Edward M. and Eleanor Wise; Matilda, Agnes, Edward, Clara, Joel (Woodmont)
Frank W. and Lillie Wood; Mary, George, Marguerite (River Road)*
Andrew and Rosa Wood (River Road)*
Lawrence (Alonzo) Wood (River Rd.)*
William D. and Matilda Wood; Marion (River Rd.)*
John Henry and Mary E. Worthmiller; Joseph Raymond (Wilson Lane)
Mrs. Annie Amelia Worthmiller (Wilson Lane)
Mrs. Weltha J. Wright (Old Georgetown Road)
George Xidias (Cedar Lane)
Edward and Cassie Hardy Young (River Road)*
Yung Kwai and Mary B.; Burnham, Elizabeth, Gertrude, Addison, Dana, Marina,Otis(H.Park)

Appendix E:

Residents of Glen Echo and Cabin John in 1915

In 1915 Samuel Dean Caldwell, who lived on Old Georgetown Road in Bethesda and was head of the roads and highways committee of the local citizens' association, issued a *Directory of the Bethesda District* which included a map of the region "showing country between Washington City and the Rockville District" (see pages 302-3). Mr. Caldwell indicated black residents, about 15% of the total in the Glen Echo area, with an asterisk (*) and minors with an "x" and identified fifty-four neighborhoods.

Here is his list of the 292 residents of Glen Echo and Cabin John areas and others who lived near the river at that time. Note that there are discrepancies in who lived where because Caldwell did not recognize Cabin John as a jurisdiction or subdivision in his list. These are the pioneers.

Aldrich, Ernest Bruce	g.e.hts.
Aldrich, Josephine Riley (Mrs. E.B.)	
Arnold, Harry C.	g.e
Arnold, --- (Mrs. H.C.)	
Bateman, Joseph M.	g.e.
Baughan, Thomas Bird	River Rd
Baughan, Miss ---	
Beekman, Dr. D.D.	g.e.hts.
Beekman, Lora M. (Mrs. D.D.)	
Beekman, Helena T.	
Belt, Fenton D.	g.e.
Bender, Louis	g.e.hts.
Benson, Charles E. P.M.	g.e.
Bissell, Miss Georgia	g.e.
Bobinger, Mrs. Lulu	g.e.
Bobinger, George Jr.	
Bock, Frank A.	Conduit Rd
Bock, ---(Mrs. F.A.)	
Bock, Ruth x	
Boswell, Edward G.	g.e.
Boswell, Mary Ann (Mrs. E.G.)	
Boswell, Charles E.	
Boswell, Louis T. x	
Boswell, Edward x	
Boswell, Frank T.	g.e.
Boswell, Rebecca (Mrs. F.T.)	
Boswell, Walter F.	
Boswell, Oliver S.	g.e.
Boswell, ---(Mrs. O.S.)	
Boswick, Mart T.	g.e.
Boush, Mrs. J. L.	g.e.
Brown, Annie V.	g.e.
Carroll, Walter C.	g.e.
Carroll, L.H. (Mrs. W.C.)	
Carroll, Walter H.	g.e.
Carroll, Wilbur S. x	
*Carter, Isiah	g.e.
*Carter, John	g.e.

*Carter, Elizabeth (Mrs. J.)	
*Carter, Samuel	g.e.
Charles, R. A.	g.e.hts.
Christian, Miss Sarah g.e.	
*Cooper, Nelson	Conduit Rd.
*Cooper, ---(Mrs.N.)	
Crehan, John E.	Conduit Rd.
Crider, S. S.	g.e.
Crider, F. W. (Mrs.S.S.)	
Crider, Ira J. x	
Cuisan, Mrs. Mathilda	g.e.hts.
Denell, Wm. Thomas	g.e.
Denell, Clara May (Mrs.W.T.)	
Denell, Wm. Theodore	
Denell, Bernard E.	
Denell, Anna L. x	
Denell, Gertrude O. x	
Denell, Mary Ellen x	
De Witt, W. E.	g.e.hts.
De Witt, Mattie B. (Mrs. W.E.)	
*Diggs, Lucinda	g.e
*Diggs, Martha	River Rd.
Dresser, Walter David	g.e.hts.
Dresser, Janie E. (Mrs. W.D.)	
Dresser, Joseph R.	
Dresser, Wm. R. x	
Dresser, George R. x	
Dresser, James H. x	
Dresser, Walter D. Jr. x	
Dresser, Mrs. Kate L.	
Duke, Bernard A.	g.e.
Duke, Mary E. (Mrs. B.A.)	
Ehrmantraut, Joseph B.	g.e.hts.
Ehrmantraut, Reverta S. (Mrs.J.B.)	
Ehrmantraut, Catherine C.	
Ehrmantraut, Josephine C.	
Ehrmantraut, Charles A. x	
Ehrmantraut, William B. x	
Ehrmantraut, Harry S. x	
Embrey, Glenn	River Rd.

Embrey, ---(Mrs. G.)

Embrey, --- x

Embrey, --- x

Emery, James A.   Mohican Lodge

Emery, Emily Hartrick (Mrs. J.A.)

Emery, Mary x

Emery, Letitia x

Emery, Alice x

Evans, Charles   Wetzell Rd.

Evans, William

Gaines, Alices (Mrs. Jos.K.) g.e.

Garret, Richard Eugene   g.e.

Garrett, Bessie (Mrs. R.E.)

Garrett, Howard x

Garrett, H. Larue   g.e.

Goodfellow, Charles   g.e.

Gosline, James T.   Conduit Rd.

*Gray, Mrs. J. H.   g.e.

*Gray, Maria   g.e.

*Gray, John W.   g.e.

*Gray, Charles Daniel g.e.

Guinip, Gertrude   g.e.

Haase, Ida B.   Canal Rd.

Hall, John Wesley   g.e.hts.

Hall, Annie C. (Mrs. J.W.)

Hall, Emmet Campbell

Hall, Mrs. Ethel Glenn

Hancock, David W.   Rock Springs

Harbert, Lewis F.   g.e.

Harbert, William H.   g.e.

Harrell, Frank   River&Wilson

Harrell, Lena (Mrs. F.)

*Harris, Peter C.   Brooks Hill

*Harris, Stella (Mrs. P.C.)

*Harris, Charles

*Harris, Edward

*Harris, Susie

*Harris, Helen

*Harris, James A.

*Harris, Annie (Mrs. J.A.)

*Harrold, Robert C.   Conduit Rd.

*Hipkins, Moses   River Rd.

*Hipkins, Charlotte (Mrs. M.)

*Hipkins, Joseph William

*Hipkins, Lizzie

*Hipkins, Lulu

*Hipkins, Agnes

Hirons, Mrs. Maybelle Rawson g.e.

Houghton, Ernest D.   g.e.

Houghton, Maria A. (Mrs. E.D.)

Houghton, Buelah x

Houghton, David x

Houghton, Livingston   x

Houghton, Arthur J.   g.e.

Houghton, Minnie A. (Mrs. A.J.)

Houghton, George W.   g.e.

Houser, Mrs. M. A.   g.e.hts.

Hubbell, Julian B.   g.e.

Humphrey, H. B.   g.e.hts.

Humphrey, ---(Mrs. H.B.)

Humphrey, Llwelyn M. x

Humphrey, Robert R. x

Humphrey, Helen W. x

Humphrey, Isabel E. x

Humphrey, Harry B. x

Husband, John L. Sr.   g.e.

Husband, Annie R. (Mrs.J.L.)

Husband, John Leonard Jr.

Husband, Maurice Francis   g.e.

Husband, Bertha (Mrs. M.F.)

Husband, Cissel J.   g.e.

Husband, Roberta (Mrs. C.J.)

Husband, William Henry

Hutchins, Lee   g.e.

*Jones, Nathan   Conduit Rd.

King, Albert Charles   Canal Rd.

King, Herbert Canal Rd.

King, Walter   Canal Rd.

Lynch, John Sr.   Canal Rd.

Lynch, Annie M. (Mrs.J.Sr.)

Lynch, John E. Jr.   Canal Rd.

Lynch, William A.   Canal Rd.

Lynch, Charles T.   Canal Rd.

McMahon, John   g.e.

Magaha, Benj. W.   River Rd.

Magaha, Charles

Magaha, John Wesley

Magaha, Wallace

Magaha, W. B.

Magaha, Hattie

Magruder, William M. g.e.hts.

Magruder, Mary E. (Mrs.Wm.M.)

Magruder,Christie A.

Magruder, Clara A.

Magruder, Nettie

Magruder, William E. x

Magruder, Harry F. x

Matthews, George W.   River Rd.

Matthews, Clara (Mrs.G.W.)

Matthews, Harry

Matthews, Florence

Maurice, Mrs. ---   g.e.

Maurice, Dorothy

Maurice, --- x

Maurice, --- x

*Moore, John W.   g.e.

Moran, James A.   g.e.

Moran, Katherine (Mrs.J.A.)

Moran, James   x
Moran, Margaret, x
Moran, Roberta   x
Moran, Pauline   x
Moran, Lewis E.   g.e.
O'Connor, Michael B. Canal Rd.
O'Connor, Nora E. (Mrs. M.B.)
O'Donoghue, Timothy   g.e.
Ogle, Annie V.   g.e.
Orndorff, Wm. Maynard   g.e.hts.
Orndorff, Harriet L. (Mrs. W.M.)
Orndorff, John M.
Orndorff, Nellie B. (Mrs. J.M.)
Otterback, Ferdinand   River Rd.
Otterbach, James   River Rd.
Randalls, William   g.e.
Richmond, Marion B.   g.e.
Richmond, ---(Mrs. M.B.)
Rickenbacher, B. P.   g.e.hts.
Rickenbacher, Hattie E.(Mrs.B.P.)
Riley, Andrew Edward   g.e.
Riley, Samuel F.   g.e.
Riley, --- (Mrs. S.F.)
Riley, Edith   x
Riley, Elsie   x
Riley, Sarah F. (Mrs. J.D.)   g.e.
Riley, James Boyd   g.e.
Riley, --- (Mrs. J.B.)
Riley, Charles Edward
Riley, M. Irene
Roach, W. H.   g.e.
Roach, Hattie M. (mrs. W.H.)
Roach, W. S.
Roach, Roscoe McK.
Rowzee, John Porter Conduit Rd.
Rowzee, Minnie (Mrs. J.P.)
Rowzee, Porter   x
Seaton, Joseph H.   g.e.
Shaffer, Charles S.   g.e.
Shaffer, --- (Mrs. C.S.)
Shaffer, Cecelia   x
Smith, Charles H.   Conduit Rd.
Smith, Charles L.
*Smothers, George   River Rd.
*Smothers, Mary (Mrs. G.)
*Smothers, Joshue   x
*Smothers, Annie   x
*Smothers, Carrie   x
*Smothers, Moses   River Rd.
*Smothers, William   River Rd.
*Smothers, Iriving   River Rd.
*Smothers, --- (Mrs. I.)
Solberg, Thorvald   g.e.hts.
Solberg, Adelaide (Mrs. T.)

*Steward, Sylvester   Canal Rd.
*Steward, Walter   Canal Rd.
Taylor, Thomas   River Rd.
Thomas, William L.   River Rd.
Thomas, Annie B. (Mrs.W.L.)
Thomas, Ethel   x
Thomas, Glennon   x
Tompkins, Mrs. Mattie J.   g.e.
*Tony, Charles   g.e.
*Tony, --- (Mrs. C.)
Toone, Joseph E.Sr.   g.e.hts
       (423 G NW D.C.)
Toone, Rosa E. (Mrs.J.E.)
Toone, T. Frederick
Toone, Joseph E. Jr.
Toone, William George
Toone, Charles A. x
Toone, John J. x
Toone, Catherine L. x
Toone, Mary Ethel x
Toone, Earl C. x
Toone, Raymond F. x
Trainor, Emma   g.e.
Trammell, John L.   g.e.
Trammell, Josephine (Mrs.J.L.)
Trammell, John L. Jr.
Vervin, Gussie   g.e.hts.
Wade, Cleveland H.   g.e.
Walker, Joseph   g.e.
Ward, Mrs. Eliza   g.e.
Ward, Otho   g.e.
Ware, H. Perry   g.e.hts.
Ware, Katherine (Mrs.H.P.)
Ware, Michael   x
*Waynes, Benjamin   Conduit Rd.
*Waynes, --- (Mrs. B.)
Wear, Joseph James   River Rd.
Wear, --- (Mrs. J.J.)
Wear, Lydia x
Wear, Hoyt x
Wear, --- x
Wear, --- x
Weaver, Mrs. Alice   River Rd.
Weaver, William E.   g.e.
Willard, James Marlin   Canal Rd.
Willard, W. W.
Winslow, Charles A.   g.e.
Wolfman, Jacob   g.e.
Wolfman, Mollie M. (Mrs. J.)
Wolfman, Loraine x
Wolfman, Martin Carl x
Woodward, Maude B.(Mrs. F. L.)g.e.

Appendix F:

How to be a pinboy (non-league division):

The job went more or less like this. You walked down the gutters between your two alleys to the pits and half sat on the low wall between the alleys while the bowlers took off their shoes and filled out a score sheet. Everybody took a few practice shots, and if Mr. Hiser was not watching, even a few practice frames. Pins were reset during this warm-up phase on a casual basis and without much hurry, but once the bowlers were ready all that fun stopped and it became a job.

As soon as the first bowler finished, you hopped down into the pit and gathered up the three balls (remember this is duck pins not that big-ball-big-pins game for sissies, like playing softball). You put the balls up on the wooden track and gave them a shove and then bent down and picked up two handsfull of pins, usually three in one hand and two in the other, but it depended on how big your hands were. Then you put your foot on the metal treadle inset at the end of the alley. It poked up ten steel pins which fit into the holes in the bottom of the wooden bowling pins. (Except during league play in the evenings, Hiser used splintered, old pins, worn or even flat on one side, until somebody complained. Then the pin boy would take the lopsided pin to him and get a slightly better one from the big box by his desk.) You held the treadle down with your foot and grabbed up the rest of the duck pins; if you were good with your feet you could scoot them up where you could reach them. You set them up on the alley and then removed your foot carefully and hoped they stood. Sometimes a wise guy would ask you to re-spot them if a pin or two wandered too far. Other times a pin would fall and take down three or four others. Cursing was not considered good form although single-word expletives did not signify. The whole operation took about thirty seconds.

Then you leapt over the wall into the other pit and did the same thing on that side since by the time you set one alley the other bowler was usually finished unless there was "wood" to clean up between shots. Subconsciously you would count the balls rolled down the other alley as you set the pins, and if there was a long pause between shots the bowler would holler "wood" at you and wait. Only a jerk would bowl with fallen pins on the alley unless he was showing off or just playing around although some guys bowled with pins in the gutter which could lead to an exciting few moments as could bowlers who lofted the ball and scattered the pins explosively. Usually you could ignore the cries of "get the wood" until you finished setting the pins. Clearing wood also gave you a chance to rest and razz the bowlers or applaud your friends' good shots. Even when you set a few strings for strangers, you could do that.

After the third ball, it was back into the pit and do it again. Lift the balls, grab the pins, stomp your foot down, set 'em up, and move out. Most pin boys liked the youngsters who only knocked down two or three pins each time, but many preferred the bowlers who worked fast and piled up the strikes and spares. A lot of juvenile duckpin bowlers carried a ball in their other hand when they threw the first one and sometime would fire the second one before the first had bounced off the back cushion.

When the four or five bowlers finished, you might get a tip or two thrown down the gutters if they were strangers. If you were setting for friends, you walked up and took off your shoes and joined the bowlers while another of your buddies went to work in the pits. That way you could bowl for eleven cents a line instead of fifteen. Of course each time you started over, everybody had to warm up again.

For league play rather than semi-social situations, pin setting was serious business, and pin boys seldom had time to even see the bowlers in action much less banter with them. A setter who cleared wood without being prodded and who was fast and careful could make two or three times what the proprietor paid. And he earned it.

Appendix G:

Ed Stock Jr. on Victory Gardening in the Bethesda *Journal* 1943

Introduced by Mrs. Bradley as "our gardening editor" whose family had been in Bethesda since before World War I, Ed Stock began his series of weekly columns in mid-February with the hope that he was addressing serious people who would not waste seed or fertilizer. "So, let only those who are tempera- mentally fitted for this kind of gardening and who possess the proper soil and sun conditions for vegetable growing consider putting their valuable time and energy to work on Victory Gardens." He stated two questions for potential gardeners to ask themselves: are they willing to work three or four times a week when the weather gets hot, and "Have I a fairly level spot of ground in **full** sun...And is this soil a fair clay loam — not the sub-soil dug out of my basement?"

In his second column, Stock wrote of the need to lighten the local clay by working in three inches of humus and adding coarse builders' sand to especially heavy soils. The War Production Board made Victory Garden plant food (3-8-7) available, but Stock urged the use of natural fertilizers when possible as he noted that almost all area gardens would need nitrogen, potash, and phosphate. He summarized: "If you are digging up a piece of your back lawn that has always grown good grass you will probably need the following materials per 100 square feet:
1/2 cubic yard (11 bushels) stable manure
1/2 cubic yard coarse sand
4 pounds poultry manure
2 pounds 0-14-7 fertilizer
5 pounds dolomitic limestone.
"Now we come to your first test as a gardener," wrote Stock on March 5, "the back-breaking job of soil preparation. If you are fortunate enough to have a place large enough to plow, your job is much lighter; if it must be hand dug, it is just plain labor. In either case the job must be done thoroughly and to a good depth." He reminded his readers to make a humus application first and then to dig that in as the soil was turned over to a depth of about 12 inches. "Right now, today, is when it should be done so that the late freezing and thawing will 'mellow' the soil. If it cannot be done before March 15 be sure that the soil is not wet when it is worked or the soil will harden and cake, making it very difficult to secure a good seed bed." By the end of March, he advised, the seed bed should be ready and fertilizer and limestone applied. "When finished the garden should be fairly level and should have a smooth, well granulated surface."

Next Stock produced four criteria for choosing what to plant: 1)most nutrition per unit of area planted, 2)crops easy to grow in our soil, 3)small space requirements, and 4)plants that have few pests. "Vegetable crops that meet all these standards, or nearly meet them, will include the following: Beans, cabbage, chard, kale, leaf lettuce, peas, spinach, tomatoes, turnips, Brussels sprouts, salisfy and endive." His reason for leaving off root crops such as carrots and beets was our heavy soil, and Stock urged adding lots of sand or sifted ashes to rows where those seeds were sown but recommended against such experimentation. The reason onions were missing had to do with a shortage of seeds and sets. "We had better leave the production of this crop to the specialists," he wrote, and corn and potatoes need more room than most back-yard gardeners had. Concentrate on high food value plants, he urged,

but "don't deny yourself a row of radishes or parsley or some other vegetable you especially like."

The next week the *Journal* printed a when-to-plant chart with other advice. "Don't rush your gardening...Frequently plantings made a little on the late side catch up and pass those that are planted too early." Stock recommended making a map of the garden and emphasized "Don't waste your seeds!" He warned against sowing seed too thickly and suggested mixing small seeds with dry sand before sowing them. Covering the seed and firming the soil over them were described with a warning that "firming does not mean pounding."

In early April, Ed Stock, now County Victory Garden chairman, suggested planting some rhubarb and strawberries and reminded his gardeners that they did not have to prepare the whole garden at once. By mid-April he had given directions for planting about half of a thirty by fifty foot garden and added that "a row or two of zinnias, marigolds or calendulas in your 'Victory Garden' are not inappropriate. With a gay dining room table you may forget there isn't any steak to eat."

On April 30 Stock wrote "Well, gardeners, the lid is off. By now we are fairly safe in planting anything." He suggested some more staggered vegetable plantings and that his fans hold off until May to put in more lima beans, tomatoes, eggplant, cauliflower, or peppers. He then turned to fertilizing with the approved 3-7-8 material and spraying or dusting using Pyrethrum and nicotine sulfate. He suggested dusting plants in the morning when the dew would act as a sticking agent. In discussing fungus and bacterial diseases, Stock emphasized the importance of weeding and thinning to produce healthy plants as well as the need to plant the right things at the right time.

By the end of May the column reached transplanting which Ed Stock called "probably the most difficult of all gardening operations." He emphasized the need to protect and harden seedlings produced in a cold frame, but if young plants were purchased, suggested getting them in the afternoon and planting them in the evening, or a cloudy or even rainy day if possible. Wrap the stem with newspaper, he wrote, and dig a hole big enough for the roots to hang down in. After the soil has been firmed around the plants and they have been watered "shade with a berry box, large flower pot, newspaper tents or any other device that will keep the hot sun and drying wind off the plants for a few days, or until they look turgid and established." And avoid fertilizer when transplanting, he warned.

The first column in June was about supporting and training plants such as tomatoes and pole beans. Stock suggested using "rough branches with the stubs left on" for beans but also described two types of trellises that could be used. For tomatoes he explained the single stem method as well as training the multiple stem plants. He suggested using strips of cloth or twine to tie the plants loosely to the stakes by looping under a leaf stem opposite the support. The next week Stock wrote a review column explaining ways to detect problems by examining early crops. He stated that most area gardens could probably use more humus before "succession crops' were planted.

"Remember, most of us are just beginning as gardeners and we are beginning on new and not well prepared soil. The results so far should not be amazing. We are learning this year; so let's profit by out mistakes and not get discouraged because John Smith, an old hand at gardening, has tomatoes before we do." Stock urged keeping a garden diary "and put everything into it. It will be wonderful winter reading and your mistakes of this year can be

750

avoided next year." Then he suggested that they start seeds for late plantings of broccoli, cauliflower, and cabbage.

By late June there was a column on the importance of thinning crops and picking things when they were ripe and in "prime condition." He also urged his readers to learn the water bath method of canning and various means of drying their crops. "Are you replanting crops where harvested crops have been removed?" he asked. He suggested rotating crops, root crops followed by leaf crops, and covering seed with sand because our soil tends to "crust and bake" in the hot weather. He added a slogan: "Keep'em hoeing, keep 'em growing, keep the Victory Gardens going."

Dry, hot weather brought problems in July. In tomatoes it was "blossom end rot" and in squash, plants that would flower but not set fruit. For both Stock prescribed irrigation until we got a good rain. He emphasized again the need to regularly spray or dust to keep down the Japanese beetles and other insect pests, and suggested that seeds be planted a little deeper and the row left a little hollow in the dry weather. Perhaps because it was so hot, Stock asked his gardeners to consider the winter use of their land and to begin planning for their late crops on part of their land and a cover of "green manure" on the rest.

Another July column centered on what Stock had learned from judging Victory Garden contests. Good planning and hard work were the unsurprising keys, he wrote. In one sideyard he found a 10 by 30 foot garden with beets, pole beans, tomatoes, lettuce and even a block of corn on one end. Even though it was shaded by the house "every vegetable in it was growing to perfection" because of good planning and soil preparation. In the last July essay he discussed three kinds of tomato wilt: physiological, which can be treated with mulching and watering, and fusarium and bacterial, which are very serious. Stock warned that if a cut stem showed a dark brown or black and slimy discoloration then the plants must be removed and burned and the soil sterilized before tomatoes can be grown there again.

The drought continued into August, and Stock's columns dealt with the need to mulch and hoe out the weeds. On August 13 he warned that the "rain will come eventually and when it does be ready for it." Hoeing out trenches between the rows and keeping the soil loose were suggested. "Have your seed ready," he wrote. He then produced a column on lawn care that seemed to conclude that crab grass in the summer and rye in the winter was probably the most reasonable compromise for our climate and soil. By the end of August he was explaining the need and methods for watering trees and shrubbery.

In September it finally rained, and Stock wrote that it was time to either rake out the garden and plant rye or save what the drought spared and plant some "turnips, spinach, kale, lettuce and radishes, of course. This is a good season for gardening; the insects are disappearing, it's cooler to work, plants make a sturdier growth — and we may get some rain." The next two columns were on the importance of humus. "To accomplish anything in horticulture the humus lesson must be learned," wrote Stock as he neared the end of the series of articles. In the final column he urged his readers to "clean up your garden before winter! That's almost like saying be sure to take a bath every Saturday Night — it's just good sanitation." After the poles and plant stems were removed, Stock advised raking and then sowing rye grass at 2 1/2 pounds per 1000 square feet. This could be done until the end of November, he wrote. He then gave advice on planting small fruits and fruit trees and on digging asparagus beds and using mulch for protection.

From The Bethesda *Journal*, Feb. 19, 1943, to Oct. 29, 1943

Appendix H:

Milestones in the building of Bethesda:

1820 - Presbyterians erect Bethesda meeting house, 1850 build second church after fire.
1829 - Turnpike (tollroad) from Georgetown to Frederick put in operation.
1862 - Darcy's Store becomes the first post office.
1871 - Post office renamed "Bethesda."
1874 - St. John's, Norwood Parish, Episcopal church founded; Grange Hall opens.
1878 - Bethesda Election District, 7th, created.
1889 - Alfred Wilson opens general store at toll gate site.
1891 - Electric railroad reaches town for the first time; Beth. Park and subdivisions follow.
1894 - First real school house since Civil War opens at Gingell's Curve.
1897 - USDA experiment station opens. (closed 1937)
1901 - Bethesda Land Co. files plat on Alta Vista.
1905 - New school opens on Wilson Lane with Masonic Lodge upstairs.
1906 - Newcomb Club founded.
1910 - B&O finally reaches Bethesda. W. E. Perry and Herbert Wilson open their stores.
1913 - Walter Tuckerman and family arrive to develop Edgemoor.
1914 - Bradley Hills development and trolley line open.
1916 - Methodist Church built in Woodmont. Imirie brothers go into garage business.
1918 - Northwest Park and Oakmont incorporated. (WSSC founded.)
1919 - Tuckerman, Stock, et al. start Bank of Bethesda.
1920 - Edgemoor tennis club organized. Census: 4,800.
1922 - Woodmont Country Club opens. Battery Park developed by Maddox and Marshall.
1924 - Community Store (Brown's) opens.
1925 - Bethesda school expanded to K-8. M. and R. B. Warren build first shopping strip.
1926 - Bank of Bethesda's new building opens. Chamber of Commerce organized and BVFD begins
1927/29/36 - Wisconsin Ave. paved (west/east/all after end of trolley).
1927 - M-NCP&P Commission established. Kenwood platted by Kennedy and Chamberlin
1928 - Tuckerman's and Sack's rows finished. B-CC Jr-Sr HS opens in Leland.
1928 - Western Suburban District created; Commissioner Dr. Benjamin Perry at County Building.
1929 - National Women's CC, Montgomery Players founded. Madonna of the Trail dedicated
1930 - First traffic light installed. Census: Bethesda has 12,000 of County's 40,000
1931 - Broadhursts take over Community P&H. Baptist Home for Children opens.
1932 - Farm Women's Market opens.
1933 - Rotary Club organized.
1934 - Lutheran mission opens. Landon School moves to McLean estate
1934 - Baptist church organized after earlier meetings.
1935 - New high school opens on East West Hyway. Trolley line closed by merged Capital Transit
1937 - Shopping center opens at Leland Street. W. P. Allen begins publishing *Tribune*.
1938 - NIH on Wilson's land, Boro/Bethesda Theater, "dime" store and new post office open.
1939 - *Journal*, second paper. Two fire departments compete. Recreation Center dedicated.
1940 - Public Library, Gifford's, Carbert's, Hot Shoppe open. Census: 26,000, County 80,000.
1941 - Several new churches opened. High school fire set by arsonist.
1942 - Naval Hospital, Jelleff's and Palais Royal open. Bradley Boulevard apartments built.
1943 - Suburban Hospital built. USO and Thrift Shop begin operation.
1944 - Malcolm Scates, Lansburgh's furniture open. Jim McAuliffe promoted to captain.
1945 - Dunnington revives First Aid Corps; Jimmy Devereux welcomed home

Appendix I:

Rocky Mountain Spotted Tick Fever

Tick fever was probably a very old Western Hemisphere disease, but cases were generally diagnosed as typhus, dengue fever or even measles until the 20th century. Lumbering operations in the Bitterroot Valley of Montana led to rapid population growth in that area in the 1880's and the call for medical help after outbreaks of smallpox, typhoid, diphtheria, tuberculosis and of the spotted or black fever which caused numerous deaths each spring.

Its symptoms: general malaise followed by terrible headaches and pain in the back and joints. High fevers, stiff necks and light sensitive eyes were common. Delirium was often reported, and capillary hemorrhages caused spots on wrists and ankles that spread to the whole body, even to the palms of the hands and soles of the feet. Most patients recovered in about two weeks, but about twenty percent died of the infection and in a few "fulminant" cases the microbe *Rickettsia rickettsii* killed before the rash appeared. The fever was particularly hard on those over forty, and for some reason the death rate was much higher along the Bitterroot.

The Montana Board of Health funded an investigation beginning in 1902 that led to Howard Taylor Ricketts' discovery of tick transmission by 1909. After failed attempts at tick eradication and much more research by both the State and the U. S. Public Health Service during which three lab workers died of the disease, Dr. Roscoe R. Spencer and entomologist Ralph R. Parker developed an effective vaccine in 1924-25. They produced their vaccine by grinding up infected ticks which they raised in captivity, obviously a potentially dangerous process. After trying it on guinea pigs, Dr. Spencer inoculated himself with "tick juice" in 1924.

By 1926, 600 people received the shots, and the supply of vaccine the Public Health Service could produce was exhausted. In 1928 Montana built a vaccine laboratory in Hamilton which was surrounded by a moat, but the Federally funded production was limited and expensive. Only twenty-five liters of the vaccine were available in 1929, but by 1935 the lab produced more than 300 liters. At first only residents of the Rocky Mountain states were offered the vaccine, but the development of CCC camps and the diagnosis of the disease in the Middle Atlantic area after an outbreak in the Virginia and Maryland suburbs of Washington, D. C., led to much greater demand than there was supply.

The infusion of Social Security funds into Public Health work made more research possible, and in 1937 microbiologist Herald R. Cox revolutionized vaccine production by growing the microbe in the yoke sacs of fertile hens' eggs. The NIH, newly ensconced in Bethesda, sent out a man to investigate, found that Cox had done what he claimed, and the new vaccine was perfected by the Infectious Diseases Division and ready for human testing in 1940. While they did not prevent the disease, both vaccines greatly lessened its effects and cut the death rate to about five percent. The Rocky Mountain Laboratory produced large quantities of spotted fever, yellow fever and typhus vaccines during World War II.

See *Rocky Mountain Spotted Fever* by the NIH's Victoria A. Harden, 1990.

Appendix J:

Acronyms, initials, abbreviations and slang:
(note in modern usage many of these have lost their periods)

A.A.U. - Amateur Athletic Union, especially in high school girls' sports

A.F. and A. M. - the Masons, Bethesda Lodge No. 204

A.M.E. - American Methodist Episcopal, African-American churches

AMS - Army Map Service, now Defense Mapping Agency

Barons - B-CC HS teams since 1940 (earlier City Slickers and Highwaymen)

B&O - the railroad, Baltimore and Ohio, a political force as well

B-CC - more usually B.C.C.H.S. at the time of this study, the public high school

Big Train, Barney - Walter Johnson of baseball's Hall of Fame

bobby soxer - female adolescent in the 1940s, fan of Sinatra, Haymes et al.

BOE - the school board, appointed at the time of this study

bottleneck - Wisconsin Ave. (355) narrowing at the Bank of Bethesda

Brown's - the Community Store on Old Georgetown at Greentree

B.S. - Blessed Sacrament, the parish, the church, the school (Shrine of the)

Bulge - Battle of the, Dec.`44, German offensive in the Ardennes

buzz bomb - V-1, German pulse-jet, pilotless, winged bomb of 1944-45

CAA- Civil Aeronautics Authority, established 1938

Call Carl - a string of garages and service stations operated by the Carls

C&0 - the canal, the Chesapeake and Ohio, which did not get to either

C.B.I. - the China-Burma-India theater of operations in WWII

C.C.C. - Civilian Conservation Corps (Reforestation Relief Act 1933)

CCDC - Citizens' Committee to Defeat the Charter in 1944

CCFAC - Dunnington's First Aid Corps, predecessor of the B-CC Rescue Squad

CCLCo - the Land Company of Newlands, Stewart et al. in Chevy Chase

CD - Civil Defense, see OCD

Charter - document describing County home rule

Chevy - the Club, the Chevy Chase Club

C.H.S. - the Columbia Historical Society, see HSW

CJVFD - Cabin John Volunteer Fire Department

C.O. or CO - commanding officer

C.S.A. - the Confederacy with its second capital at Richmond

C.T.C. - Capital Traction or Capital Transit, the trolley line and bus company

D.A.R. - Daughters of the American Revolution

D.C - Washington, D.C., also the District, downtown

D-Day - originally the date planned, now June 6, 1944, Normandy invasion

D.G.S. - District Grocery Stores, purchasing co-op of small D.C.-area groceries

District Line - usually Wisconsin and Western in this study

dogface - infantryman, G.I.

ETO - European Theater of Operations in WWII

DTMB - David Taylor Model Basin, see T.M.B, now DTRD (Research and Development)

F.E.P.C. - Fair Employment Practice Commission, `41, to curb discrimination

FHA - insurer of home loans since 1934

flattop - aircraft carrier (also Dick Tracy character)

flats - Miller's Flats between the B&O tracks and Leland Street W of Wisc. Ave.

FOI - Freedom of Information, an act to grant access to gov't. records, theoretically

Fusion - anti-Lee forces who won control of County in 1934

FWA - Federal Works Agency set up in `39 reorganization

FWM - Farm Women's Co-operative Market

gate - a hep-cat, one who swings

G.A.R. - Union Civil War veterans, the Grand Army of the Republic

G&T - a trolley line from Georgetown to Tenleytown

GEVFD - Glen Echo Volunteer Fire Department
GI - government issue, a soldier, a serviceman or, less often, service woman
G.P.O. - the Government Printing Office
HA - Navy rank, hospital apprentice, corpsman-to-be
Hatched - kept from partisan political activity or office by Hatch Act, 1939
hollow - Glen Cove area off River Road
HS - high school
HSW - The Historical Society of Washington, D.C. (former CHS)
IAABO - the basketball officials' association
Ice Palace - on Conn. at Albemarle, now a shopping center
I.R.S. - hasn't changed, the tax people of the Federal government
island hopping - Allied strategy in the Pacific in WWII
JHS - junior high school
JP - justice of the peace, lowest court level in old judicial system
kia - killed in action
Land Company - the Chevy Chase Land Company
the Lake - Chevy Chase Lake which is no more, the reference remains
L.S./M.F.T. - Lucky Strike Means Fine Tobacco ad slogan
LWV - the League of Women Voters, a voice for reform in the 1940s
Manhattan Project (Engineer District) - development of the atomic bomb
MDW - Military District of Washington
M-NCP&PC - Park and Planning, named like D.C.'s National Capital P&PC
N.I.H. - the National Institutes of Health, often the Cancer Institute
NNMC - the Bethesda Naval Hospital (National Medical Center)
N.R.A. - N.I.R.A., Blue Eagle, New Deal's National (Industrial) Recovery Act of 1933
NRHS - National Railway Historical Society, Inc.
N.T.S. - National Training School, a D.C. "reform" school
OCD - Office of Civil Defense, `42, under LaGuardia, in Bethesda under Brault
O.C.S. - Officers' Candidate School produced Army's 90-day wonders, 2nd Lts.
ODT - Office of Defense Transportation, estab. Dec. 1941
OG - Operational Group in the OSS
OPA - Office of Price Administration, rationed commodities, controlled prices
OLOL - informal reference to Our Lady of Lourdes church and school
OSS - Office of Strategic Services, spies, analysis and dirty tricks
O.U.A.M. - Order of United American Mechanics, the "Juniors" in Cabin John
O.W.I - Elmer Davis's Office of War Information (propaganda)
OWM - Office of War Mobilization (of government agencies' activities)
PAT - point after touchdown in football
patch - scrubby, overgrown, wooded area in Woodmont
PCC - President's Conference Car, the streamlined streetcars circa 1941
PE - gym class
PEPCo - the local electric company, Potomac Electric Power
POW - prisoner of war
PTA - never with periods, the Home and School Association descendant
PUC - Public Utilities Commission, rate setter among other things
P.W.A. - Works Projects Admin. helped build B-CC HS, new post office
Rec Center - the B-CC Recreation Center at the end of Norwood Drive
red barn - the Roadside Theater near Garrett Park on the Offutt place
Rosemary - the informal name for Chevy Chase Elementary
ROTC - Reserve Officers Training Corps, college Army training program
Sanitary Commission - WSSC
scuttlebutt - rumors and "the word," of naval origin
SEC - the Securities and Exchange Commission
Seventh District - Bethesda election district still
Shopping Center - the one at Leland and Wisconsin built by Hawley

Southern Society - a high school fraternity or secret society
SPARS - *Semper Paratus* Always Ready Service, women in the Coast Guard
swabjockey - sailor
T&R - a continuation of the G&T through Bethesda to Rockville, the streetcar
stag or drag - alone or with a date
Star Trophy - Kuhn Cup - for contribution to the community
Star Tourney - high school metro-area basketball championship
T.M.B. - the usual abbreviation for the David Taylor Model Basin, also DTMB
Triangle - the Woodmont area, or Mudmont as some inhabitants called it
U-boat - German submarine
U.D.C. - United Daughters of the Confederacy
U.M.W.A. - the United Mine Workers
United Democratic Organization - the public face of the Lee machine
USDA - the Department of Agriculture
USO - Bethesda's canteen for enlisted men, the United Service Organization
VD - venereal diseases
V-E Day - the end of the WWII in Europe - 8 May 1945
VFD - as a suffix, as in GEVFD, a volunteer fire department
VFW - Veterans of Foreign Wars organization
viaduct - B&O bridge over Bradley Blvd., probably designed by T. E. Hampton
V-J Day - the end of WWII against Japan - 15 August 1945
VMI - Virginia Military Institute, a college
WAACS, WACS - Women's (Auxiliary) Army Corps
WAVES - Women Appointed for Voluntary Emergency Service (US Navy)
W.C.T.U. - Women's Christian Temperance Union, powerful prohibitionists
WPB - War Production Board, controlled U.S. industry in WWII
W.P.A. - Works Progress Administration (1934) hired the unemployed
WR&ECo - the Washington Railway and Electric Company - (wreck-o)
WRECo - the trolley line to Glen Echo, a conglomerate, see WR&ECo
W.S.S.C. - the Sanitary Commission providing water and sewer connections
W.W.& G.F. - West Washington and Great Falls trolley line - to Glen Echo
WWI - the Great War, the War to End All Wars, 1914-18
WWII - "the war"
Yellowjackets - nickname of Leland JHS teams from the 1940s on
zoot suit - pleated and pegged pants with long jacket, perhaps Hispanic origin

Appendix K:

Roll of Honor - a list of the men from the Bethesda area who died in the service during the Second World War, based on reports made in local newspapers

Adams, Lt. (jg) Randal, killed while on carrier in Pacific Jan. `44, Fork Union, Duke grad, mother former Woman's Club of CC president

Adams, Sgt. Stephen, died in Hellcat crash in Bahamas, Central HS football and track, GWU, lived on Maple Ridge Road

Amussen, Lt. (jg) John Russell, killed in Calif. plane crash after winning Navy Cross, Landon grad, wife, baby, and mother in Kenwood

Bachman, Capt. Carl, MC, killed on Iwo Jima, from Minn., widow and 18-mo.-old daughter on Chevy Chase Drive

Barton, Lt. (jg) Robert, pilot, died in bomb explosion on *Hancock*, voted best personality B-CC `41, had three kills

Bell, Sgt. Richard, wounded Aug. `44, kia March `45 in ETO, on Rec Center football team, married in England

Benjamin, Pfc. Llewellyn Lee, 18, MC, killed on Peleliu Sept. `44, B-CC grad at 16 `42, father White House policeman

Bernard, Lt. Merrill Jr., AAF, died in Calif. bomber crash Oct. `43, lived on Glenwood Rd.,

Bort, Sgt. Harry Jr., 27, died in Italy March `44, Leland grad., *Star* carrier, worked at Tastee Diner, lived on Cordell

Bradley, Chief Gunners Mate Charles, 31, CG, died in sinking of escort *Leopold* March `43, D.C. policeman, left widow and daughter

Brown, Sgt. Ralph W., 22, killed in Germany in Dec. `44, educated in Mass., lived on Spring St., Chevy Chase

Buchanan, Cpl. Eldred, killed in Italy July `44, active in sports, drum major at Massanutten

Cady, Major Richard, 35, died in N. Africa in Jan. `43, with Geo. Survey since 1930, widow and two sons in Wood Acres

Canfield, Maj. Robert, shot down over Germany in Aug. `43, lived on Aberdeen Rd., Skeet Club member

Carlin, Sgt. Andrew, 27, AAF, kia Mediterranean area July `44, Navy draftsman at Carderock, had wife and daughter

Carpenter, Pvt. Collier, 20, MC, bazooka gunner, killed on Saipan June `44, left B-CC to enlist, one of Bender's right-hand men

Coleman, Sgt. Frank, 20, in B-17 crash in Iowa, B-CC, Columbia U., lived on Chatham Rd., Chevy Chase

Conrad, Capt. Doyle, 31, 29th Division, killed in France August `44, WSSC employee, nephew of Glen Echo McCuens

Corpening, Lt. (jg) Max, killed in plane crash May `44, Lehigh senior, in Canadian army before joining USN, lived on Murray Rd., CC

Dean, S/Sgt. Harry, kia Okinawa May `45, GEVFD employee, wife worked at Bell Laundry and lived with Mrs. Fahrenwald (see below)

DeVane, Lt. Enoch, MC, in Florida plane crash in Sept. `43, B-CC grad `39 "a
    quiet, serious redhead"
Dixon, Lt. Cmdr. Lewis, on minelayer *Niantonomah*, lost off France, had been
    Merchant Marine, active in Exeter Rd. citizens' assn.
Donaldson, Chase, 19, 84th Inf, 9th Army, died Apr. `45 in Germany, father
    pres. of Briggs Clarifier
Dorroh, George, died in Ky. of spinal meningitis `43, in Signal Corps, B-CC
    `43, known for clothes and pipe collection
Dowling, First Officer Noble Jr., 48, in merchant Marine 22 years, lost in sinking
    in early 1942
Draper, Lt. Norman, Navy pilot, killed in action Dec. `44
Duvall, Lt. William G., MC, plane exploded over Gulf of Mexico, B-CC grad
Eisenman, Lt. David, 22, AAF, bombardier, killed in collision of two B-17s
    over Germany on 40th mission, Wilson grad, worked for Hecht Co.
Fahrenwald, Pvt. Frank, 20, MC, n Sept. `42 on Guadalcanal, asst. pro at
    Kenwood, first County casualty
Fulks, Lt. John, senior B-24 pilot, kia over Austria Apr.`44, B-CC `38, *Tattler* staff,
    lived on St. Elmo, widow from HS homeroom, daughter
Garvin, Lt. Robert, 19, AAF, died in bomber crash in Ala, B-CC `43 on
    basketball team, active in Presby. Church, lived on Old G'town Rd.
Gibson, Pvt. Raymond, 24, killed in training accident in Tenn., Central HS
    basketball player, *Post* employee, lived on Fairfax Rd.
Grace, Lt. Cmdr. Edward Thomas, kia March `45 as CO of destroyer
    Halligan off Okinawa, parents lived on S. Chelsea Lane
Graham, S/2 William S., 20, in April `44 plane crash, B-CC pianist, Lehigh
    on scholarship, V-12 at Columbia
Guckeyson, Bill, AAF, P-47 pilot, outstanding student-athlete at B-CC `35, U.
    of Md. and West Point, mia over Germany in June 1944
Gurley, Robert, USN, in airplane accident Oct. `43, B-CC `42, remembered for his
    sax and love of jive
Gutheridge, CG radio tech Boyce, in Jan. `45 explosion of ammo ship, B-CC grad,
    both grew up at Baptist Home where mother worked
Gutheridge, MC Lt. Kenton, in Fla. plane crash in May `43, first B-CC HS grad
    killed, married one week to Florida girl
Halvorsen, MC Lt. Harold, 36, in 1942 plane crash, widow and three
    children on Del Ray in Woodmont
Hanson, Cmdr. Malcolm, 47, in Alaskan plane accident Aug. `42, Adm. Byrd's
    radio engineer, lived on Langdrum Lane with wife and five children
Harper, Lt. Cmdr. John D. Jr., lost on submarine *Shark*, wife and baby son
    with mother on Greentree Rd.
Henderson, Dr. Richard G., 32, PHS, died seeking vaccine for scrub typhus
    at NIH, wife and two children on Cedar Lane
Hollander, Pvt. Donald, 18, kia near Saarsbourgh, France, March `45,
    B-CC `44, in Army 6 mo., parents lived on Sleaford Place
Hoover, Lt. Woodward, 24, kia in Belgium Dec. `44 with 2nd Armored Div.,
    Friends grad, wife on Greenvale Rd., CC; parents on Glenbrook

Hudson, Pvt. James, 25, killed in Italy Sept. `44, on his birthday, mechanic in Bethesda, with a widow

Huntt, Pvt. Willard McC., 104th Div., killed near Leipzig Apr. 13 `45, B-CC grad., on baseball team, lived on Bradley Blvd.

Jackson, Pvt. George (Jack), 22, kia in Germany March `45, B-CC grad, worked at Cancer Institute, lived on W. Va. Ave.

Jackson, Sgt. Hugh, 9th Army, killed in action, widow and baby on Wilson La.

Jamison, Lt. William, 23, Air Transport Command, killed in CBI summer of `44, lived on Georgia St., Chevy Chase

Jennings, Cpl. William, 20, died of polio in Ariz., B-17 gunner, B-CC grad after enlisted in `43, won Soapbox Derby in `40, lived on Elgin Lane

Johnson, John W. Jr., 506th Parachute, killed in Belgium Dec. `44, lived in Glen Echo Heights,

Karr, Lt. (jg) Roger, Hellcat pilot on *Hornet*, long reported missing, wife and baby on Montgomery Lane

Kehoe, T/Sgt. Richard, AAF, killed on 44th B-24 mission in Aug. `44, B-CC grad, jazz drummer, lived on Moorland Lane

Kemeys, Pvt. Edward, MC, killed at Tulagi in Jan. `44, B-CC `42, first high school grad killed in action, from Garrett Park

Kiehl, Capt. Elmer, kia while commanding transport ship in Pacific, USNA 1920, lived on Hampden Lane, sons at Annapolis and Wilson

Kinsella, Lt. Kenneth, 8th AF navigator, missing over Germany on eighth mission, B-CC grad `38, high school singer, left wife and son

Koehler, Lt. Col. Elmer, 7th Army Field Artillery, kia, West Point `35, wife and son on Sleaford Rd.

Ligon, Lt. John, Jr., 25, co-pilot in Florida plane crash, B-CC `36, on Tattler and Pine Tree

Littlehales, Ensign James H., in patrol bomber crash off Florida in Nov. `42, D.C.schools, U.of Va., engaged, lived in Edgemoor

Loveland, Pvt. Frederick, killed in France Sept. `44

Loveland, Cpl. Raymond, killed on maneuvers in Ga. - brother Wilbur on Chestnut St. in Navy, another brother in AAF, sister in WAVES.

Lumsden, Pvt. William, 29th Inf., killed at St. Lo July `44, florist, family on West Glenbrook Rd., widow in Arlington

Magee, Ensign Adlai, died in plane accident in Florida in Oct. `43, lived on Leland St., Chevy Chase

Masincupp. Radioman 3/c Byron, lost with sub *Shark* in Nov. `44, B-CC `40, worked at Army Map Service, lived on East Ave., Chevy Chase

McKee, Lt. Robert, 23, 3rd Armored of 1st Army, kia in Germany Nov. `44, battlefield promoted, capt. of U.of Md. cadets, Andover Rd. CC

Mobley, Seaman 2/c Howard Jr., 20, died of wounds in Asian Theater of Operations, B-CC `43, "Vic" to friends

Murphy, T/Sgt. Richard, MC combat correspondent, family lived on Woodbine Street

Miller, Pfc. William G, died in Italy with the 87th, long report mia, lived on Battery Lane

Newbold, Lt. William, killed in Calif. accident July `44, Cornell, widow in
  D.C., father Glenbrook Village developer

Oliver, Ensign James Lee, 21, died in training plane crash in Calif. June `44, in
  G'Town foreign service school, lived on Cumberland Ave., CC

Perkins, Lt. George, 20, MC, in plane crash in Jacksonville May `43, Landon and
  Swathmore student

Phelps, Sgt. Frederick, 20, AAF B-25 gunner, killed over India June `44,
  McKinley HS grad, 2 bro, sister in service, Spring St., Chevy Chase

Porter, Lt. Edward, 21, AAF, B-17 co-pilot, B-CC `42, at GU when joined up,
  lived Johnson Ave., mother at Cancer Insti.

Robbins, Lt. Donald, 28, in accident at Fort Bliss, Texas, June `42, lived on N.
  Chelsea Lane

Robertson, Lt. Sam Jr., 5th Marine Div., kia on Iwo Jima Feb. `45, Md. grad. `40,
  engineer, lived on Fairmont Ave.

Ruebsam, Lt. Robert, AAF, in Oklahoma plane crash, B-CC `36, parents ran
  Wayside Shop

Sanderson, Seaman 1/c Fred, 18, dive bomber gunner killed in Fla. crash
  May `45, 3 letter man at Landon `44, lived on Chamberlin, Kenwood

Sanford, Pfc. Raymond, 21, kia June 9 `44 in invasion of France, 116th Inf, B-
  CC `41 basketball, *Pine Tree*, Va. Poly, 46th Street CC

Schmitt, Capt. Edwin, MC, 25, Wilson, U.of Md., widow in Baltimore, family
  on Ridgewood Ave., CC

Searby, Brig. Gen. Edmund, 48, killed in France Sept. `44, on Gen. McNair's
  staff, lived on Battery Lane

Shepard, Pfc. Walter, 21, kia in Italy July `44, B-CC `42, rode motorcycle
  to school, horse crazy, lived on Cumberland St., Chevy Chase

Shultz, Capt. William, 25, killed in Belgium in Dec. `44, lived on Brookeville
  Rd., wife and daughter in Tenn.

Simpson, Col. John G., 32, AAF, killed in action over Paris, McKinley and
  U.of Md. grad, FBI, widow and son on Kensington Parkway

Smith, Lt. Robert B. Jr., 24, AAF, plane crashed in Med. on 46th mission, Wilson
  and Nat. Univ. Law, lived on Albemarle St., Westmoreland

Sorrell, MC Pvt. Hardy, 19, killed on Guam in August `44, in B-CC class of `44,
  two brothers in Europe, home on Park Ave., Crestview

Stephens, Pvt. Henry, member of "lost battalion," kia Nov. `44, lived on
  Wisconsin Ave., has wife and two children in N. Carolina

Stone, Pvt. Frank P., 19, kia on Okinawa June `45, Fork Union grad,
  grandson of Lily Stone, lived on Glenmore

Syme, Maj. Samuel, 42, died in Dec. `44 on Patton's staff, D.C. lawyer, widow
  and son on 45th St., Chevy Chase

Taylor, Pvt. Sherman, 19, in Canadian Princess Pat Inf., 8th Army, kia in Italy
  May `44, Wilson HS, volunteered as senior, lived on Bradley Blvd.

Tompkins, Maj. William, 24, led heavy pontoon battalion, kia in Germany
  March `45, B-CC and Tulane, second son killed in war

Trimble, James, 3rd Marine Div., kia Iwo Jima Feb. `45, St. Albans and Duke,
  pitcher of note, mother Mrs. Sewell on Beverly Rd.

Walsh, Capt. David E., died in jeep accident in France in Oct. `45, in Army since `42, lived on Strathmore Street

Watkins, Lt. William R., 20, 8th AF fighter pilot, killed in crash in England, enlisted while at McKinley HS, family in Brookmont

Wheeler, Capt. Albert, 46, WWI vet, Army Med Corps in France, on Dr. Hospital staff, sister on Northfield

Wheeler, Lt. Stafford, kia by mine in Yugoslavia in Apr. `45, left Harvard Med School for Navy in `42

Wilcox, Rear Adm. John. lost overboard in heavy weather Apr. `42, USNA football and wrestling, WWI vet, lived on Kennedy Drive, CC

Wilson, Lt. Russell, USN, died in plane crash in Fla., served in Pacific, lived on Hesketh St., Chevy Chase

Wood, Pvt. John, 22, AAF, died in training accident in La. in Aug. `42, flight engineer, lived on Edgewood Lane

Wright, Lt. Charles, MC, died in plane crash in Calif. Jane. `43, lived with Fulks family on St. Elmo, worked for Am. Ice

Wright, Sgt. James, MC, 28, plane crash in ETO while diplomatic courier, widow lived on Chevy Chase Drive

Yon, Benjamin, 21, killed in Germany in Nov. `44, B-CC `43, worked at Army Map Service

Ziegle, Lt. Robert, AAF pilot, killed in B-29 crash on Guam returning from Tokyo bombing mission, lived on Brookeville Rd., CC

This list contains the names of forty-four enlisted men and fifty-five officers plus one PHS doctor. It is likely some men were missed in this count, and there are a few here who were barely Bethesdans. The rather disproportionately high percentage of officers is interesting and has many causes, some economic and some educational.

762

Appendix L:

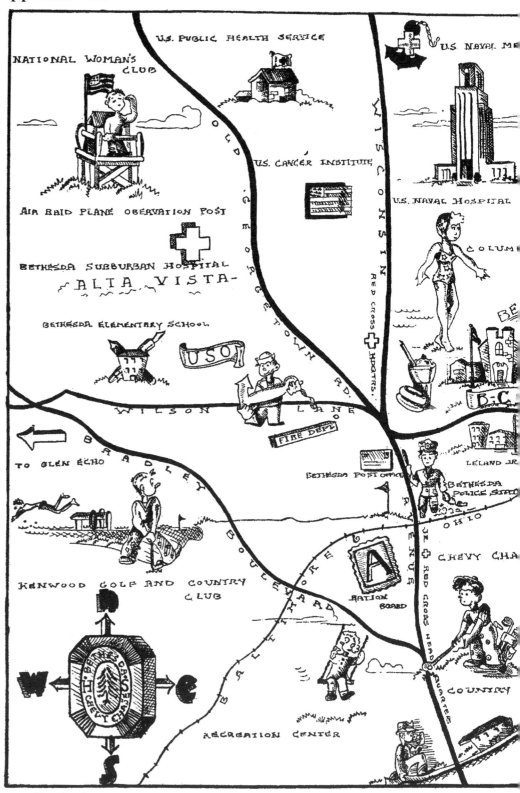

Frontisepiece cartoon by Pine Tree art editor Sheila Young for 1944 yearbook

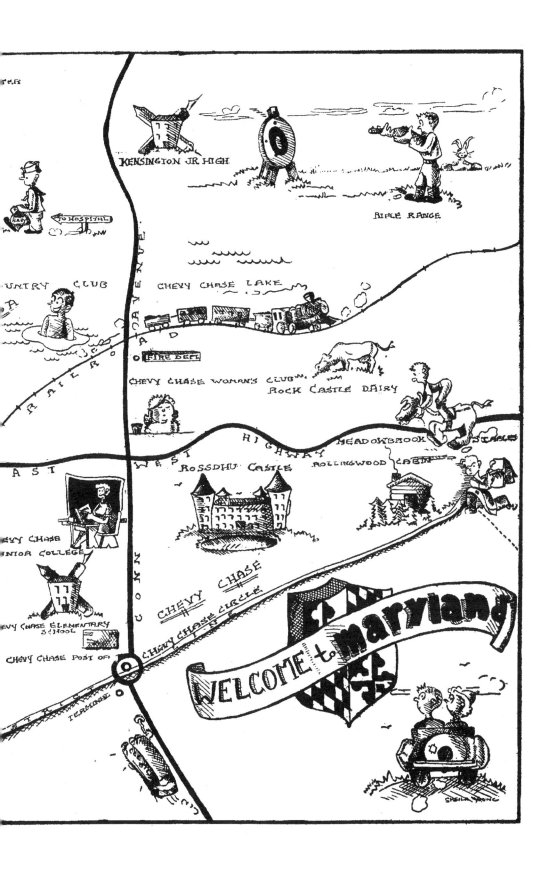

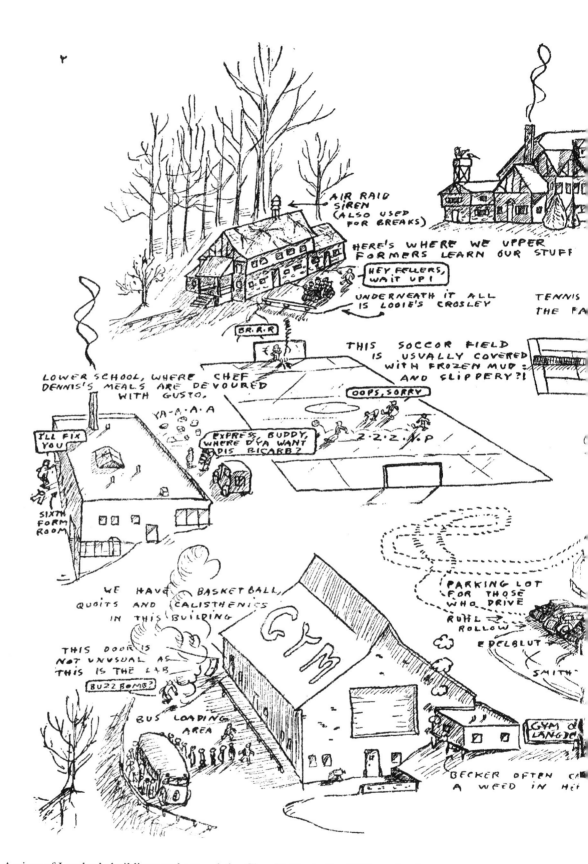

A view of Landon's buildings and grounds by Chas Hobbs in the 1945 yearbook

Appendix M:

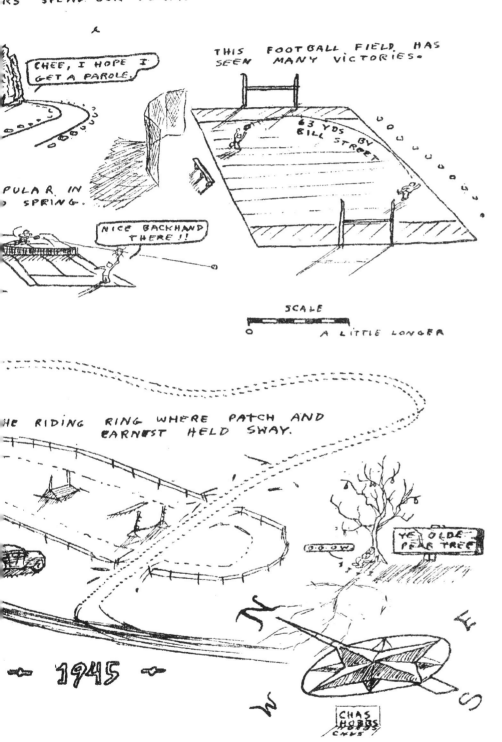

INDEX

Thielscher, Robert T., 701
Thomas J. Fisher Co, 143, 148, 185, 190
Thomas, Edward H., 142
Thomas, Henry, 172
Thomas, Henry William, 167
Thompkins, George H., 683
Thompkins, William, 683
Thompson, Connie W., 173
Thompson, Dr. Lewis, 401
Thompson, Edgar, 163
Thompson, Emma C., 409
Thompson, H. George, 336
Thompson, Les, 445
Thompson, Lyle, 396
Thompson, Mrs. Donald, 531
Thorn, A. B., 312
Thornapple Street News, 199
Thornton, Dr. William, 30
Thornton, J. E., 379
Thorpe, Day, 417, 444, 447, 454, 471, 504, 512, 526
Thorpe, Merle, 336, 418, 426
Thrift Shop, 585, 599, 613, 624, 635, 657, 673, 702
Throckmorton, Bonnie-Mason, 624
Tibbitts, James, 586
tick fever, 452, 623, 683
Tilden Gardens, 195
Tilly, Irene, 461
Tipton, Stringer, 685
tire registration, 542
Titsworth, Eleanor, 513, 671
TMB, 619, 647 see David Taylor
tobacco, 14
Tobacco Inspection Act, 4
Tofte, Hans, 565
Tohoga, 2
toilet paper, 516
Tolden, Rev. Fred A., 687
tollgate, 20
tollroads, 20
Tolson, Elizabeth, 619
tomato soup, 201
Tomlinson, J. S., 122
Too, Helen, 495
Toone, Earl C., 114
Tories, 30
tourist homes, 229
Towles, Will, 599
Town and Country Club, 312
Town of Chevy Chase, 75, 188
Town of Glen Echo, 101
traffic lights, 441, 449
trailer parks, 400
trash collection, 554, 658
Travis, Cecil, 505
Travis, Merle, 542
Trayes, Majorie, 609
Trayes, Marjorie M., 708
tree planting, 570
Tribune, 408, 422, 457, 462, 469, 471, 477, 503, 512, 526, 539, 540, 553, 589, 590, 659, 683, 703
Triest, Laura Tuckerman, 300, 307, 311, 494
Trimble, Jimmy, 458, 675
Triplett, William, 391
trolley line, 72, 100, 115, 202, 206, 253, 261, 265, 297, 362, 383
trolley, ends, 382
Troop 204, 621
Troth, Horace, 182, 195, 196
Troth, John, 196, 493
Troth, Lawrence, 188, 196, 473
Trowbridge, Betty Lou, 419
Truax, Robert, 77
Truman, Harry S, 359, 631
Trunnell, W. Kenneth., 531, 583
Tucker, Ray, 519
Tuckerman Lane, 86
Tuckerman, Edith, 300
Tuckerman, Mrs. Walter, 372, 453

Tuckerman, Walter, 172, 226, 295, 298, 300, 306, 307, 308, 311, 315, 324, 325, 326, 329, 331, 356, 358, 372
Tudor Place, 30, 31
Tuemmler, Fred, 563, 617
Tuohey, David, 123, 710
Tuohey, Dennis, 119, 124
Tuohey, Gordon, 125, 494
Tuohey, Kenneth, 527
Tuohey, Loretta, 128
Tuohey, Mary, 123
Tuohey, Norman, 119, 122
Tuohey, Thomas, 119
Tuohy, Ellen Bell, 611
Turlington,Catherine, 561
Turner Rifles, 35
Turner, Edyth, 367
turnpike, 282
Turover Lumber Co, 418
Turover, I. S., 599, 636
Tusculum Academy, 8
Tuve, Merle A., 661
Two Dollar Hole, 178
Tydings, Millard G., 257
typhoid, 40, 315

U V

U.S. Maritime Corporation, 265
Umbeck, J. Ella, 349
Uncle Frank's Folly, 152
Uncle Tom's cabin, 10
Unconditional Unionists, 47, 59
underpass, 562
Union Arch Bridge, 23, 25, 89
Union Party, 34, 49
Union Trust Co, 168
United Democratic Organization, 356, 520
Universal Military Training, 664
UNRRA, 671
Urbana, 45
USO, 476, 576, 577, 578, 583, 588, 589, 609, 611, 624, 637, 646, 658, 663, 664, 674, 682, 684, 688, 699, 708
V-E Day, 678
V-J Day, 701
V-Mail, 541
V.M.I., 50
Vacation Bible School, 449
Valley View, 164
Van Durand, Walter, 692
Van Ness, William, 305
Van Wagner, George, 480, 508, 529, 556
Vance, Annie, 79
vandalism, 685
Vandegrift, Gen. A. A., 711
Vanderwerken, Gilbert, 72
Vanemann, Chester, 538
Vannais, Leon, 405
Varela, James, 605
Vassar Circle, 112, 117
Vaughan, Eleanor, 519
Vaughan, Mrs. Lawrence M., 534
Veihmeyer, Mary, 680
Veirs, K. S., 650, 698
venereal disease, 562
Vernon Motors, 395
Veterans of Foreign Wars, 595
Veterans Service Council, 683
VFW, 500, 589, 649
Vicksburg, 47, 49
Victory Corps, 536, 555, 558, 581
Victory Garden Committee, 601
Victory Garden Corps, 561
Victory Gardens, 242, 518, 558, 559, 560, 561, 567, 578, 581, 587, 614, 662, 665, 682, 687
Viers Mill, 52
Viett, Charles H., 294
Village Hall, 160, 165, 173, 190
Village of Chevy Chase, 188, 442, 449, 477, 588, 673

Vincent, John H., 93
Vine, Ronnie, 110, 117
Virga, Joe, 377
Virginia and Truckee, 145
Visitation Convent, 324
Vogeley, Rev. Raymond, 384, 506, 687
Vogt, Allan, 405, 438, 458, 484, 518, 606
Voight, Paul, 467
Voigt, William C., 235
volleyball championship, 364
Volten, Theodore, 205
Voorhees, Austin, 562
voting machines, 457

W

W & J Sloan, 377
W. T. Galligher, 377
W.C.T.U., 97, 309
WAACs, 541
Waesche, Agnes R., 393
Waggaman, John F., 144
Wagner, Emily (Mrs. William H.), 687
wagon chase, 47
Wake Island, 505
Walhonding Road, 88, 114
Walker, Albert W., 244, 502, 524, 569, 671
Walker, Claxton, 155, 543, 556
Walker, Curtis, 376, 520
Walker, Curtis Jr., 419
Walker, Dr. Paul W., 483
Walker, Helen (Mrs. Curtis), 525
Walker, John C., 374
Walker, Louise, 419, 535, 621
Walker, Mrs. Albert W., 543
Walker, Mrs. Curtis, 568
Walker, Redford W., 188
Wallace, Charles, 477
Wallace, Francis C., 306
Wallace, Jimmy, 704
Wallace, Lew, 50
Wallace, Mrs. Gerald L., 577
Walser, Mrs. Daniel, 404
Walsh, Dr. Ralph, 78, 191, 232, 289
Walters, Henry, 390
Walton School, 390, 455, 475
Walton, Thomas Jr., 455, 492
Walton, Thomas W., 508
War of 1812, 5, 30
war refugees, 456
Ward, Horace, 542
Warner, A.J., 74, 149
Warner, Brainard H., 71, 284
Warner, Ed, 444
Warner, Josephine, 393
Warner, Mary Grace (Mrs. Edward), 673
Warner, Sam Bass, 153
Warren's Addition, 191
Warren's row, 194
Warren, M.& R.B., 191, 194
Warren, Mary, 608
Warren, Monroe, 269
Warren, Mrs. Fred G., 612
Warthen, Alfred, 351
Warthen, Willard, 187
Warwick, Harvey, 472
Washington and Georgetown Railroad, 72
Washington and Western Maryland, 74
Washington Aqueduct, 23, 25, 35
Washington Aviation Country Club, 682, 697
Washington Cathedral, 158
Washington County, 15, 68
Washington Grove, 71
Washington Hebrew Congregation, 619
Washington Hospital for Foundlings, 285
Washington Loan and Trust, 167
Washington Railway and Electric Co, 85, 87, 382 see WRECo
Washington Suburban Sanitary Commission, 314